THE CAUSES OF BEHAVIOR

Second Edition

Edited by

Allyn and Bacon, Inc.

Boston

THE CAUSES OF BEHAVIOR

Readings in Child Development and Educational Psychology

JUDY F. ROSENBLITH

Professor of Psychology
Wheaton College

WESLEY ALLINSMITH

Professor of Psychology
University of Cincinnati

1, 3, 41, 47

TO SANDRA, RONALD, BRYAN, WENDY, AND CRAIG

A NOTE ON THE COVER DESIGN

Visual acuity of infants was tested with one row of such stripes: 1/8, 1/16, 1/32, and 1/64 inch wide. Each pattern was displayed with a gray square of equal brightness, placed 10 inches from the infant's eyes. It had been established that infants preferred patterns to solid colors; so, in this test, the finest stripe pattern consistently preferred to gray showed how narrow a stripe the infant could perceive. Infants under a month old responded to the 1/8-inch stripes and infants six months old to the 1/64-inch stripes.

From Robert L. Fantz, The origin of form perception, *Scientific American*, 1961, *204* (5), 66-72 and 204; copyright © 1961 by *Scientific American, Inc.*, all rights reserved; reprinted with abridgement by permission in the first edition of *Causes of Behavior*.

Fourth Printing . . . August, 1969

Preface

A NUMBER OF UNIVERSITIES AND COLLEGES OFFER COURSES
that combine the content of educational psychology with that of child
and adolescent psychology or human development. The selections in this
book were assembled as a result of the editors' experience in teaching
such courses.

The book is organized as follows. There is an introductory section which
serves three functions. (1) It explains the organization of the book; (2)
it gives some information to help the student read and interpret the
statistics which are included in some articles; (3) it presents four selections which together give an excellent view of the range of outlooks in
the field. Each section from II through IX deals with a theme from among
the explanations of behavior emphasized by important theorists or schools
of thought about developmental psychology or human behavior. Articles
applicable to educational issues are often presented in the framework
of one of these broad avenues to the understanding of behavior. Some of
these themes are more basic and/or all-inclusive than others. A theme
that may be derivative of others is assigned a section of its own only if
the factor it emphasizes plays an important role as a determinant, either
in theory or practice. More complexly interwoven behaviors are discussed
in the section entitled Motivational Resultants (X). Although the stress of
this book is on various approaches to understanding the behavior of children rather than on educational psychology in any narrow sense, the final
section of the book (XI) does deal with research and problems which
have specific educational implications.

A book thus organized around themes in the explanation of human
behavior is obviously relevant to much of psychology. Its emphases on
the development of behavior and on behaviors of relevance to the educator
seem to the editors to make it particularly appropriate for students in
developmental psychology, educational psychology, or the combined type
of course referred to in the first paragraph.

During a period of several years the value of many of the selections
has been explored by assigning them and getting students' evaluations
of them on a number of dimensions (amount of information contained,
quality of presentation, ease of reading, amount of interest aroused, and,
all things considered, how worthwhile the student considered the reading
of the article to have been). In determining which articles selected for
the first edition ought to be replaced in settling on the content of the
second edition, we were guided by not only the availability of more
recent articles of quality but also by two sets of opinions: those of our
own students whom we polled about their experiences in reading the book
as a course assignment, and those of dozens of colleagues around the
nation who were kind enough to respond to a questionnaire we sent

to persons who had adopted the book for teaching purposes. In addition
we had the benefit of replies from several dozen professors who responded
thoughtfully to a request from our publisher, Allyn and Bacon, for
reactions to the book.

About 40 percent of the first edition's selections have been replaced
by new ones. The only other major change in this second edition is
that we have moved the section on Settings and Specific Stimuli from
ninth position to fifth. Our purpose in placing it next to the section on
Group Memberships is not only to indicate the relation between these
two sections but, even more, to clarify the contrast in the type of
determinant meant (as described in the introductions of those two
sections).

Our experience semester after semester indicates that most reading
assignments provoke a considerable variety of reactions. The article which
some students consider the most valuable of all is one which other
students rate as having limited merit. Only the rare article is rejected
by a preponderant majority of students as being too difficult, or as lacking
in worth. Such articles were, of course, eliminated. But, as a result of
the general diversity of opinion, we recognize that not all students (or
all teachers) will necessarily be pleased by each of the articles included.
We have attempted to offer a collection that changes pace frequently and
that ranges widely in topics covered, in techniques of investigation used,
in levels of difficulty, and in the views espoused by the authors. In order
to show the variety of existing methods and to convey some of the
information that exists in areas not yet subjected to precise research, we
have not hesitated to include work of investigators who, in opening up
new areas of study, have often used approaches which lack scientific rigor.

Our general orientation to the task of presenting a selection of readings
is to assume that the original material should be reproduced in its entirety.
Nevertheless, we have had to abridge some selections. In certain cases
this was done almost entirely in the interest of saving space, but without
sacrificing the points most crucial to our interest. In other cases we
considered certain portions of a particular selection too difficult for any
typical student to follow, and hence deleted those portions. In all
instances the author's agreement has been obtained. We have also taken
care to indicate all deletions so that the interested student or teacher
can check the original source if he so desires. Congruent with our interest
in completeness of content, we have usually included the original references and footnotes (our own footnotes are in italics and indicated by [Ed]).
The inclusion of references is especially important for those students who
are preparing a paper or planning and conducting a study.

We wish to express our gratitude to the authors and publishers who
have allowed us to use their material in this book. They are credited
in appropriate footnotes at the beginning of each selection. We are
also grateful to those authors and publishers who gave us permission to
reproduce materials in the trial version of this work. Burton L. White
and Richard Held deserve particular mention since they have written

a report of recent research especially for our use in this volume.

Because of their backing of our efforts in preparing the first edition, we repeat our thanks to the following individuals: Francis Keppel, former Dean of the Harvard Graduate School of Education; John W. M. Whiting, former Director of the Harvard Laboratory of Human Development; the late Harold Schlosberg, long Chairman of the Department of Psychology at Brown University; and Erich Lindemann, Chief of the Department of Psychiatry (Emeritus) at Massachusetts General Hospital. The latter supported the work of each of us during our successive roles as Coordinator of Research at the Hospital's Center for Studies in Human Development.

For support of our work on the second edition in preparing the manuscript and obtaining the necessary permissions, we are greatly indebted to the University of Cincinnati. In addition we would like to thank Paul Sprosty and Donald Heller of Wheaton College for their helpful suggestions with respect to the introductions to several of the sections of this edition.

The hundreds of students and colleagues who have given us the benefit of their reactions often made useful suggestions that went beyond standard questionnaire responses. We acknowledge their generosity. For secretarial aid we thank Christine Buelsing, Laura Dallalio, Juanita Roberts, and especially Winifred Schmedding. A final word of appreciation is owed Kathleen Staley, who for many months as a one-woman communication center shouldered responsibility that far exceeded an ordinary secretarial burden.

February, 1966

JUDY F. ROSENBLITH
WESLEY ALLINSMITH

Contents

PREFACE

I/GENERAL INTRODUCTION   1

1 / GORDON W. ALLPORT
Psychological models for guidance   6

2 / B. F. SKINNER
Behaviorism at fifty   11

3 / JEROME S. BRUNER
Freud and the image of man   19

4 / CARL R. ROGERS
Toward a modern approach to values: the valuing process
in the mature person   23

II/BIOLOGICAL BASES FOR BEHAVIOR   31

5 / FRANK A. BEACH
The individual from conception to conceptualization   35

6 / ANNE ANASTASI
Heredity, environment, and the question "how?"   45

7 / J. P. SCOTT
New directions in the genetic study of personality and intelligence   54

8 / D. G. FREEDMAN
Constitutional and environmental interactions in rearing
of four breeds of dogs   57

9 / BURTON L. WHITE AND RICHARD HELD
Plasticity of sensorimotor development   60

10 / DONALD WEATHERLEY
Self-perceived rate of physical maturation and personality in
late adolescence   71

11 / MARJORIE P. HONZIK
Prediction of behavior from birth to maturity   80

III/LEARNING AS A DETERMINANT OF BEHAVIOR   87

12 / JOHN W. M. WHITING
Theories of learning and behavior   89

13 / B. F. SKINNER
Reinforcement today   92

14 / CARL D. WILLIAMS
The elimination of tantrum behavior by extinction procedures   98

15 / FLORENCE R. HARRIS, MONTROSE W. WOLF, AND DONALD M. BAER
Effects of adult social reinforcement on child behavior   99

16 / RICHARD H. WALTERS, ROSS D. PARKE, AND VALERIE A. CANE
Timing of punishment and the observation of consequences to
others as determinants of response inhibition   107

17 / JANE LOEVINGER
Patterns of parenthood as theories of learning   119

18 / A. W. MELTON / ABSTRACTED BY A. A. LUMSDAINE AND ROBERT GLASER
The science of learning and the technology of educational methods   121

19 / ROBERT R. SEARS
A theoretical framework for personality and social behavior   123

IV/INTERPERSONAL EXPERIENCES AS
DETERMINANTS OF BEHAVIOR   131

20 / HARRY F. HARLOW AND MARGARET K. HARLOW
The effect of rearing conditions on behavior   134

21 / ROBERT R. SEARS, ELEANOR E. MACCOBY, AND HARRY LEVIN
The socialization of aggression   140

22 / ELIZABETH BING
Effect of childrearing practices on development of differential
cognitive abilities   148

23 / ALBERT BANDURA, DOROTHEA ROSS, AND SHEILA A. ROSS
A comparative test of the status envy, social power, and secondary
reinforcement theories of identificatory learning   159

24 / PAUL MUSSEN AND ELDRED RUTHERFORD
Parent-child relations and parental personality in relation to
young children's sex-role preferences   167

25 / JUDY F. ROSENBLITH
Learning by imitation in kindergarten children   179

26 / ELIZABETH DOUVAN AND JOSEPH ADELSON
The psychodynamics of social mobility in adolescent boys   186

V/SETTINGS AND SPECIFIC STIMULI AS
DETERMINANTS OF BEHAVIOR   201

27 / WILLIAM CLARK TROW, ALVIN F. ZANDER, WILLIAM C. MORSE,
AND DAVID H. JENKINS
Psychology of group behavior: the class as a group   204

28 / RONALD LIPPITT AND MARTIN GOLD
Classroom social structure as a mental health problem   211

29 / WILBUR SCHRAMM
TV as scapegoat   216

30 / W. PAUL BLAKELY
A study of seventh grade children's reading of comic books as
related to certain other variables   218

31 / LAWRENCE S. KUBIE
Introduction to "An application of psychoanalysis to education"   225

32 / HILDA TABA
Cultural deprivation as a factor in school learning   226

VI/GROUP MEMBERSHIPS AS
DETERMINANTS OF BEHAVIOR   235

33 / RICHARD DE CHARMS AND GERALD H. MOELLER
Values expressed in American children's readers: 1800-1950   238

34 / HELEN FAIGIN
Social behavior of young children in the kibbutz   245

35 / ALBERT I. RABIN
Kibbutz adolescents   257

36 / THOMAS F. PETTIGREW
Regional differences in anti-Negro prejudice   264

37 / THOMAS F. PETTIGREW
Personality and sociocultural factors in intergroup attitudes:
a cross-national comparison   273

38 / DAVID D. STEIN, JANE ALLYN HARDYCK, AND M. BREWSTER SMITH
Race and belief: an open and shut case   274

39 / GLENN TERRELL, JR., KATHRYN DURKIN, AND MELVIN WIESLEY
Social class and the nature of the incentive in discrimination learning   282

VII/AGE OR DEVELOPMENTAL STAGE AS A
DETERMINANT OF BEHAVIOR   285

40 / A healthy personality for every child   289

41 / ROBERT W. WHITE
Competence and the psychosexual stages of development   300

42 / SUSAN ISAACS
The nursery as a community   309

43 / BETTYE M. CALDWELL
The usefulness of the critical period hypothesis in the study
of filiative behavior   310

44 / JEROME S. BRUNER
Image and symbol in the development of magnitude and order   318

45 / STEPHEN M. COREY
Designing a curriculum for student development   324

46 / ANNA FREUD
Adolescence   328

47 / GORDON W. ALLPORT
Crises in normal personality development   335

VIII/SEX AS A DETERMINANT OF BEHAVIOR   341

48 / HERBERT BARRY III, MARGARET K. BACON, AND IRVIN L. CHILD
A cross-cultural survey of some sex differences in socialization   343

49 / DANIEL G. BROWN
Sex-role development in a changing culture   349

50 / IRVIN L. CHILD, ELMER H. POTTER, AND ESTELLE M. LEVINE
Children's textbooks and personality development: an exploration
in the social psychology of education   357

51 / WILLIAM J. MEYER AND GEORGE G. THOMPSON
Sex differences in the distribution of teacher approval and
disapproval among sixth-grade children   365

IX/INTELLIGENCE AS A DETERMINANT
OF BEHAVIOR   373

52 / ALFRED BINET AND THEOPHILE SIMON
Upon the necessity of establishing a scientific diagnosis of
inferior states of intelligence   375

53 / ALFRED BINET AND THEOPHILE SIMON
The development of the Binet-Simon scale   378

54 / PHILIP E. VERNON
Ability factors and environmental influences   383

55 / JEROME KAGAN, LESTER W. SONTAG, CHARLES T. BAKER AND
    VIRGINIA L. NELSON
Personality and IQ change   393

56 / LEWIS M. TERMAN
The discovery and encouragement of exceptional talent   399

57 / MICHAEL A. WALLACH AND NATHAN KOGAN
A new look at the creativity-intelligence distinction   409

X / MOTIVATIONAL RESULTANTS 421

58 / J. MC V. HUNT
Traditional personality theory in the light of recent evidence 423

59 / ROGER G. BARKER
Success and failure in the classroom 434

60 / ALBERT BANDURA AND WALTER MISCHEL
Modification of self-imposed delay of reward through exposure to
live and symbolic models 437

61 / WESLEY ALLINSMITH
Conscience and conflict: the moral force in personality 445

62 / EDITH WEISSKOPF
Intellectual malfunctioning and personality 450

63 / NEVITT SANFORD
Ego process in learning 464

64 / LILI E. PELLER
Daydreams and children's favorite books 469

65 / SANDOR FERENCZI
Stages in the development of the sense of reality 476

66 / ELEANOR E. MACCOBY
Why do children watch television? 477

67 / SEYMOUR FESHBACH
The stimulating versus cathartic effects of a vicarious
aggressive activity 481

68 / JESSE W. GRIMES AND WESLEY ALLINSMITH
Compulsivity, anxiety, and school achievement 486

69 / HARRY BEILIN
Teachers' and clinicians' attitudes toward the behavior problems of
children: a reappraisal 500

70 / PAULINE S. SEARS AND ERNEST R. HILGARD
The teacher's role in the motivation of the learner 508

XI / SPECIFIC EDUCATIONAL IMPLICATIONS 523

71 / JEROME S. BRUNER
The growth of mind 527

72 / JEROME S. BRUNER
Learning and thinking 537

73 / THOMAS G. ANDREWS AND LEE J. CRONBACH
Transfer of training 542

74 / HERBERT G. BIRCH AND HERBERT S. RABINOWITZ
The negative effect of previous experience on productive thinking   551

75 / DAVID P. AUSUBEL
The use of advance organizers in the learning and retention of
meaningful verbal material   555

76 / VERNER M. SIMS
Questioning some assumptions underlying current
achievement testing   559

77 / VERNER M. SIMS
Objective tests and teachers' measurements   563

78 / MIRIAM L. GOLDBERG
Adapting teacher style to pupil differences: teachers for
disadvantaged children   565

79 / ARTHUR A. LUMSDAINE AND IRVING L. JANIS
Resistance to "counterpropaganda" produced by one-sided and
two-sided "propaganda" presentations   576

80 / CHARLES S. MORRILL
Teaching machines: a review   581

81 / ROBERT GLASER
Instructional technology and the measurement of learning outcomes:
some questions   590

82 / A. W. MELTON
Some comments on "The impact of advancing technology on
methods in education"   594

INDEX

PSYCHOLOGY AND THE TEACHER*

. . . you make a great, a very great mistake, if you think that psychology, being the science of the mind's laws, is something from which you can deduce definite programs and schemes and methods of instruction for immediate schoolroom use. Psychology is a science, and teaching is an art; and sciences never generate arts directly out of themselves. An intermediary inventive mind must make the application, by using its originality.

The science of logic never made a man reason rightly, and the science of ethics (if there is such a thing) . . . never made a man behave rightly. The most such sciences can do is to help us catch ourselves up and check ourselves more articulately after we have made mistakes. . . .

And so everywhere the teaching must *agree* with the psychology, but need not necessarily be the only kind of teaching that would so agree; for many diverse methods of teaching may equally well agree with psychological laws. . . .

But, if the use of psychological principles thus be negative rather than positive, it does not follow that it may not be a great use, all the same. It certainly narrows the path for experiments and trials. We know in advance, if we are psychologists, that certain methods will be wrong, so our psychology saves us from mistakes. It makes us, moreover, more clear as to what we are about.

* From William James, *Talks to Teachers on Psychology* (New York: Holt, Rinehart, and Winston, Inc., 1920, first published in 1899), pp. 7-11. Reprinted by permission.

[We are grateful to Professor Gordon Hendrickson of the University of Cincinnati for calling this passage to our attention.]

I / General Introduction

Organization of the Book

IN DESCRIBING THE PURPOSES OF A PIONEERING INVESTIgation in which a number of factors relevant to the prediction of children's actions were taken simultaneously into account, John W. M. Whiting of Harvard University has written:[1]

> Various positions have been taken as to the major determinants of a child's behavior. Gesell and Piaget, taking a developmental point of view, say the most important thing to know in order to predict a child's behavior is how old he is; Freud and his followers would insist that the most important determinant of a child's behavior is his life history, especially his relationship with his father and mother; the learning theorists would insist that a knowledge of previous rewards and punishments for the particular behavior in question is what is needed. The Gestalt school, as exemplified by Lewin, Baldwin, and Barker and Wright, would take a historical approach and insist that a knowledge of the situation, that is, the setting and instigation, is the thing to have; and, of course, the anthropologists would insist that if you don't know what society the child is a member of, you can't predict a thing.

Whiting goes on to cite one more factor as possibly having some weight, namely whether the child is a male or a female. He concludes: "We suspect there is a grain of truth in each of these positions."

We believe that Whiting has put his finger on a key characteristic of the social and behavioral sciences today. Because the determinants of behavior are multiple, EACH theoretical view is more or less "true." Full understanding and precise prediction await the formula which can assign a suitable weight to each of the factors. Prior to the arrival of such a Utopian state of affairs, we can nevertheless increase our understanding of behavior by studying each of its possible determinants. We have accordingly organized this book into parts, most of which deal with a class of determinant. To the categories of determinant given by Whiting above, we have added a section on biological factors and one on intelligence. The final two parts of the book are not devoted to classes of determinants, but rather to various important *resultants* of the interaction of the determinants. A look at the table of contents will further clarify the organization of the book.

We realize that our selection of classes of determinants is not the only selection possible. Also, the classes to which we assign a label, and thus a section, are not mutually exclusive or non-overlapping. We recognize, furthermore, that some factors to which we have assigned a role as determinants are themselves a resultant of other determinants. An example is INTELLIGENCE, which may be conceived of as a resultant both of biological factors and of learning experiences. However, intelligence plays

[1] These statements are from a paper entitled "The Observation of Children's Behavior— A Cross-Cultural Approach," given by Dr. Whiting at the December 1958 Meeting of the American Association for the Advancement of Science.

an important role in educational psychology and in psychology generally; it is frequently viewed as a determinant and used as an independent variable in research studies. Consequently we have chosen to present it in that context.

In the editors' comments that precede each of the forthcoming parts, we give our description or interpretation of the material to be covered and some indication of the authors' affiliations. We also call attention to overlap with other parts. Additional readings are sometimes suggested, especially for those students who lack an adequate background for the topic under discussion or who wish to pursue the topic in greater depth.

How to Read Statistics

A number of the articles in this book present numerical findings from psychological research. In most such cases the data are accompanied by statistical statements. In this section we present some information about statistical statements which will aid in understanding the articles.[2]

The statistical tests most frequently used in these articles deal with the question of what probability exists that random error[3] or chance could have led to findings or relationships of the magnitude actually obtained. Such probability statements are a pivotal issue in statistics. The lower the probability is of obtaining a result through random error, the more confidence one can have in the finding. For example, an experimental outcome with a probability (p) of $<.05$ (less than five in a hundred) is one that would have occurred by chance less than one time in twenty. If the experiment were run a hundred times, results as extreme as those found would, on the average, occur less than five times out of the hundred if there were no systematic relation between the variables. To put it another way, even if there were no relation between the variables, findings with a p of .05 would still occur, on the average, five times out of a hundred just because of probability.

In psychological and educational research, when a finding is described as "statistically significant" the author usually means "the probability that the result is due to chance is .05 or 'better.'" A "better" probability is a lower one, e.g., .02, .01, or .001. The latter probabilities mean that

---

[2] We assume that readers are familiar with purely descriptive statistics or that their instructors will acquaint them with measures of central tendency (mean, median, mode), and with measures of dispersion (range, standard deviation), and with the basic idea of correlation. The chapter on statistics in many introductory psychology texts and the chapter "Individual differences and their measurement," pp. 489-505 of the Reference Manual in *Psychology and Teaching* by Morse and Wingo, 2nd Edition (Scott, Foresman, 1962), constitute valuable sources for review. In addition, the student is referred to the chapter on statistical thinking in Donald O. Hebb, *A Textbook of Psychology* (Saunders, 1958), for a highly readable, non-mathematical account that may aid in better understanding of statistical reasoning.

[3] "Random error," or chance, is a factor in research results in basically the same way it is in other matters; if you shuffle and deal four bridge or poker hands, you may find some rare, unlikely hands (e.g., a full house) "just by chance." Or, to take one more example, if you flip an unbiased coin ten times, you can get nine heads "just by chance." In the same way, the psychological experimenter may be "lucky" or "unlucky." Statistics provide a means of assessing this luck factor.

such a result would be obtained by chance only two times in a hundred, one time in a hundred, or one time in one thousand.

In psychological writings, the remark that a result is "significant" does not mean that it is "meaningful" or "important," but that it is STATISTICALLY significant. Of course, $p = .06$ and $p = .07$ are not much different in probability from $p = .05$. One can place almost as much confidence in them. Yet, by convention, the term "significant" is usually applied only to results that have a p value of .05 or less. Some authors give no actual probability figures when the p is greater than .05, merely labeling the results N.S. for "not significant." Others report probabilities such as .10 or .12 to indicate trends that might have reached a more acceptable "p level" if there had been more cases in the sample or if the results obtained had been a little more striking.

Two qualifications about "p values" should be understood by all students of psychology. (1) The fact that a result is significant does not rule out the possibility that it is due to chance or random error. Out of one hundred findings based on the same experiment, five (on the average) might be significant at the .05 level or better even if only chance were operating. (2) The fact that a finding is "significant" does not, as we have said before, mean that it is important. If there were a difference between the average heights of redheads and blondes, and enough women of each coloring were measured, the difference might be statistically significant, i.e., greater than is likely to be accounted for by random errors, even though the actual difference in average heights was only .1 inch. Needless to say, it would be futile under such circumstances to use the information that "redheads are taller than blondes" to predict the relative heights of a particular unknown redhead and blonde who are to be matched with a tall and a short man as blind dates.

The findings that are discussed in terms of their significance or probability level are of two major classes. One class is concerned with the significance of differences. The differences may be of various types: (a) between two different performances of the same people (e.g., between history achievement and arithmetic achievement); (b) between two groups of people measured on the same performance or characteristic (e.g., I.Q.'s of Negroes and Whites); or (c) between the results of two experimental treatments (e.g., arithmetic performance of those taught by method A and those taught by method B).

The second class of findings discussed in terms of significance levels or p values is that concerned with the degree of relationship between two variables. Such findings are assessed by correlation techniques. The Pearson product moment correlation (r) is most frequently used. In this class of findings too, a relationship may be significant without being a close or important one. To illustrate: Two indices or variables such as chronological age and score on a given test may correlate .20 with one another ($r = .20$). This may be a significant relationship ($p < .05$) if the sample on which the correlation was obtained was sufficiently large. However, the capacity to predict the test score from knowing the chronological age (or vice versa) is low indeed. The amount of variability in one factor which is controlled by the other is given by r^2 which, in this case, is .04 or 4% of the variance. In terms of our example, only 4% of the variability in test scores may be said to be controlled by chronological age.

Let us look at some examples. A child development researcher seeks to study the effects of weaning infants at various ages on the development of conscience, or on some other characteristic, at a later age. There are two research strategies he might adopt. (1) He may look for differences in conscience (or whatever variable he is concerned with) between two (or more) groups which differ in the age at which they were weaned. He would proceed to categorize all of his subjects into two or more groups in terms of the age of weaning (early *vs.* late, or early, average, and late). He would then measure a later behavior (amount of guilt at age 12, say) by some specified technique. Then he would compare the amount of guilt shown by his groups and determine whether the difference (or differences) were significant. (2) Instead of looking for differences between groups, he may look for the DEGREE OF RELATIONSHIP between the variable age of weaning and the variable amount of guilt. Age is, of course, almost automatically quantified. The data on guilt must also be expressed in quantitative form (scores, perhaps). Then the correlation between the two can be determined and the degree of relationship thus assessed. In case 1, the finding might be that there is a significant DIFFERENCE between a group weaned early and one weaned late. In case 2, a significant DEGREE OF RELATIONSHIP may be found. The actual magnitude (or size) of the difference or relationship may be large or small. If small yet statistically significant, it may be of importance for psychological theory. In such an event, the author of the study should not be misinterpreted as having shown that behaviors at age 12 (or whenever) are determined in any close and direct fashion by some particular early childhood experience taken by itself. Furthermore, the reader must always remember that even a strong degree of relationship found between two variables does not necessarily mean that one causes the other. Each might be the result of a third, unstudied factor. An example of a possible finding of this nature follows.

For instance, the number of pots and pans in home kitchens might prove to be correlated with the political preferences of the householders, with more utensils in the kitchens of Republicans. Such a finding should not be used to argue that Republicans are fonder of food, are more "oral" in their personality tendencies, or dislike eating in restaurants! If such a finding were obtained, it would probably be because, on the average, persons with more money have tended to vote for the party with the more conservative monetary policies. Thus it would be the correlation of both Republicanism and possession of kitchen utensils with a third factor, income, that would give rise to the finding. Republicanism per se would not be a cause of utensil purchases! Or vice-versa.

In addition to relationships that are so small as to be of more theoretical than practical importance, there are many which are large or important enough to have great practical utility for group prediction. This may be true despite the fact that in many individual cases they may result in forecasting failures. During World War II, for example, millions of dollars were saved by the use of psychological tests in screening candidates for pilot training. Predictions of success were far more accurate than those which could be obtained by coin-flipping or other arbitrary procedures. As a group, the trainees chosen by this means were more likely to succeed. Nevertheless, numbers of those who underwent training did not succeed. Conversely, there is evidence for believing that many of those rejected for training would have succeeded. In short, the tests were good for group prediction, but imperfect for individual prediction.[4] Readers of psychological literature who understand this distinction between group and individual prediction and who bear in mind the other qualifications cited about the meanings of statistical results will be able to avoid the most common misinterpretations of investigators' findings.[5]

Introductory Articles

Four articles are reprinted in this introductory section. It is hoped that they will serve as stimuli to thinking, and also that the student will be able to benefit from the perspective they offer on important issues.

When we sought articles that would effectively represent various orientations that exist in contemporary psychology, we found that the four we chose were all by major figures. Three of the four authors—Professors Gordon Allport, Jerome Bruner, and Carl Rogers—have been presidents of the American Psychological Association. The fourth author, Professor B. F. Skinner, is equally eminent.

Allport, Bruner, and Skinner have long been at Harvard. If nothing else, their three articles should convince readers that professors at Harvard do not always agree with one another! Professor Rogers is now a Fellow of the Western Behavioral Science Institute in LaJolla after fruitful periods at Ohio State University, the University of Chicago, and the University of Wisconsin.

We think it inadvisable to encourage students to "keep an open mind" when discovering the contrasting viewpoints so ably presented by these four authors. Better that a student choose a position, absorb it, and react in terms of it as he reads other material. With a frame of reference, he will be less confused by the heterogeneity he will find in the rest of the book and in modern psychology generally. Eventually he may renounce the position he has first chosen; the commitment should be recognized as tentative. Nevertheless, it will stand him in good stead as an anchor among shifting currents.

[4] For a good elementary discussion related to this point, see Brown and Gilhousen, *College Psychology* (Prentice-Hall, 1950), Chapter 18, "Measuring individuals," pp. 459-477.

[5] We are indebted to Professor Howard B. Lyman for suggestions about this statistics section.

1/PSYCHOLOGICAL MODELS FOR

GUIDANCE/GORDON W. ALLPORT*

HOWEVER EXCELLENT HIS NATURAL eyesight may be, a counselor always looks at his client through professional spectacles. It could not be otherwise. After all, he has invested time and money in his psychological training. Of what use is it unless it adds special prisms to his own unaided eyesight?

The lenses we wear are ground to the prescription of our textbooks and teachers. Even while we are undergraduates a certain image of the nature of man is fitted to our eyes. We grow accustomed to the image and when we become practitioners or teachers we may still take it for granted.

But every so often comes a time for optical re-examination. Perhaps the image we have is still the best fit we can get; perhaps it is not. We can tell only by examining alternative lenses. In particular I believe that three are worthy of special scrutiny:

1) MAN SEEN AS A REACTIVE BEING. Under this rubic I would include outlooks known as naturalism, positivism, behaviorism, operationism, physicalism; these are also sometimes called—mistakenly, I think—"scientific psychology."

2) MAN SEEN AS A REACTIVE BEING IN DEPTH. Here I include what is variously called psychoanalysis, psychodynamics, depth psychology.

3) MAN SEEN AS A BEING-IN-PROCESS-OF-BECOMING. This label covers recent trends known as holism, orthopsychology, personalistics, existential psychology.

These three images provide a focus not only for guidance practices, but for all other professional psychological activity whether it be teaching, research, counseling or therapy.

MAN: A REACTIVE BEING

One hundred years ago in his *Beiträge* Wilhelm Wundt mapped a program for the newly conceived science of psychology. His own view of the proper development of this science was broad and permissive, especially in the field of social psychology. But what has taken hold in the Anglo-American tradition is the experimental outlook of his *Physiologische Psychologie.* Fusing with Darwinism, Machian positivism, the quantitative outlook of Galton and his successors, as well as with techniques invented by Binet, Pavlov, Hull and others—this experimental outlook prevailed and has ground the lens that is fitted to the eyes of almost all undergraduate students of psychology. Many of us who continue in the profession feel no need for further correction in this image of man.

Seen through this lens man is no different in kind from any other living reactor; and therefore, like the paramecium or pigeon, may be studied biologically, behaviorally, mathematically. To be sure a few special concepts need to be devised to take care of the vast complexity of human behavior, but all these concepts— among them habit hierarchy, secondary reinforcement, input and output of information, and the like—are consistent with the postulates of physicalism and naturalism.

If we ask, "What does it mean to be a human being?" this school of thought replies, "Man is one more creature of nature; his behavior though complex is predictable in principle. His present state is determined by his past state. A man's consciousness is unreliable and must be distrusted, preferably disregarded altogether. We seek the general laws of nature, not personal uniqueness. We study man, not men; objective reality, not subjective."

In principle this broad positive tradition, which we all know so well, puts a desirable end to psychological naïveté. It cautions us not to believe every verbal report that comes to our ears; it warns us to be skeptical of our own naked eyesight; and from it we learn to check ourselves for observer reliability. It teaches us to use precise and repeatable methods. Because of its stress on reliable methods this favored tradition in psychology has become known as "scientific psychology." Its methods are indeed scientific; but its primary postulate—that man is simply a reactive organism—is no more scientific than any other postulate.

It is here that the counselor encounters his first difficulty. Trained in tests, statistics, and

* Gordon W. Allport, Psychological models for guidance, *Harvard Educational Review*, 1962, 32, (4), 373-381. Reprinted by permission.

experimental design, he may think, quite mistakenly, that to employ these useful aids he must also view his client as a reactive being—an exclusive product of stimulus impact, homeostasis, drive-reduction and reinforcement learning. The term "scientific" has spread like a grease spot from method to theory. Just because most of our methods evolved through the positivistic tradition does not mean that the postulates of this tradition concerning the nature of man are the only acceptable postulates for scientific psychology.

A counselor whose theoretical spectacles disclose a merely reactive being, is likely to think of his client in terms of past conditioning and potential re-conditioning; in terms of reinforcements, in terms of environmental determinism. He will assume that his client's basic motives are drive-reduction or second-order conditionings which in some shadowy way are supposed to account for all his adult interests and vocational ambitions.

The vocabulary emanating from this type of postulate is replete with terms like *reaction, response, reinforcement, reflex, respondent, reintegration*—all sorts of *re*-compounds. The reference is backward. What *has* been is more important than what *will* be. Terms such as *proaction, progress, program, production, problem-solving,* or *propriate* are characteristically lacking. One would think that the client seated opposite would *protest,* for the language of response negates the subject's immediate certainty that his life lies in the future.

The positivistic view of man as a reactor has performed a good service, shaking us out of common sense naïveté, endowing us with useful methods, and correctly informing us that man is, in *some* aspects of his being, a simple respondent to simple pressures. Its postulates are, however, questionable. It sees reality as ordered but not as personal; it sees consciousness as a nuisance; it looks at man as reactive, not proactive.

It is probably true that no counselor fully follows this creed in his daily practice. Indeed he could not do so. It is too impoverished a view of real life. When a convinced positivist attempts to fit his image of man to concrete human situations, as B. F. Skinner has done in *Walden Two,* the result strikes many of us as threadbare, even pitiable.

Probably for this reason many behaviorists (starting even as far back as E. B. Holt in *The Freudian Wish and its Place in Ethics*) attempt to combine stimulus-response with psychoanalysis. Neal Miller and John Dollard in

their *Personality and Psychotherapy* offer a good example. Man as a reactive being is combined with man as a reactive being in depth.

MAN: A REACTIVE BEING IN DEPTH

So influential is this image of man that we find it everywhere: dominant in literature, in social work, in guidance, in therapeutic practice, and in the market place. There is no need today to describe this image to any educated, or even semi-educated, American adult. Freudianism, like positivism, is our daily dish.

What I should like to do is to make clear that Freudianism (in spite of its less reliable methods) is a close kin of traditional positivism. The only change in the image of man lies in adding the depth dimension. To the long psychological vocabulary of *re*-compounds, depth psychology adds *repression, regression, resistance, abreaction, reaction formation,* and many others.

Like other simple naturalistic views of man, psychoanalysis puts its chief weight upon the press of pleasure and pain. This pressure produces in the organism a tendency to seek an equilibrium between the force of his drives and the circumstances of reality. The fact that Freud maximizes the role of sex and locates the whole constellation of reactive forces chiefly in the unconscious does not alter the essential similarity.

For Freud causation lies in the past history of the individual just as it does for the conditioned-response theorist. Both have a dismaying disregard for the person's phenomenology of the future, for his sense of personhood and sense of freedom. The ego is a reactive agent, having no energy of its own, but borrowing from the unsocialized Id.

Central to depth psychology, and important for guidance, is the doctrine of *recall* and *recovery* (two more *re*-compounds). Therapy, and presumably guidance, proceeds by disclosing to the client some buried motive, or a troublesome and repressed psychic trauma. The client's salvation, if indeed he has any, lies in this vital recall. A troublesome memory is brought to cognizable form. Presumably the result is helpful to the individual in solving his conflicts. The theory, however, does not allow for any interaction between the person and the recovered memory. Simple re-instatement is itself, as Freud says, the "pure gold" of psychoanalysis. What values a client should live by when once the re-instatement has taken place is not the "pure gold" of psychoanalysis. That all adult values are simply sublimated aim-inhibited wishes, is the central doctrine. Freud never allows for the individual's capacity to disregard his past or to reshape it freely. Indeed, since the structure of the Id never changes, the future can at best be a redirection, never a transformation, of one's purposes. What one becomes is essentially what one is, and what one was.

Among the valid portions of psychoanalysis of special use to all counselors, is the brilliant account given us by Freud and by his daughter Anna, of the defensive mechanisms of the ego. In dealing with our client we do well to follow the advice of psychoanalysis and watch for rationalizations, denials of reality through repression, and displacements of aggression. All these, and other, ego-defenses belong to the nature of man, and therefore must find a place in any theory of human personality.

But what perplexes me is why so many of the ego-processes described by psychoanalysis should be merely protective strategies. Are there no ego-processes that lead to a transformation of what is recovered? To a creative cognition? To a revised sense of personhood and a new phenomenology of the future? To Freud the person seems never to be truly proactive, seldom even active. Almost always he is seen as reactive to early fixations—perhaps to some castration threat that occurred years ago, or to some other unsocialized infant complex, especially to Oedipal fantasies. My difficulty with this image of man is summed up most tersely by the late satirist, Max Beerbohm, who said, "They were a tense and peculiar family—those Oedipuses."

There is, I am well aware, a large group of theories that derive from the psychodynamic tradition but at the same time deviate considerably from the orthodox view of reactivity-in-depth. All these theories, in my judgment, move in a desirable direction. Here I shall mention only some of the relevant authors: Adler, Jung, Hartmann, Horney, Erikson, Fromm. Still more deviant from Freud are Goldstein, Maslow, Rogers, and Robert White. These and other writers offer a type of theory that views man as a being in the process of becoming. Many of them ask the pivotal question differently from the reactivist schools of thought. And it makes a good deal of difference just how a question is asked.

A story is told about two priests. They were arguing whether it was proper to smoke and to pray at the same time. One said "Yes," the other "No."

To settle the matter they decided that both should write to the Holy Father for his opinion. Sometime later they met and compared notes. Each claimed that the Holy Father had supported his view. They were perplexed. Finally one asked, "How did you phrase your question?" The other replied: "I asked whether it was proper to smoke while one is praying; and the Pope answered, 'Certainly not, praying is serious business and permits no distractions.' And how did you phrase your question?" "Well," said the other, "I asked if it were proper to pray while smoking, and the Pope answered, 'Certainly, prayer is always in order.' "

Instead of asking Aristotle's question, "What is the place of man in Nature?" many authors today are asking St. Augustine's question, "Who am I?" This question, rephrased in the 20th Century, has opened the floodgates to a new theorizing of the broad type often labeled *existentialist*.

MAN: BEING IN THE PROCESS OF BECOMING

Seelye Bixler, former president of Colby College, tells of a student who recently remarked, "I can't tell you how much satisfaction I take in my existential despair." In some student circles despair has always been popular. To label it "existentialist" makes it doubly attractive, in fact irresistible.

But overlooking the fashionable flavor of existentialism it is surely necessary for the modern counselor to take seriously the present-day anxieties of the younger generation. No longer can youth contemplate its future under the protection of the great social stabilizers of the past. No longer can one counsel within the framework of Victorian decorum, theological certainties, or the Pax Britannica. It is obvious to us all that some sort of shattering transformation is under way. The comfortable stabilities of culture, caste, the gold standard, and military supremacy are no longer ours.

Nor are the comfortable stabilities of traditional psychology adequate. Of what use is it to invoke an impersonal theory of learning, a biological theory of motivation, and a late Victorian formula for the unconscious, when youth's problems today are acutely conscious, intensely personal, and propelling him like an unguided astronaut into an unknown future? A counselor is not equipped for his job unless he can share in some degree the apprehensions of modern youth, and sense the swampy underpinning on which youth treads. Over his desk the counselor might well tack the wisdom of the Spanish writer Unamuno, "Suffering is the life blood that runs through us all and binds us together." While not every youth who comes to the counselor is at that moment a sufferer, it is a safe assumption that he comes for guidance that will fortify him for the inevitable suffering that he will encounter in his course of life.

TENTATIVENESS AND COMMITMENT. From the existential point of view the ideal counselor will strive to develop two attitudes in his client. Taken separately they seem antithetical; but fused into a world-view they provide strength for the future. One attitude is *tentativeness* of outlook. Since certainties are no longer certain, let all dogmas be fearlessly examined, especially those cultural idols that engender a false sense of security: dogmas of race supremacy, of naïve scientism, of unilinear evolutionary progress. Let one face the worst in oneself and in the world around him, so that one may correctly estimate the hazards.

Taken by itself such tentativeness, such insightfulness, might well lead to ontological despair. Yet acceptance of the worst does not prevent us from making the best of the worst. Up to now psychologists have not dealt with the remarkable ability of human beings to blend a tentative outlook with firm commitment to chosen values. The poet Tennyson perceived the point.

> There lives more faith in honest doubt,
> Believe me, than in half the creeds.

A commitment is, as Pascal has said, a wager. One may lose it, but one may also win. Cardinal Newman warned us that our religion can never be a matter of certainty. It is at best a subjective condition of certitude which he defined as "probability supported by faith and love." Yet a mature religion, thus defined, can be infinitely sustaining and heroically motivating. Existentialism, whether theistic or atheistic, makes the same point. We have the freedom to commit ourselves to great causes with courage, even though we lack certainty. We can be at one and the same time half-sure and whole-hearted.

William James, probably America's greatest thinker, tried to teach us this lesson, but fifty years ago we were not ready for it. It is surely noteworthy that, writing as he did in a period of social stability, James saw clearly how ultimately uncertain are our foundations of value. Wealth, he saw was a false god, leading us into a national disease that has recently been called

"galloping consumption." The more we build up our material resources, the more we fear poverty. In religion, James knew, there was no certainty; yet, like Cardinal Newman, he recognized the constructive power of a mature religious commitment. Whatever ideal leads to long-range constructive consequences is psychologically sound. It is also pragmatically true. And who is to say that we have a test for truth more absolute than our own commitment in so far as it is validated by fruitful consequences?

Neither positivistic nor psychodynamic schools of thought allow for the fact that our psychological constitution permits both total tentativeness and total commitment. Such a paradox reminds us of the electron that is able to go in two opposite directions at the same time. Taken by itself tentativeness is disintegrative; commitment is integrative. Yet the blend seems to occur in personalities that we admire for their soundness and perspective. Presumably through teaching and guidance we may develop both attitudes in our youth.

Whenever the two attitudes coexist in a life we find important desirable by-products from the fusion. One is a deep sense of compassion for the lot of the human race in general and in each separate social encounter that marks our daily life. The other by-product is likewise graceful; it is the sense of humor. Humor requires the perspective of tentativeness, but also an underlying system of values that prevents laughter from souring into cynicism. As Meredith said, humor is a capacity to laugh at the things you love and still to love them.

RATIONALISM VS. IRRATIONALISM. The chief criticism made of existentialism is that it leads away from reason and exalts irrationalism. While this charge may apply to certain literary and theological trends in the existential movement I doubt that it jeopardizes the future of scientific psychology. The attitudes of tentativeness and commitment of which I speak are perfectly sound concepts—call them "intervening variables" if you wish. Indeed in so far as they reflect important states in human personality, and thus lead to improvement in understanding, prediction, and direction of human behavior, they are sounder scientific concepts than many of those we have been using.

And just what is rationalism? We venerate the ancient Greeks for their exaltation of human reason; and as psychologists we venerate Aristotle for asking the question, "What is man's place in nature." But Greek rationalism was broader than the limited, method-centered, scientism into which it has degenerated. The Greeks themselves saw a place for tentativeness and commitment within the scope of reason. The case is beautifully stated in an ancient inscription found somewhere on the coast of Greece:

> A shipwrecked sailor buried on this coast
> Bids you set sail.
> Full many a bark, when we were lost,
> Weathered the gale.

The dead sailor urges us to make the wager, take the risk, although we cannot be sure of coming through to our destination.

IMPLICATIONS FOR THEORY. What does all this mean in terms of psychological theory, and in terms of guidance? First of all it means that in order to achieve a more realistic image of man and his potentialities, we need to revise our current theories of learning and growth, of motivation and personality structure. Elsewhere (in *Pattern and Growth in Personality*, 1961) I have discussed some of the needed changes in detail, and so shall say only a few words about each.

The trouble with our current theories of learning is not so much that they are wrong, but that they are partial. They fit best the learning of animals and young children. The concepts of conditioning, reinforcement, identification, seem a bit hollow when the counselor tries to apply them to his work. They are not very helpful, for example, in explaining how a youth may learn both tentativeness of outlook and firmness of commitment. Supplementary theories in terms of organizational, biographical, and propriate learning are needed.

Except in the sense of physical maturation the concept of *growth* scarcely exists in psychology at all. Nor will it have its proper place until we have agreed upon normative standards for the maturity of personality. Up to now normative problems, except in the sense of statistical norms, are much neglected.

As for motivation and personality structure psychologists are in a state of turmoil and disagreement. That the past stages of a life do not fully explain the motivational "go" of the present, I for one am firmly convinced. Therefore we need a concept (*functional autonomy*, I think will do) to represent that portion of a life that is oriented toward the future and not toward the past. Also we need a theory of personal structure (of *personal dispositions*) to represent the important cleavages and foci of a given, concrete

personality. Such a theory will, I am convinced, carry us much further than a conception of uniform variables to which every client is forcibly ordered, whether we call these variables factors, needs, dimensions, or common traits.

Most of all we need to surrender the models that would compress human personality into the routine homeostatic situation that we find in quasi-closed systems. Human personality is a wide-open system, responsive to tangible and intangible culture, on the look-out for new ideas, and capable of asking an altogether new type of question—asked by no other creature in nature, viz., "Who am I?"

There are, I am glad to say, many psychologists who feel as strongly as I that these various types of improvement need to be made before the counselor will have a fully fashioned science of psychology to undergird his practice.

IMPLICATIONS FOR GUIDANCE. Guidance is not a matter of gimmicks, nor of rules of thumb. A guide, like a philosopher and friend, is a person who loves wisdom and loves his fellow men. True, he has skills to mark him off from the professional philosopher or the untrained friend. To some extent the counselor's present-day skills are useful. Standard tests and measurements are helpful; so too achievement records and focused interviews. Most of our devices come from researches conducted under the positivistic outlook, or (in the case of projective techniques) under the psychodynamic. While many of them are serviceable I look forward to the invention of new instruments still better suited to the study of the central or propriate aspects of single personalities.

Most important, of course, are the spectacles the counselor wears. The image should no longer be borrowed from the tradition of simple naïve reactivism. Just as centimeters, grams, seconds are outmoded in modern physics so too are simple stimulus-response connections in modern psychology. In psychology, even more than in physics, we need theory capable of dealing with fluid becoming.

The plain fact is that man is more than a reactive being, more even than a reactive being in depth. If he were comfortably fixed at these levels we could with confidence apply a uniform stencil in studying his nature. But the life process is no less paradoxical than the processes of modern physics. How can one deal with space that is both finite and unbounded, with light that is both wave and particle, with electrons that pass from orbit to orbit without traversing the space between? Similarly, a human person is both structure and process, a being both biological and noetic, a being who changes his identity even while he retains it. Small wonder that at the end of his life, the famous physicist, P. W. Bridgman, said, "The structure of nature may eventually be such that our processes of thought do not correspond to it sufficiently to permit us to think about it at all."

We need not, I think, be quite so pessimistic. Our first duty is to affirm a new and wider rationalism; that is to say, to redouble our efforts to find a more adequate image of man to guide us in fashioning a more suitable science of personality.

And what about our personal attitudes as guidance specialists or teachers? Should we not cultivate the same twin virtues that we recommend to client and student: tentativeness and commitment? We can hold our own present image of man on trial, reviewing our own past psychological training in critical perspective. At the same time we can embrace courageously our task of interpreting the wisdom of the past in such a way as to make it most available to the youthful personality who is facing an uncertain, but not uninviting, future. Tentativeness and commitment are twin ideals for both counselor and client. To my mind they lie at the heart and center of guidance, of teaching, and of living.

2 / BEHAVIORISM AT FIFTY / B. F. SKINNER*

BEHAVIORISM, WITH AN ACCENT ON the last syllable, is not the scientific study of behavior but a philosophy of science concerned with the subject matter and methods of psychology. If psychology is a science of mental life —of the mind, of conscious experience—then it must develop and defend a special methodology, which it has not yet done successfully. If it is, on the other hand, a science of the behavior of organisms, human or otherwise, then it is part of biology, a natural science for which tested and highly successful methods are available. The basic issue is not the nature of the stuff of which the world is made, or whether it is made of one stuff or two, but rather the dimensions of the things studied by psychology and the methods relevant to them.

Mentalistic or psychic explanations of human behavior almost certainly originated in primitive animism. When a man dreamed of being at a distant place in spite of incontrovertible evidence that he had stayed in his bed, it was easy to conclude that some part of him had actually left his body. A particularly vivid memory or a hallucination could be explained in the same way. The theory of an invisible, detachable self eventually proved useful for other purposes. It seemed to explain unexpected or abnormal episodes, even to the person behaving in an exceptional way because he was thus "possessed." It

*B. F. Skinner, Behaviorism at fifty, Science, 1963, 140, 3570, 951-958. Copyright 1963 by the American Association for the Advancement of Science. Reprinted with abridgement by permission. The author is Edgar Pierce Professor of Psychology at Harvard University, Cambridge, Mass. This paper . . . [was] published in Behaviorism and Phenomenology: Contrasting Bases for Modern Psychology, T. W. Wann, Ed., by the University of Chicago Press, 1964. It was presented at a symposium on behaviorism and phenomenology held at Rice University in March 1963. An earlier version was given as the R. M. Elliott lecture at the University of Minnesota in December 1962.

also served to explain the inexplicable. An organism as complex as man often seems to behave capriciously. It is tempting to attribute the visible behavior to another organism inside—to a little man or homunculus. The wishes of the little man become the acts of the man observed by his fellows. The inner idea is put into outer words. Inner feelings find outward expression. The explanation is satisfying, of course, only so long as the behavior of the homunculus can be neglected.

Primitive origins are not necessarily to be held against an explanatory principle, but the little man is still with us in relatively primitive form. He was recently the hero of a television program called "Gateways to the Mind," one of a series of educational films sponsored by Bell Telephone Laboratories and written with the help of a distinguished panel of scientists. The viewer learned, from animated cartoons, that when a man's finger is pricked, electrical impulses resembling flashes of lightning run up the afferent nerves and appear on a television screen in the brain. The little man wakes up, sees the flashing screen, reaches out, and pulls a lever. More flashes of lightning go down the nerves to the muscles, which then contract, as the finger is pulled away from the threatening stimulus. The behavior of the homunculus was, of course, not explained. An explanation would presumably require another film. And it, in turn, another.

The same pattern of explanation is invoked when we are told that the behavior of a delinquent is the result of a disordered personality, or that the vagaries of a man under analysis are due to conflicts among his superego, ego, and id. Nor can we escape from primitive features by breaking the little man into pieces and dealing with his wishes, cognitions, motives, and so on, bit by bit. The objection is not that these things are mental but that they offer no real explanation and stand in the way of a more effective analysis.

It has been about 50 years since the behavioristic objection to this practice was first clearly stated, and it has been about 30 years since it has been very much discussed. A whole generation of psychologists has grown up without really coming into contact with the issue. Almost all current textbooks compromise: rather than risk a loss of adoptions, they define psychology as the science of behavior *and* mental life. Meanwhile the older view has continued to receive strong support from areas in which there has been no comparable attempt at methodological reform. During this period, however, an effective

experimental science of behavior has emerged. Much of what it has discovered bears on the basic issue. A restatement of radical behaviorism would therefore seem to be in order.

EXPLAINING THE MIND

A rough history of the idea is not hard to trace.
· · · · · · · · · · · · · ·
The central argument [was] that behavior which seemed to be the product of mental activity could be explained in other ways. In any case, the introspectionists were prepared to challenge it. As late as 1883 Francis Galton could write (1): "Many persons, especially women and intelligent children, take pleasure in introspection, and strive their very best to explain their mental processes." But introspection was already being taken seriously. The concept of a science of mind in which mental events obeyed mental laws had led to the development of psychophysical methods and to the accumulation of facts which seemed to bar the extension of the principle of parsimony. What might hold for animals did not hold for men, because men could *see* their mental processes.

Curiously enough, part of the answer was supplied by the psychoanalysts, who insisted that although a man might be able to see some of his mental life, he could not see all of it. The kind of thoughts Freud called unconscious took place without the knowledge of the thinker. From an association, verbal slip, or dream it could be shown that a person must have responded to a passing stimulus although he could not tell you that he had done so. More complex thought processes, including problem solving and verbal play, could also go on without the thinker's knowledge. Freud had devised, and he never abandoned faith in, one of the most elaborate mental apparatuses of all time. He nevertheless contributed to the behavioristic argument by showing that mental activity did not, at least, *require* consciousness. His proofs that thinking had occurred without introspective recognition were, indeed, clearly in the spirit of Lloyd Morgan. They were operational analyses of mental life—even though, for Freud, only the unconscious part of it. Experimental evidence pointing in the same direction soon began to accumulate.

But that was not the whole answer. What about the part of mental life which a man can see? It is a difficult question, no matter what one's point of view, partly because it raises the question of what "seeing" means and partly because the events seen are private. The fact of privacy cannot, of course, be questioned. Each person is in special contact with a small part of the universe enclosed within his own skin. To take a noncontroversial example, he is uniquely subject to certain kinds of proprioceptive and interoceptive stimulation. Though two people may in some sense be said to see the same light or hear the same sound, they cannot feel the same distension of a bile duct or the same bruised muscle. (When privacy is invaded with scientific instruments, the form of stimulation is changed; the scales read by the scientist are not the private events themselves)

Mentalistic psychologists insist that there are other kinds of events uniquely accessible to the owner of the skin within which they occur which lack the physical dimensions of proprioceptive or interoceptive stimuli. They are as different from physical events as colors are from wavelengths of light. There are even better reasons, therefore, why two people cannot suffer each other's toothaches, recall each other's memories, or share each other's happiness. The importance assigned to this kind of world varies. For some, it is the only world there is. For others, it is the only part of the world which can be directly known. For still others, it is a special part of what can be known. In any case, the problem of how one knows about the subjective world of another must be faced. Apart from the question of what "knowing" means, the problem is one of accessibility.

PUBLIC AND PRIVATE EVENTS

One solution, often regarded as behavioristic, is to grant the distinction between public and private events and rule the latter out of scientific consideration. This is a congenial solution for those to whom scientific truth is a matter of convention or agreement among observers. It is essentially the line taken by logical positivism. . . .

. . . [It] is significant that P. W. Bridgman's physical operationism could not save him from an extreme solipsism even within physical science itself. Though he insisted that he was not a solipsist, he was never able to reconcile seemingly public physical knowledge with the private world of the scientist (2). Applied to psychological problems, operationism has been no more successful. We may recognize the restrictions imposed by the operations through which we can know of the existence of properties of subjective events, but the operations cannot be identified with the events themselves.

S. S. Stevens has applied Bridgman's principle to psychology, not to decide whether subjective events exist, but to determine the extent to which we can deal with them scientifically (3).

. . . .

If [as will be maintained below] seeing does not require the presence of things seen, we need not be concerned about certain mental processes said to be involved in the construction of such things—images, memories, and dreams, for example. We may regard a dream not as a display of things seen by the dreamer but simply as the behavior of seeing. At no time during a day-dream, for example, should we expect to find within the organism anything which corresponds to the external stimuli present when the dreamer first acquired the behavior in which he is now engaged. In simple recall we need not suppose that we wander through some storehouse of memory until we find an object which we then contemplate. Instead of assuming that we begin with a tendency to *recognize* such an object once it is found, it is simpler to assume that we begin with a tendency to *see* it. Techniques of self-management which facilitate recall—for example, the use of mnemonic devices—can be formulated as ways of strengthening behavior rather than of creating objects to be seen. Freud dramatized the issue with respect to dreaming when asleep in his concept of dreamwork—an activity in which some part of the dreamer played the role of a theatrical producer while another part sat in the audience. If a dream is, indeed, something seen, then we must suppose that it is wrought as such, but if it is simply the behavior of seeing, the dreamwork may be dropped from the analysis. It took man a long time to understand that when he dreamed of a wolf, no wolf was actually there. It has taken him much longer to understand that not even a representation of a wolf is there.

Eye movements which appear to be associated with dreaming are in accord with this interpretation, since it is not likely that the dreamer is actually watching a dream on the undersides of his eyelids. When memories are aroused by electrical stimulation of the brain, as in the work of Wilder Penfield, it is also simpler to assume that it is the behavior of seeing, hearing, and so on which is aroused than that it is some copy of early environmental events which the subject then looks at or listens to. Behavior similar to the responses to the original events must be assumed in both cases—the subject sees or hears—but the reproduction of the events seen or heard is a needless complication. The familiar process of response chaining is available to account for the serial character of the behavior of remembering, but the serial linkage of stored experiences (suggesting engrams in the form of sound films) demands a new mechanism.

The heart of the behavioristic position on conscious experience may be summed up in this way: seeing does not imply something seen. We acquire the behavior of seeing under stimulation from actual objects, but it may occur in the absence of these objects under the control of other variables. (So far as the world within the skin is concerned, it always occurs in the absence of such objects.) We also acquire the behavior of seeing-that-we-are-seeing when we are seeing actual objects, but it may also occur in their absence.

To question the reality or the nature of the things seen in conscious experience is not to question the value of introspective psychology or its methods. Current problems in sensation are mainly concerned with the physiological function of receptors and associated neural mechanisms. Problems in perception are, at the moment, less intimately related to specific mechanisms, but the trend appears to be in the same direction. So far as behavior is concerned, both sensation and perception may be analyzed as forms of stimulus control. The subject need not be regarded as observing or evaluating conscious experiences. Apparent anomalies of stimulus control which are now explained by appealing to a psychophysical relation or to the laws of perception may be studied in their own right. It is, after all, no real solution to attribute them to the slippage inherent in converting a physical stimulus into a subjective experience.

The experimental analysis of behavior has a little more to say on this subject. Its techniques have recently been extended to what might be called the psychophysics of lower organisms. Blough's adaption of the Békésy technique— for example, in determining the spectral sensitivity of pigeons and monkeys—yields sensory data comparable with the reports of a trained observer (4). Herrnstein and van Sommers have recently developed a procedure in which pigeons "bisect sensory intervals" (5). It is tempting to describe these procedures by saying that investigators have found ways to get nonverbal organisms to describe their sensations. The fact is that a form of stimulus control has been investigated without using a repertoire of self-observation or, rather, by constructing a special repertoire the nature and origin of which are clearly understood. Rather than describe such experiments with the terminology of introspection, we may formulate them in their proper place in an experimental analysis. The behavior of the observer in the traditional psychophysical experiment may then be reinterpreted accordingly.

MENTAL WAY STATIONS

So much for "conscious content," the classical problem in mentalistic philosophies. There are other mental states or processes to be taken into account. Moods, cognitions, and expectancies, for example, are also examined introspectively, and descriptions are used in psychological formulations. The conditions under which descriptive repertories are set up are much less successfully controlled. Terms describing sensations and images are taught by manipulating discriminative stimuli—a relatively amenable class of variables. The remaining kinds of mental events are related to such operations as deprivation and satiation, emotional stimulation, and various schedules of reinforcement. The difficulties they present to the verbal community are suggested by the fact that there is no psychophysics of mental states of this sort. That fact has not inhibited their use in explanatory systems.

In an experimental analysis, the relation between a property of behavior and an operation performed upon the organism is studied directly. Traditional mentalistic formulations, however, emphasize certain way stations. Where an experimental analysis might examine the effect of punishment on behavior, a mentalistic psychology will be concerned first with the effect of punishment in generating feelings of anxiety and then with the effect of anxiety on behavior. The mental state seems to bridge the gap between dependent and independent variables, and a mentalistic interpretation is particularly attractive when these are separated by long periods of time—when, for example, the punishment occurs in childhood and the effect appears in the behavior of the adult.

Mentalistic way stations are popular. In a demonstration experiment, a hungry pigeon was conditioned to turn around in a clockwise direction. A final, smoothly executed pattern of behavior was shaped by reinforcing successive approximations with food. Students who had watched the demonstration were asked to write an account of what they had seen. Their responses included the following: (i) the organism was conditioned to *expect* reinforcement for the right kind of behavior; (ii) the pigeon walked around, *hoping* that something would bring the food back again; (iii) the pigeon *observed* that a certain behavior seemed to produce a particular result; (iv) the pigeon *felt* that food would be given it because of its action; and (v) the bird came to *associate* his action with the click of the food dispenser. The observed facts could be stated, respectively, as follows: (i) the organism was reinforced *when* its behavior was of a given kind; (ii) the pigeon walked around *until* the food container again appeared; (iii) a certain behavior *produced* a particular result; (iv) food was given to the pigeon *when* it acted in a given way; and (v) the click of the food-dispenser *was temporally related* to the bird's action. These statements describe the contingencies of reinforcement. The expressions "expect," "hope," "observe," "feel," and "associate" go beyond them to identify effects on the pigeon. The effect actually observed was clear enough: the pigeon turned more skillfully and more frequently. But that was not the effect reported by the students. (If pressed, they would doubtless have said that the pigeon turned more skillfully and more frequently *because* it expected, hoped, and felt that if it did so food would appear.)

The events reported by the students were observed, if at all, in their own behavior. They were describing what *they* would have expected, felt, and hoped for under similar circumstances. But they were able to do so only because a verbal community had brought relevant terms under the control of certain stimuli, and this had been done when the community had access only to the kinds of public information available to the students in the demonstration. Whatever the students knew about themselves which permitted them to infer comparable events in the pigeon must have been learned from a verbal community which saw no more of their behavior than they had seen of the pigeon's. Private stimuli may have entered into the control of their self-descriptive repertoires, but the readiness with which they applied these repertoires to the pigeon indicates that external stimuli had remained important. The extraordinary strength of a mentalistic interpretation is really a sort of proof that, in describing a private way station, one is to a considerable extent making use of public information.

The mental way station is often accepted as a terminal datum, however. When a man must be trained to discriminate between different planes, ships, and so on, it is tempting to stop at the point at which he can be said to *identify* such objects. It is implied that if he can identify an object he can name it, label it, describe it, or act appropriately in some other way. In the training process he always behaves in one of these ways; no way station called "identification" appears in practice or need appear in theory. (Any discussion of the discriminative behavior generated by the verbal environment to permit a person to examine the content of his consciousness must be qualified accordingly.)

Cognitive theories stop at way stations where the mental action is usually somewhat more complex than identification. For example, a subject is said to *know* who and where he is, what something is, or what has happened or is going to happen, regardless of the forms of behavior through which this knowledge was set up or which may now testify to its existence. Similarly, in accounting for verbal behavior, a listener or reader is said to understand the *meaning* of a passage although the actual changes brought about by listening to or reading the passage are not specified. In the same way, schedules of reinforcement are sometimes studied simply for their effects on the *expectations* of the organism exposed to them, without discussion of the implied relation between expectation and action. Recall, inference, and reasoning may be formulated only to the point at which an experience is remembered or a conclusion is reached, behavioral manifestations being ignored. In practice the investigator always carries through to some response, if only a response of self-description.

On the other hand, mental states are often studied as causes of action. A speaker thinks of something to say before saying it, and this explains what he says, although the sources of his thoughts may not be examined. An unusual act is called "impulsive," without further inquiry into the origin of the unusual impulse. A behavioral maladjustment shows anxiety, but the source of the anxiety is neglected. One salivates upon seeing a lemon because it reminds one of a sour taste, but why it does so is not specified. The formulation leads directly to a technology based on the manipulation of mental states. To change a man's voting behavior we change his opinions, to induce him to act we strengthen his beliefs, to make him eat we make him feel hungry, to prevent wars we reduce warlike tensions in the minds of men, to effect psychotherapy we alter troublesome mental states, and so on. In practice, all these ways of changing a man's mind reduce to manipulating his environment, verbal or otherwise.

In many cases we can reconstruct a complete causal chain by identifying the mental state which is the effect of an environmental variable with the mental state which is the cause of action. But this is not always enough. In traditional mentalistic philosophies various things happen at the way station which alter the relation between the terminal events. The effect of the psychophysical function and the laws of perception in distorting the physical stimulus before it reaches the way station has already been mentioned. Once the mental stage is reached, other effects are said to occur. Mental states alter each other. A painful memory may never affect behavior, or it may affect it an unexpected way if another mental state succeeds in repressing it. Conflicting variables may be reconciled before they have an effect on behavior if the subject engages in mental action called "making a decision." Dissonant cognitions generated by conflicting conditions of reinforcement will not be reflected in behavior if the subject can "persuade himself" that one condition was actually of a different magnitude or kind. These disturbances in simple causal linkages between environment and behavior can be formulated and studied experimentally as interactions among variables, but the possibility has not been fully exploited, and the effects still provide a formidable stronghold for mentalistic theories designed to bridge the gap between dependent and independent variables.

METHODOLOGICAL OBJECTIONS

The behavioristic argument is nevertheless still valid. We may object, first, to the predilection for unfinished causal sequences. A disturbance in behavior is not explained by relating it to felt anxiety until the anxiety has in turn been explained. An action is not explained by attributing it to expectations until the expectations have in turn been accounted for. Complete causal sequences might, of course, include references to way stations, but the fact is that the way station generally interrupts the account in one direction or the other. For example, there must be thousands of instances in the psychoanalytic literature in which a thought or memory is said to have been relegated to the unconscious because it was painful or intolerable, but the percentage of instances in which even the most casual suggestion is offered as to why it was painful or intolerable must be very small. Perhaps explanations *could* have been offered, but

the practice has discouraged the completion of the causal sequence.

A second objection is that a preoccupation with mental way stations burdens a science of behavior with all the problems raised by the limitations and inaccuracies of self-descriptive repertoires. We need not take the extreme position that mediating events or any data about them obtained through introspection must be ruled out of consideration, but we should certainly welcome other ways of treating the data more satisfactorily. Independent variables change the behaving organism, often in ways which persist for many years, and such changes affect subsequent behavior. The subject may be able to describe some of these intervening states in useful ways, either before or after they have affected behavior. On the other hand, behavior may be extensively modified by variables of which, and of the effect of which, the subject is never aware. So far as we know, self-descriptive responses do not alter controlling relationships. If a severe punishment is less effective than a mild one, this is not because it cannot be "kept in mind." (Certain behaviors involved in self-management, such as reviewing a history of punishment, may alter behavior, but they do so by introducing other variables rather than by changing a given relation.)

Perhaps the most serious objection concerns the order of events. Observation of one's own behavior necessarily follows the behavior. Responses which seem to be describing intervening states alone may embrace behavioral effects. "I am hungry" may describe, in part, the strength of the speaker's ongoing ingestive behavior. "I was hungrier than I thought" seems particularly to describe behavior rather than an intervening, possibly causal, state. More serious examples of a possibly mistaken order are to be found in theories of psychotherapy. Before asserting that the release of a repressed wish has a therapeutic effect on behavior, or that when one knows why he is neurotically ill he will recover, we should consider the plausible alternative that a change in behavior resulting from therapy has made it possible for the subject to recall a repressed wish or to understand his illness.

A final objection is that way stations are so often simply invented. It is too easy to say that someone does something "because he likes to do it," or that he does one thing rather than another "because he has made a choice."

The importance of behaviorism as a philosophy of science naturally declines as a scientific analysis becomes more powerful because there is then less need to use data in the form of self-description. The mentalism which survives in the fields of sensation and perception will disappear as alternative techniques prove their value in analyzing stimulus control, and similar changes may be anticipated elsewhere. Cognitive psychologists and others still try to circumvent the explicit control of variables by describing contingencies of reinforcement to their subjects in "instructions." They also try to dispense with recording behavior in a form from which probability of response can be estimated by asking their subjects to evaluate their tendencies to respond. But a person rarely responds to a description of contingencies as he would respond under direct exposure to them, nor can he accurately predict his rate of responding, particularly the course of the subtle changes in rate which are a commonplace in the experimental analysis of behavior. These attempts to short-circuit an experimental analysis can no longer be justified on grounds of expedience, and there are many reasons for abandoning them. Much remains to be done, however, before the facts to which they are currently applied can be said to be adequately understood.

BEHAVIORISM AND BIOLOGY

Elsewhere, the scientific study of man has scarcely recognized the need for reform. The biologist, for example, begins with a certain advantage in studying the behaving organism, for the structures he analyzes have an evident physical status. The nervous system is somehow earthier than the behavior for which it is largely responsible. Philosophers and psychologists alike have from time to time sought escape from mentalism in physiology. When a man sees red, he may be seeing the physiological effect of a red stimulus; when he merely imagines red, he may be seeing the same effect re-aroused. Psychophysical and perceptual distortions may be wrought by physiological processes. What a man feels as anxiety may be autonomic reactions to threatening stimuli. And so on. This may solve the minor problem of the nature of subjective experience, but it does not solve any of the methodological problems with which behaviorism is most seriously concerned. A physiological translation of mentalistic terms may reassure those who want to avoid dualism, but inadequacies in the formulation survive translation.

When writing about the behavior of organisms, biologists tend to be more mentalistic then psychologists. Adrian could not understand how a nerve impulse could cause a thought. The author of a recent article on the visual space sense in *Science* (6) asserts that "the final event in the chain from the retina to the brain is a psychic experience." Another investigator reports research on "the brain and its contained mind." Pharmacologists study the "psychotropic" drugs. Psychosomatic medicine insists on the influence of mind over matter. And psychologists join their physiological colleagues in looking for feelings, emotions, drives, and the pleasurable aspects of positive reinforcement in the brain.

The facts uncovered in such research are important, both for their own sake and for their bearing on behavior. The physiologist studies structures and processes without which behavior could not occur. He is in a position to supply a "reductionist" explanation beyond the reach of an analysis which confines itself to terminal variables. He cannot do this well, however, so long as he accepts traditional mentalistic formulations. Only an experimental analysis of behavior will define his task in optimal terms. The point is demonstrated by recent research in psychopharmacology. When the behavioral drugs first began to attract attention, they were studied with impromptu techniques based on self-observation, usually designed to quantify subjective reports. Eventually the methods of an experimental analysis proved their value in generating reproducible segments of behavior upon which the effects of drugs could be observed and in terms of which they could be effectively defined and classified. For the same reasons, brain physiology will move forward more rapidly when it recognizes that its role is to account for the mediation of behavior rather than of mind.

BEHAVIORISM IN THE SOCIAL SCIENCES

There is also still a need for behaviorism in the social sciences, where psychology has long been used for purposes of explanation. Economics has had its economic man. Political science has considered man as a political animal. Parts of anthropology and sociology have found a place for psychoanalysis. The relevance of psychology in linguistics has been debated for more than half a century. Studies of scientific method have oscillated between logical and empirical analyses. In all these fields, "psychologizing" has often had disappointing results and has frequently been rejected in favor of an extreme formalism which emphasizes objective facts. Economics confines itself to its own abundant data. Political scientists limit themselves to whatever may be studied with a few empirical tools and techniques, and confine themselves, when they deal with theory, to formalistic analyses of political structures. A strong structuralist movement is evident in sociology. Linguistics emphasizes formal analyses of semantics and grammar.

Straight-laced commitments to pure description and formal analysis appear to leave no place for explanatory principles, and the shortcoming is often blamed on the exclusion of mental activities. For example, participants at a recent symposium on "The Limits of Behavioralism in Political Science" (7) complained of a neglect of subjective experience, ideas, motives, feelings, attitudes, values, and so on. This is reminiscent of attacks on behaviorism. In any case, it shows the same misunderstanding of the scope of a behavioral analysis. In its extension to the social sciences, as in psychology proper, behaviorism means more than a commitment to objective measurement. No entity or process which has any useful explanatory force is to be rejected on the ground that it is subjective or mental. The data which have made it important must, however, be studied and formulated in effective ways. The assignment is well within the scope of an experimental analysis of behav-

ior, which thus offers a promising alternative to a commitment to pure description on the one hand and an appeal to mentalistic theories on the other. To extend behaviorism as a philosophy of science to the study of political and economic behavior, of the behavior of people in groups, of people speaking and listening, teaching and learning—this is not "psychologizing" in the traditional sense. It is simply the application of a tested formula to important parts of the field of human behavior.

REFERENCES AND NOTES

1. F. GALTON, *Inquiries into Human Faculty* (London, 1883), Everyman ed., p. 60.
2. P. W. BRIDGMAN, *The Way Things Are* (Harvard Univ. Press, Cambridge, Mass., 1959).
3. S. S. STEVENS, *Am. J. Psychol.* 47, 323 (1935).
4. D. S. BLOUGH, *J. Comp. Physiol. Psychol.* 49, 425 (1956); —— and A. M. Schrier, *Science* 139, 493 (1963).
5. R. T. HERRNSTEIN and P. VAN SOMMERS, *Science* 135, 40 (1962).
6. K. N. OGLE, *ibid.*, p. 763.
7. *The Limits of Behavioralism in Political Science* (Am. Acad. Political and Social Sci., Philadelphia, 1962).

3/FREUD AND THE IMAGE OF
MAN[1]/ JEROME S. BRUNER*

BY THE DAWN OF THE SIXTH CENTURY before Christ, the Greek physicist-philosophers had formulated a conception of the physical world as a unitary material phenomenon. The Ionics had set forth a conception of matter as fundamental substance, transformation of which accounted for the myriad forms and substances of the physical world. Anaximander was subtle enough to recognize that matter must be viewed as a generalized substance, free of any particular sensuous properties. Air, iron, water, or bone were only elaborated forms, derived from a more general stuff. Since that time, the phenomena of the physical world have been conceived as continuous and monistic, as governed by the common laws of matter. The view was a bold one, bold in the sense of running counter to the immediate testimony of the senses. It has served as an axiomatic basis of physics for more than two millenia. The bold view eventually became the obvious view, and it gave shape to our common understanding of the physical world. Even the alchemists rested their case upon this doctrine of material continuity and, indeed, had they known about neutron bombardment, they might even have hit upon the proper philosopher's stone.

The good fortune of the physicist—and these matters are always relative, for the material monism of physics may have impeded nineteenth century thinking and delayed insights into the nature of complementarity in modern physical theory—this early good fortune or happy insight has no counterpart in the sciences of man. Lawful continuity between man and the animal kingdom, between dreams and unreason on one side and waking rationality on the other, between madness and sanity, between consciousness and unconsciousness, between the mind of the child and the adult mind, between primitive and civilized man—each of these has been a cherished discontinuity preserved in doctrinal canons. There were voices in each gen-

eration, to be sure, urging the exploration of continuities. Anaximander had a passing good approximation to a theory of evolution based on natural selection; Cornelius Agrippa offered a plausible theory of the continuity of mental health and disease in terms of bottled-up sexuality. But Anaximander did not prevail against Greek conceptions of man's creation nor Cornelius Agrippa against the demonopathy of the *Malleus Maleficarum*. Neither in establishing the continuity between the varied states of man nor in pursuing the continuity between man and animal was there conspicuous success until the nineteenth century.

I need not insist upon the social, ethical, and political significance of this image, for it is patent that the view one takes of man affects profoundly one's standard of the humanly possible. And it is in the light of such a standard that we establish our laws, set our aspirations for learning, and judge the fitness of men's acts. It is no surprise, then, that those who govern must perforce be jealous guardians of man's ideas about man, for the structure of government rests upon an uneasy consensus about human nature and human wants. The idea of man is of the order of *res publica*, and by virtue of its public status, it is an idea that is not subject to change without public debate. The behavioral scientist, as some nowadays insist on calling him, may propose, but it is the society at large that disposes. Nor is it simply a matter of public concern. For man as individual has a deep and emotional investment in his image of himself. If we have learned anything in the last half-century of psychology, it is that man has powerful and exquisite capacities for defending himself against violations of his cherished self-image. This is not to say that Western man has not persistently asked: "What is man that thou art mindful of him?" It is only that the question, when pressed, brings us to the edge of anxiety where inquiry is no longer free.

Two figures stand out massively as the architects of our present-day conception of man: Darwin and Freud. Freud's was the more daring, the more revolutionary, and in a deep sense, the

---

[1] This article also appeared in the July 1956 *Partisan Review* and was read earlier in the year at the Conference on Science and the Modern World View under the auspices of the American Academy of Arts and Science.

* Jerome S. Bruner, Freud and the image of man, *The American Psychologist*, 1956, *11*, 463-466. Reprinted by permission.

more poetic insight. But Freud is inconceivable without Darwin. It is both timely and perhaps historically just to center our inquiry on Freud's contribution to the modern image of man. Darwin I shall treat as a necessary condition for Freud and for his success, recognizing, of course, that this is a form of psychological license. Not only is it the centenary of Freud's birth; it is also a year in which the current of popular thought expressed in commemoration of the date quickens one's awareness of Freud's impact on our times.

Rear-guard fundamentalism did not require a Darwin to slay it in an age of technology. He helped, but this contribution was trivial in comparison with another. What Darwin had done was to propose a set of principles unified around the conception that all organic species had their origins and took their form from a common set of circumstances—the requirements of biological survival. All living creatures were on a common footing. When the post-Darwin era of exaggeration had passed and religious literalism had abated into a new nominalism, what remained was a broad, orderly, and unitary conception of organic nature, a vast continuity from the monocellular protozoans to man. Biology had at last found its unifying principle in the doctrine of evolution. Man was not unique but the inheritor of an organic legacy.

As the summit of an evolutionary process, man could still view himself with smug satisfaction, indeed proclaim that God or Nature had shown a persistent wisdom in its effort to produce a final, perfect product. It remained for Freud to present the image of man as the unfinished product of nature: struggling against unreason, impelled by driving inner vicissitudes and urges that had to be contained if man were to live in society, host alike to seeds of madness and majesty, never fully free from an infancy anything but innocent. What Freud was proposing was that man at best and man at worst is subject to a common set of explanations: good and evil grow from a common process.

Freud was strangely yet appropriately fitted for his role as architect of a new conception of man. We must pause to examine his qualifications, for the image of man that he created was in no small measure founded on his painfully achieved image of himself and of his times. We are concerned not so much with his psychodynamics, but with the intellectual traditions he embodies. A child of his century's materialism, he was wedded to the determinism and the classical physicalism of 19th-century physiology

so boldly represented by Helmholtz. Indeed, the young Freud's devotion to the exploration of anatomical structures was a measure of the strength of this inheritance. But at the same time, as both Lionel Trilling and W. H. Auden have recognized with much sensitivity, there was a deep current of romanticism in Freud—a sense of the role of impulse, of the drama of life, of the power of symbolism, of ways of knowing that were more poetic than rational in spirit, of the poet's cultural alienation. It was perhaps this romantic's sense of drama that led to his gullibility about parental seduction and to his generous susceptibility to the fallacy of the dramatic instance.

Freud also embodies two traditions almost as antithetical as romanticism and nineteenth century scientism. He was profoundly a Jew, not in a doctrinal sense but in his conception of morality, in his love of the skeptical play of reason, in his distrust of illusion, in the form of his prophetic talent, even in his conception of mature eroticism. His prophetic talent was antithetic to a Utopianism either of innocence or of social control. Nor did it lead to a counsel of renunciation. Free oneself of illusion, of neurotic infantilism, and "the soft voice of intellect" would prevail. Wisdom for Freud was neither doctrine nor formula, but the achievement of maturity. The patient who is cured is the one who is now free enough of neurosis to decide intelligently about his own destiny. As for his conception of mature love, it has always seemed to me that its blend of tenderness and sensuality combined the uxorious imagery of the Chassidic tradition and the sensual quality of the Song of Songs. And might it not have been Freud rather than a commentator of the Haftorahs who said, "In children, it was taught, God gives humanity a chance to make good its mistakes." For the modern trend of permissiveness toward children is surely a feature of the Freudian legacy, [In actuality, the respects in which Freudian writers have advocated indulgence of children are balanced by others in which they have urged parental firmness. If Freudian pronouncements gave rise to excessive leniency it is generally because they were misinterpreted. Editors' comment.]

But for all the Hebraic quality, Freud is also in the classical tradition—combining the Stoics and the great Greek dramatists. For Freud as for the Stoics, there is no possibility of man disobeying the laws of nature. And yet, it is in this lawlessness that for him the human drama inheres. His love for Greek drama and his use of it in his formulation are patent. The sense of the human tragedy, the inevitable working out of the human plight—these are the hallmarks of Freud's case histories. When Freud, the tragic dramatist, becomes a therapist, it is not to intervene as a directive authority. The therapist enters the drama of the patient's life, makes possible a play within a play, the transference,[Ed] and when the patient has "worked through" and understood the drama, he has achieved the wisdom necessary for freedom. Again, like the Stoics, it is in the recognition of one's own nature and in the acceptance of the laws that govern it that the good life is to be found.

Freud's contribution lies in the continuities of which he made us aware. The first of these is the continuity of organic lawfulness. Accident in human affairs was no more to be brooked as "explanation" than accident in nature. The basis for accepting such an "obvious" proposition had, of course, been well prepared by a burgeoning 19th-century scientific naturalism. It remained for Freud to extend naturalistic explanation to the heart of human affairs. The *Psychopathology of Everyday Life* is not one of Freud's deeper works, but "the Freudian slip" has contributed more to the common acceptance of lawfulness in human behavior than perhaps any of the more rigorous and academic formulations from Wundt to the present. The forgotten lunch engagement, the slip of the tongue, the barked shin could no longer be dismissed as accident. Why Freud should have succeeded where novelists, philosophers, and academic psychologists had failed we will consider in a moment.

Freud's extension of Darwinian doctrine beyond Haeckel's theorem that ontogeny recapitulates phylogeny is another contribution to continuity. It is the conception that in the

Ed *Transference. Misinterpretations of a therapist's statements or actions, or other misperceptions of the therapist on the part of a psychotherapeutic patient, arising from the tendency to react to the therapist as though he were some other person important in the patient's emotional life. The study by therapist and patient of these perceptual distortions is one of the ways in which patients undergoing some kinds of psychotherapy are helped to understand and control their proclivities to perceive certain people inaccurately and to behave inappropriately. The corresponding term "counter-transference" refers to distortions of the therapist about the patient. For instance, a therapist may at times respond emotionally to a female patient as though she were his daughter, sister, or mother. The well-trained therapist has become adept at noticing his own tendencies to distort. As a result, the intrusion of his personal needs upon his professional work can be minimal.*

human mind, the primitive, infantile, and archaic exist side by side with the civilized and evolved.

Where animals are concerned we hold the view that the most highly developed have arisen from the lowest. . . . In the realm of mind, on the other hand, the primitive type is so commonly preserved alongside the transformations which have developed out of it that it is superfluous to give instances in proof of it. When this happens, it is usually the result of a bifurcation in development. One quantitative part of an attitude or an impulse has survived unchanged while another has undergone further development. This brings us very close to the more general problem of conservation in the mind. . . . Since the time when we recognized the error of supposing that ordinary forgetting signified destruction or annihilation of the memory-trace, we have been inclined to the opposite view that nothing once formed in the mind could ever perish, that everything survives in some way or other, and is capable under certain conditions of being brought to light again. . . . (Freud, *Civilization and Its Discontents*, pp. 14-15).

What has now come to be common sense is that in everyman there is the potentiality for criminality, and that these are neither accidents nor visitations of degeneracy, but products of a delicate balance of forces that, under different circumstances, might have produced normality or even saintliness. Good and evil, in short, grow from a common root.

Freud's genius was in his resolution of polarities. The distinction of child and adult was one such. It did not suffice to reiterate that the child was father to the man. The theory of infantile sexuality and the stages of psychosexual development were an effort to fill the gap, the latter clumsy, the former elegant. Though the alleged progression of sexual expression from oral, to anal, to phallic, to genital has not found a secure place either in common sense or in general psychology, the developmental continuity of sexuality has been recognized by both. Common sense honors the continuity in the baby-books and in the permissiveness with which young parents of today resolve their doubts. And the research of Beach and others has shown the profound effects of infantile experience on adult sexual behavior —even in lower organisms.

If today people are reluctant to report their dreams with the innocence once attached to such recitals, it is again because Freud brought into common question the discontinuity between the rational purposefulness of waking life and the seemingly irrational purposelessness of fantasy and dream. While the crude symbolism of Freud's early efforts at dream interpretation has come increasingly to be abandoned, the conception of the dream as representing disguised wishes and fears has become common coin. And Freud's recognition of deep unconscious processes in the creative act has gone far toward enriching our understanding of the kinship between the artist, the humanist, and the man of science.

It is our heritage from Freud that the all-or-none distinction between mental illness and mental health has been replaced by a more humane conception of the continuity of these states. The view that neurosis is a severe reaction to human trouble is as revolutionary in its implications for social practice as it is daring in formulation. The "bad seed" theories, and nosologies of the 19th century, the demonologies and doctrines of divine punishment—none of these provided a basis for comparison toward human suffering comparable to that of our time.

One may argue, finally, that Freud's sense of the continuity of human conditions, of the likeness of the human plight, has made possible a deeper sense of the brotherhood of man. It has in any case tempered the spirit of punitiveness toward what once we took as evil and what we now see as sick. We have not yet resolved the dilemma posed by these two ways of viewing. Its resolution is one of the great moral challenges of our age.

Why, after such initial resistance, were Freud's views so phenomenally successful in transforming common conceptions of man?

One reason we have already considered: the readiness of the Western World to accept naturalistic explanation of organic phenomena and, concurrently, to be readier for such explanation in the mental sphere. There had been at least four centuries of uninterrupted scientific progress, recently capped by a theory of evolution that brought man into continuity with the rest of the animal kingdom. The rise of naturalism as a way of understanding nature and man saw a corresponding decline in the explanatory aspirations of religion. By the close of the 19th century, religion, to quote Morton White, "too often agreed to accept the role of a non-scientific spiritual grab-bag, or an ideological know-nothing." Elucidation of the human plight has been abandoned by religion and not yet adopted by science.

It was the inspired imagery, the proto-theory of Freud, that was to fill the gap. Success in transforming the common conception of man was not simply its recourse to the "cause-and-effect" discourse of science. Rather it is Freud's imagery, I think, that provides the clue to his ideological power. It is an imagery of necessity, if I may call it that, an imagery that combines the dramatic, the tragic, and the scientific views of necessity. It is here that Freud's intellectual heritage matters so deeply. Freud's is a theory or a proto-theory peopled with actors. The characters are from life: the blind, energic, pleasure-seeking id; the priggish and punitive superego; the ego, battling for its being by diverting the energy of the others to its own use. The drama has an economy and a terseness. The ego develops canny mechanisms for dealing with the threat of id impulses: denial, projection, and the rest. Balances are struck between the actors, and in the balance is character and neurosis. Freud was using the dramatic technique of decomposition, the play whose actors are parts of a single life—a technique that he himself had recognized in phantasies and dreams, one which is honored in his essay, "The Poet and the Daydream."

The imagery of the theory, moreover, has an immediate resonance with the dialectic of experience. True, it is not the stuff of superficial conscious experience. But it fits the human plight, its conflictedness, its private torment, its impulsiveness, its secret and frightening urges, its tragic quality.

In its scientific imagery, it is marked by the necessity of the classical mechanics. At times the imagery is hydraulic: suppress this stream of impulses, and it breaks out in a displacement elsewhere. The system is closed and mechanical, at times electrical, as when cathexes are formed and withdrawn like electrical charges. The way of thought fitted well the common-sense physics of its age.

Finally, the image of man presented was thoroughly secular; its ideal type was the mature man free of infantile neuroticism, capable of finding his own way. This freedom from both Utopianism and asceticism has earned Freud the contempt of ideological totalitarians of the Right and the Left. But the image has found a ready home in the rising, liberal intellectual middle class. For them, the Freudian ideal type has become a rallying point in the struggle against spiritual regimentation.

I have said virtually nothing about Freud's equation of sexuality and impulse. It was surely and still is a stimulus to resistance. But to say that Freud's success lay in forcing a reluctant Victorian world to accept the importance of sex-

uality is as empty as hailing Darwin for his victory over fundamentalism. Each had a far more
profound effect.

Can Freud's contribution to the common understanding of man in the twentieth century be
likened to the impact of such great physical and
biological theories as Newtonian physics and
Darwin's conception of evolution? The question
is an empty one. Freud's mode of thought is not
a theory in the conventional sense, it is a metaphor, an analogy, a way of conceiving man, a
drama. I would propose that Anaximander is the
proper parallel: his view of the connectedness
of physical nature was also an analogy—and a
powerful one. Freud is the ground from which
theory will grow, and he has prepared the
twentieth century to nurture the growth. But
far more important, he has provided an image
of man that has made him comprehensible without at the same time making him contemptible.

4/TOWARD A MODERN APPROACH TO VALUES: THE VALUING PROCESS IN THE MATURE PERSON/ CARL R. ROGERS*

THERE IS A GREAT DEAL OF CONCERN
today with the problem of values. Youth, in almost every country, is deeply uncertain of its
value orientation; the values associated with various religions have lost much of their influence;
sophisticated individuals in every culture seem
unsure and troubled as to the goals they hold
in esteem. The reasons are not far to seek. The
world culture, in all its aspects, seems increasingly scientific and relativistic, and the rigid,
absolute views on values which come to us from
the past appear anachronistic. Even more important, perhaps, is the fact that the modern
individual is assailed from every angle by divergent and contradictory value claims. It is no
longer possible, as it was in the not too distant
historical past, to settle comfortably into the
value system of one's forebears or one's community and live out one's life without ever examining the nature and the assumptions of that
system.

In this situation it is not surprising that value
orientations from the past appear to be in a state
of disintegration or collapse. Men question
whether there are, or can be, any universal
values. It is often felt that we may have lost,
in our modern world, all possibility of any general or cross-cultural basis for values. One natural result of this uncertainty and confusion is
that there is an increasing concern about, interest in, and a searching for, a sound or meaningful value approach which can hold its own in
today's world.

I share this general concern. As with other
issues the general problem faced by the culture
is painfully and specifically evident in the cultural microcosm which is called the therapeutic
relationship, which is my sphere of experience.

* Carl R. Rogers, Toward a modern approach to values: the valuing process in the mature person, *Journal of Abnormal and Social Psychology*, 1964, 68(2), 160-167. Reprinted by permission.

As a consequence of this experience I should like to attempt a modest theoretical approach to this whole problem. I have observed changes in the approach to values as the individual grows from infancy to adulthood. I observe further changes when, if he is fortunate, he continues to grow toward true psychological maturity. Many of these observations grow out of my experience as therapist, where I have had the mind stretching opportunity of seeing the ways in which individuals move toward a richer life. From these observations I believe I see some directional threads emerging which might offer a new concept of the valuing process, more tenable in the modern world. I have made a beginning by presenting some of these ideas partially in previous writings (Rogers, 1951, 1959); I would like now to voice them more clearly and more fully.

SOME DEFINITIONS

Charles Morris (1956, pp. 9-12) has made some useful distinctions in regard to values. There are "operative values," which are the behaviors of organisms in which they show preference for one object or objective rather than another. The lowly earthworm, selecting the smooth arm of a Y maze rather than the arm which is paved with sandpaper, is giving an indication of an operative value.

There are also "conceived values," the preference of an individual for a symbolized object. "Honesty is the best policy" is such a conceived value.

There is also the term "objective value," to refer to what is objectively preferable, whether or not it is sensed or conceived of as desirable. I will be concerned primarily with operative or conceptualized values.

INFANT'S WAY OF VALUING

Let me first speak about the infant. The living human being has, at the outset, a clear approach to values. We can infer from studying his behavior that he prefers those experiences which maintain, enhance, or actualize his organism, and rejects those which do not serve this end. Watch him for a bit:

Hunger is negatively valued. His expression of this often comes through loud and clear.

Food is positively valued. But when he is satisfied, food is negatively valued, and the same milk he responded to so eagerly is now spit out, or the breast which seemed so satisfying is now rejected as he turns his head away from the nipple with an amusing facial expression of disgust and revulsion.

He values security, and the holding and caressing which seem to communicate security.

He values new experience for its own sake, and we observe this in his obvious pleasure in discovering his toes, in his searching movements, in his endless curiosity.

He shows a clear negative valuing of pain, bitter tastes, sudden loud sounds.

All of this is commonplace, but let us look at these facts in terms of what they tell us about the infant's approach to values. It is first of all a flexible, changing, valuing *process*, not a fixed system. He likes food and dislikes the same food. He values security and rest, and rejects it for new experience. What is going on seems best described as an organismic valuing process, in which each element, each moment of what he is experiencing is somehow weighed, and selected or rejected, depending on whether, at that moment, it tends to actualize the organism or not. This complicated weighing of experience is clearly an organismic, not a conscious or symbolic function. These are operative, not conceived values. But this process can nonetheless deal with complex value problems. I would remind you of the experiment in which young infants had spread in front of them a score or more of dishes of natural (that is, unflavored) foods. Over a period of time they clearly tended to value the foods which enhanced their own survival, growth, and development. If for a time a child gorged himself on starches, this would soon be balanced by a protein "binge." If at times he chose a diet deficient in some vitamin, he would later seek out foods rich in this very vitamin. The physiological wisdom of his body guided his behavioral movements, resulting in what we might think of as objectively sound value choices.

Another aspect of the infant's approach to values is that the source or locus of the evaluating process is clearly within himself. Unlike many of us, he *knows* what he likes and dislikes, and the origin of these value choices lies strictly within himself. He is the center of the valuing process, the evidence for his choices being supplied by his own senses. He is not at this point influenced by what his parents think he should prefer, or by what the church says, or by the opinion of the latest "expert" in the field, or by the persuasive talents of an advertising firm. It is from within his own experiencing that his organism is saying in nonverbal terms, "This is good for me." "That is bad for me." "I like this." "I strongly dislike that." He would laugh at our concern over values, if he could understand it.

CHANGE IN THE VALUING PROCESS

What happens to this efficient, soundly based valuing process? By what sequence of events do we exchange it for the more rigid, uncertain, inefficient approach to values which characterizes most of us as adults? Let me try to state briefly one of the major ways in which I think this happens.

The infant needs love, wants it, tends to behave in ways which will bring a repetition of this wanted experience. But this brings complications. He pulls baby sister's hair, and finds it satisfying to hear her wails and protests. He then hears that he is "a naughty, bad boy," and this may be reinforced by a slap on the hand. He is cut off from affection. As this experience is repeated, and many, many others like it, he gradually learns that what "feels good" is often "bad" in the eyes of significant others. Then the next step occurs, in which he comes to take the same attitude toward himself which these others have taken. Now, as he pulls his sister's hair, he solemnly intones, "Bad, bad boy." He is introjecting the value judgment of another, taking it in as his own. To that degree he loses touch with his own organismic valuing process. He has deserted the wisdom of his organism, giving up the locus of evaluation, and is trying to behave in terms of values set by another, in order to hold love.

Or take another example at an older level. A boy senses, though perhaps not consciously, that he is more loved and prized by his parents when he thinks of being a doctor than when he thinks of being an artist. Gradually he introjects the values attached to being a doctor. He comes to want, above all, to be a doctor. Then in college he is baffled by the fact that he repeatedly fails in chemistry, which is absolutely necessary to becoming a physician, in spite of the fact that the guidance counselor assures him he has the ability to pass the course. Only in counseling interviews does he begin to realize how completely he has lost touch with his organismic reactions, how out of touch he is with his own valuing process.

Perhaps these illustrations will indicate that in an attempt to gain or hold love, approval, esteem, the individual relinquishes the locus of evaluation which was his in infancy, and places it in others. He learns to have a basic *dis*trust for his own experiencing as a guide to his behavior. He learns from others a large number of conceived values, and adopts them as his own, even though they may be widely discrepant from what he is experiencing.

SOME INTROJECTED PATTERNS

It is in this fashion, I believe, that most of us accumulate the introjected value patterns by which we live. In the fantastically complex culture of today, the patterns we introject as desirable or undesirable come from a variety of sources and are often highly contradictory. Let me list a few of the introjections which are commonly held.

Sexual desires and behaviors are mostly bad. The sources of this construct are many—parents, church, teachers.

Disobedience is bad. Here parents and teachers combine with the military to emphasize this concept. To obey is good. To obey without question is even better.

Making money is the highest good. The sources of this conceived value are too numerous to mention.

Learning an accumulation of scholarly facts is highly desirable. Education is the source.

Communism is utterly bad. Here the government is a major source.

To love thy neighbor is the highest good. This concept comes from the church, perhaps from the parents.

Cooperation and teamwork are preferable to acting alone. Here companions are an important source.

Cheating is clever and desirable. The peer group again is the origin.

Coca-Colas, chewing gum, electric refrigerators, and automobiles are all utterly desirable. From Jamaica to Japan, from Copenhagen to Kowloon, the "Coca-Cola culture" has come to be regarded as the acme of desirability.

This is a small and diversified sample of the myriads of conceived values which individuals often introject, and hold as their own, without ever having considered their inner organismic reactions to these patterns and objects.

COMMON CHARACTERISTICS OF ADULT VALUING

I believe it will be clear from the foregoing that the usual adult—I feel I am speaking for most of us—has an approach to values which has these characteristics:

The majority of his values are introjected from other individuals or groups significant to him, but are regarded by him as his own.

The source or locus of evaluation on most matters lies outside of himself.

The criterion by which his values are set is the

degree to which they will cause him to be loved, accepted, or esteemed.

These conceived preferences are either not related at all, or not clearly related, to his own process of experiencing.

Often there is a wide and unrecognized discrepancy between the evidence supplied by his own experience, and these conceived values.

Because these conceptions are not open to testing in experience, he must hold them in a rigid and unchanging fashion. The alternative would be a collapse of his values. Hence his values are "right."

Because they are untestable, there is no ready way of solving contradictions. If he has taken in from the community the conception that money is the *summum bonum* and from the church the conception that love of one's neighbor is the highest value, he has no way of discovering which has more value for *him*. Hence a common aspect of modern life is living with absolutely contradictory values. We calmly discuss the possibility of dropping a hydrogen bomb on Russia, but find tears in our eyes when we see headlines about the suffering of one small child.

Because he has relinquished the locus of evaluation to others, and has lost touch with his own valuing process, he feels profoundly insecure and easily threatened in his values. If some of these conceptions were destroyed, what would take their place? This threatening possibility makes him hold his value conceptions more rigidly or more confusedly, or both.

FUNDAMENTAL DISCREPANCY

I believe that this picture of the individual, with values mostly introjected, held as fixed concepts, rarely examined or tested, is the picture of most of us. By taking over the conceptions of others as our own, we lose contact with the potential wisdom of our own functioning, and lose confidence in ourselves. Since these value constructs are often sharply at variance with what is going on in our own experiencing, we have in a very basic way divorced ourselves from ourselves, and this accounts for much of modern strain and insecurity. This fundamental discrepancy between the individual's concept and what he is actually experiencing, between the intellectual structure of his values and the valuing process going on unrecognized within— this is a part of the fundamental estrangement of modern man from himself.

RESTORING CONTACT WITH EXPERIENCE

Some individuals are fortunate in going beyond the picture I have just given, developing further in the direction of psychological maturity. We see this happen in psychotherapy where we endeavor to provide a climate favorable to the growth of the person. We also see it happen in life, whenever life provides a therapeutic climate for the individual. Let me concentrate on this further maturing of a value approach as I have seen it in therapy.

As the client senses and realizes that he is prized as a person[1] he can slowly begin to value the different aspects of himself. Most importantly, he can begin, with much difficulty at first, to sense and to feel what is going on within him, what he is feeling, what he is experiencing, how he is reacting. He uses his experiencing as a direct referent to which he can turn in forming accurate conceptualizations and as a guide to his behavior. Gendlin (1961, 1962) has elaborated the way in which this occurs. As his experiencing becomes more and more open to him, as he is able to live more freely in the process of his feelings, then significant changes begin to occur in his approach to values. It begins to assume many of the characteristics it had in infancy.

INTROJECTED VALUES IN RELATION TO EXPERIENCING

Perhaps I can indicate this by reviewing a few of the brief examples of introjected values which I have given, and suggesting what happens to them as the individual comes closer to what is going on within him.

The individual in therapy looks back and realizes, "But I *enjoyed* pulling my sister's hair—and that doesn't make me a bad person."

The student failing chemistry realizes, as he gets close to his own experiencing, "I don't like chemistry; I don't value being a doctor, even though my parents do; and I am not a failure for having these feelings."

The adult recognizes that sexual desires and behavior may be richly satisfying and permanently enriching in their consequences, or shallow and temporary and less than satisfying. He goes by his own experiencing, which does not always coincide with social norms.

He recognizes freely that this communist book or person expresses attitudes and goals which he shares as well as ideas and values which he does not share.

He realizes that at times he experiences cooperation as meaningful and valuable to him, and that at other times he wishes to be alone and act alone.

[1] The therapeutic relationship is not devoid of values. When it is most effective it is, I believe, marked by one primary value, namely, that this person (the client) has *worth*.

VALUING IN THE MATURE PERSON

The valuing process which seems to develop in this more mature person is in some ways very much like that in the infant, and in some ways quite different. It is fluid, flexible, based on this particular moment, and the degree to which this moment is experienced as enhancing and actualizing. Values are not held rigidly, but are continually changing. The painting which last year seemed meaningful now appears uninteresting, the way of working with individuals which was formerly experienced as good now seems inadequate, the belief which then seemed true is now experienced as only partly true, or perhaps false.

Another characteristic of the way this person values experience is that it is highly differentiated, or as the semanticists would say, extensional. The examples in the preceding section indicate that what were previously rather solid monolithic introjected values now become differentiated, tied to a particular time and experience.

Another characteristic of the mature individual's approach is that the locus of evaluation is again established firmly within the person. It is his own experience which provides the value information or feedback. This does not mean that he is not open to all the evidence he can obtain from other sources. But it means that this is taken for what it is—outside evidence—and is not as significant as his own reactions. Thus he may be told by a friend that a new book is very disappointing. He reads two unfavorable reviews of the book. Thus his tentative hypothesis is that he will not value the book. Yet if he reads the book his valuing will be based upon the reactions it stirs in *him,* not on what he has been told by others.

There is also involved in this valuing process a letting oneself down into the immediacy of what one is experiencing, endeavoring to sense and to clarify all its complex meanings. I think of a client who, toward the close of therapy, when puzzled about an issue, would put his head in his hands and say, "Now what *is* it that I'm feeling? I want to get next to it. I want to learn what it is." Then he would wait, quietly and patiently, trying to listen to himself, until he could discern the exact flavor of the feelings he was experiencing. He, like others, was trying to get close to himself.

In getting close to what is going on within himself, the process is much more complex than it is in the infant. In the mature person it has

much more scope and sweep. For there is involved in the present moment of experiencing the memory traces of all the relevant learnings from the past. This moment has not only its immediate sensory impact, but it has meaning growing out of similar experiences in the past (Gendlin, 1962). It has both the new and the old in it. So when I experience a painting or a person, my experiencing contains within it the learnings I have accumulated from past meetings with paintings or persons, as well as the new impact of this particular encounter. Likewise the moment of experiencing contains, for the mature adult, hypotheses about consequences. "It is not pleasant to express forthrightly my negative feelings to this person, but past experience indicates that in a continuing relationship it will be helpful in the long run." Past and future are both in this moment and enter into the valuing.

I find that in the person I am speaking of (and here again we see a similarity to the infant), the criterion of the valuing process is the degree to which the object of the experience actualizes the individual himself. Does it make him a richer, more complete, more fully developed person? This may sound as though it were a selfish or unsocial criterion, but it does not prove to be so, since deep and helpful relationships with others are experienced as actualizing.

Like the infant, too, the psychologically mature adult trusts and uses the wisdom of his organism, with the difference that he is able to do so knowingly. He realizes that if he can trust all of himself, his feelings and his intuitions may be wiser than his mind, that as a total person he can be more sensitive and accurate than his thoughts alone. Hence he is not afraid to say, "I feel that this experience [or this thing, or this direction] is good. Later I will probably know *why* I feel it is good." He trusts the totality of himself, having moved toward becoming what Lancelot Whyte (1950) regards as "the unitary man."

It should be evident from what I have been saying that this valuing process in the mature individual is not an easy or simple thing. The process is complex, the choices often very perplexing and difficult, and there is no guarantee that the choice which is made will in fact prove to be self-actualizing. But because whatever evidence exists is available to the individual, and because he is open to his experiencing, errors are correctable. If this chosen course of action is not self-enhancing this will be sensed and he can make an adjustment or revision. He thrives on a maximum feedback interchange, and thus, like the gyroscopic compass on a ship, can continually correct his course toward his true goal of self-fulfillment.

SOME PROPOSITIONS REGARDING THE VALUING PROCESS

Let me sharpen the meaning of what I have been saying by stating two propositions which contain the essential elements of this viewpoint. While it may not be possible to devise empirical tests of each proposition in its entirety, yet each is to some degree capable of being tested through the methods of psychological science. I would also state that though the following propositions are stated firmly in order to give them clarity, I am actually advancing them as decidedly tentative hypotheses.

HYPOTHESIS I. There is an organismic base for an organized valuing process within the human individual.

It is hypothesized that this base is something the human being shares with the rest of the animate world. It is part of the functioning life process of any healthy organism. It is the capacity for receiving feedback information which enables the organism continually to adjust its behavior and reactions so as to achieve the maximum possible self-enhancement.

HYPOTHESIS II. This valuing process in the human being is effective in achieving self-enhancement to the degree that the individual is open to the experiencing which is going on within himself.

I have tried to give two examples of individuals who are close to their own experiencing: the tiny infant who has not yet learned to deny in his awareness the processes going on within; and the psychologically mature person who has relearned the advantages of this open state.

There is a corollary to this second proposition which might be put in the following terms. One way of assisting the individual to move toward openness to experience is through a relationship in which he is prized as a separate person, in which the experiencing going on within him is empathically understood and valued, and in which he is given the freedom to experience his own feelings and those of others without being threatened in doing so.

This corollary obviously grows out of therapeutic experience. It is a brief statement of the essential qualities in the therapeutic relation-

ship. There are already some empirical studies, of which the one by Barrett-Lennard (1962) is a good example, which give support to such a statement.

PROPOSITIONS REGARDING THE OUTCOMES OF THE VALUING PROCESS

I come now to the nub of any theory of values or valuing. What are its consequences? I should like to move into this new ground by stating bluntly two propositions as to the qualities of behavior which emerge from this valuing process. I shall then give some of the evidence from my experience as a therapist in support of these propositions.

HYPOTHESIS III. In persons who are moving toward greater openness to their experiencing, there is an organismic commonality of value directions.

HYPOTHESIS IV. These common value directions are of such kinds as to enhance the development of the individual himself, of others in his community, and to make for the survival and evolution of his species.

It has been a striking fact of my experience that in therapy, where individuals are valued, where there is greater freedom to feel and to be, certain value directions seem to emerge. These are not chaotic directions but instead exhibit a surprising commonality. This commonality is not dependent on the personality of the therapist, for I have seen these trends emerge in the clients of therapists sharply different in personality. This commonality does not seem to be due to the influences of any one culture, for I have found evidence of these directions in cultures as divergent as those of the United States, Holland, France, and Japan. I like to think that this commonality of value directions is due to the fact that we all belong to the same species—that just as a human infant tends, individually, to select a diet similar to that selected by other human infants, so a client in therapy tends, individually, to choose value directions similar to those chosen by other clients. As a species there may be certain elements of experience which tend to make for inner development and which would be chosen by all individuals if they were genuinely free to choose.

Let me indicate a few of these value directions as I see them in my clients as they move in the direction of personal growth and maturity.

They tend to move away from façades. Pretense, defensiveness, putting up a front, tend to be negatively valued.

They tend to move away from "oughts." The compelling feeling of "I ought to do or be thus and so" is negatively valued. The client moves away from being what he "ought to be," no matter who has set that imperative.

They tend to move away from meeting the expectations of others. Pleasing others, as a goal in itself, is negatively valued.

Being real is positively valued. The client tends to move toward being himself, being his real feelings, being what he is. This seems to be a very deep preference.

Self-direction is positively valued. The client discovers an increasing pride and confidence in making his own choices, guiding his own life.

One's self, one's own feelings come to be positively valued. From a point where he looks upon himself with contempt and despair, the client comes to value himself and his reactions as being of worth.

Being a process is positively valued. From desiring some fixed goal, clients come to prefer the excitement of being a process of potentialities being born.

Sensitivity to others and acceptance of others is positively valued. The client comes to appreciate others for what they are, just as he has come to appreciate himself for what he is.

Deep relationships are positively valued. To achieve a close, intimate, real, fully communicative relationship with another person seems to meet a deep need in every individual, and is very highly valued.

Perhaps more than all else, the client comes to value an openness to all of his inner and outer experience. To be open to and sensitive to his own *inner* reactions and feelings, the reactions and feelings of others, and the realities of the objective world—this is a direction which he clearly prefers. This openness becomes the client's most valued resource.

These then are some of the preferred directions which I have observed in individuals moving toward personal maturity. Though I am sure that the list I have given is inadequate and perhaps to some degree inaccurate, it holds for me exciting possibilities. Let me try to explain why.

I find it significant that when individuals are prized as persons, the values they select do not run the full gamut of possibilities. I do not find, in such a climate of freedom, that one person comes to value fraud and murder and thievery, while another values a life of self-sacrifice, and another values only money. Instead there seems to be a deep and underlying thread of commonality. I believe that when the human being is inwardly free to choose whatever he deeply values, he tends to value those objects, experiences, and goals which make for his own survival, growth, and development, and for the survival and development of others. I hypothesize that it is *characteristic* of the human organism to prefer such actualizing and socialized goals when he is exposed to a growth promoting climate.

A corollary of what I have been saying is that in *any* culture, given a climate of respect and freedom in which he is valued as a person, the mature individual would tend to choose and prefer these same value directions. This is a significant hypothesis which could be tested. It means that though the individual of whom I am speaking would not have a consistent or even a stable system of conceived values, the valuing process within him would lead to emerging value directions which would be constant across cultures and across time.

Another implication I see is that individuals who exhibit the fluid valuing process I have tried to describe, whose value directions are generally those I have listed, would be highly effective in the ongoing process of evolution. If the human species is to survive at all on this globe, the human being must become more readily adaptive to new problems and situations, must be able to select that which is valuable for development and survival out of new and complex situations, must be accurate in his appreciation of reality if he is to make such selections. The psychologically mature person as I have described him has, I believe, the qualities which would cause him to value those experiences which would make for the survival and enhancement of the human race. He would be a worthy participant and guide in the process of human evolution.

Finally, it appears that we have returned to the issue of universality of values, but by a different route. Instead of universal values "out there," or a universal value system imposed by some group—philosophers, rulers, priests, or psychologists—we have the possibility of universal human value directions *emerging* from the experiencing of the human organism. Evidence from therapy indicates that both personal and social values emerge as natural, and experienced, when the individual is close to his own organismic valuing process. The suggestion is that though modern man no longer trusts religion or science or philosophy nor any system of beliefs to *give* him values, he may find an organismic valuing base within himself which, if he can learn again to be in touch with it, will prove to be an organized, adaptive, and social approach to the perplexing value issues which face all of us.

SUMMARY

A description is given of the change in the value orientation of the individual from infancy to average adulthood, and from this adult status to a greater degree of psychological maturity attained through psychotherapy or fortunate life circumstances. On the basis of these observations, the theory is advanced that there is an organismic basis for the valuing process within the human individual; that this valuing process is effective to the degree that the individual is open to his experiencing; that in persons relatively open to their experiencing there is an important commonality or universality of value directions; that these directions make for the constructive enhancement of the individual and his community, and for the survival and evolution of his species.

REFERENCES

BARRETT-LENNARD, G. T. Dimensions of therapist response as causal factors in therapeutic change. *Psychol. Monogr.*, 1962, *76*, (43, Whole No. 562).

GENDLIN, E. T. Experiencing: A variable in the process of therapeutic change. *Amer. J. Psychother.*, 1961, *15*, 233-245.

GENDLIN, E. T. *Experiencing and the creation of meaning.* Glencoe, Ill.: Free Press, 1962.

MORRIS, C. W. *Varieties of human value.* Chicago: Univer. Chicago Press, 1956.

ROGERS, C. R. *Client-centered therapy.* Boston: Houghton Mifflin, 1951.

ROGERS, C. R. A theory of therapy, personality and interpersonal relationships. In S. Koch (Ed.), *Psychology: A study of a science.* Vol. 3. *Formulations of the person and the social context.* New York: McGraw-Hill, 1959. Pp. 185-256.

WHYTE, L. L. *The next development in man.* New York: Mentor Books, 1950.

II / Biological Bases for Behavior

THE LABEL "BIOLOGICAL BASES FOR BEHAVIOR" AVOIDS OLD and often sterile dichotomies, e.g., heredity versus environment or nature versus nurture. A more useful distinction is that between learned and non-learned attributes. Non-learned attributes include not only those that are genetically determined but also others such as the effects of disease and injury. Thus birth injury is not hereditary but acquired and is a biological (in this case congenital[1]) and non-learned determinant of behavior.

When the theorist who emphasizes biological determinants of behavior and the unfolding of innate or congenital potentialities seeks to explain behavior, he is likely to ask the following kinds of questions: What species of organism is this? What are the characteristics of the species? Is it a particular strain of the species? Does that strain have particular characteristics? What is the specific genetic inheritance of this individual organism? What environmental events (other than learning) have affected the organism?

Over the centuries, psychological thought has gone through periods when the predominant fashion was to consider heredity, or constitution, or—more broadly—man's biological make-up as THE all important determinant of his behavior. This included his individual behavior, and not just those behaviors characteristic of his species. The swing of the pendulum came, and it became "unfashionable" to consider any influences other than environmental experiences or individual life history as important in determining the individual's behavior. These different emphases have not been unrelated to the political thinking of the times. Democracy, with its de-emphasis of hereditary position and with its frequent companion, optimism, produced men who could see more possibility for change and improvement through control of the environment than through control of biology or heredity. Recent work with such genetic diseases as phenyl-ketonuria has shown that environmental action can alter the effects of some genetic "errors." In such an instance we see that acceptance of genetic determinism does not necessarily rule out optimism regarding the outcome.

In the present period it is fair to say that most psychologists would defend some compromise position, not claiming all importance for one or the other side of the old dichotomy. There is general recognition—in the words of the song about "love and marriage"—that "you can't have one without the other." Nevertheless, one or the other set of determinants is emphasized by various workers. Those who have been more concerned with the biological or genetic emphasis will be among those whose work is presented here.

---

[1] "Congenital"—acquired during development in the uterus or dating from birth; it is to be distinguished from "hereditary."

The first paper is by a prominent representative of the biological-comparative approach, Frank A. Beach. Now at the University of California at Berkeley after some years at Yale University, Professor Beach has made exhaustive studies of the effects of alterations of the internal and external environment of the organism upon the sexual behaviors of various species. In his paper Beach points out continuities between prenatal and postnatal growth and development. He illustrates the joint role of inherent characteristics and external influences, with an example from embryology that also gives concrete meaning to the concept of "critical periods."[2]

The second paper is by Anne Anastasi of Fordham University, one of the leading investigators and writers about "differential psychology," i.e., the psychology of individual differences. She reviews the problems of the influence of heredity and environment on behavior and poses questions about approaches to the study of HOW both influence behavior. Then comes a paper by John Paul Scott, who has recently moved to Bowling Green State University (Ohio) from the Roscoe B. Jackson Memorial Laboratory at Bar Harbor, Maine. This laboratory has done much to further the study of genetic influences on behavior, and particularly on those behaviors we call "social." Like Anastasi, who works with human subjects, Scott, who works with animals, calls attention to the fact that the use of species other than man in the study of genetic influences permits better control of both genetic and environmental factors. The next paper is a very brief report of a study done at the Jackson Laboratory by D. G. Freedman (now with the University of Chicago's Committee for Human Development). Using dogs of different breeds, Freedman dramatically illustrates the interaction of breed (genetic) and early experience in determining LATER behavior such as sociability and obeying commands.

After this comes a paper on human subjects (infants) written especially for this volume by Professors White and Held (currently at the Harvard Graduate School of Education and Massachusetts Institute of Technology respectively). It is an important exploration of the roles of the innately given mechanisms and of the role of early contact with the environment (or experience) in determining such a basic behavior as visually directed reaching. The importance of the article lies not only in the results and their implications, but in the fact that this study is one of the very few using human subjects that has shown experimental control over such a behavior in a rigorous way.[3]

At this point we present another two papers concerned exclusively with humans, one by Donald Weatherley of the University of Colorado, and one by Marjorie P. Honzik of the University of California at Berkeley. Weatherly's study derives from work done in one of the important longitudinal researches carried out in this country—the California Growth

[2] This concept is dealt with in detail by Caldwell in Section VII of this book (article No. 43).

[3] For another interesting paper concerned with genetic and acquired determinants of a visual performance (form perception), see "The Origin of Form Perception" by Robert L. Fantz, *Scientific American*, 1961, *204*, (pp. 66-72 and 204) which appeared in the first edition of this book and is in several current books of readings.

Studies. Among other contributions, these studies showed ways in which the timing of physical maturation at adolescence (genetically controlled to an important degree) influences behaviors that are commonly considered as aspects of personality. Key figures in these studies at Berkeley were Nancy Bayley, Mary Cover Jones, and the late Harold Jones. Determination of the personality traits of extreme groups of early- and late-maturers was made by Paul Mussen using one of the more common "projective techniques," the TAT or Thematic Apperception Test. In the present paper Weatherly has applied very different techniques to try to get at the questions raised by these earlier studies. Instead of an objective skeletal-age measure of maturation, the adolescents' own reports on whether they were late or early to mature were used. Instead of projective tests, "objective type" personality tests were employed. In addition, his population was slightly older when studied than were the Berkeley subjects. His investigation is thus a less intensive study of a more extensive population.[4] The high degree of congruence between the Berkeley findings and his, despite these methodological differences, underscores the importance of rate of maturation as a variable influencing personality development in boys.

The last paper in this section, that of Honzik, is labeled a book review. In addition to reviewing a book concerned with stability of behavior from birth to maturity, the article offers a cogent commentary on longitudinal studies in general and a comparison of their relevant results. With respect to this book, if certain behaviors were stable from birth to maturity one could present a strong argument (without ruling out the effects of interaction with environment) for their being biologically determined. Thus the selection is pertinent to the topic of this section. (The findings of the book emphasize sex differences, so this review could also have been placed in Section VIII.)

The reader will want to keep in mind the issues posed in these papers when reading other parts of this book, especially sections VII (Age or Developmental Stage), VIII (Sex), and IX (Intelligence). Differences between the sexes in behavior and differences among people in intelligence are products, after all, of both biology and learning. It should be noted that certain workers who have placed major emphasis on age or developmental stage (Section VII) have assumed the primacy of biological over experiential determinants. For example, much of the writing which takes its intellectual origin from either Freud or the great Swiss developmental psychologist Jean Piaget is of this type. Papers placed elsewhere in this book which bear on the topics of the present section include Harlow and Harlow (Section IV, no. 20), Robert White (VII, no. 41) and Caldwell (VII, no. 43).

The student with no background in genetics will find it helpful to read the booklet *Nature and Nurture: a Modern Synthesis* (Doubleday Papers in Psychology, 1954) by John L. Fuller of the Jackson Laboratory or the

---

[4] See Weatherly's list of references for appropriate papers reporting these various studies.

fifth edition of *Principles of Genetics* by Sinnott, Dunn, and Dobzhansky (New York: McGraw-Hill, 1958). Another readable selection is the printed version of a series of BBC lectures (*The Future Man,* Basic Books, 1959) by the British Nobel Prize geneticist, Peter Medawar. His chapters 4 and 6 are of particular interest. For contrast one might examine the views of another Nobel Laureate geneticist, Hermann J. Muller. His article "The Guidance of Human Evolution," in *Perspectives in Biology* (1959, *3*, 1-43) or the abridged version "Should we weaken or strengthen our genetic heritage?" in *Daedalus* (1961, *90*, 432-450) would be appropriate. For another general presentation and evaluation by a psychologist see *A Textbook of Psychology* (Saunders, 1958) by Donald O. Hebb. Chapter 6 entitled "Heredity, maturation, early learning" is the relevant one.

Anyone desiring a look at the newest developments in genetics should read *The Code of Life* by Ernest Borek (Columbia University Press, 1965) or "The Genetic Code" by F. H. C. Crick (*Scientific American,* 1962, *207,* 66-74). Both the book and the article are written for the educated layman, not the geneticist or biologist.

More specific than the above references is a paper by M. F. Ashley Montagu which gives an excellent picture of the interaction of genetic and environmental influences prior to the birth of the child. This paper, "Constitutional and prenatal factors in infant and child health," is in M. J. E. Senn (Ed.), *Symposium on the Healthy Personality* (Josiah Macy, Jr. Foundation, 1950). Since it is available in a number of books of readings, it is referred to rather than reproduced here.

5/THE INDIVIDUAL FROM CONCEPTION TO CONCEPTUALIZATION/FRANK A. BEACH*

INTRODUCTION

IN THE FINAL DECADE OF THE NINE-teenth century the famous European biologist, Hans Driesch, described some amazing experiments. Dr. Driesch was interested in the development of organisms, and his evidence pertained to a definitely unspectacular invertebrate, the common sea urchin. Like all other creatures, the sea urchin begins life as a single fertilized egg. Shortly after it has been fertilized, the sea urchin egg divides to form two cells. A few hours later each of these two cells redivides; and this process continues until a fully formed sea urchin has come into existence.

Herr Driesch tried out various procedures which he hoped might alter the normal course of development. To begin with, he took sea urchins in the two-cell stage of development and cut them in half, completely separating the cells from one another. He was probably astonished to discover that under optimal conditions each of these two cells divided and redivided until eventually two completely formed embryos were produced.

In later experiments Driesch found that the usual course of development of the sea urchin, as well as that of many other aquatic organisms is drastically changed when the chemical composition of the surrounding sea water is altered. By adding various inorganic salts to the normal fluid environment Driesch was able to produce a condition of cyclopia; and in other instances he caused frogs and other amphibians to grow two heads instead of one.

Half a century after Driesch had reported his discoveries, a psychiatrist, Dr. Rene Spitz, published a report concerning the physical and psychological development of 91 children reared in a foundling home. At the time of Dr. Spitz's original observations all of these children were three years old or younger. During the next two years some youngsters were adopted, but 37 per cent of the original group had died. At the end of this time the 21 survivors who still remained in the home ranged between two and four years of age.

Five of the 21 were totally unable to walk, and only five could walk unassisted. Twelve of the 21 children had not yet learned to eat alone with a spoon, and only one of the 21 was able to dress himself without help. Not a single child was completely toilet trained. Six were totally unable to talk, and only one was capable of using sentences. The marked retardation shown by these children was not limited to their behavior. Although they were all two years or older, only three of them fell within the weight range of the normal two-year-old child. Most of them had the physical appearance of children approximately half of their age.

It is most important to stress the fact that from the time of birth these children had been under excellent medical care. They had received an entirely adequate diet and had not been exposed to any unusual sources of injury or infection. The one atypical aspect of their life histories lay in the almost total lack of social stimulation during the first two years of life. Although they were fed regularly and kept clean, they never had any opportunity to play with adults, or with one another, or with inanimate toys.

In 1947 a young psychologist, Dr. Keith Hayes and his wife Catherine adopted a two-day-old chimpanzee. They named the baby Viki, and brought her up in their home just as they would a human infant. When she was three years old Viki was given a number of psychological tests. In many of these she was the equal of human children her own age, and in all of them she was highly superior to three-year-old chimpanzees that had been brought up in the regular laboratory where these animals were bred.

At first thought the observations of Driesch, of Spitz, and of the Hayeses may appear to have very little in common. But I have cited them because they all deal with the phenomena of individual development. Nor does the similarity end here. All three of these studies emphasize the fact that many aspects of development depend upon what happens to the organism during the early stages of life.

Discussions of ontogenesis traditionally sepa-

*Frank A. Beach, The individual from conception to conceptualization, in John T. Wilson *et al.*, *Psychology and The Behavioral Sciences*, Philadelphia: University of Pittsburgh Press, 1954, 82-114. Reprinted with abridgment by permission.

35

rate *prenatal* and *postnatal* differentiation and growth. It is also customary to distinguish between physical and psychological development. One aim of this address is to emphasize the similarities and continuities between prenatal and postnatal, and between physical and psychological development. It is my purpose to elucidate a few simple principles which are pertinent to the interpretation of different kinds of development occurring at different stages in the individual's life span. I shall try to show that wherever and whenever it occurs, development obeys certain common laws. All development, whether it be development of the lens of the eye, or development of abstract concepts of morality, follows an orderly and predictable course and is best understood as the product of mutual interaction between a few classes of basic factors.

EMBRYOLOGY OF THE VERTEBRATE EYE

Let us begin by considering as our first example the embryological development of that most important sensory structure, the vertebrate eye. At a time when the embryo is little more than a hollow ball, certain groups of cells begin to grow rapidly and to form what eventually will become the spinal cord and brain. Long before the cord has been fully formed it is possible to identify, in that region which will become the brain, two small, laterally placed pits or depressions. When development has proceeded a little further, these pits increase in size, balloon outward, and become the optic vesicles. With continued growth, the optic vesicles are extended closer and closer to the surface of the embryo-to-be, all the time maintaining their connection with the more central brain regions by way of the short optic stalks.

As the optic vesicles approach the surface, they change in structure and take on the shape of a two-layered cup. While the optic cups are forming, a small portion of the outer layer, that is, of the ectoderm, starts to sink inward toward the cup. This migrating group of cells forms into a hollow ball which eventually comes to rest in the cavity of the cup and forms the lens of the eye.

This is a brief and oversimplified account of one small step in normal embryological development, but it typifies the complexity and at the same time the orderliness of differentiation and growth. The sequence of changes leading up to formation of the eyecup and lens seems stereo-

typed, automatic, almost mechanical. It appears to occur identically in all embryos of the same species and presumably has been occurring in the same fashion for however many millions of years that species may have existed. How are we to account for such a complex yet regular and lawful sequence of phenomena? It was once believed that such an orderly series of events must depend exclusively upon some intrinsic properties of the various cells involved. However, a series of ingenious experiments revealed that this is not at all the case.

EXPERIMENTS ON THE LENS ORGANIZER

It is now known that the scientist can alter the normal course of development in various ways. For example, by delicate surgical methods one can remove from the surface of the embryo a small patch of tissue, which ordinarily would develop into skin of the belly wall. The next step is to insert this block of ectoderm in a position directly above the developing optic cup, having first removed the cells which normally grow there. When this is done, the tissue that originally was destined to become belly skin will form a lens. And this lens is identical to the one that would have been formed by quite different cells if the experimentalist had not interfered. It is equally feasible to induce formation of a lens in parts of the body where one would not normally grow. This can be done by removing the optic cup and transplanting it to a new location. If a growing optic cup is implanted beneath the surface of the embryo, in a region which normally would develop into skin of the back, a lens will be formed by those cells that lie directly above the transplanted optic cup.

As can be imagined, the operations involved are exceedingly delicate, and one cannot expect success in every experiment. Nevertheless, the results which I have described occur with sufficient regularity to justify the conclusion that the direction which the development of a bit of tissue may take is not determined solely by inherent characteristics of that block of tissue, but depends as well upon its location within the organism. In other words, the structures which groups of cells eventually come to form are in part dependent upon the identity of these cells' neighbors.

It must be stressed that this sort of plasticity is not unlimited. On the contrary, the tissue to be transplanted must be taken at just the right stage in its development, and the transplant must be made at a particular time when the adjacent tissues are capable of exerting their directive influences over neighboring masses of cells.

The concept of *organizer substances* has been invoked to describe the sort of phenomena that I have been talking about. It is believed that the optic cup produces a certain substance, an organizer, which exerts action upon ectodermal tissue causing it to approach the cup and to form a lens. The organizer is produced only for a limited time, and if it is to have any effect upon other cells, the optic cup must be transplanted at the appropriate time.[Ed] Of equal importance is the fact that the susceptibility of ectodermal tissue to the effects of the optic cup organizer changes through time. Cells that are too far along in their course of development can be transplanted into a region adjacent to the cup, but they will not react to the organizer.

EXPERIMENTS WITH THE PRIMARY ORGANIZER

Other embryonic organizers are known to exist. For example, the first organizer is probably one produced by a group of cells lying near that region known as the blastopore. From cells in the dorsal lip of the blastopore there comes the organizer which initiates formation of the nerve tube that eventually will become the brain and spinal cord. It has been shown that cells which would normally be involved in formation of some other part of the body can be induced to develop into a spinal cord and brain if they are transplanted into the neighborhood of the blastopore lip.

Furthermore, if tissue is taken from the dorsal lip of the blastopore and implanted elsewhere in the blastocyte, it will induce the formation of a nerve cord and brain in that new location. A classic experiment by Spemann and Mangold involved removing the dorsal lip of the blastopore from one salamander blastocyte and implanting it in a second embryo-to-be. The recipient blastocyte then contained two sources of primary organizer, the transplanted blastopore lip and its own blastopore tissue. The result was the formation of two nervous systems within the same embryo, one induced by the transplant and the other induced by the embryo's own organizer cells. Here again, as in the case of induction of the lens, it is essential that the reacting tissue be transplanted at a specific stage

in its own development; and it is also necessary that the transplantation be done while the dorsal lip tissue is actively producing the organizer substance.

The story of experimental control of embryological development is a long and fascinating one, but enough has been said to establish the point I wish to make. This is that the embryological history of any organ or organ system in the body is a joint product of the inherent characteristics of the tissues which formed that organ, and of external influences exerted upon those tissues, either through the activity of other parts of the organism, or in some cases by extra-organismal factors. Throughout the course of morphological differentiation and growth, the basic processes involved are those of interaction between cells or cell masses and their environment. Neither the intrinsic developmental capacities of the cells, nor the activity of external agents is sufficient to explain the final result. Both must always be taken into consideration and both are equally important. One subsidiary principle which is well illustrated by this evidence is that the organism and its various parts change through time with respect to the susceptibility to modification. It seems likely that every cell or group of cells passes through a critical stage of growth during which it is maximally sensitive to outside influences. Having passed this period of high susceptibility the cell or cells are no longer easily changed.

DEVELOPMENT OF VISUAL PERCEPTION

Let us turn now from the consideration of embryological development and examine the growth of sensory capacities in early life. It is well known that the newborn baby is extremely limited in his visual ability. He cannot fixate his eyes for any appreciable length of time and it seems quite clear that precise pattern vision does not develop for many weeks. Only after several months does the infant become capable of discriminating objects visually and recognizing a familiar face. A part of this gradual improvement is referrable to maturational changes in the visual apparatus. The contribution of *experience* is difficult to assess, because the infant is unable to use speech and his psychological capacities are limited. However, there is evidence proving that visual abilities which might ordinarily be put down to simple maturation are in fact heavily dependent upon early stimulation and experience.

[Ed] *I.e., there is a "critical period."*

This evidence comes from the study of adult humans after removal of congenital cataracts.[Ed] Von Senden has summarized a number of cases in which the preoperative condition of the lens was such that detailed vision had never been possible from the time of birth. Following removal of the cataract all of the patients are able to perceive the presence of a figure in the visual field. They can distinguish a figure from its background, but they cannot identify the figure or describe its shape. After a little practice most patients are able to name colors, but from this point on progress is slow and often discouraging.

Some individuals never improve beyond the ability to identify objects in terms of brightness and color. Others take months or even years to learn to identify simple geometric figures and to read separate letters and numbers. Only in rare cases do these patients master the problem of identifying complex visual patterns such as words, or outline drawings, or human faces. One woman was hospitalized for more than half a year postoperatively, and during this time she was visited daily by two physicians. Six months after the cataract had been removed this patient was totally unable to tell the doctors apart on the basis of their facial characteristics, although she could do so easily in terms of voice or other nonvisual features.

Impressive as it is, this evidence does not constitute conclusive proof of the importance of protracted visual experience for normal visual abilities. In the first place, the absence of the lens can never be completely compensated. Furthermore, these patients characteristically exhibit jerking movements of the eyes, the so-called spontaneous nystagmus. For these reasons it is highly desirable to obtain experimental data on animals in which such factors can be controlled.

This sort of evidence is now available as a result of the careful investigations of Dr. Austin Riesen. Riesen reared young chimpanzees from birth to 16 months of age in a completely darkened room. The two infants in his first experiment were brought into the light at 16 months. At this age they were unable to fixate objects in the visual field, although the normal 16-month-old chimpanzee is visually well developed. Some reflex responses to visual stimulation were present in the dark-reared apes. These reactions included pupillary constriction to bright light, startle response to sudden changes in illumination, and visual following of a large, moving target. Visual responses to complex patterns of light appeared eventually, but not until many hours had been spent in illuminated surroundings.

The chimpanzees did not respond visually to play objects or to their feeding bottles, although both of these were promptly oriented to and grasped if they touched some part of the animal's body. The apes did not blink when a blow toward the face was threatened, and if an object was brought slowly toward the face the first reaction was a startled jump when contact occurred.

Some question was raised concerning structural normality of the retinae and optic discs as a result of total absence of visual stimulation during the early phases of life; and to check this possibility a second experiment was conducted in which three more newborn chimpanzees were put into darkness. One animal was raised for seven months in complete darkness. One was allowed 90 minutes of light every day, during which time the head was covered with a white, plexiglass mask that admitted diffuse light but did not permit pattern vision. The third chimpanzee was given one and one-half hours of patterned light daily.

With minor exceptions, the behavior of the animal reared in complete darkness and the one allowed 90 minutes of unpatterned light per day was similar to that which was shown by the two animals in the original experiment. In contrast, the ape which was allowed 90 minutes of patterned light per day behaved like a normal chimpanzee. He quickly learned to avoid a large yellow- and black-striped disc after receiving one or two mild electric shocks from it; whereas the other chimpanzees were shocked from the same disc twice a day for six and nine days, respectively, before they so much as whimpered when it was shown to them. It took 13 and 15 days before these animals consistently indicated, by some sort of avoidance response, that they saw the disc when it was raised in front of their eyes.

Results of this sort, taken together with the clinical evidence from human beings, strongly suggest that early learning and experience play a very important role in the development of perception by animals and men.[Ed] It is obvious that the way a person interprets a complex vis-

[Ed] *This evidence has also been discussed by Hebb* (Organization of Behavior, *John Wiley & Sons, 1949).*

[Ed] *For new experimental evidence on the dependence of visual development in the human infant upon experience see article no. 9 by White and Held.*

ual stimulus such as a portrait or painting will depend upon his tastes and knowledge gained through experience. It is equally true, but less apparent, that the capacity to see the difference between a circle and a square is also a product of individual learning.

Another investigation conducted at the Yerkes Laboratories of Primate Biology indicates that early learning also plays a role in nonvisual behavior. In this experiment one chimpanzee was reared under conditions in which he could not use his hands or feet to manipulate objects in the environment or to touch himself. The means of prevention was to encase the extremities and distal portions of the limbs in cardboard mailing tubes which permitted limb movement but prevented manual exploration. After the tubes were removed, the animal reared in this fashion did not groom himself in normal chimpanzee style. When a tactile stimulus which he could not see was applied to some part of the body, the experimental chimpanzee failed to bring one hand to the locus of stimulation in the manner which is characteristic of normal apes. Tests which involved prevention of the use of visual cues revealed that the chimpanzee experienced great difficulty in distinguishing between stimulation of his right versus his left hand. His sitting posture was abnormal and in general the behavior was characterized by a number of deficits which seemed directly traceable to the lack of ordinary experience in the use of tactile sensations.

Dr. Arnold Gesell and his co-workers have worked out an extensive schedule describing the development of human infants. This schedule, which has been applied to large numbers of children, clearly reveals that behavioral development involves an orderly and predictable sequence of changes, and that it follows more or less the same course and has the same general tempo in all normal infants. A comparable development schedule for the chimpanzee has recently been described by Riesen and Kinder. There are marked species differences, of course, but the maturational history of the ape resembles that of the human in respect to its general predictability and consistency from individual to individual.

Postnatal progress in muscular control of bodily activity, and increasing precision of sensory-motor coordinations is as regular and consistent as is the prenatal differentiation and growth of the vertebrate embryo. An important factor in this progress is the physical maturation which brings greater strength and increased sensory

acuity. But maturation alone cannot account for many of the simplest developmental changes. The evidence I have summarized compels us to conclude that exteroceptive stimulation from the earliest age is of utmost importance; and repeated reaction to such stimulation is an indispensable influence for the development of many normal behavioral capacities. As is the case in embryonic life, normal development rests upon the interaction of intrinsic and extrinsic events and processes.

EFFECTS OF PRACTICE ON MATERNAL BEHAVIOR

It is customary to classify certain complex patterns of behavior as instinctive. The validity of this taxonomic procedure is open to serious question, but this is not an appropriate occasion on which to debate it. The instinct concept implies that certain kinds of behavior appear normally without the necessity for practice and learning. In the main, the so-called instinctive responses are reasonably constant for a given species, although they vary from species to species. Instincts are ordinarily contrasted with the habits and learned responses which are formed by the individual as a result of personal experience.

One instinctive pattern of behavior which has been studied fairly extensively in the laboratory rat is the maternal care of the young. It has been demonstrated independently by a number of investigators that female rats that have no previous experience in bearing or rearing young are capable of building a nest before the advent of the first litter, cleaning the young as they are born, keeping them together in the nest, nursing and protecting them until they reach the age of weaning.

In an experiment which I conducted a number of years ago female rats were separated from their mothers at the time of weaning and each one was reared in an individual cage where she had no contact with other animals. When they reached adulthood the females were placed with a fertile male just long enough for mating and were then returned to their isolated cages. Approximately five days before the litter was due to be born, each female was placed in a large observation cage and provided with nesting material. The majority of females readily detached paper strips which were hung from the walls of the observation cage and used them to build simple but adequate nests. As soon as the young were born the female took them between her forepaws and licked off the fetal fluids and devoured the fetal membranes. Inasmuch as I knew the entire history of each of the experimental animals I was quite sure that this behavior was properly classified as instinctive, and that it did not depend upon prior experience. More recent studies throw some question upon this naive interpretation.

Dr. Bernard Riess has conducted several experiments in which female rats were reared in an environment containing nothing which could be picked up and transported. He has found that when females of this type become pregnant and give birth to young, they build no nests and are lax in the care of their offspring. Riess's interpretation is that the normal rat has ample opportunity for experience in moving objects about the environment. When this very general sort of experience is denied the animal, there occurs a deficit in the behavior which demands precisely this kind of response. And it is true that in the early experiments, including my own, females were not prevented from doing as much transporting as they wished of food pellets, sawdust, shavings, and other materials commonly available in the living cages.[Ed]

EXPERIMENTS ON SEXUAL BEHAVIOR

The sexual behavior of animals is usually classified as instinctive or unlearned. In fact, this type of behavior has often been cited as an excellent example of what is called a "delayed instinct." It is supposed to appear automatically at puberty in response to the physiological changes which occur at this time. It is considered to be the product of physical maturation and to be independent of previous experience. The inadequacy of any such interpretation is revealed by recent experiments on the mating behavior of the laboratory rat.

Two years ago Jerome Kagan and I conducted an experiment in which male rats were reared in individual cages from the age of weaning. Some of the rats were removed from their isolated cages for a brief period each week and were placed in a large observation cage together with another young rat their own age and size. These weekly, ten-minute periods of contact represented the experimental rats' sole opportunity to form habits of social interaction with another individual of their kind.

[Ed] For other evidence of maternal laxity consequent upon unusual rearing conditions, see Harlow and Harlow, article no. 20, and Caldwell, no. 43.

When they reached sexual maturity all of the animals were tested with receptive females. The mating performance of the experimental rats was quite abnormal. They were highly excited by the presence of the estrous female and responded to her with the execution of incomplete mating attempts. At the same time, however, there occurred many playful responses of mock fighting, chasing and wrestling which are characteristic of the *immature* rat. The achievement of complete intercourse was so rare that the experimental males practically never reached the sexual climax. The infrequency of coital responses was due to the competing tendency to engage in immature, playful activities. Apparently the extremely artificial conditions of early life favored the development and retention of social habits that were inappropriate in adulthood. Presumably in *normal* development the tendency to react playfully to a second animal appears in late infancy but is gradually replaced by other forms of social interaction. The conditions of our experiment did not provide opportunity for the development of more mature types of behavior and in the absence of this essential opportunity the animals remained fixated at a prepuberal level.

This evidence suggests that abnormal experiences in early life can interfere with the development of normal sexual behavior. It does not prove that the mating of rodents depends upon sexual practice and learning. However, in the higher mammals it is quite probable that biologically-effective intercourse necessitates a considerable amount of sexual experience.

It has recently been reported by Dr. Henry Nissen that young male and female chimpanzees which are sexually mature, but have never had any heterosexual experience, are incapable of engaging in complete sexual relations. Males and females of this species which have been reared under conditions that did not permit heterosexual play do not mate when they are placed together in adulthood. It seems probable that if an indefinite period of exploration and experimentation were permitted, coitus would eventually occur; but under the controlled conditions used by Dr. Nissen, young males and females that were placed together when the female was at the height of her receptive cycle failed to engage in any primary sexual activity in the course of hours of observation. Mating responses are much more likely to occur if at least one member of the pair is sexually experienced.

It appears that normal development of sexual behavior involves both physiological maturation and behavioral experience. Neither factor alone suffices to produce the final product.

STUDIES OF IMPRINTING

One large body of evidence which emphasizes the importance of experience and early environmental stimulation in the development of social behavior is provided by the studies of the ethologists, or students of animal behavior under natural conditions. One of the first observations dealing with early social conditioning was published by Wallace Craig in 1918. Craig reported that pigeons which had been reared by parents of a different avian species preferred to mate with birds belonging to the same species as their foster parents, and were very slow to form sexual unions with individuals of their own kind.

More recently the German ornithologist, Dr. Konrad Lorenz, has described a process which he calls "imprinting." According to this hypothesis young birds of certain types form strong social attachments very shortly after they leave the egg. Under normal conditions, hatching takes place in the presence of the mother bird, and the young birds soon learn to follow and remain close to the adult female. This tendency is strengthened by virtue of the fact that the mother calls the young to food and protects them against natural enemies.

In a series of naturalistic, semi-experimental studies, Lorenz arranged to substitute himself as a foster parent. He became Father Goose to a brood of graylag goslings. The youngsters were prevented from any contact with adults of their own species and were periodically attended by Lorenz as he crawled about in the grass on his hands and knees and made gooselike noises. The result was that the newly hatched birds accepted their foster parent enthusiastically and followed him about wherever he went. Adult geese held no attractions for the adopted offspring of Dr. Lorenz, and this particular brood of birds retained the strong positive reactions to him for many months.

Other investigators have confirmed in part the initial findings of Lorenz and have shown also that imprinting is not limited to geese but can be observed in several other avian species. In addition, it is possible that a similar process operates in the early social conditioning of those species of mammals which are born at an advanced stage of development and which are by nature gregarious. For example, there are several descriptions of lambs which have been reared by hand and have had no early contact with other animals of their own species. These individuals are said to form social attachments to human beings and to be quite unsheeplike in regard to their behavior in the pasture. They tend to graze alone and do not move with the flock.

Under ordinary conditions the newborn lamb displays a very strong tendency to remain in close contact with its mother. As soon as it can get to its feet, the youngster rubs against the ewe and when she moves away, it follows immediately. At this point any enforced separation elicits immediate distress behavior in the young and the parent. Somewhat later in development the lamb may leave its mother's side briefly to investigate its environment or to play with another young sheep. Eventually the positive social response generalizes from the mother to include all other members of the flock. This orderly course of development in social behavior is dependent jointly upon inherent aspects of the sheep's behavioral capacities, and upon individual experience. The final result is a product of interaction between these two sources of influence. Furthermore, as is true in experimental embryology, susceptibility to the influence of external agents varies through time. Lambs deprived of the usual contact with other sheep in the early stages of life do not become normal sheep even though opportunity for such contact is provided at a later developmental stage.

EARLY EXPERIENCE AND COGNITIVE DEVELOPMENT IN CHILDREN

Thus far I have been speaking about the effects of early experience upon the development of perceptual functions and upon the ontogenesis of emotional, instinctual, and social behavior. Another axis of development which is of great importance is, of course, the development of intelligence or of cognitive capacities. When intelligence tests were first introduced, and the IQ was invented, there was a great deal of speculation and argument concerning the so-called *constancy* of the intelligence quotient. In the beginning, some proponents of the testing movement insisted that the intelligence test measured innate intellectual capacity and was independent of the effects of learning and experience. It has since become apparent that this extreme view is untenable, and it is questionable whether any psychological test is completely immune to the effects of certain widespread, not to say universal, forms of early life experience.

The Swiss psychologist, Piaget, has suggested that the way in which children think about the surrounding world and about themselves undergoes a regular development as the child grows older. The individual's way of thinking passes through several distinctive stages before adult ideas are attained. The theory is not that the child grasps adult ideas with different degrees of adequacy, but rather that it develops ideas which differ *qualitatively* from those of the adult.

The primary stage of thought development differs from the intermediate and final stages in that it is relatively unaffected by the culture into which the child is born. The child's primary concepts, be they concepts of names or of windstorms or any other phenomena are generated by the child himself. Primary concepts reflect the child's perception of, and reflection upon, its environment; but they are relatively unaffected by adult ideas because at this age the child is not in good contact with adult ideas, and in any event is unable to understand them.

Piaget believes that these primary ideas are arrived at independently by each succeeding generation, and eventually discarded in favor of the adult ideas favored by the particular culture in which the individual grows up. Furthermore, many of the primary ideas are the same in different cultures and in different generations. This is so because of certain assumed constants in the human psychological processes, and because of certain environmental universals, that is, certain factors and phenomena universally present in the worlds of all children.

These hypothetical environmental universals may be likened to the many constants present in the environment of the human fetus. A particular concentration of oxygen, a given amount of calcium, an essential supply of iodine—these and many other things must be available to the embryo if it is to develop normally. However, since they are almost always present, their contribution to normal growth and differentiation is easily overlooked. Only when one or another of the essential items is lacking is its essentiality apt to be recognized.

Carrying the analogy back to psychological development, we can ask the following question: If Piaget's thesis is sound, what are the cultural universals that contribute to the beginning of thought and the derivation of primary concepts? Many answers suggest themselves and one of the most obvious is the stimulation afforded all children of every society by contact with other human beings. There is some reason

to believe that this is an indispensable factor in normal psychological and perhaps even physical growth.

. . . .

[Dr. Beach next presented various observations of Spitz which have become widely known, although often challenged. Other, subsequent studies and observations have, however, corroborated certain aspects of these findings. Ed]

It seems well within the bounds of possibility that one of the universal conditions affecting human development is the impact of a considerable amount of stimulation from the environment, particularly the opportunity for social interchange with other human beings. Like the iodine content of the prenatal environment, this postnatal environmental condition is so widespread and universal that its importance is easily overlooked. If this line of reasoning is valid, the similarity between pre- and postnatal, and physical and psychological development can safely be described as fundamental and important. The gradual increase in intellectual powers is attributable, not to environmental support and direction, nor yet to inherent maturational processes, but rather to the continual interaction of both types of factors.

COGNITIVE DEVELOPMENT IN ANIMALS

If experience makes important contributions to normal intellectual development, and if experiential deficits can prevent or retard such development, it is at least conceivable that by increasing the appropriate kinds of stimulation or experience one might induce a supernormal degree of intellectual ability. This in essence is what we try to achieve with our formal educative machinery and the informal tutelage of our own children. But the effects of an "enriched" early environment are most clearly revealed in experimental studies and observations on various kinds of animals.

A number of years ago Dr. Henry Nissen studied the behavior of chimpanzees in their native habitat. One of the most interesting conclusions reached as a result of this work was that the free living chimpanzee is less well developed intellectually than is his relative who has been born and reared in the experimental laboratory. The environment in which these animals normally exist is a beneficent one. It poses relatively few problems for the individual to solve and makes minimal demands upon his learning ability. The climate is gentle and even, food is abundant, and natural enemies are scarce. Accordingly, the average chimpanzee can get along quite well without ever extending himself intellectually.

In contrast, the ape that is bred and reared in the psychological laboratory is faced with many man-made problems that never trouble his wild cousin. His food is provided, but he often has to work for his dinner, and in solving the various problems put before him by the experimentalist the animal gradually acquires a degree of sophistication which far exceeds that of the free living ape.

Comparisons of this sort suggest the interesting hypothesis that the normal or average psychological status of a given species is in part dependent upon the environmental demands placed upon all members of that species by nature. If this were true, then the possibility mentioned earlier could be investigated. It might be feasible to elevate individuals far above the norm of their species by artificially increasing the problematical aspects of the life circumstances and multiplying the situations in which learning is possible and necessary. The conditions of human life are rendered highly complex by the existence of cultural or social problems that do not confront members of other species and it is not unlikely that man's unique intellectual characteristics depend in appreciable measure upon this fact. One way of assessing the effects of this factor would be to expose the young of some other species to the same environmental opportunities and necessities which confront the growing human child. This has been attempted by several investigators; and one of the most recent and ambitious of such projects is one which I mentioned at the beginning of this address. I refer to the work of Keith and Catherine Hayes at Orange Park, Florida. Their chimpanzee, named Viki, was adopted a few days after birth and spent nearly six years in their home. Insofar as it was possible and consonant with the major purpose of the experiment, Viki was reared as a human child. The over-all plan necessitated many tests and observations to which children are not subjected. When Viki appeared to be markedly inferior in some respect, special training was usually given, to determine whether the deficiency could be overcome. During much of her life such training took place at mealtime so that she worked for most of her food.

An extensive diary has been kept of Viki's activities, and she has been compared with children and with laboratory chimpanzees in a variety of formal tests. The findings published to date do not go beyond Viki's status at three years of age. In general, she has closely paralleled the development of a normal human child, and her interest and abilities appeared in roughly the same sequence and at about the same rate. Her social behavior is that of an extrovert; she seeks the company and attention of people and is very friendly although somewhat aggressive with those who allow her to dominate them. Like human children Viki spends most of her time in play. However, her play is much more athletic and her skill far surpasses that of a child of the same age.

In *contrast* to human children, Viki is much less vocal. Unlike the three-year-old boy or girl she does not babble or chatter. She does not appear to be seriously retarded in interest or capacity to deal with concrete objects. She scribbles, cuts with shears, builds with blocks and Tinker Toys, hurls and catches balls, operates light switches and door handles, all with about the same skill and enthusiasm of most three-year-old humans. One of her favorite toys at three years of age is the telephone which she holds to her ear while dialing a few numbers at random.

Viki seems to have about as much preference for social play as do children. She leads human beings about by the hand, coaxes them to tickle her, begs for piggy-back rides, brings toys which are used in social games, and enlists human aid in exploiting new gadgets by firmly placing the human's hands at the appropriate spot. She is adept at social imitation and, just like a human child, she copies her adopted parents' routine chores. She dusts, washes dishes, sharpens pencils, saws wood, hammers and sandpapers furniture, paints woodwork, and presses photographs in books.

In an experimental analysis of her imitative behavior Viki was required to solve six problems which were also given to four human children of about the same age. Four of these six problems were presented to a laboratory raised chimpanzee nine months older than Viki. These problems in imitation involved obtaining a toy or piece of candy in various ways, such as throwing a ball at the toy to knock it down, pushing it out of a long tunnel with a rod, or by operating a light switch on the wall which released the prize magnetically from the ceiling. In other problems the incentive was placed in a box which could only be opened by using a stick to strike a distant string, by burning a nearby string with a candle flame, or by pulling three levers in a certain sequence.

The chimpanzees and children were allowed to attempt a solution first, to be sure that it could not be done readily by insight or by trial and error. Then the experimenter demonstrated the proper procedure, and allowed the subject to try again; if she was unsuccessful, additional demonstrations were given. There was little difference between the performance of Viki and the children—they usually solved these problems within a few trials. The laboratory chimpanzee solved only one, and his failure with the others seemed due, at least in part, to his lack of skill in manipulating the apparatus.

When Viki is given psychological tests that do not involve language, they indicate that her general intelligence has developed at about the same rate as that of a human child. At three years she performed with appropriate skill on such test items as form boards, peg boards, picture puzzles, block piling, and buttoning. However, she fails completely on tests of verbal intelligence. In fact, language is the one field of behavior in which a large, clear-cut, and important superiority of man over chimpanzee was found. In summarizing their first three years of observation, the Hayeses (1951 Proceedings of the American Philosophical Society, 95, p. 108) came to the following conclusion:

If we assume . . . that Viki's mental development will continue to parallel that of man to maturity— as it appears to have done for the first three years —then our results strongly suggest that the two species are much more alike, psychologically, than has heretofore been supposed. They suggest, in fact, that man's superior ability to use language may be his only important *genetic* advantage. This one genetic advantage makes further advantages possible, however, since language is a means of sharing knowledge. Intelligence depends upon three factors: the individual's innate capacity, his personal experience, and the experience he acquires second hand, through communication with others. This last factor, while unimportant to most species, makes man less dependent upon individual abilities, by providing him with a more effective "group intelligence."

In spite of the fact that Viki could not master and use language, she did develop learning and problem-solving ability to a level considerably above that of the ordinary chimpanzee. These superior attainments were due in part to the continuous stimulation and tuition provided in the home environment. Combining this evidence with the observations of Dr. Spitz leads to the conclusion that intellectual development depends upon certain nonexperiential variables, such as those that differentiate man and chimpanzee, and upon certain forms of experience occurring early in life. Serious deficiences are apt to appear if experience is impoverished; and enrichment of early experience is essential if development is to result in full achievement of the individual's potentialities.

SUMMARY AND CONCLUSIONS

I hope that I have successfully laid the groundwork for four important generalizations about development. The first generalization states that development always depends upon certain crucial external forces which act upon the developing system. The second is that development is equally dependent upon inherent characteristics of the system, including its sensitivity to environmental influences. The third is that this sensitivity or capacity for response is not constant or stable, but tends first to rise to a maximum and then to decrease and disappear so that the critical extrinsic factors can exert their normal effects only if they are present when responsivity of the reacting system is high. Later in development the same agents may be without effect. The fourth and final generalization is that all of the foregoing ones apply to all aspects of organic development, from the differentiation and growth of the embryonic neural tube to the gradual formation of basic emotional patterns and characteristic habits of thinking.

The range of phenomena, the multiplicity and variety of systems which obey the same, fundamental, ontogenetic laws is at first thought astonishing. How has it come about that development of the eye in the human embryo, and the development of primary ideas in the young child have so many features in common? The answer is that morphological and psychological development belong on the same continuum, and both represent end products of the same evolutionary process. Both have been exposed to and shaped by the selective forces or organic evolution.

These studies of development re-emphasize an oft-stated but important fact mentioned at the beginning of this address and worthy of repetition before an audience which includes specialists in several areas of biological and social science. There is no fundamental discontinuity between pre- and postnatal existence, nor between the physical and psychologic aspects of the individual.

6 / HEREDITY, ENVIRONMENT, AND THE QUESTION "HOW?"[1]/ ANNE ANASTASI*

TWO OR THREE DECADES AGO, THE socalled heredity-environment question was the center of lively controversy. Today, on the other hand, many psychologists look upon it as a dead issue. It is now generally conceded that both hereditary and environmental factors enter into all behavior. The reacting organism is a product of its genes and its past environment, while present environment provides the immediate stimulus for current behavior. To be sure, it can be argued that, although a given trait may result from the combined influence of hereditary and environmental factors, a specific difference in this trait between individuals or between groups may be traceable to either hereditary or environmental factors alone. The design of most traditional investigations undertaken to identify such factors, however, has been such as to yield inconclusive answers. The same set of data has frequently led to opposite conclusions in the hands of psychologists with different orientations.

Nor have efforts to determine the proportional contribution of hereditary and environmental factors to observed individual differences in given traits met with any greater success. Apart from difficulties in controlling conditions, such investigations have usually been based upon the implicit assumption that hereditary and environmental factors combine in an additive fashion. Both geneticists and psychologists have repeatedly demonstrated, however, that a more tenable hypothesis is that of interaction (15, 22, 28, 40). In other words, the nature and extent of the influence of each type of factor depends upon the contribution of the other. Thus the proportional contribution of heredity to the variance of a given trait, rather than being a constant, will vary under different environmental conditions. Similarly, under different hereditary conditions, the relative contribution of environment will differ. Studies designed to estimate the proportional contribution of heredity and environment, however, have rarely in-

cluded measures of such interaction. The only possible conclusion from such research would thus seem to be that both heredity and environment contribute to all behavior traits and that the extent of their respective contributions cannot be specified for any trait. Small wonder that some psychologists regard the heredity-environment question as unworthy of further consideration!

But is this really all we can find out about the operation of heredity and environment in the etiology of behavior? Perhaps we have simply been asking the wrong questions. The traditional questions about heredity and environment may be intrinsically unanswerable. Psychologists began by asking *which* type of factor, hereditary or environmental, is responsible for individual differences in a given trait. Later, they tried to discover *how much* of the variance was attributable to heredity and how much to environment. It is the primary contention of this paper that a more fruitful approach is to be found in the question "How?" There is still much to be learned about the specific *modus operandi* of hereditary and environmental factors in the development of behavioral differences. And there are several current lines of research which offer promising techniques for answering the question "How?"

VARIETY OF INTERACTION MECHANISMS

HEREDITARY FACTORS. If we examine some of the specific ways in which hereditary factors may influence behavior, we cannot fail but be impressed by their wide diversity. At one extreme, we find such conditions as phenylpyruvic amentia and amaurotic idiocy. In these cases, certain essential physical prerequisites for normal intellectual development are lacking as a result of hereditary metabolic disorders. . . .Ed

Ed *More recent evidence points to the possibility of controlling the intellectual deficiency by dietary means. See, e.g., "Treatment of phenylketonuria with a diet low in phenylalanine," by Woolf, Griffiths, and Moncrieff (Brit. J. Med., 1955, 1, 57-64).*

[1] Address of the President, Division of General Psychology, American Psychological Assocation, September 4, 1957.

* Anne Anastasi, Heredity, environment, and the question "how?" *Psychological Review*, 1958, 65, 197-208. Reprinted by permission.

A somewhat different situation is illustrated by hereditary deafness, which may lead to intellectual retardation through interference with normal social interaction, language development, and schooling. In such a case, however, the hereditary handicap can be offset by appropriate adaptations of training procedures. It has been said, in fact, that the degree of intellectual backwardness of the deaf is an index of the state of development of special instructional facilities. As the latter improve, the intellectual retardation associated with deafness is correspondingly reduced.

A third example is provided by inherited susceptibility to certain physical diseases, with consequent protracted ill health. If environmental conditions are such that illness does in fact develop, a number of different behavioral effects may follow. Intellectually, the individual may be handicapped by his inability to attend school regularly. On the other hand, depending upon age of onset, home conditions, parental status, and similar factors, poor health may have the effect of concentrating the individual's energies upon intellectual pursuits. The curtailment of participation in athletics and social functions may serve to strengthen interest in reading and other sedentary activities. Concomitant circumstances would also determine the influence of such illness upon personality development. And it is well known that the latter effects could run the gamut from a deepening of human sympathy to psychiatric breakdown.

Finally, heredity may influence behavior through the mechanism of social stereotypes. A wide variety of inherited physical characteristics have served as the visible cues for identifying such stereotypes. These cues thus lead to behavioral restrictions or opportunities and—at a more subtle level—to social attitudes and expectancies. The individual's own self concept tends gradually to reflect such expectancies. All of these influences eventually leave their mark upon his abilities and inabilities, his emotional reactions, goals, ambitions, and outlook on life.

The geneticist Dobzhansky illustrates this type of mechanism by means of a dramatic hypothetical situation. He points out that, if there were a culture in which the carriers of blood group AB were considered aristocrats and those of blood group O laborers, then the blood-group genes would become important hereditary determiners of behavior (12, p. 147). Obviously the association between blood group and behavior would be specific to that culture. But such specificity is an essential property of the causal mechanism under consideration.

More realistic examples are not hard to find. The most familiar instances occur in connection with constitutional types, sex, and race. Sex and skin pigmentation obviously depend upon heredity. General body build is strongly influenced by hereditary components, although also susceptible to environmental modification. That all these physical characteristics may exert a pronounced effect upon behavior within a given culture is well known. It is equally apparent, of course, that in different cultures the behavioral correlates of such hereditary physical traits may be quite unlike. A specific physical cue may be completely unrelated to individual differences in psychological traits in one culture, while closely correlated with them in another. Or it may be associated with totally dissimilar behavior characteristics in two different cultures.

It might be objected that some of the illustrations which have been cited do not properly exemplify the operation of hereditary mechanisms in behavior development, since hereditary factors enter only indirectly into the behavior in question. Closer examination, however, shows this distinction to be untenable. First it may be noted that the influence of heredity upon behavior is always indirect. No psychological trait is ever inherited as such. All we can ever say directly from behavioral observations is that a given trait shows evidence of being influenced by certain "inheritable unknowns." This merely defines a problem for genetic research; it does not provide a causal explanation. Unlike the blood groups, which are close to the level of primary gene products, psychological traits are related to genes by highly indirect and devious routes. Even the mental deficiency associated with phenylketonuria is several steps removed from the chemically defective genes that represent its hereditary basis. Moreover, hereditary influences cannot be dichotomized into the more direct and the less direct. Rather do they represent a whole "continuum of indirectness," along which are found all degrees of remoteness of causal links. The examples already cited illustrate a few of the points on this continuum.

It should be noted that as we proceed along the continuum of indirectness, the range of variation of possible outcomes of hereditary factors expands rapidly. At each step in the causal chain, there is fresh opportunity for interaction with other hereditary factors as well as with environmental factors. And since each interaction in turn determines the direction of subsequent interactions, there is an ever-widening network of possible outcomes. If we visualize a simple sequential grid with only two alternatives at each point, it is obvious that there are two possible outcomes in the one-stage situation, four outcomes at the second stage, eight at the third, and so on in geometric progression. The actual situation is undoubtedly much more complex, since there will usually be more than two alternatives at any one point.

In the case of the blood groups, the relation to specific genes is so close that no other concomitant hereditary or environment conditions can alter the outcome. If the organism survives at all, it will have the blood group determined by its genes. Among psychological traits, on the other hand, some variation in outcome is always possible as a result of concurrent circumstances. Even in cases of phenylketonuria, intellectual development will exhibit some relationship with the type of care and training available to the individual. That behavioral outcomes show progressive diversification as we proceed along the continuum of indirectness is brought out by the other examples which were cited. Chronic illness *can* lead to scholarly renown or to intellectual immaturity; a mesomorphic physique *can* be a contributing factor in juvenile delinquency or in the attainment of a college presidency! Published data on Sheldon somatotypes provide some support for both of the latter outcomes.

Parenthetically, it may be noted that geneticists have sometimes used the term "norm of reaction" to designate the range of variation of possible outcomes of gene properties (cf. 13, p. 161). Thus heredity sets the "norm" or limits within which environmental differences determine the eventual outcome. In the case of some traits, such as blood groups or eye color, this norm is much narrower than in the case of other traits. Owing to the rather different psychological connotations of both the words "norm" and "reaction," however, it seems less confusing to speak of the "range of variation" in this context.

A large portion of the continuum of hereditary influences which we have described coincides with the domain of somatopsychological relations, as defined by Barker et al. (6). Under this heading, Barker includes "variations in physique that affect the psychological situation of a person by influencing the effectiveness of his body as a tool for actions or by serving as a stimulus to himself or others" (6, p. 1). Relatively direct neurological influences on behavior, which have been the traditional concern of physiological psychology, are excluded from this definition, Barker being primarily concerned

with what he calls the "social psychology of physique." Of the examples cited in the present paper, deafness, severe illness, and the physical characteristics associated with social stereotypes would meet the specifications of somatopsychological factors.

The somatic factors to which Barker refers, however, are not limited to those of hereditary origin. Bodily conditions attributable to environmental causes operate in the same sorts of somatopsychological relations as those traceable to heredity. In fact, heredity-environment distinctions play a minor part in Barker's approach.

ENVIRONMENTAL FACTORS: ORGANIC. Turning now to an analysis of the role of environmental factors in behavior, we find the same etiological mechanisms which were observed in the case of hereditary factors. First, however, we must differentiate between two classes of environmental influences: (*a*) those producing organic effects which may in turn influence behavior and (*b*) those serving as direct stimuli for psychological reactions. The former may be illustrated by food intake or by exposure to bacterial infection; the latter, by tribal initiation ceremonies or by a course in algebra. There are no completely satisfactory names by which to designate these two classes of influences. In an earlier paper by Anastasi and Foley (4), the terms "structural" and "functional" were employed. However, "organic" and "behavioral" have the advantage of greater familiarity in this context and may be less open to misinterpretation. Accordingly, these terms will be used in the present paper.

Like hereditary factors, environmental influences of an organic nature can also be ordered along a continuum of indirectness with regard to their relation to behavior. This continuum closely parallels that of hereditary factors. One end is typified by such conditions as mental deficiency resulting from cerebral brain injury or from prenatal nutritional inadequacies. A more indirect etiological mechanism is illustrated by severe motor disorder—as in certain cases of cerebral palsy—*without* accompanying injury to higher neurological centers. In such instances, intellectual retardation may occur as an indirect result of the motor handicap, through the curtailment of educational and social activities. Obviously this causal mechanism corresponds closely to that of hereditary deafness cited earlier in the paper.

Finally, we may consider an environmental parallel to the previously discussed social stereotypes which were mediated by hereditary physical cues. Let us suppose that a young woman with mousy brown hair becomes transformed into a dazzling golden blonde through environmental techniques currently available in our culture. It is highly probable that this metamorphosis will alter, not only the reactions of her associates toward her, but also her own self concept and subsequent behavior. The effects could range from a rise in social poise to a drop in clerical accuracy!

Among the examples of environmentally determined organic influences which have been described, all but the first two fit Barker's definition of somatopsychological factors. With the exception of birth injuries and nutritional deficiencies, all fall within the social psychology of physique. Nevertheless, the individual factors exhibit wide diversity in their specfic *modus operandi*—a diversity which has important practical as well as theoretical implications.

ENVIRONMENTAL FACTORS: BEHAVIORAL. The second major class of environmental factors—the behavioral as contrasted to the organic—are by definition direct influences. The immediate effect of such environmental factors is always a behavioral change. To be sure, some of the initial behavioral effects may themselves indirectly affect the individual's later behavior. But this relationship can perhaps be best conceptualized in terms of breadth and permanence of effects. Thus it could be said that we are now dealing, not with a continuum of indirectness, as in the case of hereditary and organic-environmental factors, but rather with a continuum of breadth.

Social class membership may serve as an illustration of a relatively broad, pervasive, and enduring environmental factor. Its influence upon behavior development may operate through many channels. Thus social level may determine the range and nature of intellectual stimulation provided by home and community through books, music, art, play activities, and the like. Even more far-reaching may be the effects upon interests and motivation, as illustrated by the desire to perform abstract intellectual tasks, to surpass others in competitive situations, to succeed in school, or to gain social approval. Emotional and social traits may likewise be influenced by the nature of interpersonal relations characterizing homes at different socioeconomic levels. Somewhat more restricted in scope than social class, although still exerting a relatively broad influence, is amount of formal schooling which the individual is able to obtain.

A factor which may be wide or narrow in its effects, depending upon concomitant circumstances, is language handicap. Thus the bilingualism of an adult who moves to a foreign country with inadequate mastery of the new language represents a relatively limited handicap which can be readily overcome in most cases. At most, the difficulty is one of communication. On the other hand, some kinds of bilingualism in childhood may exert a retarding influence upon intellectual development and may under certain conditions affect personality development adversely (2, 5, 10). A common pattern in the homes of immigrants is that the child speaks one language at home and another in school, so that his knowledge of each language is limited to certain types of situations. Inadequate facility with the language of the school interferes with the acquisition of basic concepts, intellectual skills, and information. The frustration engendered by scholastic difficulties may in turn lead to discouragement and general dislike of school. Such reactions can be found, for example, among a number of Puerto Rican children in New York City schools (3). In the case of certain groups, moreover, the child's foreign language background may be perceived by himself and his associates as a symbol of minority group status and may thereby augment any emotional maladjustment arising from such status (34).

A highly restricted environmental influence is to be found in the opportunity to acquire specific items of information occurring in a particular intelligence test. The fact that such opportunities may vary with culture, social class, or individual experiential background is at the basis of the test user's concern with the problem of coaching and with "culture-free" or "culture-fair" tests (cf. 1, 2). If the advantage or disadvantage which such experiential differences confer upon certain individuals is strictly confined to performance on the given test, it will obviously reduce the validity of the test and should be eliminated.

In this connection, however, it is essential to know the breadth of the environmental influence in question. A fallacy inherent in many attempts to develop culture-fair tests is that the breadth of cultural differentials is not taken into account. Failure to consider breadth of effect likewise characterizes certain discussions of coaching. If, in coaching a student for a college admission test, we can improve his knowledge of verbal concepts and his reading comprehension, he will be better equipped to succeed in college courses. His performance level will thus be raised, not only on the test, but also on the criterion which the test is intended to predict. To try to devise a test which is not susceptible to such coaching would merely reduce the effectiveness of the test. Similarly, efforts to rule out cultural differentials from test items so as to make them equally "fair" to subjects in different social classes or in different cultures may merely limit the usefulness of the test, since the same cultural differentials may operate within the broader area of behavior which the test is designed to sample.

METHODOLOGICAL APPROACHES

The examples considered so far should suffice to highlight the wide variety of ways in which hereditary and environmental factors may interact in the course of behavior development. There is clearly a need for identifying explicitly the etiological mechanism whereby any given hereditary or environmental condition ultimately leads to a behavioral characteristic—in other words, the "how" of heredity and environment. Accordingly, we may now take a quick look at some promising methodological approaches to the question "how."

Within the past decade, an increasing number of studies have been designed to trace the connection between specific factors in the hereditary backgrounds or in the reactional biographies of individuals and their observed behavioral characteristics. There has been a definite shift away from the predominantly descriptive and correlational approach of the earlier decades toward more deliberate attempts to verify explanatory hypotheses. Similarly, the cataloguing of group differences in psychological traits has been giving way gradually to research on changes in group characteristics following altered conditions.

Among recent methodological developments, we have chosen seven as being particularly relevant to the analysis of etiological mechanisms. The first represents an extension of selective breeding investigations to permit the identification of specific hereditary conditions underlying the observed behavioral differences. When early selective breeding investigations such as those of Tryon (36) on rats indicated that "maze learning ability" was inherited, we were still a long way from knowing what was actually being transmitted by the genes. It was obviously not "maze learning ability" as such. Twenty—or even ten—years ago, some psychologists would have

suggested that it was probably general intelligence. And a few might even have drawn a parallel with the inheritance of human intelligence.

But today investigators have been asking: Just what makes one group of rats learn mazes more quickly than the other? Is it differences in motivation, emotionality, speed of running, general activity level? If so, are these behavioral characteristics in turn dependent upon group differences in glandular development, body weight, brain size, biochemical factors, or some other organic conditions? A number of recent and ongoing investigations indicate that attempts are being made to trace, at least part of the way, the steps whereby certain chemical properties of the genes may ultimately lead to specified behavior characteristics.

An example of such a study is provided by Searle's (31) follow-up of Tryon's research. Working with the strains of maze-bright and maze-dull rats developed by Tryon, Searle demonstrated that the two strains differed in a number of emotional and motivational factors, rather than in ability. Thus the strain differences were traced one step further, although many links still remain to be found between maze learning and genes. A promising methodological development within the same general area is to be found in the recent research of Hirsch and Tryon (18). Utilizing a specially devised technique for measuring individual differences in behavior among lower organisms, these investigators launched a series of studies on selective breeding for behavioral characteristics in the fruit fly, *Drosophila*. Such research can capitalize on the mass of available genetic knowledge regarding the morphology of *Drosophila*, as well as on other advantages of using such an organism in genetic studies.

Further evidence of current interest in the specific hereditary factors which influence behavior is to be found in an extensive research program in progress at the Jackson Memorial Laboratory, under the direction of Scott and Fuller (30). In general, the project is concerned with the behavioral characteristics of various breeds and crossbreeds of dogs. Analyses of some of the data gathered to date again suggest that "differences in performance are produced by differences in emotional, motivational, and peripheral processes, and that genetically caused differences in central processes may be either slight or non-existent" (29, p. 225). In other parts of the same project, breed differences in physiological characteristics, which may in turn be related to behavioral differences, have been established.

2) A second line of attack is the exploration of possible relationships between behavioral characteristics and physiological variables which may in turn be traceable to hereditary factors. Research on EEG, autonomic balance, metabolic processes, and biochemical factors illustrates this approach. A lucid demonstration of the process of tracing a psychological condition to genetic factors is provided by the identification and subsequent investigation of phenylpyruvic amentia. In this case, the causal chain from defective gene, through metabolic disorder and consequent cerebral malfunctioning, to feeble-mindedness and other overt symptoms can be described step by step (cf. 32; 33, pp. 389-391). Also relevant are the recent researches on neurological and biochemical correlates of schizophrenia (9). Owing to inadequate methodological controls, however, most of the findings of the latter studies must be regarded as tentative (19).

3) Prenatal environmental factors provide a third avenue of fruitful investigation. Especially noteworthy is the recent work of Pasamanick and his associates (27), which demonstrated a tie-up between socioeconomic level, complications of pregnancy and parturition, and psychological disorders of the offspring. In a series of studies on large samples of whites and Negroes in Baltimore, these investigators showed that various prenatal and paranatal disorders are significantly related to the occurrence of mental defect and psychiatric disorders in the child. An important source of such irregularities in the process of childbearing and birth is to be found in deficiencies of maternal diet and in other conditions associated with low socioeconomic status. An analysis of the data did in fact reveal a much higher frequency of all such medical complications in lower than in higher socioeconomic levels, and a higher frequency among Negroes than among whites.

Direct evidence of the influence of prenatal nutritional factors upon subsequent intellectual development is to be found in a recent, well controlled experiment by Harrell et al. (16). The subjects were pregnant women in low-income groups, whose normal diets were generally quite deficient. A dietary supplement was administered to some of these women during pregnancy and lactation, while an equated control group received placebos. When tested at the ages of three and four years, the offspring of the experimental group obtained a significantly higher mean IQ than did the offspring of the controls.

Mention should also be made of animal experiments on the effects of such factors as prenatal radiation and neonatal asphyxia upon cerebral anomalies as well as upon subsequent behavior development. These experimental studies merge imperceptibly into the fourth approach to be considered, namely, the investigation of the influence of early experience upon the eventual behavioral characteristics of animals. Research in this area has been accumulating at a rapid rate. In 1954, Beach and Jaynes (8) surveyed this literature for the *Psychological Bulletin,* listing over 130 references. Several new studies have appeared since that date (e.g., 14, 21, 24, 25, 35). The variety of factors covered ranges from the type and quantity of available food to the extent of contact with human culture. A large number of experiments have been concerned with various forms of sensory deprivation and with diminished opportunities for motor exercise. Effects have been observed in many kinds of animals and in almost all aspects of behavior, including perceptual responses, motor activity, learning, emotionality, and social reactions.

In their review, Beach and Jaynes pointed out that research in this area has been stimulated by at least four distinct theoretical interests. Some studies were motivated by the traditional concern with the relative contribution of maturation and learning to behavior development. Others were designed in an effort to test certain psychoanalytic theories regarding infantile experiences, as illustrated by studies which limited the feeding responses of young animals. A third relevant influence is to be found in the work of the European biologist Lorenz (23) on early social stimulation of birds, and in particular on the special type of learning for which the term "imprinting" has been coined. A relatively large number of recent studies have centered around Hebb's (17) theory regarding the importance of early perceptual experiences upon subsequent performance in learning situations. All this research represents a rapidly growing and promising attack on the *modus operandi* of specific environmental factors.

The human counterpart of these animal studies may be found in the comparative investigation of child-rearing practices in different cultures and subcultures. This represents the fifth approach in our list. An outstanding example of such a study is that by Whiting and

Child (38), published in 1953. Utilizing data on 75 primitive societies from the Cross-Cultural Files of the Yale Institute of Human Relations, these investigators set out to test a number of hypotheses regarding the relationships between child-rearing practices and personality development. This analysis was followed up by field observations in five cultures, the results of which have not yet been reported (cf. 37).

Within our own culture, similar surveys have been concerned with the diverse psychological environments provided by different social classes (11). Of particular interest are the study by Williams and Scott (39) on the association between socioeconomic level, permissiveness, and motor development among Negro children, and the exploratory research by Milner (26) on the relationship between reading readiness in first-grade children and patterns of parent-child interaction. Milner found that upon school entrance the lower-class child seems to lack chiefly two advantages enjoyed by the middle-class child. The first is described as "a warm positive family atmosphere or adult-relationship pattern which is more and more being recognized as a motivational prerequisite of any kind of adult-controlled learning." The lower-class children in Milner's study perceived adults as predominantly hostile. The second advantage is an extensive opportunity to interact verbally with adults in the family. The latter point is illustrated by parental attitudes toward mealtime conversation, lower-class parents tending to inhibit and discourage such conversation, while middle-class parents encourage it.

Most traditional studies on child-rearing practices have been designed in terms of a psychoanalytic orientation. There is need for more data pertaining to other types of hypotheses. Findings such as those of Milner on opportunities for verbalization and the resulting effects upon reading readiness represent a step in this direction. Another possible source of future data is the application of the intensive observational techniques of psychological ecology developed by Barker and Wright (7) to widely diverse socioeconomic groups.

A sixth major approach involves research on the previously cited somatopsychological relationships (6). To date, little direct information is available on the precise operation of this class of factors in psychological development. The multiplicity of ways in which physical traits—whether hereditary or environmental in origin—may influence behavior thus offers a relatively unexplored field for future study.

The seventh and final approach to be considered represents an adaptation of traditional twin studies. From the standpoint of the question "How?" there is need for closer coordination between the usual data on twin resemblance and observations of the family interactions of twins. Available data already suggest, for example, that closeness of contact and extent of environmental similarity are greater in the case of monozygotic than in the case of dizygotic twins (cf. 2). Information on the social reactions of twins toward each other and the specialization of roles is likewise of interest (2). Especially useful would be longitudinal studies of twins, beginning in early infancy and following the subjects through school age. The operation of differential environmental pressures, the development of specialized roles, and other environmental influences could thus be more clearly identified and correlated with intellectual and personality changes in the growing twins.

Parenthetically, I should like to add a remark about the traditional applications of the twin method, in which persons in different degrees of hereditary and environmental relationships to each other are simply compared for behavioral similarity. In these studies, attention has been focused principally upon the amount of resemblance of monozygotic as contrasted to dizygotic twins. Yet such a comparison is particularly difficult to interpret because of the many subtle differences in the environmental situations of the two types of twins. A more fruitful comparison would seem to be that between dizygotic twins and siblings, for whom the hereditary similarity is known to be the same. In Kallmann's monumental research on psychiatric disorders among twins (20), for example, one of the most convincing bits of evidence for the operation of hereditary factors in schizophrenia is the fact that the degrees of concordance for dizygotic twins and for siblings were practically identical. In contrast, it will be recalled that in intelligence test scores dizygotic twins resemble each other much more closely than do siblings—a finding which reveals the influence of environmental factors in intellectual development.

SUMMARY

The heredity-environment problem is still very much alive. Its viability is assured by the gradual replacement of the questions, "Which one?" and "How much?" by the more basic and appropriate question, "How?" Hereditary influences—as well as environmental factors of an organic nature—vary along a "continuum of indirectness." The more indirect their connection with behavior, the wider will be the range of variation of possible outcomes. One extreme of the continuum of indirectness may be illustrated by brain damage leading to mental deficiency; the other extreme, by physical characteristics associated with social stereotypes. Examples of factors falling at intermediate points include deafness, physical diseases, and motor disorders. Those environmental factors which act directly upon behavior can be ordered along a continuum of breadth or permanence of effect, as exemplified by social class membership, amount of formal schooling, language handicap, and familiarity with specific test items.

Several current lines of research offer promising techniques for exploring the *modus operandi* of hereditary and environmental factors. Outstanding among them are investigations of: (*a*) hereditary conditions which underlie behavioral differences between selectively bred groups of animals; (*b*) relations between physiological variables and individual differences in behavior, especially in the case of pathological deviations; (*c*) role of prenatal physiological factors in behavior development; (*d*) influence of early experience upon eventual behavioral characteristics; (*e*) cultural differences in child-rearing practices in relation to intellectual and emotional development; (*f*) mechanisms of somatopsychological relationships; and (*g*) psychological development of twins from infancy to maturity, together with observations of their social environment. Such approaches are extremely varied with regard to subjects employed, nature of psychological functions studied, and specific experimental procedures followed. But it is just such heterogeneity of methodology that is demanded by the wide diversity of ways in which hereditary and environmental factors interact in behavior development.

REFERENCES

1. ANASTASI, ANNE. *Psychological testing.* New York: Macmillan, (2nd ed., 1961).
2. ANASTASI, ANNE. *Differential psychology.* (3rd ed.) New York: Macmillan, 1958.
3. ANASTASI, ANNE, and CORDOVA, F. A. Some effects of bilingualism upon the intelligence test performance of Puerto Rican children in New York City. *J. educ. Psychol.*, 1953, 44, 1-19.
4. ANASTASI, ANNE, and FOLEY, J. P., JR. A proposed reorientation in the heredity-environ-
ment controversy. *Psychol. Rev.*, 1948, 55, 239-249.
5. ARSENIAN, S. Bilingualism in the post-war world. *Psychol. Bull.*, 1945, 42, 65-86.
6. BARKER, R. G., WRIGHT, BEATRICE A., MYERSON, L., and GONICK, MOLLIE R. Adjustment to physical handicap and illness: A survey of the social psychology of physique and disability. *Soc. Sci. Res. Coun. Bull.*, 1953, No. 55 (Rev.).
7. BARKER, R. G., and WRIGHT, H. F. *Midwest and its children: The psychological ecology of an American town.* Evanston, Ill.: Row, Peterson, 1955.
8. BEACH, F. A., and JAYNES, J. Effects of early experience upon the behavior of animals. *Psychol. Bull.*, 1954, 51, 239-263.
9. BRACKBILL, G. A. Studies of brain dysfunction in schizophrenia. *Psychol. Bull.*, 1956, 53, 210-226.
10. DARCY, NATALIE T. A review of the literature on the effects of bilingualism upon the measurement of intelligence. *J. genet. Psychol.*, 1953, 82, 21-57.
11. DAVIS, A., and HAVIGHURST, R. J. Social class and color differences in child rearing. *Amer. sociol. Rev.*, 1946, 11, 698-710.
12. DOBZHANSKY, T. The genetic nature of differences among men. In S. Persons (Ed.), *Evolutionary thought in America.* New Haven: Yale Univer. Press, 1950. Pp. 86-155.
13. DOBZHANSKY, T. Heredity, environment, and evolution. *Science*, 1950, 111, 161-166.
14. FORGUS, R. H. The effect of early perceptual learning on the behavioral organization of adult rats. *J. comp. physiol. Psychol.*, 1954, 47, 331-336.
15. HALDANE, J. B. S. *Heredity and politics.* New York: Norton, 1938.
16. HARRELL, RUTH F., WOODYARD, ELLA, and GATES, A. I. *The effect of mothers' diets on the intelligence of the offspring.* New York: Bur. Publ., Teach. Coll., Columbia Univer., 1955.
17. HEBB, D. O. *The organization of behavior.* New York: Wiley, 1949.
18. HIRSCH, J. and TRYON, R. C. Mass screening and reliable individual measurement in the experimental behavior genetics of lower organisms. *Psychol. Bull.*, 1956, 53, 402-410.
19. HORWITT, M. K. Fact and artifact in the biology of schizophrenia. *Science*, 1956, 124, 429-430.
20. KALLMANN, F. J. *Heredity in health and mental disorder; Principles of psychiatric genetics in the light of comparative twin studies.* New York: Norton, 1953.

21. KING, J. A., and GURNEY, NANCY L. Effect of early social experience on adult aggressive behavior in C57BL10 mice. *J. comp. physiol. Psychol.*, 1954, 47, 326-330.

22. LOEVINGER, JANE. On the proportional contributions of differences in nature and in nurture to differences in intelligence. *Psychol. Bull.*, 1943, 40, 725-756.

23. LORENZ, K. Der Kumpan in der Umwelt des Vogels. Der Artgenosse als auslösendes Moment sozialer Verhaltungsweisen. *J. Orn., Lpz.*, 1935, 83, 137-213; 289-413.

24. LUCHINS, A. S., and FORGUS, R. H. The effect of differential postweaning environment on the rigidity of an animal's behavior. *J. genet. Psychol.*, 1955, 86, 51-58.

25. MELZACK, R. The genesis of emotional behavior: An experimental study of the dog. *J. comp. physiol. Psychol.*, 1954, 47, 166-168.

26. MILNER, ESTHER A. A study of the relationships between reading readiness in grade one school children and patterns of parent-child interaction. *Child Develpm.*, 1951, 22, 95-112.

27. PASAMANICK, B. KNOBLOCH, HILDA, and LILIENFELD, A. M. Socioeconomic status and some precursors of neuropsychiatric disorder. *Amer. J. Orthopsychiat.*, 1956, 26, 594-601.

28. SCHWESINGER, GLADYS C. *Heredity and environment.* New York: Macmillan, 1933.

29. SCOTT, J. P., and CHARLES, MARGARET S. Some problems of heredity and social behavior. *J. gen. Psychol.*, 1953, 48, 209-230.

30. SCOTT, J. P., and FULLER, J. L. Research on genetics and social behavior at the Roscoe B. Jackson Memorial Laboratory, 1946-1951—

A progress report. *J. Hered.*, 1951, 42, 191-197.

31. SEARLE, L. V. The organization of hereditary maze-brightness and maze-dullness. *Genet. Psychol. Monogr.*, 1949, 39, 279-325.

32. SNYDER, L. H. The genetic approach to human individuality. *Sci. Mon., N.Y.*, 1949, 68, 165-171.

33. SNYDER, L. H., and DAVID, P. R. *The principles of heredity.* (5th ed.) Boston: Heath, 1957.

34. SPOERL, DOROTHY T. Bilinguality and emotional adjustment. *J. abnorm. soc. Psychol.*, 1943, 38, 37-57.

35. THOMPSON, W. R., and MELZACK, R. Early environment. *Sci. Amer.*, 1956, 194 (1), 38-42.

36. TRYON, R. C. Genetic differences in maze-learning ability in rats. *Yearb. nat. Soc. Stud. Educ.*, 1940, 39, Part I, 111-119.

37. WHITING, J. W. M., *et al. Field guide for a study of socialization in five societies.* Cambridge, Mass.: Harvard Univer., 1954 (mimeo.).

38. WHITING, J. W. M., and CHILD, I. L. *Child training and personality: A cross-cultural study.* New Haven: Yale Univer. Press, 1953.

39. WILLIAMS, JUDITH R., and SCOTT, R. B. Growth and development of Negro infants: IV. Motor development and its relationship to child rearing practices in two groups of Negro infants. *Child Develpm.*, 1953, 24, 103-121.

40. WOODWORTH, R. S. Heredity and environment: A critical survey of recently published material on twins and foster children. *Soc. Sci. Res. Coun. Bull.*, 1941, No. 47.

7/NEW DIRECTIONS IN THE GENETIC STUDY OF PERSONALITY AND INTELLIGENCE/J. P. SCOTT[*]

THE PROBLEM OF THE EFFECT OF heredity upon human behavior is one which concerned biologists and psychologists as soon as their fields were recognized as science. What a person does is obviously more important than his looks, and ever since the time of Galton extensive efforts have been made to find out why some people act differently from others. In spite of all this effort, the best conclusion that a recent impartial survey could report on the subject was that "the results are incapable of definitive interpretation."[1] Progress along these lines of research has apparently come to a standstill, and there is a consequent need for a fresh approach.

New ideas on human problems may come from many sources, but one of the most important of these is basic animal research. The lower animals can be studied with considerable objectivity and their greater variety of biological function inevitably leads to fresh ideas and techniques. In this article I am going to try to describe some of the new directions which are developing in animal research and indicate ways in which they might shed new light on human nature.

In recent years there has been a renaissance in the study of animal behavior, starting with the discovery by Allee, Yerkes and others that almost all animals have some degree of social life and consequently that almost all behavior has some element of social significance. A group of European biologists led by Lorenz and Tinbergen has begun to study the ways in which animals make social adjustments to each other and has concluded that a great deal of social behavior is instinctive and arises only in connection with rather specific stimuli which are called social releasers. All their results tend to emphasize the role of heredity in producing behavioral differences between species.

From this conclusion it is only a step to the idea that the important thing to study within a species is variability in fundamental traits of social behavior. Such studies are being carried out in a number of laboratories. For example, Professor William C. Young of the University of Kansas is studying genetic differences in sexual behavior of the guinea pig, and at the nearby Manhattan Agricultural College Professor A. M. Guhl is concerned with genetic differences in the fighting behavior and dominance organization of chickens. Dr. William R. Thompson of McGill University is working on variability in exploratory behavior of mice, a species which is notorious for the amount of time it spends investigating the environment. It will be seen that the essential idea is to study the genetics of a type of behavioral adjustment which has basic social importance, and this approach is constantly turning up new ideas regarding some of the old problems of intelligence and personality.

At the Jackson Laboratory a group of us have been fortunate enough to have the privilege of working with genetics and the social behavior of dogs, a species which has unique advantages for this type of research. Dogs were probably the earliest animal to be domesticated by man and have developed rich and complicated social relationships with our own species for thousands of years. Within these dog-human social relationships breeds have been selected for their ability to learn a great variety of special tasks. Beagles can be quickly taught to hunt rabbits, terriers to fight, cocker spaniels to retrieve, and sheep dogs to herd sheep. If there is any species within which heredity may produce important effects on social behavior, it should be the dog.

Starting with a broad sample of tests on emotional behavior, physiological reactions and learning capacities as well as fundamental social behavior, it has been easy for the Jackson Laboratory researchers to find emotional and motivational differences between breed populations raised in the same environment. For example, most of the dogs studied in the various breeds have a tendency to show an initial timidity in their reaction to human beings. This trait appears early in life and has to be overcome be-

[1] Anne Anastasi and J. P. Foley, *Differential Psychology*, Macmillan, 1949.

[*] J. P. Scott, New directions in the genetic study of personality and intelligence, *Eugenical News* (now *Eugenics Quarterly*), 1953, *38*, 97-101. Reprinted by permission.

fore the puppy can form a strong attachment to human beings and be taught various tasks. However, the cocker spaniels in our sample seem to show very little timidity and a strong degree of attraction to people from the very first, and this condition is maintained. With most animals it is easy to overcome timidity by proper training as a very young puppy, but this becomes increasingly difficult if the training is postponed. With the cocker spaniels such difficulty is avoided and the dog may be said to be born socialized.*

Examples of other traits which show a genetic basis can be cited: aggressiveness, sensitivity to noises, sensitivity of the heart-rate reaction to psychological stimulation, average body temperature, and so on. It will be noted that these traits, while they may profoundly alter the capacity of a dog to adjust to the dog-human social relationship—and hence to learn what he is taught—are not in themselves intellectual. This evidence is closely similar to that obtained by Tryon in an older experiment on the learning capacities of rats.

In this experiment an attempt was made to modify by selection the intelligence exhibited by rats in a maze. A mechanical maze was set up and rats were selected as parents on the basis of whether they learned the route rapidly or slowly. After six or seven generations, two widely different populations had been developed, one of which made good scores on the maze and one of which made decidedly poor ones. Fortunately, the experiment was not stopped at this point, and Tryon encouraged Searle to test these stocks on other types of problems, including such different situations as an underwater maze. The animals which had been "bright" on the original maze sometimes did very poorly, and those which had been classified as "dull" sometimes did very well on other pieces of apparatus. It was concluded that the rats had been selected not so much for differences in intelligence as differences in emotional response to the original maze apparatus; that is, the dull rats were simply those which were afraid of the maze.

Here are the results of two selection experiments, both concerned with learning abilities, one done in fields and households over a period of hundreds of years, and one done under con-

trolled laboratory conditions within a decade. It would be easy to draw the conclusion that selection for learning capacity chiefly operates on variability in emotional and motivational traits. But if still another type of experiment is considered, a deeper insight into the matter appears.

In one of the Jackson Laboratory experiments young puppies were placed within a set of barriers which gave them a variety of stimuli to escape: confinement, isolation and a food reward. If a puppy was uninterested in food there were other types of motivation present, and under these conditions the breed populations tested showed no significant differences in the average time it took them to escape. By the end of ten trials all animals rapidly came out with very minor differences in performance. The conclusion can be fairly drawn that all the animals had made an adjustment to the situation and were nearly equal in intelligence.

However, it seemed worthwhile to study the results in terms of partial rather than total adjustment. Learning can be thought of as a process, or perhaps a group of processes. Three stages can be recognized: one of initial variability in which the animal tries out in rotation the various kinds of adaptive responses which are peculiar to the species; second, a period of elimination of useless movements; finally, a period of habit formation.

When these stages were considered separately, interesting differences began to appear. The beagles, a hunting breed which might be expected to have considerable facility in dealing with natural barriers, showed on the average many mistakes in the first stage, indicating a great deal of random exploratory activity. In the second stage improvement was very rapid, and in the third the beagle showed much less tendency to form a fixed habit than did the other animals. Without lowering their efficiency, they often did the task in a slightly different way. This same type of variability has shown up in other tests, and one can see why it would be advantageous to a hunting dog. If a beagle formed a fixed habit of going down the same path through a field each day, he would not be likely to catch many rabbits. Yet the total efficiency, what we would ordinarily call intelligence, was not greatly different from the other breeds.

---

* Since the above was written, Freedman, King and Elliot (*Science*, 133, 1016, 1961) have raised cocker spaniels, in a large field, completely without socialization up until 14 weeks of age. As other breeds, these pups went completely wild, the only difference being that

they attempted to bite handlers a little less severely. Therefore, we must conclude that this breed needs a minimum amount of human contact to become socialized, but is not "born socialized."

The conclusion must be drawn that the fruitful way to analyze behavior in terms of genetics is through specific processes rather than through overall adaptation or "intelligence." This receives strong support from the study of the physiological genetics of other traits of both plants and animals. A gene can only act by modifying some physiological process, whether it be growth in the embryo or pigment formation in the adult, and clear-cut genetic results can be expected in the study of behavior only where a trait is measured which is either a physiological process or largely based on one. If behavior is measured in terms of overall adjustment, dozens and even hundreds of physiological processes are likely to be involved, and these may be organized so that a deficiency in one is cancelled by an excess in another.

Going back to Tryon's "bright" and "dull" rats, and the various breeds of dogs, it may indeed be true that emotional and motivational processes play an important role in determining differential reactions to a learning situation. But the reason why such emotional and motivational differences are easy to find is probably the simple one that they are based directly on integrated physiological processes. There is some evidence that if measurements of adaptation and "intelligence" are broken down into specific and limited processes they also give clear-cut genetic results.

The general theoretical picture is that an individual has within him a very large number of physiological processes, each independently affected by heredity and all of which may go into his behavior. Confronted with a situation or problem which requires adjustment, the individual may organize these processes in a variety of ways. The fact that he adjusts very rapidly to one special situation may have little relationship to his adjustment in another situation, where he may organize these processes (or capacities) in an entirely different way with either good or poor results.

Now, what kinds of research can fruitfully be done with the new approach? The first of these concerns animal behavior, where controlled experiments are much easier to do than with human material. The perfect experiment will probably never be done, but there are certain aims which can be enumerated:

1. Look for simple types of behavioral adjustment which are closely related to basic physiological processes.

2. Make a large number of behavioral measurements in a variety of situations. In many cases

the processes involved can be correctly identified only by correlating several measurements.

3. Look for variability in important and fundamental processes. One excellent criterion of importance is close relationship to basic types of social adjustment such as sexual behavior, fighting, parental care, and the like. Another criterion would be close association with fundamental detailed processes of learning such as habit formation.

From a genetic point of view certain other requirements should be met. The ideal genetic experiment includes two populations which are alike except for a single gene, but such a situation is rarely met. Next best are two highly inbred populations, such as are now available in house mice and may soon be available in chickens and some other domestic animals. The third choice is two separate populations, each of which contains some fixed genes and some variable ones. Such is the situation in the different breeds of dogs and other domestic animals, and also in sub-populations of wild animals like the deer-mouse *Peromyscus*. It is in this last category that some of the most interesting behavioral differences occur.

It may be predicted that some very interesting results will come out of this type of research. Evolution is now thought to proceed in terms of populations as much as individuals, and the organization of populations depends on their social behavior. Interaction between the sciences of genetics and animal behavior should soon produce new and exciting discoveries.

Finally, there are certain new lines which are indicated for human research. Boiled down, these ideas may be stated as: Look for simple types of behavior closely related to physiological processes which genes can modify. A first task would be an attempt to develop methods whereby early recognition of basic behavioral traits could be made in human infants. It should be possible to recognize the kind of emotional traits which the animal research indicates are important in behavior at a fairly early age. In this way it would be possible to give human children the kind of upbringing which would be the most beneficial for the particular capacities which they have.

In the second place it would be suggested that if the effect of genetics is to be studied in human beings a search be made for the kind of basic capacities which are little affected by training and can be measured in adults as well as children. Such things as the thresholds of emotional reactions presumably would remain relatively stable, whereas such reactions as the ability to read and form a vocabulary could be enormously affected by training.

Contrariwise, it may be suggested that genetic analysis of measures of general adaptation such as the Intelligence Quotient are not likely to give much further information at the present time. Early in the history of biological science it was sometimes assumed that the effect of heredity upon behavior might be accomplished through a simple mechanism in which a few genes modified a simple trait of intelligence or adaptability. This hope has not been realized and the actual situation appears to be one in which each individual may have dozens of capacities which are independently inherited and all of which may modify his behavior. Once the individual is faced with a situation demanding adaptation, he organizes these capacities in such a way as to produce an adjustment. Another individual with a different set of capacities may meet the same situation equally well by organizing his different capacities in another way. The task of geneticists and psychologists is to discover and measure these basic capacities. In special cases and situations these processes and capacities may strictly limit the behavior of an individual, but in most a very considerable degree of adaptability is possible.

Once these facts are known, it may be possible to again take up the problem of how genetics may modify the ability of an individual to organize his basic capacities effectively into what we call personality and intelligence. A final task will be to discover the different types of environment which are most favorable to the development of this ability in individuals with different combinations of basic capacities.

8/CONSTITUTIONAL AND ENVIRONMENTAL INTERACTIONS IN REARING OF FOUR BREEDS OF DOGS/D. G. FREEDMAN*

THE INITIAL INTENTION OF THE PRESent study was to determine the relative effects of "indulgent" and "disciplinary" modes of rearing in dogs, with particular emphasis on how each method affects the obedience of the animal at maturity. The work derived from the extensive observations of children made by D. M. Levy (1), who has shown that overindulgent rearing may lead to psychopathy, a syndrome which involves an abnormal inability to inhibit one's impulses. The study described in this report was an attempt to deal experimentally with Levy's concept. As will be seen, the results are of interest aside from their reflection on this initial hypothesis.

Eight litters of four pups each were used. These included two litters each of Shetland sheep dogs, basenjis, wire-haired fox terriers, and beagles. Following weaning at 3 weeks of age, each litter of four was divided into two pairs equated as closely as possible on the basis of sex, weight, activity, vocalizations, maturation of eyes and ears, and reactivity to a startling stimulus. Each member of one pair was there-

* D. G. Freedman, Constitutional and environmental interactions in rearing of four breeds of dogs, *Science*, 1958, *127* (3298), March 14, 585-586. Reprinted by permission.

after indulged, and each member of the other pair was disciplined, during two daily 15-minute periods from their third to their eighth week of age.

Indulgence consisted of encouraging a pup in any activity it initiated, such as play, aggression, and climbing on the supine handler. These pups were never punished. By contrast, the disciplined pups were at first restrained in the experimenter's lap and were later taught to sit, to stay, and to come upon command. When still older they were trained to follow on a leash. The pups were handled and tested individually by a single experimenter throughout the study. They lived in pairs in isolation boxes the remainder of the time, where members of in-

dulged and disciplined pairs received identical treatment. The results were as follows:

At 8 weeks of age each pup was subjected to the following test: Each time a pup ate meat from a bowl placed in the center of a room, he was punished with a swat on the rump and a shout of "no!" After three minutes the experimenter left the room and, observing through a one-way glass, recorded the time that elapsed before the pup again ate. The results over 8 days of testing are summarized in Fig. 1. Basenjis tended to eat soon after the experimenter left, the method of rearing having no statistically significant effect. Shetland sheep dogs tended to refuse the food over the entire 8 days of testing. Again, the fashion of rearing had no significant effect. Beagles and wirehaired fox terriers, however, differentiated into two significantly disparate groups, depending on the condition of rearing. The Friedman nonparametric analysis of variance (2) indicates that the indulged pups took significantly longer to return to the food than did the disciplined pups ($p = 0.001$). Thus, as measured in this test, essentially the same differences in treatment had a decisive effect upon only two breeds.

Can characteristics of the breeds explain the differences in performance on this test? It was clear that, during training, beagles and wirehaired terriers were strongly oriented to the experimenter and sought contact with him continuously. Basenjis, by contrast, were interested in all phases of the environment and often ignored the experimenter in favor of inanimate objects. Shetland sheep dogs showed yet another pattern; all became fearful of physical contact with the experimenter and tended to maintain distance from him. We see, then, that the two breeds that were highly attracted to the experimenter differentiated as a result of the mode of rearing, whereas the breeds that exhibited aloofness (basenjis) and excessive timidity (Shetland sheep dogs) did not. Apparently it was the strong (constitutional) attraction in interaction with indulgent treatment that enhanced the effectiveness of later punishment. It should be noted that basenjis and Shetland sheep dogs were not entirely unaffected by the differential treatment. The scores of *all* indulged animals were significantly different from those of their disciplined counterparts on five of ten tests administered. In general, these tests indicated that the indulged pups were more active, more vocal, less timid (although more easily inhibited with punishment) than the disciplined pups.

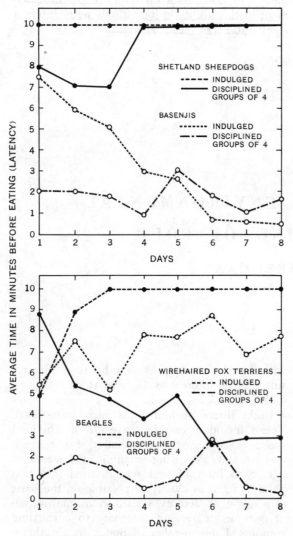

FIGURE 1 / PERFORMANCE OF 8-WEEK-OLD PUPPIES ON THE "INHIBITION-TO-EATING" TEST (SEE TEXT FOR DETAILS OF PROCEDURE).

A test of individual reactions to veterinary treatment based on vocalizations and the degree of activity during routine injections indicates that indulged pups were more vocal and active than disciplined pups in their protest ($p = 0.02$, Mann-Whitney) and that basenjis were more vocal and active than the other three breeds ($p = 0.01$, Friedman analysis of variance). It has been found at our laboratory that basenjis generally gain higher scores on this test than other breeds; hence these data suggest that similar behavior may be due in one instance to constitution (as in the basenjis) and in other instances to the conditions of rearing.

A test of the level of activity, in which the pups were observed from a hidden vantage point for 10 minutes, was administered. The testing area was 10 by 20 ft. and was demarcated into eight squares of 5 by 5 ft. each. In this setting, *disciplined* Shetland sheep dogs showed significantly less activity than any other animals ($p = 0.001$, Friedman analysis of variance). In another test the experimenter sat silently in a room for 10 minutes and recorded the amount of time the pups spent in contact with him. In this test the *indulged* Shetland sheep dogs differed significantly from all other dogs in that they rarely approached the experimenter ($p = 0.001$, Friedman analysis of vari-

ance). From these results it is clear that a specific test for a specific breed may facilitate expression of the effects of early rearing.

The conditions of rearing were continued over a second period, when the pups were 11 to 15 weeks of age, and all tests were readministered, with essentially the same results.

In the follow-up observations and tests, the indulged beagles, in contrast to all other animals, underwent dramatic changes, in time, although all animals were maintained under standard conditions. On a weekly test in which the time taken to catch each animal was recorded, these animals became exceedingly shy and wary of being caught when approached by various human beings, including the experimenter ($p = 0.05$, t test). Thus, it appears that changes in the behavior of certain animals may occur that are seemingly independent of the current environment and belatedly dependent, instead, upon the mediation of past experiences.

REFERENCES

1. D. M. LEVY, *Maternal Overprotection*. (Columbia Univ. Press, New York, 1943).

2. S. SIEGEL, *Non-parametric Statistics*. (McGraw-Hill, New York, 1956).

9/PLASTICITY OF SENSORIMOTOR DEVELOPMENT IN THE HUMAN INFANT[1,2]/

BURTON L. WHITE AND RICHARD HELD

INTRODUCTION

THE HUMAN INFANT ENGAGES IN countless episodes of sensorimotor exploration during the first months of life (1). Prominent among these behaviors is visually directed reaching (prehension) which is, in turn, dependent upon orienting, accommodating, and pursuit responses of the eyes. Achievement of these sensorimotor abilities occurs during the first half year of life. This paper, and the research effort of which it is a report, focuses on the role of experience in these fundamental aspects of development.

Two considerations have guided this research. On the one hand, we share with many other investigators an interest in the role of contact with the environment in the earliest development of infant behavior. On the other hand, we have been concerned with testing the implications of a specific theory of the development of sensorimotor coordination (2, 3). In testing for the contribution of early experience to development we are not prejudging the outcome of the complex issue of nature versus nurture. On the contrary, we are convinced that the endogenous mechanisms of development can best be delineated by increased understanding of the role of early contact with the environment.

The first steps in our research have been to trace the normal course of development of various fundamental sensorimotor behaviors such as reaching (1), exploratory activities (4), visual accommodation (5), and blink to approaching objects. Subsequently, we have systematically modified the rearing conditions of several groups of infants. For humane reasons the modifications must necessarily be mild. Consequently, we have required normative scales of sufficient detail and precision to reveal small changes in rates of development. Our initial studies were designed to assess the modifiability of these rates by introducing relatively gross environmental alterations. Future research, now in the planning stage, will be more analytical, with the identification of specific experiential factors as their goal.

During the daylight hours, the newborn infant is visually alert less than 3% of the time, but at six months of age this percentage is approaching 50% (6). At birth, aside from a rudimentary ocular centralizing reflex, the infant does not exhibit any ability to orient himself to visible targets. Yet, at six months, he skillfully pursues visible targets viewed at various distances and moving with a wide range of speeds. In addition, he reaches swiftly and accurately for visible objects nearby (1). At birth the infant's accommodative mechanism is incapable of tracking a visible object in depth, but at six months he is at least as adept and accurate as the normal adult (5). In these and other behaviors the six month old infant has attained a very high degree of competence. Does experience contribute to these developments? And, if so, in what ways?

Large individual differences in rates of infant development suggest that different rearing conditions have differential consequences. Hunt (7) has made this thesis explicit in his analysis of the implications of Piaget's sensorimotor theory (8). However, it has not been experimentally tested prior to the present work.

One systematic approach to the problem of the development of sensorimotor coordination derives from consideration of modifiability of function in the adult. Some of the errors induced by rearrangement of sensory inputs are com-

[1] At various stages, extending over the last six years, this research has received support from grant M-3657 from the National Institute of Mental Health, grant 61-234 from the Foundation's Fund for Research in Psychiatry, grant HD 00761 from the National Institute of Health, the Optometric Extension Program, grant NSG-496 from the National Aeronautics and Space Administration, grant AF-AFOSR 354-63 from the U.S. Air Force Office of Scientific Research, and the Rockefeller Foundation. The research was conducted at the Tewksbury Hospital, Tewksbury, Massachusetts. We are very grateful for the assistance of Mr. Peter Castle and Miss Kitty Riley and for the consideration and aid given by Drs. John Lu, Solomon J. Fleischman, Peter Wolff and Lois Crowell and head nurses Helen Efatathiou, Frances Craig and Virginia Donovan.

[2] This paper has been compiled in large part from an oral presentation to the American Association for the Advancement of Science, presented in Cleveland in December, 1963 by the senior author.

pletely compensated for after the subjects of these experiments have undergone prolonged experience in their normal environments (2, 16). Activity, initiated by the subject and performed in a dependably contoured surround, appears to be a necessary condition for full adaptation (9, 10, 11). The fact that accurate visual-motor function can be fully re-established suggests that the mechanism underlying the adaptation may also be involved in the original acquisition of such perceptual-motor skills. Confirmation of this speculation has come from experimental studies with animals (3). Kittens deprived solely of the opportunity for self-induced movements in the presence of a stable visual surround exhibited marked deficits in visual-motor development.

With infra-human species selective deprivation is a traditional tactic used for analyzing the role of experience. With human infants this procedure is inappropriate for obvious reasons. An alternative approach consists of selectively enriching the early experience of infants whose ordinary rearing conditions provide a comparatively bland psychological diet. The latter course is the one we have taken.

SUBJECTS

Our subjects were 63 infants born and reared in an institution because of inadequate family conditions. These infants were selected from a larger group after detailed evaluation of their medical histories[*] and those of their mothers along with relevant data on other family members whenever available. All infants included in the study were judged physically normal. Reports based on studies of institutionally-reared infants generally include a statement acknowledging atypical conditions and, in addition, such infants may congenitally constitute a non-representative sample. On the other hand, two factors make a group of such infants unusually suitable for experimental research. First, rearing conditions are virtually identical for each infant in marked contrast to the highly variable conditions for subjects reared in their own homes. Second, it is possible to systematically change rearing conditions in the institutional setting and to maintain continuous surveillance over their administration.

[*] Infants' daily records were screened under the supervision of Drs. P. Wolff and L. Crowell for signs of abnormality using standard medical criteria. Mothers' records were examined for possible genetic pathology and serious complications during pregnancy or delivery.

Figure 1 illustrates the typical crib setting for infants between the ages of one and four months. Clearly, the world of these infants is bland and uniform.

BASELINE DATA

Using standard test and observational procedures we have acquired the following information concerning infants reared under the regular hospital routine.

A. THE DEVELOPMENT OF VISUAL ATTENTION. In order to determine the sheer amount of visual exploratory activities exhibited by infants, and also to gain a thorough knowledge of their spontaneous visual-motor behavior, we initiated weekly 3-hour observation periods for each of our subjects.

Briefly, visual attention is defined as the state in which the infant's eyes are more than half open, their direction of gaze shifting at least once within any 30-second period.

Figure 2 illustrates the development of this activity from birth through 4 months (c. 120 days) of age. Each point represents the average of 2 scores taken during successive 2-week periods. It is interesting to note the correspond-

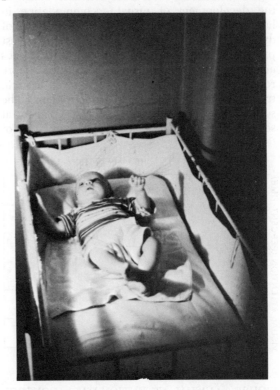

FIGURE 1.

ence between rather dramatic changes in the
visible environment and the shape of this curve.
For example, the sharp increase in slope at
about 2 months (c. 50 days) of age occurs at
about the same time as the onset of sustained
hand regard (visual regard of the hands). (See
arrow on Figure 2.) For the next 6 weeks or
so, the child spends much of his waking time
observing his fist and finger movements. The
next major change in the visible environment
occurred for these infants between 3½ and 4
months (c. 105-120 days, see vertical line on
Figure 2). They were transferred to large open-
sided cribs. The combination of greater trunk
motility, enabling them to turn from side to
side, and the more accessible visual surround
gave them more visual experience. At about this
time, the slope of the curve again shows a sharp
increase.

B. THE DEVELOPMENT OF VISUAL ACCOMMODA-
TION. Visual accommodation is the activity by
which the image of a target is focused on the
retina of the eye. This adjustment is largely
accomplished by contraction or relaxation of the
ciliary muscle which in turn changes the shape
of the crystalline lens. Prior to the present research there has been no systematic study of
the development of visual accommodation in
human infants. We have used the technique of
dynamic retinoscopy for this purpose. The test
procedure is designed to measure the subject's
accommodative ability under conditions more
relevant to normal function than those used in
traditional ophthalmological examinations. The
subject's accommodation to targets placed at
several distances is tested with eyes free of

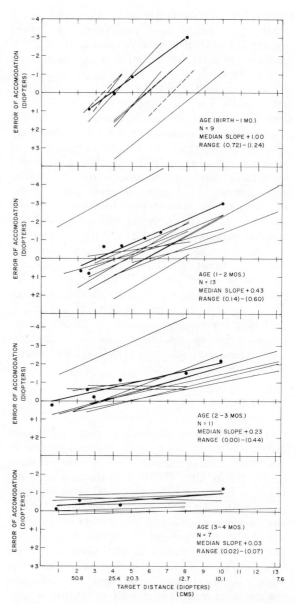

FIGURE 3* / FOUR STAGES IN THE DEVELOP-
MENT OF ACCOMMODATION IN THE FIRST 4
MONTHS OF LIFE. THE HEAVY LINES FITTED
TO THE FILLED CIRCLES ILLUSTRATE BOTH
THE PROGRESS OF A TYPICAL INFANT AND
ALSO THE CLOSENESS OF FIT OF THE LINES
TO THE PLOTTED POINTS. DURING THE FIRST
MONTH, THE DATA THAT WERE ESTIMATED
ARE REPRESENTED BY DASHED LINES. PLUS
VALUES INDICATE MYOPIC PERFORMANCE.
MINUS VALUES INDICATE DEVIATIONS IN THE
HYPEROPIC DIRECTION.

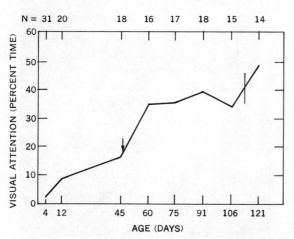

FIGURE 2 / VISUAL ATTENTION DATA—CONTROL
GROUP.

* Reprinted by permission from Harold Haynes, Burton L. White, and Richard Held, Visual Accommodation
in human infants, *Science*, 1965, *148*, 3669, 528-530.

drugs. (Routine ophthalmological examinations employ cycloplegic drugs.) He is then tested for his capacity to track the target as it is moved toward and away from his eyes. Together with Dr. Harold Haynes of Pacific University, we performed 111 dynamic retinoscopy examinations on 25 of our infants.

With the use of lenses, objective measures of accommodative performance were obtained at target distances varying from 4 to 60 inches. The infant's capacity to track the target was also tested. The instrument used was a standard Copeland streak retinoscope with a white cardboard shield mounted so as to prevent the infant from seeing the examiner's head. The results of this study are shown in Figure 3.

Perfect adjustment to changing target distance would be presented by a slope of 0.00 on the graphs (Figure 3). Complete absence of accommodative change would be indicated by a slope of + 1.00. Prior to one month of age (c. 30 days), the infant's accommodative response does not adjust to change in target distance. The system appears to be locked at one focal distance whose median value for the group is 7½ in. This is indicated by a slope value for the group of + 1.00. Occasionally, infants of this age did not remain alert long enough to allow complete calibration of their responses. In these few instances, the magnitude of error was estimated (see caption of Figure 3). Flexibility of response begins at about the middle of the second month (c. 45 days). Performance comparable to that of the normal adult is attained by the fourth month (c. 120 days), as shown by a median slope value of + 0.03.

In addition to the above measurements, eleven infants were retinoscoped while asleep in the nursery. In all eleven cases, the accommodative system was found totally relaxed. Infants less than one week of age, occasionally exhibited slow changes in accommodation, but they were in no way related to distance of the target. Older infants, when drowsy, exhibited a gradual drift of accommodation towards optical infinity suggesting that drifting seen in the first week of life is a function of level of drowsiness.

C. VISUALLY-DIRECTED REACHING. To the best of our knowledge, no previous investigator, aside

RESPONSE	OBSERVED IN	TOTAL N	MEDIAN AND RANGE OF DATES OF FIRST OCCURRENCE (DAYS)								
			20	40	60	80	100	120	140	160	180
SWIPES AT OBJECT	13	13									
UNILATERAL HAND RAISING	15	15									
BOTH HANDS RAISED	16	18									
ALTERNATING GLANCES (HAND AND OBJECT)	18	19									
HANDS TO MIDLINE AND CLASP	15	15									
ONE HAND RAISED WITH ALTERNATING GLANCES, OTHER HAND TO MIDLINE CLUTCHING DRESS	11	19									
TORSO ORIENTED TOWARDS OBJECT	15	18									
HANDS TO MIDLINE AND CLASP AND ORIENTED TOWARDS OBJECT	14	19									
PIAGET-TYPE REACH	12	18									
TOP LEVEL REACH	14	14									

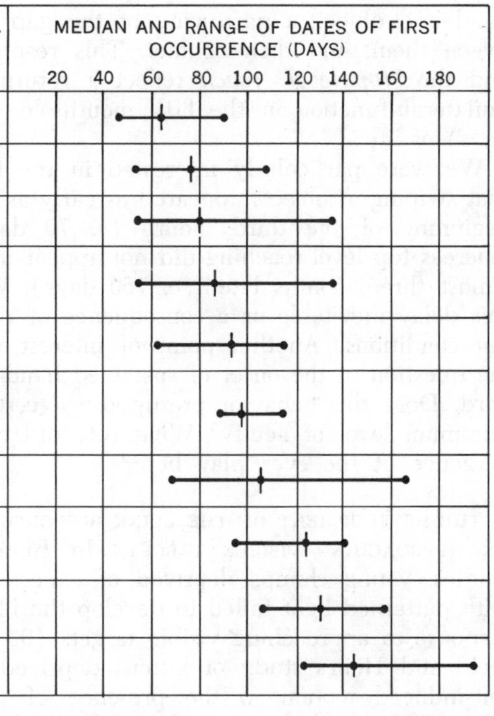

FIGURE 4* / NORMATIVE DATA ON THE DEVELOPMENT OF VISUALLY-DIRECTED REACHING. THESE DATA WERE COMPILED BY COMBINING THE SCORES OF CONTROL AND HANDLED INFANTS (WHICH DID NOT DIFFER SIGNIFICANTLY).

* From Burton L. White, Peter Castle, and Richard Held, Observations on the development of visually-directed reaching, *Child Development*, 1964, 35, 349-364. Reprinted by permission of the Society for Research in Child Development, Inc.

from Piaget (8), has studied in detail the acquisition of visually-directed reaching. However, Piaget was not centrally concerned with prehension and he observed only three subjects. Consequently, his data, though very provocative, are primarily of suggestive value.

Figure 4 depicts the results of our normative study: a 10-step analysis culminating in visually-directed reaching (1) just prior to five months (c. 150 days) of age. Moreover, by the time swiping behavior occurs, at about 2 months (c. 60 days), the infant is prepared to focus his eyes on targets (Figure 3). Convergence of the eyes as checked by clinical procedures was also found to be effective at this time. The range of accommodation increases rapidly during the period when hand regard makes its appearance.

Hands to the midline and clasp is characteristic of the bilateral behavior seen during the fourth month (c. 120 days) of life as the influence of the tonic neck reflex drops out. Torso-orienting reflects the child's growing capacities for gross motor action. What we have called a *"Piaget-type" reach* was described by Piaget as a raising of one hand to the vicinity of the object, followed by alternation of glance between hand and object, a narrowing of the gap between them, and then contact. This response and the *"top level" reach* reflect a return to unilateral function in the fifth month (c. 150 days) of life.

We were particularly interested in the fact that swiping at objects appeared as early as the beginning of the third month (c. 70 days) whereas top level reaching did not appear until almost three months later (c. 160 days). Was this delay inevitable or a consequence of rearing conditions? Another point of interest was the question of the onset of sustained hand regard. Does this behavior presuppose a certain minimum level of acuity? What role did convergence of the eyes play here?

D. THE DEVELOPMENT OF THE BLINK RESPONSE TO AN APPROACHING VISIBLE TARGET. In Riesen's studies, young chimps deprived of experience with patterned light failed to develop the blink response to approaching visible targets (9). In Held and Hein's study of kittens deprived of self-induced motion in the presence of patterned light similar deficits developed with respect to this response (3). No such studies have been done with human infants. Even normative data on the development of this function is unavailable. The literature contains several references to the palpebral response but in each

case the test circumstances combined the visual stimulus with touch or changes in air pressure as the target approached on the face.

We have performed a pilot study on 10 infants ranging in age from 1 month to 5 months of age. The apparatus we used consisted of a six inch bullseye target with ¼ in. red and white concentric rings. The object was mounted in a frame directly over the head of the supine infant. A plexiglass shield was placed 2 in. above the infant to preclude changes in air pressure as the target was dropped toward the subject. The range of target drop was from 2⅝ to 12½ in. Brightness changes were not totally prevented but the sources of light were arranged to minimize such effects. Recording procedures were also crude in this preliminary effort. One observer released the target and reported the magnitude and latency of response, the other recorded the data. The results were remarkably consistent.

The median age for the onset of blinking was 2 months (c. 60 days). The maximum target drop (12½ in.) had to be used to elicit the response and it was often slow and incomplete. By 3½ months (c. 105 days), the group exhibited very rapid and complete blinks and even occasional startles in at least 7 out of 10 trials. A target drop of but 2⅝ in. was sufficient to elicit these responses.

We have described baseline data for the development of four visual-motor functions, (A) visual attention, (B) visual accommodation, (C) visually-directed reaching, and (D) blinking to an approaching visible object. Are these developmental processes plastic? Is systematic contact with the environment instrumental in their development or does the infant simply grow into these skills?

EXPERIMENTAL RESULTS

A. FIRST MODIFICATIONS OF REARING CONDITIONS —HANDLING STUDY. Many recent studies have reported the remarkable effects of postnatal handling on the subsequent development of laboratory-reared animals (10, 11, 12). Mice, kittens and dogs given small amounts of extra early handling grew up to be "better" animals as measured by a wide variety of tests. They were superior in many physical and adaptive respects. Recent surveys of maternal deprivation studies by Yarrow (13) and Casler (14) suggest that early handling appears necessary for adequate human development. Sylvia Brody in her book, *Patterns of Mothering* (15), noted that infants who received moderate handling were consistently more visually attentive than those receiving minimal handling. Would extra handling of our subjects, who normally receive minimal amounts, result in accelerated visual-motor development?

From day 6 through day 36, nurses administered 20 minutes of extra handling each day to each infant (N = 10). Measures of overall development, physical growth, general health, the development of reaching, and visual attention were taken regularly between days 37 and 152.

No changes were found in any developmental process except the growth of visual attention. The handled group was significantly more visually attentive than controls (Figure 5). Note that the shapes of the curves are quite similar. Sustained hand regard appeared about 1 week later in the handled group (day 58) than in controls (day 50). Upon relocation in large open-sided cribs the handled group, like the control group, exhibited a sharp increase in visual attentiveness.

Aside from the relationship between handling and visual attentiveness, the major finding of this study was that an environmental modification resulted in a significant alteration in the rate of growth of visual exploratory behavior. No evidence for comparable plasticity in other visual-motor developments was found following the extra handling. It is possible that further exploration of the effects of early handling would produce still greater increases in visual exploratory behavior.

B. SECOND MODIFICATION OF REARING CONDITIONS —MASSIVE ENRICHMENT STUDY. Several recent studies seem to indicate that visual-motor performance depends to a significant extent on experience of some kind for its development. Riesen's work demonstrated that chimpanzees require exposure to patterned visual stimulation for normal visual-motor development (9). His later studies have suggested that movement within a patterned environment is also required for adequate development (9). Held and his collaborators (16, 17, 18) have repeatedly demonstrated the importance of self-induced movement in dependably structured environments for adaptation to rearranged sensory inputs in human adults. More recently, their study of neonatal kittens showed the applicability of these findings to developmental processes (3). The results of this study indicated that movement *per se* in the presence of a dependable surround was insufficient for normal visual-motor development. Kittens whose movements were *externally-produced* rather than *self-induced* did not develop normally. Self-induced movement in a dependable surround was found necessary for adequate development as well as maintenance of stable visual-motor behavior.

Our subjects are normally reared under conditions which are obviously less than optimal with respect to the types of experience discussed above. Motility is limited by soft mattresses with depressions in them as well as the supine posture in which these infants are kept. The visual surround is poorly figured. Consequently, according to our hypothesis, heightened motility in an enriched surround should produce accelerated visual-motor development.

As a first test we enriched environmental contact of a group of 19 infants in as many respects as feasible.

a. Increased tactual-vestibular stimulation. Each infant received 20 minutes of extra handling each day from day 6 through day 36.

b. Increased motility. Infants were placed in the prone posture for 15 minutes after the 6AM, 10AM, and 2PM feeding each day from day 37 through day 124. At these times, the crib liners were removed, making the ward activities visible to the child. Movements of the head and trunk in the presence of a figured visual surround resulted from the normal tendency of infants to rear their heads under such circumstances. The crib mattresses were flattened, thereby facilitating head, arm, and trunk motility.

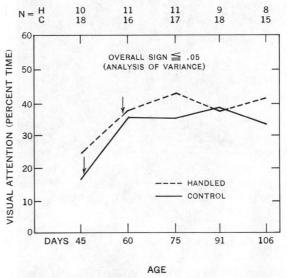

FIGURE 5 / COMPARATIVE VISUAL ATTENTION DATA.

c. Enriched visual surround. A special stabile featuring highly contrasting colors and numerous forms against a dull white background was suspended over these infants from day 37 through day 124 (see Figure 6). In addition, printed multi-colored sheets and bumpers were substituted for the standard flat white ones. These changes were designed to produce heightened visual interest and increased viewing of hand movements because of the normal tendency of infants to swipe at visible objects nearby.

Weekly measures of prehensory responses and visual attention were made. The rates of development of spontaneous behaviors related to visual-motor function such as hand regard, hands touching at the midline, mutual fingering, and torso turning were assessed from the records of the 3 hour observation periods. Performance on the Gesell tests was recorded at bi-weekly intervals to determine general developmental progress. Also, records of rate of weight gain and general health were kept.

RESULTS

1. *Hand regard and swiping*

Hand regard as such was much less frequently shown by this group as compared with controls. Instead the hands were gen-

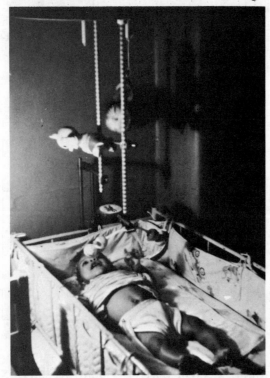

FIGURE 6.

erally first observed as they contacted portions of the experimental stabile. We called this pattern monitored stabile play and considered it together with monitored bumper play as forms of hand regard. By these criteria the onset of hand regard was delayed for some two weeks in our experimental group (N.S.—Mann-Whitney U Test). The onset of swiping was also set back, but only by some 5 days (N.S.—Mann-Whitney U Test).

Figure 7 illustrates the responses to the test object leading to reaching for this group.

2. *Prehension*

The median age for the first appearance of top level reaching was 98 days for the experimental group, an advance of some 45 days (significant at .001—Mann-Whitney U Test). Some of the types of preliminary responses reported for our control group did not occur prior to the onset of top-level reaching.

3. *Visual attention*

The course of development of visual attention was also altered dramatically in our experimental group as illustrated by Figure 8. Concurrent with the unexpected delay in the onset of hand regard, was a marked decrease in visual exploratory behavior for the first portion of the test periods. On the other hand, once the group began to engage in prehensory contacts with the stabile and figured bumpers visual attention increased sharply.

Clearly the results of this study demonstrated the plasticity of several visual-motor developments. That the onset of hand regard is in part a function of environmental factors is not a novel notion. Hand regard is an 84th day behavior on the Gesell scale. Our control infants, with virtually nothing else to view, discovered their hands at less than 60 days of age. Piaget noted that the onset of this behavior varied by as much as three months among his own children as a function of differing environmental circumstances (8). Therefore, the fact that infants provided with enriched surrounds were late in discovering their hands as compared to controls was not totally unexpected.

We were surprised that the group exhibited less visual attention during the first five weeks in the enriched visible surround. In fact, not only did they tend to ignore the stabile and

RESPONSE	OBSERVED IN	TOTAL N	MEDIAN AND RANGE OF DATES OF FIRST OCCURRENCE (DAYS)
			20 40 60 80 100 120 140 160 180
SWIPES AT OBJECT	11	14	
UNILATERAL HAND RAISING	12	13	
BOTH HANDS RAISED	12	13	
ALTERNATING GLANCES (HAND AND OBJECT)	10	11	
HANDS TO MIDLINE AND CLASP	7	10	
ONE HAND RAISED WITH ALTERNATING GLANCES, OTHER HAND TO MIDLINE CLUTCHING DRESS	5	9	
TORSO ORIENTED TOWARDS OBJECT	4	9	
HANDS TO MIDLINE AND CLASP AND ORIENTED TOWARDS OBJECT	3	9	
PIAGET-TYPE REACH	6	9	
TOP LEVEL REACH	9	9	

FIGURE 7 / THE DEVELOPMENT OF VISUALLY-DIRECTED REACHING. STUDY B—MASSIVE ENRICHMENT.

bumpers, but it is our impression that they engaged in much more crying than the control group during the same period. Starting at about 72 days of age the group as a whole began to engage in a great deal of stabile play. As we had suspected, the rattles were repeatedly swiped at thereby producing far more monitored hand and arm movements than would normally have occurred. Subsequently, in less than one month, the integration of the grasp with approach movements had been completed. Control infants had required almost 3 months for this transition.

Earlier we had noted that the course of development of visual exploratory behavior seemed to reflect the availability of interesting things to look at. We had seen that in control and handled groups the slope of the curve of visual attention increased sharply when the hands were discovered and then decreased during the next six weeks. In this experimental group it appears that for about a month starting at day 37, the enrichment was actually ineffective and perhaps even unpleasant. However, once positive responses to the surround began to occur visual attention increased sharply in striking contrast to the previous groups. At 3½ months (c. 105 days) the enriched groups exhibited much more visual activity.

C. FURTHER MODIFICATION OF THE ENVIRONMENT. Until day 37 the procedures were the same as in Study B, but instead of enrichment by prone placement and the stabile and printed sheets and bumpers, there was only one modification from day 37 until day 68. Two pacifiers were mounted on the crib rails. These devices were made to stand out visually by appending to

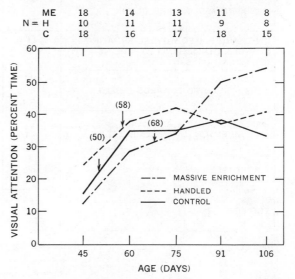

FIGURE 8 / COMPARATIVE VISUAL ATTENTION DATA.

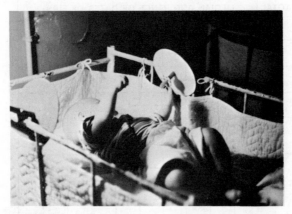

FIGURE 9.

them a red and white pattern against a flat white background (Figure 9). The objects were 6 to 7 inches away from the corneal surfaces of the infants' eyes. They were positioned so as to elicit maximum attention from a 6 to 10 week old infant (c. 42-70 days). The normal tendency of such infants is to accommodate at about 8 to 10 inches. It was assumed that the pacifiers might have the effect of orienting the infant towards the discovery of his own hands. It was further assumed that these objects might provide appropriate anchor points in space intermediate between the locus of spontaneous fixation and the ordinary path of motion of the hand extended in the tonic neck reflex posture.

At 68 days the infant was then placed in a crib with a stabile similar to that used in the previous study until he was 124 days of age. We hypothesized that these infants would be more consistently precocious in the attainment of visually-directed reaching. We also expected consistently higher visual attention from this group.

RESPONSE		OBSERVED IN	TOTAL N	MEDIAN AND RANGE OF DATES OF FIRST OCCURRENCE (DAYS)
SWIPES AT OBJECT	C+H	13	13	
	ME	11	14	
	MOD. E	14	16	
UNILATERAL HAND RAISING		15	15	
		12	13	
		13	16	
BOTH HANDS RAISED		16	18	
		12	13	
		13	16	
ALTERNATING GLANCES (HAND AND OBJECT)		18	19	
		10	10	
		12	12	
HANDS TO MIDLINE AND CLASP		15	15	
		17	10	
		10	14	
ONE HAND RAISED WITH ALTERNATING GLANCES, OTHER HAND TO MIDLINE CLUTCHING DRESS		11	19	
		5	9	
		7	14	
TORSO ORIENTED TOWARDS OBJECT		15	18	
		4	9	
		5	12	
HANDS TO MIDLINE AND CLASP AND ORIENTED TOWARDS OBJECT		14	19	
		3	9	
		4	12	
PIAGET-TYPE REACH		12	18	
		6	9	
		8	13	
TOP LEVEL REACH		14	14	
		9	9	
		13	13	

(Scale: 20 40 60 80 100 120 140 160 180)

●━━━● CONTROL AND HANDLED
●‑‑‑‑● MASSIVE ENRICHMENT
●‑·‑·● MODIFIED ENRICHMENT

FIGURE 10 / COMPARISON OF PREHENSORY RESPONSES AMONG ALL GROUPS.

RESULTS

1. *Hand regard and swiping*

In the control group the onset of sustained hand regard occurred at day 46. Infants in the handling study were slightly behind (day 58). Infants in study B were even later in this respect (day 68) supporting the idea that the discovery of the hands is, in part, a function of the availability of interesting visible objects (1). The modified enrichment of this last study seemed more appropriate for the infant during the second month of life. Study C infants exhibited sustained hand regard at day 45. It should be noted that control infants reared in bland surroundings are about as advanced in this regard. The onset of swiping responses followed the same general pattern with study C infants exhibiting this behavior earlier than all other groups (day 58: Figure 10).

2. *Prehension*

Apparently, the modified or paced enrichment of the last study was the most successful match of external circumstances to internally developing structures as indicated by the acquisition of top level reaching at less than 3 months (day 89—significantly earlier than controls at <.001—Mann-Whitney U Test).

3. *Visual Attention*

Figure 11 shows visual attention data for the subjects of the several studies. The depression of visual interest shown by study B infants from (day 37) to (day 74) has been eliminated. Curiously, although the last group was more consistently attentive than the others, the reduction of such behavior at 3½ months (c. 105 days) appeared as it had in the first two groups. It would appear that some uncontrolled variable is interacting with our various attempts at modifying the function.

CONCLUSIONS

1. THE SIGNIFICANCE OF THE AGE RANGE FROM 1½-5 MONTHS OF AGE.

The first major conclusion derivable from our research is that the age range from 1½ to 5 months (c. days 45-150) is a time of enormous importance for early perceptual-motor development. According to our findings and those of others, human infants reared under natural conditions show a dramatic

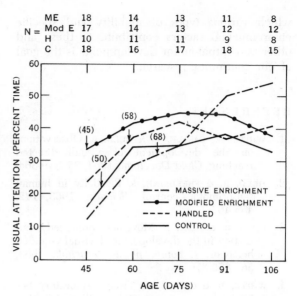

FIGURE 11 / COMPARATIVE VISUAL ATTENTION DATA.

surge in both visual activity and development at the middle of the second month of life (c. 45 days). During the next 3½ months the following events occur: (1) the development of flexible accommodative function culminating in virtually adult-like performance at 3½ months (c. 105 days), (2) discovery of the hands and gradual development of manual control by the visual system culminating in true visually-directed reaching, (3) the initiation and complete development of the blink response to an approaching visible target, (4) the initiation and complete development of visual convergence, (5) the onset of social smiling.

2. PLASTICITY IN HUMAN VISUAL-MOTOR DEVELOPMENT.

The studies reported above demonstrate that aspects of early visual-motor development are remarkably plastic. As yet we know neither the limits of this plasticity nor the range of visual-motor functions that fall within this classification. At the very least, the onset of hand regard and visually-directed reaching and the growth of visual attentiveness are significantly affected by environmental modification. Infants of both group B and C developed top level reaching in approximately 60% of the time required by the control group, a result very much in line with the theory that self-initiated movement with its visual consequences is crucial for visual-motor development. Whether or not visual accommodation, convergence, pursuit, and blinking to an approaching target share this plasticity remains to be seen. Assessment of the extent to which various types of mobility and specific environmental factors contribute to these and other perceptual-motor developments is the goal of our continuing research.

REFERENCES

1. WHITE, B., CASTLE, P. & HELD, R. Observations on the development of visually-directed reaching. *Child Develpm.*, 1964, *35*, 349-364.

2. HELD, R. & FREEDMAN, S. Plasticity in human sensorimotor control. *Science*, 1963, *142*, 455-462.

3. HELD, R. & HEIN, A. Movement-produced stimulation in the development of visually-guided behavior. *J. comp. physio. Psychol.*, 1963, *56*, 872-876.

4. WHITE, B. & CASTLE, P. Visual exploratory behavior following postnatal handling of human infants. *Percept. mot. Skills*, 1964, *18*, 497-502.

5. HAYNES, H., WHITE, R. & HELD, R. Visual accommodation in human infants. *Science*, 1965, *148*, 528-530.

6. WHITE, B. Rearing conditions and the development of visual attentiveness in human infants. Paper presented at EPA, 1965.

7. HUNT, J. MC V. *Intelligence and Experience*. New York, Ronald, 1961.

8. PIAGET, J. *The origins of intelligence in children* (2nd ed.) New York, Internat. Univ. Press, 1952.

9. RIESEN, A. H. Plasticity of behavior: psychological series. In: *Biological and Biochemical Bases of Behavior*. H. Harlow & C. Woolsey (Eds), Madison, Wis.: Univ. Wisconsin Press, 1958, 425-450.

10. DENENBERG, V. H. & KARAS, G. G. Effects of differential infantile handling upon weight gain and mortality in the rat and mouse. *Science*, 1959, *130*, 629-630.

11. LEVINE, S. Infantile experience and resistance to physiological stress. *Science*, 1957, *126*, 405.

12. MEIER, G. W. Infantile handling and development in Siamese kittens. *J. comp. physiol. Psychol.*, 1961, *54*, 284-286.

13. YARROW, L. Maternal deprivation; toward an empirical and conceptual re-evaluation. *Psychol. Bull.*, 1961, *58*, 459-490.

14. CASLER, L. Maternal deprivation; a critical review of the literature. *Monogr. Soc. Res. Child Develpm.*, 1961, *26*, 1-64.

15. BRODY, S. *Patterns of mothering*. New York, International University Press, Inc., 1951.

16. HELD, R. Exposure-history as a factor in maintaining stability of perception and coordination. *J. nerv. ment. Dis.*, 1961, *132*, 26-32.

17. HELD, R. & BOSSOM, J. Neonatal deprivation and adult rearrangement: complementary techniques for analyzing plastic sensory-motor coordinations. *J. comp. physiol. Psychol.*, 1961, *54*, 33-37.

18. MIKAELIAN, H. & HELD, R. Two types of adaptation to an optically-rotated visual field. *Amer. J. Psychol.*, 1964, *77*, 257-263.

10 / SELF-PERCEIVED RATE OF PHYSICAL MATURATION AND PERSONALITY IN LATE ADOLESCENCE[1] / DONALD WEATHERLEY [*]

IT HAS LONG BEEN RECOGNIZED THAT the timing of puberty and of the marked physical changes which herald its onset is subject to wide individual differences. It is relatively recently, however, that attention has been drawn to the differential impact on personal and social adjustment of these individual differences in the rate of physical maturation. This issue has been brought into sharp focus by a recent series of reports stemming from the California Adolescent Growth Study, a project which involved the intensive observation and testing of a group of approximately 180 boys and girls over a seven-year period (5). These reports were based on comparisons made with a variety of behavioral and personality measures of groups of extremely early and extremely late maturers (the upper and lower 20 per cent of the total Growth Study sample.)

Clear-cut results were found for boys. Both trained adult observers and peers described the late-maturing boys' behavior in less favorable terms than that of the early maturers. For example, at age 16 the late maturers were rated by adults as significantly less attractive in physique, less well groomed, less moderate in their behavior, more affected, more tense appearing, and more eager. Peers described the late maturers as more restless, less reserved, less grown-up, and more bossy (9). In brief, the tense, active, attention-seeking behavior of the late maturers contrasted sharply with the self-assured, well modulated, socially appropriate behavior manifested by the group of early maturers. Moreover, the late maturers were chosen much less frequently than early maturers for positions of leadership in their school and were much less prominent in extra curricular activities (8).

An analysis of TAT protocols obtained when the boys were 17 years old revealed personality differences consistent with the behavioral differences found between early and late maturers. These data indicated that accompanying the late maturers' less adaptive social behaviors were heightened feelings of inadequacy, negative self-conceptions, feelings of rejection and domination, and persistent dependency needs paradoxically coupled with a rebellious quest for autonomy and freedom from restraint (14).

Finally, a follow-up study (7) provided evidence that the personality differences between the early- and late-maturing boys persisted into adulthood long after physical differences between the groups had disappeared. The male subjects of the Adolescent Growth Study were administered two objective tests of personality (the California Psychological Inventory and the Edwards Personal Preference Schedule) when they had reached an average age of 33. The test results indicated that as adults the late maturers were less capable of conveying a good impression, less self-controlled, less responsible, less dominant, and more inclined to turn to others for help than were the early maturers— a pattern of personality differences quite similar to the pattern that had emerged when the groups were compared in adolescence.

The results of this series of studies on males add up to a consistent picture which makes good theoretical sense. A large, strong stature is a central aspect of the ideal masculine model in our society. Thus, it is reasonable to assume that the early attainment of the physical attributes associated with maturity serves as a social stimulus which evokes from both peers and adults a reaction of respect, acceptance, and the expectation that the individual concerned will be capable of relatively mature social behavior. Such a reaction from others serves to support and reinforce adaptive, "grown-up" actions and contributes to feelings of confidence and security in the early-maturing boys. On the other hand, the late maturer must cope with the develop-

[1] This study was supported by a grant from the Council on Research and Creative Work of the University of Colorado.

[*] Donald Weatherley, Self-perceived rate of physical maturation and personality in late adolescence, *Child Develpm.*, 1964, 35, 1197-1210. Copyright, 1964, by the Society for Research in Child Development, Inc. Reprinted by permission of the Society and the author.

mental demands of the junior high and high school period with the liability of a relatively small, immature appearing physical stature. His appearance is likely to call out in others at least mild reactions of derogation and the expectation that he is capable of only ineffectual, immature behavior. Such reactions constitute a kind of social environment which is conducive to feelings of inadequacy, insecurity and defensive, "small-boy" behavior. Such behavior once initiated may well be self-sustaining, since it is likely to only intensify the negative environmental reactions which gave rise to it in the first place. This interpretation, fully consistent with the evidence produced by the investigations of the Growth Study workers, implies that the late-maturing boy is likely to be involved in a circular psychosocial process in which reactions of others and his own reactions interact with unhappy consequences for his personal and social adjustment.

Does rate of physical maturation have the same effect on the personal-social development of girls? The early data obtained in the Adolescent Growth Study suggested that it does not— that an effect opposite to that found in boys occurs. H. E. Jones (6) reported that late-maturing girls were rated by adult judges significantly higher than early-maturing girls on a number of socially desirable traits such as sociability, leadership, cheerfulness, poise, and expressiveness. Peers also rated the late maturers in more positive terms than they did the early maturers. Moreover, the late-maturing girls were especially likely to participate in extracurricular activities at high school and hold positions of prestige in school clubs; early-maturing girls played a much less prominent role in school activities (8).

These findings imply that in contrast to the situation with boys, late physical maturation is an asset and early maturation a liability to the social adjustment of girls. Why should this be true? Mary C. Jones and Mussen (10) offered an explanation which focused upon the likely biosocial consequences of early physical maturation for girls. They pointed out that the early-maturing girl is inclined to acquire a stocky, muscular physique while the late maturer tends toward a slim, slight build, more in keeping with the feminine ideal in our society. Furthermore, the female early maturer is not only slightly out of step in physical development when compared with other girls her age, she is drastically different in physical status from her male peers of similar age, since boys in general

lag about two years behind girls in manifesting puberal growth changes. H. E. Jones (6) also noted that the parents of early-maturing girls might well be unenthusiastic about their daughters' precocious interest in the opposite sex, an interest which is likely to draw them toward social contacts with boys much older than they.

This line of reasoning led Mary C. Jones and Mussen (10) to predict that the personality development of the early-maturing girls in the Adolescent Growth Study would reflect the ill effects of an accelerated rate of growth as did their social behavior, investigated earlier. This expectation, however, was not supported by TAT data obtained when the girls were 17 years old. Although the differences found for girls between early and late maturers were not nearly as striking as those found for boys on the TAT, the differences were generally in the same direction for both sexes. The implication of the projective test data was that early-maturing members of both sexes as opposed to late maturers tend to be characterized by more adequate thought processes, a more positive self-conception, and a more relaxed, secure view of themselves and their world.

Thus in the case of girls it is necessary to somehow account for the apparent inconsistency of findings indicating that early maturation leads to less adequate social adjustment in combination with other results indicating that early maturation is associated with a more "healthy" appearing personality picture. It is possible that the personality data were unreliable, that the differences found on the TAT were artifacts of sampling or measurement error; certainly this interpretation is more reasonable than one discounting the behavior rating measures and indices of social participation on similar grounds, since the findings on the latter sets of measures were more clear-cut than the TAT results. On the other hand, it may be as Mary C. Jones and Mussen (10) suggested, that early maturation is a social disadvantage early in the adolescent period, when the behavior ratings were made, but later in adolescence when physical differences due to different rates of maturation are less marked and environmental stress presumably associated with precocious growth is reduced, the early-maturing girls relax and manifest in their personality integration the beneficial effects of their earlier start toward the assumption of an adult status.

It is obvious that additional data bearing on the relation in late adolescence between rate of physical maturation and personality attributes of girls would be helpful in choosing between these alternative explanations of the inconsistent appearing Adolescent Growth Study data. One purpose of the present study was to provide such additional data by assessing the relation between a measure of maturational rate and a variety of personality variables in girls in late adolescence. The design also permitted a between-sex comparison in order to determine whether or not rate of physical maturation had similar implications for the personality development of boys and of girls.

Another purpose of the present study was to assess once again the relation of maturational rate and personality characteristics for a group of males, considered apart from females. Although the California workers' findings for boys were generally clear-cut and consistent, the conclusions they generated rested, in one sense at least, on a quite narrow empirical base (as was also true for the less certain conclusions reached for girls). All the studies reviewed earlier involved the same small group of Ss, all of whom lived in the Berkeley, California, area. Furthermore, despite the fact that these reports have appeared relatively recently in the literature, all but the one concerning the follow-up study were based on data gathered more than two decades ago; the Growth Study Ss were, at the time the present study was undertaken, close to 40 years old—literally old enough to be the parents of today's adolescents.

It should be noted, however, that the present study was by no means a contemporary replication of earlier research; it differed in several important respects from the California investigations. The Ss in this study were on the average about two years older than were the Ss at the completion of the Adolescent Growth Study. A number of objective personality measures were used in the present study, only one of which (the Edwards Personal Preference Schedule) was used in the California research and then only in the follow-up study (7). The most noteworthy distinction between the study reported here and the previous research in this area had to do with the nature of the measure of rate of physical maturation. The California studies used an objective skeletal-age index of physical maturation as a basis for identifying early and late maturers. In the present study a simple self-report measure of relative maturational rate was used. Its use involved the assumption that adolescents have a fairly accurate idea of the relative timing of their physical maturation and can reliably report this information.

Obviously, any one or more of the factors mentioned above could be responsible for differences found between results of the present study and the findings of the California series of investigations; such differences might not be easy to interpret. On the other hand, it was felt that if the present study yielded findings with implications convergent with those generated by previous research, especially that dealing with males where prior evidence was most definitive, the generality of the conclusions reached would be strongly supported.

METHOD

The Ss were 234 male and 202 female college students enrolled in the elementary psychology course at the University of Colorado. The mean age of the girls was 19.4 ($SD=2.6$), the mean age of the boys, 19.9 ($SD=1.9$).

Early in the semester the MMPI K scale (12) and the Taylor Manifest Anxiety Scale (TMAS) (17) were administered to the Ss in large group sessions. Approximately five weeks later 96 of the boys and 92 of the girls took the Edwards Personal Preference Schedule (EPPS) (3).

In order to obtain measures reflecting degree of identification with parents and peers, the Ss were asked in the initial testing sessions to give self-ratings of the degree to which they saw themselves as similar to each of the following individuals: their mother, father, same-sex best friend, and opposite-sex best friend. These self-ratings of perceived similarity were obtained for each of the following dimensions: overall personality, intelligence, warmth, orderliness, political views, and religious views. Seven-point rating scales were used, yielding scores which ranged from one (indicating the lowest degree of perceived similarity) to seven (indicating the highest degree of perceived similarity).

Rate of physical maturation was assessed by responses to the following multiple-choice question presented to the Ss during the initial testing sessions: "With regard to your physical maturation, you would say that you matured: (a) quite early, (b) somewhat early, (c) average, (d) somewhat late, (e) quite late." These alternatives were assigned weights from one (quite early) to five (quite late) so that the choice made by each S could be represented as a numerical score. In addition, each S was categorized into one of three groups on the basis of his response to the physical maturation question. Individuals who had chosen either the alternative "quite early" or "somewhat early" were considered early maturers. Those who had chosen the alternative "average," were considered average maturers. Those who had chosen the alternatives "somewhat late" or "quite late" were categorized as late maturers.

Means of these three groups for each of the personality measures were compared by t tests, with boys and girls treated separately. This analysis was considered more suitable than a correlational analysis as a basis for describing relations between maturational rate and personality variables within each sex group because it permitted the identification of nonlinear as well as linear relations in the data.

RESULTS

In Table 1 are presented the distributions for boys and girls of responses to the item measuring perceived rate of physical maturation. The distributions for both sexes were skewed in a direction indicating that both boys and girls are more likely to see themselves as accelerated in development than retarded. For boys and girls combined, there was a significantly greater number of responses in the "somewhat early" and "very early" categories considered together than in the "somewhat late" and "very late" categories ($X^2 = 21.64$, $df = 1$, $p < .01$). While the skewness appeared slightly more marked in the distribution for girls than for boys, the distributions did not differ significantly from one another. ($X^2 = 7.31$, $df = 4$, $p > .10$).

TABLE 1 / DISTRIBUTION OF RESPONSES TO ITEM MEASURING TIMING OF PHYSICAL MATURATION.

	MALES ($N = 234$)	FEMALES ($N = 202$)
Very early	11.1%	15.8%
Somewhat early	21.4	21.8
Average	44.9	48.5
Somewhat late	19.6	12.9
Very late	3.0	1.0

Mean scores obtained by early, average, and late maturers on the personality measures are shown in Table 2. This table includes only results for personality variables on which at least one inter-group comparison revealed a difference significant at the .10 level or less.

In general, the findings for boys were highly consistent with the California Adolescent Growth Study results. The most clear-cut differences found in the present study between early-maturing boys and those who described

themselves as late maturers were on the same two EPPS variables—dominance and succorance—on which early- and late-maturing males differed when they were tested as adults in the Growth Study follow-up (7). In the present study, late maturers as opposed to early maturers scored lower on the dominance scale ($p < .05$) and higher on the succorance scale ($p < .01$). They also differed in the same direction on these variables from the group of average maturers. Thus the late maturers revealed relatively weak tendencies to lead and control others and relatively strong tendencies to seek encouragement, sympathy, and understanding from others—characteristics found previously to be associated with late maturation not only in the follow-up study mentioned above (7), but in two other investigations done as part of the California Growth Study (14, 15). It is also noteworthy that low scores on the EPPS dominance scale, and high scores on the succorance scale (i.e., the pattern characteristic of the late maturers) have been shown to be associated with scores on the Minnesota Multiphasic Personality Inventory indicative of maladjustment (13).

The late-maturing boys also obtained higher EPPS autonomy scores than did the early maturers, a difference which just failed to reach significance at the .05 level. This may at first appear to be a finding inconsistent with the implications of previous research, since the term autonomy is one often included in conceptions of the "ideal" personality. Yet a consideration of the items included in the EPPS autonomy scale (e.g., "to do things that are unconventional," "to criticize those in positions of authority," "to avoid responsibilities and obligations") points up the anti-conventional, at least mildly rebellious trends tapped by this measure. Thus the late maturers' relatively high autonomy mean score, considered in combination with their high succorance but low dominance scores suggests a prolongation of the typically adolescent independence-dependence conflict in late-maturing boys. The previous research of Mussen and Mary C. Jones (14) led them to a similar conclusion for the group of boys they studied.

If late maturers are in fact caught between competing strivings for dependency and strivings for freedom from restraint we should expect to find in them evidence of less well resolved internal conflict in the form of heightened tension and subjective distress. Two measures used in the present study are most pertinent to this

TABLE 2 / MEAN SCORES ON PERSONALITY MEASURES FOR EARLY, AVERAGE, AND LATE MATURERS.

	EARLY MATURERS	AVERAGE MATURERS	LATE MATURERS	EARLY vs. AVERAGE	AVERAGE vs. LATE	EARLY vs. LATE
				SIGNIFICANCE OF DIFFERENCES		
Males						
TMAS	6.84 (76)	6.44 (105)	8.09 (53)	ns	< .05	ns
EPPS:						
Achievement	15.40 (30)	17.44 (36)	16.96 (30)	< .10	ns	ns
Autonomy	15.17 (30)	15.69 (36)	17.17 (30)	ns	ns	< .06
Intraception	16.30 (30)	14.03 (36)	13.83 (30)	< .10	ns	< .10
Succorance	9.20 (30)	9.86 (36)	12.27 (30)	ns	< .05	< .01
Dominance	19.13 (30)	18.81 (36)	16.33 (30)	ns	< .10	< .05
Abasement	11.47 (30)	9.56 (36)	12.20 (30)	ns	< .05	ns
Endurance	10.17 (30)	13.42 (36)	10.50 (30)	< .05	< .05	ns
Perceived similarity to:						
Mother's political views	4.46 (76)	4.77 (105)	4.13 (53)	ns	< .05	ns
Mother's religious views	4.63 (76)	4.65 (105)	4.09 (53)	ns	< .10	ns
Father's political views	4.65 (68)	5.12 (100)	4.35 (51)	< .10	< .02	ns
Father's religious views	4.76 (68)	4.94 (100)	4.29 (51)	ns	< .10	ns
Boy friend's warmth	5.11 (76)	5.08 (105)	4.52 (52)	ns	< .05	< .05
Boy friend's political views	4.89 (76)	4.79 (105)	4.31 (52)	ns	< .10	< .05
Boy friend's intelligence	5.41 (76)	5.13 (105)	5.71 (52)	ns	< .05	ns
Females						
TMAS	6.91 (76)	7.46 (98)	9.54 (28)	ns	< .05	< .02
EPPS:						
Exhibition	16.38 (37)	14.96 (45)	17.00 (10)	< .05	< .10	ns
Nurturance	16.05 (37)	16.27 (45)	13.50 (10)	ns	< .10	< .10
Perceived similarity to:						
Mother's religious views	4.43 (76)	5.12 (98)	4.54 (28)	< .05	ns	ns
Father's political views	4.90 (68)	4.96 (92)	5.70 (23)	ns	< .05	< .10
Boy friend's orderliness	4.67 (76)	5.23 (97)	4.39 (28)	< .05	< .05	ns

Note: This table includes only those variables on which at least one between-group comparison was significant at the .10 level or less. The N for each cell is given in parentheses.

question, and on both the results confirmed expectations. On the TMAS and the EPPS abasement scale late-maturing boys scored higher than average or early maturers, differences which were statistically significant ($p < .05$) in the comparisons between late and average maturers. Scores on the TMAS reflect the degree of tension and manifest anxiety an individual acknowledges and have been shown to be highly correlated negatively with a measure of self-esteem (16). The abasement scale items refer to feelings of guilt, inferiority, and depression; there is evidence that high scores on this scale are associated with maladjustment (13). Of interest here also is the finding of the present study that the late-maturing males tended to score lower than the early maturers ($p < .10$) on the EPPS intraception scale (e.g., "to analyze one's motives and feelings," "to understand how others feel about problems"), suggesting that perhaps because the late maturer is, as indicated above, more likely than individuals maturing earlier to experience negative, presumably unpleasant feelings, he is less likely to develop a "psychological mindedness" in his orientation to himself and others.

On one EPPS variable—the endurance scale —a curvilinear relation with rate of maturation in boys was found; both the late and early maturers evidenced lower scores on the endurance scale (e.g., "to keep at a puzzle or problem until it is solved," "to put in long hours of work without distraction") than did the group of average maturers ($p < .05$). This is not an easy finding to interpret. The appreciable personality differences that set late and early maturers apart, however, suggest that a relative lack of persistence may have a different functional significance for early as opposed to late maturers. It may be, for example, that the late maturer as a corollary of his heightened tension and feelings of inferiority has less conviction that he will be able to succeed at tasks and thus is inclined to give up trying relatively quickly, while the early maturer is inclined to persist less than the average maturer because he is accustomed to success with less effort and seeks alternate routes to his goals when he meets a barrier. It must be recognized, however, that any such interpretation is, at this state in our knowledge, highly speculative.

The data for boys involving ratings of perceived similarity to parents and friends among various dimensions by no means revealed startling differences among the maturation groups (Table 2). Of the 72 comparisons made only 10 differences significant at the .10 level or less were found. Yet it is noteworthy that in eight of these ten instances, late maturers rated themselves less similar to parents or friends than did Ss who matured earlier. This at least suggests that late maturers are more inclined to see themselves as being different from others. A resulting sense of estrangement may contribute to the heightened subjective distress found in the late-maturing boys. This line of reasoning is consistent with the findings of previous studies which have shown that the tendency to view oneself as relatively dissimilar to others in personal characteristics is associated with relatively high anxiety (1, 2).

In previous research, no difference was found between groups of early- and late-maturing boys in degree of achievement motivation (14, 15). In the present study, boys classified as early maturers tended to obtain lower scores on the EPPS achievement scale (e.g., "to be able to do things better than others") than did the group of average maturers ($p < .10$). This may be a chance result. The high social prestige attained by the early-maturing boys who participated in the Adolescent Growth Study (8, 9) certainly does not lead one to anticipate finding a less strong achievement need in early maturers. Also of pertinence here are data obtained in connection with a study of academic over- and under-achievement in which a number of the male Ss of the present study participated (18). Thirteen

of these Ss were identified as over-achievers (i.e., their academic performance appreciably exceeded that expected on the basis of aptitude scores) and compared in terms of their scores on the measure of perceived rate of maturation with 16 Ss classified as under-achievers (i.e., their academic performance was below that expected on the basis of aptitude scores). The results indicated a tendency for the over-achievers to report an earlier physical maturation than the under-achievers ($p < .10$). This suggestion of a link between academic over-achievement and early physical maturation in males also serves to raise a question concerning the reliability of the findings of a lesser degree of striving for achievement in the early maturers. It is, of course, possible that both findings are valid: early maturers may have less strong achievement needs but because of a more efficient and effective use of their personal resources manifest a relatively higher level of success in the academic as well as the social sphere.

Turning now to the results for girls, it can be seen in Table 2 that many fewer differences were found between the maturation groups than were found for boys. The most clear-cut result was obtained on the TMAS: late-maturing girls scored higher on this measure than either the average ($p < .05$) or early maturers ($p < .02$), indicating a higher level of manifest anxiety associated with late maturation. This finding, in the same direction as TMAS results for boys, is congruent with those data obtained in the Adolescent Growth Study suggesting a less adequate personality integration in late-maturing girls (10).

Aside from these results on the TMAS, the implications of which appear to be quite meaningful, the infrequent differences among groups that were found on the EPPS and similarity rating measures do not suggest any specific personality pattern associated with either early or late maturation. The relatively few statistically significant differences which occurred in those data may well be the product of chance in view of the large total number of comparisons made. While failure to find definitive differences among groups under study may be due to a number of factors (e.g., in the present instance the relatively small number of late-maturing girls who took the EPPS reduced the probability of uncovering real differences on that measure which may exist in the population), it is pertinent to note that the previous research that attempted to trace the personality correlates of late and early maturation also produced much less clear-cut findings with girls than with boys (10).

DISCUSSION

Whenever a research strategy involves the assessment of relations between a response-inferred independent variable or variables and a response-inferred dependent variable or variables, an important question arises which must be considered before the results can be taken seriously. To what extent is it likely that the relations found between the independent and dependent variables are the artifactual products of a response bias which similarly affects the measures used to define the independent variables on the one hand and the dependent variables on the other? This question is especially pertinent in connection with the present study since the distribution of scores on the measure of self-perceived maturation—the independent variable—was skewed in a direction indicating a greater tendency for Ss to see themselves as maturing relatively early than as maturing relatively late. Frazier and Lisonbee (4) reported a similar nonsymmetrical distribution of self-rated physical maturation in tenth-grade boys and girls.

It is possible that this skewness reflects a defensive inclination on the part of at least some of the Ss to describe themselves in what they regard as more favorable terms—i.e., as being relatively advanced in physical development. Conversely, the identification of oneself as retarded in maturation could stem in part from a response bias toward self-derogation. Certainly the retrospective report of so ambiguous a characteristic as maturational rate is potentially subject to such distortions. If in fact an appreciable portion of the variance in maturation scores is due to differences among individuals in their willingness to describe themselves in unfavorable terms, then serious doubt would be cast upon the validity of the relations found in the present study between the maturation measure and those dependent measures which are also subject to influence by this sort of response bias. While the EPPS was specifically designed to minimize the effect of a bias to respond in either a socially desirable or undesirable direction, the TMAS and the similarity ratings are dependent measures certainly susceptible to such influence.

Fortunately, in the present study data were gathered that made possible an assessment of the degree to which the maturation score involved variance attributable to individual differences in willingness to describe oneself unfavorably. An estimate of each S's defensiveness was obtained by use of the MMPI K scale that was administered to all Ss. An individual characteristically inclined to distort his self-description in a derogatory direction should obtain a very low K scale score; a very high K scale score is indicative of a defensive inclination to slant one's self-description in a favorable direction.

In the present study for neither boys nor girls were there found any differences in K scale scores approaching statistical significance when the groups of early, average, and late maturers were compared. When responses to the question concerning physical maturation were converted to numerical scores, the correlations found between these scores and scores on the K scale were essentially zero both for boys ($r=.024$) and for girls ($r=.047$). This finding fails to support an argument that scores on the maturation measure were contaminated by a personality-linked response bias. Thus it is not reasonable to discount the results found in this study as merely the product of a measurement artifact.

In the case of boys, the findings of the present study are clear-cut. They indicate that the late-maturing boy of college age is less likely than his earlier-maturing peers to have satisfactorily resolved the conflicts normally attending the transition from childhood to adulthood. He is more inclined to seek attention and affection from others and less inclined to assume a position of dominance and leadership over others. Yet he is not ready to accept the dictates of authority gracefully; he is inclined, rather, to defy authority and assert unconventional behavior in a rebellious vein. In view of the evidence of these potentially competing forces at work within him, it is not surprising that the late maturer also tends to acknowledge a heightened level of subjective tension and readiness to indulge in guilt-implying self-abasement. Nor is it surprising that he tends to see himself as being different from his peers and parents.

The foregoing portrait of the late-maturing boy is, of course, misleading in that it ignores the obviously large overlap among the groups studied and the obviously appreciable individual differences within the group of late maturers. It does, however, serve to bring into focus a central conclusion to be drawn from the results of the present study: late maturation is associated with less mature appearing, less "healthy" appearing personality characteristics. The high degree of congruence between the results of this study and the results of previous studies which involved quite different procedures, measures, and subjects, underscores the generality and importance of rate of physical maturation as a variable influencing personality development in boys.

A second conclusion which can be drawn from the results of the present study, a conclusion which involves a more precise description of the nature of the relation between rate of maturation and personality in boys, has no precedent in the earlier work done as part of the California Adolescent Growth Study. These earlier investigations used an extreme-groups design in which individuals who were extremely late in maturing were compared with individuals extremely early in maturation; no comparisons were made between either of these groups and a group of individuals whose rate of maturation was average. The inclusion in the present study of the group of average maturers made possible an inference concerning the relative impact upon personality characteristics of early versus late maturation when each extreme group was compared to an average group. As an inspection of Table 2 reveals, many fewer significant differences were found when the group of early-maturing boys was compared with the group of average maturers (of a total of 41 comparisons only 1 reached significance at the .05 level or less) than when late maturers were compared with the average maturers (9 of the 41 comparisons made were significant at the .05 level or less). The early- and average-maturing groups were quite similar to one another in the personality attributes they manifested, while the late maturers were set apart from both of these groups. Thus it is clear that the relations found between rate of physical maturation and the personality characteristics measured were not in general linear ones. The implication is that while late maturation is apparently a handicap to the personality development of boys, early maturation may not be an asset; it appears rather to have an effect on personality development no different from the effect of an average rate of physical maturation.

One of the questions that prompted the present study was whether late physical maturation was a liability or an asset to the personality development of girls. The results for girls, however, were much less striking than those for boys; they do not permit a definitive answer to the question. It is clear, nevertheless, that they offer absolutely no support for the proposition that the effect of rate of physical maturation on the adequacy of personality integration in girls is the reverse of that operating in boys. On the other hand, the fact that on the TMAS the results for girls paralleled those for boys lends limited support to the alternative proposition that late physical maturation has adverse effects on personal adjustment in both sexes in late adolescence. The very slim evidence on which it is based, however, makes it necessary to emphasize the tentative nature of this conclusion.

What is perhaps more noteworthy in the findings for girls is the very fact that they were so much less dramatic than those for boys. Since previous research (10) also produced less definitive results for girls than boys, one is drawn to the conclusion that for girls as opposed to boys rate of physical maturation is a much less influential variable mediating personality development. This is not surprising. In our society the cultural sex-role prescription for males is relatively unambiguous and is one which places a high value upon attributes associated with physical strength and athletic prowess, especially in the adolescent and young adulthood years. As Lynn (11) pointed out, however, the feminine sex-role prescription is much less definite and stereotyped; consequently it is less likely to be closely tied to any specific pattern of physical attributes.

A final word is in order regarding the measure of physical maturation used in the present study. An assumption involved in the use of this measure was that individuals are both aware of the relative rate of their physical maturation and are willing to report it with reasonable accuracy. The generally high degree of congruence between the results based on the simple self-report measure used in the present study and previous findings based on an objective skeletal-age measure of physical maturation is evidence bolstering this assumption. The veridicality of such self-ratings cannot be firmly established, of course, without directly comparing the ratings with an objective measure of physical growth. Nevertheless, the present results constitute sufficient indirect evidence of the validity of the self-report measure of physical maturation to encourage the use of a measure of this sort in situations where it is impractical to obtain objective indices of maturational rate.

The present study and those done earlier have clearly established the importance of rate of physical maturation as a variable influencing personality development at least in boys; this variable deserves further study. Especially interesting would be research bearing upon the interaction of the maturation variable and variables such as social class membership, parental child-rearing practices, or peer-group social structure.

SUMMARY

On the basis of a self-report measure of rate of physical maturation, college students were categorized into groups of early, average, and late maturers and compared on a number of personality measures. Results indicated that: (a) late physical maturation represents a handicap to the personality development of boys, (b) early maturation is no greater an asset to personality development in boys than is an average rate of maturation, (c) the effects of rate of maturation on personal adjustment are much less profound in girls than boys, (d) the direction of the effects is similar in both sexes.

REFERENCES

1. CHANCE, J. E. Adjustment and prediction of others' behavior. *J. consult. Psychol.*, 1958, *22*, 191-194.

2. DAVITZ, J. R., & MASON, D. J. Manifest anxiety and social perception. *J. consult. Psychol.*, 1960, *24*, 554.

3. EDWARDS, A. L. *Manual for the Edwards Personal Preference Schedule.* Psychological Corp., 1959.

4. FRAZIER, A., & LISONBEE, L. K. Adolescent concerns with physique. *Sch. Rev.*, 1950, *58*, 397-405.

5. JONES, H. E. The California adolescent growth study. *J. educ. Res.*, 1938, *31*, 561-567.

6. JONES, H. E. Adolescence in our society. In *The family in a democratic society: Anniversary papers of the Community Service Society of New York.* Columbia Univer. Press, 1949. Pp. 70-82.

7. JONES, M. C. The later careers of boys who were early- or late-maturing. *Child Developm.*, 1957, *28*, 113-128.

8. JONES, M. C. A study of socialization patterns at the high school level. *J. genet. Psychol*, 1958, *93*, 87-111.

9. JONES, M. C., & BAYLEY, N. Physical maturing among boys as related to behavior. *J. educ. Psychol.*, 1950, *41*, 129-148.

10. JONES, M. C., & MUSSEN, P. H. Self-conceptions, motivations, and interpersonal attitudes of early- and late-maturing girls. *Child Developm.*, 1958, *29*, 491-501.

11. LYNN, D. B. A note on sex differences in the development of masculine and feminine identification. *Psychol. Rev.*, 1959, *66*, 126-135.

12. MC KINLEY, J. C., HATHAWAY, S. R., & MEEHL, P. E. The Minnesota Multiphasic Personality Inventory: VI. The K scale. *J. consult. Psychol.*, 1948, *12*, 20-31.

13. MERRILL, R. M., & HEATHERS, L. B. The relation of the MMPI to the Edwards Personal Preference Schedule on a college counseling center sample. *J. consult. Psychol.*, 1956, *20*, 310-314.

14. MUSSEN, P. H., & JONES, M. C. Self-conceptions, motivations, and interpersonal attitudes of late- and early-maturing boys. *Child. Developm.*, 1957, *28*, 243-256.

15. MUSSEN, P. H., & JONES, M. C. The behavior-inferred motivations of late- and early-maturing boys. *Child Developm.*, 1958, *29*, 61-67.

16. SIEGMAN, A. W. Cognitive, affective, and psychopathological correlates of the Taylor Manifest Anxiety Scale. *J. consult. Psychol.*, 1956, *20*, 137-141.

17. TAYLOR, J. A. A personality scale of manifest anxiety. *J. abnorm. soc. Psychol.*, 1953, *48*, 285-290.

18. WYER, R. S., WEATHERLEY, D., & TERRELL, G. Social role, aggression and academic achievement. *J. abnorm. soc. Psychol.*, in press.

11/PREDICTION OF BEHAVIOR FROM

BIRTH TO MATURITY/MARJORIE P. HONZIK*

A BOOK REVIEW OF *BIRTH TO MATURITY: A STUDY IN PSYCHOLOGICAL DEVELOPMENT*

BY JEROME KAGAN AND HOWARD MOSS

FROM BIRTH TO MATURITY IS A LONG time. It is not surprising, therefore, that longitudinal research covering the entire period of growth has been so slow in yielding its findings. And it is with a feeling of excitement that we approach the analysis of stability and change in certain personality variables for a group of young people who grew to maturity between 1929 and 1958.

Few research centers had elected to study personality development longitudinally around 1930. Notable exceptions were the Fels Research Institute's investigation which Lester Sontag, M.D., initiated in 1929 and has continued to direct for 35 years; the three independent investigations, with differing purposes, launched by the University of California's Institute of Child Welfare between 1928 and 1931—the Berkeley Growth Study, the Guidance Study, and the Oakland Growth Study (Jones, Macfarlane, and Eichorn, 1960); and the two-year investigation of Mary Shirley (1931) at the University of Minnesota's Institute of Child Welfare, with the follow-up by Neilon in 1948. The children first described by Escalona and Heider in their study of "Prediction and Outcome" (1959) and later by Lois B. Murphy in "The Widening World of Childhood" (1962) were born in the 1940's. This was also true of the children in the study by Anderson et al. (1960) of the prediction of adjustment of the school children of Nobles County over a seven-year period. More recently an investigation specifically concerned with personality development in early childhood was undertaken in this country (Chess, Thomas, Birch, and Hertzig, 1960); and a series of longitudinal growth studies have gotten under way in London (Moore, Hindley, and Falkner, 1954), Western Europe (Skard, 1960), and Africa (Geber, 1962) during the past decade. While this listing covers some of the major projects, it is well to keep in mind that the total number of individuals included in all longitudinal studies of personality development is an infinitesimal sampling of the world's peoples.

Investigations of mental growth have been more numerous than those of personality consistency and change and the results have been more definitive. It is reassuring to note that when the measuring instruments are as reliable as carefully administered intelligence tests, the results from the various centers and universities are remarkably similar (Bayley, 1949; Ebert et al., 1943; Honzik et al., 1948; Sontag et al., 1958). This fact encourages us to believe that if comparable care is used in defining and measuring behavior and personality, we may have in the next decade a verified body of facts leading to more encompassing theories of personality development.

The purpose of the Kagan and Moss investigation was, in their words, to find "the link between child and adult behavior . . . and to discover classes of stable response systems and the developmental periods during which they become manifest." They chose to look for continuity and change in "motive related behaviors, sources of anxiety, defensive behavior and modes of social interaction" rated at different age periods in childhood and in early adulthood. More specifically, they considered the stability of "passivity and dependence, aggression, fear of physical harm, achievement, sex typed activity, and spontaneity." The rationale for the choice of behavior variables was "the emphasis in current theory and research on four classes of variables: (a) behaviors aimed at attainment of culturally salient goals (i.e., motive related behaviors), (b) sources of anxiety and conflict, (c) defensive responses to anxiety arousing situations and conflicts, and (d) modes of interpersonal interaction." We propose to examine in some detail the methodology, results, and interpretations of the Kagan and Moss investigation and to compare certain of their procedures and findings with those of other longitudinal studies.

* Marjorie P. Honzik, Prediction of behavior from birth to maturity, a book review of *Birth to maturity: a study in psychological development*, by Jerome Kagan and Howard Moss (New York: Wiley, 1962). *Merrill-Palmer Quarterly of Behavior and Development*, 1965, *11* (1), 77-88. Reprinted by permission.

The reasons for this are twofold. The results are basic to personality theory, and decisions as to sampling of cases and behaviors and the nature of data analysis become magnified many times in importance when personality is considered in a time perspective. A decision to include or not to include certain individuals will color not one but all relationships. The decision to use a certain type of analysis will determine not one but the many relationships at an age and through time. And, of course, the point of view or theoretical vantage point of the investigators determine not only what they look for, and at, but how the results are interpreted; and once a course of action is taken, it has to be maintained.

Kagan and Moss used a correlational analysis in looking for continuities of behavior. In this type of analysis, the size and nature of the available sample is crucial. Although the method of selecting the Fels longitudinal sample is not described, the parents' education approximates a normal distribution. However, the major difficulty in using the described group in a correlational analysis of consistency of behavior is that "the 89 children came from 63 different families, with 19 families supplying 45 of the children." Further, 44 families had one child in the study, 12 had two children, and 7 families had three children in the group. One of the three-child families had male triplets whose zygosity is not reported. After an initial clear statement of the sample composition, the authors make no further mention of the group other than to report that 71 of the 89 subjects participated in the adult assessment. Since Pearsonian correlation coefficients constitute the sole method of describing stability and change in behavior, the inclusion of siblings of some but not all children presents a major methodological difficulty in assessing the results. If the siblings, and especially the triplets, are more alike in their behaviors than randomly selected children, the correlation coefficients may be remarkably inflated. Not only learning theory but also recent studies of the "heritability of personality dimensions" (Cattell et al., 1957; Gottesman, 1963) support this hypothesis. It would be of considerable interest to know whether the relationships would be changed if only one child from each family were selected for study. A recomputing of these materials excluding siblings would seem feasible and desirable.

The longitudinal data available at the Fels Institute for rating were observational records of the children in the natural settings of the home (in semi-annual visits), at nursery school, and at later ages in day camps and public school. One of the authors, Moss, used this rich observational material to rate 29 dimensions of behavior at four successive age periods from birth to 14 years. The age range included in each period was: birth to 3 years, 3 to 6, 6 to 10, and 10 to 14 years. One could certainly wish that the first and last of these periods had been further divided into finer age groupings. Erikson (1963), who has proposed one of the few truly developmental personality theories,[Ed] divides the age period from birth to 3 years into the three stages—"basic trust," "autonomy," and "initiative"—while he finds five more stages adequate to describe the remaining entire life span of the individual. Erikson's fourth stage, "industry vs. inferiority," coincides very nicely with Kagan and Moss's 6 to 10 year period. Of the age periods used by Kagan and Moss, the 6 to 10 year span is probably the most satisfactory.

On the other hand, giving one overall rating for years 10 to 14 for both boys and girls involves a certain discounting of the impact of puberty on behavior. There is evidence from another longitudinal investigation, the Guidance Study, that at least one of the dimensions rated by Moss, "dependence," fluctuates for girls during the age period when the largest proportion of the girls were in the pubertal cycle but does not do so during the same age span for boys (Macfarlane, Allen, and Honzik, 1954). Furthermore, it was observed that markedly dependent behavior showed a significant increase in incidence a year before menarche and declined to a much lower level at menarche. The perturbations of the dependence-independence dimension during the entire cycle of sexual maturation in girls was clear in the two independently studied groups of the Guidance Study, and it would certainly be of interest if this relationship also occurred in the Fels material.

This result is mentioned here because of its relevance to the age-period grouping and, as has been stated, the purpose of Kagan and Moss was not to portray every possible relationship but to present the continuities and discontinuities over the four specified age periods and adulthood.

One of the major strengths of this investigation is the complete independence of the adult and childhood material. Another strength lies in the fact that the senior author, Kagan, interviewed all the subjects as adults. The interviews were tape-recorded and the behavior dimensions rated by Kagan for all the subjects, and by a second psychologist for 32 subjects.

The age range of the subjects at the time of adult interview was 19 to 29 years. An effort was

[Ed] *His theory is presented in selection 40 of this book.*

made to narrow this range by interviewing the older subjects first but, nevertheless, there was an age difference of approximately 10 years between the age of the oldest and youngest subject at the time of the adult interview. This means that the interviewer was a peer of the oldest subjects but would appear as a "professor" or older man to the youngest subjects. Seventy-one per cent of the women and 56 per cent of the men were married at the time of the adult interview. While this wide age-range at the time of the adult assessments is a real difficulty, it is one which could be evaluated at some later date by considering the relation of the rated dimensions to age, marital status, number of children, etc.

The actual scales used in rating behavior either during childhood or as adults are not described, but the authors report that 7-point scales were constructed and detailed behavioral referents for scale points 1, 4, and 7 provided. A word about the variables rated and their reliabilities is in order. The titles of the variables are reported but only one end of what must be a continuum is mentioned, e.g., passivity, independence. This emphasis on one end of each scale has led to some difficulties in interpretations which will be discussed later in this report. A second psychologist rated "samples of the behaviors." The reported inter-rater reliabilities are high, which is to be expected when two psychologists have access to the same narrative material in making their ratings.

In an earlier study of the constancy of personality assessments of the Oakland Growth Study sample from 14 to 33 years, Tuddenham (1959) reported inter-interviewer agreement of .61 on the average when the two interviewers differed in sex and discussed different topics. The median reliabilities reported by Kagan and Moss when the two raters were reading the same material varied from .68 for Period I (birth to 3 years) to .85 for Period IV (10 to 14 years). Kagan and Moss state that "the dissimilarity between the adolescent and adult rating situations and the low inter-rater reliabilities were two major sources of error in (Tuddenham's) study." Tuddenham perhaps erred in his emphasis on the limitations of an outstanding investigation. The expectancies of agreement should not be the same when (1) two judges rate the same material, and when (2) the ratings of two judges, or interviewers, who have each obtained different material in different contexts from the subjects, are compared. The latter condition is more akin to a validity coefficient.

Thousands of correlation coefficients were computed for the approximately 4,500 behavior ratings. These results are well organized into tables showing continuities between Periods I (birth to 3 years), II, III, and IV (10 to 14 years) and the relation of status at each of these age-periods with that at adulthood.

The number of cases for each r is not given and the effect of differences in variability on the correlations not discussed. These would seem to be sins of omission. But one superfluous result is reported and that is the relationship for the sexes combined. A good rule might be to give the findings for the sexes separately whenever the number of cases permits, only reporting results for sexes combined when the N is small or the sex differences not significant. These technical points might be thought irrelevant in a review—except that longitudinal investigations of stability and change are now coming forth with their results in increasing numbers, and comparative evaluations are going to be hard to make unless the results are fully presented, including sample size and heterogeneity.

Kagan and Moss report that the most dramatic and consistent finding in their study was that many of the behaviors exhibited by the child during Period III (6 to 10 years) and a few during Period II (3 to 6 years) were moderately good predictors of theoretically related behaviors in early adulthood. Among the adult variables which were related to analogous behaviors during the early school years were for women, "passive withdrawal from stressful situations" and "dependency on the family"; for men, "ease of anger arousal" and "sexual behavior"; and for both men and women, "involvement in intellectual mastery," "sex role identification," and "spontaneity."

Of these variables, the persistence of "spontaneity" is most impressive since it is stable and predictive for both males and females and is neither a "sex typed" behavior nor is it an ability-related variable like achievement. Kagan and Moss consider "social interaction anxiety" to be at the opposite end of the spontaneity continuum; and they report that childhood ratings of spontaneity are predictive of spontaneity in adulthood (or "lack of adult social interaction anxiety"). They find consistency on this dimension in males from Period I (birth to 3 years) to adulthood, and in females from the 6 to 10 year period.

In at least three other longitudinal studies, investigators have reported a similar variable to be highly stable. Tuddenham (1959) reported the persistence of certain personality ratings for the young people in the Oakland Growth Study from approximately age 14 years to age 33 years, and concluded that "among the most stable variables for both sexes were several which connote spontaneity vs. inhibition." No two studies have used exactly the same variables, but in the Berkeley Growth Study a continuum which is probably highly correlated with spontaneity-inhibition is the dimension "active, extroverted vs. inactive, introverted." Bayley and Schaefer (1963) report this broad category of behavior to be the most stable and persistent of those they evaluated between birth and 18 years. In still another sample, the Berkeley Guidance Study, where the method of data collection was largely that of interviews with mothers and children over the age period 21 months to 18 years, the most consistent or stable variable of the approximately sixty considered was the dimension of "introversion vs. extroversion," and a second highly consistent dimension was "excessive reserve-spontaneity." Also in the Guidance Study sample, the most stable school behavior (according to the teachers' reports) was for boys "reserved-expressive" and for girls "somber-gay." Despite the great variation in variable description, findings of the different longitudinal studies suggest that this dimension of outgoing responsiveness versus a retractive, inward-looking response may be one of the truly stable personality dimensions. It will be of interest to all the investigators to look more carefully at the correlates of these ratings and possible determinants of this dimension over time.

The finding of Kagan and Moss that dependent behavior in girls shows a high degree of continuity is not an isolated result. In the Guidance Study (Honzik and Macfarlane, 1964) where the ratings are based on interviews with the parents and children, girls showed a greater consistency than boys on the dependent-independent continuum during the age period 4 to 16 years. Furthermore, when as 30-year-old women they checked themselves as "dependent," there was a high probability that they had been considered dependent during the middle years of childhood, and again at 15 and 16 years. What do these facts mean? Kagan and Moss believe that "congruence with traditional standards for sex-role characteristics accounts for the differential stability of behaviors of males and females." And they elaborate that "the individual's desire to mold his overt behavior in concordance with the culture's definition of sex appropriate responses is a major determinant of the patterns of continuity and discontinuity in his development."

A major flaw in this argument with respect to dependence is that the opposite end of this continuum, non-dependence or relative independence, is also predictive for the females in the Kagan and Moss study since the correlations are based on a continuum (7-point ratings). There is a correlation of .48 between passivity during the 6 to 10 years and withdrawal behavior as an adult. This means that girls with a rating of 6 or 7 on passivity in elementary school are likely to show withdrawal behavior as adults; but it also suggests that girls with ratings of 1 or 2 (very non-passive) were *not* showing withdrawal behavior as adults. This finding suggests that behavior along this continuum becomes stabilized early. The correlations do *not* show whether or not "the individual's desire to mold his overt behavior in concordance with the culture's definition of sex-appropriate responses is a major determinant of the patterns of continuity and discontinuity in his development." Only if inspection of the correlation scatters showed that there is a shift toward passivity and dependence in the females and anger arousal in males, would we be justified in concluding that the boy and girl mold their behavior in concordance with the culture's definition of sex appropriate responses.

The significant question is why are these behavioral continua maintained, and differentially so, in males and females? One possibility is that these are chance findings since they are found in one but not both sexes. However, Tuddenham (1959) found drive *aggression* to be *the* most stable of 34 variables for men, from 14 to 33 years, in the Oakland Growth Study. Dependence and passivity were not rated in the Tuddenham investigations. But the dependence-independence continuum was rated, as has been mentioned, at twelve age levels, from 4 to 16 years, in the Guidance Study and was one of the more consistent behavioral dimensions for girls but not for boys—and a high degree of consistency occurred in spite of very low correlations during the 10 to 14 year age-period when the majority of girls were pubescent.

In summary, the finding that sex appropriate or inappropriate behaviors persist was not only replicated for certain variables by Kagan and Moss, but is cross-validated in other longitudinal studies. The explanation of this sex difference is not obvious. Among the possibilities are: (1) a sex difference in variability; (2) these behavioral dimensions are constitutionally or genetically determined; (3) the environmental milieu is continuously but differentially supporting of these behavioral continua; or (4) the impact of early experiences is so overwhelming that the child's learned mode of response is maintained or continued to adulthood. The first possibility may be easily checked by looking at the variance, but the relevance of constitutional and environmental factors requires the measurement of both early response patterns and continuous measurements of the milieu.

One of the most puzzling aspects of Kagan and Moss's conclusions and interpretations is the lack of coherence between some of the findings and the theory advanced to explain their findings. They place "the construct of sex-role identification in a central position in directing the selective adoption and maintenance of several behavior domains." And yet, it seems clear that correlations showing persistence and change in behaviors are only tangentially relevant to sex-role identification. There are, of course, a number of ways of investigating the changes the boy or girl makes in his behavior to conform with traditional sex-role standards. It would not be difficult, for example, to have judges rate the characteristics of the ideal male and female and then compare the changing behaviors of the boy or girl in relation to this ideal. Kagan and Moss discuss the "hypothetical ego ideal or idealized model that embodies the essential qualities of masculinity or femininity." And they add: "Each individual has a cognitive picture of the person he would like to be and the goal states he would like to command—an idealized model of himself. . . . It would appear that the desire to be an *ideal male* or *ideal female* (italics not ours), as defined by the individual, comprises an essential component of everyman's model. Thus the position of a response on a cognitive dimension ranging from *highly masculine* to *highly feminine* is a primary determinant of its acceptability and, therefore, of its probability of occurrence."

This discussion, with italicized emphasis, of sex-role identification as "a governor of behavior" constitutes a major segment of the summary and conclusions which suggests its importance to the authors. But the extensive data were only analyzed to show "continuities or stability of behavior" over a number of age-periods and were not considered in relation to models. Nor is there any mention of mean changes in the direction of masculine or feminine behaviors among the boys and girls. There is clearly the possibility of further analysis of the 4,500 ratings to discover the extent of, or if, indeed, "sex-role identification *is* a governor of behavior."

The authors' second conclusion is that "the

early school years are a critical period" in personality development. They report that "continuity between child and adult behavior generally became manifest during the first four school years (6 to 10)." This finding is in agreement with the conclusion of Schaefer and Bayley (1963) for the Berkeley Growth Study sample, that "more enduring behavioral traits are developed during the latency period." A corollary of this finding is that prediction from the two earlier periods (birth to 6 years) is not good for a number of variables. In some instances, prediction is actually better from the 6 to 10 year period than from the 10 to 14 year period. One example is the finding that aggression-anxiety in adult males tends to be better predicted by the 6 to 10 year ratings than by the 10 to 14 year ratings. Although the sample limitations preclude a too detailed analysis of changes in the predictive power from one age-period to another, it is likely that the turbulence of adolescence may temporarily disrupt certain attitudes and personality characteristics. It is also evident that some personality constellations observed in adolescence are more highly predictive of adult personality than are the early childhood ratings. "Aggressive retaliation" in adult men is one such variable. The correlation between the adult rating of "aggressive retaliation" and "aggression to mother" during the age period birth to 3 years is .19, but by 10 to 14 years it is .47.

One of the impressive findings of longitudinal studies is the age change in relationships, and thus in prediction. This fact also points to the impossibility of assuming that predictions made from one age-period could necessarily be made from any other age-period. It may even be found that predictions vary within the adolescent period. McKee and Turner (1961) report that "drive" ratings made in adolescence are more predictive of CPI[Ed] scales in adulthood for females than males. They suggest that the basis for this difference is the later maturing of males than females. It may well be true that for some variables 12-year ratings of girls show a similar prediction to 14-year ratings of boys. In other words, biological as well as chronological age demands consideration.

The Fels data yielded many interesting sex differences in patterns of relationships. One of the most impressive sex differences occurred in the correlates of intellectual mastery: ". . . intellectually oriented men, in contrast to the intel-

[Ed] *California Personality Inventory.*

lectual women, were less competitive, more likely to withdraw to stress." This and other results lead the authors to the conclusion that "it may be unwise to pool data for males and females without first examining the data for sex differences." One of the interesting phenomena of growth data which these authors underscore is that frequently where there are no sex differences in means and standard deviations, there may be "sex differences in patterns of inter-correlations" either at an age-period or over time. (See Schaefer and Bayley, 1963, and Honzik, 1963, for comparable findings.)

One truly exciting finding in the Fels data is what Kagan and Moss have called the "sleeper effect." The authors appear to subsume two phenomena under this heading: first, the effects on later development of specific early experiences; and second, discontinuities in personality development such that behaviors manifested in infancy or early childhood may be more predictive of comparable adult behaviors than later childhood assessments of the behavior.

An example of the first type of sleeper effect is the finding that the "maternal protection of a daughter during age 0 to 3 predicted adult withdrawal from stress ($r = .52$, $p < .01$), whereas maternal protection during ages 3 to 6 or 6 to 10 showed no relation to adult withdrawal. . . ." There is a possibility that this specific result is a chance one. However, judging by reports from other longitudinal studies, as well as the Fels investigation and the observations of perceptive persons from the beginning of time, it is more than likely that certain experiences of early childhood have far-reaching effects and that these effects may not become manifest until maturity or even later adult life. Harlow's findings for monkeys (1962) [Ed] support this hypothesis. One of the rewarding research projects of the future will be the documenting more specifically of the origins of significant behaviors from the cumulative records of the various growth studies.

An example of the second type of sleeper effect—i.e., a period of discontinuity—is the finding that certain behaviors such as passivity and fear of bodily harm for the age-period birth to 3 years were more predictive of "love object dependency" in adult men than later assessments of these childhood variables. This predictive discontinuity has its counterpart in physical growth. During puberty, prediction of adult

[Ed] *For another report of Harlow's work, see selection 20 in this book.*

height is not as good as during the age-periods immediately preceding the age span when a large proportion of the youngsters are pubescent (Tuddenham, 1954). The fact of perturbations in the inter-age correlation matrices may suggest not only the periods of greater and less prediction but may also suggest the factors contributing to the continuities and discontinuities. An example of this was obtained in the Guidance Study materials, where it was noted that the age-period of lowered prediction of physical measurements in girls coincided with a period of lowered prediction in the dependence-independence continuum. This finding suggests that either the physiological changes affect the girl's behavior directly, or that the changing status of the girl approaching sexual maturity leads to a change in her dependency behavior.

In summary, there will never be a longitudinal study in which there are no methodological limitations. The investigation by Kagan and Moss has its share, some of which can still be evaluated (for example, the effect of including siblings in the correlation coefficients, and the 10-year span of the adult data). On the other hand, this developmental investigation has many strengths, including the richness of the childhood materials, high reliability of the ratings, independence of adult evaluations, and good organization of a large body of inter-relationships. The results of this investigation will be discussed for a long time and compared with those of other growth studies until the ingredients of a more adequate theory of personality growth are found. Although the behaviors rated by Kagan and Moss were derived from current theory, hypotheses were not always supported and the articulation of findings and theory is not one of the strong points of this book.

The inter-age correlations show certain continuities of behavior, some of which are cross-validated in other growth studies. One such variable is "spontaneity" which is highly persistent and may be related to an introversion-extroversion dimension which Gottesman (1963) finds "most heavily influenced by genetic factors." It is clear that behaviors which are more salient in boys such as the aggression—non-aggression continuum, and those more salient in girls, such as dependency—non-dependency, are more likely to persist. This is a significant finding in our culture where sex-appropriate behavior is so valued, but these results do not provide a clue as to *why* a child's status on sex relevant continua are likely to be maintained. Do these results mean that within sex constitutional factors are determining this continuity, or that sex appropriate or inappropriate behaviors are learned early?

In conclusion, a correlational analysis of consistency and change in relevant variables is an excellent first step—but it is just that. Having now found the areas and age-periods of continuity and change, the next steps will be more difficult but also more rewarding—the looking again at the individuals to see just when and under what conditions consistency and change take place. And when, with more knowledge and greater understanding, the picture becomes clearer, we may be led to more enlightened personality theory than is now available.

REFERENCES

ANDERSON, J. E. The prediction of adjustment over time. In I. Iscoe and H. Stevenson (Eds.), *Personality development in children*. Austin: Univer. Texas Press, 1960.

BAYLEY, NANCY. Consistency and variability in the growth of intelligence from birth to eighteen years. *J. genet. Psychol.*, 1949, 75, 165-196.

BAYLEY, NANCY, & SCHAEFER, E. S. Consistency of maternal and child behavior in the Berkeley Growth Study. Symposium on personality consistency and change. *Amer. Psychologist*, 1963, 18, No. 7.

CATTELL, R. B., BLEWETT, D. B., & BELOFF, J. R. The inheritance of personality. *Amer. J. hum. Genet.*, 1955, 7, 122-146.

CHESS, STELLA, THOMAS, A., BIRCH, H. G., & HERTZIG, MARGARET. Implications of a longitudinal study of child development for child psychiatry. *Amer. J. Psychiat.*, 1960, 117, 434-441.

EBERT, ELIZABETH, & SIMMONS, KATHERINE. The Brush Foundation Study of child growth and development. *Soc. Res. Child Develpm. Monogr.*, 1943, 8, No. 2.

ERIKSON, E. H. *Childhood and society*. (2nd ed.) New York: Norton, 1963.

ESCALONA, SIBYLLE, & HEIDER, GRACE M. *Prediction and outcome*. New York: Basic Books, 1959.

GEBER, MARCELLE. Longitudinal study and psychomotor development among Baganda children. In G. S. Nielsen (Ed.), *Child and education*. Copenhagen: Munksgaard, 1962.

GOTTESMAN, I. Heritability of personality: a demonstration. *Psychol. Monogr.*, 1963, 77, No. 9 (Whole No. 572).

HARLOW, H. The heterosexual affectional system in monkeys. *Amer. Psychologist*, 1962, 17, 1-9.

HONZIK, MARJORIE P. A sex difference in the age of onset of the parent-child resemblance in intelligence. *J. educ. Psychol.*, 1963, 54, 231-237.

HONZIK, MARJORIE P., MACFARLANE, JEAN W., & ALLEN, LUCILE. The stability of mental test performance between two and eighteen years. *J. exp. Educ.*, 1948, 17, 309-324.

HONZIK, MARJORIE P., & MACFARLANE, JEAN W. Prediction of specific behaviors and personality characteristics from 21 months to 30 years. (MS)

JONES, H. E., MACFARLANE, JEAN W., & EICHORN, DOROTHY H. A progress report on growth studies at the University of California. *Vita Humana*, 1960, 3, 17-31.

MACFARLANE, JEAN W., ALLEN, LUCILE, & HONZIK, MARJORIE P. A developmental study of the behavior problems of normal children between 21 months and 14 years. *Univer. Calif. Publ. in Child Develpm.*, 1954, Vol. 2.

MC KEE, J. P., & TURNER, W. S. The relation of "drive" ratings in adolescence to CPI and EPPS scores in adulthood. *Vita Humana*, 1961, 4, 1-14.

MOORE, T., HINDLEY, C. B., & FALKNER, F. A longitudinal research in child development and some of its problems. *Brit. Med. J.*, 1954, II, 1132-1137.

MURPHY, LOIS B. *The widening world of childhood*. New York: Basic Books, 1962.

NEILON, PATRICIA. Shirley's babies after fifteen years: a personality study. *J. genet. Psychol.*, 1948, 73, 175-186.

SCHAEFER, E. S., & BAYLEY, NANCY. Maternal behavior, child behavior, and their intercorrelations from infancy through adolescence. *Soc. Res. Child Develpm. Monogr.*, 1963, 28, No. 3.

SHIRLEY, MARY M. *The first two years: a study of twenty-five babies*. Vol. 3. *Personality manifestations*. Minneapolis. Univer. Minn. Press, 1933.

SKARD, ASE. Longitudinal observations of changing family relations. In G. S. Nielsen (Ed.), *Child and education*. Copenhagen: Munksgaard, 1962.

SONTAG, L. W., BAKER, C. T., & NELSON, VIRGINIA L. Mental growth and personality development: a longitudinal study. *Soc. Res. Child Develpm. Monogr.*, 1958, 23, No. 2.

TUDDENHAM, R. D. The constancy of personality ratings over two decades. *Genet. Psychol. Monogr.*, 1959, 60, 3-29.

TUDDENHAM, R. D., & SNYDER, MARGARET M. Physical growth of California boys and girls from birth to 18 years. *Univer. Calif. Publ. in Child Develpm.*, 1954, Vol. 1, No. 2.

III / Learning as a Determinant of Behavior

BECAUSE OF THE IMPOSSIBILITY OF GIVING ADEQUATE SPACE in a book such as this to each of the schools of thought regarding the principles of learning, we have chosen one major approach for presentation, that of reinforcement. Our reasons include the following two: (1) Reinforcement theory has played a greater role than other conceptions of the learning process in stimulating and guiding research in child psychology; (2) Educational psychology has been dominated historically by association theory, with an emphasis on contiguity and practice. This section provides balance by its emphasis on reinforcement. It focuses on the question, "What is the role of reward and punishment in determining behavior?" The theorist concerned with these principles will seek to explain behavior by asking, "What actions have been reinforced?"

The first paper in this section is by John W. M. Whiting, Professor of Anthropology at Harvard University and formerly Director of its Laboratory of Human Development. Whiting, an anthropologist-psychologist who has worked closely with Hull and the Yale learning theorists, presents a brief overview of theories of learning in relation to behavior.

The second paper is by B. F. Skinner, of Harvard, who is a leading psychologist in the field of learning.[1] He has also had a big impact on educational psychology. Like many of the earlier educational psychologists, Skinner is an association theorist but with emphasis on reinforcement. He might reject the "theorist" part of the classification, since he stresses his belief that empirical findings are more valuable than conjectures. In any case, Skinner is concerned with the role which reinforcement plays in behavior (in practical life as well as in theory or in the laboratory).[2] This is in contrast to some psychologists who have been more concerned with the role which reinforcement plays in theory.

The third paper is by Carl D. Williams of the University of Miami. It is a brief note which gives a specific example of the control of behavior (tantrums) by the control of reinforcement. The next paper demonstrates

---

[1] Other important names in the area of learning include those of three men who are now deceased. Clark L. Hull, already mentioned, was a leading behaviorist and developed the most systematized theory of his day. His name was for years almost synonymous with psychology at Yale University. Edward Chase Tolman, who was at the University of California (Berkeley) for most of the period from 1918 until his retirement in 1954, was also a behaviorist. However, his concerns were broad, and often led other workers to take into account complexities of phenomena which they might otherwise have overlooked. It has sometimes been said that where other psychologists viewed humans too much in terms of the laboratory rat, Tolman viewed his laboratory rats too much in terms of humans. Edwin R. Guthrie was the other important figure in this triad. He was less of a system-builder than the others in this group. However, in his long career at the University of Washington, he too served to mold the psychology of learning we have today.

[2] See his novel *Walden Two* (The Macmillan Co., N.Y., 1948).

the same principle on a larger subject population and in a larger social setting (nursery school). This paper was authored by a group connected (at the time) with the University of Washington (Seattle) and its laboratory preschool, of which the first author, Harris, is director. Professors Baer and Wolf are now at the University of Kansas. Still another study involving important parameters of reinforcement theory is that by Walters, Parke, and Cane. Professor Walters is at the University of Waterloo in Canada; Parke is at the University of Wisconsin; Cane is at the Lakeshore Psychiatric Hospital near Toronto. In this study they investigate effects on the child's behavior of the timing of punishment he receives and of his viewing of consequences to others who disobey.

The sixth paper is by Jane Loevinger, a psychologist interested in test theory and parenthood. She is at Washington University in St. Louis. In a somewhat whimsical fashion, she comments on the learning theories (broadly conceived) that parents use in guiding the behavior of offspring.

Several books have appeared on the topic of teaching machines in the years since Skinner wrote his classic paper in 1954.[3] One of these is *Teaching Machines and Programmed Learning: a source book,* edited by A. A. Lumsdaine, now chairman of the Psychology Department of the University of Washington, and Robert Glaser, of the University of Pittsburgh and the American Institute for Research. Their book contains an excellent appendix, consisting of an annotated bibliography and abstracts of work in the field. We reprint their abstract of an article by Arthur W. Melton, who is now at the University of Michigan after having been Technical Director of the Air Force Personnel and Training Research Center. This article is directed to the question of how the science of learning and the management of classroom learning can be mutually supporting.

The final paper in this section returns us to theoretical concerns and provides a transition between this learning section and the next section, which deals with interpersonal experiences as determinants of behavior. Indeed, this paper by Robert R. Sears shows us that two classes of determinants such as reinforcement and interpersonal events are not necessarily to be conceived of as separate or totally different. The paper focuses on the behavior of a dyadic, or two-person, unit. Since much of the learning that takes place in family and school is of this kind, the focus seems especially appropriate. Sears is one of several noted intellectual descendants of Clark L. Hull. (Ernest R. Hilgard, Neal E. Miller, and Kenneth W. Spence are among others.) Sears's specific interest has been child psychology. He is former Director of both the Iowa Child Welfare Research Station (1942-1949) and Harvard's Laboratory of Human Development (1949-1953), as well as a former president of the American Psychological Association. Since 1953 he has been at Stanford University, where he is now Dean of the School of Humanities and Sciences.

Papers which are germane to this topic, but which were not placed in this section, include the one by Freedman (No. 8), and that by Mussen

---

[3] B. F. Skinner, The science of learning and the art of teaching, *Harvard Educational Review,* 1954, *24,* 86-97. This article has been reprinted in a number of sources.

and Rutherford (24). Many of the papers in Sections VI, Group Memberships as Determinants of Behavior, and VIII, Sex as a Determinant of Behavior, are also directly related to learning. Naturally, Section XI on Educational Implications is related to learning, but the orientation there is less theoretical than that in the present section.

Students who have no background in learning or who desire to refresh their understanding might consult the appropriate section of a standard elementary text. The 36-page booklet by Fred S. Keller, *Learning: Reinforcement Theory*, (Doubleday Papers in Psychology, 1954) might also serve as a good background.

Although we have not included the work of Neal Miller, whom we mentioned as an intellectual descendent of Clark Hull, the interested student may wish to read the concise and stimulating account of his views of learning to be found in John Dollard and Neal E. Miller, *Personality and Psychotherapy* (McGraw-Hill, 1950). Part II, "Basic Principles of Learning" (pages 25-94), is the pertinent portion.

12/THEORIES OF LEARNING AND BEHAVIOR/

JOHN W. M. WHITING[*]

RESEARCH IN THE PROCESS OF LEARNing may be divided into three general areas of interest which may be referred to as *primary learning, secondary learning,* and *social learning.* Although my major interest is in the latter two, it is in the field of primary learning that the basic principles and concepts have been developed—principles upon which secondary and social learning depend. It is necessary therefore to briefly review and summarize the various theories and concepts which have been developed in the field of primary learning.

PRIMARY LEARNING

Research in primary learning has been carried on in the laboratory under carefully controlled conditions with animals as subjects. Dogs, rats, cats and pigeons have been the species most generally used. Primary drives such as hunger, thirst or pain from electric shock have been characteristically employed for motivation; relatively simple stimuli such as buzzers or lights have been preferred to more complex ones and, similarly, relatively simple responses such as salivation, maze running, or pressing a bar.

Pavlov (5) was, of course, the father of learning theory and his experiments are so well known that they need not be described. It should be pointed out, however, that he viewed learning as essentially a process of stimulus substitution. A stimulus, which he called an unconditioned stimulus, was chosen which could be counted on to evoke a response. This was then paired repeatedly with a neutral or conditioned stimulus until the latter gained power to evoke the response. It should be noted that the stimu-

[*] John W. M. Whiting, Unpublished paper, 1954, prepared for a World Health Organization study group.

lus situation was experimentally varied and the response controlled, and that contiguity between the unconditioned and the conditioned stimulus was considered to be the crucial event for learning.

In the United States quite a different view of learning was originally evolved by E. L. Thorndike (9), and developed by Hull (2), Skinner (7), N. E. Miller (3, 4), and Spence (8). This view, generally referred to as the reinforcement theory of learning, emphasizes motivation and reward. The experimental model which best expresses this view is provided by a hungry animal in a box learning to make some response (such as pressing a lever) to get a pellet of food. Rather than controlling the response and changing the stimulus as was the case in Pavlov's experimental design, the stimulus is held constant and the responses permitted to vary freely. This type of theory views learning as a process of response selection rather than stimulus substitution. Furthermore, reward following a correct performance is held to be crucial in this theory, mere contiguity between the conditioned and unconditioned stimulus is held to be insufficient.

A third view of learning is the *S-R* contiguity theory of Guthrie (1). The basic postulate of this theory is that complete learning takes place whenever a response occurs in the presence of a stimulus. Neither the presence of an unconditioned stimulus nor a reward is required. Guthrie accounts for the fact that learning is often continuous rather than a sudden "all or none" process by the fact that an organism is not perceiving all the stimuli in a situation on any given trial and gradual improvement results from more and more stimuli getting associated with the response.

The application of gestalt psychology is best exemplified by Tolman (10). Learning in Tolman's view involves changes in cognition rather than the strengthening of *S-R* connections. Vivid or salient stimuli (events) which are repeatedly perceived by an organism to be in a consistent spatial or temporal relation to one another give rise to the belief that these events will be so related in the future. Improvement in performance thus depends upon the increasing adequacy and validity of the cognitive map which guides and directs the performance.

MOTIVATION AND PERFORMANCE

Since the consequences of learning can be measured only if the organism does something, a complete theory of learning must contain principles governing performance. That is, it must concern itself with factors such as motivation, generalization and response competition as well as with acquisition. Hull has been most explicit in this regard and has assumed that the amplitude, latency, resistance to extinction and probability of occurrence of any act is a joint function of learning and motivation.[1]

Generalization is another performance principle of considerable importance. This principle is concerned with the progressive decrement in the strength of a habit as the stimuli in test situations are made more dissimilar from those present during learning. It provides a basis for some of the complex problems involved in symbolic mediation. This principle has also been used by Miller, by Sears (6), and by Whiting and Child (11), to account for the Freudian mechanisms of displacement and projection.

Response competition or conflict between simultaneously evoked habits is a final performance principle which should be mentioned. Ambivalence, insecurity and anxiety may be defined as special cases of response competition.

SECONDARY LEARNING

As the term is being used here, secondary learning refers to the special principles which govern the so-called acquired drives and acquired rewards. That is, those motives and rewards which are learned rather than innate. Since these concepts are particularly relevant to the reinforcement theory of learning, it is the followers of Hull who have done most systematic work in this area.

Acquired drives may be divided into two classes which may be termed conditioned primary drives and purposive acquired drives. Fear provides a model for the conditioned primary drive. Neutral stimuli associated with pain become danger signals which come to evoke fear. When fear has been established, the organism will learn to avoid or to escape from the dangerous situation.

The concept of purposive acquired drives is derived from the assumption that a conflict between goal expectancies produces insecurity which will motivate an organism to solve the conflict. Dependency, aggression, and achievement are examples of acquired drives which

[1] As he expresses it: $_sE_r = f(_sH_r) \times f(D)$ where $_sE_r$ is the term relating to performance, $_sH_r$ to accumulated learning, and D to current motivation.

have recently been accounted for in this manner.

Acquired rewards or token rewards are like acquired drives, learned rather than innate. It is generally held that the process of acquisition results from simple association of some neutral stimulus with some primary reward. Thus if a mother always smiles as she nurses the baby, her smile comes to be in itself rewarding. Tokens of value such as money gain their reward value in a somewhat more complicated manner, but presumably the process is not different in principle.

SOCIAL LEARNING

Culture and society provide some special circumstances or learning conditions which all children must face in growing up. Three factors in particular are important in this regard. First, rewards and punishments are administered by people, generally parents, who are perceived by the child to be similar to himself and whom he is generally taught to imitate. As a consequence, self-other discriminations, role adoption, projection, and the complicated process of identification and the internalization of values become central problems which any theory of social learning must face.

Secondly, the progressive maturation of the child from infancy to adulthood results in the child at first learning habits which he must later be forced to relinquish. For example, the child first learns to be dependent, then to be self-reliant and responsible. He may be permitted to have temper tantrums as an infant and then must learn to control his aggression as an older child. These shifts in parental attitude produce conflicts which in many instances have enduring effects.

Thirdly, all human children are brought up into a society of people who speak a language. Theories of social learning have scarcely begun to account for the implications of this fact. The transmission of systems of belief and value by formal or informal and often unintended instruction, transfer of training by verbal mediation, and the learning of the cognitive structure involved in planning are only some of the problems deriving from the symbolic behavior of human beings which an adequate theory of social learning must account for.

Justice obviously cannot be done in such a brief review to the theories here presented. Many of the fine points have had to be omitted; others have no doubt been distorted by condensation. Furthermore, many important contributors to certain facets of the learning process have not been mentioned at all. It is hoped that this review will serve as a skeleton outline of the major viewpoints held by learning theorists and the problems which face investigators concerned with learning and behavior.

A brief bibliography of important works on learning and behavior.

1. GUTHRIE, E. R. *The Psychology of Learning.* New York: Harper, 1935.

2. HULL, C. L. *The Principles of Behavior.* New York: Appleton-Century, 1943.

3. MILLER, N. E., & DOLLARD, J. *Social Learning and Imitation.* New Haven: Yale University Press, 1941.

4. MILLER, N. E. Learnable drives and rewards. In S. S. Stevens (Ed.), *Handbook of Experimental Psychology.* New York: Wiley & Sons, 1951.

5. PAVLOV, I. P. *Conditioned Reflexes.* (Trans. by G. V. Anrep) London: Oxford Press, 1927.

6. SEARS, R. R., *et al.* Some child-rearing antecedents of aggression and dependency in young children. *Genet. Psychol. Monogr.,* 1953, 47, 135-234.

7. SKINNER, B. F. *The Behavior of Organisms; an Experimental Analysis.* New York: Appleton-Century, 1938.

8. SPENCE, K. W. Theoretical interpretations of learning. In S. S. Stevens (Ed.), *Handbook of Experimental Psychology.* New York: Wiley & Sons, 1951.

9. THORNDIKE, E. L. *The Fundamentals of Learning.* New York: Teachers College, 1932.

10. TOLMAN, E. C. *Purposive Behavior in Animals and Men.* New York: Appleton-Century, 1932.

11. WHITING, J. W. M., & CHILD, I. L. *Child Training and Personality.* New Haven: Yale University Press, 1953.

13 / **REINFORCEMENT TODAY** / B. F. SKINNER*

DURING THE PAST 25 YEARS THE ROLE of reinforcement in human affairs has received steadily increasing attention—not through any changing fashion in learning theory but as the result of the discovery of facts and practices which have increased our power to predict and control behavior and in doing so have left no doubt of their reality and importance. The scope of reinforcement is still not fully grasped, even by those who have done most to demonstrate it, and elsewhere among psychologists cultural inertia is evident. This is understandable because the change has been little short of revolutionary: scarcely anything in traditional learning theory is left in recognizable form. In this paper I shall try to characterize some of the changes in our conception of reinforcement which have been forced upon us and to suggest why it has been so hard to accept them and to recognize their import.

THE ACQUISITION OF BEHAVIOR

In 1943 Keller Breland, Norman Guttman, and I were working on a wartime project sponsored by General Mills, Inc. Our laboratory was the top floor of a flour mill in Minneapolis, where we spent a good deal of time waiting for decisions to be made in Washington. All day long, around the mill, wheeled great flocks of pigeons. They were easily snared on the window sills and proved to be an irresistible supply of experimental subjects. We built a magnetic food-magazine, which dispensed grain on the principle of an automatic peanut vendor, and conditioned pigeons to turn at the sound it made and eat the grain it discharged into a cup. We used the device to condition several kinds of behavior. For example, we built a gauge to measure the force with which a pigeon pecked a horizontal block, and by differentially reinforcing harder pecks we built up such forceful blows that the base of the pigeon's beak quickly became inflamed. This was serious research, but we had our lighter moments. One day we decided to teach a pigeon to bowl. The pigeon was to send a wooden ball down a miniature alley toward a set of toy pins by swiping

the ball with a sharp sideward movement of the beak. To condition the response, we put the ball on the floor of an experimental box and prepared to operate the food-magazine as soon as the first swipe occurred. But nothing happened. Though we had all the time in the world, we grew tired of waiting. We decided to reinforce any response which had the slightest resemblance to a swipe—perhaps, at first, merely the behavior of looking at the ball—and then to select responses which more closely approximated the final form. The result amazed us. In a few minutes, the ball was caroming off the walls of the box as if the pigeon had been a champion squash player. The spectacle so impressed Keller Breland that he gave up a promising career in psychology and went into the commercial production of behavior.

Why had the pigeon learned with such surprising speed? Three points seem relevant:

1. In *magazine-training* the pigeon—that is, in getting it to respond to the sound of the magazine by turning immediately and approaching the food tray—we had created an auditory *conditioned reinforcer*. This is a great help in operant conditioning because it can follow a response instantly. When a rat runs down an alley and finds food at the end, or when a performing seal bounces a ball off its nose and is thrown a fish, behavior is reinforced under relatively loose temporal conditions. The rat may not immediately find the food, and the trainer may take a moment to throw the fish. Organisms will, of course, learn and continue to behave when reinforcement is substantially delayed, but only when certain temporal contingencies have been strengthened. Unless the gap between the behavior and the ultimate reinforcer is bridged with a sequence of conditioned reinforcers, other behavior will occur and receive the full force of the reinforcement. If the seal has time to turn toward the trainer before receiving the visual reinforcement of the approaching fish, its behavior in turning is most powerfully reinforced and may interfere with the behavior the trainer is trying to set up. Eventually a discrimination is formed so that the seal turns only after having executed the

* B. F. Skinner, Reinforcement today, *The American Psychologist*, 1958, *13*, 94-99. This article can be found also in B. F. Skinner's *Cumulative Record*, Enlarged Edition, 1961. Reprinted by permission.

proper behavior, but this can be a slow process. A delay of even a fraction of a second is sometimes important, as we have found in designing equipment for the study of operant behavior in the pigeon. When the response studied is pecking a plastic disc, the controlling circuit must act so rapidly that the sound of the magazine, as a conditioned reinforcer, will coincide with striking the disc rather than pulling the head *away* from it. This is a matter of perhaps a twentieth of a second, but such a delay produces disturbing changes in the topography of the response.

2. In early experiments on lever pressing, a quick response to the food-magazine was always set up before the lever was introduced. This was done for another reason—to permit emotional responses to the noise of the magazine to adapt out—but it must have been important in providing instantaneous reinforcement. The explicit conditioning of an auditory reinforcer was, therefore, not new; there must have been something else in the bowling experiment. In most experiments on learning an organism produces reinforcement by direct action: a rat pushes over the door of a jumping stand and discovers food, or a monkey lifts a cup and exposes a grape. Electrical circuits greatly increase the possibilities, but even then the organism is usually left to close the circuit by mechanical contact. I have elsewhere (3) described an experiment in which a rat was conditioned to pull a string to get a marble from a rack, pick up the marble with its forepaws, carry it across the cage to a vertical tube rising two inches above the floor, lift the marble, and drop it into the tube. The behavior was set up through successive approximations, but every stage was reached by constructing mechanical and electrical systems operated by the rat. In the experiment on bowling, however, we held the reinforcing switch in our hand and could reinforce any given form of behavior without constructing a mechanical or electrical system to report its occurrence. *The mechanical connection between behavior and reinforcement was greatly attenuated.*

3. But this was not new, either. Thorndike had reinforced a cat when it licked its paw, and animal trainers use hand reinforcement. The surprising result in our bowling experiment may have been due to the combination of the temporal precision of reinforcement provided by a conditioned reinforcer and the free selection of topography resulting from hand reinforce-

ment. In any event this combination must have enhanced the effect of the third, and main, feature of the experiment: the gradual *shaping up* of behavior by reinforcing crude approximations of the final topography instead of waiting for the complete response.

The technique of shaping behavior is now a familiar classroom demonstration, but the principle it demonstrates has not yet found a secure place in textbook discussions of learning. Curiously enough, the acquisition of behavior has never been directly attacked in classical research. The study of memory, from Ebbinghaus on, has not been primarily concerned with how behavior is acquired but only with how it is retained or how one form interferes with another in retention. Why does the subject sit in front of the memory drum, why does he vouchsafe anticipatory guesses, and how (not when) does he eventually arrive at that first correct response? These questions have not been the primary concern of research on memory. Animal research has almost always left the shaping of behavior to mechanical devices. In both fields the acquisition of behavior has been reported by "learning curves" or, worse, by something called *the* learning curve. When one has watched the actual shaping of behavior, it is obvious that such curves do not reflect any important property of the change in behavior brought about by operant reinforcement. They summarize the arbitrary and often accidental consequences which arise when complex and largely unanalyzed conditions of reinforcement act upon large samples of behavior. There are probably as many learning curves as there are apparatuses for the study of learning, and mathematicians will strive in vain to pull a useful order out of this chaos. Yet the prestige of the learning curve is so great that psychologists are unable to believe their eyes when the process of learning is made visible.

THE MAINTENANCE OF BEHAVIOR

An obvious fact about behavior is that it is almost never invariably reinforced. Not so obvious is the fact that the pattern of intermittent reinforcement controls the character and level of a performance. Why this is so can not be explained in a few words. Charles B. Ferster and I have recently published a fairly exhaustive account of the subject (1) in which we argue as follows.

A schedule of reinforcement is arranged by a

programming system which can be specified in physical terms. A clock is introduced into the circuit between key and magazine so that the first response made to the key after a given interval of time will be reinforced. A counter introduced into the circuit establishes a contingency in terms of number of responses emitted per reinforcement. Various settings of clock and counter and combinations of these generate almost unlimited possibilities.

A selected schedule usually generates a characteristic performance, expressed in terms of rate of responding and changes in rate. Once this has happened, the organism is characteristically reinforced at the end of a particular pattern of responding. Its behavior at the moment of reinforcement and during the period preceding reinforcement is part of the stimulating environment, aspects of which acquire control over subsequent behavior. To take a very simple example: if an organism is characteristically responding at a high rate at the moment of reinforcement, behavior at that rate becomes an optimal stimulating condition, comparable to the presence of the reinforced stimulus in a discrimination, and the probability of further responding is therefore maximal. When the organism is not responding at all, the probability is minimal. Other rates and patterns of changes in rate come to serve similar discriminative functions. Ferster and I have checked this explanation of the performances characteristic of schedules in several ways. For example, instead of letting a schedule generate a condition *most* of the time, we have added special devices to *assure* a given condition of behaving at every reinforcement. For example, when a fixed-interval performance *usually* arranges a moderately high rate at the moment of reinforcement, a special device will guarantee that reinforcements occur *only* at that rate. We have also added stimuli to the physical environment which are correlated with, and hence amplify, the aspects of the organism's behavior appealed to in such an explanation.

This, then, is what happens under intermittent reinforcement: A scheduling system sets up a performance, and the performance generates stimuli which enter into the control of the rate of responding, either maintaining the performance or changing it in various ways. Some schedules produce performances which guarantee reinforcement under conditions which continue to maintain that performance. Others produce progressive changes. Still others yield oscillations: the first performance generates conditions which eventually produce a different performance, which in turn generates conditions restoring the earlier performance, and so on.

Both the circuit and the behavior, then, contribute to the reinforcing contingencies. It follows that the effect of any circuit depends upon the behavior the organism brings to it. Some complex schedules can be studied only by taking the organism through a series of simpler schedules into the final performance. The performance, as well as the topography of a response, may need to be "shaped." This does not mean that schedule performances vary greatly because of individual histories, for only a few of the effects of schedules are not really reversible. Once a performance is reached, it usually shows a high order of uniformity, even between species. The fact that it is the *combination* of schedule and performance which generates reinforcing contingencies can easily be overlooked. A physiologist once asked to borrow one of our apparatuses to show his class the behavioral effects of certain drugs. We sent him an apparatus which reinforced a pigeon on a multiple fixed-ratio fixed-interval schedule, together with two pigeons showing beautifully stable performances. When one pigeon died through an overdose of a drug, the physiologist simply bought another pigeon and put it into the apparatus. To his surprise, nothing happened.

The same mistake is made in much traditional work on learning and problem solving. In the usual study of problem solving, for example, the experimenter constructs a complex set of contingencies and simply waits for it to take hold. This is no test of whether the organism can adjust to these contingencies with a performance which would be called a solution. All we can properly conclude is that the experimenter has not constructed an adequate succession of performances. The ability of the experimenter rather than that of the organism is being tested. It is dangerous to assert that an organism of a given species or age *can not* solve a given problem. As the result of careful scheduling, pigeons, rats, and monkeys have done things during the past five years which members of their species have never done before. It is not that their forebears were incapable of such behavior; nature had simply never arranged effective sequences of schedules.

What we have learned about the shaping of response-topography and about the techniques which bring an organism under the control of complex schedules has made it possible to study the behavior generated by arrangements of responses, stimuli, and reinforcements once classified as the "higher mental processes." An experiment can be designed in which two or more responses are emitted concurrently or in rapid alternation, under the control of multiple stimuli, often under two or more schedules of reinforcement or two or more types of reinforcement under appropriate conditions of motivation. It has been found that a schedule, or rather the stimuli present when a schedule is in force, has reinforcing or aversive properties. An organism will respond on one schedule to reach or avoid another. We can determine which of two schedules a pigeon "prefers" by comparing how fast it will respond on a variable-interval schedule to get into Schedule A with how fast it will respond on the same variable-interval schedule to get into Schedule B. The analysis of avoidance and escape behavior in the hands of Sidman, Brady, and others has made it possible to study combinations of positive and negative reinforcers in many interrelated patterns. The analysis of punishment in such terms has permitted a reformulation of the so-called Freudian dynamisms (5).

The technology resulting from the study of reinforcement has been extended into other fields of psychological inquiry. It has permitted Blough, Guttman, and others to convert pigeons into sensitive psychophysical observers. It has allowed pharmacologists and psychologists in pharmacological laboratories to construct behavioral base lines against which the effects of drugs on the so-called higher mental processes can be evaluated. It has enabled Lindsley and his co-workers to test the limits of the environmental control of psychotic subjects. And so on, in a long list. The technology is difficult. It can not conveniently be learned from books; something resembling an apprenticeship is almost necessary. Possibly we can explain the fact that psychologists in general have only slowly accepted these new methods by noting that under such conditions knowledge is diffused slowly.

Many psychologists may never wish to acquire the competence necessary for detailed research in reinforcement, but there is another application which is of broader significance. A clinical psychologist recently complained (2) that learning theory told him nothing about important aspects of human behavior. It would not explain, for example, why a man would seek "little bits of punishment in order to accept a big punishment."[Ed] He may be right in saying that learning *theory* does not tell him much, but the example he chose is just the kind of complex arrangement of contingencies which is now under intensive investigation. And he is asking for just the kind of interpretation of human affairs which is emerging from this work. The world in which man lives may be regarded as an extraordinarily complex set of positive and negative reinforcing contingencies. In addition to the physical environment to which he is sensitively attuned and with which he carries on an important interchange, we have (as he has) to contend with social stimuli, social reinforcers, and a network of personal and institutional control and countercontrol—all of amazing intricacy. The contingencies of reinforcement which man has made for man are wonderful to behold.

But they are by no means inscrutable. The parallel between the contingencies now being studied in the laboratory and those of daily life cry for attention—and for remedial action. In any social situation we must discover *who* is reinforcing *whom* with *what* and to *what effect*. As a very simple example, take the aggressive child. When two young children are left alone in a room with a few toys, conditions are almost ideal for shaping up selfish and aggressive behavior. Under these circumstances one child's reinforcement is the other child's punishment, and vice versa. When I once discussed this example with a group of teachers, one of them exclaimed: "Yes, and that's why in the nursery schools of the Soviet Union the toys are so big it takes two children to play with them!" Possibly that is one solution. Certainly there are many others. When contingencies of reinforcement are properly understood, we can not thoughtlessly allow damaging contingencies to arise or go unremedied. By taking a little thought it is now possible to design social situations which have happier consequences for everyone.

I am not saying that any one set of contingencies explains aggression in children or that it takes a long apprenticeship in reinforcement research to understand that case. It is the very existence of reinforcing contingencies which must first be recognized, and that is not always easy. Here is a slightly less obvious case. The current nationwide problem of school discipline is frequently, though possibly erroneously, attributed to progressive education. Whatever its explanation, it is a serious prob-

Ed *That is, in mourning behavior, where the pain of reliving certain experiences in the absence of a loved one is sought in the process of learning to accept the permanent loss.*

lem. How can we recapture the orderly conduct once attributed to "discipline," without reinstating all the undesirable by-products of an inhumane aversive control? The answer is: use positive reinforcement instead of punishment. But, how? A first step is to analyze the reinforcing contingencies in the classroom. In particular, what reinforcers are available to the teacher? The answer to that question is sometimes discouraging, but even in the worst possible case she can at least reinforce a class by dismissing it. The point is that she must understand that dismissal is reinforcing if she is not to throw away the small measure of power it offers her. The "natural" thing is for a teacher to dismiss the class when its conduct is most aversive to her. But this is exactly the wrong thing to do, for she then differentially reinforces the very behavior she wants to suppress. A teacher who understands reinforcement will survey the class during the final minutes of a period and choose for dismissal the moment at which things are going as well as can be expected. The effect will not be evident the first day, it may not be the second or third, and it may never be enough to solve all her problems; but a careful husbanding of small reinforcers and the nurturing of proper contingencies is a program well worth exploring.

As a final and more technical example of the use of reinforcement in interpreting human affairs, take the always interesting form of behavior called gambling. Gamblers appear to violate the law of effect because they continue to play even though their net reward is negative. Hence it is often argued that they must be gambling for other reasons. To the psychoanalyst the gambler may simply be punishing himself. Others may insist that the attraction is not money but excitement or that people gamble to get away from a humdrum life. Now, all gambling devices arrange a variable ratio schedule of reinforcement, and our explanation of the performance generated by that schedule embraces the behavior of the gambler. It happens to be relatively *excited* behavior, but this, as well as the fact that there is no net gain, is irrelevant in accounting for the performance. A pigeon, too, can become a pathological gambler, and it is unlikely that it does so to punish itself, or for the excitement, or to get away from it all.

Such expressions may not be meaningless. The complex contingencies involved in "self-punishment" may well be involved, although quantitative evidence would be needed to show this. "Getting away from it all" reminds us that some schedules are aversive. Herrnstein and Morse have shown that a pigeon can be conditioned to peck one key if this is occasionally followed by the opportunity to take time off from another key. In turning to a variable-ratio system of reinforcement, then, the gambler may well be escaping from other schedules. Moreover, a variable-ratio schedule at suitable values is reinforcing. These facts account for any behavior which brings an organism under a variable-ratio schedule, but they do not explain the performance once this schedule is in force. The conditions which prevail under the schedule are the relevant facts.

These are necessarily fragmentary examples of the contribution of an experimental analysis of intermittent reinforcement to our understanding of human behavior, but they may serve to make an important point. The relevance of reinforcement is often quite unexpected. These examples are not part of the classical field of learning; they are matters of *motivation!* One expects to see them discussed by dynamic psychologists, psychologists of personality, or psychoanalysts, not by people who study white rats and pigeons. True, learning theory has long been applied to psychotherapy, but traditional research in learning has not made a very helpful contribution. Suddenly, reinforcement takes on new dimensions. When Freud was once asked whether psychoanalysis and psychology were the same, he insisted that psychoanalysis embraced all of psychology except the physiology of the sense organs (6). This was an ambitious statement, and perhaps a similar claim for reinforcement would be equally unjustified. Yet the facts of human behavior fall to the psychoanalyst and the student of reinforcement alike for explanation. But where the analyst has studied behavior in a given environment as the manifestation of hidden (even if eventually-to-be-revealed) forces, we can now interpret the same behavior and environment as a set of reinforcing contingencies. In doing so we gain a tremendous advantage, for all terms necessary for such an analysis lie within an observable and often manipulable universe. Beyond the prediction and control made possible by recent research in reinforcement lies the broader field of interpretation. And it is a kind of interpretation so closely allied with prediction and control that positive and successful action are frequently within easy reach.

As I have suggested to psychologists in general that they will find much of interest in the modern study of reinforcement, it will be appropriate to end with a few words of caution.

1. This kind of research is difficult and relatively expensive. In our book on schedules of reinforcement, Ferster and I report on 70,000 hours of continuously recorded behavior composed of about one quarter of a *billion* responses. The personal observation of behavior on such a scale is unthinkable. The research must be heavily instrumented. The programming of complex schedules demands not only a large budget but considerable skill in relay engineering, neither of which is common in psychological laboratories.

2. It is usually single-organism research. Any other experimental method is often impossible. When an experiment on one pigeon runs to thousands of hours, it can not be repeated on even a modest group of, say, ten subjects—at least if one wants to get on with other matters. Fortunately, a statistical program is *unnecessary*. Most of what we know about the efforts of complex schedules of reinforcement has been learned in a series of discoveries no one of which could have been proved to the satisfaction of a student in Statistics A. Moreover, a statistical approach is just *wrong*. The curves we get can not be averaged or otherwise smoothed without destroying properties which we know to be of first importance. These points are hard to make. The seasoned experimenter can shrug off the protests of statisticians, but the young psychologist should be prepared to feel guilty, or at least stripped of the prestige conferred upon him by statistical practices, in embarking upon research of this sort.

3. The research is not theoretical in the sense that experiments are designed to test theories. As I have pointed out elsewhere (4), when lawful changes in behavior take place before our very eyes—or, at most, only one step removed in a cumulative curve—we lose the taste, as we lose the need, for imagined changes in some fanciful world of neurones, ideas, or intervening variables. Here again tradition throws up a roadblock. Certain people—among them psychologists who should know better—have claimed to be able to say how the scientific mind works. They have set up normative rules of scientific conduct. The first step for anyone interested in studying reinforcement is to challenge that claim. Until a great deal more is known about thinking, scientific or otherwise, a sensible man will not abandon common sense. Ferster and I were impressed by the wisdom of this course of action when, in writing our book, we reconstructed our own scientific behavior. At one time we intended—though, alas, we changed our minds—to express the point in this dedication: "To the mathematicians, statisticians, and scientific methodologists with whose help this book would never have been written."

The difficulties which have stood in the way of the advancing study of reinforcement will undoubtedly continue to cause trouble, but they will be more than offset by the powerful reinforcing consequences of work in this field. Techniques are now available for a new and highly profitable exploration of the human behavior at issue in education, commerce and industry, psychotherapy, religion, and government. A program of cultural design in the broadest sense is now within reach. Sociologists, anthropologists, political scientists, economists, theologians, psychotherapists and psychologists have long tried to reach an understanding of human behavior which would be useful in solving practical problems. In that technological race a dark horse is coming up fast. The new principles and methods of analysis which are emerging from the study of reinforcement may prove to be among the most productive social instruments of the twentieth century.

REFERENCES

1. FERSTER, C. B., & SKINNER, B. F. *Schedules of reinforcement.* New York: Appleton-Century-Crofts, 1957.

2. SHEEHAN, J. G. The marital status of psychoanalysis and learning theory. *Amer. Psychologist*, 1957, *12*, 277-278.

3. SKINNER, B. F. *The behavior of organisms.* New York: Appleton-Century-Crofts, 1938.

4. SKINNER, B. F. Are theories of learning necessary? *Psychol. Rev.*, 1950, 57, 193-216.

5. SKINNER, B. F. *Science and human behavior.* New York: Macmillan, 1953.

6. WORTIS, J. *Fragments of an analysis with Freud.* New York: Simon & Schuster, 1954.

14 / THE ELIMINATION OF TANTRUM BEHAVIOR BY EXTINCTION PROCEDURES /

CARL D. WILLIAMS*

THIS PAPER REPORTS THE SUCCESSFUL treatment of tyrant-like tantrum behavior in a male child by the removal of reinforcement. The subject (S) was approximately 21 months old. He had been seriously ill much of the first 18 months of his life. His health then improved considerably, and he gained weight and vigor.

S now demanded the special care and attention that had been given him over the many critical months. He enforced some of his wishes, especially at bedtime, by unleashing tantrum behavior to control the actions of his parents.Ed

The parents and an aunt took turns in putting him to bed both at night and for S's afternoon nap. If the parent left the bedroom after putting S in his bed, S would scream and fuss until the parent returned to the room. As a result, the parent was unable to leave the bedroom until after S went to sleep. If the parent began to read while in the bedroom, S would cry until the reading material was put down. The parents felt that S enjoyed his control over them and that he fought off going to sleep as long as he could. In any event, a parent was spending from one-half to two hours each bedtime just waiting in the bedroom until S went to sleep.

Following medical reassurance regarding S's physical condition, it was decided to remove the reinforcement of this tyrant-like tantrum behavior. Consistent with the learning principle that, in general, behavior that is not reinforced will be extinguished, a parent or the aunt put S to bed in a leisurely and relaxed fashion. After bedtime pleasantries, the parent left the bedroom and closed the door. S screamed and raged, but the parent did not re-enter the room.

Ed *Readers are cautioned that some "tantrums" involve genuine loss of self-control rather than a manipulation of the parents. The causes and treatment of such tantrums differ from those of the "tyrant-like" tantrum behavior described in this article. A helpful discussion of tantrums may be found in* Emotional Problems of Living *by O. S. English and G. H. J. Pearson (New York, W. W. Norton and Co., 3rd Edition, 1963).*

The duration of screaming and crying was obtained from the time the door was closed.

The results are shown in Fig. 1. It can be seen that S continued screaming for 45 min. the first time he was put to bed in the first extinction series. S did not cry at all the second time he was put to bed. This is perhaps attributable to his fatigue from the crying of Occasion 1. By the tenth occasion, S no longer whimpered, fussed, or cried when the parent left the room. Rather, he smiled as they left. The parents felt that he made happy sounds until he dropped off to sleep.

About a week later, S screamed and fussed after the aunt put him to bed, probably reflecting spontaneous recovery of the tantrum behavior. The aunt then reinforced the tantrum behavior by returning to S's bedroom and remaining there until he went to sleep. It was then necessary to extinguish this behavior a second time.

Figure 1 shows that the second extinction curve is similar to the first. Both curves are gen-

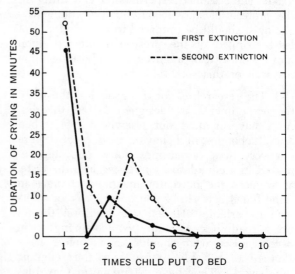

FIGURE 1 / LENGTH OF CRYING IN TWO EXTINCTION SERIES AS A FUNCTION OF SUCCESSIVE OCCASIONS OF BEING PUT TO BED.

* Carl D. Williams, The elimination of tantrum behavior by extinction procedures, *Journal of Abnormal and Social Psychology*, 1959, 59, 269. Reprinted by permission.

erally similar to extinction curves obtained with subhuman subjects. The second extinction series reached zero by the ninth occasion. No further tantrums at bedtime were reported during the next two years.

It should be emphasized that the treatment in this case did not involve aversive punishment.

All that was done was to remove the reinforcement. Extinction of the tyrant-like tantrum behavior then occurred.

No unfortunate side- or aftereffects of this treatment were observed. At three and three-quarters years of age, S appeared to be a friendly, expressive, outgoing child.

15 / EFFECTS OF ADULT SOCIAL REINFORCEMENT ON CHILD BEHAVIOR*/FLORENCE R. HARRIS, MONTROSE M. WOLF, AND DONALD M. BAER**

In a recent issue of this Journal, Horowitz (1963) *reviewed the literature concerning social reinforcement effects on child behavior. Laboratory findings concerning those factors determining reinforcer effectiveness were summarized. Now, three research workers at the University of Washington present the results of their recent and provocative work demonstrating the effectiveness of carefully worked-out contingencies of adult attention in modifying certain "problem" behaviors of children within the nursery school itself. There are unmistakable and important implications in this research for nursery school practice even though the authors prudently point to the care needed in the nursery school setting to bring childrens' behavior under the control of social reinforcement. These efforts are also preliminary, but the painstaking persistence of the Washington researchers reaffirms belief in the infinite modifiability of behavior and the potential of the nursery school teacher in this endeavor.*

WILLARD W. HARTUP, *Research Editor*

THERE IS GENERAL AGREEMENT AMONG educators that one of the primary functions of a nursery school is to foster in each child social behaviors that contribute toward more pleasant and productive living for all. However, there is no similar consensus as to precisely how this objective is to be attained. Many writers subscribe to practices based on a combination of psychoanalytic theory and client-centered therapy principles, usually referred to as a mental hygiene approach. Yet there are considerable variation and vagueness in procedures recommended, particularly those dealing with such problem behaviors as the child's hitting people, breaking valuable things, or withdrawing from both people and things. Read (1955), for example, recommends accepting the child's feelings, verbalizing them for him, and draining them off through vigorous activities. Landreth (1942) advises keeping adult contacts with the child

* These studies were supported in part by research grants from the National Institute of Mental Health (MH-02208-07) and the University of Washington Graduate School Research Fund (11-1873). The authors are also indebted to Sidney W. Bijou for his general counsel and assistance.

** Florence R. Harris, Montrose M. Wolf, and Donald M. Baer, Effects of adult social reinforcement on child behavior, *Young Children,* formerly *The Journal of Nursery Education,* 1964, *20* (1), 8-17. Reprinted by permission.

at a minimum based on his needs, backing up verbal suggestions by an implicit assumption that the suggestion will be carried out and, when in doubt, doing nothing unless the child's physical safety is involved. In addition to some of the above precepts, Taylor (1954) counsels parents and teachers to support both desirable and undesirable behaviors and to give nonemotional punishment. According to Standing (1959), Montessori advocates that teachers pursue a process of nonintervention, following careful preparation of a specified environment aimed at "canalizing the energy" and developing "inner command." Nonintervention does not preclude the "minimum dose" of instruction and correction.

Using some combination of such guidance precepts, teachers have reported success in helping some nursery school children who showed problem behaviors; but sometimes adherence to the same teaching principles has not been helpful in modifying the behavior of concern. Indeed, it is usually not at all clear what conditions and principles may or may not have been operative. All of these precepts have in common the adult behaviors of approaching and attending to a child. Therefore, it seemed to the staff of the Laboratory Preschool at the University of Washington that a first step in developing possible explicit criteria for judging when and when not to attend was to study the precise effects that adult attention can have on some problem behaviors.

This paper presents an account of the procedures and results of five such studies. Two groups of normal nursery school children provided the subjects studied. One group enrolled twelve three-year-olds and the other, sixteen four-year-olds. The two teachers of the younger group and the three teachers of the older group conducted the studies as they carried out their regular teaching duties. The general methodology of these studies was developed in the course of dealing with a particularly pressing problem behavior shown by one child at the beginning of the school year. It is worth considering this case before describing the procedures which evolved from it.

The study dealt with a three-year-old girl who had regressed to an excessive amount of crawling (Harris, Johnston, Kelley, and Wolf, 1964). By "excessive" is meant that after three weeks of school she was spending most of her morning crawling or in a crouched position with her face hidden. The parents reported that for some months the behavior had been occurring whenever they took her to visit or when friends came to their home. The teachers had used the conventional techniques, as outlined above, for building the child's "security."

Observations recorded in the third week at school showed, however, that more than 80% of the child's time was spent in off-feet positions. The records also showed that the crawling behavior frequently drew the attention of teachers. On-feet behaviors, such as standing and walking, which occurred infrequently, seldom drew such notice.

A program was instituted in which the teachers no longer attended to the child whenever she was crawling or crouching, but gave her continuous warm attention as long as she was engaging in behavior in which she was standing, running, or walking. Initially the only upright behaviors that the teachers were able to attend to occurred when the child pulled herself almost to her feet in order to hang up or take down her coat from her locker, and when she pulled herself up to wash her hands in the wash basin. Within a week of the initiation of the new attention-giving procedure, the child acquired a close-to-normal pattern of on-feet behavior.

In order to see whether the change from off- to on-feet behavior was related to the differential attention given by the teachers, they reversed their procedure, making attention once again contingent only upon crawling and other off-feet behavior. They waited for occasions of such off-feet behavior to "reinforce" with attention, while not attending to any on-feet behavior. By the second day the child had reverted to her old pattern of play and locomotion. The observational records showed the child was off her feet 80% of the class session.

To see whether on-feet behavior could be reestablished, the teachers again reversed their procedure, giving attention to the child only when she was engaging in behaviors involving upright positions. On-feet behavior rose markedly during the first session. By the fourth day, the child again spent about 62% of the time on her feet.

Once the child was not spending the greater portion of her day crawling about, she quickly became a well-integrated member of the group. Evidently she already had well-developed social play skills.

As a result of this demonstration that either walking or crawling could be maintained and that the child's responses depended largely upon the teachers' attending behaviors, the teachers began a series of further experimental analyses of the relationship between teacher attention and nursery school child behavior.

PROCEDURES

A specified set of procedures common to the next studies was followed. First, a child showing problem behavior was selected and records were secured. An observer recorded all of the child's behavior, the environmental conditions under which it occurred, and its immediate consequences under conventional teacher guidance. This was done throughout the 2½-hour school session, daily, and for several days. The records gave detailed pictures of the behavior under study. In each case, it became apparent that the problem behavior almost always succeeded in attracting adult attention.

As soon as these records, technically termed "baseline" records, of the typical behavior of the child and teachers were obtained, teachers instituted a program of systematically giving differential attention to the child. When the undesired behavior occurred, they did not in any way attend to him, but remained absorbed in one of the many necessary activities of teachers with other children or with equipment. If the behavior occurred while a teacher was attending to the child, she at once turned to another child or task in a matter-of-fact and nonrejecting manner. Concurrently, teachers gave immediate attention to other behaviors of the child which were considered to be more desirable than the problem behavior. The net effect of these procedures was that the child could gain a great deal of adult attention if he refrained from engaging in "problem behavior." If under this regime of differential attention the problem behavior diminished to a stable low level at which it was no longer considered a problem, a second procedure was inaugurated to check out the functional relationship between changes in the child's behavior and the guidance procedures followed.

The second procedure was simply to reverse the first procedure. That is, when the problem behavior occurred, the teacher went immediately to the child and gave him her full, solicitous attention. If the behavior stopped, she turned to other children and tasks, remaining thus occupied until the behavior recurred. In effect, one sure way for the child to secure adult attention was to exhibit the problem behavior.

This procedure was used to secure reasonably reliable information on whether the teachers' special program had indeed brought about the changes noted in the child's behavior. If adult attention was the critical factor in maintaining the behavior, the problem behavior should recur in stable form under these conditions. If it did so, this was evidence that adult attention was, technically speaking, a positive social reinforcer for the child's behavior.

The final stage of the study was, of course, to return to procedures in which attention was given at once and continuously for behaviors considered desirable. Concurrently, adult attention was again withheld or withdrawn as an immediate consequence of the problem behavior. As the problem disappeared and appropriate behaviors increased, the intense program of differential adult attention was gradually diminished until the child was receiving attention at times and in amounts normal for the teachers in the group. However, attention was given only on occasions of desirable behavior, and never (or very seldom) for the undesirable behavior.

CRYING AND WHINING

Following the above procedures, a study was conducted on a four-year-old boy who cried a great deal after mild frustrations (Hart, Allen, Buell, Harris, and Wolf, 1964). This child aver-

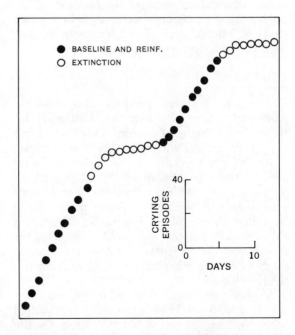

FIGURE 1 / CUMULATIVE RECORD OF THE DAILY NUMBER OF CRYING EPISODES.

aged about eight full-fledged crying episodes each school morning. The baseline observations showed that this crying behavior consistently brought attention from the teachers, in the form of going to him and showing solicitous concern. During the following days, this behavior was simply ignored. (The only exceptions to this were to have been incidents in which the child had hurt himself considerably and was judged to have genuine grounds for crying. Naturally, his hurts were to be attended to. Such incidents, however, did not occur.) Ten days of ignoring the outcries, but giving approving attention for verbal and self-help behaviors, produced a steady weakening of the crying response to a nearly zero level. In the final five days of the interval, only one crying response was recorded. The number of crying episodes on successive days is graphed in cumulative form in Fig. 1. (page 101.)

During the next ten days, crying was again reinforced whenever it occurred, the teachers attending to the boy on these occasions without fail. At first, it was necessary to give attention for mere grimaces that might follow a bump. The daily crying episodes quickly rose to a rate almost as high as formerly. A second ten-day period of ignoring the outcries again produced a quick weakening of the response to a near-zero level, as is apparent in the figure. Crying remained at this low level thereafter, according to the informal judgment of the teachers.

The same procedures were used in another study of "operant crying" of a four-year-old boy, with the same general results.

ISOLATE PLAY

Two studies involved children who exhibited markedly solitary play behavior. Extremely little of their morning at nursery school was spent in any interaction with other children. Instead, these children typically played alone in a quiet area of the school room or the play yard, or interacted only with the teachers. For present purposes, both of these response patterns will be called "isolate play." Systematic observation showed that isolate play usually attracted or maintained the attention of a teacher, whereas social play with other children did so comparatively seldom.

A plan was initiated in which the teacher was to attend regularly if the child approached other children and interacted with them. On the other hand, the teacher was not to attend to the child so long as he engaged in solitary play.

To begin with, attention was given when the child merely stood nearby, watching other children; then, when he played beside another child; and finally, only when he interacted with the other child. Teachers had to take special precautions that their attending behaviors did not result in drawing the child away from children and into interaction solely with the teacher. Two techniques were found particularly effective. The teacher directed her looks and comments to the other child or children, including the subject only as a participant in the play project. For example, "That's a big building you three boys are making; Bill and Tom and Jim (subject) are all working hard." Accessory materials were also kept at hand so that the teacher could bring a relevant item for the subject to add to the play: "Here's another plate for your tea party, Ann." In both isolate cases this new routine for giving adult attention produced the desired result: Isolate play declined markedly in strength while social play increased two- or threefold.

After about a week of the above procedure, the consequences of nonisolate and isolate play were reversed. The teachers no longer attended to the child's interactions with other children, but instead gave continuous attention to the child when he was alone. Within a week, or less, isolate play became the dominant form of activity in both cases.

The former contingencies were then reinstated: The teachers attended to social interactions by the child, and ignored isolate play as completely as they could. Again, isolate play declined sharply while social interaction increased as before. The results of one of these studies (Allen, Hart, Buell, Harris, and Wolf, 1964) are summarized in Fig. 2.

Figure 2 shows the changes in behavior of a 4½-year-old girl under the different guidance conditions. The graph shows the percentage of play time that she spent in interaction with other children and the percentage of time spent with an adult. The remainder of her time was spent alone. It is apparent that only about 15% of this child's play time was spent in social play as long as the teachers attended primarily to her solitary play. But interacting behaviors rose to about 60% of total play time when the teachers attended only to her social play. At the same time, her interactions solely with teachers, not being reinforced, fell from their usual 40% of the child's play time to about 20%. These were considered reasonable percentages for this nurs-

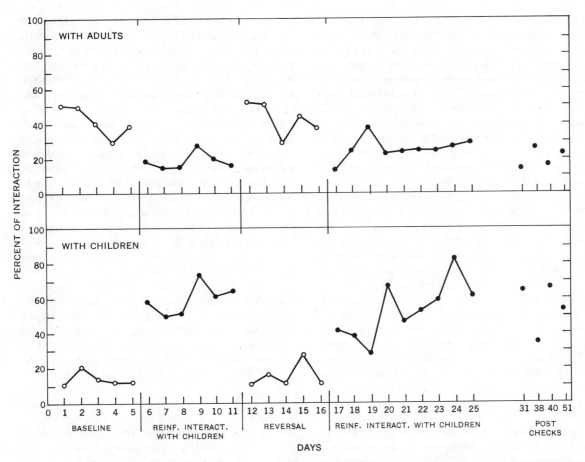

FIGURE 2 / DAILY PERCENTAGES OF TIME SPENT IN SOCIAL INTERACTION WITH ADULTS AND WITH CHILDREN DURING APPROXIMATELY TWO HOURS OF EACH MORNING SESSION.

ery school child. During Days 17 through 25 the schedule of adult reinforcement of social play was gradually reduced to the usual amount of attention, given at the usual irregular intervals. Nevertheless, the social behavior maintained its strength, evidently becoming largely self-maintaining.

After Day 25, the teachers took care not to attend too often to the child when she was alone, but otherwise planned no special contingencies for attending. Four checks were made at later dates to see if the pattern of social behavior persisted. It is apparent (Fig. 2, Post Checks) that the change was durable, at least until Day 51. Further checks were not possible because of the termination of the school year.

A parallel study, of a three-year-old isolate boy (Johnston, Kelley, Harris, Wolf, and Baer, unpub.) yielded similar results showing the same pattern of rapid behavioral change in response to changing contingencies for adult attention. In the case of this boy, postchecks were made on three days during the early months of school following the summer vacation period. The data showed that on those days his interaction with children averaged 55% of his play time. Apparently his social play was well established. Teachers reported that throughout the remainder of the year he continued to develop ease and skills in playing with his peers.

The immediate shifts in these children's play behavior may be partly due to the fact that they had already developed skills readily adapted to play with peers at school. Similar studies in progress are showing that, for some children, development of social play behaviors may require much longer periods of reinforcement.

EXCESSIVE PASSIVITY

A fifth case (Johnston, Kelley, Harris, and Wolf, unpub.) involved a boy noted for his thoroughgoing lack of any sort of vigorous play activity.

The teachers reported that this child consistently stood quietly about the play yard while other children ran, rode tricycles, and climbed on special climbing frames, trees, fences, and playhouses. Teachers also reported that they frequently attempted to encourage him, through suggestions or invitations, to engage in the more vigorous forms of play available. Teachers expressed concern over his apparent lack of strength and motor skills. It was decided to select a particular form of active play to attempt to strengthen. A wooden frame with ladders and platforms, called a climbing frame, was chosen as the vehicle for establishing this activity. The teachers attended at first to the child's mere proximity to the frame. As he came closer, they progressed to attending only to his touching it, climbing up a little, and finally to extensive climbing. Technically, this was reinforcement of successive approximations to climbing behavior. Fig. 3 shows the results of nine days of this procedure, compared to a baseline of the preceding nine days. In this figure, black bars represent climbing on the climbing frame, and white bars represent climbing on any other equipment in the play yard. The height of the bars shows the percentage of the child's play time spent in such activities. It is clear that during the baseline period less than 10% of the child's time was spent in any sort of climbing activity, but that during the course of reinforcement with pleased adult attention for climbing on the frame, this behavior greatly increased, finally exceeding 50% of the child's morning. (Climbing on other objects was not scored during this period.) There then followed five days during which the teachers ignored any climbing on the frame, but attended to all other appropriate activities. The rate of climbing on the frame promptly fell virtually to zero, though the child climbed on other apparatus and was consistently given attention for this. Another five days of reinforcement of use of the climbing frame immediately restored the climbing-frame behavior to a high stable level, always in excess of 40% of the boy's play time. After this, the teachers began an intermittent program of reinforcement for climbing on any other suitable objects, as well as vigorous active play of all sorts, in an effort to generalize the increased vigorous activity. Frame-climbing weakened considerably, being largely replaced by other climbing activities, which were now scored again as data. Activities such as tricycle-riding and running were not systematically recorded due to difficulties in reliably scoring them. It is clear from the data obtained, however, that climbing activities were thoroughly generalized by this final procedure. Checks made the following school year in another play yard indicated that vigorous climbing had become a stable part of his behavior repertoire.

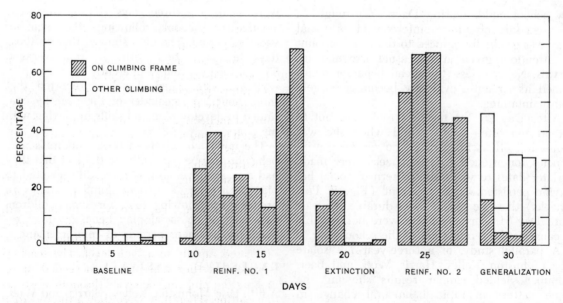

FIGURE 3 / DAILY PERCENTAGES OF TIME SPENT IN USING A CLIMBING-FRAME APPARATUS. OPEN BARS INDICATE TIME SPENT IN CLIMBING ON OTHER EQUIPMENT.

SUMMARY AND DISCUSSION

The above studies systematically examined effects of adult attention on some problem behaviors of normal preschool children. The findings in each case clearly indicated that for these children adult attention was a strong positive reinforcer. That is, the behavior which was immediately followed by a teacher's giving the child attention rose rapidly to a high rate, and the rate fell markedly when adult attention was withheld from that behavior and concurrently given to an incompatible behavior. While it seems reasonable that for most young children adult attention may be a positive reinforcer, it is also conceivable that for some children adult attention may be a negative reinforcer. That is, the rate of a behavior may decrease when it is immediately followed by the attention of an adult, and rise again as soon as the adult withdraws. Actually, for a few children observed at the preschool, it has been thought that adult attention was a negative reinforcer. This seemed to be true, for instance, in the case of the climbing-frame child. Before the study was initiated, the teachers spent several weeks attempting to make themselves positively reinforcing to the child. This they did by staying at a little distance from him and avoiding attending directly to him until he came to them for something. At first, his approaches were only for routine help, such as buttoning his coat. On each of these occasions they took care to be smilingly friendly and helpful. In time, he began making approaches of other kinds, for instance, to show a toy. Finally, when a teacher approached him and commented with interest on what he was doing, he continued his play instead of stopping, hitting out, or running off. However, since his play remained lethargic and sedentary, it was decided that special measures were necessary to help him progress more rapidly. It was the use and effects of these special measures that constituted the study. Clearly, however, adult attention must be or become positively reinforcing to a child before it can be successfully used to help him achieve more desirably effective behaviors.

Studies such as those reported here seem to imply that teachers may help many children rapidly through systematic programming of their adult social reinforcements. However, further research in this area seems necessary. Some of our own studies now in progress suggest that guidance on the basis of reinforcement principles may perhaps bring rapidly into use only behaviors which are already available within the repertory of the child. If the desired behavior requires skills not yet in the child's repertory, then the process of developing those skills from such behaviors as the child has may require weeks or months. For example, a four-year-old child who could verbalize but who very rarely spoke was helped to speak freely within several days. On the other hand, a child of the same age who had never verbalized required a lengthy shaping process that involved reinforcing first any vocalization, and then gradually more appropriate sounds and combinations of sounds. The latter study was still incomplete at the close of a year of work. The time required to develop social behaviors in isolate children has likewise varied considerably, presumably for the same reasons.

Although the teachers conducted these studies in the course of carrying out their regular teaching duties, personnel in excess of the usual number were necessary. The laboratory school was staffed with one teacher to no more than six children, making it possible to assign to one teacher the role of principal "reinforcer teacher" in a study. This teacher was responsible for giving the child immediate attention whenever he behaved in specified ways. In addition, observers were hired and trained to record the behavior of each child studied. Each observer kept a record in ten-second intervals of his subject's behavior throughout each morning at school. Only with such staffing could reinforcement contingencies be precisely and consistently administered and their effects recorded.

Unless the effects are recorded, it is easy to make incorrect judgments about them. Two instances illustrate such fallibility. A boy in the laboratory preschool frequently pinched adults. Attempts by the teachers to ignore the behavior proved ineffective, since the pinches were hard enough to produce at least an involuntary startle. Teachers next decided to try to develop a substitute behavior. They selected patting as a logical substitute. Whenever the child reached toward a teacher, she attempted to forestall a pinch by saying, "Pat, Davey," sometimes adding, "Not pinch," and then strongly approving his patting, when it occurred. Patting behavior increased rapidly to a high level. The teachers agreed that they had indeed succeeded in reducing the pinching behavior through substituting patting. Then they were shown the recorded data. It showed clearly that although patting behavior was indeed high, pinching behavior continued at the previous level. Apparently, the teachers were so focused on the rise in patting behavior that, without the objective data, they would have erroneously concluded that development of a substitute behavior was in this case a successful technique. A second example illustrates a different, but equally undesirable, kind of erroneous assumption. A preschool child who had to wear glasses (Wolf, Risley, and Mees, 1964) developed a pattern of throwing them two or three times per day. Since this proved expensive, it was decided that the attendants should put him in his room for ten minutes following each glasses-throw. When the attendants were asked a few days later how the procedure was working, they said that the glasses-throwing had not diminished at all. A check of the records, however, showed that there was actually a marked decrease. The throwing dropped to zero within five days. Presumably, the additional effort involved in carrying out the procedure had given the attendants an exaggerated impression of the rate of the behavior. Recorded data, therefore, seem essential to accurate objective assessments of what has occurred.

The findings in the studies presented here accord generally with results of laboratory research on social development reviewed in this journal by Horowitz (1963). The importance of social reinforcement was also noted by Bandura (1963) in his investigations of imitation. Gallwey (1964) has replicated the study of an isolate child discussed here, with results "clearly confirmatory of the effectiveness of the technique." Further studies in school situations that can combine the function of research with that of service seem highly desirable.

REFERENCES

ALLEN, K. EILEEN, HART, BETTY M., BUELL, JOAN S., HARRIS, FLORENCE R., & WOLF, M. M. Effects of social reinforcement on isolate behavior of a nursery school child. *Child. Develop.*, 1964, *35*, 511-518.

BANDURA, ALBERT. The role of imitation in personality development. *J. Nursery Ed.*, 1963, *18*, 207-215.

GALLWEY, MARY. Director of the Nursery School, Washington State University, Pullman, Wash., 1964. Personal communication.

HARRIS, FLORENCE R., JOHNSTON, MARGARET K., KELLEY, C. SUSAN, & WOLF, M. M. Effects of positive social reinforcement on regressed crawling of a nursery school child. *J. Ed. Psychol.*, 1964, *55*, 35-41.

HART, BETTY M., ALLEN, K. EILEEN, BUELL, JOAN S., HARRIS, FLORENCE R., & WOLF, M. M. Effects of social reinforcement on operant crying. *J. Exp. Child Psychol.* In press.

HOROWITZ, FRANCES DEGEN. Social reinforcement effects on child behavior. *J. Nursery Ed.*, 1963, *18*, 276-284.

JOHNSTON, MARGARET K., KELLEY, C. SUSAN, HARRIS, FLORENCE R., WOLF, M. M., & BAER, D. M. Effects of positive social reinforcement on isolate behavior of a nursery school child. Unpublished manuscript.

JOHNSTON, MARGARET K., KELLEY, C. SUSAN, HARRIS, FLORENCE R., & WOLF, M. M. An application of reinforcement principles to development of motor skills of a young child. Unpublished manuscript.

LANDRETH, CATHERINE. *Education of the Young Child*. New York: Wiley, 1942.

READ, KATHERINE H. *The Nursery School* (2nd ed.). Philadelphia: Saunders, 1955.

STANDING, E. M. *Maria Montessori, Her Life and Work*. Fresno: American Library Guild, 1959.

TAYLOR, KATHERINE W. *Parents Cooperative Nursery Schools*. New York: Teachers College, Columbia University, 1954.

WOLF, MONTROSE M., RISLEY, T. R., & MEES, H. L. Application of operant conditioning procedures to the behavior problems of an autistic child. *Behav. Res. Ther.*, 1964, *1*, 305-312.

16 / TIMING OF PUNISHMENT AND THE OBSERVATION OF CONSEQUENCES TO OTHERS AS DETERMINANTS OF RESPONSE INHIBITION[1] / RICHARD H. WALTERS,

ROSS D. PARKE, AND VALERIE A. CANE[*]

THE ROLE OF PUNISHMENT IN THE socialization of children has received considerable emphasis in theoretical discussions but has seldom been explored in laboratory studies. Perhaps partly for humanitarian reasons and perhaps partly because ethical and practical considerations limit the range of intensities of punishment that may be used in investigations with human subjects, psychologists have readily accepted the "legend" (Solomon, 1964) that punishment is an extremely ineffective means of controlling human behavior. In this respect most parents have probably been wiser than the "experts"; the renewed interest in punishment on the part of psychologists and the more cautious approach taken in recent theoretical discussions of this topic (e.g., Church, 1963; Solomon, 1964) are therefore welcome developments. The available research evidence strongly suggests that punishment may have very diverse (and sometimes very dramatic) effects, and that these effects are dependent on such parameters as the intensity and timing of punishment, the sequencing and scheduling of rewarding and punishing events, the strength and nature of the punished response, and the relative status of the agent and the recipient of punishment (Aronfreed, 1964; Bandura and Walters, 1963; Church, 1963; Martin, 1963; Mowrer, 1960a,b; Solomon and Brush, 1958; Solomon, 1964).

The purpose of this study was to investigate the effects of one of these parameters, the timing of punishment, on the resistance to deviation of children who, following direct punishment training, were exposed to a deviant model. Since the consequences of the responses to a social model have a considerable influence on the extent to which the model's behavior is imitated (Bandura, Ross, and Ross, 1963; Walters, Leat, and Mezei, 1963), consequences were varied in such a way as to permit an investigation, in a single experimental design, of some of the effects of both directly and vicariously experienced punishment.

TIMING OF PUNISHMENT

A theoretical basis for predicting the effects of timing of punishment has been offered by Mowrer (1960a,b). According to Mowrer, the execution of a prohibited act is accompanied by a sequence of response-produced cues, each providing sensory feedback. A punishment may be presented at any point during this sequence and result in a relatively direct association of a fear-motivated avoidance response with the response-produced cues occurring at the time that the punishment is administered. If the punishment occurs only when the deviant act has been completed, fear will be most strongly associated with the stimuli that accompany its completion and less strongly with the stimuli produced by the agent's preparatory responses. In contrast, punishment that occurs at or near the time that an act is initiated will result in a relatively strong association between the agent's preparatory responses and the emotion of fear; in this case, even the initiation of the deviant act will arouse fear that motivates incompatible prosocial or avoidance responses.

[1] This study was supported by the Public Health research grant 605-5-293 of the (Canadian) National Health Grants Program, the Ontario Mental Health Foundation grant 42, and the Defense Research Board of Canada grant 9401-24. The authors are indebted to the Superintendent of Public Schools of Waterloo and to the Principals and Staff of Northdale and Brighton Schools. Thanks are due to Patsie Hutton and Keith Barnes for assisting as observers.

[*] Richard H. Walters, Ross D. Parke, and Valerie A. Cane, Timing of punishment and the observation of consequences to others as determinants of response inhibition, *J. exp. child Psychol.*, 1965, 2, 10-30. Reprinted by permission.

Once an act has been initiated, secondary positive reinforcers associated with the instrumental behavior involved in the commission of the act may serve to maintain and facilitate the response sequence and thus to some extent counteract the inhibitory effect of punishment. Consequently, it may be argued, the earlier a punishment occurs in a deviant response sequence, the more effectively will it prevent the subsequent commission of the act.

Mowrer's account perhaps overemphasizes both the role of kinesthetic feedback and that of the emotion of fear, and underemphasizes the part played by perceptual-cognitive factors that are associated with the functioning of distance receptors. Visual and auditory cues accompanying the commission of a deviant act may be as closely associated with punishment experiences as kinesthetic feedback; since such cues are far more readily discriminable, they probably also play a more important role in the maintenance of behavioral control. This consideration does not, however, change the basic prediction generated by Mowrer's theory.

HYPOTHESIS 1. *Children who receive punishment as they begin to perform a class of responses will subsequently show greater resistance to deviation than children who receive punishment only on completion of responses of this class, provided that the deviant behavior falls in the same general category as the responses made during the punishment training session.*

CONSEQUENCES OF RESPONSES TO MODELS

Previous investigations (Bandura, 1965; Bandura *et al.*, 1963; Walters *et al.*, 1963; Walters and Parke, 1964) have demonstrated that the observation of a social model who receives punishment for a class of responses leads to response inhibition in the observer. The consequence of the model's response apparently serves as a cue signifying to the observer the nonpermissibility of the punished response within a given social context (Walters and Parke, 1964). Similarly, the observation of a reward to a model may signify the permissibility of a response class even if the rewarded response has previously been prohibited for the observer (Walters *et al.*, 1963; Walters and Parke, 1964). Under some circumstances, the observation of a model's performing a prohibited or socially disapproved act (for example, aggression) with no adverse consequences to himself may suffice as a cue to the observer that the act may be performed (Walters and Llewellyn Thomas, 1963); the inhibitions created in the observer may thus be overcome either by rewarding a model who performs the disapproved responses or simply by not punishing the model's behavior (Walters and Parke, 1964).

HYPOTHESIS 2. *Children who observe a model punished for acts that they have been prohibited from performing will show greater resistance to deviation than children who see a model rewarded or receive no punishment for these acts.*

CONSEQUENCES TO A MODEL AND OBSERVATIONAL LEARNING

Two previous studies (Bandura, 1965; Walters and Parke, 1964) have provided evidence in favor of the view that observational learning is relatively independent of the consequences of the model's responses (Bandura *et al.*, 1963). Bandura (1965) exposed nursery-school children to one of three conditions: model rewarded for aggressive behavior; model punished for aggressive behavior; and model neither rewarded nor punished for such behavior. After exposure to one of the conditions, each child was given a 10-minute free-play session, during which observers recorded the number of imitative aggressive responses displayed by the child. Children under the no-consequence and model-rewarded conditions displayed significantly more imitative aggression than children who saw the model punished. Following the observation period, the children were provided with incentives to reproduce the responses displayed by the model. The introduction of these incentives eliminated reinforcement-produced differences among the three groups of subjects.

Walters and Parke (1964) reported that observed consequences to a deviant model influenced the extent to which children engaged in imitative deviant acts. When, however, the acts in question were no longer labeled as deviant, Ss under model-rewarded, model-punished, and no-consequence film conditions did not differ in the extent to which they reproduced the model's responses; moreover, all three groups displayed significantly more imitative responses than control children who had not been exposed to a film-mediated model.

The tests for observational learning in both of the above studies do not permit an entirely satisfactory assessment of the extent to which learning had occurred through observation of the model. Although in Bandura's study some of the model's responses were highly unusual, the possibility remains that the children had already learned response patterns very similar to those displayed by the model and that the experimental manipulations served only to modify the probabilities of their performing previously learned responses. This possibility is even stronger in the case of the Walters and Parke study, since the model's responses, although distinctive, had been selected from the actual free play of a child.

In the present study, as well as having the model perform distinctive responses, the experimenters taught him to put together three educational-type toys that were difficult for a child of his (and the subjects') age to construct. The film sequence included shots of the child in the act of constructing the toys. After testing for resistance to deviation was completed, the children were required to construct the toys with which they had seen the model play. Thus, in effect, they were tested in a problem-solving task.

HYPOTHESIS 3. *Children exposed to a model performing problem-solving tasks will subsequently make a larger proportion of correct responses in performing these tasks than will children who have not been exposed to the model. The amount of observational learning will be independent of the consequences of the responses of the model.*

METHOD

SUBJECTS. Eighty kindergarten and Grade 1 boys, with a mean age of 6 years, 5 months served as Ss. The boys were randomly assigned to one of eight conditions in a 2×4 factorial design involving two timing-of-punishment conditions (early vs. late punishment) and four film conditions. Under three of the four film conditions, the children were shown a colored film sequence depicting an interaction between a 6-year-old boy and a female adult who performed a mother role; the remainder of the children saw no film.

EQUIPMENT. For the timing-of-punishment manipulations, the equipment and procedures were similar in some respects to those used by Aronfreed and Reber (1964). Nine pairs of toys (one attractive, one unattractive) were used in a series of training trials. One toy in each pair was large, well detailed, and well made, and of interest to boys (e.g., cars, guns, and trucks);

the other toy in each pair was smaller, less detailed, and in some cases sex-inappropriate (e.g., toy dishes, a bracelet, and a plastic doll).

Three film-sequences, similar to those used by Walters and Parke (1964), were prepared for the film manipulations. The sequences were identical, except for the addition of "endings" to two of the films. Complete correspondence was ensured through the use of copies of an original edited sequence. The film showed an adult female, presumably a mother, indicate to a child through a single gesture that he should not play with toys that had been set on a nearby table; the adult then sat the child in a chair beside the table, gave him a book to read, and left the room. After her departure, the child put the book aside and proceeded to play with the prohibited toys. Play continued for approximately 4 minutes. The play sequence displayed the child playing with a number of attractive toys similar to those used in the punishment-training sessions. Three of the toys had been specially selected for the purpose of testing Hypothesis 3 of this study. These were a rifle, a sword, and a truck, which were assembled, part by part, by the child-model. Shots of child constructing a toy and then playing with it were alternated with shots of the child playing with a nonconstructional toy. Altogether, nine toys were displayed, with the sequence beginning and ending with play with a toy of a nonconstructional type.

Endings were added to two of the films. The reward-movie ending showed the adult return to the room, sit beside the child, hand him toys and play with him affectionately. For the punishment-movie ending, the adult, on returning, pulled the child up from the floor, where he was playing, snatched the toy from him, spanked him, and once again sat him on the chair with the book. In the no-consequences film, the mother did not re-enter. Because children are used to seeing sound-accompanied movies in school settings, a tape recording of background music was played during the showing of the films. The recording was identical for all children.

The children were tested in a mobile laboratory, divided into an experimental room and an observation room by a partition containing two one-way vision mirrors. A diagram of the experimental arrangements is provided in Fig. 1.

On Table A were displayed three rows of toys, three toys in each row. When S was seated at one end of the table, the first row of the toys

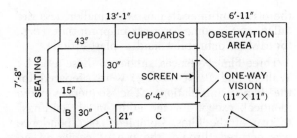

FIGURE 1 / EXPERIMENTAL ARRANGEMENTS.

was readily accessible to him, the toys in the second row were accessible if he stood up in front of the table, while the third row could be reached only if S walked around the table. A folding table (B) was used to display toys during the punishment-training session; when not in use, these toys were placed on Table C, which also held a Bolex 18-5 projector and a Uher 4000-S portable tape recorder.

PROCEDURE. The E brought S from his classroom to the mobile laboratory. She interacted with him in a relaxed and friendly manner and informed him that he was about to play a game with her. If S had been assigned to a film condition, he was also told that he would be shown a movie.

Punishment training. The S was seated behind Table B and instructed as follows:

"I'm going to put some toys out here on the table. Each time I'm going to put down two toys, and here is what I want you to do. I want you to pick the toy that you would like to play with. I want you to pick it up, hold it, and think about it for a while. Be sure you pick it up, hold it, and think about it. Now, if I ask you, I want you to tell me what the toy is or what it is used for. Do you understand?"

After S indicated that he understood the nature of the task, E continued, "Now, some of these toys are for another boy, and you're not supposed to touch them. So if you touch a toy that is for the other boy, I'll tell you. O.K.?"

Following these instructions, E uncovered the toys on Table C and commenced the punishment training. On each of nine trials E placed a pair of toys before S. The order of presentation of pairs of toys was constant for all Ss, and the position of the attractive toy was consistently alternated over the nine training trials, so that it appeared at S's left on odd-numbered trials and on his right on even-numbered trials.

Each time S selected the attractive toy, E verbally punished him by saying, "No, that's for

the other boy." For Ss in the early-punishment condition, E administered the punishment as S's hand neared the attractive toy, but before he touched it. As E spoke, she covered the forbidden toy and removed it from the table. The unattractive toy was left undisturbed for a few seconds to give S an opportunity to make the alternative choice. If he did so, he was asked to describe the toy. Almost all Ss immediately selected the unattractive toy when rebuked for choosing the attractive toy.

For Ss in the late-punishment condition, the punishment was presented only after S had picked up the attractive toy and held it for 2-3 seconds. The E took the toy from S's hand while administering the same rebuke as was used for early-punished Ss. Again S was given an opportunity to choose and describe the unattractive toy.

If, on any trial, S chose the unattractive toy first, E said, "What is it?" or "What is it used for?" Following S's description of the toy, E acknowledged the response by a simple "O.K." and removed both the toys from the table.

Resistance-to-deviation test. On completion of the punishment session the toys on Table C were covered. The S was then seated behind Table A, which contained three rows of toys, similar to, and in some cases identical with, those used in the punishment-training session. After removing the cloth covering these toys, E told all Ss, "These toys are *for the other boy* so you had better not touch them." If S was under a film condition, E added, "Now, I'm going to show you a movie." She then switched on the projector and the tape-recorded music. As soon as the movie had ended, E gave the next set of instructions. Ss under the no-film condition received these instructions immediately after being seated at Table A.

Then E said, "Before we play the game, I have to go and get something, so would you like to sit here and read this book while I am gone." (E, at this point, placed a dictionary on the table before S.) "I'm going to close the door when I go out so that nobody will come in and bother you. O.K.?"

The E now left the room for 15 minutes. On returning she took the dictionary away from S, and sat down beside him; E first said, "Have you played with any of these toys before or have you any like these at home?" No child had had previous experience with the three constructional toys.

The test for observational learning was now

commenced. The E handed S six toys, one after the other, the three constructional toys and three of the remaining toys. The latter toys were, for every S, a six-part tinker-toy set, a machine-gun, and a guitar. These three toys had each been handled in a distinctive manner by the child in the movie. The same order of presentation was used for all Ss: sword, truck, rifle, tinker-toys, guitar, machine-gun.

If S had seen a movie, E asked, as she handed him the component parts of a constructional toy, "Do you think you could put together this toy just the way the boy in the movie did?" As she handed him the tinker toy, E said, "Can you make the same thing as the little boy did in the movie?" In the case of the remaining two toys, E said, "Show me what the little boy in the movie did with this." The S was allowed a maximum of 2 minutes within which to complete each task.

For Ss under the no-film condition, the procedures were the same, but E's questions were differently worded. In the case of the constructional toys, E said, "Do you think you could put this (rifle, truck, sword) together?" As E handed S the tinker toys, she said, "What can you make with these?" Finally, in the case of the gun and guitar, E said, "Can you show me how these work?"

MEASURES. An observer, who was seated behind the one-way vision screen, recorded S's choices during the punishment-training session, thus providing a record of the number of punishments received by each S. In addition, during the test for resistance to deviation, the observer recorded on a specially prepared record sheet the times at which S touched and ceased to touch individual toys. The sheet was set up in such a way that, during the 15-minute period of E's absence from the room, the observer's only task was to record times, read from a Heuer-Century Stopwatch, in the appropriate squares which designated specific toys.

From the observer's records, the following scores were calculated: the latency of S's first deviant response, the number of times he deviated, and the total time for which he deviated. Weighted deviation scores were calculated in the following manner: a deviation involving one of the three most accessible toys was scored 1; a deviation involving one of the toys in the second row was scored 2; and S's touching a toy in the third row was scored 3. A weighted-number-of-deviations and a weighted-time score

were then obtained by multiplying the number of times S touched toys in each class, and the amount of time for which he handled them, by the appropriate weights. These scores had previously been employed by Walters et al. (1963) and Walters and Parke (1964). Since in both the earlier studies somewhat similar results were obtained with unweighted and weighted scores, only the weighted scores were utilized in this study. Weighted scores were preferred because they make use of more of the available information and reduce the number of ties in analyses based on ranking methods.

During the test for observational learning, the observer recorded S's responses to each toy. The sword was presented in five parts, and could be constructed without error if S made a sequence of four correct responses; perfect performance on the truck and rifle required sequences of six and two correct responses, respectively. For the three constructional toys, the observer recorded the number of correct responses and the number of errors made by each S. These scores were combined into a single index, proportion of correct responses, in order to test for the occurrence of observational learning among Ss who had witnessed the movie.

The child in the movie made a seven-part design with the tinker-toys; thus S could make six discriminable matching responses. In playing with the gun and guitar, the child made four additional responses that could be approximately matched by S. He placed the guitar cord over his head, played a tune by turning a crank, and tuned the instrument by means of tuning keys; in operating the machine gun, he pulled back a spring-operated lever that fired it. For each S, the observer recorded the occurrence of any of these ten possible matching responses.

Some explanation may be needed of the grouping of toys in this study. The tinker toys, although classifiable in some contexts as constructional, were not employed in the same manner as the toys used for the problem-solving tasks. No-film Ss were *not* required to make a particular design or sequence of responses with these toys; consequently, a comparison of the tinker-toy responses of no-film Ss with those of Ss under film conditions could not constitute an adequate test for observational learning.

RESULTS

RELIABILITY OF MEASURES. A second observer was present while 16 Ss were tested. Rank-order

TABLE 1 / GROUP MEANS AND MEDIANS ON THREE INDICES OF RESISTANCE TO DEVIATION.[a]

| | FILM CONDITIONS | | | | | | | |
| PUNISHMENT CONDITIONS | MODEL REWARDED | | NO CONSEQUENCE | | MODEL PUNISHED | | NO FILM | |
	MEAN	MEDIAN	MEAN	MEDIAN	MEAN	MEDIAN	MEAN	MEDIAN
Early								
Latency (seconds)	590.1	750	333.2	144.5	697.0	900	624.5	900
Weighted deviations	5.2	1	3.7	4	2.5	0	2.9	0
Weighted duration	64.5[b]	2.5	15.3	12.5	0.7	0	16.4	0
Late								
Latency (seconds)	269.0	71.5	345.6	270.5	543.1	576	299.3	141
Weighted deviations	7.4	4.5	6.8	5.5	2.7	1.5	6.2	4.5
Weighted duration	33.7	11	32.7	131	9.5	2	30.9	14

[a] $n = 10$ in each group.

[b] Mean = 11.3, excluding one extreme case.

correlation coefficients were used as indices of interrater reliability for the resistance-to-deviation measures. These correlations were 1.00, 1.00, and 0.94 for the latency, number of deviations, and duration of deviations, respectively. Reliability of scoring was above 0.94 for all three classes of responses made by S during the test for observational learning.

PUNISHMENT-TRAINING DATA. A 2×4 analysis of variance indicated that there were no significant differences among the eight groups of Ss in respect to the number of punishments received ("incorrect" choices made) during the punishment-training session. Group differences in resistance to deviation cannot therefore be attributed to this variable. The mean number of punishments received by Ss under the early-punishment and late-punishment conditions were 4.1 and 3.8, respectively.

OVER-ALL TESTS OF PREDICTED EFFECTS. The distributions of resistance-to-deviation data for some groups of Ss were markedly skewed; consequently, Table 1 gives both group medians and group means for the latency, weighted-deviations, and weighted-duration indices.

Most differences were in predicted directions. Model-rewarded and no-consequence Ss deviated more quickly, more often, and for longer periods of time than did model-punished Ss. Differences between early-punishment and late-punishment Ss were remarkably consistent across all film conditions; under each condition, the early-punishment Ss showed greater resistance to deviation.

Table 2 reports the results of nonparametric tests of main effects; it also presents the findings from over-all tests of the significance of differences among the eight groups of Ss. Eight of the nine comparisons yielded p-values of 0.05 or less; the remaining p-value fell between 0.10 and 0.05. Supplementary Mann-Whitney U-tests (Table 3) indicated that both model-rewarded and no-consequence Ss differed significantly from model-punished Ss. No-film Ss deviated to a greater extent, though not more quickly, than Ss who had seen the model punished.

SELECTED INDIVIDUAL COMPARISONS. The theoretical considerations advanced in the introduction to this paper would lead one to expect that Ss who were punished early and were also exposed to a punished model would show the

TABLE 2 / SIGNIFICANCE OF MAIN AND OVER-ALL EFFECTS.[a]

A. Model effects (Kruskal-Wallis H-tests; $df = 3$)
   Latency: $H = 6.54$; $p < 0.10$
   Weighted deviations: $H = 8.86$; $p < 0.05$
   Weighted duration: $H = 8.93$; $p < 0.05$

B. Punishment effects (Mann-Whitney U-tests)
   Latency: $z = 2.32$; $p < 0.02$
   Weighted deviations: $z = 2.67$; $p < 0.01$
   Weighted duration: $z = 2.27$; $p < 0.03$

C. Over-all effects (Kruskal-Wallis H-tests; $df = 7$)
   Latency: $H = 14.08$; $p < 0.05$
   Weighted deviations: $H = 16.74$; $p < 0.02$
   Weighted duration: $H = 14.69$; $p < 0.05$

[a] H and z corrected for ties.

TABLE 3 / COMPARISONS OF SUBJECTS UNDER FOUR DIFFERENT FILM CONDITIONS (Mann-Whitney U-tests with corrections for ties).

FILM CONDITIONS COMPARED	LATENCY		WEIGHTED DEVIATIONS		WEIGHTED DURATION	
	z	p	z	p	z	p
Model Rewarded vs. No. Consequence	0.89	n.s.	0.30	n.s.	0.72	n.s.
Model Rewarded vs. Model Punished	1.66	<0.10	2.23	<0.03	2.29	<0.03
Model Rewarded vs. No. Film	0.33	n.s.	0.30	n.s.	0.11	n.s.
No Consequence vs. Model Punished	2.53	<0.02	2.82	<0.005	2.81	<0.01
No Consequence vs. No Film	1.06	n.s.	0.51	n.s.	0.33	n.s.
Model Punished vs. No Film	1.40	n.s.	2.19	<0.05	2.13	<0.05

greatest resistance to deviation and that Ss who were punished late and were exposed to a model who did not receive punishment would show the least resistance to deviation. Table 4, which summarizes the outcomes of individual comparisons between pairs of groups, indicates that early-punishment model-punished Ss were significantly more resistant to deviation not only than late-punishment model-rewarded and late-punishment no-consequence Ss but also than late-punishment no-film Ss. Differences between the early-punishment model-punished group and the early-punishment model-rewarded and no-consequences groups, respectively, also reached

TABLE 4 / SIGNIFICANCE OF DIFFERENCES BETWEEN INDIVIDUAL PAIRS OF MEDIANS OF GROUPS (z-values, Mann-Whitney Test[a]).

	EARLY PUNISHMENT				LATE PUNISHMENT			
	MODEL REWARDED A	NO CONSEQUENCE B	MODEL PUNISHED C	NO FILM D	MODEL REWARDED E	NO CONSEQUENCE F	MODEL PUNISHED G	NO FILM H
A[b] 1		1.31	0.99	0.57	1.57*	1.57*	0.23	1.75*
2		0.55	1.58*	0.65	0.96	1.15	0.31	1.38
3		0.73	1.78*	0.48	1.00	1.23	0.31	1.49
B 1			2.14**	1.58*	0.19	0.19	1.31	0.19
2			2.39**	0.87	0.84	1.19	1.13	1.11
3			2.46**	0.52	0.23	0.69	1.16	0.65
C 1				0.53	2.38**	2.22**	1.24	2.38**
2				0.89	2.78***	2.74***	1.62*	3.33***
3				0.98	2.78***	2.78***	1.62*	3.25***
D 1					2.03**	1.64*	0.57	2.01**
2					1.72*	1.60*	0.40	1.82*
3					1.13	1.25	1.62*	1.20
E 1						0.15	1.57*	0.08
2						0.00	1.61*	0.08
3						0.27	1.61*	0.38
F 1							1.46	0.00
2							1.69*	0.11
3							1.53	0.08
G 1								1.52
2								2.14**
3								1.87*

* $p = 0.12$

** $p = 0.05$

*** $p = 0.01$

Two-tailed p-values

[a] $n = 10$ in each group. In view of the small size of samples for individual comparisons and the necessity of using a nonparametric technique, significance levels as low as 0.12 (two-tailed p-value) are indicated.

[b] 1 = latency; 2 = weighted deviations; 3 = weighted duration.

TABLE 5 / GROUP MEANS AND STANDARD DEVIATIONS OF PROPORTION OF CORRECT RESPONSES AND OF NUMBERS OF MATCHING RESPONSES.[a]

| | FILM CONDITIONS | | | | | | | |
| | MODEL REWARDED | | NO CONSEQUENCE | | MODEL PUNISHED | | NO FILM | |
PUNISHMENT CONDITIONS	MEAN	SD	MEAN	SD	MEAN	SD	MEAN	SD
Early								
Proportion correct responses	0.42	0.18	0.44	0.10	0.33	0.15	0.22	0.13
Matching responses	8.3	1.1	6.6	2.0	7.7	1.2	4.2	1.1
Late								
Proportion correct responses	0.42	0.14	0.40	0.18	0.34	0.14	0.34	0.21
Matching responses	8.0	1.1	8.1	1.6	7.1	1.1	5.2	1.0

Tests for significance of main effect of film conditions:

	MS FOR COLUMNS	ERROR	F[b]	p
Proportion correct responses	0.937	0.278	3.37	<0.025
Matching responses	45.700	1.911	23.91	<0.0001

[a] $n = 10$ in each group.
[b] $df = 3$ and 72.

or approached an acceptable level of significance. Moreover, late-punishment model-punished Ss tended to be more resistant to deviation than any of the other three late-punishment groups. In addition, differences between the early-punishment no-film group and the late-punishment model-rewarded, no-consequence, and no-film groups, respectively, reached or approached significance. Since all the above differences would be predicted from the theoretical considerations advanced earlier, the benefit of one-tailed tests might be claimed; the findings concerning the efficacy of punishment procedures then become quite impressive.

TESTS FOR OBSERVATIONAL LEARNING AND MATCHING RESPONSES. Table 5 lists group means for proportion of correct responses with the constructional toys and number of matching responses with the remaining three toys. Analyses of variance yielded significant differences attributable to the different film conditions; timing of punishment had no effect on any of the responses, nor were there any significant interactions. The F-values for the main effect of film conditions are given in Table 5. Table 6 shows the outcome of subsequent t-tests of the significance of differences between individual pairs of means for Ss under the four different film con-

TABLE 6 / SIGNIFICANCE OF DIFFERENCES BETWEEN REWARD-FILM, NO-CONSEQUENCE FILM, PUNISHMENT-FILM, AND NO-FILM GROUPS ON PROPORTION OF CORRECT RESPONSES AND NUMBER OF MATCHING RESPONSES.[a,c]

| | REWARD FILM VS. NO-CONSEQUENCE FILM | | REWARD FILM VS. PUNISHMENT FILM | | REWARD FILM VS. NO FILM | |
	t	p	t	p	t	p
Proportion correct responses	0.01	n.s.	1.50	n.s.[c]	2.68	<0.01
Matching responses	1.82	<0.10	1.70	<0.10	7.84	<0.001

| | NO-CONSEQUENCE FILM VS. PUNISHMENT FILM | | NO-CONSEQUENCE FILM VS. NO FILM | | PUNISHMENT FILM VS. NO FILM | |
	t	p	t	p	t	p
Proportion correct responses	1.50	n.s.[c]	2.68	<0.01	1.19	n.s.
Matching responses	0.11	n.s.	6.02	<0.0001	6.14	<0.0001

[a] $n = 20$ in each model group.
[b] All significance levels are based on two-tailed tests.
[c] Reward Film + No-Consequence Film vs. Punishment Film yielded $t = 1.73$; $p < 0.10$ (2 tailed).

ditions. Although there were no significant differences between any two film groups on any measure, there was some indication that the observation of punitive consequences to the model had depressed performance on the constructional toys. While the mean proportion of correct responses made by the model-rewarded and no-consequence Ss, respectively, differed significantly from that made by the no-film Ss, model-punished and no-film Ss did not significantly differ on this variable.[2] Moreover, the model-rewarded Ss tended to give more matching responses to the nonconstructional toys than did either no-consequence or model-punished Ss; however, these differences were small in comparison to the differences between Ss under film conditions and no-film Ss.

DISCUSSION

The prediction concerning timing of punishment assumed that punishment occurring at the commencement of a response sequence more effectively inhibits the initiation of the sequence than does punishment that occurs only after the sequence has been completed. Confirmation of this prediction lends weight not only to previous findings of a similar nature (Aronfreed and Reber, 1964; Black, Solomon, and Whiting,[3] Walters and Demkow, 1963), but also to theories of punishment that hold that punishment is maximally effective as an inhibitory technique when it is closely associated with the response that it is designed to suppress (Church, 1963). These theories are also supported by experiments that provide evidence for the occurrence of delay-of-punishment gradients in animal and human learning (Banks and Vogel-Sprott, 1965; Bixtenstein, 1956; Coons and Miller, 1960; Kamin, 1959; Mowrer and Ullman, 1945; Sidman, 1953; Walters, 1964).

The study leaves little doubt that judiciously timed punishment can be extremely effective in controlling human behavior. More than half the children in the early-punishment model-punished and the early-punishment no-film groups did not deviate at all; under the former of these conditions no child deviated

[2] An analysis of variance carried out with absolute numbers of correct responses yielded an F-value of 4.04 ($p < 0.02$ for 3 and 72 df). The results of individual comparisons were similar to those obtained for proportions, with the model-punished and no-film Ss not significantly differing.

[3] Cited in Mowrer (1960b).

more than twice, and the deviations that occurred were all extremely brief. Moreover, the differences between early-punishment and late-punishment no-film Ss in respect to latency and weighted number of deviations are clearly significant if the benefit of a one-tail test is claimed. Failure to find significant differences between early-punishment and late-punishment children under the individual film conditions can reasonably be attributed to the modifying effect of exposure to a deviant model whose behavior had a uniform outcome (reward, no consequence, or punishment).

In a previous study by Walters and Demkow (1963), an early-punishment group of children was interrupted by a loud, unpleasant buzzer while commencing to reach out for a toy, while a late-punishment group was interrupted immediately upon touching the toy. The difference between the two groups in the testing situation, which was similar to the one used in the present study, was quite small. Aronfreed (1964) criticized the training procedures used by Walters and Demkow on the grounds that the two temporal positions of punishment were not sufficiently separate to produce a differential effect on inhibition. The successful outcome, in the present study, of utilizing Aronfreed's procedure of permitting late-punishment children to handle a toy for a brief period before punishment is administered suggests that his criticism of Walters and Demkow was soundly based.

In the present study, late-punishment Ss were permitted to handle the attractive toys for a brief period before punishment was administered, whereas early-punished Ss were never permitted to handle these toys. Consequently, predicted differences between early-punishment and late-punishment Ss may be attributable to the classical conditioning of the approach responses of the latter Ss rather than to the establishing of avoidance responses associated with temporally and topologically different components of Ss' deviant response sequences.

In order to test the plausibility of a very similar alternative explanation of timing-of-punishment effects, Aronfreed and Reber employed a control condition. Children under this condition were asked to indicate their choice from each pair of toys merely by pointing; if the child pointed to an attractive toy, the experimenter removed both toys. The absence of a significant difference between control Ss and Ss under a late-punishment condition, in respect to proportion of deviators, permitted Aronfreed and Reber to conclude that the relatively high incidence of deviation among late-punishment Ss was not due to habituation. The classical-conditioning interpretation might be more satisfactorily investigated by permitting control children briefly to handle attractive toys without rebuke or punishment, provided that control and late-punishment Ss were equated for the number of occasions on which they handled attractive toys. The presence of a difference between control and late-punishment Ss would then strongly favor an interpretation of the reported timing-of-punishment effects in terms of avoidance learning, whereas an absence of such a difference would be consistent with an interpretation in terms of the classical conditioning of approach responses.

Comparisons of children under the model-rewarded, no-consequence, and model-punished conditions supported previous findings concerning the influence of the consequences of responses of social models on the behavior of observers. No-consequence Ss, as in the experiments of Walters and Parke (1964) and Bandura (1965), deviated as readily and as often as model-rewarded Ss, a finding that again suggests that observing a model deviate without punishment may have a disinhibitory effect on the observer.

The occurrence of disinhibitory effects under the no-consequence condition superficially resembles findings from Virginia Crandall's (1963) study of the sequencing of reinforcements. In her study, nonreward that followed direct punishment was found to function like a positive reinforcer (Bandura, 1965; Walters and Parke, 1964). However, under Crandall's non-reward condition, a nonreacting adult experimenter remained in the room with the child subjects. Moreover, a follow-up study (Crandall, Good, and Crandall, 1964) demonstrated that the omission of punishment functioned like a positive reinforcer only when the nonreacting adult was present in the room.

In child-training situations parental nonreaction to a child's misdemeanours does not inevitably serve as a cue that the behavior may continue; in fact, many parents effectively utilize nonreaction as a means of inhibiting behavior of which they disapprove. In such situations, however, parents rarely avoid displaying some emotional reaction; consequently, the child's behavior is guided by emotional-intensity cues that parents, sometimes unwittingly, provide. In other words, "nonreaction" usually implies only

that parents do not employ the customary methods of overtly rewarding or punishing a child.

Crandall's findings, together with the above considerations, suggested that it would be profitable to examine the responses of children following a film sequence identical to that used in the no-consequence condition, with the addition of a clip that displayed the mother reentering the room and standing beside the child in an impassive manner. Consequently, as a supplementary procedure, a sample of 20 children was shown a film of this kind, ten following early-punishment training and ten following late-punishment training.

After these children had been tested, they were again shown the film and questioned concerning the response of the mother to the model's playing with the toys in order to determine how the mother's nonreaction had been interpreted. The children's answers were recorded on tape and later independently classified by two raters who were not otherwise involved in the study. A third independent rating was secured in order to resolve any disagreements that occurred. If a child changed his description of the mother's behavior during questioning, his initial reaction was used for classification purposes.

Fourteen children were classified as seeing the mother as punitive, five as seeing her as rewarding or at least as not punishing the behavior, while the remaining child refused to respond during the interview. Eight of the children who saw the mother as punitive did not deviate at all, whereas all five of the children who saw the mother as nonpunitive deviated. Mann Whitney U-tests indicated that the two groups differed significantly on all measures of resistance to deviation ($p < 0.05$). While the mother-returns Ss could not be used as an intact group for comparisons with the samples used under other film conditions, the above findings lend weight to the hypothesis that observed consequences to a model may have an inhibitory or disinhibitory effect on the observers.

In this pilot investigation into the influence of nonreaction, the punishing and prohibiting experimenter did not serve as the mother in the film. It is consequently probable that the film-mother's nonresponsiveness was interpreted by the observers in terms of their own prior experiences of maternal nonreaction. In contrast, in Crandall's study, the experimenter who had administered punishments served also as the nonreacting adult; under these circumstances her nonreaction probably provided an explicit cue for the children that, within the social context of the experiment, punishment was no longer forthcoming.

The test for observational learning provided evidence that new learning does, in fact, occur through observation of a model. The constructional toys were extremely difficult for the children, none of whom had had prior experience in assembling them. Of over 100 children tested with these toys during pretesting and regular experimental sessions, not one was able to complete the assembling tasks within the time limits allowed. The differences between no-film Ss and Ss under the model-rewarded and no-consequence conditions therefore strongly favor the view that "novel" responses may be readily acquired through observational learning (Bandura and Walters, 1963).

The absolute differences between children who had observed the film model and children in the no-film condition were small; however, a single brief exposure to the model could not be expected to result in a great amount of learning. Moreover, the model had thoroughly learned the solution of the problems before the films were made and simply gave a single errorless demonstration. Had he been filmed in the process of learning to assemble the toys and making errors in doing so, the amount of learning shown by the observers may have been much more dramatic. As Herbert and Harsh (1944) have shown with cats, observational learning may be considerably enhanced if the model is observed while he acquires mastery through trial-and-error learning.

An interesting finding was that Ss under the model-punished condition performed less well on the constructional toys than did Ss under the other two film conditions. While there were clearly significant differences between Ss under each of the latter conditions and the no-film Ss, the model-punished Ss and the no-film Ss did not significantly differ. On the other hand, the model-punished Ss, like Ss under the model-rewarded and no-consequences conditions, differed significantly from no-film Ss in their handling of the tinker toys, gun, and guitar.

Since the constructional toys were specially selected to test for new learning resulting from exposure to a model, the findings for these toys could be interpreted as indicating that *learning* may, in fact, be influenced by the consequences of the responses of the model. A satisfactory theoretical explanation is difficult to find, especially since the punishment of the model occurred only after the solution of the problems had been demonstrated. Model-punished Ss may have continued to anticipate punishment even after they had been requested to handle the toys; however, the findings obtained for the nonconstructional toys, which were handled immediately after the constructional toys, do not support this interpretation. A possible explanation, consistent with the hypothesis advanced in this study, is that observation of punishment arouses emotional responses that in some way interfere with the recall of the punished behavior. Such interference may be apparent only when difficult problem-solving tasks have been demonstrated, or when the observer has himself previously experienced punishment for responses similar to those for which the model is punished.

Studies of the consequences of responses to a model (Bandura, 1965; Walters and Parke, 1964) seem, in general, to indicate that these consequences serve as cues indicating the permissibility or nonpermissibility of reproducing the model's behavior in a given social context. They thus can alter the probabilities of occurrence both of responses that existed in the observer's repertory prior to his observation of the performance of these responses by the model and of responses that he has acquired while observing the model. These probabilities can presumably be changed through alterations in the social context brought about by the provision of new incentives and deterrents, the creation or removal of a prohibition, or by subsequent observation of consequences to others who make the responses in question. The unexpectedly poor performance of the model-punished Ss on the observational-learning task requires replication before much confidence can be placed in this finding. Nevertheless, its possible implication cannot be overlooked, especially in view of the tendency of model-rewarded Ss to make more matching responses with the nonconstructional toys than Ss under the other two film conditions.

SUMMARY

Eighty Grade 1 and kindergarten children were assigned to one of eight conditions in a 2×4 factorial design involving two conditions of timing of punishment and four film conditions. Half the children under each film condition received punishment as they initiated a deviant response sequence; the remaining Ss were punished only after completing the deviation. After punishment training, Ss were assigned to one of four film conditions: film model rewarded for deviation; film model punished for deviation; no consequence to the film model; no film. Ss who received early punishment subsequently showed more resistance to deviation than Ss for whom punishment was delayed. There were significant differences among Ss under the four film conditions, with model-punished Ss showing relatively high resistance to deviation. A combination of early-punishment training and exposure to a punished model was most effective in producing inhibition. Subsequent tests with problem-solving tasks, the solution of which had been demonstrated in the films, revealed that Ss under model-rewarded and no-consequences conditions had learned from observation of the model; however, model-punished Ss did not perform significantly better in these tests than Ss who had not seen the film model.

REFERENCES

ARONFREED, J. Conscience and conduct: A natural history of the internalization of values. In M. L. Hoffman (Ed.), *Character development.* New York: Soc. Sci. Res. Council, in press.

ARONFREED, J., AND REBER, A. Internalized behavioral suppression and the timing of social punishment. *J. person. soc. Psychol.,* 1965, *1,* 3-16.

BANDURA, A. Influence of models' reinforcement contingencies on the acquisition of imitative responses. *J. person. soc. Psychol.,* 1965, *1,* 589-595.

BANDURA, A., ROSS, DOROTHEA, AND ROSS, SHEILA A. Vicarious reinforcement and imitative learning. *J. abnorm. soc. Psychol.,* 1963, *67,* 601-607.

BANDURA, A., AND WALTERS, R. H. *Social learning and personality development.* New York: Holt, 1963.

BANKS, R. K., AND VOGEL-SPROTT, MURIEL D. The effect of delayed punishment on an immediately rewarded response in humans. *J. exp. Psychol.,* 1965, in press.

BIXTENSTEIN, V. E. Secondary drive as a neutralizer of time in integrative problem solving. *J. comp. physiol. Psychol.,* 1965, *49,* 161-166.

CHURCH, R. M. The varied effects of punishment on behavior. *Psychol. Rev.,* 1963, *70,* 369-402.

COONS, E. E., AND MILLER, N. E. Conflict versus consolidation of memory traces to explain "retrograde amnesia" produced by ECS. *J. comp. physiol. Psychol.,* 1960, *53,* 524-531.

CRANDALL, VIRGINIA C. The reinforcement effects of adult reactions and nonreactions on children's achievement expectations. *Child Develpm.,* 1963, *34,* 335-354.

CRANDALL, VIRGINIA C., GOOD, SUZANNE, AND CRANDALL, V. J. The reinforcement effects of adult reactions and non-reactions on children's achievement expectations: A replication. *Child Develpm.,* 1964, *35,* 485-497.

HERBERT, J. J., AND HARSH, C. M. Observational learning by cats. *J. comp. Psychol.,* 1944, *37,* 81-95.

KAMIN, L. J. The delay-of-punishment gradient. *J. comp. physiol. Psychol.,* 1959, *52,* 434-437.

MARTIN, B. Reward and punishment associated with the same goal response: A factor in the learning of motives. *Psychol. Bull.,* 1963, *60,* 441-451.

MOWRER, O. H. *Learning theory and behavior.* New York: Wiley, 1960. (a)

MOWRER, O. H. *Learning theory and the symbolic processes.* New York: Wiley, 1960. (b)

MOWRER, O. H., AND ULLMAN, A. D. Time as a determinant in integrative learning. *Psychol. Rev.,* 1945, *52,* 61-90.

SIDMAN, M. Two temporal patterns of the maintenance of avoidance behavior by the white rat. *J. comp. physiol. Psychol.,* 1953, *46,* 253-261.

SOLOMON, R. L. Punishment. *Amer. Psychol.,* 1964, *19,* 239-253.

SOLOMON, R. L., AND BRUSH, ELINOR S. Experimentally derived conceptions of anxiety and aversion. In M. R. Jones (Ed.), *Nebraska symposium on motivation.* Lincoln: Univer. Nebraska Press, 1956. Pp. 212-305.

WALTERS, R. H. Delay-of-reinforcement effects in children's learning. *Psychonom. Sci.,* 1964, *1,* 307-308.

WALTERS, R. H., AND DEMKOW, LILLIAN F. Timing of punishment as a determinant of response inhibition. *Child Develpm.,* 1963, *34,* 207-214.

WALTERS, R. H., AND LLEWELLYN, THOMAS E. Enhancement of punitiveness through visual and audiovisual displays. *Canad. J. Psychol.,* 1963, *17,* 244-255.

WALTERS, R. H., AND PARKE, R. D. Influence of the response consequences to a social model on resistance to deviation. *J. exp. child Psychol.,* 1964, *1,* 269-280.

WALTERS, R. H., LEAT, MARION, AND MEZEI, L. Response inhibition and disinhibition through empathetic learning. *Canad. J. Psychol.,* 1963, *17,* 235-243.

17 / PATTERNS OF PARENTHOOD AS THEORIES OF LEARNING[1] / JANE LOEVINGER [*]

GERHART PIERS (IN A TALK WHICH I quote from memory) has divided methods of learning into three types: learning by reinforcement, by insight, and by identification. All three types of learning unquestionably occur, and theories of learning espoused by professional psychologists must account for those facts, whatever they take as the prototype of all learning.

Any consistent method of child-rearing contains by implication a theory of how children function, particularly how they learn. One can easily set up a correspondence between well-known patterns of parenthood and the three types of learning. Corresponding to any pattern of child-rearing there is, then, a "theory of learning," emphasizing one type of learning at the expense of others. Theories of learning held by parents are, of course, far more naive and uncomplicated than similar theories held by psychologists. To avoid confusion, the term "parental theory" may be used to distinguish the implicit learning theory.

The disciplinarian parent apparently believes that any wrong thing a child does will be continued indefinitely if the parent does not see that it is punished. While psychological research has tended to emphasize rewards as more effective than punishments as reinforcing agents, disciplinarian parents emphasize punishments as reinforcers.

Apparently insight learning is assumed to predominate by those parents, once reputed to be numerous, who believe that every demand made on a child must be rationalized and explained.

Finally, the typical permissive parent must surely believe that the socialization of his child takes place by means of the child identifying himself with the well-socialized parent.

Consider the following situation. Five-year-old Johnny is beating on his two-year-old sister Sue. Mother comes in. Let us assume that every mother will want to prevent repetition of such behavior. What will she do?

Mother One believes that if Johnny does not feel pain, he will repeat the behavior at every coincidence of impulse and opportunity. She therefore punishes him sharply, thus demonstrating her adherence to a parental reinforcement theory of learning.

Mother Two believes that Johnny can be shown how wrong his conduct is and sets about to persuade him. She believes in a parental insight theory of learning.

Mother Three believes that Johnny wants to grow up to be like his parents. If she punishes him harshly, he will learn that it is all right for the bigger one to be mean to the littler one if he or she feels like it; so his behavior is less likely to be repeated if reprimanded gently than if dealt with harshly. She believes in a parental identification theory of learning.

There is one fallacy common to all parental learning theories. Kelly (1955) points out that we are not victims of our history but only of our construction of that history. Kelly finds in that fact hope for the psychotherapist. But just as it gives hope for the therapist, it generates despair for the parent. A parent can decide to beat his child, but he cannot decide how the child will construe the beating. Nor, if he abstains from punishing, can he decide how the child will construe the abstention.

Rules for rearing children are beyond the scope of this note, indeed, beyond the competence of the writer. But one superordinate rule can safely be stated: Whatever the parent's theory of learning, the child will in fact be learning by an alternative method. Thus the son of Mother One is probably identifying with a punitive, disciplinarian adult; for the son of Mother Two it is being stamped in that beating on sister has no painful consequences; while the son of Mother Three has probably discerned, "Aha! I can get away with it." The explanation of why a child shifts his mode of learning to escape his parent's vigilant efforts at socialization is not difficult. He is attempting to defend the gratification of his impulses, and in this respect he is not altogether different from his parents.

The foregoing formulation helps to solve two

[1] Preparation of this note was supported by Research Grant M-1213 from the National Institute of Mental Health, Public Health Service.

[*] Jane Loevinger, Patterns of parenthood as theories of learning, *Journal of Abnormal and Social Psychology*, 1959, 59, 148-150. Reprinted by permission.

riddles. Why is the battle between the generations fought, generation after generation, with such vigor? And why is it that experts on child-rearing are not conspicuously more successful at the art than those less expert?

The failure of expertise in child-rearing was foreshadowed in 1909 with Freud's (1925) publication of *Analysis of a Phobia in a Five-Year-Old Boy,* for little Hans was the child of two of Freud's followers. One should not make too much of the fact. He was not necessarily the most neurotic child in Vienna, merely the one that Freud had opportunity to observe and indirectly to treat. Nonetheless, the occurrence of so severe a phobia in the child was a striking omen.

Reasons have been advanced for the failure of children of experts to be vastly superior to others in their adjustment. Without disputing or discounting those reasons, one can focus on a slightly different one. The experts know what other parents did wrong, and they avoid those errors. But while they avoid the errors of parents in other houses, their children contrive to defend their instinctual gratification against the parents in their own house. In current terms, a shift in parentmanship is countered by a shift in childmanship.

The battle between the generations is commonly accounted for by the fact that parents have need to socialize their children, and the children forever battle against the socializing process. This view is the one being elaborated here. But it is not quite the whole story. A useful way to test a theory is to see what happens in the most extreme cases. Redl and Wineman (1957) have depicted extreme cases of "children who hate." Many of the sentiments of those children, such as "Grown-ups don't want kids to have any fun," are echoed occasionally in almost all homes. But the ferocity and implacability of the war with adults is entirely disproportionate to what takes place in an ordinary household. Were their parents, then, so rigorous in their attempts at socialization? On the contrary, the parents of those children presented a picture of impulsivity no less striking than that of the children. The abuses to which the children were subjected could hardly be called punishments; they did not appear to result from any theory of how children learn but rather were crude lashing out on impulse. The picture of parent-child relations in *The Aggressive Child* is a conspicuously undesirable one, both prima facie and in terms of outcome. It

serves to demonstrate that not all parents are informed by a parental theory. The battle between the generations is never more vicious than when all pretense of representing the interests of society is dropped and it becomes the parent's impulsivity versus the child's.

A general theory of the battle between generations must account for all of the cases. It must therefore read that the child's impulse gratification conflicts with the needs of society, represented by parents, to socialize him, as well as with the parent's own impulse gratification. The normal parent, to be sure, satisfies many of his desires in and through his children. But moment by moment and day by day the needs which the children gratify are not always uppermost. The presence of an infant or child in the household necessarily imposes delay or surrender on many of the parents' wishes.

The conclusions of this discussion can be stated simply, though they do not exactly simplify life. Every consistent pattern of child-rearing embodies a theory of learning, and all those parental theories are substantially wrong. However, any parental theory is better than none.

Is it possible to base one's pattern of child-rearing on a more nearly realistic theory of learning? That is an intriguing question. In view of the adaptability of the normal child in shifting his tactics to match those of his parents, such a method would require constant reconsideration and change. Yet inconsistency, so the child-rearing experts tell us, is one of the worst faces a parent can turn to his child. Possibly, however, inconsistency got its bad name not from conscientious parents trying to outwit their children but from the label being applied to such parents as Redl and Wineman have sketched.

If, as the present discussion suggests, parental theories are more wrong than right, how does it happen that it is better to have one than not? The chief value of a parental learning theory may well be in providing a model for the child of curbing one's own impulses out of regard for the future welfare of another. The very oversimplification of parental theories may serve to make accessible to the child that his parent is acting on principle rather than on impulse. To say this is to lay emphasis on learning by identification. But probably most psychologists, whatever their professional theories, act in relation to their own children as if they expect them to learn chiefly by identification.

"All I say is by way of discourse, and nothing by way of advice. . . . I should not speak so boldly, if it were my due to be believed" (de Montaigne, 1913, p. 283).

REFERENCES

DE MONTAIGNE, M. *The essays of Michel de Montaigne.* Vol. III. C. Cotton (Trans.); W. C. Hazlitt (Ed.) London: G. Bell, 1913.

FREUD, S. Analysis of a phobia in a five-year-old boy. In *Collected papers.* Vol. III. London: Hogarth, 1925. Pp. 149-289.

KELLY, G. A. *The psychology of personal constructs.* Vol. II. *Clinical diagnosis and psychotherapy.* New York: Norton, 1955.

REDL, F., and WINEMAN, D. *The aggressive child.* Glencoe, Ill.: Free Press, 1957.

18 / THE SCIENCE OF LEARNING AND THE TECHNOLOGY OF EDUCATIONAL METHODS /

A. W. MELTON/ABSTRACTED BY
A. A. LUMSDAINE AND ROBERT GLASER*

MELTON ASSERTS THAT "THE PROPER question for consideration is not *whether* the science of learning and the management of learning in the classroom can be mutually supporting, but *how* this desirable—even necessary—relationship can be achieved." He states some of the assumptions and inferences underlying this assertion, some difficulties in the way of achieving a mutually supporting relationship, and some ways for overcoming these difficulties. Melton defines the field of learning in broad terms to encompass "all forms of relatively permanent modifications of behavior resulting from experience, with perhaps the exception of those modifications commonly identified as sensory adaptation and fatigue. This means that the science of learning must organize our knowledge and understanding of the acquisition of attitudes, motives, affective and emotional responses, mental sets, simple and complex discriminative acts, serial verbal and motor acts, motor and perceptual skills, meanings, concepts and abstractions, and various cognitive capabilities that go under such names as ideational problem solving, thinking, reasoning, decision-making, and even creative invention." He indicates that the relationship of education to psychology is analogous to the relation between engineering and the physical sciences or medical practice and the biological science. However he points out that "education is not just the straightforward application of the science of learning, any more than engineering is just a straightforward application of the physical sciences. Just as physicists discovered things that made the creation of television possible, but engineers created television, so likewise psychologists have discovered many things

* A. W. Melton, Some comments on "The impact of advancing technology on methods in education" by Dr. Simon Ramo, September 1959, unpublished; abstracted by A. A. Lumsdaine and Robert Glaser in their *Teaching Machines and Programmed Learning: A Source Book,* Washington: Department of Audiovisual Instruction, NEA, 1960. Reprinted by permission. The full article by A. W. Melton originally appeared in *Harvard Educational Review,* 1959, *29,* 96-106.

about the learning process, but educational technologists must design curricula and teaching machines that exploit that knowledge."

The relationship between basic research and application is a reciprocal one: "Thus, new discoveries in science make new achievements in technology feasible, and recognized sources of deficiency in technology guide the explorations of scientists." Melton discusses the recent relative isolation of educational technology and the science of learning, as evidenced in relatively low overlap in organizational membership and publication channels. He stresses the importance of what Glaser (1960a) has termed a *rapprochement* between educational psychology and the science of learning. Melton feels they have drifted apart partly as a result of "the lack of an explicit strategy for holding them together at the level of advanced training and research."

He draws a parallel between the needs for close interaction in the field of education with a similar interaction between basic science and application which has developed in military psychology. Among the difficulties to be met, he identifies first the immaturity of the science of learning, in which "advances in empirical generalizations and in the theoretical integration of these generalizations have resulted only in *islands* of knowledge and understanding within the science of learning"; second, the inadequacy of our present taxonomy of tasks or skills; and third, confusion concerning the proper functions of applied science or technology, on the one hand, and research on the other hand. This confusion is grounded in two misconceptions—that basic and applied research are somehow antithetical (whereas actually they are complementary), and second, that the kind of learning investigated determines whether research is basic or applied (which he points out is not true).

As requirements for a profitable working relationship between the science of learning and the technology of classroom instruction, he identifies the need for a formal statement of the relationship between the two, and a concerted planning effort in which the objective is to formulate the technological and scientific problems in particular areas of education. Such planning efforts should include identification of the present "state of the art" in the management of particular types of learning, the identifying and ordering in priority of needs for improvement in such management, the identification of which aspects of problems are amenable to basic and applied research, and identification of the needs for systematic development efforts in which the available state of the art can be employed. A third major requirement is adequate facilities and subjects for research and development studies, including ready access to school populations for analytic studies. Finally, he says, "there must be a re-examination of the training of psychologists and educational psychologists with these opportunities in mind." His general conclusion is that ". . . the present low level of interest and effort in the application to the classroom of recent advances in the science of learning is a state of affairs which can be corrected. Furthermore, it seems to me that vigorous effort to apply the necessary corrective measures to both the science of learning and the technology of education is in the best interests of a healthy science of psychology and a healthy profession of education. But over-riding all these considerations is the conviction that the full realization of the human resources of this nation cannot be achieved without a science-based management of learning processes of our children. It seems to me, therefore, that we should get on with the business, so that within a few years we can know that the goals of educational psychology are at least as well supported by educators, psychologists, educational psychologists, and all of our citizens, as are the goals of military psychology."

19 / A THEORETICAL FRAMEWORK FOR PERSONALITY AND SOCIAL BEHAVIOR[1] / ROBERT R. SEARS[*]

I WISH TO CONSIDER SOME SYSTEMATIC aspects of personality and social psychology, and to indicate what seem to me the directions further development of these fields is likely to take. Partly these directions are dictated by more general developments in psychology and the social sciences; but partly they are matters of choice, and of estimate as to what will provide us with the most effective science of human behavior.

Perhaps the most impressive thing about both these fields is the extent to which, in recent years, they have become empirical. The opinion poll, small group observational procedures, and attitude scales have contributed notably to the precision with which the actions of groups can be measured and their future behavior predicted. Similarly, in the field of personality and motivation, such devices as the TAT, doll play, behavior unit observations, and standardized interviews have become more and more effective for providing objective and quantified statements about significant variables.

From a practical standpoint, some of these methods have been extraordinarily valuable. Market surveys, studies of morale in the military services, diagnostic analyses of disturbed children, and comparative studies of techniques of teaching have yielded findings that have much improved the quality of human output. In effect, the past decade has put in the hands of any competent technician procedures which permit the empirical discovery of facts and principles that hitherto had been the province of so-called men of wisdom. For many areas of human action, intuitively skillful lucky guessing has given way to precise and replicable investigation.

THEORY

This empirical progress has been accompanied by the construction of but a minimal amount of

theory. Perhaps it could not have been otherwise. Theory does not grow in the absence of data, and until the last two decades, the data of social psychology have been meager and those of personality limited mainly to clinical observations.

Yet it is clear that further development in these fields will require an adequate theory. By a *theory* I mean a set of variables and the propositions that relate them to one another as antecedents and consequents. This involves such logical impedimenta as definitions, postulates, and theorems. And it requires the following of certain rules, such as that the definitions of variables must be mutually exclusive; that intervening variables must ultimately be reducible to operations; that the reference events specified as the consequents in theorems must be measured independently of the antecedents from which they are derived, and so on. The general procedure of theory construction is sufficiently standard that it needs no explication here.

The *findings* to be integrated are those that describe consistent relationships between behavior (or its products) and some other events. Essentially, these are the descriptive behavioral relationships that comprise the disciplines of individual and social psychology, sociology, and anthropology. Individual and group behavior are so inextricably intertwined, both as to cause and effect, that an adequate behavior theory must combine both in a single internally congruent system.

There are two main advantages of a good theory that make such a development urgent. First, it is economical in the sense that it permits many observed relationships to be subsumed under a single systematic proposition. And second, it permits the use of multiple variables and their relating principles, in combination, for the prediction of events.

These virtues have long been recognized. Several psychologists have constructed conceptual frameworks within which the facts of either social psychology or personality could be theoreti-

[1] Address of the President of the American Psychological Association at Chicago, Illinois, September 3, 1951.

[*] Robert R. Sears, A theoretical framework for personality and social behavior, *The American Psychologist*, 1951, *6*, 476-483. Reprinted by permission.

cally formulated. McDougall (11), Floyd Allport (1), and Kurt Lewin (10) provided them for social psychology; Freud (5), G. V. Hamilton (6), Lewin (9), Gordon Allport (2), and H. A. Murray (13) have done the same for personality. Examples of the application of theory construction to problems important in social psychology and personality are to be found in Festinger's work on communication (4), Miller's studies of displacement (12), and our own analyses of the projective process in parent-child relationships (7, 17, 18).

ACTION

Every theory must have a subject-matter. It must be a theory about something, obviously. A certain class of events must be selected for explication. These are the reference events, the consequents for which antecedents are discovered. The basic events to which behavior theory has reference are *actions*. This follows from the very nature of our interest in man. It is his behavior, the things he does, the ends he accomplishes, that concern us.

From a logical standpoint, a theory is of value to the extent that it orders a set of observations. There are many kinds of observations that can be and have been made of social and individual behavior. Some of these have involved inferred traits or needs; others have related to perceptions or to states of consciousness. By the criterion of logic, a theory that takes any of these phenomena as its basic reference events is acceptable.

But there is another criterion to be considered, the practical one. It is reasonable to ask what kind of events are important to us. On this score, action is clearly more significant than perception or traits. The clinician must make judgments about personality that will permit predictions of behavior. Will the patient attempt suicide? Will his performance at intellectual tasks continue to deteriorate? Will his level of social problem-solving improve under an anxiety-reduction therapy? Likewise, the teacher and the parent undertake methods of rearing a child with expectations that his actions will change in a particular direction. They want him to add more accurately, or paint more freely, or cry less violently when he is disappointed; even those changes commonly interpreted as perceptual, such as art or music appreciation, are evidenced in the form of choices as to where to go, what to look at, what to listen to.

The situation is even clearer with respect to social behavior. The social engineer is concerned with such questions as whether a certain parent-child relationship will establish habitually dependent behavior in the child, whether the eventual marriage of a courting couple will terminate in divorce or in the social facilitation of their mutual labors, whether citizens will buy bonds or vote for a Congressman, whether a group will be shattered or solidified by external opposition, i.e., whether there will be an increase or decrease in cooperative efforts and in-group aggression.

Aside from the fact that a behavior science, rather than a *need* or *perceptual* science, is of the greatest use to us, there is an evident practical advantage. Human beings deal with one another in terms of actions. The teacher has direct observation of the performance of her pupils. The parent or the husband or the foreman or the Congressman can have only inferential knowledge of the ideas or desires of those with whom he interacts. But he can describe the conditions that impinge on people and he can take note of the behavioral consequences. To put the argument briefly: actions are the events of most importance, and actions are most available to observation and measurement.

This is not to say that needs or motives, perceptions, traits, and other such internalized structures or processes are irrelevant. Any scientific system must contain both operational and intervening variables that are independent of the reference events forming the subject-matter of the system. But the choosing of such variables must depend on their contribution to a theory that will predict actions. There is no virtue in a descriptive statement that a person or a class of persons possesses such and such a trait or need unless that statement is part of a larger one that concludes with a specification of a kind of action to be performed. To describe a person as having *high emotionality* or *low sensitivity* or *diffuse anxiety* is systematically acceptable only if other variables are added that will, together with these internal personal properties, specify what kind of behavior can be expected from him under some specific circumstances.

DYNAMICS

By definition a theory of action is dynamic; i.e., it has to do with force or energy in motion. The term *dynamic* has been so abused by psychologists during the last half century, however, that its meaning is no longer clear. Perhaps it never was. But with successive "dynamic psychologies"—those of Freud, Morton Prince, Woodworth, Lewin, and a host of contemporary theorists—its meaning has been more obfuscated than ever. Sometimes it refers to a motivational approach, sometimes to a developmental, sometimes to an emphasis on unconscious processes. Mostly, I suspect, it merely means the theorist is revolting against what seem to him the stultifying structuralistic, unhuman inadequacies of his predecessors. It boils down to a self-attributed accolade for virtue, a promise to deal with important characteristics of real live people rather than dry and dusty processes.

This is a waste of a good word. By no means all modern psychological systems are dynamic; some are trait-based and some are need-based. No one would deny that combinations of habit structures do exist and do provide a kind of integrated consistency in a person's behavior. Likewise, no one would attempt to order the events of human action without variables that relate to motivation, including those kinds of motivation that cannot be verbally reported by the person himself. But there is more to dynamics than motivation. There is *change*.

Changes in behavior are of two kinds. For a theory to be dynamic, both must be systematized separately but congruently. One is ongoing action, or *performance*, and the other is learning, or *acquisition*. Obviously, no predictive statement can be made about ongoing action unless certain things are known about the person's *potentialities for action*. He has certain properties that determine what kind of behavior he will produce under any given set of circumstances. His motivation is weak or strong, he is frustrated or not in various goal-directed sequences, he has expectancies of the consequences of his behavior. Unless these are known, it is impossible to have any systematization of ongoing action. And unless the *changes* in potentialities for action are systematically ordered, there is no possibility of constructing an ongoing action theory that will enable one to predict beyond the termination of any single sequence of behavior.

The combining of these two approaches to behavior has not yet been fully accomplished. The most elaborate theory of performance, or ongoing action, is that of Kurt Lewin (9), but his field theory has never been developed to care adequately for problems of personality development (learning). Similarly, the develop-

mental theory of G. V. Hamilton (6) gave an excellent account of the acquisition of potentialities for response but did not cover so effectively the problems of ongoing action.[2]

MONADIC AND DYADIC UNITS

I have already made reference to the desirability of combining individual and social behavior into a single theoretical system. The reasons are obvious. In any social interaction, the interests, motives, habits or other psychological properties of the acting individuals determine to some degree the kind of interaction that will occur. The shy youngster is likely to have less stimulating learning experiences with his teacher than is a bolder one; the traveller in a foreign land who knows the language forms different kinds of friendships than the one who uses an interpreter. Conversely, the social milieu, the interpersonal relationships, within which a person acts determine his psychological properties. A man in a subordinate role cannot act as a leader; a child reared as the younger of two develops differently from one reared as the elder of two. Whether the group's behavior is dealt with as antecedent and the individual's as consequent, or vice versa, the two kinds of event are so commonly mixed in causal relationships that it is impractical to conceptualize them separately.

To wish for a combining theoretical framework is one thing, but to get it from psychologists is quite another. Sociologists have been more accustomed to think in such terms. The theoretical analyses of Cottrell (3) and of Parsons (15) have emphasized particularly the interactive processes. Among psychologists, Newcomb (14), with his exposition of role expectancy, and Festinger (4), in his studies of group cohesiveness, clearly exemplify the trend toward combination. In the main, however, in spite of their long prepossession with social influences on the individual, psychologists think monadi-

[2] A simple behavior sequence is shown in Figure 1. The various potentialities for action are specified by S_D (motivation) and S_{cog} (cognitive structures). In large part these characteristics are a product of learning. The successful completion of a behavior sequence is a reinforcement, and this modifies the drives and habit structures of the person in certain lawful ways, these laws being part of the body of the laws of learning. In other words, there is a change in the person's potentialities for action. It is to be noted, therefore, that although Figure 1 describes a single behavior sequence, there are two ways of ordering the events that compose it. Both refer to changes, to energy in motion. To be dynamic, a theory of behavior must encompass both.

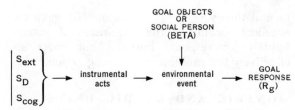

FIGURE 1 / THE MONADIC INSTIGATION-ACTION SEQUENCE.

cally. That is, they choose the behavior of one person as their scientific subject matter. For them, the universe is composed of individuals. These individuals are acted upon by external events, to be sure, and in turn the external world is modified by the individuals' behaviors. But the universal laws sought by the psychologist almost always relate to a single body. They are monadic laws, and they are stated with reference to a monadic unit of behavior.

The main variables that compose such systems have been presented diagrammatically in many ways. Some are so well known as virtually to represent signatures for the theorists who devised them. There are Tolman's schematic sow-bug, Hull's behavior sequence, Lewin's field structure, and Miller and Dollard's learning paradigm. These diagrams differ considerably in the kinds of variables they incorporate. Some emphasize reward and reinforcement; others do not. Some are time-oriented; others are descriptive of a nontemporal force field. All specify antecedent stimulus conditions and consequent actions, but in very different ways and with quite different systematic constructs. But there is one thing in common among them—they are all monadic.

But if personality and social behavior are to be included in a single theory, the basic monadic unit of behavior must be expandable into a dyadic one. A dyadic unit is one that describes the combined actions of two or more persons.[3] A dyadic unit is essential if there is to be any conceptualization of the *relationships* between people, as in the parent-child, teacher-pupil, husband-wife, or leader-follower instances. To have a science of interactive events, one must have variables and units of action that refer to such events. While it is possible to systematize some observations about individuals by using monadic units, the fact is that a large proportion of the properties of a person that compose

[3] Although the prefix means "two," the term is used here simply as the minimal instance of multiplicity. Similar principles would hold whether the interactors were two or more.

his personality are originally formed in dyadic situations and are measurable only by reference to dyadic situations or symbolic representations of them. Thus, even a monadic description of a person's action, makes use of dyadic variables in the form of social stimuli.

This is exemplified in Figure 1, a diagram of a monadic behavior sequence that, as will be seen, can be expanded into a dyadic sequence. One aspect of this figure deserves comment, the *environmental event*. This concept refers to the changes produced in the environment by the instrumental activity; these are the changes necessary for the occurrence of the goal response. The teacher trying to increase participatory activity in a class of children, for example, gets her reward when the youngsters spontaneously start a team game at recess. She makes her goal response—she has achieved her aim—when the environment changes, i.e., when the children play a team game. Or a boy is seeking approbation from his father; he hits a three-bagger; his father grins with satisfaction. The grin is the boy's environmental event in his monadically conceived action sequence.

This concept achieves importance in the present context, because it is the necessary connecting link between a monadic and dyadic systematization of behavior. The framework for such a description is shown in Figure 2. For convenience the two persons are labelled Alpha and Beta. A dyadic situation exists whenever the actions of Beta produce the environmental events for Alpha, and vice versa. The behavior of each person is essential to the other's successful completion of his goal directed sequence of action. The drives of each are satisfied only when the motivated actions of the other are carried through to completion. The nurturant mother is satisfied by the fully-loved child's expression of satiety, and the child is satisfied by the expressions of nurturance given by his mother.

It must be made clear in this connection that

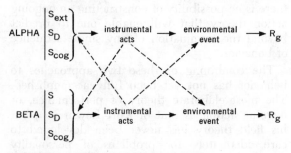

FIGURE 2 / THE DYADIC SEQUENCE.

environmental events are *only those changes in environment produced by the behavior of the person under consideration*. The stroke of lightning that splits a log for the tired woodcutter is not in this category, nor is the food given the newborn infant by his mother, nor the empty taxi that providentially appears when the rain is at its worst. These are certainly characteristics of the environment, manipulanda that govern in some ways the future behavior of Alpha, but they are not environmental events in the sense that the term is used here. They were not induced by any action of Alpha.

This is an important distinction. Unless the interaction of Alpha and Beta is based on something other than the fortuitously useful conjunction of their individual actions, there is no interdependence of each on the other. There is, in effect, no dyadic system, only a piling up of parallel monadic sequences.

The factor responsible for maintaining stability of the dyadic unit is exhibited in Figure 3. It is the *expectancy* of the environmental event, diagrammed in a notation similar to that used by Hull for the anticipatory goal response (8). In the present case, the anticipatory response is a fractional part of the reactions Alpha makes to those behaviors of Beta that constitute the environmental event. For example, if a child wants to be kissed good-night, his mother must lean toward him affectionately and kiss him. He, in turn, must slip his arms around her neck and lift his face to hers receptively. These latter movements are the ones that fractionate and become anticipatory in Alpha's behavior sequence. And as in the case of the anticipatory goal response, they elicit response-produced stimuli ($r_{ee} s_{ee}$) that become integrated into the total stimulus constellation which serves to instigate this behavior sequence on future occasions.

These anticipatory reactions to Beta's behavior are the *expectancies* that make the behavior of the two people truly interdependent. They provide the mechanism, at least within the framework of one conceptualization of the learning process, by which a dyadic behavior unit can be derived from the combining of two or more monadic units.

One can only speculate as to what variables, and what general principles, will eventually compose a dyadic behavior theory. Some of them will probably be discovered in the attempt to analyze those psychological processes that apparently result from highly particularized constellations of interpersonal relations. Identification is

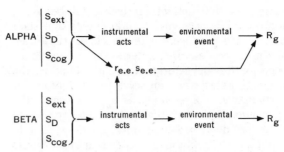

FIGURE 3 / THE DYADIC SEQUENCE WITH ANTICIPATORY RESPONSES TO THE ENVIRONMENTAL EVENT.

one such process. Reciprocal cathexis is another. A third is the process of secondary drive formation, as in the early childhood development of aggression and dependency. Other variables will likely be devised in the study of small groups. Festinger's concept of cohesiveness is a big step forward in this direction.

One way of approaching the problem would be to examine the various possibilities of reward and nonreward or punishment for Alpha and Beta. If a dyad exists on the basis of reciprocal rewards, as in the mother-child relationship, there are nevertheless possibilities of mutual interference. That is, while the dyad is held together by powerful continuing motivations and expectancies of reciprocal support, each member has the potentiality of frustrating the other. One major source of frustration is the absence of the partner, Beta, at times when Alpha needs him. Such absences would be expected to occur partly (but by no means entirely, of course) because Beta was also the partner in dyadic relationships with other people. Now, since in young children aggression and dependency are two of the major reactions to frustration, one might reach some such hypothesis as this: that the amount of aggression and dependency that characterize a mother-child interaction will be a positive function of the number of dyadic relationships in which each is a member. Or to put it in a more testable form: everything else being held constant, a child's dependency and aggressiveness toward his mother will vary with the amount of role conflict the mother has.

PERSONALITY

In this monadic-dyadic framework, personality is a description of those properties of a person that specify his potentialities for action. Such a description must include reference to motivation, expectations, habit structure, the nature of the instigators that activate instrumental behavior, and the kinds of environmental events that such actions will produce. Furthermore, all these factors must be described in terms of the dyadic aspects of the behavior that occurs. That is, the kinds of Betas who can serve as instigators for particular responses must be specified, and the environmental events that Beta creates for Alpha must be described not only as they fit into Alpha's activity but also as they fit into the whole motivational sequence of Beta.

In behavior science, personality is sometimes treated as antecedent and sometimes as consequent. As antecedent, it is part of the total matrix that must be known in order to account for either individual or dyadic action. In recent years various approaches to personality have too much depended on assumptions of fixed traits and fixed needs. This has led to measurement procedures that do not include reference to the social stimulus conditions under which the traits or needs will be expressed. As Fillmore Sanford has said, in connection with a study of leadership, there is no trait independent of the conditions that elicit it. Leadership is a quality in a person's behavior only if there are followers who react to him as a leader. Most behavior with which the personality

psychologist is concerned is either directly dyadic or is in response to symbolic representation of the dyad. Therefore, any conceptualization of the person's properties must be done with consideration of the properties of the various Betas with whom Alpha is interactive.

A simple example of the measurement problem created by these considerations arose in connection with some data on aggressive behavior collected in our laboratory (7, 17, 18). Forty preschool children were the subjects. Two main measures of aggressiveness were secured. One was overt and socially directed aggression. This measure was obtained both by teachers' rating scales and by direct observation. The other was projective or fantasy aggression displayed in doll play. By a fixed trait or need assumption, one would expect these two measures to correspond somewhat. They did—somewhat! The correlation was .13!

An analysis in terms of learning and action makes the meaning of this relationship clear. These children's mothers were interviewed concerning their methods of handling the youngsters' aggression at home. On the basis of the information it was possible to divide the children into three subgroups which had had different degrees of severity of punishment for aggression.

In Figure 4, the mother's frequency of both overt and fantasy aggression are shown for these three subgroups. It is to be noted that while the "mild" and "moderate" groups show a correspondence in amount of aggressive behavior of the two kinds, there is a radical disagreement in the "severe" punishment subgroup. These latter children, on the average, behaved rather non-aggressively in preschool, but in their doll play fantasies there was an abundance of aggression. One could ask whether these children are very aggressive or very non-aggressive. Do they have strong need for aggression or weak?

Even if these questions could be sensibly answered, which they cannot, the answers would be of little help in predicting the future aggressive behavior of these children. To accomplish the latter, which is our aim, there must be an analysis of the social stimulus conditions under which the future behavior is to be observed.

The minimum specification would be as to whether the behavior would be observed in a nursery school or in a permissive doll play experiment. With a conceptualization of the dyadic variables involved, however, it is possible to make a statement that goes beyond the narrow

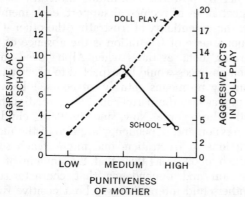

FIGURE 4 / RELATION OF INTERPERSONAL AND FANTASY AGGRESSION TO MATERNAL PUNITIVENESS. INTERPERSONAL AGGRESSION IS MEASURED BY FREQUENCY OF AGGRESSIVE ACTS OCCURRING DURING FOUR HOURS OF OBSERVATION IN PRESCHOOL; FANTASY AGGRESSION IS MEASURED BY MEAN FREQUENCY OF AGGRESSIVE ACTS OCCURRING DURING TWO TWENTY-MINUTE DOLL PLAY SESSIONS. PUNITIVENESS OF MOTHER IS BASED ON RATINGS OF INTERVIEW MATERIAL CONCERNING SEVERITY OF MOTHER'S PUNISHMENT OF CHILD'S AGGRESSIVE ACTS AT HOME. CHARTED VALUES ARE MEDIANS OF THE THREE GROUPS, SIZES OF WHICH ARE: LOW = 7, MEDIAN = 23, HIGH = 10.

confines of these two measuring situations. In this instance, the more general statements can be made that, first, the amount of aggression will be a negative function of severity of punishment, and second, with severity of punishment held constant, the amount of aggression will vary positively with dissimilarity of the dyadic situation to the original punishment situation in the home. These are strictly monadic statements, but they assume the prior existence of dyadic experiences.

The systematization of personality development requires a different approach. When personality factors are considered as antecedents to individual or group behavior, the laws of ongoing action are involved. But when personality development is the matter for study, the laws of learning are the bases. What is needed in this case is a set of principles that will describe the way in which the child's potentialities for action—that is, his drives, habits, cognitive structures, and expectancies—are changed by the experiences he has throughout his life.

This is a difficult problem, both logically and empirically. Personality is partly the product of a life-time of dyadic action which has modified the individual's potentiality for further action. The changed potentiality is therefore partly a product of his own actions. For example, in the data concerning child aggression and severity of maternal punishment for aggression, the mother's action in punishing the child was doubtless influenced in part by the amount and kind of aggression exhibited toward her by the child. Thus, the behavior that served as an antecedent to the differential display of overt and fantasy aggression by the child was contributed to by the child himself.

Logically, and practically, a good theory requires that antecedents and consequents be entirely independent of one another. It would be most satisfactory if the child did not influence the mother's behavior, and if we could then say something about the effect of severity of punishment on later behavior. One solution to this problem appears to be a careful measurement of the child's contribution to the dyadic relationship and a partialling out of that influence in the comparison of antecedent mother behavior with consequent child behavior.

The variables that appear most promising in the study of personality development come from two main sources. One is the set of definitions and postulates that compose the laws of learning. Whether the particular formulations used by Tolman, Hull, Guthrie, or Skinner are selected seems of little importance at the moment. Those of Hull and Tolman have certain *a priori* advantages, but the main point is the use of whatever laws of learning will best serve to account for changes in potentiality for action. The theoretical formulation of the research in our own laboratory stems from Hull through Miller and Dollard.

The second source of variables lies in the conceptualization of those secondary motivational systems that arise universally as a product of the dyadic relationship between mother and child (16). These include aggression, dependency, self-reliance, responsibility, the anxieties, competition, and status-seeking as well as the various consequences of the training inherent in socialization of the primary drives of hunger, sex, fatigue, and elimination. The exact forms of behavior potentiality created in each of these motivational areas are different from child to child and culture to culture. But the biological nature of man, coupled with his universal gregariousness, gives rise to various learning experiences that every human child endures in one fashion or another.

SUMMARY

In sum, it seems to me that the most promising directions now discernible in the study of social behavior and personality require a theory that has the following properties: its basic reference events must be *actions;* it must combine congruently both *dyadic* and *monadic* events; it must account for both *ongoing action* and *learning;* it must provide a description of personality couched in terms of *potentiality for action;* and it must provide principles of personality development in terms of *changes in potentiality for action.*

REFERENCES

1. ALLPORT, F. H. *Social psychology.* Boston: Houghton-Mifflin Co., 1924.

2. ALLPORT, G. W. *Personality; a psychological interpretation.* New York: Henry Holt, 1937.

3. COTTRELL, L. S. The analysis of situational fields in social psychology. *Amer. Sociol. Rev.,* 1942, 7, 370-382.

4. FESTINGER, L. Informal social communication. *In* L. Festinger et al. *Theory and experiment in social communication.* Ann Arbor: Research Center for Group Dynamics, 1950.

5. FREUD, S. *General introduction to psychoanalysis.* New York: Boni & Liveright, 1920.

6. HAMILTON, G. V. *Objective psychopathology.* St. Louis: C. V. Mosby, 1925.

7. HOLLENBERG, E., and SPERRY, M. Some antecedents of aggression and effects of frustration in doll play. *Personality,* 1951, *1,* 32-43.

8. HULL, C. L. Goal attraction and directing ideas conceived as habit phenomena. *Psychol. Rev.,* 1931, *38,* 487-506.

9. LEWIN, K. *A dynamic theory of personality.* New York: McGraw-Hill, 1935.

10. LEWIN, K. Constructs in psychology and psychological ecology. *Univ. Ia. Stud. Child Welf.,* 1944, *20,* 1-29.

11. MC DOUGALL, W. *An introduction to social psychology.* London: Methuen, 1908.

12. MILLER, N. E. Theory and experiment relating psychoanalytic displacement to stimulus-response generalization. *J. abn. soc. psychol.,* 1948, *43,* 155-178.

13. MURRAY, H. A. *Explorations in personality.* New York: Oxford Univ. Press, 1938.

14. NEWCOMB, T. M. *Social psychology.* New York: Dryden Press, 1950.

15. PARSONS, T. *The Social system.* Glencoe, Illinois: The Free Press, 1951.

16. SEARS, R. R. Personality development in contemporary culture. *Proc. Amer. Philos. Soc.,* 1948, *92,* 363-370.

17. SEARS, R. R. Relation of fantasy aggression to interpersonal aggression. *Child Develpm.,* 1950, *21,* 5-6.

18. SEARS, R. R. Effects of frustration and anxiety on fantasy aggression. *Amer. J. Orthopsychiat.,* 1951, *21,* July.

IV / Interpersonal Experiences as Determinants of Behavior

THE NATURE OF A PERSON'S EXPECTATIONS OF OTHERS, HIS ways of gaining satisfaction, of expressing his feelings, and of resolving emotional conflicts (in mature or less mature ways), the content and fervor of his ideals, and the extent of his inhibitions and guilt feelings— ALL are formed in an interpersonal context. Those who emphasize interpersonal determinants are indebted to Sigmund Freud far more than to any other theorist, a debt Bruner made clear in an opening selection of this book. Although psychoanalytic theory today represents a gradual modification and differentiation of Freud's views, his recognition of the formative impact of emotional relationships in the family stands solidly as a cornerstone of today's conceptions of personality development.

The influence of the family is not limited to the tie with father and mother. A child's gratifications and deprivations, his loves and enmities in relation to figures other than the parents may be crucial. Which relationships are important depends upon the composition of the particular family group and the roles taken by the different members.

Intense and prolonged hatreds or affectional bonds occurring in childhood may even be forgotten in adulthood, and yet they may color the person's perceptions of other people, especially in circumstances that arouse inner conflict. A man who has had chronic trouble with a brother, unmitigated by sufficient happy experiences, is likely to have difficulties when a competitive situation arises with a peer at work. Such difficulties may lead not only to discomfort, but also to inappropriate behavior. The woman whose relation with her mother was unsatisfactory is likely to have problems in getting along with an older woman who employs her. If the picture is further complicated by unresolved difficulties the older woman had with *her* younger sister, both the supervisor and employee may behave in such distorted ways that a total impasse is reached. In such ways the emotional cares of childhood may live on to burden adult associations in work, marriage, and parenthood.

The first approach to gaining knowledge about such interpersonal determinants of behavior was the CLINICAL one of Freud and his successors, the approach still used by most psychiatrists and social workers as well as by some psychologists. Hypotheses are generated from a series of cases. Such cases are usually of patients undergoing treatment for emotional tensions or for bodily disorders that represent symptoms of inner conflict. The body of theories and hypotheses that have grown out of such clinical studies offers a fertile field to the empirical researcher who can make the controlled investigations needed in order to test, and enrich or correct, the hard-won theoretical formulations. All articles in this section offer the results of empirical rather than clinical research, yet in each case it was clinical work that initially gave rise to the ideas now being pursued by replicable methods more suited to verification of hypotheses. At the present stage of the scientific study of human personality and behavior, clinical studies are an indispensable counterpart to the empirical ones in providing guidelines for further investigations.

Our first selection describes ways in which the social, sexual, and parental behaviors of adult monkeys were affected by varying degrees of social contact and mothering in their early lives. The article is by Harry Harlow, famous for his work with primates at the University of Wisconsin and a former president of the American Psychological Association. Dr. Harlow's collaborator in this study is his wife, Dr. Margaret Kuenne Harlow, a child psychologist.

Next comes a report of findings about the ways in which parents deal with children's aggressiveness. It is from a study done at the Harvard Laboratory of Human Development when all three authors were there. Sears (See III) and Maccoby are now at Stanford, where she is Director of the Laboratory of Human Development. Harry Levin is at Cornell University's Laboratory for Research on Language Skills in the Department of Child Development and Family Relationships, another of the outstanding centers of research and training in child and adolescent psychology.

The third selection is by Elizabeth Bing of Stanford University, who studied two groups of fifth-grade children equal in overall ability, contrasting those higher in verbal ability with those whose aptitudes were greater in the numerical or spatial realms. She finds substantial differences between the groups in the child-rearing to which they were exposed.

The next three articles deal with aspects of the identification process by which children acquire allegiance to certain values and model themselves after their parents in various respects. The educational implications of identificatory learning are implicit in the following statement by Edward Joseph Shoben, Jr.:

> Psychologically, it seems sound to argue that the essential curriculum for each school child at any given time is not what is on paper in the curriculum supervisor's office. It is much more likely to be the way he perceives his teacher. The curriculum, after all, is only a statement of what the pupil is to learn. His learning proceeds through the vital and basic mediation of the teacher. What he learns, therefore, is in significant degree a function of how he reacts to and interprets the mediating adult. . . .[1]

The first of our selections on identification is by Albert Bandura of Stanford University in collaboration with Dorothea and Sheila Ross. The second is by Paul Mussen and Eldred Rutherford of the University of California at Berkeley. The third was done at Harvard's Laboratory of Human Development by Judy Rosenblith. This article replaces one based on the same study and by the same author that was included in the earlier edition of this book.

[1] The Shoben paper, called, "Viewpoints from related disciplines: learning theory," is from an issue of *Teachers College Record* (1959, 60, 272-282) devoted to the topic: "What Shall the Schools Teach?" Reprinted by permission.

The study of adolescent mobility by Elizabeth Douvan and Joseph Adelson is an outgrowth of an investigation at the University of Michigan's Survey Research Center. In addition to the value of its substantive content, it serves to illustrate the kind of study that can be conducted using refinements of public opinion survey techniques.

The papers by Loevinger (III, 17) and Sears (III, 19) could very appropriately have been placed in this section. So could others such as that of Faigin (VI, 34).

Readers who are interested in pursuing the topic of interpersonal influences from the viewpoint of psychoanalytic psychiatry and psychology will enjoy spending an evening with Dorothy W. Baruch's book *One Little Boy* (Julian Press, 1952). Another book which we have found to be very well liked by many students is *Emotional Problems of Living* by O. S. English and G. H. J. Pearson (Third Edition, Norton, 1963). Although written dogmatically—that is, as though psychoanalytic ideas are 100 per cent right and impervious to time and further investigation— their book conveys rich insights into the inner lives of children. It also deals with the ways in which such inner lives constitute a major component in determining children's and adults' behavior. For those interested in material beyond that in English and Pearson on specific problems which face caretakers of children and youth, *A Manual of First Aid for Mental Health in Childhood and Adolescence* by Green and Rothenberg (Julian Press, 1953) is valuable.

Those desiring more exposure to the type of data and approach used in the Sears, Maccoby and Levin material on aggression might well enjoy reading about other areas of parental and child behavior in their book *Patterns of Child Rearing* (Row, Peterson, 1957). Readers may also wish to browse through journals such as *Child Development*, the *Merrill-Palmer Quarterly of Behavior and Development*, and the *Journal of Experimental Child Psychology*.

20 / THE EFFECT OF REARING CONDITIONS ON BEHAVIOR* / HARRY F. HARLOW AND MARGARET K. HARLOW**

A WEALTH OF CLINICAL EVIDENCE shows that human children who have never had adequate maternal care or who have been separated from adequate maternal care within some critical stage, suffer disturbance and delay or even irreparable damage in terms of subsequent personal-social development. The importance of maternal ministrations in the child's development is further supported by many clinical investigations and by some limited experimental data.

Personality malfunctions that have been attributed to maternal inadequacy include such syndromes as marasmus, hospitalism, infantile autism, feeble-mindedness, inadequate maternal responsiveness, and deviant or depressed heterosexuality. If these disorders are the results of maternal inadequacy, only research with human subjects can establish the conditions and kinds of maternal behavior that produce them. Unfortunately, experiments critical to the resolution of these problems cannot be done with human subjects. We cannot rear babies in illuminated black boxes during the first half-year, year, or two years of their lives. We cannot have mothers rear their children in isolation from other children and from adults for the first two, four, or eight years. We dare not have human children reared with either no mothers or inadequate mothers while providing them with maximal opportunity to interact with age-mates, either identically reared or differentially reared. Yet these are the kinds of experiments which are required if we are to assess the effects of maternal variables unconfounded with other experiential variables on the child's personal-social deveopment.

Most clinical investigations have given primary attention to the effects of maternal privation, defined as absence or inadequacy of maternal responsiveness, or to maternal deprivation, defined as infant separation after the infant has established profound, or at least adequate, maternal attachments. Relatively little attention has been given to the effects of the absence or inade-quacy of opportunity for the child to interact with other children and to form adequate affectional patterns with and for them. We know that it is important for the child to form effective infant-mother affectional patterns, but it also is likely that he must form effective child-child affectional patterns if he is to attain normal personal-social, sexual, and parental patterns. Obviously these affectional systems are not independent. It is possible, but by no means a certainty, that at the human level, normal child-child affection requires previous affectional bonds between mother or mother-figure and child. It is certain that the mother plays an important role in the formation of peer affections by providing for and encouraging associations between infants or children, or by preventing or discouraging such associations. Human mothers may also markedly influence the nature and course of child-child relationships.

Psychoanalytic theory, which looks for temporal reduction and temporal primacy, will ascribe primary importance to the earliest causes and conditions whether or not these are of greatest importance. Initial traumas have a false clarity as causative agents since they are not confounded by preceding events, whereas the role of all subsequent events is confounded by the role of these events operating during previous experience. Yet primacy in time need not, and often should not, be equated with primacy in importance.

EFFECTS OF TOTAL SOCIAL DEPRIVATION ON MONKEYS

Six years ago we took two newborn rhesus monkeys, one male and one female, and subjected them to total social deprivation for the first two years of life. Each was placed in a solid, illuminated cage such that it never saw any other animal—monkey or human—even though it was tested for food responsiveness and learning by remote-control techniques. During isolation these

* Presented to a forum of the Menninger School of Psychiatry, December 4, 1961.

** Harry F. Harlow and Margaret K. Harlow, The effect of rearing conditions on behavior, *Bulletin of the Menninger Clinic*, 1962, 26, #5, 213-224. Reprinted by permission.

monkeys adapted to solid food slowly and learned with great difficulty, but they were found to have normal weight and good coats when removed—there were no signs of marasmus. At the conclusion of the two years' isolation, they were tested for social responsiveness to each other and to normal monkeys smaller and younger than themselves. They did not respond to each other and either froze or huddled in a corner when abused by the younger animals. Placed together in a cage in a room with many caged monkeys, they showed withdrawal from this new external world, and in the more than two years they lived together, they remained abnormally frightened, showed minimal interaction, and engaged in no sex activities. In follow-up social tests at four years of age with smaller and weaker monkeys, they made no effort to defend themselves except for one brief episode with one of the pair, after which it curled into a ball and passively accepted abuse. The potential for social behaviors in these animals had apparently been obliterated.

We have preliminary, incomplete data on the effects of such total social deprivation confined to a six-month period and are obtaining other data on the effects of such deprivation over a twelve-month period. The results to date indicate severe but not complete withdrawal from external environmental stimulation. Repeated testing in our playroom situation, shown in Figure 1, reveals that one of these monkeys is almost totally unresponsive socially and the other only occasionally engages in brief, infantile-type social interactions. Normally, the playroom is a highly stimulating situation for monkeys. It is 8 feet high with 36 square feet of floor space, and it contains multiple stationary and mobile toys and tools, flying rings, a rotating wheel, an artificial tree, a wire-mesh climbing ramp, and a high, wide ledge, offering opportunities to explore and play in a three-dimensional world.

We also have data on eight monkeys subjected to total social isolation from other monkeys during the first 80 days of life. Although they neither saw nor contacted nor heard other monkeys, they did see and contact human experimenters, who removed them from their isolation boxes and tested them repeatedly on learning problems after the second week of life. A year later these animals appear to be normally responsive to external environmental stimulation and they are socially responsive to each other when tested in the playroom. This social responsiveness as measured by the appearance of increasingly

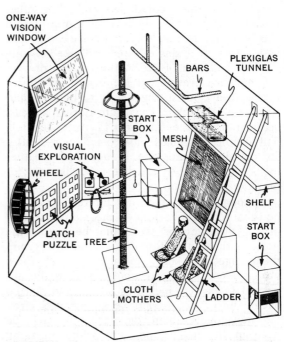

FIGURE 1.

complex play patterns has become qualitatively normal, but probably it is depressed somewhat quantitatively. Whether there will be subsequent effects on heterosexual and maternal behavior remains for future observation.

If we assume a rough developmental ratio of four to one for monkey to man, the results on these eight monkeys are not completely in accord with human clinical data, which at best are only roughly comparable to our experimental situation. Social isolation up to eight or ten months of age is reported to endanger or impair the personal-social development of human infants. It may be that the stimulation and handling of the monkeys in the learning experiments played a positive role in preparing them for subsequent exposure to a monkey environment, thus minimizing the isolation effects. It is also possible that the human infant is more susceptible than the monkey infant to damage from social isolation.

EFFECTS OF EARLY PARTIAL SOCIAL DEPRIVATION

We have data on various groups of monkeys raised from the day of their birth without their mothers and without any monkey companionship at least through the first half-year. One group of 56, now ranging in age from five to eight years, was raised in individual bare wire cages where they could see and hear other monkeys, but not touch them. A group of four was similarly housed for up to five years, but had access to a single wire surrogate* during the first half-year of life. A third group of over 100 monkeys was raised identically except for access to a cloth surrogate† or to both a cloth surrogate and a wire surrogate during at least six months of the first year.†† Approximately half of these animals have been housed after six months or one year of age with another monkey of like age and like or unlike sex for part or all the time since.

Although there may be differences in the personal-social behaviors of the monkeys comprising these groups, we cannot be sure at the present time, and for this reason we group them together. Many members of all three groups have developed what appear to be abnormal behaviors, including sitting and staring fixedly into space, repetitive stereotyped circling movements about the cage, clasping the head in the hands and arms while engaging in rocking, autistic-type movements, and intrapunitive responses of grasping a foot, hand, arm, or leg and chewing or tearing at it with the teeth to the point of injury.

The sex behavior of the six oldest wire-cage-raised monkeys was first measured by Mason‡ in 1960 and compared with that of rhesus monkeys of equal age which had lived in the wild during most of the first year of life. All the wild-raised monkeys, male and female, showed normal sex behavior, characterized in the male by dorsoventral mounting, clasping the legs of the female by the feet, and holding the buttocks by the hands. The females in turn sexually presented themselves by elevating their buttocks and tails, lowering their heads, and frequently looking backward without threatening. No laboratory-raised male or female showed normal sex behavior. Attempted mounting by the male was random in

* A wire surrogate mother is a bare, welded wire cylindrical form surmounted by a wooden head with a crude face and supported semiupright in a wooden frame.

† A cloth surrogate differs from the wire surrogate in that the wire cylinder is cushioned with a sheathing of terry cloth.

†† Harlow, H. F.: The Nature of Love. *Amer. Psychologist* 13:673-685, 1958. Harlow, H. F.: Love in Infant Monkeys. *Sci. Amer.* 200:68-74, 1959.

‡ Mason, W. A.: The Effects of Social Restriction on the Behavior of Rhesus Monkeys: I. Free Social Behavior. *J. Comp. Physiol. Psychol.* 53:582-589, 1960.

regard to body part, and the most frequent pattern was grasping a side of the female's body and thrusting laterally. The female's patterns were totally disordered and often involved sitting down and staring aimlessly into space. Although none of these animals was sexually mature, heterosexual positioning in both male and female normally develops during the second year.

Attempts to breed the cage-raised monkeys approximately two years later also ended in complete failure. When the oldest wire-cage-raised females were between five and seven years of age and the oldest surrogate-raised females were between three and five years, repeated attempts were made to breed 11 of the wire-cage-raised females and four of the cloth-surrogate-raised females with highly selected males from our breeding colony. The females were placed in the large breeding cages during estrus, and if no fighting ensued within 15 minutes, they were left overnight. Eventually one wire-cage-raised female and three cloth-surrogate females became pregnant. Although observation did not reveal clear-cut differences in the behavior of these two groups, the differences in pregnancy approach significance in spite of—or possibly because of—the greater immaturity of the cloth-surrogate-raised females. Actually, no female, impregnated or not, demonstrated a normal pattern of sexual behavior. Many females tried to avoid the males; some actually threatened the males and would probably have been injured had our males not been carefully screened. When the males approached and positioned the females, the females usually collapsed and fell flat on the floor. Impregnation of the four females was achieved only through the patience, persistence, knowledgeability, and motor skill of the breeding males.

We have subsequently tested many wire-cage- and surrogate-mother-raised males and females with experienced breeding females and experienced breeding males, respectively, in a large 8-foot by 8-foot by 8-foot room especially designed for breeding studies. All the males have continued to show the disorganized and inappropriately oriented sexual responsiveness which we have already described, and no male has ever appropriately mounted our experienced and cooperative breeding-stock females, let alone achieved intromission.

With a single exception we have never seen normal, appropriate sexual posturing in our wire-cage- or surrogate-raised females. The females do not approach the males, nor do they groom or present. One cloth-surrogate-raised female was not impregnated throughout six mating sessions, and during this time she began to respond positively and appropriately to the males and eventually developed a normal, full-blown pattern of sexual presentation and sexual posturing during copulation.

EFFECTS OF MATERNAL CONDITIONS

Direct comparison of the effects of being raised by real monkey mothers and cloth surrogate mothers on subsequent personal-social development has been measured by the use of our playpen test situation. In two playpen situations babies were housed with their real mothers, and in a third setup the babies were housed with cloth mothers. The playpen, whose floor plan is given in Figure 2, consists of large living cages each housing a mother and an infant and adjoining a compartment for the playpen. A small opening in each living cage restrains the mother, but gives the infant continuous access to the adjoining playpen compartment. During two daily test sessions, each an hour in length, the screens between playpen compartments were raised, permitting the infant monkeys to interact as pairs during the first six months and as both pairs and groups of four during the second six months. Two experimenters independently observed and recorded the behavior exhibited during test sessions.

The infants raised by real monkey mothers were more socially responsive to each other than were the infants raised by the cloth surrogates. They showed a wider range of facial expressions, and, probably of paramount importance, they developed simple interactive play patterns earlier than the surrogate-raised monkeys and achieved a level of complex play patterns not achieved by the surrogate-raised monkeys during an 18-month test period.

All the male, mother-raised infants have at one time or another responded sexually toward the mother with pelvic thrusting and in at least two cases by dorsoventral mounting. In three cases pelvic thrusting to a female was observed before 50 days of age and in a fourth case, before 100 days of age. Only two (one male and one female) cloth-surrogate-raised monkeys were observed to show pelvic thrusting to the surrogate, and this occurred initially at approximately 100 days of age. Frequency of this sexual play was much higher toward real mothers than toward surrogates. In both situations maximal frequency

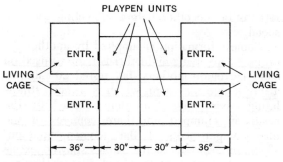

FIGURE 2.

occurred at about five months and then declined, apparently being superseded by thrusting directed toward other infants.

Surrogate babies and mothered babies showed no significant differences in first-observed, infant-directed thrusting, but the actual mean score of the surrogate group was lower. The frequency of sexual play was higher for the real-mothered babies than for the surrogate babies. Finally, seven of eight mother-raised monkeys showed appropriate adult-form sex behaviors during the first 18 months, including ankle clasp by the males, whereas adult-oriented sex behavior was not observed in the cloth-surrogate-raised babies.

There is every reason to believe that normal mothering facilitates the development of heterosexual behavior in rhesus monkeys. This may be in part the result of direct contacts with the mother growing out of the intimate bonds between mother and child. One must not, however, underestimate the importance of the role which the real mother apparently plays, indirect though it is, in stimulating the infants to associate with other infants. This is accomplished from the third month on by discouraging the infant from constant clinging as it matures. From time to time the mother restrains the infant's approaches or cuffs it if it nips her or pulls her hair. The chastised infant seeks the companionship of other babies until the storm subsides—the other mothers by this time generally reject all but their own babies—and in the infant-infant interchanges, strong affectional bonds develop along with behaviors, sexual and nonsexual, appropriate to the sexes.

In the present study, as in all ordinary human situations, there is confounding in the roles played by the mother-infant affectional systems and the infant-infant and peer-peer affectional systems in determining later behavior. We expect to resolve this in part by raising two groups of monkey babies with real mothers, but denying them any opportunity to interact with other infants for six months in the one group and 12 months in the other before subjecting them to social testing.

Some information is supplied by another experiment involving eight rhesus babies raised on cloth surrogate mothers, but tested 20 minutes a day in the playroom, which is a more stimulating environment than that afforded by the relatively cramped and bare confines of the play compartments of the playpen situation. These surrogate-mothered babies showed excellent and appropriately timed play behaviors and very early came to assume both sexual and nonsexual behaviors appropriate to males and females. The males threatened, the females did not; the males initiated rough-and-tumble play, but not the females. Males chased males and males chased females, but females practically never chased males and seldom chased females. By a year of age considerable appropriate male and female sex behavior had occurred, and full and complete copulation, other than insemination, was repeatedly observed in the two males and two females on which observations were continued during the second year of life.

It is obvious that we must not underestimate the importance and role of the infant-infant affectional system as a determiner of adolescent and adult adjustments. It is more than possible that this system is essential if the animal is to respond positively to sheer physical contact with a

peer, and it is through the operation of this system, probably both in monkey and man, that sexual roles become identified and, usually, acceptable.

The role of the mother in the formation of the adult personality is obviously important, but the exact mechanics are open for experimentation. The most tender and intimate associations occur at a stage in which the monkey infant and human infant can to a considerable extent be molded. Monkey and human mother both have the obligation of gradually dissolving the intense physical bonds which characterize the early mother-child relationship. For the monkey mother it is easy and natural—when the infant becomes mature enough and strong enough to become bothersome, she rejects or punishes it and the baby retreats for a time. Subsequently, she welcomes the baby back. Independence is gradually established. For the human mother, with her more complicated motivational systems and her complex culture, it may be difficult to achieve this gradual separation. The overprotective mother is a well-known clinical extreme in the human problem of weaning the infant and child emotionally. Probably the surrogate monkey mother is a parallel of the overprotective human mother, failing usually to equal the normal mother in rearing socially and sexually adjusted monkeys because, at least in part, she is ever available to provide comfort and security. She never discourages contact and thereby never encourages independence in her infant and affectional relationships with other infants and children. The normal state of complete dependency necessary in early infancy is prolonged until it hinders normal personal-social development.

As we have already pointed out, four of our laboratory-raised females never had real mothers of their own, one being raised in a bare wire cage and three with cloth surrogates. The first week after the birth of the baby to the wire-cage-raised female, the mother sat fixedly at one side of the cage staring into space, almost unaware of her infant or of human beings, even when they barked at and threatened the baby. There was no sign of maternal responses, and when the infant approached and attempted contact, the mother rebuffed it, often with vigor, as shown in Figure 3.

The next two unmothered mothers constantly rebuffed the approaches of their infants, but, in addition, frequently engaged in cruel and unprovoked attacks. They struck and beat their babies, mouthed them roughly, and pushed their faces

FIGURE 3.

into the wire-mesh floor. These attacks seemed to be exaggerated in the presence of human beings, and for this reason all formal testing was abandoned for three days for the third unmothered mother because we feared for the life of the infant. The fourth unmothered mother ignored and rejected her infant but did not exhibit excessive cruelty.

In strong contrast to the frailty of the maternal affectional system was the vigor and persistence of the infants' bondage to the mother—time after time, hour after hour, the infants returned, contacted, and clasped the mother in spite of being hit, kicked, and scraped unceremoniously off the mother's body, as shown in Figure 4. The physical punishment which these infants took or sought for the privilege of brief contact even to the back or side of the mother's body testified to the fact that, even in infants, attachment to the mother may be prepotent over pain and suffering. One could not help but be reminded of children, removed from indifferent or cruel, indigent and alcoholic parents, whose primary insistent wish is to return home.

The degree to which monkey data are generalizable to the human being will remain an unsolved dilemma. Nevertheless, we are so struck by the many apparent analogies that we are tempted to say the monkey experiments give us faith in the human clinical observations.

SUMMARY

Infant rhesus monkeys have been reared starting on the first day of life in a variety of situations, including total isolation; partial isolation, either in individual bare wire cages in a colony room for two years or longer, or in individual wire cages with access to one or two mother surrogates for at least the first six months; and in situations with real or surrogate mothers plus contact with other infants for the first year or two of life.

Total isolation for two years resulted in failure to display social or sexual behavior in the next two years, spent in a joint living cage. Results on six months of such isolation are still being gathered and suggest severe, but not complete, social

FIGURE 4.

deficits. Only mild effects have been observed thus far in monkeys isolated through the first 80 days of life.

Partial isolation has produced behavioral aberrations in many monkeys and sexual inadequacy in all males and in all but one female. Four females were impregnated, in spite of inadequate posturing, and proved to be completely inadequate mothers.

Infants raised by live mothers were more advanced in social and sexual behavior than infants raised by surrogate mothers in a controlled playpen situation. The mother's role is not entirely clear, however, because in a more stimulating playroom situation, surrogate-mothered babies have shown normal social and sexual behavior.

Over all, it appears that the longer and the more complete the social deprivation, the more devastating are the behavioral effects. Further research is needed to evaluate the relative contributions of live mothers and infant companions to later adjustment.

21/THE SOCIALIZATION OF AGGRESSION/

ROBERT R. SEARS, ELEANOR E. MACCOBY

AND HARRY LEVIN[*]

AGGRESSION, AS THE TERM IS COMmonly used, means behavior that is intended to hurt or injure someone. Most human adults have quite a repertory of acts that fit this definition. Some of these are bold and violent, others sly and attenuated. Some are accompanied by rage or annoyance; others are done coldly and seemingly, to the perpetrator, without emotion. The complexity and subtlety of adult aggression is the end product of two or three decades of socialization by the individual's parents and peers, however, and bears little resemblance to the primitive quality of the infant's action patterns, from which it developed.

To understand the problem of aggression in child rearing, one does well to remind himself firmly that man is a mammal, and that there are certain kinds of behavior which characterize all mammals. The two that are most relevant to the problem of aggression are *fighting* and the *expression of rage.*

From the lowest quadruped to the highest biped, physical attack is used for defense. Techniques vary, depending on the sharpness of hooves, the strength of jaws, and the presence of specialized weapons like antlers. Man, being the most intelligent and inventive of all, makes use of many of the other species' techniques and adds a host of new ones that, happily, no other animal has ever dreamed of. He can bite like a dog, claw like a cat, kick like a stallion, trade insults like a howling monkey, squeeze like a gorilla; and he constructs his own clubs, blow-pipes, knives, and guns to make up for his lack of antlers and horns. The evolutionary continuity becomes crystal clear in any TV wrestling match.

In spite of this ingenuity, however, physical fighting is not the commonest form of human aggression. *Injury* is a broad term, and the socialization process develops many motives that can be thwarted. Interference with any of these motives causes pain or anguish, and if this was the intention, the interfering act was truly aggressive.

Defensive fighting is usually accompanied by expressions of rage. The older child or adult, who can report his feelings, may recognize his desire to hurt, and be very aware of his angry emotion. But this quality of aggression is attenuated, too, in the process of socialization, and there are many forms of hurt that an adult inflicts with little emotional arousal.

In a civilized society adults are rarely beaten or knifed or lashed. More often, they are hurt by attacks on their pride or status, their desire for social approval, or their feelings of affection for their families and friends. These kinds of hurt can be far more serious and more prolonged than most physical hurts. The withholding of affection by a loved spouse, for example, can have the meaning of pain that goes far beyond that from broken legs or crushed fingers. Nor do injuries that come through sheer accident, the vagaries of nature, hurt like injuries to self-esteem. Contrast them with the gratuitous insult from an admired and intimate friend, or the malicious gossip that one is "slipping" at his job, or the suggestion by a neighbor that one has been a failure in child rearing, or the rejection of a young girl seeking membership in a college sorority. And it is a strong and seasoned old man who can recall without pain his first failure as a lover—and his mistress's amusement.

Not all injuries are so great as these, of course. There are tongue-lashings that do not hurt—much—and insults that are shrugged off. There are the little obstinacies in one's friends, and the non-cooperative indifferences of one's working associates. There are the irritants of family living —a tired and sassy child, a grumpy and complaining husband, a daughter who dawdles. Since all these cause discomfort, they can be forms of aggression. Whether they are in fact, however, depends on whether the discomfort they engender was *designed* by the perpetrator to hurt someone else.

Not all acts that hurt are intended to do so. Even sophisticated and sensitive adults some-

[*] Robert R. Sears, Eleanor E. Maccoby, and Harry Levin, The socialization of aggression, excerpts from Chapter 7, Sears, Maccoby, and Levin, *Patterns of Child Rearing* (Evanston, Illinois: Row, Peterson & Co., 1957). Reprinted by permission.

times fail to anticipate the effects of what they do. The unanswered letter can seem a slight; the unasked question can be interpreted as indifference. With children, the problem is especially noticeable in the manipulation of physical forces. A child's innocently swinging stick only too easily turns into a painful club, the experimental bombing into a brother's broken toys.

Since these hurts are obviously unintentional, they do not qualify as *aggression* in the technical sense of the word. There are certain borderline examples, however, that are hard to be sure about. There are acts that sometimes are and sometimes are not aggressive. Most mothers consider obedience of some importance, for they use much verbal guidance in instructing and controlling their children. The children know their mothers want compliance with directions, and hence willful disobedience is widely recognized as a form of aggression. Now if a child has been told to pick up his clothes a dozen times, and if he has remembered to do this the last half-dozen times, his mother may look suspiciously at his motives if he forgets the thirteenth time. Did he just forget? Or was he angry and disobedient? People differ considerably in the degree to which they perceive an aggressive intent in the behavior of others, and what one mother calls carelessness another will call disobedience.

If we disregard borderline cases and accidents, however, there is still a great deal of human behavior that is designed to hurt. Such activity develops early in life and is a disrupting influence on family living. Later it becomes a problem for the peer group. . . .

All human societies, even all colony-living subhuman primates, have rules to limit the kinds and direction of aggression that may be expressed. The most fundamental of these is the high degree of prohibition on in-group fighting. The closer together people live, the more interdependent they are, the less they dare be aggressive toward one another. Free fighting and antagonism within the household—whether it be a nomad's hut or a suburbanite's four-bedrooms-and-two-baths—could only lead to wreckage of the family unit. Hence, all societies require that only very attenuated forms of aggression be expressed among family members, and that, within the parent-child relationship, aggression be expressed only downward. One mother described this principle with great clarity:

I. How do you handle it (if he strikes you)?
M. I don't allow it. I slap him and punish him for it, and explained that he was never to raise his hand to anyone older than himself, that he must respect older people—his mother and father especially. Never! But they do attempt it, of course; but I do think it should be checked right away.
I. How did you handle this?
M. I would just put him right in his room. Just take hold of him right at the moment and put him right in his room, and say "You mustn't do that! You never should hit your mother and father, ever; they're always right." I always make a big issue out of it.
I. That your mother and father are always right?
M. Always right; "You must never raise your hand to your mother or father."

Not all mothers felt as strongly as this one did, and different societies have different degrees of tolerance for in-family aggression, but the prohibition exists in some degree in all known societies.

Outside the family, limitations are less severe in most societies. As will be seen later, the mothers in this present study were less concerned—more permissive—about fighting between their own children and neighbor youngsters than about sibling quarreling. There were a number of instances in which mothers felt children must be encouraged to fight, to protect their own interests. Even so, there is still a good deal of necessary restriction on the more severe forms of aggression, no matter toward whom they are directed.

To insure the firm establishment of these rules, many mothers feel they must begin the control of aggression very early in the child's life. A newborn infant is not particularly dangerous, even to himself, but he represents a potential threat nevertheless. The family, indeed the whole society, has a delicate balance; the forces of aggression are being kept in check, and co-operation and love are out-weighing non-co-operation and hate. The baby is an alien who does not know all the rules. He lacks knowledge of when to hit and when not to. He has no skill at securing compliance by a *little* hurting. He cannot be counted on to channelize, to displace, or to attenuate his aggressions. He must be taught them if he is to be an acceptable member of society. . . .

PUNISHMENT AND ANXIETY

The mother's almost automatic aggressive response to her child's aggression creates a special problem in child-rearing tactics that does not seem to arise nearly so seriously in connection with other areas of child behavior. Unless a mother is busy, or annoyed to start with, dependency is likely to elicit nurturance from her, and an expression of affection will evoke its like. But aggression, being a frustration to its object, has a strong tendency to evoke counter-aggression or punishment. After all, the mother was once a child herself and learned the same ways of reacting that her child is now learning.

This built-in relationship between the aggressor and his victim has an important consequence. It means that every child grows up with the experience of being punished in some degree for his aggressive behavior. The extent and severity of such punishment differs greatly from one child to another, of course, depending on the tolerance of his parents and siblings. It is our impression, however, that the average child in our sample received more actual *punishment* (as distinguished from *non-reward*) for aggressive behavior than for any other kind of changeworthy action.

One significant effect of punishment is the production of anxiety. If the punishment is repeated many, many times through early childhood, situations that provoke aggressive feelings gradually come to arouse anxiety, too—anxiety over the danger of being punished for aggression. Eventually, the aggression itself, or the accompanying feeling of being angry, becomes sufficient to arouse anxiety. In such cases the anxiety may properly be called aggression-anxiety.

The formation of such a reaction has two kinds of consequences that are relevant to the socialization process. One is the uneasiness and discomfort that become connected with the arousal of aggressive impulses. By and large, adults in our culture do not tolerate aggression comfortably, neither their own nor that displayed by others. It evokes too much anxiety; this may be reflected in feelings of worry, dislike, avoidance, guilt, or moral disapproval. They cannot feel fully comfortable when they are angry. They are in conflict—ambivalent—about their own impulses. The carrying through of an aggressive act is often followed not simply by the catharsis or satisfaction that one would expect from a successful action (assuming the action accomplished the intended results), but also by feelings that arise from the undercurrent anxiety. These may be shame, embarrassment, guilt, regret, self-deprecation, or even just plain fear of retaliation. A mother's uneasiness and conflict often make difficult a calm use of reason in deciding how to handle a child's aggressive actions.

A second consequence of punishment and its

ensuing anxiety is the development, by the child, of techniques for avoiding punishment. The child who is consistently punished for swearing is likely to cease the practice in his parent's presence. This does not necessarily mean he will stop swearing, for punishment seems usually to have a rather localized inhibiting effect. The impulse to be aggressive is not reduced, but only the overt aggressive act that was punished. The total impulse to aggression is made stronger than ever, for the punishment is itself an additional frustration. . . .

We can turn now to the findings from our interviews. In this chapter we will describe first the ways in which the mothers handled aggression, with respect to both permissiveness and punishment. It will be seen that there was some consistency in individual mothers' attitudes, and we will indicate what some of the other personality characteristics were that were commonly associated with gentle or severe handling. Finally, we will examine the relation between these child-rearing practices and the mothers' own reports of their children's aggressiveness to discover what procedures seemed to influence such behavior. . . .

THE MOTHERS' PERMISSIVENESS FOR AGGRESSION

In the discussion so far we have talked of aggression as a changeworthy form of behavior, particularly that directed toward the parents. This is a generalization, however, that hides a multitude of individual differences among the mothers. As might easily be predicted from what has been said of aggression-anxiety, parents differ greatly from one another in the amount of aggression they can tolerate. Some set great store by a completely non-aggressive child others accept the inevitability of a certain amount of aggression even as late as age five; a few believe aggression is such a natural quality of early childhood behavior that they simply ignore all but the most violent episodes. . . .

In our interviews, the mothers described the ways in which children get on adult nerves, found ingenious devices for expressing annoyance or getting revenge, and in general created the social and emotional havoc that goes with anger. They also expressed their own attitudes toward their children's aggression, and gave descriptions of how this changeworthy behavior was handled. With respect to aggression of children toward their parents, the mothers were asked:

Sometimes a child will get angry at his parents and hit them and kick them or shout angry things at them. How much of this sort of thing do you think parents ought to allow in a child of (his, her) age? How do you handle it when (child's name) acts like this?

[Ed CASE A

M. I think he's at the age right now where you're apt to get quite a lot of it. I think as they get a little bit older, you can stop and reason with them, but right now I think that they get pretty angry at times and they do say things. And afterwards they're sorry for it, so I let him say it and it's over with, and afterwards I might say, "You weren't very nice to Mummy," and he'll generally admit it.

CASE B

I. In what ways do you get on each other's nerves?

M. I think our mutual tempers, as much as anything, as he has one, and so have I. I attempt to control it, so for instance I can understand things that he does. He gets very angry and he goes upstairs and throws things, and I can understand that perfectly. I don't know whether I was ever allowed to or whether I ever did throw things, but I wanted to, so that heaving things into the closet, I can easily understand; so that kind of thing doesn't aggravate me the way it would somebody else, and the same way with getting very angry at me. I never mind that as much, because I also get angry at him, and if I am going to, he has got to be allowed that privilege also.

CASE C

M. Well, she'll say, "I don't like you." She seldom says, "I hate you," or "I don't like you anymore," or something like that. I have let her go up to now because I feel she's just getting it out of her system. If it isn't too loud, or if she isn't too angry about it, I just let it go. If it's something that I can't turn my back on, if it's something that she's so angry about that she won't stop, then I speak to her. Otherwise she'll say, "Well, I don't like you." And I say, "Well, that's all right," or something like that. I don't pay too much attention to it because I know that she doesn't actually mean it. She means it because she isn't getting what she wants, and she doesn't mean it actually.

If she kicked me or if she slapped me, I'd slap her back. I just told her that it doesn't feel good to get slapped. If she didn't want to get slapped herself, not to slap other people. The reaction would be the same in anyone that got slapped—they wouldn't like it.

Ed *The material in brackets, ending on page 144, is an edited version taken from Maccoby, Newcomb, and Hartley (eds.),* Readings in Social Psychology *(Holt, 1958).*

CASE D

M. They never should allow him to hit them back. If he hits them, they should hit him right back. If you let him get away with it once he will always want to get away with it.

I. How do you handle it when he acts like this?

M. If he hits me I hit him back twice as hard, and if he does it again, I just get my paddle I have, and I give it to him again, and then he stops.

I. How do you handle it if he is deliberately disobedient?

M. I take off his clothes and he's in for the day and he's not to play with anything—not even his toys or anything that belongs to him—he's not to touch anything—he's to leave things alone and stay in bed.

CASE E

M. That is something I will not tolerate—my child has never done it. I mean, they have done it once in a while, both of them, but I would absolutely not tolerate it.

I. How did you teach them not to do this?

M. I don't know—I guess I just told them once, in no uncertain terms, that it was something that was never done, and I have never had any trouble with it; and if I did, I don't know just how I would cope with it, because I wouldn't stand for it.

I. How much of this sort of thing do you think a parent ought to allow?

M. I don't think they should allow it at all. I think a child should be allowed to express himself, and all that, but I don't think there is ever an exception for a child to hit his parents.

Responses of these kinds, together with much other relevant material elsewhere in the interview, enabled us to rate each mother on two dimensions: (1) her *permissiveness* for aggression, directed by the child toward herself and (2) the amount (and severity) of *punishment* she had administered to the child for such aggression. Under the heading of permissiveness we included not only the mother's stated values as to whether aggression should be allowed but also her behavior toward the child, *i.e.,* whether she actually *did* allow it or whether she always tried to take measures to prevent or stop it.

As might be expected, the two scales were correlated. That is, the mothers who were permissive about aggression, tended to use little punishment, while the nonpermissive mothers used quite a bit. But the correlation was only —.46, a low enough value to warrant considering the two dimensions separately. The two scales did not correlate more closely because there were a number of mothers who did not permit aggression from their children, but stopped it by other means than punishment.

Surprisingly, there were also a number whom we rated both quite permissive and highly punishing. In this latter group were some mothers who felt they *should* allow their children to display aggression; but they could restrain their own impulses to suppress the child's aggression only so long, and then they would blow up. When the punishment came, it was likely to be severe.

In this sample of 379 normal mothers, we found that a majority were most accurately rated at the *nonpermissive* end of our permissiveness scale. The social norm prevailing in these families was one of little tolerance about parent-directed aggression from children, although there was considerable variation in the severity with which this value was enforced.

It is of some interest to note that parents allowed somewhat more aggression from their sons than from their daughters, and that working-class parents were less permissive about aggression than parents at the middle-class level.

EFFECTS ON CHILDREN'S AGGRESSION

We turn now to a consideration of the child's aggressiveness, and will then address ourselves to the question: Does the amount of overt aggression a child displays at home have any relation to the values parents hold about aggression and the techniques they have employed in dealing with the child's aggression?]

THE SOURCES OF AGGRESSION IN THE HOME

What makes a child aggressive and quarrelsome? Among these youngsters, there were a few whose mothers could recall almost no angry behavior around home, but this was not the case for most of them. In spite of the general aura of prohibition, the majority of the youngsters had displayed many varieties and combinations of angry emotional response. Some children were more aggressive toward one parent than the other, some quarreled mainly with siblings and were pleasant toward the parents, some expressed themselves openly, and some relied chiefly on non-co-operation for their expression.

Nearly all the mothers gave fairly detailed reports of the typical forms of aggression their children displayed. It was thus possible to make a rating of *amount of aggression exhibited in the home* (excluding that toward siblings). . . .

These ratings can be compared with the mothers' reports of child-rearing practices to discover what characteristics of the latter were associated with high or low degree of reported aggression by the child.

The measures of the mothers' practices and the children's reactions were not independent. Both came from the mother herself. We cannot be certain in any particular case, therefore, that we have secured an unbiased report of the child's actual behavior. It is possible that some quality in a given mother—for instance, a sense of despair about her effectiveness as a child rearer—might lead her to give an exaggerated report about her child's aggressiveness. If we find, as we do, that mothers who felt little confidence in themselves had more (reportedly) aggressive children, we cannot tell whether this finding results from exaggerated reports by these mothers, or whether there was actually something about their behavior toward children that evoked more child aggressiveness. It would not be surprising if both were true, for the same qualities of her personality that influence her perception of the child may also induce a characteristic set of responses in him. . . .

Permissiveness and punishment. There is a constant tug of war in a child's behavior between the instigation and the inhibition of aggression. On one hand there are frustrations, threats, or other stimulating situations that tend to evoke aggressive action; on the other, there are warnings that inhibit aggression, and there are instigators to competing responses that the mother finds more desirable than aggression. One of the major research problems in the investigation of the socialization process is the discovery of just what kinds of maternal behavior fall into these classifications. What does the mother do that excites aggression in her child? What does she do that inhibits it?

The two scales of *permissiveness for aggression* and *severity of punishment for aggression* are the most obviously relevant dimensions to examine first. What should we expect of their relation to the reported amount of aggression the child shows in the home? Permissiveness, by definition, is an expression of the mother's willingness to have the child perform such acts. A simple and straight-forward prediction is that children with permissive mothers will be more aggressive than children with non-permissive mothers. Similarly with punishment: if we assume that this method of discipline establishes in the child a fear of behaving aggressively, then the more punitive the mother is, the more the child should avoid being aggressive. These two predictions fit together nicely. The scales for *permissiveness* and *punishment* are correlated—.46; that is, to some degree the more permissive mothers tended to be less severe in their punishment.

In point of fact, however, one of the predictions is right and the other is wrong. It is true that high *permissiveness* is associated with high aggression. The correlation is + .23. But *punishment* works just the other way: the more severe the punishment, the more aggression the child showed. The correlation is +.16. Both these correlations are small, but they are significant, and they are artificially reduced by the negative correlation between the permissiveness and punitiveness scales. Their true importance is substantially greater, as will be seen in the next section.

We interpret these findings in this way. When a mother adopts a permissive point of view about aggression, she is saying to her child, in effect, "Go ahead and express your angry emotions; don't worry about me." She gives few signals in advance that would lead the child to fear to be aggressive. On the contrary, her attitude is one of expectancy that he *will* be, and that such behavior is acceptable. It is scarcely surprising that the child tends to fulfill her expectations. The non-permissive mother, however, does something quite different. She has an attitude that aggression is wrong, that it is not to be tolerated, and an expectancy (often very subtly expressed) that the child will not behave in such undesirable ways. When he is aggressive, she does something to try to stop it—sometimes by punishment, sometimes by other means. He, also, fulfills his mother's expectations. This dimension of permissiveness, then, is a measure of the extent to which the mother prevents or stops aggression,

the non-permissive extreme being the most common.

Punishment is apparently a somewhat different matter. It is a kind of maternal behavior that occurs *after* the child's aggression has been displayed. The child has already enjoyed the satisfaction of hurting or of expressing anger—and so has had a reinforcement for aggressive action. But then he gets hurt in turn. He suffers further frustration. This should, and on the average does, incite him to more aggression. If the punishment is very severe, he may gradually learn to fear the consequences of his own actions, and the particular acts that get most repeatedly punished may be inhibited. But the total frustration is increased, and hence the total amount of aggression displayed in the home is higher. The dimension called *severity of punishment for aggression toward parents*, then, is one measure of the amount of painful frustration that is imposed on the child without direct guidance as to what would be a more acceptable form of behavior.

It is evident from this analysis that the mothers who were most permissive but also most severely punitive would have the most aggressive children; those who were most non-permissive but least punitive would have the least aggressive ones. As may be seen in Table VII:8, this was the case for both sexes. The children of mothers in the other two groups were in between.

These findings are similar to those of an earlier study (Sears *et al.*, 1953) in one respect. In that research, 40 children were observed in nursery school. The amount of aggression they showed there was compared with their mothers' reports of the severity of punishment for aggression that they suffered at home. In that study, too, high aggression was found to be associated with severe punishment, especially in the boys. There was some indication that the most severely pun-

TABLE VII:8 / PERCENTAGE OF HIGHLY AGGRESSIVE CHILDREN IN SUBGROUPS DIVIDED ACCORDING TO WHETHER MOTHER WAS IN UPPER OR LOWER HALF OF THE DISTRIBUTION ON PERMISSIVENESS AND SEVERITY OF PUNISHMENT FOR AGGRESSION TOWARD PARENTS.

	HIGHLY AGGRESSIVE *			
	BOYS		GIRLS	
SUBGROUP	PER CENT	N †	PER CENT	N
Low permissiveness and low punishment	3.7	27	13.3	30
Low permissiveness and high punishment	20.4	51	19.1	47
High permissiveness and low punishment	25.3	81	20.6	63
High permissiveness and high punishment	41.7	36	38.1	22

* By "*highly aggressive*" is meant that the child was rated by one or both raters as being in one of the two highest levels of aggression; these are scale points 4 and 5 in Table VII:7.

† Number of cases.

ished girls had become quite passive and inhibited. They displayed little activity of any kind, including aggression. When activity level was taken into consideration, they tended to be more like the boys, i.e., the more severely punished girls were *relatively* more aggressive than the less severely punished. It is interesting to note the similarity between the present findings and the earlier study, because in that research the measure of child aggression was entirely independent of the measures of child-rearing practices.

A word of caution must be said here about the interpretation of our results. We have shown that the mothers who punished their children most severely for aggression tended to report that their children displayed more than the average amount of aggression toward their parents. We have implied in our discussion that the maternal behavior *caused* the child behavior. It is entirely possible, of course, that the correlation could be explained as a parental response to the child's pre-existing temperament. That is, some children may have been born with a higher level of aggressive impulses than others, and the more aggressive the child naturally was, the more his parents were forced to punish him for aggression. We have chosen to interpret the matter the other way around: that punishment by the mother bred counter-aggression in the child. Our reason is that permissiveness was also associated with aggression, and we cannot see why aggression in the child should elicit permissiveness in the mother.

Our interpretation must be tentative, however, for the other explanation of the results cannot be ruled out without further research. It is quite possible, of course, that a circular process develops: the parent's punishment makes the child aggressive, this aggression leads to further punishment, and so on. Which came first, to set the whole thing in motion, is a problem we cannot solve with our existing information. . . .

Our findings suggest that the way for parents to produce a non-aggressive child is to make abundantly clear that aggression is frowned upon, and to stop aggression when it occurs, but to avoid punishing the child for his aggression. Punishment seems to have complex effects. While undoubtedly it often stops a particular form of aggression, at least momentarily, it appears to generate more hostility in the child and lead to further aggressive outbursts at some other time or place. Furthermore, when the parents punish—particularly when they employ physical

punishment—they are providing a living example of the use of aggression at the very moment they are trying to teach the child not to be aggressive. The child, who copies his parents in many ways, is likely to learn as much from this example of successful aggression on his parents' part as he is from the pain of punishment. Thus, the most peaceful home is one in which the mother believes aggression is not desirable and under no circumstances is ever to be expressed toward her, but who relies mainly on non-punitive forms of control. The homes where the children show angry, aggressive outbursts frequently are likely to be homes in which the mother has a relatively tolerant (or careless!) attitude toward such behavior, or where she administers severe punishment for it, or both.

These conclusions will certainly not astonish anyone who has worked professionally with children and their parents. Social workers, psychologists, teachers, psychiatrists, and probation officers have seen the twin effects of permissiveness and punishment many times in their own experience. What is important in the present report is the demonstration with this group of families. When one works with a few cases, particularly when most of them are quite deviant from the general population, one often has some uncertainty as to whether the relationships he sees would apply to a more normal group. Here is as normal a group of American mothers and their children as one could want for these purposes. The principles hold good.

There is another aspect to the matter worth emphasizing, however. The effects of these two aspects of control may already be known by professionals, but, even with a demonstration of this sort, they will not find ready acceptance by many others. There are two reasons.

First, *punishment is satisfying* to the parent. When a child aggresses toward his mother, he angers her, interferes with what she is doing, with her peace of mind, with her dignity and self-respect. Aggression hurts. It is meant to. And it produces in the mother the appropriate stimulation to retaliate in kind. Combined with her sense of obligation to rear her child properly, this retaliation comes out in a way she thinks of as "punishment"—that is, a form of aggression designed to have a good *training* effect on its recipient. As will be seen in a later chapter, many mothers have developed strong beliefs that punishment is a helpful method of control. (Sometimes it is, too.) These beliefs are essential to the peace of mind of such mothers. Without the conviction that "punishment is *good* for my child," these mothers would be forced to view their own behavior as retaliatory, aggressive, childish—in short, contemptible. This would not long provide a tolerable self-image. It is to be expected, then, that our demonstration of the deleterious effect of severe punishment of aggression will not be an easy finding for many people to swallow.

A second matter has to do with permissiveness. The difficulty grows out of the problem of punishment. During the last three decades there has developed, among the more literate and sensitive part of the American people, an uneasy recognition that punishment sometimes eliminates a few specific responses, but leaves a strongly hostile drive bottled up within the child. There is evidence to support this belief. With this consideration in mind, and an urgent desire to provide better mental hygiene for their children, not a few parents have developed what almost amounts to a cult of being permissive about aggression. Their aim is to avoid repression, to permit the child easier and freer expression of his impulses, and thus to prevent the development of aggression-anxiety, with its accompanying displacements, projections, and sometimes uncontrollable fantasies.

This aim is good, both for the children and the society they will compose, but whether it can be achieved by a high degree of permissiveness for expression of aggression toward the parents is a question. Does a permissive attitude, with the consequent freer expression of aggression, decrease the strength of projective fantasies? There is no indication in our own data that it does. Each of the children in the present study was tested with two 20-minute sessions of doll play. The children of the more non-permissive half of the group of mothers showed little if any more fantasy aggression under these circumstances than the children of the more permissive half. This finding is in sharp contrast to that with respect to punishment; the children of the more severely punishing mothers displayed quite significantly more fantasy aggression than the children of the less severely punishing ones (Levin and Sears, 1956). Permissiveness does not seem to decrease fantasy indications of aggressive impulses.

Permissiveness does increase the amount of aggression in the home, however, and it is worth considering what this does to the child himself. An angry child is not usually a happy child, nor is he one who receives affection and willing companionship from others. He is a source of discomfort to family and peers, and probably receives a certain amount of retaliation. He upsets his siblings, raises the level of frustration imposed on his parents, and inevitably has an increase, to some extent, of his own aggression-anxiety. There seems little advantage in all this, either to the child himself or to his parents.

These comments may seem to encourage a conclusion that parents will find it to their advantage to be somewhat non-permissive of aggression that is directed toward themselves. This can be a dangerous conclusion if the kind of permissiveness we mean is not clearly understood.

Therefore, let us be as clear as possible about the aspect of permissiveness we have in mind. A child is more likely to be non-aggressive if his parents hold the value that aggression is undesirable and should not occur. He is more likely to be non-aggressive if his parents prevent or stop the occurrence of aggressive outbursts instead of passively letting them go on, but prevent them by other means than punishment or threats of retaliation. If the parents' non-permissiveness takes the form of punishing the child (and thus leading the child to *expect* punishment) for aggressive behavior, then non-permissiveness will not have the effect of reducing the child's aggression. On the contrary, the instant that punishment enters, all the consequences of punishment that have been discussed earlier may be anticipated, including that of increasing the child's level of aggression.

One cautionary point: we are not suggesting that parents should band together in omnipotent suppression of every justifiable angry response the child makes. The right to be angry without fear or guilt is as inalienable as any other, and more important than some. But since anger interferes with constructive action in the face of many, if not most, problem situations that the child and his family face, parents are understandably anxious to keep it within reasonable bounds; and our interest has been in showing what parental actions are likely to have the desired effects and what actions are likely to have undesired side-effects.

22 / EFFECT OF CHILDREARING PRACTICES ON DEVELOPMENT OF DIFFERENTIAL COGNITIVE ABILITIES[1] / ELIZABETH BING[*]

INDIVIDUAL DIFFERENCES IN COGNI-tive development have come to be considered the result of interactions between a child's life experiences and the set of genes with which he has been endowed. Relations have been found between cognitive abilities and perceptual and cognitive style on one side and personality traits on the other side, and some investigators have made efforts to identify antecedent conditions in the home which might be responsible for differences in children's personality as well as cognitive development. Thus "democratic homes" (1, 2), "maternal acceleration" (18), and a "warm, positive family atmosphere" (17) have been reported to increase the rate of growth of children's intelligence, especially verbal ability. Results of investigations of the effect of institutionalization and prolonged hospitalization of infants, summarized by McCarthy (15, pp. 584-585), uniformly indicate retardation in language development. On the other hand, there has been suggestive evidence that certain conditions favor disproportionately the development of verbal ability and possibly impede the development of nonverbal skills, like numerical and spatial ability. Suggested as antecedents for such differential development in favor of verbal ability were "growth restricting" childrearing practices (24), such as parental overlimitation and excessive control, "maternal overprotection" (14), "emphasis on verbal accomplishment" (13), and a "demanding discipline with emphasis on academic achievement" (11). Similarly, overanxious discipline (11) and tense parent-child relationships (10) were postulated to be responsible for low nonverbal, especially spatial, ability in children. While the consistently found superiority of boys over girls in spatial ability may be considered innate (5, 6, 8, 9), there has been suggestive evidence that this may be the result of differences in roles assigned to males and females in our culture (4, 7, 19, 22).

Most of these studies, while yielding intriguing leads, failed to measure children's verbal and nonverbal abilities with relatively "pure" tests. Also, these studies investigated primarily parents' present-day childrearing behavior and did not attempt to investigate the very early mother-child relationships. Furthermore, the sole measure of parents' behavior used was the interview of the parent.

In the present study, specifically designed tests were used to measure children's verbal and nonverbal abilities, such as spatial and numerical, as well as their total IQ in order to identify groups of children with discrepant abilities. An effort was made to investigate not only present, but also early childrearing practices as far as they may be assumed to be antecedents to differential cognitive development in children. And, finally, the mother's actual mode of interaction with the child was observed in a fairly structured situation.

From the theoretical considerations and available research findings, it was assumed that childrearing practices which stimulate, reward, and encourage verbal or nonverbal abilities should increase either one of these abilities and that fostering dependency should favor verbal ability while at the same time depressing nonverbal ability, whereas fostering independence should have the opposite effect. While not consistent over all age groups, some studies indicate female superiority in verbal and male superiority in numerical ability (12). It was therefore thought worthwhile to test the hypothesis that emphasis on sex-typing should reinforce verbality as a sex-appropriate trait in girls and spatial and numerical ability in boys.

An interview and questionnaire were designed to obtain information on the variables which were assumed to be more strongly represented in high verbal or in high nonverbal groups, and the following predictions were made:

[1] This paper is based on a doctoral dissertation submitted to Stanford University. The writer wishes to express her appreciation to Dr. Lucy Rau and Dr. Eleanor Maccoby for their help and generous assistance with this project.

[*] Elizabeth Bing, Effect of childrearing practices on development of differential cognitive abilities, *Child Develpm.*, 1963, 34, 631-648. Copyright: 1963, by the Society for Research in Child Development, Inc. Reprinted by permission of the Society and the author.

148

[Nine predictions, five about verbal ability, two about nonverbal ability, and two about both, in relation to mothers' behaviors fostering dependency and independence, were made to be checked from interview and questionnaire data. Seven predictions were made relevant to observation sessions in which the child did both verbal and performance tasks with the mother present and able to interact. These predictions will become apparent in the context of the results and discussion, hence are not detailed here. Ed]

METHODS AND PROCEDURES

SUBJECTS. The subjects of the sample consisted of 60 mothers who had children who were in the fifth grade and had discrepant cognitive abilities. The selection was made from a total of 1214 children representing the universe of fifth grade children in the public school system of Redwood City and San Carlos, two communities in the San Francisco Bay Area.[2] The basic discrepancy that was of interest for the purpose of the study was the comparison of high verbal children with low verbal children of similar IQ, the complementary nonverbal abilities being either spatial or numerical ability.

Verbal and nonverbal mental abilities were partly assessed on the basis of results of the Thurstone's SRA Primary Mental Abilities for ages 7 to 11 (Form AH) which was administered to all fifth grade children in their classrooms. The scores obtained by each child on the verbal, spatial, and numerical parts of this test were supplemented by scores from the Iowa Achievement Test or the California Mental Maturity Test. Cases with total PMA scores below 125, cases with visual or hearing impairment, cases from foreign language homes, and cases whose "high" ability was below the population median, and those whose "low" ability was above the population median were dropped from the sample.

With this selection procedure the following four major groups could be established: 16 high verbal boys, 16 low verbal boys, 12 high verbal girls, and 16 low verbal girls. The contrasting ability was spatial ability for one half and numerical ability for the other half of these groups with the exception of the group of the 12 high verbal girls. Eight of these were low in space

and four were low in number.[3] Cases of girls with high verbal, low number ability were surprisingly difficult to find.[4]

Only four cases which should have been included in the final sample of 60 were lost and replaced by comparable cases. In two of these cases the experimental conditions were spoiled by the presence of the fathers, and in two cases the mothers were not available for the interview.

The groups were fairly well equated on "general intelligence," as measured by total PMA score; analysis of variance did not reveal any significant differences between means for the groups. Furthermore, differences between group averages with respect to socioeconomic status of the family and with respect to parents' education were not significant.

MEASUREMENT OF ANTECEDENT VARIABLES

Questionnaire. The mother was asked to fill in a questionnaire which consisted of 20 groups of questions referring to factual material in relation to the mother's caretaking activity of the child, the child's first verbal and nonverbal accomplishments, kinds of toys, number of story-books, and the mother's as well as her husband's interest in reading and manual activities. The mother was also asked to estimate age levels at which she thought the average child would have usually learned a variety of listed behaviors, some of these based on Winterbottom's scale (23), such as feeding himself, keeping room tidy, shopping for own clothing, crossing busy street, etc.

On the basis of a previously constructed rating scale, a total of 16 dimensions representing possible antecedent variables was rated. Some of the scales could be objectively scored according to a specified point system; in cases where the answer could be given in numerical form, the number was regarded as the score, transformed into a standard score in accordance with the total frequency distribution; for other scales, five fairly specific levels were indicated ranging from a high level of 5 to a low level of 1.

Three raters were used for the ratings. They did not know to which group the case belonged and assignments were made in such a way that

---

[2] The cases were selected from a larger pool of cases which had already been sampled for a more comprehensive research project on correlates of differential cognitive abilities in children (16).

[3] An analysis of the data according to whether the compensating ability was spatial or numerical was made, and results are reported in the doctoral dissertation on which this article is based.

[4] The reasons for this are to be found in Maccoby and Rau (16).

each one of the three raters double rated at least 10 cases with each of the other two raters.

Interview. The interviews with the mothers were semi-structured with open-ended questions similar to the type developed by Sears, Maccoby, and Levin (20) and by Bandura and Walters (3). It was attempted to cover in the interviews the child's early history as well as the present with respect to the mother's behavior regarding her relationship with the child, verbal stimulation provided by her, fostering dependency or independence in the child, verbal freedom allowed, permission for object experimentation, emphasis on sociability, academic achievement and sex-typing, and restrictiveness. The interviews lasted from 1 to 2 hours, were tape recorded, and conducted by one graduate student in psychology and the author. Neither of the two interviewers knew to which group the mother belonged.[5]

Three graduate students in psychology and the author rated the interviews from the tape recordings according to preconstructed rating scales comprising 41 dimensions. Most of these scales were 5-point scales, specifying five different levels of behavior or attitudes. All 60 interviews were rated by various combinations of two of the four raters, and none of the raters knew to which group the case belonged.

Interaction situation. Either before or after the interview, the child was called in and the mother was asked to read some verbal problem questions to the child, and, following the completion of this task, the child was requested by the observer to perform two nonverbal tasks.

While seemingly the child's performance was the focus of attention, the situation was devised to obtain firsthand observational data on the mother's mode of interaction with the child. The situation was so constructed that the mothers could demonstrate a great variability of behavior, from no intervention at all to a high degree of helping, pressuring, or disapproving types of behavior.

For the verbal task, a comprehension type test was used. It contained five problem situations which were rather difficult for 10-year-old children to answer satisfactorily. The questions were also worded in such a way that several solutions were possible. Two of the questions required the child to give reasons to explain a fact; the rea-

[5] One of the investigators engaged in the larger research project distributed the cases between the two interviewers in such a way that each had an approximately equal representation of cases from each group in her interview sample.

sons being manifold, it gave the mother an opportunity to prompt, encourage, or pressure the child to improve his answer. (Example: Why should children not be out in the street alone at night?)

The first of the nonverbal tasks consisted of putting together a complicated jigsaw puzzle (commercially available, Kwazy Quilt, Tryne, No. 114). The child had to fit the colored pieces together into a pattern following a model. At the same time, the mother was provided with a model which showed the placement of all pieces more clearly than the child's model did, thus putting the mother in a position where she was able to help and could do so as much as she wanted to and in whatever way she chose. The other nonverbal task was the Healy Picture Completion Test, in which the child was requested to put the block with the best fitting picture detail in a large picture with recessed spaces for the blocks. While there is always one "best" solution, there are also other adequate solutions. This situation provided the mother again with the opportunity to assist or pressure the child for improvement of his solution. The two performance tasks gave the mother an opportunity for helping the child not only with verbal means, but also with a variety of physical ways of assisting, like actually moving pieces into place or handing the appropriate piece to the child.

In order to have the interaction situations as comparable as possible, the following procedures were adhered to:

After mother and child were comfortably seated side by side at the table opposite to the observer, the following instructions were given:
"Since (child's name) happens to be in this project, we know a little bit how he is learning at school. However, we know very little about how he and children in general are learning in the home. We have here a number of fairly hard tasks. Let's suppose these are problems that (child's name) has brought home and is supposed to solve. I would like you to have (child's name) do these tasks in whatever way you think would give him a chance to do his best. Here are some questions that I would like you to read to (child's name) and later on we have some puzzles to do. Now pretend that I am not here and go ahead as you would at home."

The observer handed to the mother the question sheet which contained five problem tasks. After mother and child had finished these tasks, the observer asked the child to do a puzzle with the help of a model, and the mother was given the more clearly marked model; both were told that the mother's copy made the solution of the problem easier. After completion of the puzzle or after 10 minutes, whichever was earlier, the Healy Picture Completion Test was presented with standardized instructions. After 10 minutes or after completion of this task, the observer commended the child for his efforts and ended the session. Whenever during the procedure the mother asked the observer any question about her participation in the situation, he said: "You can enter into this as much or as little as you feel like." The whole procedure usually lasted about half an hour, and most children seemed to like the novelty of the situation.

The mother's behavior with the child during the verbal and nonverbal tasks was analyzed according to pre-established categories which were thought to represent different degrees and manners of stimulating and helping the child with his tasks. The following nine categories could be distinguished for both verbal and performance tasks: Focusing, Approval, Encouragement, Prompting, Giving answers (instead of letting child answer), Pressure for improvement, Disapproval, Withholding help, and Helping after request from child. One category covering the number of questions the mother asked the experimenter was devised as yielding a possible measure of the mother's dependency needs, or at least her need for more structure. Three additional categories were established for the nonverbal tasks, dealing with the mother's physical help-giving behavior, such as the mother's own handling of puzzle pieces, showing of her own copy to child, and the time elapsed until the mother made her first help-giving response. This resulted in a total of 22 categories.

The scoring was done by the person who conducted the interview. For five cases of the sample the alternate interviewer was also present and scored the behavior independently so that the reliability of the scoring was established on the basis of these five sample cases in addition to five pretesting cases which were double scored.

RELIABILITIES OF RATINGS. As a measure of the reliabilities of the ratings for the questionnaire and the interview, the percentage of cases with perfect agreement between two raters and the percentage of cases with 1 and with more than 1 point difference was computed for every scale. Perfect agreement of ratings ranged from 62 to 100 per cent of the cases for the questionnaire scales and from 48 to 88 per cent for the interview scales. Agreement within 1 point ranged

from 89 to 100 per cent for questionnaire scales and from 87 to 100 per cent for the interview scales.

The percentage of cases showing perfect agreement between two scorers for the various categories of the interaction situation ranged from 50 to 100, and agreement within 1 point ranged from 80 to 100 per cent.

CORRELATIONAL ANALYSIS AND COMBINATION OF VARIABLES. From the questionnaire, the interview, and the interaction situation, a total of 79 variables was obtained. In cases where variables were assumed to belong to the same complex of behavior, but to represent different aspects of it, the scores of these variables were combined if the variables also actually showed a correlation of at least .26 which corresponds to the .05 level of significance for our sample of 60 cases. As a result of these combinations, the 16 questionnaire and 41 interview variables were reduced to a total of 34 variables and the 22 interaction categories or variables to a total of 15.

The differences between the means of all variables for the high verbal children as compared to the low verbal children and for the high verbal boys and girls as compared to the low verbal boys and girls had to be tested for significance. This was done by the t technique for testing differences between independent means for small samples. For two variables showing extremely skewed distributions, the chi square method for testing the significance of the differences between the distributions for two contrast groups was used.

RESULTS

INTERVIEW AND QUESTIONNAIRE. Of the 34 single and combined variables of the interview and questionnaire, 10[6] were found to distinguish significantly between high and low verbal groups (see Table 1).

ANTECEDENTS OF VERBAL ABILITY.

1. *Verbal stimulation and interest shown by mother.* For the early childhood period, a combination of measures relating to the child's early verbal stimulation (amount of playtime mother had with infant, verbal stimulation of infant, mother's responsiveness to child's early questions, taking young child on outings, early reading to child; tutoring before school; interest

[6] Three additional variables distinguished between high and low number groups.

TABLE 1 / SIGNIFICANCE OF DIFFERENCES BETWEEN MEANS OF HIGH VERBAL AND LOW VER-
BAL GROUPS FOR BOYS ($N = 32$) AND GIRLS ($N = 28$) AND SEXES COMBINED ($N = 60$) ON ALL
VARIABLES DISTINGUISHING BETWEEN THESE GROUPS.

	BOYS			GIRLS			SEXES COMBINED		
	HIGH	LOW	p	HIGH	LOW	p	HIGH	LOW	p
INTERVIEW AND QUESTIONNAIRE VARIABLES									
Early verbal stimulation	44.1	34.4	<.001	38.9	33.6	ns	41.9	34.0	<.001
Memory for early accomplishments	19.1	14.4	>.05*	16.0	12.6	ns	17.8	13.5	.02*
Number of story books	36.3	23.9	>.05	37.0	24.2	ns	36.6	24.1	<.05
Punishment for poor speech	5.4	5.8	ns	4.7	6.1	<.05	5.1	6.0	ns
Participation in meal conversations	6.4	4.3	<.01	6.4	6.1	ns	6.4	5.2	<.05
Criticism for academic achievement	7.6	6.4	<.05	6.7	5.3	<.05	7.2	5.8	<.01
Permissiveness for object experimentation and lack of restrictions	17.6	22.2	<.05	18.5	15.9	ns	18.0	19.0	ns
Anxiety arousal in cautiousness training	4.9	3.9	>.05	4.3	3.8	ns	4.6	3.8	<.05
Father's reading time	12.0	15.6	ns	14.1	6.3	<.001	12.9	11.0	ns
Father's strictness	5.3	4.4	ns	6.1	4.6	ns	5.6	4.5	.05*
SITUATION VARIABLES									
Helping on verbal and non-verbal tasks†	404.7	386.7	ns	438.0	388.1	<.01	419.0	387.4	<.01
Helping on nonverbal tasks‡	157.7	142.7	<.05	166.3	143.9	<.01	161.4	143.3	<.01
Approval on nonverbal tasks	47.9	48.4	ns	56.2	47.9	<.05	51.4	48.1	ns
Focusing on verbal tasks	48.4	48.4	ns	55.0	49.3	<.01	51.3	48.8	ns
Pressure for improvement on nonverbal tasks	47.6	50.7	ns	54.8	47.2	<.05	50.5	47.8	ns
Pressure for improvement on verbal and nonverbal tasks	99.6	99.7	ns	105.2	96.1	<.05	102.0	97.9	ns
Help after request	3.0	3.3	ns	6.1	1.7	<.01	4.3	2.5	<.05
Child's bids for help	4.1	3.7	ns	6.8	2.3	<.01	5.3	3.0	<.05
Withholding help and disapproval	4.6	3.3	ns	4.4	1.9	<.05*	4.5	2.6	<.05*
Mother questions observer	2.2	1.6	ns	3.1	1.7	<.05	2.6	1.6	>.01

NOTE.—All tests are one-tailed unless p value is followed by an asterisk.

† Combination of eight categories: focusing, prompting and encouragement, approval, giving answers on both verbal and on nonverbal tasks.

‡ Combination of three categories: focusing, prompting and encouragement, and giving answers on nonverbal tasks.

shown in child's good speech habits) differentiated on a highly significant level between high verbal and low verbal groups for boys and for sexes combined as predicted, $p < .001$ in favor of more verbal stimulation during infancy occurring with high verbal than with low verbal groups. While for the girls, taken by themselves, the mean of this variable was higher for the high verbal than for the low verbal group, the difference was not large enough to be significant.

Using the number of memories that a mother was able to report on her baby's early verbal and nonverbal accomplishments as a measure of importance attached to these and as an indirect measure of attention given to the child, it was found that this variable, also, was significantly higher for high verbal groups, if boys and sexes combined were considered. However, the difference, while in the expected direction, did not reach significance for girls.

For the period after school age, the specific measures hypothesized to differentiate between HiV and LoV groups were (a) number of story books and (b) use of encyclopedia and "word-games" played by family. Only with regard to story books, the hypothesis was confirmed for boys and sexes combined.

Caution is needed in interpreting the higher

number of story books in the HiV group as an antecedent to the child's high verbal ability. The possession of a greater number of books by age 10 may be a consequence of the child's high verbal interest and ability. It is interesting to note that Milner (17) found a greater number of story books among her high verbal 6-year olds, an age level at which being exposed to story books can be considered as an antecedent condition to a greater extent, since the child's reading ability has hardly developed.

2. *Verbal freedom.* Two of the seven scales assumed to measure different aspects of verbal freedom differentiated significantly between groups as predicted. Punishment for poor speech differentiated significantly in favor of LoV as compared to HiV girls, and amount of meal conversation distinguished HiV from LoV groups significantly for boys and for sexes combined. None of the differences on the measures dealing with permissiveness or punishment for verbal aggression, permissiveness to listen and participate in adult conversation, and freedom for democratic discussion to discuss "adult" topics was significant.[7]

3. *Emphasis on academic achievement.* The hypothesis that verbal ability should be associated with emphasis on academic achievement was confirmed when criticism for poor academic achievement was taken as a separate measure, but not for a combination of this measure with rewarding academic achievement, level of schooling desired by parents, and amount of present tutoring. Criticism for poor academic achievement, taken by itself, discriminated significantly between HiV and LoV groups for boys, girls, and for sexes combined, the means of criticism of poor academic achievement being higher for all high verbal groups.

4. *Sex-role differentiation and parent's own verbal interest.* It was hypothesized that, for girls, verbal ability should be positively associated with mother's emphasis on the girl's adopting a feminine role and sex-appropriate behavior and with father's relative strictness and that for both sexes it would be associated with like-sex parent's amount of time spent reading

to the child. The hypothesis with respect to father's strictness was partly confirmed; significant results were obtained though not predicted for girls with respect to father's reading time. None of the other variables of this cluster distinguished significantly between groups.

While mothers of the high verbal group girls reported on the average that their husbands were stricter than themselves, this difference failed to reach significance. However, further analysis of the data indicated that, for those of the HiV girls whose low ability was space, the difference was significant at the .05 level, the stricter father being associated with the HiV girl group.

One assumption had been that the mother's perception of the father as the "Master" would enhance the masculinity of the male role and implicitly the feminine role of the girl in the family and might reveal the importance that the mother attaches to appropriate sex-typing and thereby strengthening girls' verbal ability. This was borne out with respect to the HiV-LoS girls and their contrast group.

The fact that father's reading time discriminated highly in favor of high verbal ability only for girls and not for boys was just as surprising as the fact that mother's reading time did not differentiate between any of the groups. The latter fact may be due to lower dispersion of scores of reading time for mothers. The assumption that with respect to verbal and nonverbal ability children would model themselves after the like-sex parent was not borne out. Many of the mothers' behavior patterns and attitudes that were investigated through the interview seemed to influence boys' cognitive development, but not girls'; on the other hand, of the very few behavior patterns pertaining to fathers that were evaluated, two proved to be significantly associated with girls' cognitive development. This points to the possible importance of the influence of the opposite-sex parent on the child's cognitive development. Such an influence is hard to account for in terms of our present knowledge of personality development, but merits further investigation.

ANTECEDENTS OF NONVERBAL ABILITY

1. *Nonverbal stimulation and freedom of exploration.* It was hypothesized that nonverbal ability should be associated with opportunity and freedom for exploration and object experimentation at preschool age and at present. This hypothesis was confirmed with respect to boys

[7] It appeared, in retrospect, that the variable "democratic discussion" related less to the freedom to talk than to the child's freedom not to have to join in the family's undertakings and to be free from authoritarian family control. This variable may then reflect a certain aspect of independence granted to the child. An analysis of the data comparing HiV-LoN with LoV-HiN children revealed that the HiN group was higher than the LoN group on this variable, $p < .10$ for a two-tailed test.

for a combination of the measures of permissiveness for object experimentation at preschool age, availability to child of tools, gadgets, and objects for experimentation at present, and lack of restrictions indoors and outdoors. It was not confirmed for the measures of number of toys at preschool age and strictness of time schedules.

While the number of toys that children have before school age did not seem to be a significant antecedent to nonverbal cognitive development, the freedom the children have in playing with these toys and in exploring their environment was the condition that discriminated significantly between HiV and LoV groups of boys, the greater freedom being associated with the low verbal boys who are high either in space or number.

2. *Sex-role differentiation and parent's own nonverbal interest.* It was hypothesized that nonverbal ability should be positively associated for boys with mother's emphasis on the boy's adopting a masculine role and sex-appropriate behavior and for both sexes with parents' time spent with child in arts, crafts, hobbies, and do-it-yourself activities. None of these hypotheses was confirmed.

DEPENDENCY-INDEPENDENCE. It was hypothesized that verbal ability was associated with mother's behavior fostering dependency and nonverbal ability with behavior fostering independence. Dependency-fostering behavior was measured by (a) encouragement of emotional dependency and lack of punishment for dependency; (b) permissiveness for instrumental dependency; (c) anxiety arousal in cautiousness training; (d) continuity of mother-child relationship; and (e) continuity of caretaking activity. One of these five measures, anxiety arousal in cautiousness training, differentiated between the high and low verbal group, greater anxiety arousal being associated with the HiV group for boys and sexes combined.

The assumption was thus borne out, at least for boys, that the mother who tried to impress the child more with the potential dangers of the environment would make the child more anxious, insecure, and dependent and thus less capable of dealing with cognitive tasks presumably requiring more independence, such as arithmetic and spatial relations.

Behavior fostering independence was measured by (a) earliness of age at which mothers expect the achievement of independence by child in different areas; (b) pressure for respon-

sibilities; (c) permissiveness to spend allowance freely; and (d) a combined scale of permissiveness for independence, pressure for independence, and lack of protectiveness. None of these four measures distinguished between High verbal and Low verbal groups as predicted.[8]

The result that some of the variables, like pressure for responsibility and pressure for independence, which were considered to belong to the cluster of variables fostering independence did not differentiate between the groups is probably due to the fact that there is no linear relation between these variables and independence. An excess of pressure for mature behavior may lead to more manifestations of dependency. Similarly, permissiveness for dependency on the part of the parent does not necessarily show a linear relation with dependency behavior in the child. It may also be useful in future studies to distinguish between "independence" in the sense of self-help and "independence" in the sense of self-determination. Conditions which foster dependency or independence are varied, subtle, and extremely difficult to measure through one standardized interview. It might very well be that the observational method proved to be more sensitive and apt to pick up differences between mothers with respect to the dependency-independence dimension.

INTERACTION SITUATION

Six of the seven hypotheses were essentially confirmed. One hypothesis was not only confirmed, but the opposite of the stated hypothesis was confirmed (*see* Table 1).

1. The hypothesis that high verbal mothers should be more active in all categories of help-

---

[8] Further analysis of the dependency-independence variables according to whether the compensating ability was space or number revealed that two of the measures of this dimension, while not distinguishing between high verbal and low verbal groups as a whole, distinguished between HiV-LoN and LoV-HiN groups. This was similar to the findings with respect to the variable "democratic discussion" or freedom from authoritarian family control. Greater permissiveness for instrumental dependency was significantly associated with the HiV-LoN group, and the objectively scaled score for the earliness of independence age was also significantly associated with this group. In retrospect, it appeared that this scale was rather a measure of pressure for achievement than of genuine expectancy of independence in the sense of self-determination. In contrast to the mothers of the HiV-LoN children, the LoV-HiN group mothers expected independence or, rather, achievement later, but tended on the average to let the child struggle more by himself with difficult tasks.

giving behavior (focusing, encouragement, approval, prompting and answering problems for child) was confirmed, at least when these categories were combined. The differences were significant at the < .01 level for girls and for sexes combined. However, the differences were not significant for boys alone. When the help-giving behavior on the nonverbal tasks alone was considered, the differences in favor of the high verbal mothers were highly significant for the same groups, in addition to a difference at the < .05 level for the boys. On the other hand, if one considers some of the help-giving activities on the verbal tasks alone, they did not yield significant differences. This was true for approval and for the combination of focusing and prompting and giving answers, where the differences for the means were for all groups in the predicted direction, but did not reach significance. However, with respect to helping the child focus on the verbal task as a separate variable, the mothers of HiV girls were significantly higher on this behavior category than the mothers of the LoV girls.

2. The hypothesis that high verbal group mothers should be higher in pressure for improvement was confirmed for HiV girls as compared to LoV girls. This held true for nonverbal tasks as well as for the combination of verbal and nonverbal tasks, but not for verbal tasks alone.

3. The hypothesis that high verbal group mothers should give help more often after request was confirmed for girls and sexes combined. There were no differences for any of the boys' groups. The number of times a mother helped a child after request was partly a function of the child's asking for help. It appeared that the child who had learned to expect an answer, at least intermittently, would ask more questions. The child's asking questions in the observed interaction situation may then be partly a measure of the mother's past (unobserved) behavior in interaction with the child; this category may thus reflect not so much temporary behavior specific to the experimental situation, but rather usual interaction patterns between mother and child.

Considering, then, differences in the children's behavior, the high verbal groups of girls and sexes combined asked for help significantly more often than the respective low verbal groups. No significant differences were found for boys. An analysis of these data by sex indicated that the total group of girls, on the average, did not ask their mothers for help significantly more often than the boys.

4. The hypothesis that high nonverbal mothers should disapprove and withhold help more often was not only not confirmed, but the observed differences were significant in the opposite direction. High verbal group mothers disapproved and withheld help more often. This was true for girls and sexes combined, while the difference for boys was in the same direction but failed to reach significance. On this measure of "negative" interaction, just as on "help after request," a measure of "positive" interaction, high verbal mothers scored significantly higher. It appears, therefore, that what is important seems to be the degree of interaction between mother and child rather than its content.

5. As predicted, high verbal group mothers asked the observer more questions. This was true for girls' mothers with respect to HiV as compared to LoV groups. Again, no significant differences were found for boys' mothers. It was thought that the mother's need to ask questions about procedure would be a measure of one aspect of her dependency needs. That this measure yielded significant results for girls' mothers, but not for boys' mothers, came as a surprise, but was consistent with results for the other categories where mother's behavior was found to be significant mainly for girls' discrepancy groups.

6. The hypothesis that high verbal group mothers should give more physical help was confirmed when the chi square method of analyzing the data instead of the comparison of means was used. Twelve of the 32 LoV group mothers abstained completely from giving any physical help as compared to four of the 28 HiV group mothers ($X^2 = 4.19$; $df = 1$), a difference significant at the < .05 level for a one-tailed test.

7. The hypothesis that on performance tasks HiV mothers should give help sooner was also confirmed, when they were compared with LoV mothers for the whole sample as to whether they waited 30 seconds or less (8 HiV and 6 LoV), 30 seconds to 5 minutes (15 HiV and 12 LoV), or more than 5 minutes (5 HiV and 14 LoV) before helping physically. The difference was significant ($X^2 = 4.73$; $df = 2$) at the .05 level for a one-tailed test.

The pattern of behavior of the high verbal girls' mothers was thus quite different from the behavior of the low verbal group. The HiV mothers showed on the average more positive and negative interaction with the child, the child asking more often for help and getting the help part of the time. Most of the help was given without being requested by the child, and these mothers helped their children, especially on the performance tasks, in all categories of helping behavior. Their motivation might very well have been their eagerness for the child to do well on the tasks, since these were also the mothers who, on the average, pressured their children more for improvement of responses than the mothers of the high nonverbal children. While thus attempting to help their children, these mothers of high verbal children revealed themselves to be rather controlling and pressuring while the mothers of the high nonverbal group left their children more on their own and interfered less with their responses.

COMPARISON OF RESULTS OF INTERVIEW AND INTERACTION SITUATION

Comparing the results of the interview with those of the interaction situation, it appeared that the interview variables that distinguished significantly between groups did so mainly for boys, while the observation situation variables did so mainly for girls.

Several possible explanations for this discrepancy have to be considered. One is the difference in means and variability for the whole group of girls as compared to the whole group of boys. Comparing all the help-giving activities in the interaction situation, one finds that the means on these variables were consistently, though not significantly, higher for the girls than for the boys. The lower means for boys, in addition to smaller range and less variability of the help-giving variables, could partly explain the fact that the situation measures failed to distinguish between the boys' discrepant abilities groups. (An observation of a father and son interaction might have been more revealing of differences between boys' groups.) However, this explanation does not hold for the interview. The interview variables which differentiated the ability groups for boys and not for girls did not show consistent differences in means and variability.

Another possible explanation for the difference between results from interview variables and situation variables may be found in the time factor. Most interview variables refer to the child's early history, while the situation variables refer essentially to present behavior. Could one assume that it is at an early age that child training practices influence boys' cognitive development but that girls' cognitive development is differentially enhanced by parents' attitudes and behavior at a later time during childhood? This would contra-

dict what we know about the relative stability of specific abilities (21). Yet, one cannot exclude the possibility that the significant antecedents during infancy for the development of verbal ability may not be identical for boys and girls. Kagan, also, has suggested that different agents may be responsible for the degree of development of different cognitive styles in boys and in girls (10). It may be that early verbal stimulation is more decisive for the development of verbal ability in boys. In this connection, it is interesting to note that Levy (14), who found maternal overprotection associated with high verbal ability, had almost exclusively boys in his sample.

There is one further reason that might be considered for the differential significance of the interview and situation data for boys and for girls. The validity of the interview as a measurement may be greater for boys than for girls. If it can be assumed that mothers feel more responsible about the development of their daughters than their sons (partly because of a culturally accepted feeling, "like father, like son"), then one might expect more defensiveness on the part of the mothers of the LoV girls than of LoV sons. While mothers were quite aware of their children's verbal ability, since it is reflected in reading ability and vocabulary, they were less aware of their children's spatial ability. There was therefore no reason for the mothers of the HiV-LoSpace girls defensively to enhance the role of nonverbal stimulation provided for their daughters. Yet, being often aware of their daughters' low verbal ability, some of the LoV girls' mothers may have tended to exaggerate the verbal stimulation they gave to them.

At the present time, there is not enough evidence to explain definitely the lack of more complete consistency between the results from the interview and the interaction situation.

IMPLICATION OF RESULTS

Considering all the results which indicate that the HiV groups have received more and earlier help, physical or verbal, on nonverbal tasks as well as verbal tasks, a possible question arises about interpreting the mother's behavior as an antecedent to the child's cognitive functioning. One might argue that mothers of the HiV group whose children are low in space or number have developed a pattern of helping their children more on performance tasks because their children showed more difficulties with such problems. However, one of our nonverbal tasks, the

Healy Picture Completion, did not involve spatial ability. Furthermore, if the child's ability had consistently determined the mother's degree of help-giving behavior, the mothers of high verbal children would have presented verbal tasks to them without any admonishment, realizing that their children have little difficulty with verbal tasks. Nevertheless, mothers of HiV girls scored significantly higher on "focusing" their children's attention on these verbal tasks than mothers of LoV girls.

We therefore felt entitled to interpret the mother's behavior in the interaction situation as a sample of the kind of behavior which in the past was antecedent to the child's cognitive development.

The data do not support the contention that a child develops a particular ability because his parents are selectively training him in it. Rather, the high level of interaction between mother and child must produce some intervening conditions which enhance verbal more than number or spatial performance.

The essential condition for the development of verbality is probably the close relationship with an adult, and verbal ability is fostered by a high degree of interaction between mother and child. In contrast, the development of number ability requires, above all, concentration and ability to carry through a task by oneself. Similarly, spatial ability is probably developed through interaction with the physical rather than the interpersonal environment. A marked pattern of help seeking and help giving interferes with the development of an independent and self-reliant attitude, which may be the intervening condition for a high degree of development of spatial and numerical ability.

It seems therefore likely that the mother of a child in the HiV-Low nonverbal group is much more emotionally involved with her child, having given more attention and stimulation to the baby, but tending to pressure, restrict, and control the child more later than the low verbal, high nonverbal mother.

SUMMARY

It was the purpose of this study to examine the differences in mothers' childrearing practices and in their behavior with their children in relation to differences in children's cognitive development.

The subjects were 60 mothers of fifth grade children of either high or low verbal ability with similar total IQ, the compensating nonverbal ability being spatial or numerical ability.

A comparison of the high with the low verbal groups on an interview, questionnaire, and a mother-child interaction situation showed the following significant differences:

In accordance with predictions, high verbal group mothers (whose children were low in either spatial or number ability) gave their children more verbal stimulation during infancy and early childhood, remembered a greater number of their children's early accomplishments, let their children participate more in meal conversations, punished them less for poor speech, bought more story books for them, and criticized them more for poor academic achievement, used anxiety arousal more in cautiousness training, showed less permissiveness with object experimentation, had more restrictions, and perceived their husbands as stricter than themselves. Contrary to predictions, not the mother's but the father's reading time was very significantly higher for the high verbal girls' group.

With respect to the interaction session, as predicted, high verbal group mothers were found to be higher than low verbal mothers in all categories of helping behavior, in pressure for improvement, in giving help after request by child, in asking the observer more questions, in giving more physical help, and in giving such help sooner. Contrary to the prediction, high verbal mothers were also higher on withholding help and on disapproval than the low verbal mothers.

The findings led to the general conclusion that discrepant verbal ability is fostered by a close relationship with a demanding and somewhat intrusive mother, while discrepant nonverbal abilities are enhanced by allowing the child a considerable degree of freedom to experiment on his own.

REFERENCES

1. BALDWIN, A. L. *Behavior and development in childhood.* Dryden, 1955.

2. BALDWIN, A. L., KALHORN, J., & BREESE, F. H. Patterns of parent behavior. *Psychol. Monogr.,* 1945, *58,* No. 3 (Whole No. 268).

3. BANDURA, A., & WALTERS, R. H. *Adolescent aggression.* Ronald, 1959.

4. BIERI, J. Parental identification, acceptance of authority, and within sex differences in cognitive behavior. *J. abnorm. soc. Psychol.,* 1960, *60,* 76-79.

5. BIERI, J., BRADBURN, W. M., & GALINSKY, M. D. Sex differences in perceptual behavior. *J. Pers.,* 1958, *26,* 1-12.

6. EMMET, W. C. Evidence of a space factor at eleven and earlier. *Brit. J. Psychol.*, 1949, 2, 3-16.

7. GARDNER, R. W., HOLZMAN, P. S., KLEIN, G. S., LINTON, H. B., & SPENCE, D. P. Cognitive control: a study of individual consistencies in cognitive behavior. *Psychol. Issues*, 1959, 1, No. 4.

8. HERZBERG, F., & LEPKIN, M. A study of sex differences on the primary mental abilities test. *Educ. psychol. Measmt.*, 1954, 14, 687-689.

9. HOBSON, J. R. Sex differences in primary mental abilities. *J. educ. Res.*, 1947, 41, 126-132.

10. KAGAN, J., & MOSS, H. A. The psychological significance of styles of conceptualization. Draft of paper presented at a conference on basic cognitive process in children, sponsored by the Social Science Research Council, Minneapolis, Minnesota, April 21-23, 1961.

11. KENT, M., & DAVIS, D. R. Discipline in the home and intellectual development. *Brit. J. med. Psychol.*, 1957, 30, 27-34.

12. KUCKENBERG, L. Effects of early father absence on subsequent development of boys. Unpublished doctoral dissertation, Harvard Univer., 1962.

13. LEVINSON, B. M. Cultural pressure and WAIS scatter in a traditional Jewish setting. *J. genet. Psychol.*, 1958, 93, 277-286.

14. LEVY, D. M. *Maternal overprotection.* Columbia Univer. Press, 1943.

15. MC CARTHY, D. Language development in children. In L. Carmichael (Ed.), *Manual of child psychology.* (2nd Ed.) Wiley, 1954. Pp. 492-630.

16. MACCOBY, E. E., & RAU, L. Differential cognitive abilities. Contract No. 1040, USOE, manuscript in preparation, 1962.

17. MILNER, E. A study of the relationships between reading readiness on grade one school children and patterns of parent-child interactions. *Child Develpm.*, 1951, 22, 95-112.

18. MOSS, H. A., & KAGAN, J. Maternal influences on early IQ scores. *Psychol. Rep.*, 1958, 4, 655-661.

19. PETTIGREW, T. F. The measurement and correlates of category width as a cognitive variable. *J. Pers.*, 1958, 26, 532-544.

20. SEARS, R.R., MACCOBY, E. E., & LEVIN, H. *Patterns of child rearing.* Row, Peterson, 1957.

21. SONTAG, L. W., BAKER, C. T., & NELSON, V. L. Mental growth and personality development: a longitudinal study. *Monogr. Soc. Res. Child Develpm.*, 1958, 23, No. 2 (Serial No. 68).

22. WALLACH, M. A., & CARON, A. J. Attribute criteriality and sex-linked conservatism as determinants of psychological similarity. *J. abnorm. soc. Psychol.*, 1959, 59, 43-50.

23. WINTERBOTTOM, M. R. The relation of childhood training in independence to achievement motivation. Unpublished doctoral dissertation, Univer. of Michigan, 1953.

24. WITKIN, H. A. The perception of the upright. *Sci. Amer.*, 1959, 200, 50-56

23/A COMPARATIVE TEST OF THE STATUS ENVY, SOCIAL POWER, AND SECONDARY REINFORCEMENT THEORIES OF IDENTIFICATORY LEARNING[1]/

ALBERT BANDURA, DOROTHEA ROSS,[2] AND SHEILA A. ROSS[*]

ALTHOUGH IT IS GENERALLY ASSUMED that social behavior is learned and modified through direct reward and punishment of instrumental responses, informal observation and laboratory study of the social learning process reveal that new responses may be rapidly acquired and existing behavioral repertoires may be considerably changed as a function of observing the behavior and attitudes exhibited by models (Bandura, 1962).

The latter type of learning is generally labeled "imitation" in behavior theory, and "identification" in most theories of personality. These concepts, however, are treated in the present paper as synonymous since both encompass the same behavioral phenomenon, i.e., the tendency for a person to match the behavior, attitudes, or emotional reactions as exhibited by actual or symbolized models. While the defining properties of identification are essentially the same in different personality theories, a host of divergent learning conditions have been proposed as the necessary antecedent variables for matching or identificatory behavior (Bronfenbrenner, 1960; Freud, 1946; Freud, 1924, 1948; Kagan, 1958; Klein, 1949; Maccoby, 1959; Mowrer, 1950; Parsons, 1955; Sears, 1957; Whiting, 1960).

In the experiment reported in this paper predictions were derived from three of the more prominent theories of learning by identification, and tested in three-person groups representing prototypes of the nuclear family. In one condition of the experiment an adult assumed the role of controller of resources and positive reinforcers. Another adult was the consumer or recipient of these resources, while the child, a participant observer in the triad, was essentially ignored. In a second treatment condition, one adult controlled the resources; the child, however, was the recipient of the positive reinforcers and the other adult was assigned a subordinate and powerless role. An adult male and female served as models in each of the triads. For half the boys and girls in each condition the male model controlled and dispensed the rewarding resources, simulating the husband dominant family; for the remaining children, the female model mediated the positive resources as in the wife dominant home. Following the experimental social interactions the two adult models exhibited divergent patterns of behavior in the presence of the child, and a measure was obtained of the degree to which the child subsequently patterned his behavior after that of the models.

According to the *status envy theory* of identification recently proposed by Whiting (1959, 1960), where a child competes unsuccessfully with an adult for affection, attention, food, and care, the child will envy the consumer adult and consequently identify with him. Whiting's theory represents an extension of the Freudian defensive identification hypothesis that identificatory behavior is the outcome of rivalrous interaction between the child and the parent who occupies an envied consumer status. While Freud presents the child as in competition with the father primarily for the mother's sexual and affectional attention, Whiting regards any forms of reward, material and social, as valued resources around which rivalry may develop. The status envy theory thus predicts that the highest degree of imitation by the child will occur in the experimental condition in which the rivalrous adult consumes the resources desired by

[1] This investigation was supported by Research Grant M-5162 from the National Institutes of Health, United States Public Health Service.

The authors are indebted to Beverly Busching, Malka Yaari, Nancy Wiggins, and John Steinbruner, who assisted in collecting the data.

[2] This research was carried out while the junior author was the recipient of an American Association of University Women International Fellowship for postdoctoral research.

[*] Albert Bandura, Dorothea Ross, and Sheila A. Ross, A comparative test of the status envy, social power, and secondary reinforcement theories of identificatory learning, *J. abnorm. soc. Psychol.*, 1963, 67, #6, 527-534. Reprinted by permission.

the child, with the consumer adult serving as the primary object of imitation.

In contrast to the envy theory, other writers (Maccoby, 1959; Mussen & Distler, 1959; Parsons, 1955) assume that the controller, rather than the consumer, of resources is the main source of imitative behavior. The *power theory* of social influence has received considerable attention in experimental social psychology, though not generally in the context of identification theories.

Social power is typically defined as the ability of a person to influence the behavior of others by controlling or mediating their positive and negative reinforcements. French and Raven (1959) have distinguished five types of power based on expertness, attractiveness, legitimacy, coerciveness, and rewarding power, each of which is believed to have somewhat differential effects on the social influence process. For example, the use of threat or coercion, in which the controller derives power from his ability to administer punishments, not only develops avoidance behavior toward the controller but also decreases his attractiveness and hence his effectiveness in altering the behavior of others beyond the immediate social influence setting (French, Morrison, & Levinger, 1960; Zipf, 1960). The use of reward power, in contrast, both fosters approach responses toward the power figure and increases his attractiveness or secondary reward value through the repeated association of his attributes with positive reinforcement. Attractiveness is assumed to extend the controller's power over a wide range of behavior (French & Raven, 1959).

In the present investigation power based upon the ability to dispense rewards was manipulated experimentally. In accordance with the social power theory of identification, but contrasting with the status envy hypothesis, one would predict that children will reproduce more of the behavior of the adult who controls positive reinforcers, than that of the powerless adult model, and that power inversions on the part of the male and female models will produce cross-sex imitation.

The *secondary reinforcement theory* of identification, which has been alluded to in the discussion of social power through attractiveness, has been elaborated in greatest detail by Mowrer (1950, 1958). According to this view, as a model mediates the child's biological and social rewards, the behavioral attributes of the model are paired repeatedly with positive reinforcement and thus acquire secondary reward value. On the basis of stimulus generalization, responses which match those of the model attain reinforcing value for the child in proportion to their similarity to those made by the model. Consequently, the child can administer positively conditioned reinforcers to himself simply by reproducing as closely as possible the model's positively valenced behavior. This theory predicts that the experimental condition in which the child was the recipient of positive reinforcements will yield the highest imitation scores with the model who dispensed the rewards serving as the primary source of imitative behavior.

METHOD

SUBJECTS.   The subjects were 36 boys and 36 girls enrolled in the Stanford University Nursery School. They ranged in age from 33 to 65 months, although the variability was relatively small with most of the ages falling around the mean of 51 months.

An adult male and female served as models in the triads so as to reproduce possible power structures encountered in different types of family constellations. A female experimenter conducted the study for all 72 children.

DESIGN AND PROCEDURE.   The subjects were assigned randomly to two experimental groups and one control group of 24 subjects each. Half the subjects in each group were males, and half were females.

High rewarding power was induced experimentally through the manipulation of material and social reinforcements, and the use of verbal structuring techniques. While accompanying the child to the experimental room, for example, the experimenter informed the child that the adult who assumed the role of controller owned the nursery school "surprise room," as well as a fabulous collection of play materials. After introducing the child to the controller, the experimenter asked whether the child may play in the surprise room. The controller explained that he was on his way to his car to fetch some of his most attractive toys, but the experimenter and the child could proceed to the room where he would join them shortly. As the controller left, the experimenter commented on how lucky they were to have access to the controller's play materials.

On the way to the experimental room they met the other adult who insisted on joining them but the experimenter informed her that she would have to obtain permission from the controller since he owned the room, and it was doubtful whether sufficient play materials were available for both the adult and the child. This brief encounter with the other adult was designed primarily to create the set that rewards were available to one person only and thereby to induce rivalrous feelings over the controller's resources.

As soon as the experimenter and the child arrived in the experimental room, they sat down at a small table and played with the few Lincoln Logs and two small cars that were provided. A short time later the other adult appeared and announced that the controller also granted her permission to play in the room.

The controller then entered carrying two large toy boxes containing a variety of highly attractive masculine and feminine toys, a colorful juice dispensing fountain, and an ample supply of cookies. As soon as the controller appeared on the scene, the experimenter departed.

For children in the Adult Consumer condition, the adult who assumed the role of consumer requested permission to play with the articles and the controller replied that, since the child appeared to be occupied at his table, the consumer was free to use the play materials. This monopolistic move by the consumer adult left the child stranded at a table with two relatively uninteresting toys. During the 20-minute play session, the controller offered the consumer, among other things, miniature pinball machines, mechanical sparkling toys, kaleidoscopes, dolls, and actively participated with the consumer in dart games and other activities. To add to the credibility of the situation, both the controller and consumer devoted most of their attention to articles, such as the pinball machine and dart game, which could be used in adult appropriate activities. Throughout the interaction the controller was most helpful, supportive, and generous in dispensing social reinforcers in the form of praise, approval, and positive attention. The consumer, in turn, commented frequently on the controller's highly attractive resources so as to further enhance the controller's rewarding status. The consumer also verbalized considerable positive affect characteristic of a person experiencing positive reinforcements.

Approximately half way through the session, the controller remarked, "Say, you look hungry. I have just the thing for you." He then brought forth the soda fountain dispenser, poured colorful fruit juices into paper cups and served them to the consumer along with a generous supply of cookies. While the consumer was enjoying his snack, the controller turned on a "TV-radio" that played a nursery melody while a revolving dial displayed a series of storybook scenes.

Toward the end of the session, the controller informed the consumer that he will be leaving on a shopping trip to San Francisco that afternoon, and asked the consumer if there was anything special she would like him to buy for her. The consumer requested a super two-wheel bicycle, a high status object among the nursery school children. The controller promised to purchase the bicycle along with

any other items the consumer might think of before the controller departed for the city.

The procedure for the Child Consumer condition was identical with that described above except the child was the recipient of the material rewards and the social reinforcement. During the session the other adult sat at the opposite end of the room engrossed in a book, and was totally ignored by the controller. In discussing the prospective San Francisco shopping trip, the controller mentioned to the child that he was planning to visit some toy stores in the city that afternoon, and asked for suggestions of attractive toys he might purchase for future play sessions with children.

For half the boys and girls in each treatment condition the male model controlled and dispensed the resources, simulating the husband dominant family; for the remaining children the female model mediated the positive resources as in the wife dominant home.

At the completion of the social interaction session the controller announced that he had a surprise game in his car that the three of them could play together. The controller then asked the other adult to fetch the experimenter to assist them with the game, and as soon as the adult departed, the controller removed the toys and assembled the imitation task apparatus.

IMITATION TASK. The imitation task was essentially the same two-choice discrimination problem utilized in an earlier experiment (Bandura & Huston, 1961), except the response repertoires exhibited by the models were considerably extended, and the procedure used in the acquisition trials was somewhat modified.

The apparatus consisted of two small boxes with hinged lids, identical in color and size. The boxes were placed on stools approximately 4 feet apart and 8 feet from the starting point. On the lid of each box was a rubber doll.

As soon as the other adult returned with the experimenter, the controller asked both the child and the experimenter to be seated in the chairs along the side of the room, and the other adult to stand at the starting point, while the controller described the game they were about to play. The controller then explained that the experimenter would hide a picture sticker in one of the two boxes and the object of the game was to guess which box contained the sticker. The adults would have the first set of turns, following which the child would play the guessing game.

The discrimination problem was employed simply as a cover task that occupied the children's attention while at the same time permitting observation of the models as they performed divergent patterns of behavior during the discrimination trials in the absence of any set to attend to or learn the responses exhibited by the models.

Before commencing the trials, the controller invited the other participants to join him in selecting a "thinking cap" from hat racks containing two identical sets of four caps, each of which had a different colored feather. The controller selected the green feathered hat, remarked, "Feather in the front" and wore the hat with the feather facing forward. The other model selected the yellow feathered hat, commented, "Feather in the back," and placed the hat on her head with the feather facing backward. The child then made his choice from the four hats in the lower rack and it was noted whether he matched the color preference, hat placement, and the verbal responses of the one or the other model.

The models then went to the starting point, the child returned to his seat, and the experimenter loaded both boxes with sticker pictures for the models' trials.

During the execution of each trial, each model exhibited a different set of relatively novel verbal and motor responses that were totally irrelevant to the discrimination problem to which the child's attention was directed. At the starting point the controller stood with his arms crossed, but at the experimenter's warning not to look, the controller placed his hands over his eyes, faced sideways, and asked, "Ready?" The other model stood with his arms on his hips, then squatted with his back turned to the boxes, and asked, "Now?"

As soon as the experimenter gave the signal for the first trial, the controller remarked, "Forward march" and began marching slowly toward the designated box repeating, "March, march, march." When he reached the box he said, "Sock him," hit the doll aggressively off the box, opened the lid and yelled, "Bingo," as he reached down for the sticker. He then remarked, "Lickit-sticket," as he pressed on the picture sticker with his thumb in the upper-right quadrant of a 24×24 inch sheet of plain white paper that hung on the wall immediately behind the boxes. The controller terminated the trial by replacing the doll facing sideways on the container with the comment, "Look in the mirror," and made a final verbal response, "There."

The other model then took her turn and performed a different set of imitative acts but equated with the controller's responses in terms of number, types of response classes represented, structural properties, and interest value. At the starting point, for example, she remarked, "Get set, go" and walked stiffly toward the boxes repeating "Left, right, left, right." When she reached the container she said, "Down and up," as she lay the doll down on the lid and opened the box. She then exclaimed, "A stickeroo," repeated, "Weto-smacko," and slapped on the sticker with the open hand in the lower-left quadrant of the sheet of paper. In terminating the trial, the model lay the doll on the lid of the container with the remark, "Lie down," and returned with her hands behind her back, and emitted the closing remark, "That's it."

The two sets of responses were counterbalanced by having the models display each pattern with half the subjects in each of the three groups.

The models performed alternately for four trials. At the conclusion of the fourth trial the controller explained that he had to check some materials in his car and while he and the other model were away the child may take his turns. Before they departed, however, the experimenter administered a picture preference test in which the models were asked to select their preferred picture from six different stickers pasted on a 5×8 inch card, after which the child was presented a similar card containing an identical set of stickers and requested to indicate his preference.

In addition to the introductory block of four trials by the models, the child's 15 total test trials were interspersed with three two-trial blocks by the models. The models were always absent from the room during the child's test series. This procedure was adopted in order to remove any imagined situational restraints against, or coercion for, the child to reproduce the models' responses. Moreover, demonstrations of delayed imitation in the absence of the model provide more decisive evidence for learning by means of imitation.

The models always selected different boxes, the right-left position varying from trial to trial in a fixed irregular order, and the controller always took the first turn. Although the models received stickers on each trial, the child was nonrewarded on one third of the trials in order to maintain his interest in the cover task.

At the beginning of each of the blocks of subjects' trials, the experimenter administered the picture preference test and the selection of stickers that matched the models' choices was recorded. In addition, on the eighth trial the models removed their hats and hung them in different locations in the room. If the child removed his hat during the session and placed it along side one or the other of the model's hats, this imitative act was also scored.

At the completion of the imitation phase of the experiment, the children were interviewed by the experimenter in order to determine whom they considered to be the controller of resources, and to assess their model preferences. The latter data were used as an index of attraction to the models. In addition, for the children in the adult consumer condition, the session was concluded by providing them the same lavish treatment accorded their adult rival.

Children in the control group had no prior social interaction with the models but participated with them in the imitative learning phase of the study. The experimenter assumed complete charge of the procedures and treated the models as though they were naive subjects. This control group was included primarily to determine the models' relative effectiveness as modeling stimuli. In addition, the models alternated between subjects in the order in which they executed the trials so as to test for the possibility of a primacy or a recency of exposure effect on imitative behavior.

IMITATION SCORES. The imitation scores were obtained by summing the frequency of occurrence of the postural, verbal, and motor responses described in the preceding section, and the hat, color, and picture preferences that matched the selections of each of the two models.

The children's performances were scored by three raters who observed the experimental sessions through a one-way mirror from an adjoining observation room. The raters were provided with a separate check list of responses exhibited by each of the two models, and the scoring procedure simply involved checking the imitative responses performed by the children on each trial. In order to provide an estimate of interscorer reliability, the performances of 30% of the children were recorded simultaneously but independently by two observers. The raters were in perfect agreement on 95% of the specific imitative responses that they scored.

RESULTS

The control group data revealed that the two models were equally effective in eliciting imitative responses, the mean values being 17.83 and 20.46 for the male and female model, respectively; nor did the children display differential imitation of same-sex ($M = 20.30$) and opposite-sex ($M = 17.92$) models. Although children in the control group tended to imitate the second model ($M = 22.21$) to a somewhat greater extent than the one who performed first ($M = 16.08$) on each trial, suggesting a recency of exposure effect, the difference was not of statistically significant magnitude ($t = 1.60$).

Table 1 presents the mean imitation scores for children in each of the two experimental triads. A $2 \times 2 \times 2 \times 2$ mixed factorial analysis of variance was computed on these data in which the four factors in the design were sex of child, sex of the model who controlled the resources, adult versus child consumer, and the controller versus the other model as the source of imitative behavior.[3] As shown in Table 2, the findings of this study clearly support the social power theory of imitation. In both experimental treatments, regardless of whether the rival adult or the children themselves were the recipients of the rewarding resources, the model who possessed rewarding power was imitated to a greater degree than was the rival or the ignored model ($F = 40.61$, $p < .001$). Nor did the condition combining resource ownership with direct reinforcement of the child yield the highest imitation of the model who controlled and dispensed

[3] The assistance of Eleanor Willemsen with the statistical computations is gratefully acknowledged.

TABLE 1 / MEAN NUMBER OF IMITATIVE RESPONSES PERFORMED BY SUBGROUPS OF CHILDREN IN THE EXPERIMENTAL TRIADS.

SUB- JECTS	OBJECTS OF IMITATION			
	MALE CONTROLLER	FEMALE CONSUMER	FEMALE CONTROLLER	MALE CONSUMER
Girls	29.00	9.67	26.00	10.00
Boys	30.17	18.67	22.33	16.17
Total	29.59	14.17	24.17	13.09
	CONTROLLER	IGNORED	CONTROLLER	IGNORED
Girls	22.00	16.17	31.84	22.17
Boys	29.17	16.67	26.83	34.50
Total	25.59	16.42	29.34	28.34

the positive rewards. The latter finding is particularly surprising since an earlier experiment based on two-person groups (Bandura & Huston, 1961), demonstrated that pairing of model with positive reinforcement substantially enhanced the occurrence of imitative behavior. An examination of the remaining significant interaction effects together with the postexperimental interview data suggest a possible explanation for the discrepant results.

The differential in the controller-other model imitation was most pronounced when the male model was the controller of resources ($F = 4.76$, $p < .05$), particularly for boys. In fact, boys who were the recipients of rewarding resources mediated by the female model tended to favor the ignored male as their object of imitation. In the postexperiment interview a number of boys in this condition spontaneously expressed sympathy for the ignored male and mild criticism of the controller for not being more charitable with her bountiful resources (for example, "She doesn't share much. John played bravely even though she didn't even share. . . . She's a bit greedy.").

As a partial check on whether this factor would tend to diminish the differential imitation of the two models, six children—three boys and three girls—participated in a modified Child Consumer treatment in which, halfway through the social interaction session, the ignored adult was informed that he too may have access to the playthings. He replied that he was quite content to read his book. This modified procedure, which removed the rivalry and the exclusion of the model, yielded four times as much imitation of the controller relative to the model who was ignored by choice.

The significant triple interaction effect indicates that the differential in the controller-other model imitation was greatest when the same-sex model mediated the positive reinforcers, and this effect was more pronounced for boys than for girls.

The data presented so far demonstrate that manipulation of rewarding power had produced differential imitation of the behavior exhibited by the two models. In order to assess whether the

TABLE 2 / SUMMARY OF THE ANALYSIS OF VARIANCE OF THE IMITATION SCORES.

SOURCE	df	MS	F
Between subjects	47	310.17	
Sex of subjects (A)	1	283.59	<1
Sex of controller model (B)	1	128.34	<1
Adult versus child consumer (C)	1	518.01	1.61
A × B	1	23.01	<1
A × C	1	1.76	<1
B × C	1	742.59	2.31
A × B × C	1	21.10	<1
Error (b)	40	321.49	
Within subjects	48	113.24	
Controller versus other model (D)	1	2,025.84	40.61***
A × D	1	297.51	5.96*
B × D	1	237.51	4.76*
C × D	1	396.09	7.94**
A × B × D	1	256.76	5.15*
A × C × D	1	19.52	<1
B × C × D	1	23.02	<1
A × B × C × D	1	184.00	3.69
Error (w)	40	49.88	

* $p < .05$.
** $p < .01$.
*** $p < .001$.

dispensing of positive reinforcers in the prior social interaction influenced the overall level of matching responses, the imitation scores in each of the three groups were summed across models and analyzed using a Sex × Treatment design.

The mean total imitative responses for children in the Child Consumer, Adult Consumer, and the Control group were 50.21, 40.58, and 37.88, respectively. Analysis of variance of these data reveals a significant treatment effect ($F = 3.37$, $.025 < p < .05$). Further comparisons of pairs of means by the t test, show that children in the child rewarded condition displayed significantly more imitative behavior than did children both in the Adult Consumer treatment ($t = 2.19$, $p < .05$), and those in the Control group ($t = 2.48$, $p < .02$). The Adult Consumer and Control groups, however, did not differ from each other in this respect ($t = .54$).

The model preference patterns were identical for children in the two experimental conditions and consequently, the data were combined for the statistical analysis. Of the 48 children, 32 selected the model who possessed rewarding power as the more attractive, while 15 preferred the noncontrolling adult. The greater attractiveness of the rewarding model was significant beyond the .05 level ($x^2 = 5.34$). The experimental triad in which boys were the recipients of positive reinforcers while the male model was ignored, and the female consumer-girl ignored subgroup, contributed the highest preference for the non-controlling adult.

In addition to the experimental groups discussed in the preceding section, data are available for 9 children in the Adult Consumer condition, and for 11 children in the Child Consumer treatment who revealed, in their postexperiment interviews, that they had actually attributed rewarding power to the ignored or the consumer adult despite the elaborate experimental manipulations designed to establish differential power status. A number of these children were firmly convinced that only a male can possess resources and, therefore, the female dispensing the rewards was only an intermediary for the male model (for example, "He's the man and it's all his because he's a daddy. Mommy never really has things belong to her. . . . He's the daddy so it's his but he shares nice with the mommy. . . . He's the man and the man always really has the money and he lets ladies play too. John's good and polite and he has very good manners.") This view of resource ownership within the family constellation was often directly reinforced by the mothers (for example, "My mommy told me and Joan that the daddy really buys all the things, but the mommy looks after things."). Children who attributed the resource ownership to the consumer or ignored female model had considerable difficulty in explaining their selection (for example, "I just knowed it does. . . . I could tell, that's how."), perhaps, because the power structure they depicted is at variance with the widely accepted cultural norm.

As shown in Table 3, models who were attributed rewarding power elicited approximately twice as many matching responses than models who were perceived by the children as possessing no control over the rewarding resources. Because of the small and unequal number of cases in each cell, these data were not evaluated statistically. The differences, however, are marked and quite in accord with those produced by the experimentally manipulated variations in power status.

TABLE 3 / IMITATION AS A FUNCTION OF ATTRIBUTED REWARDING POWER TO THE MODELS.

TREATMENT CONDITION	OBJECTS OF IMITATION			
	FEMALE CONTROLLER	MALE NONCON- TROLLER	MALE CONTROLLER	FEMALE NONCON- TROLLER
Adult consumer	24.0	12.3	29.8	14.6
Child consumer	18.2	6.7	35.5	16.2

DISCUSSION

To the extent that the imitative behavior elicited in the present experiment may be considered an elementary prototype of identification within a nuclear family group, the data fail to support the interpretation of identificatory learning as the outcome of a rivalrous interaction between the child and the adult who occupies an envied status in respect to the consumption of highly desired resources. Children clearly identified with the source of rewarding power rather than with the competitor for these rewards. Moreover, power inversions on the part of the male and female models produced cross-sex imitation, particularly in girls. The differential readiness of boys and girls to imitate behavior exhibited by an opposite-sex model are consistent with findings reported by Brown (1956, 1958) that boys show a decided preference for the masculine role, whereas, ambivalence and masculine role preference are widespread among girls. These findings probably reflect both the differential cultural tolerance for cross-sex behavior displayed by males and females, and the privileged status and relatively greater positive reinforcement of masculine role behavior in our society.

Failure to develop sex appropriate behavior has received considerable attention in the clinical literature and has customarily been assumed to be established and maintained by psychosexual threat and anxiety reducing mechanisms. Our findings strongly suggest, however, that external social learning variables, such as the distribution of rewarding power within the family constellation, may be highly influential in the formation of inverted sex role behavior.

Theories of identificatory learning have generally assumed that within the family setting the child's initial identification is confined to his mother, and that during early childhood boys must turn from the mother as the primary model to the father as the main source of imitative behavior. However, throughout the course of development children are provided with ample opportunities to observe the behavior of both parents. The results of the present experiment reveal that when children are exposed to multiple models they may select one or more of them as the primary source of behavior, but rarely reproduce all the elements of a single model's repertoire or confine their imitation to that model. Although the children adopted many of the characteristics of the model who possessed rewarding power, they also reproduced some of the elements of behavior exhibited by the model who occupied the subordinate role. Consequently, the children were not simply junior-size replicas of one or the other model; rather, they exhibited a relatively novel pattern of behavior representing an amalgam of elements from both models. Moreover, the specific admixture of behavioral elements varied from child to child. These findings provide considerable evidence for the seemingly paradoxical conclusion that imitation can in fact produce innovation of social behavior, and that within the same family even same-sex siblings may exhibit quite different response patterns, owing to their having selected for imitation different elements of their parents' response repertoires.

The association of a model with noncontingent positive reinforcement tends to increase the incidence of imitative behavior in two person groups (Bandura & Huston, 1961), whereas the addition of a same-sex third person who is denied access to desired rewards may provoke in children negative evaluations of the rewarding model and thereby decreases his potency as a modeling stimulus. These two sets of data demonstrate how learning principles based on an individual behavior model may be subject to strict limitations, since the introduction of additional social variables into the stimulus complex can produce significant changes in the functional relationships between relevant variables.

SUMMARY

Predictions derived from 3 prominent theories of identificatory learning were tested in 3-person groups representing prototypes of the nuclear family. In 1 condition an adult assumed the role of controller of positive reinforcers. Another adult was the consumer of these resources, while the child, a participant observer in the triad, was essentially ignored. In a 2nd treatment condition, one adult controlled the rewarding resources; the child, however, was the recipient of the positive reinforcers, while the other adult was assigned a subordinate and powerless role. Following the experimental social interactions the 2 adult models exhibited divergent patterns of behavior in the presence of the child, and a measure was obtained of the degree to which the child subsequently patterned his behavior after that of the models. Children imitated primarily the model who possessed rewarding power rather than the competitor for the rewards. Moreover, power inversions on the part of the male and female models produced cross-sex imitation, particularly in girls.

REFERENCES

BANDURA, A. Social learning through imitation. In M. R. Jones (Ed.), *Nebraska symposium on motivation: 1962*. Lincoln: Univer. Nebraska Press, 1962. Pp. 211-269.

BANDURA, A., & HUSTON, ALETHA C. Identification as a process of incidental learning. *J. abnorm. soc. Psychol.*, 1961, *63*, 311-318.

BRONFENBRENNER, U. Freudian theories of identification and their derivatives. *Child Develpm.*, 1960, *31*, 15-40.

BROWN, D. G. Sex-role preference in young children. *Psychol. Monogr.*, 1956, *70*(14, Whole No. 421).

BROWN, D. G. Sex-role development in a changing culture. *Psychol. Bull.*, 1958, *55*, 232-242.

FRENCH, J. R. P., JR., MORRISON, H. W., & LEVINGER, G. Coercive power and forces affecting conformity. *J. abnorm. soc. Psychol.*, 1960, *61*, 93-101.

FRENCH, J. R. P., JR., & RAVEN, B. The bases of social power. In D. Cartwright (Ed.), *Studies in social power*. Ann Arbor, Mich.: Institute for Social Research, 1959. Pp. 150-167.

FREUD, ANNA. *The ego and the mechanisms of defense*. New York: International Univer. Press, 1946.

FREUD, S. The passing of the Oedipus-complex. In, *Collected papers*. Vol. 2. London: Hogarth Press, 1924. Pp. 269-282.

FREUD, S. *Group psychology and the analysis of the ego*. London: Hogarth Press, 1948.

KAGAN, J. The concept of identification. *Psychol. Rev.*, 1958, *65*, 296-305.

KLEIN, MELANIE. *The psycho-analysis of children*. London: Hogarth Press, 1949.

MACCOBY, ELEANOR E. Role-taking in childhood and its consequences for social learning. *Child Develpm.*, 1959, *30*, 239-252.

MOWRER, O. H. Identification: A link between learning theory and psychotherapy. In, *Learning theory and personality dynamics*. New York: Ronald Press, 1950. Pp. 69-94.

MOWRER, O. H. Hearing and speaking: An analysis of language learning. *J. speech hear. Disord.*, 1958, *23*, 143-152.

MUSSEN, P., & DISTLER, L. Masculinity, identification, and father-son relationship. *J. abnorm. soc. Psychol.*, 1959, *59*, 350-356.

PARSONS, T. Family structure and the socialization of the child. In T. Parsons & R. F. Bales (Eds.), *Family, socialization, and interaction process*. Glencoe, Ill.: Free Press, 1955. Pp. 35-131.

SEARS, R. R. Identification as a form of behavioral development. In D. B. Harris (Ed.), *The concept of development*. Minneapolis: Univer. Minnesota Press, 1957. Pp. 149-161.

WHITING, J. W. M. Sorcery, sin, and the superego: A cross-cultural study of some mechanisms of social control. In M. R. Jones (Ed.), *Nebraska symposium on motivation: 1959*. Lincoln: Univer. Nebraska Press, 1959. Pp. 174-195.

WHITING, J. W. M. Resource mediation and learning by identification. In I. Iscoe & H. W. Stevenson (Eds.), *Personality development in children*. Austin: Univer. Texas Press, 1960. Pp. 112-126.

ZIPF, SHEILA G. Resistance and conformity under reward and punishment. *J. abnorm. soc. Psychol.*, 1960, *61*, 102-109.

24/PARENT-CHILD RELATIONS AND PARENTAL PERSONALITY IN RELATION TO YOUNG CHILDREN'S SEX-ROLE PREFERENCES[1,2]/

PAUL MUSSEN AND ELDRED RUTHERFORD[*]

ACCORDING TO CLASSICAL PSYCHOAN-alytic theory, the identification process originates in the child's hostility toward his like-sexed parent and consequent fear of that parent's retaliation. In contrast, the more recently formulated developmental identification hypothesis considers the process to be motivated by warmth and affection toward that parent, whose characteristics and responses are then taken on as a "total pattern" (2, 13, 18, 22, 28, 29).

Most of the available evidence supporting this latter hypothesis has been derived from studies of boys' identification with their fathers. If the hypothesis has general validity, however, it should apply equally well to the girl's identification with her mother. This hypothesis would not predict, as classical psychoanalytic theory does, that the process is more confused, complex, and slower for girls than for boys (18, 22, 28).[3]

The primary purpose of the present investigation was to test the developmental identification

[1] This study was supported by the National Institute of Mental Health, United States Public Health Service, under Research Grant M-3217.

[2] The authors wish to express their appreciation to A. B. Campbell, Assistant Superintendent of Schools of Berkeley, Frank Wylde, Principal of the Jefferson School, and Mrs. Sue Callan, Mrs. Georgia Johnson, Mrs. Virginia Allison, Miss Marcia Morgen, and Mrs. Ruth Lockwood, first grade teachers, for their cooperation in this study.

[3] In fact, Sears et al. have argued that the opposite is true, stating: ". . . We are inclined to believe that the boy's shift [from identification with the mother to identification with the father] retards the smooth development of the [identification] process. His gradual adoption of a new model is doubtless somewhat frustrating to him, and puts him in a state of conflict as to whom he should act like. Thus we might expect not only that boys in their sixth year would be less fully identified with their fathers than girls with their mothers, but that they would have a less complete identification with the adult role in general than girls would have. Also, this means they would show less indication of high conscience, as well as other signs of identification, than girls" (28, p. 384).

hypothesis further to determine its general validity and its usefulness in understanding the process of the girl's identification with her mother. A major aspect of the basic design paralleled that of two earlier studies of the antecedents of father identification in kindergarten boys (20, 21) in which masculinity was found to be related to perceptions of the father as more rewarding and nurturant and also the more powerful source of punishment.

In addition to testing the developmental identification hypothesis, the study was designed to permit investigation of the association between certain parental variables not directly related to that hypothesis and one criterion of identification with the same-sexed parent, the development of appropriate sex-role preference. For the sake of simplicity of presentation, the hypotheses tested may be categorized in terms of the relation between sex-role preference and (a) parent-child relationships, (b) parental personality characteristics, and (c) parental encouragement of appropriate sex-typing. A series of hypotheses with parallel versions for boys and girls was formulated.

1. *Hypotheses concerning parent-child relationships.* This category includes the most central hypotheses of this study, those derived from the developmental identification hypotheses. More specifically it was hypothesized that femininity (female sex-role preference) in little girls —generally assumed to be a product or manifestation of identification with the mother—is related to rewarding, nurturant, and affectionate relationships with that parent (hypothesis Ia). Mother-daughter relationships were evaluated, first, from the child's point of view, by means of projective doll play, and secondly, from the mother's account of her interactions with her daughter, given in response to interview questions.

Since most of the research was conducted in a coeducational public grammar school, data on

167

boys were also collected. It was therefore possible to achieve something that is rare in research in personality and development: a replication (but with more subjects) of an earlier study and thus additional independent checks on the developmental, defensive, and role-taking hypotheses of identification as applied to boys. All the hypotheses received some support in the earlier study (20). The developmental hypothesis states that masculinity in young boys is related to positive, affectionate father-son relationships (hypothesis Ib).

②️ *Hypotheses concerning consequents of parental personality structure*. Both theory and empirical findings suggest that certain aspects of parental personality structure would have facilitative effects on the child's appropriate sex identification. Thus it was hypothesized that self-acceptance on the part of the like-sexed parent would promote femininity in girls (hypothesis IIa) and masculinity in boys (hypothesis IIb). The prediction is based on the assumption that the parent who accepts himself (or herself) is satisfied with his own sex role and is therefore more likely than the parent who is not self-accepting to reward responses replicating his (her) own. Helper found that children were more likely to emulate the characteristics of a mother who approved of herself (i.e., accepted herself) as a model for her children (12). Mc-Candless has pointed out that, if the girl's mother is successful and, hence, self-accepting, "she provides the best available model for the appropriate sex role" (16, p. 347). The same kind of reasoning probably applies to the boy, i.e., a self-accepting father provides the best model for the son.

In addition, self-acceptance on the part of the opposite-sexed parent may contribute to the development of appropriate sex-typing of his (her) child's behavior. Assuming that self-acceptance is related to approval of—and respect for—others, the self-accepting mother or father is more likely than the parent who lacks this characteristic to approve of his opposite-sexed child's sex-appropriate responses, rewarding and encouraging them. Thus, it is hypothesized that the mother's self-acceptance would be related to the boy's masculinity of interests (hypothesis IIIa), while the father's self-acceptance would be similarly related to the girl's femininity of interests (hypothesis IIIb).

On the basis of learning theory, it was hypothesized that, in general, more masculine fathers and more feminine mothers would foster their daughters' femininity (hypothesis IVa) and their sons' masculinity (hypothesis IVb). The rationale underlying these hypotheses was twofold. First, it was assumed that highly feminine women and masculine men are good models for their like-sexed children and provide more distinctive cues for their children's sex-appropriate responses and attitudes. Secondly, it seems plausible to assume such parents are more cognizant of those interests and responses that are sex-appropriate and those that are inappropriate. They might then be expected to reward sex-appropriate responses, thus increasing their frequency and intensity, and to discourage and punish sex-inappropriate behavior.

③️. *Hypothesis concerning parental encouragement of sex-typed behavior*. Parents may directly encourage their child's participation in activities (games, hobbies, etc.) traditionally engaged in by members of the child's own sex and may even participate in such activities with the child. By doing this, they make it clear to the child that they approve and perhaps expect certain kinds of behavior while others are considered inappropriate. They delineate for the child the distinctive cues of sex-typed behavior and, simultaneously, differentially reward such behavior, thus increasing its habit strength. By generalization, other sex-appropriate responses, not specifically rewarded, may also become more intense and frequent. It was therefore hypothesized that strong parental encouragement of participation in sex-appropriate activities would implement the feminization of girls (hypothesis Va) and the masculinization of boys (hypothesis Vb).

METHOD

Psychoanalytic theory holds that identification with the like-sexed parent follows resolution of the Oedipus complex which takes place around the age of 5 or 6 years. Moreover, it is generally agreed that the child becomes increasingly aware of his sex identification at this time—e.g., "at the kindergarten-first grade level, the little girl is faced with the inevitability of her femininity" (16, p. 347). For these reasons, first grade children, between 5 and 6 years of age, would seem to be ideal subjects for the study of the familial antecedents of sex-typing of behavior and interests.

Femininity and masculinity of interests were assessed by means of the IT scale, a projective test of sex-role preference (3) which was administered to 57 girls and 46 boys in the first grade of a middle class public school. In this test, the child is first given a card with a figure drawing unstructured as to sex and referred to as IT. He is then presented with groups of pictures of toys, objects, and activities and asked to choose, from among these, the things that IT would like. The underlying assumption of the test is that "the child will project himself or herself into the IT figure on the basis of his own sex-role preference and will attribute to IT the child's own role preference" (3, p. 5). Scores ranged from 0 (exclusively feminine choices) to 84 (exclusively masculine choices).

To designate male and female subjects high and low in sex-typing, the distributions of the IT scale scores, for each sex separately, were dichotomized at the median. The 29 girls with scores ranging from 0 to 70 were considered high in femininity (i.e., low in masculinity), while the other 28 girls, whose scores were over 70, were considered low in femininity (relatively high in masculinity). Among the boys, the highly masculine group, 24 subjects, scored more than 81 on the IT scale, while the 22 considered low in masculinity had scores ranging between 19 and 80.

DOLL PLAY.   About a week after the IT test was administered, each subject was tested individually in a structured doll play situation involving a mother doll, a father doll, and a child doll of the subject's own sex. The subject was asked to use the dolls in playing out, and thus completing, nine incomplete stories designed to elicit the child's attitudes toward, and perceptions of, his (her) parents.[4] The following is illustrative:

The child wants a certain toy. He can't reach it. He goes into the living room to get help. Both Mommy and Daddy are busy reading. What happens?

In telling the stories, which were completely recorded, the child could depict either father or mother as nurturant and/or punitive. The following scores were derived from the children's stories: Mother Nurturance (MN) and Father Nurturance (FN) scores were the total number of stories in which the mother or father, respectively, gave the child in the story help, care, comfort, or attention. Total Nurturance (TotN) score was the sum of the MN and FN scores. Mother Punishment (MP) and Father Punish-

ment (FP) scores were the number of stories in which the mother and father disciplined, spanked, criticized, or in any way punished the child. Mother Power (MPow) and Father Power (FPow) scores were the number of stories involving either nurturant or punitive relationships with the mother or father, i.e., MN plus MP, and FN plus FP.[5]

MOTHER INTERVIEWS.   The other, perhaps more objective, source of information on parent-child relationships consisted of interviews with the mothers, but for many reasons, it was possible to interview only 19 mothers of girl subjects—11 mothers of highs and eight mothers of lows. The interviews consisted of 32 open ended questions, some of them with suggested probes, adapted and somewhat modified from the interview schedules used by Sears, Maccoby, and Levin (28). These dealt with various aspects of mother-daughter relationships such as restrictions and demands on the child, types of discipline used, warmth and affection, punitiveness, and the child's dependence, and conscience development. Interviews lasted between one and two hours and were conducted by trained interviewers who asked the questions in a prescribed order using the exact wording given in the schedule. All interviews were electrically recorded.

Following completion of the interviews, a trained rater listened to the recordings and then rated each of them on 19 scales taken from Appendix B of *Patterns of Child Rearing*, e.g., warmth of mother to child, acceptance-rejection, and child's conscience (28).[6] It should be noted that neither the interviewer nor the rater were informed of the real purpose of the research and knew nothing about the subjects beforehand. Consequently, neither the interviews nor the ratings could be biased by any knowledge of hypotheses or of the method of selecting the interviewees.

ASSESSMENT OF PARENTAL PERSONALITY.   In order to test hypotheses IIa, IIb, IIIa, IIIb, IVa, and IVB as simply and directly as possible, two scales

[4] Dittoed copies of the full set of nine stories and the interview question may be obtained by writing to the authors.

[5] Since the scoring categories were very explicitly defined, interrater agreement was high. Two scorers agreed in over 90 per cent of their scores for 10 protocols (90 stories).

[6] The two interview raters were trained in scoring comparable interviews with other mothers, but based on the same questions, before they scored the interviews involved in this study. On these "practice" ratings, they achieved 91 per cent agreement, based on five interview protocols.

of the California Psychological inventory, the Femininity and Self-Acceptance scales, were mailed to both parents of each of the subjects. The femininity scale purports to measure femininity of interest and attitudes, while the self-acceptance assesses "factors such as sense of personal worth, self-acceptance, and capacity for independent thinking and action" (11, p. 12).

The inventories were completed and returned by 32 girls' mothers (14 mothers of highs, 18 mothers of lows) and by 30 girls' fathers (14 fathers of highs, 16 fathers of lows). Among the parents of the boys, 22 mothers (8 of highs, 14 of lows) and 18 fathers (7 of highs, 11 of lows) returned the tests.

MEASUREMENT OF PARENTAL ENCOURAGEMENT OF APPROPRIATE SEX-TYPED ACTIVITIES. All the parents of the subjects were also sent a "play and games list," a list of 50 well known sex-typed children's games, play activities, and hobbies, taken from a list of activities that had been shown to differentiate significantly between the preferences of the two sexes (25). Parents were instructed to complete the questionnaires separately and independently, indicating, for each activity, whether they had "actually played the game with their child," "encouraged the child to play the game," or "discouraged the child from playing the game."

The responses to each item (game or activity) were scored in terms of the child's sex. If the parent indicated that he actually played a girls' game with his daughter or a boys' game with his son, the item was scored + 2. Each indication of

simple encouragement of the child's playing a sex-appropriate game or participating in a sex-appropriate activity was scored + 1, while "discouraging the child" from an activity or game appropriate to his sex was scored −2. The sum of the scores on the 50 items constituted the parent's "encouragement of appropriate sex-typed behavior" score. This score was used in testing hypotheses Va and Vb dealing with parental encouragement of the child's sex-typed activities and behavior.

RESULTS

Verification of the major hypotheses involved comparing the highs and lows in sex-typing of interests in relevant variables derived from doll play, maternal interviews (in the case of the girl subjects only), parental scores on the CPI, and parental responses to the "play and games" questionnaires. In the interests of simplicity of exposition, the results of the comparisons of the two groups of boys, including the replication of the Mussen and Distler study (20), will be presented first. In general, the present findings on boys substantiate those of the earlier study and may therefore serve as a point of reference for the evaluation and interpretation of the data relevant to the process of identification in girls.

ANALYSIS OF BOY'S DOLL PLAY RESPONSES. The mean scores of the variables evaluated from the doll play responses of the high and low masculinity groups of boys are given in Table 1. In general, these findings clearly substantiate those of the Mussen-Distler study (20).

TABLE 1 / MEAN SCORES OF BOYS HIGH AND LOW IN MASCULINITY ON FAMILY PERCEPTION (DOLL PLAY) VARIABLES.

VARIABLE	HIGH MASCULINITY GROUP (N = 24)	LOW MASCULINITY GROUP (N = 22)	t	p*
Father Nurturance (FN)	1.3	.8	1.66	.05
Mother Nurturance (MN)	.9	1.3	1.33	ns
They Nurturance (TN)	.3	.4	.18	ns
Total Nurturance (TotN)	2.5	2.5	.24	ns
Father Punishment (FP)	2.3	1.7	1.33	< .10
Mother Punishment (MP)	1.4	1.6	.41	ns
They Punishment (TP)	.6	.6	.00	ns
Total Punishment (TotP)	4.3	3.9	.67	ns
Father Power (FPow)	3.6	2.5	2.19	< .025
Mother Power (MPow)	2.3	2.9	1.10	ns

* In evaluating the significance of differences in this and the following tables, p values were calculated in terms of a one-tail test when there was *specific* prediction (from hypothesis) about the direction of the difference between the groups. Otherwise, two-tail tests were used.

The present data, like those of the earlier study, demonstrate that boys with highly masculine interests told significantly more stories involving father nurturance—i.e., scored higher on the average in Father Nurturance (FN) than boys low in masculinity. These data, then, provide further evidence supportive of the developmental hypothesis, showing that "young boys are more likely to identify strongly with their fathers, and thus to acquire masculine interests, if they perceive their fathers as highly nurturant and rewarding" (20, p. 353).

Table 1 also reveals that there was a tendency (reliable only at the 10 per cent level) similar to that discovered in the other study (reliable at the 6 per cent level, in that instance) for the highly masculine boys to have higher mean Father Punishment (FP) doll play scores than the less masculine boys. This is in accord with what was predicted on the basis of the defensive identification hypothesis which holds that identification with the father is based on perceptions of him as punitive, threatening, and hostile. However, in both studies, the evidence supportive of this hypothesis was much less impressive than that confirming the developmental identification hypothesis.

Since the Father Power (FPow) score was composed of the Father Nurturance (FN) and Father Punishment (FP) scores, the highly masculine boys, of course, received higher scores in this variable, i.e., perceived their fathers as more powerful, than the other group. This may be regarded as support for the role-taking hypothesis of identification which maintains that sex role learning depends upon the amount of the child's interaction with the identificand and the latter's power or control over the child.

In summary, the findings of the present investigation—involving a larger sample of subjects than the Mussen and Distler study (20) and a different definition of high and low masculinity status (above and below the median score for the entire group rather than extreme scores)—in essence replicated those of the earlier study. In both studies, the most salient variables appeared to be the father's nurturant and (to a less marked degree) punitive qualities, the substantially father-identified (i.e., those with strongly sex-typed interests) tending to view their fathers as possessing more of both.

The present results are also consistent with those of other studies in showing that, for boys, sex-typing of interests is more directly related to perceptions of their fathers than to feelings about their mothers. Thus, as Table 1 shows, none of the mother-child interaction variables, derived from the doll play, significantly differentiated the high and low masculinity groups.

ANALYSIS OF CPI AND PLAY AND GAMES LIST DATA OF BOYS' PARENTS. The data collected from the parents failed to confirm any of the hypotheses concerning the relations between boys' sex-role preferences and parental personality characteristics (hypotheses IIb, IIIb, and IVb) or parental encouragement of sex-appropriate activities (hypothesis Vb). There was no evidence that sex-typing of parental interests and attitudes (high masculinity of fathers and high femininity of mothers) or parental self-acceptance, as measured by the CPI, fostered high degrees of masculinity in the sons. Moreover, neither the fathers nor mothers of the highly masculine boys differed significantly from the other parents in their responses to the "play and games" list. Hence these hypotheses were rejected.

It may be concluded that the boy's perception of his father as a nurturant and powerful individual is of paramount importance in his development of masculinity, but there is no evidence that his parents' personality structures, particularly degree of sex-typing and self-confidence, have any significant influence. Moreover, parental encouragement of their son's participation in masculine activities does not seem to have a significant effect on the youngster's sex-role preferences. In other words, it appears that, if a father is warm and nurturant in his relationships with his son, the latter is likely to become highly masculine, even if the father himself is not highly masculine or lacks a high degree of self-acceptance or even if he does not encourage his son to participate in traditionally masculine activities. On the other hand, a ruggedly masculine, self-confident father who has poor relationships with his son is not likely to produce a highly masculine son, even if he actively attempts to stimulate his son's participation in typical male activities.

ANALYSIS OF GIRLS' DOLL PLAY RESPONSES. The means of the doll play scores of the girls low and high in femininity, used in testing hypothesis Ia, are presented in Table 2. As indicated in the table, the groups differed significantly in Mother Nurturance (MN) scores, the mean score of the highly feminine girls in this variable being significantly higher than that of the girls low in femininity. The finding is entirely consistent with, and supports, the developmental identifica-

TABLE 2 / MEAN SCORES OF GIRLS HIGH AND LOW IN FEMININITY ON FAMILY PERCEPTION (DOLL PLAY) VARIABLES.

VARIABLE	HIGH FEMININITY GROUP (N = 29)	LOW FEMININITY GROUP (N = 28)	t	p°
Mother Nurturance (MN)	1.5	1.1	1.65	.05
Father Nurturance (FN)	.8	.5	1.34	ns
They Nurturance (TN)	.2	.3	.21	ns
Total Nurturance (TotN)	2.6	1.9	2.12	< .05
Mother Punishment (MP)	2.4	2.0	1.14	ns
Father Punishment (FP)	1.9	1.9	.07	ns
They Punishment (TP)	.6	.7	.11	ns
Total Punishment (TotP)	4.9	4.6	.30	ns
Mother Power (MPow)	3.9	3.0	1.93	< .05
Father Power (FPow)	2.7	2.5	.18	ns

° *See* footnote to Table 1.

tion hypothesis which holds that girls will identify strongly with their mothers—and consequently become more feminine—if they perceive their mothers as warm, nurturant, affectionate, and rewarding.

As the data summarized in Table 2 show, highly feminine girls, compared with girls low in femininity, regarded their mothers as significantly more powerful (i.e., obtained higher scores in MPow). This finding seems analogous to the finding that highly masculine boys scored significantly higher in FPow than the other boys. There is a major difference between the findings for the two sexes, however. The highly masculine group's high FPow scores were due to the group's significantly, or nearly significantly, higher scores in *both* components of the FPow—i.e., in Father Nurturance (FN) and Father Punishment (FP). The highly feminine group's significantly higher Mother Power scores, on the other hand, are almost entirely attributable to the higher scores in only one of the components of that score, Mother Nurturance (MN). The two groups of girls did not differ significantly in the Mother Punishment (MP) variable. It may therefore be concluded that the development of a high degree of femininity is importantly influenced by the girl's perceptions of her mother as an important, warm, and gratifying person, but not by the extent to which she is perceived as punitive and threatening.

It may be tenably assumed that strong fear of loss of maternal love would be reflected in perceptions of the mother as harsh and punitive. If this is true, then, according to the defensive identification hypothesis, highly feminine girls would obtain relatively higher Mother Punish-

ment (MP) scores than the other girls. This was not the case; the defensive identification hypothesis, as applied to girls, received no support from these data.

While the mean score of the highly feminine girls in Father Nurturance (FN) was greater than that of the other group, the difference was not statistically significant. Since the Total Nurturance (TotN) score is essentially a composite of the Mother Nurturance (MN) and Father Nurturance (FN) scores, the mean score of the highly feminine girls in this variable was, of course, also significantly higher, the difference being attributable primarily to the group difference in MN.

ANALYSIS OF MATERNAL INTERVIEWS. These interviews were designed to elicit information on mother-daughter relationships from the mother's point of view, similar to the information obtained on father-son relationships in the Mussen-Distler study (21). The interview protocols were rated on 19 variables, taken from the Sears, Maccoby, and Levin study (28). These included: warmth of mother to child; acceptance-rejection; mother's use of withdrawal of love, scolding, physical punishment, deprivation, and reasoning as disciplinary techniques; restrictions imposed upon the child and expectancy of good conduct; child's conscience, tendency to admit guilt.

Only one of the 19 rating variables significantly differentiated the two groups. While it is true that one significant difference might have been expected on the basis of chance alone, it is interesting to note that the differentiating variable, "warmth of mother to child," is of paramount theoretical importance. The mean rating for the highly feminine group in this variable was 4.1, while for the other group, it was 3.4 ($t = 1.75$, $p. < .05$). As predicted on the basis of the developmental identification hypothesis, young girls were more likely to identify with their mothers, and thus to acquire appropriately sex-typed interests and responses, if their mothers were warm, rewarding, and affectionate. Thus the finding from the interview reinforces the doll play Mother Nurturance (MN) finding and further supports the developmental identification hypothesis.

The interview data, like those from doll play, failed to provide any confirmation for the defensive identification hypothesis and, in fact, contained some suggestive evidence contradictory to that hypothesis. While none of the interview punishment variables was significantly differentiating, there was a slight, statistically nonsignificant tendency for the mothers of the girls low in femininity to be rated higher in "use of withdrawal of love as a disciplinary technique" (mean rating for mothers of the highs was 1.8, for mothers of the lows 2.4; $t = 1.51$, $p < .20$ for two-tail test). If the defensive identification hypothesis is valid, and if it assumed that frequent use of this technique[7] is likely to evoke fear of loss of maternal love, it would be expected that extensive use of this technique would produce high mother-identification and, consequently, high femininity in the daughter. According to these results, however, a high degree of use of this technique by the mother, if it has any effect, tends to produce *less* femininity in the daughter.

There were some striking parallels between these interview findings and those derived from a study of childrearing antecedents of masculine

[7] It has been suggested that withdrawal of love is regarded as extremely harsh punishment by girls (4).

identification in kindergarten boys (21). Maternal interviews in that study showed that, compared with the other fathers, the fathers of highly masculine boys were warmer and more affectionate toward their sons, a finding analogous to the group differences in maternal warmth in the present study. Moreover, the mothers of the highly feminine girls did not differ significantly from the other mothers with respect to the punishment variables, and the fathers of the two groups of boys were not found to differ in degree of punitive or threatening treatment of their sons (although it will be recalled that in doll play there was a tendency for the highly masculine boys to portray their fathers as more punitive) (20, 21).

ANALYSIS OF CPI RESULTS OF GIRLS' PARENTS. It has been hypothesized that, compared with the other parents, the parents of highly feminine girls would be more self-accepting and self-assured individuals (hypotheses IIa and IIIb), with appropriately sex-typed interests, opinions, and orientations (hypothesis IVa). The hypotheses were tested by comparing the self-acceptance and femininity (in reverse, masculinity) scale scores of the CPI inventories completed by the two groups of parents. Parental scores in these scales are summarized in Table 3.

As that table shows, hypothesis IIa was clearly confirmed. As predicted, the mothers of the highly feminine girls scored significantly higher than the other mothers in the CPI self-acceptance scale, indicating that they possess greater self-confidence, self-assurance, and "capacity for independent thinking and action." The relation between the mothers' security and self-confidence and the daughters level of femininity may be interpreted in several ways. Perhaps mothers with these characteristics are more able than less

TABLE 3 / MEAN SCORES ON PERSONALITY MEASURES (CPI) OF PARENTS OF GIRLS HIGH AND LOW IN FEMININITY.

VARIABLE	HIGH FEMININITY GROUP ($N = 15$)	LOW FEMININITY GROUP ($N = 16$)	t	p^*
SELF ACCEPTANCE				
Mother	22.1	18.5	2.82	$< .005$
Father	19.8	21.7	1.35	ns
FEMININITY				
Mother	24.2	24.1	.26	ns
Father	16.7	18.7	1.35	$< .10$

* *See* footnote to Table 1.

secure mothers to maintain warm, affectionate relationships with their daughters, thus fostering their daughter's femininity. Or, mere possession of these characteristics—which must be evident to the child—may make her a stable, successful, and, consequently, desirable model for the daughter to emulate. These explanations are, of course, not mutually exclusive and both of them may be valid.

The data did not provide any evidence supportive of hypothesis IVa as it applied to mothers. The mothers of highly feminine girls were not found to be more feminine than the mothers of the other girls. It may be inferred that girls are likely to express a high degree of female sex-role preference if their mothers are warm, nurturant, and self-accepting (self-confident), though not necessarily highly feminine. The nature of the mother-child relationships and the mother's personal security are basic determinants of the girl's acquisition of feminine orientations, but the degree of the mother's femininity in itself does not appear to exert an important influence. In other words, so far as we are able to determine, the differences between the two groups of girls in the degree of feminine sex-role preference cannot be attributed to differences in the quantity or intensity of sex-appropriate characteristics or cues presented by their mothers, for the two groups of mothers are approximately equal in this respect. Rather it may be assumed that the more feminine little girls are more strongly motivated than the others to imitate their mothers' behavior as a consequence of their allegiance to that parent. This may have either or both of the following consequents. The feminine cues presented by the mother may have greater vividness or be more distinctive for the girl (i.e., she pays closer attention to them) and hence she is more likely to assimilate more of these characteristics into her own role behavior. Or, being strongly motivated to imitate her mother, she may also emulate the behavior of

other women, some of whom present more highly feminine models than the mother does. In terms of this latter explanation, it may be suggested that the daughter who is securely identified as a female does not need to duplicate her mother's behavior *in toto* but finds other appropriate, sometimes more feminine, models among others in her environment.

While the two groups of fathers did not differ significantly from each other in either the CPI Femininity or Self-Acceptance scales (Table 3), there was a trend consistent with, and supportive of, that part of hypothesis IVa which concerns the girls' fathers. The fathers of the highly feminine group tended to be more masculine in interests and orientations (scored more masculine, or lower, on the Femininity scale) than the fathers of the other group. Perhaps more highly masculine fathers are more aware of the behaviors appropriate for both sexes and, consequently, are better able to discriminate and reward appropriately sex-typed responses in their daughters, thus encouraging and promoting their feminization.

ANALYSIS OF PARENTAL RESPONSES TO PLAY AND GAMES LIST. The parents' direct encouragement of their daughters' participation in sex-appropriate play and activities (hypothesis Va) was measured by the play and games list score. The data are summarized in Table 4.

Contrary to what was predicted on the basis of hypothesis Va, the scores of the mother of the highly feminine girls on this questionnaire did not differ significantly from those of the other mothers. Hypothesis Va, as it relates to the mothers of the girls, was therefore refuted. In brief, the two groups of mothers appeared to be alike in the extent to which they participated with their daughters—and encouraged participation—in feminine games and activities. Apparently the mothers of highly feminine girls provide good models and in subtle ways motivate their daugh-

TABLE 4 / MEAN SCORES ON ENCOURAGEMENT OF SEX-APPROPRIATE BEHAVIOR BY PARENTS OF GIRLS HIGH AND LOW IN FEMININITY.

VARIABLE: PLAY AND GAMES LIST	HIGH FEMININITY GROUP		LOW FEMININITY GROUP		*t*	*p**
	N	MEAN	*N*	MEAN		
Mother	14	31.9	17	32.2	.13	*ns*
Father	11	29.0	15	19.9	1.97	<.05

* *See* footnote to Table 1.

ters to emulate them. According to these data, they accomplish this primarily by interacting warmly and affectionately with their daughters and by revealing their security and self-confidence, rather than by being highly feminine in interests and orientation or by directly stimulating the girl's participation in sex-appropriate female activities.

Hypothesis Va as it related to the fathers of the girls was supported, however. The fathers of the highly feminine group apparently provide much more encouragement and stimulation of their daughters' participation in sex-appropriate activities, scoring significantly higher, on the average, on the play and games list than the fathers of the other girls (Table 4). Clearly, these fathers play an important and direct role in steering their daughters into feminine role preferences.

DISCUSSION

The results on boys' father-identifications—and consequent appropriate sex-typing of their behavior—are essentially in agreement with those of previous studies. An unexpected finding was that, for girls, the process of identification with the like-sexed parent—assessed in terms of degree of appropriate sex-role preference—appears to be much more complexly determined and contingent upon a greater number of antecedent conditions. This was somewhat surprising in view of the fact that much current psychological theorizing emphasizes that the establishment of appropriate sex identification is as difficult—or perhaps more difficult—for boys as for girls (2, 18, 22, 28).

According to the data of this study, the most crucial determinant of the development of masculinity in young boys is the nature of the father-son relationship. Appropriate sex-role preference in boys was found to be directly correlated with nurturant, affectionate relationships with the father, a finding fully consistent with the developmental identification hypothesis and the conclusions of other studies (19, 20, 21, 26). There was also a tendency for highly masculine boys to perceive their fathers as punitive and threatening, a finding supportive of the defensive identification hypothesis. In general, it may be concluded that the boy who sees his father as a highly salient and powerful person in his life—instrumental in both rewarding and punishing him—is likely to develop highly sex-appropriate responses. Except for those pertain-

ing to father-son relationships, none of the hypotheses about the acquisition of masculine sex-role preference was supported in the present study. That is, according to these data, appropriate sex-typing of boys was not influenced by the boys' relationships with their mothers, the personality structures of their parents (self-acceptance and relative degrees of masculinity or femininity), or parental encouragement of specifically sex-typed activities.

The acquisition of femininity by young girls is not so simply determined, however. In a way that is analogous to the boys' development of masculine interests, a positive mother-daughter relationship is of paramount importance in the girl's establishment of appropriate sex-role preference. In addition to this factor, however, aspects of the parents' personality structure—e.g., high degree of maternal self-acceptance and self-confidence—appear to be conducive to the establishment of a high degree of femininity in the daughter. Furthermore, while the mother's personality and interrelationships with her son seem to have little influence on the boy's sex-role preference, the father's personality and behavior appear to be important factors in the daughter's development of femininity. The father's possession of a high degree of masculinity of interests and attitudes and his active encouragement of the girl's participation in appropriate sex-typed activities tend to foster the girl's development of appropriate sex-role preference.

From a synthesis of these data it may be inferred that the boy who loves his father (regards him as nurturant) and perceives him as a powerful person is highly motivated to incorporate some of that parent's behavior and personal qualities, including his sex-typed characteristics and interests. By generalization, he tends to view other men in the same way and emulates their behavior, thus reinforcing his masculine identification. This may occur even though the parents do not strongly encourage, or give direct tuition in, masculine activities and even though the father is not an outstanding model of masculinity or personal security.

It seems that the boy, being strongly motivated to become masculine—initially as a consequence of his positive feelings toward his father—maintains, and probably increases, this motivation. Under these conditions, there is little need for his parents to present clear-cut models of sex-typing or excellent personal adjustment or to exert strong pressure toward masculinizing him. In brief, given positive father-son relationships, no specific family socialization techniques are required for the boy's achievement of a high level of male typing.

The process of female typing in the little girl, while directly related to mother-daughter relationships, is also facilitated by the presence of a highly adequate mother as the feminine model and a father who tends to be aware of the behavior expected of a young girl, encouraging his daughter to act in feminine ways (i.e., to participate in girls' games).

It may be concluded that, in the development of the young child's appropriate sex-typing, the girl's family must play more forceful and direct roles as teachers and socializers than the boy's. The reasons for this are not clear, but we may speculate that the boy receives more assistance and support from the general social environment in the process of establishing appropriate sex-role behavior than the girl does. This may be true for several reasons. For one thing, in American culture—particularly in the middle class group from which most of these subjects come—maleness (being a male and acting like one) is relatively highly valued, while being a female and behaving in feminine ways are relatively less valued and rewarded (15). Evidence for this comes from the finding that, when asked, boys seldom, if ever, state that they wish they were girls, while girls frequently state that they wish they were boys (30). Moreover, masculine characteristics are rated as more desirable by children and adults of both sexes (17). Moreover, among nursery school children, boys identify significantly more strongly with their fathers than with their mothers, while girls often identify with both mother and father (5). Boys generally become firmly sex-typed in their behavior earlier than girls do (24). From these facts it may be inferred that society strongly motivates the boy to acquire his own sex-role characteristics and rewards him for acquiring them. The girl is not so strongly motivated in this way to become feminine and is less likely to be highly rewarded for it if she does.

Moreover, as common observation attests, behavior considered appropriate for boys is more clear-cut and well-defined, and boys' violations of approved behavior are more likely to elicit punishment and hence to be extinguished. For example, young boys can wear cowboy outfits and play ball but would be severely ridiculed if they wore dresses or played with dolls. Little girls, on the other hand, can wear either outfit and play either game without suffering such harsh social criticism. In short, boys can acquire masculine behavior and interests relatively more simply than girls can assimilate femininity, partially because the cues for sex-appropriate masculine behavior are more distinct, easier to discriminate, and hence easier to learn.

From the point of view of learning theory, the role of the parents in masculinizing their sons is primarily that of providing initial motivation to acquire masculine characteristics and behavior. The general social-cultural milieu further implements the masculinization by presenting numerous, well articulated, and distinct cues for the male sex role and rewards the boy for learning these. If the boy is already highly motivated to learn this kind of behavior as a consequence of his relationships with his father, he will not have difficulty acquiring these behaviors.

For girls, the social-cultural milieu gives less support in the assimilation of her sex role. Due to the relatively lesser value of the feminine role in middle class American culture and the relative paucity and nondistinctiveness of cues associated with the female sex role among young children, her parents must assist her in several ways if she is to achieve a high degree of femininity. More specifically, parents are forced to assume three feminizing functions with their daughters, only one of which is like the parents' role in masculinizing boys. They must evoke motivation to acquire femininity, and, in addition, they help the feminizing process by presenting some cues for discriminating the sex roles and by directly encouraging the girls to adopt at least certain kinds of behavior characteristic of the feminine role.

It is also possible that, for young boys, masculinization is facilitated by their tendency to have higher activity levels and greater freedom of movement. These probably permit them to seek out and establish more numerous and intense social relationships outside the home than girls do. Some of the boy's peers and friends are likely to be excellent models of masculine behavior, and, by imitating these people, the boy's own appropriate sex-typing will be strengthened. Young girls, having more limited freedom to make contacts outside the home, may find fewer good models of sex-appropriate behavior to emulate. For this reason, the establishment of a high degree of sex-typing in girls may be relatively less influenced by factors outside the home than the masculinization of boys and more importantly affected by parental personality structure and direct efforts at sex-typing.

The data of the present study are consistent with at least one aspect of psychoanalytic theory, for they indicate that, as that theory maintains, the achievement of sex-identification is more complicated for girls than for boys. The greater difficulty involved in feminine than in masculine sex-typing may, however, be plausibly—and probably more parsimoniously—attributed to certain features of the social structure that promote the boys' acquisition of appropriate sex-role behavior more than they do the girl's.

It is impossible to know, without empirical tests, the extent to which findings such as these can be generalized. The results might have been different if other criteria of strength of identification were used. For example, it is possible that the achievement of a high degree of same-sex parental modeling, another criterion of identification (as distinguished from sex identity, the criterion used here), is in fact more complex for boys than for girls in our society. It is at least possible that different manifestations of identification are related to different processes. Thus, as Mowrer has suggested (18), sex typing may depend on developmental identification while conscience development or parental modeling may depend on defensive identification.

SUMMARY

This study was designed to test several hypotheses dealing with boys' father-identifications and girls' mother-identifications as these are reflected in the degree of appropriate sex-role preference. The sex-role preference of 46 first grade boys and 57 first grade girls was determined by means of the IT scale. Boys above the boys' median masculinity score and girls above the median for femininity (i.e., below the median for masculinity) were considered to have developed high degrees of appropriate sex-role identification while the others were considered low in this dimension.

The major hypotheses concerned the relations between parent-child interactions and identification with the like-sexed parent. Doll play techniques provided the basis for assessing the subjects' perceptions of their parents. Analysis of these data substantially supported the developmental identification hypothesis for both sexes. That is, compared with members of their own sex low in appropriate sex-role identification, highly masculine boys and highly feminine girls

perceived their like-sexed parents as significantly warmer, more nurturant, and more affectionate. Maternal interviews with the girls' mothers buttressed the doll play findings, the mothers of the highly feminine girls being rated significantly higher than the other mothers in "warmth toward the child." Among the boys—but not among the girls—there was also evidence supportive of the defensive identification hypothesis, for the highly masculine group tended to perceive their fathers as more punitive as well as more rewarding.

The other hypotheses investigated were related to parental characteristics — specifically mothers' femininity, fathers' masculinity, and self-acceptance—and parental encouragement of the child's participation in sex-appropriate activities as antecedents of high degrees of sex-typing. These were evaluated from parental questionnaires which included the CPI Femininity and Self-Acceptance scales and a play and games list in which the parent indicated whether he (she) encouraged or discouraged his (her) child's participation in certain typically male and female activities.

There was no evidence that high masculinity of fathers, femininity of mothers, parental self-acceptance, or encouragement of their son's participation in masculine activities had any significant effect on the boy's masculinization. Apparently the boy's perceptions of his father as a nurturant and powerful individual are crucial in his development of masculinity, but his parents' personality structure and their pressures toward sex-typing him are not significantly influential.

The young girl's feminization, on the other hand, appears to be facilitated by several factors in addition to warm mother-daughter relationships. Thus, the mothers of highly feminine girls were found to be significantly more self-accepting, but not more feminine or more encouraging of their daughters' participation in feminine activities, than the mothers of girls low in femininity.

Fathers of the highly feminine girls also appear to play a vastly important role in their daughters' feminization. Compared with the fathers of girls low in femininity, these fathers tended to be more masculine and gave their daughters significantly more encouragement to participate in feminine activities. It may be concluded that the feminization of young girls involves a greater number of, and more complex, determinants than does the masculinization of boys. In the development of the child's appropriate sex-typing, the girl's family appears to play more forceful and direct roles as teachers and socializers than the boy's. It is suggested that this is true because the male role is more highly valued in middle class American culture and because behavior considered appropriate for the boy is more clear-cut and well-defined. In short, it may be that the boy receives more assistance and support from the general social environment in the process of sex-typing than the girl does.

REFERENCES

1. BRONFENBRENNER, U. The study of identification through interpersonal perception. In R. Tagiuri & L. Petrullo (Eds.), *Person perception and interpersonal behavior*. Stanford Univer. Press, 1958. Pp. 110-130.

2. BRONFENBRENNER, U. Freudian theories of identification and their derivatives. *Child Develpm.*, 1960, *31*, 15-40.

3. BROWN, D. G. Sex role preference in young children. *Psychol. Monogr.*, 1956, *70*, No. 14 (Whole No. 421).

4. BURTON, R. V., MACCOBY, E. E., & ALLINSMITH, W. Antecedents of resistance to temptation in four-year-old children. *Child Develpm.*, 1961, *32*, 689-710.

5. EMMERICH, W. Parental identification in young children. *Genet. Psychol. Monogr.*, 1959, *60*, 257-308.

6. FREUD, A. *The ego and the mechanisms of defense*. International Universities Press, 1946.

7. FREUD, S. The passing of the Oedipus-complex. In *Collected papers*. Vol. II. London: Hogarth Press, 1949. Pp. 269-282.

8. FREUD, S. On narcissism; an introduction. In *Collected papers*. Vol. IV. London: Hogarth, 1925. Pp. 30-59.

9. FREUD, S. *Group psychology and the analysis of the ego*. London: Hogarth Press, 1949.

10. FREUD, S. Some psychological consequences of the anatomical distinction between the sexes. In *Collected papers*. Vol. V. London: Hogarth, 1950. Pp. 186-197.

11. GOUGH, H. G. *The California Psychological Inventory*. Consulting Psychology Press, 1957.

12. HELPER, M. M. Learning theory and the self-concept. *J. abnorm. soc. Psychol.*, 1955, *51*, 184-194.

13. KAGAN, J. The concept of identification. *Psychol. Rev.*, 1958, *65*, 296-305.

14. LEVIN, H., & SEARS, R. R. Identification with parents as a determinant of doll play aggression. *Child Develpm.*, 1956, *27*, 135-153.

15. LYNN, D. B. A note on sex differences in the development of masculine and feminine identification. *Psychol. Rev.*, 1959, *66*, 126-135.

16. MC CANDLESS, B. R. *Children and adolescents*. Holt, Rinehart, & Winston, 1961.

17. MC KEE, J. P., & SHERRIFFS, A. C. The differential evaluation of males and females. *J. Pers.*, 1957, *25*, 356-371.

18. MOWRER, O. H. Identification: A link between learning theory and psychotherapy. In *Learning theory and personality dynamics*. Ronald, 1950. Pp. 573-616.

19. MUSSEN, P. Some antecedents and consequents of masculine sex-typing in adolescent boys. *Psychol. Monogr.*, 1961, *75*, 2, (Whole No. 506).

20. MUSSEN, P., & DISTLER, L. Masculinity, identification, and father-son relationships. *J. abnorm. soc. Psychol.*, 1959, *59*, 350-356.

21. MUSSEN, P., & DISTLER, L. Child rearing antecedents of masculine identification in kindergarten boys. *Child Develpm.*, 1960, *31*, 89-100.

22. PARSONS, T. Family structure and the socialization of the child. In T. Parsons & R. F. Bales (Eds.), *Family, socialization, and interaction process*. Free Press, 1955. Pp. 35-131.

23. PAYNE, D. E., & MUSSEN, P. H. Parent-child relations and father identification among adolescent boys. *J. abnorm. soc. Psychol.*, 1956, *52*, 358-362.

24. RABBAN, M. Sex-role identification in young children in two diverse social groups. *Genet. Psychol. Monogr.*, 1950, *42*, 81-158.

25. ROSENBERG, B. G., & SUTTON-SMITH, B. The measurement of masculinity and femininity in children. *Child Develpm.*, 1959, *30*, 373-380.

26. SEARS, P. S. Child-rearing factors related to playing of sex-typed roles. *Amer. Psychologist*, 1953, *8*, 431. (Abstract)

27. SEARS, R. R. Identification as a form of behavior development. In D. B. Harris (Ed.), *The concept of development*. Univer. of Minnesota Press, 1957. Pp. 149-161.

28. SEARS, R. R., MACCOBY, E. E., & LEVIN, H. *Patterns of child rearing*. Row, Peterson, 1957.

29. STOKE, S. M. An inquiry into the concept of identification. In W. E. Martin & C. B. Stendler (Eds.), *Readings in child development*. Harcourt, Brace, 1954. Pp. 227-239.

30. WEST, J. *Plainville, U.S.A.* Columbia Univer. Press, 1945.

25/LEARNING BY IMITATION IN KINDERGARTEN CHILDREN[1]/JUDY F. ROSENBLITH[*]

THIS STUDY ASKS FOUR MAIN QUES-tions: (a) Does having a model lead to significantly greater improvement in learning than additional experience only? (b) Is the extent of a child's learning by copying an adult "leader" or model affected by the sex of that leader (considered, especially, in relation to the child's sex)? (c) Does the way in which the leader treats the child immediately before the copying session affect learning? (d) Is there an interaction between the "sex" and "treatment" variables?

The problem of imitation examined in an experimental framework has received its most extensive treatment in Miller and Dollard's book *Social Learning and Imitation* (4). They demonstrated that the tendency to imitate is acquired in rats and children, and that the operations of reinforcement are necessary for the establishment of imitative tendencies.

Schein (8) attempted to test the assertions of Miller and Dollard with adult Ss. Studying the effect of reward on adult imitative behavior, he found that a significant number of Ss "learned" to imitate a model when such imitation was rewarded. He also found that the imitative response generalized to a similar but new situation. Since the absolute level of imitation was not high, Schein speculated about motives (e.g., "imitation is equivalent to cheating") which might have been operative to demand that his adult Ss not imitate. Such motives all appeared less apt to be present in young children than in adults. Also, Schwartz (9) found more imitation in 9- and 10-year-olds than in 15- and 16-year-olds, suggesting that more imitation might be expected in kindergarten Ss.

Miller and Dollard classified imitation into three categories of behavior: *same* behavior, *matched-dependent* behavior, and *copying*. They asserted that all three behaviors are learned via

the principles of instrumental conditioning. Learning by imitation is linked to their concept of copying in which one person learns to model his behavior on that of another. They further asserted that all three kinds of imitative learning respond to the same conditions.

In this study there was no attempt to teach the child to copy. There was reliance on the child's having learned to make imitative responses as a result of past experience in the processes of socialization. Generalization of this established learning to imitate is what was looked for. As Miller and Dollard have said: "An analysis in terms of learning principles indicated that the factor of generalization should play an important role in the processes determining the degree to which any leader will be reacted to as a prestigeful model" (4, p. 166). Thus, generalization to a male model from significant males in the child's life was expected, and similarly for a female model. Since the child has very little contact with the particular adults who serve as models, it was assumed that the degree to which the model is effective does stem from such generalization. Nevertheless, rewards were not excluded from the situation. The leader to be imitated or copied was not only prestigeful by virtue of age and size, but the leader's skill was emphasized by verbally rewarding his correct performance. The child was also verbally rewarded when his performance was a sufficiently close copy of the leader's (i.e., was correct).

This problem can also be examined in the theoretical framework of identification theory. Doing so poses the question of whether an adult leader of the same sex as the child might not be a more effective model for imitative behavior for 5-year-old children.

Miller and Dollard, in commenting that sex-typing may belong to a list of social conditions that may enhance or inhibit imitation or the tendency to imitate, do not tell at which age level this factor should become important. It is, however, not unreasonable to assume that at kindergarten age most children have had more reinforcement for imitating a female and hence that a female model should be more effective for

[1] This paper is based on a dissertation submitted to Harvard University in partial fulfillment of the requirements for the Ph.D. The author would like to express gratitude to Dr. Wesley Allinsmith for his encouragement and counsel. This research was aided by a grant to the Laboratory of Human Development from the Public Health Service.

[*] Judy F. Rosenblith, Learning by imitation in kindergarten children, *Child Develpm.*, 1959, 30, 69-80. Reprinted by permission of the Society for Research in Child Development.

both sexes. Such a view would be congruent with that expressed by Miller and Dollard or by contiguity theorists with regard to the secondary reward value which people acquire.

Most identification theories, on the other hand, would lead one to expect that a good deal of identification has taken place by the kindergarten age. Thus, one would expect that a leader of the same sex as the child should be the most effective, with considerable individual fluctuation due to differences in the stage of identification that has been reached.

Another aspect of identification theories leads to a consideration of the role of threat in the formation of identification (Freud, castration threat; Fromm, threat from authoritarian father). Mowrer (5) posits two kinds of identification. The first is developmental, it is with the mother for both sexes, threat does not play a role in it, and it is related to the learning of skills. The second kind of identification is a later form. It is with the parent of the same sex and threat may play a role. Mowrer calls this kind defensive identification, and says that it is related to character learning and is well under way by kindergarten age. In line with these considerations one might expect differences in the amount of identification shown or generalized (hence in the effectiveness of the adult as a model for copying) according to the presence or absence of an implied threat in the adult-child relation. The contingency or uncertainty-reduction theory of effectiveness of secondary rewards would lead to the same set of expectations.

These considerations led to the following experimental manipulations: (a) the adult leader was attentive to the child for the entire period prior to the copying session for some Ss, and (b) the adult withdrew attention from the child after half of the period and stayed withdrawn for the remainder of the period prior to the copying session for other Ss. Such withdrawal presumably constitutes a mild threat to the child's relation to the adult.

The present study was not intended to provide an *experimentum crucis* for deciding the merits of the above theories, but only to shed light on these problems.

PROCEDURE

The Ss were 120 kindergarten children from two public schools in a Boston suburb composed of middle and upper-middle class residents. Each child was brought individually from the class-

room to the experimental room by the E in order to "play a game." In this initial session the child was tested using the Porteus Maze Test (6); this test was administered with slight modifications in the instructions and procedure to make it more suitable to the age of the children.[2] The Porteus Test contains one maze for each year from 3 through 11. Two trials were allowed on each of these as in the Porteus Test. There are also mazes for 12- and 14-year-olds and adults. Porteus allows four trials for each of these mazes. In this experiment only two trials were allowed since the 5-year-old Ss who reached the 12-year-old level or above were apt to be frustrated by four trials on such difficult mazes and want to quit the "game." The Porteus criteria for discontinuing testing were used, i.e., failure on two consecutive or on two out of three consecutive age levels.

On the basis of level of performance in this initial session children were assigned to one of four groups. Group 1 consisted of those who passed only the first two mazes, (i.e., the 3- and 4-year mazes). Group 2 consisted of those who passed a total of three or four of the mazes. Group 3 passed five mazes, and Group 4 passed six or more of the mazes. Children from each group were then assigned to each of the treatments.

One to three weeks after this initial session the child was brought from his room by E to "have a second turn at the game." This will be referred to as the copying session. Just before arriving at the experimental room, E said to each child who was not in a control group: "You know what? I have someone else here to play the game with us." E and child then entered the room and E introduced the child to the other adult by first names. E then explained to the child that she had something to do for a while and invited the child and the other adult to go to another table in the room and play with the toys on it until E was ready to play the game.[3] The child was seated facing the table of toys and the adult at the adjacent side facing the child and/or table.

It should be noted that E essentially was treat-

---

[2] Copies of the exact procedure may be seen in (7).

[3] The toys on the table were chosen for their masculine and feminine identification potential. E was actually recording the child's behavior as the child played with the toys. Ratings of these protocols for masculine and feminine identification will be examined later. The toys included shaving set and make-up kit, carpenter tools and kitchen utensils, and a family of dolls, among others.

ing the other adult in the same manner as the child. *E* did nothing to enhance the adultness or maleness (or femaleness) of the leaders except to reward their proficiency. They were not called Mr. or Mrs. and not described as fathers or mothers. However, they were adult and they were proficient at the task. During the play period the leader behaved as an adult interested in the play of the child and not as another child playing.

The experiment was first run using a male for a leader. The treatments or conditions were: (I) Male leader with a child of the same sex, leader attentive to child throughout the 10-minute period that preceded the copying session proper. (II) Male leader with a child of the same sex, leader attentive to the child for 5 minutes, then leader said: "I'm sorry, I can't play with you any more, I have to read a book." Leader then turned his chair so his back was toward the child and read a book for 5 minutes. (III) Control *Ss*, males, who were brought to the room by *E* and who immediately received two additional trials at each maze previously failed, until the criterion for discontinuing testing was reached. (IV) Male leader with a child of the opposite sex, attentive throughout (as in I). (V) Male leader with a child of the opposite sex, withdrew attention after 5 minutes (as in II). (VI) Control *Ss*, females, tested in the same fashion (as in III). The entire design was then repeated using a female leader.

In treatments I, II, IV, and V, at the end of the 10-minute period *E* said: "I'm ready to play the game now." Adult leader and child moved to the *E*'s table. They took adjacent seats at the table on the side opposite *E* and facing her with the adult to the right of the child. *E* then said to the child: "You've played this game with me before. —— (adult) wasn't here when we played then, so how would it be if you take turns and give —— (adult) the first turn?" (We might note here that no child ever argued with the suggestion of taking turns.) The adult was then given the first maze which the child failed previously and the same instructions that the child had received. The leader did the maze correctly at a rather slow pace and with pauses at choice points accompanied by some visual search. The child watched during this period and then was given a turn at the same maze. To ensure that the child was watching the entire performance, the adult paused when he was not and only continued when the child had again turned his attention to the maze. There were two such trials on each maze failed initially (unless the child passed it correctly on the first trial, in which case there was only one), until the criterion for discontinuing testing was reached. This yields a design in which there are six treatments (including controls) and four replications (by initial level of performance). The part of the study using the male leader was started at one school and completed at the second. The repetition with the female leader was started at the second school and completed at the first.

The number of *Ss* decided on for each cell was based on the distribution of passes obtained by the children in the first school. Since the second school had a different distribution of passes (fewer children with a high number of passes), the number of children from groups 3 & 4 of initial performance level in each cell was decreased from 3 to 2, thus dropping the total N from an anticipated 132 to 120 (*see* Table 1).

TABLE 1 / EXPERIMENTAL DESIGN (Number of Ss in each cell is shown).

INITIAL PERFORMANCE GROUPS	MALE Ss			FEMALE Ss			
	A†(I)	WA†(II)	C†(III)	A(IV)	WA(V)	C(VI)	
MALE LEADER*							
1	3	3	3	3	3	3	18
2	3	3	3	3	3	3	18
3	2	2	2	2	2	2	12
4	2	2	2	2	2	2	12
	10	10	10	10	10	10	60

* The entire design is repeated with a female leader.

† A stands for leader attentive throughout, WA, for withdraws attention for last half of period, and C, for controls in this and all subsequent tables.

TABLE 2 / NUMBER OF NEW PASSES OBTAINED BY Ss IN THE VARIOUS CELLS.

INITIAL PERFORMANCE GROUPS	MALE Ss			FEMALE Ss		
	A(I)	WA(II)	C(III)	A(IV)	WA(V)	C(VI)
MALE LEADER						
1	7	6	5	5	4	2
2	9	12	8	9	6	6
3	4	6	1	4	4	2
4	6	7	1	4	5	2
Total	26	31	15	22	19	12
FEMALE LEADER						
1	6	2	4	4	1	1
2	10	4	6	6	3	4
3	8	4	2	3	3	4
4	6	4	1	3	5	3
Total	30	14	13	16	12	12
Total	56	45	28	38	31	24

The data to be analyzed here, in investigating the amount of learning by imitation, are the number of new mazes passed ("new passes") in the second or copying session.

RESULTS

Since the distribution of the number of new passes is not normal, and since the number of mazes passed forms only an ordinal scale, the results will be examined using nonparametric statistics.

The data in Table 2 refer to the over-all experimental design, i.e., to both the male and female leader experiments. If one applies Friedman's X^2r (9) to these data, one finds the p values[4] shown in Table 3. The differences found justify separate examination of pairs of treatments.

[4] All p values reported in this paper are for a two-tailed test.

Before doing so, it is interesting to examine the data according to the sex of Ss and of leaders. Table 3 shows the p values of X^2r calculated for the various combinations of sex of Ss and of leader. Male leader and male Ss show more influence of these manipulations.

Examination of pairs of treatments by a method described by Wilcoxon (11) shows that boys and girls who are control Ss do not differ significantly, although there is a tendency for the control boys to improve more than the control girls. This tendency is close to the .05 level for those whose initial performance placed them in level 1. The remaining results of these comparisons are presented in Table 4. In summary it can be seen that: (a) having a model is more effective than merely having additional trials; (b) girls seem less sensitive to the experimental manipulations than are boys; (c) the female leader was less effective than the male leader; (d) attention is more effective than withdrawal of attention.

TABLE 3 / COMPARISON OF TREATMENTS EXAMINED BY THE FRIEDMAN X^2r.

	p VALUES	
TREATMENTS COMPARED	MALE LEADER	FEMALE LEADER
Total Table (Conditions I through VI)	.01	.09
Treatments—controls not included (Conditions I, II, IV, V)	.06	.052
Conditions involving male Ss (Conditions I, II and III)	.04	.05
Conditions involving female Ss (Conditions IV, V and VI)	.15	.80

TABLE 4 / COMPARISONS OF PAIRS OF TREATMENTS USING THE WILCOXON RANKING METHOD.

p VALUES*

COMPARISON†	MALE LEADER		FEMALE LEADER	
	MALE Ss	FEMALE Ss	MALE Ss	FEMALE Ss
A plus WA vs C	.01 (A&WA)	.01 (A&WA)	ns (A&WA)	ns (A&WA)
A vs C	.10 (A)	.05>p>.02 (A)	.10 (A)	ns (A)
WA vs C	.05 (WA)	.10>p>.05 (WA)	ns (WA)	ns (WA)
A vs WA	ns (WA)	ns (A)	ns (A)	ns (A)
A plus WA vs C (by initial performance groups)				
Group 1	ns (A&WA)	.05 (A&WA)	ns (C)	ns (C)
Group 2	.05 (A&WA)	ns (A&WA)	ns (C)	ns (A&WA)
Group 3 and 4	.05>p>.02 (A&WA)	ns (A&WA)	.01 (A&WA)	ns (A&WA)

* Exact p values or p values larger than the .10 level are not available in the published tables. "ns" is used to indicate that p is greater than .10, i.e., is not significant.

† The abbreviations in the parentheses indicate which side of the comparison gave the superior performance

Certain qualifications of these general statements are found in the detailed results. The finding concerning the effectiveness of the male and female leaders cannot be labeled a sex difference without further replication since it is possible that individual characteristics of the leaders rather than their immediately perceptible sex characteristics were responsible. In any event, these rather major effects of sex (of both leader and child) which operate in a way that cuts across the original experimental design make the next step of analysis less apt to yield significant results.

The next step was to examine the two experiments together. Since the Ss were not randomly assigned to treatments across both sexes of leader, some justification for combining the data is probably needed. Both leaders did have Ss from both schools, though not equal proportions of Ss from each. The control Ss in both replications showed no significant difference; in

fact, the rank totals are 412 for the first group and 408 for the second. It thus seems reasonable to conclude that the two populations are similar enough to justify combining them for comparisons.

Analyzing the data in this way, the design yields five conditions: opposite sex attentive, opposite sex withdraws attention, same sex attentive, same sex withdraws attention, and controls. If these treatments are examined over the four replications provided by initial level groups, the X^2r is 8.85, which (with 4 df) has a p value between .06 and .07. As in the earlier analysis, the boys show a significant effect of treatments (p is .02) and the girls do not (p is .15). An extension of the Kruskal-Wallis technique[5] yields an analysis of variance the results of which are shown in Table 5.

[5] This extension of the Kruskal-Wallis analysis of variance was suggested to the author by Dr. R. Hyman of the Department of Social Relations at Harvard.

TABLE 5 / KRUSKAL-WALLIS ANALYSIS OF VARIANCE AS EXPANDED BY HYMAN.

SOURCE OF VARIATION	H	df	APPROXIMATE p
Among subcells	36.6	39	ns (.5)
Treatments	7.87	4	.10
Levels of initial performance	7.13	3	.07
Sex of Ss	3.00	1	.09
Sex × Levels	.72	3	ns (.85)
Levels × Treatments	8.4	12	ns (.75)
Sex × Treatments	7.43	4	.11
Sex × Treatments × Levels	2.05	12	ns (.99)

DISCUSSION

The difference between the results for the male leader and the female leader are striking, as are the differences between the results for boys and girls. The fact that the boys tended to show more improvement than the girls may provide more ceiling for finding differences between treatments for the boys. However, such differences between boys and girls remain puzzling since they had been equated for pretest performance. Although there was no significant difference between boys and girls as controls, the consistent superiority of all Ss with a male leader is noted ($p < .05$ that they differ from controls by chance, but $p < .10$ that Ss with the female leader do). Hartup (3) found that boys learned a concept formation task more quickly than girls. He speculated that the blocks involved were more salient for boys than for girls. (Note: The mazes used as a subtest on WISC correlate most highly with block design and object assembly, about .48). Publications on the Porteus Test fail to give any information on sex differences that sheds any light on this problem.

One should also note that the level of performance on the pretest is a significant source of variation. Thus, it is wise to control for level of pretest performance in a study such as the present one. The fact that levels did not enter into any significant interaction term mitigates this conclusion. It does, however, seem (see Table 4) more profitable to look for certain effects of treatments at particular levels rather than in a random population or a representative one.

Now one can turn to the questions raised at the beginning of the paper.

1. Does having a model have a significant effect on the amount of improvement? The answer to this question is yes.

2. Is one sex of leader more effective in evoking learning by imitation? In particular the question raised was whether a female leader or a leader of the same sex as the child would be more effective. Actually the male leader was more effective for both sexes, though only significantly so for the girls. One possible explanation for this finding might lie in the fact that an adult male is more unusual in the school setting, hence has more reward value. Gewirtz and Baer (2), in studying the effectiveness of a social reinforcer (approval) in conjunction with social deprivation, found that the effectiveness of the isolation was qualified by an interaction which

indicated that the woman was less effective relative to the man under the condition where Ss were tested immediately on removal from the play group than the condition where Ss were tested after a 20-minute period of total isolation. Our situation would seem to be closer to the former condition. Perhaps the whole school setting is one of social deprivation in respect to adult males who play a role in the life of kindergarten children. In summary, there is an effect of sex of leader, but it is not the effect anticipated from either of our theoretical approaches.

3. Does an implied threat to the relation between the child and the adult operate to enhance identification and thus enhance learning by imitation? For boys there was a tendency for those from whom the male leader withdrew attention to do better. They were not significantly better than boys with an attentive male leader; but they were better than controls at the .05 level, while the male leader attentive group were better than controls at only the .10 level. For girls, however, the effectiveness of the leader of the same sex withdrawing attention does not appear. With the female leader, as with the male, girls tend to do better when they have attention throughout.

The failure to find a relation between implied threat and better learning for girls with a female leader is particularly puzzling in view of Hartup's findings (3). In his study he found that 4-year-old girls learned a simple concept formation task twice as fast when the woman for whom they were doing it had been very nurturant for 5 minutes and then had sat "busy" at her desk for 5 minutes. This quicker learning was not shown for the 4-year-old boys in general. There are a number of differences that could account for the discrepancy: (a) He used 4- instead of 5-year-olds. (b) His task was presented by the person who withdrew instead of by a third person. (c) There were differences in the task (his Ss learned the concept that determined which of four blocks is the "right" one, ours the way to do a maze). (d) Our results also might be idiosyncratic to our female leader.[6] Hartup used two females and found no significant differences between them. (e) The nurturance which his leaders interrupted was of a more active kind

[6] We did a spot check using another female leader for 4 children (2 boys and 2 girls, all at the same initial level of performance). It is suggestive that there was no apparent difference between results for these 4 children and a comparable 4 from our female leader experiment.

(getting down on the floor and playing with the child). The possible effects of the last four differences are very difficult to speculate about. There is, however, an interesting question we might raise concerning the first point. There are reasons to expect on the basis of Freudian thinking that a girl changes her primary object from mother to father at about age 4. If that is the case, the girl may be particularly sensitive to threat from females at that age. Boys presumably do not change until resolution of the Oedipus complex, well into the fifth year on the average. In that case, 5-year-old boys might be particularly sensitive to threat from males. This interpretation would be congruent with both Hartup's and our findings. Very general support for this idea may be found by examining the data for all girls and boys in the sample who are under 5 years, 3 months, in comparision with all those who are over 5 years, 7 months. We find that the older boys improve significantly more than the younger ($p = .02$), while the older girls do not improve significantly more than the younger ($p > .10$). Unfortunately, there are too few cases to enable us to look at the operation of the attention and withdrawal of attention variables within these age subgroups.

In summary, there is equivocal evidence for threat having the effect of enhancing performance where boys with the male leader are concerned, but in no other case.

4. Is there an interaction between the sex and treatment variables? Yes. This answer must be qualified by saying that we cannot be certain whether it is the sex of the leaders or other personal characteristics which account for some of the interactions. Further replications are needed to settle this issue. However, one should bear in mind that generalization from adults significant in the child's life was expected to be more important than the personal characteristics of the leaders to whom the Ss were exposed for only a brief span of time. Also, Hartup's failure to find differences between two female adults in their effect on the children, and the lack of differences in our own small check are signs which indicate that this is a reasonable view.[7]

On the basis of the data, boys and girls both respond better to attention from the opposite sexed leader than to withdrawal. Boys, and not girls, tend to do better after withdrawal of attention from the leader of the same sex. As indicated above, the differential functioning of threat may be, in part at least, a function of the age of the Ss. The rank orders of effectiveness of treatments for the over-all design is given in Table 6.

SUMMARY

The effectiveness of learning by imitation was studied in a context which permitted examination of a number of variables relevant to learning and identification theories. These were: (a) the effectiveness of having a leader or model as contrasted with experience in the absence of a model; (b) the effectiveness of the sex of the leader and of the leader's sex in relation to that of the child; (c) the effectiveness of the adult leader who gives attention to the child for the entire period preceding the imitation, as contrasted with the adult who pays attention to the child for half the time and withdraws attention for the remaining half.

In general, having a model was more effective than merely having additional trials. There were important differences between the effectiveness of the male leader and the female leader. The male leader was, in general, more effective.

[7] Additional evidence of this kind is provided by Bishop (1), who found that when children were brought into a play room situation with a neutral adult (female) they reacted in the same way they had earlier reacted to their mothers with respect to aggressive stimuli, cooperation, noncooperation and resistance.

TABLE 6 / RANK ORDERS OF AMOUNT OF IMPROVEMENT.

	SS-A	SS-WA	OS-A	OS-WA	C
Boys	3 (26)	1 (31)	2 (30)	5 (14)	4 (15)
Girls	3 (17)	4 (12)	1 (21)	2 (19)	5 (11)

NOTE.—SS-A stands for leader of same sex—attentive throughout;
    SS-WA stands for leader of same sex—withdraws attention;
    OS-A stands for leader of opposite sex—attentive throughout;
    OS-WA stands for leader of opposite sex—withdraws attention;
    C stands for controls, additional experience with no leader.
Figures in parentheses represent the number of new passes obtained by all subjects in that cell.

There were also important differences between boys and girls. Boys showed more improvement. Girls seemed less sensitive to the experimental manipulations. There was a tendency for attention to be more effective than withdrawl of attention except in the case of boys with a male leader. The specific findings were examined in detail and their relation to current theories discussed. Analysis of variance on the male and female leader parts of the study combined showed effects of: (a) treatments, (b) sex of Ss, (c) initial or pretest level of Ss' performance on the mazes, and (d) interaction between the sex of Ss and the treatments.

REFERENCES

1. BISHOP, BARBARA M. Mother-child interaction and the social behavior of children. *Psychol. Monogr.*, 1951, 65, No. 328.

2. GEWIRTZ, J. L., & BAER, D. M. Does brief social "deprivation" enhance the effectiveness of a social reinforcer ("approval")? *Amer. Psychol.*, 1956, 11, 428-429.

3. HARTUP, W. W. Nurturance and nurturance-withdrawal in relation to the dependency behavior of preschool children. *Child Develpm.*, 1958, 29, 191-201.

4. MILLER, N. E., & DOLLARD, J. *Social learning and imitation.* New Haven: Yale Univer. Press, 1941.

5. MOWRER, O. H. *Learning theory and personality dynamics.* New York: Ronald, 1950.

6. PORTEUS, S. D. *The Porteus Maze Test and intelligence.* Palo Alto: Pacific Books, 1950.

7. ROSENBLITH, JUDY F. Imitation in kindergarten children. Unpublished doctoral dissertation, Radcliffe College, 1958.

8. SCHEIN, E. H. The effect of reward on adult imitative behavior. *J. abnorm. soc. Psychol.*, 1954, 49, 389-395.

9. SCHWARTZ, N. An experimental study of imitation. The effects of reward and age. Senior honors thesis, Radcliffe College, 1953.

10. SIEGEL, S. *Nonparametric statistics for the behavioral sciences.* New York: McGraw-Hill, 1956.

11. WILCOXON, F. Individual comparisons by ranking methods. *Biometrics Bull.*, 1945, 1, 80-83.

26/THE PSYCHODYNAMICS OF SOCIAL MOBILITY IN ADOLESCENT BOYS/

ELIZABETH DOUVAN AND JOSEPH ADELSON*

THERE IS A LARGE AND GROWING BODY of literature on social mobility, and the significance of the topic is generally acknowledged; so it is surprising to find that only limited attention has been given to studying the motivational sources of mobility. What we do find is a general disposition to treat *upward* mobility in a vaguely invidious fashion. It would seem that, in this country, the Horatio Alger tradition and the "dream of success" motif (6) have been pervasive and distasteful enough to have alienated, among others, a good many social scientists. The upwardly aspiring individual has apparently become associated with the pathetic

* Elizabeth Douvan and Joseph Adelson, The psychodynamics of social mobility in adolescent boys, *Journal of Abnormal and Social Psychology*, 1958, 56, 31-44. Reprinted by permission.

seeker after success or with the ruthless tycoon. This image of success is, much of it, implicit—assumption and attitude, and not quite conviction—but it seems to have dominated the thinking of our intellectual community.

Or so it has been until recently. Newer empirical findings have encouraged a more differentiated view of mobility. We begin to get some sense that varying motivations may underlie social striving; we become aware that the direction, the rapidity, and the absolute extent of mobility may reflect differing psychodynamic sources and thus require separate analytic treatment.

In this paper, a first effort is made to explore and clarify one problem in this complex area—to analyze some of the psychic accompaniments of upward and downward mobility strivings among adolescent boys. In the following section, a theory of the personality determinants of mobility is presented; the paper as a whole is devoted to testing some of these formulations.

THEORETICAL CONSIDERATIONS

UPWARD MOBILITY. We can distinguish at least three separate patterns of motivation which are implicit in discussions of upward social mobility: fear of failure, ambivalence toward success, and hope of success.

The first pattern—perhaps the most common image of the mobile individual—is of the desperately scrambling philistine, exhausted in his pursuit of status. He has defined his identity and personal worth exclusively by the criteria of success. Perhaps a typical genetic source of this pattern has been described by Ackerman and Jahoda (1). Competitiveness is taught by the family: "Most of the mothers of our cases . . . apparently did not tell their children 'be happy' but rather 'make money'. . . ." "Success is measured by comparison with others rather than by actual acheivement. . . . There are always some who have done better, who have more money and more social prestige; and there is always the danger of being pushed down the social ladder by a competitor" (1, pp. 88-89).

In the second pattern—ambivalence toward success—the dynamics are more complex. The individual aspiring upward is here seen as responding to the dominance and prestige of the more privileged stratum through a defensive identification with this group and by denying and decrying his own background and status. The genetic sources of this choice of mechanism

may be sought in the aspirer's early encounters with authority and status in the original family setting. We discover in the family scene a harsh and forbidding parent, one who allows the child no hostility; we find a child who has accommodated to parental strength through identification. In this formulation, we see the mobile individual showing many of the characteristics of the "authoritarian personality": a conscious over-idealization of the parent and of authority together with unconscious rebellion and hostility, rigidity, conformity, and anti-intraception. As regards mobility, we find the following dynamics: the motive for upward aspiration arises out of the need to emulate the parents; at the same time mobility arouses conflict since it implies a struggle with this powerful authority figure (2).

Without question, both of these mobility types occur (perhaps frequently) in our society. Yet the recent literature on mobility has suggested that the most common pattern is the one we have called "hope of success" (7). Here we find interest in success directed by a rational ego: the individual who can mobilize his energies effectively, whose aspirations are realistic. The mobility goals are moderate or, in those cases where aspiration is toward a substantial status move, they are nevertheless realistic in view of the individual's talents.

We find a family milieu which encourages autonomy, is not obsessed by status, yet accepts and transmits without ambivalence the culturally central value of achievement. Moreover, the shifts in identity required do not implicate the child in conflict: the family has provided or permitted the child a model for identity consistent with the goal of mobility.

In a society which holds upward mobility to be a central value, which provides opportunity for it, and in which it is, apparently, a very common occurrence, we can expect that the dominant motivational pattern informing upward aspiration is not a defensive one—does not necessitate a personally damaging flight from one's past; rather, we would expect it to accompany effective ego functioning and successful socialization by a family which is transmitting a cultural value of which it approves.[1]

---

[1] One may speculate about those social situations in our culture where upward aspiration necessitates a good deal of emotional stress or induces personal conflict. Generally, we would say, these are situations where a change in status requires a decisive modification of behavior or necessitates a sharp shift in identity models. A number of such situations come to mind:

DOWNWARD MOBILITY. What about the adolescent boy whose aspirations are downward in direction? Here we have someone whose goals are atypical; indeed, they contradict directly a strongly held cultural value. To be sure, the same novelistic tradition which associates upward mobility with Babbittry has sometimes offered us a sentimental image of the downward mobile type, presenting him as an unfettered, romantically sullen child of nature. Our own view is considerably darker.

We see downward aspiration as representing, in many areas, the psychodynamic opposite of upward mobility. If we are correct, these adolescents are demoralized, alienated, anomic. An ambivalent relationship to the parents produces an impoverished ego, vulnerability to conflict, a failure to internalize general cultural values. Ambivalence is, of course, an almost universal outcome of the socialization process; but we conjecture that it is especially acute among the downward mobile. We expect to find a relationship to the parents which is infantile, that is, dependent and hostile. Dependency and aggression accompany, reinforce, and conceal each other. The child who is captured in an infantile tie to his parents has too much of his energy committed in ambivalence; ego functions remain immature and conflict-ridden; the ego is unable to cope adequately with impulses, internalized morality, and the more complex aspects of reality. At its best, the ego enforces a harmony among the psychic institutions and the outside world. But the downward mobile boy, if our formulation is correct, is at the mercy of his impulses, which continually threaten to overwhelm brittle controls. The superego drives are equally primitive and frightening; parental prohibitions are not sufficiently internalized, in part because of their very intensity; superego functioning is consequently immature, in that there is an inadequate fusion of ego and super-

ego processes; the superego stands at some distance from the ego, so that questions of morality are not so much matters of right and wrong as of escape and pursuit. As regards the ego's operations vis-a-vis the outer world, we do not hypothesize that the downward mobile show any gross pathology of reality testing. And yet we feel that the more complex and articulated ego processes—judgment, rapport, control, time-binding—are poorly or unevenly developed.

HYPOTHESES. In the research reported here, a study of the mobility aspirations of adolescent boys, we test a number of hypotheses based on these conceptions of the sources of mobility strivings. Specifically, the following predictions were made about upward- and downward-aspiring boys.[2]

1. *Energy Level.* The upward-mobile boys possess a high degree of available energy for use in social and work activities. Downward-mobile boys, on the other hand, show a diminished vitality.

2. *Achievement Mode.* The boys aspiring to higher status show a pervasive achievement orientation and a secure sense of their own effectiveness in reaching goals. The downward mobile are less oriented toward achievement and dominated by a concern with security.

3. *Orientation Toward the Future.* The time perspective of the upward mobile tends to be extended, while the downward mobile tend to have a constricted orientation in time.

4. *Personal Standards.* The upward mobile boys manifest well internalized moral values and standards of personal behavior. Internalization is relatively incomplete among the downward mobile.

5. *Autonomy.* The upward aspiring display a precocious independence from the family, and a strong sense of autonomy in choosing values and goals. Downward mobile boys, on the other hand, are tied in a dependent relationship to the family.

6. *Orientation Toward the Self.* Upward-mobile boys are realistic in assessing themselves, and show a high degree of self-confidence. The downward aspiring reveal ambivalence toward the self and a lack of poise in social situations.

7. *Family Milieu.* In this area, our predictions were firmer and more specific about the

---

(a) where the status change involves a concomitant ethnic (including religious) shift; (b) where it involves a gross movement up the status ladder; (c) where there has been a limited opportunity to learn the status behavior of the higher status group; (d) at certain points in the status continuum, where the defining criteria of the higher status group are realistically difficult to achieve; e.g., in the movement from lower-upper to upper-upper status in those cases where a defining criterion is ancestry; (e) where the group-of-origin is ambivalent or hostile to the mobility of its members, necessitating a decisive abandonment of the past as a condition of mobility. Under these conditions, mobility upward will require an unusually high degree of personal motivation.

[2] In this paper we will use the terms "upward aspiring" and "upward mobile" interchangeably. It should be clear that we do not assume that upward aspiration will necessarily lead to successful social mobility.

downward mobile group. Previous research (3) led us to expect a pattern of ambivalent dependency in the downward mobile boys' relations with their families. Rebellion and rejection of parental values combined with a strong dependency stem from inconsistent and punitive treatment at the parent's hand: in short, we anticipated an authoritarian family setting.

In addition to these specific predictions, we were interested in inquiring whether the relationship to the family, in upward mobile boys, is characterized by an ambivalent rejection of family values or by a conflict-free differentiation of the self from the family.

METHOD

SUBJECTS. The data for our analysis derive from a national sample survey of adolescent boys conducted by the Survey Research Center.[3] The sample for the total study consisted of a thousand boys in the 14- to 16-year range selected by probability sampling methods. Each boy was given a personal interview at school by a member of the research center's field staff. Open-ended questions and projective questions were used, and interviews lasted from one to three hours.

In the present analysis, we have used as the base sample the interviews taken with urban nonfarm youth whose fathers' occupations fell in any of the following categories: small business owners, self-employed artisans, white collar, sales, and clerical workers, skilled and semi-skilled manual workers. The reason for excluding the sons of men occupying positions at the two extremes of the skill hierarchy becomes apparent when the mobility measure is discussed.

MOBILITY ASPIRATION. Each of our youthful respondents was asked the following questions:

A. What kind of work would you like to do as an adult?

B. Are you pretty sure about this or do you think you're just as likely to go into something else?

Each boy's aspiration was classed on the occupational scale and compared to his father's posi-

[3] The survey was sponsored by the Boy Scouts of America. The complete questionnaire used in the study has been deposited with the American Documentation Institute. Order Document No. 5422 from ADI Auxiliary Publications Project, Photoduplication Service, Library of Congress, Washington 25, D.C., remitting in advance $1.75 for 35 mm. microfilm or $2.50 for 6 by 8 in. photocopies. Make checks payable to Chief, Photoduplication Service, Library of Congress.

TABLE 1 / DISTRIBUTION OF ASPIRATION TYPES BY FATHER'S OCCUPATION.

	FATHER'S OCCUPATION			
ASPIRATION	1 PROFESSIONAL, MANAGERIAL (N = 136)	2 WHITE COLLAR[a] (N = 183)	3 MANUAL SKILLED[b] (N = 335)	4 MANUAL UNSKILLED (N = 70)
	%	%	%	%
Upward		46	58	84
Stable	67	29	34	16
Downward	33	25	08	

Note.—Ten per cent of the total urban sample of boys was lost in the process of rating the boy's aspiration in relation to father's occupation. These were Ss who had not decided what they wanted to be, who gave vague answers, or who wished to be farmers.

[a] This category includes small business owners in addition to sales and clerical workers.

[b] This category includes both skilled and semi-skilled workers.

tion to determine whether it was equivalent to or higher or lower than the father's job in the hierarchy of skills and status.

The distribution of aspiration types by father's occupation is presented in Table 1 for all urban youth in the original sample. An obvious fact is illustrated in this table. Boys whose fathers currently occupy jobs in the top category are by definition limited to equivalent or lower status aspirations, just as those whose fathers are unskilled workers are barred from downward aspiration.

Because of this limitation on the relative freedom of direction in the aspirations of boys from families in Groups 1 and 4, and because we were interested ultimately in both upward and downward mobility, the sample was restricted to those boys from the two middle categories. The aspiration behavior of boys from the extreme groups may reflect in part a statistical artifact. That is, assuming that by chance a certain proportion of boys will aspire to a status-skill level different from the parent's, the direction of deviation is automatically determined for boys in Groups 1 and 4. In the middle groups, on the other hand, deviation is possible in either direction, and the selection of one or the other type should reflect certain specific motivational factors. One might maintain that the fact of aspiring to a level other than the father's in itself reflects unique psychological characteristics, but since the direction of deviation is a focus of our present concern, opportunity for choice in both directions was controlled.[4]

RESULTS

In the following pages we show contrasts among upward, downward, and stable groups. In most cases, we find linear relationships between status aspiration and other variables: the upward mobile are particularly high or low on a variable, the downward mobile are at the opposite extreme, and the stable group falls somewhere in between. Occasionally we find that either the upward or downward aspiring group clearly distinguishes itself from the other two groups. And in a few relationships, the stables stand out, the linear relationship gives way to a curvilinear one.

Since our predictions all concern the mobility categories and there was uncertainty about the exact position of the stable group, chi square was used to test the significance of variation among the three groups.

ENERGY LEVEL. We see here a sharp contrast between upward and downward subjects (Ss): while the upward mobile boy is unusually lively and energetic, the downward aspirer is inactive and apathetic. On all of our measures, the upward group reveals a high commitment of energy to social and recreational pursuits, and yet not at the expense of work involvement; they also seem to show a spirited and enthusiastic love of activity. The downward mobile boy, in contrast, shows an impoverished vitality: he does not participate energetically or enthusiastically in recreational activities.

Looking first at boys' memberships in organizations (Table 2, Item 1), we find that three quarters of the upward mobile Ss belong to some organized group; while slightly less than half of the downward aspiring boys report membership. The upward mobile also have a relatively high proportion of multiple memberships, compared to the other two groups. A similar relationship appears in the area of general leisure activities:

[4] The group used for analysis consisted of 335 boys from working-class background and 183 from white-collar families. Since the upward mobile group contained a disproportionate number of boys from blue-collar backgrounds, we ran all mobility analyses separately for the two broad occupational groups (Categories 2 and 3 in Table 1). Relationships were of approximately the same order within each of these groups. Analysis is presented for the combined group in order to avoid complicating tables unnecessarily, but in all cases relationships reported also held within each of the two background groups.

TABLE 2 / RELATIONSHIPS BETWEEN MOBILITY ASPIRATION AND INDICES OF LEVEL OF ENERGY.

ITEM	MOBILITY			X^{2*}	p LEVEL
	UP-WARD (N = 277) %	STABLE (N = 168) %	DOWN-WARD (N = 73) %		
1. Number of group memberships[a]					
a. none	25	33	52	26.91	.01
b. one	32	38	22		
c. two	23	20	17		
d. three or more	20	09	09		
2. Number of leisure activities					
a. fewer than 20	52	65	67	11.65	.01
b. 20 or more	48	35	33		
3. Dating					
a. do date	66	59	52	5.67	.10-.05
b. do not date	34	41	48		
4. Employment					
a. have jobs	49	47	51	.44	.90
b. do not have jobs	51	53	49		
5. Leisure reading					
a. do not read	17	27	25	7.93	.05
b. fiction-novels, mysteries	32	23	11	12.31	.01
c. travel and adventure	31	20	18	10.52	.01
d. technical, scientific	09	04	01	11.13	.01
e. sports and hobby books	10	09	04	2.44	.30-.20
f. history, biography	08	07	05	.27	.90-.80
g. animal stories	05	04	05	.73	.70-.50
h. comics, joke books	21	26	27	1.95	.50-.30
i. newspapers, magazines	19	16	19	.96	.70-.50
6. Proportion of activities enjoyed					
a. fewer than half	45	41	59	6.09	.05
b. one half or more	55	59	41		
7. Additional activities desired					
a. suggest activity	63	31	10	87.67	.01
b. do not suggest activity	37	69	90		

almost half the upward mobile report having tried twenty or more separate activities while only about one quarter of the downward mobile fall in this category; the stable group is approximately midway between the other two (Table 2, Item 2). There is a small difference in dating, the upwards being slightly more likely, and the downwards least likely to date (Table 2, Item 3).

Although they more commonly engage in leisure pursuits, the aspiring boys are not significantly different from others in having job commitments. One might expect that the reason the downward-aspiring boys play less is that they work more. But this does not seem to be the case (Table 2, Item 4), the three groups being approximately equal in the percentage who hold jobs. The more active social life of the upward mobile boy represents an increment in total activity rather than a substitute for work activity. The upward mobile boy is more likely to report leisure reading. He has a more diversified reading pattern, and his reading includes more demanding material. The downward aspiring boy much less often reads novels and mysteries, travel and adventure stories, and technical, scientific literature. Stable boys fall between the other two groups on all specific categories of reading, but are like the downward mobile in the proportion of nonreaders. The single case in which the trend favors the downward mobile boys is in the category "comics, joke books" (Table 2, Item 5).

Upward mobile boys are not only more active currently but also seem to be more enthusiastic about their activities and more receptive to new experiences. After our Ss had checked the leisure pursuits they had experienced within last year, they were asked to check the ones they had especially enjoyed. In general, the two indices bear a low negative relation to each other, that is, boys who do more things are more selective in naming those they "particularly enjoy." Despite this tendency for a negative association, we find that the upward aspiring boys (who take part in more leisure activities) are nevertheless enthusiastic about the things they do. They are like the stables in the proportion of their leisure pursuits that they designate as particularly enjoyable; while the downward mobile, who have tried relatively few leisure activities, are much less enthusiastic about these few (Table 2, Item 6).

° Unless noted, the chi square was derived from a 3 × 2 table with two degrees of freedom.

ᵃ In this case, the chi square was derived from a 3 × 2 table with six degrees of freedom.

When asked if there are other activities they would like to try, aside from those appearing on the list, almost two-thirds of the upward group name something else they would enjoy. This responsiveness contrasts sharply to the other groups: a third of the stable group, and only one tenth of the downward group suggest any additional unlisted activities that appeal to them (Table 2, Item 7).

ACHIEVEMENT MODE. We expected that the degree of striving reflected in a boy's job aspiration would be part of a general achievement orientation, that upward occupational aspiration would be associated with the pattern of behavior which McClelland et al. (7) have termed the "achievement syndrome," and that the upward mobile boy would show concern with achievement as against security and would be interested in meeting self-imposed standards of excellence. The downward aspiring boy, on the other hand, should show the same lack of vigor, the same constriction in setting other goals that we have seen in his choice of a future occupation.

The most direct evidence on these points is found in response to other questions in the occupation area. The Ss were asked to choose among criteria for judging the attractiveness of a job, to choose the two most and the two least important dimensions. Compared to the stable and downward groups, upward mobile boys stress interesting work and have a less dominating concern about security. They are highest of all three groups in desire for status achievement. The downward mobile also strongly wish for status, but their status drive is not bound to a demand for interest in the content of the job; rather, they would most like to have status combined with security. The answers of our stable group are interesting on this item; relatively unattracted by status and fame, they stress security and interesting work (Table 3, Item 1).

When we ask boys to rationalize their own job choices, the upward aspiring S emphasizes interest in the work itself, while the downward mobile more often adduces the ease of the work, or the ease of obtaining employment in the field (Table 3, Item 2).

It would seem, then, that the upward mobile Ss are more willing to yield security for the sake of achievement. In answer to a forced-choice question: "Which would you rather have—a job where you're sure you won't be laid off or one you can't be so sure of but where you have a chance to be a big success?" the striving boys

TABLE 3 / RELATIONSHIPS BETWEEN MOBILITY ASPIRATION AND INDICES OF ACHIEVEMENT MODE.

| | MOBILITY | | | | |
ITEM	UP-WARD (N = 277) %	STABLE (N = 168) %	DOWN-WARD (N = 73) %	X^2 [*]	p LEVEL
1. Job criteria selected[a]					
a. interesting work	56	51	33	15.74	.01
b. status achievement	44	28	36	22.15	.01
c. security	50	59	65	5.84	.10
2. Reasons for job choice[a]					
a. status	20	09	03	11.65	.01
b. ease of job or ease of obtaining job	04	12	32	15.27	.01
c. interest of work	70	78	58	5.99	.05
3. Preference: success or security					
a. success	52	35	33	12.00	.01
b. security	48	65	67		
4. Savings					
a. do save	30	21	18	6.16	.05
b. do not save	70	79	82		
5. Education plans					
a. beyond high school	69	42	12	140.06	.01
b. not beyond high school	31	58	88		

[*] Unless noted, the chi square was derived from a 3×2 table with two degrees of freedom.

[a] Categories here are not exhaustive. Tests are run on the presence or absence of particular answers.

choose the challenging, less secure job significantly more often than boys in either of the other groups (Table 3, Item 3).

Achievement orientation is often inferred from the willingness to forego immediate gratification for long-term goals. One indication of this appears in answer to the question, "What do you spend your own money for?" The boys who aspire high are more likely to say they save their resources for education or other long term goals (Table 3, Item 4). As we would expect, boys aspiring to higher occupations also reveal more extensive educational plans than do other boys (Table 3, Item 5).

ORIENTATION TOWARD THE FUTURE. The upward mobile boys have an extended time perspective and a marked interest in attaining adult status; while the downward group shows constriction in time, as in other aspects of the life space. We asked our Ss what decisions they would have to make in the next few years; the answers were rated for the breadth of time perspective. The upward aspiring boys are more likely to mention decisions in the more distant future, such as adult roles and goals. The downward mobile more often name immediate decisions, those within the high school period (Table 4, Item 1).

In answer to the question "What things that you do—at home, in school, or with your friends—make you feel important and useful?" The upward striving boy more often states instances in which he has assumed adult roles. He is less likely than the downward mobile S to mention peer acceptance as a source of self-esteem. An interesting finding here is that the stable group is highest of all three in choosing "belonging, being part of a group," one of the few occasions where this group does not fall somewhere between the other two. We suggest, though very tentatively, that this may reflect a concern with maintaining stable interpersonal ties.

We may also point to the apparently greater social maturity of the upward mobiles. As we have seen, they are somewhat more likely to date. They are also more eager for heterosexual social activities; when asked to choose between an all-boy or a coed social club, the upward aspiring less often prefer the former (Table 4, Item 3).

THE INTERNALIZATION OF PERSONAL STANDARDS. Another point of difference between the groups concerns the internalization of standards. Upward mobile boys consistently show a more complete internalization of personal controls. Downward mobile boys show a tendency to externalize standards and to rebel against them.

A set of projective pictures showed an adolescent boy in conflict between a promise made to his parents (to be home at a certain time) and peer pressure (to stay out later). Our Ss were asked what the boy would do and how he would feel about it.

In all of our groups, approximately two thirds of the respondents say that the boy will go home. However, the motives attributed to the boy differ sharply. The upward mobile boys more often have the boy go home because "he promised" or because "his parents trust him," whereas the

TABLE 4 / RELATIONSHIPS BETWEEN MOBILITY ASPIRATION AND INDICES OF ORIENTATION TOWARD THE FUTURE.

ITEM	MOBILITY UP-WARD (N = 277) %	STABLE (N = 68) %	DOWN-WARD (N = 73) %	X^2*	p LEVEL
1. Time perspective on decisions[b]					
a. within high school	17	18	29	5.21	.10
b. beyond high school	78	73	77	1.75	.50
c. distant future	53	51	26	16.51	.01
2. Sources of self-esteem[b]					
a. assuming adult role	31	23	16	6.91	.05
b. belonging, being part of a group	46	56	32	11.34	.01
c. being accepted by peers	03	07	14	10.90	.01
d. nothing	04	08	11	6.39	.05
3. Preference for co-ed or all-boy club[a]					
a. all-boy	39	48	59	10.60	.05
b. neutral	23	16	14		
c. coed	38	36	27		

* Unless noted, the chi square was derived from a 3 × 2 table with two degrees of freedom.

[a] In this case, the chi square was derived from a 3 × 2 table with four degrees of freedom.

[b] Categories here are not exhaustive of responses given to open questions, and more than one response was often given. Tests are run on the presence or absence of particular answers.

TABLE 5 / RELATIONSHIPS BETWEEN MOBILITY ASPIRATION AND INDICES OF INTERNALIZATION OF PERSONAL STANDARDS.

ITEM	MOBILITY UP-WARD (N = 277) %	STABLE (N = 168) %	DOWN-WARD (N = 73) %	X^2*	p LEVEL
1. Reaction to parent-peer conflict[a]					
a. adheres to promise because of sense of trust	37	19	16	24.03	.01
b. Adheres to promise because of fear of punishment	04	06	14	6.38	.05
2. Honesty with parents					
a. would tell parents	55	42	44	9.15	.05
3. Conditions for breaking a rule[a]					
a. emergency	18	10	10	6.56	.05
b. boy mature enough	11	07	01	6.49	.05
c. rebellion	10	14	22	10.11	.01
d. impulse	05	11	16	11.41	.01
e. parental authority absent	05	10	27	31.50	.01
4. Unbreakable rule					
a. no unbreakable rule	03	17	21	10.85	.01

* Unless noted, the chi square was derived from a 3 × 2 table with two degrees of freedom.

[a] Categories here are not exhaustive of responses given to open questions, and more than one response was often given. Tests are run on the presence or absence of particular answers.

downward say he will go because of a fear that the parents will find out and punish the transgression (Table 5, Item 1).

Regardless of their responses to these questions, all Ss were asked: "If the boy decided to stay with his friends awhile, do you think he'd tell his parents about it later?" The upward aspiring group answer "yes" more frequently than other boys (Table 5, Item 2).

Another series of questions concerned boys' conceptions of and general reactions to rules. Here, again, the upward mobile group reveals a greater degree of internalization. When asked why a boy might break a rule, they focus on un-

controllable emergency situations and those in which a boy is old enough (i.e., responsible enough) to guide his own behavior. On the other hand, the downwards more frequently give responses fitting the categories of "rebellion against the parent," "irresistible impulse," and "when parental authority is not present" (Table 5, Item 3). When asked what kind of a rule they would never break, upward mobile Ss more often men-

TABLE 6 / RELATIONSHIPS BETWEEN MOBILITY ASPIRATION AND INDICES OF AUTONOMY.

| ITEM | MOBILITY | | | X^2* | p LEVEL |
| | UP-WARD | STABLE | DOWN-WARD | | |
	(N = 277) %	(N = 168) %	(N = 73) %		
1. Independence in allocating funds					
a. no-independence	01	01	19	59.27	.01
2. Advice on decisions					
a. interjects own opinions	30	21	03	24.69	.01
3. Intimacy of friendship					
a. can be as close as family relationship	59	54	34	9.92	.01
4. Role of adult leader[a]					
a. helper	58	51	38	9.71	.01
b. decision maker	40	43	51	3.67	.20
5. Authority reliance					
a. high	38	47	54	6.06	.05
b. moderate	62	53	47		
6. Adult ideal[a]					
a. family member	41	50	55	5.99	.05
b. unrelated adult acquaintance and composite	31	24	18	6.74	.05

* Unless noted, the chi square was derived from a 3×2 table with two degrees of freedom.

[a] Categories here are not exhaustive of responses given to open questions, and more than one response was often given. Tests are run on the presence or absence of particular answers.

tion those which involve responsibility to others; they less frequently say that there is no rule or no rule that comes to mind, which they wouldn't break (Table 5, Item 4).

AUTONOMY. We saw earlier that the striving boys are interested in assuming adult-like roles, those, that is, in which they themselves are responsible for their behavior and for a job. We see here a seemingly greater drive towards independence and responsibility. In contrast, the downward mobile, though they show signs of rebellion against the parents, are also more dependent on them.

In one series of items, our Ss were asked whose advice they would prefer to take on particular problems—their parents' or friends'. The issues ran from such central ones as what time to be in at night to matters of taste, such as personal grooming. While there were no very striking differences in the proportions who would heed their parents on any of these topics, one interesting difference appears in the proportion of boys who inject a note of independence while discussing these issues. Thirty per cent of the striving group spontaneously assert that they would follow their own ideas on at least one of the six issues, and only three per cent of the downwards give such a response (Table 6, Item 2).

We find another indication of independence from the family in response to the question, "can a friend ever be as close as a family member?" The upward mobile Ss most often agree to this idea (Table 6, Item 3).

When our Ss are asked what the role of a club leader ought to be, we again find that the aspiring boys desire independent direction of their behavior. They limit the leader's function to that of a helper (Table 6, Item 4). A coder rating based on this question and on one which asked the S to describe an adult leader he had liked, revealed that the downward mobile S is more authority reliant than other boys (Table 6, Item 5).

Finally, a crucial index of independence from the family is yielded when Ss are asked to choose an adult ideal. As we would expect, the stable group, which includes all boys who choose the same occupation as the father's, also has the largest proportion of boys who choose the father as an ideal. The upwards more often choose a model outside the family, or describe a composite of characteristics from several people. More often than other boys, downward mobiles say there is no adult they wish to be like. And despite the fact that they choose the father less often than stable boys, they give the largest proportion of within-family models of any group, particularly choosing grandfathers and uncles. Here again we can observe the ambivalence of the downward mobile boys; though they are covertly rebellious toward family authority, they cling to within-family models. Another way of viewing this finding is to see in it a reflection of the downward mobile boys' narrowed and immature life space. Havighurst (4) has found that the tendency to choose within-family models characterizes the earlier years of adolescence. Our downward mobile boys retain the more infantile, more restricted image of the adult world.

The upward mobile boys, on the other hand, tend to a certain precocity in the loosening of family ties. Yet we have seen in the previous section on internalization that this is not associated with rebellion from or rejection of the family. Further evidence along these lines appears in the discussion of family milieu.

Until now evidence has been presented bearing on the *sense* of autonomy. Some other data suggest that these differences are related to the objective degree of autonomy permitted upward and downward boys by their parents. We asked: "What are your parents' ideas about the way you spend your money?" One fifth of the downward mobile respondents replied that they do not have funds of their own but ask their parents for money as they need or want some special thing. In the upward mobile group, fewer than one per cent gave this answer (Table 6, Item 1). Since there is no difference between the groups with respect to actual spending of money, we may infer that the difference resides in the *control* of spending.

ORIENTATION TOWARD THE SELF.   Upward mobile boys show a high degree of self-acceptance, and a confidence in social situations. The downward mobile is more ambivalent toward himself and more unsure and conflicted in social interaction.

Interviewers rated boys on a number of variables, among which were self-confidence, humour, and the clarity with which they organized and presented their opinions and attitudes. We may interpret these ratings, with caution, as reflecting the boy's social skill and ability to handle himself in social interaction with an adult. On each of the ratings, the upward mobile are high; they are more self-assured, show humour more often, and are better organized in the interview. The downward mobile are relatively unconfident, humourless, and disorganized (Table 7, Items 1, 2, and 3).

We find signs of self-rejection and demoralization in the downward mobile boys' answers to the question, "What would you like to change about yourself if you could—about your looks or your life or your personality?" They more often desire changes so gross or so central as to indicate alienation from the self; and they more often wish for changes that are unlikely to occur. The upward mobile boy more often refers to changes he has the power to effect himself. He is more realistically critical of himself, and less self-rejecting (Table 7, Item 4).

FAMILY MILIEU.   The reader may recall that we felt far more confident of our predictions about the downward than the upward mobile in this area. We believed that the downward group would show a pattern of ambivalence towards the parent, a mingling of dependency and hostility; and we further held that this pattern would arise out of inconsistent, overly harsh methods of discipline. We did not, however, feel we could make any specific statement about the

TABLE 7 / RELATIONSHIPS BETWEEN MOBILITY ASPIRATION AND INDICES OF ORIENTATION TOWARD THE SELF.*

	MOBILITY				
	UP-WARD	STABLE	DOWN-WARD	X^{2}*	p
ITEM	$(N = 277)$ %	$(N = 168)$ %	$(N = 73)$ %		LEVEL
1. Self-confidence[a]					
a. high	30	23	18	7.93	.10
b. average	52	57	57		
c. low	18	20	25		
2. Humour					
a. present	74	67	58	7.14	.05
b. absent	26	33	42		
3. Organization of ideas[a]					
a. high	60	53	50	7.31	.10
b. average	22	27	20		
c. low	18	20	30		
4. Desired changes[b]					
a. self reject-ing, major	04	10	15	6.36	.05
b. changes that are impos-sible	06	07	23	11.33	.01
c. changes within boy's own power	37	29	05	14.10	.01

* Unless noted, the chi square was derived from a 3×2 table with two degrees of freedom.

[a] In these cases, the chi square was derived from a 3×3 table with four degrees of freedom.

[b] Categories here are not exhaustive of responses given to an open question, and more than one response was often given. Tests are run on the presence or absence of particular answers.

TABLE 8 / RELATIONSHIPS BETWEEN MOBILITY ASPIRATION AND INDICES OF FAMILY MILIEU.

| ITEM | MOBILITY | | | X^2* | p LEVEL |
	UP- WARD (N = 277) %	STABLE (N = 168) %	DOWN- WARD (N = 73) %		
1. Punishment[a]				19.12	.01
a. physical	02	08	15		
b. deprivational	66	69	65		
c. psychological	32	23	20		
2. Portrayal of parental figures				11.59	.01
a. harsh	27	35	48		
b. non-harsh	73	65	52		
3. Disagreements with parents				6.39	.05
a. have disagreements	66	56	49		
b. do not have disagreements	34	44	51		
4. Parents' attitudes toward way boy spends money				8.58	.05
a. disapproval	19	16	05		
b. no disapproval	81	84	95		
5. Leisure activities with parents[a]				17.23	.01
a. share many	19	11	09		
b. share some	73	74	68		
c. share none	08	15	23		

* Unless noted, the chi square was derived from a 3 × 2 table with two degrees of freedom.

[a] In these cases, the chi square was derived from a 3 × 3 table with four degrees of freedom.

upward mobile: here we were interested in discovering what we could about the family milieu, in particular whether upward aspiration is associated with a rejection of family values, or a defensive identification with a forbidding parental authority, or by that relatively amiable relationship to the parent which permits the growth of autonomy.

To begin with, we find that deprivation seems to be the dominant method of discipline for all groups; differences here are not significant. Striking differences appear, however, in the relative frequency of "psychological" and "corporal" methods of punishment. Only one in fifty of the upwards say that their parents use physical punishment; approximately one in ten of the stables and one in seven of the downwards report this method. In contrast, the use of "psychological" techniques (such as "given a good talking to") occurs in more than one quarter of the upward mobile responses, about one in five of the stables, and only one in eighteen of the downwards (Table 8, Item 1). We find that the parents of the upward aspirers avoid the harshest method of punishment; the "psychological" methods, which we suspect encourage the child's internal controls, are infrequently used by the parents of downward mobile boys.

Are our mobile Ss presenting an over-idealized picture of their families? We looked for the pattern of repressed hostility and surface idealization which has been shown to characterize defensive identifiers (2, 5, 9). But our data reveal that the opposite is true: in the projective materials—where the Ss are not discussing their own parents and where they have an opportunity to discharge repressed hostility without danger—the upward aspiring portray parents as less harsh than do the other groups (Table 8, Item 2). And as we shall see, they are more aware of differences between themselves and their parents. They more commonly report that their parents have some "old-fashioned ideas, or ideas they disagree with" (Table 8, Item 5), and that their parents in some respect disapprove of the way in which they spend their own money (Table 8, Item 6). We saw previously (Table 6, Item 3) that they are not likely to feel that family relationships are necessarily more intimate than friendships; and they less often choose an ideal adult from within the family group (Table 6, Item 6). The upward mobile boys are, then, more sensible of differences with parents.

Do the aspiring boys have a detached rather than congenial relationship to their parents? The single bit of evidence on this question suggests that this is not the case: they more often report engaging in leisure activities with their parents (Table 8, Item 5).

The downward mobile boy's family relationship is, as we expected, marked by ambivalence: the pattern is one of conscious idealization, accompanied by unconscious suspicion and hostility.

We have already seen that the parents of this group are more often severe in their punishment. And in this group we find evidence of repressed hostility: in the projective stories, the downward mobile boys picture parental figures as both harsh and suspicious (Items 3 and 4, Table 8). Yet consciously they are more likely to deny differences with their parents. Some of our findings on autonomy have shown this; and in addition we find that these boys most often say they have no disagreements with their parents (Table 8, Item 5), and they least often say their parents disapprove of their handling of funds (Table 8, Item 6). The downward mobile boy shares leisure activities with his parents somewhat less than do boys in the other two groups (Table 8, Item 7).

ALTERNATIVE HYPOTHESES.   Before we discuss the possible meanings of these findings, we must consider briefly alternative hypotheses which might account for them. These are: (a) An age differential among the three groups; thus, the upward aspiring Ss might have given "little boy" job hopes, while the non-mobile group presented more mature aspirations; (b) a difference among the groups in frame of reference, so that the upward aspirers may have understood the interviewer to be asking for "fantasy" aspirations while other boys took the question to mean "realistic expectations; (c) objective differences in the social status of the groups: perhaps the upward mobile boys' families are at the upper end of their group in income or education, and so provide their sons with an objectively greater opportunity for mobility; (d) a difference in intelligence among the groups.

First, on the question of realism. There were in our total sample fewer than one per cent of the boys who gave as their job choices distinctly "little boy" or "glamour" occupations. Among boys in the mobility analysis sub-sample, there were no aspirations listed which were obviously or totally based on ideas of glamour. When the boys are asked how sure they feel about the job they've chosen, we find that very few of them say they're not at all sure; more important, the variation that does occur is not related to the type of aspiration they express. Boys in the three groups show approximately equal certainty that they will *get* the jobs for which they are aiming (Table 9, Item 1).

Furthermore, we find a difference in educational plans, one which is appropriate for the difference in job aspirations; this indicates at least a minimal degree of realism in our Ss understanding of work preparation (Table 3, Item 5).

The groups differ neither in age (Table 9, Item 2) nor in present socioeconomic status. The upward mobile boys are not from homes which

TABLE 9 / RELATIONSHIP OF MOBILITY ASPIRATION TO AGE, CERTAINTY ABOUT ASPIRATION, FAMILY INCOME, FATHER'S EDUCATION AND INTELLIGENCE.

	MOBILITY				
ITEM	UP-WARD	STABLE	DOWN-WARD	X^2*	p LEVEL
	(N = 277) %	(N = 168) %	(N = 73) %		
1. Certainty about aspiration					
a. high	57	58	54	3.22	.70
b. moderate	34	33	33		
c. low	09	09	13		
2. Age					
a. fourteen	33	29	31	1.94	.80
b. fifteen	30	36	33		
c. sixteen	37	35	36		
3. Family economic status[a]					
a. high average	32	35	31	2.76	.70
b. average	53	49	52		
c. low	15	16	17		
4. Father's education					
a. grade school	32	27	25	3.07	.70
b. high school	50	58	55		
c. college	18	15	20		
5. Verbal ability					
a. high	25	11	03	33.92	.01
b. average	69	75	74		
c. low	06	14	23		

* Unless noted, the chi square was derived from a 3×3 table with four degrees of freedom.

[a] The measure used for economic status was the Remmers House and Home Scale.

are higher economically or in educational background (Table 9, Items 3, 4).

The two rough measures of intelligence available both show the striving group to be somewhat superior. The upward aspiring boy is more likely to report leisure reading (Table 2, Item 5) and he is rated by coders as more facile verbally (Table 9, Item 5). The downward mobile are rated low on verbal skills, but their reading pattern does not differ significantly from that of the stable group ($x^2 = .10$; $p > .90$ with 1 df). We will defer a consideration of this until the discussion.

DISCUSSION

We may interpret our data on the upward aspiring boy in relation to ego structure and functioning. We did not, of course, make a direct investigation of intrapsychic processes; furthermore our understanding of "normal" ego functioning is, at present, limited and tentative. Nevertheless, it may be of some interest to attempt a formulation of our results in the current vocabulary of ego psychology.

Among upward aspiring boys we find a high level of diversified activity, suggesting that energy is available to the ego for focused use in work and play. We may infer that the antecedent condition for this accessibility is in the ego's having at its disposal a relatively high degree of neutralized energy. If we assume that both groups, mobile and non-mobile, do not differ in primary energy resources, we may conjecture that the aspiring Ss have less energy tied to the resolution of conflict, and consequently gain in neutralized, disposable energy.[5]

Another sign of the comparative effectiveness of ego functioning among aspiring boys is seen in the greater degree of cohesion among the three major systems within the personality. On the one hand, ego processes in the mobile boy are less likely to be imperiled by the breakthrough of impulses. (When would a boy break a rule?); on the other hand, he is less likely to show evidence of an excessively punitive superego. The greater degree of internalization of moral values among aspiring boys suggests a more harmonious articulation between the ego and super-ego systems. Our data show that this integration is not purchased at the expense of an unusual quantity of guilt.

A consideration of the intelligence factor is relevant here. Although we had no direct measure of intelligence, we saw that the upward mobile boys read more and read more difficult things; and they are judged on the basis of the interview to be more verbally skilled. In all likelihood there *is* an intellectual difference among our groups; one plausible interpretation of many of our findings is that they merely reflect group differences in IQ. We feel, however, that such a formulation assumes an overly simple causal sequence—for one thing it fails to clarify the mechanisms which mediate between IQ and other indices of successful ego functioning. A good deal of recent data points to a high degree of association be-

tween intelligence and variables which indicate effective ego functioning. The direction of causality and connection among those variables is by no means understood. Furthermore, to explain our data as a function of intelligence alone would not allow us to generate predictions in the area of family relations. If we assume, however, that our data are best understood by positing differences in intrapsychic organization—and particularly in ego structure and functioning—we may then posit specific expectations about family milieu.

We would expect—on the basis of the higher energy level and the more refined control of impulsivity among upward mobile Ss—that they have relatively good relationships within the family and have successfully resolved infantile object ties. We mean by this that there is a relative absence both of covert hostility toward the parents, and of overt dependence upon them, together with a relatively high degree of objectivity about family relations.

We have seen that this is, in fact, the case. The mobile boy asserts (and probably has been encouraged toward) greater independence of judgment and behavior. It will be recalled that he expresses a desire for equalitarian rather than dependent relationships with adults. He frequently uses his own convictions as authority in making decisions.

The aspiring boy more often admits differences between himself and his family. He seems able to assert the legitimacy of an autonomous self-definition—to the extent, at least, of selecting an ego ideal outside the family setting.

The independence we have observed has not occurred through rebellion from or rejection of the family. Despite their ability to differentiate themselves from their parents, the upward aspirers give evidence of a congenial relationship with them. They share their leisure activities; in response to a projective measure they reveal relatively little covert hostility toward parental figures.

Their parents are, in fact, comparatively lenient; they are more likely to employ mild and essentially verbal discipline and use physical punishment infrequently.

We have seen, then, that the upward aspiring boy is characterized by a high energy level, the presence of autonomy, and a relatively advanced social maturity. These attributes may be viewed as derivatives of a generally effective ego organization, one which has developed out of the successful resolution of infantile object-ties and conflicts. We would expect, on theoretical grounds,

[5] Cf. Rapaport (8, p. 353): "In other words, the amount of energy which the person can dispose by investing it in objects, by becoming interested in activities, even when essential drive-aims and drive-objects are in abeyance, is an indicator of ego-autonomy and ego strength."

that this development would be most likely to occur in a family setting where the parents allow the child a nonambivalent connection with them, where autonomy can emerge without conflict. As we have seen, the data we have suggest that this is the case.

We have already presented, in the introductory section, our view of the internal psychic processes which characterize downward mobile boys. From the specific perspective of ego functioning, we see an apparent blocking or impoverishment of energy which should, ideally, be available to the ego. We may infer that neutralization is not being successfully accomplished. There is a relatively poor articulation among the psychic systems: impulses threaten the ego's integrity; the superego seems overly severe and yet incompletely incorporated. These boys seem humourless, gauche, disorganized—relatively so, at least. Perhaps the most telling and poignant datum which the study locates is their response to the possibility of personal change, their tendency to want to change intractable aspects of the self, and the degree of alienation revealed by their desire to modify major and fundamental personal qualities. As we have seen, this pattern is associated with a certain quality of family interaction: the boy gives evidence of an ambivalent tie to the parents, a mixture of overt dependency and covert aggression. One of the determinants of this ambivalence, we may infer on theoretical grounds, is in the parents' relatively punitive style of discipline which fails to establish self-governing controls in the child.

A final point concerning the mechanisms through which the differing aspirations become established: In the case of upward aspiration we assume a direct connection between the socialization process and the aspiration to social mobility. That is, we assume that the parents transmit the value on mobility during socialization, and that the child incorporates this as part of a complex of values which includes autonomy and general achievement. In contrast, we conjecture that the process in downward aspiration may be more indirect: the rebellion engendered by an ambivalent family atmosphere may be directly expressed in a rejection of general social goals; or we may have a diffuse demoralization which causes (and prepares the child for) failure and isolation in social situations. In turn, these failures result in a general narrowing of goals, and a retreat from success; a central expression of this is the lowering of occupational goals.

SUMMARY

We have only recently begun to recognize that prevalent views of the dynamics of mobility, based as they are largely on literary sources and on extreme instances, require refinement and differentiation. The paper begins by distinguishing varieties of mobility behavior. There is presented a model of the psychodynamics of upward and downward aspiration, which is tested with data from a national sample of adolescent boys. The general formulation holds that upward mobility is found among boys with effective, autonomous, ego functioning; downward mobility is seen as a symptom of demoralization. Psychoanalytic ego theory provides the framework from which we make specific predictions of differences in the areas of activity level, achievement mode, time perspective, internalization of values, autonomy, self-esteem, and family milieu. The findings reveal sharp differences, in the predicted directions, between upward and downward aspiring groups.

REFERENCES

1. ACKERMAN, N. W., and JAHODA, MARIE. *Anti-Semitism and emotional disorder.* New York: Harper, 1950.

2. ADORNO, T. W., FRENKEL-BRUNSWICK, ELSE, LEVINSON, D., and SANFORD, N. *The authoritarian personality.* New York: Harper, 1949.

3. GOUGH, H. *Personal communication,* 1955.

4. HAVIGHURST, R. J., ROBINSON, MYRA Z., and DORR, MILDRED. The development of the ideal self in childhood and adolescence. In J. Seidman (Ed.), *Readings in adolescence.* New York: Dryden Press, 1953.

5. HOFFMAN, M. L. Some psychodynamic factors in compulsive conformity. *J. abnorm. soc. Psychol.,* 1953, 48, 383-393.

6. LYNN, K. S. *The dream of success.* Boston: Little, Brown, 1955.

7. MC CLELLAND, D. C., ATKINSON, J. W., CLARK, R. A., and LOWELL, E. L. *The achievement motive.* New York: Appleton-Century-Crofts, 1953.

8. RAPAPORT, D. *Organization and pathology of thought.* New York: Columbia Univer. Press, 1953.

9. SARNOFF, I. Identification with the aggressor: Some personality correlates of anti-Semitism among Jews. *J. Pers.,* 1952, 20, 199-218.

V / Settings and Specific Stimuli as Determinants of Behavior

IN THIS CLASS OF DETERMINANT WE INCORPORATE VARIOUS situational influences. Immediate INSTIGATIONS such as another person's act with reference to oneself are only one part of a stimulus situation. A second aspect is the SETTING: "Where did it happen?" People act differently in differing contexts; the gymnasium evokes orders of response seldom seen in the classroom, the parlor, or the church. It is not just that basketball is played in a gym rather than a classroom, but that in the gym, additional behaviors appear, e.g., boisterousness, joking, or—in some individuals—unaccustomed restraint and shyness. Such shyness might not be suspected as part of the person's repertoire if he were seen only in other settings.

Setting is not a question solely of location; a setting can change even when the place remains the same. A classroom when the teacher is out of the room is not likely to remain psychologically the same environment if the absence becomes prolonged. Indeed, change in the amount of structure—either in the clarity of expected behavior or in the extent of external control—often causes marked alterations in response. (For instance, some persons who are free of anxiety during the week suffer from "weekend neurosis" when deprived of the routine of their workday lives.) Research on classroom atmosphere attempts to study the effects of different emotional climates in one type of setting.

Still another influence is the impact of the various FACE-TO-FACE GROUPS with which an individual deals personally—his recreational cronies; his employees, employers, and competitors at work; his family at home.[1] These groups comprise a series of social systems, changes in any of which can broadly affect a person's behavior. A man's troubles in the office or a boy's anxieties in school are betrayed by actions at home. Conversely, conflict at home may damage scholastic performance. A worsening state of affairs at home may heighten the importance, to man or boy, of his boon companions outside the family. Improvements at school, e.g., a new teacher generous with praise for a girl responsive to praise, may reduce the rate of outbursts at home. It is these kinds of face-to-face relations that are dealt with in this section. The wider social systems, involving cultural and institutional memberships, are discussed under Section VI, Group Memberships. Hoping to help students see more clearly the distinction between that section and this, we have put the two next to each other, changing the position of this section from IX, in the first edition, to V in the present edition.

Kurt Lewin's application of a gestalt viewpoint to understanding human social behavior stands as a landmark in the history of psychological thought.

[1] The latter was partly covered under Interpersonal Experiences in Section IV, but here we deal with the immediate relationships rather than home social learnings of the past.

The research on group dynamics which he spawned continues to push back conceptual horizons. More recently such authors as Roger Barker and Herbert Wright have been demonstrating the alterations in behavior that accompany changes in setting. Now leading psychiatrists such as Erich Lindemann are studying the effects of face-to-face social systems on the eruption of mental illness, especially when an "emotional hazard" such as a point of ROLE TRANSITION (see introduction to Section VII) occurs in a social system that puts undue stress on a particular individual or fails to support him in accustomed ways. Some people will show neurotic responses in any setting, but others become disturbed solely because the role relationships in which they are involved are organized in ways "unhealthful" for them. In such cases, the most appropriate treatment may be that which attempts to make changes IN THE SOCIAL SYSTEM without necessarily treating the patient directly.

The first three authors of the initial article presented, Trow, Zander, and Morse, are at the University of Michigan. Dr. Jenkins is at Temple University. The four describe many of the classic findings of research on group dynamics and suggest educational applications. The second article also reflects the influence of the Research Center for Group Dynamics at Michigan, where Lippitt and Gold did their study. Professor Lippitt is currently Program Director of the Center for Research on Utilization of Scientific Knowledge. Their study lends emphasis to the importance of the group context in which classroom learning occurs.

The next two selections discuss the effects of mass media on children. The first, dealing with television, consists of a review by Wilbur Schramm of a British study on the effects of television. Dr. Schramm is Director of the Institute for Communication Research at Stanford University, and he has written or edited five books on mass communication. The Institute has done the largest study of mass communication in relation to children that has yet been made in North America (*Television in the Lives of Our Children*, Stanford University Press, 1961). The data come from the United States and Canada, and the children range from very early ages up to the end of high school (another paper on children and television is that of Maccoby (X, 66) in this volume.

The second article on mass media as stimuli is by W. Paul Blakely of Drake University. His study of the effects of comic books should be considered in relation to the selection in Part VIII by Child, Potter, and Levine (No. 50) as well as in relation to Peller's discussion of children's literature (X, 64).

Next is a passage by Lawrence Kubie, a prominent psychiatrist and psychoanalyst, in which he expresses his faith that a new kind of classroom climate can reduce neurotic interference with the learning process. We might have placed in this section, too, the study in Part VIII by Meyer and Thompson, (No. 51), since the frequency of disapproval expressed toward male pupils by female teachers may indicate that an inhospitable climate exists for many boys in American schools. A somewhat related study demonstrating the different effects of two teaching methods is described in Part X in the article by Grimes and Allinsmith (No. 68). It contrasts structured *vs.* unstructured classroom approaches. Still another paper that might have been assigned to this section is that of Goldberg (XI, 78) on adapting teacher style to pupil differences.

We close Part V with Hilda Taba's article on school learning among the culturally disadvantaged, recognizing that the plight of children whose families are in the lowest income bracket (the "disorganized working class" or "lower-lower class") is as much a matter of group membership (Section VI) and deficiencies of interpersonal experience (Section IV) as it is of setting and specific stimuli.

27/PSYCHOLOGY OF GROUP BEHAVIOR: THE CLASS AS A GROUP/WILLIAM CLARK TROW,

ALVIN F. ZANDER, WILLIAM C. MORSE, AND DAVID H. JENKINS*

SOCIAL PSYCHOLOGY HAS BEEN EXPERIencing a marked development in recent years; and because of the many implications for learning situations, those tilling the educational fields should be alert to the new points of view and new findings which are emerging. This statement does not imply that individual educational psychology is to be discarded, but rather that it is now directly complemented by the basic socio-psychological concept of the group and the consideration of intra-group relationships. As long as sociologists confined their attention largely to such social groupings as crowds and mobs, criminals and delinquents, the family, and to census groups with racial and nationality characteristics, the help they could furnish to the classroom teacher was relatively slight. But with the development of field theory and the study of interaction of individuals in a face-to-face group, and more specifically with the coming of the Iowa studies of democratic, autocratic and *laissez-faire* leadership, followed by the energetic labors of those in the field of group dynamics, the picture has changed. To this has been added the later Freudian influence in the mental hygiene movement, its expansion in the area of inter-personal relationships, and the exploitation of such treatment techniques as those of group work and play therapy. We are forced to ask ourselves whether the school class is a group, and, if it is, what this should mean to educational psychologists whose task it is to introduce teachers to the principles which should aid them in developing the best possible environment for learning in their classrooms.

DEVELOPMENTAL BACKGROUND AND CONCLUSIONS FROM RESEARCH

It should be recognized at the outset that educational psychology has from the beginning devoted itself almost exclusively to modifying the responses of individuals to more or less separate stimuli. The principles of learning, derived from the performances of laboratory animals and sometimes of children, though the results were brought together statistically, have been applied to the individual learner; and his performance has been tested by presenting him with a series of tasks to perform, and measuring his success in performing them. To describe the educational psychology of the past and the present in this way is not to belittle it. Tremendous improvements have been made in instructional materials and methods as a consequence of this view. We can well feel proud of the contributions of our colleagues and wish for their continuance, for there is much more to be done. After all, individuals are individuals, and they are probably here to stay!

The single-line, teacher-pupil relationship, however, has other sources than the psychological laboratory. There seem to have been changing patterns in our educational assumptions as to the most effective and desirable learning situations for the pupil. At one time the tutorial arrangement, the scholar and the single student in a face-to-face relationship, was felt to be most nearly ideal. And it may be for certain kinds of learning. But the practical situation in our public schools has not, of course, permitted this kind of teacher-pupil ratio; so we tried to make our classes of twenty-five or more pupils into twenty-five simultaneous one-to-one relationships. At any rate we followed this pattern, in our classwork, of teacher control, assignment, and class discussion, all dependent on the teacher-pupil-teacher-pupil kind of interaction. In this tradition we not only have emphasized the importance of the individual pupil and of the subject-centered curriculum, but also of individualized instruction, and the child-centered school.

This arrangement tended to be strengthened

* William Clark Trow, Alvin F. Zander, William C. Morse, and David H. Jenkins, Psychology of group behavior: the class as a group, *Journal of Educational Psychology*, 1950, *41*, 322-338. Reprinted with abridgement by permission.

by virtue of the fact that it provided a more direct system of control. Any break in the line, with consequent spontaneous interaction among pupils, might well mean that the teacher had lost that control which he felt it necessary to maintain. If the class were allowed to become an interacting group, the behavior of the pupils would presumably not be contributing to the learning goals which the teacher had in mind. Thus, "groupiness" implied "bad discipline."

Two factors have probably contributed to the movement away from this tutorial conception of our classrooms: the increasing interest and attention being given to social learning, and the awareness that the classrooms are, potentially at least, social situations. With the acceptance of the broader social goals of learning, no longer restricted to scholarly and intellectual activities alone, dependence on the tutorial tradition began to lessen, and the potentialities of the class as a medium for instruction in social learning became clearer.

The point where modern social psychology can offer desirable additions to the individualized approach lies in a recognition of the complex nature of what has in the past been rather loosely referred to as the stimulus situation when this situation is largely made up of other persons. The exploration of this phenomenon, and of the function of perceptual and conceptual processes in relation to it, is the chief contribution of the gestalt psychologists, whose point of view the late Kurt Lewin was largely responsible for bringing over into the interaction field of social psychology. Teachers have long known that pupils responded to other stimuli than the words of wisdom emanating from behind the teacher's desk. But the teacher's task was to eliminate such distraction so far as possible. And while this is still often desirable, we are now interested in these other stimuli also, in the interactions of the pupils among themselves and with the teacher. We are asking, what are the implications of viewing the class not merely as a number of individuals in the same room, but as a group? . . .

A number of assertions from recent research in group dynamics have both theoretical and practical value for the field of educational psychology and teaching methods. This list is not exhaustive and there will be no attempt to describe the nature of the studies from which these data are derived. Many of these findings are from laboratory investigations with groups, but a sufficient number of them were obtained in

field-experiment settings to indicate that work of this nature can readily be done in the actual classroom setting, as well as in the laboratory. Some of these assertions are well-tested and validated. Others are less well proven. All of them have relevance and promise for educational psychology.

1. The attitudes of an individual have their anchorage in the groups to which he belongs. Present evidence makes it apparent that many attitudes can be changed more easily by making changes in certain properties of the group than by directly teaching the individuals, as individuals, even in a classroom audience situation.[9, 10]

2. The conduct and beliefs of pupils is regulated in large measure by the small groups within a classroom, such as friendship cliques, and the cohesive groups of students within a school. These groups demand conformity from their members to certain group standards, and the more cohesive the group, the greater is its power over the member.[2, 5]

3. In some instances failure to learn may be advantageously conceptualized as resistance to change, using resistance here in the same sense as the therapist uses it in his relationships with a patient.[†] For example, the group standards developed by persons who were learning a motor task quite similar to a previously perfected one, and who were simply told what they were to do, were entirely different from the group standards developed in a group in which the learners participated in a discussion and made group decisions about the necessity for, and the nature of, the new task to be learned. Those who participated in the discussion learned much more, more rapidly, and with much less aggression and resentment toward the persons inducing them to make this change.[2, 17]

4. When frustrations are met, highly cohesive groups maintain their effort in movement toward the group goal much more vigorously and effectively than do groups of low cohesiveness.[6]

5. Groups, especially those similar to classroom groups, can be disrupted into separate cliques; or this threat of disruption can be eliminated, by the alteration of forces which determine the attractiveness of the group for the members. (For example, helping them to become aware of the strength of attraction they have for each

---

† It should be noted, however, that failure to change may not be due to such "resistance." There may be an inadequate set, unsatisfactory motivation, inability to comply with the demands of the goal or a rational non-acceptance of a new position.

other, or the degree to which membership in the group provides a way to achieve things they value highly.) This condition can be brought about most easily when the members become aware of the forces influencing them, but it can also be effected by an outsider, such as a teacher, who adroitly helps the group to change the impact and strength of these forces surrounding and within their group.[16]

6. The training of persons for effective social action such as performance in school or civic service, can lead to greater effectiveness of effort by the trainees if they are members of a group which is being trained to work as a group, than will result if they are merely individuals in an audience situation.[11]

7. The amount of interaction among students in a class is determined in part by group factors. For example, in highly cohesive groups arriving at a decision that has general approval, the person whose viewpoint is too different from that of the rest will be rejected—that is, ignored. In a less well knit group, in which the discussion is not directed to a group decision, the deviate member is likely to get more comments directed to him than the person whose ideas are quite similar to those of the rest of the group.[15]

8. When the members see themselves competing for their own individual goals which make coöperative effort impossible, there is disruption of the ready communication of ideas, the coordination of efforts and the friendliness and pride in one's group which are basic to class harmony and effectiveness. The competitive grading system commonly used today is an illustration in that it creates mutually exclusive goals among the members of a class group.[3, 4]

9. The group climate or style of group life can have an important influence on the members' personalities. One such style of group life can develop hostile, obedient, uncreative "goldbrickers"; another can produce confused, purposeless, competitive drifters; and still another can mould coöperative, flexible, purposeful, turn-taking, we-spirited persons. The group climate that produces such effects is created by the resultant of a number of group properties which can be combined in various ways, among which are the leadership style of the teacher or that of those who function most as group leaders, the degree of cohesiveness, which has already been mentioned, the group-member skills, the suitability of the group process for the task in hand, the techniques employed by the teacher to satisfy his ego and other needs, and the

tension-release patterns used by the group.[12, 18]

10. The reasons for the occasional failure of project methods, and other teaching procedures which depend upon effectively functioning groups often lie in the ineffective use of group problem-solving methods, or in the unskillful handling of group procedures. Groups can help themselves to mature and improve their ability as a learning or producing team by diagnosing their own failures and planning ways of repairing their own deficiencies. Students of group development have devoted much attention to methods of group diagnosis, ways of presenting the findings to a group, and methods for alleviating a group's procedural difficulties.

11. Certain forms of classroom behavior may be recognized as mechanisms developed for relieving tensions somewhat similar to those employed by an individual in relieving his tensions. For example, they employ patterns of group behavior which help avoid difficult tasks or unpleasant situations. These mechanisms are often difficult to identify since they may either be wrongly perceived by the teacher as signs that the group is keeping busy, or they may be accepted as the usual troubles one gets into by the use of committee methods.[13]

12. Difficulties in the transfer of verbal learning to social behavior can often be overcome by the use of that form of role-playing referred to as reality practice, in which the participants try-out the behavior they are expected to use in a situation from which all threat has been removed. Inhibition blindnesses, or fears of "learning" certain content, or behaving in unaccustomed ways can be removed by the use of a "cultural-island," a situation where new group standards are generated while away from the source of the inhibitions. This procedure is effectively used in excursions, conferences, summer camps, and other group activities in which the person is under the pressure of group standards that are different from those at home, and so he dares to adopt forms of behavior which might be quite desirable for him, but which he might hesitate to try out in his accustomed environment for fear of adverse criticism.[7]

Thus we can safely accept the view that group phenomena definitely affect the progress of learning, as well as the kind of learning that takes place. The educational significance of this view derives from the fact that the pupil's attitudes as well as his behavior patterns are modifiable. Increased motivation in participating in the classroom activities, and consequently in learning, derives from several different potential sources in a group atmosphere where good mental hygiene prevails.

Three such potential sources of increased motivation will be considered. The first of these sources lies in the method of *goal determination*—the extent to which the goals of the class are determined by the entire group including both pupils and teachers, in a truly co-participant sense. When this procedure is followed, the child will feel that he has some control over his own destiny and, therefore, is able to accept the group goals which he helped select as being his own personal goals. They are things which he himself wants to do and, therefore, he is more likely to follow through on them. The absence of such codetermined objectives does not mean the absence of group standards, but some of these standards are not likely to be the ones which the teacher would choose, or the ones which best promote learning. Such group standards as the "gentlemen's mark" of C, and the group rejection of the student who is too "eager," are familiar to all. Thus group standards in a classroom may inhibit good learning as well as accelerate it.

The second source of increased motivation lies in the extent to which the teachers and the pupils build a *supportive atmosphere* in the classroom, one which helps each child to realize that he is an accepted group member. When this condition maintains, each child has his own "area of freedom," within which he is free to make his own decisions. This area can often be much wider than is ordinarily supposed by teachers who are constantly making pupils' decisions for them. Although the group may not approve of everything a pupil does, it still accepts him as a person. In this kind of an atmosphere the child is able to develop a greater feeling of security with his fellows. In addition—and this is the important contribution to learning—he is likely to feel freed from personal threat and criticism and, therefore, more willing to go ahead and try new things without fear, realizing that if he fails he will not be rejected either by the class or by the teacher. Thus failure can be a very positive learning experience because, once the emotional threat is removed, the child can look at his abilities and limitations far more objectively and with greater awareness of what next steps are required for his learning. It would seem that little learning can occur if the child is denied positive opportunities to make errors.

A third potential source of increased motivation lies in the extent to which the various members of the class are accepted as *participating members*. When they are so accepted, each can benefit from the knowledge, skills, and abilities of all the other members. They are no longer dependent primarily or solely on the teacher for all information and guidance. Besides offering the possibility of the development of broader understandings, this gives to each pupil the opportunity to be a contributor to the group, and the classroom becomes, then, a situation for mutual exchange, for mutual sharing. Research is beginning to show the increased productivity of groups which have this coöperative pattern of relationship.[3] Goal determination by the group, a supportive atmosphere, and a participating membership, then, constitute three conditions of group organization of great effectiveness in developing motivation which contribute to the promotion of effective learning.

THE ROLES OF A TEACHER

What can the teacher do to develop and maintain these conditions conducive to learning? There are three fundamental roles which cover the things a teacher does. Actually these are not discrete parts of the teacher's job, but they do carry quite different implications. The roles that will be discussed are the following: (1) the instructional role, (2) the role of the democratic strategist, and (3) the role of the therapist. Following this, we will ask how the teacher selects the proper role, and how the actual operation of this role can be evaluated.

First, the *instruction role*. It is obvious that the concept of what a teacher should do has changed over the years. To the Hoosier schoolmaster the matter was quite simple. He was the drill sergeant. The cadence of recitation was akin to the sound of marching feet. As master of the drill, he called the steps. This teacher also held the role of academic authority; not only did he choose the school experiences, but he was also revered for his great storehouse of information. His very person was the embodiment of learning, and he was categorically right. This fundamental instructional role has mellowed with the years. Now the teacher does not always have to know. He operates as an adult with superior learning to be sure, but serves more as a resource person explaining, telling, and demonstrating. His drillmaster's uniform has been exchanged for the Socratic garb, for his instruction is more concerned with fostering the students' power to think and reason. This major "informational role" of the teacher is often discussed and is perhaps quite well understood. But it should be clear that this role itself is not exclusively the property of the teacher. At times, especially as the content of the course falls within the experience of the students, the class members share or take over the instructional role. As we come to understand more about the dynamics of the classroom, we realize that the way in which this role is handled by the teacher has important effects on the total learning situation.

A second major role which the teacher must play is that of *democratic strategist*. This has been discussed by other writers under the heading of "group formation." With the goal of pupil participation the teacher must provide the occasion for the introduction of processes to facilitate teacher-pupil planning. To play this role successfully two things are required: a high regard for democratic values, and their implications, and a high level of psychological insight into group factors and individual personality. In the role of a democratic strategist, the teacher helps the group utilize various methods of progress evaluation, and the information about their progress which they secure. He further helps them see and clarify their accomplishments, blocks, and failures, as well as the values in democratic group action. Thus, the task is more than that of being merely an exponent of democratic education. This role becomes one of activating democratic processes by helping the class to experience democratic goals and relationships in the design of their everyday classroom experiences.

Understanding the dynamic forces which are affecting the class as a group and those which the techniques bring into play makes possible a contribution to democratic learning because our democratic ethics have established the educational goals and values. Techniques are selected in terms of their potentiality for contributing to the democratic goals of the group at the particular time. It should be pointed out that on the basis of a different set of ethics for the same conditions in a group, different techniques would be selected in order to achieve the goals determined by these differing ethics. However, since it is a contribution toward democratic learning that is desired, it is essential that teachers become as skilled as possible in understanding and working with their classroom groups. For a lack of such skill is likely to result in conditions which are quite the opposite of democratic, even though

democratic techniques were supposedly being used. Democratic techniques do not exist *per se;* a technique is democratic only to the extent that it serves as a means to help the group achieve its democratic goals at a particular time. For example, the democratic technique of voting has been used as a very effective method of imposing some small minority opinion on the group.

A third important role of the teacher can be subsumed under the title of *therapist*—a combination of clinician and group worker. Lest someone remonstrate at this obligation, let him be reminded that, willingly or not, every teacher plays this role. Sometimes it is somewhat separate from other functions, but more often it is embedded in the classroom life while other functions predominate. No teacher avoids being a group worker, although some are more successful than others and some do crude jobs to be sure. The role of therapist implies group management to the end of helping all of the children toward individual and social adjustment. This means a degree of permissiveness, the establishment of rapport with each child, and the conduct of the work without the teacher's ego becoming involved. Such masterful, objective, "impersonal" human relationships are hard to come by. No one person is able to meet the differential needs of thirty-five or more children and serve as a cushion to soften the blows of harsh reality dealt out by the child's peer culture. But one tries. To do this the teacher must so act as to be the implicit embodiment of an acceptable code of behavior. Time and time again the mores of mental hygiene are illustrated as the teacher relates to the children, to their feelings and to their problems.

It is through the supportive atmosphere previously discussed that the teachers' therapeutic work is carried on. In a conflict situation pupils may come to the teacher as a judge or decision maker. The case need not be handled arbitrarily, but it must be handled. Teachers can never be neutrals but are continually interpreting "the law" as it applies in individual cases. In the therapist role, the teacher shares insights concerning human behavior, helps to get at causes of conflict and to find methods of resolving it. Sometimes the teacher serves this end by just being a friend, or he may provide, or himself be, an example with whom the child can identify in the Freudian sense. At any rate, the teacher must be an expert in human relations, understanding both the group and the individual.

In general teachers play this role least adequately of all. They tend toward being moralists, policemen, or punitive agents expecting good character to be developed by decree. While we have much to learn in applying the therapist role to the teacher, we already understand enough to know that such a playing of the role spells failure. The reason for such failure may often be that the teacher, having personal needs, tends to exploit the situation to satisfy these needs. We have in mind the need to be loved, the desire to avoid conflict, or pressures from latent hostility as examples. A very common attitude is the desire for dependency, where the teacher is happy if the students remain attached and dependent. Redl[14] has written a very interesting paper approaching this from a slightly different angle in which he shows how teachers tend to orient the whole atmosphere so that it plays into a masochistic or sadistic syndrome, to take only two examples. This is a complicated study in depth psychology, fraught with controversy. But it is not without point to us.

SITUATION AND CHOICE OF ROLE

From the point of view we have been discussing, it will be seen that there is no single complex of roles a teacher plays. The different legitimate objectives of a classroom demand different emphases. Certainly groups of children differ in their leadership qualities, and other individual and group factors need to be studied and understood. The question the teacher would then ask is: "What technique will contribute most effectively, in terms of the dynamics of my class at this time, to the goals and values which are held by the class (or myself, depending on who determines the goals)?" Two things are needed in selecting the techniques: (1) a knowledge of the dynamics of the technique itself, and (2) a knowledge of the goals and values of the group.

Knowledge about groups will help materially in gaining an understanding of the dynamics of a particular technique, and of the kinds of forces in the group which it brings into play in a positive (or negative) manner under specified conditions. To know these dynamics is important. Otherwise the teacher may fall into the trap of thinking that certain techniques are "good" per se, forgetting that a technique will contribute to the group only as it is able to draw on the positive forces present in the group at the time. If the condition of the group is different at a particular time, the "good" technique may bring out all that is "bad" in the group, causing him to wonder why it didn't work, or to blame the group for "not cooperating."

SOME TYPICAL CUES FOR ROLE CHANGES

How is it possible to determine which role to play at a particular time? What are the characteristics of a group which will serve as cues for shifting roles? One such cue is group "apathy." If the group is lethargic and passive, one must start searching for reasons. Is it the course content? The teaching methods? A general atmosphere of repression? Children who do not become boisterous at times are living under the control of teachers who are misers of freedom.

Another cue is to be found in the rapidity of "spread of disorder." In a group with adequate morale and goal involvement, disturbances do not spread easily. If one child upsets the room, individual work with that child is, of course, indicated. But more important is the signal it gives about the group condition. If a "bad actor" is a source of rapid contagion, the bond of common purpose must be weak indeed. This condition may be caused by such a simple thing as the need for a change of activity due to a requirement for over-long attention to a specific task. It may be a tension for muscle discharge, or it may go far beyond this to a fundamental dissatisfaction with the teacher behavior.

Other cues for further diagnosis and role modification include the presence of isolates, cliques, scapegoating, exclusiveness, extreme competitiveness, and the like. How much do teachers know about diagnosing these things? Indeed, how much help can educational psychologists give? Once the teacher really understands the situation and appreciates its deeper aspects, the role complex to meet the situation can usually be found. The task of the educational psychologist is to see that teachers are so trained that they will understand the dynamics of that situation.

Understanding more about the dynamics of groups helps the teacher in a variety of ways toward increasing his effectiveness in the roles that are appropriate in different situations. As more is learned about the theory and research on groups, new ways of thinking about the classroom situation will at first be gained, ways which may have been overlooked before. The importance of effective communication will come to be recognized in giving instructions and in expressing ideas. The relationships between the various pupils in the class will be studied, how they feel about each other, and the leader-group relationships, and gradually the teacher will become aware of his own behavior in the class and the kinds of effect it has on the pupils.

Of course, it is not easy to take one's knowledge into the classroom and become immediately aware of these complex interrelationships. Often it takes considerable training in observation and experience to be able to see, especially at the time it is happening, what is occuring in the group and what its casual relationships and potential effects are. The transition from "book learning" to "observation skill" is a difficult one to make, but it must be made if knowledge about groups is to contribute to teaching effectiveness . . . .

REFERENCES

1. WILLIAM C. BAGLEY. *School Discipline.* New York: Macmillan. 1917.

2. LESTER COCH and JOHN R. P. FRENCH, JR. "Overcoming Resistance to Change." *J. Human Relations,* Vol. I, 4, 1948.

3. MORTON DEUTSCH. "An Experimental Study of the Effects of Cooperation and Competition upon Group Process." *J. Human Relations,* Vol. II, 3, 1949.

4. ———. "A Theory of Cooperation and Competition." *J. Human Relations,* Vol. II, 2, 1949.

5. LEON FESTINGER, KURT BACK, and STANLEY SCHACHTER. *Social Influence* (pre-publication book manuscript, mimeographed). Chapter VI, "The Operation of Group Standards" and Chapter X, "A Theory of Group Structure and Group Standards."

6. JOHN R. P. FRENCH, JR. "Organized and Unorganized Groups under Fear and Frustration." *Iowa Studies in Child Welfare, Studies in Vector and Topological Psychology,* Vol. XX, 1944.

7. CHARLES E. HENDRY, RONALD LIPPITT, and ALVIN ZANDER. *Reality Practice as Educational Method.* Psychodrama Monographs, No. 9, 1944, p. 36. *Sociometry,* May 1944.

8. DAVID JENKINS. "Feedback and Group Self-evaluation." *J. Social Issues,* Vol. IV, 2, 1948.

9. KURT LEWIN. "Group Decision and Social Change." In Newcomb and Hartley, *Readings in Social Psychology.* New York: Henry Holt, 1947, pp. 330-344.

10. ———. *Resolving Social Conflicts.* New York: Harper Bros., 1948. Chapter IV.

11. RONALD LIPPITT. *Training in Community Relations.* New York: Harper Bros., 1949, p. 286.

12. RONALD LIPPITT and R. K. WHITE. "An Experimental Study of Leadership and Group Life." In Newcomb and Hartley, *Readings in Social Psychology.* New York: Henry Holt, 1947, pp. 315-329.

13. T. MAIN and M. NYSWANDER. *Some Observations on the Third National Training Laboratory in Group Development.* (mimeographed)

14. FRITZ REDL. "Group Emotion and Leadership." *Psychiatry.* Vol. V, 4, 1942, pp. 573-596.

15. STANLEY SCHACHTER. *Deviation, Rejection, and Communications.* Doctoral dissertation, University of Michigan, 1950.

16. JOHN THIBAUT. *The Relationship of Group Cohesiveness to Inter-Group Status Differences.* Doctoral Dissertation, Massachusetts Institute of Technology, 1949.

17. ALVIN ZANDER. "Resistance to Change—Its Analysis and Prevention," *Advanced Management,* Vol. XV, 1 Jan. 1950, pp. 9-12.

18. ———. "Within the Bonds of Freedom." *Childhood Education,* Vol. XXIV, 1, Sept. 1947.

28/CLASSROOM SOCIAL STRUCTURE AS A MENTAL HEALTH PROBLEM/

RONALD LIPPITT AND MARTIN GOLD[*]

ONE OF THE TWO MOST IMPORTANT and influential environments for the child is the classroom in which he lives during a part of each day. His relations with his teacher and with his peers are two major aspects of his school environment. These relations have a variety of important meanings for the child: "What is expected of me?" "What can I do and what can't I do?" "What will happen if . . . ?" "Who do I like?" "Who don't I like?" "Who likes me?" "Who doesn't?" "Who does the teacher like?" "Who's the strongest?" As clarification emerges about the meaning of such important questions, relations in the classroom develop a stable pattern or structure, which we are calling the classroom socio-emotional structure. Stratification becomes clear about those who are looked up to and down on in various ways. Each child finds he has a position, or several positions, in this socio-emotional structure. This social structure becomes a dominant aspect of his school environment and of his total life situation. His position in this structure becomes a very important determinant of his personal mental health situation, and of his motivation and ability to participate in classroom interaction.

This paper reports a research exploration of the development and maintenance of the classroom socio-emotional structure in a sample of 39 elementary classrooms.[1] The paper also explores some of the mental health correlates of the child's position in this socio-emotional structure, which in turn suggest focal points for diagnosis of socio-emotional problems in the classroom situation and formulation of therapeutic strategy in working toward the improvement of classroom mental health.

[1] The research reported in part in this paper was supported by Grant M-919 of the National Institute of Mental Health. Principal investigators were Ronald Lippitt, Robert Fox, and Douglas Blocksma. Sidney Rosen was Project Director. A book is in preparation reporting the total research program.

THE DEVELOPMENT OF THE SOCIO-EMOTIONAL STRUCTURE OF THE CLASSROOM

To what degree can we really talk about a social structure in the classroom? How much consensus is there among classmates about who belongs where in the structure? How stable is the structure over time?

All of the children in all of the 39 elementary school classrooms rated all their classmates on a four point scale, indicating the degree to which the ratee was perceived as able to get the others to do what he wanted them to do. The resulting stratification is called the social power structure of the classroom. . . .

Not only is there high consensus about who belongs where in the social structure, but there is high stability of the structure from early in the school year to the middle of the school year and to the end of the school year. Looking first at the social power structure we find that for the first, second, and third graders there is an average classroom correlation (Pearson r) of .73 between the social structure in early October and in the middle of January; between January and May the average correlation is .72; and from early fall until the end of the school year, the correlation in the primary grades is .63. All of the individual correlations are highly significant. For the fourth, fifth, and sixth grades the average correlations are similar except that the correlation between early October and May is .75. The structures concerning who is liked and disliked and who is regarded as expert and inexpert in classroom activities have an even higher stability, with most of the correlations being above .80. The evidence is clear that the interpersonal social structure of the classroom forms rapidly and maintains a high degree of stability throughout the school year. The same children remain in positions of low power and isolation or dislike throughout the year, and the same children stay at the top of the totem pole.

But are the same children at the top and the bottom of all the totem poles? A partial correla-

[*] Ronald Lippitt and Martin Gold, Classroom social structure as a mental health problem, *Journal of Social Issues*, 1959, *15* (1), 40-49. Reprinted with slight abridgement by permission.

tion program was carried out for four different social structures in each classroom; the social power structure, the affective (like and dislike) structure, the expertness structure, and the coerceability (ability to use physical coercion) structure. These analyses were summarized separately for younger and older classrooms in the elementary grades, and also for the beginning and end of the year. We find that with the other variables controlled there is still a high relationship between the power structure and the affect structure, a correlation of .57 at the beginning of the school year and .65 at the end of the year. The correlation is significantly higher for older than for younger boys (.44 as compared to .69). There is a smaller but significant relationship between the power structure and the expertness structure (.21 in October and .29 in May). The relationship of the coercion structure to the power structure increases from a zero relationship in the fall to an average correlation of .27 in the spring, although there is a great variability between groups in this relationship, and the relationship is accounted for to a great extent by the boys in each classroom rather than the girls. There is a significant relationship (.40) between the affect structure and the expertness structure in the fall which drops somewhat during the school year (.21 in May).... It is clear then that the children are making differentiations in their judgments of one another, and that being highly liked or being perceived as expert are both significant paths to social influence in the socio-emotional structure of the group.

But how do the children really think about each other when they have a chance to freely apply their own descriptive and evaluative labels? Are these dimensions we have been measuring really the central dimensions of the interpersonal structure as far as the children are concerned, or have they been somewhat imposed by measurement procedures? Gold (1958) has explored this question in a substudy of 152 children in kindergarten through the sixth grade. In a preliminary study he had fairly lengthy interviews with 21 children representing all the grade levels exploring with open ended questions their perceptions of their peers. From these interviews emerged seventeen characteristics or properties of children which seem to be matters of some concern as peers describe each other. These items fell into four areas: expertness characteristics (e.g. smart, has good ideas, good at making things); physical characteristics (e.g. fighting ability, strength, appearance); socio-emotional characteristics (e.g. friendliness, fun to be with,

doesn't tease); and "associational" characteristics (e.g. likes to do same things I do). These open ended interviews clearly confirmed the previous researches in camp settings (Polansky, Lippitt & Redl, 1950) concerning the salience of the dimensions of socio-emotional structuring studied in the classroom groups. In a second part of the study specific low power and high power children were compared as to their possession of the valued characteristics. Gold found that the children gave the highest value to socio-emotional characteristics, but also placed a high value on expertness and the lowest value on physical prowess. It was also found that highly valued characteristics were attributed significantly more often to children who were high in the power structure of the classroom group. It seems clear that children do perceive each other in terms of these characteristics, and that these characteristics are evaluated in such a way that they become resources relevant to the acquiring of high or low position in the social structure of the group.

MENTAL HEALTH CORRELATES OF POSITION IN THE CLASSROOM SOCIAL STRUCTURE

Let's turn from the perceptions of peers to the judgments and assessments of adults. Adults in the school environment who have an interest in mental health tend to perceive children in terms of adjustment and deviancy along similar socio-emotional dimensions. We might expect, therefore, that there would be some relationship between perceptions and evaluations by peers and mental health assessments by adults. Two explorations of this question have been carried out as part of a larger study. Douglas (1958) conducted a study of the responses of 115 children to frustration in a series of story completion situations where a child is frustrated by a loved adult. In these situations children use various types of psychological defenses against the expression of their feelings of aggression toward powerful loved adults. Working within a theoretical framework developed by Miller (Miller & Swanson, 1959), Douglas coded the primitivity or maturity of the defenses used by the children in coping with frustrating situations. Partialing out the effects of intelligence and age, Douglas found that the children who are lowest in the socio-emotional structure of the classroom more often used the most primitive defense of denial in the face of conflict than those children high in being liked and influential, who were more apt to use more mature defenses showing relatively minor distortions of the reality situation. In terms of clinical judgments, the use of the more primitive defenses is a symptom of poorer mental health in coping with conflict situations.

In a study of seven elementary classrooms, Echelberger (1959) analyzed cumulative teacher ratings of children on the Haggerty-Olson-Wickman Behavior Rating Schedule (1930). This schedule yields five scores: behavior problem symptoms, problems in intellectual functioning, problems of physical characteristics, social adjustment problems, and problems of emotional temperament. Echelberger correlated the position of the child in the socio-emotional structure in the classroom with the behavior problems scale (e.g. cheating, temper outbursts, truancy), the social adjustment scales (e.g. shyness, relation to authority, assertiveness), and the emotional adjustment scales (e.g. cheerfulness, excitability, suspiciousness). The tabulation below reports some relevant correlations (those .26 and greater are significant at the .05 level or better).

In every case it can be noted that the more influential and more popular children impress their teachers with a significantly more favorable mental health picture. They show fewer behavior problem symptoms, greater social adjustment, and more stable emotionality.

Jennings (1943) has proposed that an important dimension of personality health is the ability to make and maintain social connections, to have the capacity for friendships with others. In this context we might expect that the amount of positive affection, as compared to negative affect, which a child feels toward his peers might be considered a mental health criterion. In our classrooms each child indicated how much he liked or disliked other children in the class on a four point scale, with ratings 1 and 2 indicating two degrees of liking the other, and points 3 and 4 indicating two degrees of intensity of dislike. The tabulation below indicates that in the older grades the children in high status positions express more positive affect in their ratings of peers than do low status children. (The differences of 8 per cent are significant beyond the .02 level.) Through the course of the school year, this difference becomes greater, the low status children increasing the proportion of negative feelings toward their fellow classmates.

TABLE 2 / COMPARISON OF MEAN PERCENTAGES OF LIKING CHOICES (SPRING) MADE BY HIGH AND LOW POWER CHILDREN, BY GRADE AND SEX.

	HIGH STATUS		LOW STATUS	
	MEAN	N	MEAN	N
Kindergarten to Grade 3				
Boys	60%	(79)	62%	(83)
Girls	60	(82)	61	(67)
Grades 4 to 6				
Boys	72	(103)	64	(77)
Girls	70	(73)	62	(78)

Direct observation of the children interacting in the classroom supports this conclusion about negative and positive affect. We recorded on quantitative behavior schedules an hour of classroom interaction in a standardized situation a few weeks after the school year began. The children participated in four activities designed to maximize the need for cooperation and coordination with others. Each child interacted with every other child in the classroom in at least one of the activities. The data from these observations permit typing each child in terms of a behavioral output pattern. In the tabulation below we can see that those behavior patterns which indicate aggressive-assertive or passive-hostile activity output are more frequently characteristic of the low power children in the classroom social structure. Low status children tend to behave in ways that are likely to disrupt interpersonal friendships and also classroom functioning. (Differ-

TABLE 1 / CORRELATIONS (PEARSON r) OF SOCIOMETRIC RATINGS WITH SELECTED H.O.W. RATINGS, BY GRADE.

GRADES	N	BEHAVIOR PROBLEMS	SOCIAL ADJUSTMENT	EMOTIONAL ADJUSTMENT
1-3	64			
Power x		−.28	.26	.21
Popularity x		−.46	.36	.27
4-6	72			
Power x		−.31	.36	.41
Popularity x		−.29	.35	.38

TABLE 3 / COMPARISONS OF PERCENTAGES OF LOW POWER WITH OTHER CHILDREN IN BEHAVIOR OUTPUT TYPE CATEGORIES.

BEHAVIOR OUTPUT TYPE CATEGORIES	LOW POWER ($N = 311$)	OTHER ($N = 654$)
1. Active-assertive, friendly	14%	25%
2. Active-assertive, unfriendly	27	22
3. Neutral or mixed	27	28
4. Passive, friendly	22	21
5. Passive, unfriendly	10	4
	100%	100%

ences of 5 per cent are significant beyond the .05 level.)

To summarize, then, we can say that children in low positions in the socio-emotional structure of the classroom tend to have mental health difficulties which are reflected both in inner psychological processes, in interpersonal relationship difficulties, and in behavior patterns which disrupt the life of the classroom group.

THE IMPACT OF THE CLASSROOM MILIEU ON THE CHILD'S MENTAL HEALTH SITUATION

It becomes very important to consider the question: do the on-going processes of the classroom tend to aggravate or to alleviate the mental health problems of children low in the socio-emotional structure of the classroom? Looking first at the meaning of the on-going relationship with peers, we find that children who are low in the social structure have a continuing experience of social failure and rejection. For example, the success of each child's attempts to influence his peers during the standardized activity situation proved to be significantly correlated with his position in the social structure. Those low in the social structure experienced more failure of their own attempts and were more dominated by the behavior of others. This correlation increased during the course of the school year. Some of the low status children reacted to these behaviors from their peers by more withdrawal, and others reacted by more aggressive-assertive efforts to improve their position, which only resulted in still more failure.

That the children are sensitive to this incoming feedback from their peers is revealed by the self-evaluation index, which is a combination of self ratings on the social power and liking scales. The tabulation below indicates that children's self-evaluations tend to correspond to the feelings expressed by peers. (Differences between high and low power means are significant by T-test beyond the .05 level, except among the younger boys.) The younger boys seem to be less sensitive to the feelings of others about them, although their ratings also indicate some awareness of their status. It may be that they are more prone to make defensive self ratings to help them cope with their unhappy position in the group.

It is quite apparent to the children's teachers that high and low status pupils are treated differentially by their peers. We asked the teachers in the experimental classrooms to rate each child on the relative amount of warmth he received

TABLE 4 / COMPARISONS OF MEAN SELF-EVALUATION SCORE (FALL) OF HIGH AND LOW POWER CHILDREN, BY GRADE AND SEX.

	HIGH POWER		LOW POWER	
	MEAN	N	MEAN	N
Kindergarten to grade 3				
Boys	3.47	(79)	3.86	(83)
Girls	3.23	(82)	3.91	(67)
Grades 4 to 6				
Boys	3.76	(103)	4.53	(77)
Girls	3.74	(73)	4.35	(78)

from others. These ratings were significantly correlated with the peer ratings of social power and likeability. The correlations were considerably higher in the spring than in the fall.

But peers are only part of the classroom milieu. The teacher is an important part of the environment. What about her contribution?

Part of our study included observations of a sample of classroom activities by a team of graduate student observers. Each observer watched an individual elementary school child for an hour at a time, recording (1) with whom the child interacted and who initiated the interaction; (2) the affective quality of the interaction, whether friendly, neutral or unfriendly; (3) whether the content of the interaction was primarily social or was concerned with the performance of a learning activity. None of the observers had any knowledge of the pupils' social status in the classroom. Each child was observed by two different observers. There were 318 child hours of observation in the sample of classrooms. Part of the analysis deals with pupil-teacher interactions which can be summarized only briefly here.

It will be noted from Table 5 (p. 215) that teachers pay attention to the social behavior, rather than the performance behavior, of low status pupils more often than of high status pupils. Evidently this aspect of their behavior leads to social evaluation and response more frequently on the teacher's part, just as it does for classmates. How the teacher responds depends on whether she is interacting with a low status girl or boy. Low status boys tend to receive more criticism than their high status boy classmates; but low status girls receive more support. In Table 6 we see that teachers were friendly more often toward low status girls than other girls, but more often neutral or unfriendly toward low status boys. Differences in children's behavior probably evoke these different responses from teachers. Looking at the data on the children's approaches to their teachers, we note that low status girls are actively affectionate in their approaches while

TABLE 5 / COMPARISON OF PERCENTAGES OF TEACHER INTERACTION WITH HIGH AND LOW POWER CHILDREN, BY SEX.

	N	SOCIAL BEHAVIOR EVALUATION	PERFORMANCE EVALUATION	TOTAL CONTENT TALLIES	SUPPORTIVE REMARKS	CRITICAL REMARKS	TOTAL SUPPORTIVE-CRITICAL TALLIES
Girls:							
High	43	16%	84%	104	57%	43%	104
Low	44	24%	76%	116	73%	27%	116
Boys:							
High	37	22%	78%	102	62%	38%	103
Low	35	30%	70%	176	42%	58%	176

TABLE 6 / COMPARISON OF AFFECTIVE QUALITY OF TEACHERS' INTERACTIONS WITH HIGH AND LOW POWER PUPILS, BY SEX.

	N	TEACHERS' APPROACHES TO PUPILS			TOTAL TEACHERS' APPROACHES	PUPILS' APPROACHES TO TEACHERS			TOTAL PUPILS' APPROACHES
		FRIENDLY	NEUTRAL	UNFRIENDLY		FRIENDLY	NEUTRAL	UNFRIENDLY	
Girls:									
High	43	32%	48%	19%	99	29%	66%	5%	111
Low	44	36%	51%	14%	111	49%	49%	2%	100
Boys:									
High	37	36%	47%	18%	118	20%	66%	14%	64
Low	35	28%	52%	20%	167	17%	74%	9%	118

low status boys do not show such positive affect. From other data we can infer that low status girls are not only more warm in their relations with the teachers, but are relatively passive and withdrawing, while low status boys are more aggressive and troublesome than their higher status classmates.

This brief discussion of teachers' behavior should not be construed to mean that the teachers involved in the study were "playing favorites." Rather, we think that teachers, faced with the task of teaching youngsters in classroom groups and necessarily having to maintain order to do so, must respond critically to disruptive behavior, and respond quite naturally with affection to little girls who seem to be asking for it and apparently getting little from their peers. But, we must ask, what are the implications of these findings for evaluating the classroom as a mental health milieu? What solutions to mental health problems do low status boys find from the generally critical and rejecting classroom relationships; or low status girls, who depend upon their relationships to teachers in the absence of satisfying give and take with their peers?

IMPLICATIONS FOR DIAGNOSTIC FOCUS AND THERAPEUTIC STRATEGY

When we try to close in on the locus of pathology which maintains and aggravates the unhealthy situation of certain children in the classroom group, it is apparent that the difficulties are created and maintained by a circular social process contributed to by the individual child, by his classmates, and by the teacher. If we focus on the individual child who is in difficulty we see that he contributes to the unhealthy situation by (1) his negative self evaluation and his response to this; (2) his hostility toward others; (3) his unskilled and unrealistic behavior output of assertive aggressiveness or withdrawing noncontribution; (4) his insensitive and defensive reception of feedback from others which might potentially give him more guidance for his own behavior.

If we look at the rest of the group as a source of difficulty for the individual child we see that there is (1) a very rapid evaluative labelling of a child and a strong tendency to maintain this evaluative consensus in spite of further information about the individual child as stimulus; (2)

very inadequate skills of the group in providing the member with feedback which communicates sympathetic guidance rather than rejection or ignoration; and (3) a lack of group standards concerning the acceptance and support of deviancy.

If we look at the role of a teacher and her contribution to the situation we note (1) a lack of teaching effort focussed on developing personal attitude and group standards about good human relations; (2) a lack of interpersonal grouping practices and other procedures guided by mental health goals; (3) a lack of clear presentation of constructive behavior patterns toward low status children which could be imitated by her other pupils.

The conversion of these diagnostic insights into a mental health strategy is a challenging task. How much can one do by working directly outside the classroom group with the children in need of help, to assist them to initiate changes in the social process? How much can be done by working directly with the high power children who have the most influence on the socio-emotional structure of the classroom? What can be done by helping teachers to initiate curriculum content and training procedures which will have a direct influence on the socio-emotional structure of the class? These are the questions we are exploring with our collaborating classrooms.

REFERENCES

DOUGLAS, VIRGINIA. *The Development of Two Families of Defense.* Unpublished doctoral dissertation, University of Michigan, 1958.

ECHELBERGER, EDNA. *Relationships between Personality Traits and Peer Status.* Unpublished doctoral dissertation, University of Michigan, 1959.

GOLD, MARTIN. Power in the Classroom. *Sociometry,* 1958, *21,* No. 1.

HAGGERTY-OLSON-WICKMAN. *Behavior Rating Schedule.* New York: World Book Company, 1930.

JENNINGS, HELEN HALL. *Leadership and Isolation.* New York: Longman's Green and Company, 1943.

MILLER, DANIEL, and SWANSON, GUY E. *Inner Conflict and Defense.* New York: Henry Holt and Company, 1960.

POLANSKY, NORMAN, LIPPITT, RONALD, and REDL, FRITZ. The use of near-sociometric data in research on group treatment processes. *Sociometry,* 1950, *13,* No. 1, 39-62.

29/TV AS SCAPEGOAT/WILBUR SCHRAMM*

GEOFFREY GORER HAS POINTED OUT that each time when mass communication has acquired another medium, older people have blamed the new medium for all the defects they see in the young. Thus movies, radio, and television have all been accused of corrupting the youth, and so likewise have forms of older media such as dime novels (at the end of the last century) and comic books (in our own time).

Yet when researchers or commissions have tried to ferret out the mischief these new media are supposed to be doing, their results are predominantly negative. Nobody has yet been able to demonstrate that the effects of these devices

* Wilbur Schramm, TV as Scapegoat, a review of "Television and the Child: An Empirical Study of the Effect of Television on the Young" by Hilde T. Himmelweit, A. N. Oppenheim, and Pamela Vance (New York: Oxford University Press, for the Nuffield Foundation, 1958), *Contemporary Psychology,* 1959, *4,* 357-358. Reprinted by permission.

on children's social behavior, mental or physical health, or intellectual well-being has been either very bad or very good or very important.

Now here is another such study financed by the Nuffield Foundation in England and put through by three psychologists who are or have been at the University of London. Dr. Himmelweit is in charge of social psychology at the London School of Economics and is currently chairman of the social psychology section of the British Psychological Society. Dr. Oppenheim is a lecturer in social psychology at the London School of Economics and also has been involved in a considerable amount of work in abnormal psychology. Miss Vance is a graduate in psychology from London University, now engaged in research in commercial motivation in Great Britain.

This book is distinguished by being the most extensive and thorough study of television and children yet published. More precisely, it is a number of studies. The most important of these are two field surveys: one, of children in Norwich before and after television came to that city; the other, of children who viewed television and children who did not, in four English cities, Bristol, Portsmouth, Sunderland, and London.

Let us look first at the four-city study. This is designed in a factorial pattern, meaning that certain variables are to be represented by cells of equal size. Four such variables were chosen: age (10–11 and 13–14), sex, intelligence quotient (115 or over, 100–114, and below 100), and social class (father's occupation was used as a gross measure by which to distinguish between lower and middle class; there were no upper-class children in the sample). Since viewers and nonviewers were to be represented equally, 48 cells would have to be represented. The experimenters wished to have 40 children in each cell of the design, requiring, therefore, an n of 1920. Furthermore, they wanted every viewer matched with a nonviewer in age (6 months), sex, intelligence (6 points), and occupation (one position on the Hall-Jones scale).

Even after drawing a total sample of 4,838 they still found it impossible to fill all the cells in the design, and therefore relaxed the restrictions somewhat. They finally resorted to weighting the sample by duplicating the cards of randomly chosen subjects in the unfilled cells. They also ran into a mammoth job of analysis, sorting with a deck that included 40 Hollerith cards for every subject. Because of the cumbersome nature of their data, they were able, for example, to analyze only 336 diaries, instead of 1920.

Despite these difficulties, they worked with admirable rigor and produced a great quantity of data from skillful and searching questions. Because of their design, they could easily and reliably compare across variables, although they could not extrapolate to any population, as they could have done, for example, if they had designed their experimental sample within a representative sample. Very wisely, however, they supplemented the large study with the Norwich study, which was small—56 pairs of 10–11-year-olds, 129 pairs of 13–14-year-olds—but highly useful in showing that many of the behaviors associated with television-viewing existed in children before they got television. These two were supplemented by a series of smaller studies, including an examination of the content of some programs, diaries kept by mothers, observation of children watching television, and so forth.

The net result is a mountain of information, previously unavailable, on how English children in two age-groups view television. They view it very much as do U.S. children, although apparently for a little less time. Brighter children view TV less than duller children. They prefer adult over children's programs, commercial television over BBC. Their tastes in television are parallel to their tastes in other things.

But how about the effects? Televison makes children go to bed about 20 minutes later, on the average. Beyond that, the results are significant in what the authors do *not* find, rather than in what they do. Television may make the duller children a bit better informed and, by displacing more useful sources, may slightly reduce the level of information of the brighter, thus contributing to a leveling of the population. TV gives bright children a quicker start on learning in the pre-school years, but this difference seems to iron out later. There is no evidence of harmful physical effects. There is no indication that TV introduces a harmful amount of aggression, or fear, or makes a previously well-behaved child into a juvenile delinquent, or an undisturbed child into a disturbed one. It may feed a disturbance that already exists or give criminal suggestions to a budding criminal; and this effect may be more alarming than it sounds, inasmuch as the "addicts" to television turn out in a high proportion of cases to be the maladjusted, disturbed children. But if they were not in front of the television set, they would probably be at the movies or poring over a comic or pulp.

Is this the whole story of the effect on children of an activity to which they give an average of two hours a day, or are we missing something? Two suggestions seem pertinent. For one thing, the significant effects of television, if any, are probably long-term effects. They have to do with the child's view of his environment, his values, his tendency to stereotype, and so on. By controlling two hours a day, television must also control the storage of some of the things children know and value, and on which they act. But our research designs, for the most part, have been ill-adapted to sorting out these very long-term effects. Furthermore, television operates through a family of other variables. Compared to the influence of the home, the peer group, the values of the culture, and the child's own abilities and qualities, television (even if we could clearly isolate its effect) must be a relatively small determinant. These authors insist that the object of our concern should be not *how long* a child watches television, but rather *what* he sees. Perhaps, in fact, a better way to ask the question "what does television do to children?" is "what do children do with television?" For it is clear that what the child brings to the program and the needs that he meets by using it will determine in large part television's residual effects upon him.

30/A STUDY OF SEVENTH GRADE CHILDREN'S READING OF COMIC BOOKS AS RELATED TO CERTAIN OTHER VARIABLES/W. PAUL BLAKELY*

A. INTRODUCTION

SPECULATION ABOUT ALLEGED DANgers as well as possible benefits of the ubiquitous comic books to their numerous youthful readers, has been widespread and vehement. There is less empirical data than the important status and serious implications of this problem would seem to warrant. Gunnar Dybwad, Executive Director of the Child Study Association of America, speaking before the United States Senate Subcommittee Investigating Juvenile Delinquency in 1954, declared that: "The absence of any definitive studies of the effects of comic reading on children's emotions and/or behavior has been a serious handicap to us as to everyone dealing with this problem." (3) The Senate Subcommittee itself, in its Interim Report issued in 1955, noted "with some surprise that little attention has been paid by educational and welfare agencies to the potential dangers, as well as benefits, to children presented by the growth of the comic book industry." (1)

The purpose of the present study has been to identify among a specific group of children, subgroups whose reading of comic books falls into various categories as to amount and as to type; then to measure as well as possible among these children certain variables upon which the reading of comic books has been alleged to have a bearing; and to determine whether the subgroups differ on the average with respect to these variables as measured.

* W. Paul Blakely, A study of seventh grade children's reading of comic books as related to certain other variables, *Journal of Genetic Psychology*, 1958, 93, 291-301. Reprinted by permission.

B. RELATED LITERATURE

It is rather easy to find literature in which this problem is discussed in terms of clinical or case-study material, or in terms of "expert opinion." It is more difficult, as already implied, to find reports of experimental data.

Dr. Frederic Wertham, in his status as practicing psychiatrist, has commanded a wide audience with various pronouncements condemning comic books. Citing case material on children with reading difficulties whom he has found to be "addicted" to the reading of comic books, for example, he infers a causal connection (8).

Sperzel, in an experimental study involving use of comic books in the classroom, found no effects on reading ability (7). Luckiesh and Moss have cited statements of ophthalmologists that some children appear to suffer from eyestrain attributable to reading the comics, but have noted at the same time the lack of evidence available (2).

Witty has made inferences about comic reading and educational achievement in a group of Evanston-Chicago-Milwaukee children he studied, reporting that a subgroup who read the most comic books received almost the same average school marks as one who read the fewest (9). Heisler (5) studied 600 elementary and junior high school children and for each school grade level, made a number of comparisons between a group who read no comic books and one of equal or nearly equal size who read the most. Evidences of differences in school achievement, adjustment, and ownership of library-type books were neither consistent nor of a generally recognized significance level.

Concerning adjustment and behavior, Dr. Wertham (8) says that his clinical data obtained by a number of standard techniques show factors in the psychological patterns of children which require other than conventional Freudian explanations, and correspond to material in comic books. He cites as an example, an injury-to-the-eye motif.

Josette Frank (4) in 1948 reported a symposium of psychiatric and psychological opinion, concluding that there was agreement that "the radio programs, movies and comics do not in themselves *create* fears, but for certain children and under various conditions, do precipitate or stimulate anxieties lying beneath the surface ready to be awakened."

Wolfe and Fiske studied a relatively small group of children intensively and found certain unhealthy characteristics associated with reading the comic books as "fans," that is, with excessive intensity (10).

Hoult (6) studied 235 boys and girls, ages 10 through 17, who had been arrested for juvenile delinquency, in comparison with a matched group of controls. He categorized comic books as harmful, questionable, and harmless according to their general content (e.g., crime and gangsterism, animated animal cartoons), and found that his delinquent subjects reported reading more titles in the first two categories than the non-delinquents, but no more in the third.

C. THE PRESENT STUDY: POPULATION AND METHOD

The population chosen for the present study consisted of 12 class sections of seventh grade children in two public junior high schools in an Iowa city of about 100,000 population. Complete data were obtained for 323 children, except that one of the coöperating schools withheld a group of children from the achievement testing program so that achievement test scores were available on only 281.

The city is one which thrives on industry and trade. The schools in the study draw from populations which are not atypical in the city. An unselected list of parents' occupations as reported by the children in the study follows: printer, supermarket manager, tool-grinder, worker in sales department of radio-manufacturing company, truckdriver, dock foreman, traveling salesman, crane operator, dishwasher (mother), painter, electrician, design engineer, roofer, and college instructor.

As a measure of comic book reading, three questionnaires were constructed, each labeled *Junior High Interest Questionnaire*, and administered at intervals of about one month beginning early in September, 1956. Among the questions on each, the child was asked to list the titles of all comic books he had read "within the past week," and in any case where he had read the same title more than once, to put the number of times just following the title. The question about comic book reading, in each case, was placed among others about various interests and activities in an effort to avoid the possibility of putting the responding child "on his guard"; that the study was particularly concerned with comic book reading was not divulged.

From the questionnaires was computed for each child his total comic book *frequency*—that is, the total number of titles reported read multiplied by the number of times for each. (For example, having read *Donald Duck* 2 times and *Tarzan* once would constitute a frequency of 3.)

For each child was also computed a *comic book type score*. Each title which appeared in the most recent classification of the Cincinnati Committee on Evaluation of Comic Books was considered accordingly, as rating "No Objection," "Some Objection," or "Objectionable." For titles not on the most recent list, earlier lists were consulted. Some titles found on none of these lists were classified by the investigator, applying as best he could the criteria set forth by the Committee in its 1956 leaflet. It was impossible to classify 7.31 per cent of the reported frequency, which were ambiguous or could not be identified; these titles were ignored in computing the comic book type score. The complete list of titles reported, with their classifications, appears in the writer's doctoral dissertation, which is in the library of the State University of Iowa, and on file with University Microfilms, Ann Arbor, Michigan.

The comic book type score for each child was computed by the formula

$$T = \frac{(N \times 2) + (S \times 1) + (B \times 0)}{N + S + B} \times 10$$

where T = type score; N = frequency of "No Objection" titles; S = frequency of "Some Objection" titles; and B = frequency of "Objectionable" titles.

As a measure of "legitimate" reading, each questionnaire also asked the child to list all books of the type obtainable at a library, which he had read "within the last month," and after each, to specify where he had obtained it—public library, school library, home, etc.

As an intelligence test as independent of reading as possible, The Lorge Thorndike Intelligence Test, Non-Verbal Series, Level 4, Form A was administered.

The *SRA* Junior Inventory, Form S was chosen as a measure of various phases of adjustment. The checking of problems on the Inventory as "big" or "middle-sized" has been taken as indicative of the child's concern about his adjustment in the respective area. Checking a problem as "little" or "not a problem" might, of course, indicate conscious or unconscious reluctance to admit the problem, as well as the non-existence of the problem for the child concerned. Therefore, the scores derived by counting the number of checks in "big" and "middle-sized"

boxes must be taken as indicative of the child's *perception* (quantitatively) of his problems. For each child, the total score on the inventory was thus computed, as well as the subscores "About Me and My School," "About Me and My Home," "My Health," "About Myself," "Getting Along With Other People," and "Things in General"; and a subscore for a category of items selected throughout the inventory taken to be indicative of "personal adjustment."

As a measure of behavior and behavior-related characteristics observable to others, teachers of the children filled out the Haggerty-Olson-Wickman Behavior Rating Schedules, A and B. Schedule A consists of a list of behavior problems in their order of frequency as reported for a group of elementary school children, with statistical weights assigned on the basis of seriousness and frequency. In Schedule B are five-point graphic rating scales for traits studied in relation to the behavior problems of Schedule A among the standardizing group; thus a high score on Schedule B is taken to be suggestive of behavior-problem proneness.

The Stanford Achievement Test, Advanced Battery, Form J, was administered during the school year as part of the regular program of the coöperating schools. Grade norm scores for the children in the study were taken as follows: reading (average of Paragraph Meaning and Sentence Meaning); average of Language and Spelling; and general school achievement status (average of Language, Spelling, Arithmetic Reasoning, Arithmetic Computation, and Social Studies).

The intelligence test, the *SRA* Junior Inventory, and Questionnaires 1 and 2 were administered by the investigator during school periods allotted him for the purpose. Questionnaire 3 and the Stanford Achievement Test were administered, and the ratings on the Haggerty-Olson-Wickman Schedules made, by coöperating school personnel.

D. PARENT INTERVIEWS

Hoping to be able to make an assessment of the truth of the children's answers to the questionnaires, the investigator visited the homes of 35 of them. The 35 were initially chosen by taking every tenth name from an alphabetized list of all children who responded to the first questionnaire. When an interview could not be completed after a second call at a home (because no one was found at home), the next name in order was substituted.

The parents were asked questions about their children's comic book and library book reading, along with others about television viewing and other activities. It soon became apparent that an estimate of their children's weekly reading of comic books is difficult for many parents to make. Likewise, much of the library book reading was found to take place in the school, and the parents were unable to report it very accurately. A product-moment correlation coefficient of 0.42 was obtained, for the 35 cases, between the average weekly frequency of comic book reading computed from each child's three questionnaires, and the parents' estimates of "number of comic books read each week." A coefficient of 0.43 was obtained between the average monthly number of library books reported read by the children, and a parent estimate of library books obtained monthly, on the average, from the public library plus "other sources."

Many of the parents interviewed obviously felt it reflected on their child-rearing to admit their children were readers of comic books. This, plus the fact that the children were asked actually to list titles of comic books and library type books read, is taken as justifying the conclusion that there is probably greater error in the parents' estimate than in the figure derived from the children's reports.

E. RESULTS OF THE STUDY

1. COMPARISONS BASED ON COMIC BOOK FREQUENCY GROUPS. The children participating in the study were divided into subgroups according to total reported comic book frequency, for purposes of a series of comparisons. An attempt was made to keep subgroups of maximum size possible while at the same time maintaining categories descriptive as to frequency of comic book reading. Table 1 shows the subgroupings used; it will be noted, for example, that "Light Readers" reported reading frequency of from one to six comic books during the three weeks covered by the questionnaires, or an average frequency of not more than two per week.

Comparisons among the subgroups so derived, with respect to the other measures, which are regarded as dependent variables, were made by the simple analysis of variance, using a .05 coefficient of risk. The comparisons are shown in Table 2.

Where the obtained F meets the chosen criterion of significance, the t-test has been applied between the various pairs of means. The following differences in reported library-book reading were thus found to be significant: Subgroups III over I and IV over I (.01 level); and IV over II (.05 level).

When the same set of analyses of variance were applied to the sexes separately, and F of 4.83 (significant at .01 level, $df = 3,168$) was obtained for boys alone in reported library-book reading; and significant t's were found in testing the fol-

TABLE 1 / THE SUBGROUPS ACCORDING TO TOTAL REPORTED COMIC BOOK FREQUENCY FOR THREE NON-CONSECUTIVE WEEKS.

SUBGROUPS	N[1]	RANGE	MEAN	SD
Boys				
I. Non-readers	43 (30)	0	0	0
II. Light readers	35 (32)	1-6	3.26	1.63
III. Moderate readers	55 (46)	7-21	12.95	4.23
IV. Heavy readers	39 (34)	22 or more	44.18	27.76
Total	172 (142)		14.82	21.44
Girls				
I. Non-readers	33 (27)	0	0	0
II. Light readers	46 (44)	1-6	3.48	1.53
III. Moderate readers	54 (51)	7-21	12.07	3.96
IV. Heavy readers	18 (17)	22 or more	39.67	27.44
Total	151 (139)		10.11	15.41
Total				
I. Non-readers	76 (57)	0	0	0
II. Light readers	81 (76)	1-6	3.38	1.58
III. Moderate readers	109 (97)	7-21	12.51	4.12
IV. Heavy readers	57 (51)	22 or more	42.75	27.75
Total	323 (281)		12.62	19.01

[1] Figures in parentheses are reduced N's used for achievement test comparisons.

TABLE 2 / COMPARISONS AMONG COMIC BOOK FREQUENCY SUBGROUPS (SEXES COMBINED).

| | SUBGROUP MEANS | | | | | |
MEASURE	I	II	III	IV	df	F
Lorge-Th.						
Non-V *IQ*	99.53	102.73	102.81	102.40	3,319	1.55
Library Book						
Rdg. (3 mo.)	4.00	5.14	5.73	6.68	3,319	5.12[1]
SRA Jr. Inv.						
Home	2.20	2.31	2.59	3.26	3,319	1.30
People	1.46	2.48	2.28	3.00	3,319	1.91
School	8.50	7.67	7.89	8.35	3,319	0.28
Self	2.50	3.24	3.28	2.95	3,319	0.62
Th. Gen.	4.59	4.98	5.31	6.18	3,319	0.99
Health	1.93	2.22	2.44	2.75	3,319	0.86
Pers. Adj.	2.45	2.91	2.89	3.07	3,319	0.28
Total	21.18	22.89	23.80	26.49	3,319	0.65
Hag-Ol-Wick						
Sch. A	11.42	7.52	11.87	13.95	3,319	1.30
Sch. B	66.34	65.35	67.60	67.07	3,319	0.29
St. Achvt.						
Reading	9.01	8.95	8.99	9.14	3,277	0.10
Lang-Sp	8.52	8.56	8.31	8.32	3,277	0.37
5 Subtests	8.47	8.45	8.34	8.28	3,277	0.27

[1] Significant at .01 level.

TABLE 3 / THE SUBGROUPS ACCORDING TO COMIC BOOK TYPE SCORES.[1]

SUBGROUP	N[2]	RANGE	MEAN	SD
Boys				
I. Non-readers	43 (30)	——	——	——
II. All "No Obj."	50 (44)	(All have scores of 20)		
III. Few "S.O.," "Obj."	46 (37)	16-19	17.67	1.06
IV. Most "S.O.," "Obj."	33 (31)	0-15	11.15	4.34
Total readers	129 (112)	0-20	16.91	4.19
Girls				
I. Non-readers	33 (27)	——	——	——
II. All "No Obj."	70 (66)	(All have scores of 20)		
III. Few "S.O.," "Obj."	30 (29)	16-19	17.50	1.06
IV. Most "S.O.," "Obj."	18 (17)	0-15	12.94	2.63
Total readers	118 (112)	0-20	18.29	2.75
Total				
I. Non-readers	76 (57)	——	——	——
II. All "No Obj."	120 (110)	(All have scores of 20)		
III. Few "S.O.," "Obj."	76 (66)	16-19	17.61	1.07
IV. Most "S.O.," "Obj."	51 (48)	0-15	11.98	3.92
Total readers	247 (224)	0-20	17.57	3.64

[1] For derivation, see text.

[2] Figures in parentheses are reduced *N*'s used for achievement test comparisons.

TABLE 4 / COMPARISONS AMONG COMIC BOOK TYPE SCORE SUBGROUPS (SEXES COMBINED).

| | SUBGROUP MEANS | | | | | |
MEASURE	I	II	III	IV	df	F
Lorge-Th.						
Non-V. *IQ*	99.53	103.39	101.54	103.00	3,319	2.00
Library Book						
Rdg. (3 mo.)	4.00	5.73	5.71	5.90	3,319	3.51[1]
SRA Jr. Inv.						
Home	2.20	2.33	3.11	2.73	3,319	1.20
People	1.46	2.08	2.79	3.14	3,319	2.59
School	8.50	7.53	8.84	7.47	3,319	0.88
Self	2.50	3.08	3.51	2.96	3,319	0.76
Th. Gen.	4.59	4.58	6.45	5.77	3,319	2.38
Health	1.93	2.32	2.57	2.55	3,319	0.65
Pers. Adj.	2.45	2.63	3.18	3.29	3,319	0.66
Total	21.18	21.93	27.26	24.61	3,319	1.26
Hag-Ol-Wick						
Sch. A	11.42	9.83	12.12	11.64	3,319	0.24
Sch. B	66.34	64.81	66.59	72.55	3,319	2.20
St. Achvt.						
Reading	9.01	8.89	9.15	9.09	3,277	0.31
Lang-Sp	8.52	8.40	8.63	7.94	3,277	1.51
5 Subtests	8.47	8.37	8.43	8.24	3,277	0.27

[1]Significant at .05 level.

TABLE 5 / COMPARISONS AMONG GIRLS' COMIC BOOK TYPE SCORE SUBGROUPS, *SRA* JUNIOR INVENTORY, "THINGS IN GENERAL."

SUBGROUPS	MEANS	DIFFERENCES		
		I	II	III
I	5.36	I	II	III
II	4.30	1.06		
III	7.57	2.21	3.27[2]	
IV	6.50	1.14	2.20	1.07

F (df = 3,147) = 2.80.[1]

[1] Significant at .05 level.
[2] Significant at .01 level.

lowing differences: Subgroups III over I, IV over II, and IV over III (.05 level); and IV over I (.01 level). Thus for boys, and for the sexes combined, reported readership of library-type books tends to increase as does frequency of comic book reading. The subgroup means for library book readership for girls clearly followed the same pattern, but not to the chosen level of significance.

With the exception noted, the comparisons made among subgroups who differ in frequency of comic book reading show no corresponding, average differences in the measures applied.

2. COMPARISONS BASED ON COMIC BOOK TYPE SCORE GROUPS. A second arrangement of subgroups has been made according to comic book type scores, as shown in Table 3. Again, factors of both maximum subgroup size and descriptiveness

of category were considered. However, the range of type scores in Subgroup IV is necessarily wider than might be desirable, because of the considerable negative-skewedness of the type-score distribution. It will be noted that Subgroup I, "Non-readers," is the same subgroup so-used in the comparison based on frequency.

Results of the simple analysis of variance as applied to this arrangement of subgroups, with respect to the various measures applied, may be observed in Table 4. Again, the lack of significant differences is much greater than their presence. It will be noted that the tendency of comic book readers to be greater readers of library books, by their own report, at least, persists without respect to the "type" of comic books read.

When the series of analyses were applied to the type-score subgroups, sexes separately, one further difference emerged. The girls in Subgroup III score higher on problems related to "Things in General" than do those in Subgroup II (see Table 5). This category of items in *SRA* Junior Inventory, Form S, is rather miscellaneous; the one outstanding characteristic seems to be a lack of skills or "know-how": "I need to learn how to use the library"; "I want to learn how to dance"; "I wish I could take music lessons"; "I wonder what my real abilities are." It is probably not justified to invest too much concern in this one significant difference which appears among so many possible ones (maybe this is an error of rejection which the .05 coefficient of risk implies will occur 5 per cent of the time in the long run). However, it should be noted that girls in type-score Subgroups III or IV, or both, also have higher observed means than those in Subgroups I and/or II (not at the chosen level of significance) in *SRA* total, "People," "Self," "Health," and "Personal Adjustment," and in the Haggerty-Olson-Wickman schedules.

F. CONCLUSIONS

Within the limitations inhering in the method and population of the study, the following conclusions have been drawn:

1. Seventh grade children who differ in comic book reading, either as to type (as defined) or as to frequency, do not differ correspondingly in tested reading ability.

2. Such children, so grouped, do not differ correspondingly in achievement in language and spelling as measured by a standardized test.

3. Such children, so grouped, do not differ correspondingly in general school achievement as measured by an average of five subtests of a standardized test.

4. Such children, so grouped, do not differ correspondingly in behavior problem status, or in traits related to behavior problem status, as observed and rated by their teacher.

5. Such children, so grouped, are not significantly different from each other, correspondingly, in intelligence.

6. Seventh grade children who read comic books read more library books than do those who read no comic books. The difference tends to be in proportion to the frequency of comic book reading, and to exist for all "qualities" of comic book reading as defined by the Cincinnati Committee. Although the difference is not significant in the case of girls alone, their subgroup means clearly follow the same pattern as those for boys and they appear to contribute to the significance level for the combined sexes.

7. Seventh grade boys who differ in comic book reading, either as to type (as defined) or as to frequency, do not differ correspondingly in reported recognition of their own personal problems.

8. Seventh grade girls who read some comic books of the type regarded by the Cincinnati Committee as rating "Some Objection" or "Objectionable" are more troubled than are those who read entirely comic books of the "No Objection" type, by some personal problems. The difference is statistically significant in the *SRA* Inventory subdivision, "Things in General," which seems in general concerned with need for knowledge, skills, and experience. There is a suggestion, not otherwise statistically substanti-

ated, that girls whose reading of comic books falls into these "objectionable" categories may be a somewhat less well-adjusted group than others. The point is highly inconclusive.

10. The data as analyzed provide only very meager evidence (and this in the case of girls only) that the type of criteria applied in classifying comic books according to type or "quality" identify comic books the reading of which has observable, immediate concomitants in the variables studied for seventh grade children.

Finally, it may be well to emphasize that this study does not purport to have disproved the existence of all the ills allegedly attendant upon the reading of comic books. It is a serious matter to endanger the morals, the mental health, or the normal progress of development of children. It is also a serious matter to interfere with popular access to the media of communication—certainly too serious to be undertaken casually. Those who would do either of these two things ask us to engage in a calculated risk of large proportions. Upon those proposing either type of risk it would seem incumbent to marshal justifying evidence. The results of this study for the most part *fail* to *support* curtailment of children's access to comic books.

REFERENCES

1. EDUCATIONAL DIGEST. Comic books and juvenile delinquency. *Educ. Dig.*, 1955, *21*, 8-10.

2. DEBOER, J. J. Using modern channels of communication: Magazines. *Elemen. Eng.*, 1950, *27*, 107-125.

3. DYBWAD, G. Statement to the Senate Subcommittee. *Child Stud.*, 1954, *31*, 38-41.

4. FRANK, J. Chills and thrills in radio, movies, and comics. *Child Stud.*, 1948, *25*, 42-48.

5. HEISLER, F. A comparison of comic book and non-comic book readers of the elementary school. *J. Educ. Res.*, 1947, *40*, 458-464.

6. HOULT, T. F. Comic books and juvenile delinquency. *Social. & Soc. Res.*, 1949, *33*, 279-284.

7. SPERZEL, E. Z. The effect of comic books on vocabulary growth and reading comprehension. *Elemen. Eng.*, 1948, *25*, 109-113.

8. WERTHAM, F. *Seduction of the Innocent.* New York: Rinehart, 1954.

9. WITTY, P. Reading the comics: A comparative study. *J. Exper. Educ.*, 1941, *10*, 105-109.

10. WOLFE, K. M., and FISKE, M. The children talk about comics. In Lazarsfeld, P. F., and Stanton, F. N., (Eds.), *Communications Research 1948-1949.* New York: Harper, 1949.

31/INTRODUCTION TO "AN APPLICATION OF PSYCHOANALYSIS TO EDUCATION"/

LAWRENCE S. KUBIE*

THROUGHOUT OUR EDUCATIONAL SYStem a realization is growing that both intellectual development and creativity will continue to be seriously hampered unless we find out how to make emotional maturation a part of education. Consequently educators are preoccupied increasingly with the difficult problems attendant on the attempt to introduce self-knowledge-in-depth into the main stream of formal education. They recognize that if this is to be done at all, it must start in the kindergarten and continue throughout the elementary grades, grammar school, high school, college and graduate years.

"Progressive education" was one of the early efforts in this direction. Originally, however, this involved a misapplication to education processes of techniques which are sometimes essential in formal psychotherapy. The predictable failures of these well-meant but inept efforts caused the climate of education to swing back temporarily to an opposite extreme, i.e., back to the old-fashioned techniques of drill and grill, and more drill and more grill.

A newer realization of the full complexity of these problems is now developing, i.e., that there is an incessant interaction between universal but subtly masked neurotic mechanisms and the educational process, and that as a result of this interplay education is blocked and distorted. The relationship between the two is evidently so close, that both must be solved if either is to be solved.

This does not, however, force us to the impossible conclusion that every teacher must be an analytically trained psychotherapist or that every school child must be psychoanalyzed. It brings us rather to conclude that all education should be conducted in an atmosphere in which the universal and recurrent emotional disturbances and repressive tendencies of childhood can be resolved as soon as they arise, and before they become chronic. The child's fifth freedom is the right to know what he feels; but this does not carry with it any right to act out his feelings blindly. This will require a new mores for our schools, one which will enable young people from early years to understand and feel and put into words all the hidden things which go on inside of them, thus ending the conspiracy of silence with which the development of the child is now distorted both at home and at school. If the conspiracy of silence is to be replaced by the fifth freedom, children must be encouraged and helped to attend to their forbidden thoughts, and to put them into words, i.e., to talk out loud about love and hate and jealousy and fear, about curiosity over the body, its products and its apertures; about what goes in and what comes out; about what happens inside and what happens outside; about their dim and confused feelings about sex itself; about the strained and stressful relationships within families, which are transplanted into schools. All of these are things about which school must help children to become articulate in the schoolroom.

Once any child becomes free in this sense then his great preconscious creative capacity will be freed from the retarding weight of pedestrian, literal, conscious processes, and at the same time from the distortions which arise out of neurotogenic and psychotogenic unconscious processes.

---

* Lawrence S. Kubie, Introduction to Richard M. Jones, *An Application of Psychoanalysis to Education*, 1960, pp. vii-viii. Reprinted by permission of the authors and the publisher, Charles C. Thomas.

32/CULTURAL DEPRIVATION AS A FACTOR IN SCHOOL LEARNING[1]/HILDA TABA*

THE TERM "CULTURALLY DEPRIVED child" suggests only a variation on a theme. It denotes a group of children who previously were called problem children, retarded, slow learners, underprivileged, and under-achievers. It is hoped that this new appellation is more than just another euphemism, that it indicates both a new statement of the problem we are facing and a new approach to it. The previous designations described only the difficulties of such a group in school. "Cultural deprivation" points to a possible cause of the phenomenon.

For some sort of a theoretical orientation, four questions need to be asked about this theme: (1) What is the situation? (2) What are the social and psychological factors which account for it? (3) What is the educational problem? (4) What is the task of the schools?

THE SITUATION

Two developments seem to be responsible for the present interest in cultural deprivation as a factor in school learning. One, curiously enough, is a consequence of our success in achieving an educational goal dictated by the democratic ideal. The fact that school attendance approaches the 100 per cent limit of the school-age group represents a fulfillment of this ideal of providing education for all the children of all of the American people. But this attainment also creates another phenomenon with which our schools seemingly are not prepared to cope. As the percentages of the age groups attending school increase, school also draws increasingly from the "bottom of the pile." The able, the adjusted, and the motivated, the upper 30 per cent in ability, have always been in school. Extension of school attendance can only add students from the lower end of the span: the emotionally and the physically handicapped, the less willing and able, and the less motivated, those less able to cope with the school culture and its expectations, or

even hostile to what school represents. The result is that the school population becomes more heterogeneous in practically every conceivable respect.

The second development is the increasing migration from the rural areas into the great industrial cities. These large centers draw people both from the rural areas of the United States and from other countries: Negroes and Puerto Ricans in the East; Spanish-Americans, Mexicans, and Indians in the Southwest; and marginal farmers and hillbillies everywhere (Jenks, 1962). The 1950 U.S. census figures indicate that of this population 25 per cent have either themselves migrated from foreign countries or have foreign-born parents. (Bureau of Census, 1956).

Many of these people are actually making a jump from the Eighteenth to the Twentieth century in one generation. This transition involves a difficult adaptation, for it represents not only a shift from a simpler culture into a more complex one but also into a society which is mechanized, anonymous, and alienated. Recently the debilitating effect of unemployment or the threat of it has been added. In this culture individuals and families are cut off from familiar contact; there are few sources for advice and support for what one is, and little reinforcement for the values these groups brought with them. In addition, in urban centers, these migrants are hemmed in in encapsulated environments which prevent opportunities to learn the larger culture in which they exist. Instead the city surrounds them with the hedonism of slum life, and with a dangerous freedom born of anonymity which permits license without teaching the limits and controls.

These conditions create the problems facing the schools in the great cities: an increasing heterogeneity and an increasing social distance between the school culture and that of the home and the neighborhood. The greater the social distance, the greater also the difficulty in using the means of learning that the school provides, the likelihood of hostility to school, and the resistance to what it teaches.

Among the children from such conditions the usual difficulties that plague the public school in

[1] A revision of a lecture presented at The Merrill-Palmer Institute, March, 1963.

* Hilda Taba, Cultural deprivation as a factor in school learning, *Merrill-Palmer Quarterly of Behavior and Development*, 1964, *10*, 147-159. Reprinted by permission.

large cities are magnified. The pupils show generally poor performance. They have a high proportion of failure, of drop-outs, of reading and learning disabilities, and innumerable life-adjustment problems. Sexton's tables of correlations between income and education show that the lower income groups show a consistently lower performance on practically every index: they have lower I.Q.'s, achievement, and grades; poorer health; and are beset with deficiencies in reading and language, the two chief tools on which success in school depends. The yield of merit scholars by professions and income levels dramatizes this discrepancy. In producing merit scholars the professors' families are at the top, and especially so the sons and daughters of librarians. This group produces 234 merit scholars per 12,672 families. At the lowest end are the laborers. They produce one merit scholar per 3,581,370 families (Sexton, 1961). Since it seems reasonable to assume that potentiality is distributed much more evenly than the incidence of merit scholarships suggests, one must look for some other factors at work.

Meanwhile, quantitatively, the problem is increasing. According to Riessman (1962) in 1950 fourteen large cities had one culturally deprived child in ten; in 1960 there was one in three; and the prediction is that in 1970 there will be one in two. Fifty per cent of the children in schools in these cities will come from environments that can be described as culturally deprived. Deutsch (1962) suggests, in addition, that at least in elementary schools anywhere from 40 to 70 per cent of the students will be from minority groups.

These conditions also indicate the new proportions of the problem which confronts the public schools: the task of providing adequate and equal educational opportunities not only for the few exceptions from the rule, but for masses of students who do not or cannot respond to its curriculum and instruction. This means that a large proportion of future citizens will grow up not only poorly equipped academically, but that the effectiveness of the school as a socializing agent is diminished also. Social distance between the school culture and the home culture results in the inability to use the means of learning that the school provides, generates hostility to school, and resistance to what it teaches.

This is not news. In 1950, Allison Davis made a dramatic impact on the audience at the White House Conference on Education by declaring that 40 per cent of children go through school untouched by it, except for acquiring a meager literacy. As characters, as persons, as possessors of academic competency, they might just as well not have been in school. From this population we get disproportionate contributions to delinquency, particularly among the brighter ones because their genius and energy turns to organizing delinquent activities in order to express their anti-social feelings.

THE PSYCHOLOGICAL MEANING OF CULTURAL DEPRIVATION. It is one thing to recognize the difficulties. It is another matter to build a theoretical understanding of the causes of these difficulties and the psychological dynamics which underlie them. A sound theoretical basis for educational programs must be based on the understanding of the culture of the groups that feel the critical impact of cultural deprivation.

The relationship between cultural background and school learning is not simple and not too well understood. More or less adequate research is available on social-class differences in values, behavior patterns, and aspirations. We know, for example, that the homes of these children have a limited educational tradition and, hence, also little "know-how" about the school and its expectation. Not only are the parents themselves uneducated, they also have a meager understanding of the requirements for success in school. Therefore, they cannot help their children with academic content, skills in conduct, or in kindling aspiration for continued education.

Generally, also, the parents of these children have low ambitions for the educational careers of their children. And what ambitions they have, they cannot communicate for lack of proper models or because they are in the dark about the operational steps or means necessary for preparing the child to take advantage of the available learning opportunities. Negro boys, for example, tend to have no model of a successful male. Consequently, they have no psychological framework which suggests that effort can result at least in the possibility of achievement (Deutsch, 1962).

This phenomenon has been described in numerous studies. Kahl (1953), for example, compared the college aspirations of the "common man's" sons with sufficient ability to qualify for college work, with boys from the middle or upper-middle class families on the same ability level. Scarcely any of the parents in the "common man" group perceived a college education as an objective for their sons. Those who had aspirations did not know what was needed to realize them. The author observed a similar phenomenon in an all-white, lower-class eighth grade in an eastern industrial city. While the parents who were interviewed about their ambitions for their children indicated interest in college, these ambitions were vague and planless (Taba, 1955). These facts, probably, still hold in spite of the recent rise in the level of aspirations, especially among the Negroes.

Culturally disadvantaged children also lack the skills and the habits necessary for meeting the expectations of conduct in school. The author has observed first-grade classrooms where the children did not even distinguish one piece of paper from another one. They might tear out a page from one book to make a marker for another, then cherish a piece of toilet paper. They had had no training in disciplined group behavior, such as the middle-class child gets around the dinner table, because they seldom had dinner as a family group. Consequently, they lacked the habits and skills necessary for reading in groups. The teacher reported her bafflement at the fact that these children sat down obediently enough, but soon would go each about his own business.

The stories these children dictated about their families provided the clues. There were recurring examples of such behavior, especially when facing a conflict. When father gets mad he "goes away and stays all night"; when brother gets mad "he goes to a baseball game"; when mother gets mad she "takes us to the movies and doesn't bring us back."

Similar observations abound about difficulties with speaking or being spoken to in groups, and such virtues cherished in school as cleanliness, punctuality, and orderliness. Instead of being perceived by teachers as functional habits learned at home and in the neighborhood, behaviors which are inappropriate by middle-class standards are treated as malicious conduct to be corrected by appropriate punishment.

Another series of difficulties result from lack of readiness for the learning tasks in school. Children from such homes and neighborhoods may be potentially able, but developmentally retarded so far as learning to read and to master the content of school subjects is concerned.

Since schools can measure only the functioning capacity, individual potentiality is a vague quality about which we know little. It is obvious that individual potentiality is an unmarketable commodity if the child has no means of developing it, or if there are no ways of identifying it. Our instruments identify only a particular limited kind of potentiality, namely, the capacity to ma-

nipulate verbal symbols and abstractions. These are precisely the accomplishments which are the least stimulated in the culturally deprived environment.

Recently some observations have emerged regarding the role of stimulus deprivation in intelligence and learning. Studies of intelligence point out that intelligence is a product of a transaction between an individual and the environmental stimulation. For example, Miner (1957) describes intellectual stimulation as a product of the interrelationship of three factors: individual potential, motivation, and environmental stimulation. Individual potential is presumably evenly distributed among all groups of people and is probably greater than we have as yet learned how to release. Environmental stimulation involves more than the degree, complexity, and variation of the environment. It also involves motivation, or the extent to which the environment affects the individual's responses. Different individuals respond to different cues in the same environment. The variations in these responses are generated in part by the individual's motivation and in part by the availability of adult mediation in facilitating conceptualization. A potentially rich environment may therefore be functionally unstimulating and, in reverse, a limited environment may be highly stimulating if it is exploited to the fullest. Variety in stimulation combined with mediation tends to sharpen and to force the accommodating modification in the mental structure.

Deutsch (1962) points out that the greater the variety of stimulation and the number of situations which challenge modification of conceptualization, the more mobile and differentiated the mental structure becomes. In other words, the more the child hears, sees, and interprets, or is being helped to interpret, the more likely he will want to see and hear, and the more he will get from what he sees and hears. The greater the variety of reality situations with which the child has coped the greater his ability to cope (Deutsch, 1962). Any of these conditions—limited environment, a lack of systematic and ordered interpretation and mediation, or a limited motivation (or a combination of them)—may bring about stimulus deprivation and with it a deficiency in the development of intelligence.

Some researchers suggest that the conditions of life in slums tend to be meager in all these aspects. Deutsch points out that slum life provides a minimum range of stimulation and of opportunity to manipulate objects or to experiment with them in an orderly manner. Restriction in the range of the variety of input limits the output in expression, and reduces precision and the ability to perceive relationships or other abstract qualities, such as size, shape, distance, and time (Deutsch, 1962).

The lack of mediation, in addition, reduces the opportunities to link experience with interpretation of it, i.e., with the ability to convert objects and events to verbal symbols, to explore causal relationships, and to form abstractions.

Examination of the diary materials of lower-class children in city slums confirms this. These diaries describe the typical day, characterized by a rapid shift from one activity to another one, by lack of attention to one thing. One is impressed with the meagerness of experiences with abstraction. For example, dinner-time, which is the only time when parents and children are together, if they are together at all, tends to be spent on two things: to mete out the punishments for infractions committed the day before, and to allocate the chores to be done. In one group of 25 eighth graders, only one family used dinner-time to describe what happened to them as persons during the day (Taba, 1955). Bernstein (1960) points out, further, that the lower-class conversations are limited to the immediate instant and generally do not include time sequences, relationships between concepts, logical sequences, or causal relationships.

Thus, the problem of deficiency is not limited to non-verbality or bilingualism. It includes also the level of cognitive skills and of relationships expressed in whatever language is used. This combination of non-verbal orientation and an absence of conceptualization alone may very well account for what we call low intelligence.

Recently the possibility has been suggested that early stimulation may be crucial in laying the psychological foundation for the capacity to process information. If this should be true, early stimulus deprivation may create a lifelong handicap in response capacity and in the assimilating and manipulating of facts and ideas (Hebb, 1949; Hunt, 1961).

The factors and conditions described above create deficiencies in the skills and the mental equipment necessary for success in school tasks: the ability to distinguish the meaning of one word from that of another; the capacity to handle the abstractions which organize the physical, geographical, and geometric characteristics of the environment; and the capacity for sustained attention.

Cognitive deficiencies alone, no matter how serious, might be easier to correct, if it were not for the additional complications of emotional characteristics and attitudes. The psychologists describe a syndrome of feelings and attitudes which the majority of culturally deprived children tend to share, as follows: both the family climate and experience tend to induce a feeling of alienation; their self concept is low; they question their own worth, fear being challenged, have a desire to cling to the familiar, and have many feelings of guilt and shame; there is a limited trust in adults; they tend to respond with trigger-like reactions, are hyperactive, and have generally a low standard of conduct; and they usually show apathy and lack of responsiveness. It is difficult for them to form meaningful relationships (Krogman, 1956).

These tendencies translate themselves into an additional orientation which is difficult for teachers to understand: a negative attitude toward school, teachers, and achievement; the tendency to seek immediate gratification over and above any long-range purposes; the freer use of violence in solving conflicts than is permissible in a school setting. Some of this conduct, such as fighting, plays havoc in school and is therefore a great cause for disciplinary action and misinterpretation. Haystack, a seventh grader, stated the difference between the teacher's perception and that of a slum child rather neatly when he said: "Teachers are funny, they are so afraid of a leetle beet of fighting." What Haystack described as a "little bit of fighting" was a regular gang war.

Discrepancies exist also between the motivating devices used in school and the motivational patterns. Achievement as a means of making further education possible is relatively little understood. Getting by rather than getting ahead is, therefore, the rule. Hence, grades, promotions, and all other external similar incentives used by the schools will not work nearly as well as expected.

FACTORS IN SCHOOL EXPERIENCE

The experience in school adds to the difficulties described above. Variations in background naturally create a discrepancy between the cognitive, perceptual, and emotional development of the child and the school expectations and curriculum. The differences in the meanings involved in the content of the curriculum and the meanings which the children from a deviant background attach to the verbal cues of that content is one example of this discrepancy and, therefore, also one factor in the deficiency in academic performance. This discrepancy is more than a deficit in skills. It is a discontinuity between the conceptual scheme developed and meanings acquired in previous experience and that employed or implied in the curriculum and teaching. The description of one fourth-grader of what a policeman means to him is a vivid illustration of this discontinuity (Taba, 1955).

To tell the truth, I don't like policemen, because one day I was walking on Broad Street and I saw a police car on Western Avenue. There were no police there. I waited for a while. Soon the police came out of the house. They had a man and a girl with them. The man and the girl were put in the police car, and taken away to the jail. I don't know what they had done, but the reason I don't like cops is because they are so rough when they arrest people. They didn't have to push the girl down when they put her in the car.

Yes, I would have run home if a cop had stopped me fighting in the street, because I am afraid of a cop. I did run away once and hid in my house. I was playing on the roofs of some houses with some other boys and the ball went through a skylight and broke it. The cops heards us and chased us. I ran home, but some boys must have told him, for he came to my house and rang the doorbell. I wouldn't let him in and nobody else was home. He said that if I didn't let him in he was going to come in through the window and get me. I knew I had to open the door then. He said, "Why'd you break that skylight for?" "I ain't been out. I been right here like my father told me." He said, "You are lying, boy, because I saw you run." I kept right on lying and he left. I was afraid, just shaking, and I felt like busting out crying, but the cop didn't know that. He thought I was tough.

The above image of the "cop" is very different from the one which the teacher was using in talking about policemen as "community helpers."

Similar discontinuities exist in the meanings of such terms as cooperation and control. A considerable proportion of material which describes family life, homes, human relations, or the work of the world consists of content which is alien to the experience of these children. For example, when a teacher in a semi-rural, lower-class area showed the pictures of the homes in primers and asked whether they knew these homes, a loud "No" arose in response. Yet, when asked to describe the homes they knew, the descriptions were both sensible and differentiated. They talked of large families who had to live in small houses, and the problems that this situation cre-

ated. They could describe adequately a variety of homes, including trailers and shacks. They were just not acquainted with white houses with green shutters, in front of which stood a smiling mother with a starched white apron welcoming a father returning home carrying a briefcase. Naturally, such alien content makes the mastery of reading skills vastly more difficult.

The differences between the social learning of the children from culturally deviant backgrounds and the schools create also severe acculturation problems, which further affect their academic performance. It is difficult for any person to span two cultures. For the first-grader from a culturally deviant environment, the spanning of two cultures represents a difficult enough task to be described as culture shock. The psychological consequences of this shock could be mild or severe, depending on the distance between his particular culture, his expectations, his level of understanding, and those of the school. If the discontinuities in the demands of the two contending cultures are mild they may only impede the socialization power of the school. If they are severe they may lead to disorganization or neurotic behavior (Allinsmith and Goethals, 1956).

The problem of acculturation is still more difficult for the minority children, for in their case the problems of isolation, language, conduct, and the difficulties with academic content converge. Elam (1960) describes cases resulting in a total incapacity to respond. Writing about the Puerto Rican children in New York, he describes the consequences of the acculturation shock which causes them to cease responding altogether. They evade responsibility because to function is to fail. The safest thing is not to respond at all. Milder cases are observed in which children "tune out" when directions are given.

School often adds to the difficulty by failing to recognize the problem, to diagnose the gaps, and by demanding too abrupt a transition, by paying too little attention to the role school life plays in facilitating acculturation.

Finally, there is the problem of the hidden I.Q., which is created by the nature of the tests used for diagnosing ability, for grouping, and for setting expectations. Since it is well known that generally the children from culturally deprived areas earn lower I.Q.'s, and since it seems difficult to believe that the potential ability is distributed according to economic or social privilege, the appropriateness of the measures of ability has been questioned. Guilford (1956) has attacked the concept of I.Q. as a single ability and points out that intelligence tests results do not reflect either cultural or personal variations, because they are compounded of too narrow a range of abilities. Sigel (1963) says that such tests have limited usefulness, because the "rightness" of the response is determined by the cultural conventions assumed by the testmaker. This imposition of a cultural convention is the case when Mexican children with no experience with saucers pair the cup with the table, instead of with the saucer, and are marked wrong—even though the pairing is perfectly logical in the light of their experience. Thus the culturally biased choice of the test content, together with the limitation in the mental systems represented in the performance required, produces the phenomenon of a hidden I.Q. and undiscovered potential. As Eells and Haggard suggest, the I.Q. may be described as the cement which fixes the individual to the class of his birth (Eells, 1953; Haggard, 1954).

These deficiencies in the background and the problems encountered in the school compound themselves into a vicious circle. Culturally deprived children come to school with acculturation problems, an ill-developed capacity to differentiate and to conceptualize experience, and less well-developed verbal articulation than the school work requires. This results in lower performance on ability tests, which leads to designating them as slow learners or low achievers. This reduces the already low self-esteem and self-expectation. Meanwhile, these children are required to learn the most crucial skill—reading—at a point at which the acculturation problems are at their peak. The first-graders from culturally deprived homes thus carry a double load in their first school year: that of mastering a new skill, while handicapped with problems of acculturation and lack of readiness for reading. Naturally, it is impossible for them to master either task adequately.

Moreover, the "socialization" process is carried on in the school in a manner which induces conflict between the child and his home. In effect, this process requires him to deprecate both himself and his parents, his way of life and the values which he has invested with feelings and emotional identification, and on which, therefore, his self-esteem rests.

The net result is that these students are labelled uneducable and treated as such. Little is expected of them and little is offered. The students, in turn, expect little and get little. Comparatively speaking, such students

"get dumber" as they grow older. By the fifth grade they are three years behind. This, in turn, adds to lowering of self-expectation and generates hostility to school, teachers, and the whole business of learning. This is probably the dynamics which turns those children who in kindergarten are described as curious, cute, affectionate, warm, independently dependent, and mischievous, into the ones described in the fourth grade as alienated, withdrawn, angry, passive, and apathetic (Deutsch, 1962). Something is happening in this three-year interval for which the school itself is responsible.

THE TASK OF THE SCHOOL

The contemplation of the above facts redefines the task of the school. First and foremost is the task of developing a better understanding of the implications of the social and psychological dynamics of cultural deprivation, and the translation of this understanding into educational programs: the training of teachers and administrators, and the planning of curriculum and instruction.

Another important requirement is to recognize the complexity and seriousness of the problem. One is distressed to observe the repeated efforts to effect a "cure" by crash programs which depend on some simple single device, such as remedial reading, counseling, visits to the opera, or reciting poetry in old English. If there is a principle governing the program-building for these children, it is that no single device will suffice for a complexity of factors has produced the problem.

Educators also need to realize that the lack of success in school for certain groups of children suggests a two-way cause: the factors residing in the backgrounds of the children and the factors residing in the school program. Usually, the efforts to diagnose the problems have overemphasized the first and overlooked the second. Somehow, the fact has escaped our attention that the basic features of our curriculum and instructional methods were formulated when only the most able and willing constituted the school populations. Therefore, the programs tend to stress remedial measures ahead of the possibility of revising the fundamental approach to curriculum and teaching in order to effect prevention.

A careful diagnosis of the emotional dynamics and the cognitive styles of deviate children is necessary for effective program building in many different ways, irrespective of whether or not we regard the objective to be to enable these children to adopt the middle-class ways. Sufficient knowledge of the cognitive styles is needed to provide optimum opportunities for learning. The understanding of the emotional dynamics is indispensible for treating these children as individuals, and as human beings with positive qualities, instead of as so many minuses and gaps. This knowledge also is essential to finding proper ways for eliminating the blocks to learning. These are tasks that should have priority over the remedial programs to correct disabilities in skills.

If the double burden of dealing simultaneously with acculturation problems and learning is to be avoided, supplementary experience in early education seems almost a necessity. Administratively, this possibility may be implemented by an ungraded sequence in the first few years, by an addition of a pre-school year devoted to the task of filling the gaps in experience, or by postponing the learning of reading. Such an addition stands a chance of preventing the formation of a negative attitude towards learning, and a lowering the self-esteem. It is possible, moreover, that the separation of these tasks would do more to improve the level of achievement than any single measure.

Unlocking the hidden potentiality requires a more radical change in the program. Both the materials and the methods of teaching need to be brought into line with the psychological realities of these children. At least in the primary grades, the content of curriculum needs to be in tune with their out-of-school experience or else derived from experiences provided by the school. Producing reading material in school in the form of stories written about some gripping and exciting experiences is not beyond possibility, as demonstrated by one first grade which produced enough stories on one trip to San Francisco harbor to last for an entire year. The stories were, in fact, well written, beautifully illustrated, included poetry, and used a precise as well as a beautiful vocabulary. Evidently, the use of this material eliminated the problem of motivation to read: children were observed coming to school and reading the stories (covering three walls) before they even removed their coats (Landis, n.d.).

Research on the cognitive style and language patterns cited above suggests also the need to capitalize on materials and tasks using operational and concrete, rather than verbal, stimuli. To cultivate mental activity without the hindrance of poor language development indicates

the value of using audio-visual materials developed with the purpose of providing for concrete thought operations through manipulation and experimentation with objects and processes. In effect, this would amount to providing a greater variety of modes of learning. In addition to learning from books, provisions are needed for examining objects and processes and emphasizing analysis, comparison, and precision in verbal description to cultivate the mental structures with which to turn later to books.

A considerable shift may be needed in the motivational devices also. The research on motivational patterns suggests the futility of emphasis on external rewards and the need for stressing the kindling of curiosity, the opportunities for experiencing one's power over the materials, and other intrinsic motivating devices.

It is surprising to note that in spite of considerable evidence of the efficacy of "belonging" in school life as a factor in enhancing learning and staying power, so little has been done in the current programs for the culturally deprived toward creating fuller participating in school life and forms of grouping and of learning which enhance interaction and a sense of belonging. Opportunities for interaction which are present within a sufficient heterogeneity in cultural background and ability would permit some learning of the culture across the shoulder, so to say. The learning of the common culture is too often made difficult when this learning has to be accomplished across the social distance, from verbal exhortations, and not from models and examples. Wisely designed cultural heterogeneity in classrooms probably would do much to reduce the cultural deprivation by providing models for motivation, conduct, ways of thinking, and aspirations—as well as for language patterns.

All this adds up to a conception of education as a countervailing agent. In today's climate, which emphasizes excellence and "no-nonsense" disciplined learning, the idea that school be a countervailing force may not be too popular. It is much easier to assume that if Moore at Yale[Ed] can teach the three-years-olds to read, early training in reading for all children is not only possible but also desirable. Yet, for culturally deprived children, school must be supple-

[Ed] *Professor Moore is now at the University of Pittsburgh. Further information on his approach is contained in J. Hellmuth (Ed.) The Special Child in Century 21, 1964, Special Child Publications, pp. 87-138. This material was also issued from the Responsive Environment Foundation, Inc., 20 Augur Street, Hamden, Conn.*

mentary and counteract their social learning if they are to have an equal opportunity to learn. School must fill the gaps left by social learning at home and mend the conflict between the culture of the home and of the school.

REFERENCES

ALLINSMITH, W. & GOETHALS, G. W. Cultural factors in mental health; an anthropological perspective. *Rev. educ. Res.*, 1956, *26*, 433-438.

BERNSTEIN, B. Language and social class. *Brit. J. Sociol.*, 1960, *11*, 271-276.

DEUTSCH, MARTIN. The disadvantaged child and the learning process: Some social, psychological, and developmental considerations. Paper presented at Ford Foundation work conference on curriculum and teaching in depressed urban areas. Teach. Coll., Columbia Univer., July, 1962.

EELLS, K. Some implications in school practice of the Chicago studies of cultural bias in intelligence tests. *Harvard educ. Rev*, 1953, *23*, 284-297.

ELAM, S. L. Acculturation and learning problems of Puerto Rican children. *Teach. Coll. Rec.*, 1960, *61*, 258-264.

GUILFORD, J. P. The structure of intelligence. *Psychol. Bull*, 1956, *53*, 267-293.

HAGGARD, E. A. Social status and intelligence. *Genet. Psychol. Monogr.*, 1954, *49*, 141-186.

HEBB, D. O. *Organization of behavior*. New York: Wiley, 1949.

HUNT, J. MC V. *Intelligence and experience*. New York: Ronald Press, 1961.

JENKS, C. Slums and schools. *The New Republic*, Sept. 10, 17, 1962.

KAHL, J. A. Educational and occupational aspirations of "common man's boys." *Harvard educ. Rev.*, 1953, *23*, 186-203.

KROGMAN, JUDITH. Cultural deprivation and child development. *High Points*, 1956, *38*.

LANDIS, ONEIDA. Teaching children to think. Yolo County Schools, Woodland, Calif. (Mimeo)

MINER, J. B. *Intelligence in the United States.* New York: Springer, 1957.

RIESSMAN, FRANK. *The culturally deprived child.* New York, Harper, 1962.

SEXTON, PATRICIA. *Education and income.* New York: Viking, 1961.

SIGEL, I. E. How intelligence tests limit understanding of intelligence. *Merrill-Palmer Quart.*, 1963, *9*, 39-57.

TABA, HILDA. *Curriculum development: theory and practice.* New York: Harcourt Brace, 1962.

TABA, HILDA. *With perspective on human relations.* Washington, D.C.: American Council on Education, 1955.

VI / Group Memberships as Determinants of Behavior

ANOTHER IMPORTANT DETERMINANT OF BEHAVIOR concerns the groups and institutions or organizations to which an individual belongs or with which he identifies himself. Face-to-face groups such as the family, whose impact is largely a matter of interpersonal influence (see Section IV), are not included here, nor do we refer to the classroom or playground groups, which were covered under settings and specific stimuli in Section V. Rather, we deal with (1) the society or culture in which a man is reared; (2) his connections with various organizations and societal institutions; (3) his economic and other role relations with his fellow men; (4) the "reference groups" to which he belongs or with which he is identified, including his membership in a caste, a social class, an ethnic or national group, his political leanings, his religious affiliation, and his residence in a rural or urban area. Because the fields of sociology, of social or cultural anthropology, and of social psychology are in large part represented by this topic, the selections included here are merely illustrative of some realms of possible inquiry. [1] Such growing sub-disciplines as educational sociology and educational anthropology will increasingly demand study in their own right. In fact, W. W. Charters and N. L. Gage have produced a book of *Readings in the Social Psychology of Education* (Boston: Allyn and Bacon, 1963). The student especially interested in this area will find other useful papers in this collection.

The first paper in this section is by Richard deCharms, of Washington University in St. Louis, with the collaboration of Gerald Moeller. The authors examine effects of one kind of group to which people belong, the one determined by the time or era in which the person grows up. They show ways in which the content of school books written for American children has changed since 1800. The changes have corresponded with changes in the nature of the economy, implying a reciprocal influence between the nature of the economic behaviors required in the society and the values or motives held (and imparted to the next generation).

---

[1] It may be helpful to give a rough idea of the differing preoccupations of the principal disciplines mentioned. By and large, anthropologists are concerned with differences between societies, sociologists study differences between groups in the same society, and psychologists are interested in differences among individuals in the same group. Although there is increasing overlap of interests among all three fields, there are characteristic distinctions in viewpoint. The fact that most adult Americans use alarm clocks might be called to our attention by an anthropologist because of variations among peoples or cultures in technological development and/or in attitudes toward time and toward work. He might contrast behaviors of Americans with those of Italians or of Zulus. A sociologist might investigate attitudes toward time and work among religious or economic groups within a culture, comparing the groups to discover differences and seek explanations of them. Either psychologists or sociologists might investigate changes in such attitudes between the ages of 14 and 24 or differences between sorority members and non-members in their views and habits. Only psychologists would seek meaning in the fact that Suzie Snoozy neglects to set her alarm clock at night.

The paper by Helen Faigin (Antonovsky) focuses on social behaviors of very young children. The groups under study were two kibbutzim, or collective settlements, in Israel which had different political and educational orientations. Comparisons were made between the behaviors of the children in the two kibbutzim. Also some very general contrasts were noted between the behavior of kibbutz-reared children and that generally noted for Western children reared in individual homes.

The third paper is by Albert I. Rabin of Michigan State University. He reports a study of differences between those Israeli adolescents who have grown up in the kibbutzim and those who have grown up in individual families. The behaviors under consideration were chosen for their relevance to aspects of psychoanalytic theory. Such study of cultural groups very different from one's own enables one to assess the universality of behavior. If behaviors that appear universal in one's own group prove to be truly universal or world-wide, it may be that they are determined by the biological nature of the organism, although social factors common to all men could be the cause. If they are seen not to be universal, the role of learning factors is underscored. Because Freud propounded his theory of psychosexual development as a universal and biologically-rooted theory, it has been of great interest to psychologists to test universality of behaviors by studying children from family structures not found in Western Europe and North America. [2]

The fourth selection, by Thomas F. Pettigrew (now at Harvard but formerly at the University of North Carolina), addresses itself to still another type of behavior, "white" persons' attitudes toward Negroes. The group memberships under consideration in this article (residence in the North *vs.* residence in the South) can be called subcultural. Pettigrew is not asking the relatively simple question of whether those in the South are more prejudiced than those in the North. Rather, he questions whether the factors that are related to (and possibly causative of) prejudice are the same in both cultures. Just as other studies of special groups help to answer questions regarding the universal, and perhaps biological, nature of certain behaviors, this study helps us view the question of whether a behavior (prejudice) is universally related to, or caused by, a particular set of determinants (of personality or socio-cultural factors). Appended to this Pettigrew selection is the summary of another article by the same author. It compares two regions or cultures that are further apart geographically (South Africa *vs.* southern United States), but which share an atmosphere of strong racial conflict. Taken together, these articles make a strong case for the need for more than one theory of prejudice or for a multifaceted theory. Such a theory or theories must take into account not only interpersonal relationships (including child-rearing) but also group memberships (including characteristics of the locale).

---

[2] For other material on differences in development and especially on differences in human relationships related to more extreme differences in family structures, see: Anna Freud and Sophie Dann, "An Experiment in Group Upbringing" from *The Psychoanalytic Study of the Child,* Vol. VI (International Universities Press, Inc., 1951); and William Goldfarb, "The effects of psychological deprivation in infancy and subsequent stimulation," *American Journal of Psychiatry* (1945, *102,* 18-33).

Next is an article from the University of California at Berkeley by David Stein, Jane Allyn Hardyck, and M. Brewster Smith. It reveals a major underlying determinant of racial prejudice, at least among the teen-agers studied: their assumption—when they lack further information—that persons of a different race hold different values and beliefs.

Last is an article by Glenn Terrell, now Dean of the College of Arts and Sciences at the new Chicago Circle campus of the University of Illinois, and two coauthors. They examine still another kind of behavior (speed of learning) in relation to both the kind of incentive used (reinforcement) and the group membership (here, social class) of the children. The findings have obvious implications for those who teach children; teachers inevitably use certain types of incentive, but often do so without regard for such attributes of the children as their social class background with the attendant values and reinforcement histories.

Four articles in this book that might have been assigned to this section are: Taba (V, 32), Barry, Bacon, and Child (VIII, 48), Daniel Brown (VIII, 49), and Vernon (IX, 54).

For other material on the influence of group membership on behavior (though not necessarily the behavior of children) see *Readings in Social Psychology*, edited by Maccoby, Newcomb and Hartley (Holt, 1958). The sections on Reference Groups, Social Stratification, Role and Role Conflict, and Leadership are most appropriate. However, individual selections of particular relevance also occur in other sections.

33/VALUES EXPRESSED IN AMERICAN CHILDREN'S READERS: 1800-1950[1]/

RICHARD deCHARMS AND GERALD H. MOELLER *

STUDENTS OF CULTURAL CHANGE within the United States seem to have reached some agreement as to a trend observable within the last century. This trend, which deals with some of the basic values of our culture, may be seen as a change from what Weber (1930) called "the Protestant ethic" to what has been called the "social ethic" (Whyte, 1956). Specifically, the dominant value of individual salvation through hard work, thrift, and competition is seen as being replaced by "a belief in the group as the source of creativity; a belief in 'belongingness' as the ultimate need of the individual; and a belief in the application of science to achieve the belongingness" (Whyte, 1956, p. 7). In Reisman's (Riesman, Glazer, & Denney, 1950) terminology the basic trend is from inner-direction to other-direction.

Actually this process is circular in the sense that the cultural change is probably accompanied by a change in values which starts a new cycle. The psychologist likes to conceive of the basic variables in human behavior as being internally determined and thus breaks this circle and concentrates on motives as basic.

The aim of the present paper is to investigate psychological variables which it seems logical to predict will be associated with the cultural changes observed in the United States over the last century and a half.

McClelland (1955) has noted striking similarity between his concept of the person with high achievement motivation and Riesman's inner-directed character type. McClelland defines achievement motivation as "success in competition with a standard of excellence" (p. 43). According to Riesman et al. (1950) "the drive instilled in the child is to *live up to ideals* and to

test his ability to be on his own by continuous experiments in self-mastery" (p. 59). For the other-directed person "making good becomes almost equivalent to making friends" (Riesman et al., 1950, p. 66). This sounds very much like the person with high affiliation motivation. Atkinson (1958) defines affiliation motivation as "concern . . . over establishing, maintaining, or restoring a positive affective relationship with another person. This relationship is most adequately described by the word friendship" (p. 206).

Assuming that achievement motivation is a basic component of the inner-directed character type, and that affiliation motivation is a basic component of the other-directed character type, in the context of Riesman's cultural change thesis, one would predict a decline in over-all achievement motivation and an increase in affiliation motivation in the last century of United States history. Strauss and Houghton (1960) have found evidence giving some support to these hypotheses in the period since 1924 in a study of 4-H club journals. A meaningful relationship should also be found between achievement orientation and economic and technological change according to McClelland (1955).

A further aspect of Riesman's thesis is that the stage of inner-direction is preceded by a stage of tradition-direction. During this stage strict moral codes demand behavioral conformity of the individual. The change from a tradition-directed society to an inner-directed society involves a secularization in the sense that the individual must prove himself worthy as in Weber's (1930) Protestant ethic, rather than be told what to do by categorical imperatives. One might thus predict more reliance on moral teaching early in the history of the United States.

The objective measurement of cultural orientations or values is always difficult, especially if an attempt is to be made to tap the values of the past. An intriguing attempt to measure the motives of an ancient culture has been reported by McClelland (1958). He has developed a method

[1] This study was carried out under Contract Nonr-816 (11) between the Office of Naval Research and the Small Groups Laboratory, Social Science Institute at Washington University.

We wish to thank David C. McClelland and Raymond E. Callahan for critical comments on an earlier version of the paper.

* Richard deCharms and Gerald H. Moeller, Values expressed in American children's readers: 1800-1950, *Journal of Abnormal and Social Psychology*, 1962, 64, 136-142. Reprinted by permission.

238

of assessing achievement motivation in a culture by content analysis of literary products of the culture. Using this tool he found striking confirmation for his hypothesis that achievement motivation preceded the economic and technological development of Athenian civilization in classical Greece, a culture also discussed by Riesman.

McClelland's measure of motivation was developed originally to assess the motives of individuals (McClelland, Atkinson, Clark, & Lowell, 1953). The extension of it to apply to cultures raises questions as to what is being measured. McClelland (1958) has argued that his content analysis of documents produced by the culture will give a measure of the level of specific types of motivation within the culture if the documents are carefully selected to reduce effects of other obviously important variables. The best support for this argument derives from a study which demonstrated that content analysis of American Indian folk tales relates to content analysis of stories obtained from individuals in the manner used originally to validate the measure for studying individual motives (McClelland & Friedman, 1952).

It is obvious that a measure which has been shown to be related to individual motives would be expected to reflect the motives of the writer of any document chosen from a culture. In order to use such a measure as an indication of cultural orientation one does not have to assume that the motive score of an individual author is a measure of the cultural orientation alone. One must, however, assume that a portion of the score is a measure of the cultural orientation. The problem of reducing idiosyncratic components in the measure of cultural orientation becomes one of (a) sampling randomly many authors (b) under as similar conditions as possible (i.e., writing similar material) and (c) choosing materials which should place few restrictions on the author's fantasy.

All of the above advantages can be obtained by careful sampling of stories written for children's readers. In addition, the stories are actually written to be used in transmitting cultural values, and information on how widely they have been used gives at once some indication of cultural acceptance of the values contained in the book and of the extent of its influence. An example of the use of children's readers to assess values in many cultures has been presented by McClelland (1961).

The schema presented above predicts a relationship between cultural achievement orientation and behavior of the members of the culture which would lead to technological advance. Just as one might predict that an individual with high achievement motivation might strive for some unique accomplishment, one might also predict that a culture with strong achievement orientation would produce many inventions. A measure of the inventiveness of the culture at various periods in history might be obtained from the number of patents issued per population, and one could predict a relationship between this and a measure of cultural achievement orientation.

HYPOTHESES. The present study is an attempt to plot the incidence of achievement and affiliation imagery and moral teaching in a sample of children's readers from 1800 to the present. In addition, achievement imagery is to be related to data on the number of patents issued per population.

Hypothesis I. The incidence of achievement imagery in a sample of children's readers selected over the period 1800-1950 will decrease over the time period.

Hypothesis II. The incidence of affiliation imagery in the same sample of readers will increase over the time period.

Hypothesis III. The incidence of moral teaching in the sample will decrease over the time period.

Hypothesis IV. The incidence of achievement imagery will be positively related to the number of patents issued, corrected for changes in population.

The hypotheses assume, with Riesman, that the nineteenth century in the United States was dominated by the inner-directed character type. Riesman is not specific as to dates, but it would appear that the early period of the century witnessed the transition from the tradition-directed character type and that the United States has recently been in transition from an inner-directed phase to an other-directed phase.

METHOD

A bibliography of reading textbooks with copyright dates ranging from 1800 to 1952 was compiled. An attempt was made to procure at least four books from each 20-year period beginning in 1800. Readers were excluded which were not in wide use[2] during the period or which were used by religious affiliated schools. In the more recent periods from which more than four books were available, the choice of books was made randomly. In the periods in which fewer than four books were available the sample from each book was enlarged in so far as possible. Generally, the sample from each book was obtained by scoring every third page.

It was found that the number of words per page was sufficiently similar throughout the total sample to allow use of the page itself as the scoring unit. In order to equate for number of pages available the score was the number of pages containing imagery per 75 pages sampled. A raw score was thus computed for every 75 pages sampled (i.e., 25 pages scored).

The readers chosen for the study were, generally speaking, at a fourth grade level. During the nineteenth century many readers were designed in ways which had no relevance to grade level or, as in some cases, grade level was quite different from that of contemporary American readers in which the vocabulary is based on standard word lists. In some instances it was necessary to use the Dale and Chall (1948) formula[3] for predicting readability to determine whether the readers might be allowed in the study.

The pages selected from each book were scored independently by two scorers as to whether the page contained (a) achievement imagery, (b) affiliation imagery, or (c) a category called moral teaching. Achievement and affiliation imagery were scored according to the procedure outlined in Atkinson (1958). The subcategories usually scored in this procedure were not scored. The category Moral Teaching was developed and defined as explicit or implicit statements of judgment between right and wrong from the point of view of the author. The following (McGuffey, 1857) are examples of items which were scored for moral teaching:

The little boy took care of his faithful dog as long as he lived and never forgot that we must do good to others, if we wish them to do the same to us (p. 42).

[2] Evidence of "wide use" was fairly easy to establish in readers published after 1850 since the McGuffey readers and the readers of the major book companies enjoyed national popularity as official texts of large school systems. Prior to 1850 Johnson (1904) and Nietz (1961) provided lists of historical texts from which to choose. In the first two decades of the sample the only secular texts available were used.

The following criteria were used in this order to establish "wide use": Evidence (often cited in later editions) of number of copies sold; several editions of the same book; and knowledge of use by large school systems.

[3] This readability formula which utilizes a word list and sentence length for determining grade level of reading materials was used because of evidence of its applicability to middle grade reading matter and high correlations with other formulae and criteria of readability (Chall, 1958).

Now that is the way with a great many thoughtless, quick tempered people. They try to find fault with somebody or something else, and get into a passion, and perhaps do mischief, when, if they would but reflect a little, it is their own dear selves who ought to bear the blame (p. 47).

Scorer reliabilities, based on presence of imagery only, were consistently high (Achievement Imagery = 94%, Affiliation Imagery = 96%, Moral Teaching = 97%).

The number of patents issued by the United States Patent Office and the United States Census figures were taken from governmental documents (United States Department of Commerce, 1960) and a patent index was compared by dividing the number of patents granted in a 20-year period by the population reported in the midyear of that period and multiplying by one million. This results in an index of patents issued per one million population during the period.

There are two methodological flaws in the procedure which it was felt might have had an effect on the results. In the first place, the technique of blind scoring was not employed. The scoring was done directly from the book and it was therefore probable that the scorer knew the date of the book. The effect of this knowledge cannot be assessed. A second methodological flaw lies in the sampling procedure. Systematic samples were taken from each book and the books were chosen as representative and in wide use. However, since each score was based on 75 pages of text, the individual values of certain authors might have unduly influenced the results in the case where only a few books were available for a 20-year period.

In order to correct these methodological flaws it was decided to repeat the study with a drastically smaller sample. A sample of 6 pages was chosen at random from each book. The sampling of books followed the same criteria as those used in the first sample. Four books were selected from each period except the periods 1800-1819 and 1820-1839 where only two were available. The books from these two periods were double sampled. Scores on each variable were assigned to each book giving four scores for each of the eight periods thus resolving the ambiguities of sampling in the first study.

The sample had to be drastically cut since the pages were typed and coded for blind scoring. (A total of 192 pages were scored independently by two scorers in the replication whereas 2,375 pages were scored in the first study.) The same number of typed lines were taken starting with each page which had been drawn randomly.

Whenever available different books were selected for the second sample. It was anticipated that since this was a much smaller sample than the first the results would not be as statistically significant. It was felt that general trends in the same direction would validate the statistically significant findings of the first sample. Actually, plots of the results of the two studies are almost identical and statistical significance was reached in most instances in the second study, although, as anticipated, the probability levels were not as great as in the first. This comparison of the two replications gives greater confidence in the results of the first study. The data presented here come from the first study. Statistical analyses will be presented for both studies.

RESULTS

Table 1 presents the mean imagery scores for achievement, affiliation, and moral teaching in each of the 20-year periods. Figures 1 and 2 are graphic presentations of these data.

Hypothesis I predicted a consistent decrease in achievement imagery. The data (see Table 1 and Figure 1) show a sharp decline since 1890, but a steady increase from 1800 to the peak at about 1890. The second sample showed almost an identical curve with consistent increase up to about 1890 and then a sharp decline. The data of both samples show a significant relationship between amount of imagery and date (First sample, $F = 8.09$, $df = 7/87$, $p < .0005$; Second sample, $F = 2.62$, $df = 7/24$, $p < .05$).

Hypothesis II predicted a consistent increase in affiliation imagery from 1800 to the present. The data in Table 1 and Figure 2 show no consistent increase but do show a general trend with an unexpected drop in 1950 to the 1890 level. Analysis of variance shows a significant relationship ($F = 2.41$, $df = 7/87$, $p < .05$) but the variance was heterogeneous. The Kruskal-Wallis

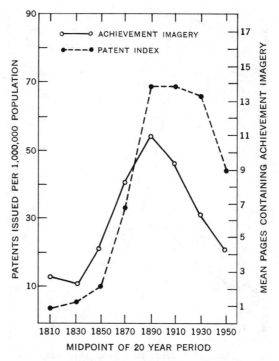

FIGURE 1 / MEAN NUMBER OF PAGES (OUT OF 25) CONTAINING ACHIEVEMENT IMAGERY AND THE PATENT INDEX.

(see Siegal, 1956) analysis of variance of ranks also shows a significant relationship ($p < .01$). In addition, a rank correlation (Kendall's tau) between affiliation imagery and date equals $+ .61$ ($p < .03$).

The data from the second sample show the same general trend with greater variability. The correlation drops below significance and analysis of variance does not reach significance.

Hypothesis III predicts a decrease in moral teaching from 1800 to the present. The data show a striking confirmation (First sample, $F = 101.9$, $df = 7/87$, $p < .0005$, heterogeneous variance; Second sample, $F = 6.95$, $df = 7/24$, $p < .0005$, variance homogeneous).

Hypothesis IV predicts a relationship between the amount of achievement imagery during a specific period and the index of patents issued per population. Figure 1 shows this relationship in graphic form. A striking relationship is apparent. The rank correlation (tau) here is $+ .79$ ($p < .003$). The correlation in the second sample is $+ .68$ ($p < .02$).

DISCUSSION

Achievement imagery and patent index. The data on achievement imagery do not confirm the

TABLE 1 / MEAN SCORES FOR ACHIEVEMENT IMAGERY, AFFILIATION IMAGERY, AND MORAL TEACHING IN THE FIRST SAMPLE OF READERS.

20-YEAR MID-POINT	N[a]	ACHIEVEMENT IMAGERY $\overline{X}$	σ^2	AFFILIATION IMAGERY[b] $\overline{X}$	σ^2	MORAL TEACHING[b] $\overline{X}$	σ^2
1810	3	2.67	4.5	3.33	2.5	16.00	22.0
1830	4	2.50	1.7	4.25	11.7	16.75	9.7
1850	12	4.42	13.4	6.00	24.4	12.42	11.2
1870	3	8.33	2.5	6.33	25.5	6.00	1.0
1890	16	11.06	13.5	5.13	4.7	4.19	4.9
1910	10	9.40	5.1	6.70	12.0	4.50	2.7
1930	15	6.33	19.6	9.33	6.1	1.00	0.7
1950	32	4.25	14.8	5.50	12.7	0.06	0.1

[a] Number of samples of 25 pages scored. The raw score was the number of pages (out of 25) containing imagery.

[b] Variance heterogeneous. In no case were the variances heterogeneous in the second sample.

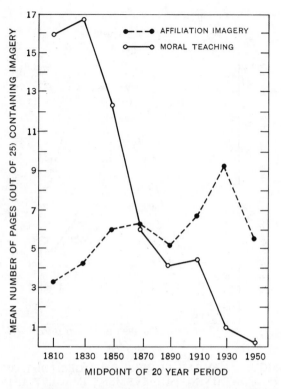

FIGURE 2 / MEAN NUMBER OF PAGES (OUT OF 25) CONTAINING AFFILIATION IMAGERY AND MORAL TEACHING IMAGERY.

original hypothesis which was obviously too simple. There are clear indications in both samples that achievement imagery increases to a peak around the turn of the present century and has steadily declined since then. This relationship is supported by the strikingly similar data from the patent index. The number of patents granted was used in preference to the number of applications for patents for two reasons: no record was kept of patents applied for until 1840 (this would have cut 39 years from the patent population measure) and the very fact that a patent is issued is indicative of the "uniqueness" of the patent. Unique accomplishment is one of the criteria for scoring achievement imagery (Atkinson, 1958).

Affiliation imagery. The data from both samples tend to confirm the hypothesis of increasing affiliation imagery, although the results were not statistically significant in the second sample. Certain aspects of the difference in type of affiliation imagery through time are noteworthy. Much of the early and middle nineteenth century readers' affiliation imagery, though widely scattered, was quite unsophisticated as shown by the following (Parker & Watson, 1857) example:

I love my dear little brother and I am pleased when I see him happy. I did not intend to disobey you, dear father, and I hope you will not be displeased with me for what I have done (p. 75).

The discussion of the joys of giving to others continued unabated for the next page and a half. In contrast, affiliation imagery in the period from 1920 was considerably more subtle.

It was more difficult to score affiliation imagery in the earliest books in the study and it was in this period that interrater reliability was lowest. The difficulty lay in differentiating true affective affiliation imagery from a culturally sanctioned form of address. Thus, "dear son," "dear father," and "my dear" were not scored unless affect was also demonstrated since this was often mere conventionally approved formalism.

It is possible that this scoring difficulty could account for the results found. This, in combination with the fact that the results were not significant in the second sample, suggests caution in interpretation of these results.

Moral imagery. The decline in the religious-moral emphasis in textbooks has long been noted by various researchers. Hart (1933), in analyzing selected popular magazines of the period from 1900 to 1930, found evidence of a general decline in the status of religion and religious sanctions. These findings are in general accord with the results of the present study. In the case of the school readers it may be argued that the diminishing frequency of moral references is a result of the secularization of the schools during the nineteenth century.

It should be noted that the first schools in the colonies were church-sponsored and, in many instances, the minister of the church also served as teacher to the children. His primary purpose was not general education but simply to teach the pupils to read the Bible. The shift from church-sponsored to the public-sponsored and supported schools began about the time of the American Revolution and continued through most of the nineteenth century. However, since all the books in the present study were prepared for public schools, the decrease in moral teaching imagery indicates the cultural trend toward secularization which affected the management of the schools and was reflected in the books written for the schools even after they had become nominally secular.

The antecedent conditions of changes in values such as demonstrated here are very complex. As noted earlier, theorists such as Riesman et al. (1950) stress the importance of psychological factors (character type) which lead to the examination of child rearing practices. Economic historians stress political and economic factors (Rostow, 1960). The historical evidence is probably easier to marshal to support the economic interpretation.

The findings of the present study fit very well the conceptual paradigm of Rostow (1960) who stresses the economic factors. He has developed a general model of the stages of economic growth which distinguishes (a) precondition for take-off, (b) the take-off, (c) the drive to maturity, and (d) the age of high mass consumption.

In the United States, Rostow (1960) found that the traditional or agricultural society lasted until about 1840. The take-off occurred from 1843 to 1860. This appears to be the take-off period for achievement orientation also (see Figure 1). During the next period from 1860 to 1900, called by Rostow the drive to maturity, "some ten to twenty per cent of the national income was steadily invested, permitting industrial output regularly to outstrip the increase in population" (p. 9). The United States, according to Rostow's data and reasoning, reached technological maturity around 1900. This date is extremely close to the high points of achievement imagery and patent measures.

Rostow's (1960) preconditions for take-off are technological developments which might set the stage for increased social mobility, a factor mentioned by Riesman et al. (1950) as affecting child rearing practices. Rostow feels that during this period the idea that economic progress is possible and necessary for such ends as national dignity becomes prevalent in the culture and men come forward who are willing to mobilize savings, take risks, and engage in entrepreneurial activity.

The latter aspects have a distinctly psychological flavor. Men who take risks and engage in entrepreneurial activity are those who have high achievement motivation (McClelland, 1958). Recently economists have noted the importance of motivation and personality structure in economic growth. Thus Hagen (1958) discusses the role of the need for achievement, for autonomy, for aggression, for dominance, for affiliation, and for dependence in the beginning of economic growth. These motivational variables interact with economic and political variables to produce cultural changes.

As noted in the introduction, evidence for the importance of psychological factors such as motives and values in cultural change and economic growth has been presented by McClelland (1955, 1958, 1961). There are, moreover, studies which have made a start in uncovering the relationship between child rearing practices and achievement and affiliation motivation. Briefly, achievement motivation appears to be associated with early parental stress on independence training and mastery, coupled with a warm acceptance of the child (Winterbottom, 1958). Affiliation motivation is related to maternal acceptance and to parental stress on interpersonal involvement of the child (Gall, 1960).

These findings appear to be in accord with Riesman's analysis of the child rearing practices which lead to the inner- and other-directed types. The parent rearing a child in the period of transition to inner-direction must equip him with a "gyroscope" which will fit him to remain on course in a society where it is impossible to foretell, due to increasing social mobility, what role he will be called upon to play. He must be equipped to be self-reliant and independent. These are the aspects which Riesman sees in nineteenth century child rearing. The antecedents of achievement motivation seem clear.

On the other hand, with increasing urbanization and population density which result from technological advance, the child is no longer pushed to be independent, but learns the importance of other individuals in the environment. He must be taught to win approval. Although Riesman's argument is more complicated than this, the child rearing practices which he sees in contemporary United States culture seem to be ones which might lead to affiliation motivation.

In summary we propose that motivation, or cultural orientation, be conceived of as an intervening variable standing between antecedent environmental factors associated with economic and political changes and consequent behavior resulting in cultural changes such as technological growth. Such an analysis should give increased explanatory power, since it is probable that motivation is a function of factors other than economic changes. For instance, cultural values affect child rearing practices and hence motives (McClelland, Rindlisbacher, & deCharms, 1955). Thus two cultures undergoing similar economic or political change may react quite differently due to the intervening variables of values, child rearing practices, and motives.

SUMMARY

Content analysis of children's readers from schools in the United States demonstrated a rise in achievement imagery from 1800 to about 1900 and then a steady decline. The achievement imagery curve was related to an index of the number of patents issued. A steady decline over the period 1800-1950 was found in the amount of moral teaching in readers. There was tentative indication of an increase in affiliation imagery.

The over-all picture presented by the data corresponds very well with certain cultural trends pointed out by students of cultural change. The data illustrate an interesting technique for obtaining objective data to investigate cultural historical hypotheses.

REFERENCES

ATKINSON, J. W. *Motives in fantasy, action, and society.* Princeton: Van Nostrand, 1958.

CHALL, JEANNE. Readability: An appraisal of research and application. *Bur. educ. Res. Monogr. Ohio St. U.,* 1958, No. 34.

DALE, E., & CHALL, JEANNE. A formula for predicting readability. *Educ. res. Bull.,* 1948, 27, 11-20, 37-54.

GALL, H. S. The development of affiliation motivation. Unpublished doctoral dissertation, University of North Carolina, 1960.

HAGEN, E. E. How economic growth begins: A general theory applied to Japan. *Publ. opin. Quart.,* 1958, 12, 373-390.

HART, H. Changing social attitudes and interests. In, *Recent social trends in the United States.* New York: McGraw-Hill, 1933. Pp. 382-442.

JOHNSON, C. *Old-time schools and school-books.* New York: Macmillan, 1904.

MC CLELLAND, D. C. Some social consequences of achievement motivation. In M. R. Jones (Ed.), *Nebraska symposium on motivation: 1955.* Lincoln: Univer. Nebraska Press, 1955. Pp. 41-65.

MC CLELLAND, D. C. The use of measures of human motivation in the study of society. In J. W. Atkinson (Ed.), *Motives in fantasy, action, and society.* Princeton: Van Nostrand, 1958. Pp. 518-552.

MC CLELLAND, D. C. *The achieving society.* Princeton: Van Nostrand, 1961.

MC CLELLAND, D. C., ATKINSON, J. W., CLARK, R. A., & LOWELL, E. L. *The achievement motive.* New York: Appleton-Century-Croft, 1953.

MC CLELLAND, D. C., & FRIEDMAN, G. A. A cross-cultural study of the relationship between child-rearing practices and achievement motivation appearing in folk tales. In G. E. Swanson, T. M. Newcomb, & E. L. Hartley (Eds.), *Readings in social psychology.* (2nd ed.) New York: Holt, 1952. Pp. 243-249.

MC CLELLAND, D. C., RINDLISBACHER, A., & DE-CHARMS, R. Religious and other sources of parental attitudes toward independence training. In D. C. McClelland (Ed.), *Studies in motivation.* New York: Appleton-Century-Croft, 1955. Pp. 389-397.

MC GUFFEY, W. H. *New fourth eclectic reader.* New York: Wilson, Hinkle, 1857.

NIETZ, J. A. *Old textbooks.* Pittsburgh: Univer. Pittsburgh Press, 1961.

PARKER, R. G., & WATSON, J. M. *The national second reader.* New York: Barnes, 1857.

RIESMAN, D., GLAZER, N., & DENNEY, R. *The lonely crowd.* New Haven: Yale Univer. Press, 1950.

ROSTOW, W. W. *The stages of economic growth.* Cambridge: Cambridge Univer. Press. 1960.

SIEGAL, S. S. *Nonparametric statistics for the behavioral sciences.* New York: McGraw-Hill, 1956.

STRAUSS, M. A., & HOUGHTON, L. J. Achievement, affiliation, and cooperation values as clues to trends in American rural society, 1924-1958. *Rural Sociol.,* 1960, 25, 394-403.

UNITED STATES DEPARTMENT OF COMMERCE. *Historical statistics of the United States colonial times to 1957.* Washington: 1960.

WEBER, M. *The Protestant ethic.* (Trans. by T. Parsons) New York: Scribner's, 1930.

WHYTE, W. H. *The organization man.* Garden City: Doubleday, 1956.

WINTERBOTTOM, M. R. The relation of need for achievement to learning experiences in independence and mastery. In J. W. Atkinson, (Ed), *Motives in fantasy, action, and society.* New York: Van Nostrand, 1958. Pp. 453-478.

34/SOCIAL BEHAVIOR OF YOUNG CHILDREN IN THE KIBBUTZ[1]/ HELEN FAIGIN[*]

THE SYSTEM OF COLLECTIVE EDUCA-tion followed in the *kibbutzim* (collective settlements)[2] in Israel provides a unique opportunity for the study of the effects on personality development and social behavior of a pattern of socialization that stresses group living and the importance of peer relationships from the very beginnings of life. The study reported here is an exploratory investigation of the social relationships among children of toddler age growing up in this setting.

Within the system of collective education, the children are reared in groups from birth through adolescence. They live in their own houses apart from their parents and are cared for by a *metapelet* (children's caretaker) whose responsibility it is to care for and socialize the children. The role of the *metapelet* (plural, *metaplot*) changes with the age of the children and as the children grow older, teachers and the children themselves assume some of the roles which the *metapelet* had performed earlier. The children spend two to three hours every afternoon with their parents and most of the day on Saturday, the day of rest. Whereas the *metapelet* (especially in the early years) has responsibility and authority for the socialization of the children, the role of the parents is to be "good friends" with the children. The parents' role as disciplinary agents is negligible.

Toddlers' groups were chosen as the special focus of the study in order to determine whether under these special conditions of group-living social interaction between children and group identification can be learned in very young children. Most studies and observations of children in western societies indicate that children interact with one another to a very small degree and for short lengths of time until approximately the age of three years. There is little concept of group or group identification at a younger age. The children are oriented for the most part to

themselves and to the significant adults in their environment. The development from a biological to a social being is a slow and gradual process. Do children living in groups from birth in this type of setting learn to interact with each other at an earlier age; do they begin to feel themselves as part of a group and develop close relationships with one another earlier than children reared in families? These were the primary questions investigated in this study. A secondary point of emphasis was the role of the *metapelet* and her relationship with the children.

METHOD

THE SAMPLE. The study was carried out in two settlements, in each of which three groups of toddlers were observed. The children ranged in age from 19 to 38 months at the time the study was begun. The groups were divided according to age, with an age span of five to six months within each group. All groups consisted of six children.

The two settlements had been in existence for approximately twenty years at the time of the study. The members of both *kibbutzim* are of European origin and have the same general educational level. Each of the *kibbutzim* belongs to a different *kibbutz* movement[3] and can be said to be typical to a certain degree of the educational philosophies and practices of that particular movement. The differences in educational orientation may be summarized in terms of the greater degree of deliberate educational stimulation and the more structured setting of *Kibbutz* S, as compared with the greater freedom allowed the child in *Kibbutz* M.

METHOD OF OBSERVATION. Observations were made on the children at regular intervals over a period of six months. Systematic observations were made on the aggressive and dependent

[1] This research was supported by the Committee for Research on Collective Education of Seminar Hakibbutzim.

[2] For description of the *kibbutz* setting and the system of Collective Education, see (2, 6, 7).

[3] Each *kibbutz* is a member of a *kibbutz* movement which coincides in general with a political party. Each movement has certain political, social and educational ideologies which distinguishes it from the other movements. For fuller detail see Spiro (7).

[*] Helen Faigin, Social behavior of young children in the kibbutz, *Journal of Abnormal and Social Psychology*, 1958, *56*, 117-129. Reprinted by permission.

behavior of each individual child[4] in various activities: free play, organized play, meal time, and getting up in the afternoon. In all, there were three hours of systematic observation made on each child in ten- or fifteen-minute time units. Specific time periods were allotted to each activity. Observations were made, also, upon each group as a whole in the above noted activities and, in addition, getting up in the morning, going to sleep in the afternoon and evening, on walks, at shower time, etc. In this way, the children were observed in all the daily routines. In addition, both formal and informal discussions were held with the *metaplot,* parents, and the person or persons responsible for organizing and directing educational practices with young children in each of the settlements.

NATURE OF THE DATA. Systematic observations of dependent and aggressive behavior of the children were made in terms of predetermined categories to be described, so as to permit statistical analysis of the frequency of different response categories.

Most of the observations were made by the writer. Help was obtained for a short period of time from two assistants in order to establish reliability of observation.[5] The reliability of observation of the various categories of aggressive responses ranged from 70 to 95 per cent, using the formula:

per cent agreement =

$$\frac{\text{number of agreements of two observers}}{\text{number of agreements plus number of disagreements}}$$

Agreement on total aggression was 92 per cent. The reliability of the dependency categories ranged from 75 to 97 per cent. Agreement on total dependency was 90 per cent.

[4] There were six children in each group, but the individual child sample included only those children born in the *kibbutz.* This made a total of 31 children: five children from five of the groups, and six children in one of the groups.

[5] These assistants were seminary students, who were given special training in the observation and recording of aggression and dependency, including ten hours each of observing dependency and aggression in groups of children of similar age but not in the research sample, during free play activity. The data on reliability summarized here were obtained from ten hours of joint observation by the author and an assistant. Of the five hours that each assistant observed with the author, three hours of observation were made during the free play period. Observations were divided quite equally among the three groups of children.

The data on group behavior were obtained from consistent rather than systematic observations. Full records were kept of the occurrences of responses of the various categories of social behavior observed. Special care was taken not to generalize from one instance of unusual or interesting behavior but to generalize only from types of behavior that occurred with some frequency over the entire period of observation. These data were used for descriptive purposes. All data on the behavior of the children are based on these two types of observation. Information was thus obtained on the day-to-day activities of the children, the patterns of interaction among them, and their interaction with the *metapelet.*

The data obtained from formal and informal discussions with *metaplot* and educators were used as background material and as a basis for assessing their attitudes toward the educational system and the problems, general and specific, that arise in taking care of very young children.

THE DAILY ROUTINE

The daily routine in the toddlers' house is quite similar in the two *kibbutzim,* but the daily program is somewhat more set and routinized in *Kibbutz* S than in *Kibbutz* M. The children wake up in the morning at about 6:00 or 6:30. There is a period of free play before breakfast usually inside the house. After breakfast there is again free play; the children usually play outside while the *metapelet* cleans up the house. After this the children usually go on walks around the settlement, visiting various work branches, go swimming in the summer, have their mid-morning snack, play again around the house, and then have lunch. In *Kibbutz* S, almost every morning after the walk, or in place of it, the children spend about half an hour in concentrated activity known as "work": in general, some creative or constructive activity, such as drawing, building, or reading. Emphasis is placed on working well and quietly. This morning "work" period tends to become a routinized daily activity when the children are about 24-27 months old. In *Kibbutz* M, concentrated activity is an almost daily occurrence in the oldest (3-year) group and occurs once in a while in the younger groups. The concept of "work" is not employed and there is not as much emphasis on quiet concentrated activity.

The children eat lunch at about 11:00 A.M. and then go out and play in the yard while the *metapelet* cleans up. After this they shower and take their afternoon nap, which usually lasts around two hours. The children are washed, dressed, and given a snack, and then go off to their parents. In *Kibbutz* M, the children have their evening meal at this time. The reason for this will be explained below.

The children spend two to three hours with the parents and siblings. The parents (one or both) bring the children back to the children's house. In *Kibbutz* S, the children have their evening meal, and the *metapelet* puts them to bed. In *Kibbutz* M, the parents bring the children back to the children's house and put them to sleep. In both *kibbutzim*, the children sleep in the houses all night without any adult with them. A night watchwoman, who is assigned to the children's houses, walks about in the area and looks after any children that cry or have any particular problems.

THE ROLE OF THE METAPELET

The role of the *metapelet* of the toddlers includes a large number of duties and responsibilities; the *metapelet* functions as housekeeper, caretaker, socializing agent, and teacher. She does all the things that a mother usually does and has been delegated the responsibility and authority for rearing the children. Her evaluation as a *metapelet* is in terms of how well the children in her care develop. A close attachment exists between the children and the *metapelet*, and the children will often go to visit the *metapelet* who worked with them at this age when they are older and she no longer works with them.

THE METAPELET AS HOUSEKEEPER. One of the *metapelet's* duties is to keep the children's house clean and in order. She washes the floors, the dishes, makes the beds, takes care of the laundry and in general keeps the house in order. To this task the *metapelet* devotes more or less time depending upon the age of the children, upon her own interests, her efficiency as a housekeeper, and how she herself defines her role.

THE METAPELET AS CARETAKER.

Physical care of the children. The *metapelet* feeds, washes, bathes, and clothes the children. She takes care of them when they are ill, calls the doctor if necessary, does all that is necessary for their general health.

Emotional care of the children. This is the

area around which many of the problems of collective education are centered. There is much discussion, both by parents and by *metaplot*, about whether or not the children get enough individual attention. Since the group is composed of six children, the problem of balancing individual needs against group needs often arises. There are special courses for *metaplot*, and many discussions are held about the emotional needs of the young child in an effort to help with the problem arising in this area. The *metapelet* usually tries to give the child as much attention as he demands; the children who demand more usually receive more. The *metapelet* often spontaneously hugs and kisses the children when she is bathing and dressing them, holds their hands when they go for a walk, and kisses them when she puts them to sleep. There are individual differences among the *metaplot* in "warmth" and "motherliness" which influence the amount of attention and affection that they express toward the children.

There exists some conflict about the *metapelet's* infringing on the parents' loving role. The *metapelet* often rationalizes her feelings of not giving the children enough individual attention by saying that they get enough from their parents. On the other hand, the parents tend to resent the child's strong attachment to the *metapelet*.

THE METAPELET AS SOCIALIZING AGENT. Among the important duties of the *metapelet* is the socialization of the basic disciplines. Weaning is done by the mother, but after this the responsibility is largely the *metapelet's*. She teaches the children to eat by themselves, toilet trains them, teaches them to wash and dress themselves, answers their questions about sex, permits and limits their expression of aggression, and in general makes demands upon them in all areas of behavior.

Eating. The children begin eating by themselves at about one year of age. At this time, little fuss is made about the child smearing the table or his face. There are very few feeding problems. Since the children tend to imitate one another, learning to eat in a group seems to make the process easy and quick.

Toilet training. Toilet training is begun when the child is about eighteen months old. The children sit down in a group together, each on his own pot. The company of the other children and the presence of the *metapelet* seem to make toileting one of the activities of the daily routine. In each of the youngest groups (under two years of age) there were two children who did not always make a bowel movement in the pot. All the children in the other groups were bowel trained. Most of the children, even in the youngest groups, usually urinated in the pot during the day; occasional accidents occurred when the child was involved in his play. Two children in the oldest groups (two-and-a-half to three years) occasionally wet at night, the others were all dry. In the middle groups (two to two-and-a-half years) most of the children occasionally wet at night, but none wet every night. In the youngest groups (under two years), there were four children who wet every night, the rest, occasionally.

Sex training. There is no separation of the sexes in the groups. The children sleep, bathe, and go to the toilet together. The children masturbate sometimes when sitting on the pot, when standing about doing nothing, and occasionally when upset. The children masturbate each other occasionally. The *metapelet* usually pays no attention to the child's masturbation, but occasionally tries to distract him by getting him interested in some activity.

Independence training. The children begin to try to dress themselves by about the age of two years. There is no direct pressure for them to do so, but they are highly praised for their attempts in this direction. They eat alone at an early age, and in general are encouraged to do things by themselves. They are praised for their achievements. Emphasis is placed on "being big." There is somewhat more emphasis on independence in *Kibbutz* S than in *Kibbutz* M.

Control of aggression. The problem of aggression is discussed later in detail. In general, the *metapelet* does not interfere in quarrels between the children, only in cases when a child is getting badly hurt. The general attitude is that the children should have the opportunity for working through their quarrels by themselves.

Discipline. Physical punishment is taboo in the *kibbutz*. Discipline can be characterized, in general, in terms of explaining and trying to win the child over by suggestion or persuasion. A very effective technique is to separate the child from the other members of the group until he is ready to behave properly. Other members of the group often join in and suggest that the "erring" child be deprived of something or they tell him what to do.

The children are very cooperative in general with regard to the demands made upon them, and there are no real disciplinary problems in these groups. Disobedience and disciplinary problems arise much more frequently when the child is with his parents. The general atmosphere within the groups is permissive, and few demands for obedience are made upon the child. There is a tendency to conform to group demands and pressures.

THE METAPELET AS EDUCATOR. Education as used here refers to the active teaching and stimulating of the children as opposed to the subtle, barely conscious teaching of attitudes and relationships. The *metapelet's role* as educator is greatly stressed in *Kibbutz* S, whereas in *Kibbutz* M it is hardly considered a part of her role with these young children.

The *metapelet* in *Kibbutz* S also sees guiding and educating the parents in how to handle their children as an important part of her task.

THE CHILDREN'S GROUPS

The children's groups are described in terms of the general tendency toward group identification, the quality and types of interaction, and the effects of group living on the social development of the children.

IDENTIFICATION WITH THE GROUP. There seems to exist a certain strong "we group" feeling in all of the children's groups. This was evident in their supporting each other whenever criticized or attacked by children from another group. All toys, furniture, and space within the children's house were referred to as "ours" as opposed to "theirs." There were many instances of out-group aggression, and the group united to support its own members. The children often did not permit children from other groups to play with their toys or to come into their house. Whenever a child was absent from a group activity, his absence was noted and mentioned. For example, when a group goes for a walk, even the youngest groups always see to it that all the children are present before going off, without any prompting from the *metapelet*. One of the favorite games of the children was playing on a carousel. They always made room for the members of their own group, but would not permit children from other groups to join them.

The concept of "we" and "ours" was well developed in the children by the age of two. All activities and property connected with the children's house were referred to by the children as "ours," whereas anything that a child had or did in his parents' room was referred to as "mine." A child might bring candy from his parents' room to the children's house and it was up to him whether or not he would distribute it; if he did, he usually did so with much ceremony. The general idea is that this is mine and I am sharing it with you. He does not have to share, however, and no pressure is put upon him to do so by the *metapelet*. The attitude toward things around the children's house, however, was quite different. Here, the expected thing was to share—everything is *ours*. Even when a child had a coveted toy which he did not want to give to another child—he would not say "this is mine"—he would say, "but I had it first."

The children in one group would often brag about the things they had done or the property they had in their house to children of another group. "We have a nice house and you don't," "we went for a walk and you didn't," and the children of the other group would retort in kind.

If a child was hit or teased by a child from another group, the other children in his group would always rise to his defense no matter what the reason was for the quarrel. The children in a given group would often adopt the same attitudes toward things: such and such food is good, such and such is not, such and such toy is good, such and such is not, such and such person is good, such and such is not.

When a child did not want to do something—for example, eat, help clean up, look at a book, in general to do the same activity as the rest of the group—the *metapelet* would usually say, "If you don't want to you don't have to, you can go out and play." This was reacted to by the children as punishment and they joined in the activity.

The children often imitated one another at mealtime and in many of the group activities. Often when the *metapelet* helped a child eat or dress, this child would tell her to help the other children also.

In *Kibbutz* S, this group orientation and identification was more verbalized both by the *metapelet* and by the children. The *metapelet* very consciously talked about the group, in many ways encouraged the development of the concept "we" and "ours." In *Kibbutz* M, this was done much less consciously, but the group feeling exists. A favorite game of the children in the oldest group in *Kibbutz* M, when the observer was present, was to ask her to write down their names. Each child would ask to have his name and the names of all the other children in the group written down. No child ever omitted the name of any of the other children in the group. In both settlements, the children always made sure that everyone was present at mealtime, and at all group activities, such as going for walks and concentrated activity such as reading, drawing, and making things out of plastilina. This making sure that everyone is present was more frequent and consistent in *Kibbutz* S.

The more conscious awareness and expression of group feeling in *Kibbutz* S than in *Kibbutz* M seems attributable mainly to two factors: (*a*) the greater general awareness and articulation in the *Kibbutz* S movement of inculcating the ideology of group living in the young children and (*b*) in *Kibbutz* M, the groups break up at the age of three to three-and-a-half to go to separate kindergartens and come together again only in the second grade—whereas in *Kibbutz* S the group continues to stay together.

SOCIAL PARTICIPATION IN THE CHILDREN'S GROUPS. Much of the time the children spend playing separately, and yet together. Each child is involved in his own particular activity, but plays in the vicinity of the other children. Each child looked around from time to time to see if the others were present and would often point out to the others what he was doing. If any child was not present, the other children would inquire as to this child's whereabouts.

Even in the youngest groups the children often played games together such as peek-a-boo in a group or just two or three of them together. They often imitated one another, crawled on the floor, or pretended that they were dogs. Often two or three children would evolve some game which might go on as long as 15 minutes. In the youngest group, when they played in twos and threes, the specific children changed from activity to activity and from game to game. In the two older groups, certain friendships had formed and there were often two or three children who usually played together. There began to be a trend toward pairing off or forming smaller groups within the group. This was observed mostly during free play.

In the youngest groups, "play together"—aside from general group activities such as going for walks or riding on the carousel—

usually involved looking at things such as grass or insects together—and laughing, playing peek-a-boo, imitating animals, and occasionally building things together. In the middle groups, the children often build things together and play more involved games such as picking and exchanging flowers, exchanging toys, and building canals together out of sand and water. In the oldest group, the children built things together, and there was also quite a bit of imaginative play in which the children took on roles of adults. The most popular of these games in the oldest groups in both *kibbutzim* was playing mother, father, and baby. The same game would be continued by the same group of children day after day, during some of the free play time. Usually, the same child would play the same role each day; sometimes there would be shifts in the child who played a particular role. It is interesting to note, however, that this imaginative play centered on the family, not on the children's group and the *metapelet*. Occasionally, the children played doctor and similar games, but the family group was most popular. Further investigation of this problem in terms of analysis of the children's play might prove rewarding in getting at the kinds of relationships these children have with their families as compared to children growing up in private families.

GROUP VALUES. One of the important values expressed by the children both in their behavior and verbally in all the groups in both settlements is sharing and taking turns. This was apparent especially with regard to food, and playthings such as paper, crayons, and plastilina. The children knew that they would each get some and that they had to wait their turn. How much the children learned in this area was especially evident when a new child came into the group who had not learned to share and wait his turn. The other children explained to him and often pounced on him when he did not behave properly.

In *Kibbutz* S there was also much stress put upon being big and strong and independent, and on doing "constructive" things—"working" quietly and making things. The "big" and independent child can take care of himself, can dress himself, and doesn't cry when he gets hurt. In *Kibbutz* M, children were praised for these things, but there was little stress placed on them.

Values expressed with regard to fighting and displaying affection are discussed later.

The children's groups, even the youngest, play an important part in setting standards for behavior and in controlling the behavior of group members. Often the children's statements of encouragement or discipline were direct imitations of the words of the *metapelet*; sometimes they were inventions of the children themselves. Whichever they were they were used at the appropriate times and carried the weight of sanctions. The children to whom the statements were addressed responded in accordance with them.

In the youngest groups in both settlements, most statements of social control referred to eating and toilet training. Sometimes they also referred to matters of disobedience and aggression. For example, when one of the children made a bowel movement on the floor the other children in the group looked at him and they all said, "Haggai did a BM, Haggai did a BM, not on the floor, Haggai, not on the floor." At another time the children were sitting around the table eating soup. One of the children said the soup was hot, so another child said to her "It's not hot, taste it and you'll see, it's not hot." At times, this control took the form of action rather than words. One of the children had been hitting another child; the second child was crying. All the rest of the children in the group came over and hit the first child.

In the older groups in both *kibbutzim* this control covers all areas of behavior. Sometimes the older children told the younger children how to behave. Below are several examples of statements used by the children in the two older groups to control each other's behavior. First, statements referring to eating:

One of the children isn't eating. Another child says, "Why aren't you eating—I'll feed you." He held him by the arm and fed him.

When one of the children did not want to eat her soup, another child said to her, "It will cool off soon, then you should eat it, when it cools off."

One of the children wanted the observer to write his name, but he hadn't yet eaten his lunch. One of the other children said, "She won't write it for you until you eat." All the other children joined in and told him that first he had to eat and then she (the observer) would write his name.

One of the children wanted to play with nails. Two of the other children told the *metapelet*, "Don't give him any nails yet, he hasn't finished eating."

Statements referring to aggression:

Two children were standing in the house looking out the window. They saw another child hitting a baby. One said to the other, "One mustn't hit babies." Then he called out to the child outside, "You mustn't hit the baby."

One child said to another, "I'm going to hit you." The second child said. "Why do you want to hit me?" The first child then said, "I won't hit you" and hit the table instead.

One child hit another. A third child came over and hugged the child who had been hit and said, "Who hit you?" He then told that child that he must not hit the other child again.

One child hit another. The second child said, "Why are you hitting me? I'm not hitting you." The first child stopped hitting.

One child hit another. A third child told the child who had hit, "How many times do I have to tell you not to hit other children."

SOCIAL CONTROL.   Statements referring to being careful:

One of the children put a pin in his mouth. Another child told him, "You mustn't put a pin in your mouth—you'll get a sore." She took the pin away from him.

On sharing:

Two children were fighting over who was to sit by the steering wheel in an auto. A third child said: "Giladi, that belongs to all of you, to Yisrael too, he can sit there, too, both of you can." They both sat down beside the steering wheel.

The children from a very early age have thus taken over the values of the culture in which they are being reared and use these actively in setting standards for each other's behavior. Not only are these social control statements used but they carry weight in controlling behavior of the children. So the group operates as a socializing agent upon its members from a very young age. In many instances the forms of social control expressed and exercised by these young children seemed to have the quality of "punishment by reciprocity" and to carry the notions of "equality" and "solidarity" as these concepts are used by Piaget (4). These children are much younger than the age at which the idea of distributive or equalitarian justice is thought to develop, but perhaps the conditions of group living tend to induce the development of cooperation, equality, and group solidarity at a very early age. A more focussed study of the methods of social control used by very young children would seem highly desirable.

It is interesting to compare these observations with the use of rules by three-year-old middle-class nursery school children studied by the same investigator (1) in a small city in the United States. Two interesting differences may be noted. The American three-year-olds tended to use more rules about property, that is, about toys and play space, than rules of interaction, how to behave. In the *kibbutz* group, the children although younger tend to use more rules about social interaction than property. This difference would seem to follow from the fact that the *kibbutz* children live and interact with one another to a much greater extent than do nursery school children. The other interesting difference concerns the nature of the property rules. The American nursery school children used rules referring to this being "mine"—"I had it first, you can't have it"—whereas the *kibbutz* children's property rules refer to sharing, "This is ours, this belongs to all of us." The social control methods used by these very young children thus appear to reflect the values of the society in which they grow up: one a society in which private property is highly valued, the other in which there is communal ownership and no private ownership.

RELATIONS BETWEEN THE CHILDREN.   The affective ties between the children are very strong. They do not approach the intensity of relations observed among siblings outside the *kibbutz*, and yet they are much more intense than that of friendships among other Israeli children of this age who play together. In spite of the fact that much of the time the children play by themselves, they almost always play in the vicinity of the other children and are carefully attuned to the movements of the other children. They are aware of the presence and absence of the other children, know what they are doing, respond immediately to the crying and fighting of the other children.

Many of the *metaplot* and parents have some doubts about whether or not children of this age should be living in groups. They talk about the "struggle for existence" which goes on among the children. They say that there is too much fighting and that the strong, more aggressive children hold the power and can get what they want, whereas the weaker, less aggressive children have a hard time holding their own and have to give in to the stronger. This is only partially the case. There is much fighting and crying and the stronger children often do hit the weaker children and take the toys away from them. On the other hand, the children often comfort each other when they are upset or crying. When a child is crying because he has been hurt or because a toy was taken away from him, very often the aggressor will come over and pat the child, tell him he will not hurt him again and perhaps return the toy he has taken or give him another in exchange. If the child who has been the aggressor does not comfort the hurt child, other children in the group will do so.

In each of the two youngest groups there was one extremely aggressive child. These children very often hit the other children and took toys from them with seemingly no provocation, at least no provocation apparent in the situation. The other children tended to avoid them, and from time to time would gang up on the aggressive child. In the two older groups in each of the *kibbutzim* there was no child who could be called extremely aggressive, in the sense of showing behavior similar to the two children in the youngest groups.

In none of the groups was there a domineering or bossy child who would try to tell all the others what to do. During the course of the observation, a new child came into one of the groups who tried to boss the other children around. She quickly learned that she could not do this. The other children either paid no attention to her or fell upon her as a group and beat her. In a very short time this behavior disappeared.

There was no child in any of the groups who could be called the leader. At different times different children played leadership roles in given activities, but no child played this role consistently. Leadership was always in the hands of the *metapelet*. Often when older children would come to visit, an older sibling of one of the children in the group, this older child

would take a leader role, organize some activity and the children in the group would follow this leadership.

SYSTEMATIC OBSERVATIONS OF AGGRESSION AND DEPENDENCY

AGGRESSION. It is difficult to give a general picture of the frequency or types of aggression expressed by the children in the two settlements. Systematic observations were made of the frequency of various types of aggression expressed by the children during free play. Each child was observed at four different periods of 15 minutes each. Nothing can be said about whether children in *kibbutzim* display more or less aggression than children growing up in private families, since there are no comparative data. The data have been analyzed to compare the children in the two *kibbutzim*, with special emphasis on the different educational practices, and to compare the different age groups within each *kibbutz*.

The aggression shown by the children was broken down into various types of aggression. The data on the frequency of all types of aggression recorded are shown in Table 1.

Physical aggression. Physical aggression is defined in terms of hitting for the purpose of hitting or hurting. There were no statistically significant differences between the children in the two *kibbutzim* in the frequency of use of physical aggression as can be seen from Table 1. Within the *kibbutzim* the only significant difference between age groups was found in *Kibbutz* M in which the children in the oldest group exhibited significantly less physical aggression than the children in the middle age

TABLE 1 / MEAN AGGRESSIVE RESPONSES FOR THREE GROUPS OF CHILDREN IN EACH KIBBUTZ.[a]

MEAN NUMBER OF RESPONSES PER CHILD DURING FOUR
15-MINUTE PERIODS OF OBSERVATION

CATEGORY	KIBBUTZ M				KIBBUTZ S			
	GRP. A[a] (N = 5)	GRP. B (N = 5)	GRP. C (N = 5)	ALL GRPS. (N = 15)	GRP. A (N = 6)	GRP. B (N = 5)	GRP. C (N = 5)	ALL GRPS. (N = 16)
Physical aggression	4.2	3.4	1.2	2.9	2.5	2.4	2.6	2.5
Instrumental aggression	1.0	3.4	1.8	2.1	4.3	1.0	1.0	2.2
Defense of toys	0.2	0.8	1.4	0.8	0.5	0.8	3.0	1.4
Defense of self	0.2	0.8	0.6	0.5	0.2	1.2	1.2	0.8
Aggression to objects	1.2	2.0	0.0	1.0	2.8	2.0	3.8	2.5
Verbal aggression	0.0	0.0	2.0	0.7	0.0	0.2	0.8	0.3
Aggression to smaller children	0.0	0.8	2.2	1.0	0.0	0.4	2.8	1.0
Disobedience	0.4	1.0	0.4	0.6	0.3	0.4	1.8	0.8
Total aggression	7.2	12.2	9.6	9.7	10.7	8.4	17.0	11.9
(SD)	(6.2)	(6.8)	(7.2)	(6.6)	(11.2)	(5.8)	(11.5)	(10.6)

[a] In each case, Group A is composed of the youngest children, Group C of the oldest.

group. The highest frequency of expression of physical aggression was by a child in the youngest group in *Kibbutz* M, one of the very aggressive children previously described, for whom 15 units of physical aggression were recorded in the hour's observation. For many of the children, 6 out of 31, no physical aggression was recorded during the hour period, and for nine children only one instance of physical aggression. Thus, about half the children (15 out of 31) expressed very little or no physical aggression.

Instrumental aggression. Instrumental aggression is defined in terms of hitting or pushing in order to attain some other goal, such as a toy, play space, or attention. Table 1 shows the frequency of expression of instrumental aggression. There were no significant differences between the *kibbutzim* or between the various age groups. The highest frequency of instrumental aggression was recorded for one of the previously described aggressive children, in the youngest group in *Kibbutz* S, 20 units. For 13 children, no instances of instrumental aggression were recorded, and for five children only one instance of instrumental aggression was recorded. Thus, for 18 out of 31 children there was practically no instrumental aggression expressed.

Other forms of aggression. The frequency of occurrence of the other categories of aggression (defense of toys, defense of self, aggression toward objects, verbal aggression, aggression toward younger children, and disobedience) is so small that not much can be said about it except to note its lack of occurrence.

Total aggression. Total aggression includes all forms of aggression, the total scores for the various types of aggressive responses. There were no significant differences in the frequency scores of total aggression (Table 1) between the two *kibbutzim*, between boys and girls, or among the different groups. There were large individual differences in the frequency of occurrence of aggressive responses as reflected in the large *SD*'s, presented in Table 1, with a range from 1 to 39 in the frequency of total aggression.

These wide individual variations would seem to indicate that the instigation to aggression is due to factors other than or in addition to the frustrations inherent in group living. It was observed that not only did the individual *metaplot* respond differently in general to the aggressive responses of the children and by their patterns

of relationship instigate more or less aggression, but each *metapelet* responded differently to each individual child when he responded aggressively. Some children were encouraged to respond aggressively, some discouraged from this, and some "just got away with it." Although the *metaplot* tend to practice a "hands off" policy, they were frequently inconsistent in their reactions to the aggressive responses of individual children. The presence or absence of the *metapelet* at the time of occurrence of aggressive responses adds to the factor of inconsistency. In addition, the children themselves respond differently to one another in reaction to aggression directed toward them. The family constellation, too, probably has an important effect on the child's tendency to respond aggressively. It was noted, however, that children who are less aggressive in the group are more aggressive in the parents' room and vice versa.

DEPENDENCY. The dependency behavior expressed by the children was observed and recorded systematically as was aggressive behavior. Under the general heading of dependency the following types of behavior were recorded: crying, showing affection toward adults (other than the *metapelet* and observer), showing affection toward the observer, showing affection to the *metapelet*, showing affection toward children, instrumental dependency, i.e., asking help to do something, seeking attention or approval for making or doing something, and thumbsucking. The frequencies with which these responses occurred in the various groups in the two *kibbutzim* may be seen in Table 2.

Expressing affection was categorized under dependency since it is also a means of seeking attention and affection. Affection is expressed by responses such as touching, holding, or being near. The nature of these responses inevitably induced a response of a similar type from the other person—thus the child's giving and seeking attention could not be separated.

Dependency toward adults. The one consistent difference that appeared in all the categories of dependent behavior (except affection toward children and displaying achievements) was that between the children of the youngest groups in the two *kibbutzim*. In total dependency toward adults, the children in the youngest group in *Kibbutz* S showed higher scores than the children in the youngest group in *Kibbutz* M.[6] This same

[6] All differences mentioned are statistically significant at the .05 level of confidence using the *t* test, unless otherwise stated.

TABLE 2 / MEAN DEPENDENCY RESPONSES FOR THREE GROUPS OF CHILDREN FROM EACH KIBBUTZ

MEAN NUMBERS OF RESPONSES PER CHILD DURING FOUR
15-MINUTE PERIODS OF OBSERVATION

	KIBBUTZ M				KIBBUTZ S			
CATEGORY	GRP. A[a] (N = 5)	GRP. B (N = 5)	GRP. C (N = 5)	ALL GRPS. (N = 15)	GRP. A (N = 6)	GRP. B (N = 5)	GRP. C (N = 5)	ALL GRPS. N = 16
Crying	10.6	3.4	2.8	5.6	4.7	4.0	2.4	3.8
Affection to adults	1.8	7.2	6.8	5.3	5.8	9.0	8.0	7.5
Affection to observer	8.0	9.0	14.2	10.4	21.3	8.8	6.4	12.8
Affection to *metapelet*	0.8	4.2	6.4	3.8	2.8	9.4	8.4	6.6
Instrumental dependency	0.4	0.6	5.8	2.3	1.3	1.6	1.2	1.3
Displaying achievements	0.0	0.6	2.8	1.1	0.0	2.6	0.6	1.0
Total dependency to adults	21.6	25.0	39.0	28.5	35.8	35.4	27.0	32.9
Affection to children	1.0	5.6	4.0	3.5	1.3	2.0	4.0	2.4
Thumbsucking[b]	7.2	6.2	2.0	5.1	1.5	6.0	1.2	2.8
Total dependency	22.6	30.6	43.0	32.1	37.3	37.5	31.0	35.3
(SD)	(10.4)	(5.0)	(17.4)	(15.2)	(9.5)	(20.6)	(19.0)	(16.9)

[a] In each case, Group A is composed of the youngest children, Group C of the oldest.
[b] Not included in total dependency score.

type of difference was found in the separate categories of affection toward adults, toward *metapelet*, toward observer (.10 level of confidence) and instrumental dependency (.10 level of confidence). In contrast, the children in the youngest group in *Kibbutz* M cried more frequently (.10 level of confidence) and sucked their thumbs more frequently (.10 level of confidence) than did the children in the youngest group in *Kibbutz* S.

These apparently inconsistent findings probably can best be understood in terms of the differences in educational orientation in the two *kibbutzim*. It will be remembered that *Kibbutz* S was described as stressing educational stimulation more at an early age, whereas *Kibbutz* M tends to stress a great deal of freedom and permissiveness, letting the child develop at his own rate. One of the consequences of this difference is that the *metapelet* in *Kibbutz* S spends more time with the children during free play and hence they direct their dependency responses toward her. In contrast, the children in *Kibbutz* M tend to cry more unheeded and suck their thumbs since the *metapelet* is not around. There is less opportunity to direct dependency responses toward adults. In general, the children in the youngest group in *Kibbutz* S seemed to develop at a faster rate than the children in *Kibbutz* M. They seemed to be more aware of adults, more aware of their surroundings, played more, and spoke earlier than the children in *Kibbutz* M. These differences in rate of development seem to level off in the two older groups where the same differences do not occur.

Differences were found between the oldest groups in the two *kibbutzim* in two categories: displaying achievements and instrumental dependency. Here the children of *Kibbutz* M more frequently displayed this behavior than the children of *Kibbutz* S, contrary to what might have been expected. A possible explanation is that the *metapelet* of the oldest group in *Kibbutz* S usually praised the achievements of the children without their asking for it. The difference between the two groups on instrumental dependency is more easy to understand. As noted previously, the *metapelet* in *Kibbutz* S encourages and demands more independence on the part of the children than the *metapelet* of *Kibbutz* M. She urges them to do things by themselves rather than to ask for help. She often refuses help when the children ask for it, telling them instead to try to do whatever they wanted by themselves.

Dependency toward children. There is a general tendency for the amount of affection and dependency expressed toward children to increase with age. That is, the children in the youngest groups showed affection to other children less frequently than the children in the older groups. There were differences between the two *kibbutzim* only in the middle groups. The children of the middle group in *Kibbutz* M showed more affection and dependency toward other children than the similar age children in *Kibbutz* S. It is not clear why this difference should appear in the middle groups and not in the oldest groups. When the amount of affection expressed toward children was compared with the amount of affection expressed toward the *metapelet*, there were no differences found except in the middle group in *Kibbutz* S. Here the children expressed affection toward the *metapelet* significantly more frequently than toward other children. We would expect to find differences in the youngest groups, but this is not the case.

RELATIONSHIP BETWEEN DEPENDENCY AND AGGRESSION. In terms of overall scores, the children in both *kibbutzim* expressed significantly more dependent than aggressive responses ($t = 6.95$). There is a significant negative relationship ($r = -.73$) between the frequency scores of aggression and dependency. That is, the children who are more aggressive are less dependent, and the children who are more dependent are less aggressive. Most studies of nursery school children indicate a general low but positive relationship between dependency and aggression. Lois Murphy (3) in a classical study on sympathy and aggression in young children finds a positive relationship between these two types of responses. In a study reported by Sears *et al.* (5) there tends to be a low positive correlation between these two types of responses. These studies were made on older children than those observed here. Perhaps at this age dependency and aggression are alternative responses to frustration and the children who have been successful in using one or the other type of response tend to persist in its use. If we look at each group separately we note that in all groups, except the middle group in *Kibbutz* M, there is a negative correlation between total aggression scores and total dependency scores. The correlations range from $-.09$ to $-.72$. In the middle group in *Kibbutz* M, there is an unexplained positive correlation ($+ .82$) between the frequency of occurrence of these two types of responses.

When analysis is limited to the aggressive and dependent responses expressed toward other children, there is no relationship ($r = + .12$) between the occurrence of each of these responses. In the groups taken separately, however, there is, in four out of the six cases, a high positive correlation ($.55-.93$) between the expression of aggression and dependency toward children. The children show aggression toward each other with significantly greater frequency than they show dependency ($t = 2.00$), in contrast to the findings with respect to total scores. Not unexpectedly, the children thus tend to respond to other children more frequently with aggression and toward adults with dependency. In the groups considered separately, the chil-

dren in the youngest group in each *kibbutz* are more frequently aggressive toward one another than they are affectionate, whereas in the two older groups the frequency of these two responses does not differ significantly. At the younger ages, the children are probably more affectionate toward adults as the source of their main satisfactions and care, and are aggressive toward other children since other children do not satisfy their needs; if anything, their peers are probably more likely to frustrate and interfere with need satisfaction. The process of learning to be affectionate toward other children is presumably a more complicated process involving the development of identification with one's peers and of capacities and skills of helping one another out.

SUMMARY AND CONCLUSIONS

An exploratory study of the social development of children of toddler age growing up in *kibbutzim* has been described. Since these children live together in groups practically from birth, the setting is propitious for studying the extent and limits of social interaction among very young children. A secondary point of emphasis was the role of the *metapelet* (children's caretaker) and her relationship with the children.

The sample consisted of three groups of children from each of two *kibbutzim*. The children ranged in age from 19 to 38 months at the time the study was begun. Observations were made on the children for a period of six months. Systematic observations were made on the individual children, general observations were made on each group, and discussions were held with the *metaplot* and educators.

The first part of the report deals with a description of the daily routine of the children. Differences between the *kibbutzim* in degree of deliberate educational stimulation and of freedom vs. structure in the setting were seen as having consequences in the relative amount of time the *metaplot* from the two *kibbutzim* spend with the children.

Accompanying differences in the behavior of the children in the two *kibbutzim* were noted mainly in the youngest groups. The children in the youngest group in *Kibbutz* S showed more dependency responses toward adults, whereas the children in *Kibbutz* M tended to suck their thumbs more often and to cry more frequently. The youngest children in *Kibbutz* S seemed to develop at a faster rate in terms of being aware of their surroundings, more aware of adults, playing more, and speaking earlier. These differences tended to level off in the older groups where no differences of this sort were noted. The children in *Kibbutz* S tended to verbalize group identification and being "big" more than the children in *Kibbutz* M, but no differences were noted in other behavioral indices of these factors except that in *Kibbutz* M the children in the oldest group had higher instrumental dependency scores than the children in *Kibbutz* S.

The role of the *metapelet* is discussed in some detail, in terms of her role as housekeeper, caretaker, and socializer of the children.

The main body of the study is concentrated on the relations among the children. There is a strong group identification, frequent use of the terms "we" and "ours" as against "theirs." Competition exists between groups rather than within groups. Each group defends its members from attack by other groups. There is not a very high degree of social participation among the children, especially in the youngest groups, but the children always play in the presence of the others, and the absence of any child is noted by the other children. The children tend to control each other's behavior by telling each other how to behave. There is a tendency to conformity to group standards. Problems of discipline are negligible. Treatment of sex play and masturbation is very permissive. Toilet training and eating habits seem to be learned with a minimum of conflict.

There are wide individual differences in the frequency of aggressive responses. The frequency of dependent responses is significantly higher than the frequency of aggressive responses, and children who are aggressive tend not to be dependent and vice versa. Children tend to be more aggressive than affectionate toward each other, especially in the youngest groups, and to be as frequently affectionate as aggressive in the older groups. There is a positive relationship between aggression and affection expressed toward other children.

The results of this study indicate, then, that group identification, sharing, and group control of individual behavior can be learned by very young children under conditions of group living. Caution is in order in generalizing from these results in view of the lack of comparative data on similar age children growing up in private families, and of the fact that children in only two *kibbutzim* were studied.

REFERENCES

1. FAIGIN, HELEN. The frequency and types of rules used by preschool children in their social interaction. Unpublished master's thesis, State University of Iowa, 1948.
2. IRVINE, ELIZABETH E. Observations on the aims and methods of child rearing in communal settlements in Israel. *Hum. Relat.*, 1952, 5, 247-275.
3. MURPHY, LOIS B. *Social behavior and child personality.* New York: Columbia Univer. Press, 1937.
4. PIAGET, J. *The moral judgment of the child.* New York: Harcourt, Brace, 1932.
5. SEARS, R. R., WHITING, J. W. M., NOWLIS, V., and SEARS, PAULINE S. Some child rearing antecedents of aggression and dependency in young children. *Genet. Psychol. Monogr.*, 1953, 47, 135-234.
6. SPIRO, M. E. Education in a communal village in Israel. *Amer. J. of Orthopsychiat.*, 1955, 25, 283-293.
7. SPIRO, M. E. *Kibbutz: Venture in Utopia.* Cambridge, Mass.: Harvard Univer. Press, 1956.

TWO PREVIOUS REPORTS BEFORE THE meetings of the American Orthopsychiatric Association were concerned with comparisons, along several psychological dimensions, between different age groups of Kibbutz-reared children and their non-Kibbutz age peers. Our findings were that the infants in the Kibbutz setting lagged in some aspects of their development behind the non-Kibbutz infants (9). However, no residues of this slower start in ego development were noted in the comparative study of Kibbutz ten-year-olds. As a matter of fact, it appeared that these children gave indications of more mature ego development than the ten-year-olds raised outside the Kibbutz structure (8). In a subsequent report (11) we have also pointed out that the Kibbutz educational setting does not affect adversely the children's attitudes to parents and family. On the contrary, the findings were that more Kibbutz children had positive attitudes to the family than did the non-Kibbutz controls.

In the present paper we will follow the pattern or design of the previous studies and report its application to groups of adolescents. We shall attempt a comparison between Kibbutz and non-Kibbutz adolescents with respect to a number of pertinent and relevant psychological variables. More specifically, we shall address ourselves to two broad questions: 1) Are the gains in ego strength observed in Kibbutz preadolescents, as measured by our instruments, also maintained during the adolescent period? 2) What are the qualitative differences in terms of fantasy content and inferred dynamics, in social and family interrelationships, in heterosexual attitudes, and in goals and future perspectives, between the Kibbutz-reared adolescents and a similar age group reared in the conventional family setting?

PROCEDURE

In order to try to obtain some answers to these questions two groups of 30 Kibbutz and 25 non-Kibbutz 17-year-olds, roughly equally divided between the sexes, were examined by means of several projective methods.[1] The Kibbutz children were drawn from four different Kibbutzim, while the non-Kibbutz adolescents resided in three different villages of the conventional variety. All subjects were at the time pupils of the twelfth grade in their local high schools. Group and individual examinations took place in special rooms designated for the purpose in the school buildings through the cooperation of the local authorities.

The projective techniques employed were: the Rorschach, the Sentence Completion Test, which was an expanded version of the one used with the younger children (11), and the Thematic Apperception Test. The Rorschach was administered individually, while the other two tests were administered in small groups.

Limitations of space would prevent us from reporting the complete results obtained with each of these methods. Consequently, only the data which are more or less directly relevant to the questions which we have raised in the introductory section of this paper will be summarized and discussed. Thus, only some of the Rorschach indices will be included; the response patterns to several of the 52 incomplete sentences will be noted; and the analysis of TAT cards 1, 2, and 4 only will be reported.

RESULTS

THE RORSCHACH TEST. The first aspect of this test that may be noted is that of productivity, i.e., the number of responses given to the ink-blots. The median number of responses for both groups combined is 31, which is consistent with the usual expectancies. However, the Kibbutz group tended to be more productive. Sixty-two per cent of the Kibbutz subjects exceeded the 31 responses, whereas only 36 per cent of the non-Kibbutz group did so. This difference approaches statistical significance ($p = .08$).

Another interesting index is "first reaction time." This refers to the time it takes the subject to give a response after the card is presented. On eight of the ten cards the average first reaction time of the Kibbutz adolescent is shorter than that of the parallel group. In the remaining two (V and VII) the difference is negligible in

---

[1] The numbers of individual tests vary somewhat owing to absence or incompleteness of record in a few instances.

TABLE 1 / MEDIAN REACTION TIMES FOR THE RORSCHACH CARDS (IN SECONDS).

	I°	II	III	IV	V	VI	VII	VIII	IX	X
Kibbutz	6.8	12.2	11.0	17.0	8.0	20.0	16.5	11.5	22.5	24.8
Non-Kibbutz	19.0	17.0	11.5	19.5	7.0	37.5	16.0	12.0	32.5	30.0

° Difference significant at the .02 level.

the opposite direction. Moreover, the differences on the first card are very significant statistically ($p = .02$). Generally, the Kibbutz group reacts more immediately, with less anxiety and inhibition (see Table 1).

Since Rorschach's movement response is assumed to reflect fantasied behavior, we followed the notion that some need is expressed in its content. As our guide in classifying the movement content, we followed Kaplan (6), who employed Murray's classification of needs. We utilized only 8 of the 17 categories listed by Kaplan, for only a negligible number of responses was classifiable in the omitted categories (see Table 2).

The most outstanding difference between the groups is with respect to the "play" category. Nearly 70 per cent of the Kibbutz subjects have it in their records as compared with 32 of the non-Kibbutz adolescents. The other differences are less striking. The non-Kibbutz group includes more individuals who utilize the "aggression" category, and the Kibbutz youngsters have more in the "orality" category. However, the differences on these and the remaining categories are not statistically significant.

Lastly, an index of what may be called "general adjustment" was applied to the Rorschach data. Davidson (3) reported a series of "signs of adjustment," based on the Rorschach, which she

TABLE 2 / THEMAS REPRESENTED IN THE MOVEMENT (M) RESPONSES OF THE RORSCHACH RECORDS OF THE TWO GROUPS.

NEEDS	NO. OF SUBJECTS		PERCENTAGES	
	K	NK	K	NK
Play°	18	7	69	32
Achievement	7	7	27	32
Aggression	4	7	15	32
Activity	12	8	46	36
Cognizance	6	5	23	23
Affiliation	5	4	19	18
Orality	5	1	19	4.5
Passivity	17	14	65	63

° $Chi^2 = 6.80$; $p < .005$.

found useful in her investigations. We employed 15 of the suggested 17 signs; these are least susceptible to subjective judgment. The range of adjustment signs for individuals in both groups is from 4 to 11. The average number of signs for the Kibbutz and non-Kibbutz group is 8.04 and 7.95 respectively. This is obviously a small and insignificant difference. The two groups do not differ on this index of adjustment or lack of emotional disturbance.

If we are to summarize the Rorschach data only provisionally, for we shall return to integrate them with the findings on the other tests, we can state as follows: The Kibbutz adolescents are more productive and less inhibited in responding to the test; they emphasize more play and orality themes and less aggression themes in the content; their over-all adjustment, i.e., freedom from signs of deviation, is similar to that of the control group.

THE SENTENCE COMPLETION TEST. This instrument is an extended version of the test used with the ten-year-olds (11) and was obtained from the same source (13). The 52 sentence roots deal with 13 different areas—four sentences for each area. Consonant with our present limited objectives, we shall deal with 6 of these areas in the present context—Family, Father, Mother, Sexuality, Goals, and Future.

The first three areas were assessed globally, i.e., the four completions in each area were rated as a whole in terms of the positiveness of the attitude which they express. The results are based on a combination of the ratings of two judges working independently. See Table 3.

No significant differences between the groups with respect to the incidence of "positiveness" of attitude to Family, Father and Mother were reflected in the findings. Very similar proportions of both groups indicate positive attitudes in these three areas. In terms of relative numbers, more of the Kibbutz adolescents indicate positive attitudes to Father and Mother. This is a mere trend, however, since the differences are not great enough to be statistically significant.

In the area of sexuality one sentence (out of four) yielded significant group differences. The

TABLE 3 / GLOBAL COMBINED RATINGS OF FAMILY, FATHER AND MOTHER AREAS BASED ON SENTENCE COMPLETION RESPONSES.

	FAMILY		FATHER		MOTHER	
	POSITIVE	OTHER	POSITIVE	OTHER	POSITIVE	OTHER
Kibbutz	11	17	12	16	14	14
Non-Kibbutz	11	13	9	15	8	17

TABLE 4 / SIGNIFICANT DIFFERENCES BETWEEN THE GROUPS ON FUTURE AND GOALS ITEMS.

ITEM 16			ITEM 29			ITEM 30		
	K	NK		K	NK		K	NK
School	14	3	Personal ambition	7	14	Long range	12	18
Other	10	12	Other	18	9	Trivial	12	4
Chi^2	5.40			5.42			4.98	
p	$<.02$			$<.02$			$<.03$	

sentence reads: "If I had sexual relations. . . ." The vast majority of the Kibbutz group rejected this idea unequivocally. "I would discontinue" or "Not at my age" were some of the most frequent responses. About one third of the non-Kibbutz adolescents also rejected the idea. However, most of them indicated positive or neutral attitudes to this hypothetical possibility. The differences between the groups were highly significant statistically ($p<.01$).

In the areas of Future and Goals, three of the eight items yielded interesting and significant differences between the two groups (see Table 4). On item 16 ("I would be definitely satisfied if . . .") more of the Kibbutz group are concerned about being "a good pupil" or "if I am permitted to continue to study," whereas the non-Kibbutz subjects stated more specific goals—"if I were able to be a pilot," for example. On item 29 ("My secret ambition in life . . .") more of the non-Kibbutz group indicate specific personal ambitions ("to be a successful farmer" or "to be a literary man"), while the Kibbutz adolescents are less specific ("continue living in the Kibbutz") or deny having such ambitions altogether. In a similar vein, responses to item 30 ("One of these days, I . . .") show that the non-Kibbutz group have by-and-large long-range goals, being a teacher, building a farm, etc. Half of the Kibbutz group have similar long-range perspectives, but the other half mention short-range or trivial aims, such as going home, climbing a mountain, and so on. Even the greater interest of the Kibbutz group in school (see item 16) is not an expression of any specific long-range goals; there is no implication of preparation for something specific.

A provisional summary of this material would seem to indicate that the Kibbutz adolescents do not differ from the controls with respect to intrafamilial attitudes, that they reject sexual relations at an early age, and that their goals and future aspirations are less specific (and probably less mature) than those of their non-Kibbutz peers.

THE THEMATIC APPERCEPTION TEST. Since we did not have a direct measure of the intellectual level of our subjects, we attempted to use the TAT stories, written by them, as a basis for such an evaluation. A psychologist,[2] a native Israeli, was asked to classify the complete records without knowing to which group they belonged. On the basis of facility in the use of language and style, he placed the subjects in three categories—below average, average and superior. The Kibbutz adolescents were nearly evenly divided between the superior and the other two categories combined. Only 5 of the non-Kibbutz group placed in the superior category, while the remaining 18 subjects were put in the average or below average categories (see Table 5).

Productivity on the three TAT cards, in terms of word count per story, was also calculated. The Kibbutz group was on the average consistently more productive, on each card, than the control group. These findings are quite consistent with the higher Rorschach productivity referred to above.

In comparing the content of the TAT stories, i.e., the fantasy material of the subjects, we

[2] The author is grateful to Dr. Joshua Levy for his assistance with this aspect of the study.

TABLE 5 / PRODUCTIVITY AND ESTIMATES OF INTELLIGENCE BASED ON TAT STORIES.

	PRODUCTIVITY (MDN. NO. WORDS)			INTELLIGENCE (SUBJECTS RATED)		
	CARD 1	CARD 2	CARD 3	LOW	AVERAGE	SUPERIOR
Kibbutz	94	102	90	2	11	10
Non-Kibbutz	84	60	55	3	15	5

attempted to employ some of the categories reported in normative studies with adults (4, 12). However, with our small samples of adolescents this was only partially applicable. The final classifications that evolved were most meaningful for, and were dictated by, the material itself.

Card 1. Murray (7) describes this picture as that of "a young boy [who] is contemplating a violin which rests on a table in front of him."

The stories in response to this card were analyzed in terms of the dominant characteristics of the hero and in terms of the major themes contained in them. The vast majority of the Kibbutz adolescents describe the hero as "a child who has a violin" or "a pupil." Most of the non-Kibbutz adolescents see either a talented child or one who is in the process of obtaining a violin despite economic limitations. Most of the non-Kibbutz themes involve ambition and high motivation for achievement whereas the Kibbutz themes involve more ambivalence about practice and rejection of the musical endeavor altogether. They view playing the violin as not self-motivated, but as a result of pressure exercised by parents and teachers. Examples of the two types of stories are as follows:

Kibbutz—Card 1. Violin pupil—not anxious about playing. His parents are pressing him to do this. He is before some boring exercise. He has no desire to play. He is thinking of his friends' games outside.

At the end the pupil will begin to understand the music and love playing, although it will not become the center of his life.

Non-Kibbutz—Card 1. In this picture I see a lad with ambitions and stirrings to be a great violinist. The lad played and played, then got tired and put the violin on top of the music. He is looking at the music notes and the violin and is thinking that these two things are his entire life. Slowly he sinks into thought and pictures his future for himself.

Card 2. "Country scene: in the foreground is a young woman with books in her hand; in the background a man is working in the fields and an older woman is looking on."

The "latent stimulus demand" of this picture, according to Henry (5), involves the "eliciting feelings toward interpersonal interaction, toward parent-child relations, and toward heterosexual relations"; also "the contrast between the new and the old . . . girl going off for education as opposed to the farm folk." Wittenborn (15) states that it "may reveal yearnings for independence, ambition . . . the conflict of the socially mobile student."

The relationship between the characters portrayed in the stories and the themes involved were of paramount interest in the present context. More than 90 per cent of the non-Kibbutz adolescents see blood relationships between two or all characters; most often they are seen as members of one family. This is in contrast with the Kibbutz group; 64 per cent of this group see such a relationship. The themes are even more revealing of the differences between the groups. (See Table 6.)

About two thirds (68%) of the non-Kibbutz stories on this card have conflict as their major theme—conflict with parents or internal conflict over leaving the farm and going to the city, over changing occupational status, etc. Less than one fifth of the Kibbutz adolescents project this theme in their stories. They merely describe the pastoral scene, but comparatively rarely see conflict between "new and old," farm and city, and so on.

Examples of contrasting stories follow:

Kibbutz—Card 2. Illana loved to go out every evening to the field and landscape to be acquainted with and know and feel the country, the soil the fatherland. As usual, also, this evening Illana went up among the rocks on the side of the village, at twilight, looking as she is absorbed in thoughts and ideas. The village is peaceful and quiet; tractors and machines do not disturb the peace and quiet. And the thoughts flow and well up in her—thoughts of love and tenderness—love for the entire world, nature, quiet and peace, for the plowing horse and the man who is walking in his footsteps and for his and everybody's landscape—for all the country folk in the world. How beautiful!

Non-Kibbutz—Card 2. The family is a simple agricultural family and have no connection with education. Agriculture is the magic of the life of the family. But the daughter is dissatisfied with such a narrow outlook. She leaves agriculture and turns to

TABLE 6 / CHARACTERS AND MAJOR THEMES IN TAT STORIES (PERCENTAGES OF GROUPS).

DESCRIPTION OF HERO AND MAJOR THEMES IN
RESPONSE TO CARD 1

HERO			THEME		
	K	NK		K	NK
Talented child	4	26	Ambition-motivation	17	65
Tries to obtain violin	17	56	Ambivalence-rejection	61	17
Has violin	78	17	Other (incl. damage to violin)	22	17

IDENTIFICATION OF CHARACTERS AND MAJOR THEMES
IN RESPONSE TO CARD 2

CHARACTERS			THEME		
	K	NK		K	NK
Members of one family	55	68	Conflict over aspirations	18	64
Not related	36	9	Economic frustration	5	9
Two related	9	23	Description	68	18
			Love triangle	9	9

CHARACTERS AND MAJOR THEMES IN RESPONSE TO CARD 4

CHARACTER			THEMES			ACTION		
	K	NK		K	NK		K	NK
Husband and wife	35	47	Infidelity	10	52	Prevent separation	35	74
Two in love	35	47	Aggression	50	11	Prevent aggression	40	21
Fellow and girl	30	5	Rejection of love	30	5	Embrace	25	5
			Miscellaneous	10	32			

the city. The father terminated his relations with her and does not speak to her. He is tired of all the persuasion which was useless, but mother has not yet given up—looking at father and daughter. She is hoping for an answer from both of them. The daughter does not give in, leaves home and goes away.

Card 4. "A woman is clutching the shoulders of a man whose face and body are averted as if he were trying to pull away from her." There is also a hazy image of another woman in the background, not mentioned in the standard description in the manual.

Henry (5) feels that "attitudes toward heterosexual relationship are . . . of course the central issue of importance in this card." "Refusal to see the sexual implications of this picture," according to Wittenborn (15), "is particularly indicative of a type of immature psychosexual adjustment common in young men."

Some differences in the nature of the main characters portrayed may be noted. Ninety-five per cent of the non-Kibbutz stories specify the relationship of the man and the woman as "married" or "in love." This is true to a lesser degree in the Kibbutz stories, of which 70 per cent delineate this relationship, but 30 per cent mention no close relationship—just "a fellow and a girl." (See Table 6—part 3.)

The differences become more salient when we turn our attention to the themes involved. More than half of the non-Kibbutz stories deal with the issue of infidelity. This theme is represented to a negligible extent (10%) in the Kibbutz stories. Instead, half of the stories have aggression as their major theme, and 30 per cent deal with outright rejection of love and heterosexuality (usually male rejecting female). The "action" involved parallels closely the themes described. The following are two kinds of stories which correspond to the contrasts just discussed:

Kibbutz—Card 4. He is a worker and she is on a farm. They met after a short time that they have not seen each other. They met accidentally at the entrance to one of the movies which described prostitution. They went into the movie with their thoughts. After it is over the woman asks the man to kiss her; she sees it in the film, she sees the couples kissing each other. But, something else entirely different than joy pierces the mind of the worker. He is not joyous, but analyzes and thinks about the problems in the movie—the problem of unemployed workers who find their satisfaction by going to houses of ill fame. Can that go on for long? No—I will change the situation. I will unite the workers around the condition of their brethren. I will bring out workers full of consciousness among them.

Non-Kibbutz—Card 4. In this picture the man

is seen between the arms of his wife and the arms of sin. We see him at home.

When he got married he considered himself happy and loved his wife very much; but, accidentally, on one occasion he met a dancer in a cheap club; she attracted him and he fell in love with her. His wife, who felt that something is the matter, tried to stop him and he, still in love with her, did not know what to decide. In the picture we see them together; he wants to go and meet the other one and his wife is holding him back. We see the prostitute in the background, the one he fell in love with, as if she is coming out of his head. It is impossible to know what he will decide.

The major trends elicited from the TAT stories may now be pulled together. The Kibbutz adolescents appear to be less achievement oriented and less motivated. Their stories tend to be less populated with family-related characters. They also see less conflict between the parents and their children. There is also a greater tendency to reject heterosexuality altogether and also not to see infidelity as a possible problem.

Perhaps important sex differences may also be gleaned from these data. However, this will take us too far afield. We shall address ourselves to this issue on another occasion.

COMMENT

We shall attempt to gather the several strands of evidence and try to integrate them, see their dynamic interrelationship and relate the differences that have evolved from the material to known differences in the experiences of the two groups of adolescents.

We may note, especially from the Rorschach data, that there are no marked differences between the groups with respect to over-all "adjustment." There are a few deviant and tense individuals in both groups, but the over-all picture with respect to what we might infer as ego development is essentially the same for the vast majorities of Kibbutz and non-Kibbutz adolescents. The evidence points to a greater degree of spontaneity (productivity on Rorschach and TAT; first reaction times) in the Kibbutz group. Moreover, there is also some justification for rating the Kibbutz adolescents somewhat higher on the continuum of intellectual development. The quality of the Kibbutz *Mosad* (high school) and the relatively sophisticated intellectual atmosphere in most Kibbutzim must be in part responsible for this fact.

Two problems which are part of the *Sturm und Drang* period of adolescence have been stressed by various authors (1, 14)—heterosexuality and independence or emancipation. With respect to the first problem, we note a fairly consistent puritanical trend in the Kibbutz group. Whether it is immaturity or suppression is a question not easily settled. There are three sources of information that may be considered. In the first place there is some evidence of the lesser oedipal intensity in Kibbutz children (10); also, that little emphasis on sexual segregation is placed in Kibbutz rearing—boys and girls sleep in the same rooms, take showers together, etc. Finally, with all that, there are fairly rigid rules involving adult disapproval and group ostracism with respect to sex play and premarital sexual intercourse. Thus, there is relatively little of the sexual curiosity noted in adolescents who are not brought up in the Kibbutz (14); less of it is involved in the fantasy of the Kibbutz adolescents as noted in the TAT. Fewer Kibbutz adolescents deal with love and sex in their stories of card 4. The picture has less potency·for them in this respect; thus, they include more themes of aggression and the role of the woman as the peacemaker. In most stories of Kibbutz adolescents in which heterosexuality is the major theme, rejection occurs, probably because of the cultural taboos.

Because of the relative independence of the children from their parents from the very beginning, in the Kibbutz setting, the issue of emancipation is not a crucial one. Thus, very few Kibbutz adolescents see the conflict between the generations, between agriculture and culture and education, which is noted by the majority of the non-Kibbutz respondents to card 2 of the TAT. This fact, perhaps, accounts for the tendency of the Kibbutz group to involve fewer parents and relations in their TAT stories. The parental figures are less fraught with conflict and less represented in fantasy. The relatively conscious attitudes to the parents as expressed in the Sentence Completion Test are, by and large, positive and not different from those of the control group.

In considering the data relative to goals and ambitions, two major differences between the two groups, emanating from differences in the family vis-à-vis the socioeconomic structure of the settlements, should be scrutinized. In the first place, as Eisenstadt (3) has pointed out, there is a discontinuity of roles in the Kibbutz rearing process from childhood to adulthood. By that is meant that until the child becomes eligible for membership in the Kibbutz (following graduation from high school) he virtually has no economic responsibilities. Whatever work he does is primarily educational—not "work" in the economic sense of the adult. Thus, in this respect there is a discontinuity in roles in the Kibbutz as contrasted with the continuity in the role of the village child who begins to participate in the adult economic workaday world at a relatively young age.

Another relevant difference is that Kibbutz education is geared toward perpetuation of the Kibbutz, i.e., membership in it. This means general personality attributes, but no specific occupational specialization or achievement in the broader "outside" world. This is in contrast with the village child who is reared in the tradition of "rugged individualism" and is preparing for a competitive society.

Bearing these points in mind, the contrast between the groups regarding ambitions, goals, and future perspective becomes readily understood. The high emphasis on play in the Rorschach movement content, less emphasis on long-range goals and specific occupational aspirations reflected in the sentence completion material, and the low incidence of themes of ambition and motivation in response to TAT card 1, are all characteristics of the Kibbutz sample which converge on the same point. It involves a shortening of the future perspective as a personal outlook, for the longer future perspective is dependent primarily on the social context and structure, on the peer group, on the collectivity as a whole—the Kibbutz.

If we were to attempt the delineation of a composite picture of the Kibbutz adolescent, we could state that he has an adequately developed ego, is probably above average in intelligence, and is on fairly good terms with his parents, who, however, do not figure importantly in his fantasy, and with whom he is in relatively little conflict. He is relatively less concerned with heterosexuality than the non-Kibbutz age peers and consciously accepts the taboos of his society upon premarital or premature sex play and sexual intercourse. He is not very ambitious or achievement oriented in the world of occupations; in this respect his childhood is prolonged. His goals are not very specific, for they do not require precise definition by the society, and for the social structure, which he expects and is expected to perpetuate.

SUMMARY

In an attempt to tease out some of the psychological differences between Kibbutz-reared adolescents and adolescents (controls) reared in the conventional family and social setting, three projected techniques (Rorschach, Sentence Completion and TAT) were administered to two parallel groups of 17-year-olds. From the data presented, it was concluded that the Kibbutz adolescent is at least as well adjusted as his non-Kibbutz counterpart; there is some evidence that he is more spontaneous and at least as intelligent. The Kibbutz adolescent does not seem to differ from the control with respect to positiveness of attitude to parents; also, he tends to be less in conflict with them and to involve them less in his fantasy productions. He is more rigidly concerned with taboos on premarital sexuality, less self-motivated and less "ambitious" in our conventional sense.

The results were discussed and related to differences in life experience, stemming from differences in the social structure, to which the two groups have been exposed.

REFERENCES

1. AUSUBEL, D. P. *Theory and Problems of Adolescent Development.* New York: Grune & Stratton, 1954.

2. DAVIDSON, HELEN H. *A Measure of Adjustment Obtained from the Rorschach Protocol.* J. Proj. Tech., 14: 31-38, 1950.

3. EISENSTADT, S. N. *Studies in Social Structure: I. Age Groups and Social Structure—A Comparison of Some Aspects of Socialization in the Cooperative and Communal Settlements in Israel.* Jerusalem, April, 1950.

4. ERON, L. D. *A Normative Study of the Thematic Apperception Test.* Psychol. Monogr., 64: No. 9, 1950.

5. HENRY, W. E. *The Analysis of Fantasy.* New York: Wiley, 1956.

6. KAPLAN, B. A. *A Study of Rorschach Responses in Four Cultures.* Papers of the Peabody Museum, 42: 2, 3-44, 1954.

7. MURRAY, H. A. *Thematic Apperception Test Manual.* Cambridge, Mass.: Harvard Univ. Press, 1943.

8. RABIN, A. I. *Personality Maturity of Kibbutz (Israeli Collective Settlement) and Non-Kibbutz Children as Reflected in Rorschach Findings.* J. Proj. Tech., 21: 148-153, 1957.

9. ———. *Infants and Children Under Conditions of "Intermittent" Mothering in the Kibbutz.* Am. J. Orthopsychiatry, 28: 577-586, 1958.

10. _____. *Some Psychosexual Differences between Kibbutz and Non-Kibbutz Israeli Boys.* J. Proj. Tech., 22: 328-332, 1958.

11. _____. *Attitudes of Kibbutz Children to Family and Parents.* Am. J. Orthopsychiatry, 29: 172-179, 1959.

12. ROSENZWEIG, S., and EDITH FLEMING. *Apperceptive Norms for the Thematic Apperception Test II. An Empirical Investigation.* J. Pers., 17: 483-503, 1949.

13. SACKS, J. M., and S. LEVY. "The Sentence Completion Test," in *Projective Psychology* (L. E. Abt and L. Bellak, Eds.), pp. 357-402. New York: Knopf, 1950.

14. SPIRO, M. E. *Children of the Kibbutz.* Cambridge, Mass.: Harvard Univ. Press, 1958.

15. WITTENBORN, J. R. *Some Thematic Apperception Test Norms and a Note on the Use of the Test Cards in Guidance of College Students.* J. Clin. Psychol., 5: 157-161, 1949.

36/REGIONAL DIFFERENCES IN ANTI-NEGRO PREJUDICE[1]/ THOMAS F. PETTIGREW*

ABUNDANT EVIDENCE HAS BEEN ADvanced in support of the widespread belief that white Southerners are typically more prejudiced against Negroes than are whites in the North (Hyman & Sheatsley, 1956; Myrdal, 1944; Prothro, 1952; Samelson, 1945; Sims & Patrick, 1936; Stouffer, Suchman, DeVinney, Star, & Williams, 1949). But does this heightened hostility represent (a) more externalizing personality potential for prejudice among Southerners,[2] (b) the effects of different cultural norms and pressures, or (c) both of these?

Virtually no work has been focused specifically on this question, but the scant, indirect evidence available suggests that sociocultural and social adjustment factors—not externalizing personality factors—may be the crucial correlates of the stronger anti-Negro attitudes of most Southerners. Roper (1946, 1947), for example, twice found the South to be one of the least anti-Semitic regions in the nation, and Prothro (1952) noted that two-fifths of his white adult Louisiana sample harbored intensely unfavorable attitudes toward Negroes together with favorable attitudes toward Jews. Yet if such externalization variables as authoritarianism

[1] The author wishes to express his appreciation to Gordon W. Allport for his encouragement and advice, to Herbert C. Kelman for his theoretical and editorial suggestions, and to Charles LaMonte for his interviewing assistance. The project was supported by a grant from the Laboratory of Social Relations of Harvard University.

[2] "Externalizing personality potential" refers to one of the three functions of attitudes delineated by Smith, Bruner, and White (1956): externalization, social adjustment, and object appraisal. "Externalization occurs when an individual, often responding unconsciously, senses an analogy between a perceived environmental event and some unresolved inner problem . . . [and] adopts an attitude . . . which is a transformed version of his way of dealing with his inner difficulty." Attitudes can play a social adjustment role by contributing to the individual's identification with, or differentiation from, various reference groups. And attitudes can serve an object appraisal function by aiding in the process of understanding "reality" as it is defined by the culture.

* Thomas F. Pettigrew, Regional differences in anti-Negro prejudice, *Journal of Abnormal and Social Psychology*, 1959, 59, 28-36. Reprinted by permission.

were the crux of the problem, the South would be highly anti-Semitic as well as anti-Negro, and Southerners who are prejudiced against Negroes would be typically prejudiced against Jews too.

Furthermore, the prejudice-prone personality supposedly arises from a family pattern marked by harsh domineering parents who reveal little understanding of and affection for their children. (Adorno, Frenkel-Brunswik, Levinson, & Sanford, 1950; Harris, Gough, & Martin, 1950.) There is no evidence, however, that such a family pattern is more prevalent in the South than in the North (Davis, Gardner, & Gardner, 1941; Dollard, 1937). Thus it is not surprising that the few white Southern samples that have been administered the F scale have yielded means that fall well within the range of means reported for non-southern groups by the California investigators. (Adorno et al., 1950; Milton, 1952; Smith & Prothro, 1957.)[3]

Prothro (1954) has summed it up. "The small amount of evidence already available in the South suggests that factors other than personality type enter into the 'American dilemma.' But here again the need is for more research below the Mason-Dixon line."

The present research is an investigation into anti-Negro prejudice in the southern and northern United States, using identical instruments on comparable groups in the two regions. The study focuses upon the following central hypothesis: *The anti-Negro prejudice complex of the South is more related to sociocultural and social adjustment factors and less related to externalizing personality factors than in the North.* Specific hypotheses derived from this basic hypothesis are presented together with the results that pertain to them.

METHOD

During the summer of 1955, two experienced interviewers employed standard public opinion polling techniques in eight towns varying in population from 4,000 to 14,000, four in each region. The white adult respondents were selected by simple random procedures from recently published town directories. Seventy-four per cent of the original sample was located, and of these only 8% refused to be interviewed. The final sample's 186 Southerners were slightly younger, slightly less educated, and more often native born than the 180 Northerners polled

—all differences existing between the regions taken as wholes.

The eight communities were not chosen randomly. Since all of them had new directories, they were probably more prosperous and industrial than average. In addition, the southern localities, located in North Carolina and Georgia, were selected to have Negro population ratios ranging from 10–45%. The northern towns, all located in New England, each had less than 1% Negroes.

The interview schedule contained three Likert scales. A 10-item instrument of authoritarianism (F scale), an 8-item scale of anti-Semitism (A-S scale), and a 12-item measure of anti-Negro prejudice (N scale) were presented both orally and on cards interspersed among numerous filler items concerning mass media participation and background questions. The poll purported to be concerned with the effects of the mass media on public opinion, and it seemed largely due to this guise that the blatantly phrased prejudice statements caused no interview break-offs. Background items ascertained not only age, educational level, and occupation, but also political party identification, military service, father's occupation, and church affiliation and attendance.

The F, A-S, and four items of the N scale were drawn from the investigations of the authoritarian personality.[4] These measures produced with the present sample adequate Spearman-Brown corrected split-half reliabilities of + .86, + .82, and + .88 respectively. The A-S and N scales were further divided into "stereotyped-belief" (s-b) and "exclusion-discrimination" (e-d) subscales. A typical stereotyped-belief N statement is, "Most Negroes are happy-go-lucky and irresponsible," and a typical exclusion-discrimination N item is "Most Negroes scarcely deserve the right to vote."

RESULTS

TESTS OF THE SPECIFIC HYPOTHESES. The first hypothesis was that more anti-Negro prejudice—both stereotyped-belief and exclusion-discrimination aspects—exists in the southern sample. Table 1 shows that this prediction is supported at a high level of significance. The Southerners' opinions contrast most sharply with those of the Northerners on the exclusion-discrimination statements. Item analyses indicate that all 12 N items separate the two regions at the .001 level, but the two most discriminating items deal explicitly with racial segregation.[5]

[3] If one stretches his definition of the South to include Oklahoma (and the author does not), then Christie and Garcia's (1951) study becomes the lone exception to this statement.

[4] The California statements used are: for the F scale, Items 1, 8, 13, 18, 21, 26, 27, 31, 37, and 42 on pages 255-57; for the A-S scale, Items 3, 4, 13, 15, 22, and 24 on pages 68-69, and Items 4 and 15 on page 70; and for the N scale, Items 8, 31, and 34 on page 105, and Item 14 on page 117 (Adorno et al., 1950).

[5] Detailed analyses of six of these N scale items together with the results of specific questions concerning school desegregation asked in this same study have been published previously (Pettigrew, 1957).

TABLE 1 / REGIONAL DIFFERENCES IN ANTI-NEGRO PREJUDICE AND AUTHORITARIANISM.[a]

SCALE	NORTHERN SAMPLE		SOUTHERN SAMPLE		t	p
	MEAN	SD	MEAN	SD		
Total N scale	4.49	1.54	6.64	1.93	+11.81	<.001
Ns-b subscale	5.07	1.47	6.88	1.91	+10.11	<.001
Ne-d subscale	3.90	1.69	6.28	1.99	+12.40	<.001
F scale	6.18	1.46	6.19	1.96	.05	n.s.

[a] Scale scores can vary between 0 and 10. They were calculated on the basis of +4 for agree strongly, +3 for agree, +2 for undecided, +1 for disagree, and 0 for disagree strongly for each item, and then the total scale scores were collapsed into 11 categories for machine analysis. Thus, the higher the score, the greater is the amount of prejudice or authoritarianism.

No difference was predicted to occur between the regions in F scale means. As we see in Table 1, virtually no difference does result.[6] Though considerably more anti-Negro, the southern sample is not more authoritarian in orientation.

The third hypothesis predicted that there would be a closer relationship between the Ne-d and Ns-b subscales in the South than in the North. A difference appears in the expected direction, but does not quite attain statistical significance. Ne-d and Ns-b correlate + .617 in the northern sample and + .711 in the southern sample ($p < .06$), but some difference might have been expected in this direction simply because of the larger variance in the southern data (Table 1).

Following directly from the central hypothesis was the prediction that when education and age are held constant, the relationship between authoritarianism and anti-Negro prejudice is closer in the North than in the South.[7] Table 2 summarizes the relevant data. The results do not support the hypothesis, but rather indicate that F and N correlate to similar degrees in both regions.[8] The slightly higher southern correla-

[6] With a different scoring system used, these F scale means are not directly comparable to those published by Adorno et al (1950).

[7] Education and age must be controlled in such relationships, because they have been shown to be correlates not only of prejudice (Allport, 1954; Harding, Kutner, Proshansky, & Chein, 1954; Hyman & Sheatsley, 1956) but also of authoritarianism (Christie, 1954; MacKinnon & Centers, 1956).

[8] Bass (1955), Christie, Havel, and Seidenberg (1958), and others have shown that item form contributes in part to the correlations between such unidirectional Likert scales as those used in this study. Part of this form variance is probably eliminated from the present relationships with the partialling out of both age and education. In any case, the present concern is the difference between the correlations of the two regions and not their absolute magnitudes.

tions again probably reflect the restricted variances of the northern sample on both the N and F scales (Table 1).

Another specific hypothesis deals with the generalization of prejudice in the two regions, a phenomenon typical of ethnocentric personalities (Adorno et al., 1950; Allport, 1954; Harding, Kutner, Proshansky, & Chein, 1954; Hartley, 1946). With age and education partialled out again, anti-Semitism and anti-Negro prejudices were expected to correlate more highly in the North than in the South. Table 3 reveals that again there are no differences between the regions. Externalization factors, as measured by both the F and A-S scales, appear to operate in similar ways in the North and South.[9]

The final hypothesis concerns sex differences in prejudice. On the assumption that women, the "carriers of culture," reflect the mores more directly than men, it was predicted that females would be more anti-Negro than men in the South, but not in the North. The results of Table 4 lend support to these expectations. No significant differences appear between the sexes in the North—though females tend to be slightly more prejudiced. In the South, as predicted, women are considerably more anti-Negro than men, particularly in an exclusion-discriminatory manner. Item analyses indicate that the three N statements significantly separating the sexes in the South are all e-d items. Southern women in the sample oppose the equal voting, employment, and educational rights of Negroes more than southern men in the sample. Not all of these sex differences in the South can be attributed to southern mores, however; Table 4 shows that on the F scale females received significantly higher scores than males in the South.

FURTHER ANALYSES OF THE DATA. In order to test the importance of sociocultural and social adjustment factors in the two regions, matched pair designs controlling for education and age (and usually sex) were employed with a number of social variables.[10] Political party identification, military service, church attendance, and social mobility were all analyzed for their effects on N, F, and A-S scores to learn if these factors are more important in the South than in the North.

[9] Correlations between the N and A-S scales are considered as evidence for the externalizing aspect of prejudice because only anti-Negro attitudes are positively sanctioned by southern culture (Roper: 1946, 1947). Thus for a southerner to be intolerant of both Negroes and Jews strongly suggests that these attitudes serve largely a function of externalization—not of social adjustment—for him.

[10] All matches were made with a tolerance of one year in formal education completed and of five years in chronological age. When more than one respondent could be matched in a pair, the one used was selected randomly.

TABLE 2 / CORRELATIONS BETWEEN ANTI-NEGRO PREJUDICE AND AUTHORITARIANISM WITH AGE AND EDUCATION HELD CONSTANT.[a]

VARIABLES	NORTHERN SAMPLE	SOUTHERN SAMPLE	z	p
Total N scale and F scale	+.27	+.34	0.73	n.s.
Ns-b subscale and F scale	+.29	+.29	0.00	–
Ne-d subscale and F scale	+.25	+.35	1.05	n.s.

[a] All six of these partial correlations are significantly different from zero correlation at better than the .01 level.

Table 5 presents the political identification results for 62 northern pairs and 36 southern pairs matched for education and age. No significant differences are found on the N, F, and A-S scales between northern respondents who identify themselves as independents rather than as Democrats or Republicans. In the South, however, the political independents are considerably more tolerant of Negroes than party identifiers. This difference is not a function of sex, since the 28 same-sex pairs also provide a discrepancy attaining the same level of significance. The southern pairs also tend to differ on the F and A-S scales—independents being somewhat less authoritarian and anti-Jewish.

Male veterans during or since World War II were matched on age and education with male nonveterans and yielded the results provided in Table 6. While veterans in both of the regional samples show a slight tendency to be more authoritarian, the southern veterans are markedly less anti-Negro than other southern males. By contrast, the northern veterans are somewhat more intolerant of Negroes than other northern males.

Respondents who had attended church within the week were matched on education and age with others

TABLE 3 / CORRELATIONS BETWEEN ANTI-SEMITISM AND ANTI-NEGRO PREJUDICE WITH AGE AND EDUCATION HELD CONSTANT.[a]

VARIABLES	NORTHERN SAMPLE	SOUTHERN SAMPLE	z	p
Total A-S scale and N scale	+.55	+.58	0.42	n.s.
A-Ss-b subscale and N scale	+.49	+.52	0.37	n.s.
A-Se-d subscale and N scale	+.51	+.47	0.50	n.s.

[a] All six of these partial correlations are significantly different from zero correlation at better than the .001 level.

TABLE 4 / SEX DIFFERENCES IN ANTI-NEGRO PREJUDICE AND AUTHORITARIANISM.

SCALE	MEANS		t	p
	FE-MALES	MALES		
NORTHERN SAMPLE				
Total N scale	4.56	4.41	0.65	n.s.
Ns-b subscale	5.09	5.06	0.15	n.s.
Ne-d subscale	4.03	3.76	1.20	n.s.
F scale	6.28	6.08	0.92	n.s.
SOUTHERN SAMPLE				
Total N scale	6.83	6.43	1.42	<.08
Ns-b subscale	7.00	6.74	0.93	n.s.
Ne-d subscale	6.55	5.96	2.03	<.03
F scale	6.47	5.98	2.09	<.05[*]

[*] Unlike the one-tailed tests for the predicted N scale differences, this F scale test employed a two-tailed test of significance.

who had not attended church within the month. Table 7 shows that no differences occur between these groups in the North, but church attenders in the southern pairs tend to be significantly more anti-Negro and authoritarian than nonattenders. These differences hold up when only the results for same-sex pairs are considered.

Previous research by Chein (Harding et al., 1954) having suggested the necessity of holding separate the major religious groupings to understand the rela-

TABLE 5 / POLITICAL PARTY IDENTIFICATION AND SCALE SCORES.[a]

SCALE	MEANS		t	p
	INDE-PENDENTS	IDEN-TIFIERS		
NORTHERN SAMPLE[b]				
Total N scale	4.26	4.37	0.44	n.s.
F scale	5.90	6.08	0.77	n.s.
Total A-S scale	3.92	3.92	0.00	–
SOUTHERN SAMPLE[c]				
Total N scale	5.67	7.11	4.54	<.001[*]
F scale	5.44	5.92	1.46	<.20
Total A-S scale	3.17	3.86	1.79	<.10

[a] A political identifier is a respondent who considers himself either a Democrat or Republican; an independent specifically refers to himself as such.

[b] 62 pairs matched on education and age (51 same-sex pairs).

[c] 36 pairs matched on education and age (28 same-sex pairs).

[*] This same level of significance is maintained for the 28 same-sex pairs.

TABLE 6 / MILITARY SERVICE AND SCALE SCORES.[a]

SCALE	MEANS		*t*	*p*
	VETER-ANS	NON-VETER-ANS		
NORTHERN SAMPLE[b]				
Total N scale	4.32	3.57	1.83	<.10
F scale	6.11	5.58	1.33	<.20
Total A-S scale	2.50	2.50	0.00	—
SOUTHERN SAMPLE[c]				
Total N scale	4.47	6.33	3.30	<.01
F scale	6.13	5.87	0.65	n.s.
Total A-S scale	3.53	4.33	1.52	<.20

[a] Only veterans during or since World War II were employed in these matches.

[b] 19 male pairs matched on education and age.

[c] 15 male pairs matched on education and age.

TABLE 7 / CHURCH ATTENDANCE AND SCALE SCORES.[a]

SCALE	MEANS		*t*	*p*
	ATTEND-ERS	NONAT-TENDERS		
NORTHERN SAMPLE[b]				
Total N scale	4.36	4.73	1.31	n.s.
F scale	6.31	6.09	1.09	n.s.
Total A-S scale	4.20	4.25	0.21	n.s.
SOUTHERN SAMPLE[c]				
Total N scale	7.28	6.38	2.65	<.02[d]
F scale	6.69	6.13	2.03	<.05[e]
Total A-S scale	5.28	4.69	1.47	n.s.

[a] An attender is defined as one who has been to church within the week; a nonattender has not been within the month.

[b] 55 pairs matched on education and age (50 same-sex pairs).

[c] 39 pairs matched on education and age (31 same-sex pairs).

[d] For the 31 same-sex pairs, *t* becomes 3.20 (*p* <.01).

[e] For the 31 same-sex pairs, *p* remains at the same level.

TABLE 8 / NORTHERN CHURCH ATTENDANCE BY RELIGION AND SCALE SCORES.[a]

SCALE	MEANS		*t*	*p*
	ATTEND-ERS	NONAT-TENDERS		
PROTESTANTS[b]				
Total N scale	4.05	5.19	3.16	<.01[c]
F scale	5.62	6.10	1.03	n.s.
Total A-S scale	2.95	3.33	0.74	n.s.
CATHOLICS[d]				
Total N scale	4.38	4.00	0.74	n.s.
F scale	6.62	6.54	0.17	n.s.
Total A-S scale	3.62	2.92	0.97	n.s.

[a] An attender is defined as one who has been to church within the month; a nonattender has not been within the month.

[b] 21 pairs matched on education and age (12 same-sex pairs).

[c] For the 12 same-sex pairs, *t* becomes 2.39 (*p* <.05).

[d] 13 pairs matched on education, age, and sex.

TABLE 9 / DOWNWARD MOBILITY AND SCALE SCORES.[a]

SCALE	MEANS		*t*	*p*
	DOWN-WARDS	STA-BLES		
NORTHERN SAMPLE[b]				
Total N scale	6.20	4.50	2.62	<.05
F scale	6.00	6.50	1.25	n.s.
Total A-S scale	4.30	2.80	1.72	<.15
SOUTHERN SAMPLE[c]				
Total N scale	3.57	6.42	6.67	<.001
F scale	6.14	6.14	0.00	—
Total A-S scale	2.17	3.67	1.77	<.20

[a] Downwardly mobile individuals have a manual occupation, but their fathers held a nonmanual occupation; stable workers also hold a manual job, but their fathers held manual jobs too.

[b] 10 pairs matched on education and age (8 same-sex pairs).

[c] 7 pairs matched on education and age (6 same-sex pairs).

tionship between church attendance and anti-Negro attitudes, separate analyses were made of the Catholic and Protestant groups in the North. A redefinition of church attender was necessary for these tests; attenders within the month were compared with nonattenders within the month. The small number of Jews in both regional samples and of Catholics in the southern sample made further analyses impractical.

Table 8 shows that when age and education are controlled the northern Protestant attenders are con-siderably more tolerant of the Negro than nonattend-ers, but they are not significantly less anti-Semitic or authoritarian. No differences appear between the Catholic attending and nonattending pairs.

Following Greenblum and Pearlin (1953), mobil-ity was defined in terms of generational shifts be-tween manual and nonmanual occupations. Thus downward mobility is recorded when a respondent reports that he (or her husband) holds a manual occupation when his father held a nonmanual job.

TABLE 10 / UPWARD MOBILITY AND SCALE SCORES.[a]

SCALE	MEANS		t	p
	UP-WARDS	STA-BLES		
NORTHERN SAMPLE[b]				
Total N scale	4.20	4.07	0.31	n.s.
F scale	6.13	6.19	0.09	n.s.
Total A-S scale	3.29	3.36	0.15	n.s.
SOUTHERN SAMPLE[c]				
Total N scale	5.75	5.18	1.59	<.20
F scale	5.93	5.71	0.51	n.s.
Total A-S scale	3.68	3.32	0.86	n.s.

[a] Upwardly mobile individuals have a nonmanual occupation, but their fathers held a manual occupation; stable nonmanual respondents also hold nonmanual jobs, but their fathers held nonmanual jobs too.

[b] 15 pairs matched on education, age, and sex.

[c] 28 pairs matched on education, age, and sex.

With matches on age and education again, the comparisons between the downwardly mobile and the stable manual workers (whose fathers were also manual workers) can be seen in Table 9. As noted in previous research (Bettelheim & Janowitz, 1950; Greenblum & Pearlin, 1953), the downwardly mobile in the northern sample tend to be both more anti-Negro and anti-Semitic—though not more authoritarian. With the few southern pairs, however, this trend is reversed. Equal on F scale means, the stable manual workers are more prejudiced—particularly against the Negro—than the downwardly mobile in the southern sample.

The upwardly mobile are compared with stable nonmanual respondents in Table 10. With age and education controlled, the only difference approaching significance involves upward mobility in the South. Southerners in the sample with nonmanual employment whose fathers had held manual employment tend to be slightly more anti-Negro than other nonmanual Southerners.

Matched pair designs were not necessary to test the effects of two additional social variables: education and the Negro-white ratio of a community. Education proves to be a potent factor in southern attitudes toward the Negro. The results in Table 11 indicate that education correlates more highly with the N scales—particularly the stereotyped-belief subscale—among the southern interviewees. That this higher correlation is not largely a function of differential variance in the two regional samples (Table 1) is suggested by the relationships between education and the F and A-S measures. Though these scales also have larger SDs in the South than in the North, they do not relate to education in the manner that the N scales do: F and education are associated to a similar degree in the two regions and

A-S and education are somewhat more closely associated in the North than in the South.

The final variable tested is the percentage of Negroes living in a southern community. Table 12 shows the discrepancies in scale scores between the two low ratio areas polled in the South (10 and 18% Negroes) and the two high ratio areas (38 and 45% Negroes). Though not different in either authoritarianism or anti-Semitism, the respondents in the high Negro percentage localities are significantly more anti-Negro—particularly in their exclusion-discriminatory attitudes.

TABLE 11 / CORRELATIONS BETWEEN EDUCATION, PREJUDICE, AND AUTHORITARIANISM.[a]

VARIABLES	NORTH-ERN SAMPLE	SOUTH-ERN SAMPLE	z	p
Total N scale and education	− .30	− .47	1.90	<.06
Ns-b subscale and education	− .26	− .51	2.81	<.01
Ne-d subscale and education	− .31	− .47	1.80	<.08
F scale and education	− .38	− .45	0.80	n.s.
Total A-S scale and education	− .40	− .26	1.49	<.15

[a] These product-moment correlations were developed by measuring education in terms of years of formal schooling completed. All significance levels are based on two-tailed tests.

TABLE 12 / NEGRO RATIO AND SOUTHERN SCALE SCORES.[a]

SCALE	MEANS		t	p
	LOW RATIO SOUTHERN TOWNS	HIGH RATIO SOUTHERN TOWNS		
Total N scale	6.25	6.97	2.95	<.01
Ns-b subscale	6.54	7.16	2.21	<.03
Ne-d subscale	5.86	6.63	2.78	<.01
F scale	6.15	6.23	0.31	n.s.
Total A-S scale	3.82	3.68	0.50	n.s.

[a] The two low ratio towns have 10% and 18% Negroes respectively; the two high ratio towns have 38% and 45% Negroes respectively. All significance tests are based on two-tailed tests.

DISCUSSION

The central hypothesis of the study consists of two parts: (a) the increased importance of sociocultural and social adjustment factors and (b) the decreased importance of externalization factors in southern compared to northern attitudes toward the Negro. The first of these predictions is supported by the data, the second must be modified. Social variables are more significant in the South, but such an externalization variable as authoritarianism is equally relevant in both regions for the samples polled.

SOCIOCULTURAL AND SOCIAL ADJUSTMENT FACTORS AND ANTI-NEGRO PREJUDICE. The anti-Negro norms of the South are reflected on the personality level in social conformity. The maintenance of negative attitudes toward Negroes becomes a mechanism of social adjustment for the white Southerner. And, as the data indicate, conformity is associated with intolerance, deviance with tolerance.

Conformity. Four types of southern respondents, whose positions in the social structure should be associated with conformity to the culture's dictates, proved to be more intolerant of Negroes than their counterparts: females, political party identifiers, church attenders, and the upwardly mobile.

Though the females score higher on F, cultural factors are also important in the southern sex discrepancy in prejudice (Table 4). Women are more comforming to the norms and expectations of the culture than men. Thus, in the present data, they are more faithful attenders of church than men, behavior that meets the demands of small-town life. Moreover, the sharpest sex divergence in the South occurs on the e-d subscale of the N—the same subscale that distinguishes best between the total northern and southern samples (Table 1) and between the low and high Negro ratio communities in the South (Table 12). Southern women therefore reflect that aspect of anti-Negro feeling that is more characteristic of the southern region as a whole and of the intensely anti-Negro areas of the South in particular. No significant sex differences appear in the North, where the women conform to a culture that allows greater tolerance of Negroes.

The intolerance of political party identifiers in the South is further evidence of the power of southern mores (Table 5). In a small southern town, where politics is everybody's game, identifying with a major political party is—at least in part—conforming, and steadfastly remaining an independent is deviating from the norm.[11] Conformity in the political realm, then, is related to

conformity in the ideological realm. And again the North has no such difference.

The greater prejudice of southern churchgoers serves partly an externalization function—as indicated by their higher F scores—and partly a social adjustment function (Table 7). Going to church in a small town in the "Bible Belt" South is definitely conforming to community norms; and these norms also definitively prescribe attitudes toward Negroes. By contrast, Protestant attendance in the North is related to tolerance (Table 8).

The upwardly mobile form another group of conformers. Forced to be keenly attuned to their culture's dominant ideologies in their successful climb up the social ladder, these Southerners tend to be more prejudiced against Negroes than their nonmanual colleagues (Table 10). No such difference occurs in the northern data.

Cultural deviance. It is a common finding of research on prejudice in Western society that unconventional people have a tendency to be tolerant of out-groups. This relationship is particularly evident in the southern data. Several types of deviants have been discussed as the opposites of conformers—political independents and nonattenders of church. Other potential deviants are the downwardly mobile, veterans, and the highly educated.

As in other northern studies (Greenblum & Pearlin, 1953; Bettelheim & Janowitz, 1950), downward mobility is positively related with bigotry in the northern sample (Table 9). But a striking reversal occurs in the southern sample. Perhaps in a region that emphasizes status and family background, that draws a sharp distinction between "poor whites" and "respectable whites," and that cherishes its aristocratic traditions (Cash, 1941; Davis et al., 1941; Dollard, 1937), the downwardly mobile Southerner learns to reject much of his culture. And rejecting the culture's stress on status and tradition makes it easier to reject also the culture's dictates concerning the Negro.

The tendency of northern veterans to be somewhat more hostile toward Negroes than northern nonveterans is perhaps due to the introduction to southern culture that many of them received while training in one of the numerous military installations in the South (Table 6). On the other hand, southern veterans have experienced in the service their first equal status contact with Negroes and their first exposure to nonsouthern ways of life. And, with the culture's hold on them loosened, these veterans' Negro attitudes tend to change.

---

[11] Being a Republican in these southern communities is not as deviant as one might imagine. Three of the four southern towns polled have favored some Republican candidates in recent elections.

Like the southern veterans, the highly educated in the South have had the opportunity to encounter nonsouthern ideas and values. Thus, while education is an important negative correlate of prejudice in the North, it becomes unusually crucial in the South (Table 11).

Negro ratio. These consistent social relationships in the southern data have been interpreted in terms of conformity and deviance from the narrowly prescribed mores of small town southern life. A final finding provides further evidence for such an analysis. Not only are Southerners living in low Negro ratio towns significantly more tolerant of the Negro than Southerners living in high ratio towns, but there are no externalization differences between them (Table 12). That is, their F and A-S scores are not different. Moreover, they differ most on the e-d subscale of the N—the same subscale that most clearly distinguishes the two regional samples as wholes (Table 1).

EXTERNALIZING PERSONALITY FACTORS AND ANTI-NEGRO PREJUDICE. The differences between the regional samples in attitude toward the Negro cannot be explained in terms of differences in externalizing personality potential for prejudice; their F scale means are quite similar (Table 1). And, contrary to the central hypothesis, externalization factors as indexed by F scores are of equal importance in the anti-Negro attitudes of the northern and southern respondents. The correlations in the two regions between the N scale and either the F scale (Table 2) or the A-S scale (Table 3) do not differ significantly.

These results indicate the existence in the South of a large number of culturally intolerant individuals who subscribe to the typical regional attitudes concerning the Negro but who are not authoritarians. As the South's norms regarding the Negro continue to change, these *latent liberals* can be expected to mirror these changes in their own attitudes.

SUMMARY AND CONCLUSIONS

Public opinion polling techniques were employed with 366 randomly selected respondents in eight roughly matched communities in the North and South to investigate anti-Negro prejudice. The restricted nature of the small town samples limits their generality, but the tentative results offer a broad hypothesis for more representative future research: *in anti-Negro prejudice, externalizing personality findings are of equal importance in the North and South, and sociocultural and social adjustment factors are considerably more important in the South and account for the sharp differences in the regions.*

The hypothesis has several implications for prejudice theory. Areas like the South with heightened prejudice against a particular outgroup should not necessarily be thought of as harboring more authoritarianism; the special conflict may represent the operation of particular historical, cultural, and social factors. Indeed, this type of analysis has already been applied to the Union of South Africa (Pettigrew, 1958).

A second implication concerns the current racial desegregation process. The success of this movement in the South, this hypothesis contends, does not depend on changing the deeply ingrained orientations of authoritarian personalities; rather, it rests on the effectiveness with which racial integration now going on in the South can restructure the mores to which many latent liberal Southerners conform.

A final implication involves the role of psychological analysis in the study of prejudice. While psychological work has concentrated almost entirely on the externalization function of prejudice (e.g., the frustration-aggression and the authoritarian personality research), the social adjustment function of prejudice is paramount in the South. This does not mean, as Rose (1956) has argued, that the psychological approach is of little value in explaining the heightened intolerance of the South. Rather, this hypothesis suggests that future advances in the psychology of prejudice will come when the direct personality concomitants of cultural pressures are isolated and better understood.

REFERENCES

ADORNO, T. W., FRENKEL-BRUNSWIK, ELSE, LEVINSON, D. J., and SANFORD, N. *The authoritarian personality.* New York: Harper, 1950.

ALLPORT, G. W. *The nature of prejudice.* Cambridge, Mass.: Addison-Wesley, 1954.

BASS, B. M. Authoritarianism or acquiescence? *J. abnorm. soc. Psychol.,* 1955, 51, 616-623.

BETTELHEIM, B., and JANOWITZ, M. *Dynamics of prejudice.* New York: Harper, 1950.

CASH, W. J. *The mind of the South.* New York: Knopf, 1941.

CHRISTIE, R. Authoritarianism re-examined. In R. Christie and Marie Jahoda (Eds.), *Studies in the scope and method of "The authoritarian personality."* Glencoe, Ill.: Free Press, 1954.

CHRISTIE, R., and GARCIA, J. Subcultural variation in authoritarian personality. *J. abnorm. soc. Psychol.*, 1951, *46*, 457-469.

CHRISTIE, R., HAVEL, J., and SEIDENBERG, B. Is the F scale irreversible? *J. abnorm. soc. Psychol.*, 1958, *56*, 143-159.

DAVIS, A., GARDNER, B., and GARDNER, MARY. *Deep South*. Chicago: Univer. Chicago Press, 1941.

DOLLARD, J. *Caste and class in a southern town*. New Haven: Yale Univer. Press, 1937.

GREENBLUM, J., and PEARLIN, L. I. Vertical mobility and prejudice: A socio-psychological analysis. In R. Bendix and S. M. Lipset (Eds.), *Class, status and power*. Glencoe, Ill.: Free Press, 1953.

HARDING, J., KUTNER, B., PROSHANSKY, H., and CHIEN, I. Prejudice and ethnic relations. In G. Lindzey (Ed.), *The handbook of social psychology*. Vol. II. Cambridge, Mass.: Addison-Wesley, 1954.

HARRIS, D. B., GOUGH, H. G., and MARTIN, W. E. Children's ethnic attitudes: II. Relationship to parental beliefs concerning child training. *Child Developm.*, 1950, *21*, 169-181.

HARTLEY, E. L. *Problems in prejudice*. New York: Kings Crown Press, 1946.

HYMAN, H. H., and SHEATSLEY, P. B. Attitudes toward desegregation. *Scient. Amer.*, 1956, *195*, 35-39.

MACKINNON, W. J., and CENTERS, R. Authoritarianism and urban stratification. *Amer. J. Sociol.*, 1956, *41*, 610-620.

MILTON, O. Presidential choice and performance on a scale of authoritarianism. *Amer. Psychologist*, 1952, *7*, 597-598.

MYRDAL, G. *An American dilemma*. New York: Harper, 1944.

PETTIGREW, T. F. Desegregation and its chances for success: Northern and southern views. *Soc. Forces*, 1957, *35*, 339-344.

PETTIGREW, T. F. Personality and sociocultural factors in intergroup attitudes. A cross-national comparison. *J. conflict Resolution*, 158, *2*, 29-42.

PROTHRO, E. T. Ethnocentrism and anti-Negro attitudes in the deep South. *J. abnorm. soc. Psychol.*, 1952, *47*, 105-108.

PROTHRO, E. T. Social psychology of the South: Challenge without response. *J. soc. Issues*, 1954, *10*, 36-43.

ROPER, E. United States anti-Semites. *Fortune*, 1946, *33*, 257-260.

ROPER, E. United States anti-Semites. *Fortune*, 1947, *36*, 5-10.

ROSE, A. M. Intergroup relations vs. prejudice: Pertinent theory for the study of social change. *Soc. Probl.*, 1956, *4*, 173-176.

SAMELSON, BABETTE. The patterning of attitudes and beliefs regarding the American Negro: An analysis of public opinion. Unpublished doctoral dissertation, Radcliffe College, 1945.

SIMS, V. M., and PATRICK, J. R. Attitude towards the Negro of northern and southern college students. *J. soc. Psychol.*, 1936, *7*, 192-204.

SMITH, C. U., and PROTHRO, J. W. Ethnic differences in authoritarian personality. *Soc. Forces*, 1957, *35*, 334-338.

SMITH, M. B., BRUNER, J. S., and WHITE, R. W. *Opinions and personality*. New York: Wiley, 1956.

STOUFFER, S. A., SUCHMAN, E. A., DEVINNEY, L. C., STAR, SHIRLEY A., and WILLIAMS, R. M., JR. *The American soldier: Adjustment during army life*. Vol. I of *Studies in social psychology in World War II*. Princeton: Princeton Univer. Press, 1949.

37/PERSONALITY AND SOCIOCULTURAL FACTORS IN INTERGROUP ATTITUDES: A CROSS-NATIONAL COMPARISON/T. F. PETTIGREW[*]

SUMMARY AND CONCLUSIONS[Ed]

Finely interwoven personality and sociocultural variables together form the foundation upon which a broad and satisfactory theory of racial prejudice must be built. Neither set of factors can be neglected, but a heuristic separation between the relatively culture-free externalization factors and social factors aids analysis. The present paper uses this distinction to interpret prejudice data from two parts of the world with tense racial conflict—the Union of South Africa and the southern United States.

Externalization factors such as authoritarianism are associated with prejudice in both the South African and the southern samples at levels roughly comparable with other areas. Data from the South African students hint, however, that susceptibility to conform may be an unusually important psychological component of prejudice in regions where the cultural norms positively sanction intolerance. In addition, there is no indication in either of these samples that there is any more externalizing personality potential for prejudice in these areas than in more tolerant parts of the globe.

The extensive racial prejudice of the South African and southern groups seems directly linked with the antiblack dictates of the two cultures. Sociocultural factors which reflect the mores consistently relate to prejudice—place of birth, political party preference, upward mobility, and ethnic-group membership in the South African data and sex, church attendance, social mobility, political party identification, armed service, and education in the southern data. The pattern is clear: conformity to South African or southern mores is associated with racial intolerance, while deviance from these mores is associated with racial tolerance.

[Ed] *Only the summary and conclusions of this full length article are presented here. They are designed as a supplement to the preceding article.*

Taken together with other published work, these limited results suggest a broad, cross-national hypothesis:

In areas with historically imbedded traditions of racial intolerance, externalizing personality factors underlying prejudice remain important, but sociocultural factors are unusually crucial and account for the heightened racial hostility.

Should future, more extensive, research support such a hypothesis, its implications for prejudice theory would be considerable. Regions or peoples with heightened prejudice against a particular outgroup would not necessarily be thought of as harboring more authoritarianism; the special conflict may reflect the operation of particular historical, cultural, and social factors. Such a prospect may be encouraging to many action programs—efforts which typically are more successful at changing a person's relation to his culture than they are at changing basic personality structure. Desegregation is a case in point. The success of the movement in the South does not depend—this hypothesis would contend—on changing the deeply ingrained orientations of prejudice-prone personalities; rather, it rests on the effectiveness with which racial integration now going on in the South can restructure the mores to which so many culturally intolerant southerners conform.

A second implication of the hypothesis is that personality factors such as authoritarianism and susceptibility to conform cannot be overlooked in understanding bigotry even in parts of the world like the Union of South Africa and the southern United States. Most psychological approaches to prejudice, it has been noted, are concerned chiefly with the externalization function of attitudes. Perhaps, as the object-appraisal and social-adjustment functions of attitudes are studied in more detail, the direct personality concomitants of cultural pressures will be isolated and better understood.

* Thomas F. Pettigrew, Personality and sociocultural factors in intergroup attitudes: a cross-national comparison, *Journal of Conflict Resolution*, 1958, 2, 29-42. Summary and conclusions reprinted by permission.

38/RACE AND BELIEF: AN OPEN AND SHUT

CASE[1]/DAVID D. STEIN, JANE ALLYN HARDYCK, AND

M. BREWSTER SMITH*

ONE OF THE MANY IDEAS PRESENTED in *The Open and Closed Mind* (Rokeach, 1960) is that prejudice may be in large part the result of perceived dissimilarity of belief systems. That is, Rokeach, Smith, and Evans (1960) contend that the prejudiced person does not reject a person of another race, religion, or nationality because of his ethnic membership per se, but rather because he perceives that the other differs from him in important beliefs and values. He reports two studies in which subjects were asked to rate pairs of stimulus individuals on a 9-point scale, defined at the ends by the statements, "I *can't* see myself being friends with such a person" and "I can *very easily* see myself being friends with such a person." In one experiment, the stimulus individuals were white or Negro; in the other they were Jewish or gentile. Racial and religious attitudes and general beliefs of the stimulus individuals were also varied. In this situation, it was found that the friendship preferences expressed were determined primarily on the basis of congruence in beliefs rather than on racial or religious grounds.

Triandis (1961) took issue with this position, stating that:

People do not exclude other people from their neighborhood, for instance, because the other people have different belief systems, but they do exclude them because they are Negroes [p. 186].

He has reported results contrary to Rokeach's contention regarding the primacy of belief congruence over race as a determinant of prejudice. Since he objected to Rokeach's use of the single criterion of friendship as the measure of prejudice, he employed a social distance scale of 15 items. For his manipulation of belief congruence, he used "same philosophy" or "different philosophy" as determined by the subjects' most and least preferred of Morris' (1956) "13 ways

to live." Stimulus individuals in the study were varied in race, religion, and occupational status as well as in philosophy. He obtained a "race effect" that accounted for about four times as much variance, in terms of the percentage of the total sum of squares, as any of the other three effects singly, although all four main effects were highly significant.

Rokeach (1961) replied with the objection that the long and involved passages of Morris' "ways to live" could not be equated with belief systems as he defined them; the "ways to live" were too vague and were not salient to the subjects. He concluded that the results of Triandis' study were therefore irrelevant to the point at issue. In a more recent study, Byrne and Wong (1962) essentially supported Rokeach's position, employing personal feelings of friendliness and willingness to work together in an experiment as dependent variables.

The present study was designed with the intent of reconciling these disparate findings. It seemed reasonable to assume that there might be some truth in each position, and that the large differences between the results obtained by Rokeach et al. and by Byrne and Wong, on the one hand, and by Triandis, on the other, followed primarily from the methods used.

In the design of the present study, our first concern was that of making our "stimulus individuals" appear real to our subjects. In Rokeach's studies, pairs of individuals, described in very sketchy fashion, were presented in such a way that it was rather obvious to the subject that a choice was to be made between race and belief. In Triandis' study, there was less of a suggestion of choice, but the descriptions were equally sketchy and the measure of belief was, indeed, very vague. Our intent has been, following an improved procedure devised by Byrne (1961), to present to our subjects, as nearly as is possible on paper, realistic stimulus individuals. In this study, as in Byrne and Wong (1962), stimulus individuals were varied in race and in the similarity of their beliefs to those pre-

[1] This paper may be identified as Publication A-26 of the Survey Research Center, University of California, Berkeley.

* David D. Stein, Jane Allyn Hardyck, and M. Brewster Smith, Race and belief: an open and shut case, *Journal of Personality and Social Psychology*, 1965, *1*, (4) 281-289. Reprinted by permission.

viously expressed by the subjects. This procedure makes it possible to elicit absolute rather than comparative judgments so as to minimize self-consciously ideological responses. As our dependent variables, we employed both a measure of friendly feelings and a social distance scale, on which responses to each individual item could be separately analyzed.

METHOD

The sample consisted of 23 male and 21 female white teen-agers in two ninth grade classes of a California high school. The subjects, all of whom were 14 years of age, came mainly from working class homes in a nonmetropolitan industrial community. They participated in the study during their advisory periods.[2]

At the beginning of the period, the experimenter introduced himself as "a research worker from the University of California" and handed out a mimeographed booklet to each student, by name. The instructions were printed on the front page of the booklet and read as follows:

As you remember, a few months ago we asked you to answer some questions concerning your interests and attitudes about yourself, your friends, and certain groups of teenagers. You may also recall that there were some questions asking you to give first impressions about people when you knew only a few things about them, such as the person's religion or type of job. We are very much interested in how people form these impressions.

In fact, we would like to know how you would feel about some teenagers who took the same questionnaires as you did, but in other parts of the country. Therefore, we have taken some of their answers and presented them on the following pages.

We want you to look at the descriptions of *four* teenage boys [girls] and then answer some questions about how you feel toward them. The four teenagers will be called: TEENAGER I, II, III, and IV. If you have any questions, please raise your hand and the research worker will help you. Be sure to read everything carefully.[3]

As the instructions indicate, 2 months prior to this study the students had filled out the pretest version of a questionnaire being developed for a large-scale study of teen-age attitudes towards minority groups.[4]

[2] We would like to thank Wayne Henderson, his teaching staff, and the students at Pacifica High School, Pittsburg, California, for their cooperation in this research, and Herbert Weissman who served as experimenter in one classroom.

[3] Male subjects answered questions about boys; female subjects answered questions about girls. Wording throughout the questionnaire was adapted to the sex of the subject.

[4] This study of teen-age attitudes is a part of a 5-year program of research on various aspects of anti-Semitism being conducted at the Survey Research Center of the University of California under the general direction of

A value scale on the pretest questionnaire had asked the students, "Do you think teenagers in general *ought* to . . ." about each of 25 items. Five response alternatives were provided, ranging from "Strongly feel they should" to "Strongly feel they shouldn't." The students' own responses to these items on the pretest provided the basis for the manipulation of belief congruence in the present study (Figure 1).

For each of the subjects, two "stimulus teen-agers" were constructed who were like him in values, and two were constructed who were unlike him, following a procedure similar to that used by Byrne (1961). One "like" stimulus teen-ager was made up whose responses were identical with those given by the subject. In order to avoid raising the suspicions of the subjects, the other "like" teen-ager was made to differ slightly from the first by moving the responses to six items, chosen at random, one step on the 5-point scale.[5] Each "unlike" teen-ager was created by choosing at random three of the items the subject had answered "Strongly feel they should" and changing them to "feel they shouldn't." Three more modest alterations were made as well, depending on the subject's original pretest response pattern.[6]

Besides the information on how the stimulus teen-agers had "answered" the value items, the subjects were given the sex, grade and program in school, last year's grades, and race of the teen-ager (Figure 2). For half the subjects, this additional information preceded that on values throughout the booklet, and for the other half, the value scale information was presented first. The sex and grade in school were always the same as that of the subject, the program in school was college preparatory, and grades were "about a B average." Only race was varied. Thus, by combining like and unlike responses on the value scale with "Negro" and "white," four stimulus teen-agers were created. These will be referred to as white-like, white-unlike, Negro-like, and Negro-unlike. These four were presented in eight different orders, the only restriction on ordering being that like and unlike teen-agers were alternated.

Charles Y. Glock. The research is supported by a grant to the Survey Research Center from the Anti-Defamation League of B'nai B'rith. We gratefully acknowledge our indebtedness to the Anti-Defamation League, but this organization is not to be held responsible for our intepretations.

[5] A check of responses to the question, "How much like you is this teen-ager?" showed that responses to an "exact-like" stimulus teen-ager differed somewhat from those to a "modified-like" teen-ager ($t = 1.76$, $p < .05$, one tailed test). Since half of the white-like stimulus teen-agers were "exact like" and half of each were "modified like," this difference cannot have affected our results.

[6] A pilot study revealed that more drastic changes than the ones finally used made the stimulus teen-agers appear unreal. Details of procedure for constructing the stimulus teen-agers may be had by writing to the first author listed.

On this page and the one facing it are the answers given by TEENAGER I. After you have looked over the answers and have a good picture of what you think this person is like, turn the page and answer the questions about how you feel toward this person.

Every teenager has his own ideas about how his fellow students ought to be. We would like you to tell us, for each of the items on the list below, whether or not you think teenagers in general ought to be like that, and how strongly you feel about it.

"Do you think teenagers in general *ought* to . . ."	STRONGLY FEEL THEY SHOULD	FEEL THEY SHOULD	DON'T CARE	FEEL THEY SHOULDN'T	STRONGLY FEEL THEY SHOULDN'T
1. Try to please their parents by the things they do.	⚬ ⚬	⚬	0	–	– –
2. Have school spirit; know what's going on in school and take part in activities.	⚬ ⚬	⚬	0	–	– –
3. Be able to express their feelings freely and "let themselves go."	⚬ ⚬	⚬	0	–	– –
4. Try to get average grades, not go "all out" for "A's."	⚬ ⚬	⚬	0	–	– –
5. Be intelligent, be able to think clearly about things.	⚬ ⚬	⚬	0	–	– –
6. Be well groomed, keep themselves neat and attractive.	⚬ ⚬	⚬	0	–	– –
7. Have good taste in clothes.	⚬ ⚬	⚬	0	–	– –
8. Be concerned about other people, *not* be self-centered.	⚬ ⚬	⚬	0	–	– –
9. Be modest, *not* try to draw attention to themselves.	⚬ ⚬	⚬	0	–	– –
10. Be good at athletics.	⚬ ⚬	⚬	0	–	– –
11. Be sincerely religious.	⚬ ⚬	⚬	0	–	– –
12. Have respect for other students' wishes and beliefs; *not* be bossy.	⚬ ⚬	⚬	0	–	– –
13. Let everybody have his fair say in running things in the school.	⚬ ⚬	⚬	0	–	– –
14. Be honest and trustworthy.	⚬ ⚬	⚬	0	–	– –
15. Be generally friendly and sociable, mix with different kinds of students.	⚬ ⚬	⚬	0	–	– –
16. Treat other students as equals, *not* be conceited or snobbish.	⚬ ⚬	⚬	0	–	– –
17. Be quiet and well behaved in school, *not* get into fights.	⚬ ⚬	⚬	0	–	– –
18. Follow all the rules and laws that have been made by those in authority.	⚬ ⚬	⚬	0	–	– –
19. Stay in groups where they are welcome, *not* be "social climbers."	⚬ ⚬	⚬	0	–	– –
20. Live up to strict moral standards.	⚬ ⚬	⚬	0	–	– –
21. Be good at expressing their opinions.	⚬ ⚬	⚬	0	–	– –
22. Be good at dancing.	⚬ ⚬	⚬	0	–	– –
23. Be able to stick to hard problems, try to do well in school work.	⚬ ⚬	⚬	0	–	– –
24. Go along with what most other students do and stand for, *not* be too different.	⚬ ⚬	⚬	0	–	– –
25. Stand on their own feet, work for things, not seek special favors.	⚬ ⚬	⚬	0	–	– –

FIGURE 1 / EXAMPLES OF INFORMATION CONCERNING VALUES PROVIDED TO DESCRIBE A "STIMULUS TEEN-AGER." (UNDERLINED RESPONSES REFLECT THE SUBJECT'S OWN RESPONSES FROM THE PRETEST QUESTIONNAIRE.)

TEENAGER I

1. Sex   M   Grade   9

2. What program are you taking in school? (If undecided, mark the program you think you will take.)
   0 _____ Vocational
   1 _____ Commercial
   2 ___X___ College preparatory
   3 _____ General
   4 _____ Other _____ (write in)

3. Last year, what kind of grades did you get?
   0 _____ about an A average   4 _____ about a C average
   1 _____ between an A & B average   5 _____ between a C & D average
   2 ___X___ about a B average   6 _____ about a D average
   3 _____ between a B & C average   7 _____ below a D average

4. What is your race?
   0 ___X___ white   1 _____ Negro   2 _____ Oriental
   3 _____ other (What? _____)

FIGURE 2 / EXAMPLE OF INFORMATION, OTHER THAN VALUES, PROVIDED TO DESCRIBE A WHITE-LIKE OR WHITE-UNLIKE STIMULUS TEEN-AGER.

As the subject opened his booklet, he was confronted with the description of one of the four stimulus teen-agers, called Teenager I. The subject read this first description, at his own speed, and then turned to the next pair of pages and answered three questions. One of these served as a check on the manipulation of belief congruence, and the other two were measures of friendliness and social distance towards the stimulus teen-ager. The questions will be discussed in more detail under Results. The subject then went on to read the description of Teen-agers II, III, and IV and in turn to answer the questions about them. When he had finished, usually in 20-25 minutes, he turned over his booklet and waited for the rest of the class to complete their booklets.

RESULTS AND DISCUSSION

CHECK ON THE MANIPULATION OF BELIEF CONGRUENCE. One question answered by the subjects about each of the four stimulus teen-agers was the following:

How much like you would you say Teenager X is?
   0 ____ as much like me as any teenager I can think of
   1 ____ very much like me
   2 ____ a little like me
   3 ____ a little unlike me
   4 ____ very much unlike me
   5 ____ as much unlike me as any teenager I can think of

The subjects' responses to this question served as a check on the manipulation of similarity between the subject and the stimulus teen-agers. Mean responses to this question, for each of the four stimulus teen-agers, may be found in Table 1. It is clear that the white-like (1.63) and Negro-like (1.91) teen-agers are seen as more like the subjects than are the white-unlike (2.76) and Negro-unlike (3.27) teen-agers. The mean of responses to both like teen-agers combined (3.56) differs from the mean of responses to both unlike teen-agers (6.05) at well beyond the .001 level ($t = 6.99$). All individual like-unlike comparisons also yield t values significant at beyond the .001 level (p values reported henceforth are all two-tailed). From these data we may conclude that the manipulation of similarity or dissimilarity between the subjects and the stimulus teen-agers has been successful.

"FRIENDLINESS" QUESTION. The first question the subject answered about each stimulus teen-ager was the following:

If you met this teenager for the first time, what would your immediate reaction be?
   I think I would feel:
   0 ____ quite friendly
   1 ____ a little friendly
   2 ____ nothing either way
   3 ____ a little unfriendly
   4 ____ quite unfriendly

This question was intended to be a nearly pure measure of "affect"; that is, a measure of the subject's overall reaction to each stimulus teen-ager. The mean responses with respect to each of the teen-agers are given in Row 1 of Table 1. Subjects would feel most friendly towards the white-like teen-ager (.59), followed by the Negro-like (.83), white-unlike (1.69), and Negro-unlike (1.86) teen-agers. An analysis of variance[7] using McNemar's (1955, p. 330)

[7] All analyses of variance reported follow this model.

TABLE 1 / MEAN RESPONSE TO STIMULUS TEEN-AGERS.

QUESTION	N	STIMULUS TEEN-AGER			
		WHITE-LIKE	WHITE-UNLIKE	NEGRO-LIKE	NEGRO-UNLIKE
1. "How friendly"[a]	42	.59	1.69	.83	1.86
2. Social distance scale total score[b]	44	9.84	5.90	7.81	5.54
2A. Individual items on social distance scale[c]					
Invite home to dinner	44	.82	.36	.39	.20
Go to party to which this person was invited	44	1.00	.80	.93	.70
Go to same school	44	1.00	.91	1.00	.91
Have as member of social group	44	.91	.32	.82	.48
Have as speaking acquaintance	44	.91	.59	.91	.59
Live in same apartment house with this					
person and his (her) family	44	.89	.45	.43	.27
Eat lunch at school with	44	.93	.57	.84	.57
Sit next to in class	44	.98	.70	.93	.73
Close personal friend	44	.80	.27	.59	.32
Work on committee with	44	.93	.68	.91	.73
Date my sister (brother)	44	.68	.25	.09	.05
3. "How much like you?"[a]	43	1.63	2.76	1.91	3.27

[a] For these questions, a low score signifies greater friendliness and perceived similarity, respectively.
[b] Scoring: 1 for "yes," 0 for "no"; 11 points possible.
[c] Scores run from 0 to 1. A mean of 1.0 signifies endorsement of the item by everyone.

TABLE 2 / ANALYSIS OF RESPONSES ON THE "FRIENDLINESS" SCALE TOWARDS VARIOUS STIMULUS TEEN-AGERS ($N = 35$).

STIMULUS TEEN-AGER	M[a]	σ^2	COMPARISON	CORRELATION	t BETWEEN MEANS	t BETWEEN VARIANCES
Negro-like	.91	.48	Negro-like versus Negro teen-ager	.15	2.08*	2.31*
Negro teen-ager[b]	1.34	.99	Negro teen-ager versus Negro-unlike	.62***	2.88**	<1
Negro-unlike	1.80	1.13	Negro-like versus Negro-unlike	.29	4.68***	3.01**

[a] A low score indicates greater friendliness towards the stimulus teen-ager.
[b] From pretest questionnaire.
   *$p<.05$.
   **$p<.01$.
   ***$p<.001$.

Case XIV mixed model reveals that belief congruence accounts for a much larger part of the variance of responses than does race, although the effects for both race and belief are significant. (F for the belief effect $= 37.72$, $p<.001$; F for the race effect $= 5.21$, $p<.05$.) This result, of course, is consistent with Rokeach's theory.

This question was also asked, in a somewhat different format, on the "pretest" questionnaire mentioned earlier. At that time subjects were asked to respond to a list of many different individuals, of which one was "A Negro teen-ager." Of the subjects in the present experiment, 35 answered this item on the pretest. An interesting finding emerges when we compare responses to "A Negro teen-ager," with no other information, with responses to Negro-like and Negro-unlike in the present study.

A rather obvious expectation is that the mean of responses to "A Negro teen-ager" should fall between the means for Negro-like and Negro-unlike. This is the case. Means for those subjects present on both occasions ($N = 35$) are given in Table 2. (They are .91, 1.34, and 1.80 for Negro-like, Negro teen-ager, and Negro-unlike, respectively.) Subjects feel significantly more friendly towards the Negro-like teen-ager than towards the Negro teen-ager ($t = 2.08$, $p <.05$) and significantly more friendly towards the Negro teen-ager than towards the Negro-unlike teen-ager ($t = 2.88$, $p<.01$).

One should also expect that subjects' responses to the Negro teen-ager should correlate moderately both with responses to Negro-like and Negro-unlike. This should be the case unless, for some reason, subjects have an expectation that Negro teen-agers in general are either like them or unlike them. Again referring to Table 2, we note that the correlation between Negro-like and Negro teen-ager is .15 and the correlation between Negro-like and Negro-unlike is .29. Neither of these correlations is large enough to be considered significantly different from zero. (The *CR* for the correlation of .29 reaches the .09 level of significance.) The correlation between Negro teen-ager and Negro-unlike, however, is .62, significant at beyond the .001 level, and also significantly different from the other two correlations, at the .01 and .05 levels, respectively.

These differences would seem to demonstrate an important point: namely, when our white subjects are given no information at all about a Negro teen-ager, they apparently assume that he is different from them in values and react towards him accordingly. It should be noted here, referring again to Table 2, that the variance of responses to the Negro-like teen-ager is significantly smaller than the variance of the other two distributions. Some caution must be exercised in the interpretation of the differences between the correlations for this reason. Our data from the question "How much like you would you say Teenager X is?" add further information, however. On that question, the subjects perceived the Negro stimulus teen-agers to be significantly less like them than were the white teen-agers, even when given the same information about both. The mean of responses to Negro-like and Negro-unlike teen-agers combined was 5.33, while the mean for like and unlike white teen-agers was 4.44 (*t* for this difference is 3.29, *p*<.01). That is, with belief similarity held constant, the subjects perceived that the white stimulus teen-agers were more like them, given *identical* information about the whites and Negroes. These results parallel findings reported by Byrne and Wong (1962, p. 247, Table 1), in which white subjects attributed greater similarity of attitudes to unknown whites than to unknown Negroes. Our data further indicate the expectation held by the subjects that a Negro teen-ager, simply by virtue of his being a Negro, will be different from them. It seems likely that their propensity to react negatively towards the Negro is based on this expectation, or, equally compatible with the obtained relationship, for persons sharing the anti-Negro prejudices endemic in American society, the sheer fact that a person is Negro marks him as significantly "different," however similar he may be in other respects.

SOCIAL DISTANCE SCALE. Our major measure of reactions to the four stimulus teen-agers was the following "teen-age social distance scale":

Everyone has his own preferences about the people he wants to associate with. There are probably some people with whom you would be willing to be very good friends, and others whom you would just as soon not ever be with. We would like you to tell us how close a relationship you think you would be willing to have with TEENAGER X. Check the blank under "yes" for each statement you agree with, and the blank under "no" for each statement you disagree with for TEENAGER X. Guess if you aren't really sure.

I think I would be willing:
Yes No
— — to invite this person home to dinner
— — to go to a party to which this person was invited
— — to go to the same school with this person
— — to have this person as a member of my social group or club
— — to have this person as one of my speaking acquaintances
— — to live in the same apartment house with this person and his family
— — to eat lunch with this person in school
— — to sit next to this person in class
— — to have this person as a close personal friend
— — to work on a committee at school with this person
— — to have this person date my sister [brother]

This social distance scale, which was devised for the pretest questionnaire, was patterned after that of Triandis. Items were changed, omitted, and added to make the scale suitable for teen-age subjects; for example, no negative items were used, on the assumption that they would not discriminate between the subjects. Total scores on the scale were obtained by simply summing responses to the 11 items, each scored "1" for "yes" and "0" for "no."

TABLE 3 / ANALYSIS OF VARIANCE OF TOTAL SOCIAL DISTANCE SCALE SCORES.

SOURCE	SS	df	F
Individuals (A)	528.11	43	—
Race (B)	62.64	1	7.20*
Belief (C)	423.46	1	48.51**
A × B	374.11	43	<1
A × C	375.29	43	<1
B × C	30.28	1	<1
A × B × C	9,225.11	43	—
		175	

*p<.02.
**p<.001.

TABLE 4 / SOCIAL DISTANCE SCALE ITEM COMPARISONS WITH RESPECT TO BELIEF AND RACE (N = 44).

ITEMS IN SOCIAL DISTANCE SCALE	t FOR BELIEF[a]	t FOR RACE[b]
1. Invite home to dinner	4.57**	5.00**
2. Go to party to which this person was invited	4.30**	2.00
3. Go to same school	2.57*	<1
4. Have as member of social group	7.75**	<1
5. Have as speaking acquaintance	4.92**	<1
6. Live in same apartment house	5.36**	4.92**
7. Eat lunch at school with	4.92**	<1
8. Sit next to in class	4.00**	<1
9. Close personal friend	6.15**	1.23
10. Work on committee with	3.75**	<1
11. Date my sister (brother)	4.80**	6.67**

[a] Based on the difference in mean response to like and unlike stimulus teen-agers, regardless of race: (white-like+Negro-like)−(white-unlike+Negro-unlike).

[b] Based on the difference in mean response to white and Negro stimulus teen-agers, regardless of whether like or unlike: (white-like+white-unlike)−(Negro-like +Negro-unlike).

*$p<.02$.

**$p<.001$.

Responses to the social distance scale were analyzed in two ways. First, an analysis of variance of the total scores was computed; results are presented in Table 3. As in the analysis of the "friendliness" question, belief accounts for by far the largest amount of the variance, although effects for both race and belief are highly significant. (F for race $= 7.20$, $p<.02$; F for belief $= 48.51$, $p<.001$.) Then, t tests for both race and belief effects were calculated for each of the 11 items. That is, each subject's responses to the two Negro stimulus teen-agers were combined. The t between the means of these scores evaluates the race effect. The belief effect was tested similarly, by combining responses to the two like teen-agers and comparing the mean of these scores with the mean of the summed responses to the two unlike teen-agers.

The t-test analysis, presented in Table 4, adds more specific information concerning the areas in which race and belief effects are strongest. It is clear that belief has a very strong effect on all 11 items. All but one of the differences between responses to like and unlike teen-agers are significant at beyond the .001 level; the difference on the item concerning "Go to the same school" is significant at the .02 level. The race effect, however, appears to be specific to three items:

"Invite him home to dinner," "Live in the same apartment house," and "Have him date my sister [brother]." These 3 items on which the race effect is significant at beyond the .001 level seem to be "sensitive areas," ones in which there is widespread resistance, in American society, to Negro-white contacts. Rokeach (Rokeach et al., 1960) has stated that his theory applies "insofar as psychological processes are involved . . . [p. 135]." As an example of institutionalized racial prejudice outside the framework of his theory he later states "the southern white bigot would not want his daughter to marry the 'good' Negro any more than the 'bad' one [p. 165]." In Rokeach's sense, the present "sensitive" items would seem to fall in the latter category. Clearly, an empirical definition of institutional prejudice in terms of an obtained "race effect" would be circular and meaningless. For purposes of future research, we would suggest two criteria for situations that may be expected to produce a "race effect": intimacy of contact and presence of others—in this case parents—who are the enforcers of social norms. At present, all we can state from our empirical finding is that a belief effect is strong on all the items, whereas a race effect occurs on items that appear to involve publicly visible relationships that are "sensitive" or controversial by prevailing cultural standards.

One further set of data is available, from the pretest, which provides an important comparison with the results of the social distance scale in the present study. On the pretest, subjects were asked to respond, on the same "teen-ager social distance scale," to stimulus teen-agers who resembled quite closely the stimulus individuals used by Triandis. "Same or different philosophy" and "same or different religion" which he used as variables were omitted. Our stimulus teen-agers were all stated to be Christians, and var-

TABLE 5 / ANALYSIS OF VARIANCE OF TOTAL SOCIAL DISTANCE SCALE SCORES, PRETEST DATA.

SOURCE	SS	df	F
Individuals (A)	408.77	36	−
Race (B)	283.95	1	45.50*
Status (C)	134.33	1	28.52*
A × B	224.80	36	<1
A × C	169.42	36	<1
B × C	10.28	1	<1
A × B × C	8,695.45	36	−

*$p<.001$.

ied only in race, white versus Negro, and in status. For the status variable, program in school and grades were varied. The teen-agers were thus described as either "in the college preparatory program getting Bs" or "in the vocational program getting failing grades." Again, there were four stimulus teen-agers: white, low status; white, high status; Negro, low status; and Negro, high status.

The results of the analysis of variance of total scores on the social distance scale, in response to these four stimulus teen-agers, are given in Table 5. In this case, there is a very large race effect ($F = 45.50$, $p < .001$), about twice as large as a smaller, but still highly significant status ($F = 28.52$, $p < .001$), in terms of percentage of variance explained. These results, obtained on 37 of the 44 subjects used in the later study, resemble quite closely those obtained by Triandis. When belief is not a variable, as in these data, or when the belief effect is weakened by the ambiguity of the information provided, as in Triandis' data, both race and status account for appreciable portions of the variance, with race being by far the more important variable.

The explanation for all of these data, it would seem, is to be found in a very simple fact. Individuals make judgments about others on the basis of all of the relevant information they possess. If little information is provided, and a judgment is demanded, it is made on the basis of inferences from past experiences or information obtained from others. That first impressions are seldom accurate is due to the fact that very little information is available, and the person must be judged on the basis of some known group membership. The correlations presented earlier, between responses to Negro-like, Negro teen-ager, and Negro-unlike, seem to indicate that the inference made by most subjects about a Negro teen-ager, in the absence of other information, is that he is *unlike* them.

If the foregoing interpretation is correct, the very large race effects obtained by Triandis and also demonstrated in the pretest data are easily accounted for. The subjects are forced to guess at the belief systems of the stimulus individuals, and their guess is that the Negro is unlike them. Our subjects in this situation respond with a very large "race effect." When essentially the same subjects were provided, in the later study, with actual information about the belief systems of the stimulus individuals, they no longer had to guess, and they responded primarily, though

not exclusively, in terms of the information about belief congruence with which they had been provided.

CONCLUSIONS

The data presented strongly support Rokeach's theory that the variable of belief congruence accounts for a major portion of the variance in prejudice, if it does not tell the "whole truth" about it. The teen-age subjects in this study, when given extensive information concerning the belief systems of stimulus teen-agers, react primarily in terms of similarity of beliefs and only very secondarily in terms of race. This was the case in an analysis of total scores on a social distance scale, and in an analysis of "friendliness" responses. Strong "race effects" were obtained on "sensitive" items on the social distance scale, perhaps reflecting institutionalized areas of prejudice, and on total social distance scores when information concerning belief systems was not provided.[8]

Not only do our results support Rokeach's contention regarding the primacy of belief congruence, but they also account for the discrepancy between the findings reported by Rokeach et al. (1960) and by Byrne and Wong (1962), on the one hand, and those reported by Triandis (1961), on the other. When subjects are forced to evaluate stimulus individuals in terms of their beliefs, then belief congruence is more important than race. But when the belief component is not provided, spelled out in considerable detail, subjects will react in racial terms on the basis of assumptions concerning the belief systems of others, and of emotional or institutionalized factors. The practical implications of these results are obvious. If people of different races encounter one another under conditions favoring the perception of belief congruence (as, for example, in equal-status contacts), then racial prejudice should be substantially reduced.

SUMMARY

In a test of Rokeach's contention that prejudice is the result of perceived dissimilarity of belief systems, 44 white 9th graders completed a "teen-age social distance scale" for 4 "stimulus teen-agers," presented as, respectively, white or Negro, and like or unlike the respond-

[8] Current research by one of the authors (DDS) replicates these findings for white ninth grade subjects in an Eastern school system in which there were substantial numbers of Negro students.

ent in values, in relation to Ss' own responses 2 mo. earlier. Ss also indicated how friendly they would feel toward each. When information was provided on values, similarity of belief accounted for much more variance than the race effect, which was also significant; other data indicate a strong race effect in the absence of such information. Ss' earlier responses to an otherwise undescribed "Negro teen-ager" correlated substantially with their responses to an unlike but not to a like Negro teen-ager.

REFERENCES

BYRNE, D. Interpersonal attraction and attitude similarity. *Journal of Abnormal and Social Psychology,* 1961, *62,* 713-715.

BYRNE, D., & WONG, T. J. Racial prejudice, interpersonal attraction, and assumed dissimilarity of attitudes. *Journal of Abnormal and Social Psychology,* 1962, *65,* 246-253.

MC NEMAR, Q. *Psychological statistics.* New York: Wiley, 1955.

MORRIS, C. *Varieties of human value.* Chicago: Univer. Chicago Press, 1956.

ROKEACH, M. (Ed.) *The open and closed mind.* New York: Basic Books, 1960.

ROKEACH, M. Belief versus race as determinants of social distance: Comment on Triandis' paper. *Journal of Abnormal and Social Psychology,* 1961, *62,* 187-188.

ROKEACH, M., SMITH, PATRICIA W., & EVANS, R. I. Two kinds of prejudice or one? In M. Rokeach (Ed.), *The open and closed mind.* New York: Basic Books, 1960. Pp. 132-168.

TRIANDIS, H. C. A note on Rokeach's theory of prejudice. *Journal of Abnormal and Social Psychology,* 1961, *62,* 184-186.

39/SOCIAL CLASS AND THE NATURE OF THE INCENTIVE IN DISCRIMINATION LEARNING[1]/

GLENN TERRELL, JR., KATHRYN DURKIN, AND MELVIN WIESLEY[*]

PREVIOUS RESEARCH HAS SUGGESTED interesting differences in the relative effectiveness of material and nonmaterial incentives for children of different social-class backgrounds. In an experiment involving the solution of a series of tasks, Douvan (1956) found that middle-class subjects (Ss) maintained approximately the same level of achievement motivation when told they had reached a norm as when they were promised a sum of money. The motivation of lower class Ss, on the other hand, dropped significantly when the material reward was absent. Terrell and Kennedy (1957) found that children, a preponderance of whom were from a rural background, require significantly more trials to learn a "larger-than" response when given only a light flash as an indication of a correct response than when given a series of material incentives, including candy, praise, token, and reproof. In a similar experiment performed with middle-class children, Terrell (1958) found that children assigned to the light flash condition learned somewhat faster than those who received candy.

[1] The writers wish to thank Nevin J. Platt and all of the teachers of Fairview school, without whose cooperation this experiment could not have been performed.

[*] Glenn Terrell, Jr., Kathryn Durkin, and Melvin Wiesley, Social class and the nature of the incentive in discrimination learning, *Journal of Abnormal and Social Psychology,* 1959, 59, 270-272. Reprinted by permission.

From the foregoing, it would be predicted that an interaction exists between social class and the nature of the incentive. Specifically, it was believed that a nonmaterial incentive is as effective as a material incentive for middle-class Ss, whereas, for lower-class Ss a material incentive is more effective than a nonmaterial one. The present experiment was designed to test this belief. It is important to note that while Douvan studied the relationship between these variables using a measure of motivation as a criterion variable, this paper is a report of a discrimination learning experiment, involving an acquisition measure as a dependent variable.

METHOD

SUBJECTS. There were 12 Ss in each of the following age categories: 5-, 6-, 10-, and 11-year-olds, with an equal number of boys and girls in each age group. The school from which Ss for this experiment were drawn very appropriately contains children from a wide variety of social-class backgrounds. Warner's Index of Status Characteristics (Warner, Meeker, & Eels, 1949) was the measure used to define class position. In the present study, all Ss designated as middle class fell into either the upper-middle or the lower-middle classes of Warner's schema, while Ss with scores placing them in Warner's upper-lower and lower-lower classes constituted the lower class.

MATERIALS. The apparatus for the problem has been described in detail elsewhere (Terrell, 1957). There were three pairs of three-dimensional geometric figures in the shape of cubes, cones, and cylinders. The small member of each stimulus set had a basal area of 4 sq. in., while the large member had a basal area of 8 sq. in. These stimuli are hereafter referred to as the training stimulus sets. A third cube with a basal area of 16 sq. in. was used in a transposition test, along with the 8 sq. in. cube. These stimuli are hereafter referred to as the test stimuli. The order of presenting the stimuli and the position of the positive, large-size, stimulus were randomized alike for each S.

Additional apparatus consisted of a 16 x 24 x 4 in. box which contained the batteries and circuits necessary to operate a signal light. Two jacks and two push-button mounts were on top of the box. The stimuli were placed into the jacks on each trial. Locked onto the rear edge of the box was a 10 x 16 x 1/4 in. panel board which contained the signal light. The circuits were arranged so that a correct response, pushing the button at the base of the large stimulus, caused the light to go on.

DESIGN. There were two experimental groups. Following each correct response, one group of Ss received a nonmaterial reward, a light flash, while the Ss of the other group received a material reward, a small piece of candy in addition to the light flash. Within each of the two levels of social class, Ss were randomly assigned to the two incentive conditions, making a total of 12 Ss in each treatment-level combination.

PROCEDURE. The Ss were tested individually. Each S received the following instructions:

This is a game where I want you to try to choose one of these (E points to the training stimulus sets), and push the button in front of the one you choose. If you are right, this little light will go on. If you are wrong, the light will not go on. Now remember, the game is to see how quickly you can learn to choose the one that makes the light go on.

The last sentence was repeated after every tenth trial. Immediately after reaching a criterion of 9 of 10 correct responses, each S was given a four-trial transposition test on the test stimuli. The same differential incentive conditions employed during the acquisition trials were continued during the test trials.

RESULTS AND DISCUSSION

The original design called for an analysis of variance of the mean number of trials to the criterion and mean number of transposition responses. All Ss except one transposed on every trial, making an analysis of transposition data useless. In the case of the number of trials to the criterion, the homogeneity and normality assumptions were far from met. Also, the criterial means and variances were correlated. For these reasons, it seemed advisable to subject these data to a nonparametric test. Wilson's (1956) chi-square technique makes possible the test of hypotheses concerning main and interaction effects ordinarily tested by a two-way analysis of variance.

Table 1 contains the training means and SDs. As can be seen from this table, a striking interaction exists between social class and the type of incentive. Middle-class children learn more quickly when given a nonmaterial incentive than when given a material incentive, while the reverse is true of lower-class children. The over-all means for social class are identical, while the difference between over-all incentive means is negligible.

TABLE 1 / MEANS AND SDs OF TRIALS TO CRITERION IN TRAINING (EACH TREATMENT GROUP N = 20).

| CLASS | MATERIAL INCENTIVE | | | | | |
| | PRESENT | | ABSENT | | TOTAL | |
	MEAN	SD	M	SD	M	SD
Middle	7.91	8.33	3.50	2.58	5.70	6.72
Lower	3.41	3.02	8.00	5.15	5.70	4.80
Total	5.66	6.66	5.75	4.65		

Table 2 contains frequencies above and below the median for each of the incentive-class combinations in number of trials to the criterion. All analyses and subsequent discussion are based on the data of Table 2. The predicted interaction is apparent in this table, and to a significant degree. The chi-square value for interaction is 5.17, which with one degree of freedom reaches significance at about the .03 significance level.[2]

TABLE 2 / FREQUENCIES ABOVE AND BELOW THE MEDIAN IN NUMBER OF TRIALS TO CRITERION FOR EACH INCENTIVE-CLASS COMBINATON.

| | INCENTIVE | | | |
| | MIDDLE CLASS | | LOWER CLASS | |
	MA-TERIAL	NON-MA-TERIAL	MA-TERIAL	NON-MA-TERIAL
Above median	6	7	5	12
Below median	6	5	7	0

The direction of the interaction is the same for ages 5 and 6 as well as for ages 10 and 11. No analyses of interaction effects were made for these ages independently, since the frequencies were very small. The chi-square test for main effects of class was nonsignificant, while the test of main effects of incentive was significant at the .05 level. There was a significant tendency for Ss assigned to the material incentive condition to learn more quickly than those Ss assigned to the nonmaterial incentive treatment. This finding is rendered rather meaningless in view of the significant interaction present in this experiment.

Several interesting implications arise from this experiment. There is evidence to indicate that parents of middle-class children place a greater emphasis on learning for learning's sake than do parents of lower-class children (Davis, 1944; Erickson, 1947). Additional evidence in support of this hypothesis was found in the aforementioned experiment by Terrell (1958), in which middle-class Ss indicated in a questionnaire given to them following the experiment that they would rather "do something for the fun of it" than to be "promised or given something for doing it." It would appear that the most important feature in the learning of middle-class Ss is merely some indication that they are progressing. It is strikingly apparent in Table 2, however, that the presence of a material incentive is very important to lower-class Ss. It is possible

that the lower-class child is too preoccupied with obtaining the material, day-to-day necessities of life to have the opportunity to learn the value of less material, symbolic incentives. Davis (1941, 1943) suggests such a possibility. Additionally, since it is likely that the lower-class child generally is more deprived of the specific material incentive, candy, used in the present study, this deprivation may result in an intensification of his desire for candy. It would be interesting to know whether or not the same results would be obtained in experiments employing other material incentives such as toys, clothing, movie tickets, and the like.

Finally, there is a possibility that the middle-class child is more adept than the lower-class child at engaging in effective imaginative activity during learning.[3] If this be the case, it would seem that the middle-class child would learn more effectively under a symbolic, nonmaterial type incentive than lower-class children. Research bearing on this point is currently being conducted by the senior author.

[3] The writers are indebted to Howard E. Gruber for this interesting suggestion.

REFERENCES

DAVIS, A. American status systems and the socialization of the child. *Amer. sociol. Rev.*, 1941, 6, 345-354.

DAVIS, A. Child training and social class. In R. G. Barker, J. S. Kounin, and H. F. Wright (Eds.), *Child behavior and development.* New York: McGraw-Hill, 1943.

DAVIS, A. Socialization and adolescent personality. *Adolescence, Forty-third Yearbook, Part I.* Chicago: National Soc. for Study of Education, 1944.

DOUVAN, E. Social status and success striving. *J. abnorm. soc. Psychol.*, 1956, 52, 219-223.

ERICKSON, MARTHA C. Social status and child rearing practices. In T. M. Newcomb and E. L. Hartley (Eds.), *Readings in social psychology.* New York: Holt, 1947. Pp. 494-501.

TERRELL, G. The role of incentive in discrimination learning in children. *Child Develpm.*, 1958, 29, 231-236.

TERRELL, G., and KENNEDY, W. A. Discrimination learning and transposition in children as a function of the nature of the reward. *J. exp. Psychol.*, 1957, 53, 257-260.

WARNER, W. L., MEEKER, M., and EELS, K. *Social class in America.* Chicago: Science Research Associates, 1949.

WILSON, K. V. A distribution-free test of analysis of variance hypotheses. *Psychol. Bull.*, 1956, 53, 96-101.

[2] Yates' correction was applied to the computation of the main effects of social class and incentive conditions.

VII / Age or Developmental Stage as a Determinant of Behavior

THERE ARE A NUMBER OF WAYS A THEORIST CAN USE THE age of a person to predict his actions. 1) He may consider chronological age by itself to be an important determinant. 2) He may consider that the stage of development reached is a crucial determinant of behavior. 3) He may believe that certain ages or periods are critical. A period may be critical in two senses: a) if certain experiences or learnings do not take place at that time, development cannot proceed properly; or, b) certain experiences occurring at that time have more serious negative consequences than if they occurred either earlier or later.

It is very likely that, when pressed, no workers would maintain that chronological age per se is the important determinant. We can characterize as "maturationists" a number of authors who believe that psychological characteristics appear in a predictable sequence, but who also believe that the absolute age for reaching a given stage of development varies among individuals. Despite their explicit statements on the importance of such individual variations, some "authorities" have written in such a fashion that their readers have focused on absolute ages. This tends to occur either as a result of the author's describing the "typical" behaviors for given ages (e.g., Gesell) or from the author's giving age labels to the stages he discusses (e.g., Piaget).

Some of the most important workers whose thinking is (or was) dominated by a belief in the sequential orderliness of development are: Jean Piaget[1] and the late Arnold Gesell, both mentioned above; and Myrtle McGraw and the late Heinz Werner. They have all tended to assume that the contrasts they find between younger and older human beings are found in the development of all individuals. Because Gesell believed that the attributes he saw as unfolding sequentially were biologically determined, we have also commented on his work in Section II (Biological Bases for Behavior).

Psychoanalytic theory has a developmental aspect in its concept of psychosexual stages.[2] Although the stages themselves are considered to be biologically determined, an important role is accorded to life experiences in creating the behaviors held characteristic of a developmental stage. Inherited capacities appearing in accordance with chronological maturation interact with interpersonal influences to produce behavior. Consequently a change in either the inherited capacities or the interpersonal experiences

---

[1] For a detailed view of Piaget's contributions see the book by John H. Flavell, *The Developmental Psychology of Jean Piaget*, D. Van Nostrand Co., Inc., Princeton, New Jersey, 1963.

[2] The term "psychosexual stages" refers to stages in the socialization of pleasure needs, and is not limited to "sexual" in the American use of the term.

can alter the outcome of the interaction. Thus individual differences, which have been of little interest to Piaget and Gesell, are accounted for in psychoanalytic theory by variations not only in hereditary tendencies, but also in emotional histories.

We have not attempted to organize the selections in this section on exactly the lines dictated by these theoretical concerns. Instead, the section commences with two general papers which span a range of stages of development. Both of these owe much of their intellectual heritage to the psychoanalytic approach. Next we present an examination of the critical period idea.

Our first selection, "A healthy personality for every child," is an account adapted for a White House conference from the writings of Erik Erikson. Erikson is a psychoanalyst noted for his clinical studies of children and for his theoretical work enlarging and enriching Freud's developmental concepts. The book *Childhood and Society* (W. W. Norton and Co., Inc., N.Y., 1950, rev. 1963) is probably Erikson's best known work. Recently he produced a study of Martin Luther (*Young Man Luther*, Norton, N.Y., 1958). Long at the University of California in Berkeley, Erikson has been Professor of Human Development at Harvard University since 1960.

Robert W. White, author of the second selection, is in Harvard's Department of Social Relations. He is author of the widely used text *The Abnormal Personality* (Ronald, 3rd ed., 1964). In his article he comments on Erikson's elaboration of Freud's developmental stages. He suggests a new motivational dimension, competence, that he would add to the body of theory about ego psychology. Many lines of evidence have been brought to bear in support of this concept, which is advanced also by J. McV. Hunt (X, 58) and others, each in his own terminology. Piaget has particularly influenced the people who have been concerned with this motivational problem.

The short selection printed next is by Susan Isaacs, a British child analyst whose writing focused on the inner life and emotional needs of very young children.

Bettye Caldwell's article examines the usefulness of the critical period hypothesis and points out the criteria for an adequate test of the hypothesis. It details the kinds of facts needed to establish the existence of critical periods in humans on a sound basis rather than as mere loose analogies to ethological and embryological findings. The author is a developmental psychologist at the Upstate New York Medical Center.

The child's development of the concepts of magnitude and order, a topic extensively investigated by Piaget, is dealt with in the next article by Jerome S. Bruner (see the Introductions to Sections I and XI for information on Professor Bruner). He is interested in the psychological processes that lead the child to the formation of concepts rather than in the fact that at a certain stage the child has a given concept. Since the present section is concerned with age or stage as a variable, it seems appropriate to quote Bruner on this topic, from another source, as an introduction to the paper reprinted here. In "Education as Social Invention"[3] he states:

"Consider now our understanding of the nature of human ontogenetic development. Several important conclusions stand out . . .

"The first is that mental growth is not a gradual accretion either of associations or of stimulus-response connections or of means-end readinesses or of anything else. It appears to be much more like a staircase with rather sharp risers, more a matter of spurts and rests than of anything else. The spurts ahead in growth seem to be triggered off when certain capacities begin to unfold. And certain capacities must be matured and nurtured before others can be stimulated into being. The sequence of their appearance is highly constrained. But these steps or stages or spurts or whatever you may choose to call them are *not* very clearly linked to age; certain environments can slow the sequence down, others move it along faster. In the main, one can characterize these constrained sequences as a series of prerequisites. It is not until the child can hold in mind two features of a display at once, for example, that he can deal with their relationship—as in a ratio.

"The steps or stages have been variously described by a variety of investigators working in centers as various as Geneva, Moscow, Paris, London, Montreal, Chicago, and Cambridge, but they seem to have an interesting likeness, even though the proposed dynamism varies. . . .

"What comes out of this picture, rough though I have sketched it, is a view of human beings who have developed three parallel systems for processing information and for representing it—one through manipulation and action, one through perceptual organization and imagery, and one through the symbolic apparatus. It is not that these are "stages" in any sense, but rather emphases in development . . . In the end, the mature organism seems to have gone through a process of elaborating three systems of skills that correspond to the three major tool systems to which he must link himself for full expression of capacities—tools for the hand, for the distance receptors, and for the process of reflection."

The next article by Stephen M. Corey, formerly at the University of Chicago and now at Teachers College, Columbia University, discusses problems of adolescent students. The particular orientation is toward the question of how to design a curriculum that takes these problems into account.

An article by Anna Freud of London, England, follows. Her contributions to psychoanalytic theory are probably exceeded only by those of her father, Sigmund Freud. Pursuing the same theme as Corey, but emphasizing personality differences *among* adolescents in coping with the stresses of this age period in Western society, Anna Freud brings us a recent, enriched version of her long-famed descriptions of adolescent defenses against anxiety and guilt. She closes her article with an important discussion of the normalcy of adolescent difficulties.

In the last article of this section Gordon W. Allport deals with crises in the personality development of "normal" college students. Professor Allport, of Harvard University (who was described in the introduction to Section I), deals with his topic in terms of autobiographical materials supplied by his students. His discussion is not from a Freudian point of view. Vicissitudes of adjustment to college, motherhood, etc., have a lesson for preventive work in the field of mental health. A study of the transition

[3] Bruner, J. S., "Education as social invention," *The Journal of Social Issues*, 1964, *20*, 21-33 (pp. 24-26).

points in life may permit forecasting (or at least early recognition of) periods of emotional difficulty which then may be palliated, often in fairly simple ways. Examples of such role changes are: getting a new brother or sister, entering school, developing sexually in early adolescence, leaving home in late adolescence, and experiencing major changes in adulthood (entering military service, marrying, being pregnant, giving birth, moving, changing jobs, and being bereaved). Indeed, the relatively fixed age, within our society, of some of these role changes may contribute to the apparent relation of developmental periods to chronological age.

The reader who is not acquainted with the writings of anthropologists on the topic of the normalcy of adolescent difficulties may wish to refer to Margaret Mead's paper "Adolescence in Primitive and Modern Society" in Maccoby, Newcomb, Hartley (Eds.) *Readings in Social Psychology* (Henry Holt and Co., Inc., 1958). A classic paper in a similar vein is Ruth Benedict's "Continuities and Discontinuities in Cultural Conditioning." It has been reprinted in at least two collections of readings and should be readily available to readers.

Additional articles that relate to phases of development appear elsewhere in this book. Three which deal with adolescence are the Weatherley paper in Section II (10), the Douvan and Adelson article in Section IV (26), and the Rabin paper in Section VI (35).[4]

---

[4] There are, of course, whole books of readings (as well as texts) devoted to adolescence. Among them the recent *Studies in Adolescence* (New York: Macmillan, 1963) edited by Robert Grinder represents many of the same viewpoints as the present volume.

40/A HEALTHY PERSONALITY FOR EVERY CHILD*

MANY ATTEMPTS HAVE BEEN MADE TO describe the attributes of healthy personality. They have been put succinctly as the ability to love and the ability to work. A recent review of the literature suggests that the individual with a healthy personality is one who actively masters his environment, shows a unity of personality, and is able to perceive the world and himself correctly. Clearly, none of these criteria applies to a child. It seemed to us best, then, to present for the Conference's consideration an outline that has the merit of indicating at one and the same time the main course of personality development and the attributes of a healthy personality.

This developmental outline was worked out by Erik H. Erikson, a psychologist and practicing psychoanalyst who has made anthropological field studies and has had much experience with children. It is an analysis that derives from psychological theory, to which is added knowledge from the fields of child development and cultural anthropology. The whole is infused with the author's insight and personal philosophy.

In each stage of child development, the author says, there is a central problem that has to be solved, temporarily at least, if the child is to proceed with vigor and confidence to the next stage. These problems, these conflicts of feeling and desire, are never solved in entirety. Each shift in experience and environment presents them in a new form. It is held, however, that each type of conflict appears in its purest, most unequivocal form at a particular stage of child development, and that if the problem is well solved at that time the basis for progress to the next stage is well laid.

In a sense personality development follows biological principles. Biologists have found that everything that grows has a groundplan that is laid out at its start. Out of this groundplan the parts arise, each part having its time of special ascendancy. Together these parts form a functioning whole. If a part does not arise at its appointed time, it will never be able to form fully, since the moment for the rapid outgrowth of some other part will have arrived. Moreover, a part that misses its time of ascendancy or is severely damaged during its formative period is apt to doom, in turn, the whole hierarchy of organs. Proper rate and normal sequence is necessary if functional harmony is to be secured.

Personality represents the most complicated functioning of the human organism and does not consist of parts in the organic sense. Instead of the development of organs, there is the development of locomotor, sensory, and social capacities and the development of individual modes of dealing with experience. Nevertheless, proper rate and proper sequence are as important here as in physical growth, and functional harmony is achieved only if development proceeds according to the groundplan.

In all this it is encouraging for parents and others who have children in charge to realize that in the sequence of his most personal experiences, just as in the sequence of organ formation, the child can be trusted to follow inner laws of development, and needs from adults chiefly love, encouragement, and guidance.

The operation of biological laws is seen, also, in the fact that there is constant interplay between organism and environment and that problems of personality functioning are never solved once and for all. Each of the components of the healthy personality to be described below is present in some form from the beginning, and the struggle to maintain it continues throughout life.

For example, a baby may show something like "autonomy" or a will of his own in the way he angrily tries to free his head when he is tightly held. Nevertheless, it is not until the second year of life that he begins to experience the whole conflict between being an autonomous creature and a dependent one. It is not until then that he is ready for a decisive encounter with the people around him, and it is not until then that they feel called upon to train him or otherwise curb his free-questing spirit. The struggle goes on for months and finally, under favorable circumstances, some compromise between dependence and independence is reached that gives the child a sense of well-being.

---

* A Healthy Personality for Every Child: A digest of the Fact Finding Report to the Midcentury White House Conference on Children and Youth, 1951, 6-25.

The sense of autonomy thus achieved is not a permanent possession, however. There will be other challenges to that sense and other solutions more in keeping with later stages of development. Nevertheless, once established at two or three years of age, this early sense of autonomy will be a bulwark against later frustrations and will permit the emergence of the next developmental problem at a time that is most favorable for its solution.

So it is with all the personality components to be described. They appear in miniature early in life. The struggle to secure them against tendencies to act otherwise comes to a climax at a time determined by emergence of the necessary physical and mental abilities. There are, throughout life, other challenges and other responses but they are seldom so serious and seldom so decisive as those of the critical years.

In all this, it must be noted in addition, there is not the strict dichotomy that the analysis given below suggests. With each of the personality components to be described, it is not all or nothing: trust *or* mistrust, autonomy *or* doubt, and so on. Instead, each individual has some of each. His health of personality is determined by the preponderance of the favorable over the unfavorable, as well as by what manner of compensations he develops to cope with his disabilities.

THE SENSE OF TRUST

The component of the healthy personality that is the first to develop is the sense of trust. The crucial time for is emergence is the first year of life. As with the other personality components to be described, the sense of trust is not something that develops independent of other manifestations of growth. It is not that the infant learns how to use his body for purposeful movement, learns to recognize people and objects around him, and also develops a sense of trust. Rather, the concept "sense of trust" is a short-cut expression intended to convey the characteristic flavor of all the child's satisfying experiences at this early age. Or, to say it another way, this psychological formulation serves to condense, summarize, and synthesize the most important underlying changes that give meaning to the infant's concrete and diversified experience.

Trust can exist only in relation to something. Consequently a sense of trust cannot develop until the infant is old enough to be aware of objects and persons and to have some feeling that he is a separate individual. At about three months of age a baby is likely to smile if somebody comes close and talks to him. This shows that he is aware of the approach of the other person, that pleasurable sensations are aroused. If, however, the person moves too quickly or speaks too sharply the baby may look apprehensive or cry. He will not "trust" the unusual situation but will have a feeling of uneasiness, of mistrust, instead.

Experiences connected with feeding are a prime source for the development of trust. At around four months of age a hungry baby will grow quiet and show signs of pleasure at the sound of an approaching footstep, anticipating (trusting) that he will be held and fed. This repeated experience of being hungry, seeing food, receiving food, and feeling relieved and comforted assures the baby that the world is a dependable place.

Later experiences, starting at around five months of age, add another dimension to the sense of trust. Through endless repetitions of attempts to grasp for and hold objects, the baby is finally successful in controlling and adapting his movements in such a way as to reach his goal. Through these and other feats of muscular coordination the baby is gradually able to trust his own body to do his bidding.

The baby's trust-mistrust problem is symbolized in the game of peek-a-boo. In this game, which babies begin to like at about four months of age, an object disappears and then reappears. There is a slightly tense expression on the baby's face when the object goes away; its reappearance is greeted by wriggles and smiles. Only gradually does a baby learn that things continue to exist even though he does not see them, that there is order and stability in his universe. Peek-a-boo proves the point by playful repetition.

Studies of mentally ill individuals and observations of infants who have been grossly deprived of affection suggest that trust is an early-formed and important element in the healthy personality. Psychiatrists find again and again that the most serious illnesses occur in patients who have been sorely neglected or abused or otherwise deprived of love in infancy. Similarly, it is a common finding of psychological and social investigators that individuals diagnosed as a "psychopathic personality" were so unloved in infancy that they have no reason to trust the human race and, therefore, no sense of responsibility toward their fellow men.

Observations of infants brought up in emotionally unfavorable institutions or removed to hospitals with inadequate facilities for psychological care support these findings. A recent report says: "Infants under six months of age who have been in an institution for some time present a well-defined picture. The outstanding features are listlessness, emaciation and pallor, relative immobility, quietness, unresponsiveness to stimuli like a smile or a coo, indifferent appetite, failure to gain weight properly despite ingestion of diets which are entirely adequate, frequent stools, poor sleep, an appearance of unhappiness, proneness to febrile episodes, absense of sucking habits."[1]

Another investigation of children separated from their mothers at six to twelve months and not provided with an adequate substitute comes to much the same conclusion: "The emotional tone is one of apprehension and sadness, there is withdrawal from the environment amounting to rejection of it, there is no attempt to contact a stranger and no brightening if a stranger contacts him. Activities are retarded and the child often sits or lies inert in a dazed stupor. Insomnia is common and lack of appetite universal. Weight is lost, and the child becomes prone to current infections."[2]

Most significant for our present point, these reactions are most likely to occur in children who up to the time of separation at six to nine months of age had a happy relation with their mothers, while those whose relations were unhappy are relatively unaffected. It is at about this age that the struggle between trusting and mistrusting the world comes to a climax, for it is then that the child first perceives clearly that he and his environment are things apart. That at this time formerly happy infants should react so badly to separation suggests, indeed, that they had a faith which now was shattered. Happily, there is usually spectacular change for the better when the maternal presence and love are restored.

It is probably unnecessary to describe the numerous ways in which stimuli from without and from within may cause an infant distress. Birth is believed by some experts to be a painful experience for the baby. Until fairly recently doctors were likely to advise that babies be fed on schedule and that little attention be paid to their cries of hunger at other times. Many infants spent many of the waking hours of the first four months doubled up with colic. All of them had to be bathed and dressed at stated times, whether they liked it or not. Add to these usual discomforts the fact that some infants are handled rather roughly by their parents, that others hear angry words and loud voices, and that a few are really mistreated, and it will not be difficult to understand why some infants may feel the world is a place that cannot be trusted.

In most primitive societies and in some sections of our own society the attention accorded infants is more in line with natural processes. In such societies separation from the mother is less abrupt, in that for some time after birth the baby is kept close to the warmth and comfort of its mother's body and at its least cry the breast is produced. Throughout infancy the baby is surrounded by people who are ready to feed it, fondle it, otherwise comfort it at a moment's notice. Moreover, these ministrations are given spontaneously, wholeheartedly, and without that element of nervous concern that may characterize the efforts of young mothers made self-conscious and insecure by our scientific age.

We must not exaggerate, however. Most infants in our society, too, find smiles and the comfort of mother's soft, warm body accompanying their intake of food, whether from breast or bottle. Coldness, wetness, pain, and boredom—for each misfortune there is prompt and comforting relief. As their own bodies come to be more dependable, there is added to the pleasures of increasing sensory response and motor control the pleasure of the mother's encouragement.

Moreover, babies are rather hardy creatures and are not to be discouraged by inexperienced mothers' mistakes. Even a mother cat has to learn, and the kittens endure gracefully her first clumsy efforts to carry them away from danger. Then, too, psychologists tell us that mothers create a sense of trust in their children not by the particular techniques they employ but by the sensitiveness with which they respond to the children's needs and by their over-all attitude.

For most infants, then, a sense of trust is not difficult to come by. It is the most important element in the personality. It emerges at the most vulnerable period of a child's life. Yet it is the least likely to suffer harm, perhaps because both nature and culture work toward making mothers most maternal at that time.

THE SENSE OF AUTONOMY

The sense of trust once firmly established, the struggle for the next component of the healthy

[1] Harry Bakwin, "Emotional Deprivation in Infants," *Journal of Pediatrics*, October, 1949, 35, 512-529.

[2] John Bowlby, M.D., Summary of Dr. René Spitz's observations, unpublished manuscript.

personality begins. The child is now twelve to fifteen months old. Much of his energy for the next two years will center around asserting that he is a human being with a mind and will of his own. A list of some of the items discussed by Spock under the heading, "The One Year Old," will serve to remind us of the characteristics of that age and the problems they create for parents. "Feeling his oats." "The passion to explore." "He gets more dependent and more independent at the same time." "Arranging the house for the wandering baby." "Avoiding accidents." "How do you make him leave certain things alone?" "Dropping and throwing things." "Biting humans." "The small child who won't stay in bed at night."

What is at stake throughout the struggle of these years is the child's sense of autonomy, the sense that he is an independent human being and yet one who is able to use the help and guidance of others in important matters. This stage of development becomes decisive for the ratio between love and hate, between cooperation and wilfulness, for freedom of self-expression and its renunciation in the make-up of the individual. The favorable outcome is self-control without loss of self-esteem. The unfavorable outcome is doubt and shame.

Before the sense of autonomy can develop, the sense of trust must be reasonably well-established and must continue to pervade the child's feeling about himself and his world. Only so dare he respond with confidence to his new-felt desire to assert himself boldly, to appropriate demandingly, and to hurl away without let or hindrance.

As with the previous stage, there is a physiological basis for this characteristic behavior. This is the period of muscle-system maturation and the consequent ability (and doubly felt inability) to coordinate a number of highly conflicting action patterns, such as those of holding on and letting go, walking, talking, and manipulating objects in ever more complicated ways. With these abilities come pressing needs to use them: to handle, to explore, to seize and to drop, to withhold and to expel. And, with all, there is the dominant will, the insistent "Me do" that defies help and yet is so easily frustrated by the inabilities of the hands and feet.

For a child to develop this sense of self-reliance and adequacy that Erikson calls autonomy, it is necessary that he experience over and over again that he is a person who is permitted to make choices. He has to have the right to choose, for example, whether to sit or whether to stand, whether to approach a visitor or to lean against his mother's knee, whether to accept offered food or whether to reject it, whether to use the toilet or to wet his pants. At the same time he must learn some of the boundaries of self-determination. He inevitably finds that there are walls he cannot climb, that there are objects out of reach, that, above all, there are innumerable commands enforced by powerful adults. His experience is much too small to enable him to know what he can and cannot do with respect to the physical environment, and it will take him years to discover the boundaries that mark off what is approved, what is tolerated, and what is forbidden by his elders whom he finds so hard to understand.

As problems of this period, some psychologists have concentrated particularly on bladder and bowel control. Emphasis is put upon the need for care in both timing and mode of training children in the performance of these functions. If parental control is too rigid or if training is started too early, the child is robbed of his opportunity to develop, by his own free choice, gradual control of the contradictory impulses of retention and elimination.

To others who study child development, this matter of toilet training is but a prototype of all the problems of this age-range. The sphincters are only part of the whole muscle system, with its general ambiguity of rigidity and relaxation, of flexion and extension. To hold and to relinquish refer to much more than the bowels. As the child acquires the ability to stand on his two feet and move around, he delineates his world as me and you. He can be astonishingly pliable once he has decided that he wants to do what he is supposed to do, but there is no reliable formula for assuring that he will relinquish when he wants to hold on.

The matter of mutual regulation between parent and child (for fathers have now entered the picture to an extent that was rare in the earlier stage) now faces its severest task. The task is indeed one to challenge the most resourceful and the most calm adult. Firmness is necessary, for the child must be protected against the potential anarchy of his as yet untrained sense of discrimination. Yet the adult must back him up in his wish to "stand on his own feet," lest he be overcome by shame that he has exposed himself foolishly and by doubt in his self-worth. Perhaps the most constructive rule a parent can follow is to forbid only what "really matters" and, in such forbidding, to be clear and consistent.

Shame and doubt are emotions that many primitive peoples and some of the less sophisticated individuals in our own society utilize in training children. Shaming exploits the child's sense of being small. Used to excess it misses its objective and may result in open shamelessness, or, at least, in the child's secret determination to do as he pleases when not observed. Such defiance is a normal, even healthy response to demands that a child consider himself, his body, his needs, or his wishes evil and dirty and that he regard those who pass judgment as infallible. Young delinquents may be produced by this means, and others who are oblivious to the opinion of society.

Those who would guide the growing child wisely, then, will avoid shaming him and avoid causing him to doubt that he is a person of worth. They will be firm and tolerant with him so that he can rejoice in being a person of independence and can grant independence to others. As to detailed procedures, it is impossible to prescribe, not only because we do not know and because every situation is different but also because the kind and degree of autonomy that parents are able to grant their small children depends on feelings about themselves that they derive from society. Just as the child's sense of trust is a reflection of the mother's sturdy and realistic faith, so the child's sense of autonomy is a reflection of the parents' personal dignity. Such appears to be the teaching of the comparative study of cultures.

Personal autonomy, independence of the individual, is an especially outstanding feature of the American way of life. American parents, accordingly, are in a particularly favorable position to transmit the sense of autonomy to their children. They themselves resent being bossed, being pushed around; they maintain that everybody has the right to express his opinion and to be in control of his affairs. More easily than people who live according to an authoritarian pattern, they can appreciate a little child's vigorous desire to assert his independence and they can give him the leeway he needs in order to grow up into the upstanding, look-you-in-the-eye kind of individual that Americans admire.

It is not only in early childhood, however, that this attitude toward growing children must be maintained. As was said at the outset, these components of the healthy personality cannot be established once and for all. The period of life in which they first come into being is the most crucial, it is true. But threats to their maintenance occur throughout life. Not only parents, then, but everybody who has significant contact with children and young people must respect their desire for self-assertion, help them hold it within bounds, and avoid treating them in ways that arouse shame or doubt.

This attitude toward children, toward all people, must be maintained in institutional arrangements as well. Great differences in educational and economic opportunity and in access to the law, discrimination of all kinds are threats to this ingredient of mental health. So, too, may be the over-mechanization of our society, the depersonalization of human relations that is likely to accompany large-scale endeavor of all kinds.

Parents, as well as children, are affected by these matters. In fact, parents' ability to grant children the kind of autonomy Americans think desirable depends in part on the way they are treated as employees and citizens. Throughout, the relation must be such as affirms personal dignity. Much of the shame and doubt aroused in children result from the indignity and uncertainty that are an expression of parents' frustrations in love and work. Special attention must be paid to all these matters, then, if we are to avoid destroying the autonomy that Americans have always set store by.

THE SENSE OF INITIATIVE

Having become sure, for the time being, that he is a person in his own right and having enjoyed that feeling for a year or so, the child of four or five wants to find out what kind of person he can be. To be any particular kind of person, he sees clearly, involves being able to do particular kinds of things. So he observes with keen attention what all manner of interesting adults do (his parents, the milkman, the truck driver, and so on), tries to imitate their behavior, and yearns for a share in their activities.

This is the period of enterprise and imagination, an ebullient, creative period when phantasy substitutes for literal execution of desires and the meagerest equipment provides material for high imaginings. It is a period of intrusive, vigorous learning, learning that leads away from the child's own limitations into future possibilities. There is intrusion into other people's bodies by physical attack, into other people's ears and minds by loud and aggressive talking. There is intrusion into space by vigorous locomotion and intrusion into the unknown by consuming curiosity.

By this age, too, conscience has developed. The child is no longer guided only by outsiders;

there is installed within him a voice that comments on his deeds, and warns and threatens. Close attention to the remarks of any child of this age will confirm this statement. Less obvious, however, are experts' observations that children now begin to feel guilty for mere thoughts, for deeds that have been imagined but never executed. This, they say, is the explanation for the characteristic nightmares of this age period and for the over-reaction to slight punishment.

The problem to be worked out in this stage of development, accordingly, is how to will without too great a sense of guilt. The fortunate outcome of the struggle is a sense of initiative. Failure to win through to that outcome leaves the personality overburdened, and possibly over-restricted by guilt.

It is easy to see how the child's developing sense of initiative may be discouraged. So many of the projects dreamed up at this age are of a kind which cannot be permitted that the child may come to feel he is faced by a universal "No." In addition he finds that many of the projects are impossible of execution and others, even if not forbidden, fail to win the approval of the adults whom he has come to love. Moreover, since he does not always distinguish clearly between actuality and phantasy, his over-zealous conscience may disapprove of even imaginary deeds.

It is very important, therefore, for healthy personality development that much leeway and encouragement be given to the child's show of enterprise and imagination and that punishment be kept at a minimum. Boys and girls at this stage are extraordinarily appreciative of any convincing promise that someday they will be able to do things as well, or maybe better, than father and mother. They enjoy competition (especially if they can win) and insistence on goal; they get great pleasure from conquest. They need numerous examples of the kinds of roles adults assume, and they need a chance to try them out in play.

The ability that is in the making is that of selecting social goals and persevering in the attempt to reach them.

If enterprise and imagination are too greatly curbed, if severe rebukes accompany the frequently necessary denial of permission to carry out desires, a personality may result that is over-constricted. Such a personality cannot live up to its inner capacities for imagination, feeling, or performance, though it may over-compensate by immense activity and find relaxation impossible.

Constriction of personality is a self-imposed constriction, an act of the child's over-zealous conscience. "If I may not do this, I will not even think it," says conscience, "for even thinking it is dangerous." Resentment and bitterness and a vindictive attitude toward the world that forces the restriction may accompany this decision, however, and become unconscious but functioning parts of the personality. Such, at least, is the warning of psychiatrists who have learned to know the inmost feelings of emotionally handicapped children and adults.

This developmental stage has great assets as well as great dangers. At no time in life is the individual more ready to learn avidly and quickly, to become big in the sense of sharing obligation and performance. If during this preschool period the child can get some sense of the various roles and functions that he can perform as an adult, he will be ready to progress joyfully to the next stage, in which he will find pleasurable accomplishment in activities less fraught with phantasy and fear.

There is a lesson in this for later periods of personality development as well. As has been said before, these conflicts that come to a head at particular periods of a child's life are not settled once and for all. The sense of initiative, then, is one that must be continually fostered, and great care must be taken that youngsters and young people do not have to feel guilty for having dared to dream.

Just as we Americans prize autonomy, so too do we prize initiative; in fact, we regard it as the cornerstone of our economic system. There is much in the present industrial and political mode of life that may discourage initiative, that may make a young person think he had best pull in his horns. What these tendencies are and what they may do to youngsters and to their parents, who too must feel free if they are to cultivate the sense of initiative in their children, is a subject that warrants much serious discussion.

THE SENSE OF ACCOMPLISHMENT

The three stages so far described probably are the most important for personality development. With a sense of trust, a sense of autonomy, and a sense of initiative achieved, progress through the later stages is pretty well assured. Whether this is because children who have a good environment in their early years are likely to continue to be so favored, or whether it is because they have attained such strength of personality that they can successfully handle later difficulties, research has not yet made clear. We do know that nearly all children who get a good start continue to develop very well, and we know that some of those who start off poorly continue to be handicapped. Observations of this sort seem to support psychological theory in the conclusion that personality is pretty well set by about six years of age. Since, however, some children develop into psychologically healthy adults in spite of a bad start, and since some who start well run into difficulties later, it is clear that much research is needed before this conclusion can be accepted as wholly correct.

To return to the developmental analysis, the fourth stage, which begins somewhere around six years of age and extends over five or six years, has as its achievement what Erikson calls the sense of industry. Perhaps "sense of accomplishment" would make the meaning clearer. At any rate, this is the period in which preoccupation with phantasy subsides, and the child wants to be engaged in real tasks that he can carry through to completion. As with the other developmental stages, there are foreshadowings of this kind of interest long before six years of age. Moreover, in some societies and in some parts of our own society children are trained very early to perform socially useful tasks. The exact age is not the point at issue. What is to be pointed out is that children, after a period characterized by exuberant imagination, want to settle down to learning exactly how to do things and how to do them well.

In contrast to the preceding stages and to the succeeding ones, this stage does not consist of a swing from a violent inner upheaval to a new mastery. Under reasonably favorable circumstances this is a period of calm, steady growth, especially if the problems of the previous stages have been well worked through. Despite its unspectacular character, this is a very important period, for in it is laid a firm basis for responsible citizenship. It is during this period that children acquire not only knowledge and skills that make for good workmanship but also the ability to co-operate and play fair and otherwise follow the rules of the larger social game.

The chief danger of this period is the presence of conditions that may lead to the development of a sense of inadequacy and inferiority. This may be the outcome if the child has not yet achieved a sense of initiative, or if his ex-

periences at home have not prepared him for entering school happily, or if he finds school a place where his previous accomplishments are disregarded or his latent abilities are not challenged. Even with a good start the child may later lapse into discouragement and lack of interest if at home or school his individual needs are overlooked—if too much is expected of him, or if he is made to feel that achievement is beyond his ability.

It is most important for health of personality, therefore, that schools be conducted well, that methods and courses of instruction be such as will give every child the feeling of successful accomplishment. Autobiographies of juvenile delinquents show time and again a boy who hated school—hated the fact that he was marked out as stupid or awkward, as one who was not as good as the rest. Some such boys find in jobs the sense of accomplishment they miss at school and consequently give up their delinquent ways. Others, however, are handicapped in job finding and keeping by the very fact that in school they did not develop the sense of industry; hence they have work failure added to their other insecurities. Nor is delinquency the only or the most likely outcome of lack of success in school. Many children respond in a quieter way, by passive acceptance of their inferiority. Psychologically they are perhaps even more harmed.

Our Puritan tradition maintains that children will not work except under the spur of competition, so we tend to fear the suggestion that all should succeed. To help children develop a sense of accomplishment does not mean, however, merely giving all of them good marks and passing them on to the next grade. Children need and want real achievement. How to help them secure it, despite differences in native capacity and differences in emotional development, is one of the school's most serious challenges.

School, of course, is not the only place in which children at this stage of development can secure the sense of industry. In work at home there are many opportunities for a child to get a feeling of mastery and worthwhile endeavor. Rural youth groups and their urban counterparts cater to this need, and many recreation programs put as much emphasis on work as on play. School, however, is the legally constituted arrangement for giving instruction to the young, so it is upon teachers that the professional responsibility for helping all children achieve a sense of industry and accomplishment rests.

In addition to aiding personality development in this way, teachers have many opportunities for reconfirming their pupils' sense of trust, autonomy, and initiative or for encouraging its growth in children who have been somewhat hampered by previous life experiences. Teachers cannot work alone, of course, either in aiding a child in the development of new capacities or in strengthening old ones. Jointly with parents and others they can do much, not only for children of already healthy personality but also for many whose development has been handicapped.

THE SENSE OF IDENTITY

With the onset of adolescence another period of personality development begins. As is well known, adolescence is a period of storm and stress for many young people, a period in which previous certainties are questioned and previous continuities no longer relied upon. Physiological changes and rapid physical growth provide the somatic base for the turmoil and indecision. It may be that cultural factors also play a part, for it has been observed that adolescence is less upsetting in some societies than in others.

The central problem of the period is the establishment of a sense of identity. The identity the adolescent seeks to clarify is who he is, what his role in society is to be. Is he a child or is he an adult? Does he have it in him to be someday a husband and father? What is he to be as a worker and an earner of money? Can he feel self-confident in spite of the fact that his race or religion or national background makes him a person some people look down upon? Over all, will he be a success or a failure? By reason of these questions adolescents are sometimes morbidly preoccupied with how they appear in the eyes of others as compared with their own conception of themselves, and with how they can make the roles and skills learned earlier jibe with what is currently in style.

In primitive societies adolescents are perhaps spared these doubts and indecisions. Through initiation rites, often seemingly cruel in character, young people are tested out (and test themselves out) and are then welcomed into a socially recognized age category in which rights and duties and mode of living are clearly defined. In our society there are few rituals or ceremonies that mark the change in status from childhood to youth. For those who have religious affiliations, confirmation, joining the church, may serve this purpose in part, since the young people are thereby admitted, in this one segment of their lives at least, to the company of adults. Such ceremonies serve, in addition, to reaffirm to youth that the universe is trustworthy and stable and that a way of life is clearly laid out.

Graduation ceremonies might play a part in marking a new status were it not that, in present-day America, status is so ill defined. What rules of law and custom exist are too diverse to be of much help. For example, legal regulations governing age of "consent," age at which marriage is permitted, age for leaving school, for driving a car, for joining (or being required to join) the Army or Navy mark no logical progressions in rights and duties. As to custom, there is so much variation in what even families who live next door to each other expect or permit that adolescents, eager to be on their way, are practically forced into standardizing themselves in their search for status. In this they are ably abetted by advertisers and entertainers who seek their patronage, as well as by well-meaning magazine writers who describe in great detail the means by which uniformity can be achieved.

In this urge to find comfort through similarity, adolescents are likely to become stereotyped in behavior and ideals. They tend to form cliques for self-protection and fasten on petty similarities of dress and gesture to assure themselves that they are really somebody. In these cliques they may be intolerant and even cruel toward those they label as different. Unfortunate as such behavior is and not to be condoned, intolerance serves the important purpose of giving the group members at least the negative assurance that there is something they are not.

The danger of this developmental period is self-diffusion. As Biff puts it in *The Death of a Salesman*, "I just can't take hold, Mom. I can't take hold of some kind of a life." A boy or girl can scarcely help feeling somewhat diffuse when the body changes in size and shape so rapidly, when genital maturity floods body and imagination with forbidden desires, when adult life lies ahead with such a diversity of conflicting possibilities and choices. Whether this feeling of self-diffusion is fairly easily mastered or whether, in extreme, it leads to delinquency, neurosis or outright psychosis, depends to a considerable extent on what has gone before. If the course of personality development has been a healthy one, a feeling of self-esteem has accrued from the numerous experiences of succeeding in a task and sensing its cultural meaning. Along with this, the child has come to the conviction that he is moving toward an understandable future in which he will have a definite role to play. Adolescence may upset this assurance for a time or to a degree but fairly soon a new integration is achieved, and the boy or girl sees again (and with clearer vision) that he belongs and that he is on his way.

The course is not so easy for adolescents who have not had so fortunate a past or for those whose earlier security is broken by a sudden awareness that as members of minority groups their way of life sets them apart. The former, already unsure of themselves, find their earlier doubt and mistrust reactivated by the physiological and social changes that adolescence brings. The latter, once secure, may feel that they must disavow their past and try to develop an "American" personality.

Much has been learned and written about the adolescent problems of the boys and girls whose early personality development has been impaired. How they can be helped, if their disorders are not too severe, is also fairly well known. The full implications of these findings for parents, teachers, and others who would guide youth are still to be worked out but, even so, there is considerable information.

Less well understood are the difficulties and the ways of helping adolescents who grew up in cultures that are not of the usual run. These boys and girls may have been privileged in having had a childhood in which there was little inhibition of sensual pleasures, and in which development proceeded by easy, unselfconscious stages. For them, difficulties arise if their parents lose trust in themselves or if their teachers apply sudden correctives, or if they themselves reject their past and try to act like the others. The new role of middle-class adolescent is often too hard to play. Delinquency or bizarre behavior marks the failure.

How to reach these boys and girls, how to help them attain their desire, is a matter not well understood. It is clear, however, that they should not be typed by pat diagnoses and social judgments, for they are ever ready to become the "bums" that they are called. Those who would guide them must understand both the psychology of adolescence and the cultural realities of the day. There is trust to be restored and doubt and guilt and feelings of inferiority to be overcome. The science of how to do

this is still pretty much lacking, though here and there teachers, clergymen, probation officers and the like are highly successful in the task.

Hard though it be to achieve, the sense of identity is the individual's only safeguard against the lawlessness of his biological drives and the authority of an over-weening conscience. Loss of identity, loss of the sense that there is some continuity, sameness, and meaning to life, exposes the individual to his childhood conflicts and leads to emotional upsets. This outcome was observed time and again among men hard pressed by the dangers of war. It is clear, then, that if health of personality is to be preserved much attention must be given to assuring that America makes good on its promises to youth.

THE SENSE OF INTIMACY

After the sense of identity, to a greater or less extent, is achieved it becomes possible for the next component of the healthy personality to develop. This is the sense of intimacy, intimacy with persons of the same sex or of the opposite sex or with one's self. The youth who is not fairly sure of his identity shies away from interpersonal relations and is afraid of close communion with himself. The surer he becomes of himself, the more he seeks intimacy, in the form of friendship, love and inspiration.

In view of the early age at which boy and girl attachments are encouraged today, it may seem strange to put the critical period for the development of the sense of intimacy late in adolescence. The explanation is that, on the one hand, sexual intimacy is only one part of what is involved, and, on the other, boy-girl attachments of earlier age periods are likely to be of a somewhat different order. Regarding the latter point, it has been observed by those who know young people well that high-school age boys and girls often use each other's company for an endless verbal examination of what the other thinks, feels, and wants to do. In other words, these attachments are one means of defining one's identity.

In contrast to this use of friendship and companionship, boys and girls late in adolescence usually have need for a kind of fusion with the essence of other people and for a communion with their own inner resources. If, by reason of inadequacies in previous personality development, this sense of intimacy cannot be achieved, the youth may retire into psychological isolation and keep his relations with people on a formal, stereotyped level that is lacking in spontaneity and warmth or he may keep trying again and again to get close to others, only to meet with repeated failure. Under this compulsion he may even marry, but the role of mate is one he can rarely sustain, for the condition of true two-ness is that each individual must first become himself.

In this area of personality development as in the others, cultural factors play a part in sustaining or in discouraging the individual in his development. American culture is unusually successful in encouraging the development of the feelings of independence, initiative, industry, and identity. It is somewhat less successful in the area of intimacy, for the culture's ideal is the subordination of sexuality and sensuality to a life of work, duty, and worship.

Consequently, American adolescents are likely to be unsupported by their parents and to find little confirmation in story or song for their desire to sense intimately the full flavor of the personality of others. In many of them, then, the sense of intimacy does not develop highly and they have difficulty in finding in close personal relations the outlet for tension that they need.

There is some evidence that a change in conventions and customs in this respect is in the making, however. Too abrupt change in any such cultural matter is not to be urged, but it is to be hoped that gradual, frank discussion can bring about gradual alteration in attitude and overcome the dangers inherent in the traditional rigidity.

THE PARENTAL SENSE

"Parental sense" designates somewhat the same capacity as that implied in the words, creativity or productivity. The individual has normally come to adulthood before this sense can develop fully.

The parental sense is indicated most clearly by interest in producing and caring for children of one's own. It may also be exhibited in relation to other people's children or by a parental kind of responsibility toward the products of creative activity of other sorts. The mere desire for or possession of children does not indicate that this component of the healthy personality has developed. In fact, many parents who bring their children to child guidance clinics are found not to have reached this stage of personality development.

The essential element is the desire to nourish and nurture what has been produced. It is the ability to regard one's children as a trust of the community, rather than as extensions of one's own personality or merely as beings that one happens to live with.

Failure to develop this component of the healthy personality often results in a condition which has not been adequately categorized clinically. Although a true sense of intimacy has not developed, the individual may obsessively seek companionship. There is something of egotism in this as in his other activities, a kind of self-absorption. The individual is inclined to treat himself as a child and to be rivalrous with his children, if he has any. He indulges himself, expects to be indulged, and in general behaves in an infantile or immature manner.

There are both individual and social explanations of the failure to develop an adequate parental sense. Individually, the explanation may be found in the inadequate development of the personality components previously described. In some people this failure goes far back. Because of unfortunate experiences in childhood they did not arrive at a firm sense of trust, autonomy, and the rest. In others it is only inadequacies in later stages, especially in the development of the sense of intimacy, that are at fault.

Socially, as has been suggested throughout this analysis, healthy personality development depends upon the culture's ideals and upon the economic arrangements of the society. In order that most people may develop fully the sense of being a parent, the role of parent, both mother and father, must be a respected one in the society. Giving must rank higher than getting, and loving than being loved. The economy must be such that the future can be depended upon and each person can feel assured that he has a meaningful and respected part to play. Only so can most individuals afford to renounce selfish aims and derive much of their satisfaction from rearing children.

THE SENSE OF INTEGRITY

The final component of the healthy personality is the sense of integrity. In every culture the dominant ideals, honor, courage, faith, purity, grace, fairness, self-discipline, become at this stage the core of the healthy personality's integration. The individual, in Erikson's words, "becomes able to accept his individual life cycle and the people who have become significant to it as meaningful within the segment of history in which he lives."

To continue Erikson's description, "Integrity thus means a new and different love of one's parents, free of the wish that they should have been different, and an acceptance of the fact that one's life is one's own responsibility. It is a sense of comradeship with men and women of distant times and of different pursuits, who have created orders and objects and sayings conveying human dignity and love. Although aware of the relativity of all the various life styles that have given meaning to human striving, the possessor of integrity is ready to defend the dignity of his own life style against all physical and economic threats. For he knows that, for him, all human dignity stands or falls with the one style of integrity of which he partakes."

The adult who lacks integrity in this sense may wish that he could live life again. He feels that if at one time he had made a different decision he could have been a different person and his ventures would have been successful. He fears death and cannot accept his one and only life cycle as the ultimate of life. In the extreme, he experiences disgust and despair. Despair expresses the feeling that time is too short to try out new roads to integrity. Disgust is a means of hiding the despair, a chronic, contemptuous displeasure with the way life is run. As with the dangers and the solutions of previous periods, doubt and despair are not difficulties that are overcome once and for all, nor is integrity so achieved. Most people fluctuate between the two extremes. Most, also, at no point, either attain to the heights of unalloyed integrity or fall to the depths of complete disgust and despair.

Even in adulthood a reasonably healthy personality is sometimes secured in spite of previous misfortunes in the developmental sequence. New sources of trust may be found. Fortunate events and circumstances may aid the individual in his struggle to feel autonomous. Imagination and initiative may be spurred by new responsibilities, and feelings of inferiority be overcome by successful achievement. Even late in life an individual may arrive at a true sense of who he is and what he has to do and may be able to win through to a feeling of intimacy with others and to joy in producing and giving.

Evidence of such changes is found in the case records of psychiatrists and social workers. Common sense observation attests that similar changes in health of personality are sometimes accomplished without benefit of any form of psychotherapy. Much remains to be learned about this, however, especially about how life itself may serve as therapeusis.

For the healthy personality development of children and youth it is necessary that a large proportion of adults attain a sense of integrity to a considerable degree. Not only parents but all who deal with children have need of this quality if they are to help children maintain the feeling that the universe is dependable and trustworthy. Integrity is relatively easily attained and sustained when the culture itself gives support, when a meaning to life is clearly spelled out in tradition and ceremony, and roles are clearly defined. Our culture, with its rapidly changing technology and its diversity of value standards, leaves much for the individual to work out for himself. In the American dream, however, and the Judaeo-Christian tradition on which it is based there are values and ideals aplenty. In the interest of the welfare of children and youth, in order that a generation of happy individuals and responsible citizens be reared, it is highly important that these values and ideals be brought into prominence and that the promise of American life be kept.

41/COMPETENCE AND THE PSYCHOSEXUAL STAGES OF DEVELOPMENT/ROBERT W. WHITE[*]

THE PURPOSE OF THIS PAPER IS TO reconsider a part of psychoanalytic theory, the part that deals with stages of emotional development. It will be necessary first, however, to show why I think it important to look again at a theory that has survived nearly half a century of critical onslaught and that enjoys enduring high esteem among clinicians. This will require a short exposition of the concept of competence and of certain related concepts which I have discussed at length elsewhere (1959). As you will see, my use of these concepts puts me at variance with theories that make drive the necessary condition for activity and learning; at variance, therefore, with Freud's theory of instincts. The concept of competence, moreover, leads to an idea of the ego that is different from the one we usually find in discussions of psychosexual stages. Freud's theory of these stages undoubtedly occupies a secure historical position. It will stand in the history of thought as an astonishing first approximation to a theory of growth in its dynamic aspects. Nevertheless, I believe that the time has come when its continued use will only block further insights. The theory that illuminated us all as a first approximation may only hinder us in reaching those closer approximations that always mark the forward steps in a scientific pilgrimage.

In broadest outline, Freud's theory is that the most important features of childhood development, the ones that are fateful for emotional well-being and for the shape of personality, have their motive power in sexual energy or libido. Conceiving sexuality broadly to include the obtaining of pleasure from various zones of the body, he postulated a maturational se-quence whereby first the mouth, then the anal zone, finally the genitals become the dominant source of libidinal gratification. Aggressive impulses, fused with libidinal ones, enter importantly during the anal stage and from then on, but the movement from one stage to another is determined biologically by the sequence of libidinal changes. The latency period[Ed] and the final genital stage likewise come into existence through developments strictly in the sphere of sexual energy. Thus it is possible to speak of psychosexual stages, and Freud intended the double adjective to be taken quite literally. It is libido, he said, that makes demands upon the mind, that calls forth psychic activity, that constitutes the motivating force behind the development of the mental apparatus (Freud, 1905, 1908, 1913, 1923).

The great virtue of this theory lies, of course, in its gathering and ordering of the confusingly diverse facts of development. For the first three and the last stages it provides us with a model or prototype of behavior: the infant at the breast, the child on the toilet, the phallic child concerned about genital impulses toward family members, the physically mature adult in the heterosexual relation. It tells us, moreover, that these prototypes are truly basic, that events in these situations are really the most important things that happen, so that if we know just these aspects of a person's history we know all that counts. Each prototype involves not only libidinal and aggressive energies but also frustrations, anxieties, defenses, ego developments, and relations with other people. But all these other things are brought to pass by the instincts, and we are thus permitted to place them in a subordinate relation to the central libidinal events. The theory thus achieves a heroic simplification. Right or wrong, it rescued us historically from a tangled mass of facts and made it possible for the first time to think coherently about emotional development.

Freud's ideas on this subject were completed nearly forty years ago. His ideas concerning the

[Ed] LATENCY PERIOD = *The period of life corresponding roughly to the kindergarten and elementary school years when, in the psychoanalytic conception, children have gained control of—or are less preoccupied than formerly with—their body-pleasure needs and primitive impulsiveness. Oral, anal, and sexual interests are said to be less evident or more disguised, i.e., to be relatively "latent," remaining so until the resurgence of sexuality in adolescence.*

[*] Robert W. White, Competence and the psychosexual stages of development, reprinted from *Nebraska Symposium on Motivation, 1960,* 97-104, 106-108, 133-138, by permission of the author and the University of Nebraska Press. Copyright © 1960 by the University of Nebraska Press. Library of Congress Catalog Card Number 5311655. Mfg. in the United States of America.

libido itself, a highly mobile and general source of energy, look anything but plausible in the light of recent research on motivation. Many psychoanalysts, however, retain the libido model as a working tool, finding that it greatly helps them to understand their patients' problems. Other workers have proposed more or less extensive revisions in the theory of development. In the writings of Horney (1939), Thompson (1950), and Fromm (1947), for instance, emphasis is shifted sharply from instinctual roots to human relations, especially those between child and parents. These neo-Freudians treat motivation in an offhand, pluralistic way, with perhaps special accent on security and anxiety. Development really turns, they believe, on a series of crises in parent-child relations, crises which arise because the parents, acting both for themselves and for the culture, make successive demands upon the infant that put the relation under strain. (The libido model is thus displaced in favor of an interpersonal model.)

One might suppose that this change of model would sweep away the prototypes provided by psychosexual theory. But the fact is that only Sullivan (1953) has seriously attempted to revise the scheme of crises in strictly interpersonal terms. With most of the revisionists the oral, anal, phallic, and genital prototypes live on, either quite literally or in such guises as "neurotic trends" and "character orientations." The familiar stages, no longer libidinal, are still considered to be crucial. This situation is most clearly recognized by (Silverberg (1952), who translates Freud's stages into *"areas of experience . . . presented to the children of western civilization by parents performing the task of acculturating their offspring."* Each area has its typical problem: deprivation in the oral area; obedience, conformity, and rebelliousness in the anal; rivalry and genitality in the phallic area. It is thus contended that the prototypes originally provided by libido theory are adequate models for the crucial events in the child's interpersonal development. Feeding, toilet training, and the Oedipal triangle are still the fateful battlefields of growth.

The thesis of this paper can be set forth at this point in the form of two propositions. I shall contend, first, that *the child's emotional development cannot be adequately conceptualized by an exclusive libido model,* no matter how liberally we interpret this concept. Second, I shall try to show that *when the prototypes derived from libido theory are translated into interpersonal terms they still do not constitute*

adequate models for development. The best of these prototypes is undoubtedly the feeding child of the oral stage, who cuts a prominent figure even in Sullivan's revision, but from then on the models simply miss part of the significant problems of growth. In particular they fail to embody the development of competence, and they tend to direct attention away from certain crises in the growth of the child's sense of competence. This weakness is attested most eloquently by the lack of a clear-cut model for the latency period, when competence is a central theme. What is needed, I shall argue, is a clearly conceived *competence model* that can be used throughout the stages. Sexual and interpersonal models will be needed too, but we can never do justice to emotional development until we work up a competence model to put beside them.

COMPETENCE AND SENSE OF COMPETENCE

By presenting my theme in this way I have placed a great burden on the word "competence," and I must now give this concept a fuller introduction. Let me say at the outset that it is not something I have invented. It has been distilled from the writings of a great many workers in animal psychology, child development, research on personality, and psychopathology—workers whose only common quality is a certain disenchantment with prevailing concepts of drive. It is a way of saying what I believe many voices have been saying, especially during the last twenty years. Among those who have moved in this direction, it seems to me, are Erikson, Hartmann, and other workers who are trying to carry psychoanalytic ego psychology forward from the point at which Freud left it. I am therefore not trying to promote a novel idea, but rather to find suitable expression for a concept which, suppressed for a time by the immensely popular drive theories, has lately begun to throw out restless derivatives in every direction.

Competence means fitness or ability. The competence of an organism means its fitness or ability to carry on those transactions with the environment which result in its maintaining itself, growing, and flourishing. Some parts of the environment must if possible be fought off, but other parts can safely be enjoyed, and still others can be ingested and transformed into materials for self-maintenance and growth. Some organisms are born more or less fully equipped with patterns of behavior that produce effective interactions with favorable surroundings. This is not the case with the higher animals, least of all with man, who has to learn almost everything that is useful in dealing with his world, yet who immeasurably surpasses all other living creatures in his ultimate ability to subdue and transform the environment to his own use. Man's prowess as a learner has long been an object of wonder. How does he do it, and when does he get it all done?

Theories in which drive is the central motivational concept deal quite simply with this problem. Drives arise from lacks and deficits. They are powerful and persistent internal stimuli which arouse the organism from homeostatic bliss and promote activities that ultimately eliminate the deficit, thus reducing the drive. Reduction of drive supplies the selective principle whereby patterns of behavior are retained or discarded. Our knowledge of the world and our competence in dealing with it are thus acquired in the course of satisfying our constantly recurring needs. We learn what helps us to reduce drives.

There have recently been some startling departures from this orthodoxy—not, as one might suppose, among soft-headed students of personality, but in the very heartland of hard-headedness, the animal laboratory. In a series of experiments Sheffield and others (1950, 1951, 1954) have shown that instrumental learning can take place without drive reduction, indeed under circumstances where one can suppose only that drive level is being increased. Olds and Milner (1954) have found a connection between reinforcement and the electrical stimulation of certain areas of the brain. A whole series of workers, including Harlow (1953), Butler (1958), Montgomery (1954), Berlyne (1950), and Myers and Miller (1954), have pointed out that animals show persistent tendencies toward activity, exploration, and manipulation even when all known primary drives have been satiated. Clearly the original drive model, based on hunger and other internal deficits, stands in need of extensive revision.

One way of accomplishing this revision is to postulate new drives not hitherto included in the list. In addition to hunger, sex, and the avoidance of pain we must attribute an exploratory drive and perhaps an activity drive to the higher animals, even a manipulative drive to those forms that have free use of the forelimbs. These new drives are like the older ones, it is argued, in that they provoke activity

and lead to the reinforcement of instrumental learning. I find myself unable to climb aboard this drive bandwagon because I am so impressed by the differences between the old and new drives. Exploration and manipulation have nothing to do with deficits, they appear to arise in the nervous system without visceral stimulation, and they produce instrumental learning without any sign of consummatory response or drive reduction. (Call them drives if you are fixated on that term, but remember that in doing so you have destroyed the original conception of drive, including Freud's conception of the instincts.) Remember that you are separating drives from visceral deficits and somatic cravings, so that hunger and sex must be treated as special cases rather than as prototypes for the whole idea. But if you do remember these things, what good are you getting out of the concept of drive? I prefer to leave the word in its excellent original meaning so that we can look with a fresh eye at the adaptive significance of activity, manipulation, and exploration.

The theory that we learn what helps us to reduce our viscerogenic drives will not stand up if we stop to consider the whole range of what a child must learn in order to deal effectively with his surroundings. He has much to learn about visual forms, about grasping and letting go, about the coordination of hand and eye. He must work out the difficult problem of the constancy of objects. He must put together an increasingly varied repertory of skilled acts such as locomotion and the use of words. He must learn many facts about his world, building up a cognitive map that will afford guidance and structure for his behavior. It is not hard to see the biological advantage of an arrangement whereby these many learnings can get under way before they are needed as instruments for drive reduction or for safety. An animal that has thoroughly explored its environment stands a better chance of escaping from a sudden enemy or satisfying a gnawing hunger than one that merely dozes in the sun when its homeostatic crises are past. Seen in this light, the many hours that infants and children spend in play are by no means wasted or merely recuperative in nature. Play may be fun, but it is also a serious business in childhood. During these hours the child steadily builds up his competence in dealing with the environment.

Careful study of exploratory play, even in the first year of life, shows it to have the characteristics of directedness, selectivity, and persistence. Piaget's observations (1952) make it plain that the child seeks opportunities to investigate his surroundings and will go to no little trouble to find them. My proposal is that activity, manipulation, and exploration, which are all pretty much of a piece in the infant, be considered together as aspects of competence, and that for the present we assume that one general motivational principle lies behind them. The word I have suggested for this motive is effectance because its most characteristic feature is seen in the production of effects upon the environment. At first these effects may consist of any changes in sensory input that follow upon activity or exertion, but before long the child becomes able to intend particular changes and to be content only with these. The experience that goes with producing such changes I have designated as the feeling of efficacy. Effectance is to be conceived as a neurogenic motive, in contrast to a viscerogenic one. It can be informally described as what the sensori-neuro-muscular system wants to do when it is not occupied with homeostatic business. Its adaptive significance lies in its promotion of spare-time behavior that leads to an extensive growth of competence, well beyond what could be learned in connection with drive reduction.

This, then, is the new motivational base from which I want to reconsider the stages of psychosexual development. But I must make it clear that my procedure will not consist merely of introducing a neglected motive and fighting for its recognition against the claims of sexuality and aggression. If the problem could be so easily solved, it would have been solved long ago. The difficulty is that effectance does not pursue a separate life. It does not typically come into sharp, decisive conflict with drives. It can be mobilized alone, as in the child's play or in the adult's fascination with puzzles, but it is often mobilized in close connection with other needs. The feeling of efficacy can be experienced alone, but it is often merged with other satisfactions, as when, for example, a campus Don Juan reduces his sexual drive while also congratulating himself on the success of his technique of seduction. Because of this high tendency toward fusion it is not profitable to carry on the analysis of later development in terms of effectance and feelings of efficacy. Competence is built up out of all kinds of interactions with the environment, including those due to effectance alone and those due to much more complex patterns of motives. Our interest from here on will be in competence and its very important subjective aspect, which I am calling sense of competence. And we shall not find it profitable to look for the sense of competence as if it were a separate thing in personality; rather, we must become aware of the aspect of competence in a wide variety of actions and experiences.

Sense of competence can be seen as the cumulative product of one's history of efficacies and inefficacies. It comes to operate in new behavior as a kind of set: we judge whether or not we can jump over a brook or carry out a proposed task. It also comes to be much cherished, so that we feel truly elated at new proofs of our ability and deeply humiliated when we cannot do something we supposed was within our power. The sense of competence thus has strong motivational backing, doubtless from a variety of sources. Its importance in personality will be more readily apparent if we bear in mind that it applies to interactions with people as well as to dealings with the inanimate environment. Just as the child explores his physical surroundings, finding out what he can do with objects and what they will do to him, so he investigates his human environment, learning what he can make people do and what he can expect of them. Sense of social competence may well be the more important of the two, though I think we should beware of the current fashion of discussing personality as if it grew in a physical vacuum where tumbles and bumps, victories of locomotion, and struggles with refractory objects are held to exist only insofar as they elicit social responses. We do not live exclusively in a social environment, but we live there importantly, and it is often harder to develop a stable sense of one's social competence than to know what one can accomplish with material objects.

COMPETENCE AND EGO PSYCHOLOGY

I should like now to indicate the relation between these ideas and some of the recent advances in psychoanalytic ego psychology. As you will see, there is a great deal of similarity when we talk on the level of general concepts. There are also many common implications for the psychosexual stages, though only Erikson has tried to reconsider these stages in a systematic way. . . .

[We omit here some material about writers other than Erikson.]

It is in the work of Erikson (1950, 1959) that one finds the most far-reaching attempt to extend the range of ego psychology. Erikson's eight stages in the development of the ego constitute, it seems to me, a major advance in psychoanalytic theory. For the first time the latency period is given a significance of its own. Likewise for the first time the problems of growth are seen as continuing beyond young adulthood when haply the goal of genital primacy has been achieved. But the most important step is the systematic relating of the child's unfolding capacities to his encounters with the social environment. Erikson sees early development as a process of mutual regulation between child and parents. The child's changing capacities and the parents' changing demands lead to a series of decisive encounters, the outcomes of which are fateful for future growth. Later on, these encounters involve the social environment more broadly conceived; in this way, Erikson achieves the social relatedness that is the virtue of neo-Freudian theories without falling into their vice of losing touch with the biological roots of behavior.

Erikson's description of development is remarkably inclusive. In his concept of zones he retains the essence of libido theory, though with a somewhat altered meaning. With the concept of mutual regulation he draws in the best features of the interpersonal model. With his idea of modes he introduces competence, describing at each stage the motor and cognitive capacities that determine the character of the crisis. Erikson's account therefore seems to have everything the heart could desire. But it has one thing I wish it did not have, namely, an implied close connection between zones and modes which I think can lead only to confusion.

In recasting libido theory Erikson undertakes to avoid the scientific crudeness of Freud's formulation by a generous broadening of the biological base. Zonal sensitivities are but part of the picture; the progression from oral to anal to phallic stages is determined by a general ripening of sensory-motor capacity as a whole. The concept of mode captures these broader possibilities. Thus the oral stage, called "oral-sensory," is dominated by the incorporative mode, which means that everything the infant does, even his visual and tactile exploration, has the character of a taking in of experience. The anal stage, renamed "muscular-anal," represents more advanced prowess in motor and manipulative control. It is dominated by the retentive and eliminative modes, which show themselves alike in bowel functions and in the familiar manipulative sequence characterized by grasping and a little later by letting go and throwing away.

Likewise the "locomotor-genital" stage brings to full flower the intrusive mode, which includes "the intrusion into other bodies by physical attack; the intrusion into other people's ears and minds by aggressive talking; the intrusion into space by vigorous locomotion; the intrusion into the unknown by consuming curiosity" (Erikson, 1950, p. 83). Erogenous zones and neuromuscular competence are thus seen as strictly isomorphic, set in the same patterns of interaction with the environment.

My discontent with this idea comes from my belief that in trying to put the stages of development on a broader base Erikson has not sufficiently disengaged himself from the old libidinal prototypes. He wants to assign significance to the growth of competence, but he describes this growth in generalizations carried over directly from the original theory. Incorporation, retention, elimination, and intrusion precisely describe the zonal impulses demanded by straight libido theory. Erikson then asks us to believe that these modes successively characterize virtually all the important things a young child does in the course of growth. This seems to me rather dubious, and I prefer a different strategy for finding out about it. It seems to me safer to treat visual exploration, manipulation, locomotion, and the many other aspects of competence as functions developing in their own right, more or less autonomously, without any presumed relation to zonal pleasures or presumed similarity to zonal impulses. By using the competence model in this way we can protect ourselves from unwarranted generalizations while yet leaving the facts free to tumble back into the old psychosexual stages if that is how they really look.

Let us proceed to re-examine the stages in the light of what I have said about effectance, feeling of efficacy, competence, and sense of competence, and let us see what happens. . . .

THE FINAL GENITAL STAGE

We come now to the last stage in psychosexual development, the stage at which newly strengthened sexual impulses bring about the possibility of genital primacy. In view of the great length of this paper you will be happy to hear that I shall have few words to say about the final stage. The plot is already clear. A prolonged fifth act would add little to whatever impact it may already have made. Obviously I would have words of praise for the more orthodox description of adolescence as given, for instance, by Anna Freud (1937, 1958), Bernfeld

(1938), and Helene Deutsch (1944). Obviously there is great illumination in the treatment of this period as a time of increased instinctual drive and threat to established patterns of ego control. Certainly it is fruitful to look upon some aspects of adolescent behavior as a struggle to maintain and expand one's defenses. You would expect me also to mention some merit in the interpersonal model as developed, for instance, by Sullivan (1953), who described the task of late adolescence as that of establishing "a fully human or mature repertory of interpersonal relations." But then you would predict complaints on my part about the neglect of competence and the failure of the two models to capture whole ranges of behavior that are essential for full understanding. To spell out what you can so easily anticipate would be a bad anticlimax, and it would be a pity to lend an air of anticlimax to anything as dramatic as adolescence and genital primacy.

Perhaps the one thing I should do is to indicate the kinds of behavior in adolescence that I consider important, well handled by a competence model, and neglected by libido and interpersonal models. Since the adolescent is reaching adult size, strength, and mental development, the behavior in question lies in the realm of serious accomplishment—serious in the terms either of the youth culture or of adult society. I am referring to the adolescent equivalent of what Erikson calls a *sense of industry* in the latency period, and I see this problem as continuing rather more strongly after puberty than seems to be implied in Erikson's account. No doubt I bring to this judgment an occupational bias different from that of a therapist. My professional life is spent among late adolescents whose sexual problems and social relations have for the most part not overwhelmed them. We talk together about their plans for study, their abilities and limitations, their struggles with materials to be learned and skills to be attained, their occupational leanings, career plans, and concerns about modern society as the scene of their future endeavors. We talk, in other words, mostly about their competence, and I do not believe that understanding is fostered by interpreting these concerns too much as displacements of instinctual drives, defense mechanisms, or interpersonal relations. They are real.

Adolescents today learn how to drive cars. Some of them learn to compete against adult records in sports, occasionally breaking them. Some of them become part of the football, band, and cheerleader complex that plays such an important part in community entertainment. Some of them try their hands at building workable radio sets, at scientific exploration, at editing newspapers, at writing stories and verse, at musical and dramatic performances, at political activity. Some of them with fewer opportunities or talents put their maturing bodies to heavy work or their maturing minds to white-collar office jobs. All this belongs in the sphere of work, and work, as Schilder (1942) so cogently argued, is importantly a phenomenon of competence. These happenings create many crises, many defeats, many victories for the sense of competence. Once again there are large spheres in which the adolescent can be suffering losses or making gains in ego strength. In theorizing about the subject we must not foreclose the possibility that these developments significantly affect what happens in the erotic and interpersonal realms.

I shall say no more about this stage of development except to launch my last complaint against the models bequeathed us by psychosexual theory. The model proffered by libido theory is that of heterosexual relations, and their ideal form is embodied in the concept of genital primacy. It is not argued, of course, that we all successfully become genital primates, but the ideal type serves to indicate the problems of the period. The sexual act itself plays a prominent part in genital primacy, reminding us that Freud's oft-mentioned broadened conception of sex sometimes touched base again in what no one has ever denied to be sexual. In libidinal terms, the regular discharge of genital tensions serves also to drain some of the energy from pregenital tensions, thus making the control and sublimation of the latter an easy problem for the ego. Erikson (1950) prefers "to put it more situationally: the total fact of finding, via the climactic turmoil of the orgasm, a supreme experience of the mutual regulation of two beings in some way breaks the point off the hostilities and potential rages caused by the oppositeness of male and female, of fact and fancy, of love and hate. Satisfactory sex relations thus make sex less obsessive, overcompensation less necessary, sadistic controls superfluous." Erikson's further account of what "the utopia of genitality" should include—mutual trust and a willingness to share lives in the interest of securing a happy development for the children—is something I commend to you all as an uncommonly beautiful statement of what we should aspire to in family life. It is an interpersonal statement as well as a libidinal one. I like it so well that I am sorry to point out that it has only the slightest relation to competence and to that other sphere of human concern—work.

Unfortunately the climactic turmoil of the orgasm is completely the wrong model for work. This is not to say that good sexual relations may not sometimes free a person from gnawing hates and doubts that have interfered with his capacity to work. But the emphasis of the idea of orgastic potency and mutuality is on an essential loss of ego, a drowning of all other considerations in the immense involuntary experience of the sexual relation. He who takes the ego to bed with him will never get a gold star for genital primacy. The orgastic model has virtue for certain human activities requiring a temporary submergence of self, such as inspiration, creative imagination, and thoroughly relaxed play. But it will never do for the serious, stable, lasting concerns of human life, the realm that I am trying to designate as work. This is the sphere in which the ego must always keep a firm hand on the helm.

Work requires a certain constancy of effort. There must be sustained endeavor with control of wayward impulses that distract from the requirements of external reality and social roles. There must be a capacity for persistent return to tasks, sometimes dull in themselves, that form part of the job requirement or that belong in a long-range plan to achieve remote goals. There must be a quality of reliability, so that one keeps promises and lives up to the obligations one has assumed. Even the fashion for being spontaneous and natural, even the bright vision of self-fulfilling work in Fromm's (1955) sane society, even Marcuse's (1955) fantasy of a nonrepressive civilization in which all work becomes libidinal pleasure cannot exorcize the true and somewhat stern nature of reality. And even Ernst Kris (1952), no enemy of psychoanalytic theory, reminded us that artistic creation required, in addition to a phase of inspiration, a second phase characterized by "the experience of purposeful organization and the intent to solve a problem." When we call an artist "merely competent" it is a weak form of praise, but if he were "merely inspired," without a certain rather high minimum of competence, we would never even see or hear his products.

I should like to close with a short coda on the words "merely competent." I particularly do not want to be misunderstood concerning the part to be assigned to competence and the sense of competence in human development. As a simple and sovereign concept it will never do. A person developed wholly along lines of competence, with no dimensions of passion, love, or friendliness, would never qualify for maturity. Competence is not intended to describe such experiences as enjoying food, immersing oneself in a sexual relation, loving children, cherishing friends, being moved by natural beauty or great works of art; nor is it designed to swallow up the problems created by aggression and anxiety. This is what I meant by saying that the competence model must always be used in conjunction with other models that do full justice to such things as hunger, sexuality, and aggression. It may hurt one's desire for logical simplicity to suppose that several models are needed to understand a problem. Yet I think no one can claim a probability that human nature was designed in the interests of logic.

It is my conviction, in short, that Freud's discoveries were of epoch-making importance, that psychoanalytic ego psychology has taken effective steps to fill out some of the undeveloped parts of Freud's theories, and that Erikson in particular has accomplished a synthesis that promises good things for future understanding of the growth of personality. But I also believe that our understanding cannot be rounded out by stretching Freud's concepts in a vain attempt to cover everything, or by calling everything interpersonal as if body and material world did not exist. We should add to the picture a meticulous consideration, at every level, of the growth of the child's capacity both for action and for understanding. We should try to be as shrewd in detecting the vicissitudes of the sense of competence as Freud was with sexuality, aggression, and defense. It is to encourage such a development that I have had so much to say about the concept of competence.

SUMMARY

Even an idea as monumental as Freud's theory of the psychosexual stages of development can come to have an adverse effect upon scientific progress if it is believed too literally too long. Libido theory provided a series of models for critical phases in emotional growth: feeding, toilet training, the Oedipus situation, latency, and the adult heterosexual relation. These models are largely preserved in revisions of Freud, though changed to interpersonal terms, and they continue to dominate the thinking of workers in psychoanalytic ego psychology. In this paper it is maintained that the models are in certain respects inadequate and misleading. In particular, they encourage us to neglect a range of facts which is ordered here under the concept of competence. If these facts are slighted, it is held, there can be little hope of further progress in psychoanalytic ego psychology or in closing the gap between this and other theories of development.

The concept of competence subsumes the whole realm of learned behavior whereby the child comes to deal effectively with his environment. It includes manipulation, locomotion, language, the building of cognitive maps and skilled actions, and the growth of effective behavior in relation to other people. These acquisitions are made by young animals and children partly through exploratory and manipulative play when drives such as hunger and sex are in abeyance. The directed persistence of such behavior warrants the assumption of a motivation independent of drives, here called effectance motivation, which has its immediate satisfaction in a feeling of efficacy and its adaptive significance in the growth of competence. Effectance motivation can be likened to independent ego energies in the psychoanalytic scheme. The child's actual competence and his sense of competence are built up from his history of efficacies and inefficacies, and sense of competence is held to be a crucial element in any psychology of the ego.

It is proposed that libidinal and interpersonal models for critical points in development be supplemented by a competence model. For the oral stage this means taking serious account of the growth of manipulative prowess and experimentation as seen both in the child's many hours of play and in his zeal for self-help in feeding. For the anal stage it means attributing importance to negativism in the sphere of giving and receiving commands, an early crisis in social competence, and to the enormous growth of motility with its constant influence upon self-esteem. Neither development is adequately implied in the anal-erotic model. For the phallic stage it means detecting the consequences of growth in locomotion, linguistic understanding, and imagination; it also means noticing the child's waxing ability to comprehend and try out various social roles, in many of which he receives encouragement. The Oedipus model, with its foreordained inexplicable defeat, cannot be considered typical for the period. During latency the chief developments are in the sphere of competence; this is clear in Erikson's account of the sense of industry and Sullivan's of competition and compromise. For the final

genital stage the competence model invites us to take seriously the adolescent's continuing concern with sense of industry and with social competence, problems that confront him with new crises in their own right. The heterosexual relation does not provide an adequate model for all the serious concerns of this stage of life, nor can they be fully conceptualized in terms of instinctual drive and defense.

In short, the competence model is held to supplement in significant ways the models of development derived from psychoanalysis. By directing attention to action and its consequences and to the vicissitudes of the sense of competence, it should help to speed the construction of an adequate ego psychology.

REFERENCES Ed

BERLYNE, D. E. Novelty and curiosity as determinants of exploratory behavior. *Brit. J. Psychol.*, 1950, *41*, 68-80.

BERNFELD, S. Types of adolescence. *Psychoanal. Quart.*, 1938, 7, 243-253.

BUTLER, R. A. Exploratory and related behavior: A new trend in animal research. *J. indiv. Psychol.*, 1958, *14*, 111-120.

DEUTSCH, HELENE. *The psychology of women*, Vol. I. New York: Grune & Stratton, 1944.

ERIKSON, E. H. *Childhood and society.* New York: Norton, 1950.

ERIKSON, E. H. Identity and the life cycle: selected papers. *Psychol. Issues*, 1959, Monograph 1.

FREUD, ANNA. *The ego and the mechanisms of defence.* (Trans. by C. Baines.) London: Hogarth, 1937.

FREUD, ANNA. Adolescence. *Psychoanal. Stud. Child*, 1958, *13*, 255-278.

FREUD, S. *Three contributions to the theory of sex.* (1905). (Trans. by A. A. Brill.) New York and Washington: Nerv. and Ment. Dis. Pub. Co., 1930.

FREUD, S. Character and anal erotism (1908). *Collected papers.* (Trans. under supervision of J. Riviere.) New York: Basic Books, 1959. Vol. II, 45-50.

FREUD, S. The predisposition to obsessional neurosis (1913). *Collected papers.* (Trans. under supervision of J. Riviere.) New York: Basic Books, 1959. Vol. II, 122-131.

FREUD, S. The infantile genital organization of the libido (1923). *Collected papers.* (Trans. under

Ed *For a more extensive list of references, see original paper.*

supervision of J. Riviere.) New York: Basic Books, 1959. Vol. II, 244-249.

FROMM, E. *Man for himself*. New York: Rinehart, 1947.

FROMM, E. *The sane society*. New York: Rinehart, 1955.

HARLOW, H. F. Mice, monkeys, men, and motives. *Psychol. Rev.*, 1953, *60*, 23-32.

HORNEY, KAREN. *New ways in psychoanalysis*. New York: Norton, 1939.

KRIS, E. *Psychoanalytic explorations in art*. New York: International Univer. Press, 1952.

MARCUSE, H. *Eros and civilization*. Boston: Beacon Press, 1955.

MONTGOMERY, K. C. The role of the exploratory drive in learning. *J. comp. physiol. Psychol.*, 1954, *47*, 60-64.

MYERS, A. K., and MILLER, N. E. Failure to find a learned drive based on hunger; evidence for learning motivated by "exploration." *J. comp. physiol. Psychol.*, 1954, *47*, 428-436.

OLDS, J., and MILNER, P. Positive reinforcement produced by electrical stimulation of septal area and other regions of rat brain. *J. comp. physiol. Psychol.*, 1954, *47*, 419-427.

PIAGET, J. *The origins of intelligence in children.* (Trans. by M. Cook.) New York: International Univer. Press, 1952.

SCHILDER, P. *Goals and desires of men.* New York: Columbia Univer. Press, 1942.

SHEFFIELD, F. D., and ROBY, T. B. Reward value of a non-nutritive sweet taste. *J. comp. physiol. Psychol.*, 1950, *43*, 471-481.

SHEFFIELD, F. D., ROBY, T. B., and CAMPBELL, B. A. Drive reduction vs. consummatory behavior as determinants of reinforcement. *J. comp. physiol. Psychol.*, 1954, *47*, 349-354.

SHEFFIELD, F. D., WULFF, J. J., and BACKER, R. Reward value of copulation without sex drive reduction. *J. comp. physiol. Psychol.*, 1951, *44*, 3-8.

SILVERBERG, W. V. *Childhood experience and personal destiny.* New York: Springer, 1952.

SULLIVAN, H. S. *The interpersonal theory of psychiatry.* New York: Norton, 1953.

THOMPSON, C. *Psychoanalysis: evolution and development.* New York: Hermitage, 1950.

WHITE, R. W. Motivation reconsidered: The concept of competence. *Psychol. Rev.*, 1959, *66*, 297-333.

42/THE NURSERY AS A COMMUNITY/SUSAN ISAACS[*]

ONE OF THE BIGGEST SOURCES OF trouble for the little child is precisely that at the time when his need to make things better is the most intense and urgent, his skill in doing this is so much less than the ease with which he can destroy. At eighteen months and two years it is so easy to dirty, to knock things down, to make a mess with one's food, to scream and shout. It is so difficult, indeed almost impossible, to make things clean, to build and draw, even to speak or sing in a way that brings pleasure to oneself or others. Many children are overcome by the sense of the insufficiency of the good within them to counterbalance the bad; and this despair very largely rests on this real lack of skill and knowledge. This, again, is why children so often have to play at being bigger and wiser and cleverer than they are. They have to be on top of things in imagination because they do not know how to achieve in reality. Provided their faith is kept alive, however, this contrast lessens step by step. One of the biggest changes that occurs in the child between one and four years of age is the growth in confidence in his own skill and in the possibility of real achievement,

whether in making things or speaking or giving pleasure to others. Everything we can do to further the child's development of bodily skill, or artistic expression, of confidence in his power to help others and gain pleasure from their company, will aid his struggle with the destructive forces inside himself, and carry him out of the despair that confirms him in his destructiveness and defiance. Tantrums and obstinacies and night terrors thus gradually get less, not so much by the direct comfort we give to the child at the time, as by the indirect support against the very source of these things, which he gains by his normal growth in the arts of life. Much could be said about the immense psychological value of the little child's play, and of all his impulses to learn and to do. Many of you are already familiar with the remarkable changes in health and peace of mind which a good nursery school will effect for the child of three or four years. It does this by means of providing the right materials and the right opportunities for the child's own normal impulses to skill and achievement, thus giving him a profound reassurance against his inner doubts and difficulties and depressions.

[*] Susan Isaacs, The nursery as a community, from John Richman (ed.), *On the Bringing Up of Children* (New York: Robert Brunner, 1952).

43/THE USEFULNESS OF THE CRITICAL PERIOD HYPOTHESIS IN THE STUDY OF FILIATIVE BEHAVIOR[1]/BETTYE M. CALDWELL*

WHEN ONE IS CONCERNED WITH LIFE processes, every time period is somehow critical, in that it must occur, be reacted to, and be assimilated into the life history of the organism. Yet for the person whose orientation to behavior study is developmental, the vaguely stated "critical period hypothesis" is likely to have considerable appeal. Some of this may stem from the pleasing dactylic rhythm of the term itself, some from the exciting connotation of developmental brinksmanship. What the hypothesis lacks in rigor of definition, it gains in semantic elasticity which enables it to be stretched, with varying degrees of tension, into almost any theoretical framework. It is equally at home in embryology, experimental teratology, psychoanalysis, educational theory, ethology, and genetic psychology. Acceptance of the concept by the experimentalists has given it respectability; its social and clinical implications have given it prestige. But, unless pragmatic considerations are also met, respectability and prestige will not indefinitely support a scientific construct.

In this paper I shall propose certain refinements which, it is hoped, will increase the utility of the hypothesis without in any way aspersing it. Then, in considering the problem of criterion behavior, I shall discuss a response measure which may have usefulness in heralding, in the human infant, the terminal points of a critical period for attachment or *filiative behavior*. Finally, I shall suggest a research strategy which, with respect to early human social behavior, should eventually make possible a definitive answer to the question raised by this symposium.

REFINING THE HYPOTHESIS

SINGULAR OR PLURAL? In this symposium there has been a tendency to speak of *the* critical period hypothesis, but, of course, that is a simplification and a misnomer. Rather, there can be many hypotheses about developmental periods which are critical, with respect to certain forms of behavior (*e.g.*, "imprinting," "motor development," "learning," "language facility," "formation of affectional bonds," etc.). Conceivably a critical period hypothesis could be stated—and perhaps should be—for every investigation in which "antecedent-consequent relationships" are sought.

In embryology, where the concept had its origin, there is no direct reference to behavioral events, but rather to time periods of maximum sensitivity or indifference, to chemical forces acting upon the cellular mass. Scott, *et al.* (1958, 1950), popularizing the term perhaps more than any other group, have been concerned largely with the socialization process and the differential impact of certain socializing experiences. Holding events constant, they have varied time and thus identified in various mammalian species, periods of relatively greater significance for social behavior. McGraw (1946) asserted that there are periods during which motor activity is particularly sensitive to practice effects. She designated these as critical periods, but did not highlight the term.

Traces of the hypothesis can also be seen in Havighurst's (1952) concept of developmental tasks. Watson and Caldwell (1959) have pointed out that the developmental aspects of Freudian theory could be recast into a critical period framework. And, finally, the all-embracing concept of "educational readiness" is an implicit critical period hypothesis. Relating as it does to the learning process, the readiness version is not too different from the current statement of the hypothesis advanced by the imprinters (Hess, 1959b, 1958; Jaynes, 1957).

Thus, the critical period hypothesis, though generally spoken of in the singular, does not, in and of itself, refer to a limited class of behaviors, as does, say, the "frustration-aggression"

[1] This paper was part of a symposium entitled, "Is the critical period hypothesis useful?" presented at the 1961 meeting of the American Psychological Association. Other participants included Dorothy Eichorn, Harry F. Harlow, Austin Riesen, and Robert R. Sears.

* Bettye M. Caldwell, The usefulness of the critical period hypothesis in the study of filiative behavior, *Merrill-Palmer Quarterly of Behavior and Development*, 1962, 8 (4), 229-242. Reprinted by permission.

hypothesis. The only necessary common denominator in these diverse applications of the concept is a developmental orientation, a research design in which time is one of the independent variables. It seems appropriate to call attention to this rather obvious point, lest failure to establish a critical period for one type of behavior be used as evidence to refute the general utility of the hypothesis rather than to deny its relevance in a specific behavioral context.

BEYOND OR DURING? Currently the critical period hypothesis seems to be used in two distinct ways: (a) a critical period *beyond* which a given phenomenon will not appear (*i.e.,* a point in time which marks the onset of total indifference, or resistance, to certain patterns of stimulation); and (b) a critical period *during* which the organism is especially sensitive to various developmental modifiers, which, if introduced at a different time in the life cycle, would have little or no effect (*i.e.,* a period of maximum susceptibility).

At the embryological level, there are many data to support the first or "beyond" version of the hypothesis. For instance, it can be shown (Hamburger, 1954) that cell transplants, done *prior* to a certain critical time, will develop in conformity with the region to which they are transplanted; the same kind of transplant, done *after* the terminal point of the critical period is passed, will result in misplaced development of the organ, which would normally have emerged in the region from which the transplanted cells were taken.

The second, or "during" version of the critical period hypothesis is also impressively supported at the cellular level. Vulnerability, as a function of time, has been demonstrated repeatedly by embryologists, in the experimental production of a host of congenital anomalies. The teratogen may vary but the timing must be precise. As Warkany (1947) states it, "Periods exist in which the organs are vulnerable, while at other times, they are immune to external factors." Embryologically, the hypothesis has more substance than a random time assignment; it has been demonstrated that the organ systems most affected are those which are showing maximum cellular proliferation at the time the stressor is introduced, while those which have passed or not quite reached the maximally proliferative stage are spared (Hamburger, 1947).

Scott (1958) asserts that, with respect to social behavior, the "beyond" version of the

critical period hypothesis is no longer an hypothesis, but is, rather, an established generalization; to wit, there is a period early in life during which primary social relationships are established, and beyond which they either cannot be established or else will appear in distorted form. Such a categorical statement about human social behavior would be hazardous at this point, as most students of animal behavior have recognized.

Bowlby (1952) amasses empirical research and clinical data to support a "during" version of the hypothesis, in which maternal care is compared to the chemical "organizer" of embryonic development:

In dealing here with the embryology of the human mind one is struck by a similarity with the embryological development of the human body, during the course of which undifferentiated tissues respond to the influence of chemical organizers. If growth is to proceed smoothly, the tissues must be exposed to the influence of the appropriate organizer at certain critical periods. In the same way, if mental development is to proceed smoothly, it would appear to be necessary for the undifferentiated psyche to be exposed during certain critical periods to the influence of the psychic organizer— the mother (p. 63).

Much of Bowlby's concern, however, is with the "beyond" statement of the hypothesis (*i.e.,* with the critical period beyond which deprivation of maternal care will result in permanently impaired offspring).

In calling attention to these two variations on a single theme, the author does not intend to imply that they are unrelated. Often the terminus of a sensitive critical period is assumed to designate also the critical point beyond which certain behaviors will not occur, an assumption which is not always justified. For example, Hess (1959b) has suggested that 13-16 hours after hatching is the critical period for imprinting in the duck; but this period of maximum sensitivity is not immediately succeeded by one of indifference. Modification of the organism with drugs (Hess, 1960, 1959c, 1957), or modification of the procedure (Jaynes, 1957) will result in a prolongation of the sensitive period.

In a recent study by Freedman, *et al.* (1961), the optimal period for socializing dogs was found to be 7-9 weeks. However, adequate socialization was possible through 13 weeks, beyond which the animal showed almost no response to the socializing procedure. Thus, in this instance, termination of the period of maximal sensitivity occurred several weeks before onset of the period of continuing resistance. It also seems likely that in other organisms and in other kinds of behaviors, one is not justified in assuming that the end of the period of maximum sensitivity automatically coincides with the beginning of the period of total indifference or resistance, the point beyond which the organism is unmodifiable with respect to a given behavioral parameter.

NOMOTHETIC OR IDIOGRAPHIC? One further refinement of the critical period hypothesis pertains to inter-individual variability with respect to the onset and termination of sensitive periods. Even though a given critical period might, in itself, be extremely narrow, this does not mean that the onset of the period in different individuals would be equally narrow. That is, life age as measured from the moment of birth, and developmental or maturational age are not necessarily identical, a fact commonly recognized in comparisons between premature and full-term human infants.

A recent study by Gottlieb (1961) demonstrates this point in reference to Peking ducklings. No critical period for imprinting could be established in terms of post-hatch age, but more imprinting occurred on the 27th gestational day than any other. Undoubtedly this is a generally acknowledged fact, but one which seems often ignored as, for example, when Gray (1958) speculates about whether the critical period for the development of filial behavior in the human infant, is before or after six months.

Scott (1958) has emphasized that identification of critical periods in any single animal or breed of animals can best be achieved through an understanding of the pattern of neurophysiological changes which will facilitate new forms of social behavior. Because of the relative inaccessibility of the major sensory systems to external stimulation during the neonatal and transition periods, he discounts the permanent influence of social events occurring therein. However, between approximately three and seven weeks of age, changes in heart rate and EEG functioning give evidence of the possibility of establishment of neural connections between cortex and hypothalamus. As a consequence of these neurophysiological changes, this should be an especially sensitive period for the development of social responses; behaviorally, that is what they have observed. However, he stresses the fact that there are discernible differences in

the rate of maturing of these different systems, and equally important individual differences. He estimates the variability to be approximately three to four days on either side of the average date of onset of a particular natural period, adding, "This means that when experimental procedures are employed in which time is the experimental variable, close attention must be paid to the breed and the state of individual development. Two litters of puppies of exactly the same chronological age could give completely different results" (p. 51). On the basis of the fact that the human life span is approximately six times that of the dog, he estimates that the variability of equivalent periods in the human infant—should they be determined—might be approximately six weeks.

CRITICAL PERIODS IN
HUMAN FILIATIVE BEHAVIOR

In the realm of human social behavior, the most frequent application of the critical period hypothesis seems to have been in the area of attachment behavior—what I have here termed "filiative" behavior. Dressed in both versions of the critical period hypothesis, the theoretical questions asked pertain to whether (1) there are periods during which the human infant is maximally sensitive to the social contacts with its mother, and during which affectional bonds are most easily cemented; and (2) whether, in the absence of mother-infant contact during the sensitive period, a durable infant-mother attachment can ever be established.

Many persons have been struck by the similarity between the emergence of the exclusive infant-mother affectional bond and the attachment behavior—(i.e., imprinting)—experimentally induced in various precocial[Ed] birds and mammals. The word currently used to describe this attachment is "filial" behavior, in that the imprinted bird will demonstrate certain aspects of species-typical filial responses—chiefly physical proximity or active pursuit—to the imprinting object, regardless of whether this object is an inanimate replica of the parent, a human adult, or something like a green cube moving about within the animal's visual field.

Early experiments (Lorenz, 1954; Ramsay, 1951) on imprinting suggested that the filial response to a neutral object could not be elicited unless the imprinting was carried out soon after

Ed "Precocial" refers to birds able to run when newly hatched.

hatching. Most subsequent research has pointed toward a critical period of maximum susceptibility, though there is some difference of opinion about a critical point beyond which the response cannot be obtained. For a recent review covering much of this research, the reader is referred to Moltz (1960).

SUGGESTIONS FROM CLINICAL DATA. The identification in experimental animals and birds of critical periods for filial behavior has led to a wealth of speculation about comparable periods in the human infant. Most of these estimates have been based upon clinical studies of infants and children in whom the normal limits of mother-infant behavior were exceeded—generally, institutionalized or hospitalized children. A review of the literature containing one or another tentative postulation shows that a fairly wide age spread has been covered, ranging roughly from three months to five years. In some of Goldfarb's studies (1955, 1949) one might conclude that age three is a terminus, but in one study (Goldfarb, 1943) a compound of age at institutionalization, plus length of institutionalization, essentially defined the critical period. Bowlby's (1952) affectionless psychopaths were found to have been deprived after six months in some cases, but after twelve months in a majority of cases. The Spitz studies (1946, 1945) are usually interpreted as suggesting that the second six-month period of the first year is more critical than the first six months, but he apparently changed his thinking somewhat, and concluded that serious damage was often done by changes of mother as early as three months (Bowlby, 1952). Gray (1958), considering the clinical literature, plus suggestions from animal studies, proposes that a critical period should range roughly from six weeks to six months. Scott, over the years, has grown increasingly wary about a possible critical period for socialization of the human infant. In 1950, he suggested that it might range from about 15 months to three years (Scott, 1950). In 1958, perhaps overwhelmed by the clinical literature, he was more cautious, suggesting that it might be as early as one month or six weeks or as late as 5-6 months.

Yarrow (1963) has data from what may be the only carefully designed prospective study attempting to secure information on this issue. In this project, the effects of change in mother-figure, during infancy, on personality development are being investigated. Ninety-six cases placed in adoptive homes at different periods during the first year of life have now been fol-

lowed for varying lengths of time. Criteria of the infant's reaction include maternal interviews and tests, and observations of the infants both immediately prior to and immediately following adoptive placement.

Findings to date indicate that some infants show disturbance as early as three months, and that 86 per cent of the cases placed at six months do so. All children placed at seven months or beyond reacted with extreme disturbance. Progressively more severe disturbance was found at each month interval from three to 12 months. Analysis of individual cases seemed to suggest that a superficial relationship with the temporary foster mother was associated with mild or no disturbance, whereas, an intense relationship was associated with more severe disturbance. These data, of course, pertain only to immediate post-placement response.

SELECTING A RELEVANT CRITERION MEASURE. These approaches to a designation of a critical period for filiative behavior are essentially negative; that is, they are based on cases in which a relationship either did not have an opportunity to develop, or else was disrupted after a time. One difficulty in approaching the problem in a positive way is that it is difficult to define filiative behavior during the infancy period. There is probably no other species in which the direction of effort in the mother-infant diad is so unidirectional. No matter how much one might want to wax poetic about the struggle to develop and maintain independent breathing, elimination, etc., the human neonate pretty well "has it made." He doesn't have to get up and start scurrying about after the mother, or get on his feet and find the udder or teat for himself. Even freshly hatched tree-nesting birds, rather dependent creatures at first, must quickly learn to "open" and "gape" at the proper time, or else the parental food offering is likely to go into another hungry mouth, or to the bottom of the nest. Hess (1959a, 1959b) maintains that amount of effort involved is one of the variables associated with strength of imprinting in the duck, with stronger imprinting occurring in response to greater amounts of effort. And, since the human infant exerts so little effort to demonstrate his attachment, we are sometimes "at a loss" to demonstrate it. We have no highly objective, readily observed response—like dashing off down a runway after a green cube, or walking over to the side of a male model decoy, to mention two of the criteria used in recent experiments on imprinting. Yet, if following during the immediate postnatal period is really an instance of filial behavior—as is generally interpreted—then we do indeed have such a response to observe in the human infant. We have *following*.

In view of the attention given the following response by ethologists and experimental psychologists, it is puzzling that so little attention has been paid to it in the human infant. Gray (1958) who has made some provocative speculations about imprinting in the human infant, disregards following and proposes instead that the smiling response is the motor equivalent of following in subprimate species. Since only speculation is possible at this stage, I am going to speculate that the motor equivalent of following is "following" (*i.e.*, visual pursuit). In many ways, the distance receptors of the human infant facilitate a type of contact with his principal caretaker that is not too different from the artificial laboratory situation for eliciting imprinting in precocial birds. Control of the oculomotor muscles develops quickly, and with them the young infant makes very effective pursuit movements. Scanning and searching of the maternal face are commonly reported observations during breast or bottle feeding sessions. Most mothers, and all manufacturers of expensive equipment for slightly older infants, know that the waking infant is likely to be more contented if somehow maintained in a vertical or near-vertical posture—"So he can see," the alert mother will tell you.

Regardless of whether he sees, he indeed looks; and if his looked-at object moves, he follows. To offer more technical data, Graham, Matarazzo, and Caldwell (1956) and Wolff (1959) have demonstrated visual fixation and short pursuit in the human newborn; Griffiths (1954) scores fleeting regard of the examiner's face at one month; Cattell (1940) and Gesell (1941) place the item of "following a moving person with the eyes" at two months. Thus, in a social habitat with limited territory, the human infant at a very early age can follow the parent object. Later, when independent locomotion by any means has been established, the filiated infant adds total body movements to those of his eyes, and strives to maintain physical proximity, as well as visual contact, with the maternal object. In evolutionary terms, it is not hard to understand how the following response is adaptive; the infant, who maintains close proximity to his mother, has a greater likelihood of surviving, whether in a territory occupied by predatory beasts, or by electrical outlets, plastic bags, and abandoned refrigerators.

In a brilliant and provocative paper, Bowlby (1958) has called attention to the following response as one of five "component instinctual responses" likely to be involved in cementing the affectional bond between mother and infant (the others being sucking, clinging, crying, and smiling). In fact, he accords following a higher status than the oft-studied sucking response. Using essentially the choice model of Hess (1958), the author is currently collecting data on some parameters of the following response in infants. Early returns demonstrate that the human infant does not initially follow any one person with the precision of the chicks of Gray and Howard (1957). After having been imprinted to one or the other of those experimenters, 10 of the 12 chicks correctly chose their own imprinter when given a choice between the two. It may be that some infants show the same exclusive pattern of following; only a great deal of empirical data will answer that question. At present, we know that, over a period of months, most infants *do* develop a preference for the mother as a followed object. This may simply be due to the fact that, in the natural environment, the mother is likely to be the most available following object. If so, this would permit social reinforcement to strengthen what may well be initially an unlearned response. The same sort of process undoubtedly operates with respect to the genesis of smiling and of vocalization, as demonstrated in the studies of Brackbill (1958) and Rheingold, Gewirtz, and Ross (1959).

Regardless of the process by which it is strengthened, once the choice for a specific person has been established, then we might say that the following response has matured. This maturation may offer an extremely important clue for the identification of critical attachment periods within a given infant. That is, the appearance of efficient visual pursuit of any human figure should herald the beginning of the critical period. Then, the abandonment of indiscriminate following and the distinct preference for a single followed object—that is, the mother—should signal the termination of this period. Add to this formula, if you will, the early onset of indiscriminate smiling and the later onset of stranger anxiety (or discriminated smiling), and you will have a larger set of variables in terms of which to make predictions.

One way of describing this interactive process is as a series of discrimination learning trials for the infant. Early in the process, he may respond to isolated stimulus characteristics possessed by the mother—(*e.g.*, the capacity to move around, a pair of eye-dots to release smiling, etc.)—but, by no means unique to her. Toward the end of his learning period, he is undoubtedly responding to far more subtle cues and to constellations of cues in such a way that individuals not possessing the total constellation (everyone except the mother) will be rejected. Viewed in this way, the critical period is simply "the length of the learning period required for the establishment of the discriminated filiative response."

There are many intriguing speculations possible, if one accepts the tenability of this explanation; furthermore, they are all amenable to experimental verification or refutation. For example, once this discriminated learning is successful, has the infant moved into a period of resistance—(*i.e.*, a "beyond which" critical period)—to the establishment of a new filiative attachment, should transfer (adoption, foster home placement, etc.) be necessary? One inference which can be drawn from Yarrow's data, namely that infants transferred out of a good foster mother relationship react more negatively than those where the infant-mother relationship is superficial, suggests that this may well be so. Or, on the other hand, is transfer from one maternal object to another safe so long as the learning has not yet reached criterion? The fact that the following response matures at different rates in different infants may help to explain the many different estimates of the time point beyond which new attachments are formed with difficulty, if at all. It is logical to assume that such learning would be more difficult in "polymatric" interpersonal environments; that is, the infant in an institution cared for by several mothers, rather than one mother, has a much more difficult discrimination program than the infant reared in a "monomatric" household.

CRITICAL PERIODS OR EVENTS? This sketch of the kinds of response measures which might be useful in identifying a critical period for filiative behavior helps to anchor the hypothesis more firmly in a behavioral context. That is, the period is critical because of the events that occur therein, because of the state of the organism at that time, and because of the sequence in which the developmental events occur. These same boundaries might occur at three months and nine months in one child, or four weeks

and three months in another. This suggests that it is dangerous to emphasize the *period* too strongly. Probably critical periods for filiative behavior will show general uniformity from one infant or child to another; just as "most" children walk at around a year, talk a half a year later, and so on. But, as mentioned earlier, the wide individual differences in the maturation or learning of significant life functions, ought to caution us that time units do not seem to mean the same thing from one individual to another. Behavior is probably a more accurate signal of the time period the infant has reached than the time period is of the behavior to be expected.

THE CRITICAL PERIOD FOR DETERMINING THE CRITICAL PERIOD? When we are concerned with child behavior, we have the tendency to assume that the penultimate state—or even the antepenult—is the ultimate one. Often, in our well-designed studies, a short time period for evaluation is all that is available. On subsequent evaluations, Yarrow's cases (1960) may have changed significantly. A child deprived of an intense mother-child relationship during infancy may, in later childhood, be affectionless and unattached. Yet, it is entirely possible that this same child will be found to have certain adaptive characteristics for some later point in the developmental cycle. The same point also applies in reverse; early adaptability does not insure future adjustment.

Much developmental learning must be quickly unlearned. For example, the baby for whom finger feeding and the swallowing of solid foods represent a triumph, must soon learn to wrap those fingers around a spoon, or still later to thrust and retrieve with a fork. Likewise, intense affiliative behavior to a specific person must weaken and be replaced by other attachments. The failure of an intense mother-child relationship to weaken is as maladaptive, both ontogenetically and phylogenetically, as courtship behavior from goose to human. Thus, when we scan for significant critical periods, we must not fail to consider ultimate (adult) as well as penultimate criteria. And when we are concerned with infant-mother affiliation, I can think of no better test period—at least not for females—than the period of mothering.

The most intriguing bit of current data relating to this point comes from Harlow (1961). The cloth mother-surrogates, so beautifully engineered and so effective for providing contact comfort and security for monkeys during their infancy and early childhood, seem to have been totally inadequate from the standpoint of fostering the normal species pattern of heterosexual and maternal behavior. That is, monkeys reared on the surrogates do not engage in species-modal heterosexual and mating behavior. At the time of this report, only three of the surrogate-reared monkeys have been impregnated and delivered infants, and their maternal behavior is described as bizarre and totally inadequate. Two of them were either abusive or indifferent, or both, to their infants, while the third was forced into a *little* mothering behavior by an infant willing to endure incredible physical punishment in order to attain maternal contact. To borrow Harlow's inimitable comments on these findings, ". . baby love is strong and wonderful, but one simply cannot trust mothers."

TESTING THE HYPOTHESIS

At this point, I am almost ready to offer my answer to the question raised by our symposium. In order for such an answer to be possible, it seems that we need to proceed along three lines:

1. Encouragement of an experimental teratology of behavior, using animals. Actually this is being done in admirable quantities—witness the work of members of this panel, Scott and his group, and many others too numerous to mention. Many behavioral teratogens, or antiteratogens, have been employed experimentally, and this vast body of data needs to be collated and integrated. Experiments on animal adoptions, imposed separations, surrogate mothers, gentling and handling, the effects of drugs, and so on, are all relevant. Obviously, such animal research could not answer specific questions about critical periods in human development, if we continue to orient the hypothesis *only* in terms of time. If, however, we posed questions more in terms of critical events, or sequences of events, then such research would help us to answer the question of whether such periods do exist, the amount of variability to be expected within a given species, and so on.

2. Epidemiological studies of relevant behavioral manifestations in humans. There are probably lurking around in old file cabinets, a wealth of clinical and social data which could and should be analyzed within a critical periods framework. Many a social agency must have in its files material for a retrospective and less elegant version of the Yarrow study. Both retrospective and short-term epidemiological studies should be encouraged initially. Some critical periods may emerge as the result of an almost random search for possibly related stressors and behavioral effects, plus the interaction effects, as these are geared into the time machine of the life history. An interesting example of this approach is the finding by Wagenheim (1959) of an association in boys between measles contracted around the age of two and subsequent reading disability.

3. Prospective differential studies of human development. Retrospective studies can never be definitive, and in many of our investigations of the development of social behavior, we can never be experimental. Such studies need more than a one-point evaluation period. Only if repeated evaluations can be arranged, can the question of reversibility—which is crucial to the critical period hypothesis—be dealt with adequately.

SUMMARY

This paper has been concerned with formulating an answer to the question, "Is the critical period hypothesis useful in the study of filiative behavior of the human infant?" In general an affirmative answer has been implied, in that the hypothesis highlights an important fourth dimension for behavior theories (*i.e.*, serves as a reminder that time, or timing, cannot be overlooked as a variable in making predictions about behavior). However, in order for the hypothesis to serve behavior theory as more than an orienting framework, certain refinements seem warranted:

1. We should be careful to distinguish the sensitive version from the resistance version of the hypothesis and not assume that the end of one marks the beginning of the other.

2. We should emphasize the events which make any given period critical, the sequence in which they occur, and the behavioral criteria which are to serve as proof of the criticality.

3. Prior to the designation of any one or more time periods as critical, we should make certain that a full range of possible time periods has been sampled.

In conclusion, the author cannot resist paraphrasing Orwell to propose that all periods are critical, only some are probably more critical than others.

REFERENCES

BOWLBY, JOHN. The nature of the child's tie to his mother. *Int. J. Psychoanal.*, 1958, *39*, 1-23.

BOWLBY, JOHN. Maternal care and mental health. Geneva, Switzerland, World Health Organization, 1952, 194.

BRACKBILL, YVONNE. Extinction of the smiling response in infants as a function of reinforcement schedule. *Child Developm.*, 1958, 29, 115-124.

CATTELL, PSYCHE. *The measurement of intelligence of infants.* New York: Psychological Corporation, 1940.

FREEDMAN, D. G., KING, J. A. & ELLIOT, O. Critical period in the social development of dogs. *Science*, 1961, 133, 1016-1017.

GESELL, ARNOLD & AMATRUDA, CATHERINE S. *Developmental diagnosis: normal and abnormal child development.* New York: Paul Hoeber, 1941.

GOLDFARB, WILLIAM. Emotional and intellectual consequences of psychologic deprivation in infancy: a revaluation. In Hoch, P. H., and Zubin, J. (Eds.), *Psychopath. Childh.* New York: Grune and Stratton, 1955, 105-119.

GOLDFARB, WILLIAM. Rorschach test differences between family-reared, institution-reared, and schizophrenic children. *Amer. J. Orthopsychiat.*, 1949, 19, 624-633.

GOLDFARB, WILLIAM. Infant rearing and problem behavior. *Amer. J. Orthopsychiat.*, 1943, 13, 249-265.

GOTTLIEB, GILBERT. Developmental age as a baseline for determination of the critical period in imprinting. *J. comp. physiol. Psychol.*, 1961, 54, 422-427.

GRAHAM, FRANCES K., MATARAZZO, RUTH G. & CALDWELL, BETTYE M. Behavioral differences between normal and traumatized newborns: II. Standardization, reliability, and validity. *Psychol. Monogr.*, 1956, 70 (21), (Whole No. 428), 17-33.

GRAY, P. H. Theory and evidence of imprinting in human infants. *J. Psychol.*, 1958, 46, 155-166.

GRAY, P. H. & HOWARD, K. I. Specific recognition of humans in imprinted chicks. *Percept. mo. Skills*, 1957, 7, 301-304.

GRIFFITHS, RUTH. *The abilities of babies.* New York: McGraw-Hill, 1954, 229.

HAMBURGER, V. Trends in experimental neuroembryology. In *Biochemistry of the developing nervous system*, 1954, 52-73.

HAMBURGER, VIKTOR & HABEL, KARL. Teratogenic and lethal effects of influenza -A and X- mumps viruses on early chick embryos. *Proc. Soc. exper. biol. and Med.*, 1947, 66, 608-617.

HARLOW, HARRY F. Personal communication, 1961.

HAVIGHURST, R. J. *Developmental tasks and education.* New York: Longmans, Green, 1952, 100.

HESS, E. H. Effects of drugs on imprinting behavior. In L. M. Uhr and J. G. Miller, (Eds.), *Drugs and behavior.* New York: John Wiley & Sons, 1960, 268-271.

HESS, E. H. Two conditions limiting critical age for imprinting. *J. Comp. physiol. Psychol.*, 1959a, 52, 515-518.

HESS, E. H. Imprinting. *Science*, 1959b, 130, 133-141.

HESS, E. H., POLT, J. M. & GOODWIN, ELIZABETH. Effects of carisoprodol on early experience and learning. In J. G. Miller, (Ed.), *The pharmacology and clinical usefulness of carisoprodol.* Detroit: Wayne State Univer. Press, 1959c, 51-65.

HESS, E. H. Imprinting in animals. *Scient. Amer.*, 1958, 198 (3), 81-90.

HESS, E. H. Effects of meprobamate on imprinting in waterfowl. *Ann. New York Acad. Sci.*, 1957, 67, 724-732.

JAYNES, J. Imprinting: the interaction of learned and innate behavior: II. The critical period. *J. comp. physiol. Psychol.*, 1957, 50, 6-10.

LORENZ, K. Z. The companion in the bird's world. *Auk*, 1954, 245-273.

MC GRAW, MYRTLE B. Maturation of behavior. In L. Carmichael (Ed.), *Manual of child psychology.* New York: John Wiley & Sons, 1946, 332-369.

MOLTZ, HOWARD. Imprinting: empirical basis and theoretical significance. *Psychol. Bull.*, 1960, 57, 291-314.

RAMSAY, A. O. Familial recognition in domestic birds. *Auk*, 1951, 68, 1-16.

RHEINGOLD, HARRIET L., GEWIRTZ, JACOB L., & ROSS, HELEN W. Social conditioning of vocalizations in the infant. *J. comp. physiol. Psychol.*, 1959, 52, 68-73.

SCOTT, J. P. Critical periods in the development of social behavior in puppies. *Psychosom. Med.*, 1958, 20, 42-54.

SCOTT, J. P. & MARSTON, MARY-'VESTA. Critical periods affecting the development of normal and maladjustive social behavior of puppies. *J. genet. Psychol.*, 1950, 77, 25-60.

SPITZ, R. A. Hospitalism: a follow-up report. In O. Fenichel, *et al.* (Eds.), *The psychoanalytic study of the child.* New York: Int. Univer. Press, 1946, 2, 113-117.

SPITZ, R. A. Hospitalism. In O. Fenichel, *et al.* (Eds.), *The psychoanalytic study of the child.* New York: Int. Univer. Press, 1945, 1, 54-74.

WAGENHEIM, LILLIAN. Learning problems associated with childhood diseases contracted at age two. *Amer. J. Orthopsychiat.*, 1959, 29, 102-109.

WARKANY, J. Etiology of congenital malformations. *Advances in Pediatrics*, 2, 1947, 1-63.

WATSON, R. I. *The psychology of the child.* New York: John Wiley & Sons, 1959.

WOLFF, P. H. Observations on newborn infants. *Psychosom. Med.*, 1959, 21, 110-118.

YARROW, L. J. Research in dimensions of early maternal care. *Merrill-Palmer Quarterly of Behavior and Development*, 1963, 9, 101-114.

44/IMAGE AND SYMBOL IN THE DEVELOPMENT OF MAGNITUDE AND ORDER/JEROME S. BRUNER[*]

I SHOULD LIKE TO DISCUSS THE DEVEL-
opment of the concepts of magnitude and
order in the child from the point of view not
so much of the nature and form of the child's
accomplishments, as represented by solutions to
mathematical problems involving these ideas,
but rather from the point of view of the operations the child uses in attempting to determine
magnitude and to discover or impose order.
How does the child go about the task of estimating magnitudes of various kinds and how
does he search for and find regularity in what
at first might seem to him to be disorder? I
shall give rather short shrift to the symbolic
or mathematical form that describes the child's
solutions—Professor Piaget has done that job
superbly well—and concentrate instead upon
the psychological processes involved. This is in
no sense intended as a criticism of the Geneva
approach, which seeks to translate the child's
problem solving activities into a more economical restatement in logical terms. I would,
however, like to redress a balance. I am among
those who have felt that there has been insufficient emphasis upon the *psychological* processes that lead a child to solve problems in
mathematics or physics by the use of certain
naive theoretical models. For it does not suffice
as psychological description to note only that
a child, at a certain stage, uses, say, nominal
and ordinal scaling and has not grasped either
the idea of equality of interval or the concept
of zero, while later these appear. By the same
token, description is incomplete when we note
only that a child grasps the idea of invariance
across transformations where before he did not.
The power of Piaget's approach is that he has
made us aware of these beautiful formal or
syntactic regularities in the child's behavior. I
have sensed, however, that he has been more
concerned with clarification of these findings in
epistemological and mathematical terms than in
terms of psychological processes. But his powerful techniques of formal description have also
made it possible for us to examine more carefully the means whereby the child achieves the
scientific and logical notion he brings to bear
on his problem solving.

I had better say now rather than later what
I mean by psychological processes, for I have
nothing particularly highbrow in mind. I mean,
quite simply, a description of some intervening
variable between input of information and emis-
sion of behavior that accounts for the fact that
response does not map uniquely on the nature
and change in the stimulus. To take a concrete
case, if the apparent size of an object moving
away from the observer in a rich context does
not change with the size it displaces on the
retina, then we have the task of explaining the
processes that mediate between stimulus variation and perceptual invariance. We set forth a
theory of constancy to account for the formal regularity. Or if we ask a child which of
two containers is fuller, one being a two-quart
beaker containing one quart, the other a two-
pint container containing a single pint, and at
one age children say that the former is fuller
and a year later they say that both are equally
full, then we search for the process that led
them in one case to treat the concept "fuller"
in absolute measure and, in the later case, in
relative measure. What psychological processes
lead a child to use a system of measure and
then to change it? A formal description of the
two systems of measure, however valuable it
may be, does not specify psychological process.
I hope this matter will become clearer as we
go along.

Let me begin by taking a very simple case
of order: a two-dimensional matrix. Suppose we
present the child the following task. Nine beakers are laid out on a surface evenly divided
into a three-by-three grid. The glasses vary
three degrees in height and three degrees in
diameter—as in Figure 1. We familiarize the
child with the matrix by removing first one
glass, then two, and then three at a time, asking
him to replace them. All the children (we studied 10 children at each age from five through
seven) can do this. We also get them to tell
us how the glasses in the rows and columns
are different and how they are alike, principally to sample their language. Then we scramble the glasses, and ask the child to construct
something like what was there before. After

[*] An unpublished address to the XVIIth International Congress of Psychology (Washington, D. C., 1963). Reprinted by permission.

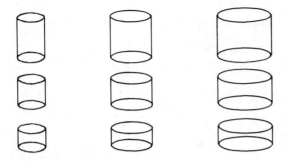

FIGURE 1 / MATRIX PROCEDURE.

that, we reconstitute the matrix and scramble it again, but this time we place one glass on the board—it is the glass that was at the southeast corner before, but it is now placed in the southwest corner. We ask the child whether he can build something like what was there before, only this time he must leave the glass where it has been placed. In order to succeed, in short, he must transpose the matrix.

That is the experiment. The results are surprising from one point of view. On the first task, fives, sixes, and sevens do the task equally well, making very few errors. But on the transposition task, there is a striking difference. Very few of the youngest children succeed; the oldest children do as well with the transposition task as they do with the original. Figure 2 contains the results.

Consider for a moment the behavior of the five-year-olds. In the original task, they, like their older confreres, uniformly produce a matrix of glasses that is positioned identical to the original display. It is as if the children were copying an image. Now comes the transposition. The younger children attempt to move the displaced glass back to its old position, or some of them simply rebuild the original as best they can, putting another glass right over the one that has been displaced. Or, some of them will attempt something that looks like edge-matching to the displaced glass, but then fall into the reconstruction of the original pattern. They do not appear to know how to proceed. The seven-year-old is much more likely to see the transposition problem as a problem; he mumbles to himself, is obviously figuring out something that has to do with ordering the two variables jointly. Almost always, he lays the glasses down next to a glass that was put down before, giving himself maximum perceptual guidance. He has a terminus in mind, but he has step-by-step guides enroute. He is very slow at the task.

I have chosen this example for a particular reason. I think there is a discontinuity in the behavior of the younger and older children having to do with the techniques they are using in processing the information they must deal with. The difference is psychologically crucial. In one case, children are dealing with the display in terms of an organization of information that has the properties of a picture or image; in the second, transposed, case the properties of that image have in some degree been translated into a code or set of rules that can be operated upon to produce transformations that include transpositions in space. The two systems of representing information have quite different design features, and an understanding of the difference between them leads, I think, to an appreciation of what is involved in the internalization of language as an instrument of thought. But before we turn to that matter, let me mention several more observations on children in the period between four and ten, better to elucidate the issues that need explanation.

Let me cite next an experiment by Frank.[1] She was concerned with the kinds of psychological factors that might account for conservation and her experiment begins with the standard conservation procedure. There were 40 children, 10 at each age from four through seven; all were from a suburban school near Boston. Two standard beakers are first used to establish an equality in the amount of water in each. Then the contents of one of them is poured into a taller, thinner beaker and the child is asked whether the two vessels now

[1] Mlle. Francoise Frank, "Perception and Language in Conservation," in Jerome S. Bruner, *Studies in Cognitive Growth* (in preparation).

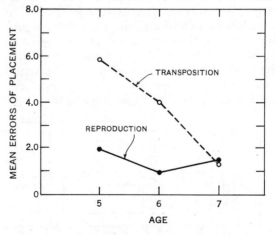

FIGURE 2 / RECONSTRUCTION OF MATRIX.

contain the same amounts of water or whether one has more than the other. A further test for conservation is also made in which the contents of one of the standard beakers is poured into six small beakers, and so on. After this pretest Mlle. Frank's experiment proper begins. Two standard beakers are used, part filled an equal amount. A third, empty beaker is introduced, wider but of the same height as the two standards, and now the three beakers are covered by a screen, except for their tops, as in Figure 3, which shows only one of the standard beakers. The experimenter pours from one of the standard beakers into the wider beaker, and the child is asked, without seeing the water, which has more to drink, the standard beaker or the new beaker. The results are contained in Figure 4. In comparison with the unscreened pretest, there is a striking increase in correct equality judgement, call it conservation if you will. The fours jump from 0% to 50%, the fives from 20% to 90%, and the sixes and sevens from 50% to 100%. Virtually all the children who are correct, whatever the age, justify their judgement by noting that "it's the same water," or "you only poured it." No child mentions anything about compensation of height and diameter; none speaks of reversibility.

Now the screen is removed. All the four-year-olds regress back to their earlier, pretest behavior. The perceptual display overwhelms them and they come out universally with the judgement that the wider beaker has less water. But virtually all of the five-year-olds stick to the judgement they made when the screen was present, and all of the sixes and sevens. The reasons given by children who stick to the conservation judgement after removal of the screen often refer to the distinction between appearance and reality—as one six-year-old put it, "it looks like more to drink, but it is only the same because it is the same water and it was only poured from here to there." Some few mention the fact that if you poured it back, it would look the same as before—reversibility—but none invokes compensation as an argument.

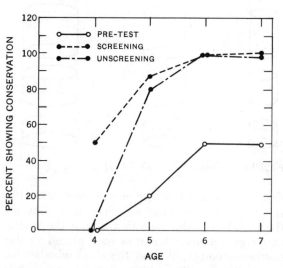

FIGURE 4 / CONSERVATION AND SCREENING.

A quarter-hour later, a post-test for conservation is conducted, identical with the pretest. The results are in Figure 5. The fours are untouched; none of them grasps the idea of invariance any better than before. But with the fives, 70% now show conservation as compared with 20% before, and among the six- and seven-year-olds, conservation increases from 50% to 90%. Control groups, repeating a conservation test some time later the same day, show little change.

How shall we interpret these findings? Let me explore the distinction between "what something looks like" and "what something is." It is a distinction that presupposes two modes of reckoning, the first perceptual and the second involving operations upon the input of perception. The results of the two modes of operation are then compared. What are these operations? Perhaps, as Professor Piaget suggests, the child, at a given point in growth, converts his sensory-motor coordinations into an internalized and reversible symbolic form that has certain crucial logical properties. Can we say anything further psychologically about the two systems and how one is 'changed' into the other?

FIGURE 3 / SCREENING PREDICTION AND FEED-BACK.

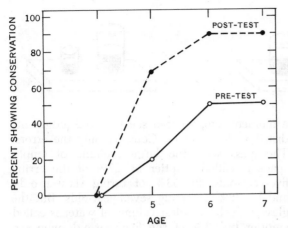

FIGURE 5 / AFTER-EFFECTS OF SCREENING.

Let me approach the matter in the following way. To distinguish how something looks from how something is, in any domain involving magnitude and order, requires that there be parallel systems of information processing. One of them—the look of things—involves the type of activity that we usually speak of as perceptual organization, with its laws of unit formation, grouping, assimilation and contrast, adaptation, level, and such economical transformations, to use Attneave's term,[2] as we are able to master. The other—the conceptual status we call "reality"—involves the translation of perceptual organizations into the terms of a symbol system that has rules for forming, transforming, and verifying propositions. What is unique and powerful about a symbol system is that its rules can generate propositions that do not make literal sense, indeed that violate sense impressions. In the case of the last experiment, the symbol system has a rule of invariance that "the same thing" remains the same thing in *amount* when it is transferred in position. We know from an experiment of Nair's on five-year-olds[3] (40 of them, from a suburban kindergarten) that when water is poured in full view from a rectangular beaker into one that is greater in length and width, most children will say that it is the same water, but more than half of them will then go on to say that

there is less of it (pointing to its lower water level in the new beaker). In the Frank experiment, shielded from the visual sense of the display, the children are able to establish a linguistic rule first and then use it to reinterpret a sense impression.

Let me now turn to an experiment[4] where it is possible to distinguish further the ways in which information is processed and how one must be wary about leaving the matter at the level of logical description. There are 30 children at each age from five through seven. They have the task of saying which of two glasses in a pair is fuller and which is emptier. Children of all three ages have no trouble calling the following display equal (Figure 6a) or saying that the appropriate glass is fuller in the next display (Figure 6b). Now we complicate the task a little. We use pairs of glasses of unequal volume. Under these circumstances, we often find that a child says of a pair of glasses that A is fuller than B and then goes on to say that A is emptier than B as well. Or he calls two vessels equally full and then says that one of them is emptier, and so on. This seemed extraordinary, for it is such a patent contradiction. Ordinarily, one expects errors to be of a type such that if one erroneously says A is fuller than B, one then says that B is emptier than A.

What was the more astonishing was that if one examined errors made by children of ages five through seven, the proportion of errors that were contradictory *increased* with age rather than, as one might have expected, decreased. Let us examine the matter for a moment, since it sheds some light on our problem.

Take, for example, pairs of glasses of unequal volume, each member of the pair filled halfway to the top (Figure 7). Now, only 7% of the five- and six-year-olds say that the pairs are both equally full and equally empty. The sevens do better, but not strikingly: 16% are correct. Consider how the errors distribute themselves over the three ages. Some 27% of the errors of the fives are contradictions, 52% of those of the sixes, and 68% of the errors of the sevens.

[2] F. Attneave, "Some Informational Aspects of Perception," *Psychol. Rev.*, 61 (1954), 183-193.

[3] Patricia Nair, "An Experiment in Conservation," Report of the Center for Cognitive Studies.

[4] Jerome S. Bruner and Helen Kenney, "The Development of the Concepts of Order and Proportion in Children," in Jerome S. Bruner, *Studies in Cognitive Growth* (in preparation).

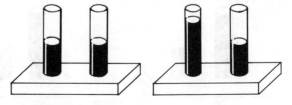

FIGURE 6 (a AND b).

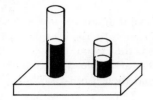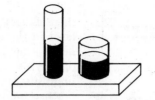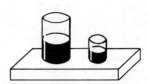

FIGURE 7 (a, b, AND c).

What accounts for the increase in contradiction? There are two alternative interpretations open. One is that the older children are less concerned with consistency, which seems rather far-fetched in view of what else we know. The other is that logical contradiction is a by-product of something else, of the criteria that children of different ages use in judging what is fuller and what emptier.

A close examination of the bases of judgement quickly confirms the latter view. All the children in the age range we have studied use pretty much the same criteria for judging fullness, and these criteria are based on directly observable sensory indices rather than upon proportion. That glass is judged fuller that has the greater volume of water, and the favored indication of greater volume is water level, or where that is equated, then width of glass will do, and when width and water level are the same, then height of glass will prevail. But now consider the judgments made by the three age groups with respect to which glass in each pair is *emptier*. The older children have developed an interesting consistency based on an appreciation of the complementary relation of filled and empty space—albeit an incorrect one. For them "emptier" means the glass that has the largest volume of unfilled space, just as "fuller" meant the glass that had the largest volume of filled space. In consequence, their responses seem logically contradictory. For the glass that is judged fuller also turns out to be the glass that is judged emptier—given a large glass and a small glass, both half full. The younger children, on the other hand, equate emptiness with "littleness": that glass is emptier that gives the impression of being smaller in volume of liquid. If we take the three pairs of glasses mentioned

a moment ago, we can see how the judgments distribute themselves. Consider only the errors. The glass with the larger volume of empty space is called emptier by 27% of the erring five-year-olds, by 53% of erring six-year-olds, and by 72% of erring seven-year-olds. But the glass with the smallest volume of water is called emptier by 73% of the five-year-olds who err, 47% of the sixes, and only 28% of the sevens. When the children are asked for their reasons for judging one glass as emptier, there is further confirmation: most of the younger children justify it by pointing to "littleness" or "less water" or some other aspect of diminutiveness. And most of the older children justify their judgments of emptiness by reference to the amount of empty space in the vessel.

The phenomenon becomes particularly amusing when the children are presented with beakers of uneven volume, with each member of the pair filled to the brim, and asked as before which one is fuller and which emptier. The pairs used are shown below in Figure 8. The handling of full and empty is now forced onto a new footing, for the glasses contain no empty space. As for full judgments—both correct and incorrect judgments are based on a directly apprehended cue: "both up to the top" for correct judgments, or "more water," "higher water level," etc., for incorrect. The sevens do better than the fives or sixes—six in ten correct *versus* four in ten. But the judgments of emptiness are strikingly different. The proportion of correct judgements rises steadily from 57% at age 5 to 84% at age 7. And the reason is quite plain. Since the younger subjects equate emptiness with diminutiveness it is not surprising that some four in ten of them call the beaker with the smaller volume of water "emptier," a tendency that drops steadily to 2% by age 7.

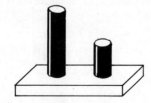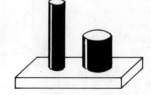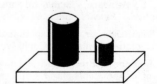

FIGURE 8 (a, b, AND c).

Again, contradiction is the by-product. The older children are prepared to call a larger, filled volume fuller, as are the younger ones. But the older ones then assert, on the grounds that neither container has any empty space at all, that both are equally empty. And so a contradiction emerges. The young, true to their simpler rule of equating big with full and small with empty, emerge as consistent, if wrong. And so while only 33% of the errors of the five-year-olds contain contradictions, the proportion increases to 50% at age 6, and 72% at age 7.

How shall we interpret these findings? Let me suggest that what is involved is a translation difficulty in going from the perceptual or ikonic realm to the symbolic. If you ask children of this age whether something can be fuller and also emptier, they will smile and think that you are playing riddles. They are aware of the contrastive nature of the two terms. Indeed, even the very young child has a good working language for the two poles of the contrast: "all gone" for completely empty and "spill" or "tippy top" for completely full. Recall too that from five to seven, there is perfect performance in judging which of two identical beakers is fuller and emptier. The difference between the younger and the older child is in the number of attributes that are being attended to in situations involving fullness and emptiness: the younger child is attending to one—the volume of water; the older to two—the volume of filled space and the volume of empty space. The young child is applying a single contrast pair—like full-empty —to a single feature of the situation. The older child can attend to two features, but he does not yet have the means for relating them to a third, the volume of the container *per se*. To do so, involves being able to deal with a relation in the perceptual field that does not have a "point-at-able" or ostensive definition. Once the third term is introduced—the volume of the glass— then the symbolic concept of proportion can come to "stand for" something that is not present perceptually. The older child is on the way to achieving the insight, in spite of his contradictions. We have tried to train children in this experiment by giving them discriminaton practice in judging which of two members of a pair has the higher water level, and which glass was higher, but it was to no avail. We think that what is required is not so much discrimination training in the presence of displays, but some means of developing and activating appropriate symbolism for dealing with the sense impressions when they are encountered.

One last comment on the issue of appropriate symbolism. In the matrix experiment described earlier, we examined the language used by children who succeeded and those who failed in building the transposed matrix. Following a lead worked out jointly with Professor Inhelder, we separated the children according to the way they described the difference between glasses that were alike in height but different in diameter and vice versa. The first kind of usage is *dimensional*: one is "tall" the other "short." The second is *global*: one is "big" and the other "little." And the third is *confounded*, where the first two are confused: one is "tall" and the other "little." Confounded language is highly associated with failure in the transposition task, not at all with the simple construction task. We also searched for a relation between use of the comparative form and performance on the task: whether one said big*ger* and littl*er* rather than big and little. We found none. Inhelder and Sinclair,[5] on the other hand, have found that the comparative form is associated with whether or not the child has grasped the idea of conservation of volume. It is difficult to discern exactly how one might establish relationships between spontaneous language use and the extent to which children utilize linguistic distinctions for processing the testimony of their senses, but surely these leads are suggestive of one way of approaching the task.

Let me conclude by returning to the general point made at the outset. The form of a solution achieved by a child can certainly be described compactly and usefully in terms of the logical operations involved, and one can state when the child is or is not using a four-group or the sixteen binary propositions, as Inhelder and Piaget have so brilliantly done.[6] But what is equally important is that we examine the psychological response tendencies that underlie or lead to the logic or theory of the child. We have been at great pains to examine, for example, the nature of logical contradiction in one experiment. Close inspection reveals that it has little to do with the child's "logical" operations concerning consistency *per se,* but rather with how he uses language to order experience. Or in another case, we have looked to the classical conservation study which, logically, is said to depend

[5] B. Inhelder and M. Sinclair, Private Communication.

[6] Barbel Inhelder and Jean Piaget, *The Growth of Logical Thinking*. London: Routledge & Keegan Paul, Ltd., 1958.

upon whether the child is able to grasp the logical concept of compensation—that volume of a liquid remains invariant if its height increases and its diameter decreases to a compensatory degree. We found no explicitly verbalized reason based on compensation in the forty children studied in great detail both behaviorally and linguistically. What we did find, and it is what leads to the child's logical (or illogical) stance was a tendency for children to use perceptual estimation procedures based on ordering the preceptual magnitude of immediately apprehendable cues in a visual display. When the children were activated linguistically before encountering the displays, activated in a linguistic system that contains rules for the maintenance of identity, the perceptual estimating tendency was substantially reduced. Or in the case of the matrix, the ability to handle a double-

classification problem appeared to be a function of whether the children had an image for copying—up to the point where it was necessary to transpose the matrix and then the image failed. At that point, an ordering rule became necessary and judging from the manner in which the children placed the glasses on the matrix, it is likely that the process involved was edge-matching rather than true double classification.

I would urge that what is needed now is a much closer look at the kinds of information processes that lead the child to various logical consistencies. The logical consistencies that we find can most certainly guide the search for processes. I hope that it is obvious that a logical description of different stages of development, all by itself, is scarcely a substitute for a detailed psychological description of how the child grows.

45/DESIGNING A CURRICULUM FOR STUDENT DEVELOPMENT/ STEPHEN M. COREY[*]

EVERY RESPONSIBLE SECONDARY-school educator I know insists that the needs and interests of adolescents must be considered in designing a secondary-school curriculum. Similarly, the great majority of secondary-school educators claim that teaching in the high schools would be better if teachers and administrators had a penetrating understanding of the way adolescent youngsters grow and develop. There are many arguments, usually heated and sometimes enlightening, about the relative amount of attention that should be paid to the personal

needs of teen-age boys and girls. Some say that the concerns of adolescents should be given maximum weight in building the secondary-school curriculum. Others say that, while these concerns are important, they are apt to be ephemeral and transitory, and major attention should be directed to selecting and organizing those aspects of the cultural heritage which must be learned. Despite these arguments, there is general agreement that the way adolescents develop must be taken into account.

It is exceedingly fortunate that few high-

[*] Stephen M. Corey, Designing a curriculum for student development, *The Bulletin of the National Association of Secondary-School Principals*, March, 1948, *32*, 101-110. Copyright: Washington, D. C. Reprinted with abridgement by permission.

school teachers or administrators claim, as do many university professors, that knowledge of subject matter is all that is necessary for good teaching. Extensive familiarity with the facts and generalizations of science, of physical science, and of the various humanistic studies is a necessary condition but not a sufficient condition for effective high-school instruction. Sufficient conditions obtain only when there is added to the teachers' mastery of "subject matter" a sympathetic understanding of the personal needs and interests and wants of adolescent boys and girls. Unless both types of competency characterize high-school instruction, pupils will learn very little of benefit to them.

CONSIDERING PUPILS' NEEDS AND INTERESTS

This does not mean that teen-age youngsters are unique. Everybody in the world learns only when he believes his learning will enable him to get something that he personally wants. This fact is frequently lost sight of in schools because they do not represent voluntary learning organizations in the sense that an adult education program is usually voluntary. Rarely does an adult educator state explicitly, or even imply, this belief: "We will give them what is good for them whether they like it or not." The reason is that, if such an attitude were acted upon, the adults would stay away from the adult education program in large numbers.

School is different, though. Pupils cannot stay away. They can, strictly speaking, but the consequences are so unpleasant as to mean that a school must literally be intolerable before youngsters will stay away from it and accept the various types of punishment in which truancy results.

Compulsory education is not an unmixed blessing. It sometimes acts as a deterrent to the improvement of curriculums. As long as society requires that pupils attend particular schools, one excellent test of their value is precluded. The test I have in mind is the natural test of the worth of any activity; namely, the number of people who voluntarily choose to participate in it. Schools suffer from the sickness that is apt to characterize any monopoly. In most communities there is only one high school that a particular youth can attend. I have often thought that considerable advantage might be gained if, in every city where there were at least two high schools youth might choose to which one they want to go. I recognize that certain difficulties

would be involved, but, if the enrollment of one of these two high schools—or, if not the enrollment, the number indicating they wanted to attend—were 2700, whereas only 300 chose the second, an inquiry would be in order. . . .

To design a curriculum that takes into account the developmental needs of adolescent boys and girls requires that we learn a great deal about adolescents. This is difficult learning. For one thing, our age stands in the way. I recently heard an argument between an adolescent boy and his father. The boy wanted to go with the gang and do a lot of things that the father thought silly. The father finally said: "I can't understand why you want to do those things." The boy answered, rather hopelessly: "You're too old to know." That was an insightful remark. Unless we make a strenuous effort, most of us are too old to learn about adolescents.

If someone invited me to design, in some detail, a high-school curriculum based on the developmental needs of adolescents, I would refuse the invitation. If I were asked, however, to recommend what might be done to assure, in due course, a curriculum that would more nearly meet the needs of adolescents I would say: "Do everything possible to encourage teachers and administrators to learn as much as they can about teen-age boys and girls." . . .

CURRICULUM BUILDING A GRADUAL PROCESS

. . . LEARN THE PSYCHOLOGY OF ADOLESCENCE. In general there are three different ways for adults who work in high schools to increase their understanding of teen-age boys and girls. The most common method is to read articles and books about the psychology of adolescence. This method undoubtedly has some value, but the benefits of reading as a method of learning are probably greatly exaggerated. . . .

RECALL YOUR OWN ADOLESCENCE. Another interesting way to get insight into what is going on in the minds of teen-age youngsters is to try to recall one's own adolescence. This is helpful, but it is also hard and humiliating. I recently heard a group of men teaching in secondary schools talk for a couple of hours about the Halloween pranks they played as boys. Yet when it was reported that one of the high-school youngsters did something that, judged objectively, was nowhere near so bad, these men were furious. Not long ago I was able to eavesdrop on the conversation between a dean of girls and a very attractive high-school sophomore who apparently had said rather forthrightly that she thought boys were more important than algebra. The dean of girls was indignant at this "childish" conclusion, but, when the dean herself and I were students at the University of Illinois, it was clear from her behavior that she thought boys were more important than almost anything else. Even then she probably paid too much attention to her studies, because she got a degree but no husband. Maybe this explains her inability to understand the high-school girl.

STUDY YOUR PUPILS.   The third and best way to gain more insight into what makes secondary-school youngsters tick is to study the ones who are around the high school day after day. It is surprising how many teachers and administrators can spend forty years teaching secondary-school boys and girls and yet know almost nothing about them. This is possible because in most high schools few rewards are given for understanding youth. The rewards go to those who are able to teach the most subject matter and maintain the best discipline. Few secondary-school administrators have been inventive and ingenious in providing ways and means for teachers to work together reaching a better understanding of teen-age boys and girls. When such provisions are not made, teachers probably are correct in inferring that their "superiors" put little premium on such understanding. . . .

One of the best books I have read on this subject was published by the American Council on Education. It is called *Helping Teachers to Understand Children*. This book makes it clear that it is not easy to help an entire faculty reach such understanding. The book also makes clear that before a curriculum which takes the facts of adolescent development into account can be implemented, the teachers must themselves learn about adolescents. . . .

DEVELOPMENTAL TASKS

Whenever teachers do study their own pupils, watching them thoughtfully and trying to draw generalizations from what is seen, they learn that in ever so many ways teen-age youngsters are alike. They are all struggling with some exceedingly important developmental lessons that have to be learned during adolescence. I am not talking about lessons in the sense of assignments high-school teachers habitually require. I am talking about developmental lessons that boys and girls must learn if they are to make a reasonably adequate adjustment to their cul-

ture. I want to spend the next few minutes talking about some of these developmental lessons or developmental tasks. I am convinced that at least one of the major responsibilities of any secondary school is to help boys and girls to become better in achieving these tasks. A curriculum designed for adolescent development would make them the center of attention.

Everyone who has watched youth grow up, whether he be a father or a mother or a teacher, realizes that it is during adolescence that boys and girls first become very much aware of their own bodies. During early and middle childhood, arms and legs and faces are more or less taken for granted. Children use their developing bodies, but they do not notice them particularly. Along about age eleven, twelve, or thirteen, however, and usually some eighteen months to two years earlier for girls, boys and girls become quite conscious of what is going on within their bodies, and of the way their bodies and faces look to others.

Now adults are apt to be impatient with adolescents for paying so much attention to the way they look. The spindly fourteen-year-old boy who wants to look manly and puts four or five handkerchiefs under each shoulder is apt to be ridiculed by his father. This is the case, even though the father himself wears a well-tailored coat with greatly exaggerated shoulders. The boy's mother may scold him for being childish even though she practices some deceitful modification of her natural contours. The problem the boy was struggling with was a real one for him. He was trying to come to terms with his body. Within fairly narrow limits, everyone has to accept his own body and appearances. Adolescents are particularly anxious because they have to accept a new body and new faces in the rapid and dramatic changes in their contours and appearances.

I wish that high-school teachers and administrators could realize how crucial appearances are to many boys and girls. The boy, who is exceedingly and constantly embarrassed because he has acne, has his mind on that problem much of the time. The same is true of the girl who is in anguish because she is some thirty pounds overweight or thirty pounds underweight. Some of you may remember your early adolescence. I ate six yeast cakes a day for several months the first time I had pimples on my face. It took me that long to find anyone sufficiently interested in my welfare to point out to me that eating half a dozen candy bars a day might have something to do with my complexion. Nothing I was learning in school gave me any insight into this serious problem.

A second important developmental task adolescent boys and girls must learn involves working out new relationships to their age mates. Probably the most important and most difficult of these relationships are those involved in playing the proper sex role. Preadolescent groups most commonly are single sex groups. During that period, boys and girls are somewhat contemptuous of one another. When adolescence comes, however, their attitudes change decidedly and they want to be mutually attractive. Even a superficial observer of high-school society cannot help but conclude that ever so many youth spend most of their time trying to learn what to do to be more attractive to the opposite sex.

It is common knowledge that these sexual adjustments are difficult for American youth for a number of reasons. In the first place, while they mature physiologically along about the age of fifteen, sixteen, or seventeen, a very large number of boys and girls cannot behave consistently with this physiological maturity for six or seven years. Society won't let them, if they are in the middle class as most high-school pupils are. This situation makes for a great deal of strain.

A second reason for the difficulty high-school children have making wholesome heterosexual adjustments is that many of their parents won't give them helpful counsel for fear of losing face. A mother, who might be able to talk realistically to her daughter about the pleasures and hazards of pre-marital love making is reluctant to do so. This would risk the fiction of parental perfection, narrowly defined, that most fathers and mothers try to perpetuate. Unmarried high-school teachers are even in a more compromising position. They are not supposed to know much about sex other than what comes out of books, and anyone can read. The consequence is that high-school boys learn about heterosexual relations from each other or from pornographic literature. Both of these sources are interesting, but neither is dependable. The unrest of high-school boys and girls about sexual matters is genuine and the problem is important. The ignorance of adults in this area is reflected in our divorce courts. There is little to indicate that this generation of adolescents will be much better than we are—such is this world's sadness.

A third developmental task or series of problems that adolescent youngsters face as they try to grow up involves the new relationships they must develop to their parents and to other adults. This problem does not cause only fathers and mothers a great deal of difficulty. During adolescence many youngsters become rebellious toward all symbols of authority, including teachers. This is a factor in the relationship of high-school boys and girls to teachers and principals and sometimes to police officers. Adults of whom boys and girls really are fond and whom they have learned to respect are usually influential. The great majority of adults are not in this category, however, and teen-age youth are resistant not only to suggestion but also to authority as well.

This is as it should be. If young people are to become adults, they must escape from the domination of older people who constantly are telling them what to do. We older people like to tell adolescents what to do. It makes us feel powerful. We rationalize by claiming that teen-age youngsters have immature judgment, which is true by definition, and then we do everything we can to keep them from maturing.

As high-school youngsters try to be grown up, they frequently mistake the form for the substance—they mistake the symbol for the real thing. This is disturbing to adults. Girls feel like women if they use a lot of make-up, do their hair right, stay out late at night, and choose their friends without parental interference. Many boys feel like men if they swear, smoke, drink beer, stay out late, dash around in a car, and "sass" their teachers. These ways of being men and women are not good ways, but the desire to be grown up is natural and worthy.

Boys and girls must become men and women. They must develop self reliance, a sense of responsibility, and independence. They must learn to live on their own. They need practice trying to work out their destinies, and they must be permitted to suffer the consequences of their mistakes; or at least most of them. . . .

I never visit a secondary school and watch the boys and girls mill through the corridors as they go from class to class without feeling humble in my ignorance as to what really is going on in their minds. I feel so often that the gap between them and me is almost unbridgeable. On the other hand, I know of no better exercise for a secondary-school teacher or administrator than to work hard at the job of trying to find out what it is boys and girls value and think important. It is only through understanding these aspects of adolescent life that teaching can be made vital and meaningful. It is only through such understanding that a curriculum can eventually be designed and built for student development.

46/ADOLESCENCE[1] / ANNA FREUD*

I. ADOLESCENCE IN THE PSYCHOANALYTIC THEORY

INTRODUCTION.   I return to the subject of adolescence after an interval of twenty years. During this time much has happened in analytic work to throw added light on the problems concerned and to influence the conditions of life for young people, whether normal or abnormal. Nevertheless, in spite of partial advances, the position with regard to the analytic study of adolescence is not a happy one, and especially unsatisfactory when compared with that of early childhood. With the latter period, we feel sure of our ground, and in possession of a wealth of material and information which enables us to assume authority and apply analytic findings to the practical problems of upbringing. When it comes to adolescence, we feel hesitant and, accordingly, cannot satisfy the parents or educational workers who apply for help to us and to our knowledge. One can hear it said frequently that adolescence is a neglected period, a stepchild where analytic thinking is concerned.

[1] The content of this paper is based on material collected in the Hampstead Child-Therapy Clinic with the aid of grants by The Field Foundation, Inc., New York, The Foundations' Fund for Research in Psychiatry, New Haven, Connecticut, The Ford Foundation, New York, The Psychoanalytic Foundation, Inc., and The Grant Foundation, Inc., New York.

These complaints, which come from two sides, from the parents as well as from the analytic workers themselves, seem to me to warrant closer study and investigation than they have received so far. . . .

II. CLINICAL APPLICATIONS

What follows is an attempt to apply at least some of our hard-won insights to three of the most pressing problems concerning adolescence.

IS THE ADOLESCENT UPSET INEVITABLE? There is, first, the ever recurrent question whether the adolescent upheaval is welcome and beneficial as such, whether it is necessary and, more than that, inevitable. On this point, psychoanalytic opinion is decisive and unanimous. The people in the child's family and school, who assess his state on the basis of behavior, may deplore the adolescent upset which, to them, spells the loss of valuable qualities, of character stability, and of social adaptation. As analysts, who assess personalities from the structural point of view, we think otherwise. We know that the character structure of a child at the end of the latency period represents the outcome of long drawn-out conflicts between id and ego forces. The inner balance achieved, although characteristic for each individual and precious to him, is preliminary only and precarious. It does not allow

* Anna Freud, Adolescence, *Psychoanalytic Study of the Child*, 1958. Reprinted by permission of International Universities Press and the author.

for the quantitative increase in drive activity, nor for the changes of drive quality which are both inseparable from puberty. Consequently, it has to be abandoned to allow adult sexuality to be integrated into the individual's personality. The so-called adolescent upheavals are no more than the external indications that such internal adjustments are in progress.

On the other hand, we all know individual children who as late as the ages of fourteen, fifteen or sixteen show no such outer evidence of inner unrest. They remain, as they have been during the latency period, "good" children, wrapped up in their family relationships, considerate sons of their mothers, submissive to their fathers, in accord with the atmosphere, ideas and ideals of their childhood background. Convenient as this may be, it signifies a delay of normal development and is, as such, a sign to be taken seriously. The first impression conveyed by these cases may be that of a quantitative deficiency of drive endowment, a suspicion which will usually prove unfounded. Analytic exploration reveals that this reluctance to "grow up" is derived not from the id but from the ego and superego aspects of the personality. These are children who have built up excessive defenses against their drive activities and are now crippled by the results, which act as barriers against the normal maturational processes of phase development. They are, perhaps more than any others, in need of therapeutic help to remove the inner restrictions and clear the path for normal development, however "upsetting" the latter may prove to be.

IS THE ADOLESCENT UPSET PREDICTABLE? A second question which we are asked to answer frequently concerns the problem whether the manner in which a given child will react in adolescence can be predicted from the characteristics of his early infantile or latency behavior. Apart from the more general affirmative answer given by Ernest Jones (1922), only one among the authors named above has made clear and positive assertions in this respect. Siegfried Bernfeld (1923), when discussing his protracted type of male adolescence and its characteristics, established the links between this form of puberty and a specific type of infantile development based on the following three conditions: (a) that the frustration of infantile sex wishes has been shattering for the child's narcissism; (b) that the incestuous fixations to the parents have been of exceptional strength and have been maintained throughout the latency period; (c) that the superego has been established early, has been delineated sharply from the ego, and that the ideals contained in it are invested with narcissistic as well as with object libido.

Other and less precise answers to the same question are scattered through the literature. We find the opinion that, in the majority of cases, the manifestations of the adolescent process are not predictable since they depend almost wholly on quantitative relations, i.e., on the strength and suddenness of drive increase, the corresponding increase in anxiety causing all the rest of the upheaval.

I suggested in another place (1936) that adolescence brings about occasionally something in the nature of a spontaneous cure. This happens in children whose pregenital activities and characteristics remained dominant throughout latency until the increase in genital libido produces a welcome decrease in pregenitality. This latter occurrence, on the other hand, can be matched by a corresponding one which produces the opposite effect: where phallic characteristics have remained dominant during latency, the increase in genital libido produces the effect of an exaggerated and threatening aggressive masculinity.

It seems to be generally accepted that a strong fixation to the mother, dating not only from the oedipal but from the preoedipal attachment to her, renders adolescence especially difficult. This latter assertion, on the other hand, has to be correlated with two recent findings of a different nature which we owe to work done in our Hampstead Child-Therapy Clinic. One of these findings is derived from the study of orphaned children who were deprived of the relationship to a stable mother figure in their first years. This lack of a mother fixation, far from making adolescence easier, constitutes a real danger to the whole inner coherence of the personality during that period. In these cases adolescence is preceded frequently by a frantic search for a mother image; the internal possession and cathexis of such an image seems to be essential for the ensuing normal process of detaching libido from it for transfer to new objects, i.e., to sexual partners.

The second finding mentioned above is derived from the analyses of adolescent twins, in one case children whose twin relationship in infancy had been observed and recorded in minute detail (Burlingham, 1952). In their treatments it transpired that the "adolescent revolt" against the love objects of infancy demands the breaking of the tie to the twin in no lesser degree than the breaking of the tie to the mother. Since this libidinal (narcissistic as well as object-directed) cathexis of the twin is rooted in the same deep layer of the personality as the early attachment to the mother, its withdrawal is accompanied by an equal amount of structural upheaval, emotional upset, and resulting symptom formation. Where, on the other hand, the twin relationship survives the adolescent phase, we may expect to see a delay in the onset of maturity or a restrictive hardening of the character of the latency period similar to the instances mentioned above in which the childhood love for the parents withstands the onslaught of the adolescent phase.

To return to the initial question: it seems that we are able to foretell the adolescent reactions in certain specific and typical constellations but certainly not for all the individual variations of infantile personality structure. Our insight into typical developments will increase with the number of adolescents who undergo analysis.

PATHOLOGY IN ADOLESCENCE. This leaves us with a third problem which, to my mind, outweighs the preceding ones so far as clinical and theoretical significance are concerned. I refer to the difficulty in adolescent cases to draw the line between normality and pathology. As described above, adolescence constitutes by definition an interruption of peaceful growth which resembles in appearance a variety of other emotional upsets and structural upheavals.[3] The adolescent manifestations come close to symptom formation of the neurotic, psychotic or dissocial order and merge almost imperceptibly into borderline states, initial, frustrated or fully fledged forms of almost all the mental illnesses. Consequently, the differential diagnosis between the adolescent upsets and true pathology becomes a difficult task.

For the discussion of this diagnostic problem I leave most other authors in the field to speak for themselves and summarize my own impressions based on past and present clinical experience.

In 1936, when I approached the same subject from the aspect of the defenses, I was con-

cerned with the similarity between the adolescent and other emotional disturbances rather than with the differences between them. I described that adolescent upsets take on the appearance of a neurosis if the initial, pathogenic danger situation is located in the superego with the resulting anxiety being felt as guilt; that they resemble psychotic disturbances if the danger lies in the increased power of the id itself, which threatens the ego in its existence or integrity. Whether such an adolescent individual impresses us, then, as obsessional, phobic, hysterical, ascetic, schizoid, paranoid, suicidal, etc., will depend on the one hand on the quality and quantity of the id contents which beset the ego, on the other hand on the selection of defense mechanisms which the latter employs. Since, in adolescence, impulses from all pregenital phases rise to the surface and defense mechanisms from all levels of crudity or complexity come into use, the pathological results—although identical in structure—are more varied and less stabilized than at other times of life.

Today it seems to me that this structural description needs to be amplified, not in the direction of the similarity of the adolescent to other disorders but in that of their specific nature. There is in their etiology at least one additional element which may be regarded as exclusive to this period and characteristic for it: namely that the danger is felt to be located not only in the id impulses and fantasies but in the very existence of the love objects of the individual's oedipal and preoedipal past. The libidinal cathexis to them has been carried forward from the infantile phases, merely toned down or inhibited in aim during latency. Therefore the reawakened pregenital urges, or—worse still—the newly acquired genital ones, are in danger of making contact with them, lending a new and threatening reality to fantasies which had seemed extinct but are, in fact, merely under repression.[4] The anxieties which arise on these grounds are directed toward eliminating the infantile objects, i.e., toward breaking the tie with them. Anny Katan (1937) has discussed this type of defense, which aims above all at changing the

___

[3] Adolescence, of course, is not the only time in life when alterations of a physiological nature cause disturbances of mental equilibrium. The same happens in later years in the climacterium; and recently, Grete L. Bibring has given a convincing description of similar damage to the equilibrium of mental forces during pregnancy.

[4] An important clinical instance of this can be found in adolescent girls with anorexia nervosa. Here the infantile fantasies of oral impregnation receive added impetus from the new real possibilities of motherhood opened up by genital development. Consequently, the phobic measures adopted against the intake of food on the one hand and identification with the mother on the other hand are overemphasized to a degree which may lead to starvation.

persons and the scene of conflict, under the term of "removal." Such an attempt may succeed or fail, partially or totally. In any case, I agree with Anny Katan that its outcome will be decisive for the success or failure of the other, more familiar line of defensive measures which are directed against the impulses themselves.

A number of illustrations will serve to clarify the meaning of this assumption.

(I) *Defense Against the Infantile Object Ties.*
Defense by Displacement of Libido. There are many adolescents who deal with the anxiety aroused by the attachment to their infantile objects by the simple means of flight. Instead of permitting a process of gradual detachment from the parents to take place, they withdraw their libido from them suddenly and altogether. This leaves them with a passionate longing for partnership which they succeed in transferring to the environment outside the family. Here they adopt varying solutions. Libido may be transferred, more or less unchanged in form, to parent substitutes, provided that these new figures are diametrically opposed in every aspect (personal, social, cultural) to the original ones. Or the attachment may be made to so-called "leaders," usually persons in age between the adolescent's and the parents' generation, who represent ideals. Equally frequent are the passionate new ties to contemporaries, either of the same or of the opposite sex (i.e., homosexual friendships) and the attachments to adolescent groups (or "gangs"). Whichever of these typical solutions is chosen, the result makes the adolescent feel "free," and revel in a new precious sense of independence from the parents who are treated, then, with indifference bordering on callousness.

Although the direction taken by the libido in these instances is, in itself, on lines of normality, the suddenness of the change, the carefully observed contrast in object selection, and the overemphasis on the new allegiances mark it as defensive. It represents an all too hasty anticipation of normal growth rather than a normal developmental process.

It makes little further difference to the emotional situation whether the libidinal flight is followed by actual flight, i.e., whether the adolescent also "removes" himself bodily from his family. If not, he remains in the home in the attitude of a boarder, usually a very inconsiderate one so far as the older and younger family members are concerned.

On the other hand, the withdrawal of cathexis from the parents has most decisive consequences for the rest of the defensive processes. Once the infantile objects are stripped of their importance, the pregenital and genital impulses cease to be threatening to the same degree. Consequently, guilt and anxiety decrease and the ego becomes more tolerant. Formerly repressed sexual and aggressive wishes rise to the surface and are acted on, the actions being taken outside the family in the wider environment. Whether this acting out will be on harmless, or idealistic, or dissocial, or even criminal lines will depend essentially on the new objects to which the adolescent has attached himself. Usually the ideals of the leader, of the adolescent group, or of the gang, are taken over wholeheartedly and without criticism.

Adolescents of this type may be sent for treatment after their actions have brought them into conflict with their schools, their employers, or the law. As far as psychoanalytic therapy is concerned, they seem to offer little chance for the therapeutic alliance between analyst and patient without which the analytic technique cannot proceed. Any relationship to the analyst and, above all, the transference to him would revive the infantile attachments which have been discarded; therefore the adolescent remains unresponsive. Also, the escape from these attachments has suspended the feeling of internal conflict, at least temporarily; consequently, the adolescent does not feel in need of psychological help. A. Aichhorn had these points in mind when he maintained that adolescents of the dissocial and criminal type needed a long period of preparation and inner rearrangement before they could become amenable to analytic treatment. He maintained that the latter would be successful only if, during this preparation in a residential setting, the adolescent made a new transference of object love, reawakened his infantile attachments, internalized his conflicts once more, in short, became neurotic.

To try and analyze an adolescent in his phase of successful detachment from the past seems to be a venture doomed to failure.

Defense by Reversal of Affect. A second typical reaction to the same danger situation, is, although less conspicuous outwardly, more ominous in nature inwardly.

Instead of displacing libido from the parents —or, more likely, after failing to do so—the adolescent ego may defend itself by turning the emotions felt toward them into their opposites. This changes love into hate, dependence into revolt, respect and admiration into contempt and derision. On the basis of such reversal of affect the adolescent imagines himself to be "free" but, unluckily for his peace of mind and sense of conflict, this conviction does not reach further than the conscious surface layer of his mind. For all deeper intents and purposes he remains as securely tied to the parental figures as he has been before; acting out remains within the family; and any alterations achieved by the defense turn out to his disadvantage. There are no positive pleasures to be derived from the reversed relationships, only suffering, felt as well as inflicted. There is no room for independence of action, or of growth; compulsive opposition to the parents proves as crippling in this respect as compulsive obedience to them can prove to be.[5] Since anxiety and guilt remain undiminished, constant reinforcement of defense is necessary. This is provided in the first place by two methods: denial (of positive feeling) and reaction formations (churlish, unsympathetic, contemptuous attitudes). The behavioral picture that emerges at this stage is that of an uncooperative and hostile adolescent.

Further pathological developments of this state of affairs are worth watching. The hostility and aggressiveness, which serve as a defense against object love in the beginning, soon become intolerable to the ego, are felt as threats, and are warded off in their own right. This may happen by means of projection; in that case the aggression is ascribed to the parents who, consequently, become the adolescent's main oppressors and persecutors. In the clinical picture this appears first as the adolescent's suspiciousness and, when the projections increase, as paranoid behavior.

Conversely, the full hostility and aggression may be turned away from the objects and employed inwardly against the self. In these cases, the adolescents display intense depression, tendencies of self-abasement and self-injury, and develop, or even carry out, suicidal wishes.

During all stages of this process, personal suffering is great and the desire to be helped intense. This, in itself, is no guarantee that the adolescent in question will submit to analytic therapy. He will certainly not do so if treatment is urged and initiated by the parents. Whenever this happens, he will consider analysis as their tool, extend his hostility or his suspicions to include the person of the analyst, and refuse

cooperation. The chances are better if the adolescent himself decides to seek help and turns to analysis, as it were, in opposition to the parents' wishes. Even so, the alliance with the analyst may not be of long duration. As soon as a true transference develops and the positive infantile fantasies come into consciousness, the same reversal of affect tends to be repeated in the analytic setting. Rather than relive the whole turmoil of feelings with the analyst, many adolescent patients run away. They escape from their positive feelings, although it appears to the analyst that they break off treatment in an overwhelmingly strong negative transference.

Defense by Withdrawal of Libido to the Self. To proceed in the direction of increasing pathology:

Withdrawal of libido from the parents, as it has been described above, does not, in itself, decide about its further use, or fate. If anxieties and inhibitions block the way toward new objects outside the family, the libido remains within the self. There, it may be employed to cathect the ego and superego, thereby inflating them. Clinically this means that ideas of grandeur will appear, fantasies of unlimited power over other human beings, or of major achievement and championship in one or more fields. Or, the suffering and persecuted ego of the adolescent may assume Christ-like proportions with corresponding fantasies of saving the world.

On the other hand, the cathexis may become attached to the adolescent's body only and give rise there to the hypochondriacal sensations and feelings of body changes that are well known clinically from initial stages of psychotic illness.

In either case analytic therapy is indicated as well as urgent. Treatment will dispel the appearance of severe abnormality if it reopens a path for the libido, either to flow backwards and recathect the original infantile objects, or to flow forward, in the direction described above, to cathect less frightening substitutes in the environment.

What taxes the analyst's technical skill in these cases is the withdrawn state of the patient, i.e., the problem of establishing an initial relationship and transference. Once this is accomplished, the return from narcissistic withdrawal to object cathexis will relieve the patient, at least temporarily.

I believe there are many cases where the analyst would be wise to be content with this partial success without urging further treat-

[5] S. Ferenczi has pointed to this effect of "compulsive disobedience" many years ago.

ment. A further, and deeper, involvement in the transference may well arouse all the anxieties described above and, again, lead to abrupt termination of the analysis due to the adolescent's flight reaction.

Defense by Regression.   The greater the anxiety aroused by the object ties, the more elementary and primitive is the defense activity employed by the adolescent ego to escape them. Thus, at the extreme height of anxiety, the relations with the object world may be reduced to the emotional state known as "primary identification" with the objects. This solution with which we are familiar from psychotic illnesses implies regressive changes in all parts of the personality, i.e., in the ego organization as well as in the libido. The ego boundaries[6] are widened to embrace parts of the object together with the self. This creates in the adolescent surprising changes of qualities, attitudes and even outward appearance. His allegiance to persons outside himself betrays itself in these alterations of his own personality (i.e., his identifications) rather than in an outflow of libido. Projections, together with these identifications, dominate the scene and create a give-and-take between the self and object which has repercussions on important ego functions. For example, the distinction between the external and internal world (i.e., reality testing) becomes temporarily negligible, a lapse in ego functioning which manifests itself in the clinical picture as a state of confusion.

Regression of this kind may bring transitory relief to the ego by emptying the oedipal (and many of the preoedipal) fantasies of their libidinal cathexis.[7] But this lessening anxiety will not be long-lived. Another and deeper anxiety will soon take its place which I have characterized on a former occasion (1951) as the fear of emotional surrender, with the accompanying fear of loss of identity.

(II) Defense Against Impulses. Where the defenses against the oedipal and preoedipal object ties fail to achieve their aim, clinical pictures emerge which come nearest to the borderline toward psychotic illness.

The "Ascetic" Adolescent.   One of these, the "ascetic" adolescent, I have described before as fighting all his impulses, preoedipal and oedipal, sexual and aggressive, extending the

defense even to the fulfillment of the physiological needs for food, sleep, and body comfort. This, to me, seems the characteristic reaction of an ego, driven by the blind fear of overwhelming id quantities, an anxiety which leaves no room for the finer distinctions between vital or merely pleasant satisfactions, the healthy or the morbid, the morally permitted or forbidden pleasures. Total war is waged against the pursuit of pleasure as such. Accordingly, most of the normal processes of instinct and need satisfaction are interfered with and become paralyzed. According to clinical observation, adolescent asceticism is, with luck, a transitory phenomenon. For the analytic observer it provides precious proof of the power of defense, i.e., of the extent to which the normal, healthy drive derivatives are open to crippling interference by the ego.

On the whole, analytic treatment of the ascetic type does not present as many technical difficulties as one would expect. Perhaps, in these individuals, defense against the impulses is so massive, that they can permit themselves some object relationship to the analyst and, thus, enter into transference.

The "Uncompromising" Adolescent.   Another, equally abnormal adolescent, is described best as the "uncompromising" type. The term, in this instance, does refer to more than the well-known conscious, unrelenting position adopted by many young people who stand up for their ideas, refuse to make concessions to the more practical and reality-adapted attitudes of their elders, and take pride in their moral or aesthetic principles. "Compromise," with these adolescents, includes processes which are as essential for life as, for example, the cooperation between impulses, the blending of opposite strivings, the mitigation of id strivings by interference from the side of the ego. One adolescent whom I observed in analysis did his utmost, in pursuit of this impossible aim, to prevent any interference of his mind with his body, of his activity with his passivity, his loves with his hates, his realities with his fantasies, the external demands with his internal ones, in short, of his ego with his id.

In treatment this defense was represented as a strong resistance against any "cure," the idea of which he despised in spite of intense suffering. He understood correctly that mental health is based in the last resort on harmony, i.e., on the very compromise formations which he was trying to avoid.

---

[6] See P. Federn (1952) and, following him, T. Freeman et al. (1958).

[7] See in this connection M. Katan (1950).

III. THE CONCEPT OF NORMALITY IN ADOLESCENCE

Where adolescence is concerned, it seems easier to describe its pathological manifestations than the normal processes. Nevertheless, there are in the above exposition at least two pronouncements which may prove useful for the concept: (1) that adolescence is by its nature an interruption of peaceful growth, and (2) that the upholding of a steady equilibrium during the adolescent process is in itself abnormal. Once we accept for adolescence disharmony within the psychic structure as our basic fact, understanding becomes easier. We begin to see the upsetting battles which are raging between id and ego as beneficent attempts to restore peace and harmony. The defensive methods which are employed either against the impulses, or against the object cathexis, begin to appear legitimate and normal. If they produce pathological results, this happens not because of any malignancy in their nature, but because they are overused, overstressed, or used in isolation. Actually, each of the abnormal types of adolescent development, as it is described above, represents also a potentially useful way of regaining mental stability, normal if combined with other defenses, and if used in moderation.

To explain this last statement in greater detail: I take it that it is normal for an adolescent to behave for a considerable length of time in an inconsistent and unpredictable manner; to fight his impulses and to accept them; to ward them off successfully and to be overrun by them; to love his parents and to hate them; to revolt against them and to be dependent on them; to be deeply ashamed to acknowledge his mother before others and, unexpectedly, to desire heart-to-heart talks with her; to thrive on imitation of and identification with others while searching unceasingly for his own identity; to be more idealistic, artistic, generous, and unselfish than he will ever be again, but also the opposite: self-centered, egoistic, calculating. Such fluctuations between extreme opposites would be deemed highly abnormal at any other time of life. At this time they may signify no more than that an adult structure of personality takes a long time to emerge, that the ego of the individual in question does not cease to experiment and is in no hurry to close down on possibilities. If the temporary solutions seem abnormal to the onlooker, they are less so, nevertheless, than the hasty decisions made in other cases for one-sided suppression, or revolt, or flight, or withdrawal, or regression, or asceticism, which are responsible for the truly pathological developments described above.

While an adolescent remains inconsistent and unpredictable in his behavior, he may suffer, but he does not seem to me to be in need of treatment. I think that he should be given time and scope to work out his own solution. Rather, it may be his parents who need help and guidance so as to be able to bear with him. There are few situations in life which are more difficult to cope with than an adolescent son or daughter during the attempt to liberate themselves.

IV. SUMMARY

In the foregoing papers the author has reviewed and summarized some of the basic literature on adolescence, as well as her own views on the subject. Her former description of the defensive processes in adolescence has been amplified to include specific defense activities directed against the oedipal and preoedipal object ties.

BIBLIOGRAPHY

AICHHORN, A. (1925), *Wayward Youth.* New York: Viking Press, 1948.

BERNFELD, S. (1923), Über eine typische Form der männlichen Pubertät. *Imago*, IX.

BURLINGHAM, D. (1952), *Twins.* New York: International Universities Press.

FEDERN, P. (1952), *Ego Psychology and the Psychoses.* New York: Basic Books.

FREEMAN, T., CAMERON, L. J. and MC GHIE, A. (1958), *Chronic Schizophrenia.* New York: International Universities Press.

FREUD, A. (1936), *The Ego and the Mechanisms of Defense.* New York: International Universities Press, 1946. See Chapters X and XI.

FREUD, A. (1951), A Connection between the States of Negativism and of Emotional Surrender (Horigkeit). Paper read at the International Psycho-Analytical Congress, Amsterdam, August 1951. Summary in *Int. J. Psa.*, XXXIII, 1952, p. 265.

JONES, E. (1922), Some Problems of Adolescence. *Papers on Psycho-Analysis.* London: Bailliere, Tindall & Cox, fifth edition, 1948.

KATAN-ANGEL, A. (1937), The Role of Displacement in Agoraphobia. *Int. J. Psa.*, XXXII, 1951.

KATAN, M. (1950), Structural Aspects of a Case of Schizophrenia. *This Annual*, V.

47/CRISES IN NORMAL PERSONALITY
DEVELOPMENT/GORDON W. ALLPORT*

THERE IS ONE TRICK EVERY TEACHER knows: When trapped in a state of ignorance throw the question back to the class. Without suspecting the teacher's predicament, bright students will often rescue him.

This is the strategy I employed to learn something about crises in normal personality development. I passed along the assignment to my class of 100 captive undergraduates, and they obligingly provided me, through their own autobiographical writing, with the insights that I articulate now. Parenthetically, let me say that in my opinion no teacher or counselor has the right to require intimate autobiographical documents from students. Yet when given a completely free choice, the large majority will choose to write in the autobiographical vein. For the few who would find the experience too threatening, it should not be prescribed.

. . . .

It is in middle and late adolescence, . . . according to Erikson (3), that the identity crisis is in the ascendance.[Ed] The young person seems to be moving from past childhood into present adulthood in a jerky manner. Development is not continuous like a hill; rather, it is episodic like a flight of stairs. It is this episodic or crisis character of development that brings both challenge and opportunity to the guidance officer.

NATURE OF CRISIS

What precisely is a "crisis"? It is a situation of emotional and mental stress requiring significant alterations of outlook within a short period of time. These alterations of outlook frequently involve changes in the structure of personality. The resulting changes may be progressive in the life or they may be regressive. By definition, a person in crisis cannot stand still; that is to say, he cannot redact his present traumatic experience into familiar and routine categories or em-

ploy simple habitual modes of adjustment. He must either separate himself further from childhood and move toward adulthood, or else move backward to earlier levels of adjustment which may mean becoming disorganized, dropping out of school, escaping from the field, developing hostilities and defenses, and in general becoming a thorn in the flesh of the teacher, the parent, the counselor, the dean, and occasionally of the police. Sometimes, following a crisis, the adolescent will become stabilized anew after four or five weeks of severe disorganization; but in many cases the trauma retards development for a year or more, and may even leave a lifelong scar.

Turning now to my data, drawn from college undergraduates, we ask first about the phenomenology of crisis. What does it "feel" like to the student? Common is a sense of numbness and apathy. Upon entering college, the youth finds fewer strict role-prescriptions than at home. He is no longer tied to his domestic filial role, to the highly structured routine of high school, to his siblings, to his church connections, to his teen-age sub-cultures. He has left his possessions behind—his stamp collection, his television, his girl friends, his boy friends. All his familiar roles are in suspension. As one student writes,

The complete freedom of college is itself a crisis. For the first time I live in close contact with people who are not members of my family. They don't even resemble people I have known before. They have different opinions, different origins, and different emotions. I feel numbed by it all.

Interestingly enough, this sense of hollowness does not necessarily have its maximum effect during the freshman year. The excitement of new scenes and especially frequent correspondence with and visits back to the home town keep the silver cord intact. The student feels that he should prove to his parents, teachers, friends, that he can master the college environment and thus please them and win their approval as he has done in the past. The im-

[Ed] *Erikson's views are stated at the beginning of this section in the article based on his work (no. 40).*

* Gordon W. Allport, Crises in normal personality development, *Teachers College Record*, 1964, *66* (3), 235-241. Reprinted, with slight abridgement, by permission.

335

pending crisis has not yet overwhelmed him (or her—for what I am saying is as true for college girls as for boys).

It is the sophomore year that seems (from my data) to be the year of crisis *par excellence*. Suddenly it becomes no longer tolerable to live one's life for the edification of people "back home." The time has come for the child of the past to be separated once and for all from the adult of the present. Here are typical phenomenological statements of this stage of the crisis:

I feel I have been dragged into something against my will.

I feel like a rat in a maze.

I want to be a law unto myself, but cannot.

It seems suddenly that the decisions I make must be valid for the rest of my life.

To shake off parental norms and values seems to me the most important thing I must do.

The life of the past and the life of the future seem suddenly to be at cross purposes. There is often an intolerable feeling of suspended animation. Recrystallization is not yet possible. The youth is waiting still to make a choice of careers, a suitable marriage, and to find an integrative philosophy of life which his diverse college courses are too discordant to supply.

APATHY AND ANXIETY

It is small wonder that apathy and a paralysis of will often occur. But apathy is only a mask for anxiety. The whole framework of life is disturbed. Whereas the majority of students contrive gradually to build a new framework in spite of, or perhaps because of, the goads of anxiety, yet a large minority cannot cope with the situation unaided.

From my data, I would estimate that three-quarters are able to take the progressive road in creating their new frame of existence. About one-quarter cannot immediately do so. Proof of this point is that the dropout rate during undergraduate years is surprisingly high—over 20 per cent at Harvard, about three-quarters of the cases representing voluntary withdrawals (2). The dropouts present a special problem of guidance. Blaine and McArthur (2) write,

The drop-outs as a group ultimately do quite well if properly handled. We attempt to establish a relationship, however brief or tenuous, with these students, not so much to prevent their leaving school, but rather in the hope of giving them some insight into the determinants of their difficulties so that

their dropping out can be ultimately converted into a meaningful constructive experience instead of mere failure.

After a year or two of constructive work elsewhere, the majority of voluntary dropouts return to college and graduate. But they could not have met their crisis by remaining in the environment that was the context of their conflict.

The regressive road is surprisingly common. Among eventual dropouts, but also among other students, we find such self-destroying behavior as quitting classes, a compulsion to do trivial things, playing bridge until four A.M., drinking bouts, feelings of unreality, fugues, and general debauchery. The candid documents received startle me a bit by the extent of plain juvenile delinquency among my innocent-appearing students:

One student finding himself unable to handle his conflicts over choice of career and over friction with his roommate, indulged in plagiarism on a term paper in such a way that he would be caught and forcibly separated from college. In this case a wise instructor, catching him in the transgression, turned the occasion into constructive counseling, forgave the deed, and put the lad onto the progressive rather than regressive road.

Here I venture a theoretical digression. The problem, as I see it, is one of interiorizing motivation. To put it in a student's words: "I am fed up with having everybody else cheer me on. I want to work to please myself rather than others, but I don't know how to do it." This plaintive statement points to a serious dilemma in our educational process. In school, the child is rewarded and punished by good grades and bad grades. Even in college, As and Bs are pats on the back, Ds and Fs are punishments. To gain love, the student must read books and toe the academic line. Finally, he obtains his degree (which is a symbol of academic love) and is freed from this external form of motivation. What then happens?

We know that a shockingly high percentage of college graduates rarely or never read another book after receiving their bachelor's degree. Why should they? Their love now comes from their employer, their wife, their children, not from the approval of parents and teachers. For them, intellectual curiosity never became a motive in its own right. External rewards are appropriate props in early childhood. But we educators, being limited by current inadequate theories of learning, do not know how to help the student free himself from the props of reward and develop a functionally autonomous zeal for learning. With our slavish dependence on reinforcement theory, I think it surprising that we arouse as much internal motivation as we do. In any event, we cannot be proud of the many educational cripples who after graduation, lacking the routine incentive of college, sink into intellectual apathy.

CRISIS AREAS

The counselor or teacher, of course, cannot wait for better theories of learning. He is confronted here and now with crises in the concrete. Four areas of conflict, judging from my data, are especially common.

INTELLECTUAL CRISES. First, there are students whose problem is one of intellectual malplacement. Among my cases, a large number report that in primary and secondary school they were too bright for their class. The penalty is one of boredom lasting down into college work, which they still do not find challenging enough for their abilities. At the same time, double promotions in elementary and high school are not a solution. To be placed with older children often creates social difficulties far more serious than boredom. In fact, the evil consequences reported from double promotion are so numerous that we should challenge this particular solution of the bright child's dilemma.

The opposite type of intellectual crisis is also common. It is the deep disturbance that often results in college from intensified competition. It is statistically impossible for most students to maintain the same relative superiority in college that they enjoyed in high school. While this fact does not trouble the majority, it is a critical experience for those who depend on scholarship aid or who frame their self-image almost entirely in terms of scholarly preeminence. They are suffering a severe narcissistic wound.

SPECIFIC INFERIORITIES. A second area of crisis is the old, familiar "inferiority complex." Besides the sense of intellectual inferiority just described, we encounter deep disturbance due to physical handicaps or to plain physical appearance, with resulting shyness, loneliness, and misery. To be poor at athletics creates a crisis for males, probably more acute in high school than in college. To be a member of a minority group likewise creates an inevitable crisis somewhere along the line. Here again I suspect the major adjustments and defenses are prepared before the college age. Occasionally, the inferiority concerns guilt due to moral lapses. One student is still haunted by her dishonesty which enabled her to pass a certain course three years ago. She has felt miserable ever since about this critical experience and badly needs a means of expiation.

In this connection we may speak of religious crises. While they are uncommon in my sample, Havens (5) estimates that at any given time 12 per cent of college students have a critical concern, and sometimes acute crises, due to their religious conflicts. I suspect the concern is even more widespread, but since it pertains to one's whole ground of being, it is seldom configurated as a specific crisis at a given moment of time.

Another area, seldom mentioned but surely important, is the ideological crisis of modern society as a whole. Youth is inevitably worried, as are adults, by our uncertain future. Elsewhere I have discussed the withdrawal of American youth from their social and political context (4). Both the earlier and present data show an almost exclusive concern among American youth with their own lives. Compared with autobiographies of youth in other cultures, the American documents are far more self-centered, more privatistic. They are too baffled to articulate their distress, and so take refuge in their private concerns.

SEX AND FAMILY[Ed]

SEX CONFLICTS. Needless to say, our candid discussions of crises frequently, in fact usually, report acute sex conflicts. Extremely common are breakups in boy-girl relationships which are usually taken as a disaster only slightly less fatal than the end of the world. Such breakups are so recently experienced that college students do not realize that they will, in spite of their present feelings, eventually make a good recovery.

We should face the fact that at least in the early years of college life crises in the sexual sphere are for the most part frankly genital in their reference. The biological drive is so powerful that the youth is concerned with it almost

[Ed] *In order to interpet the material which follows, the reader should know that the majority of students in this study were males.*

by itself. Its integration into mature love, into marriage, into career plans, into an embracing philosophy of life, exceeds his present capacity. He is likely to think that genitality by itself is maturity. Sexual gratification is frankly the aim, often with devastating consequences. At this stage of development, the students have much to say about sex and little to say about mature love.

FAMILY CONFLICTS. I have left until last the most pervasive area of conflict and crisis. I am referring, of course, to the situation that exists between every adolescent and his parents. It is not enough to say that adolescent rebellion against the parents is the rule. Of course it is; but my documents show that the whole history of the relationships from the time of earliest memories is important. Almost any irregularity in normal family life is felt bitterly and may trouble a student even into adulthood. A mother who is neglectful or self-centered, or perhaps overpossessive and neurotic, leaves traumatic traces in the child's life. A father who is ineffectual and weak, or cruel, or absent (if only for wartime service) leaves the child with a lasting feeling of protest.

One document of unusual maturity notes that many college students seem to need their parents as scapegoats. They find it comfortable to blame parents for their own shortcomings. Perceiving that their parents are not all-powerful, all-wise, and all-perfect, they can say, "Well, no wonder I am having a hard time growing up; they didn't raise me right." Thus, an adolescent, having no genuine ground for complaint, may yet soak himself in self-pity, not being mature enough to relate his restricted image of his parents to the totality of human nature—not yet ready to appreciate the fact that his parents, considering human limitations, may have done a good job. Even if the job was not especially good, the adolescent seems not yet able to appreciate his parents' good intentions as an important value in their own right. From talking with many parents, I hazard the hypothesis that normally it is not until the age of 23 that a child encounters his parents on a mature, adult-to-adult basis.

This brief account of crises emanating from the parent-child relationship leads me to a final point. My students were required to discuss their crises from the point of view of personality theory. They were free to employ any of the theories they were studying in my course. Most of them took Freud. (I may add that

the reason was not because Freud was their instructor's favorite author.)

THE CONDITIONS OF THEORY

Now my observation is this: Their Freudian interpretations seemed to fit well if and when the family situation in early life was disturbed. When the father was absent or ineffectual, when the mother was notably aggressive, when there was deliberate sex stimulation within the family—in such cases, it seems that the Oedipal formula provides a good fit, together with all its theoretical accoutrements of identification, superego conflict, defense mechanisms, castration threats, and all the rest.

When, on the other hand, the family life is reasonably normal and secure, a Freudian conceptualization seems forced and artificial. If we say, by way of rough estimate, that 60 per cent of the students try a Freudian conceptualization of their own cases, about 10 per cent turn out to be wholly convincing and theoretically appropriate. The remaining 50 per cent appear to be somehow contrived and badly strained.

I am wondering whether the same ratio might be applicable to cases that come to counselors. If a counselor or a therapist approaches every client or patient with the preconceived belief that his life must fit a Freudian frame of conceptualization, he may win in a minority of the cases, but lose in the majority.

Even where a Freudian approach is clearly justified, exclusive adherence to it may distract the counselor from many significant developments within the life—for example, from the present functional significance of religious and aesthetic values, from the competence and interests that extend beyond the neurotic core, from the client's conscious plans for the future, and from his "will to meaning" and existential concern with life as a whole.

Every person concerned with guidance, or for that matter with teaching, needs as background some general theory of the nature of human personality (1).[Ed] Our tendency, I fear, is to draw our theories from the realm of illness and deviance. It is somehow tempting to apply psychiatric rubrics to all personalities, for psychiatric rubrics are vivid, incisive, dramatic, and easy. Our conceptual banners bear such sloganized concepts as Oedipal complex, character disorder, identity diffusion, schizoid, act-

[Ed] *The article cited here is to be found in Section I of this book (no. 1).*

ing out, and maybe an array of dimensions drawn from the Minnesota Multiphasic Personality Inventory. All such concepts, of course, have their proper place. But personality theory for guidance and teaching needs also to be woven of less lurid fabrics.

Youth, whatever neurotic threads may lie in his nature, is busy with his realistic perceptions, with his gradual learning and quiet coping, with the slow extension of selfhood, with noncritical failures and successes, with developing a generic conscience and a personal style of life. Even in the throes of crisis, he seeks in undramatic ways to consolidate his gains and continue on the path of becoming. A theory of personality adequate to undergird the art of guidance will keep such nondramatic facts in mind. Crises in normal personality development are important, but so too is the slow growth of each youth's unique style of life.

REFERENCES

1. ALLPORT, G. W. Psychological models for guidance. *Harvard educ. Rev.*, 1962, *32*, 373-381.

2. BLAINE, G. B., & MC ARTHUR, C. C. Emotional *problems of the student.* New York: Appleton-Century-Crofts, 1961.

3. ERIKSON, E. *Childhood and society.* New York: Norton, 1950.

4. GILLESPIE, J. M., & ALLPORT, G. W. *Youth's outlook on the future.* New York: Doubleday, 1955.

5. HAVENS, J. A study of religious conflict in college students. *J. sci. Stud. Relig.*, 1963, *3*, 52-69.

VIII / Sex as a Determinant of Behavior

UNDER MANY CONDITIONS KNOWING A PERSON'S GENDER IS important if one seeks to predict how he or she will behave. As an explanatory concept sex has been the center of considerable controversy. Are behavioral sex differences rooted in the contrasting biological makeup of males and females? Are they determined by differences in the ways boys and girls are taught to act in conformity to the role of each sex (as culturally prescribed or as viewed by the particular parents)?

Anthropologists have contributed some answers. The contrasts between males and females observed in certain societies are different from the contrasts in others. By providing us with knowledge of the range of behaviors adopted by each of the sexes in various cultures, anthropologists have shown us that certain behaviors are clearly not determined by biological sex. The work of Margaret Mead on this topic (e.g. *Male and Female*, Morrow, 1949) is well known.

The anthropological evidence that many or most sex differences are learned has led some psychologists to act as though sex differences did not really exist—i.e., as if they were not "real," ONLY learned. They even formed their research samples by including males and females together as though sex would not affect the results. Interest in sex differences has undergone a revival, partly because analysis of research data separately for the two sexes has frequently revealed that girls and boys have responded to the experimental conditions disparately or even oppositely. At the 1961 meeting of the American Psychological Association, a psychologist (Dorothy Eichorn of the University of California at Berkeley) commented on the basis of some of her work: "If you want to predict the behavior of a male, you must know the male. If you want to predict the behavior of a female, you must know the situation." This statement implies not only that there are differences between males and females, but that to explain or predict the behavior of males requires a different theory from that required for females.

As a product of both biological attributes and learning, sex differences may be created or molded in a variety of ways: 1. Certain behaviors may have been reinforced more in one sex than in the other; 2. Interpersonal experiences may be different according to one's sex; or 3. Individuals may belong to groups which have members of only one sex and which mold their behavior accordingly.

To rephrase, *sex* as an explanatory concept can be *biological* (Section II), or it can be an intermediate variable in such explanatory systems as those stressing *learning* (Section III), *interpersonal experiences* (Section IV), *settings and instigations* (Section V), or *group memberships* (Section VI).

From whichever of these standpoints one conceives of sex, it may play a role as a variable in relation to other factors given emphasis in this book, such as intelligence, motivational and perceptual resultants, and educational implications (Sections IX, X, and XI). Papers in various sections of this book have analyzed or discussed research data in terms of each sex separately. Some workers have limited their studies to one sex of subject. Such a decision may be dictated by theoretical or by practical concerns. Some theoretical issues are best answered by study of one sex of subject; discrepant findings for the two sexes may be difficult to deal with in theoretical terms; and the money to permit study of a sample large enough to be analyzed for each sex separately is often lacking.

The papers in the present section focus upon sex as an intermediate variable. All of these papers were in the earlier edition of this book. The fact that new articles are not included does not reflect a lack of work in the area, but a stage of the field where it is hard to see what the significant new contributions are. The first article, from Yale University, is by Herbert Barry III, Margaret K. Bacon and Irvin L. Child. They give some cross-cultural perspective on socialization practices for the two sexes, thus exemplifying a type of anthropological contribution referred to above. This article is based on material from the Human Relations Area Files developed at Yale University. The files contain information about the living practices of human beings in societies around the globe and are an important source of data for testing hypotheses in psychology and child development as well as for anthropology.

The second article by Daniel G. Brown, who is at the United States Air Force Hospital at Forbes Air Force Base in Kansas, also has a cultural orientation. Here the special emphasis is on the learning of sex roles in our contemporary and changing culture.

The last two articles have special relevance to problems in education. The first of them, by Irvin L. Child of Yale University's Department of Psychology, Elmer H. Potter (now Ethelyn H. Klatskin) of the Yale Medical School Department of Pediatrics, and Estelle M. Levine, points out some of the incidental "teaching" that occurs in schools (via text books) with respect to the definition of sex roles. The second of these, by William J. Meyer of the University of Rochester and George G. Thompson of Ohio State University, deals with another aspect of the schoolchild's life in which the differential treatment of the sexes is important. Dr. Thompson is the author of one of the most widely used child psychology texts, and is coauthor of a recent text in educational psychology. Both articles may help us to keep in mind the fact that what is taught is not always limited to that which was intended.

For a sociologist's view of sex patterning of behavior in our culture, see Talcott Parsons' "Age and Sex in the Social Structure of the United States," which appears in his *Essays in Sociological Theory* (The Free Press, 1949) and has been reprinted in other readings.

In several sections of the book we have called attention to the fact that an article is relevant to the issue of sex differences.

48/A CROSS-CULTURAL SURVEY OF SOME SEX DIFFERENCES IN SOCIALIZATION[1]/

HERBERT BARRY III, MARGARET K. BACON,

AND IRVIN L. CHILD[*]

IN OUR SOCIETY, CERTAIN DIFFER-ences may be observed between the typical personality characteristics of the two sexes. These sex differences in personality are generally believed to result in part from differences in the way boys and girls are reared. To the extent that personality differences between the sexes are thus of cultural rather than biological origin, they seem potentially susceptible to change. But how readily susceptible to change? In the differential rearing of the sexes does our society make an arbitrary imposition on an infinitely plastic biological base, or is this cultural imposition found uniformly in all societies as an adjustment to the real biological differences between the sexes? This paper reports one attempt to deal with this problem.

DATA AND PROCEDURES

The data used were ethnographic reports, available in the anthropological literature, about socialization practices of various cultures. One hundred and ten cultures, mostly nonliterate, were studied.[2] They were selected primarily in terms of the existence of adequate ethnographic reports of socialization practices and secondarily so as to obtain a wide and reasonably balanced geographical distribution. Various aspects of socialization of infants and children were rated on a 7-point scale by two judges (Mrs. Bacon

and Mr. Barry). Where the ethnographic reports permitted, separate ratings were made for the socialization of boys and girls. Each rating was indicated as either confident or doubtful; with still greater uncertainty, or with complete lack of evidence, the particular rating was of course not made at all. We shall restrict the report of sex difference ratings to cases in which both judges made a confident rating. Also omitted is the one instance where the two judges reported a sex difference in opposite directions, as it demonstrates only unreliability of judgment. The number of cultures that meet these criteria is much smaller than the total of 110; for the several variables to be considered, the number varies from 31 to 84.

The aspects of socialization on which ratings were made included:

1. Several criteria of attention and indulgence toward infants.

2. Strength of socialization from age 4 to 5 years until shortly before puberty, with respect to five systems of behavior; strength of socialization was defined as the combination of positive pressure (rewards for the behavior) plus negative pressure (punishments for lack of the behavior). The variables were:

(a) Responsibility or dutifulness training. (The data were such that training in the performance of chores in the productive or domestic economy was necessarily the principal source of information here; however, training in the performance of other duties was also taken into account when information was available.)

(b) Nurturance training, i.e., training the child to be nurturant or helpful toward younger siblings and other dependent people.

(c) Obedience training.

(d) Self-reliance training.

(e) Achievement training, i.e., training the child to orient his behavior toward standards of excellence

[1] This research is part of a project for which financial support was provided by the Social Science Research Council and the Ford Foundation. We are greatly indebted to G. P. Murdock for supplying us with certain data, as indicated below, and to him and Thomas W. Maretzki for suggestions that have been used in this paper.

[2] Most of the societies we used are listed by name in H. Barry III, I. L. Child, and M. K. Bacon, Relation of child training to subsistence economy, *American Anthropologist*, 1959, *61*, 51-63.

[*] Herbert Barry III, Margaret K. Bacon, and Irvin L. Child. A cross-cultural survey of some sex differences in socialization, *Journal of Abnormal and Social Psychology*, 1957, *55*, 327-332. Reprinted by permission.

in performance, and to seek to achieve as excellent a performance as possible.

Where the term "no sex difference" is used here, it may mean any of three things: (a) the judge found separate evidence about the training of boys and girls on this particular variable, and judged it to be identical; (b) the judge found a difference between the training of boys and girls, but not great enough for the sexes to be rated a whole point apart on a 7-point scale; (c) the judge found evidence only about the training of "children" on this variable, the ethnographer not reporting separately about boys and girls.

SEX DIFFERENCES IN SOCIALIZATION

On the various aspects of attention and indulgence toward infants, the judges almost always agreed in finding no sex difference. Out of 96 cultures for which the ratings included the infancy period, 88 (92%) were rated with no sex difference by either judge for any of those variables. This result is consistent with the point sometimes made by anthropologists that "baby" generally is a single status undifferentiated by sex, even though "boy" and "girl" are distinct statuses.

On the variables of childhood socialization, on the other hand, a rating of no sex difference by both judges was much less common. This finding of no sex difference varied in frequency from 10% of the cultures for the achievement variable up to 62% of the cultures for the obedience variable, as shown in the last column of Table 1. Where a sex difference is reported, by either one or both judges, the difference tends strongly to be in a particular direction, as shown in the earlier columns of the same table. Pressure toward nurturance, obedience, and respon-

sibility is most often stronger for girls, whereas pressure toward achievement and self-reliance is most often stronger for boys.

For nurturance and for self-reliance, all the sex differences are in the same direction. For achievement there is only one exception to the usual direction of difference, and for obedience only two; but for responsibility there are nine. What do these exceptions mean? We have re-examined all these cases. In most of them, only one judge had rated the sexes as differently treated (sometimes one judge, sometimes the other), and in the majority of these cases both judges were now inclined to agree that there was no convincing evidence of a real difference. There were exceptions, however, especially in cases where a more formal or systematic training of boys seemed to imply greater pressure on them toward responsibility. The most convincing cases were the Masai and Swazi, where both judges had originally agreed in rating responsibility pressures greater in boys than in girls. In comparing the five aspects of socialization we may conclude that responsibility shows by far the strongest evidence of real variation in the direction of sex difference, and obedience much the most frequently shows evidence of no sex difference at all.

In subsequent discussion we shall be assuming that the obtained sex differences in the socialization ratings reflect true sex differences in the cultural practices. We should consider here two other possible sources of these rated differences.

1. The ethnographers could have been biased in favor of seeing the same pattern of sex differences as in our culture. However, most anthropologists readily perceive and eagerly report novel and startling cultural features, so we may expect them to have reported unusual sex differences where they existed. The

TABLE 1 / RATINGS OF CULTURES FOR SEX DIFFERENCES OF FIVE VARIABLES OF CHILDHOOD SOCIALIZATION PRESSURE.

VARIABLE	NUMBER OF CULTURES	BOTH JUDGES AGREE IN RATING THE VARIABLE HIGHER IN		ONE JUDGE RATES NO DIFFERENCE, ONE RATES THE VARIABLE HIGHER IN		PERCENTAGE OF CULTURES WITH EVIDENCE OF SEX DIFFERENCE IN DIRECTION OF		
		GIRLS	BOYS	GIRLS	BOYS	GIRLS	BOYS	NEITHER
Nurturance	33	17	0	10	0	82%	0%	18%
Obedience	69	6	0	18	2	35%	3%	62%
Responsibility	84	25	2	26	7	61%	11%	28%
Achievement	31	0	17	1	10	3%	87%	10%
Self-reliance	82	0	64	0	6	0%	85%	15%

distinction between matrilineal and patrilineal, and between matrilocal and patrilocal cultures, given prominence in many ethnographic reports, shows an awareness of possible variations in the significance of sex differences from culture to culture.

2. The two judges could have expected to find in other cultures the sex roles which are familiar in our culture and inferred them from the material on the cultures. However, we have reported only confident ratings, and such a bias seems less likely here than for doubtful ratings. It might be argued, moreover, that bias has more opportunity in the cases ambiguous enough so that only one judge reported a sex difference, and less opportunity in the cases where the evidence is so clear that both judges agree. Yet in general, as may be seen in Table 1, the deviant cases are somewhat more frequent among the cultures where only one judge reported a sex difference.

The observed differences in the socialization of boys and girls are consistent with certain universal tendencies in the differentiation of adult sex role. In the economic sphere, men are more frequently allotted tasks that involve leaving home and engaging in activities where a high level of skill yields important returns; hunting is a prime example. Emphasis on training in self-reliance and achievement for boys would function as preparation for such an economic role. Women, on the other hand, are more frequently allotted tasks at or near home that minister most immediately to the needs of others (such as cooking and water carrying;) these activities have a nurturant character, and in their pursuit a responsible carrying out of established routines is likely to be more important than the development of an especially high order of skill. Thus training in nurturance, responsibility, and, less clearly, obedience, may contribute to preparation for this economic role. These consistencies with adult role go beyond the economic sphere, of course. Participation in warfare, as a male prerogative, calls for self-reliance and a high order of skill where survival or death is the immediate issue. The childbearing which is biologically assigned to women, and the child care which is socially assigned primarily to them, leads to nurturant behavior and often call for a more continuous responsibility than do the tasks carried out by men. Most of these distinctions in adult role are not inevitable, but the biological differences between the sexes strongly predispose the dis-

tinction of role, if made, to be in a uniform direction.[3]

The relevant biological sex differences are conspicuous in adulthood but generally not in childhood. If each generation were left entirely to its own devices, therefore, without even an older generation to copy, sex differences in role would presumably be almost absent in childhood and would have to be developed after puberty at the expense of considerable relearning on the part of one or both sexes. Hence, a pattern of child training which foreshadows adult differences can serve the useful function of minimizing what Benedict termed "discontinuities in cultural conditioning" (1).

The differences in socialization between the sexes in our society, then, are no arbitrary custom of our society, but a very widespread adaptation of culture to the biological substratum of human life.

VARIATIONS IN DEGREE OF SEX DIFFERENTIATION

While demonstrating near-universal tendencies in direction of difference between the socialization of boys and girls, our data do not show perfect uniformity. A study of the variations in our data may allow us to see some of the conditions which are associated with, and perhaps give rise to, a greater or smaller degree of this difference. For this purpose, we classified cultures as having relatively large or small sex difference by two different methods, one more inclusive and the other more selective. In both methods the ratings were at first considered separately for each of the five variables. A sex difference rating was made only if both judges made a rating on this variable and at least one judge's rating was confident.

In the more inclusive method the ratings were dichotomized, separately for each variable, as close as possible to the median into those showing a large and those showing a small sex difference. Thus, for each society a large or a small sex difference was recorded for each of the five variables on which a sex difference rating was available. A society was given an over-all classification of large or small sex difference if it had a sex difference rating on at least three variables and if a majority of these ratings agreed in being large, or agreed in being small. This method permitted classifi-

[3] For data and interpretations supporting various arguments of this paragraph, see Mead (2), Murdock (3), and Scheinfeld (6).

cation of a large number of cultures, but the grounds for classification were capricious in many cases, as a difference of only one point in the rating of a single variable might change the over-all classification of sex difference for a culture from large to small.

In the more selective method, we again began by dichotomizing each variable as close as possible to the median; but a society was now classified as having a large or small sex difference on the variable only if it was at least one step away from the scores immediately adjacent to the median. Thus only the more decisive ratings of sex difference were used. A culture was classified as having an over-all large or small sex difference only if it was given a sex difference rating which met this criterion on at least two variables, and only if all such ratings agreed in being large, or agreed in being small.

We then tested the relation of each of these dichotomies to 24 aspects of culture on which Murdock has categorized the customs of most of these societies[4] and which seemed of possible significance for sex differentiation. The aspects of culture covered include type of economy, residence pattern, marriage and incest rules, political integration, and social organization. For each aspect of culture, we grouped Murdock's categories to make a dichotomous contrast (sometimes omitting certain categories as irrelevant to the contrast). In the case of some aspects of culture, two or more separate contrasts were made (e.g., under form of marriage we contrasted monogamy with polygyny, and also contrasted sororal with nonsororal polygyny). For each of 40 comparisons thus formed, we prepared a 2×2 frequency table to determine relation to each of our sex-difference dichotomies. A significant relation was found for six of these 40 aspects of culture with the more selective dichotomization of overall sex difference. In four of these comparisons, the relation to the more inclusive dichotomization was also significant. These relationships are all given in Table 2, in the form of phi coefficients, along with the outcome of testing significance by the use of x^2 or Fisher's exact test. In trying to interpret these findings, we have also considered the nonsignificant correlations with other variables, looking for consistency and inconsistency with the general implications of the significant findings. We have

[4] These data were supplied to us directly by Professor Murdock.

TABLE 2 / CULTURE VARIABLES CORRELATED WITH LARGE SEX DIFFERENCES IN SOCIALIZATION, SEPARATELY FOR TWO TYPES OF SAMPLE.

VARIABLE	MORE SELECTIVE SAMPLE		MORE INCLUSIVE SAMPLE	
	∅	N	∅	N
Large animals are hunted	.48*	(34)	.28*	(72)
Grain rather than root crops are grown	.82**	(20)	.62**	(43)
Large or milking animals rather than small animals are kept	.65*	(19)	.43*	(35)
Fishing unimportant or absent	.42*	(31)	.19	(69)
Nomadic rather than sedentary residence	.61**	(34)	.15	(71)
Polygyny rather than monogamy	.51*	(28)	.38**	(64)

* $p < .05$.

** $p < .01$.

Note.—The variables have been so phrased that all correlations are positive. The phi coefficient is shown, and in parentheses, the number of cases on which the comparison was based. Significance level was determined by x^2, or Fisher's exact test where applicable, using in all cases a two-tailed test.

arrived at the following formulation of results:

1. Large sex difference in socialization is associated with an economy that places a high premium on the superior strength, and superior development of motor skills requiring strength, which characterize the male. Four of the correlations reported in Table 2 clearly point to this generalization: the correlations of large sex difference with the hunting of large animals, with grain rather than root crops, with the keeping of large rather than small domestic animals, and with nomadic rather than sedentary residence. The correlation with the unimportance of fishing may also be consistent with this generalization, but the argument is not clear.[5]

[5] Looking (with the more inclusive sample) into the possibility that this correlation might result from the correlation between fishing and sedentary residence, a complicated interaction between these variables was found. The correlation of sex differentiation with absence of fishing is found only in nomadic societies, where fishing is likely to involve cooperative activity of the two sexes, and its absence is likely to mean dependence upon the male for large game hunting or herding large animals (whereas in sedentary societies the alternatives to fishing do not so uniformly require special emphasis on male strength). The correlation of sex differentiation with nomadism is found only in nonfishing societies; here nomadism is likely to imply large game hunting or herding large animals, whereas in fishing

Other correlations consistent with the generalization, though not statistically significant, are with large game hunting rather than gathering, with the hunting of large game rather than small game, and with the general importance of all hunting and gathering.

2. Large sex difference in socialization appears to be correlated with customs that make for a large family group with high cooperative interaction. The only statistically significant correlation relevant here is that with polygyny rather than monogamy. This generalization is, however, supported by several substantial correlations that fall only a little short of being statistically significant. One of these is a correlation with sororal rather than nonsororal polygyny; Murdock and Whiting (4) have presented indirect evidence that co-wives generally show smoother cooperative interaction if they are sisters. Correlations are also found with the presence of either an extended or a polygynous family rather than the nuclear family only; with the presence of an extended family; and with the extreme contrast between maximal extension and no extension of the family. The generalization is also to some extent supported by small correlations with wide extension of incest taboos, if we may presume that an incest taboo makes for effective unthreatening cooperation within the extended family. The only possible exception to this generalization, among substantial correlations, is a near-significant correlation with an extended or polygynous family's occupying a cluster of dwellings rather than a single dwelling.[6]

---

societies nomadism evidently implies no such special dependence upon male strength. Maximum sex differentiation is found in nomadic nonfishing societies (15 with large difference and only 2 with small) and minimum sex differentiation in nomadic fishing societies (2 with large difference and 7 with small difference). These findings further strengthen the argument for a conspicuous influence of the economy upon sex differentiation.

[6] We think the reverse of this correlation would be more consistent with our generalization here. But perhaps it may reasonably be argued that the various nuclear families composing an extended or polygynous family are less likely to develop antagonisms which hinder cooperation if they are able to maintain some physical separation. On the other hand, this variable may be more relevant to the first generalization than to the second. Occupation of a cluster of dwellings is highly correlated with presence of herding and with herding of large rather than small animals, and these economic variables in turn are correlated with large sex difference in socialization. Occupation of a cluster of dwellings is also correlated with polygyny rather than monogamy and shows no correlation with sororal vs. nonsororal polygyny.

In seeking to understand this second generalization, we feel that the degree of social isolation of the nuclear family may perhaps be the crucial underlying variable. To the extent that the nuclear family must stand alone, the man must be prepared to take the woman's role when she is absent or incapacitated, and vice versa. Thus the sex differentiation cannot afford to be too great. But to the extent that the nuclear family is steadily interdependent with other nuclear families, the female role in the household economy can be temporarily taken over by another woman, or the male role by another man, so that sharp differentiation of sex role is no handicap.

The first generalization, which concerns the economy, cannot be viewed as dealing with material completely independent of the ratings of socialization. The training of children in their economic role was often an important part of the data used in rating socialization variables, and would naturally vary according to the general economy of the society. We would stress, however, that we were by no means using the identical data on the two sides of our comparison; we were on the one hand judging data on the socialization of children and on the other hand using Murdock's judgments on the economy of the adult culture. In the case of the second generalization, it seems to us that there was little opportunity for information on family and social structure to have influenced the judges in making the socialization ratings.

Both of these generalizations contribute to understanding the social background of the relatively small difference in socialization of boys and girls which we believe characterizes our society at the present time. Our mechanized economy is perhaps less dependent than any previous economy upon the superior average strength of the male. The nuclear family in our society is often so isolated that husband and wife must each be prepared at times to take over or help in the household tasks normally assigned to the other. It is also significant that the conditions favoring low sex differentiation appear to be more characteristic of the upper segments of our society, in socioeconomic and educational status, than of lower segments. This observation may be relevant to the tendency toward smaller sex differences in personality in higher status groups (cf. Terman and Miles, 8).

The increase in our society of conditions favoring small sex difference has led some people to advocate a virtual elimination of sex differences in socialization. This course seems likely to be dysfunctional even in our society. Parsons,

Bales, *et al.* (5) argue that a differentiation of role similar to the universal pattern of sex difference is an important and perhaps inevitable development in any social group, such as the nuclear family. If we add to their argument the point that biological differences between the sexes make most appropriate the usual division of those roles between the sexes, we have compelling reasons to expect that the decrease in differentiation of adult sex role will not continue to the vanishing point. In our training of children, there may now be less differentiation in sex role than characterizes adult life—so little, indeed, as to provide inadequate preparation for adulthood. This state of affairs is likely to be especially true of formal education, which is more subject to conscious influence by an ideology than is informal socialization at home. With child training being more oriented toward the male than the female role in adulthood, many of the adjustment problems of women in our society today may be partly traced to conflicts growing out of inadequate childhood preparation for their adult role. This argument is nicely supported in extreme form by Spiro's analysis of sex roles in an Israeli kibbutz (7). The ideology of the founders of the kibbutz included the objective of greatly reducing differences in sex role. But the economy of the kibbutz is a largely nonmechanized one in which the superior average strength of men is badly needed in many jobs. The result is that, despite the ideology and many attempts to implement it, women continue to be assigned primarily to traditional "women's work," and the incompatibility between upbringing or ideology and adult role is an important source of conflict for women.

NOTE ON REGIONAL DISTRIBUTION. There is marked variation among regions of the world in typical size of sex difference in socialization. In our sample, societies in North America and Africa tend to have large sex difference and societies in Oceania to have small sex difference. Less confidently, because of the smaller number of cases, we can report a tendency toward small sex differences in Asia and South America as well. Since most of the variables with which we find the sex difference to be significantly correlated have a similar regional distribution, the question arises whether the correlations might better be ascribed to some quite different source having to do with large regional similarities, rather than to the functional dependence we have suggested. As a partial check, we have

tried to determine whether the correlations we report in Table 2 tend also to be found strictly within regions. For each of the three regions for which we have sizable samples (North America, Africa, and Oceania) we have separately plotted 2 x 2 tables corresponding to each of the 6 relationships reported in Table 2. (We did this only for the more inclusive sample, since for the more selective sample the number of cases within a region would have been extremely small.) Out of the 18 correlations thus determined, 11 are positive and only 3 are negative (the other 4 being exactly zero). This result clearly suggests a general tendency for these correlations to hold true within regions as well as between regions, and may lend further support to our functional interpretation.

SUMMARY

A survey of certain aspects of socialization in 110 cultures shows that differentiation of the sexes is unimportant in infancy, but that in childhood there is, as in our society, a widespread pattern of greater pressure toward nurturance, obedience, and responsibility in girls, and toward self-reliance and achievement striving in boys. There are a few reversals of sex difference, and many instances of no detectable sex difference; these facts tend to confirm the cultural rather than directly biological nature of the differences. Cultures vary in the degree to which these differentiations are made; correlational analysis suggests some of the social conditions influencing these variations, and helps in understanding why our society has relatively small sex differentiation.

REFERENCES

1. BENEDICT, RUTH. Continuities and discontinuities in cultural conditioning. *Psychiatry*, 1938, *1*, 161-167.

2. MEAD, MARGARET. *Male and female.* New York: Morrow, 1949.

3. MURDOCK, G. P. Comparative data on the division of labor by sex. *Social Forces*, 1937, *15*, 551-553.

4. MURDOCK G. P., and WHITING, J. W. M. Cultural determination of parental attitudes. The relationship between the social structure, particular family structure and parental behavior. In M. J. E. Senn (Ed.), *Problems of infancy and childhood: Transactions of the Fourth Conference*, March 6-7, 1950. New York: Josiah Macy, Jr. Foundation, 1951. Pp. 13-34.

5. PARSONS, T., BALES, R. F., *et al. Family, socialization and interaction process.* Glencoe, Ill.: Free Press, 1955.

6. SCHEINFELD, A. *Women and men.* New York: Harcourt, Brace, 1944.

7. SPIRO, M. E. *Kibbutz: Venture in Utopia.* Cambridge: Harvard Univer. Press, 1956.

8. TERMAN, L. M. and MILES, CATHERINE C. *Sex and personality.* New York: McGraw-Hill, 1936.

49 / SEX-ROLE DEVELOPMENT IN A CHANGING CULTURE[1] / DANIEL G. BROWN*

ONE OF THE MORE SIGNIFICANT PSYchosocial developments of contemporary American society would appear to be the relatively fluid state of the sex roles of individuals. Within a single generation, significant changes have taken place in the traditional conceptions of what is masculine and what is feminine. Whether such changes have been abrupt enough to be considered a cultural revolution or sufficiently gradual to be simply degrees of cultural variation is difficult to judge. In either case, however, this changed and changing cultural pattern has a number of implications and possible effects that bear directly on individual, group, and institutional behavior. In this connection such questions as the following might be asked: What are some of these changes that have taken place in the sex roles? Have such changes been more pronounced in the feminine role than in the masculine role? How have these changes affected the life adjustment of individ-

uals? And the relationships of the sexes with each other? What about the effect on boys and girls at the present time and in the years ahead? These are just a few of the problems in the area of masculinity-femininity development and adjustment that need to be studied and investigated.

The present paper is primarily directed toward a consideration of the nature and theoretical implications of sex-role development in children.

DIFFERENTIATION OF SEX AND SEX ROLE

As a starting point, consideration might be given to the age at which the child becomes aware of biological sex differentiation per se as well as when the child becomes aware of the essential meaning of "masculine" and "feminine," i.e., sex-role behavior.[2] At what age for example is the average child able to distinguish himself or her-

[1] This paper was read at a symposium on "Psychological Implications of Changing Sex Roles," at the annual meeting of the APA, New York, September, 1957. Acknowledgement with thanks is made to Ruth E. Hartley, City College of New York, and to G. D. Ofiesh, United States Air Force Academy, for helpful suggestions concerning this paper.

[2] The concept, *sex role* refers to those psychological characteristics and behavioral patterns that are typical of one sex in contrast to the other sex. The sex role of a person consists of the behavior that is socially defined and expected of that person because of his or her status as a male or female.

* Daniel G. Brown, Sex-role development in a changing culture, *Psychological Bulletin*, 1958, 55, 232-242. Reprinted by permission.

self as a boy or girl? Evidence suggests that between two thirds and three fourths of children by the age of three are able to make this basic distinction (12, 13, 31).

Evidence also suggests that sex-role differentiation is a gradual process, probably beginning in the second year of life and becoming definitely established by the age of three (18, 30, 31). By or during the fifth year most children make a clear differentiation between the more obvious biological cues of maleness and femaleness and psychological cues of masculinity and femininity (1, 3, 9, 12, 13, 18, 20, 21, 26, 30, 31). As in the other aspects of psychological development there are undoubtedly wide individual differences in the clarity with which differences between the sexes are perceived by children.

In any event, whatever the exact age in a particular case, it seems safe to conclude that preschool children as a group become fully aware of the fact that the world is divided into two groups of people and that, depending on whether one belongs to one group or the other, different behavior patterns are expected accordingly. At an early age, then, children are being conditioned to and are actively acquiring their sex roles. One of the most important considerations here has to do with the *meaning* and *significance* to the child of the earliest perceptions of structural and sex-role differences between boys and girls. What does it mean to a child to become aware of his sex for the first time, and gradually, his sex role? For the child to feel safe, secure, and satisfied in his emerging sexual identity would appear to be one of the most important conditions in his entire development.

SEX-ROLE PREFERENCE IN CHILDREN

Related to the factor of age in sex and sex-role differentiation in children is the phenomenon of sex-role preference. Does preference for one sex role over the other parallel the developing awareness of the difference between the masculine and feminine roles? Or does preference come later, only after the child has been exposed sufficiently to the differential treatments accorded boys in contrast to girls? The origin and earliest occurrence of sex-role preference is a problem that awaits research investigation. That definite preferences exist in young children for one or the other sex role, however, has been reasonably well demonstrated by several studies (1, 3, 9, 21, 26). This problem has been investigated by the present writer by means of a

technique known as the *It Scale for Children* (2), a scale composed of 36 picture cards, three by four, of objects and figures typically associated with the masculine or feminine roles in our culture (e.g., preferring to play with a tractor rather than a doll; wearing a dress rather than trousers; preferring to be a boy rather than a girl, etc.). A child-figure called "It," relatively ambiguous as to sexual identity, is used in administering the scale by having each child make choices for It, rather than the child himself or herself making the choices directly. Results based on the use of the It Scale with children between the ages of about 3½ and 11½, most of whom were from middle class homes, show that beginning with the young preschool group (ages 3½ to 5½) and extending through the fourth grade (ages 9½ to 10½) boys express a stronger preference for the masculine role than girls do for the feminine role (1, 3, 17, 21). For example, at the kindergarten and third-grade levels, about 85% and 95% of the boys respectively indicate that It would rather be an "Indian Chief" than an "Indian Princess." And when asked which shoes It would rather "dress up and play house in," about 75% and 95% of the kindergarten and third-grade boys respectively chose men's rather than women's shoes.

Girls between the ages of 3½ and 6½ are quite heterogeneous as a group: some are predominantly feminine, choosing practically all of the feminine alternatives; others are predominantly masculine, and still others are "in-betweens," choosing both masculine and feminine alternatives. Taken as a group, for example, 50% express a preference for It "playing grownups" with cosmetic articles and 50% with shaving articles.

After about the sixth year and extending through the ninth year, most girls show a very strong preference for masculine in contrast to feminine things. For example, between 60% and 70% of the girls in the first, second, third, and fourth grades indicate that It would rather work with "building" tools than with "cooking and baking" utensils.

It is not known whether girls in the fifth grade and beyond (age group from about 10 to 11 and older) become less masculine in preference. Brown's study (3) of fifth-grade subjects indicated a definite feminine changeover in girls, but Hogan (19) failed to find any such change in the preference patterns of either fifth- or sixth-grade subjects. The whole problem of change in sex-role preference in relation to age needs further and more intensive study.

In contrast to girls, boys *at all ages* show a strong preference for the masculine role. This preference is evident in the youngest group (ages 3½ to 5½) and becomes even stronger until it reaches a near maximum at about the age of eight and thereafter. Thus, between 90% and 95% of boys in the second, third, fourth, and fifth grades indicate that, given a choice, It would rather wear a shirt and trousers than a dress.

SEX-ROLE PREFERENCE IN CHILDREN COMPARED TO ADULTS

To what extent are the sex-role preference patterns of children similar to those of adults? For comparative purposes the Parental Role section of the It Scale may be used (3). This section involves asking the child whether It would rather be a mother or a father. Results from this section may be summarized as follows: From about 80% to 95% of boys at all ages from kindergarten through the fifth grade express a preference for It becoming a father, only 3% to 20% for It becoming a mother. On the other hand, in the case of girls from kindergarten through the fourth grade only about 25% to 45% express a preference for It becoming a mother, while between 55% and 75% for It becoming a father.

These results in the case of children are quite consistent with studies of adults in our culture which asked men and women: "Have you sometimes wished you were of the opposite sex?" or "If you could be born over again, would you rather be a man or a woman?" or "Have you ever wished that you belonged to the opposite sex?" Results may be summarized as follows: only between 2% and 4% of adult men compared to between 20% and 31% of adult women recall *consciously* having been aware of the desire to be of the opposite sex (10, 11, 34). And in Puerto Rico only 33% of a group of adult female students compared to about 93% of male students indicated they would prefer to be female and male respectively if they "could come to life again after death" (28). This lopsided preference for being male in preference to being female is also reflected in a recent survey of several hundred university students at Ohio State University who were asked whether they would rather have a male or female child in their family if they could have only one child (8). The results showed that 91% of the men and 66% of the women students expressed a preference for a male child. When both groups

are combined, boys were preferred by approximately 75% and girls by only 25% of these students.

A significant problem connected with these findings concerns the psychological effect on large numbers of women who openly admit having preferred to be male. How does such awareness affect the self-concept of a girl or woman? The result, according to White (35) is to undermine a woman's respect for herself as a woman and to derogate the feminine role in general.

An important anthropological analysis in connection with sex differences in acceptance of appropriate sex roles would be a *cross-cultural* comparison of the percentage of men compared to women who had preferred to be of the opposite sex. Compared to those cultures, for example, where male domination reaches exaggerated proportions, very different results might be expected among the Burmese (7), Ojibwa Indians (33) and Tchambuli (23) where females have relatively high status and a favorable position in their society.

FACTORS RELATED TO MASCULINE ROLE PREFERENCE

What factors are functionally related to the much greater preference that boys show for the masculine role than girls show for the feminine role and for the definite preference that many girls show for the masculine role? Although this is a problem in relation to which much research is needed, several conditions or factors may be suggested as contributory.

First, there is the emphasis by Freud on the *anatomical difference* between males and females, the effect of which is supposed to make the boy proud of his status and the girl dissatisfied with hers. Having versus not having a penis allegedly "explains" why girls as well as boys prefer to be boys.

Another attempt to account for sex differences in role preference is the emphasis by Adler on *sociocultural advantages* that go with being male in contrast to being female. The little girl may early perceive the greater prestige and numerous privileges connected with the masculine role. This would tend to arouse envy and drive her in the direction of wanting that which she does not have, namely, masculine status. Adler introduced the concept of "masculine protest" to refer to this phenomenon. That our culture has been and still is masculine-centered and masculine-oriented is obvious. The superior position and privileged status of the male permeates nearly every aspect, minor and major, of our social life. The gadgets and prizes in boxes of breakfast cereal, for example, commonly have a strong masculine rather than feminine appeal.[3] And the most basic social institutions perpetuate this pattern of masculine aggrandizement. Thus, the Judeo-Christian faiths involve worshipping God, a "Father," rather than a "Mother," and Christ, a "Son," rather than a "Daughter."

A third factor relative to the difference between the sexes in role preference is the *greater latitude* of the girls compared to the boys in sex-role development. It appears somewhat paradoxical that, although restricted much more in practically all other respects, girls are allowed *more* freedom than boys in sex role learning. This is, however, simply consistent with the idea that masculine status is so superior to feminine status that many girls are not even discouraged from striving to attain the former. For a girl to be a tomboy does not involve the censure that results when a boy is a sissy. With little, if any, embarrassment or threat, girls may show strong preference for the masculine role; this is not true in the case of boys.

Further evidence of the fact that girls in contrast to boys not only have much more opportunity to pattern their behavior after the model of the opposite sex but in many cases actually do so is cited by Cunningham (6). She reports on a group of fourth- and fifth-grade students who, when asked to describe what they consider to be some of the "pressing problems in human relations" included the following: "How can I stop my sister from being a tomboy?" Other examples that may be cited include:

1. *Clothing.* Girls may wear shirts and trousers with little or no social disapproval, but boys do not wear skirts or dresses; in fact, men who wear feminine clothing, i.e., transvestites, do so at the risk of severe social censure and even legal punishment.

2. *Names.* Many girls are given masculinized names such as Jackie, Stephanie, Billie, Pauline, Jo, Roberta, Frankie, etc., but few boys are given feminized names.

3. *Toys and Play Activities.* Girls may play with any or all of the toys typically associated with boys (e.g., cars, trucks, erector sets, guns, etc.) but boys are discouraged from playing

with toys that are considered feminine (e.g., dolls, dishes, sewing materials, etc.).

Goodenough (14, p. 318) has commented on the greater freedom of girls in sex-typed play as follows: "A boy is not likely to be a Dale Evans, but a girl often becomes Roy Rogers, or any of his masculine colleagues. Boys are rarely glamour girls, but many little girls fall eagerly into the roles of space men, or masculine rough riders."

Based on research findings that show boys consistently making more appropriate sex-typed choices than girls, Rabban (26) and Hurlock (20) conclude that "boys are more aware of sex-appropriate behavior than girls." Rather than being "more aware" than girls, however, it is the relative lack of flexibility of boys in sex-role choices that probably accounts for some of the difference between boys and girls in this regard. Boys simply do not have the same freedom of choice as girls when it comes to sex-typed objects and activities. In this connection, Hartley[4] raises the question as to whether or not results of studies of sex-role preference in children, rather than measuring role preference as such, might not simply reflect the fact that girls are given much and boys little opportunity for variation in expressing preferences for sex-typed objects and activities. This is a good point and should be explored further.

As to the basis of the narrow, rigid sex-typing pattern in males, Goodenough (14) presents evidence that suggests fathers show *greater concern* than mothers for sex-appropriate behavior in their children. In other words, father is more likely than mother to insist that "junior" look and talk and act like a *man.* This pattern, which would tend to have greater impact on the boy than the girl, is consistent with findings presented in the present paper, showing boys are much more likely than girls to make sex-appropriate choices.

Related to these differences in sex roles in childhood appears to be a parallel difference in adult occupational roles. Even though women traditionally have been subject to various kinds of vocational and economic discrimination, it is still true that a woman may and does enter a "masculine" vocation or profession, e.g., bus driver, engineer, lawyer, etc., with less social disapproval or concern as to one's sex-role "normality" than a man who enters a "feminine" field, e.g., hair stylist, dress designer, nurse, etc. The census in 1950, for example, revealed

---

[3] Typical examples include military equipment, cowboy paraphernalia, police badges, airplanes, boats, trains, spaceships, marbles, yo-yos, miniature auto license plates, etc.

[4] Personal communication from Ruth E. Hartley.

that women are now in all of the 446 occupations reported by the census. Among the 16,000,000 American women employed, there are "lady" carpenters, sailors, tractor drivers, pilots, telephone linesmen, locomotive engineers, lumbermen, firemen, and even stevedores and longshoremen!

SEX-ROLE IDENTIFICATION AND SEX-ROLE PREFERENCE

In dealing with the complex problem of sex-role behavior it seems particularly important to distinguish between sex-role identification and sex-role preference (1). *Identification* is the basic process in which a child, at first involuntarily, and later consciously, learns to think, feel, and act like members of one sex in contrast to the other sex. *Preference* refers to the tendency to adopt the sex role of one sex in contrast to that of the other sex, the former being perceived as more desirable and attractive. With this distinction in mind it is possible to delineate three major sex-role patterns: (*a*) Identification with and preference for the sex role of one's own sex, e.g., a girl may identify with and prefer the feminine role; (*b*) Identification with the sex role of one's own sex but preference for the sex role of the opposite sex, e.g., a girl may identify with the feminine role but prefer the masculine role; (*c*) Identification with the sex role of the opposite sex but preference for the sex role of one's own sex, e.g., a girl may identify with the masculine role but prefer the feminine role. Of the two processes, identification appears to be primary, while preference is more or less secondary relative to sex-role behavior. In normal development the two form a single, integrative process.

In view of the finding that masculine role preference appears to be widespread among girls, it might be hypothesized that conflict or confusion will be conspicuous in their sex role development. Thus, the fact that girls are destined for feminine functions in adulthood, yet envy and attempt to emulate the masculine role in childhood would tend to produce ambivalence and a lack of clarity in the feminine role (16, 24, 31). On the basis of a study of sex-role learning in five-year-olds, for example, Fauls and Smith (9) refer to the "lack of clear definition" of a sex role in the case of female children. Related to this is the contradiction between the sex-role identification of many girls with the feminine model and the tendency for them to prefer the masculine role.

On the other hand, boys do not necessarily escape difficulties in sex-role development. Even though the culture greatly favors the male, the fact that boys must shift *from* an original identification-attachment with the mother *to* an identification with the father may create difficulties for boys that girls do not experience (30). Thus, Sears (30) reports that six-year-old boys have not identified with their fathers as well as girls have with their mothers. On the basis of extensive observations of children in preschools, Hartley arrives at a conclusion similar to that of Sears and, in addition, raises the question as to whether many boys really experience their fathers in their paternal role. She also questions whether many boys even picture themselves as "future fathers" (18).

It is also true that a considerable number of boys get overly exposed to the feminine model in early life when the mother is much more prominent in the life of the child than the father. This is especially likely to occur if for any reason the father is psychologically distant or a predominantly negative figure for the son and there is no adequate substitute.

According to Parsons (25) and Gorer (15) a major effect of the situation in which the father is typically away most of the time while the mother is around continually exemplifying the feminine model is to facilitate the role development of the girl and to complicate the role development of the boy. These writers seem to emphasize the *quantity* of the parent-child relationship rather than the *quality* of such a relationship. In other words, the degree that the child respects, admires and loves the parent may be much more significant than the sheer amount of contact, per se.[5]

SEX-ROLE DEVELOPMENT AND ADULT SEXUAL ADJUSTMENT

A boy who incorporates the basic features of the feminine model via predominant identification with the mother intrinsically will feel most comfortable in the feminine role, which to him is "normal" and "natural." Such a boy will show a "feminine protest," i.e., he will protest any restriction of his desire and effort to become thoroughly feminine. He will often plead and even demand the freedom to adopt the feminine role (27). This is the developmental pattern in childhood that seems to provide the

[5] Acknowledgement is made to L. E. Dameron for making this point in discussion with the writer.

basis for sex-role inversion in adulthood. In fact, inversion refers precisely to the adoption of the basic behavior patterns that are characteristic of the opposite sex (4a).

In cases of males that do not involve a relatively complete inversion of sex role but do show considerable feminine identification, the result may be boys who become rebellious and develop strong defensive reactions in the form of extreme aggressiveness as a means of attempting to counteract their underlying inverted tendencies. MacDonald (22) has presented a number of cases of "effeminate" boys who developed pathological aggressive reactions.

Although direct evidence is limited it appears that the child's eventual sexual orientation and adjustment in adolescence and adulthood bears a direct relationship with the nature of his sex-role development in childhood. Adult sexual behavior, at least in part, appears to be an outgrowth of the individual's underlying sex role. Thus, a normal male is one who has identified with, incorporated, and prefers the masculine role; his sexual desire for the female is one aspect of this role. A boy who has identified with, incorporated, and prefers the feminine role will most likely desire a male as a sexual partner in adulthood in keeping with the inverted role pattern. The problem of normal and inverted sex-role development has been discussed in another paper (4).

SEX-ROLE CONVERGENCE: A NEW CULTURAL PATTERN EMERGING?

Despite the fact that boys, much more than girls, show a concern for behaving along sex-appropriate lines, there has been considerable change in the direction of both masculine and feminine roles becoming broader, less rigidly defined, less sex-typed, and more overlapping with each other. As Seward (32, p. 175) observes, "Today in the post-World War II United States, there is a good deal less self-consciousness about sex roles and probably more freedom of choice for the individual than ever before." In line with this observation is a new course in domestic arts for eighth-graders in a public school in Jersey City, New Jersey, in which boys learn how to cook, sew, and become "efficient housewives," and in which girls learn how to handle "man-sized tools," do woodwork, plumbing repairs, and become the "man-of-the-house." This course is described as so successful that the sexes may be switched in all

eighth-grade homemaking and shop courses in the Jersey City system. The same type of course has been established recently in a junior high school in St. Petersburg, Florida. And in the public senior high schools in Denver, Colorado, courses in cooking for boys, metal crafts and lathe work for girls, and child care and training for both boys and girls are offered.

Other indications of the trend toward increasing similarity of sex roles include: (a) similarity of educational experiences of girls and boys from kindergarten through the secondary school system; (b) husbands doing the dishes, cleaning the house and carrying out other domestic tasks historically considered exclusively "feminine"; (c) wives holding down jobs outside the home, many of which have been traditionally "masculine"; and (d) the apparel of boys and men that emphasize color, softness, and more delicate features along with the adoption by girls and women of all kinds of "masculine" clothing, hair styles, etc.

Mead (24) and Seward (32) have pointed out that this greater flexibility in sex-role learning makes for increased interfamily variability and, hence, increasing cultural diversity in this regard. Is it still possible, in our culture for example, to speak of *the* feminine role or *the* masculine role? Or is it necessary to refer to various *roles?* Thus, within a single neighborhood, the role of the husband-father in one home involves almost absolute control, while the role of the wife-mother is strictly subservient and dependent. Next door, the dominating control of the family may be maintained by the wife-mother, while the husband-father is little more than a financially convenient "boarder." Across the street there may be hostile competitiveness and a continual "power struggle" between the husband-father and the wife-mother, each at times emerging "victorious," the other "defeated." And, in still another home, the respective roles of husband-father and wife-mother are largely complementary and equalitarian rather than hierarchical. What must be the effect of these very different parental role patterns on the sex-role identifications and preferences of children who are developing in these respective familial environments? For example, how is the process by which a boy becomes like his father (i.e., "a man") influenced by the various role structures in such families? It is plausible that degree of ease and normality or difficulty and abnormality is directly related to the particular parental role relationships. Intensive study in this area is very much needed.

Finally, on a culture-wide level, the rapid changes in the sex roles of the Japanese during the past decade might be cited.[6] Among other contributing factors, the cultural diffusion stemming from American occupation of Japan has brought about far-reaching changes, particularly in the feminine role. In a country that gave rise to the expression "as unimportant as a Japanese woman," the traditional and relatively complete subordination of the female to the male appears to be on the way out and is being replaced by a status of women that is beginning to approach that of men. This trend is reflected not only in the fact that women can now vote, an unheard of practice ten years ago, but also in the hopes and aspirations of Japanese children as revealed in their drawings. When asked to draw pictures depicting what they wanted to be when they were grown, many girls drew pictures of teachers, secretaries, industrial workers, beauticians, scientists, etc.

A somewhat parallel development to that in Japan has been taking place in Germany during the past decade or so.[7] Here, too, feminine status has undergone marked change in the direction of greater freedom and opportunity for women in the educational and economic spheres. A continuing sociopsychological analysis of such significant and rapid changes in the feminine sex role of the Japanese and Germans should be very informative and valuable, especially in terms of the impact on the present and future generation of children.

SUMMARY

The young child, as early as the second year of life, begins to distinguish between male and female and between masculine and feminine. Preference for one sex role or the other also begins to emerge early in the life of the child, probably by the third year. Beginning at the kindergarten level and extending through the fourth grade, boys show a much stronger preference for aspects of the masculine role than girls show for aspects of the feminine role. In fact, a majority of girls in Grades 1 through 4 express greater preference for masculine things than for feminine things. These results are based on the It Scale for Children, a masculinity-femininity projective technique for use with young children.

[6] *Life Magazine,* March 29, 1954, *36,* 89-95.
[7] *Life Magazine,* May 10, 1954, *36,* 107-112.

The finding that girls more than boys show a preference for the role of the opposite sex is paralleled by studies of adults in our culture which reveal that between five and twelve times as many women as men recall having wished they were of the opposite sex.

As to the basis of masculine role preference in both sexes, three factors are mentioned: (a) the Freudian emphasis on the anatomical differences between males and females; (b) the Adlerian emphasis on sociocultural favoritism of the male compared to the female; and (c) the fact that the girl has more latitude than the boy in expressing a preference for sex-typed objects and activities.

A child may identify with and prefer the sex role appropriate to his own sex; or he may identify with and prefer the sex role of the opposite sex; or he may identify with one sex role and prefer the other. A distinction between sex-role identification and sex-role preference is emphasized.

In some ways girls would appear to have a more difficult time than boys in sex-role development; in other ways the development of boys would seem to be more complicated. The general problem of sex differences in ease of masculinity-femininity development is discussed.

Adult sexual adjustment or maladjustment is related to the nature and outcome of sex-role development in childhood.

There are definite signs that a convergence of the two sex roles gradually is taking place in our society. This cultural trend is evident in the increasing overlap between things and activities formerly considered "exclusively masculine" or "exclusively feminine." A major effect of this emerging cultural pattern is widespread inter-family variability in the sex roles of family members.

Finally, attention is called to the rapid changes in the feminine sex role in Japan and Germany during the past ten years. Emphasis is placed on the need for a continuing sociopsychological analysis of sex-role development in such changing cultures as those of the Japanese and Germans as well as that of our own.

REFERENCES

1. BROWN, D. G. Sex-role preference in young children. *Psychol. Monogr.,* 1956, *70,* No. 14 (Whole No. 421).

2. BROWN, D. G. *The It Scale for Children.* Grand Forks, North Dakota: Psychological Test Specialists, 1956.

3. BROWN D. G. Masculinity-femininity development in children. *J. consult. Psychol.*, 1957, *21*, 197-202.

4. BROWN, D. G. The development of sex-role inversion and homosexuality. *J. Pediat.*, 1957, *50*, 613-619.

4a. BROWN, D. G. Inversion and Homosexuality. *Amer. J. Orthopsychiat.*, 1958, Vol. 28, 424-429.

5. CONN, J. H., and KANNER, L. Children's awareness of sex differences. *J. Child Psychiat.*, 1947, *1*, 3-57.

6. CUNNINGHAM, RUTH, ELZI, ANNA, HALL, J. A., FARRELL, MARIE, and ROBERTS, MADELINE. *Understanding group behavior of boys and girls.* New York: Bureau of Publications, Teachers College, Columbia Univer., 1951.

7. DEIGNAN, H. G. *Burma: gateway to China.* Washington, D. C.: Smithsonian Institution, 1943.

8. DINITZ, S., DYNES, R. R., and CLARKE, A. C. Preference for male or female children: traditional or affectional. *Marriage Fam. Living*, 1954, *16*, 128-130.

9. FAULS, LYDIA B., and SMITH, W. D. Sex-role learning of five-year-olds. *J. genet. Psychol.*, 1956, *89*, 105-117.

10. FORTUNE SURVEY, *Fortune*, August, 1946.

11. GALLUP, G. *Gallup poll.* Princeton: Audience Research Inc., June, 1955.

12. GESELL, A., HALVERSON, H. M., THOMPSON, H., ILG, F. L., CASTNER, B. M., AMES, L. B., and AMATRUDA, C. S. *The first five years of life: the preschool years.* New York: Harper, 1940.

13. GESELL, A., ILG, FRANCES L., LEARNED, J., and AMES, L. B. *Infant and child in the culture of today: The guidance of development in home and nursery school.* New York: Harper, 1943.

14. GOODENOUGH, EVELYN W. Interest in persons as an aspect of sex difference in the early years. *Genet. Psychol. Monogr.*, 1957, *55*, 287-323.

15. GORER, G. *The American people.* New York: Norton, 1948.

16. GRAY, SUSAN W. Masculinity-femininity in relation to anxiety and social acceptance. *Child Develop.*, 1957, *28*, 203-213.

17. HANDY, G. D. The sex-role preference scale for children: a study of the It-figure. Unpublished master's thesis, Univer. Denver, 1954.

18. HARTLEY, RUTH, FRANK, L. K., and GOLDENSON, R. M. *Understanding children's play.* New York: Columbia Univer. Press, 1952.

19. HOGAN, R. A. Children's sex-role preference with the It-figure. Unpublished master's thesis, Univer. Denver, 1957.

20. HURLOCK, ELIZABETH B. *Developmental psychology.* New York: McGraw-Hill, 1953.

21. LOW, WILLABE P. Sex of the examiner in relation to sex-role preferences in kindergarten children. Unpublished master's thesis, Univer. Denver, 1957.

22. MACDONALD, MARTHA W. Criminally aggressive behavior in passive effeminate boys. *Amer. J. Orthopsychiat.*, 1938, *8*, 70-78.

23. MEAD, MARGARET. *Sex and temperament in three primitive societies.* New York: New American Library, 1935.

24. MEAD, MARGARET. *Male and female.* New York: Morrow, 1949.

25. PARSONS, T. Age and sex in the social structure of the United States. *Amer. sociol. Rev.*, 1942, 7, 604-616.

26. RABBAN, M. Sex-role identification in young children in two diverse social groups. *Genet. Psychol. Monogr.*, 1950, *42*, 81-158.

27. RONGE, P. H. The "feminine protest." *Amer. J. indiv. Psychol.*, 1956, *12*, 112-115.

28. SANCHEZ-HIDALGO, E. [The feeling of inferiority in the Puerto Rican female.] *Rev. Asoc. Maestros, P. R.*, 1952, *11* (6), 170-171; 193.

29. SCHEINFELD, A. *Women and men.* New York: Harcourt, Brace, 1944.

30. SEARS, R. R., MACCOBY, ELEANOR E., and LEVIN, H. *Patterns of child rearing.* Evanston, Illinois: Row, Peterson, 1957.

31. SEWARD, GEORGENE H. *Sex and the social order.* New York: McGraw-Hill, 1946.

32. SEWARD, GEORGENE H. *Psychotherapy and culture conflict.* New York: Ronald, 1956.

33. SHAW, F. J., and ORT, R. S. *Personal adjustment in the American culture.* New York: Harper, 1953.

34. TERMAN, L. M. *Psychological factors in marital happiness.* New York: McGraw-Hill, 1938.

35. WHITE, L., JR. *Educating our daughters.* New York: Harper, 1950.

50/CHILDREN'S TEXTBOOKS AND PERSONALITY DEVELOPMENT: AN EXPLORATION IN THE SOCIAL PSYCHOLOGY OF EDUCATION/

IRVIN L. CHILD, ELMER H. POTTER, AND ESTELLE M. LEVINE*

INTRODUCTION

IN THE APPLICATION OF PSYCHOLOGY to the study of formal education in our society, attention has been directed primarily at intellectual aspects of education. A few notable studies, such as those by the Character Education Inquiry (1) and by Jones (2), have been concerned with the development of ideals and morals in the school situation. But for the most part, psychologists have directed their attention to the study of intellectual aptitudes and achievements—their measurement, the factors influencing them, and their predictive value.

Yet intellectual achievements and aptitudes are only one aspect of the child's behavior that schools are capable of influencing. Also of tremendous importance is another aspect: the motives that children develop, the ways they learn to satisfy their motives, the expectations they acquire about the consequences of trying to satisfy their motives in various ways. It is around this motivational aspect of the educational process that this study is centered.

The motivational influences of education are significant both in themselves and in relation to intellectual development. They are important in themselves because education should be directed at training children to become well-adjusted and responsible adults as well as adults equipped with intellectual skills. But a person's very acquisition of information and understanding, and most of all the use he will make of it, depends upon motivational aspects of his personality. Hence the attainment of the intellectual aims of education is itself dependent upon the motives developed in children. This study represents, then, one of several beginnings that have been and are being made in the social

psychology of education in our society—the study of the role of the educational system in shaping not merely the intellect but the general personality of the child.

The specific objective of this study is the analysis of certain content of the world of ideas which confronts children in the process of education, from the point of view of the probable effect of that content on the motivation of their behavior. Just what that means will be made clear through the discussion, in the rest of this chapter, of the way the content was analyzed.

SELECTION OF MATERIAL

THE BOOKS CHOSEN. The material chosen for analysis consisted of certain portions of the content of general readers intended for use in the third grade. Printed material was selected, rather than the content of what was said by teachers in classrooms, because of the accessibility of printed material, and because a manageable sample of it must of necessity reflect accurately certain educational practices in the country at large. The choice of the third-grade level was made on the grounds of convenience for the purpose of this study: textbooks for the first and second grades have such very simple content that few passages are susceptible of the kind of analysis that we have undertaken, while readers from the fourth grade up, on the other hand, begin to have such complex material that the analysis would be more laborious and less reliable.

We chose for our purpose all of the general third-grade readers we were able to find which had been published since 1930. (Excluded were third-grade readers intended primarily to teach special topics such as science, social studies, or

* Irvin L. Child, Elmer H. Potter, and Estelle M. Levine, Children's textbooks and personality development: An exploration in the social psychology of education. *Psychological Monographs*, 1946, *60*, No. 3, pp. 1-7, 43-53. Reprinted with abridgement by permission.

arithmetic, and one reader which deviated greatly from all the others in containing considerable material on religion.) In all, 30 books were included in the analysis.

SELECTION OF CONTENT FROM THE BOOKS. . . . The general criterion for selection was that the story contain characters in action, since the child's behavior would be affected only by his generalizing from that of individuals in the sto-

TABLE 1 / CATEGORIES OF BEHAVIOR EMPLOYED IN ANALYZING THE CONTENT OF THIRD-GRADE READERS, WITH THE NUMBER OF THEMA IN WHICH EACH CATEGORY WAS FOUND.

CATEGORY[Ed]	NUMBER OF THEMA IN WHICH IT APPEARS
Objectless behavior	
Activity	264
Passivity	89
Sentience	82
Elation	55
Behavior primarily in relation to things and events	
Cognizance	351
Achievement	221
Construction	75
Imaginality	31
Acquisition	177
Retention	33
Order	43
Altruistic social behavior (generally leading to simultaneous gratification of other person's needs)	
Affiliation	364
Nurturance	266
Succorance	176
Deference	184
Egoistic social behavior (generally competing with other person's needs)	
Aggression	206
Dominance	152
Recognition	175
Autonomy	122
Rejection	21
Avoidance behavior	
Harmavoidance	212
Blamavoidance	72
Infavoidance	38

[Ed] *For definition of terms, see Glossary at end of article.*

ries to his own behavior. This resulted in the exclusion of [some] types of material . . . but the material analyzed included well over three quarters of the content of the books. Altogether, 914 stories were analyzed.

A story is often, however, a cumbersome and complex unit for analysis and comparision. . . . The unit for analysis, therefore, was not the story but the *thema*. A thema is a sequence of psychological events consisting of (1) a situation or circumstances confronting a person, (2) the behavior (internal and external) with which the person responds, (3) the consequences of the behavior as felt by the person himself (3). In the 914 stories used, 3409 thema were found and analyzed, an average of almost 4 thema per story. In the presentation of quantitative data in the rest of this monograph, the number of thema is always the basic quantity dealt with.

METHOD OF ANALYSIS

. . . SUMMARY OF PROCEDURE. The outline of the analysis given above will now be briefly summarized, together with some indication of the actual technique used in recording the data.

The first step was to read each story in a given book and determine whether it was suitable for the purposes of the analysis. If it was suitable, the second step was to identify all the separate thema in the story that fitted the pattern of analysis. When these thema were identified, a file card was prepared for each one. It was labeled appropriately to identify the story and the book and then the following information was entered on it:

(1) The type of story
(2) Whether the character was central or antisocial
(3) The classification of the character according to age, sex, humanity, etc.
(4) The behavior displayed, classified according to Murray's system of needs (3)
(5) Notes on the circumstances surrounding the behavior
(6) The classification of the consequences of the behavior.

OVERALL FINDINGS AND DISCUSSION

CULTURAL FORCES INFLUENCING PERSONALITY. The observations that have been reviewed on the treatment of various categories of behavior in children's readers can leave no doubt that this treatment is such as to encourage the development of certain motives and to discourage others. A tabulation of the percentage of reward, punishment, and no consequence for the various categories of behavior, presented in Table 2, brings out this general point quite clearly. The categories are arranged here in order of relative frequency of reward, and this order may be taken as one indication of the degree of encouragement or discouragement of the development of each one. In considerable part, of course, this order reflects general cultural norms —for example, in the high value placed on affiliation, nurturance and cognizance, and in the frequent punishment of aggression, retention and rejection. To this extent the analysis of the contents of the readers does not stand alone but is useful as symptomatic of probable characteristics of other kinds of content of the world of ideas that reach children—what teachers say to them in classes, morals that their parents point up to them, the content of stories they read elsewhere.

But the entire impact of cultural forces on personality manifested in these readers is not shown in a simple listing of the treatment of the several categories separately. There are also certain generalities which can be found running through the whole series of categories, generalities about particular ways of achieving ends which are most likely to lead to success or to failure.

Perhaps the most striking case of this sort is the repeated reward of effort or work as a way of reaching goals. In the discussion of acquisition, it was shown that effortful ways of acquiring things are the most frequently rewarded; similar observations were made in connection with achievement and construction. Even in the case of the relatively objectless need for activity, the more purposeful instances of activity which require more work are more frequently rewarded. Here certainly are some of the forces leading to the development of a motive to work or put forth effort. This motive is sometimes very important in adults or older children, and may activate them for a long time, even when the effort leads to no external reward. It needs explanation, because of marked contrast with the general tendency for human beings and other organisms to avoid work or effort when it is not necessary. The motive is doubtless developed in large part through social learning, and we have in this reading matter an example of the kinds of social influences that lead to its development.

Another special emphasis is on the acquisition of skills, on learning. This is, of course, evident in the first place from the high frequency of cognizant behavior and its high proportion of reward. It also appears in the treatment of achievement; there it was observed that the most frequently rewarded mode of achievement was by the acquisition of new skills, even more frequently rewarded than achievement through the display of skills formerly acquired.

TABLE 2 / PERCENTAGE OF REWARD, PUNISHMENT, AND NO CONSEQUENCE FOR EACH CATEGORY OF BEHAVIOR (IN ALL OF THE 3409 THEMA WHICH WERE ANALYZED).

CATEGORY OF BEHAVIOR	PERCENT OF THEMA IN WHICH THE BEHAVIOR IS REWARDED	PERCENT OF THEMA IN WHICH THE BEHAVIOR IS PUNISHED	PERCENT OF THEMA IN WHICH BEHAVIOR RESULTS IN NO CONSEQUENCE (I.E., NEITHER REWARDED NOR PUNISHED)
Construction	96	1	3
Sentience	96	4	0
Elation	95	4	1
Cognizance	86	9	5
Succorance	84	10	6
Affiliation	82	8	9
Nurturance	82	5	12
Achievement	80	10	9
Recognition	79	13	8
Activity	74	9	16
Dominance	74	16	8
Blamavoidance	71	15	14
Imaginality	71	6	23
Order	70	2	28
Acquisition	64	31	3
Passivity	54	26	20
Deference	52	10	38
Harmavoidance	49	39	12
Autonomy	48	40	12
Retention	42	48	10
Aggression	35	52	11
Rejection	14	62	24
Infavoidance	8	74	18
All categories	71	17	12

Despite the emphasis on learning, there is in these third-grade readers little encouragement of intellectual activity as such. The cognizance is usually directed at simple isolated information rather than a quest for understanding. Sentience, as it appears in the readers, is only rarely concerned with esthetic appreciation which goes beyond the admiration of simple man-made objects or of nature. Activity is ordinarily physical, and in only one case intellectual in nature. The achievements, even those involving the acquisition of a skill, can in most cases hardly be spoken of as intellectual. Similarly in constructive behavior: only one story about construction concerns a non-material product, a poem.

It should be noted, moreover, that the acquisition of skills or knowledge which is rewarded is generally that which is dependent upon persons in a superior position—for example the gaining of knowledge by children through questioning parents or teachers. In this sense, too, there is less emphasis on intellectual activity than might appear, since there is relatively little encouragement of original thinking on the part of the central character.

A distinction is also made between satisfying needs in socially approved ways, which tends to be rewarded, and satisfying them in disapproved ways, which tends to be punished. For example, in the case of retention, retention which is defined as socially or individually useful and permissible, such as saving money, is rewarded; on the other hand, retention which is defined as selfish is punished. Similarly for recognition: there is heavy reward for exhibiting one's capacities so long as social rules are followed; but when rules are broken, as by exhibiting oneself at the wrong time or making claims about one's powers that are not justified, then the behavior is punished. Dominance and aggression provide examples of other modes of behavior where social rules set down certain conditions as making the behavior permissible and certain other conditions as not. In these cases the conditions have to do with what other needs, if any, are served at the same time; if dominance or aggression does not serve some other approved purpose, or if it serves other disapproved purposes such as selfish acquisition or retention, it is punished.

PROBLEMS OF ADJUSTMENT. In the ways that have just been indicated, material such as that in the readers provides lessons to children, encouraging or discouraging the development of motives in a way that on the whole is likely to lead to more satisfactory adjustment in our society. But at the same time there are certain respects in which this material is failing to contribute to good adjustment.

A major defect of the readers from this point of view is what might be called their unrealistic optimism. Behavior directed at affiliation and nurturance, for example, is almost always rewarded in the readers. There are very few cases of failure. It is impossible to compare the proportion of success here with that obtaining in children's everyday life. Yet from the point of view of contributing to the solution of problems of everyday life, failures ought to receive a larger proportion of attention, for it is they that pose problems.

It may indeed be true that the encouragement of affiliative and nurturant needs in this reading is of little consequence, because the much stronger pressures from the real environment are already working in that same direction, and the contribution from here can be little more. But there is a very great opportunity for reading matter, such as in these textbooks, to point up possible solutions for frustrations often encountered by the child in seeking for gratification of these needs. In that case, such reading matter should include a larger number of accounts of how children get around obstacles in their attempts to satisfy affiliative and nurturant needs—stories in which expression of these needs first meets with punishment or rebuff and only attains success when some new method of approach more suited to the environment is hit upon.

For children who have encountered failure in their everyday life, the easy attainment of goals such as nurturance and affiliation in the readers may be so unrealistic as to have little effect in strengthening their desire for such goals. Suggestions as to how these needs may be satisfied despite serious difficulties might, on the other hand, through their realism to such children, contribute to strengthening the needs.

A similar sort of unrealism was commented on in the discussion of infavoidance. While the content of these readers might do a great deal towards strengthening a desire for achievement in competitive success, there is very little about those children—perhaps the majority—who frequently experience failure in competition, and few suggestions about how such children can find some satisfactory way of adjusting to their failure. Such material might be more beneficial than what is actually found in contributing to the better adjustment of those children whose present adjustment is unsatisfactory.

A similar failure to make positive suggestions is found in the treatment of aggression and acquisition. Here are two needs, certainly universally present in children, which lead to serious problems of adjustment because of their frequent interference with desires of other and more powerful persons.

Children's reading matter might be quite useful in furthering satisfactory adjustment if it were able to pose models for the child of ways to satisfy these needs when they are prevented from the most direct and immediately satisfactory expression. While there are certainly some incidents which might be useful in this way, the general tendency in the readers is, instead, for these needs simply to be overlooked in the child characters. It is as though the writers were inclined to solve problems of aggression and acquisition in children by trying to convince children that they do not have these needs, that they are experienced only by adults, animals and supernatural creatures. To a certain extent the child's real social environment may be cooperating with the readers in this direction, through a tradition that children do not hate or covet and are basically nice unless they are led to be otherwise. But the fact probably is that every child does hate and does covet, and that in his efforts to do so he is being repeatedly rebuffed by the more powerful persons in his environment. Those persons are apt often not to have the psychological insight necessary for redirecting these interests of the child into channels where they can have more success. Here then is a valuable potential role of children's reading matter.

Another possible inadequacy of the reading matter, one much more difficult to judge, is concerned with maturity. It is notable in the content of these readers that independent action initiated by child characters, and indeed by anyone, is more likely to be punished than similar behavior which is performed under the direction of a superior. Cognizance, for example, is rather frequently punished when it is undertaken on the child's own initiative and leads to pursuit of knowledge directly by the child's own exploratory behavior, whereas it is almost always rewarded if knowledge is gained through dependence upon authority. Autonomous behavior, too, is generally punished except in the case where the kind of autonomy is that desired by the child's elders. (There is an exception to this in the case of nurturance, which is more often rewarded when it is spontaneously initiated by the character himself.)

There can be no doubt that if children continue to be trained in this way as they grow older, the effect on their potentialities as adults will be a bad one. It may indeed be that a considerable proportion of adult maladjustment in marriage and occupational life is due to the discouragement of autonomy and independence by the educational system up to the point where an adolescent or young adult leaves it. On the other hand, it may of course be argued that the amount of independence encouraged by the content of these readers is quite appropriate for the particular age level at which the readers are directed. Certainly the development towards autonomy must be a gradual process and a considerable amount of dependence on superiors is necessary, not only at this age but on into adult life. For this reason it is impossible to make a conclusive judgment about the wisdom of this aspect of the content of the readers.

DIFFERENTIAL TREATMENT OF THE SEXES. Perhaps the most striking single finding of this study is the extent to which a differentiation is made between the roles of male and female in the content of these readers. To the extent that boys identify with male characters, and girls with female characters, this difference both in itself and as a reflection of facts that hold true of many other sources of influence on children, must have a profound significance on the differential development of personality in the two sexes.

Some of the differentiation can be seen in the mere frequency with which the two sexes appear among the characters displaying the various categories of behavior. Female characters, for example, are relatively more frequent among those displaying affiliation, nurturance, and harmavoidance. On the other hand, females are less frequent, relatively, among characters displaying activity, aggression, achievement, construction, and recognition. Girls and women are thus being shown as sociable, kind and timid, but inactive, unambitious and uncreative.

This picture is further added to by considering the relative proportion of male and female characters among the subsidiary characters who are objects related to the satisfaction of the needs of the central characters. The most important findings here refer to nurturance and cognizance. The persons nurtured by a central character are in the majority female, suggesting that females are in a relatively helpless position. The persons who supply information to central characters who are seeking for knowledge are, in contrast, predominantly male. It will be recalled that even among unrelated adults who supply knowledge to children, the majority are male despite the obvious fact that the most important such persons of the real environment are the child's teachers, who are mostly women. Males, in short, are being portrayed as the bearers of knowledge and wisdom, and as the persons through whom knowledge can come to the child.

In all of these respects, a distinction in role is being made between the sexes which may indeed have a certain validity as of our society of the present time, but which seems much more a survival of former practices. The many schoolgirls who will at some future time have to make their own living are failing, if they identify with female characters, to receive the same training in the development of motives for work and achievement that boys are receiving. To the extent that this distinction is characteristic of many other aspects of the training the child receives from his environment, it should cause little wonder that women are sometimes less fitted for creative work and achievement than men of similar aptitude, for there is certainly much difference in the motivational training they receive for it. It has been a common assumption that the education of the two sexes is virtually the same in American public schools, except for differences in vocational training. Here is clear evidence that the education is not the same, even at early levels of grammar school and even when the boys and girls are mixed together, as they usually are, in the same classroom. Not only does the informal training of boys and girls at home and in the community differ, but even the formal education they are receiving in the classroom differs.

It has been shown in several instances that the differential treatment of the sexes goes further than mere correspondence with this stereotype of different categories of behavior as being more conspicuous in a particular sex. There are several striking instances where females are shown as being definitely inferior from a moral point of view. In the discussion of passivity it was shown that female characters are portrayed as lazy twice as often, relatively, as male characters. In the discussion of acquisition it was seen that female characters are shown as acquiring in socially disapproved ways much more often, relatively, than males, and much less frequently by the most approved routes of work and effort.

In view of the social values of our society, it can also be said that the facts already cited above are relevant here. Insofar as female characters are shown as not often achieving, con-

structing, obtaining recognition or engaging in activity, they are being shown in an unfavorable light by the general standards of our society. But on the other hand, in that female characters are being shown as more frequently affiliative, nurturant, or unaggressive, they may perhaps be said to be receiving the more favorable treatment. While it is not true, then, that female characters are uniformly shown in a more unfavorable light, the balance is certainly in that direction.

The most striking single fact of all, however, about the difference between the sexes is that female characters do simply tend to be neglected. Of all the central characters in all these thema (excluding central characters who consist of a group of mixed sex), 73% are male and only 27% are female. Male characters are thus over two and a half times as frequent as female ones. The same tendency is found, though not so strikingly, in the characters who are objects of, or cooperators in, the satisfaction of the needs of the central characters; here the proportion of males is 63% and of females 37%.

There can be no excuse for this greater attention to males in the claim that males have achieved more in society and hence that there is more to write about them. These stories are, with few exceptions, not about individuals of outstanding achievement but simply about the life of everyday people. The implication of this difference for a girl is that being female is a pretty bad thing, that the only people even in everyday life who are worth writing about or reading about are boys and men. If the content of these readers is typical of other social influences, small wonder that girls might develop for this reason alone an inferiority complex about their sex.

DIFFERENTIAL TREATMENT OF ADULTS AND CHILDREN. The human characters in the stories were readily divisible into two groups according to age—adults and children. The treatment of these two groups differed markedly, and in ways that raise interesting problems about the effect of these stories on the children who read them.

There are, first of all, great differences in the relative frequency of the various categories of behavior. Children are much lower than adults in the incidence of aggression and acquisition. In adults, aggression and acquisition are the most frequently appearing categories of behavior, whereas in children these two are of very low incidence. . . .

That children are shown as more socialized is demonstrated also by the relative frequency of different kinds of rewards. It was noted in connection with several categories of behavior, especially affiliation and nurturance, that children are shown as more frequently receiving only internal rewards. This generalization holds true for all of the behavior in the readers taken as a whole. A summary of the percent of each type of reward in all four types of character is presented in Table 3. . . .

TABLE 3 / KINDS OF REWARDS FOR ALL CATEGORIES OF BEHAVIOR: PERCENTAGE DISTRIBUTION IN EACH CHARACTER TYPE.

CHARACTER TYPE	PERCENTAGE DISTRIBUTION OF KINDS OF REWARD IN EACH CHARACTER TYPE			
	INTERNAL	SOCIAL	MATERIAL	AUTOMATIC
Children	34	23	36	6
Adults	16	26	53	4
Animals	24	18	50	8
Fairies	16	34	43	8

Now internal rewards are dependent upon socialization, for they are rewards that a person administers to himself because he is well socialized, because he is able to feel good or virtuous at having done the right thing, even if no reward is offered by an external agency.

That children are shown as more socialized than adults, perhaps points up more clearly than anything else the role that the content of these readers must be more or less consciously intended to play in the moral education of children. If the readers are intended for inculcating proper behavior in children, then it must seem only natural at first glance that it is the child characters who especially should be shown as displaying the desired forms of behavior. But a serious question may be raised as to whether the readers are likely to accomplish the purpose in this way. A more sophisticated consideration of the probable effect of the content of these readers would suggest that there is considerable probability that children pattern their behavior more after that of the adult characters than after that of the child characters. There is ample reason to suppose that children imitate adults, especially their parents, much more than they do their age-mates, and particularly with reference to deep-seated motivational tendencies. If this be true, then for purposes of the moral education of the children who read these stories, the adult characters should be shown as at least as well socialized as the child characters.

Whether this criticism is justified does, of course, depend upon factual determination of whether children are more likely to be influenced by the behavior portrayed in adult characters than in child characters. But on general psychological grounds, this does seem so likely as to give the criticism considerable weight. . . .

TREATMENT OF ANIMALS AND FAIRIES.   Animals are the central characters in 17% of the thema, ranking second to child characters in frequency. Their behavior can be expected to influence the children reading about them not only because of the frequency of their occurrence, but also because most of them are shown as young animals who appear in a parent-child relationship. They are usually portrayed as anthropomorphic characters endowed with speech, and their relationship to the physical and social environment closely approximates the subordinate position in which children also find themselves.

The pattern of their behavior is in most instances similar to that of children: they, like the child characters, are shown as rewarded for dependent, socially conforming behavior. There are a few striking exceptions to this parallelism, however. The major differences in child and animal behavior are in the more frequent occurrence of aggression among animals (where it ranks second in frequency), and also of autonomy. . . . Their aggression is also usually of the more undesirable form, unprovoked aggression, while their instances of autonomy are most frequently instances of disobedience to authority. These, as has been pointed out, are the most frequently punished forms of aggression and autonomy.

To a certain extent, then, animal characters seem to furnish an outlet for the expression in child-like characters of aggressive and rebellious tendencies. Since these needs are predominantly punished, the animal characters serve the function of teaching the lesson that whenever asocial tendencies are expressed, they are punished. Thus they have a double purpose: they remove the necessity of showing child characters as exhibiting undesirable behavior, while at the same time yielding an object lesson as to the results of such behavior should it be manifested. It is as though the writers felt that, to a child reading animal stories, the behavior is detached enough from the child so that he would not copy it, and yet plausible enough for him to accept the moral that aggressive and autonomous asocial behavior leads to certain punishment. . . .

Indirectly, then, the readers do admit the existence of aggression in young persons (i.e., young animals or young fairies). Yet here, too, there is little constructive suggestion as to how to handle such tendencies. When characters are shown as aggressive, punishment follows, without an indication of suitable substitute outlets.

SIGNIFICANCE OF VARIOUS STORY TYPES. . . . It is apparent [however] that the various types of stories do serve a function, and that this is related to the types of characters appearing in them. For the stories represent various degrees of realism in portraying behavior, from the prosaic everyday story, through the idealized hero and the humanized animal story, to the frankly unrealistic fairy story. It is significant, therefore, that most of the behavior of the children is portrayed against a realistic, everyday background. For if the children are able to differentiate between the real and the unreal, they will tend to be more influenced by behavior which is possible for them. And even where they do not make this distinction, the very fact that such behavior more closely resembles theirs is likely to make for greater generalization to their own behavior. It is important to note, therefore, that the pattern of behavior for children in the readers, which was summarized earlier in this chapter, is the one pattern of behavior for any character type that is most consistently presented realistically. It is reinforced and emphasized by the medium of its presentation—the everyday story. . . .

Fairy stories . . . [permit] the expression of antisocial egoistic behavior in an unreal situation where the reader will be less likely to copy it. It is probably also true, however, that presentation of such behavior in very unrealistic circumstances fails to contribute to a child's learning ways for handling the similar anti-social tendencies he must cope with in everyday life. In this respect, it is consistent with the whole treatment of children's behavior in the readers that these categories of behavior which are handled unrealistically within themselves, are further treated so by having them displayed primarily in an unrealistic situation.

The total picture of adult behavior is also somewhat clarified by noting how very often it is placed in the unrealistic setting of the fairy story. It will be remembered that adults are frequently shown as conforming less often to socially approved behavior than are children. The interpretation of this pattern is less ambiguous when it is noted that it frequently occurs in the fairy story. In fact, the relative frequency of the various categories of behavior in the fairy story corresponds quite closely to their relative frequency in the adult characters. Again the fairy stories are apparently serving as an outlet for the expression of anti-social needs, in situations where children will be less likely to generalize from the behavior. . . .

Since animal stories are composed almost exclusively of animal characters, the interpretation of them is similar to that for the characters: they permit the expression of rebellious and asocial tendencies in a situation where the child will not be very likely to copy such undesirable behavior. . . .

BIBLIOGRAPHY Ed

1. HARTSHORNE, H. and MAY, M. A. *Studies in deceit.* New York: Macmillan, 1928.

2. JONES, V. *Character and citizenship training in the public schools.* Chicago: Univ. Chicago Press, 1936.

3. MURRAY, H. A., *et al. Explorations in personality.* New York: Oxford Univ. Press, 1938.

GLOSSARY

COGNIZANCE. Refers to behavior that evinces an "inquiring attitude . . . To explore (moving and touching). To ask questions. To satisfy curiosity. To look, listen, inspect. To read and seek knowledge." One of the needs listed by Murray.°

CONSTRUCTION. Refers to behaviors of organizing and building. One of the needs listed by Murray.°

DEFERENCE. "To admire and willingly follow a superior . . . To co-operate with a leader. To serve gladly." One of the needs listed by Murray.°

INFAVOIDANCE. "To avoid failure, shame, humiliation, ridicule. To refrain from attempting to do something that is beyond one's powers. To conceal a disfigurement." One of the needs listed by Murray.°

NURTURANCE. "To nourish, aid or protect a helpless [person]. To express sympathy. To 'mother' a child." One of the needs listed by Murray.°

SENTIENCE. ". . . refers to the inclination for sensuous gratification, particularly from objects in contact with the body: taste sensations and tactile sensations." One of the needs listed by Murray.°

SUBBORANCE. "To seek aid, protection, or sympathy. To cry for help. To plead for mercy. To adhere to an affectionate, nurturant parent. To be dependent." One of the needs listed by Murray.°

Ed *See original for more extensive bibliography, including the books analyzed.*

° Henry A. Murray *et. al., Explorations in Personality* (New York: Oxford University Press, 1938), pp. 77-83.

51/SEX DIFFERENCES IN THE DISTRIBUTION OF TEACHER APPROVAL AND DISAPPROVAL AMONG SIXTH-GRADE CHILDREN/

WILLIAM J. MEYER AND
GEORGE G. THOMPSON°

THIS STUDY WAS DESIGNED TO INVEStigate the relative frequency of women teachers' approval and disapproval evaluations of sixth-grade male as contrasted with female pupils. The relevant data for this study were obtained by means of two independent techniques: thirty hours of direct observation of teacher-pupil interactions in each of three classrooms; and, the use of a modification of the "Guess Who?" technique to determine if the children themselves were aware of any sex differences in their teachers' approval and disapproval evaluations.

There is considerable agreement among psychologists that the use of approval by the teacher results in better learning and probably in better over-all adjustment (Hurlock, 1924; Ojemann and Wilkinson, 1939). Some studies (Olson and Wilkinson, 1938; Snyder, 1947) have shown that personal maladjustments in teachers have deleterious effects on the adjustment level of the children in their classes.

In a series of studies by Anderson and Brewer (1945, 1946) and Anderson, Brewer, and Reed (1946), using a sample of kindergarten-age children, the data indicate that teachers typically use statements of a dominative nature in their interactions with the children in their classes. Anderson further reports that the teachers in his study tended to levy most of their dominative and/or integrative overtures on only a few pupils to the relative neglect of the other children in the classroom. Further evidence of this nature is reported in a study by deGroat and Thompson (1949) using four sixth-grade classrooms. In addition to reporting inequities in teacher approval and disapproval they also found that teachers give more praise to the youngsters who are brighter, better adjusted and higher achievers. The more poorly adjusted and the duller children were observed by these investigators to receive more disapproval from their teachers.

The purpose of the present investigation is to shed more light on the ways in which teachers respond toward the pupils in their classrooms. Extensive research findings have been reported in the literature[1] which consistently show that boys are more aggressive and generally more "unmanageable" than girls. It is our hypothesis that this "masculine" behavior will result in male pupils receiving a larger number of dominative, or punitive, contacts than girls from their teacher, who is usually a woman from the middle socio-economic stratum of our society. That is, we feel that the behavior of boys in the typical classroom is of such a nature as to make it less acceptable to teachers who probably attempt to perpetuate certain middle-class standards of what "good" classroom behavior should be. We believe that girls usually display behavior more in conformity to the standards perceived as "good" by the average elementary school teacher and will therefore receive fewer disapproval contacts and more approval contacts from their teachers.

Assuming that the above hypotheses are supported by the data we would also predict that children of elementary school age will recognize, and take for granted, that boys receive more disapproval and blame from their teachers than girls.

[1] Goodenough (1931); Hayes (1943); Radke (1946); Sears (1951); Tuddenham (1952).

° William J. Meyer and George G. Thompson, Sex differences in the distribution of teacher approval and disapproval among sixth-grade children, *Journal of Educational Psychology*, 1956, 47, 385-396. Reprinted by permission.

EXPERIMENTAL PROCEDURE

In order to test the hypothesis that boys receive a larger number of dominative, or disapproval, evaluations from their teachers than do girls, teacher-pupil interaction within three sixth-grade classrooms were recorded for a total sample of thirty hours per classroom. These time samples of classroom behavior were spread over an entire school year. Among other things being studied, interactions between teachers and pupils were classified into two categories: (a) praise contacts (teacher initiated interactions with a child in which she verbally expressed approval of some behavior which the child had displayed), and (b) blame contacts (teacher initiated interactions with a child in which she verbally expressed disapproval for some bit of behavior which the child had displayed). Observer agreement for the praise classification ranged from eighty-four to one hundred per cent with a median of approximately ninety-two per cent. Observer agreement for the blame classification ranged from fifty-seven to one hundred per cent, with a median of approximately ninety-three per cent.

In an attempt to cast some light on children's perceptions of any sex differences in teacher disapproval, a modified "Guess Who?" approach was employed. The "Guess Who?" approach used in this study required each child to nominate fellow class members for a number of situations in which children are receiving approval or disapproval from their teacher for some behavior. (See deGroat and Thompson [1949] for a more complete description of these scales and information about their reliabilities.) The behavior descriptions were selected on the basis of their familiarity to children and contain a fairly representative sample of situations in which children typically receive either approval or disapproval from their teachers. Each child was required to list the names of four of his classmates whom he thought fitted each of the behavior descriptions most adequately.

RESULTS

Fisher's t test was used to determine the reliability of the obtained sex differences.[2] The difference between disapproval contacts received by boys and by girls from their teachers was statistically significant in each of the three classrooms. As predicted, the boys received the larger number of disapproval contacts. These differences may be interpreted according to our hypothesis as supporting the notion that teachers are responding with counter-aggression to the greater expression of aggression by boys. The results obtained in analyzing the teachers' praise contacts with boys and girls are presented in Table 2.

[2] This test assumes that the samples being compared are homogeneous with respect to their variances. Frequently this assumption had to be rejected in some of the group comparisons. In such cases a more conservative test of significance was used which makes some allowance in the error term for heterogeneity of variance. This technique is presented in detail in Cochran and Cox (1950).

TABLE 1 / SEX DIFFERENCES IN FREQUENCY OF TEACHERS' DISAPPROVAL CONTACTS.

	CLASSROOM A		CLASSROOM B		CLASSROOM C	
	BOYS	GIRLS	BOYS	GIRLS	BOYS	GIRLS
N	10	9	12	14	17	16
Mean	11.10	2.67	10.75	2.79	10.06	1.44
S.D.	7.62	2.18	9.27	2.42	14.42	1.59
t	3.20[b]		3.11[b]		2.37[a]	
F	12.22[b]		14.67[b]		130.36[b]	
$t_{.01}$[c]	3.30		3.10		2.92	

a Significant at the five per cent level.
b Significant at the one per cent level.

c See footnote 2.

TABLE 2 / SEX DIFFERENCES IN FREQUENCY OF TEACHERS' APPROVAL CONTACTS.

	CLASSROOM A		CLASSROOM B		CLASSROOM C	
	BOYS	GIRLS	BOYS	GIRLS	BOYS	GIRLS
N	10	9	12	14	17	16
Mean	9.90	9.67	10.50	5.50	3.71	2.69
S.D.	6.10	7.65	5.33	2.53	2.95	1.99
t	0.074		2.50[a]		1.15	
F	1.57		4.43[b]		2.19	
$t_{.05}$[c]	—		2.19		—	

a Significant at the five per cent level.
b Significant at the one per cent level.

c See footnote 2.

The only statistically significant differences obtained for this variable was in school B. However the boys received more praise than the girls in each of the classrooms. It may be that the teachers are attempting to reinforce any positive behavior that the boys may display. Or this tendency to praise boys more than girls may reflect compensatory behavior for guilt feelings created in the teacher by her excessive aggressiveness towards boys. Either interpretation, or any one of the several others that could be offered, is highly speculative.

The data presented above are based on the extensive observations of an objective observer who played no functional role in the classrooms. The data presented in the following section reflect the teachers' approval and disapproval contacts as viewed by their pupils.

''GUESS WHO?'' DATA

Analysis of the "Guess Who?" data was performed along the same lines as the data obtained by direct observation. A comparison of the pupils' nomination of their peers on the disapproval items revealed statistically significant differences between boys and girls for two of the three schools. This can be interpreted as showing that the boys are viewed by the girls as well as by their male peers as being involved in more situations which evoke disapproval from their teachers.

Analysis of the children's responses to the items related to teacher approval produced no significant differences between boys and girls.

A final analysis of the "Guess Who?" data was performed in an attempt to determine how boys as contrasted with girls perceived the teacher's approval and disapproval biases. The choices made by the boys and by the girls for the approval and disapproval items were separately analyzed. It seemed unreasonable to use the t test in this situation because of the unequal numbers of boys and girls in the classroom. Therefore the groups were equated by converting the frequencies of nominations to percentages and working with percentage differences.

The results of the statistical analysis of boys' nominations on the disapproval items show that boys respond as if they usually received more blame from teachers than do girls. It would appear that boys are quite sensitive to the disapproval of their teachers. Table 5 shows that the girls also respond as if boys receive more teacher disapproval.

There is little consistency in the nominations made by the boys for the praise items. In schools B and C the boys react as though they typically receive more praise than girls, although this difference is not statistically significant. In contrast to the boys' responses, the girls feel that they receive more praise, particularly in school B where the difference is statistically significant. These results might be interpreted as meaning that children fail to recognize any definite dichotomy in the teacher's distribution of praise contacts.

TABLE 3 / SEX DIFFERENCES IN CHILDREN'S NOMINATIONS FOR TEACHER DISAPPROVAL.

	CLASSROOM A		CLASSROOM B		CLASSROOM C	
	BOYS	GIRLS	BOYS	GIRLS	BOYS	GIRLS
N	10	9	12	14	17	16
Mean	21.60	5.33	42.33	9.71	33.82	5.18
S.D.	13.33	5.68	43.06	8.13	55.87	8.26
t		3.39[b]		2.79[b]		2.03
F		5.51[b]		28.07[b]		19.21[b]
$t_{.01}$[c]		3.26		3.10		—

[b] Significant at the one per cent level.   [c] See footnote 2.

TABLE 4 / SEX DIFFERENCES IN CHILDREN'S NOMINATIONS FOR TEACHER APPROVAL.

	CLASSROOM A		CLASSROOM B		CLASSROOM C	
	BOYS	GIRLS	BOYS	GIRLS	BOYS	GIRLS
N	10	9	12	14	17	16
Mean	11.00	34.33	23.58	31.42	23.71	21.60
S.D.	12.93	32.64	18.51	25.08	35.75	25.70
t		2.09		0.856		0.242
F		6.376[b]		1.835		19.35
$t_{.01}$[c]		—		—		—

[b] Significant at the one per cent level.   [c] See footnote 2.

TABLE 5 / CHOICES MADE BY BOYS AND GIRLS ON TEACHER DISAPPROVAL ITEMS.

	CLASSROOM A				CLASSROOM B				CLASSROOM C			
	BOYS CHOOSING		GIRLS CHOOSING		BOYS CHOOSING		GIRLS CHOOSING		BOYS CHOOSING		GIRLS CHOOSING	
	B	G	B	G	B	G	B	G	B	G	B	G
N	8	9	8	9	14	12	14	12	17	16	17	16
%	89.77	10.23	83.09	16.91	88.37	11.63	73.05	26.95	88.70	11.20	82.21	17.79
CR	5.60[b]		3.64[b]		6.10[b]		2.65[b]		7.03[b]		4.84[b]	

[b] Significant at the one per cent level.

TABLE 6 / CHOICES MADE BY BOYS AND BY GIRLS ON TEACHER APPROVAL ITEMS.

	CLASSROOM A				CLASSROOM B				CLASSROOM C			
	BOYS CHOOSING		GIRLS CHOOSING		BOYS CHOOSING		GIRLS CHOOSING		BOYS CHOOSING		GIRLS CHOOSING	
	B	G	B	G	B	G	B	G	B	G	B	G
N	8	9	8	9	14	12	14	12	17	16	17	16
%	36.98	63.01	34.07	65.92	56.95	43.04	24.58	75.42	57.56	42.43	46.22	53.77
CR	1.11		1.38		0.72		3.01[b]		0.88		0.44	

[b] Significant at the one per cent level.

DISCUSSION

The general findings of this study support the hypothesis that the male pupil receives reliably more blame from his teacher than the female pupil. Moreover, the boys recognize that they are the recipients of a higher incidence of teacher disapproval. We feel that these data lend indirect support to the notion that "masculine" behavior is not tolerated by the typical teacher who in turn attempts to inhibit such behavior by means of punishment.

Davis and Havighurst (1947) have discussed at length the divergence of cultural mores between lower-class children and their middle-class teachers. Their work may best be summarized in the assertion that the goals defined by the middle-class teacher do not receive reinforcement from the lower-class child's peer group or from his family. Teacher initiation of punishment for "misbehavior" only serves to reinforce an already existing dislike for school and further leads to peer group reinforcement. A similar (but by no means identical) interpretation appears relevant to the present discussion. Our society's definitions of acceptable male and female behavior are divergent particularly with respect to aggression. For example Radke (1946) in her monograph on the relationship of parental authority to child behavior reports that the fathers in her sample felt that

aggressive, assertive behavior on the part of boys was less undesirable than the identical behavior in girls (and in many cases was deemed highly desirable). The mothers felt that aggression was unacceptable behavior in either sex but in general they were in agreement that aggressive behavior is more unacceptable in girls. In another study specifically related to the notion that aggressive behavior is more unacceptable in the female culture is a study by Sears, Pintler, and Sears (1946). These writers predicted that in father-absent homes, wherein the child is brought up by the mother, boys would be less aggressive than in father-present homes in which the boy models his behavior after the father. The results of their study support the "sex-typing" hypothesis as presented above. Bach (1946) reports similar evidence in support of the "sex-typing" hypothesis.[3] Apparently the social mores of the typical female teacher, at least with respect to aggressive, assertive behavior, are in sharp contrast to the behavioral tendencies of the typical male youngsters. The behavioral tendencies of the female child are, however, in close agreement with those of her teachers. We feel that the above

[3] Though there is insufficient evidence at this time, the present writers feel that the factor of innate sex differences in aggressive tendencies should not be overlooked. See Beach (1948) for suggestive findings.

generalization accounts to a high degree for the data reported in this study. Our argument becomes somewhat stronger when the work of Wickman (1938) and a follow-up study by Mitchell (1942) are included in the discussion. These investigators found that teachers perceive aggressive non-conforming behavior as more serious than withdrawal behavior. More recently Kaplan (1951-1952) has reported that the aggressive child was deemed annoying to almost three-quarters of the teachers in his sample. The present investigation suggests that perhaps teachers react to the aggressive behavior of children with counter-aggression, a vicious circle for both pupil and teacher.

Consistent with the above interpretation is the larger amount of variation found among the male pupils as contrasted with the female pupils. In a culture such as ours in which the father is away from the home during most of the child's waking hours (and in some instances pays only cursory attention to the youngster when at home), it appears obvious that both the male and female child are more directly influenced by the mother. Many boys, however, will be influenced more by their fathers and peer culture than by the mother because of identification with the masculine rôle in our culture. Our belief is that these more "masculine" boys are the ones who receive the greater share of teacher disapproval. Such an interpretation appears consistent with the work of Sears, Pintler, and Sears (1946) and Bach (1946).

The foregoing discussion has certain implications for the student of child development and education. If our interpretation of the teacher and male-pupil relationship is accurate, then the fact that boys dislike school more than girls is understandable. The daily punishment received by the boy for behavior he really does not consider "bad" must certainly be anxiety producing. If the anxiety created in the school situation becomes sufficiently intense, it seems reasonable that tension reduction can be achieved by means of avoiding school. It is known that more boys leave school at an earlier age than girls (Tanenbaum, 1939-1940).

Perhaps of even more importance is the effect of this teacher-disapproval generated anxiety on the general personality adjustment of male pupils. It is unfortunate that we do not have evidence on the changes in adjustment level of the children in our sample, but studies by Ojemann and Wilkinson (1939) and others indicate that consistent teacher dominance has deleterious effects on the adjustment of children. We can only speculate as to the nature of these adjustment problems but such behavioral manifestations as nervousness, withdrawal and lack of self-confidence are a few of the known symptoms.

We feel that the consistent trends in our findings imply that teachers' negative attitudes towards their male pupils arise from a lack of appreciation for the term "normal" male child. In our culture, aggressive outgoing behavior is as normal in the male as quiescent nonassertive behavior is in the female. The teacher who attempts to thwart this behavior by means of threats and punishment can only meet with frustration since the boy is confronted with a conflicting social code. A more reasonable plan to follow would seem to be one in which the excess energy and tensions of the male child could be discharged on some constructive activity. Planned physical education classes will do much to dissipate aggressive needs in a socially acceptable manner. Perhaps most important of all, however, is the knowledge that some degree of aggressive behavior is a normal part of development in both boys and girls and should be treated not as a personal threat to the teacher but as sign of "normal" social and personality development.

SUMMARY

The purpose of this study was to investigate sex differences in teacher distribution of approval and disapproval among three sixth-grade classrooms. Data relevant to the children's perceptions of their teachers' attitudes towards boys and girls were also collected. Using the discrepancies in attitude between males and females in our culture toward aggressive behavior as the basic underlying variable, the hypothesis was offered that boys, who are more aggressive and nonconforming than girls, would receive more disapproval contacts from their teachers than girls. Girls being quiescent and more conforming than boys would as a consequence receive more approval from their teachers than boys. We further hypothesized that both boys and girls will be aware of the differences in their teachers' attitudes towards them.

In order to test the foregoing hypothesis three sixth-grade teachers and their pupils were directly observed for a total of thirty hours per classroom. All teacher initiated contacts of an approval or disapproval nature were recorded. The measurement of the children's perceptions of teacher attitude was accomplished by means of a variation of the "Guess Who?" technique. The pupils were asked to list the names of four students who best fitted a series of statements of a teacher approval nature and of disapproval nature. Analysis was made of the number of children of each sex chosen for the approval items and for the disapproval items.

Statistical analysis of the data clearly supports our hypothesis with respect to male pupils. In all three schools the boys received reliably more disapproval from their teachers than the girls. We also found that both the boys and the girls nominated more boys for the disapproval items than girls. This difference was statistically reliable. With respect to the second hypothesis concerning girls, the data did not yield any clear-cut differences. If any trend was present it was in a direction opposite to that predicted. These results indicated that the teachers in our sample tended to have fewer contacts with the girls in their classrooms.

The results of this investigation were interpreted as being consistent with the notion of a sex difference in attitude towards aggressive behavior. The conclusion was drawn that teachers attempt to "socialize" the male child by means of dominative counter-aggressive behavior. The negative consequences of this situation for the child are discussed.

GUESS-WHO? SCALE.

Directions: In this booklet are some word pictures of members of your class. Read each statement and write down the names of the people whom you think the description fits. *Remember*—

1. Several people may fit one picture. You may write down after each description as many names as you think belong there.
2. The same person may be mentioned for more than one word-picture.
3. If you cannot think of anyone to match a particular word-picture go on to the next one.
4. Write the first and last names of the people chosen, not their nicknames or initials.
5. Do not use your own name.

1. Here is someone whose work is often put up on the bulletin board.[4]
2. Here is someone whose work is often pointed out as being very neat.
3. Here is someone whom the teacher often scolds for whispering.
4. Here is someone who is often praised for good writing on all papers handed in.

[4] Each item has four lines.

5. Here is someone whom the teacher often scolds for disturbing the class in some way (shooting paper wads, chewing gum, etc.).
6. Here is someone who is often scolded by the teacher because he or she pays little attention to what is going on in class.

REFERENCES

1. ANDERSON, H. H., and BREWER, J. E. "Effects of Teachers' Dominative and Integrative Contacts on Children's Classroom Behavior," *Applied Psychology Monograph No. 8.* Stanford, Calif.: Stanford University Press, 1946.

2. ANDERSON, H. H., BREWER, J. E., and REED, M. F. "Studies of Teachers' Classroom Personalities: III. Follow-up studies of the effects of dominative and integrative contacts on children's behavior," *Applied Psychology Monograph No. 11.* Stanford, Calif.: Stanford University Press, 1946.

3. BACH, G. R. "Father-Fantasies and Father-Typing in Father Separated Children," *Child Development*, 17:63-80, 1946.

4. BEACH, F. A. *Hormones and Behavior.* New York: Paul B. Hoeber, 1948.

5. DAVIS, W. A., and HAVIGHURST, R. J. *Father of the Man: How Your Child Gets His Personality.* Boston: Houghton Mifflin, 1947.

6. DE GROAT, A. F., and THOMPSON, G. G. "A Study of the Distribution of Teacher Approval and Disapproval among Sixth-Grade Pupils," *Journal of Experimental Education*, 18:57-75, 1949.

7. GOODENOUGH, F. L. "Anger in Young Children," *Child Welfare Monograph No. 9.* Minneapolis: Univ. of Minnesota Press, 1931.

8. HAYES, M. L. "A Study of the Classroom Disturbances of Eighth Grade Boys and Girls," *Teachers College Contributions to Education*, 871:139, 1943.

9. HURLOCK, E. "The Value of Praise and Reproof as Incentives for Children," *Archives of Psychology*, 11: No. 71, 1924.

10. KAPLAN, L. "The Annoyances of Elementary School Teachers," *Journal of Educational Research*, 45:649-665, 1951-52.

11. MITCHELL, J. C. "A Study of Teachers' and of Mental-Hygienists' Ratings of Certain Behavior Problems of Children," *Journal of Educational Research*, 36:292-307, 1942.

12. OJEMANN, R., and WILKINSON, F. R. "The Effect on Pupil Growth of an Increase in Teacher's Understanding of Pupil Behavior," *Journal of Experimental Education*, 8:143-147, 1939.

13. OLSON, W., and WILKINSON, M. "Teacher Personality as Revealed by the Amount and Kind of Verbal Direction Used in Behavior Control," *Educational Administration and Supervision, 24:*81-93, 1938.

14. RADKE, M. J. "The Relation of Parental Authority to Children's Behavior and Attitudes," *Child Welfare Monograph No. 22.* Minneapolis: Univer. of Minnesota Press, 1946.

15. SEARS, P. S. "Doll Play Aggression in Normal Young Children: Influence of Sex, Age, Sibling Status, Father's Absence," *Psychological Monographs, 65:*42, 1951.

16. SEARS, R. R., PINTLER, M. H., and SEARS, P. "Effect of Father Separation on Preschool Children's Doll Play Aggression," *Child Development, 17:*219-243, 1946.

17. SNYDER, W. "Do Teachers Cause Maladjustment?", *Journal Exceptional Children, 14:*40-46, 1947.

18. TENENBAUM, S. "Uncontrolled Expressions of Children's Attitudes toward School," *Elementary School Journal, 40:*670-768, 1939-40.

19. TUDDENHAM, R. D. "Studies in Reputation: I. Sex and Grade Differences," *Psychology Monographs, 66:*58, 1952.

IX / Intelligence as a Determinant of Behavior

INTELLIGENCE AND THE MEASUREMENT OF INTELLIGENCE have been primary concerns of many psychologists, especially those in the field of education. Intelligence is one of the key variables in influencing the outcome of education and in determining the nature of the training that should be given. The problems of intelligence and its measurement are related to biological issues. Biological bases for intelligent behavior are discussed by Scott and by Anastasi in Section II. Indeed, historically the question of hereditary *vs.* experiential determinants has dominated discussions of intelligence. Not content to think of intelligence as merely that which is measured by intelligence tests, many psychologists (as well as lay people) have tended to reify intelligence and then to engage in lengthy discussions about the degree to which "it" is innately or biologically determined. Recently, psychologists have found it more fruitful to think in terms of INTELLIGENT BEHAVIORS rather than "intelligence" and to turn attention to the interactions of heredity and environment in determining intelligent behaviors.

This section of the readings begins with two excerpts from the writing of the pioneer figures in the measurement of intelligence—the French physicians and psychologists Alfred Binet and Theophile Simon. We have called Binet a psychologist not only because of his study of intelligence, but also because he founded the first psychological laboratory in France (Sorbonne, 1889). In addition to studying medicine, Binet had earlier studied law, and also worked in a famous biological laboratory. Simon, who was the physician at a hospital for the insane, became President of the Society for the Psychological Study of the Child after Binet's death. Their two papers are included not only for their historical interest, but also to show the sophistication or "modernity" of many of their thoughts and their awareness of issues that have frequently been lost sight of since that time.

These excerpts are followed by a paper from one of Britain's leading figures in the field of intelligence testing. Its author, Philip E. Vernon, is from London University's Institute of Education. Like the American pioneer in testing, L. L. Thurstone, he sees a role for various specific factors in "intelligence." Unlike Thurstone, Vernon attaches principal interest to a general intellectual factor (g).[1] Another theme in Vernon's article is the influence of culture or subculture on intelligence. This topic is also repre-

---

[1] The student interested in theories of intelligence might also refer to the booklet "Intelligence: Statistical Conceptions of Its Nature" by L. G. Bischof (Doubleday Papers in Psychology, 1954). A more personality-oriented approach can be found in the booklet "Intelligence: A Dynamic Approach" by Erika Fromm and Lenore Hartman (Doubleday Papers in Psychology, 1955).

sented indirectly in papers which deal with the "culturally deprived" child (Taba's paper, Section V, no. 32, and Goldberg's, Section XI, no. 78).

The next article, by Jerome Kagan, Lester W. Sontag, Charles T. Baker, and Virginia L. Nelson, addresses itself to the interactions between personality and intelligence in terms of I.Q. change. Their paper is from The Fels Research Institute for the Study of Human Development, the locus of one of the earliest-begun and broadest longitudinal studies. The techniques used by Kagan *et al* to assess personality are two well-known projective techniques—the Rorschach Ink Blots and the TAT or Thematic Apperception Test. Professor Kagan is now at Harvard University's Department of Social Relations.

There follows a paper by Lewis M. Terman, a former president of The American Psychological Association, which gives a further view of testing in this country. The general framework stresses the importance of discovering and making use of talent—a concern which has received considerably more emphasis in the post-Sputnik era. Terman himself devoted most of his life (he died in 1956) to the longitudinal study of the gifted. He developed many kinds of tests in the process of furthering the study of the especially promising. The Stanford-Binet Test, which (together with the two Wechsler Tests—WISC and WAIS—) is a mainstay of individual testing of intelligence in the United States, derives its name from the fact that Terman and his colleagues at Stanford University developed the most widely used American forms of the Binet-Simon Test.

One of the issues raised by Terman is related to the topic of "readiness." Gesell, Piaget, McGraw and other "maturationists" have all influenced educational thinking about the problem of "readiness" to learn. We would like to stress further the incidental point of Terman that it is important not to make the child wait until long after he is ready. Although not explicitly addressed to the topic, the paper by Terman helps to point out the inadequacy of chronological age as a basis for deciding readiness for education.

The final paper in this section is addressed to a topic which has aroused great interest in recent years—creativity. Some of the important issues that have been raised include these questions: (1) Are there aspects of cognitive functioning which might properly be called "creativity" and which differ from our traditional concept of intelligence? (2) If so, what are the correlates of these distinct aspects of cognitive functioning, and how do the correlates differ? (3) Does our schooling tend to inhibit creativity in its efforts to impart knowledge to the child? Numerous articles and books have appeared recently reporting studies of these topics. Some of the investigations have been sharply criticized for inadequacies in method or in the interpretation of the findings. We have chosen a paper concerned with the first two questions raised above, "A new look at the creativity-intelligence distinction" by Michael A. Wallach of Duke University and Nathan Kogan of the Educational Testing Service. It is based on a chapter from their important new book, *Modes of Thinking in Young Children: A Study of the Creativity-Intelligence Distinction* (New York: Holt. Rinehart and Winston, 1965).

52/UPON THE NECESSITY OF ESTABLISHING A SCIENTIFIC DIAGNOSIS OF INFERIOR STATES OF INTELLIGENCE/

ALFRED BINET AND THEOPHILE SIMON[*]

WE HERE PRESENT THE FIRST ROUGH sketch of a work which was directly inspired by the desire to serve the interesting cause of the education of subnormals.

In October, 1904, the Minister of Public Instruction named a commission which was charged with the study of measures to be taken for insuring the benefits of instruction to defective children. After a number of sittings, this commission regulated all that pertained to the type of establishment to be created, the conditions of admission into the school, the teaching force, and the pedagogical methods to be employed. They decided that no child suspected of retardation should be eliminated from the ordinary school and admitted into a special class, without first being subjected to a pedagogical and medical examination from which it could be certified that because of the state of his intelligence, he was unable to profit, in an average measure, from the instruction given in the ordinary schools.

But how the examination of each child should be made, what methods should be followed, what observations taken, what questions asked, what tests devised, how the child should be compared with normal children, the commission felt under no obligation to decide. It was formed to do a work of administration, not a work of science.

It has seemed to us extremely useful to furnish a guide for future Commissions' examination. Such Commissions should understand from the beginning how to get their bearings. It must be made impossible for those who belong to the Commission to fall into the habit of making haphazard decisions according to impressions which are subjective, and consequently uncontrolled. Such impressions are sometimes good, sometimes bad, and have at all times too much the nature of the arbitrary, of caprice, of indifference. Such a condition is quite unfortunate because the interests of the child demand a more careful method. To be a member of a special class can never be a mark of distinction, and such as do not merit it, must be spared the record. Some errors are excusable in the beginning, but if they become too frequent, they may ruin the reputation of these new institutions. Furthermore, in principle, we are convinced, and we shall not cease to repeat, that the precision and exactness of science should be introduced into our practice whenever possible, and in the great majority of cases it is possible.

The problem which we have to solve presents many difficulties both theoretical and practical. It is a hackneyed remark that the definitions, thus far proposed, for the different states of subnormal intelligence, lack precision. These inferior states are indefinite in number, being composed of a series of degrees which mount from the lowest depths of idiocy, to a condition easily confounded with normal intelligence. Alienists have frequently come to an agreement concerning the terminology to be employed for designating the difference of these degrees; at least, in spite of certain individual divergence of ideas to be found in all questions, there has been an agreement to accept *idiot* as applied to the lowest state, *imbecile* to the intermediate, and *moron* (*débile*) to the state nearest normality. Still among the numerous alienists, under this common and apparently precise terminology, different ideas are concealed, variable and at the same time confused. The distinction between idiot, imbecile, and moron is not understood in the same way by all practitioners. We have abundant proof of this in the strikingly divergent medical diagnoses made only a few days apart by different alienists upon the same patient.

Dr. Blin, physician of the Vaucluse Asylum, recently drew the attention of his fellow physicians to these regrettable contradictions. He states that the children who are sent to the

[*] This article first appeared in *L'Annee Psychologique, XI* (1905), 163-190. The present text is taken from the translation by Elizabeth S. Kite, published in 1916 by Williams and Wilkins Co., Baltimore, under the auspices of The Training School at Vineland, New Jersey, under the title *The Development of Intelligence in Children.*

colony come provided with several dissimilar certificates. "One child, called imbecile in the first certificate, is marked idiot in the second, feeble-minded (*débile*) in the third, and degenerate in the fourth." M. Damaye, former house surgeon of Dr. Blin, adds this observation: "One would have only to look through several folders of records belonging to children of the colony, in order to collect almost the same number of different diagnoses." Perhaps this last affirmative is a little exaggerated, but a statistical study would show the exact truth on this point.

We cannot sufficiently deplore the consequence of this state of uncertainty recognized today by all alienists. The simple fact, that specialists do not agree in the use of the technical terms of their science, throws suspicion upon their diagnoses, and prevents all work of comparison. We ourselves have made similar observations. In synthesizing the diagnoses made by Mr. Bourneville upon patients leaving the Bicetre, we found that in the space of four years only two feeble-minded individuals have left his institution although during that time the Bureau of Admission has sent him more than thirty. Nothing could show more clearly than this change of label, the confusion of our nomenclature.

What importance can be attached to public statistics of different countries concerning the percentage of backward children if the definition for backward children is not the same in all countries? How will it be possible to keep a record of the intelligence of pupils who are treated and instructed in a school, if the terms applied to them, feeble-minded, retarded, imbecile, idiot, vary in meaning according to the doctor who examines them? The absence of a common measure prevents comparison of statistics, and makes one lose all interest in investigations which may have been very laborious. But a still more serious fact is that, because of lack of methods, it is impossible to solve those essential questions concerning the afflicted, whose solution presents the greatest interest; for example, the real results gained by the treatment of inferior states of intelligence by doctor and educator; the educative value of one pedagogical method compared with another; the degree of curability of incomplete idiocy, etc. It is not by means of *a priori* reasonings, of vague considerations, of oratorical displays, that these questions can be solved; but by minute investigation, entering into the details of fact, and considering the effects of the

treatment for each particular child. There is but one means of knowing if a child, who has passed six years in a hospital or in a special class, has profited from that stay, and to what degree he has profited; and that is to compare his certificate of entrance with his certificate of dismissal, and by that means ascertain if he shows a special amelioration of his condition beyond that which might be credited simply to the considerations of growth. But experience has shown how imprudent it would be to place confidence in this comparison, when the two certificates come from different doctors, who do not judge in exactly the same way, or who use different words to characterize the mental status of patients.

It might happen that a child, who had really improved in school, had received in the beginning the diagnosis of moron (*débile*), and on leaving, the prejudicial diagnosis of imbecile, simply because the second doctor spoke a different language from the first. If one took these certificates literally, this case would be considered a failure. On the contrary, the appearance of amelioration would be produced if the physician who delivered the certificate of dismissal had the habit of using higher terms than the one who furnished the certificate of entrance. One can even go further. The errors which we note, do not necessarily emanate from the disagreement of different physicians. It would suffice for the same physician to deliver the two certificates, if he did not employ for each one the same criterion; and it would certainly be possible for him to vary unconsciously after an interval of several years if he had nothing to guide him but his own subjective impressions. Might not the same thing also happen if his good faith as a physician happened to be in conflict with the interests of the institution which he directed? Might he not unconsciously as it were, have a tendency to lower the mental status of patients on entering and to raise it on dismissal, in order to emphasize the advantages of the methods which he had applied? We are not incriminating anyone, but simply calling attention to methods actually in use which, by their lack of precision, favor the involuntary illusions of physicians and relatives, in a word, of all those who, having an interest in the amelioration of the condition of the defective child, would have a tendency to confound their desires with the reality.

Perhaps someone will raise an objection and say this uncertainty has no special application to diagnosis of the degrees of mental debility; it is also to be found in mental pathology and, in a general way, in the diagnosis of all maladies; it is the result of the empirical nature which is characteristic of clinical studies. It might be added, that, if anyone took the trouble to make a statistical study of the divergence in the diagnosis of different physicians upon the same patient, it would probably be found that the percentage of disagreement is very great in all branches of medicine.

We believe it worth while to examine their objection because it permits us to enter more deeply into the analysis of the question. The disagreements of practitioners might come from three very different classes of causes:

1. Ignorance, that is, the lack of aptitude of certain physicians. This is an individual failure, for which abstract science is not responsible. It is certain that, even when the symptoms of a disease are absolutely clear, such a physician might fail to recognize them through incapacity. There are many accountants who make mistakes in calculation, but these errors do not discredit mathematics. A physician might not be able to recognize a "p.g." if he is himself a "p.g."

2. The variable meaning of terms. Since the same expression has a different sense according to the person who uses it, it is possible that the disagreement of diagnosis may be simply a disagreement of words, due to the use of different nomenclature.

3. Lack of precision in the description of the symptoms which reveal or which constitute a certain particular malady; different physicians do not examine the same patient in the same manner and do not give the symptoms the same importance; or, it may be they make no effort to find out the precise symptoms, and no effort to analyze carefully in order to distinguish and interpret them.

Of these three kinds of error, which is the one that actually appears in the diagnosis of inferior states of intelligence? Let us set aside the first. There remain the faults of nomenclature, and the insufficiency of methods of examination.

The general belief seems to be that the confusion arises wholly from an absence of a uniform nomenclature. There is some truth in this opinion. It can be proved by a comparision of terms used by authors belonging to the different countries. Even in France the terms differ somewhat according to the physician, the order of the admitted subdivisions not being rigorously followed. The classification of Magnan is not that of Voisin, and his, in turn, differs from that of Bourneville. Undoubtedly it would be a good work to bring about a unification of this nomenclature as has been done for the standard of measurements and for electric units. But this reform in itself is not sufficient and we are very sure that they deceive themselves who think that at bottom this is only a question of terminology. It is very much more serious. We find physicians who, though using the same terminology, constantly disagree in their diagnosis of the same child. The examples cited from M. Blin prove this. There the doctors had recourse to the terminology of Morel, who classifies those of inferior intelligence as idiots, imbeciles and *débiles*. Notwithstanding this use of the same terms, they do not agree in the manner of applying them. Each one according to his own fancy, fixes the boundary line separating these states. It is in regard to the facts that the doctors disagree.

In looking closely one can see that the confusion comes principally from a fault in the method of examination. When an alienist finds himself in the presence of a child of inferior intelligence, he does not examine him by bringing out each one of the symptoms which the child manifests and by interpreting all symptoms and classifying them; he contents himself with taking a subjective impression, an impression as a whole, of his subject, and of making his diagnosis by instinct. We do not think that we are going too far in saying that at the present time very few physicians would be able to cite with absolute precision the objective and invariable sign, or signs, by which they distinguish the degrees of inferior mentality.

53/THE DEVELOPMENT OF THE BINET-SIMON SCALE/ALFRED BINET AND THEOPHILE SIMON*

NEW METHODS FOR THE DIAGNOSIS OF THE INTELLECTUAL LEVEL OF SUBNORMALS[1]

OUR PURPOSE IS TO BE ABLE TO MEASure the intellectual capacity of a child who is brought to us in order to know whether he is normal or retarded. We should, therefore, study his condition at the time and that only. We have nothing to do either with his past history or with his future; consequently we shall neglect his etiology, and we shall make no attempt to distinguish between acquired and congenital idiocy; for a stronger reason we shall set aside all consideration of pathological anatomy which might explain his intellectual deficiency. So much for his past. As to that which concerns his future, we shall exercise the same abstinence; we do not attempt to establish or prepare a prognosis and we leave unanswered the question of whether this retardation is curable, or even improvable. We shall limit ourselves to ascertaining the truth in regard to his present mental state. . . .

We shall set the unstable aside, and shall consider only that which bears upon those who are backward in intelligence. . . .

Lastly, we should say a word upon our manner of studying those whom alienists call idiots but whom we here call of inferior intelligence. The exact nature of this inferiority is not known; and today without other proof, one very prudently refuses to liken this state to that of an arrest of normal development. It certainly seems that the intelligence of these beings has undergone a certain arrest; but it does not follow that the disproportion between the degree of intelligence and the age is the only characteristic of their condition. There is also in many cases, most probably a deviation in the development,

a perversion. The idiot of fifteen years, who, like a baby of three, is making his first verbal attempts, can not be completely likened to a three-year old child, because the latter is normal, but the idiot is not. There exists therefore between them, necessarily, differences either apparent or hidden. The careful study of idiots shows, among some of them at least, that whereas certain faculties are almost wanting, others are better developed. They have therefore certain aptitudes. Some have a good auditory or musical memory, and a whole repertoire of songs; others have mechanical ability. If all were carefully examined, many examples of these partial aptitudes would probably be found.

Our purpose is in no wise to study, analyze, or set forth the aptitudes of those of inferior intelligence. That will be the object of a later work. Here we shall limit ourselves to the measuring of their general intelligence. We shall determine their intellectual level, and, in order the better to appreciate this level, we shall compare it with that of normal children of the same age or of an analogous level. The reservations previously made as to the true conception of arrested development, will not prevent our finding great advantage in a methodical comparison between those of inferior and those of normal intelligence.

To what method should we have recourse in making our diagnosis of the intellectual level? No one method exists, but there are a number of different ones which should be used cumulatively, because the question is a very difficult one to solve, and demands rather a collaboration of methods. It is important that the practitioner be equipped in such a manner that he shall use, only as accessory, the information given by the parents of the child, so that he may always be able to verify this information, or, when necessary, dispense with it. In actual practice quite the opposite occurs. When the child is taken to

[1] From *L'Anee Psychologique*, XI (1905), 191-244.

* This article first appeared in two articles in *L'Annee Psychologique*, XI (1905) and *XIV* (1908). The present text is an abridgement of the translation by Elizabeth S. Kite, published in 1916 by Williams and Wilkins Co., Baltimore, under the auspices of The Training School at Vineland, New Jersey, under the title *The Development of Intelligence in Children*. Footnote references are to the original article from which each section in the present test is taken.

378

the clinic the physician listens a great deal to the parents and questions the child very little, in fact scarcely looks at him, allowing himself to be influenced by a very strong presumption that the child is intellectually inferior. If, by a chance not likely to occur, but which would be most interesting some time to bring about, the physician were submitted to the test of selecting the subnormals from a mixed group of children, he would certainly find himself in the midst of grave difficulties, and would commit many errors especially in cases of slight defect.

The organization of methods is especially important because, as soon as the schools for subnormals are in operation, one must be on his guard against the attitude of the parents. Their sincerity will be worth very little when it is in conflict with their interests. If the parents wish the child to remain in the regular school, they will not be silent concerning his intelligence. "My child understands everything," they will say, and they will be very careful not to give any significant information in regard to him. If, on the contrary, they wish him to be admitted into an institution where gratuitous board and lodging are furnished, they will change completely. They will be capable even of teaching him how to simulate mental debility. One should, therefore, be on his guard against all possible frauds.

In order to recognize the inferior states of intelligence we believe that three different methods should be employed. We have arrived at this synthetic view only after many years of research, but we are now certain that each of these methods renders some service. These methods are:

1. *The medical method,* which aims to appreciate the anatomical, physiological, and pathological signs of inferior intelligence.

2. *The pedagogical method,* which aims to judge of the intelligence according to the sum of acquired knowledge.

3. *The psychological method,* which makes direct observations and measurements of the degree of intelligence.

From what has gone before it is easy to see the value of each of these methods. The medical method is indirect because it conjectures the mental from the physical. The pedagogical method is more direct; but the psychological is the most direct of all because it aims to measure the state of the intelligence as it is at the present moment. It does this by experiments which oblige the subject to make an effort which shows his capability in the way of comprehension; judgment, reasoning, and invention.

THE PSYCHOLOGICAL METHOD. The fundamental idea of this method is the establishment of what we shall call a measuring scale of intelligence. This scale is composed of a series of tests of increasing difficulty, starting from the lowest intellectual level that can be observed, and ending with that of average normal intelligence. Each group in the series corresponds to a different mental level.

This scale properly speaking does not permit the measure of the intelligence, because intellectual qualities are not superposable, and therefore cannot be measured as linear surfaces are measured, but are on the contrary, a classification, a hierarchy among diverse intelligences; and for the necessities of practice this classification is equivalent to a measure. We shall therefore be able to know, after studying two individuals, if one rises above the other and to how many degrees, if one rises above the average level of other individuals considered as normal, or if he remains below. Understanding the normal progress of intellectual development among normals, we shall be able to determine how many years such an individual is advanced or retarded. In a word we shall be able to determine to what degrees of the scale idiocy, imbecility, and moronity correspond.

The scale that we shall describe is not a theoretical work; it is the result of long investigations, first at the Saltpetriere, and afterwards in the primary schools of Paris, with both normal and subnormal children. These short psychological questions have been given the name of tests. The use of tests is today very common, and there are even contemporary authors who have made a specialty of organizing new tests according to theoretical views, but who have made no effort to patiently try them out in the schools. Theirs is an amusing occupation, comparable to a person's making a colonizing expedition into Algeria, advancing always only upon the map, without taking off his dressing gown. We place but slight confidence in the tests invented by these authors and we have borrowed nothing from them. All the tests which we propose have been repeatedly tried, and have been retained from among many, which after trial have been discarded. We can certify that those which are here presented have proved themselves valuable.

We have aimed to make all our tests simple, rapid, convenient, precise, heterogeneous, holding the subject in continued contact with the experimenter, and bearing principally upon the faculty of judgment. Rapidity is necessary for this sort of examination. It is impossible to prolong it beyond twenty minutes without fatiguing the subject. During this maximum of twenty minutes, it must be turned and turned about in every sense, and at least ten tests must be executed, so that not more than about two minutes can be given to each. In spite of their interest, we were obliged to proscribe long exercises. For example, it would be very instructive to know how a subject learns by heart a series of sentences. We have often tested the advantage of leaving a person by himself with a lesson of prose or verse after having said to him, "Try to learn as much as you can of this in five minutes." Five minutes is too long for our test, because during that time the subject escapes us; it may be that he becomes distracted or thinks of other things; the test loses its clinical character and becomes too scholastic. We have therefore reluctantly been obliged to renounce testing the rapidity and extent of the memory by this method. Several other equivalent examples of elimination could be cited. In order to cover rapidly a wide field of observation, it goes without saying that the tests should be heterogeneous.

Another consideration. Our purpose is to evaluate a level of intelligence. It is understood that we here separate natural intelligence and instruction. It is the intelligence alone that we seek to measure, by disregarding in so far as possible, the degree of instruction which the subject possesses. He should, indeed, be considered by the examiner as a complete ignoramus knowing neither how to read nor write. This necessity forces us to forego a great many exercises having a verbal, literary or scholastic character. These belong to a pedagogical examination. We believe that we have succeeded in completely disregarding the acquired information of the subject. We give him nothing to read, nothing to write, and submit him to no test in which he might succeed by means of rote learning. In fact we do not even notice his inability to read if a case occurs. It is simply the level of his natural intelligence that is taken into account.

But here we must come to an understanding of what meaning to give to that word so vague and so comprehensive, "the intelligence." Nearly all the phenomena with which psychology concerns itself are phenomena of intelligence; sensation, perception, are intellectual manifestations as much as reasoning. Should we therefore bring into our examination the measure of sensation after the manner of the psycho-physicists? Should we put to the test all of his psychological processes? A slight reflection has shown us that this would indeed be wasted time.

It seems to us that in intelligence there is a fundamental faculty, the alteration or the lack of which, is of the utmost importance for practical life. This faculty is judgment, otherwise called good sense, practical sense, initiative, the faculty of adapting one's self to circumstances. To judge well, to comprehend well, to reason well, these are the essential activities of intelligence. A person may be a moron or an imbecile if he is lacking in judgment; but with good judgment he can never be either. Indeed the rest of the intellectual faculties seem of little importance in comparison with judgment. What does it matter, for example, whether the organs of sense function normally? Of what import that certain ones are hyperesthetic, or that others are anesthetic or are weakened? Laura Bridgman, Helen Keller and their fellow-unfortunates were blind as well as deaf, but this did not prevent them from being very intelligent. Certainly this is demonstrative proof that the total or even partial integrity of the senses does not form a mental factor equal to judgment. We may measure the acuteness of the sensibility of subjects; nothing could be easier. But we should do this, not so much to find out the state of their sensibility as to learn the exactitude of their judgment.

The same remark holds good for the study of the memory. At first glance, memory being a psychological phenomenon of capital importance, one would be tempted to give it a very conspicuous part in an examination of intelligence. But memory is distinct from and independent of judgment. One may have good sense and lack memory. The reverse is also common. Just at the present time we are observing a backward girl who is developing before our astonished eyes a memory very much greater than our own. We have measured that memory and we are not deceived regarding it. Nevertheless that girl presents a most beautifully classic type of imbecility.

As a result of all this investigation, in the scale which we present we accord the first place to judgment; that which is of importance to us is not certain errors which the subject commits, but absurd errors, which prove that he lacks judgment. We have even made special provision to encourage people to make absurd replies. In spite of the accuracy of this directing idea, it will be easily understood that it has been impossible to permit of its regulating exclusively our examinations. For example, one can not make tests of judgment on children of less than two years when one begins to watch their first gleams of intelligence. Much is gained when one can discern in them traces of coordination, the first delineation of attention and memory. We shall therefore bring out in our lists some tests of memory; but so far as we are able, we shall give these tests such a turn as to invite the subject to make absurd replies, and thus under cover of a test of memory, we shall have an appreciation of their judgment.

MEASURING SCALE OF INTELLIGENCE.

General Recommendations. . . . We here give the technique of each question. It will not suffice simply to read what we have written in order to be able to conduct examinations. A good experimenter can be produced only by example and imitation, and nothing equals the lesson gained from the thing itself. Every person who wishes to familiarize himself with our method of examination should come to our school. Theoretical instruction is valuable only when it merges into practical experience. Having made these reservations, let us point out the principal errors likely to be committed by inexperienced persons. There are two: the first consists in recording the gross results without making psychological observations, without noticing such little facts as permit one to give to the gross results their true value. The second error, equally frequent, is that of making suggestions. An inexperienced examiner has no idea of the influence of words; he talks too much, he aids his subject, he puts him on the track, unconscious of the help he is thus giving. He plays the part of the pedagogue, when he should remain psychologist. Thus his examination is vitiated. It is a difficult art to be able to encourage a subject, to hold his attention, to make him do his best without giving aid in any form by an unskillful suggestion.

THE DEVELOPMENT OF INTELLIGENCE IN THE CHILD[1]

. . . This measurement is taken by means of a series of tests, the gradation of which constitutes what we call a "Measuring Scale of Intelligence." It is important, above all, to set forth these tests with sufficient precision to enable

[1] From *L'Annee Psychologique*, XIV (1908), 1-90.

anyone to repeat them correctly who will take the trouble to assimilate them.

Classification of the Tests According to Age. We here give the series of tests ranged according to the ages at which the majority of children succeed in them. This constitutes our measuring scale of intelligence. [*Descriptions of the tests, given in a later section of Binet and Simons' article, are not included in these readings.—*Editors]

THREE YEARS[Ed]
Show eyes, nose, mouth
Name objects in a picture
Repeat 2 figures
Repeat a sentence of 6 syllables
Give last name

FIVE YEARS
Compare 2 boxes of different weights
Copy a square
Repeat a sentence of 10 syllables
Count 4 sous
Put together two pieces in a game of "patience"

SEVEN YEARS
Indicate omissions in drawings
Give the number of fingers
Copy a written sentence
Copy a triangle and a diamond
Repeat 5 figures
Describe a picture
Count 13 single sous
Name 4 pieces of money

NINE YEARS
Give the date complete (day, month, day of the month, year)
Name the days of the week
Give definitions superior to use
Retain 6 memories after reading
Make change, 4 sous from 20 sous
Arrange 5 weights in order

ELEVEN YEARS
Criticize sentences containing absurdities
Place 3 words in 1 sentence
Find more than 60 words in 3 minutes
Give abstract definitions
Place disarranged words in order

THIRTEEN YEARS
Paper cutting
Reversed triangle
Give differences of meaning

THE USE OF THE MEASURING SCALE OF INTELLIGENCE. . . . One question remains to be examined. To what purpose are these studies? In reading the reflections which we have inter-

[Ed] *Even-numbered years are omitted.*

spersed in the course of our treatise, it will be seen that a profound knowledge of the normal intellectual development of the child would not only be of great interest but useful in formulating a course of instruction really adapted to their aptitudes. We fear that those who have drawn up the programs actually in force, are educated men who in their work have been led more by the fancies of their imaginations than by well-grounded principles. The pedagogical principle which ought to inspire the authors of programs seems to us to be the following: the instruction should always be according to the natural evolution of the child, and not precede it by a year or two. In other words the child should be taught only what he is sufficiently mature to understand; all precocious instruction is lost time, for it is not assimilated. We have cited an example of it in regard to the date, which is taught in the Maternal School, but which is not known and assimilated before the age of nine years. This is only one example, but it is eloquent; it shows the error of what has hitherto been done; it suggests a method which will enable us to improve upon the past,—a method less literary, less rapid, and even extremely laborious, for it demands that one establish by careful investigations the normal evolution of a child's intelligence, in order to make all our programs and methods of instruction conform to that evolution, when it is once known. If by this labor we have succeeded in showing the necessity for a thorough investigation conducted after this plan, our time has not been lost. But we are far from flattering ourselves that we have inaugurated a reform. Reforms in France do not succeed except through politics, and we cannot readily imagine a secretary of state busying himself with a question of this kind. What is taught to children at school! As though legislators could become interested in that!

It now remains to explain the use of our measuring scale which we consider a standard of the child's intelligence. Of what use is a measure of intelligence? Without doubt one could conceive many possible applications of the process, in dreaming of a future where the social sphere would be better organized than ours; where every one would work according to his known aptitudes in such a way that no particle of psychic force should be lost for society. That would be the ideal city. It is indeed far from us. But we have to remain among the sterner and the matter-of-fact realities of life, since we here deal with practical experiments which are the most commonplace realities.

We are of the opinion that the most valuable use of our scale will not be its application to the normal pupils, but rather to those of inferior grades of intelligence. . . .

During the past year one of us examined 25 children who for various reasons had been admitted to Sainte-Anne and later confined at the Bicetre, at Saltpetriere, or at other places. We applied the procedure of our measuring scale to all these children, and thus proved that *three of them were at age in intelligence, and two others were a year advanced beyond the average.*

On reflection, these cases should not surprise us; and it is not necessary to be in touch with questions of mental medicine to inveigh against arbitrary segregation. One ought to confine a child of normal intelligence, or even of super-normal, if he has epilepsy, or irresistible impulses which constitute a danger to his neighbors or to himself. But it is none the less true that the doctors who were obliged to diagnose these cases, have had to judge the degree of intelligence of these children; it is very interesting to show the errors of diagnosis which have been committed in this regard. To two of these children who showed normal intelligence we regret to say that the term *mental debility* had been applied without consideration. The third had received the term, truly extraordinary of its kind, of *"enfant idiot."* The child was named T——, aged seven years. A doctor had written concerning him, "Idiotic, with attacks of furious anger. Wishes to bite. Does not know how to read or write." This last is a little too naive. Since the normal child does not know how to read and write at seven years, to be astonished that T—— who is just seven is still illiterate, is like reproaching a three year old baby for not knowing how to play the piano. Finally, one of these children who was a year in advance, was classed as a moron; and as to the other nothing was said concerning his mentality. Nothing could show more clearly, that with the means which it has at its command, the mental clinic is not in a position to diagnose correctly a child's intelligence.

In terminating this account, it will suffice to make a very brief allusion to the appreciation of penal responsibility; there also our scale will render service. . . .

We suggest to [experts before tribunals] that they should use the six differentiating tests that we have described above. By the methodical employment of these tests, they will arrive at precise and controllable conclusions, which at the same time cannot help but enhance in the mind of the judges the value of the medico-legal appraisement of the alienists.

These examples to which we could add many others show that the methods of measuring the individual intelligence have not a speculative interest alone; by the direction, by the organization of all the investigations, psychology has furnished the proof (we do not say for the first time but in a more positive manner than ever before), that it is in a fair way to become a science of great social utility.

54/ABILITY FACTORS AND ENVIRONMENTAL INFLUENCES[1]/PHILIP E. VERNON[*]

ALTHOUGH I HAVE NOT, LIKE SOME previous lecturers, had the privilege of close professional contacts with Dr. Bingham, apart from friendly meetings at International Congresses, I have always admired *Aptitudes and Aptitude Testing* (Bingham, 1937) as one of the most sound and comprehensive treatments of the topic. During World War II it was a main textbook for the British military psychologists and personnel selection officers whom we trained for allocation of recruits to suitable trades. Bingham and Moore's (1931) *How to Interview* is likewise still a valuable text for occupational psychologists. And on looking up Dr. Bingham's career, I was delighted to find that his first love was the psychology of music and that he eventually came to vocational and military testing via educational psychology, for these are the areas in which I too have chiefly been interested.

In *Aptitudes and Aptitude Testing*, Walter VanDyke Bingham (1937) clearly attaches major importance to general intelligence, as I wish to do today. But he took no doctrinaire theoretical position on the nature of intelligence, being content to define it as the ability to solve new problems, which he recognized as the product of endowment + growth + opportunity. He admitted, too, that intelligence is complex, that there might be different intelligences for dealing with different kinds of problems, though he did not commit himself as to which main types should be distinguished. He tended rather to classify aptitudes in terms of the main kinds of jobs for which people might be selected.

I want, then, to ask again what are the most useful psychological dimensions or factors under which the vocational psychologist can conceptualize people, and how do these originate? What can research tell us of the environmental influences that chiefly contribute to individual differences in these abilities? I intend to argue the case for a model, or structure, of ability factors which, even 3 years ago, might have been considered by most American psychometrists as hopelessly old-fashioned. This is the model based on g, the general intellectual factor, plus major and minor group factors. Thurstone's scheme of multiple primary abilities is preferred

[1] The Walter VanDyke Bingham Lecture given at Purdue University, April 21, 1965.

[*] Philip E. Vernon, Ability factors and environmental influences, *American Psychologist*, 1965, *20*, 723-733. Reprinted with slight abridgement by permission.

TABLE 1 / DIFFERENTIAL ATTITUDE TESTS: MEDIAN CORRELATIONS WITH SCHOOL GRADES AMONG SEVERAL CLASSES OF NINTH–TWELFTH-GRADE BOYS.

	ENGLISH	MATHS	SCIENCE	SOCIAL STUDIES
Verbal reasoning	.49	.33	.54	.48
Numerical computation	.48	.47	.52	.46
Abstract reasoning	.32	.32	.42	.32
Space	.26	.26	.34	.24
Mechanical comprehension	.21	.19	.40	.21
Clerical speed and accuracy	.22	.16	.24	.21
Spelling	.44	.28	.36	.36
Sentences (English usage)	.50	.32	.45	.43

Note.—Four highest coefficients in each column are underlined.

by almost all psychometrists, though apparently it is seldom adopted by counselors or others who use tests for reaching practical decisions. Despite Thurstone's and Guilford's assurance that general intelligence is too vague and heterogeneous a construct to be worth measuring—we should break it down into its components and measure each individual's profile of factors—most practicing psychologists in schools, clinics, and industry happily go on using the familiar group or individual tests of intelligence. The main concessions they make to the factorist are to obtain separate linguistic and quantitative scores in some academic aptitude tests, and separate verbal and performance scores in the Wechsler scales. When I visited some military psychological establishments in 1957, I was told more than once that military psychologists could not ignore g. Try as they would to find differential tests for different army trades, intercorrelations were always so high that recruits appeared to be differentiated more by all-round level of ability than by type of ability, that is to say, by g rather than by factor profile. Table 1 provides another instance, extracted from the Psychological Corporation's follow-up studies of the Differential Aptitude Tests. True, these are not pure factor tests, but their aim is to give differential predictions for different educational courses or jobs. I have underlined the four highest validity coefficients in each column, and you will see that the pattern of coefficients for different school courses is sickeningly similar. Verbal and Reasoning tests, that is those which are most typical of the conventional general intelligence test, together with the Numerical test, tend to give the best correlations throughout, and only to a limited extent do Space and Mechanical tests add something to the prediction of ability in science courses.

Currently there seems to be greater recognition of the failure of multiple-factor profiles to fulfil their promise, and scepticism over the proliferation of factors. In 1962 Lloyd Humphreys came out in favor of something very similar to the British g + group-factor model, and last year Quinn McNemar (1964) trenchantly criticized the American multiple factorist's "fragmentation of ability, into more and more factors of less and less importance . . . [p. 872]." A general intelligence factor seems unavoidable since substantial positive intercorrelations are found when any cognitive tests are applied to a fairly representative population. But at the same time intelligence has many aspects which can usefully be represented, as Thurstone did, in terms of partially distinct though overlapping primary factors. The trouble arises because any one of these major primaries can be endlessly fractionated, depending simply on the number and variety of different tests in that area which the psychometrist can think up and, I would add, on the homogeneity—the restriction in the range of g—in the tested population. I would entirely agree with Humphreys (1962) that it is useful to superimpose on the hierarchical group-factor model Guttman's notion of facets. Test intercorrelations are affected not only by test content but by the form or technique of the test, its speededness, level of difficulty of the items, whether multiple-choice or creative response, whether analogies, series, or classifications, and so forth. These facets, which are seldom of much diagnostic interest, have been variously referred to as method factors (Campbell & Fiske, 1959), formal factors and work attitudes (Vernon, 1958), instrument factors (Cattell, 1961), and response sets (Cronbach, 1950).

HIERARCHICAL GROUP-FACTOR THEORY

Figure 1 gives the best indication I can manage of the factors that emerge most consistently when large and varied test batteries are applied to representative samples of adolescents or young adults (Vernon, 1961). I admit, of course, that there is no one final structure, since so much depends on the population tested, its heterogeneity and educational background, the particular tests chosen, and the techniques of factorization and rotation employed. I have followed British usage in naming the factors by small letters to differentiate them from the corresponding American primaries from which the g element has not been removed.

After removing the general factor (whether by group-factor technique or by rotation of centroid factors), the positive residual correlations always fall into two main groups—the verbal-educational (*v:ed*) group and the spatial-practical-mechanical group. The *v:ed* factor usually yields additional minor fluency and divergent thinking abilities—scholastic and *n* or number subfactors. Likewise the *k:m* complex includes perceptual, physical, and psychomotor, as well as spatial and mechanical factors, which can be further subdivided by more detailed testing. In addition there seem to be various cross-links: For example clerical tests usually combine verbal ability and perceptual speed, *p;* likewise math and science depend both on number and spatial abilities, *n* and *k*.

Sometimes an inductive reasoning ability (also very relevant to science) can be distinguished, though most of the common variance of reasoning tests is apt to be absorbed into g. At a still lower level in the hierarchy come what are usually referred to as specific factors, though of course any specific can be turned into an additional narrow group factor by devising additional tests.

Now despite certain differences of analytic technique and interpretation of factors, the hierarchical model and the multiple-factor model are fundamentally in agreement. It is just as legitimate to start, as it were, from the bottom upwards—that is to say, to extract the primaries—and from their intercorrelations calculate the second-order factors, and if need be a third-order factor, corresponding to our major group factors and g. . . .

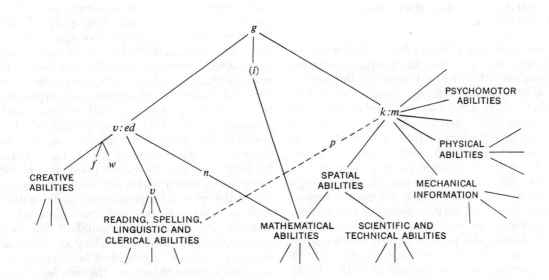

FIGURE 1 / DIAGRAM OF THE MAIN GENERAL AND GROUP FACTORS UNDERLYING TESTS RELEVANT TO EDUCATIONAL AND VOCATIONAL ACHIEVEMENTS.

From the point of view of the practical tester, the hierarchical model seems more logical since, in making educational or vocational decisions, he can cover most of the ground just by applying g or g + v tests, and then supplement by spatial-mechanical, clerical, number, or other group-factor tests where relevant. In other words, measures of factors which are higher in the hierarchy generally have better external va-

lidity, or more generalizability (Cronbach, Rajaratnam, & Gleser, 1963) to capacities of everyday life; whereas many of the published primary factors seem to be so narrow, so specific to the particular test material, as to have no practical use. This is true, for example, of Thurstone's and other rote memory factors. The user is tempted, even encouraged, to regard them as measuring memorizing ability which is likely to be highly relevant to school learning. In fact they usually correlate with scholastic achievement only insofar as they have not been purified of g and v. Similarly a large proportion of Guilford's numerous factors of intellect have failed to show any external validity which could not be accounted for by their g, v, and space content, though I would agree that some of his originality and creativity factor tests may cover a little fresh ground.

Perhaps the basic source of disagreement is that Thurstone and Guilford regarded primary factors almost as fundamental components or chemical elements of the mind, which in combination go to make up all the important human capacities; whereas Godfrey Thomson (1939), Cyril Burt (1940), and I have always tried to keep in mind that factors are primarily classifications of similar tests. And just because a lot of tests appear to involve memorizing or whatever, and intercorrelate positively, this does not prove that they are good measures of the memorizing that children do in school.

PSYCHOLOGICAL ORIGINS OF FACTORS

At the same time g theory has its difficulties, in particular that g is not, as Spearman believed, determinate—that is to say, one and the same g whatever cognitive tests one likes to apply. Psychologically it is the all-round level of our thinking skills; while statistically it is merely the average of a battery of tests of intellectual capacities which are so diverse that the group factors or facets involved in each separate test mostly cancel one another out. Hence although we know what kinds of tests are most saturated with g, it can still vary according to the particular measures the psychologist likes to use. Perhaps, though, this is not a serious disadvantage, since it is what one would expect in the light of the psychological contributions of Hebb (1948) and Piaget (1950), Ferguson (1954) and Hunt (1961).

All of these writers point to the need to get away from the notion of intelligence as a definite entity, an autonomous mental faculty, which simply matures as children grow up. Rather we have to think of it in terms of a cumulative formation of more and more complex and flexible schemata (Piaget's term) or phase sequences (Hebb), or what Miller, Galanter, and Pribram (1960) call plans, which develop through interaction between the growing organism and its environment. They depend both upon environmental stimulation and on active exploration and experiment (Piaget's accommodation and assimilation); i.e., they are formed and organized by use. This implies, to a much greater extent than Piaget seems to have recognized, that they also depend upon personality and motivational factors, organic and social drives, curiosity and interests; and that they are channelled by family, cultural, and educational pressures. Intelligence, then, refers to the totality of concepts and skills, the techniques or plans for coping with problems, which have crystallized out of the child's previous experience. Most representative of these, as Ferguson points out, are the thinking skills which have been overlearned and which are transferable to a wide variety of new situations. Although, of course, each person's accumulation of skills is different, all persons who have been brought up within a fairly homogeneous culture can reasonably be compared at any set of tasks which that culture values and which it likes to include within its conception of intelligence. But obviously, also, the whole structure, from perceptual and linguistic schemata upwards, may differ markedly in other cultures. The group of skills which we refer to as intelligence is a European and American middle-class invention: something which seems to be intimately bound up with puritanical values, with repression of instinctual responses and emphasis on responsibility, initiative, persistence, and efficient workmanship. It is a kind of intelligence which is specially well adapted for scientific analysis, for control and exploitation of the physical world, for large-scale and long-term planning and carrying out of materialistic objectives. It has also led to the growth of complex social institutions such as nations, armies, industrial firms, school systems, and universities, though it has been notably less successful in working out solutions of group rivalries or providing harmonious personal adjustment than have the intelligences of some more primitive cultures. Other cultures have evolved intelligences which are better adapted than ours for coping with problems of agricultural and tribal living. The aboriginal in the Australian desert and the Eskimo in the Far North have many schemata far more efficient than our own. Again subcultures such as our lower working class, or rural groups, develop rather different intelligence.

How about ability factors other than g? It seems entirely plausible that different kinds of skills, or those applied to different kinds of problems, should group together and yield the various group or primary factors that the mental tester discovers. But any reification of such clusters into entities or basic faculties of mind, or what Spearman calls an oligarchic system, is to be deplored. The grouping depends mainly on what cultural and educational pressures dictate. Thus it is very natural, at least in Western cultures, that all the skills bound up with language and school should show a common factor over and above g, and that all contrasted skills of a noneducational type should show a different factor. Likewise we can envisage a whole host of minor group factors arising from the overlapping of schemata involved in similar tasks.

CROSS-CULTURAL TESTING

Let me now turn to the second half of my title—namely, the environmental influences or other causal agencies that underly the development of different patterns of abilities. Here, too, the adoption of the hierarchical model simplifies our problem. It would be extraordinarily difficult to inquire into the agencies associated with a large number of Thurstone's primary factors, with Rote Memory, Induction, Fluency, etc., let alone with Guilford's 60 or more factors, since there would be so much overlapping. It seems more feasible to explore the agencies contributing to general intelligence, and those particularly relevant to verbal-educational and to spatial-practical factors—the group factors that carry a lot of everyday-life variance, and to proceed from there to find out what we can about contributory influences to minor factors of, say, creativity, number, art, music, athletic ability, etc., holding intelligence constant.

I would urge that this is a major responsibility of applied psychology in the second half of the twentieth century. If we are to help the newly developing, nontechnological nations of Africa, Asia, South America, and elsewhere, we must know more about the environmental and other handicaps which retard the development of those abilities that are needed for technological advancement (cf. Schwarz, 1961; Vernon, 1962). We want to assist them in selecting children who will make good professionals, teachers, commercial and political leaders, and technicians, and to tell them what factors of diet and health, cultural tradition and family upbringing, and schooling most require attention if they are to produce sufficient highly skilled personnel.

It is in the controversial area of cross-cultural testing that I am at the moment carrying out a series of small-scale researches, supported by the Association for the Aid of Crippled Children. My wife and I have applied a varied battery of tests, mostly individual, to a reference group of 100 11-year-old boys in England, to 50 boys of the same age in Jamaica, and to 90 Canadian Indians and Eskimos; and I hope to sample some African and other cultural groups later. I am confining myself to boys because, as Schaefer and Bayley (1963) point out, the long-term effects of upbringing are more clear-cut than in girls. Also I am working with groups which, by 11 years of age, have acquired enough English to understand oral instructions. Now I am well aware of the difficulties of cross-cultural testing which Anastasi (1958), for example, has discussed; and indeed it follows from what was said earlier that there is no such thing as a culture-free or culture-fair test. But insofar as the developing nations are aiming to achieve viable technological civilizations, they will need Western-type intelligence. Thus it is entirely legitimate to compare their standing with that of Europeans or Americans on tests which are known to sample abilities relevant to Western-type achievements. Moreover, insofar as the contrasted cultures provide a much wider range of environments than commonly occur within Western societies, their test scores should throw a clearer light on the determinants of abilities.

DETERMINANTS OF TEST PERFORMANCE

Let us broadly distinguish the following classes of determinants:[2]

A. Genetic factors which are nonobservable and nonmeasurable, though we know that they exist since foster children or orphans continue to show some resemblance to their true parents who have had nothing to do with their upbringing. Presumably individuals differ in some quality of the plasticity of the nervous system which makes possible the building up of any schemata or plans; and it may well be that there are genetic differences contributing to linguistic and spatial aptitudes which tend to be sex linked. Certainly there are genetic factors in musical and possibly in mathematical and other talents,

[2] Note the parallel between this classification and Hebb's Intelligence A and B. Elsewhere (Vernon, 1955), I have coined the term "Intelligence C" to refer to actual test results, i.e., to the particular sampling of Intelligence B which an intelligence test provides. Intelligence C also differs from B on account of the facets or instrument factors mentioned above; in other words it is distorted by the C type of determinant.

however much environment also contributes. One cannot rule out the possibility of genetic differences in aptitudes among ethnic groups or so-called races, but I would agree with the United Nations Educational, Scientific, and Cultural Organization manifesto that we cannot prove them; and they are likely to be small compared with environmentally produced differences.

B.   An enormous amount of research, using very varied approaches, has helped to pinpoint the major environmental handicaps to mental development, and I will try to sketch this briefly under nine main headings.

1. *Physiological and nutritional factors.* These mainly operate during pregnancy and parturition (cf. Stott, 1960); though certain diseases and malnutrition may also be important later insofar as they lower the energy and activity level that the growing child needs to explore his environment and seek out self-stimulating experiences.

2. *Perceptual deprivation in the preschool years is suggested by Piaget's and Hebb's work.* This may well operate in such situations as Spitz (1945) and Wayne Dennis (1960) describe, but would hardly seem important in most cultural groups where nature provides plenty of sticks, stones, water, and human contacts. I would rather emphasize conceptual deprivation during the school years when parents fail to answer questions, encourage curiosity, and provide books, TV, and other types of experience (cf. Bloom, 1964).

3. *Repression of independence and constructive play, either through overprotection, arbitrary subjection, or conformity to tribal traditions.* This is very noticeable in West Indian and African societies, and seems to be linked particularly with deficit in spatial abilities, in 3-dimensional perception (cf. Hudson, 1962), and in technical skills. My recent studies with Eskimo boys reveal a strong contrast.

4. *Family insecurity and lack of planfulness,* In families living at the subsistence level, immediate gratification of hunger and sex needs naturally takes precedence over long-term, purposive planning—the Pleasure Principle over the Reality Principle—and discourages the development of internal controls and rational thinking. In our own culture, Schaefer and Bayley (1963) have shown the ill effects of parental anxiety, irritability, punitiveness, and rejection on later intellectual as well as social traits.

5. *Female dominance.* In many cultures, including the West Indian though not the Canadian Indian or Eskimo, the father may take little part in child rearing, and there is a lack of masculine models with whom the boy can identify. According to Witkin's (Witkin, Dyk, Faterson, Goodenough, & Karp, 1962; Witkin, Lewis, Hertzman, Machover, Meissner, & Wapner, 1954) and some other findings, this may favor verbal at the expense of spatial abilities.

6. *Education in the underdeveloped countries is often defective, brief or irregular, starved of materials.* Teachers may be poorly qualified and they may follow highly formal and mechanical methods, discouraging any intellectual initiative. Yet at the same time even bad education contributes greatly to the development of nonverbal as well as verbal abilities when the average home provides no intellectual stimulation.

7. *Linguistic handicaps are almost universal in these societies.* There may be a variety of dialects, or a debased and simplified pidgin or Creole; yet English, or sometimes French, is the main medium of instruction, especially for higher education. Unless the child can acquire complete facility in this second language he is likely to be backward in conceptual development and thinking skills, and this too seems to be reflected in nonverbal reasoning as well as in linguistic tests.

8. *The conceptual and grammatical structures of the native language may differ markedly from those of English, so that the classifications or relations demanded by a Western-type test may be quite unfamiliar, although the non-Western child can very well classify, relate, and abstract in concrete situations.* Again he may never have acquired the ability to interpret pictures as portraying 3-dimensional objects (cf. Biesheuvel, 1952).

9. *Adult role and adolescent aspirations.* Here there is little definite evidence. But it is reported of some North American Indian and other cultures that children show fairly normal intellectual development till adolescence, but then, when they realize the depressed status of their minority culture—the absence of opportunity for progress and advancement—apathy sets in. To adapt Gordon Allport's description of personality as "Becoming," intelligence may depend on the future as well as on the past. It is interesting to speculate whether a Western adult does not also cease growing intellectually at 20, 30, 50, or later when he reaches his peak of aspiration and curiosity.

C. This group of determinants obviously overlaps in practice with the B group. But it refers to those characteristics of the test which frequently distort the results of unsophisticated testees, and which could be fairly effectively controlled by appropriate modifications of the form of the test and its administration. Schwarz (1961) has laid down a useful series of principles for getting across Western-type tests to African subjects which, in effect, amounts to teaching them the required mode of response before giving the test. I would still question whether any multiple-choice group test such as Schwarz uses, especially any involving time limits, is suitable for cultures with such different modes of thought and such different attitudes to competition, to working on one's own, or to working at speed.[3] Thus I preferred in my own work to rely more on individual, free-response tests, given like the Terman-Merrill, so that one can expand explanations as necessary and try to ensure that motivation is adequate.

While I hope that this summary of determinants and handicaps provides some clarification, the interpretation of cross-cultural data is still extremely tricky, for test results alone tell us little about what determinants are operating in any particular test. Whiting and Whiting (1960) point out that we may be unaware of the crucial parameters in an unfamiliar culture, and Irvine (1965) argues that different sources of variance may be operating: A particular test may be measuring essentially different things in different cultural contexts. For example, amount and quality of schooling may have very little effect on nonverbal tests like Progressive Matrices, Porteus Mazes, or Draw-a-Man in Western cultures, but may have much greater effects in societies where intellectual stimulation by the home is lacking. However one can hope to make some progress: (a) by contrasting a number of different cultures, (b) by applying factor analysis within each culture to see how the abilities group and what differences occur in factor patterns, (c) by obtaining assessments of major determinants within each culture and observing their correlations with the various test scores or factors.

[3] It is only fair to point out that Schwarz is not concerned with cross-cultural comparisons, but with devising tests which will give useful predictions within African cultures. Thus a speeded test, say, may actually be more predictive of suitability for technical jobs in a culture where speed plays little part in conventional living.

SOME RESULTS OBTAINED IN ENGLAND AND THE WEST INDIES

Table 2 indicates the main results of group factor analyses among my English and Jamaican subjects; loadings are shown merely by + or ++ signs, as the detailed figures are available elsewhere (Vernon, 1965). It may be seen that the general pattern is similar in the two groups, though there are some differences in the content of particular tests. In the English group there are a large educational and a subsidiary linguistic factor, a large perceptual-spatial factor, and some separation of the more practical performance tests. With the smaller numbers in the Jamaican sample, these subsidiary factors are less clear-cut, and the only sign of a practical factor is in Porteus Mazes and Formboard. The educational factor is definitely more pervasive, entering not only into verbal but also most of the paper-and-pencil perceptual tests. Probably it represents general sophistication in understanding instructions and coping with symbolic material, whether verbal or pictorial. The best general factor tests—Piaget, Matrices, and Concept Formation—are those involving the simplest oral instructions and creative responses.

The median Jamaican performance in each test was expressed as a deviation quotient relative to the English distribution, and it will be seen that these figures range from 94 for Spelling down to 68 for Formboard, i.e., from .4 σ to 2.1 σ below the English mean. Performance is generally best on the more mechanical attainments, though very weak on vocabulary and on information learning which involve verbal comprehension. The quotients for perceptual tests, including Draw-a-Man, are also mainly around 85–90, and the most serious deficits are in verbal and nonverbal induction, Kohs Blocks, and Formboard—that is in g and practical-spatial abilities. This bears out my point that no test can be regarded as culture fair. Jamaican boys actually score better on conventional verbal intelligence and achievement tests, despite their linguistic handicap, than they do on tests which would appear to be purer measures of g, or of what Cattell (1963) refers to as fluid ability. I suspect that the same result would be found among Negroes in the United States.

Within each group the environmental variables listed in Table 3 were assessed on the basis of semistructured interviews with the boys and reports from the teachers. Time and expense did not permit home interviews, and in any case I was more interested in home and

TABLE 2 / MAIN FACTOR LOADINGS OF TESTS GIVEN TO ENGLISH AND WEST INDIAN ELEVEN-YEAR BOYS.

TESTS	MEAN WEST INDIAN DEVIATION QUOTIENT	ENGLISH FACTORS					WEST INDIAN FACTORS			
		g	EDUCA-TIONAL	VERBAL	PER-CEPTUAL	PRAC-TICAL	g	v:ed	PER-CEPTUAL	PRAC-TICAL ?
Arithemetic Achievement	84	++	+				++	+		
Spelling	94	+	+				+	+		
Memorizing lists of words	91	+	+		+		+	+		
English comprehension, usage, spelling	82	+	+	+			+	+		
Vocabulary, group multiple choice	83	+	+	+			+	+		
Vocabulary, individual Terman-Merrill	72	+	+	+			+		−	
Memorizing oral information	72	+	+				+	+		
Abstraction, verbal induction	?75	++	+							
Piaget, arithmetic-orientational	} 86	++					+	+	+	
Piaget, visualization-conservation		+			+	+	++			
Matrices, nonverbal induction	75	++					++			
Concept formation, sorting test	90	+		+			++			
Porteus Mazes	91	+					+	+		+
Vernon Formboard	68	+			+	+	+		+	+
Kohs Blocks (WISC-Jahoda)	75	++			+	+	++	+	+	
Goodenough Draw-a-Man	91	+			+	+	+	+	+	
Gottschaldt (Embedded) Figures	88	+			+		+		+	
Reproducing Designs (Bender-Gestalt and Terman-Merrill)	87	+			+		+	+	+	
Picture Recognition, 3-D Perception	?85	+			+		+	+		

Note.— + indicates loadings of psychological interest, almost all statistically significant; ++ represents loadings of .70 or over. In the second column, certain quotients are preceded by "?" where the identical test was not given to the two groups and an approximate estimate was made.

schooling over the past few years than in the kind of details of early upbringing that Sears, Maccoby, and Levin (1957), Prothro (1961), and others have studied. I would certainly not claim high reliability for these assessments, yet they yielded some quite substantial and plausible correlations with the ability factors. The cultural level of the home is clearly the most significant single influence—more important than socioeconomic rating; and in the Jamaican group, but not the English, it affects perceptual as well as general and educational abilities. Linguistic background is similar, and the planfulness or rationality of the home is particularly associated with g factor. Curiously the unbroken home or nuclear family pattern gives slight negative correlations with g in both groups, though positive with other factors.[4]

[4] No explanation can be offered for the slight negative association of schooling with g in the English group. In both groups it appears to contribute to spatial as well as to educational development.

Encouragement of initiative, independence, and maturity seems more important in the Jamaican than the English group though it did not relate, as I had hypothesized, to perceptual-practical ability. But male dominance definitely linked with some aspect of this factor.

During the past 2 months I have been working with groups of boys in Indian reservations in Southern Alberta and Eskimos in the Mackenzie Delta in Arctic Canada. The results are not yet fully scored, let alone analyzed, but they do already bring out one important point —that different groups at similar levels of acculturation, and with similar language difficulties, may show very different patterns of scores. The Eskimos are just about equal to Jamaican standards in written English, though much behind in Arithmetic, probably because less stress is laid in Canadian schools on mechanical drill. The Indian boys do somewhat less well on achievement tests; their linguistic handicap is generally greater since less English is spoken

TABLE 3 / CORRELATIONS OF ABILITY FACTORS WITH ENVIRONMENTAL VARIABLES AMONG ENGLISH AND WEST INDIAN ELEVEN-YEAR BOYS.

ENVIRONMENTAL ASSESSMENTS	ENGLISH FACTORS					WEST INDIAN FACTORS			
	g	EDUCATIONAL	VERBAL	PERCEPTUAL	PRACTICAL	g	v:ed	PERCEPTUAL	PRACTICAL ?
Length and regularity of schooling	−.15	.31		.21		.23	.19	.26	
Family pattern: unbroken versus broken home	−.11	.30			.14	−.17	.24	.15	+
Stable home background versus frequent shifts						.14	.17		+
Economic: parents' job, housing, equipment	.38	.18	.24			.27	.28		+
Cultural stimulus: books in home, education of relatives, parent interest in education	.56	.29	.16			.33	.46	.25	
Male dominance and identification versus female overprotection or dominance					.39	.25		.27	
Initiative and maturity encouraged in play and household activities	.13			.13		.27	.16		+
Planfulness: rational home climate versus impulsive, emotional, arbitrary	.32	.26				.32			
Linguistic background	.49	.31	.24			.47	.41	.28	
Child's health, physical development, and nourishment							.21	.19	

Note.—As explained above, no clear practical group factor was established in the West Indian sample. However, Porteus Mazes and Formboard gave substantial positive residual correlations with certain variables, indicated by +.

in their homes or at school. Like the Jamaicans they are most retarded in oral understanding and vocabulary.

Both groups score much higher than the Jamaicans on Kohs Blocks and other spatial tests, with a mean quotient of 88 instead of 75; and the Eskimos come up very well also on the inductive reasoning tests—Abstraction and Matrices. Now economic conditions are extremely poor in all three groups, and there is similar family instability and insecurity. Thus it seems reasonable to attribute the better performance of Eskimo and Indian groups to the greater emphasis on resourcefulness in the upbringing of boys, perhaps combined with their strong masculine identification. True, the traditional hunting-trapping life is rapidly disappearing and the majority of parents are wage earning or on relief, but the children are still brought up permissively and encouraged to explore and hunt. Moreover, a subgroup of the Eskimos who came from the most isolated Arctic communities scored better on all three of the tests just mentioned than did those who lived in closer contact with whites and had become more acculturated.

Data such as these do not, of course, necessarily prove causality. Thus the correlation between cultural level of the home and intellectual development in the child might arise because brighter parents, who have brighter children, also provide them with better cultural and educational stimulation. Clearly the cross-sectional survey needs to be complemented by longitudinal and, if possible, direct experimental studies. We are on the verge of extremely exciting advances in the understanding and control of intellectual and personality development through such varied approaches as social learning and reinforcement theory, direct observation and follow-up of children, socioanthropological studies, and work such as I have described with mental tests and factor analysis. But I would not claim to have done more than to have scratched the surface, and to have raised many more problems than I have solved.

REFERENCES

ANASTASI, A. Differential psychology. New York: Macmillan, 1958.

BIESHEUVEL, S. The study of African ability. African Studies, 1952, 11, 45-58, 105-117.

BINGHAM, W. VAN D. Aptitudes and aptitude testing. New York: Harper, 1937.

BINGHAM, W. VAN D., & MOORE, B. V. How to interview. New York: Harper, 1931.

BLOOM, B. S. Stability and change in human characteristics. New York: Wiley, 1964.

BURT, C. *The factors of the mind.* London: Univer. London Press, 1940.

CAMPELL, D. T., & FISKE, D. W. Convergent and discriminant validation by the multitrait-multimethod matrix. *Psychological Bulletin,* 1959, *56,* 81-105.

CATTELL, R. B. Theory of situational, instrument, second order, and refraction factors in personality structure research. *Psychological Bulletin,* 1961, *58,* 160-174.

CATTELL, R. B. Theory of fluid and crystallized intelligence: A critical experiment. *Journal of Educational Psychology,* 1963, *54,* 1-22.

CRONBACH, L. J. Further evidence on response sets and test design. *Educational and Psychological Measurement,* 1950, *10,* 3-31.

CRONBACH, L. J., RAJARATNAM, N., & GLESER, G. C. Theory of generalizability: A liberalization of reliability theory. *British Journal of Statistical Psychology,* 1963, *16,* 137-163.

DENNIS, W. Causes of retardation among institutional children: Iran. *Journal of Genetic Psychology,* 1960, *94,* 47-59.

FERGUSON, G. A. On learning and human ability. *Canadian Journal of Psychology,* 1954, 8, 95-112.

HEBB, D. O. *The organization of behavior.* New York: Wiley, 1948.

HUDSON, W. Pictorial perception and educational adaptation in Africa. *Psychologia Africana,* 1962, *9,* 226-239.

HUMPHREYS, L. G. The organization of human abilities. *American Psychologist,* 1962, *17,* 475-483.

HUNT, J. MC V. *Intelligence and experience.* New York: Ronald Press, 1961.

IRVINE, S. H. Testing abilities and attainments in Africa. *British Journal of Educational Psychology,* 1965, *35,* in press.

MC NEMAR, Q. Lost: Our intelligence? Why? *American Psychologist,* 1964, *19,* 871-882.

MILLER, G. A., GALANTER, E., & PRIBRAM, K. H. *Plans and the structure of behavior.* New York: Holt, 1960.

PIAGET, J. *The psychology of intelligence.* London: Routledge & Kegan Paul, 1950.

PROTHRO, E. T. *Child-rearing in the Lebanon.* Cambridge: Harvard Univer. Press, 1961.

SCHAEFER, E. S., & BAYLEY, N. Maternal behavior, child behavior and their intercorrelations from infancy through adolescence. *Monographs of the Society for Research in Child Development,* 1963, *28,* No. 87.

SCHWARZ, P. A. *Aptitude tests for use in the developing nations.* Pittsburgh, Pa.: American Institute for Research, 1961.

SEARS, R. R., MACCOBY, E. E., & LEVIN, H. *Patterns of child rearing.* Evanston, Ill.: Row, Peterson, 1957.

SPITZ, R. A. Hospitalism: An inquiry into the genesis of psychiatric conditions in early childhood. *Psychoanalytic Studies of Children,* 1945, *1,* 55-74.

STOTT, D. H. Interaction of heredity and environment in regard to "Measured Intelligence." *British Journal of Educational Psychology,* 1960, *30,* 95-102.

THOMSON, G. H. *The factorial analysis of human ability.* London: Univer. London Press, 1939.

VERNON, P. E. The assessment of children. In University of London Institute of Education, *Studies in education.* Vol. 7. London: Evans, 1955. Pp. 189-215.

VERNON, P. E. Educational testing and test-form factors. (Res. Bull. 58-3) Princeton, N. J.: Educational Testing Service, 1958.

VERNON, P. E. *The structure of human abilities.* (2nd ed.) London: Methuen, 1961.

VERNON, P. E. Intellectual development in non-technological societies. In G. Nielsen (Ed.), *Proceedings of the XIV International Congress of Applied Psychology.* Vol. 3. *Child and education.* Copenhagen: Munksgaard, 1962. Pp. 94-105.

VERNON, P. E. Environmental handicaps and intellectual development. *British Journal of Educational Psychology,* 1965, *35,* in press.

WHITING, J. W. M., & WHITING, B. B. Anthropological study of child rearing. In P. H. Mussen, *Handbook of research methods in child development.* New York: Wiley, 1960. Ch. 27.

WITKIN, H. A., DYK, R. B., FATERSON, H. F., GOODENOUGH, D. R., & KARP, S. A. *Psychological differentiation: Studies of development.* New York: Wiley, 1962.

WITKIN, H. A., LEWIS, H. B., HERTZMANN, M., MACHOVER, K., MEISSNER, P. B., & WAPNER, S. *Personality through perception.* New York: Harper, 1954.

55/PERSONALITY AND IQ CHANGE[1]/

JEROME KAGAN, LESTER W. SONTAG,

CHARLES T. BAKER, AND VIRGINIA L. NELSON[*]

RESEARCH ON MENTAL DEVELOPMENT during the last twenty years has indicated that a child's IQ score does not necessarily remain constant with age (2, 3, 4, 10). Several reports (9, 10, 12) suggest that changes in environmental conditions can depress or raise IQ level and it is sometimes implied that these changes may be explained by recourse to personality variables. The purpose of this paper is to demonstrate that changes in IQ during childhood are correlated with certain personality predispositions as inferred from projective test data. The personality variables under study include (a) need for achievement, (b) competitive strivings, (c) curiosity about nature, and (d) passivity.

Performance on an IQ test is assumed to be a function of at least two major variables: the variety of skills and abilities the person brings to the test situation and his motivation to perform well on the test (2, 6). Since the IQ scores of some children change markedly during the school years, it seems plausible to assume that those children who show marked increases in IQ have a very strong motivation to acquire or develop the various intellectual skills tapped by an IQ test and to perform well in a testing situation. It is suggested that need for achievement, competitive strivings, and curiosity about nature motivate the acquisition and improvement of cognitive abilities and by so doing facilitate increases in tested IQ.

The social environment often awards praise and recognition for intellectual accomplishment, and school age children with a high need for achievement might seek to gratify this need through intellectual activity. Thus it was predicted that children showing marked increases in IQ would produce more achievement imagery on the TAT than those with minimal gains in IQ.

Secondly, the school environment emphasizes competitive intellectual activity, and children with strong competitive needs would be highly motivated to acquire the intellectual skills which result in successful competition with one's classmates. Thus it was predicted that children showing IQ gains would show more competitive strivings than children displaying minimal gains in IQ. In choosing an index of competitive strivings, besides the related measure of TAT achievement fantasy, it was decided to use aggressive content on the Rorschach. The bases for this choice rested on the assumptions that (a) incidence of aggressive imagery reflected degree of aggressive motivation and (b) competition was a socially accepted form of aggressive behavior. For in competition, as in aggression, the child desires to defeat another individual and assert his superiority over him. The population of children in this study is predominantly middle class and apt to place strong inhibitions on direct overt expression of aggression. Therefore, there would be a tendency for the individual with high aggressive motivation to seek socially accepted channels for aggressive expression such as competitive activity with peers. Thus it was predicted that children showing IQ gain would report more Rorschach aggressive content than those with minimal gain because of their greater competitive predisposition.

A third motive that might facilitate a child's acquisition of knowledge and skills in dealing with the environment could be curiosity about nature. Interest in birth, death, sexual anatomy, and other processes of nature is a frequent phenomenon in young children. It is suggested that the more intense this curiosity the greater the motivation to acquire the habits which would gratify this motive. Since reading, questioning, and manipulating the environment are effective behavioral methods of gratifying one's curiosity, it might be expected that the highly curious

[1] This investigation was supported in part by a research grant (PHS M 1260) from the National Institute of Mental Health of the National Institutes of Health, United States Public Health Service. The writers wish to thank Dr. Seymour B. Sarason for his critical reading of the manuscript.

[*] Jerome Kagan, Lester W. Sontag, Charles T. Baker, and Virginia L. Nelson, Personality and IQ change, *Journal of Abnormal and Social Psychology*, 1958, 56, 261-266. Reprinted by permission.

child would be more likely to develop these skills and therefore apt to gain in IQ score. The TAT measure used to evaluate curiosity was presence of themes of interest in nature and its phenomena. For the Rorschach, it was hypothesized that concern with the body might reflect, in part, heightened interest in natural processes, and it was suggested that anatomy content might be more frequent for children who showed marked IQ gains than for those with minimal increases in IQ. It is recognized that many clinical psychologists regard anatomy content in adults as indicative of psychopathology. This study is concerned with the correlates of IQ gain rather than psychopathology, and it is not implied that children who show increases in IQ are completely free of conflict. Secondly, it was felt that the determinants of anatomy content for children might be different from those which produce this content in adults.

A final prediction dealt with the predisposition to behavioral passivity. The children who show IQ gains have been characterized as having high need achievement, competitive strivings, and curiosity about the environment. This constellation of motives implies that when these children are confronted with a problem, they would have a tendency to attack and attempt to solve the problem rather than withdraw from the situation or seek help. On this basis, it was predicted that children who showed IQ gains would be less likely than those with minimal IQ increases to characterize their TAT heroes as passive in attitude or behavior.

The Fels Research Institute is uniquely equipped to test these ideas about IQ change since it has continuous longitudinal information on the development of a sample of normal children. These data include intelligence and projective tests, observations of the children, and reports on the parent-child interaction. In a recent study, Sontag, Baker, and Nelson (11) related personality information on a sample of children with changes in IQ and found that those children who showed marked increases in IQ were rated as more competitive, more likely to display self-initiated behavior and less passive than those who showed decreases in IQ. The TAT and Rorschach protocols were not utilized in making these personality ratings, and the results from this study served as a major stimulus for the present investigation.

METHOD

A sample of 140 Fels subjects (Ss), 70 of each sex, were chosen for study because a fairly complete

record of test information was available on them. From ages 2-1/2 to 6, the Stanford-Binet intelligence test (1916 or 1937 revision) was administered to most Ss twice yearly, on their birthdays and six months after their birthdays. From ages 6 to 12, most Ss received alternately Form L or Form M of the 1937 revision annually on or near each S's birthday. All of the tests were administered by one of the authors (VLN). The mean IQ of the Fels population is near 120, with standard deviation varying from 14 to 20 IQ points.

In order to obtain groups of Ss who showed the most change in IQ score from ages 6 to 10, a smoothed longitudinal plot of each S's IQ was prepared by averaging the mean of three consecutive test scores around each age. This procedure is explained in detail in other reports (1, 10, 11). This technique tends to eliminate erratic variations in IQ and hopefully furnishes a more valid measure of IQ changes. Then each S's smoothed IQ at age 6 was subtracted from his smoothed IQ at age 10, and this distribution of differences, positive if S gained in IQ and negative if S lost in IQ, was divided into quartiles. This report deals with the projective test information on those S's in the two extreme groups: those who increased and those who decreased the most in IQ score. These will be called Group A, the IQ ascenders, and Group D, the IQ descenders, respectively. There was no significant difference between the mean IQ of the two extreme quartiles at age six, the means being 119 and 116 for Groups A and D respectively. The average amount of increase in IQ for Group A was larger (plus 17 points) than the corresponding decrease for the members of Group D (minus 5 points) and while 46 per cent of Group D lost five or more points, every child in Group A gained 10 or more points during the years 6 through 10. The mean IQ of the entire sample of 140 tends to increase slightly from ages 6 to 10, probably as a result of practice effects with the same test. Since every S in Group D showed a decrease in IQ, it might be inferred that the members of Group D did not benefit from practice and familiarity with the test, and it is probably more accurate to view Group D Ss in this light rather than as Ss who showed marked decreases in IQ score.

The projective tests used in the analysis were the Rorschach and selected TAT pictures. Two factors governed the choice of the TAT cards which were analyzed. Because the protocols were gathered over a period of years, there was not complete comparability for all Ss for the number of cards administered. Secondly, the specific hypotheses of the study dictated the cards chosen for analysis and Cards 1, 3 BM, 3 GF, 5, 6 BM, 12 F, 14, and 17 BM were selected for analysis. The age at which the TAT protocols were administered ranged from 8-9 to 14-6 with median at 11-6 and 80 per cent of the protocols obtained between the ages of 11 and 12. The age at which the Rorschachs were administered ranged from 6-5 to 13-6 with median at 10-5 and 63 per cent of the sample having had the test between ages

10 and 11. Since the Rorschach and TAT were administered by different examiners there was no comparability with respect to inquiry or probing. Thus, the analysis of both the Rorschach and TAT were restricted to the S's spontaneous verbalization to the stimulus before any questions or inquiry were conducted by the examiner. The protocols were scored for the following fantasy categories.

1. *Need achievement on the TAT*. Achievement imagery on the TAT was scored according to the definition of McClelland et al. (8); and themes involving a reference to competition with a standard of excellence were scored achievement imagery.

2. *Rorschach aggression*. The definition of aggressive content on the Rorschach included (*a*) people, animals, or creatures engaged in physical or verbal aggression, e.g., fighting or quarreling, (*b*) explosive objects or explosions, e.g., volcanoes, bombs exploding, fireworks, and (*c*) objects or animal parts normally regarded as instruments of aggression, e.g., spears, rifles, clubs, guns, knives, horns, and claws.

3. *Intellectual curiosity about nature*. For the TAT, curiosity was defined in terms of themes in which someone is interested in the processes or phenomena of nature. Curiosity on the Rorschach was restricted to anatomy or X-ray responses of internal organs or boney parts, e.g., stomach, backbone, ribs.

4. *Passivity*. Because of the limited amount of thematic material in the spontaneous performance, themes of passivity were limited to stories in which the central figure was described as sleepy, tired, or resting.

The fantasy categories were independently scored by the senior author and an assistant without knowledge of the S's IQ scores.[2] Reliability was very high because of the limited amount of content scored for each response and the objectivity of the definitions. Percentage of agreement for the three TAT categories was 95 per cent and for the two Rorschach categories 99 per cent.

RESULTS

Although there was a total of 70 Ss in the two extreme quartiles, not all of the Ss had Rorschach or TAT data for the age range under study. Table 1 shows the distribution of Ss, by sex and direction of IQ change, for the TAT and Rorschach analyses. Because there are approximately twice as many boys as there are girls in Group A, all comparisons were first made separately by sex and results were only combined if the direction of the result for both boys and girls in the same IQ group was in the predicted direction.

1. *Need Achievement*. All achievement themes, save one, occurred to Cards 1 and 17 BM. The typi-

[2] The writers wish to thank Mary Schnurer for her assistance in assessing the reliability of the scoring.

TABLE 1 / DISTRIBUTION OF Ss BY SEX AND DIRECTION OF IQ CHANGE USED IN THE ANALYSIS OF THE TAT AND RORSCHACH.

| | TAT | | RORSCHACH | |
GROUP	BOYS	GIRLS	BOYS	GIRLS
Group A	22	11	22	10
Group D	10	20	9	18
Both groups	32	31	31	28

TABLE 2 / PERCENTAGE OF Ss REPORTING ACHIEVEMENT IMAGERY TO CARDS 1 AND 17 BM.

| TAT CARD | GROUP A | | | GROUP D | | |
	BOYS	GIRLS	BOYS AND GIRLS	BOYS	GIRLS	BOYS AND GIRLS
Card 1	36.4	50.0	40.6	27.3	15.0	19.4
Card 17 BM	36.4	30.0	34.4	0.0	15.0	9.7
Cards 1 and 17 BM	22.7	10.0	18.8	0.0	0.0	0.0

cal achievement story to Card 1 concerned a boy who wanted to master the violin and/or become a famous violinist, while the typical achievement theme to 17 BM involved competitive activity with regard to rope climbing. Table 2 shows the percentage of Ss in each group reporting achievement imagery plots to Cards 1, 17 BM, and to both pictures.

For both Cards 1 and 17 BM, more male and female Ss in Group A report achievement imagery than the boys or girls of Group D. For Card 1, the difference between Group A and Group D girls is reliable at the .03 level; the difference for boys is in the predicted direction but not significant. For Card 17 BM, the difference between Group A and Group D boys is significant ($P = .03$) and in the predicted direction for girls. All P values are for one tail and were evaluated using the exact method suggested by Fisher (5). When the sexes were pooled, comparisons between Groups A and D were significant not only for Cards 1 and 17 BM separately but also for the number of Ss telling achievement imagery to both Cards 1 and 17 BM ($P < .10$, .03, and .01 respectively). Thus, the Ss who showed increases in IQ were more prone to structure Cards 1 and 17 BM in terms of achievement oriented behavior than the Ss in Group D.

2. *Aggressive Content on Rorschach*. There was no significant difference between Groups A and D or between boys and girls with respect to the mean number of responses per protocol, and the mean for the entire sample was 27 responses. There was no difference between Group A and Group D girls with respect to percentage of each group reporting one or more aggressive responses per protocol (30.0 per

cent for Group A versus 33.0 per cent for Group D). However, the difference between Group A and D boys approached significance with 59.1 per cent of the former and 22.2 per cent of the latter reporting one or more aggressive images ($P = .07$). Thus, the prediction of a correlation between IQ increase and aggressive imagery held only for the boys. Because of the tentativeness of this result and the more speculative nature of the hypothesis relating competitive striving and aggressive content, an attempt was made to validate this finding by analyzing a later Rorschach protocol for the boys in Groups A and D. Not all of the boys had Rorschachs administered to them at a later age, and only 15 Ss in Group A and five in Group D were available for analysis. The median ages at the time of administration were 13-8 and 15-0 for Groups A and D respectively, and there was no significant difference in the lengths of the protocols of the two groups. The results were in the same direction for 86.7 per cent of Group A, and 20.0 per cent of Group D reported one or more aggressive images, and this difference is highly significant ($P = .01$).

3. *Intellectual Curiosity.* The only TAT card eliciting curiosity plots was Card 14, and the typical theme described a person gazing at or interested in the stars or the heavens. Table 3 shows the percentage of each group telling such themes to Card 14.

Both the boys and girls in Group A told more themes of interest in the stars or heavens than the males and females in Group D ($P = .14$, $P = .10$, respectively) and combining of the sexes yielded a highly significant difference between Groups A and D ($P < .01$).

4. *Anatomy and X-Ray Responses on the Rorschach.* There was no difference between Group A and Group D girls reporting one or more anatomy responses (30.0 per cent versus 38.9 per cent for Groups A and D respectively). For the boys, 31.8 per cent of Group A and 0.0 per cent of Group D reported anatomy or X-ray imagery, a difference that approached significance ($P = .06$). This finding was also validated on the same sample of 20 boys that was used to check the differences in aggressive content. The results were in the same direction with 60.0 per cent of Group A and 20.0 per cent of Group D reporting anatomy content ($P = .15$).

5. *Passivity.* Card 3 BM accounted for most of the passivity themes and the groups were compared with respect to the incidence of stories to Card 3 BM in which the central figure was sleepy, tired, or resting. Table 4 shows the percentage of each group telling such themes. Both the boys and girls in Group D showed more passivity themes than the boys and girls in Group A. Although only the difference for the girls was significant ($P = .06$), when the sexes were pooled the difference was highly reliable ($P < .03$).

Cards 3 GF, 5, 6 BM, and 12 F did not furnish data relevant to the hypotheses under test and these results are not summarized.

TABLE 3 / PERCENTAGE OF Ss REPORTING THEMES OF CURIOSITY TO CARD 14.

SEX	GROUP A	GROUP D
Boys	40.9	18.2
Girls	30.0	5.0
Boys and girls	37.5	9.7

TABLE 4 / PERCENTAGE OF Ss REPORTING THEMES OF PASSIVITY TO CARD 3 BM.

SEX	GROUP A	GROUP D
Boys	9.1	27.3
Girls	10.0	45.0
Boys and girls	9.4	38.7

DISCUSSION

In the main, the hypotheses about the differences between Groups A and D have been verified. Boy and girl ascenders produced more TAT achievement imagery and curiosity about nature than Group D children and male ascenders displayed more aggressive content on the Rorschach than the boys in Group D. The higher incidence of aggressive imagery for the boys who gained in IQ was interpreted as reflecting stronger competitive motivation. Finally, the Ss in Group D were presumed to have a more passive orientation since they were more likely to perceive the ambiguous figure on Card 3 BM as sleeping or tired. The relation between Rorschach anatomy content and IQ gain was the most tentative finding.

The results are interpreted as indicating that high motivation to achieve, competitive strivings, and curiosity about nature may motivate the acquisition of intellectual skills and knowledge which, in turn, facilitates increases in tested IQ. If one accepts the generally assumed notion that boys are more competitive and achievement oriented than girls, the fact that there were twice as many boys in Group A as there were girls supports the present interpretation. A recent study using the Edwards Personal Preference Schedule found that high school boys obtained higher need achievement scores than high school girls (7).

These results are not interpreted as indicating that strong achievement, competitive, and curiosity motives are the only variables involved in producing gains in IQ. The Ss in this study are all average or above in IQ and there is not adequate sampling of children with lower IQ levels. One would not expect Ss with low IQs or language handicaps to suddenly show an interest in reading despite achievement needs or intellectual curiosity. The child who spends increased time reading because of a heightened interest in natural processes must have already learned the basic reading skills so that his behavior is not a difficult or unlikely choice for him.

Similarly, needs for achievement and successful competition should only motivate attempts at improvement of intellectual abilities in a social milieu where praise, recognition, and superior status are awarded for such accomplishment. That is, achievement-oriented children from homes in which intellectual activity was praised would probably be more likely to master intellectual skills than achievement-oriented children from homes in which such accomplishment was not rewarded. In a cultural environment where athletic ability, fighting prowess, or success with the opposite sex was highly valued, one might expect the child to choose these behavioral channels to gratify his achievement and competitive needs. The parents in the Fels population are predominantly middle class and tend to place importance on intellectual accomplishment. A large majority of the parents have attended college, and since enrollment in the Fels program is voluntary it might be inferred that only parents who valued knowledge and scientific pursuits would be predisposed to become part of the research population. Thus, the children under study tend to come from homes which value intellectual ability.

Study of the educational attainment of the parents of the Ss in Groups A and D revealed no significant difference between the groups with respect to the percentage of families in which both parents attended college (57.1 per cent for Group A versus 42.9 per cent for Group D; $P >$ .30). Although there is a slight difference favoring the educational level of Group A families, the difference was not dramatic. There may be important differences between Groups A and D with respect to the differential encouragement of intellectual achievement, but measurement of these differences would probably require variables more refined than educational level of the parents. However, even though parental emphasis on intellectual activity may increase the child's desire to improve his cognitive skills, the child's predisposition to adopt or rebel against parental values should selectively influence his motivation to strive for intellectual accomplishment. Thus, the type of relation between parent

and child may be an important factor in this process.

Finally, there is the possibility that genetic and/or constitutional variables may play a role in facilitating marked IQ changes. There is considerable data indicating that genetic factors influence IQ level but less evidence relevant to the role of these variables in producing childhood increases in IQ score. For most of the children in our population, IQs tend to level off during the ages 6-10 and most of the marked changes in level occur during the preschool years. However, the exact relationship between genetic variables and IQ change has yet to be determined. The phenomenon of IQ increase during the school years is admittedly complex and it is not implied that the child's motives are the major factor. However, it is suggested that personality needs may influence this process. Perhaps the most accurate generalization is that for middle-class children with average or above IQ levels, strong achievement, competitive, and curiosity needs may facilitate IQ gains by motivating the child to master intellectual skills.

A final implication of these findings is that they add indirect evidence for the usefulness of the Rorschach and TAT as research instruments. Validation of a predicted relationship between TAT achievement imagery and IQ gain increases one's confidence in the hypothesis that TAT plots can serve as an index of achievement-oriented tendencies. The results of the Rorschach analysis suggest that aggressive content may be an index of an individual's aggressive predispositions but not necessarily a measure of his tendency to express direct, physical aggression. Although Sontag, Baker, and Nelson (11), using behavioral observations, rated the boys in Group A as more competitive than those in Group D, there was no difference between these groups with respect to intensity or incidence of direct verbal or physical aggression or destruction of property. We have assumed that competition is a socially approved form of aggressive behavior and the higher incidence of aggressive content for Group A boys was presumed to be a result of their more intense competitive strivings. Some clinicians who use projective tests are too prone to focus on predictive statements about direct, physical aggression when confronted with a protocol containing aggressive content. One is apt to overlook the fact that the individual may have alternative behavioral channels for expression of aggressive motives.

SUMMARY

For a group of 140 boys and girls in the Fels Research population on whom continuous Binet IQ data were available, a distribution of IQ change was obtained by subtracting each S's smoothed IQ at age 6 from his smoothed IQ at age 10. This distribution of differences was divided into quartiles, and the Rorschach and TAT protocols of the upper (maximum increase in IQ) and lower (maximum decrease in IQ) quartiles were analyzed and compared. The results showed that in comparing the Ss who showed IQ increases with those showing IQ decreases, the former had, on the TAT, significantly more (a) achievement imagery on Cards 1 and 17 BM and (b) themes of curiosity about nature on Card 14, and significantly fewer themes of passivity on Card 3 BM. For the boys only, more of the Ss who increased in IQ had anatomy responses and aggressive imagery on the Rorschach. The results were interpreted as indicating that high need achievement, competitive striving, and curiosity about nature are correlated with gains in IQ score because they may facilitate the acquisition of skills that are measured by the intelligence test.

REFERENCES

1. BAKER, C. T., SONTAG, L. W., and NELSON, VIRGINIA L. Specific ability in IQ change. *J. consult. Psychol.*, 1955, *19*, 307-310.

2. BAYLEY, NANCY. Mental growth in young children, *Yearb. Nat. Soc. Stud. Educ.*, 1940, *39*, (II), 11-47.

3. BAYLEY, NANCY. Consistency and variability in the growth in IQ from birth to eighteen years. *J. genet. Psychol.*, 1949, *75*, 165-196.

4. BRADWAY, KATHERINE. IQ constancy on the Revised Stanford-Binet from the preschool to the junior high school level. *J. genet. Psychol.*, 1944, *65*, 197-217.

5. FISHER, R. A. *Statistical methods for research workers.* (5th ed.) Edinburgh: Oliver & Boyd, 1934.

6. HAGGARD, E. A., DAVIS, A., and HAVIGHURST, R. J. Some factors which influence performance of children on intelligence tests. *Amer. Psychol.*, 1948, *3*, 265-266.

7. KLETT, C. J. Performance of high school students on the Edwards Personal Preference Schedule. *J. consult. Psychol.*, 1957, *21*, 68-72.

8. MCCLELLAND, D. C., ATKINSON, J. W., CLARK, R. A., and LOWELL, E. L. *The achievement motive.* New York: Appleton-Century-Crofts, 1953.

9. RICHARDS, T. W. Mental test performance as a reflection of the child's current life situation: A methodological study. *Child Develpm.*, 1951, *22*, 221-233.

10. SONTAG, L. W., BAKER, C. T., and NELSON, VIRGINIA L. Personality as a determinant of performance. *Amer. J. Orthopsychiat.*, 1955, *25*, 555-562.

11. SONTAG, L. W., BAKER, C. T., and NELSON, VIRGINIA L. Mental growth and personality development. *Monogr. Soc. Res. Child Develpm.*, in press.

12. WELLMANN, BETH L., and MC CANDLESS, B. R. Factors associated with Binet IQ changes of preschool children. *Psychol. Monogr.*, 1946, *60*, No. 2 (Whole No. 278).

56/THE DISCOVERY AND ENCOURAGEMENT OF EXCEPTIONAL TALENT/

LEWIS M. TERMAN*

The following remarks were made by Professor E. C. Tolman, introducing Professor Lewis M. Terman in the first Walter Van Dyke Bingham lecture at the University of California at Berkeley, March 25, 1954:

Tonight we honor, and give thanks to, the memory of Walter Van Dyke Bingham. As Chairman of this country's first Department of Applied Psychology at the Carnegie Institute of Technology; as one of the two succeeding small groups of expert psychologists who developed the intelligence and classification tests used in the two World Wars; and as one who, in many prominent and key positions both in government and in industry, devoted almost his entire professional activity to the problems of the selection, management, and encouragement of personnel, Walter Bingham nonetheless remained profoundly disturbed at our prodigious waste of talent —at our society's failure to discover and encourage potential leaders.

And so at his death he left a memorandum desiring that money from his estate be used to support a series of annual lectures on "The Discovery and Development of Exceptional Abilities and Capacities." These lectures, for which we are grateful, are Walter Bingham's continuing contribution toward a better, a more free, and a more happy society.

The lectures are to be given at different universities and by those individuals who have made significant contributions to the problem of discovering and fostering high ability. This is the first lecture. And it is more than right that Professor Lewis M. Terman should have been chosen as the first lecturer. For Lewis Terman, in his development of the Stanford-Binet test and in his study of the gifted children, has made this country's outstanding research contribution to the problem of the discovery and understanding of intelligence.

At the close of the lecture, Mrs. Bingham, whom we have the honor of having with us tonight, will present two illuminated scrolls, one to the University of California, selected by a committee of the American Psychological Association as the locale for the first lecture (this scroll will be received by Dean Alva R. Davis in the name of the University); and one to Professor Terman, selected by the same committee as the first lecturer.

I take great professional and personal pleasure in introducing Lewis M. Terman, Professor Emeritus of Psychology, Stanford University, who will speak on "The Discovery and Encouragement of Exceptional Talent."

I AM DEEPLY SENSIBLE OF THE HONOR of being invited by the American Psychological Association, through its special committee, to give the initial lecture in the Walter V. Bingham Lectureship series.

I am especially happy that Chancellor Kerr and the psychology department of the University of California graciously acceded to my request that the address be given here, where I have many friends and where so much notable research has been done on the mental, physical, and personality development of children; where such famous experiments have been made on the purposive behavior of rats, both gifted and dull; where authoritarian minds have been so exhaustively probed; and where the recently established Institute of Personality Assessment is engaged in such promising investigations.

Before beginning my lecture I should like to pay tribute to the life work of the late Walter Van Dyke Bingham, at whose request this lectureship was established by Mrs. Bingham. Born in Iowa in 1880, young Walter early demonstrated his exceptional gifts by skipping both the third and fourth grades and by graduating from high school at the age of 16. As a freshman in college he was the youngest in his class and the only one to make a straight A record. After graduating from Beloit College he taught in high schools for four years, then entered the graduate school of the University of Chicago and in 1908 won his doctorate in psychology with honors. From 1908 to 1910 he was instructor at Teachers College and assistant to Edward L. Thorndike. In 1910 he was appointed assistant professor at Dartmouth to teach all their classes in psychology, but when he left there five years later the staff included an instructor and two full professors, all selected by Dr. Bingham. His rare ability to recognize exceptional talent is indicated by the fact that both of these professors became college presidents.

* Lewis M. Terman, The discovery and encouragement of exceptional talent, *American Psychologist*, 1954, 9, 221-230. Reprinted by permission.

From 1915 to 1924 Dr. Bingham was professor of psychology and head of the division of applied psychology at the Carnegie Institute of Technology, and it was here that he found the opportunity he had long wanted to promote large-scale investigations in applied psychology. The faculty he assembled for that purpose was one of the most distinguished ever brought together anywhere in this country. Among them were J. B. Miner, L. L. Thurstone, Walter Dill Scott, Kate Gordon, and E. K. Strong. Three others appointed as consultants were F. L. Wells, G. M. Whipple, and Raymond Dodge. It was this faculty that, under the wise leadership of Dr. Bingham, laid the solid foundation for vocational and industrial psychology in America.

When our country entered the war in 1917, nearly all of the Carnegie group were soon engaged in psychological work either for the Surgeon General or for the War Department or for both. Dr. Bingham was a member of Yerkes' committee of seven that devised the army mental tests, in 1917-18 was a member of the Committee on Classification of Personnel (the committee charged with devising and administering vocational tests in all the army camps), and in 1918-19 was Lt. Colonel in the Personnel Branch of the Army General Staff.

During World War II even greater service was rendered by Dr. Bingham as chief psychologist for the Office of Adjutant General from 1940 to 1946. In this capacity he and his committee were responsible not only for the Army General Classification Test that was administered to the many millions of inductees, but also for advising on the entire program of psychological services in the armed forces. In this capacity too he was in position to influence the selection of men best qualified to head the various branches of military psychology. I have no doubt that the extraordinary success of the work accomplished by psychologists during the war was largely due to his leadership and to his judgment of men.

If time permitted, I should like to tell you about his more than 200 publications, about the great variety of problems they dealt with, and the contributions they made in several fields of psychology, but I am sure that if Dr. Bingham were here he would want me to get on with our scheduled program.

I have often been asked how I happened to become interested in mental tests and gifted children. My first introduction to the scientific problems posed by intellectual differences occurred well over a half-century ago when I was a senior in psychology at Indiana University and was asked to prepare two reports for a seminar, one on mental deficiency and one on genius. Up to that time, despite the fact that I had graduated from a normal college as a Bachelor of Pedagogy and had taught school for five years, I had never so much as heard of a mental test. The reading for those two reports opened up a new world to me, the world of Galton, Binet, and their contemporaries. The following year my MA thesis on leadership among children (10) was based in part on tests used by Binet in his studies of suggestibility.

Then I entered Clark University, where I spent considerable time during the first year in reading on mental tests and precocious children. Child prodigies, I soon learned, were at that time in bad repute because of the prevailing belief that they were usually psychotic or otherwise abnormal and almost sure to burn themselves out quickly or to develop postadolescent stupidity. "Early ripe, early rot" was a slogan frequently encountered. By the time I reached my last graduate year, I decided to find out for myself how precocious children differ from the mentally backward, and accordingly chose as my doctoral dissertation an experimental study of the intellectual processes of fourteen boys, seven of them picked as the brightest and seven as the dullest in a large city school (11). These subjects I put through a great variety of intelligence tests, some of them borrowed from Binet and others, many of them new. The tests were given individually and required a total of 40 or 50 hours for each subject. The experiment contributed little or nothing to science, but it contributed a lot to my future thinking. Besides "selling" me completely on the value of mental tests as a research method, it offered an ideal escape from the kinds of laboratory work which I disliked and in which I was more than ordinarily inept. (Edward Thorndike confessed to me once that *his* lack of mechanical skill was partly responsible for turning *him* to mental tests and to the kinds of experiments on learning that required no apparatus.)

However, it was not until I got to Stanford in 1910 that I was able to pick up with mental tests where I had left off at Clark University. By that time Binet's 1905 and 1908 scales had been published, and the first thing I undertook at Stanford was a tentative revision of his 1908 scale. This, after further revisions, was published in 1916. The standardization of the scale was based on tests of a thousand children whose IQ's ranged from 60 to 145. The contrast in intellectual performance between the dullest and the brightest of a given age so intensified my earlier interest in the gifted that I decided to launch an ambitious study of such children at the earliest opportunity.

My dream was realized in the spring of 1921 when I obtained a generous grant from the Commonwealth Fund of New York City for the purpose of locating a thousand subjects of IQ 140 or higher. More than that number were selected by Stanford-Binet tests from the kindergarten through the eighth grade, and a group mental test given in 95 high schools provided nearly 400 additional subjects. The latter, plus those I had located before 1921, brought the number close to 1,500. The average IQ was approximately 150, and 80 were 170 or higher (13).

The twofold purpose of the project was, first of all, to find what traits characterize children of high IQ, and secondly, to follow them for as many years as possible to see what kind of adults they might become. This meant that it was necessary to select a group representative of high-testing children in general. With the help of four field assistants, we canvassed a school population of nearly a quarter-million in the urban and semiurban areas of California. Two careful checks on the methods used showed that not more than 10 or 12 per cent of the children who could have qualified for the group in the schools canvassed were missed. A sample of close to 90 per cent insured that whatever traits were typical of these children would be typical of high-testing children in any comparable school population.

Time does not permit me to describe the physical measurements, medical examinations, achievement tests, character and interest tests, or the trait ratings and other supplementary information obtained from parents and teachers. Nor can I here describe the comparative data we obtained for control groups of unselected children. The more important results, however, can be stated briefly: children of IQ 140 or higher are, in general, appreciably superior to unselected children in physique, health, and social adjustment; markedly superior in moral attitudes as measured either by character tests or by trait ratings; and vastly superior in their mastery of school subjects as shown by a three-hour battery of achievement tests. In fact, the typical child of the group had mastered the school subjects to a point about two grades beyond the one in which he was enrolled, some of them three or four grades beyond.) Moreover,

his ability as evidenced by achievement in the different school subjects is so general as to refute completely the traditional belief that gifted children are usually one-sided. I take some pride in the fact that not one of the major conclusions we drew in the early 1920's regarding the traits that are typical of gifted children has been overthrown in the three decades since then.

Results of thirty years' follow-up of these subjects by field studies in 1927-28, 1939-40, and 1951-52, and by mail follow-up at other dates, show that incidence of mortality, ill health, insanity, and alcoholism is in each case below that for the generality of corresponding age, that the great majority are still well adjusted socially, and that the delinquency rate is but a fraction of what it is in the general population. Two forms of our difficult Concept Mastery Test, devised especially to reach into the stratosphere of adult intelligence, have been administered to all members of the group who could be visited by the field assistants, including some 950 tested in 1939-40 and more than 1,000 in 1951-52. On both tests they scored on the average about as far above the generality of adults as they had scored above the generality of children when we selected them. Moreover, as Dr. Bayley and Mrs. Oden have shown, in the twelve-year interval between the two tests, 90 per cent increased their intellectual stature as measured by this test. "Early ripe, early rot" simply does not hold for these subjects. So far, no one has developed postadolescent stupidity!

As for schooling, close to 90 per cent entered college and 70 per cent graduated. Of those graduating, 30 per cent were awarded honors and about two-thirds remained for graduate work. The educational record would have been still better but for the fact that a majority reached college age during the great depression. In their undergraduate years 40 per cent of the men and 20 per cent of the women earned half or more of their college expenses, and the total of undergraduate and graduate expenses earned amounted to $670,000, not counting stipends from scholarships and fellowships, which amounted to $350,000.

The cooperation of the subjects is indicated by the fact that we have been able to keep track of more than 98 per cent of the original group, thanks to the rapport fostered by the incomparable field and office assistants I have had from the beginning of the study to the present. I dislike to think how differently things could have gone with helpers even a little less competent.

The achievement of the group to midlife is best illustrated by the case histories of the 800 men, since only a minority of the women have gone out for professional careers (15). By 1950, when the men had an average age of 40 years, they had published 67 books (including 46 in the fields of science, arts, and the humanities, and 21 books of fiction). They had published more than 1,400 scientific, technical, and professional articles; over 200 short stories, novelettes, and plays; and 236 miscellaneous articles on a great variety of subjects. They had also authored more than 150 patents. The figures on publications do not include the hundreds of publications by journalists that classify as news stories, editorials, or newspaper columns; nor do they include the hundreds if not thousands of radio and TV scripts.

The 800 men include 78 who have taken PhD degree or its equivalent, 48 with a medical degree, 85 with a law degree, 74 who are teaching or have taught in a four-year college or university, 51 who have done basic research in the physical sciences or engineering, and 104 who are engineers but have done only applied research or none. Of the scientists, 47 are listed in the 1949 edition of *American Men of Science*. Nearly all of these numbers are from 10 to 20 or 30 times as large as would be found for 800 men of corresponding age picked at random in the general population, and are sufficient answer to those who belittle the significance of IQ differences.

The follow-up of these gifted subjects has proved beyond question that tests of "general intelligence," given as early as six, eight, or ten years, tell a great deal about the ability to achieve either presently or 30 years hence. Such tests do not, however, enable us to predict what direction the achievement will take, and least of all do they tell us what personality factors or what accidents of fortune will affect the fruition of exceptional ability. Granting that both interest patterns and special aptitudes play important roles in the making of a gifted scientist, mathematician, mechanic, artist, poet, or musical composer, I am convinced that to achieve greatly in almost any field, the special talents have to be backed up by a lot of Spearman's *g*, by which is meant the kind of general intelligence that requires ability to form many sharply defined concepts, to manipulate them, and to perceive subtle relationships between them; in other words, the ability to engage in abstract thinking.

The study by Catharine Cox of the childhood traits of historical geniuses gives additional evidence regarding the role of general intelligence in exceptional achievement. That study was part of our original plan to investigate superior ability by two methods of approach: (*a*) by identifying and following living gifted subjects from childhood onward; and (*b*) by proceeding in the opposite direction and tracing the mature genius back to his childhood promise. With a second grant from the Commonwealth Fund, the latter approach got under way only a year later than the former and resulted in the magnum opus by Cox entitled *The Early Mental Traits of Three Hundred Geniuses* (1). Her subjects represented an unbiased selection from the top 510 in Cattell's objectively compiled list of the 1,000 most eminent men of history. Cox and two able assistants then scanned some 3,000 biographies in search of information that would throw light on the early mental development of these subjects. The information thus obtained filled more than 6,000 typed pages. Next, three psychologists familiar with mental age norms read the documentary evidence on all the subjects and estimated for each the IQ that presumably would be necessary to account for the intellectual behavior recorded for given chronological ages. Average of the three IQ estimates was used as the index of intelligence. In fact two IQ's were estimated for each subject, one based on the evidence to age 17, and the other on evidence to the mid-twenties. The recorded evidence on development to age 17 varied from very little to an amount that yielded about as valid an IQ as a good intelligence test would give. Examples of the latter are Goethe, John Stuart Mill, and Francis Galton. It was the documentary information on Galton, which I summarized and published in 1917 (12), that decided me to prepare plans for the kind of study that was carried out by Cox. The average of estimated IQ's for her 300 geniuses was 155, with many going as high as 175 and several as high as 200. Estimates below 120 occurred only when there was little biographical evidence about the early years.

It is easy to scoff at these post-mortem IQ's, but as one of the three psychologists who examined the evidence and made the IQ ratings, I think the author's main conclusion is fully warranted; namely, that "the genius who achieves highest eminence is one whom intelligence tests would have identified as gifted in childhood."

Special attention was given the geniuses who had sometime or other been labeled as backward in childhood, and in every one of these cases the facts clearly contradicted the legend. One of them was Oliver Goldsmith, of whom his childhood teacher is said to have said "Never was so dull a boy." The fact is that little Oliver was writing clever verse at 7 years and at 8 was reading Ovid and Horace. Another was Sir Walter Scott, who at 7 not only read widely in poetry but was using correctly in his written prose such words as "melancholy" and "exotic." Other alleged childhood dullards included a number who disliked the usual diet of Latin and Greek but had a natural talent for science. Among these were the celebrated German chemist Justus von Liebig, the great English anatomist John Hunter, and the naturalist Alexander von Humboldt, whose name is scattered so widely over the maps of the world.

In the cases just cited one notes a tendency for the direction of later achievement to be foreshadowed by the interests and preoccupations of childhood. I have tried to determine how frequently this was true of the 100 subjects in Cox's group whose childhood was best documented. Very marked foreshadowing was noted in the case of more than half of the group, none at all in less than a fourth. Macaulay, for example, began his career as historian at the age of 6 with what he called a "Compendium of Universal History," filling a quire of paper before he lost interest in the project. Ben Franklin before the age of 17 had displayed nearly all the traits that characterized him in middle life: scientific curiosity, religious heterodoxy, wit and buffoonery, political and business shrewdness, and ability to write. At 11 Pascal was so interested in mathematics that his father thought it best to deprive him of books on this subject until he had first mastered Latin and Greek. Pascal secretly proceeded to construct a geometry of his own and covered the ground as far as the 32nd proposition of Euclid. His father then relented. At 14 Leibnitz was writing on logic and philosophy and composing what he called "An Alphabet of Human Thought." He relates that at this age he took a walk one afternoon to consider whether he should accept the "doctrine of substantial forms."

Similar foreshadowing is disclosed by the case histories of my gifted subjects. A recent study of the scientists and nonscientists among our 800 gifted men (15) showed many highly significant differences between the early interests and social attitudes of those who became physical scientists and those who majored in the social sciences, law, or the humanities. Those in medical or biological sciences usually rated on such

variables somewhere between the physical scientists and the nonscientists.

What I especially want to emphasize, however, is that both the evidence on early mental development of historical geniuses and that obtained by follow-up of gifted subjects selected in childhood by mental tests point to the conclusion that capacity to achieve far beyond the average can be detected early in life by a well-constructed ability test that is heavily weighted with the g factor. It remains to be seen how much the prediction of future achievement can be made more specific as to field by getting, in addition, measures of ability factors that are largely independent of g. It would seem that a 20-year follow-up of the thousands of school children who have been given Thurstone's test of seven "primary mental abilities" would help to provide the answer. At present the factor analysts don't agree on how many "primary" mental abilities there are, nor exactly on what they are. The experts in this field are divided into two schools. The British school, represented by Thomson, Vernon, and Burt, usually stop with the identification of at most three or four group factors in addition to g, while some representing the American school feed the scores of 40 or 50 kinds of tests into a hopper and manage to extract from them what they believe to be a dozen or fifteen separate factors. Members of the British school are as a rule very skeptical about the realities underlying the minor group factors. There are also American psychologists, highly skilled in psychometrics, who share this skepticism. It is to be hoped that further research will give us more information than we now have about the predictive value of the group factors. Until such information is available, the scores on group factors can contribute little to vocational guidance beyond what a good test of general intelligence will provide.

I have always stressed the importance of *early* discovery of exceptional abilities. Its importance is now highlighted by the facts Harvey Lehman has disclosed in his monumental studies of the relation between age and creative achievement (8). The striking thing about his age curves is how early in life the period of maximum creativity is reached. In nearly all fields of science, the best work is done between ages 25 and 35, and rarely later than 40. The peak productivity for works of lesser merit is usually reached 5 to 10 years later; this is true in some twenty fields of science, in philosophy, in most kinds of musical composition, in art, and in literature of many varieties. The lesson for us from Lehman's statistics is that the youth of high achievement potential should be well trained for his life work before too many of his most creative years have been passed.

This raises the issue of educational acceleration for the gifted. It seems that the schools are more opposed to acceleration now than they were thirty years ago. The lockstep seems to have become more and more the fashion, notwithstanding the fact that practically everyone who has investigated the subject is against it. Of my gifted group, 29 per cent managed to graduate from high school before the age of 16½ years (62 of these before 15½), but I doubt if so many would be allowed to do so now. The other 71 per cent graduated between 16½ and 18½. We have compared the accelerated with the nonaccelerated on numerous case-history variables. The two groups differed very little in childhood IQ, their health records are equally good, and as adults they are equally well adjusted socially. More of the accelerates graduated from college, and on the average nearly a year and a half earlier than the nonaccelerates; they averaged higher in college grades and more often remained for graduate work. Moreover, the accelerates on the average married .7 of a year earlier, have a trifle lower divorce rate, and score just a little higher on a test of marital happiness (14). So far as college records of accelerates and nonaccelerates are concerned, our data closely parallel those obtained by the late Noel Keys (3) at the University of California and those by Pressey (9) and his associates at Ohio State University.

The Ford Fund for the Advancement of Education has awarded annually since 1951 some 400 college scholarships to gifted students who are not over 16½ years old, are a year or even two years short of high school graduation, but show good evidence of ability to do college work. Three quarters of them are between 15½ and 16½ at the time of college entrance. A dozen colleges and universities accept these students and are keeping close track of their success. A summary of their records for the first year shows that they not only get higher grades than their classmates, who average about two years older, but that they are also equally well adjusted socially and participate in as many extracurricular activities (17). The main problem the boys have is in finding girls to date who are not too old for them! Some of them have started a campaign to remedy the situation by urging that more of these scholarships be awarded to girls.

The facts I have given do not mean that all gifted children should be rushed through school just as rapidly as possible. If that were done, a majority with IQ of 140 could graduate from high school before the age of 15. I do believe, however, that such children should be promoted rapidly enough to permit college entrance by the age of 17 at latest, and that a majority would be better off to enter at 16. The exceptionally bright student who is kept with his age group finds little to challenge his intelligence and all too often develops habits of laziness that later wreck his college career. I could give you some choice examples of this in my gifted group. In the case of a college student who is preparing for a profession in science, medicine, law, or any field of advanced scholarship, graduation at 20 instead of the usual 22 means two years added to his professional career; or the two years saved could be used for additional training beyond the doctorate, if that were deemed preferable.

Learned and Wood (7) have shown by objective achievement tests in some 40 Pennsylvania colleges how little correlation there is between the student's knowledge and the number of months or years of his college attendance. They found some beginning sophomores who had acquired more knowledge than some seniors near their graduation. They found similarly low correlations between the number of course units a student had in a given field and the amount he knew in that field. Some with only one year of Latin had learned more than others with three years. And, believe it or not, they even found boys just graduating from high school who had more knowledge of science than some college seniors who had majored in science and were about to begin teaching science in high schools! The sensible thing to do, it seems, would be to quit crediting the individual high school or the individual college and begin crediting the individual student. That, essentially, is what the Ford Fund scholarships are intended to encourage.

Instruments that permit the identification of gifted subjects are available in great variety and at nearly all levels from the primary grades to the graduate schools in universities. My rough guess is that at the present time tests of achievement in the school subjects are being given in this country to children below high school at a rate of perhaps ten or twelve million a year, and to high school students another million or two. In addition, perhaps two million tests of intelligence are given annually in the elementary and high schools. The testing of college students began in a small way only 30 years ago; now almost every college in the country requires applicants for admission to take some kind of aptitude test. This is usually a test of general aptitude, but subject-matter tests and tests of special aptitudes are sometimes given to supplement the tests of general aptitude.

The testing movement has also spread rapidly in other countries, especially in Britain and the Commonwealth countries. Godfrey Thomson devised what is now called the Moray House test of intelligence in 1921 to aid in selecting the more gifted 11-year-olds in the primary schools for the privilege of free secondary education. This test has been revised and is given annually to about a half million scholarship candidates. The Moray House tests now include tests of English, arithmetic, and history. In 1932 the Scottish Council for Research in Education (18) arranged to give the Moray House test of intelligence (a group test) to all the 90,000 children in Scotland who were born in 1921, and actually tested some 87,000 of them. The Stanford-Binet tests have been translated and adapted for use in nearly all the countries of Europe and in several countries of Asia and Latin America. Behind the Iron Curtain, however, mental tests are now banned.

I have discussed only tests of intelligence and of school achievement. There is time to mention only a few of the many kinds of personality tests that have been developed during the last thirty-five years: personality inventories, projective techniques by the dozen, attitude scales by the hundred, interest tests, tests of psychotic and predelinquent tendencies, tests of leadership, marital aptitude, masculinity-femininity, et cetera. The current output of research on personality tests probably equals or exceeds that on intelligence and achievement tests, and is even more exciting.

Along with the increasing use of tests, and perhaps largely as a result of it, there is a growing interest, both here and abroad, in improving educational methods for the gifted. Acceleration of a year or two or three, however desirable, is but a fraction of what is needed to keep the gifted child or youth working at his intellectual best. The method most often advocated is curriculum enrichment for the gifted without segregating them from the ordinary class. Under ideal conditions enrichment can accomplish much, but in these days of crowded schools, when so many teachers are overworked, underpaid, and inadequately trained, curriculum enrichment for a few gifted in a large mixed class

cannot begin to solve the problem. The best survey of thought and action in this field of education is the book entitled *The Gifted Child*, written by many authors and published in 1951 (16). In planning for and sponsoring this book, The American Association for Gifted Children has rendered a great service to education.

But however efficient our tests may be in discovering exceptional talents, and whatever the schools may do to foster those discovered, it is the prevailing *Zeitgeist* that will decide, by the rewards it gives or withholds, what talents will come to flower. In Western Europe of the Middle Ages, the favored talents were those that served the Church by providing its priests, the architects of its cathedrals, and the painters of religious themes. A few centuries later the same countries had a renaissance that included science and literature as well as the arts. Although presumably there are as many potential composers of great music as there ever were, and as many potentially great artists as in the days of Leonardo da Vinci and Michaelangelo, I am reliably informed that in this country today it is almost impossible for a composer of *serious* music to earn his living except by teaching, and that the situation is much the same, though somewhat less critical, with respect to artists.

The talents most favored by the current *Zeitgeist* are those that can contribute to science and technology. If intelligence and achievement tests don't discover the potential scientist, there is a good chance that the annual Science Talent Search will, though not until the high school years. Since Westinghouse inaugurated in 1942 this annual search for the high school seniors most likely to become creative scientists, nearly 4,000 boys and girls have been picked for honors by Science Service out of the many thousands who have competed. As a result, "Science Clubs of America" now number 15,000 with a third of a million members—a twenty-fold increase in a dozen years (2). As our need for more and better scientists is real and urgent, one can rejoice at what the talent search and the science clubs are accomplishing. One may regret, however, that the spirit of the times is not equally favorable to the discovery and encouragement of potential poets, prose writers, artists, statesmen, and social leaders.

But in addition to the over-all climates that reflect the *Zeitgeist*, there are localized climates that favor or hinder the encouragement of given talents in particular colleges and universities. I have in mind especially two recent investigations of the differences among colleges in the later achievement of their graduates. One by Knapp and Goodrich (4) dealt with the undergraduate origin of 18,000 scientists who got the bachelor's degree between 1924 and 1934 and were listed in the 1944 edition of *American Men of Science*. The list of 18,000 was composed chiefly of men who had taken a PhD degree, but included a few without a PhD who were starred scientists. The IBM cards for these men were then sorted according to the college from which they obtained the bachelor's degree, and an index of productivity was computed for each college in terms of the proportion of its male graduates who were in the list of 18,000. Some of the results were surprising, not to say sensational. The institutions that were most productive of future scientists between 1924 and 1934 were not the great universities, but the small liberal arts colleges. Reed College topped the list with an index of 132 per thousand male graduates. The California Institute of Technology was second with an index of 70. Kalamazoo College was third with 66, Earlham fourth with 57, and Oberlin fifth with 56. Only a half-dozen of the great universities were in the top fifty with a productivity index of 25 or more.

The second study referred to was by Knapp and Greenbaum (5), who rated educational institutions according to the proportion of their graduate level in the six-year period from 1946 to 1951. Three kinds of awards were considered: a PhD degree, a graduate scholarship or fellowship paying at least $400 a year, or a prize at the graduate level won in open competition. The roster of awardees they compiled included 7,000 students who had graduated from 377 colleges and universities. This study differs from the former in three respects: (*a*) it deals with recent graduates, who had not had time to become distinguished but who could be regarded as good bets for the future; (*b*) these good bets were classified according to whether the major field was science, social science, or the humanities; and (*c*) data were obtained for both sexes, though what I shall report here relates only to men. In this study the great universities make a better showing than in the other, but still only a dozen of them are in the top fifty institutions in the production of men who are good bets. In the top ten, the University of Chicago is third, Princeton is eighth, and Harvard is tenth; the other seven in order of rank are Swarthmore 1, Reed 2, Oberlin 4, Haverford 5, California Institute of Technology 6, Carleton 7, and Antioch 9. When the schools were listed separately for production of men

who were good bets in science, social science, and the humanities, there were eight that rated in the top twenty on all three lists. These were Swarthmore, Reed, Chicago, Harvard, Oberlin, Antioch, Carleton, and Princeton.

The causes of these differences are not entirely clear. Scores on aptitude tests show that the intelligence of students in a given institution is by no means the sole factor, though it is an important one. Other important factors are the quality of the school's intellectual climate, the proportion of able and inspiring teachers on its faculty, and the amount of conscious effort that is made not only to discover but also to motivate the most highly gifted. The influence of motivation can hardly be exaggerated.

In this address I have twice alluded to the fact that achievement in school is influenced by many things other than the sum total of intellectual abilities. The same is true of success in life. In closing I will tell you briefly about an attempt we made a dozen years ago to identify some of the nonintellectual factors that have influenced life success among the men in my gifted group. Three judges, working independently, examined the records (to 1940) of the 730 men who were then 25 years old or older, and rated each on life success. The criterion of "success" was the extent to which a subject had made use of his superior intellectual ability, little weight being given to earned income. The 150 men rated highest for success and the 150 rated lowest were then compared on some 200 items of information obtained from childhood onward (14). How did the two groups differ?

During the elementary school years, the A's and C's (as we call them) were almost equally successful. The average grades were about the same, and average scores on achievement tests were only a trifle higher for the A's. Early in high school the groups began to draw apart in scholarship, and by the end of high school the slump of the C's was quite marked. The slump could not be blamed on extracurricular activities, for these were almost twice as common among the A's. Nor was much of it due to difference in intelligence. Although the A's tested on the average a little higher than the C's both in 1922 and 1940, the average score made by the C's in 1940 was high enough to permit brilliant college work, in fact was equaled by only 15 per cent of our highly selected Stanford students. Of the A's, 97 per cent entered college and 90 per cent graduated; of the C's, 68 per cent entered but only 37 per cent graduated. Of those who graduated, 52 per cent of the A's but only 14 per cent of the C's graduated with honors. The A's were also more accelerated in school; on the average they were six months younger on completing the eighth grade, 10 months younger at high school graduation, and 15 months younger at graduation from college.

The differences between the educational histories of the A's and C's reflect to some degree the differences in their family backgrounds. Half of the A fathers but only 15 per cent of the C fathers were college graduates, and twice as many of A siblings as of C siblings graduated. The estimated number of books in the A homes was nearly 50 per cent greater than in the C homes. As of 1928, when the average age of the subjects was about 16 years, more than twice as many of the C parents as of A parents had been divorced.

Interesting differences between the groups were found in the childhood data on emotional stability, social adjustments, and various traits of personality. Of the 25 traits on which each child was rated by parent and teacher in 1922 (18 years before the A and C groups were made up), the only trait on which the C's averaged as high as the A's was general health. The superiority of the A's was especially marked in four volitional traits: prudence, self-confidence, perseverance, and desire to excel. The A's also rated significantly higher in 1922 on leadership, popularity, and sensitiveness to approval or disapproval. By 1940 the difference between the groups in social adjustment and all-round mental stability had greatly increased and showed itself in many ways. By that time four-fifths of the A's had married, but only two-thirds of the C's, and the divorce rate for those who had married was twice as high for the C's as for the A's. Moreover, the A's made better marriages; their wives on the average came from better homes, were better educated, and scored higher on intelligence tests.

But the most spectacular differences between the two groups came from three sets of ratings, made in 1940, on a dozen personality traits. Each man rated himself on all the traits, was rated on them by his wife if he had a wife, and by a parent if a parent was still living. Although the three sets of ratings were made independently, they agreed unanimously on the four traits in which the A and C groups differed most widely. These were "persistence in the accomplishment of ends," "integration toward goals, as contrasted with drifting," "self-confidence," and "freedom from inferiority feelings." For each trait three critical ratios were

computed showing, respectively, the reliability of the A-C differences in average of self-ratings, ratings by wives, and ratings by parents. The average of the three critical ratios was 5.5 for perseverance, 5.6 for integration toward goals, 3.7 for self-confidence, and 3.1 for freedom from inferiority feelings. These closely parallel the traits that Cox found to be especially characteristic of the 100 leading geniuses in her group whom she rated on many aspects of personality; their three outstanding traits she defined as "persistence of motive and effort," "confidence in their abilities," and "strength or force of character."

There was one trait on which only the parents of our A and C men were asked to rate them; that trait was designated "common sense." As judged by parents, the A's are again reliably superior, the A-C difference in average rating having a critical ratio of 3.9. We are still wondering what self-ratings by the subjects and ratings of them by their wives on common sense would have shown if we had been impudent enough to ask for them!

Everything considered, there is nothing in which our A and C groups present a greater contrast than in drive to achieve and in all-round mental and social adjustment. Our data do not support the theory of Lange-Eichbaum (6) that great achievement usually stems from emotional tensions that border on the abnormal. In our gifted group, success is associated with stability rather than instability, with absence rather than with presence of disturbing conflicts —in short with well-balanced temperament and with freedom from excessive frustrations. The Lange-Eichbaum theory may explain a Hitler, but hardly a Churchill; the junior senator from Wisconsin, possibly, but not a Jefferson or a Washington.

At any rate, we have seen that intellect and achievement are far from perfectly correlated. To identify the internal and external factors that help or hinder the fruition of exceptional talent, and to measure the extent of their influences, are surely among the major problems of our time. These problems are not new; their existence has been recognized by countless men from Plato to Francis Galton. What is new is the general awareness of them caused by the manpower shortage of scientists, engineers, moral leaders, statesmen, scholars, and teachers that the country must have if it is to survive in a threatened world. These problems are now being investigated on a scale never before approached, and by a new generation of workers in several related fields. Within a couple of decades vastly more should be known than we know today about our resources of potential genius, the environmental circumstances that favor its expression, the emotional compulsions that give it dynamic quality, and the personality distortions that can make it dangerous.

REFERENCES

1. COX, CATHARINE C. *The early mental traits of three hundred geniuses*. Vol. II of *Genetic studies of genius*, Terman, L. M. (Ed.). Stanford: Stanford Univer. Press, 1926.

2. DAVIS, W. Communicating science. *J. atomic Scientists*, 1953, 337-340.

3. KEYS, N. The underage student in high school and college. *Univer. Calif. Publ. Educ.*, 1938, 7, 145-272.

4. KNAPP, R. H., and GOODRICH, H. B. *Origins of American scientists*. Chicago: Univer. of Chicago Press, 1952.

5. KNAPP, R. H., and GREENBAUM, J. J. *The younger American scholar: his collegiate origins*. Chicago: Univer. of Chicago Press, 1953.

6. LANGE-EICHBAUM, W. *The problem of genius*. New York: Macmillan, 1932.

7. LEARNED, W. S., and WOOD, B. D. The student and his knowledge. *Carnegie Found. Adv. Teaching Bull.*, 1938, No. 29.

8. LEHMAN, H. C. *Age and achievement*. Princeton: Princeton Univer. Press, 1953.

9. PRESSEY, S. L. *Educational acceleration: appraisals and basic problems*. Columbus: Ohio State Univer. Press, 1949.

10. TERMAN, L. M. A preliminary study in the psychology and pedagogy of leadership. *Pedag. Sem.*, 1904, *11*, 413-451.

11. TERMAN, L. M. Genius and stupidity: a study of some of the intellectual processes of seven "bright" and seven "dull" boys. *Pedag. Sem.*, 1906, *13*, 307-373.

12. TERMAN, L. M. The intelligence quotient of Francis Galton in childhood. *Amer. J. Psychol.*, 1917, *28*, 209-215.

13. TERMAN, L. M. (Ed.), et al. *Mental and physical traits of a thousand gifted children*. Vol. I of *Genetic studies of genius*, Terman, L. M. (Ed.). Stanford: Stanford Univer. Press, 1925.

14. TERMAN, L. M., and ODEN, M. H. *The gifted child grows up*. Vol. IV of *Genetic studies of genius*, Terman, L. M. (Ed.). Stanford: Stanford Univ. Press, 1947.

15. TERMAN, L. M. Scientists and nonscientists in a group of 800 gifted men. *Psychol. Monogr.*, 1954, *68*, in press.

16. WITTY, P. (Ed.) *The gifted child*. Boston: Health, 1951.

17. *Bridging the gap between school and college*. New York: The Fund for the Advancement of Education, 1953.

18. *The intelligence of Scottish children*. Scottish Council for Research in Education. London: Univer. of London Press, 1933.

"I think that children are more intelligent and less experienced than most parents realize. I have tried to treat my son as if he were a beloved companion with whom I was traveling in a country where I had been before and he had not."

Frederick Lewis Allen
(quoted in *Reader's Digest*,
February 1959, page 28)

57/A NEW LOOK AT THE CREATIVITY-INTELLIGENCE DISTINCTION[1]/

MICHAEL A. WALLACH AND NATHAN KOGAN[*]

FOR SEVERAL YEARS WE HAVE BEEN concerned with two modes of thinking in young children, which, it turns out, bear directly upon what has assumed the proportions of a controversy in recent psychological history. The nature of the controversy might be put somewhat as follows: Is there an aspect of cognitive functioning which can be appropriately labled "creativity" that stands apart from the traditional concept of general intelligence? A close appraisal of the quantitative findings available on this subject led us to a pessimistic answer. We shall pass some of these findings quickly in review. Our examination of this literature opened up to us, however, the possibility of a valid distinction between creativity and intelligence that had not, in our view, been sufficiently pursued and developed. The next step, therefore, was empirical research in terms of this distinction. Finally, if creativity and intelligence could be validly distinguished, we were interested in studying the possible psychological correlates that might distinguish individual differences on these two dimensions considered jointly. Specifically, we were concerned with correlates in such areas as the child's observed behavior in school and play settings, his aesthetic sensitivities, his categorizing and conceptualizing activities, his test anxiety and defensiveness levels. We can, of course, give but an overview of this work. For a complete presentation, see Wallach and Kogan (1965).

We began with a simple question: Does the relevant psychological literature support the as-sumption of a unified dimension of individual differences describing more and less creative cognitive behavior? To put this question another way, can one demonstrate the existence of greater and lesser degrees of a cognitive capability that is like intelligence in regard to being a pervasive, broad dimension, but yet is independent of intelligence, and which can appropriately be labeled "creativity?" It is clear that to talk of "creativity" is to imply a referent different from that of the general intelligence concept. If that is not intended, then the creativity label becomes quite superfluous. The typical evidence that we found on this issue led, however, to an opposite conclusion. Let us consider an example.

The volume by Getzels and Jackson (1962), *Creativity and Intelligence,* is perhaps the best known of recent efforts in the field. Five alleged tests of creativity were administered to large samples of students ranging in class from sixth grade through the end of high school. Four of the five creativity tests correlated significantly with IQ for the girls, and all five of these tests correlated significantly with IQ for the boys. Consider next the relationships among the instruments in the creativity battery—that is, the question of whether they define a unitary dimension of individual differences. The Getzels-Jackson results showed that the five creativity tasks are virtually no more strongly correlated among themselves than they are correlated with intelligence. To give some averages, for boys the mean correlation is .26 between the creativity battery and IQ, and is .28 among the tasks in the creativity battery; in the case of the girls, the corresponding mean correlations are .27 and .32. In sum, the creativity measures correlated with intelligence on the order of .3, and also correlated with each other on the order of .3. There is no evidence, in short, for arguing that the creativity instruments are any more strongly related to one another than they are related to general intelligence. The inevitable conclusion is that little warrant exists here for talking about creativity *and* intelligence as if these terms re-

[1] The research reported herein was supported through the Cooperative Research Program of the Office of Education, United States Department of Health, Education, and Welfare, Project No. 1316B. This paper was presented in abridged form at a symposium, "Current Issues in Creativity Research," sponsored by Division 15 of the American Psychological Association, Los Angeles, California, September, 1964. The material is adapted with the permission of the publisher from *Modes of Thinking in Young Children: A Study of the Creativity-Intelligence Distinction*, by M. A. Wallach and N. Kogan. New York: Holt, Rinehart and Winston, 1965.

[*] Michael A. Wallach and Nathan Kogan, A new look at the creativity-intelligence distinction, *Journal of Personality*, 1965, *33*, 348-369.

fer to concepts at the same level of abstraction. The creativity indicators measure nothing in common that is distinct from general intelligence. Inspection of the creativity battery reveals a quite varied range of materials, including measures of the ability to devise mathematical problems, to compose endings for fables, to detect embedded geometric figures, to think up word definitions, and to imagine uses for an object.

Comparable examination of other research reports in the literature forced us to the same kind of conclusion. Our survey included the study of findings reported by Torrance and his co-workers (e.g., Torrance, 1960; 1962; Torrance & Gowan, 1963), Guilford and his collaborators (e.g., Guilford & Christensen, 1956; Wilson, Guilford, Christensen, & Lewis, 1954), Cline, Richards, and Needham (1963), Cline, Richards, and Abe (1962), Barron (1963), and Flescher (1963). To give but one more example of the kind of outcome obtained, consider a recent study by Cline, Richards, and Needham (1963). With high school students as Ss and seven creativity measures, the average correlation for boys between the creativity indexes and an IQ measure is .35, while it is .21 among the various creativity tests. For girls, the average correlation between the creativity tests and IQ is .33, while it is .24 among the seven creativity measures. Again and again in reviewing the research in this area, the evidence led to the conclusion that the various creativity measures utilized are almost as strongly, equally strongly, or even more strongly related to general intelligence than they are related to each other. The evidence in hand thus seemed not to permit the very type of conceptualization that Getzels and Jackson (1962) and other researchers were proposing: namely, that there exists a pervasive dimension of individual differences, appropriately labeled "creativity," that is quite distinct from general intelligence. We should note that this same critical point has been made by Thorndike (1963) in a recent article.

Appropriate wielding of Occam's razor at this juncture thus dictated the tough-minded conclusion that little of any generality was being measured here beyond differences in the traditional notion of intelligence. Let us pose two issues, however, that made it seem premature to let the matter go at that. First, a potpourri of abilities was being assessed in the good name of "creativity"; second, all of the work that we had seen failed to consider the implications of the social psychology of the assessment situation

within which measurement of "creativity" was attemped. Consider each of these points in turn.

If we return to the introspections of highly creative artists and scientists, one major focus emerges. The majority of the available introspective accounts have in common a concern with associative freedom and uniqueness. These accounts consistently stress the ability to give birth to associative content that is abundant and original, yet relevant to the task at hand rather than bizarre. The writer's classical fear of "drying up" and never being able to produce another word, the composer's worry over not having another piece of music within him, the scientist's concern that he won't be able to think of another experiment to perform—these are but indications of how preoccupied creative individuals can become with the question of associative flow. Introspections about times of creative insight also seem to reflect a kind of task-centered, permissive, or playful set on the part of the person doing the associating. Einstein refers to "associative play" or "combinatory play." The person stands aside a bit as associative material is given freedom to reach the surface.

We would propose that the essentials of the creative process may be contained in the two elements just considered: first, the production of associative content that is abundant and that is unique; second, the presence in the associator of a playful, permissive task attitude. Given a task clear enough that bizarre associative products do not readily occur, and given a permissive context within which the person works, two variables should permit us to index individual differences in creativity: the number of associations that the person can generate in response to given tasks, and the relative uniqueness of the associations that he produces.

One implication of this view is that productivity and uniqueness of associates should be related variables. Defining uniqueness as a relative infrequency of a given associative response to the task at hand for a sample of Ss, we would then expect stereotyped associates to come earlier and unique associates to come later in a sequence of responses. Such an expectation would also be consistent with recent work by Mednick (e.g., 1962). If unique associates tend to come later in time, then it becomes clear also that an appropriate assessment context will require freedom from the pressure of short time limits, and perhaps freedom from any temporal pressure at all. The postulated need for a permissive, playful attitude also implies the desirability of freedom from time pressure. Such temporal freedom is one aspect of what a permissive situation would involve. Permissiveness further connotes a relative lessening of valuational pressures—that is, a focus upon the task rather than upon the self, a relaxed entertaining of the possible rather than tense insistence upon an answer that must be correct if one is not to lose face. The Taoists, as discussed by Rugg (1963), have called such a relaxed attitude a state of "letting things happen." Clearly, we are describing a type of situation in which the individual does not feel that he is being tested, and hence does not feel that what he does will have a bearing upon his self-worth in the eyes of others.

The foregoing analysis of creativity hence suggests a concentration of assessment attempts in the area of associational processes, in contrast to the quite heterogeneous types of tasks that have received the "creativity" label in studies of the kind touched upon earlier. This theoretical analysis also suggests that the assessment context must be quite different from the kind utilized in the studies that we have reviewed; there should be freedom from time pressure and there should be a playful, game-like context rather than one implying that the person is under test. Interestingly enough, the kind of context present in the case of all of the studies on creativity that we reviewed earlier has borne strong connotations that a test or examination is at issue; the creativity procedures invariably have been referred to as "tests," they have been administered to large groups of students in a classroom, and temporal constraint has been present—either explicitly, through the use of relatively brief time limits, or implicitly, through the use of group administration procedures. In all of this work, there has been the evident assumption that a testing context, with its implication that the respondent is being evaluated in terms of some success-failure criterion, is quite appropriate for studying creativity. The associative approach to creativity that we have taken, however, with its emphasis upon an attitude of playful entertaining of possibilities in a task-centered rather than ego-centered environment, suggests otherwise.

At this point we were ready to begin some experimentation of our own. Following the prescriptions just stated, could one empirically define a dimension of individual differences that concerned the ability to produce many cognitive associates, and many that are unique?

Would this dimension possess a substantial degree of generality across differences in types of tasks—for example, verbal vs. visual kinds of procedural formats? Such a contrast was of special interest since the general intelligence concept is defined with respect to a kind of ability that manifests itself in visual (performance) as well as verbal types of tasks, and we were presuming to assess a characteristic possessing approximately the same level of generality as conventional intelligence. Finally, and most important, would the foregoing dimension of associational ability be independent of individual differences in the traditional area of general intelligence? If research findings could provide affirmative answers to these questions, then, and only then, would one be in a position to talk about a kind of thinking ability appropriately labeled *creativity*, with the evident implication of a characteristic different from general intelligence, but yet a characteristic which also possesses a substantial degree of generality across task variations.

Our work, conducted with 151 children comprising the entire fifth-grade population of a suburban public school system in a middle class region, took great pains to establish a game-like, non-evaluational context for the administration of procedures. The *E*s, two young women, were introduced as visitors interested in children's games, and spent two initial weeks with each class gaining rapport with the children. This initial period of familiarization also provided the basis for observations leading to ratings of the children's behavior on various dimensions, to be discussed later. Great effort was expended in communicating to the children that the presence of the *E*s did not concern examinations or tests. The teachers and principals, furthermore, did their utmost to dissociate the *E*s from any concern with intellectual evaluation. Finally, it was our view that the establishment of a game-like context required the *E*s to work individually with each of the 151 children. We sedulously avoided group administration with its academic testing implications.

Five procedures formed the basis for our exploration of creativity in these children. They concerned the generation of five kinds of associates. Two variables were measured in the case of each: uniqueness of associates, and total number of associates. Some of the procedures were verbal, others were visual in nature. One verbal procedure, for example, requested the child to generate possible instances of a verbally specified class concept, such as "round things," or "things that move on wheels." Here and for every other creativity procedure, the child is given as much time on each item as he desires. Number of unique responses to an item is defined as the number of responses given by only one child in the sample of 151 to the item in question. Total number of responses offered to an item is, of course, self-defining. For "round things," for example, "life savers" is a unique response, while "buttons" is not. Another verbal procedure requests the child to think of possible uses for various objects presented orally, such as "shoe" or "cork." "To trap a mouse in," is a unique use suggested for "shoe," while to throw at a noisy cat" is not. A third verbal procedure asks the child to propose possible similarities between two objects specified in verbal terms. For instance, one pair is "train and tractor," another is "milk and meat." A unique response to "milk and meat" was "they are government-inspected," while "they come from animals" was not unique. The visual procedures, in turn, request the child to think of possible interpretations or meanings for each of various abstract visual patterns and line forms.

These procedures obviously owe a debt to the Guilford group. They are administered, however, in a carefully constructed game-like context, with each child taken individually and encouraged to spend as much time as he wishes, in a relaxed atmosphere, on every item. These administration arrangements were very different from those employed by the Guilford group. It should be emphasized, furthermore, that the use of a game-like context did not lead to a violation of the task constraints present in the various items of the procedure. Bizarre or inappropriate responses were exceedingly rare.

To assess the traditionally demarcated area of general intelligence, ten indicators were utilized. These included verbal and performance subtests from the Wechsler Intelligence Scale for Children (Wechsler, 1949); the School and College Ability Tests, which provide measures of verbal and quantitative aptitude (Cooperative Test Division, 1957a; 1957b); and the Sequential Tests of Educational Progress, which provide yardsticks of achievement in various academic content areas (Cooperative Test Division, 1957c; 1957d; 1959).

The ten creativity indicators—a uniqueness and a productivity measure for each of five procedures—proved to be highly reliable, in terms of both split-half and item-sum correlations. The reliabilities of the ten intelligence instruments, in turn, are known to be quite

high. We now were in a position, therefore, to study the dimensionality of the creativity and intelligence indexes. The findings were as follows. Whether examining results for the sample as a whole, or separately for the 70 boys and the 81 girls, the ten creativity measures proved to be highly intercorrelated, the ten intelligence measures proved to be highly intercorrelated, and the correlation *between* the creativity and the intelligence measures proved to be extremely low. To provide an idea of the correlational magnitudes involved, the average correlation among the ten creativity measures is on the order of .4; the average correlation among the ten intelligence indicators is on the order of .5; and the average correlation between these two sets of measures is about .1.

We may conclude, therefore, that a dimension of individual differences has been defined here which, on the one hand, possesses generality and pervasiveness, but which, on the other hand, nevertheless is quite independent of the traditional notion of general intelligence. This new dimension concerns a child's ability to generate unique and plentiful associates, in a generally task-appropriate manner, and in a relatively playful context. It is a considerable surprise that such a dimension should prove to be quite independent of general intelligence, and it seems indeed appropriate to label this dimension "creativity." The independence of this dimension from general intelligence seems all the more intriguing for two reasons: first, the creativity procedures almost inevitably call upon verbal facility in some degree, and verbal facility is a very basic element of the general intelligence concept; second, the independence in question is found for elementary school children, and one would expect young children to show less differentiation in modes of cognitive functioning than adults.

In a sense, all that has been described thus far constitutes a prelude. Having isolated a mode of thinking in children that is pervasive, independent of intelligence, and appropriately described as a dimension of individual differences in "creativity," we now wish to understand its psychological significance. The appropriate research strategy at this point seemed to require consideration of individual differences on the creativity and the intelligence dimensions taken *jointly*. That is, a child's location had to be defined with respect both to general intelligence and to creativity as we have conceived of it. It was necessary, in other words, to compose four groups of children within each sex: those high in both creativity and intelligence, those high in one and low in the other, and those low in both. In order to define these groups, a single creativity index score and a single intelligence index score were obtained for each child. These index scores were the summed standard scores of the ten measures in each respective domain. The distributions of creativity index scores and of intelligence index scores then were dichotomized at their respective medians, within sex, to yield the groups that exemplified the four possible combinations of creativity and intelligence levels. The two sexes, incidentally, were quite similar with regard to the distributions of these index scores. Since all cases were retained, rather than just the extremes, it is evident that the procedure used for composing creativity and intelligence combinations was a conservative one.

Consider now some of the psychological differences that we found to distinguish children who are both creative and intelligent, creative but not intelligent, intelligent but not creative, and neither creative nor intelligent.

To begin with, we turn to the behavior of these several groups of children in the school environment. The two Es made independent ratings of the children along specifically defined behavioral dimensions during an initial two weeks of observation in each class. This work was carried out prior to any further contact with the children, so that the ratings could not be influenced by the performances of the children on the various experimental procedures used in our research. Furthermore, no other possible sources of information about the children were made available to the raters during the observation period. In short, every effort was made to insure that the ratings would be unbiased.

It should also be mentioned that these rating dimensions possess high inter-rater reliability, a very important point that the use of two independent observers permitted us to establish. Without this kind of reliability, investigation of individual differences on these behavioral dimensions would have been fruitless.

The judges rated each child's status on a given dimension in terms of a nine-point scale. For example, one characteristic was defined in terms of the following question: "To what degree does this child seek attention in unsocialized ways, as evidenced by such behavior as speaking out of turn, continually raising his hand, or making unnecessary noises?" The first, third, fifth, seventh, and ninth points on the rating scale

for this question were given the verbal labels "never," "seldom," "sometimes," "usually," and "always," respectively. Other questions rated in the same manner included: "To what degree does this child hesitate to express opinions, as evidenced by extreme caution, failure to contribute, or a subdued manner in a speaking situation?" "To what degree does this child show confidence and assurance in his actions toward his teachers and classmates, as indicated by such behavior as not being upset by criticism, or not being disturbed by rebuffs from classmates?" "To what degree is this child's companionship sought by his peers?" "To what degree does this child seek the companionship of his peers?"

The preceding questions were focused upon issues of social behavior. Several questions of an achievement-centered nature also were included. These inquired about such matters as the following: "How would you rate this child's attention span and degree of concentration for academic school work?" "How would you rate this child's interest in academic school work, as indicated by such behavior as looking forward to new kinds of academic work, or trying to delve more deeply into such work?" For these questions, the first, third, fifth, seventh, and ninth points of the rating scales were labeled "poor," "below average," "average," "good," and "superior," respectively.

Let us look in some detail at the results for the girls. Those high in both creativity and intelligence show the least doubt and hesitation of all the groups, show the highest level of self-confidence, and display the least tendency toward depreciation of oneself and one's work. Concerning companionship, these girls are sought out by their peers more eagerly than is any other group, and this high intelligence-high creativity group also seeks the companionship of others more actively than does any other group. There is reciprocity in social relationships for the members of this group. With regard to achievement, this group shows the highest levels of attention span, concentration, and interest in academic work. In all of these respects, the high-high group obviously is reflecting highly desirable modes of conduct in both the social and the achievement spheres. Interestingly enough, however, this group also is high in regard to disruptive, attention-seeking behavior. The high-high children may well be brimming over with eagerness to propose novel, divergent possibilities in the classroom, in the face of boredom with the customary classroom routines. Against the context of classroom programs that emphasize equal participation by class members and academic values that are likely to center around the traditional intelligence dimension, the cognitive behavior reflected in high creativity levels in the case of these girls may well possess a nuisance value and exert a rather disruptive effect in the classroom situation.

Consider next the group high in creativity but low in intelligence. In many respects it turns out that this group is at the greatest disadvantage of all in the classroom—and, indeed, under more of a disadvantage than the group which is low in both creativity and intelligence. Those of high creativity but low intelligence are the most cautious and hesitant of all the groups, the least confident and least self-assured, the least sought after by their peers as companions, and in addition are quite avoidant themselves of the companionship of others. There is a mutuality of social avoidance in the case of these girls. In the academic sphere, they are the most deprecatory of their own work and the least able to concentrate and maintain attention. In terms of the ratings for disruptive attention-seeking, however, these girls are high, and in this one respect similar to the high creativity-high intelligence group. Most likely, however, the attention-seeking of these two groups is quite different in quality, given the highly different contexts of other behaviors in the two cases. While the disruptive behaviors of the high-high group suggest enthusiasm and overeagerness, those of the high creative-low intelligent group suggest an incoherent protest against their plight.

It affords an interesting comparison to turn next to the group low in both intelligence and creativity. These girls actually seem to be better off than their high creativity-low intelligence peers. The low-low group possesses greater confidence and assurance, is less hesitant and subdued, and is considerably more outgoing toward peers in social relationships than is the high creative-low intelligent group. The low-low group members appear to compensate for their poor academic performances by activity in the social sphere, while the high creative-low intelligent individuals, possessing seemingly more delicate sensitivities, are more likely to cope with academic failure by social withdrawal and a retreat within themselves.

Finally, we turn to the group high in intelligence but low in creativity. As in the case of the high-high group, these girls show confidence and assurance. In terms of companionship patterns, however, an intriguing difference emerges. While sought quite strongly as a companion by others, the girl in this group tends not to seek companionship herself. She also is least likely to seek attention in disruptive ways and is reasonably hesitant about expressing opinions. Attention span and concentration for academic matters, in turn, are quite high. The impression that emerges, then, is of a girl who is strongly oriented toward academic achievement, is somewhat cool and aloof in her social behavior but liked by others anyway, and is unwilling to take the chance of overextending or overcommitting herself; there is a holding back, a basic reserve.

These results make it clear that one needs to know whether creativity in a child is present in the context of high or low intelligence, and one needs to know whether intelligence in a child is present in conjunction with high or low creativity. It is necessary to consider a child's joint standing on both dimensions. One must seriously question, therefore, the Getzels and Jackson (1962) procedure of defining a "high creative" group as children who are high in creativity *but* low in intelligence, and defining a "high intelligent" group as children who are high in intelligence *but* low in creativity. If one wishes to establish generalizations about the nature of creativity and of intelligence as distinct characteristics, one cannot afford to ignore those children who are high in both and who are low in both.

Let us consider now some evidence in a different area—that of conceptualizing activities. This evidence will cast light on differences among the groups of boys. In one of our procedures, the child was asked to group pictures of everyday physical objects, and was requested to give the reason for his grouping in each case. Among the 50 objects pictured were, for example, a rake, a screwdriver, a telephone, a lamppost, a candle. The groupings were to be carried out in terms of putting together things that seem to belong together. When this phase was completed, reasons for grouping were obtained. These reasons later were content-analyzed—blindly, of course, with respect to the identities of the children—and the reliability of the content analysis system was evaluated by having all materials scored by two independent judges. Reliability was found to be quite high. Consider briefly now one of the content-analysis distinctions employed.

We were interested in contrasting relational or thematic reasons for grouping with reasons based upon abstracted similarities among the objects. In the latter type of reason, every object in the group is an independent instance of the label applied, whether the labels refer to shared physical properties or to shared conceptual properties. An example of the physical-descriptive type of category would be the label, "hard objects," for a group consisting of a lamp-post, a door, and a hammer. An example of the conceptual-inferential type of category would be the label, "for eating," in the case of a group containing a fork, a spoon, a cup, and a glass. By a relational or thematic type of reason, on the other hand, we refer to a label deriving from the relationship among the objects in the group; no single object is an independent instance of the concept, but rather all of the objects in the grouping are required in order to define it. An example of a thematic category is the label, "getting ready to go out," for a group consisting of a comb, a lipstick, a watch, a pocketbook, and a door.

The distinctions just made derive from work carried out by Kagan, Moss, and Sigel (1960, 1963), with certain modifications necessitated by the nature of the stimuli. It has typically been assumed by these investigators as well as by others that responding on a relational or the-matic basis represents an intellectually inferior manifestation. This may well be true when the stimuli to be grouped are few in number and their thematic characteristics highly salient, as has been the case in the studies just cited. The-matizing under such circumstances may repre-sent a passive, global approach to the materials provided. In the procedure that we employed, however, a large number of stimuli—50 in all—were present, and their nature as well as the instructional context were such as to reduce markedly the *Eindringlichkeit* or prominence of thematic relationships. The child was encour-aged to group in terms of abstractions, since the instructions implied to him that similarity be used as the basis for sorting. In addition, the objects were commonplace physical things, and there were many of them. Under these circum-stances, it might well be the case that relational or thematic grouping would constitute a free-wheeling, unconventional type of response to the given task, in contrast to the more customary practice of sorting the objects in terms of com-mon elements, whether such elements be physi-cal or conceptual. Constraints arising from the nature of the stimuli would be considerably stronger in the case of groupings based upon shared physical or conceptual properties. Group-

ings based on relationships or themas, on the other hand, would permit greater free play for the evolving of unique combinations of stimuli. With these considerations in mind, let us turn to some results.

The findings for males point to a particularly clear phenomenon. The group of high intelli-gence but low creativity stands out as avoiding the use of thematic or relational bases for group-ing. Rather, they concentrate on conceptual common elements. For whatever reasons—and the reasons may differ in the case of different groups—the other three groups are more willing to indulge in thematic forms of conceptualiz-ing. It is the high intelligence-low creativity group that shows a disproportionate avoidance of thematizing. Such a finding reinforces the hypothesis that thematic responding may, under the conditions of the present procedure, repre-sent a more playful, imaginative approach to the grouping task than does strict common-element sorting.

To suggest that the low incidence of thema-tizing by the high intelligence-low creativity group is evidence for an avoidance reaction, however, is to imply a further distinction. In principle, a low incidence could reflect either an inability to thematize or an avoidance of it. In another experimental procedure, however, we assessed the ability of the children to inte-grate a set of words into a unified theme in story telling: that is, in this new task, thematizing was required of the child. Under such conditions, the high intelligence-low creativity group the-matizes as well as the group high in both cre-ativity and intelligence. It is when the option not to thematize is available that thematizing drops out of the behavior of the high intelligent-low creative group. Such evidence, then, sug-gests that we are dealing with a disinclination to thematize on the part of this group, not an inability to thematize.

It has typically been proposed in work on cognitive development (e.g., Bruner & Olver, 1963) that the most mature cognitive function-ing involves inferential abstraction—the kind of organizing that would be reflected in terms of sorting objects on the basis of shared conceptual properties. Thematizing has been considered a developmentally primitive response. Our find-ings suggest, however, that a more critical con-sideration may be the relative balance between conceptual-inferential and thematizing tenden-cies. Consider the results for the various groups of boys on the sorting task in somewhat more detail. For both of the high creativity groups, the relative incidence of thematizing *and* inferential-conceptual grouping is fairly high. For the high intelligence-low creativity group, the relative incidence of thematizing is quite low, while the relative incidence of inferential-conceptual sorting is quite high. Finally, for the low intelligence-low creativity group, the relationship is reversed; the incidence of thematizing is high, while the incidence of inferential-conceptual sorting is relatively low.

In sum, the creative boys seem able to switch rather flexibly between thematizing and inferential-conceptual bases for grouping; the high intelligence-low creativity boys seem rather inflexibly locked in inferential-conceptual categorizing and strongly avoidant of thematic-relational categorizing; finally, the low intelligence-low creativity boys tend to be locked within thematic modes of responding and relatively incapable of inferential-conceptual behavior. Parenthetically, it might be well to offer the reminder that the incidences of thematic and inferential-conceptual groupings both can be high since there also exists the third scoring category of grouping in terms of common physical elements.

When we consider some of our data concerning sensitivity to the expressive potential of visual materials, a result similar to the thematizing findings is obtained for the high intelligence-low creativity group of girls. With line drawings of stick figures in various postures as stimuli, various emotional states were proposed to the child as possibilities for one or another figure, and the child indicated a willingness or disinclination to entertain each possibility. Let us focus our attention upon two kinds of affective labels for each stick figure: a label constituting a highly likely, conventional suggestion, and a label representing a quite unlikely, unconventional possibility. Unconventional and likely emotional attributions for the various stick figures were defined with reference to the consensus of adult judges. Each of some 24 stick figures was offered to the child with one affective label upon each presentation. A different type of label would be proposed each time a given figure was presented, and a given figure was repeated only after all the others had been shown. More inappropriate and more appropriate kinds of labels for the various figures would be offered on a random schedule. Note that a choice is never forced between these two classes of emotional attributions. Each presentation involves one stick figure and one label, with the child requested to accept or reject the

label as a descriptive possibility. The child thus is free to accept appropriate and unconventional emotional attributions, to reject both kinds, or to accept one kind and reject the other.

The main results with this procedure for the girls were as follows. Although the four groups did not differ in regard to their acceptance of appropriate or likely affective attributions for the stick figures, they differed in a particular way regarding acceptance of the unconventional attributions—the group high in intelligence but low in creativity exhibited a conspicuously low level of such acceptance. Although the rate of acceptance of such attributions by the other three groups was generally quite low (about 5 per cent), the high intelligence-low creativity group accepted virtually none at all. The comparability among the groups regarding acceptance of appropriate attributions acts as a control, indicating that the differential acceptance behavior just described relates to the entertainment of unconventional attributions in particular, rather than simply to the acceptance of any kind of affective labels. Furthermore, there is no relationship between degree of acceptance of unconventional and of appropriate attributions. It is safe to conclude, therefore, that an acquiescence or "yea-saying" response set cannot account for the differential acceptance of unconventional attributions.

The implications of the present findings appear to be quite similar to the thematizing results considered before in the case of the boys. In both cases, the high intelligence-low creativity group is intolerant of unlikely, unconventional types of hypothesizing about the world. This particular group appears conspicuously loath to "stick its neck out," as it were, and try something that is far out, unconventional, and hence possibly "wrong." It is of particular interest that the high intelligence-low creativity group of girls avoids entertaining the possibility of unconventional emotional attributions under the present experiment's conditions. Recall that the entertainment of such possibilities has no effect upon the availability for acceptance of the likely and highly appropriate possibilities; it is not an "either–or" situation. The high intelligence-low creativity girls seem to be so attuned to error that even where appropriate responses are not sacrificed, they refuse to deviate from a critical standard of "correctness."

Consider next some of the other findings in the domain of expressive sensitivity. Included in this domain were tasks requiring free descriptions of stimuli with implicit emotive significance. We content analyzed these free descriptions in order to determine the extent to which a child would confine his descriptions to comments upon the physical and geometric characteristics of the various stimuli, as contrasted with the extent to which he would "go beyond" such physical categories and discuss the affective or expressive connotations of such materials. In the case of both sexes, the ability to range beyond the physical and into the realm of affective content tended to be maximal in the group high in both creativity and intelligence. That creativity and intelligence both could contribute to such physiognomic sensitivity—responsiveness to "inner" feeling states on the basis of perceivable externals—suggested that two processes could be jointly involved in the display of this sensitivity. On the other hand, the capacity to make inferential translations from one mode of experience to another seems to be reflective of the general intelligence concept; on the other hand, the associational freedom implied by the creativity concept evidently enhances the range of experience available for making inferential linkages.

Let us turn now to some evidence on how the children describe themselves with respect to general anxiety symptoms and to those symptoms experienced under the stress of tests or examinations. Consider the findings for the boys. Standard materials for assessing manifest anxiety and test anxiety were employed, deriving from the work of Sarason, Davidson, Lighthall, Waite, and Ruebush (1960). The results are suggestive of a Yerkes-Dodson function. They are of the same nature for both general manifest anxiety and test anxiety. The level of anxiety is lowest for the group that is high in intelligence but low in creativity. Anxiety level is middling for the two groups that are high in creativity, regardless of intelligence level. Finally, anxiety level is highest for the group that is low in intelligence and low in creativity. The allusion to the Yerkes-Dodson law is made since creativity is found to be maximal in the presence of an intermediate level of anxiety. If anxiety is either too low or too high, then creativity is reduced. Just as interesting, however, are the particular conditions under which anxiety level is lowest. It is the group high in intelligence but low in creativity who, by self-report, are least anxious. At the other end of the dimension, with the highest anxiety scores, stands the group low in both intelligence and creativity.

What are the implications of these findings?

First of all, they force us to question whether creativity should be conceptually associated with a state of maximal freedom from anxiety symptoms. It is not those children who are lowest in anxiety level, but those who report a moderate degree of anxiety, whom we find to be most creative in their thinking processes. Traditional conceptions of mental health place considerable emphasis upon anxiety as a debilitator of cognitive performance and as a signal of inappropriate or ineffective adjustment. This no doubt is true when anxiety reaches quite high levels. We need only remember that the strongest degree of anxiety is found in the most cognitively deprived group of children—those who are low both in general intelligence and creativity. However, it may also be the case that a modicum of anxiety is reflecting more the presence of sensitivity to internal states than the presence of disturbance. This should not be construed, of course, as acceptance of the old saw that neuroticism breeds creativity. However, the data in hand do suggest that it is equally unrealistic to assume that the most creative children are the happiest children. There may well be elements of obsessiveness present in the kind of associative freedom that leads to high creativity status. A playful contemplation of the possible, but also an obsessive, task-centered reluctance to put a problem aside may be involved in the production of many associates and of a large number of unique associates. Creativity need not be all sweetness and light, therefore, but may well involve a tolerance for and understanding of sadness and pain. To think otherwise is to fall prey to the rather widespread American stereotype that suffering is always a bad thing and is to be avoided at all costs.

One possible cost of the avoidance of suffering is evident in the group whose levels of general anxiety and of test anxiety are lowest—the group high in intelligence but low in creativity. This result may well stem from the fact that the group in question is the most closely attuned to the demands of the classroom environment. In that environment, traditionally defined intelligence and its manifestations in the form of high academic achievement most likely are heavily rewarded, while creativity may well be viewed as more of a disruption than a boon. The mode of operation of the high intelligence-low creativity child, therefore, may be such as to minimize the sources of possible conflict between himself and the school environment and to maximize the sources of reward from that environment. It is not surprising that such a close fit between individual and social context would be reflected in a minimal level of anxiety.

From the kinds of results that have been passed in review, pictures begin to emerge concerning the psychological nature of the children in the four cognitive groupings: high creativity-high intelligence, high creativity-low intelligence, low creativity-high intelligence, and low creativity-low intelligence. In addition to our quantitative studies, clinical accounts describing various children in the sample also have been prepared, and these clinical materials have tended to reinforce the conclusions derived from the experimental work. The case studies can be summarized in terms of the generalizations presented below. These will also serve to underline the major points of congruence between the clinical and the experimental sources of information concerning the four creativity and intelligence groupings.

High creativity-high intelligence: These children can exercise within themselves both control and freedom, both adult-like and child-like kinds of behavior.

High creativity-low intelligence: These children are in angry conflict with themselves and with their school environment, and are beset by feelings of unworthiness and inadequacy. In a stress-free context, however, they can blossom forth cognitively.

Low creativity-high intelligence: These children can be described as "addicted" to school achievement. Academic failure would be perceived by them as catastrophic, so that they must continually strive for academic excellence in order to avoid the possibility of pain.

Low creativity-low intelligence: Basically bewildered, these children engage in various defensive maneuvers ranging from useful adaptations such as intensive social activity to regression such as passivity or psychosomatic symptoms.

In conclusion, this presentation has traced in outline form the history of our research on two modes of thinking in young children; modes which constitute quite different, but yet quite pervasive, dimensions of individual differences. Our work progressed from the definition and operationalization of the cognitive types in question to an investigation of their correlates in such areas as observable social and achievement-relevant behaviors, ways of forming concepts, physiognomic sensitivities, and self-described levels of general anxiety and test anxiety. From the findings obtained, it seems fair to conclude

that the present definition of creativity denotes a mode of cognitive functioning that matters a great deal in the life of the child. Most critical of all for advancing our understanding is a consideration of the child's *joint* status with regard to the conventional concept of general intelligence and creativity as here defined.

REFERENCES

BARRON, F. *Creativity and psychological health.* Princeton, N. J.: Van Nostrand, 1963.

BRUNER, J. S., & OLVER, ROSE R. Development of equivalence transformations in children. In J. C. Wright and J. Kagan (eds.), Basic cognitive processes in children, *Monogr. soc. Res. Child Developm.,* 1963, *28,* No. 2 (Serial No. 86), pp. 125-141.

CLINE, V.B., RICHARDS, J. M., JR., & ABE, C. The validity of a battery of creativity tests in a high school sample. *Educ. Psychol. Measmt,* 1962, *22,* 781-784.

CLINE, V. B., RICHARDS, J. M., JR., & NEEDHAM, W. E. Creativity tests and achievement in high school science. *J. appl. Psychol.,* 1963, *47,* 184-189.

COOPERATIVE TEST DIVISION. *Cooperative school and college ability tests: Technical report.* Princeton, N. J.: Educational Testing Service, 1957. (a)

COOPERATIVE TEST DIVISION. *SCAT: Directions for administering and scoring.* Princeton, N. J.: Educational Testing Service, 1957. (b)

COOPERATIVE TEST DIVISION. *Cooperative sequential tests of educational progress: Technical report.* Princeton, N. J.: Educational Testing Service, 1957. (c)

COOPERATIVE TEST DIVISION. *STEP: Directions for administering and scoring.* Princeton, N. J.: Educational Testing Service, 1957. (d)

COOPERATIVE TEST DIVISION. *Cooperative sequential tests of educational progress: Teacher's guide.* Princeton, N. J.: Educational Testing Service, 1959.

FLESCHER, I. Anxiety and achievement of intellectually gifted and creatively gifted children. *J. Psychol.,* 1963, *56,* 251-268.

GETZELS, J. W., & JACKSON, P. W. *Creativity and intelligence.* New York: Wiley, 1962.

GUILFORD, J. P., & CHRISTENSEN, P. R. A factor-analytic study of verbal fluency. *Rep. psychol. Lab.,* No. 17. Los Angeles: Univer. Southern California, 1956.

KAGAN, J., MOSS, H. A., & SIGEL, I. E. Conceptual style and the use of affect labels. *Merrill-Palmer Quart.,* 1960. *6,* 261-278.

KAGAN, J., MOSS, H. A., & SIGEL, I. E. Psychological significance of styles of conceptualization. In J. C. Wright & J. Kagan (eds.), Basic cognitive processes in children. *Monogr. soc. Res. Child Develpm.*, 1963, *28*, No. 2 (Serial No. 86), pp. 73-112.

MEDNICK, S. A. The associative basis of the creative process. *Psychol. Rev.*, 1962, *69*, 220-232.

RUGG, H. *Imagination.* New York: Harper and Row, 1963.

SARASON, S. B., DAVIDSON, K. S., LIGHTHALL, F. F., WAITE, R. R. & RUEBUSH, B. K. *Anxiety in elementary school children.* New York: Wiley, 1960.

THORNDIKE, R. L. Some methodological issues in the study of creativity. In *Proceedings of the 1962 invitational conference of testing problems.* Princeton, N. J.: Educational Testing Service, 1963, pp. 40-54.

TORRANCE, E. P. Educational achievement of the highly intelligent and the highly creative: Eight partial replications of the Getzels-Jackson study. (Research Memorandum BER-60-18.) Minneap-

olis: Bureau of Educational Research, Univer. Minnesota, 1960.

TORRANCE, E. P. *Guiding creative talent.* Englewood Cliffs, N. J.: Prentice-Hall, 1962.

TORRANCE, E. P., & GOWAN, J. C. The reliability of the Minnesota tests of creative thinking. (Research Memorandum BER-63-4.) Minneapolis: Bureau of Educational Research, Univer. Minnesota, 1963.

WALLACH, M. A., & KOGAN, N. *Modes of thinking in young children: A study of the creativity-intelligence distinction.* New York: Holt, Rinehart and Winston, 1965.

WECHSLER, D. *Wechsler intelligence scale for children: Manual.* New York: Psychological Corp., 1949.

WILSON, R. C., GUILFORD, J. P., CHRISTENSEN, P. R., & LEWIS, D. J. A factor-analytic study of creative-thinking abilities. *Psychometrika*, 1954, *19*, 297-311.

X / Motivational Resultants

HERE WE DEAL WITH PSYCHOLOGICAL CONDITIONS, STATES, or processes that influence human behavior. Included are such topics as conscience and conscientiousness; level of aspiration and need for achievement; intellectual efficiency (ability to use one's intelligence rather than degree of intelligence); capacity for sublimation in resolution of inner conflict; tendency to experience anxiety and its effect on school performance; and various other personality traits. We refer to these motivational and perceptual attributes as "resultants" because they clearly are caused or affected by a combination of the determinants described in the foregoing parts of the book.

The first article presented is very broad in scope and reviews a great deal of material. The next eleven papers might, in most instances, have been placed in a section labeled personality. However, they are included in Part X (Motivational Resultants) not only because we consider them resultants of a number of other determinants, but also because we are especially concerned with the motivational aspects or effects of the personality characteristics under discussion.

In the opening article J. McVicker Hunt describes recent evidence that is leading to new understanding about motivation and personality. A prominent author and editor in psychology and former president of the American Psychological Association, Hunt is a professor at the University of Illinois.

In the second paper Roger G. Barker, of the University of Kansas, discusses level of aspiration and problems of failure and success in school. Dr. Barker is one of the important Gestalt psychologists active in the field of child psychology. It is largely his influence that led us to see the need for a section of this book devoted to "settings" (Section V).

The crucial capacity of the mature person to give up a small reward now for a larger one later has been phrased in various ways—postponing satisfaction, delaying gratification, tolerating frustration. Albert Bandura and Walter Mischel of Stanford University describe investigations of this capacity in the third selection. This is one of a series of studies of delay of reinforcement in which Mischel has been involved. Bandura's ingenious work in studying imitative behavior is represented in Section IV (no. 23).

Another resultant of several kinds of influence is "conscience," the ideals to which a person owes private allegiance, with the accompanying self-exhortations and self-prohibitions. The article by Allinsmith describes the key importance of internalized moral values for understanding the dynamics of personality.

Next comes a review by Edith Weisskopf (now Weisskopf-Joelson) of Purdue University. She discusses the many ways intellectual functioning may be adversely affected by personality factors stemming from a variety of determinants.

The selection following is by Nevitt Sanford, now at Stanford University. Editor of *The American College* (John Wiley & Sons, 1962), Sanford has long been concerned with personality development at the college age, a topic he studied at Vassar and elsewhere. Here he discusses the implications of educational experience for personality growth at all age levels. One of his themes is the importance of the enjoyment of fictional material in books and other media as a route to mature behavior and creative thinking. The next article, by Lili Peller, deals with a related matter. Peller is a lay analyst in New York and a member of the faculty of the Philadelphia Association for Psychoanalysis. She describes the latent meanings she discerns in the plots of children's books—meanings of the kind which account for the satisfaction readers gain from literature.

Adding a footnote to discussion of the meanings of children's literature, we quote the conclusion of a classic paper written by one of the pioneers of psychoanalytic theory, the late Sandor Ferenczi.

A less psychoanalytically oriented selection dealing with the meanings to children of fiction and fantasy is the paper about television, by Eleanor Maccoby of Stanford University. (She is identified in the Introduction to Section IV.) An article presenting evidence related to Maccoby's topic is that by Seymour Feshbach of the University of California at Los Angeles, who has been investigating stimulating versus cathartic effects of vicarious aggressive activity. Additional selections bearing on television and on other sources of fictional entertainment appeared in Part V, *Settings and Specific Stimuli.*

The next article in this section is by Jesse Grimes, now associated with the Reading Laboratory in the Newton (Massachusetts) City Schools, and Wesley Allinsmith. It gives evidence that children's scholastic achievement depends upon the relation between teaching method used and the personality make-up of the children. The authors argue that someday classroom placement of students of all ages may take personality as well as ability into account, with instructional techniques gauged accordingly.

The paper by Harry Beilin reviews a considerable literature on the attitudes of teachers as contrasted with those of mental health professionals about the criteria of maladjustment among pupils. In addition to the wealth of interesting facts to be found in this selection, attention is called to the possibility that there OUGHT to be a difference in the attitudes of these two professions, since their roles are different. Dr. Beilin teaches at Brooklyn College.

In the final article in the section, Pauline Sears of Stanford University and Ernest Hilgard, also a professor there and former president of the American Psychological Association, summarize evidence about the teacher's role in the motivation of the learner.

58/TRADITIONAL PERSONALITY THEORY IN THE LIGHT OF RECENT EVIDENCE[1]/

J. McV. HUNT[*]

KNOWLEDGE OF PERSONS HAS BEEN disturbingly static over the centuries. Those changes which have occurred have all too often come like the swings in the pendulum of opinion. Knowledge within this domain of persons and of conduct has been too little touched by that cumulative dynamic process of science which followed the Renaissance and which transformed forever the shape of knowledge and understanding within other domains.

Yet, a science of persons and of conduct has been one of the serious hopes of this century. Critics of this hope have been quick to point out, nevertheless, how those propositions about persons, their development, and their conduct that have been passing for a science of persons have derived from such arts of practice as psychotherapy and from the naturalistic observation of administrative behavior rather than from controlled investigation. They have noted how schools of conviction about such matters have contended and debated with one another without controlled evidence ever entering the discourse. They have also noted how hard it is actually to apply the experimental method, which has become the chief source of controlled evidence elsewhere, in the domain of persons and their life histories. They have wondered, therefore, if this hope for a science of persons may not be in vain.

Although science does ultimately yield a body of relatively definitive knowledge about a domain, it is in essence less this definitive knowledge that is science than the dynamic, self-corrective process of ongoing inquiry. This process of science, to quote Conant (1947, p. 37), consists in the "development of [I would prefer the phrase *creating of*] conceptual schemes" where the relative validity of competing concepts is tested against concept-directed observations so that "new concepts arise from . . . these observations [and experiments]." It has been common for many critics to contend that the failure of this dynamic yeast of science to get underway within our knowledge of persons results from the vagueness of the conceptual schemes which pass for personality theory. I wish to counter that any beliefs definite enough to make observed phenomena surprising or incredible constitute a suitable starting point. Moreover, a majority of personologists have been sharing a number of beliefs which are sufficiently definite to render a good many of the observations made since World War II, and some made earlier, very surprising and so incredible that they call for revision of these beliefs. My purpose in this paper is to state five of these beliefs and to synopsize some of the observations which they make surprising.

ARE PERSONALITY TRAITS THE MAJOR SOURCE OF BEHAVIORAL VARIANCE?

According to the first of these beliefs, the source of most of the variation in behavior resides within persons. Psychoanalysts, clinicians generally, personologists, and students of individual differences have shared this belief. Moreover, they have shared it in opposition to those social psychologists—their thought rooted in the work of C. H. Cooley (1902), George Herbert Mead (1934), and W. I. Thomas (see Volkart, 1951)

[1] The first version of this paper was prepared for presentation at the International Congress of Psychology (Washington, D.C., August 30, 1963). Later versions were presented at the Academic Exercises Celebrating the Dedication of the Allan Memorial Institute of Psychiatry at McGill University in Montreal (November 10, 1963), as an invited address for a meeting of the Arizona State Psychological Association in Tucson (February 5, 1964), as a public address at the Educational Testing Service in Princeton, N.J. (March 12, 1964), and as the invited dinner-address for a meeting of the Illinois Psychological Association in Chicago (October 30, 1964). Here revising stops. (Supported by a Public Health Service Research Career Award MH k6-18,567.)

[*] J. McV. Hunt, Traditional personality theory in the light of recent evidence, *American Scientist*, 1965, 53, 1, 80-96. Reprinted by permission.

—who have contended that the major source of the variation in behavior resides in the "situation."

In this context, individual differences have been conceived typically after the fashion of static dimensions and have been called traits. Those who have attempted to measure personality traits, however, have all too often found even the reliability and validity coefficients of their measures falling within a range of 0.2 and 0.5. If one takes the square of the coefficient of correlation as a rough, "rule-of-thumb" index of the proportion of the variance attributable to persons, it would appear to be limited to somewhere between 4 and 25% of the total. This is incredibly small for any source which is considered to be *the* basis of behavioral variation, but we personologists have blamed our instruments rather than our belief in the importance of static dimensional traits. Such results, when coupled with the opposition of the social psychologists, suggest the desirability of a direct attempt to determine the relative amounts of common-trait variance attributable to persons, to the modes-of-response which serve as indicators of the traits, and to situations.

Norman Endler and Alvin Rosenstein, two of my former students, and I have attempted this for the trait of *anxiousness* (Endler, Hunt, and Rosenstein, 1962). We asked our subjects to report the degree (on a five-step scale) to which they had manifested a sample of 14 modes-of-response which are commonly considered indicative of anxiety. These included, for instance, "Heart beats faster," "Get an 'uneasy feeling,'" "Emotions disrupt action," "Feel exhilarated and thrilled," "Need to urinate frequently," "Mouth gets dry," "Seek experiences like this," "Experience nausea," and "Have loose bowels." We asked our subjects to report the degree to which they had manifested each of these modes-of-response in each of a sample of 11 specified situations. This sample of situations included, for instance, "Going to meet a [blind] date," "Crawling along a ledge high on a mountain side," "Getting up to give a speech before a large group," "Sailing a boat on a rough sea," "Being alone in the woods at night," "Going into an interview for a very important job," and "Entering a final examination in an important course."

When we made a three-way analysis of variance of these quantified reports of response, the largest main source came from the modes-of-response. This finding in itself is trivial, for one might expect an individual to "get an 'un-

easy feeling'" to an extreme degree in many situations without ever having "loose bowels" in any. Far from trivial, however, is the fact that the second largest main source came from the situations. In one sample of Illinois sophomores, with the middle 70% on a measure of anxiousness removed, the mean square for situations (152) was 3.8 times that for persons (40); and in another sample of unselected Penn State freshmen, the mean square for situations (244) was somewhat more than 11 times that for persons (21).

When we have recited these facts to our colleagues, some of them have criticized our comparing of mean squares. Nevertheless, they have typically paid us the compliment of staring in disbelief. Such a reaction implies that personality theory has contained at least one proposition sufficiently definite to be the basis for incredibility of observational evidence. The compliment derives from the implication that we have apparently found evidence, the inappropriateness of comparing mean squares notwithstanding, which is sufficiently relevant to the belief in static trait-dimensions to be surprising. We admitted that the generality of our findings could not be inferred from comparing mean squares. Rather, the generality of our findings would have to derive from their reproducibility with other samples of modes-of-response, with other samples of situations, with other samples of subjects, and with other personality traits. If these results should prove to be reproducible in general, as I have defined general, they imply that our brethren from social psychology have had a conceptual slant which is more nearly congruent with reality than has been the slant of us personologists.

On the other hand, like many disputes in the history of science, this one is based on what is, in a sense, a pseudo-question. Behavioral variance is due primarily to neither persons nor situations. Although a comparison of mean squares for situations and for subjects may have surprise or shock value, actually the mean square for the situational source is a composite of the variances from situations *per se*, from the interaction of situations-by-subjects, from the interaction of situations-by-modes-of-response, from the triple interaction, and from the residual. Also, the mean square for subjects is a similar composite. If one employs the equations of Gleser, Cronbach, and Rajaratnam (1961) to partition these various sources properly, one finds that the modes-of-response do contribute about one-fourth of the variance, again a trivial point. But one also finds that neither situations nor subjects contribute substantially. Typically, neither contributes 5% of the total, and for subjects this is what would be expected from the reliability and validity coefficients for tests of personality traits. The simple interactions contribute nearly a third of the total variance (about 10% each), and the triple interaction with residual contributes about the final third. Thus, main sources, simple interactions, and triple interaction with residual each contribute about a third of the total variance (Endler and Hunt, 1964). Three-way analyses of variance for some 15 samples of subjects with three forms of the S-R Inventory have served to indicate that the percentages of total variance from these various main sources and interactive sources are quite stable. While increasing the variability of situations increases the percentage of variance from situations, the increase is only one from something of the order of 2 or 5% to something of the order of 7 or 8%. Thus, it is neither the individual differences among subjects, *per se*, nor the variations among situations, *per se*, that produce the variations in behavior. It is, rather, the interactions among these which are important.

In the words of a Vermont farmer once quoted by Henry A. Murray, "people is mostly alike, but what difference they is can be powerful important." I am now guessing to be "powerful important" the variations in the meanings of situations to people and the variations in the modes-of-response they manifest. These results imply that, for either understanding variations of behavior or making clinical predictions, we should be looking toward instruments that will classify people in terms of the kinds of responses they make in various categories of situations. Osgood has provided us with the Semantic Differential, an important method of assessing the interaction between people and situations (Osgood, Suci, and Tannenbaum, 1957). Perhaps our own approach may also be helpful.

IS ALL BEHAVIOR MOTIVATED?

The second belief which I wish to confront with evidence from recent investigation concerns personality dynamics or, particularly, motivation. It has most commonly taken the form of the assertion that "all behavior is motivated." In this form, which either originated with or was popularized by Freud, the assertion is indeed too vague to provide a basis for observational surprise, but Freud (1900, 1915), such physiologists as Cannon (1915), and such modern behavior theorists as Hull (1943), Miller and

Dollard (1941), and Mowrer (1960), have all shared in filling out the statement so that it has come to say, "all behavior is motivated by painful stimulation, homeostatic need, sexual appetite, or by acquired drives, *i.e.*, originally neutral stimuli which have been associated with painful stimuli, homeostatic need, or sex in the organism's past experience."

This is the well-known drive-reduction theory. According to this theory, the aim or function of every instinct, defense, action, habit, or phantasy is to reduce or to eliminate either stimulation or excitation within the nervous system. Once the assertion gets this form, it can readily provide the basis for observational surprise, for it implies that, in the absence of such motivation, organisms will become quiescent.

They do not become quiescent. I have reviewed these surprising observations elsewhere (1960, 1963a). It has been contended that I have reviewed them *ad nauseam*, so let me be brief here. These observations derive from the studies of play in children by Bühler (1928) and in animals by Beach (1945) and others, the studies of monkeys and chimpanzees manipulating puzzles by Harlow (1950) and by Harlow, Harlow, and Meyer (1950), the studies of spatial exploration in rats by Berlyne (1960) and by Nissen (1930), the studies of spontaneous alternation of rats in a T-maze by Montgomery (1953, 1955), the finding that monkeys will learn various things merely to get a peek at a new scene by Butler (1953), the studies of human beings under conditions of homogeneous input by Bexton, Heron, and Scott (1954), and the now classic studies by Hebb (1946) which found that fear in chimpanzees will occur with encountering something familiar in an unfamiliar guise.

Such evidence, however, has recently been given theoretical recognition in several unfortunate fashions. One of these is drive-naming. The literature is now full of drives (manipulative, exploratory, curiosity, etc.) and of needs (stimulus, change, etc.). This naming of new motives which merely describe the activities they are designed to explain, helps little. Moreover, in motive-naming, we are revisiting the instinct-naming which McDougall (1908) popularized early in this century but which was discredited just after World War I. We should know better.

A second unfortunate fashion of theoretical recognition is naming motives in terms of their telic significance. I refer to the "urge to mastery" promulgated by Ives Hendrick (1943) and to the concept of "competence motivation" proposed by Robert White (1959) in his excellent review of the evidence concerned. Unfortunately, concepts of telic significance seem to me to provide no means of developing hypotheses about antecedent-consequent relationships that can be tested against observations.

A third unfortunate. fashion of theoretical recognition has consisted of postulating spontaneous activity. Some activity can be said to be spontaneous, from a descriptive standpoint, as Hebb has pointed out to me. But this does not make spontaneity a useful explanation, and I am indebted to my colleague, L. I. O'Kelly, for noting that postulating spontaneous activity as an explanation may be just as useless as postulating a list of instincts and drives, and for precisely the same reasons.

As I see it, these various lines of evidence combine to indicate that a system and a mechanism of motivation inheres within the organism's informational interaction with its environmental circumstances. I have described this mechanism elsehwere (Hunt, 1963a). The news of its existence was, I believe, one of the implicit messages of that now classic book entitled *The Organization of Behavior* (Hebb, 1949). This message has since been made explicit, and it has been confirmed by various lines of evidence.

It is no easy matter to characterize properly what it is in the informational interaction with circumstances that is essential. I have termed it "incongruity" (Hunt, 1963a). By this term, I have intended to designate the discrepancy between the incoming information of the moment and that information already coded and stored within the brain in the course of previous encounters with the category of circumstances concerned. Berlyne (1960) uses the term "collative variables" and sees these underlying "arousal potential"; Festinger (1957) speaks of "cognitive dissonance"; Hebb (1949) has referred the matter to a stage of development in cortical organization; Munsinger and Kesson (1964) and Eckblad (1963), a Norwegian psychologist, are calling it "uncertainty." The role of arousal in this informational organism-environment interaction is also a moot point (see Hunt, 1963a). Whether there is one factor or several in it is another moot point. Nathan Isaacs, in Britain, likes to distinguish between novelty, for discrepancies between input and that already stored in mere information processing, and incongruity, where inputs are discrepant from established commitments and plans

(personal communication). He may well be correct.

Whatever the essential character of this informational organism-environment interaction and its relationship to arousal turns out to be, there appears to be an optimum amount of it for each organism at any given time. I suspect that this optimum is to a considerable degree a function of experience, and that it may obey Helson's (1959) notion of the adaptation level. When a situation offers too much, *i.e.*, when the inputs from a situation are too incongruous with the information already coded and stored, the organism withdraws as illustrated by Hebb's (1946) fearful chimpanzees, and by some of the human beings whom Festinger (1957) has found to be avoiding or discrediting information dissonant with their commitments and plans. On the other hand, when a situation offers too little incongruity, *i.e.*, when the inputs from a situation are too similar to the information already in storage, boredom results, and the organism withdraws from that situation to seek another one offering more incongruity, stimulus-change, novelty, dissonance, uncertainty, or what-have-you. It is this seeking of incongruity which is apparently illustrated by the college students in the McGill experiments of Bexton, Heron, and Scott (1954) who refused to remain under conditions of homogeneous input even though they were paid $20 a day. It is this seeking of incongruity which is also illustrated by the fact that Butler's (1953) monkeys will learn merely in order to get a peek at the world outside their monotonous cage-situations, and by that early study of Nissen's (1930) in which rats left their familiar nests and crossed an electrified grid (one of Worden's obstructions) to get to a Dashiell maze filled with objects fresh and novel to them. This work of Nissen's never got into the textbooks, probably because it was too dissonant with the traditional propositions about motivation presented therein.

This line of conceptualizing has still largely unacknowledged implications for our traditional notions of both psychodynamics and psychological development. Both Sigmund Freud (1926) and Anna Freud (1936) conceived of the mechanisms of defense as serving to protect a person from anxiety. Sigmund Freud, at least in his later days when he came to see repression as a consequence of anxiety rather than as its source, saw anxiety originating from castration threats, Oedipal anxieties, and other overwhelmingly intense experiences of painful stimulation. The fact that Hebb (1946) has found chimpanzees withdrawing from sources of input which could never have been associated with painful stimulation (by virtue of the fact that the infants had been reared under observation in the Yerkes Laboratory), coupled with the fact that Festinger (1957) and his students have found human subjects utilizing various strategies to avoid dissonant information, and coupled again with the fact that evidence dissonant with prevailing theories—like that of Nissen's early study—seldom gets into the textbooks, suggest that the mechanism of defense may sometimes, or may even typically, function chiefly to protect individuals from information too incongruous with that which they already have coded in the storage or with that already involved in their commitments and plans. Probably the most important category of stored information for this theoretical context is that concerning the self, as the theorizing of Hilgard (1949) and as the clinical observations and theorizing of Rogers (1951) and George Kelly (1955) would indicate. I dare not take the time to elaborate; here it must be enough to point a direction.

Within the domain of psychological development, it is generally believed that the existence of fears implies that the feared sources of input, when they are not themselves painful, have been associated in the past with painful stimulation. But separation anxiety (or perhaps *separation grief* is a better term) typically appears in infants who are least likely to have had the disappearance of a familiar adult associated with painful stimulation or intense homeostatic need. Moreover, this separation anxiety or grief does not develop while infants are still very young and at a stage of life when the painful stimulation from colic and homeostatic need would be most likely to be prominent. Instead, as the observations of Anna Freud and Burlingham (1944) have indicated, separation grief becomes prominent and prolonged only during the latter part of the first year and during the second year. It is significant to note that this is the time, according to the observations of Piaget (1936), that objects are beginning to have permanence. This emerging permanence of objects implies that some kind of coded template must have been gradually established within the brain-storage in the course of repeated encounters with these objects. Again, I dare not take time to elaborate. My main point is to bring to your attention these indications that there is a highly important system of moti-

vation which is inherent in the organism's informational interaction with the environment and that it has a developmental basis in experience quite different from that of the now traditional acquired drives. I tend to think of this kind of motivation as "intrinsic motivation," a term which distinguishes it from the motivation deriving from painful stimulation, homeostatic need, and sexual appetite, all of which are extrinsic to the organism's informational interaction with the environment.

ARE EMOTIONAL FACTORS SO MUCH MORE IMPORTANT THAN COGNITIVE FACTORS IN PSYCHOLOGICAL DEVELOPMENT?

The third belief which I wish to discuss in the light of recently uncovered evidence is also motivational and dynamic, but it is developmental as well. Freud probably did more to emphasize the importance of infantile experience in psychological development than anyone else in the history of thought. Freud's (1905) theory of psychosexual development put the emphasis on the fate of the instinctive modes of infantile pleasure-striving, *i.e.*, sucking, elimination, and genitality. Freud's influence has led to the very widespread belief among personologists that these extrinsic motivational or emotional factors are much more important in development than are cognitive factors. This minimization of the importance of cognitive and perceptual factors in early infantile, or preverbal, development has been abetted, moreover, by the beliefs in fixed intelligence and predetermined development so widely held among the earlier students of individual differences in intelligence.

Recent evidence indicates, perhaps, that just about the opposite should hold. Reviews of those relatively objective studies of the effects of the emotional factors pointed up in the theory of psychosexual development have generally tended to depreciate the importance of those factors (see Child, 1954; Hunt, 1946, 1956; Orlansky, 1949). Every study finding significant effects can be matched with another which does not. Moreover, the better controlled the study, the less likely is it to have found significant effects. Similarly, while infantile feeding-frustration in rats appeared to increase eating speed and hoarding in adulthood (Hunt, 1941; Hunt, *et al.*, 1947), thereby lending support to the importance of extrinsic motivational factors, these studies have not always been reproducible so far as the effect on hoarding is concerned

(Marx, 1952; McKelvey and Marx, 1951). More-over, having done the first of these studies, perhaps I should admit that I probably misin-terpreted the facts anyway. Of course, it is still true that painful stimulation can inhibit eating and drinking and that prolonged failure to eat and drink can kill an organism. On the other hand, the studies of the effects of variations in the richness of early perceptual experience in animals have regularly shown (Forgays and Forgays, 1952; Forgus, 1954, 1955a, 1955b; Hymovitch, 1952) substantial effects on adult problem-solving. These studies have stemmed from Hebb's theorizing, and the first of the kind (Hebb, 1947) compared the performances of pet-reared rats with those of cage-reared rats in the Hebb-Williams (1946) test of animal intelligence. The pet-reared animals proved much superior to their cage-reared litter-mates. Thompson and Heron (1954) have made a similar experiment with dogs, and the evidence of the superiority of the pet-reared dogs over their cage-reared litter-mates is even more striking than that for rats. The fact that the evidence from dogs is stronger than that from rats suggests that the importance of early ex-perience, and particularly the importance of early cognitive or perceptual experience, prob-ably increases up the phylogenetic scale as that portion of the brain without direct connection to sensory input or motor outlet increases rela-tive to the portion which does have direct sensory and/or motor connections (i.e., with the size of what Hebb [1949] has termed the A/S ratio). Moreover, there is direct evidence that such effects can be generalized from ani-mal subjects to human beings in studies by Goldfarb (see 1955 for summary) which indi-cate that being reared in an orphanage, where the variety of circumstances encountered is highly restricted, results at adolescence in lower intelligence, less ability to sustain a task, less attentiveness, and more problems in interper-sonal relations than being reared in a foster home. Moreover, those findings of Dennis (1960) that 60% of the two-year-olds in a Teheran orphanage, where changes in ongoing stimulation were minimal, were not yet sitting up alone and that 85% of the four-year-olds were not yet walking alone, serve to dramatize how very much the factor of variety of circum-stances encountered in infancy can affect the rate of development—even the rate of develop-ment of posture and locomotion.

As I see it, these various lines of evidence combine to indicate that cognitive experience—

or, more precisely, the organism's informational interaction with the environment—can be as important for psychological development as emotions based on the fate of instincts, and perhaps it is typically more important. In cor-ollary fashion, these same bits of evidence would also appear to indicate that we have been wrong in our widespread belief that it is the intellectual characteristics of a person which are most nearly fixed by the genotype and that the emotional characteristics of a person are highly subject to substantial environmental influence. Although the life history is of considerable im-portance in the development of both types of characteristics, it appears that it may be the intellectual variety which is the more subject to substantial effects of environmental encoun-ters, particularly those coming in early infancy.

MUST EMOTIONAL ATTACHMENTS DERIVE FROM GRATIFICATION OF LIBIDINAL OR HOMEOSTATIC NEEDS?

According to a fourth belief commonly held by personologists, the emotional attachments to objects, persons, and places—called cathexes in psychoanalytic terminology—derive from their association with the gratification of libidinal or homeostatic needs. In his *Three Contributions to the Theory of Sex*, Freud (1905) not only assumed a separation of libidinal from nutri-tional needs, but he also attributed all object-cathexes to libidinal energy (see p. 553, p. 611, and p. 743 footnote 2). These points, coupled with Freud's (1915) conception of instinct, ap-pear to indicate that he attributed all emotional attachments to libidinal gratification, as he de-fined it. As I (Hunt, 1946) pointed out nearly 20 years ago, any such generalization is contra-dicted by the wide variety of studies in which preference for objects, persons, and places has been changed by association with food reward (see, e.g., Mowrer, 1960; Razran, 1938a, 1938b; Williams, 1929; Williams and Williams, 1943) or by association with success in goal-achievement (see Mierke, 1933; Nowlis, 1941; Rosenzweig, 1933).

More recently, it has been generally believed that such emotional attachment derives from the association of objects, persons, and places with homeostatic gratification. And so it is some-times, but Harlow's (1958) work indicates that association with homeostatic gratification is far from the whole story. In his studies, you will recall, monkey babies, when frightened, went for solace to the soft surrogate-mothers covered with padded terry-cloth rather than to the wire surrogate-mothers on which they had sucked to gratify their need for food.

Nor can softness of contact be the whole story, for behavioral criteria defining emotional attachment appear to have another basis. Infants of various species appear to approach, to seek, and to take delight in objects which are becoming recognizably familiar in the course of repeated encounters (see Hunt, 1963b), and they show varying degrees of distress as these objects escape their perceptual ken. Piaget (1936) has described how his children came to make what is clearly an "intentional effort" to keep interesting spectacles within perceptual range. Anyone who has ever jounced an infant on his knee and stopped his motion only to find the infant starting a similar motion of his own, is familiar with this intentional effort of the infant to hold on to an interesting spectacle. One gathers from Piaget's (1936) observations that these interesting spectacles very commonly consist of objects or persons that are becoming familiar through repeated encounters. In an exploratory study of this phenomenon, Dr. Ina Uzgiris and I have got evidence consonant with this idea that the young human infant prefers a mobile which has been hanging over his crib to another mobile which he has never encountered before (Hunt and Uzgiris, 1964). Here, the term *prefers* is based on looking time. When the familiar mobile has been withdrawn for a time and is then returned with another unfamiliar one beside it, the infant looks more at the familiar than at the unfamiliar one. Similar phenomena of emotional attachment are to be found in animals. Since it is following an object and distress at its escape from perceptual ken that characterizes the one major component of what the ethologists (Heinroth, 1910; Lorenz, 1935; Thorpe, 1944) call "imprinting," it intrigues me to consider that this effort to follow and to keep interesting spectacles within view and the distress at losing them in lower mammals and birds may be a special case of this more general principle of emotional attachment deriving from recognitive familiarity. If this be sensible, and I believe it is, one can then relate the marked variation in the number of encounters required to establish such recognitive emotional attachments to Hebb's A/S ratio. There appears to be a progression in the number of encounters or in the amount of exposure time required, from two or three hours in the grey-leg goose through two or three days in the

sheep or deer, some two weeks in the monkey infant, and some six or so weeks in the chimpanzee infant, to some six or so months in the human infant. Maternal attachment appears to be another special case of this same principle, but it is well contaminated also with skin contacts and with the gratification of homeostatic need. In all probability, fear of strangers is a direct derivative comparable to the fear of the familiar in an unfamiliar guise found in adult chimpanzees by Hebb (1946) and already mentioned.

But following is alone no indication of emotional delight. Evidence of the delight comes from the infant's smile and laugh of recognition. Spitz (1946) and others have considered smiling to be a social response, one based, presumably, on the fact that the human face is repeatedly associated with homeostatic gratification, but Piaget's (1936) observations and those of my colleague, Dr. Uzgiris, indicate that the infant will smile and show laughing delight at the appearance of various objects which are merely becoming familiar with repeated encounters (Hunt, 1963b).

Such observations and considerations strongly suggest that recognitive familiarity is in itself a source of emotional attachment, and this attachment is attested further by the fact that separation grief always concerns familiar objects and persons and by the fact that such grief is but transient in infants too young to have established object permanence. In a sense, this is a further elaboration of the importance of that intrinsic system of motivation which inheres in the organism's informational interaction with the environment.

DO ENCOUNTERS WITH PAINFUL STIMULATION IN INFANCY RESULT IN SENSITIVITY AND PRONENESS TO ANXIETY?

According to a fifth belief, which we may call the "trauma theory of anxiety," encounters with painful stimulation or strong homeostatic need inevitably leave a young child or a young animal prone to be sensitive and anxious in most situations. This trauma theory assumes the conditioning conception of fear. Thus, it is presumed that the various sources of inputs present immediately before and during encounters with painful stimulation will acquire the capacity to evoke the autonomic and central emotional features incorporated within the total response to painful stimulation.

In spite of Hebb's (1946) strong evidence to the contrary, most clinicians of all professions act as if *the only source* of anxious emotional disturbance were this association of originally neutral sources of input with pain. Recently, however, another source of evidence dissonant with this widely held belief has been the investigations of the effects of shocking infant animals before they are weaned. Although there may well be both species and strain differences in some of these effects, as indicated by reports —based on studies using mice as subjects— which deviate from those which I am about to mention (see Hall, 1934; Lindzey, *et al.*, 1960), rats shocked in infancy have been repeatedly found as adults to be less fearful than rats which have been left unmolested in the maternal nest. This is to say that they urinated less and defecated less in, were less hesitant to enter, and were more active in unfamiliar territory than were rats which had been left unmolested in the maternal nest (see Deneberg, 1962; Levine, 1959, 1961).

In two other investigations, moreover, rats shocked before weaning, with sufficient intensity to keep them squealing continually for three minutes each day, have been found as adults to require stronger shocks to instigate escape-activity than do rats left unmolested (Goldman, 1964; Griffiths, 1960). Finally, in a very recent study by Salama, one of my own students, rats shocked daily from their 11th through their 20th day were found to show much less "fixative effect" of shock after the choice-point in a T-maze than did rats left unmolested in the maternal nest or than did rats either gentled or handled for this same period (Salama and Hunt, 1964).

Let me explain this last experiment briefly. Some 16 years ago, Farber (1948) reported a study of "fixation" which showed that rats intermittently shocked just after the choice-point on their way to one of the goal-boxes in a T-maze, where they were fed, required substantially more unrewarded trials to give up going to that goal-box than did rats merely given food-reward in it. Salama (1962) has replicated this finding and found the mean number of unrewarded trials to be 20.7 for the shocked animals but only 2.8 for those merely given food-reward. He has gone further; he has compared the number of unrewarded trials required for rats shocked in infancy to give up the goal-box with the numbers required by rats gentled and handled. The means for those gentled (21.4) and for those handled (17.58) differed little

from the mean for those left unmolested in the maternal nest (20.7), but the mean for those shocked (9) approximates only half the means for these other groups, and it differs significantly ($p < 0.001$) from these and from the unmolested group not shocked after the choice-point.

It is very interesting in connection with these studies that Holmes (1935) has found the children of lower-class backgrounds from a day-care center to be less fearful than children of an upper-middle-class background from a nursery school. Holmes' study was conducted in 1935, right in the midst of the Great Depression, when children of lower-class parents could be expected to have encountered more painful stimulation and homeostatic need than children of the upper-middle class. This result suggests that the findings from these animal studies may well generalize to human beings.

It is clear from the evidence that all of these studies tend to disconfirm the present formulation of the trauma theory of anxiety based on the conditioning principle as the only experiential basis for anxiousness. They also suggest that encounters with painful stimulation may serve instead to raise what Helson (1959) calls the adaptation level for painful stimulation and thereby to reduce its aversiveness. The force of such evidence is hardly yet sufficient to warrant—and certainly not sufficient to call for —a change in child-rearing practices, for trauma is also a fact. There are varieties of early experience that leave infants prone to be sensitive and anxious, but we cannot yet clearly specify their nature. Perhaps it should be remembered in connection with this evidence, however, that the Spartan culture survived for several centuries while holding to a belief that infants should be exposed to cold and to painful stimulation to prepare them to bear the dire exigencies of later life.

SUMMARY

I have been calling your attention to the fact that, vague as the propositions in traditional personality may have been, some have been sufficiently definite to provide those who have believed them with an experience of surprise or incredulity when they have encountered some of the observations deriving from investigation, largely from that investigation done since World War II.

I have cited five beliefs which have served as a basis for such surprise: (1) that personality traits are the major sources of behavioral variance; (2) that all behavior is motivated; (3) that emotional factors are much more important than cognitive factors in psychological development; (4) that emotional attachments derive from gratification of libidinal or homeostatic needs; and (5) the trauma theory of anxiousness, that encounters with painful stimulation in infancy always result in sensitivity and proneness to anxiety.

I have synopsized some of the evidence which these beliefs make surprising, and I have indicated some new interpretations which have implications for further investigation. In the light of these developments, perhaps the hope for a science of persons is not in vain. Perhaps the yeastful and self-corrective dynamic of science has at last found its way into knowledge of persons and of personality development.

REFERENCES[2]

BEACH, F. A., 1945. Current concepts of play in animals. *Amer. Natur.*, 79, 523-541.

BERLYNE, D. E., 1960. *Conflict, arousal, and curiosity.* New York: McGraw-Hill.

BEXTON, W. H., HERON, W., and SCOTT, T. H., 1954. Effects of decreased variation in the sensory environment. *Canad. J. Psychol.*, 8, 70-76.

BÜHLER, K., 1928. Displeasure and pleasure in relation to activity. In M. L. Reymert (Ed.), *Feelings and emotions: the Wittenberg symposium.* Worcester, Mass.: Clark Univ. Press. Ch. 14.

BUTLER, R. A., 1953. Discrimination learning by rhesus monkeys to visual exploration motivation. *J. comp. physiol. Psychol.*, 46, 95-98.

CANNON, W. B., 1915. *Bodily changes in pain, hunger, fear, and rage.* New York: Appleton, 1929.

CHILD, I. L., 1954. Socialization. In G. Lindzey (Ed.), *Handbook of social psychology.* Cambridge, Mass.: Addison-Wesley. Ch. 18.

CONANT, J. B., 1947. *On understanding science.* New York: The New American Library (Mentor No. 68), 1951.

COOLEY, C. H., 1902. *Human nature and the social order.* New York: Scribner's.

DENENBERG, V. H., 1962. The effects of early experience. In E. S. E. Hafez (Ed.), *The behavior of domestic animals.* London: Balliere, Tindall, & Cox. Ch 6.

DENNIS, W., 1960. Causes of retardation among institutional children: Iran. *J. genet. Psychol.*, 96, 47-59.

---

[2] The date following the name(s) of the author(s), which is used to identify the reference in the body of the text, is, to the best of my knowledge, the date of the original publication. When a date appears at the end of a reference, it serves to identify the edition or republication available to me.

ECKBLAD, G., 1963. The attractiveness of uncertainty. *Scand. J. Psychol.*, 4, 1-13.

ENDLER, N. S., and HUNT, J. MC V., 1964. Sources of variance in reported anxiousness as measured by the S-R Inventory. (Mimeographed prepublication.)

ENDLER, N. S., HUNT, J. MC V., and ROSENSTEIN, A. J., 1962. An S-R Inventory of anxiousness. *Psychol. Monogr.*, 76, No. 17, 1-33.

FARBER, I. E., 1948. Response fixation under anxiety and non-anxiety conditions. *J. exp. Psychol.*, 38, 111-131.

FESTINGER, L., 1957. *A theory of cognitive dissonance.* Evanston, Ill.: Row, Peterson.

FORGAYS, D. G., and FORGAYS, JANET W., 1952. The nature of the effect of free environmental experience in the rat. *J. comp. physiol. Psychol.*, 45, 322-328.

FORGUS, R. H., 1954. The effect of early perceptual learning on the behavioral organization of adult rats. *J. comp. physiol. Psychol.*, 47, 331-336.

FORGUS, R. H., 1955a. Influence of early experience on maze-learning with and without visual cues. *Canad. J. Psychol.*, 9, 207-214.

FORGUS, R. H., 1955b. Early visual and motor experience as determiners of complex maze-learning ability under high and reduced stimulation. *J. comp. physiol. Psychol.*, 48, 215-220.

FREUD, ANNA, 1936. *The ego and the mechanisms of defense.* (Trans. by Cecil Baines.) New York: International Universities Press, 1946.

FREUD, ANNA, and BURLINGHAM, DOROTHY, 1944. *Infants without families.* New York: International Universities Press.

FREUD, S., 1900. The interpretation of dreams. In A. A. Brill (Trans. & Ed.), *The basic writings of Sigmund Freud.* New York: Modern Library, 1938.

FREUD, S., 1905. Three contributions to the theory of sex. In A. A. Brill (Trans. & Ed.), *The basic writings of Sigmund Freud.* New York: Modern Library, 1938.

FREUD, S., 1915. Instincts and their vicissitudes. *Collected Papers*, 4, 60-83. London: Hogarth, 1927.

FREUD, S., 1926. *Hemmung, Symptom und Angst.* (Trans. as *The problem of anxiety*, by H. A. Bunker.) New York: Norton, 1936.

GLESER, G. C., CRONBACH, L. J., and RAJARATNAM, N., 1961. Generalizability of scores influenced by multiple sources of variance. Mimeographed Technical Report, Bureau of Educational Research, Univ. of Illinois.

GOLDFARB, W., 1955. Emotional and intellectual consequences of psychologic deprivation in infancy: a re-evaluation. In P. H. Hoch and J. Zubin (Eds.), *Psychopathology of childhood.* New York: Grune & Stratton, 105-119.

GOLDMAN, JACQUELIN R., 1964. The effects of handling and shocking in infancy upon adult behavior in the albino rat. *J. genet. Psychol.*, *104*, 301-310.

GRIFFITHS, W. J., JR., 1960. Effects of isolation and stress on escape thresholds of albino rats. *Psychol. Rep.*, *6*, 623-629.

HALL, C. S., 1934. Emotional behavior in the rat. I. Defecation and urination as measures of individual differences in emotionality. *J. comp. Psychol.*, *18*, 385-403.

HARLOW, H. F., 1950. Learning and satiation of response in intrinsically motivated complex puzzle performance by monkeys. *J. comp. physiol. Psychol.*, *43*, 289-294.

HARLOW, H. F., 1958. The nature of love. *Amer. Psychol.*, *13*, 673-685.

HARLOW, H. F., HARLOW, M. K., and MEYER, D. R., 1950. Learning motivated by a manipulation drive. *J. exp. Psychol.*, *40*, 228-234.

HEBB, D. O., 1946. On the nature of fear. *Psychol. Rev.*, *53*, 259-276.

HEBB, D. O., 1947. The effects of early experience on problem-solving at maturity. *Amer. Psychologist*, *2*, 306-307.

HEBB, D. O., 1949. *The organization of behavior*. New York: Wiley.

HEBB, D. O., and WILLIAMS, K., 1946. A method of rating animal intelligence. *J. genet. Psychol.*, *34*, 59-65.

HEINROTH, O., 1910. Beitrage zur Biologie, namentlich Ethnologie und Physiologie der Anatiden. *Verhl, Internat. Ornith. Congr.*, *5*, 589-702.

HELSON, H., 1959. Adaptation level theory. In S. Koch (Ed.), *Psychology, a study of a science. Vol. 1. Sensory, perceptual, and physiological formulations*. New York: McGraw-Hill, 565-621.

HENDRICK, I., 1943. The discussion of the "instinct to master." *Psychoanal. Quart.*, *12*, 561-565.

HILGARD, E. R., 1949. Human motives and the concept of the self. *Amer. Psychologist*, *4*, 374-382.

HOLMES, FRANCES B., 1935. An experimental study of children's fears. In A. T. Jersild and Frances B. Holmes (Eds.), *Children's fears*. New York: Teachers College, Columbia Univ. (*Child Develpm. Monogr.*, *20*.)

HULL, C. L., 1943. *Principles of behavior*. New York: Appleton-Century.

HUNT, J. MC V., 1941. The effects of infantile feeding-frustration upon adult hoarding in the albino rat. *J. abnorm. soc. Psychol.*, *36*, 338-360.

HUNT, J. MC V., 1946. Experimental psychoanalysis. In P. L. Harriman (Ed.), *Encyclopedia of psychology*. New York: Philosophical Library.

HUNT, J. MC V., 1956. Psychosexual development, the infant disciplines. Mimeographed paper written as a chapter for *Behavioral science and child rearing*, as yet unpublished.

HUNT, J. MC V., 1960. Experience and the development of motivation: some reinterpretations. *Child Develpm.*, *31*, 489-504.

HUNT, J. MC V., 1961. *Intelligence and experience*. New York: Ronald.

HUNT, J. MC V., 1963a. Motivation inherent in information processing and action. In O. J. Harvey (Ed.), *Motivation and social interaction: the cognitive determinants*. New York: Ronald Press. Ch. 3.

HUNT, J. MC V., 1963b. Piaget's observations as a source of hypotheses concerning motivation. *Merrill-Palmer Quart.*, *9*, 263-275.

HUNT, J. MC V., SCHLOSBERG, H., SOLOMON, R. L., and STELLAR, E., 1947. Studies of the effects of infantile experience on adult behavior in rats. I. Effects of infantile feeding frustration on adult hoarding. *J. comp. physiol. Psychol.*, *40*, 291-304.

HUNT, J. MC V., and UZGIRIS, INA C., 1964. Cathexis from recognitive familiarity: an exploratory study. (To appear in the volume of studies honoring J. P. Guilford.)

HYMOVITCH, B., 1952. The effects of experimental variations in early experience on problem solving in the rat. *J. comp. physiol. Psychol.*, *45*, 313-321.

KELLY, G. A., 1955. *The psychology of personal constructs*. New York: Norton. 2 vols.

LEVINE, S., 1959. The effects of differential infantile stimulation on emotionality at weaning. *Canad. J. Psychol.*, *13*, 247-253.

LEVINE, S., 1961. Psychophysiological effects of early stimulation. In E. Bliss (Ed.), *Roots of behavior*. New York: Hoeber.

LINDZEY, G., LYKKEN, D. T., and WINSTON, H. C., 1960. Infantile trauma, genetic factors, and adult temperament. *J. abnorm. soc. Psychol.*, *61*, 7-14.

LORENZ, K., 1935. Der Kumpan in der Umwelt des Vögels. *J. Ornith.*, *83*, 137-214; 289-413. (Cited by W. H. Thorpe, Jr., in *Learning and instinct in animals*. London Methuen, 1956.)

MARX, M. H., 1952. Infantile deprivation and adult behavior in the rat: retention of increased rate of eating. *J. comp. physiol. Psychol.*, *45*, 43-49.

MC DOUGALL, W., 1908. *Social psychology*. Boston: Luce.

MC KELVEY, R. K., and MARX, M. H., 1951. Effects of infantile food and water deprivation on adult hoarding in the rat. *J. comp. physiol. Psychol.*, *44*, 423-430.

MEAD, G. H., 1934. *Mind, self, and society*. Chicago: Univ. Chicago Press.

MIERKE, K., 1933. Über die Objectionsfähigkeit und ihre Bedeutung fur die Typenlehre. *Arch. gest. Psychol.*, *89*, 1-108.

MILLER, N. E., and DOLLARD, J., 1941. *Social learning and imitation*. New Haven: Yale Univ. Press.

MONTGOMERY, K. C., 1953. Exploratory behavior as a function of "similarity" of stimulus situations. *J. comp. physiol. Psychol.*, *46*, 129-133.

MONTGOMERY, K. C., 1955. The relation between fear induced by novel stimulation and exploratory behavior. *J. comp. physiol. Psychol.*, *48*, 254-260.

MOWRER, O. H., 1960. *Learning theory and behavior*. New York: Wiley.

MUNSINGER, H. L., and KESSEN, W., 1964. Uncertainty, structure, and preference. (Unpublished manuscript.)

NISSEN, H. W., 1930. A study of exploratory behavior in the white rat by means of the obstruction method. *J. genet. Psychol.*, 37, 361-376.

NOWLIS, H. H., 1941. The influence of success and failure on the resumption of an interrupted task. *J. exp. Psychol.*, 28, 304-325.

ORLANSKY, H., 1949. Infant care and personality. *Psychol. Bull.*, 46, 1-48.

OSGOOD, C. E., SUCI, G. J., and TANNENBAUM, P. H., 1957. *The measurement of meaning.* Urbana: Univ. Illinois Press.

PIAGET, J., 1936. *The origins of intelligence in children.* (Trans. by Margaret Cook.) New York: International Universities Press, 1952.

RAZRAN, G. H. S., 1938a. Conditioning away social bias by the luncheon technique. *Psychol. Bull.*, 35, 693.

RAZRAN, G. H. S., 1938b. Music, art, and the conditioned response. (Paper read at Eastern Psychol. Assoc., April.)

ROGERS, C. R., 1951. *Client-centered therapy.* Boston: Houghton-Mifflin.

ROSENZWEIG, S., 1933. Preferences in the repetition of successful and unsuccessful activities as a function of age and personality. *J. genet. Psychol.*, 42, 423-441.

SALAMA, A. A., 1962. Fixation in the rat as a function of infantile shocking, handling, and gentling. Unpublished doctoral dissertation, Univ. Illinois.

SALAMA, A. A., and HUNT, J. MC V., 1964. "Fixation" in the rat as a function of infantile shocking, handling, and gentling. *J. genet. Psychol.*, 105, 131-262.

SPITZ, R. A., 1946. The smiling response: a contribution to the ontogenesis of social relations. *Genet. Psychol. Monogr.*, 34, 67-125.

THOMPSON, W. R., and HERON, W., 1954. The effects of restricting early experience on the problem-solving capacity of dogs. *Canad. J. Psychol.*, 8, 17-31.

THORPE, W. H., JR., 1944. Some problems of animal learning. *Proc. Linn. Soc. Lond.*, 156, 70-83.

VOLKART, E. H., 1951. *Social behavior and personality: the contributions of W. I. Thomas to theory and social research.* New York: Social Science Research Council.

WHITE, R. W., 1959. Motivation reconsidered: the concept of competence. *Psychol. Rev.*, 66, 297-333.

WILLIAMS, K. A., 1929. The reward value of a conditioned stimulus. *Univ. Calif. Publ. Psychol.*, 4, 31-35.

WILLIAMS, S. B., and WILLIAMS, E., 1943. Barrier-frustration and extinction in instrumental learning. *Amer. J. Psychol.*, 56, 247-261.

59/SUCCESS AND FAILURE IN THE CLASSROOM/ROGER G. BARKER°

OF THE NUMEROUS ROLES WHICH THE classroom teacher plays, that of dispenser of success and failure is undoubtedly the most impressive and worrisome to the pupils, and one of the most crucial for their present and future adjustment. It is also the role in which many teachers meet their severest conflicts; to fail John or not to fail him, whichever is done, frequently leaves feelings of guilt and anxiety. Clearly an understanding of the conditions and effects of success and failure would be of greatest value to teachers.

When does a child experience success? When does he experience failure? In what ways do these experiences affect behavior? Do the schools make it possible for children to achieve a sufficient number of important success experiences? If not, what can be done about it? A small but very important body of verified knowledge is now available bearing upon these crucial questions. In this article only a very small segment of these data can be presented.

Professor Kurt Lewin, then at the University of Berlin, and his student Ferdinand Hoppe initiated an experimental approach to these questions in the late 1920's.[1] Hoppe first considered the fundamental problem of when a person experiences success and when failure. He presented his adult subjects with simple motor and intellectual tasks such as hanging sixteen rings upon as many hooks as they passed upon a rapidly moving belt, and solving puzzles. During each trial with the tasks, Hoppe observed the subjects secretly and after the completion of each trial he interviewed them thoroughly in an effort to find out the circumstances under which they experienced success and failure. One result was clearly apparent: the experiences of success and failure were unrelated to the actual achievements of the individual. One subject might experience success when he placed four rings on the hooks; another experienced failure when he placed fifteen correctly. In addition, for a particular person, the achievement experi-

enced as success (or failure) continually changed; at one time a single ring correctly placed might give rise to an experience of success, while on a later occasion the placing of six rings would result in an experience of failure. These findings led Hoppe to a conclusion which seems very obvious once it is stated, but one that is so fundamental that it has very wide implications: *the occurrence of success and failure experiences is independent of actual achievement; it is determined, rather, by the goals, expectations and aspirations of the person at the time of the action.* These expected achievements Hoppe called *the level of aspiration.*

It is obvious that the level of aspiration is important for on it depends the occurrence of success and failure. Hoppe therefore directed his study to the effects of success and failure experiences on the level of aspiration. He found that after success the level of aspiration is usually raised (i.e. a new and higher goal is set after a lower one is achieved), and that after failure the level of aspiration is usually lowered (i.e. a new and lower goal is set after a high one has not been achieved). He found, in other words, that the level of aspiration shifts in such a way that, whatever the actual achievement of the person, the frequency of his success and failure experiences remains fairly constant. This means that the level of aspiration operates as a mental hygiene factor of great significance. It constitutes a sort of governor; it protects the person against continual failure on the one hand, and against easy achievements which do not give the feeling of success, on the other hand. This fact is behind the frequent observation that feelings of success accompany the process of achieving but disappear after attainment.

Sometimes, however, this mechanism is thrown out of balance and it fails to perform this protective function. In some cases, aspirations are maintained consistently above achievement. The individual is then subjected to continual failure with its disastrous consequences for adjustment and happiness. In other cases, aspirations are placed consistently below

[1] Hoppe, F., "Erfolg und Misserfolg," *Psychol. Forsch.,* 1930, *14,* 1-62.

° Roger G. Barker, Success and failure in the classroom, *Progressive Education*, 1942, *19*, 221-224. Reprinted by permission.

434

achievement with resulting lack of ambition, exaggerated caution, broken morale, cynicism, etc. In both instances very serious personal and social difficulties may develop. It is of the greatest importance, therefore, to determine why the level of aspiration does not function protectively for these persons.

Hoppe suggested that the level of aspiration is set as a compromise between two conflicting tendencies: (1) the desire to avoid the hurt accompanying failure, operating to force aspirations safely below the level of achievement; and (2) the desire to succeed at the highest possible level, operating to push goals above achievement levels. Subsequent investigations suggested that the latter tendency derives from social pressures to do what is most highly approved by society, irrespective of a realistic assessment of one's own capabilities. This conflict between fear of failure and desire to maintain goals that are socially approved results, usually, in a level of aspiration at or near the upper limit of one's ability range.

If this interpretation is correct, it would be expected that an increase in social pressure should alter the level of aspiration. This is, in fact, the case. Subsequent investigations have shown that pupils at the low end of the class achievement distribution aspire, on the average, above the level of their achievement possibilities (and therefore experience failure), while those at the upper end of the achievement distribution set their aspirations below their level of achievement (and therefore experience success).[2]

Although the differences between aspiration and achievement are not great in a quantitative sense, they are psychologically very important. So far as success and failure are concerned, "a miss is as good as a mile." This difference in relation of aspiration to achievement appears to mean that the social pressures of the school situation may operate to throw off-balance the protective mechanism of the level of aspiration, thus subjecting children to exaggerated failure and success experiences.

It is not difficult to understand why these pressures arise in many schools. Social acceptability in an intimate group such as a school class requires a high degree of conformity to group standards in all sorts of public behavior. The first step in achieving such acceptability is to set goals in accordance with the group standards. In schools where evaluation is largely on the basis of academic achievements this means that poor students are forced, by the social pressure of the classroom, to set goals they cannot achieve or else to admit that they are mavericks; both are undesirable alternatives from a mental hygiene viewpoint. There is pressure upon bright students, also, to set their goals in conformity with the achievements of their roommates, rather than with their own.

Adults on the other hand are infrequently subjected to such pressures for long periods of time, for adults are able with considerable success to hide from others certain crucial symbols of their divergence from what is considered good or desirable (such as age, income, family background), and they are able to withdraw when the pressures become too great. Furthermore, achievement in most adult activities is not estimated with the precision that is attempted in many schools. Doctors, lawyers, plumbers and bakers can vary within a considerable range of effectiveness and no one is wiser; they are still adequate. This gives a fundamental security which is denied to pupils who are frequently and publicly evaluated, i.e., acclaimed or humiliated by an authority from whose decisions there is no recourse and in a group from which there is no escape.

Middle-class pupils are unusually sensitive to these pressures. They are, in effect, subjected to the demands of a single dominating institution, for the family supports the demands of the school. This means that the pressures, the demands, the rewards, the punishments, the successes and the failures of the school are frequently of overwhelming importance to these children. No one with influence will question the righteousness of the school's verdicts or the correctness of its values. If the school is one in which the rewards are all centered about a very limited variety of achievements, for example academic achievements, the child who is relatively dull or uninterested in academic activities must experience continual failure. He will fail even though he is kind, or good looking, or has a sense of humor or has physical prowess, even though he is full of energy, graceful, courageous, friendly or with mechanical abilities. He will fail in school even though these behavior characteristics are very highly valued by many other institutions, until in adolescence he be-

2 Hilgard, E. R., E. M. Sait, and G. A. Magaret, "Level of aspiration as affected by relative standing in an experimental social group," *J. Exper. Psychol.,* 1940, *27,* 411-421.
Anderson, H. H. and H. F. Brandt, "Study of motivation involving self-announced goals of fifth grade children and the concept of level of aspiration," *J. Soc. Psychol.,* 1939, *10,* 209-232.

comes sufficiently independent to establish affiliations with other groups which do reward
nonacademic achievement.

Compared with life outside school, many
schools distribute success and failure in an extremely unrealistic way. Adults, for example,
are inevitably influenced by various pressures,
and rewarded according to conflicting values of
a variety of institutions and social groups (family, vocation, clique, church, lodge, union, etc.),
and these influences are likely to be of somewhat equal potency in their lives. This means
that the adult can to some extent balance the
failures in one region of his life by successes in
other regions. The effects of vocational failures
may be mitigated by successes in family and
recreational relationships where quite different
achievements are valued. In schools that emphasize academic achievement, this kind of balancing is impossible for middle-class children.

What is the consequence of the chronic failure and success that many schools enforce upon
great numbers of pupils? We do not know a
great amount from scientific experiment but
what we do know is very suggestive.

Sears studied the level of aspiration of a group
of fifth grade children who had long histories of
chronic school failure in reading and arithmetic,
and another group with equally consistent histories of school success in reading and arithmetic.[3] She found that the children who had experienced continual success set their aspirations
at a realistic level, i.e., at a level where success
was frequently achieved. The children with a
history of chronic failure, on the other hand, set
their aspirations with little regard for their
achievements. Of those in this latter group, some
children apparently lived almost exclusively in

[3] Sears, P. S., "Levels of aspiration in academically successful and unsuccessful children," *J. Abnor. and Soc.
Psychol.*, 1940, 35, 498-536.

terms of their aspirations, ignoring completely
the fact that their achievements were entirely
out of line with their expectations. In these
cases the desire for respectability may have
forced the children to an imaginary world where
the mere gesture of achieving by setting high
goals was accepted in lieu of real achievement.
The seriousness of this behavior is sufficiently
obvious to need no special emphasis. The institutionalized person for whom a gesture is sufficient to convince him he is Napoleon has
traveled further along the same path.

The cases where the children failed to set
goals even at the level of their poor achievement may involve withdrawal from the activity
in any except a very peripheral sense; they may
be cases of extreme caution or they may represent attempts to depreciate the importance of
the activity by refusing to take it seriously. None
of these outcomes of educational effort are
desirable.

What can schools do to avoid throwing out of
gear the protective mechanism of the level of
aspiration with the resulting unfortunate consequences for the success and failure experiences
of pupils? The answers are implied in the discussion, but they may be summarized as follows:

(1) broaden the basis for evaluating pupils;

(2) reduce to a minimum the prominence of
the relative standing of the pupils;

(3) allow maximum freedom to pupils to set
their own goals and to alter them as their success and failure experiences require; i.e., make
success possible at all levels of achievement;

(4) reduce the dominance of the teacher.

These conditions can be achieved in different
ways. It is interesting to note, however, that
they can hardly be avoided if democratic teaching procedures are used, if the interests of the
child are followed and if group undertakings
are an important part of school activities.

60/MODIFICATION OF SELF-IMPOSED DELAY OF REWARD THROUGH EXPOSURE TO LIVE AND SYMBOLIC MODELS[1]/ ALBERT BANDURA AND WALTER MISCHEL[*]

THEORY AND RESEARCH RELATING TO the process of internalization and the development of self-control have been largely confined to resistance to deviation and the occurrence of self-punitive or restitutive responses following transgression (Aronfreed, 1964). Equally important and perhaps even more prevalent behavioral manifestations of self-control are the manner in which persons regulate the self-administration of highly rewarding resources over which they have control (Bandura & Kupers, 1964; Kanfer & Marston, 1963), and their willingness to defer immediate rewards in favor of delayed, more highly valued reinforcers (e.g., Mischel & Gilligan, 1964; Mischel & Metzner, 1962).

In recent years there have been numerous investigations into behavioral manifestations of willingness to defer immediate gratification. These studies have typically employed a research paradigm in which subjects are confronted with real choices between immediately available but less valued rewards, as opposed to delayed but more valuable reinforcers (e.g., Mahrer, 1956; Mischel, 1958, 1961c). Results from this procedure provide evidence that delay responses are relatively stable, tend to increase with age, and are systematically related to other theoretically relevant variables usually subsumed under "ego-strength" constructs (e.g., Mischel, 1961b, 1961c, 1965). It has likewise been demonstrated that delay responses can be increased by direct training through raising the probability that the delayed reward is forth-

coming (Mahrer, 1956; Mischel & Staub, 1965), or by decreasing the delay interval (Mischel & Metzner, 1962). Relevant data are lacking, however, on the effects of social-learning variables that might be expected to play an influential role in the establishment of delay-of-reward behavior.

It is generally assumed that the acquisition and maintenance of the various forms of self-controlling responses are primarily achieved either through direct aversive stimulation (Aronfreed, 1964), or by means of complex intrapsychic mediational processes when immediate gratification is unavailable (Freud, 1946). Directly experienced rewarding and punishing response consequences are undoubtedly important factors in the development and maintenance of self-controlling responses. However, a number of recent studies have demonstrated that response inhibition (Bandura, 1965; Bandura, Ross, & Ross, 1963; Walters, Leat, & Mezei, 1963) and the contingent self-regulation of reinforcers (Bandura & Kupers, 1964; Bandura & Whalen, 1966; Marston, 1965; Mischel & Liebert, 1966) can be readily transmitted vicariously without the mediation of direct reinforcement. In accord with the theory of vicarious learning, it is plausible to hypothesize that self-imposed delay of reward is likewise influenced by the delay patterns displayed by social models. Indeed, some suggestive evidence for the influence of parental modeling in the development of children's willingness to delay rewards is provided in a study by Mischel (1958) who found that children from the Trinidadian Negro subculture, in which immediate self-reward is the prevailing gratification pattern, displayed a greater preference for immediate rewards than children of Trinidadian Indians, who characteristically exhibit self-denying delayed-gratification behavior.

[1] This investigation was supported by Research Grants M-5162 and M-6830 from the National Institutes of Health, United States Public Health Service.

The authors are indebted to Ruthe Burg, who assisted with various phases of this project, and to Nicholas Anastasiow, Palo Alto Unified School District, for his aid in arranging the research facilities.

[*] Albert Bandura and Walter Mischel, Modification of self-imposed delay of reward through exposure to live and symbolic models, *Journal of Personality and Social Psychology*, 1965, *3*, 5, 698-705. Reprinted by permission.

It is often mistakenly assumed that vicarious or imitative learning is essentially limited to younger age groups and to stimulus situations in which real-life models exhibit, intentionally or unwittingly, the desired social-response patterns. While undoubtedly much observational learning is fostered through exposure to live models (Bandura, 1962, in press; Bandura & Walters, 1963), once a person has developed an adequate verbal repertoire, increasing reliance is generally placed on symbolic models presented in the form of oral or written behavioral descriptions, pictorial displays, or through a combination of verbal and pictorial devices. The influence of verbally presented normative models in shaping and controlling social behavior has been abundantly documented in the research in experimental social psychology (Berg & Bass, 1961; Hovland, Janis, & Kelley, 1953). There have been, however, no systematic comparative studies of the relative magnitude and stability of changes in social behavior as a function of exposure to real-life and symbolic modeling cues. Consequently, the present investigation studied the relative efficacy of both live and verbally presented symbolic models in modifying children's delay-of-reward behavior.

In the experiment reported in this paper children who exhibited predominantly either delayed-reward or immediate-reward patterns of behavior were assigned randomly to one of three treatment conditions. One group of children observed live adult models who exhibited delay-of-reward responses counter to the group's self-gratification pattern; a second group was similarly exposed to a model displaying the opposite delay-of-reward behavior with the exception that the modeling cues were presented in written form, while a third group had no exposure to any models. Immediately following the experimental procedures the children's delay-of-reward responses were measured in the absence of the model. In order to test the generality and stability of changes in delay behavior, the subjects were reassessed by a different experimenter in a different social setting approximately 1 month after completion of the experimental phase of the study.

It was predicted that the modeling procedures would alter the children's delay-of-reward behavior in the direction of their model's response dispositions. Since an actual performance is apt to provide substantially more relevant cues with greater clarity than can be conveyed by a verbal description, it was also expected that live models would prove more efficacious than symbolic models in modifying children's self-imposed delay tendencies.

The maintenance of response patterns established through vicarious experiences is highly dependent upon reinforcement-related variables (Baer & Sherman, 1964). In view of the absence of any information concerning the naturalistic reinforcement contingencies that were operative during the relatively long period of time elapsing between the post-exposure and the generalization test phases of the experiment, no predictions were advanced regarding group differences based on the terminal assessment.

METHOD

SUBJECTS. The subjects were 60 boys and 60 girls selected from the fourth and fifth grades of three elementary schools in the Stanford vicinity.

DESIGN AND PROCEDURE.

Preexperiential assessment of delay-of-reward responses. In the initial phase of the experiment approximately 250 children were administered in their classroom groups a series of 14 paired rewards, in each of which they were asked to select either a small reward that could be obtained immediately, or a more valued item contingent on a delay period ranging from 1 to 4 weeks. The group administration (Mischel & Gilligan, 1964) proceeded in the following manner: Children were provided individual booklets containing on each page a brief description of a given set of paired objects and the associated time interval. After the experimenter had displayed both rewards and explained the temporal contingency, the children were instructed to record their choice, and to turn the page in preparation for the next set of items. The subjects were also advised to choose carefully and realistically because in *one* of the choices they would actually receive the item they selected, either on the same day or after the prescribed delay period, depending upon their recorded preference.

Half of the sets of paired rewards involved small amounts of money (e.g., $.25 today, or $.35 in 1 week), while the remaining items included edibles (e.g., small bag of salted peanuts today, or a can of mixed nuts in 2 weeks), children's magazines, and various play materials (e.g., small rubber ball today, or a large rubber ball in 2 weeks).

From the total pool of subjects those falling in the extreme top and bottom 25% of the delay-score distribution, computed separately for boys and girls, were selected for the succeeding phases of the experiment. The *low-delay* group consisted of 60 children, 30 boys and 30 girls, who displayed a marked preference for immediate reward (mean percentage of immediate choices = 83); in contrast, the group of 60 *high-delay* children exhibited a consistent pattern of delay behavior (mean percentage of delay choices = 93). The subjects in each of these two groups were then randomly assigned to one of three treatment conditions, with 10 boys and 10 girls in each subgroup (Table 1).

Experimental treatments. Approximately 4 weeks elapsed between the initial assessment of the children's delay behavior and the experimental phase of the study. Two female experimenters, each working with a different male and female model, conducted the experimental treatments.

In order to help create the set that the two phases of the experiment were unrelated, the teachers announced to their classes that a new group of experimenters from Stanford University would be conducting a similar, but independent, project concerned with object preferences of different groups of both children and adults.

The subjects were brought individually from their classrooms to the experimental room where the experimenter explained that the adults had been invited to appear at the school, since it was difficult on weekdays to see them in their various places of employment. To insure that the model was endowed with adequate prestige, the adults were described as recent college graduates. All children who were assigned to the experimental treatments observed same-sex models.

For children in the *live-model* condition, the adult entered shortly after the child was seated and introduced himself to the experimenter and to the subject. In order to further increase credibility, the experimenter described the choice procedure to the model in considerable detail as though he were a naive subject. The instructions stated the objects would be presented in pairs and in each case the subjects were to select either a less valued item that could be obtained immediately, or a more valued object conditional on a specified delay period. The participants were also informed that they would in fact receive 1 of their 14 choices.

On the pretext of the model's "busy schedule," the experimenter first administered the items to the model while the child waited for his turn. The model's paired rewards included such adult-appropriate items as chess sets, paperback books, hi-fi magazines, gourmet candy bars, jars of instant coffee, and monetary choices. Although the items differed from those subsequently administered to the children, the delay intervals necessary for attaining the more valuable rewards were similar in both sets of items. During the modeling phase the experimenter displayed each pair of items to the model who then indicated his choices verbally.

With high-delay children, the model consistently selected the immediately available rewards and in several instances commented briefly, according to a

TABLE 1 / SUMMARY OF THE EXPERIMENTAL DESIGN.

EXPERIMENTAL GROUP	PHASE 1 ASSESSMENT OF PREEXPERIMENTAL DELAY BEHAVIOR	PHASE 2 EXPERIMENTAL TREATMENTS	PHASE 3 POSTTREATMENT MEASUREMENT OF DELAY BEHAVIOR	PHASE 4 TEST FOR THE GENERALITY AND STABILITY OF DELAY BEHAVIOR
High delay				
I (N = 20)	Administration of 14 paired rewards (Set A)	Live model exhibits an immediate-reward pattern	Administration of 14 paired rewards (Set B)	Administration of 14 paired rewards (Set A)
II (N = 20)	Same	Symbolic model of immediate-reward pattern presented in written form	Same	Same
III (N = 20)	Same	No model present	Same	Same
Low delay				
IV (N = 20)	Same	Live model exhibits a delayed-reward pattern	Same	Same
V (N = 20)	Same	Symbolic model of delayed-reward pattern presented in written form	Same	Same
VI (N = 20)	Same	No model present	Same	Same

prearranged script, on the benefits of immediate self-reward (e.g., "Chess figures are chess figures. I can get much use out of the plastic ones right away.") In addition, after the fourth item, the model casually summarized his immediate-gratification philosophy of life as follows: "You probably have noticed that I am a person who likes things now. One can spend so much time in life waiting that one never gets around to really living. I find that it is better to make the most of each moment or life will pass you by." While the model periodically extolled the virtues of immediate self-gratification, he carefully refrained from depracating delay behavior; otherwise, it would be impossible to determine whether any changes in the children's behavior were a function of positive modeling of immediacy, or the modeling of negative attitudes toward postponement of gratification.

With low-delay children the procedure was identical to that described above except the model consistently selected the more valued delayed rewards. The model likewise commented periodically on the virtues of self-imposed delay (e.g., "The wooden chess figures are of much better quality, more attractive and will last longer. I'll wait two weeks for the better ones."), and expounded his postponement-of-gratification philosophy of life in the following manner: "You have probably noticed that I am a person who is willing to forego having fewer or less valuable things now, for the sake of more and bigger benefits later. I usually find that life is more gratifying when I take that carefully into account."

In both of the above experimental treatments, the models departed immediately upon completion of the choice task so as to remove situational pressures on the children to adopt the models' self-rewarding dispositions.

In the symbolic-model condition, the experimenter explained to the child that the adult who was scheduled for the same time had to leave early and consequently, he had already made his selections. In addition, the subject was told that children and adults are typically seen simultaneously to expedite matters; therefore, in order to keep the conditions as similar as possible for all participants, he would first be shown the paired items that were administered to the adult together with his recorded preferences and comments. The child was then handed the answer booklet in which were written both the model's choices and accompanying philosophy-of-life commentaries. The experimenter then exhibited each choice pair sequentially while the subject read the corresponding verbal accounts of the model's behavior.

In the *no-model-present* condition the children were informed that, because of scheduling difficulties, no adult would be present, but in order to insure intersubject comparability the items between which adults ordinarily make choices would be shown. The experimenter then simply displayed the series of paired objects. This procedure was adopted

in order to control for any effects that mere exposure to a set of reinforcers might have on children's subsequent delay behavior.

Postexposure assessment of delay behavior. Immediately following the above procedures each child was individually administered his own set of 14 paired items. The rewarding objects in the latter series differed from those employed in the initial phase of the experiment, but the money items were the same since pretesting revealed that subjects were unable to recall the exact amounts and temporal intervals involved. In order to maintain realistic choice behavior on all items, the specific payoff objects were varied randomly among the children. They were thus unable to predict which one of their choices they were likely to receive even if some prior communication between subjects had occurred.

Test for generalization and stability of altered delay patterns. Between 4-5 weeks after the experimental treatments all children were readministered the initial set of 14 items within their classroom settings utilizing the same group procedure described earlier. The same experimenter who had conducted the preexperimental measurement of delay responses presided over the follow-up assessment. Considering the relatively long temporal intervals separating the various phases of the study, the variation in experimenters, and the fact that in the terminal assessment children recorded their pref-

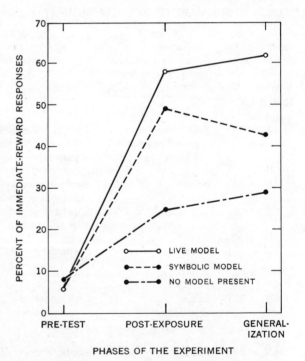

FIGURE 1 / MEAN PERCENTAGE OF IMMEDIATE-REWARD RESPONSES BY HIGH-DELAY CHILDREN ON EACH OF THREE TEST PERIODS FOR EACH OF THREE EXPERIMENTAL CONDITIONS.

erences privately in the context of their natural classroom situation, it was assumed that the follow-up data would provide a particularly stringent test of both the generality and the stability of modeling effects.

Dependent measures. Changes in the subjects' behavior were measured in terms of the relative number of delayed responses produced by the low-delay groups and conversely, the number of immediate responses displayed by children in the high-delay groups at each of the three phases of the experiment.

RESULTS

Figure 1 shows the mean percentage of immediate-reward responses produced by the high-delay children on each of the test periods as a function of treatment conditions.

Analysis of variance of these data (Table 2)[Ed] reveals that the main effects of modeling and experimental phases are highly significant sources of variance. In addition, the two modeling procedures proved to be differentially effective at the immediate postexposure and the later generalization phases of the experiment.

Further comparisons by the t test of pairs of means across experimental phases (Table 3) show that high-delay children in all three conditions not only altered significantly their delay-of-reward behavior in favor of immediate gratification, but also maintained the response changes long after the experimental interventions.

Moreover, comparisons between groups at each of the test phases (Table 4) reveal that children who had been presented either live or symbolic models differed substantially in their postexposure delay behavior from the no-model controls, with the live-model condition yielding the greatest differences. It should also be noted that while the live and symbolic models were equally effective within the immediate social-influence setting, the changes in delay responses induced by the live model were significantly more stable over time. This is shown in the finding that high-delay children who had observed the live model continued to display in the generalization test a significantly higher level of immediate-reward responses than children in either the symbolic model or the control groups, which did not differ significantly from each other.

The corresponding set of data for low-delay children exposed to models exhibiting a prefer-

Ed *Tables 2 and 5 are omitted.*

TABLE 3 / COMPARISON OF PAIRS OF MEANS ACROSS EXPERIMENTAL PHASES.

TREATMENT CONDITIONS	PRETEST VERSUS POST-EXPOSURE TEST t	PRETEST VERSUS GENERALI-ZATION TEST t	POST-EXPOSURE TEST VERSUS GENERALI-ZATION TEST t
Immediate-reward treatment			
Live model	7.13***	7.87***	0.64
Symbolic model	4.76***	4.07***	0.69
No model control	2.77**	3.37**	0.60
Delayed-reward treatment			
Live model	6.96***	4.32***	3.09**
Symbolic model	5.93***	3.41**	1.34
No model control	4.82***	1.99	1.93

** $p < .01$.
*** $p < .001$.

TABLE 4 / COMPARISON OF PAIRS OF MEANS BETWEEN TREATMENT CONDITIONS FOR HIGH-DELAY CHILDREN EXPOSED TO IMMEDIATE-REWARD MODELS.

EXPERIMENTAL PHASES	LIVE MODEL VERSUS SYMBOLIC MODEL t	LIVE MODEL VERSUS CONTROL t	SYMBOLIC MODEL VERSUS CONTROL
Postexposure test	<1	3.41***	2.46**
Generalization test	2.52***	4.22***	1.70

** $p < .01$.
*** $p < .001$.

ence for more valued delayed reinforcers is presented graphically in Figure 2.

Analysis of variance of these scores (Table 5)[Ed] reveals that the children's willingness to delay gratification increased substantially across the phases of the experiment.

Although the overall differences between the three experimental groups were not of statistically significant magnitude, it is evident from supplementary analyses (Table 3) that the two conditions employing modeling procedures were chief contributors to enduring increases in delay behavior. Within-treatment comparisons disclose that both forms of modeling produced highly significant temporary and long-term increases in

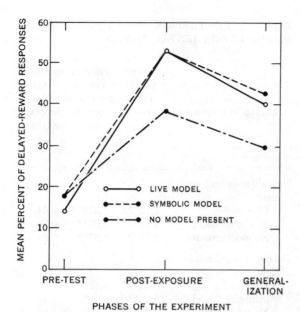

FIGURE 2 / MEAN PERCENTAGE OF DELAYED-REWARD RESPONSES BY LOW-DELAY CHILDREN ON EACH OF THREE TEST PERIODS FOR EACH OF THREE EXPERIMENTAL CONDITIONS.

self-imposed delay of reward. On the other hand, although the no-model control subjects exhibited a temporary change, their subsequently assessed delay behavior did not differ significantly from their preexperimental level. Unlike the findings based on the high-delay children, however, the low-delay subjects were not differentially affected by the live as compared to the symbolic model. Another noteworthy difference between the two sets of data is the finding that experimentally induced immediate-reward responses generally remained more stable over time (see Figure 2 and Table 3) than did self-imposed delay behavior.

DISCUSSION

The results of the present investigation provide further support for the influential role of modeling variables in the social transmission of self-controlling responses. Children who had shown a predominantly delayed-reward pattern displayed an increased preference for immediate and less valued rewards as a function of observing models favoring immediate gratification; conversely, subjects who had exhibited a marked disposition toward immediate rewards displayed an enduring increased willingness to wait for more highly valued delayed reinforcers following exposure to models displaying high-delay behavior.

Although in all subgroup comparisions the live model produced changes of greater magnitude than those induced by the verbally presented symbolic model, both forms of modeling procedures were essentially equally efficacious within the immediate social-influence setting. With high-delay children, however, the symbolic model yielded relatively weaker long-term effects. There are several possible explanations for the fact that similar long-term differences between modeling conditions were not obtained based on findings from low-delay subjects. This discrepancy may partly reflect the effects of differential reinforcement contingencies characteristically associated with high- and low-delay behavior. In social training in our culture self-imposed delay-of-reward behavior is actively modeled, encouraged, and generously rewarded by socialization agents, whereas immediate self-gratification is negatively reinforced on many occasions. To the extent that adoption by high-delay children of immediate self-gratification responses requires some reduction of previously established inhibitions, it would be expected that actual observation of a moderately prestigeful adult exhibiting low-delay behavior would have stronger disinhibitory cue value than a verbal description of his responses. This factor, if operative, would suggest that predictions about the relative efficacy of live and symbolic models should consider not only the number and clarity of modeling cues associated with different modes of presentation, but also the possibly greater inhibitory or disinhibitory influence of performances by live models.

An alternative explanation, and one that accounts for other obtained differences, is in terms of the temporal variations in reinforcement invariably associated with immediate- and delayed-reward responses. There is considerable empirical evidence that behavior can be more effectively maintained by immediate reinforcement than by delayed rewards (Renner, 1964). Consequently, self-imposed delay behavior, which is accompanied by less favorable reinforcement conditions, would be harder to establish and even more difficult to maintain in the absence of intervening positive reinforcements. This interpretation would help to explain both the greater stability of changes in immediate-compared to delayed-reward behavior among subjects in the no-model conditions, and the larger decrement in delay responses among subjects whose behavior was being altered in the direction of delayed gratification. It will be recalled that, of the three groups in the latter condition, only the live-model treatment yielded a statistically significant decrement in terminal delay behavior. Although subjects in the latter group continued to exhibit a higher level of delay behavior than they displayed in the pre-experimental phase, nevertheless difficulty in maintaining the newly acquired behavior in the prolonged absence of the model, reduced the possibility of obtaining significant differences between modeling conditions. These overall findings point to the necessity for supporting newly established self-control behavior, particularly when it is associated with less optimal reinforcement conditions as in the case of self-imposed denial of readily available rewarding resources.

The results of this study also provide an interesting contrast between traditional psychoanalytically based theories of personality and those derived from principles of social learning. According to the psychoanalytic theory of delay behavior (Freud, 1946; Singer, 1955), aroused impulses press for immediate discharge of tension through overt motoric activity. As a function of repeated association of tension reduction with goal objects, and development of greater ego organization, absence or imposed delay of satisfying objects results in the substitution of hallucinatory satisfactions, and other thought processes that convert free cathexes into "bound cathexes." The capacity to delay or inhibit motor discharge by substituting cathected ideational representations presumably reflects the gradual shift from primary-process activity to reality-oriented secondary-process thinking.

The psychoanalytic approach thus leads one to seek determinants of delay behavior in terms of hypothetical internal events in the form of ego organizations and energy-binding ideations. In contrast, social-learning theory, as illustrated in both the findings of the present experiment, and those to which reference was made earlier, views manipulable social-stimulus events as the critical determinants of self-controlling behavior.

SUMMARY

In a comparative test of the relative efficacy of live and symbolic models for modifying delay-of-reward behavior, groups of children with marked preferences for either immediate but less valued rewards, or more valuable delay reinforcers, were assigned randomly to 1 of 3 experimental conditions. One group observed live models who exhibited delay behavior that was counter to the children's pattern; a second group was presented essentially the same modeling cues except in symbolic verbal form; while a third group had no exposure to any models. Changes in Ss' delay-of-reward behavior were measured immediately following exposure to the modeling procedures, and reassessed approximately one month later within a different stimulus situation. Both live and symbolic models produced substantial modifications in delay-of-reward behavior within the immediate social-influence setting, but the changes induced in high-delay children through exposure to symbolic models were less stable over time.

REFERENCES

ARONFREED, J. Conduct and conscience: A natural history of internalization. Unpublished manuscript, University of Pennsylvania, 1964.

BAER, D. M., & SHERMAN, J. A. Reinforcement control of generalized imitation in young children. *Journal of Experimental Child Psychology*, 1964, 1, 37-49.

BANDURA, A. Social learning through imitation. In M. R. Jones (Ed.), *Nebraska symposium on motivation: 1962.* Lincoln: Univer. Nebraska Press, 1962. Pp. 211-269.

BANDURA, A. Influence of models' reinforcement contingencies on the acquisition of imitative responses. *Journal of Personality and Social Psychology*, 1965, 1, 589-595.

BANDURA, A. Vicarious processes: A case of no-trial learning. In L. Berkowitz (Ed.), *Advances in experimental social psychology.* Vol. 2. New York: Academic Press, in press.

BANDURA, A., & KUPERS, CAROL J. Transmission of patterns of self-reinforcement through modeling. *Journal of Abnormal and Social Psychology*, 1964, 69, 1-9.

BANDURA, A., ROSS, DOROTHEA, & ROSS, SHEILA A. Vicarious reinforcement and imitative learning. *Journal of Abnormal and Social Psychology*, 1963, 67, 601-607.

BANDURA, A., & WALTERS, R. H. *Social learning and personality development.* New York: Holt, Rinehart, & Winston, 1963.

BANDURA, A., & WHALEN, CAROL K. The influence of antecedent reinforcement and divergent modeling cures on patterns of self-reward. *Journal of Personality and Social Psychology*, 1966, in press.

BERG, J. A., & BASS, B. M. (Eds.) *Conformity and deviation.* New York: Harper, 1961.

FREUD, S. Formulations regarding the two principles in mental function. In *Collected Papers.* Vol. 4. London: Hogarth Press, 1946. Pp. 13-21.

HOVLAND, C. I., JANIS, I. L., & KELLEY, H. H. *Communication and persuasion.* New Haven: Yale Univer. Press, 1953.

KANFER, F. H., & MARSTON, A. R. Conditioning of self-reinforcing responses: An analogue to self-confidence training. *Psychological Reports*, 1963, *13*, 63-70.

MAHRER, A. R. The role of expectancy in delayed reinforcement. *Journal of Experimental Psychology*, 1956, *52*, 101-106.

MARSTON, A. R. Imitation, self-reinforcement, and reinforcement of another person. *Journal of Personality and Social Psychology*, 1965, *2*, 255-261.

MISCHEL, W. Preference for delayed reinforcement: An experimental study of a cultural observation. *Journal of Abnormal and Social Psychology*, 1958, *56*, 57-61.

MISCHEL, W. Delay of gratification, need for achievement, and acquiescence in another culture. *Journal of Abnormal and Social Psychology*, 1961, *62*, 543-552. (a)

MISCHEL, W. Father-absence and delay of gratification: Cross-cultural comparisons. *Journal of Abnormal and Social Psychology*, 1961, *63*, 116-124. (b)

MISCHEL, W. Preference for delayed reinforcement and social responsibility. *Journal of Abnormal and Social Psychology*, 1961, *62*, 1-7. (c)

MISCHEL, W. Research and theory on delay of gratification. In B. A. Maher (Ed.), *Progress in experimental personality research*. Vol. 2. New York: Academic Press, 1965, in press.

MISCHEL, W., & GILLIGAN, CAROL. Delay of gratification, motivation for the prohibited gratification, and responses to temptation. *Journal of Abnormal and Social Psychology*, 1964, *69*, 411-417.

MISCHEL, W., & LIEBERT, R. M. Effects of discrepancies between observed and imposed reward criteria on their acquisition and transmission. *Journal of Personality and Social Psychology*, 1966, in press.

MISCHEL, W., & METZNER, R. Preference for delayed reward as a function of age, intelligence, and length of delay interval. *Journal of Abnormal and Social Psychology*, 1962, *64*, 425-431.

MISCHEL, W., & STAUB, E. Effects of expectancy on working and waiting for larger rewards. *Journal of Personality and Social Psychology*, 1965, *2*, 625-633.

RENNER, K. W. Delay of reinforcement: A historical review. *Psychological Bulletin*, 1964, *61*, 341-361.

SINGER, J. L. Delayed gratification and ego development: Implications for clinical and experimental research. *Journal of Consulting Psychology*, 1955, *19*, 259-266.

WALTERS, R. H., LEAT, MARION, & MEZEI, L. Inhibition and disinhibition of responses through empathetic learning. *Canadian Journal of Psychology*, 1963, *17*, 235-243.

61/CONSCIENCE AND CONFLICT: THE MORAL FORCE IN PERSONALITY[1,2]/

WESLEY ALLINSMITH[*]

THE CHARACTERISTICS OF ONE'S moral code determine how often and in what life situations inner conflict is aroused, influence the ways such conflict is experienced, and set limits on the techniques that can be used to resolve it. The goal of this paper is to convey the theoretical richness of the topic and to clarify some of the research implications. Therefore, we give only a brief outline of our empirical work on the acquisition of moral needs; details of the latter are presented elsewhere (1, 2). Instead, we describe a number of the problems we have encountered in the development of our investigations. The paper closes with a discussion of some hypothetical interrelationships between moral standards and other facets of personality.

In using the concept of "moral needs" we refer to the *internalized* standards, the "voice of conscience," rather than simply societal rules or role expectations to which people may give lip-service without really subscribing. It is common to use the term "superego" in this connection. "Superego" refers to certain learned needs in a person that provide internal reward and punishment regardless of whether the person's actions also provoke positive or negative reactions from other people.

If this definition is accepted, it has meaning for the way we do research. In most actual life situations there is usually a good possibility that an antisocial act will have environmental as well as internal repercussions. As a result, we usually cannot tell from observing a man's behavior how much his inhibitions are motivated by fear or wish for praise, and how much by inner moral forces. Similarly, we cannot tell to what extent his disturbance following a misdeed is caused by fear rather than guilt feeling. In research on superego we need evidence of conformity to a standard regardless of reality pressures, or of guilt following violation of the standard regardless of reality pressures. In practice, this ordinarily means that we have to create experimentally a plausible circumstance that permits a tempted subject to violate his norm without fear of discovery. There must be neither an *external* advantage to him from conformity, nor an external disadvantage for infraction.

This principle of eliminating risk of getting caught in a moral violation is one of the minimal prerequisites for defining moral standards in accordance with our theoretical conception. It will make easier the task of describing other prerequisites if we first concretize our work by illustrating the kind of research design used and by giving the gist of our findings.

We used a story-completion device as our measure of guilt (1). In each story-beginning the hero violates a commonly held moral standard; for example, he disobeys his mother or has hostile thoughts about a friendly male authority figure. The story is so phrased that the infraction either cannot be detected or cannot be attributed to him unless of course he gives himself up or gives himself away, acts which would in themselves be evidence of a guilt reaction.

Subjects were 112 junior high school boys from a wide range of economic backgrounds in Detroit. Factors such as age, intelligence, religion, race, and ethnicity were controlled. The boys were asked to finish each of the stories, and we coded intensity of guilt from the story-endings. Since we were interested in relating

[1] This paper was presented originally at the Biennial Conference of the Society for Research in Child Development at Robert Allerton Park, University of Illinois, in April 1955, as part of a symposium entitled "Research on Conflict and Personality."

[2] The viewpoints expressed here were developed and the study mentioned was done in the course of participating in a larger project. Other investigators, who were concerned with aspects of conflict and defense different from those stressed herein, collected additional data on the same subjects. The larger project was directed by Daniel R. Miller and Guy E. Swanson of the University of Michigan, and was supported, in part, by a grant from the National Institute of Mental Health, U. S. Public Health Service. A fuller report of the methods and empirical findings stemming from an application of some of the concepts in this paper has appeared in a book (1).

[*] Wesley Allinsmith, Conscience and conflict: the moral force in personality, *Child Development*, 1957, 28, 469-476. Reprinted by permission of the Society for Research in Child Development and the author.

childhood experiences to intensity of guilt, we interviewed the mothers of the boys in their homes concerning the boys' upbringing.

In order to test whether events early in life are factors in moral development, we asked the mothers about their sons' weaning and toilet training. In addition, we inquired into current disciplinary practices. From their reports, we divided the group into those who tended to attack the children directly and those who used "psychological" measures such as reasoning with the child and appealing to his love for the parents.

Our results indicate that it is possible to predict from certain experiences in infancy the moral feelings of children 12 years later. We found significant relationships between intensity of guilt over hostile thoughts and the variables of age of completion of weaning and age of bowel training. Current disciplinary procedures also seem to be connected with guilt over hostile thoughts. The over-all direction of the results indicates associations between high guilt about aggression and early weaning, early bowel training, and psychological discipline.[Ed] The discipline finding has since been corroborated with a sample of adults (2). But in analyzing the items concerning disobedience of the mother, the results provided us with a puzzling contradiction to the findings for guilt over aggression. High guilt over disobedience was associated with *late* rather than early weaning and *late* rather than early bowel training. A possible interpretation is that guilts in different moral areas may have different developmental origins and that it is unjustified to use a single measure of "guilt" in advancing hypotheses about the genesis of superego. Incidentally, social class was worthless as a predictor of guilt over both disobedience and hostile thoughts.

What are some of the problems in method that had to be resolved in order to do this kind of research? First there is the problem of control of substantive *content*: that is, whether the standard concerns anger, stealing, disobedience or some other value area. A second dimension of moral needs that has to be controlled is the *height* of the standard. This refers to the degree of impulse-expression permitted. For example, one person might be guilty for stealing a three-cent stamp but another might experience no guilt unless he stole a whole sheet of stamps. The *breadth* of a standard is a third dimension

that has to be controlled. This takes into account the range of situations in which the standard applies. A broad standard might state, "You must never steal under any circumstances." A narrower one might be, "You must not steal *except* from the rich, or when starving."

A fourth dimension is the *severity* of the standard. Two boys might each have a standard which forbids stealing anything over a dime from one's mother, but if each stole 50 cents, one of them might be much more remorseful than the second. In such a case, the standards are the same in moral area (theft), the same in height (prohibition of anything over a dime), and the same in breadth (from the mother), but differ in intensity—what we call the severity.

In the research we have briefly described we wished to study this last variable, severity. We chose as our measure the intensity of guilt in the subjects' story-endings. In order to be able to interpret the results, we had to keep content, height, and breadth constant. For this purpose, we found the story-completion type of test very satisfactory, since the beginnings can be expanded to include all the details necessary to specify the exact nature of the moral violation as well as to eliminate convincingly any risk of the hero's getting caught. To illustrate the importance of controlling moral area, height, and breadth, suppose we asked a child to finish a story which reads, "Henry steals some money from a man asleep in the park. Nobody sees him do it." Height is not held constant; we cannot know how much money each child imagines it to be. Nor is breadth controlled, because we have not specified anything about the man who is the victim or about the motive for Henry's action in stealing. If we used such an item, we could not be sure of the meaning of the results. Different degrees of guilt in the story-endings might reflect not differences in severity but varying interpretations by the children of the test item.

We have now raised two of the primary considerations in investigating internalized moral needs, the principle of elimination of risk to the violator, and the principle of controlling such factors as height and breadth. A third issue is that there must be some feasible way of measuring guilt. Once a coding scheme was devised, guilt phenomena could be coded reliably and not too arduously from the story-endings. But there is a major complication in inventing a coding scheme for detecting guilt. If subjects were always obliging enough to experience guilt in the form of conscious self-blame they would

[Ed] *Caution is called for, however, in the interpretation of these findings because of curvilinearity in the distributions* (1).

be very helpful to researchers. Unfortunately, they are sometimes unaware of guilt reactions because of defenses which they use to avoid unpleasant feelings. When guilt has been pushed out of awareness, it cannot appear as manifest remorse in the story-endings.

How can remorse be recognized when it has been defended against? The way we resolved this dilemma was to assume that since danger of external repercussions has been ruled out by the experimental design, any indication in a subject's story of pain, anxiety, or misfortune experienced by the hero following transgression may justifiably be interpreted as a superego reaction. For example, moral violators may show entirely unrealistic fear of being caught. This is a common defense against guilt in our culture: to avoid awareness of his own self-blame, a person externalizes the conflict by projecting his standards, seeing *someone else* as wishing to blame or punish him. In terms of this reasoning, a man who has misbehaved secretly and becomes afraid that lightning will strike him is as clearly guilt-ridden as the person who says his conscience bothers him. Still other evidences of guilt are attempts to make reparation, to confess, to provoke punishment from others or to punish oneself. As examples of self-punishment, in our data, the heroes often shot or stabbed themselves "by accident" or deliberately banished or otherwise deprived themselves.

In discussing the research problems we have been facing, we have mentioned several aspects of moral needs. Next we shall discuss briefly both some additional research implications of the dimensions already covered, and the possible fruitfulness of a few other dimensions our group has conceptualized.

In mentioning content, height, breadth, and severity up to now, we have indicated the possibility of studying each of these individually. One could also assess their interrelations. In mapping the constellation of a person's moral needs, it would be necessary to know, for example, that his standards are high and broad, but not severe, in the content area of stealing, and high and severe, but not broad, in respect to sexual inhibitions. Thus in comparing groups, one might want to predict that people with particular child-rearing experiences, or particular religious affiliations, will have distinctive patternings of height, breadth, and severity in given moral areas. Undoubtedly the standards of some individuals are severe in many content areas. Presumably, when some of these standards are contradictory, the conflict is intense since there is no basis for giving one value precedence over another. If telling a lie is as bad as hurting someone's feelings, a person may have difficulty using white lies. It may be healthier to have some hierarchization of moral needs with respect to severity.

Similarly, if within one moral area different heights are associated with very similar degrees of severity—if an adolescent boy becomes nearly as guilty for insulting his father as he would be for murdering him or nearly as guilty for kissing a girl as he would for having premarital intercourse—then discrimination of the relative permissibility of various actions is impaired and the person's adjustment handicapped.

Let us move on to a new aspect of the moral forces. A very fascinating problem is raised by workers like Flugel (6), Fromm (8), and Riesman (11) who have emphasized the fact that some people are "other-directed," taking as their ethical guide the views of peers or leaders rather than inner standards of their own. Among the possible explanations of such behavior there are at least three that concern the nature of the moral needs: (a) The other-directed person may have *no internalized standards.* To borrow a metaphor from Riesman (11) and Murphy (10), he has no gyro stabilizer to keep him upright through upheavals in the environment. As a result he is influenced solely by expediency. Some anthropologists (3, 9) believe that certain societies (e.g., Japan) are "shame" rather than "guilt" cultures. In shame cultures people respond to external coercion, to role expectations, but have no conscience. (b) A second explanation of other-direction is that the person is "heteronomous" (5). This means that he has *only one internalized standard,* that of doing what is demanded. He is guilty if he does not conform to role requirements, but no kind of action is abhorrent if his peers or leader urge it. (c) Finally, a person who conforms to others' wishes and takes his cues from them may be a very guilt-ridden person—one, consequently, with low self-esteem—who is *oversensitive to approval and disapproval because of his need to defend against his own guilts.* He "projects his superego" (6) so that he sees others as the ones who know what the standards should be. In that way he can avoid awareness that the standards are parts of his own needs. If he then violates one of his own (unconscious) standards, he tries to find someone who will condone the behavior or forgive it or who has done likewise. Seeing that person as approving the behavior constitutes a denial of his own blame-worthiness. When no one can be found who approves, the guilty person may find a disapproving superego figure whom he fears and needs to placate. In this way he can continue to see the standard as external and avoid awareness of the intrapsychic conflict. Both varieties of projection of the superego—seeking someone who will approve or someone who will disapprove—lead to dependence on opinions of others. There are several variables implicit in the foregoing discussion and a number of research problems. We have explored the possibility of measuring one of the variables, defense against guilt, and have found promising leads in our data. For example, many subjects react to violation with fear rather than conscious guilt even when the chance of being caught has been eliminated.[4]

There are at least four more aspects of moral needs that can be measured. The first is the *perceived source* of standards. To find out whether they see their standards as "own" or "induced" forces, we asked the junior high school boys how they know whether a contemplated action is right or wrong. Some boys told us they "just know," but others, relying apparently on a more external guide, say that in making a moral decision they "think what mother would say." Our results indicate that type of perceived source is related to social class and other indices of social position.

Like or *dislike* of conscience is another aspect that could be studied. Some people feel burdened by their standards; others take pride in them. One instance of this rejection of standards is the rebelliousness of the adolescent, who may do his best to deny to himself any allegiance to the parents' values. Dislike of conscience may be one of the conditions giving rise to a tendency to defend against guilt.

A related factor is that of the relative *emphasis on ideals as opposed to prohibitions*. Some persons may experience their self-admonitions chiefly in the form of "don'ts." Others may

phrase theirs in more positive terms: "do well" rather than "don't fail"; "be honest" instead of "don't lie and steal." Conceivably, negative emphasis may be associated with dislike of conscience as well as with the ways the parents have exhorted and rewarded or warned and blamed the child.

Vigilance is still another factor that can be investigated. Some people are on guard all the time—moral needs are salient for them so that these individuals have to serve as "vigilantes" in watching out for possible ethical lapses in their own behavior and often in the actions of others.

With regard to all the dimensions we have mentioned, the degree of generality of each over various moral areas and the interrelations of the factors would need to be determined for a full description of the organization and functioning of a person's moral needs.

However, much broader research problems emerge when we consider moral needs in the context of the entire control system of the personality—that is, in relation to the skills that enable an individual to defer pleasure for greater ultimate gain, to think before acting, to anticipate external dangers, and to defend himself against the internal danger of being overwhelmed by tension from unsatisfied needs. Let us say here that the theoretical formulation we are about to present is offered as a set of hypotheses and arbitrary definitions that may be fruitful for deriving testable propositions and designing research, not as assertions that have already been tested experimentally. In thinking about inner conflict and its implications for personality, we believe there are three chief reasons for taking into account the individual's moral needs. The first of these is that moral needs are so often a factor in *causing* conflict. It is true that a person may experience a conflict that does not involve internalized moral standards. He may be torn between a wish for gratification of some sort and an external danger, such as the prospect of parental disapproval. But external dangers can often be evaded, whereas, when the individual's own moral needs are opposed to his wishes, there is an internal danger of *self*-disapproval that cannot be dodged. In our society, if not in all societies, important conflicts commonly have internalized moral components.

The second reason for concerning ourselves with moral needs is that the *outcome* of conflict is largely determined by them. As a result of the moral forces within him, a person must either control himself, often distorting his per-

---

[4] An alternative to interpreting unrealistic fear after moral violation as defense against guilt was pointed out to me by John W. M. Whiting and his research group in the Laboratory of Human Development at Harvard. A very angry person with no outlet for the feeling may through projection of the anger perceive others as wanting to punish him even when there is no unconscious guilt. The distinction between the two interpretations can be made experimentally but may prove difficult to uphold in observations of real-life situations or in evaluating interview data that is limited to subjects' reports of their conscious reactions to moral transgressions.

ceptions defensively to cope with the tension he feels, or else he must suffer the guilt which will accompany a violation of his standards. If the moral needs are more powerful than the temptation, the person will inhibit himself, but having an unsatisfied wish, is likely to use defense mechanisms to allay the resulting tension. He will be able to avoid defending only if an adequate substitute satisfaction can be found, or if his personality organization is strong enough to stand the feeling of frustration (unfortunately, no one is this mature at all times). If the temptation is more pressing than the moral needs, the individual seeks gratification, but becomes guilty, and this too may lead to defense. In the latter case we speak of defense against guilt to distinguish the circumstance from defense against impulse. As students of personality, our second reason, then, for being interested in moral needs is that they motivate delay of gratification and the use of defenses, and they cause guilt.

Our third reason is that quite apart from determining the fact that defensive distortions are used, the moral aspects of personality cause individual differences in ways and frequency of defending—that is, in characteristic ways of resolving conflict. To put it another way, the nature of a person's moral needs affects what has often been called his "character structure." In the first place, of course, the particular impulses or guilts a person defends against are determined by the substantive content of his moral needs. One person tends to become disturbed and defend primarily because of the unacceptability to him of his hostile feelings or behaviors, another because of sexual wishes or sexual activities. The *frequency* of defense is affected by the height of the standards. If a person's standards in the area of aggression are so high as to forbid the expression of even a little bit of anger toward an authority figure, then every time that person's employer is irritating, the person will have to defend.

Another consideration in predicting frequency of defense is the breadth of the standards. If one must avoid anger not only toward father-figures but also toward mother-figures, brother-figures, cousin-figures, inferiors, children, and dogs, then there are many situations in which one may have to defend. Frequency of defense is influenced by still another aspect, the severity of the standards. The more intense the guilt a person will experience for a violation, the more likely he is to defend against the forbidden impulse, and if temptation overcomes him

and infraction occurs, the more likely he will be to defend against guilt.

In addition to determining the content of the impulses or guilts defended against and to affecting the frequency of defense, the nature of the moral needs influences *which defenses are used.* Some defense mechanisms may be ruled out because they involve behaviors that are morally unacceptable to the individual. For instance, the defense of restriction of the ego (7) may be unavailable to a person who would define it as "quitting." Some mechanisms may come to be used more readily because they are especially suited to warding off those particular impulses or guilts with which the individual is concerned. Theorists (e.g., 7) have speculated that repression may be of particular value in coping with sexual desires, and other processes of distortion may be of more use against anger. Where height, breadth, or severity of a given standard necessitates frequent defense, those mechanisms will be more relied upon which afford a constant protection, although at the expense of a more lasting change in the personality. An example is "reaction formation" ("reactive alteration of the ego") (7). When this defense is used against anger, the person becomes incapable of the affect, even when it is appropriate to the situation. He is always kind, and the angrier he becomes unconsciously, the kinder he becomes on the surface. The more severe the internalized prohibitions, the more reaction formation will take on the generalized form of a character trait (4).

Thus, quite in addition to the intrinsic interest and importance of moral needs, the fact that they are so relevant for the theory of defense mechanisms and inner conflict argues that their investigation will pay dividends.

REFERENCES

1. ALLINSMITH, W. The learning of moral standards. In Miller, D. R. & Swanson, G. E. *Inner Conflict and Defense.* New York: Henry Holt, 1960, 141-176.

2. ALLINSMITH, W., AND GREENING, T. C. Guilt over anger as predicted from parental discipline: a study of superego development. *Amer. Psychologist*, 1955, *10*, 320. (Abstract)

3. BENEDICT, RUTH F. *The chrysanthemum and the sword.* Boston: Houghton Mifflin, 1946.

4. FENICHEL, O. Outline of clinical psychoanalysis. *Psychoanal. Quart.*, 1932, *1*, 545-652.

5. FENICHEL, O. *The psychoanalytic theory of neurosis.* New York: Norton, 1945.

6. FLUGEL, J. C. *Man, morals and society.* New York: International Universities Press, 1945.

7. FREUD, ANNA. *The ego and the mechanisms of defence.* New York: International Universities Press, 1946.

8. FROMM, E. *Man for himself.* N.Y.: Rinehart, 1947.

9. HSU, F. L. K. Suppression versus repression; a limited psychological interpretation of four cultures. *Psychiatry,* 1949, *12,* 223-242.

10. MURPHY, G. Personality. N.Y.: Harper, 1947.

11. REISMAN, D. *The lonely crowd.* New Haven: Yale Univer. Press, 1950.

62/INTELLECTUAL MALFUNCTIONING AND PERSONALITY/EDITH A. WEISSKOPF*

IT IS ONE OF THE TRADITIONAL TASKS of the psychologist to evaluate the intellectual potentialities of individuals. The traditional tool for such evaluation is the intelligence test. At the same time, experience with the use of intelligence tests has shown that this instrument has serious limitations. If, for instance, of two individuals with the same IQ, one behaves considerably more "intelligently" outside the test situation than the other one, it becomes evident that intelligent behavior is affected by factors which may not be measured by traditional intelligence tests.[1] More specifically, these factors are thought to be personality traits, such as persistence, emotional stability, curiosity, etc. However, it would be erroneous to say that these personality factors affect the degree to which an individual behaves intelligently outside the test situation without ever influencing the scores on intelligence tests. That psychometric performance also may be influenced by personality factors is a tacit assumption made by clinical

[1] The statement that the term "intelligence" as used in the field of intelligence testing has a different meaning from the same term as used in everyday language expresses the same idea in different words.

psychologists (62) and corroborated by various studies which submit the components of intelligence to factorial analysis (3, 9, 61).

Thus, a child with a comparatively high IQ, who functions on a low academic level, may be handicapped by personality factors unfavorable for high academic achievement. In this case, these unfavorable personality factors depress the individual's academic achievement more than they depress his psychometric performance. Stoddard (58) indicates that the nature of the psychometric situation prevents certain personality factors from having an effect on test scores, while the same factors may be of potent influence on intellectual achievement outside the test situation. The ability to concentrate one's effort and interest over a long period of time on a problem, for example, is a factor which may have little effect on psychometric performances, since each problem in such performances requires only a very short amount of time. On the other hand, the ability to make a persistent effort may be an important factor affecting intellectual achievement outside the test situation. In other cases, nonintellective factors may depress test scores as much as they depress per-

* Edith A. Weisskopf, Intellectual malfunctioning and personality, *Journal of Abnormal and Social Psychology,* 1951, *46,* 410-423. Reprinted by permission.

formance outside the test situation. For example, this is the case with certain individuals who are described as being pseudofeebleminded. The test scores of such individuals fall within the feebleminded range. Their behavior outside the test situation is in agreement with the test scores, i.e., on a defective level. Yet, there may be indicators in these individuals' performance on tests and projective techniques as well as in their present and past behavior outside test situations which make the clinician suspect that nonintellective personality factors rather than low intellectual ability are responsible for the defective behavior. Such suspicion is, of course, of great practical importance to the clinician, since unfavorable personality traits may yield to therapeutic effort. Thus, in studying nonintellective factors inhibiting intellectual functioning, the psychologist should not limit himself to cases where he finds a discrepancy between psychometric score and performance outside the test situation.

It will be noted that no attempt has been made, thus far, to draw, by definition, a line of demarcation between intellective and nonintellective factors. Wechsler says "personality traits *enter into* the effectiveness of intelligent behavior and, hence, into any global concept of intelligence itself" (62, p. 82). If this is the case, the question may arise how these personality traits can be distinguished from "intellective" factors. Probably the only way to distinguish the two kinds of factors is by enumeration, not by definition. We speak traditionally of the ability to do arithmetical computation or to grasp spatial relationships as intellective factors, while we do not include curiosity under the same heading. The recognition that intelligent behavior is influenced by every aspect of the personality may induce the psychologist to do away completely with any line of demarcation between intellective and nonintellective factors.

Part of the psychological literature on nonintellective factors affecting intelligence deals with the correlation of personality traits as measured by personality tests with intelligence as measured by intelligence tests (43). This is a perfectly legitimate and fruitful approach. But this approach should not exclude another type of approach, in which the problem of total personality and intelligence is not seen as a correlational investigation between isolated traits but as a causal investigation of the effect of various aspects of the case history of individuals on their intellectual functioning. The intelligence of individuals is studied as affected by parent-child relationship, and by the complicated dynamic interaction of impulses and defense mechanisms, by the vicissitudes of psychosexual development, and the like. It is highly important that we psychologists, the traditional evaluators of intelligence, should give this dynamic approach to the study of intelligence the emphasis it deserves.

It is the purpose of this article to survey some of the dynamic personality factors as this is a survey of case studies of individuals rather than large-scale statistical investigations. The individuals studied are handicapped in intellectual functioning by emotional factors. In some cases psychotherapy has greatly increased their intellectual efficiency. Here, as in so many instances, the study of abnormal personalities serves as a magnifying glass to help us take notice of factors which are present to a lesser degree in the normal personality. The same emotional factors which cause pathological intellectual blocking in some individuals may, by being present in different degrees, become responsible for quantitative and qualitative differences in intelligence within the normal range.

Another fruitful and "magnifying" source for getting acquainted with the influence of personality factors on intelligence are case studies of geniuses, i.e., of individuals with whom such factors play a strongly enhancing rather than a blocking role. However, such studies are not included in the present paper.

This article is a discussion of some emotional factors which have been identified in the course of intensive study of individuals as possible blocks for the unhampered functioning of cognition. In most cases a combination of these etiological factors, rather than one single factor, is responsible for intellectual blocking.

ETIOLOGICAL FACTORS[2]

LACK OF PARENTAL REWARD. It is well known that the emotional relationship of parents with their children may influence the children's intellectual efficiency. Thus, parental rejection may be a factor which blocks the child in the progress of his intellectual development. There are various possible connections between parental rejection and learning disabilities. The author has pointed out one connection in a previous treatment (63), the main points of which are as follows:

[2] The sections in the following discussion are somewhat overlapping.

Learning processes of any kind and at any age are connected with frustration of more or less serious degree. The child feels frustrated when he has to learn to drink from a cup instead of a nipple. It is frustrating, too, for him to adjust the functioning of his bowels to the demands and taboos of the society in which he lives. Also, the acquisition of knowledge and skills at school is frustrating to a certain degree. What is it, then, that makes children put up with all the thwarting "do's and dont's" which are impressed on them? It is obvious that children could never be induced to put on the tight corset of cultural demands unless they are given some reward which makes it worth while for them. Maybe the most powerful reward is love and approval, especially when given by the parents or parent substitutes. Thus, if the child develops intellectually, if he learns to master the three R's and to acquire the skill which enables him to perform the little tricks required by psychometric scales, he does it partly in exchange for approval, love, and security.[3] If he does not get this reward because he has no parents or parent substitutes, or because the responsible adults fail to give love and security, he may fail to learn what is expected from him by society and to develop intellectually in the desired direction. This is usually an unconscious psychological mechanism rather than conscious malingering. Such a child appears dull to the superficial observer. However, he may actually be like a good businessman, who does not deliver the merchandise unless the price has been paid; sometimes it is smart to be dull.

Thus, if we encounter parents who seem to reject their children because they are dull and do not get along at school, we find frequently that the cart has been put before the horse. The children may be rejected because they are dull, but they may be dull because they are rejected.

DESIRE TO PUNISH THE PARENTS. In our culture the most potent satisfiers of children's needs, namely the parents, are, at the same time, the most potent frustrators. Such a culture can be expected to create a frequent desire in children to punish their parents. This desire may be present even though the relationship between the parents and children is a "normal" one. It may become strongly enhanced by such maladaptive factors as domination, neglect, etc.

[3] This statement does not negate heredity as a factor in the determination of intellectual differences. However, this article is concerned with the effect of environmental rather than hereditary factors.

Because of societal taboos and the child's dependence on his seemingly powerful, omnipotent parents, the hostile impulses of children against their parents remain frequently unconscious. For the same reason, punishing actions against the parents have often to be undertaken in an indirect, camouflaged manner whereby the connection between the action and its punishing significance may remain entirely unconscious. The refusal to eat, or to defecate regularly, is often an unconscious way of punishing parents, characteristic for the preschool child, but often carried on far beyond the first years of life, and even into adulthood. The refusal to develop intellectually—for example, to progress at school—may have the same unconscious significance (4, 5, 6, 52). The following example illustrates the above.

Shirley, an 18-year-old girl, was referred to the author for psychotherapy because of her inability to meet the academic requirements of a junior college. Her Wechsler-Bellevue IQ was 120. She showed considerable blocking in her social relationships. She was overcome with feelings of despair and anxiety whenever she was in social contact with contemporaries, but she felt perfectly at ease with her parents and their friends. Her academic difficulties at school, however, were probably not a mere outcome of her inability to associate with people of her own age, since she exhibited the same blocking towards academic achievement when taking individual instructions from a tutor. Shirley's mother underwent psychotherapy simultaneously with Shirley. She was a woman who had great difficulties in accepting a feminine role. Her marriage and pregnancy forced her to give up her aim of getting graduate academic training and becoming a lawyer. She unconsciously resented Shirley for this reason. When Shirley reached school age and proved to have good intellectual endowment, her mother transferred her professional ambitions from herself to her daughter, hoping that Shirley would get a higher education and reach the goal which she herself had to give up. Shirley's father was a pediatrician and very fond of children. He wanted to have another child, a desire which met with strong resistance on the part of the mother. Shirley remained the only child. The father's arguments in favor of having a second child centered especially around the idea that Shirley's development might suffer by her being the only child. The mother tried to pacify her feelings of guilt about the matter by making herself believe that Shirley would associate with many other children and never be lonely on account of her onliness. Thus, the mother had two main ambitions for her daughter. She wanted her to get a higher education, and she wanted her to be a sociable person who is surrounded by and enjoys the company of a large number of contemporaries.

It is remarkable that Shirley blocked in exactly the activities which were most important to her mother, namely, in her association with contemporaries and in her intellectual growth. In the course of Shirley's therapy it became apparent that behind a façade of extreme submission she harboured a tremendous amount of resentment against her mother. The material brought out in the course of her treatment suggested that the two main symptoms of her neurosis were partially determined by her unconscious desire to hit her mother's two most sensitive spots.

Edith Buxbaum (12) cites another case where learning difficulties appear to be a device to punish the parents.

A girl with academic difficulties was constantly admonished by her mother to study. The girl stated that her mother thought she was unable to do her school work without constant nagging. In the course of treatment the therapist advised the mother to stop any kind of interference with the girl's learning process. The mother followed this advice and stopped nagging, whereupon the girl remarked that she would now show her mother how wrong she was to think that her daughter would only progress in school under constant nagging. From then on the girl made good progress. The author comments that the girl was apparently able to make progress, or not to make progress, in order to spite her mother.

DESIRE FOR SELF-PUNISHMENT. Like many other neurotic symptoms, intellectual blocking may be brought about by an unconscious desire for self-punishment and, thus, for atonement of guilt feelings (5). These guilt feelings may stem from some of the sources discussed in this paper, or from other sources. The fact that a very high prestige premium is put on intellectual achievement in certain strata of society facilitates the use of learning disabilities as a self-punishing device.

Individuals whose intellect serves in the function of self-punishment frequently torture themselves through many other devices besides failure; for example, by compulsive pedantry in their intellectual work, through exaggeratedly long studying hours, etc. (7, 34, 38).

DESIRE FOR MASOCHISTIC GRATIFICATION. Intellectual blocking may be unconsciously enjoyed as a masochistic pleasure by the afflicted individual. The desire to obtain such masochistic gratification may be among the etiological factors of pseudostupidity (30, 32, 39). As is well known, this desire may be a factor in the etiology of many other psychological disorders.

DESIRE TO MAINTAIN AN INFANTILE LEVEL OF GRATIFICATION. Intellectual malfunctioning may be a manifestation of a conscious resistance against growing up. Every step which the child undertakes in his development toward maturity brings about the necessity to forego more infantile gratifications. Thus, developmental progress is often accompanied by considerable nostalgia. Growing up means losing the privilege of entertaining sweet, dependent, protected relationships which are based on self-centered receiving rather than on a give-and-take basis. For example, the satisfaction of passive, irresponsible sucking at the mother's breast has to be given up, first for the sake of more active, less convenient cup-and-spoon feeding, which lacks the intimate physical contact with the mother and burdens the child with heavy responsibility, and much later for the strenuous and inconvenient activity of making a living. Intellectual growth, too, means renouncement of the satisfaction of dependent needs. Learning to read may mean to a child not being read to (32); learning to think may mean not being thought for; learning to orient himself in his environment may mean not being guided and protected. The child who is excessively afraid of losing infantile gratifications may block in his intellectual development (39, 44, 51).

Mahler-Schoenberger (44) reports on an 18-year-old boy suffering from pseudoimbecility. His behavior was seriously retarded. He walked with a shuffling gait like an automaton and sat with his arms listlessly hanging at his side. His mother and his siblings felt toward him as towards a small child and treated him accordingly. They exchanged kisses and caresses with him, a form of behavior in which they could not have indulged if the patient were a normal 18-year-old boy. Mahler-Schoenberger considers the desire of obtaining such infantile gratification one of the etiological factors of the boy's neurosis.

In this connection it may be interesting to note that clinical workers are frequently concerned as to whether the mentally retarded child will encounter rejection by his parents and whether the parents will show favoritism towards the normal siblings. The opposite danger is discussed less frequently, namely, that the parents, especially the mother, may develop an unduly strong attachment toward the defective child, so that the normal sibling may be at a disadvantage. In many ways mentally retarded children may offer certain libidinal satisfactions to parents which the normal child cannot supply, namely, complete, helpless dependence without the threat of a second childbirth, i.e., of a painful separation from the child at the time of adolescence. Such helplessness may satisfy the parents' need to protect, or to dominate. In a more indirect manner it may also satisfy the parents' dependency needs, since it offers them the possibility of identifying with a completely dependent individual. The parents may, thus, enjoy the care of a feebleminded child directly and vicariously. In this manner, *true* mental retardation may offer certain libidinal satisfactions to the child and to his parents. *Pseudo*retardation, on the other hand, may be caused by the unconscious desire of the child to gain such satisfaction, and unconsciously encouraged through the same desire in the parents.

A graduate student of the author who worked in an institution for the feebleminded remarked jokingly that if he would ever adopt a child, it would have to be a Mongolian imbecile. The remark was, of course, not serious, but humorous in a grim way. However, a genuine emotion may have given rise to his statement, namely, the sweet feeling of attachment which many adults experience towards creatures who are and will forever remain helpless. It is known that Mongolians with their characteristic clinging behavior often become the favorites of institutional staff members.

The previous discussion also throws some light on the problems of children who show intellectual regression, such as deterioration of speech, reading, or other mental skills, at the time of the birth of a younger sibling. At that time the advantages of the infant's way of life and the futility of trying to capture the parents' attention by "academic sophistication" seems especially apparent to the older child. If the child could express his feelings, he would say something like, "Why did I have to go through all the troubles of growing up, when this helpless and stupid baby receives so much affection?"

In this connection it may be enlightening to compare the attitude of adults toward children of very superior intelligence and toward less intelligent children. We often find that superior children are to a lesser degree recipients of adults' protective warmth. Many adults are inclined to handle superior children with objective detachment. Thus, the unconscious desire to avoid such curtailment in warmth and affection may result in intellectual blocking with children of superior ability. Gumpert (27) says

about the American woman that "she would rather be loved than respected" (p. 163). The same may be true for some children of superior intellect.

DISPLACEMENT OF ATTITUDES TOWARD ORAL AND ANAL IMPULSES UPON INTELLECTUAL PROCESSES. The well-adjusted infant gets great satisfaction from the intake of food. The mouth seems to be the most important organ of his body. He may develop a variety of attitudes toward oral gratification, depending on the person who feeds him and the manner in which he is fed and weaned. His oral development may proceed unhampered or be subject to various disturbances. For example, he may fail to experience the normal satisfaction of feeding due to the absence of a secure emotional relationship with the mother or due to various other factors. In this case he may refuse the normal amount of food intake. In many instances, drinking and eating may become a tool by the help of which the child rewards or punishes his mother, or food intake may turn into an antidote against anxiety and insecurity. In the latter case the child may eat an excessive amount of food.

Similarly, defecation is an important source of pleasure for the child. During an early period in his life he likes to smell, touch, and smear his bowel movements. He may be as proud of his feces as an adult individual is proud of personal achievement. His mother usually indicates to him that it is a prerequisite for friendly acceptance in the family and society to acquire a somewhat negative attitude toward anal activities and anal products. She also trains him to limit his defecation to specific times and conditions. The well-adjusted child is able to give up his anal freedom without too much frustration in order to please his mother. However, the anal development can also undergo various disturbances. This may occur if the relationship between mother and child is an unfavorable one, so that the child is unable to give up anal pleasures for her sake. If, for example, she tries to enforce toilet training in a hostile, rigid, and nonsympathetic manner, the normal development may be seriously endangered. The child may become overcompliant or rebellious. In the former case he may adjust as far as overt behavior is concerned, but "boil inside" about the environment's impingement upon "his private life." In the latter case he may refuse to conform to anal etiquette and annoy his mother by developing training difficulties. Constipation, for example, is at times a form of protest which enjoys great popularity among toddlers. No wonder, since it fulfills so many purposes at the same time. It is a symbolic expression of the child's unwillingness to give, a method of punishing the mother, a way of getting attention and feelings of power, and a secret device to increase anal stimulation.

Needless to say, the attitudes toward orality and anality which are acquired during early childhood may persist into adulthood (1, 2, 21). The gourmet, the drunkard, the worrier about digestion, the ulcer patient, the chronically constipated individual are examples of continuations of oral or anal conflicts. However, attitudes toward oral or anal matters can also be displaced upon certain other fields. Experience has taught us that displacement is often facilitated by similarity between the person, object, or situation *from* which displacement takes place, and the person, object, or situation *upon* which the individual displaces (49). For example, attitudes toward parents are more often displaced upon older persons in an authoritarian position than upon younger subordinates. Thus, attitudes towards orality and anality are most likely displaced upon activities which possess certain similarities with drinking, eating, and defecating. Intellectual activities show such similarities. Learning is similar to drinking and eating inasmuch as it is an intake and assimilation process. In reading and in listening to lectures, knowledge is taken in and assimilated. Intellectual activity is also a giving-out process, and as such it resembles defecation. Writing, answering the teachers' questions, etc., are examples of this aspect of intellectual work. According to psychoanalytic theory, various disturbances of oral and anal development may thus be displaced upon intellectual activities, and such displacement may result in intellectual disturbances (1, 2, 4, 25, 32, 36, 37, 55, 56, 59). In this manner, the refusal to take food may be transformed into the inability to grasp and assimilate subject matter. Likewise, the tendency to be constipated, when displaced upon intellectual functions, may result in unwillingness or inability to express ideas, for example, to answer questions, to recite in class, etc.[4]

[4] According to the psychoanalytic school, speech disturbances may be caused by oral as well as anal displacement. Speaking is performed with the mouth and, thus, invites oral displacement. On the other hand, it is an expulsion process and, therefore, lends itself to anal displacement.

If the displaced oral and anal disturbances have orig-

Moreover, the similarity of intellectual activities to pregenital (oral and anal) sexual activities may make the individual feel guilty about intellectual work, and such guilt may block mental development.[5]

One of Bornstein's (7, p. 393), intellectually blocked patients made the following statement: "I lack milk for my brain, for my thinking" (translated by the present author). The remark may indicate a possible connection between orality and mental retardation in this case.

Chidester and Menninger (15) report on a boy, Henry, who received psychoanalytic treatment at the Southard School from the age of 12 to the age of 15 years. When treatment was begun, his IQ on the 1916 Binet was 65. In the course of therapy the IQ rose to 90. Oral and anal displacement was, according to the author's interpretation, one of the emotional factors responsible for his intellectual malfunctioning. He was especially weak in arithmetic and writing. He would irritate his teachers by his extreme slowness in giving answers. Before he underwent treatment he spoke so slowly that it sometimes took him 15 minutes to complete a sentence. However, he was a good and eager reader. His intellectual pattern was one of taking in without giving out. The same pattern could be observed also in nonacademic situations. His relationship to other children was one of taking without giving. He requested gifts from them, took their possessions, asked questions, but never volunteered any information. He had the habit of collecting old cans and other odd objects, which he never used. Instead, he liked to hoard them in his room and was deeply upset if anybody tried to remove them.

That Henry displaced oral attitudes upon the reading process was suggested by various indications. He was, for example, occasionally punished by being prevented from reading the newspaper. He stated that he then felt "as mad as a hungry bear" (p. 621). At such occasions he would look for discarded food in garbage cans. The interpretation that Henry's resistance against speaking or writing is connected with anal retention gains probability from the fact that he exhibited so many adjustment patterns characteristic of the anal retention phase, such as hoarding. Similarly, he expressed his resistance against his analysis in a passively stubborn, rather than in an actively aggressive, manner. During periods of resistance he

inated as a response to lack of emotional reward, as protest against growing up, or as a device to punish the parents, then we find an overlapping between the first, second, and fifth sections above and the present section of this paper. However, learning difficulties can arise as an effect of the previously discussed factors without the detour of oral and anal displacement.

[5] For such cases, the present section of this paper overlaps with the section immediately below.

refused to groom himself. He also became constipated frequently and remained in the bathroom for
hours even though there was a line of children
waiting outside. All these are characteristically anal
forms of behavior. One day he made an interesting
statement with the purpose of explaining his reluctance to communicate with other people in and
outside the school situation. He said he was hesitant to express ideas since that meant giving them
away; the more you said, the less you retained for
yourself. In his magical thinking he seemed to
equate the expression of ideas with the expulsion
of matter.

DISPLACEMENT[6] OF INHIBITIONS FROM SPECIFIC,
THREATENING ASPECTS OF COGNITION TO INTELLEC-
TUAL ACTIVITY IN GENERAL.

*Inhibitions caused by guilt feelings. (a) Sex-
ual curiosity.* In certain strata of society the
attitude of adults towards children's sexual
knowledge is, in many ways, diametrically the
opposite of their attitude toward other kinds of
knowledge. This rather obvious fact becomes
especially apparent if we examine the literature
on sex education written for parents and teachers of young children. Many authors, for example, make statements to this effect:
A frank way of discussing the facts of life
will, they say, stop the child's curiosity and interest in these matters and will put an end to
his preoccupation and his questions. Now let
us compare this alleged aim of sex education
with the aim of any other branch of education.
Is there any other field in which the teacher
aims at squelching the children's intellectual
thirst, at suffocating interest and curiosity, and
at stopping further questions? On the contrary,
educators measure the success of their teaching not so much according to the amount of
knowledge or information they transmit, but
according to the interest they create. Questions,
stimulated curiosity, attempts to make further
investigations are considered criteria of success
in teaching. Thus, the aims of sex education
appear to be the exact opposite of the aims of
education in any other field (26).
It is no wonder that many children develop
guilt feelings about their knowledge and curiosity concerning sexual matters. According to
psychoanalytic theory, such guilt feelings do
not always remain limited to knowledge about

---

[6] In many instances where the term "displacement" is
used in this paper, it would be more correct to use the
term "displacement or stimulus generalization" since the
exact nature of the mechanism cannot be determined.
(See Miller [49] regarding the distinction between the
two mechanisms.)

sex. Again, displacement upon similar stimuli
may take place, i.e., the guilt feelings may
spread to intellectual activity in general. Since
the guilt is irrational, it usually remains unconscious, but may result in serious blocking of intellectual functioning (6, 52).

The author treated an 11-year-old boy who was
making poor progress at school. His school achievement improved considerably after treatment for several months. The main topic of conversation during
the counseling sessions was "the facts of life." The
boy had very drastic misconceptions about reproduction. His foster parents had never given him any
sex information. He had acquired most of his
knowledge from an older boy, whom he met secretly, against the wish of his foster parents. He
considered the conversations about sex which he
carried on with this boy as "bad." The treatment
sessions taught him that it was not necessarily bad
to talk, to know, or to be curious about sex. This
relief of his guilt feelings about a specific type of
knowledge may be one of the factors which decreased his blocking against school work.

Sylvester and Kunst (60) report about an
interesting fantasy of a boy with a reading
disability.

He daydreamed that his father had invented a
big machine and had cautioned the boy to stay
away from it. It was a dangerous machine which
made terrific noises. However, the boy disregarded
his father's warning and looked at the machine.
As an effect of this disobedience, he was forced to
run with closed eyes for many years so that the
machine could not catch him. He then pretended
in his daydream that *he* was the inventor of the
machine, and that he was not permitted to make
any further inventions. The fantasy suggests that
the boy feels guilty about curiosity, knowledge,
and intellectual creativity, and that he believes it
is safest to "keep his eyes closed." Since the boy is
suffering from a reading disability, guilt may be
one of the etiological factors of his difficulty.

Thus, the conventional parental reasoning—
that if curiosity about sexual matters is suppressed, children will turn their thinking "to
more wholesome and constructive matters"—
may be a fallacy. In many cases the results may
be the opposite from what the parents expect
(see 56).

(b) Aggression and sadism. The above discussion indicates that intellectual blocking may result from guilt feelings about a specific *kind* of
knowledge and subsequent displacement upon
intellectual work in general. Similarly, guilt
feelings about a specific *aspect* of knowledge

may develop and be displaced upon intellectual functioning in general. For example, the aggressive and sadistic aspect of thinking may, thus, become an instigator of learning difficulties (5, 6, 8, 22, 32, 33, 37, 38, 39, 40, 41, 54).

There are various connections between the acquisition of knowledge, and aggression and sadism. One possible connection becomes apparent during preschool age, when the toddler tears apart toys, such as dolls, or living creatures, such as beetles, in order to investigate what is inside. Also the desire to know what is inside the human body may become associated with the aggressive desire to tear apart and to destroy.

Sylvester and Kunst (60) report about an eight-year-old boy who was placed in a subnormal room at school even though he was of superior intelligence. His behavior during play therapy suggested strong aggression against the mother. He stated that the mother doll did not want to carry her baby since the baby might kick her. Finally the boy tied the baby doll to the mother doll's arm in order to prevent him from kicking. It also became apparent that the boy was filled with strong curiosity as to what was in his mother's body. During his play with dolls, he expressed the desire to tear the mother doll apart in order to see what was inside. Thus, intellectual curiosity and aggression were closely associated in the boy's personality structure. Furthermore, the situation was aggravated by the fact that the mother was seriously sick. The boy's magical thinking made his own aggressive desires responsible for her disease. In this manner, his guilt feelings were greatly increased. Finally, displacement of guilt from the aggressive aspect of "wanting to know" to intellectual functioning in general took place, and the boy developed a serious learning disability.

Aggression and intellectuality may become associated in various other ways. Intellective learning, for example, has a strong competitive aspect in certain strata of society. With some individuals competition may become the main motive for learning. Competition, however, implies aggression. Again, guilt feelings about competitive aggression may be displaced upon learning in general. Guilt feelings about competition are especially likely to arise in a culture where cooperative and competitive ideals are taught simultaneously. While tribes such as the Mundugumor stress competition and tribes such as the Arapesh preach mainly cooperative ideals (48), Western civilization finds itself in between the two contradictory ideals of competition and cooperation. Both attitudes are taught simultaneously. Thus, Western man is quasi forced to go out in the rain without getting wet. Indoctrinated with the ideal of competition, he finds it difficult to cooperate, and his training in cooperation makes him feel guilty about competitive activities.

In addition, some of the words used synonymously with "intelligent" and "stupid" suggest an association between intelligence and aggression in people's thinking, for example, the terms "sharp" and "dull." Similarly, Landauer (35) points out that the German word "albern," meaning stupid, is derived from the obsolete word "alvari," meaning good or friendly.

Since intellectual work is related to a higher degree to the masculine role in our culture than to feminine activity, women often use their intellect as a device to compete aggressively with men. If such competition becomes the major motivating factor of intellectual endeavor, the ensuing guilt may become a serious block to progress.

Especially strong guilt feelings about competitive aggression are likely to arise in the Oedipus situation and in sibling rivalry, since the victims of aggression in these situations are people who should be loved, and not hated, according to the mores of our society. Thus, it is not surprising that the etiology of pseudostupidity is often connected with Oedipal hatred (4, 7) and aggressive competition against siblings (37, 40, 41).

Bornstein (7) reports a case of a 12½-year-old girl with whom Oedipal competition resulted in guilt and intellectual retardation. Learning, for this girl, was partially motivated by the desire to gain the affection of her father and of men in general. She was convinced that her mother and teacher were afraid of her competition for the attention of men and, therefore, did not want her to progress intellectually. The girl interpreted any encouragement she received from her mother or teacher as an insincere, strategic device designed to give her a false belief of achievement in order to prevent her from further striving.

Thus, it seems that intellectual endeavor may become associated with, and work in the service of, various impulses. The fate of intellectuality will then depend upon the fate of these impulses. If the intellect functions "in the service" of aggression, and if the individual feels guilty about aggression and tends to repress it, the servant intellect may share the fate of his master—and intellectual blocking may result.

Inhibitions caused by failure. Serious failure in specific intellectual endeavors may result in inhibition of intellectual functioning in general (32).

A child may be unsuccessful in his first attempts to master academic subject matter, not due to lack of intellectual endowment, but due to more extraneous factors such as a bad teacher, or a visual or auditory defect. The discouraging experience may condition the child in such a manner that he remains intellectually blocked even after all obstacles have been removed, e.g., after he has been placed with a better teacher or after his physical defects have been corrected.

According to psychoanalytic theory, such blocking is especially frequently instigated by children's failures in their investigations about sexual matters. These investigations are especially liable to meet with failure, since most adults tend to increase the obstacles of such endeavors or, at least, not to offer much constructive help. Moreover, his own psychosexual immaturity often prevents the young thinker from finding the truth. Instead, he may lose himself in a maze of contradictory hunches and fantastic sexual theories (8, 18, 23). Such "first failure" may have "a crippling effect forever after" (23, p. 68).

Inhibitions caused by miscellaneous other threats. Guilt about knowing and the threat of failure are not the only factors which can cause negative attitudes toward specific types of cognition. Knowledge may become threatening in many other ways. In such cases also, the individual may avoid a specific piece of knowledge, and the avoidance response may become displaced upon other or all intellective activity.

A ten-year-old boy was referred for psychiatric treatment because of various neurotic disturbances. When his mother was pregnant with his sister, he had denied to himself the coming of the child, even though informational and observational clues should have led him to the correct conclusion. He patterned his behavior to the slogan, "What I don't know doesn't hurt me." Displacement of this response was a partial cause of his reading disability, according to the author's interpretation (60).

Also, Freud's little Hans may have become a victim of "protective stupidity" when he said about his baby sister that "her widdler [penis] is still quite small" (24, p. 155), since the knowledge that girls do not possess penises may be of considerable threat to boys (see 51). In a sarcastic footnote to little Hans's remark, Freud draws a parallel between Hans's error and an erroneous statement made by philosophers:

We can go a step further in vindicating little Hans's honour. As a matter of fact, he behaved no worse than a philosopher of the school of Wundt. In the view of that school, consciousness is the invariable characteristic of what is mental, just as in the view of little Hans a widdler is the indispensable criterion of what is animate. If now the philosopher comes across mental processes, the existence of which has to be inferred, but about which there is not a trace of consciousness to be detected—for the subject, in fact, knows nothing of them, although it is impossible to avoid inferring their existence—then, instead of saying that they are unconscious mental processes, he calls them *semi-conscious.* The widdler is still very small (24, p. 155)!

Just as in Hans's case, the difficulty of the philosopher to accept fully the concept of the unconscious may be a defense against threatening insight. Hermann (28) illustrates a similar kind of blocking, using Semmelweis' great discovery of the causes of childbed fever as an example. Semmelweis was bewildered by his observation that many more women died in a maternity ward attended by physicians than in a ward attended by midwives. Finally he found the explanation: the physicians examined their patients after they had conducted autopsies and, thus, killed them by infecting them. This understanding led to the introduction of prophylactic measures against childbed fever. Semmelweis' colleagues showed considerable resistance against the new discovery. Semmelweis was ignored, ridiculed, and even fired from his position (16). Such resistance may be partly due to the fact that the knowledge of having killed some of their patients, even though inadvertently, was highly threatening to many gynecologists. One of Semmelweis' young collaborators was especially strongly affected by this threat. He had treated a cousin of his some time before the discovery was made. The woman had died from childbed fever. Semmelweis' discovery made it clear to the young doctor that he had killed his own cousin. He committed suicide. One could speculate that the young doctor, even though he was aware of all the necessary premises, could hardly have discovered the cause of childbed fever himself, since the threat of the discovery would have resulted in blocking.

The statement that a stimulus might remain unrecognized because it is threatening may seem a paradox, since it is hard to conceive how an individual could respond to a characteristic of a stimulus, namely its threatening nature, without previous recognition of the stimulus.

However, clinical observation of this phenomenon is in agreement with various experimental findings. Postman, Bruner, and McGinnies (53), for example, found that subjects recognize tachistoscopically exposed stimulus words less quickly when these words are connected with areas on which the subject puts little value than when they are connected with highly valued areas. Thus, a scientist may recognize words such as "logical" more quickly than words such as "wealthy." The question arises how this scientist would "know" that the exposed word belonged to an area of low value, and therefore build up defenses against the word before he was able to read it. A similar riddle arises in McGinnies' study (47), where it was found that subjects show significantly stronger GSR's during the *pre*-recognition phase of emotion-evoking words such as "whore" as compared to neutral words such as "apple" (see 11, 46). The protective stupidity of individuals who don't become aware of threatening material, as well as the paradoxical results of these experimental investigations, are covered by Bruner and Postman's statement that "the threshold for affective avoidance response is frequently lower than the threshold for veridical report" (10, p. 27). In other words, subjects respond to "emotional tones" of stimuli before they recognize other characteristics of the stimulus situation.

It is tempting to speculate on the implications of "protective stupidity" for clinical research. Some clinicians are especially attracted by research topics which are closely connected with their own unresolved personal problems. Thus, stuttering clinicians may become interested in speech defects, etc. Such personal involvement in the area of one's research may become a serious block. As is well known, insight into the etiological factors of his own neurotic disturbances may be threatening to the individual. Therefore, any material contributing to such insight may be repressed. The removal of such repression usually encounters considerable resistance and often requires deep-reaching and time-consuming psychotherapeutic procedures. Consequently, if a scientist engages in research to discover psychological phenomena in other individuals which are closely related to his own repressions, he may encounter considerable difficulties. Like the previously discussed clinical cases, he may become a victim of protective blocking. Much of the pseduo-efficiency and pseudoexactness of psychological research may be an expression of the unconscious desire to avoid discovery rather than to achieve it, i.e., to seek security in a blind alley and, at the same time, "cheat the ego" into mistaking the blind alley for a road leading to the goal. Some investigations of this kind remind one of the following cartoon:[7] An elderly woman is seen copying a painting in an art gallery. The huge picture shows a nude and luscious nymph courted by a faun; an incidental little bird is seen in the corner of the painting. The copyist, disregarding the essence of the original, copies the bird only, with perfect technique, in an exacting and painstaking manner.

On the other hand, personal involvement in the area of one's research may be a strong incentive and have a constructive effect on the progress of research. This is especially the case when the type of repression discussed in the previous paragraphs is absent or incomplete.

Personal involvement may affect the psychotherapist in a similar manner as the research worker. When a patient discusses conflictive topics which correspond to repressed problem areas in the therapist's personality, the therapist may unconsciously block the patient's progress, e.g., by diverting him to less threatening topics (42).

DESIRE TO POSSESS "A MAGIC CAP OF INVISIBILITY" (44). When analyzing the previously mentioned 18-year-old pseudoimbecile (44), Mahler-Schoenberger calls the boy's intellectual retardation "a magic cap of invisibility." Thereby she postulates a possible etiological factor of his disturbance. The term "magic cap of invisibility" refers to the "tarnkappe" in the Niebelungen Saga, which made Siegfried invisible and enabled him, thus, to engage in various kinds of socially unacceptable behavior without being discovered. By the help of his cap of invisibility he could witness situations from which he would otherwise be barred, remaining unnoticed by others. Similarly, Mahler-Schoenberger's patient is made "invisible" by his pseudoimbecility, i.e., invisible as an adult male with normal impulses. This invisibility makes it possible for him to obtain surreptitious gratifications from which normal adults are usually excluded. For example, he is able to satisfy his curiosity about his brothers' sexual life. One brother and his sweetheart, a married woman, engage in heavy necking in the presence of the patient, who is considered too dull to understand. For the same reason, the patient is permitted to enter the bedroom where another

---

[7] The source of this cartoon could not be identified.

brother and his bride are in bed with each other. According to Mahler-Schoenberger, this gain obtained from the retardation is one of the etiological factors responsible for the boy's pseudofeeblemindedness.

More generally speaking, children may gain various satisfactions of their curiosity by wearing the "magic cap of stupidity." They may attempt purposely to appear naive in order to encourage adults in carrying on conversations about tabooed knowledge in their presence. If, instead of conscious suppression of the behavioral manifestations of understanding, repression of actual understanding takes place, "the magic-cap mechanism" becomes an etiological factor of intellectual blocking.

Jones gives a vivid description of children's attempt to appear stupid in order to gain forbidden information:

"When a mother chats with her intimate friend over various private topics, frequently the child will resort to the strangest devices in order to stay in the room and listen to the conversation. Then when someone remarks him, and by her looks insinuates a doubt as to the propriety of conversing in his presence, he will interrupt his innocent crooning over his toys and indulge in exaggeratedly foolish antics, to disarm as it were, the suspicions of the company —by convincing them of his thorough simple-mindedness and innocence" (31, p. 484).

By using "the magic-cap mechanism" of pseudostupidity, the individual can get away with the expression of other unacceptable impulses besides sexual curiosity, e.g., with the expression of aggression (20, 31, 32, 35). Landauer (35) reports about two children who showed much interest in the fact that a woman living on the floor above them was expecting a baby. On the day the woman gave birth to the baby, the children broke a window in their own apartment. The mother asked who had done it. She received the reply that the window had been broken by the stork, who had mistakenly tried to enter through the window of their apartment instead of flying into the apartment upstairs. At this reply the mother broke out in laughter. The children were not punished for the breakage.

DESIRE TO AVOID SELF-EVALUATION. Some individuals fail intellectually because they do not make any effort to succeed. Such "lazy" individuals are often extremely ambitious. Their ambition may be so strong that they could not bear to become aware of their limitations. Since they do not make any effort to succeed, they can avoid getting a realistic and possibly disappointing conception of their capacity. Thus their laziness enables them to excuse their failure and to cling to the magical belief that they would be champions if they would care to participate in the contest (6, 17).

DESIRE TO BE THE RECIPIENT OF LOVE RATHER THAN OF ENVY AND AGGRESSION.[8] The desire to succeed and the desire to be liked by one's fellow men are frequently incompatible. Success in climbing the ladder of achievement is often accompanied by loss of love. The successful individual may endanger himself by becoming the target of envy and aggression. Such envy and aggression against a successful person may be attitudes which are actually existing, or they may be projections on the part of the successful individual. In other cases actually existing aggression may be exaggerated in the recipient's perception through the mechanism of projection. Three kinds of projection, as described by Cattell (14), may be at work to produce such distortion. One is projection in the psychoanalytic sense, a mechanism by which individuals attempt to remain unaware of their own ego-alien impulses by ascribing them to the outside world. Thus, especially people who themselves have strongly competitive, aggressive attitudes which they cannot accept, may perceive their fellow men as more aggressive than they actually are. Another type of projection is called by Cattell, "Projection of Press Required by Emotional State" (PRES projection). When this mechanism is at work, the individual may be fully aware of his own attitudes. However, he distorts his perception of the outside world in a way which helps him to justify his own feelings. Thus, Murray (50) found that girls whose anxiety had been aroused experimentally, perceived photographs of faces as being more hostile than they had perceived them before the arousal of anxiety. Similarly, the hostile competitor may justify his uncooperative attitude toward his fellow men by perceiving them as more hostile than they actually are. Or he may expect hostility as a retaliation for his own feelings and, thus, perceive expected rather than actual hostility. Finally, Cattell distinguishes a further type of projection, "Naive Inference from Personal Ex-

[8] This section is, in many ways, closely related to the section, "Desire to Maintain an Infantile Level of Gratification." However, it is believed that the emphasis under these two headings is sufficiently different to justify separate discussion.

perience" (NIPE projection). People with limited knowledge about their fellow men may naively assume that all individuals have attitudes similar to their own. This type of projection may also be applicable to the hostile competitor's view of the world around him. He may naively shape his perception of other individuals according to his own image.

Thus, the successful competitor may experience discomfort due to perceived hostility, regardless of whether his perception is realistic or distorted. He may attempt to avoid discomfort by avoiding achievement (29, 54).

A very bright student of the author excelled in class by her stimulating contributions to the discussion, and by the quality of her written work. However, after a few weeks of class work her contributions dropped noticeably in quality and quantity. In conversation with the author she stated that several remarks made by her colleagues were reported to her, indicating that her intellectual superiority made her unpopular with her classmates. Thus, she decided to control her behavior at school in such a way that she would appear less outstanding. We would hesitate to designate this girl as a case of intellectual blocking, because her plan not to excel was conscious, intentional, and reversible through deliberate decision. However, the study of individuals' attitudes toward success in intellectual activities or in any other field indicates that the tendency to "hold back" in order to avoid hostility can lie anywhere on a continuum from complete conscious intention to entirely unconscious blocking. For example, "holding back" may start as a consciously planned maneuver and later develop into an automatic, uncontrollable habit.

Brilliant, well-educated, and sophisticated young women occasionally engage in diplomatic malingerings when associating with men in social situations such as dates. They try to hide their knowledge and sophistication in order not to be threatening to their companion and, thus, to enjoy the pleasures of unambivalent male affection rather than to be frustrated by the ambivalent emotional relationship of competitors and the pseudo-triumph of Pyrrhic victory (32). In other cases, the expectation of loss of gratification may automatically inhibit their intellectual development, without conscious planning or even against conscious planning. Every step which a man undertakes toward vocational success makes him more desirable as a love object, but every step undertaken by a woman in the same direction may make her less desirable

as a partner for love and marriage. This conflict between two goals may become an etiological factor for the automatic inhibition of activity directed toward either goal.

The role played by the innocent, unsophisticated fool in myth, fairy tale, and fiction may serve as an illustration of the statement that intellectual blocking may be caused by fear of hostility. The fool in folk literature and other fiction is often an appealing figure, loved by everybody, envied by nobody (35). Since he is at the bottom of the ladder already, nobody can push him down.

CONCLUSION

The above is a discussion of some connecting bonds between intelligence and total personality. The discussion claims neither completeness nor originality. The emotional factors affecting thought processes covered in this paper have been described by others. However, the treatment of these topics is scattered through the psychiatric and psychological literature and interwoven with various other material. The author considered it a worth-while undertaking to extract pertinent material from various sources in order to present a more systematic discussion of intellect and total personality. Moreover, much of the subject matter surveyed in this paper is, in its original source, expressed in the often highly esoteric language of psychoanalysis, and interwoven with other psychoanalytic material which may be less acceptable to psychologically trained clinicians. In the author's opinion the above presentation discusses important aspects of intelligence, with emphasis on dynamic connections rather than quantitative comparisons. This approach has been relatively neglected by psychological investigators. Yet the objective research training of the academic psychologist is badly needed for the study of these aspects. Most emotional factors affecting intelligence have been ascertained "intuitively" rather than by objective methods. It will require all the ingenuity of psychologists to plan research designs which corroborate or disprove some of the "hunches" discussed in this paper.

REFERENCES

1. ABRAHAM, K. Contributions to the theory of the anal character. In *Selected papers*. London: Hogarth, 1927.

2. ABRAHAM, K. The influence of oral erotism on character formation. In *Selected papers*. London: Hogarth, 1927.

3. ALEXANDER, W. P. Intelligence, concrete and abstract. *Brit. J. Psychol. Monogr. Suppl.*, 1935, *6*, No. 19.

4. BERGLER, E. Zur Problematik der Pseudodebilität. *Int. Z. Psychoanal.*, 1932, *18*, 528-538.

5. BLANCHARD, PHYLLIS. Reading disabilities in relation to difficulties of personality and emotional development. *Ment. Hyg.*, N. Y., 1936, *20*, 384-413.

6. BLANCHARD, PHYLLIS. Psychoanalytic contribution to the problem of reading disabilities. *Psychoanal. Stud. Child.*, 1946, *2*, 163-187.

7. BORNSTEIN, BERTA. Zur. Psychogenese der Pseudodebilität. *Int. Z. Psychoanal.*, 1930, *16*, 378-399.

8. BORNSTEIN, BERTA. Beziehungen zwischen Sexual-und Intellektentwicklung. *Z. psychoanal. Pädag.*, 1930, *4*, 446-454.

9. BROWN, W. M. Character traits as factors in intelligence test performance. *Arch. Psychol.*, N. Y., 1923, *10*, No. 65.

10. BRUNER, J. S., and POSTMAN, L. Perception, cognition, and behavior. *J. Personality*, 1949, *18*, 14-31.

11. BRUNER, J. S., and POSTMAN, L. On the perception of incongruity: A paradigm. *J. Personality*, 1949, *18*, 206-223.

12. BUXBAUM, EDITH. Uber schwierige, insbesondere faule Schuler. *Z. psychoanal. Pädag.*, 1930, *4*, 461-466.

13. CATTELL, R. B. Temperament tests. I. Temperament. *Brit. J. Psychol.*, 1933, *23*, 308-329.

14. CATTELL, R. B. Projection and the design of projective tests of personality. *Character & Pers.*, 1944, *12*, 177-194.

15. CHIDESTER, LEONA, and MENNINGER, K. A. The application of psychoanalytic methods to the study of mental retardation. *Amer. J. Orthopsychiat.*, 1936, *6*, 616-625.

16. DE KRUIF, P. *Men against death.* New York: Harcourt, Brace, 1932.

17. FREUD, ANNA. *The ego and the mechanisms of defence.* London: Hogarth, 1937.

18. FREUD, S. Three contributions to the theory of sex. In *The basic writings of Sigmund Freud.* New York: Modern Library, 1938.

19. FREUD, S. *A general introduction to psychoanalysis.* Garden City, N. Y.: Garden City Pub. Co., 1938.

20. FREUD, S. On the psychopathology of everyday life. In *The basic writings of Sigmund Freud.* New York: Modern Library, 1938.

21. FREUD, S. Character and anal eroticism. In *Collected papers, Vol. II.* London: Hogarth, 1949.

22. FREUD, S. The predisposition to obsessional neurosis. In *Collected papers, Vol. II.* London: Hogarth, 1949.

23. FREUD, S. On the sexual theories of children. In *Collected papers, Vol. II.* London: Hogarth, 1949.

24. FREUD, S. Analysis of a phobia in a five-year-old boy. In *Collected papers, Vol. III.* London: Hogarth, 1949.

25. GLOVER, E. Notes on oral character formation. *Int. J. Psycho-Anal.*, 1925, *6*, 131-154.

26. GRUENBERG, SIDONIE M. *We, the parents.* New York: Harper, 1939.

27. GUMPERT, M. *First papers.* New York: Duell, Sloan and Pearce, 1941.

28. HERMANN, I. Begabtheit und Unbegabtheit. *Z. psychoanal. Pädag.*, 1930, *4*, 408-416.

29. HORNEY, KAREN. *The neurotic personality of our time.* New York: Norton, 1937.

30. JACOBSOHN, EDITH. Lernstörungen beim Schulkind durch masochistische Mechanismen. *Int. Z. Psychoanal.*, 1932, *18*, 242-251.

31. JONES, E. Simulated foolishness in hysteria. *Papers on Psychoanal.* London: Wood, 1913.

32. KLEIN, E. Psychoanalytic aspect of school problems. *Psychoanal. Stud. Child.*, 1949, *4*, 369-390.

33. KLEIN, MELANIE. A contribution to the theory of intellectual inhibition. *Int. J. Psycho-Anal.*, 1931, *12*, 206-218.

34. LAFORGUE, R. Die Mechanismen der Selbstbestrafung und ihr Einfluss auf den Character des Kindes. *Z. psychoanal. Pädag.*, 1930, *4*, 104-114.

35. LANDAUER, K. Zur psychosexuellen Genese der Dummheit. *Z. Sexual Wissenschaft und Sexual-politik*, 1929, *16*, 12-22.

36. LISS, E. Libidinal fixations as pedagogic determinants. *Amer. J. Orthopsychiat.*, 1935, *5*, 126-131.

37. LISS, E. Emotional and biological factors involved in learning processes. *Amer. J. Orthopsychiat.*, 1937, *7*, 483-488.

38. LISS, E. Learning: Its sadistic and masochistic manifestations. *Amer. J. Orthopsychiat.*, 1940, *10*, 123-128.

39. LISS, E. Learning difficulties. *Amer. J. Orthopsychiat.*, 1941, *11*, 520-523.

40. LISS, E. The failing student. *Amer. J. Orthopsychiat.*, 1941, *11*, 712-717.

41. LISS, E. Examination anxiety. *Amer. J. Orthopsychiat.*, 1944, *14*, 345-348.

42. LORAND, S. *Technique of psychoanalytic therapy.* New York: Int. Univ. Press, 1946.

43. LORGE, I. Intelligence and personality as revealed in questionnaires and inventories. *Yearb. nat. Soc. Stud. Educ.*, 1940, *39*, Pt. I, 275-281.

44. MAHLER-SCHOENBERGER, MARGARET. Pseudoimbecility: A magic cap of invisibility. *Psychoanal. Quart.*, 1942, *11*, 149-164.

45. MC CARTHY, DOROTHEA. Personality and learning. *Amer. Coun. Educ. Stud.*, 1948, Ser. I, No. 35.

46. MC CLEARY, J., and LAZARUS, R. Autonomic discrimination without awareness. An interim report. *J. Personality*, 1949, *18*, 171-179.

47. MC GINNIES, E. Emotionality and perceptual defense. *Psychol. Rev.*, 1949, *56*, 244-251.

48. MEAD, MARGARET (ed.). *Cooperation and competition among primitive peoples.* New York: McGraw-Hill, 1937.

49. MILLER, N. E. Theory and experiment relating psychoanalytic displacement to stimulus response generalization. *J. abnorm. soc. Psychol.*, 1948, *43*, 155-178.

50. MURRAY, H. A. The effect of fear upon estimates of the maliciousness of other personalities. *J. soc. Psychol.*, 1933, *4*, 310-329.

51. OLDEN, CHRISTINE. Headline intelligence. *Psychoanal. Stud. Child.*, 1946, *2*, 263-269.

52. PEARSON, G. H. J., and ENGLISH, O. S. *Common neuroses of children and adults.* New York: Norton, 1937.

53. POSTMAN, L., BRUNER, J. S., and MC GINNIES, E. Personal values as selective factors in perception. *J. abnorm. soc. Psychol.*, 1948, *43*, 148-153.

54. SCHMIDEBERG, MELITTA. Intellektuelle Hemmungen und Aggression. *Z. psychoanal. Pädag.*, 1930, *4*, 467-477.

55. SCHMIDEBERG, MELITTA. Intellectual inhibition and disturbances in eating. *Int. J. Psycho-Anal.*, 1938, *19*, 17-22.

56. SCHMIDT, VERA. Die Entwicklung der Wisstriebes bei einem Kinde. *Imago. Lpz.*, 1930, *16*, 246-289.

57. SPEARMAN, C. *The abilities of man.* New York: Macmillan, 1927.

58. STODDARD, G. D. *The meaning of intelligence.* New York: Macmillan, 1947.

59. STRACHEY, J. Some unconscious factors in reading. *Int. J. Psycho-Anal.*, 1930, *11*, 322-331.

60. SYLVESTER, EMMY, and KUNST, MAY S. Psychodynamic aspects of the reading problem. *Amer. J. Orthopsychiat.*, 1943, *13*, 69-76.

61. WEBB, E. Character and intelligence. *Brit. J. Psychol. Monogr. Suppl.*, 1915, *1*, No. 3.

62. WECHSLER, D. Cognitive, conative, and non-intellective intelligence. *Amer. Psychologist*, 1950, *5*, 78-83.

63. WEISSKOPF, EDITH A. The influence of mental hygiene on intellectual development. *Publ. Welf. Ind.*, 1945, *55*, 8, 19-20.

63/EGO PROCESS IN LEARNING/NEVITT SANFORD[*]

I WOULD LIKE TO CONSIDER THE AC-tivities of the ordinary classroom as a means of promoting psychological health and development in children. . . .

Without a doubt, education, psychological health, and adequately paced development are salutary things by which to be characterized. . . .

THE MEANING OF EDUCATION

To maintain the separateness of [these] concepts, the term education must be restricted to its traditional, and somewhat narrow, meaning: the inculcation in the individual of the cultural heritage. The process of education, when we use the term in this sense, is primarily a matter of transmitting symbols. And this, I take it, is what happens most characteristically in the classroom.

If we define education in this way, it is clear that a person can be highly educated but at the same time unhealthy—in the sense of being neurotic. He can carry on his neurotic activities in an educated way, perhaps using symbols of high culture. . . .

Health can be defined as the capacity for dealing in some more or less adaptive fashion with the problems and strains that life offers. We do not define it in terms of what is most common in the statistical sense, or in terms of freedom from symptoms or freedom from suffering, even though these things might actually favor the development of future capacity for coping. We can't define it strictly as stability because, as Dr. Gerald Caplan has shown, much of the instability to be observed in young people can be understood as the beginning of a new and possibly quite healthy adaptation. On the other hand, where there is adequate adaptative capacity, there is probably a fundamental stability, in that the individual can adapt or deal with present strains while somehow remaining fundamentally himself.

. . . .

This leaves us, then, the concept of development, or optimum development, or high levels of development—all of which may be defined as how close we come to the maximum realization of our human potentials.

. . . .

My task then is to consider how education in the narrow sense, i.e., activities involving books, classrooms, blackboards, the use of teaching materials, visual aids, teaching machines, and television, *can* actually contribute to the development of personality. We have seen that it does not necessarily do so. In approaching this task, we must go, a little way at least, into the theory of personality and its development.

First to be emphasized is the idea that the personality functions as a whole. This is not just a slogan. We must not permit educators categorically to separate the intellectual or the cognitive from the rest of the personality. Conceptually, of course they may do this. Cognition, feeling, emotion, action, and motivation are easily separated by abstraction, but no one of these can function independently of the others. This point is of great importance to me because during the time I have been involved in the study of colleges and of students I have been told many times by teachers: "We'll take care of the intellect, and you psychologists can take care of personality development, if you're interested in that sort of thing."

It is not difficult to show that intellectual performances and intellectual development depend on events in the personality as a whole. All we need do is consider some of the familiar emotional barriers to learning in school. Since this is the stock in trade of the school psychologist, I need not dwell upon it. Instead, I would argue that the facts which the teacher who accents intellect is eager to have a student learn will *not* be learned unless these facts are in some way integrated with the fundamental purposes of the individual. Facts, if they are not to remain inert but are to be retained and put to use later on, must be related to the emotional and motivational processes of the person.

THE MYTH OF DISEMBODIED INTELLECT

I have wondered where educators got the idea of the disembodied intellect, and have had to conclude that it probably arrived via the psychologists. In their efforts to arrive at general

* Nevitt Sanford, Ego process in learning, in Nadine M. Lambert, *et al.*, *The Protection and Promotion of Mental Health in Schools*, Public Health Service Publication #1226, Mental Health Monograph #5, U.S. Department of Health, Education, and Welfare, 1964, pp. 22-30. Reprinted with abridgement by permission.

laws, the psychologists have abstracted—and isolated experimentally—such processes as perceiving, learning, and emotion and have demonstrated relationships between variations in these processes and external stimuli.

It is widely believed that knowledge of this kind can somehow be applied in school. But it cannot in fact be directly applied, because in any schoolroom situation there are a great many variables operating. The vaunted general laws of psychology—laws of perceiving considered without reference to the perceiver, or laws of learning that do not refer to the learner—are not really very general. If a new variable is introduced, the demonstrated relationship changes and, since in any life situation there are always more variables than could possibly be controlled in a laboratory situation, the generality of the laws is bound to be quite limited.

Lifting learning out of its living context in this way contributes heavily, I think, to the dullness of much of the educational psychology that is taught to unwary graduate students. It is not always made clear that cognitive changes in the person influence functioning in the rest of him so that cognitive development is all of a piece with emotional and characterological development. Yet undoubtedly development after the age of about two—after the acquisition of language—is very much a cognitive matter.

THEORIES OF DEVELOPMENT

There is a fundamental notion that development in general occurs in response to some kind of strain, that a challenge must be present if the individual is to generate a new kind of response or adaptive device. When such a device is generated, we say that development has occurred, for the personality is now expanded: something new has been added.

This view of the matter puts the emphasis upon intervention from outside the individual. Not much that is psychologically interesting can be said to happen as a result of a natural unfolding. After the child has developed a few mechanisms for dealing with his problems, further development is not likely to occur unless the challenges put to him are of such intensity, and of such quality, that his old adaptive mechanisms won't suffice. Yet if the challenge is too severe, there is the likelihood that he will fall back on primitive devices which, though they might serve for the moment, are in the long run maladaptive.

Denial [Ed(1)] and repression [Ed(2)] are such devices. They enable the individual to manage strains of the moment, but they are modes of adaptation that are at once unfavorable to later development and difficult to modify. The child or the older student can learn from a crisis, but not if it is so severe—and the people around so unhelpful—that he is forced to fall back upon primitive devices that have served in the past.

Children, by and large, inevitably have to deal with enough strains so that we need not spend much time thinking of ways to challenge them. But as the child grows and acquires a larger and larger repertory of adaptive devices, and thus finds support for his natural hope that he can deal with any new situation without having to change, we then must begin thinking of situations that will challenge this young person so that he will continue to develop. Yet we need to be careful about our efforts to manage crises. It is possible that the effort may so well prepare the individual for a crisis that the crisis never really occurs, and nothing happens to induce developmental changes.

Implicit in what I have been saying are some assumptions concerning goals of development. Development involves expansion and differentiation in all the major areas of the personality, integration within each of these areas, and integration among the areas. With respect to the impulse life of the individual, it seems that one developmental task is to find ways for obtaining emotional satisfaction that are in accord with the requirements of the real world and of society.

As soon as we speak about the requirements of society, we remind ourselves that individuals are social beings, and that they become further socialized in the course of their development. They all have some kind of conscience, primitive or otherwise. A further developmental task would be the enlightenment of this conscience —a state of affairs in which the requirements of conscience are in accord with the individual's best thought and judgment, and not simply rigid rules adopted automatically in childhood. With higher development there is greater en-

Ed(1) *"Denial" is a defense mechanism by which a person unconsciously eliminates or interrupts awareness of anxiety-arousing realities by focusing in his imagination (denial in fantasy) or in his actions (denial in word and deed) on pleasant or reassuring matters. An extreme case is some schizophrenics' retreat into a dream world in which they really believe.*

Ed(2) *See footnote 8 in Peller's article, #64 in this book (p. 475).*

lightenment and hence, greater individualization of conscience. It is this, most essentially, that makes the conscience dependable. "Best thought and judgment" of course refers to the major processes of control, those ego functions according to which the individual gains mastery of the environment and control over himself.

In all of these kinds of development, cognitive processes have an important and perhaps crucial role. And for this, psychotherapy is no substitute. Expanding the major areas of the person, making the individual capable of responding to more and more aspects of the world, and enabling him to do more and more kinds of things—these are not benefits to be gained directly from psychotherapy or even psychological counseling. These things have to be acquired through education.

EDUCATION AS INTERVENTION

We come, then, to education—an "outside intervention" that expands and frees the impulse life. Here the accent is on the cultivation of the life of the imagination. The individual must be able to deal with his problems in his imagination, if he is not to be restricted always to concrete action or to sensation.

Let us consider first the negative side of this. It has been suggested that alcoholics cannot really enjoy movies or television, not because they do not want to be away from the bottle that long, but because they are incapable of participating with satisfaction in collective fantasies. They are too addicted, one might say, to their own version of reality which is based on sensation. This is a severe handicap. One thinks of this handicap also in the case of delinquency.

The point came home to me when I first read James T. Farrell's "Studs Lonigan," a vivid treatment of young people with no inner resources. Meeting on the street in the evening they could think of nothing to do that did not involve overt sexual or aggressive action. The motion picture "Marty" made the point again; young males met each day after work and asked each other, "Now what will we do tonight?"—and there was no answer. This is the kind of impoverishment we constantly find in people who do not know how to read or have not learned to enjoy reading or who cannot deal with problems in the realm of imagination. It is interesting to note the difference between Studs Lonigan and his friend, Danny O'Neill, who went on to become a scholar and writer. Danny was at home reading, or being read to, while most of the boys in his neighborhood were out in the streets doing what boys insist on doing. Danny, of course, could do in his imagination all kinds of things that Studs and his friends couldn't even dream of.

On the positive side, there is evidence of the vast importance for the individual of developing early imaginative experiences. In my own observations at Vassar College, for example, it was clear that "good" students—those who performed very well academically and showed signs of creativity—differed from other students in what they had to say about their play as children. The "good" students had more often played alone, made up games to play, had engaged in play-acting, and enjoyed imaginary companions, had read and been read to. In other words, for these more creative students, the life of the imagination was allowed to be, or by some accident became, important in childhood; they went on from there to scholarship and an interest in the things of the mind.

In this connection it may be noted that in assessment studies of graduate students in the natural sciences there has been a strong indication that the outstanding students are distinguished by their broader interests and greater esthetic sensitivity.

According to theory—and a theory to which I subscribe and am advancing—the individual who has learned to use his imagination is not merely in touch with his impulse life; his impulse life has itself expanded. The way this happens, in my view, is that the symbols of our culture become available to the individual, enabling him to deal with his basic impulses through fantasy and through his imaginative participation in literature, plays, movies, TV, and various other art forms.

The enormous importance of this can be appraised by noting that knowledge has had two basic functions in human history: the practical function of enabling us to master our "real" environment and the imaginative function by which we may extend the real world and enrich it by getting beyond sensation and the immediate situation. The imaginative function may, of course, also favor withdrawal from reality, but this special—ultimately pathological—phenomenon need not detain us at this moment. The point to be accented is that a fantasy starting as a way of expressing a basic impulse becomes a plan, and a plan is necessary for any kind of intelligent action.

THE DEVELOPMENT OF IMAGINATION

Education in the nations of the West, and especially in the United States today, tends to put the accent overwhelmingly on the practical aspects of knowledge, to the neglect of the imaginative aspects. But our concern here is with development, and my main point is that in development the individual needs the kind of knowledge that expands and differentiates his impulse life. This is to be accomplished through making available to him the symbols of our culture. From this point of view, then, culture is the friend of impulse rather than its enemy.

The basic theory, of course, comes from Freud. It was his notion that in the infant a frustration of a need is followed immediately by an image of something that would be gratifying. This is the primary process. Fantasy, dreams, autism thus come naturally to the child, and this is the stuff of which poetry and art and other creative products are made. The generation of images is in itself gratifying to the child —despite admonitions from his elders against "idle fantasy." The kind of reading that was really gratifying to us as children was usually something that our teachers and parents didn't want us to read. That much gratification of our impulses was considered suspect. But it is to be hoped that this kind of gratification can be available to everyone in the present generation of children through reading what has been judged esthetically "good," because culture, and particularly "high" culture, is the means, *par excellence*, for the gratification of the human being's most primitive emotional needs, once the necessary symbols have been acquired.

This, then, is how the individual may expand, and release the impulse life. By making the cultural world available to him and teaching him symbols and how to use them, we enable him to perform symbolically all kinds of psychological functions that would be impossible if he were restricted to transactions with "real" things. One might say that this is the only way in which civilized adults can gratify the infantile needs which are still very much with them and which demand to be satisfied in some way.

In the highest forms of intellectual, artistic and scholarly endeavor, which are rewarding in various concrete and adult ways, there is always some expression of the most primitive emotional needs. The beauty of it is that by doing this kind of work a man can find gratification for some of his most infantile cravings.[Ed] Not all of us can do something about our Oedipus com-

plex by writing a story about it. But we *can* try to deal with our problems imaginatively.

Of course one can go from this to the general issue of taste, and the question of what is "good" at various stages of the individual's development. From the present point of view, taste would be just the right balance between impulsive gratification on the one hand and the requirements of convention on the other. In really good literature there is always a strong element of passion and primitiveness. This is why good literature is so often banned; but at the same time, for a piece of writing to be classed as art, it must conform well enough— *just* well enough—with the demands of convention so that a sophisticated person can enjoy it.

THE IMPORTANCE OF READING

All of this has implications for practice. Above all, children must be taught to enjoy reading. It is sad to contemplate how many of them read without enjoyment—because they have been taught, not that reading is a glorious means of satisfying their impulses, but that it is primarily a duty. Teachers must somehow counteract this prevailing notion. I would say that the first developmental task, the first educational task, is to teach *every* child to enjoy reading, to enjoy making up stories, and to enjoy imaginative work. If this isn't done, there's hardly any use troubling with the many other educational tasks that come later. In personality development, first things must come first.

It is not difficult to teach children to enjoy imaginative work, even though the earlier spontaneous imaginative life that all children know has been dampened by the adults around them. I have had the experience of trying to get Thematic Apperception Test stories out of 10-year-old boys. At first, confronted with the task of making up a story about a picture, they denied that it could be done. But I found that if I stayed with them, coaxed them to say *something*, and then used what they had said as a basis for more coaxing, they could finally produce what would pass as a story. The next production came a little easier—and so on. I would say that almost any child can be persuaded to forget earlier prohibitions against being imaginative.

When children are beginning to read, it prob-

[Ed] *The process of symbolically gratifying primitive needs such as hostile wishes or longings for bodily pleasures is called "sublimation." As an instance, the phrase "to attack one's work" expresses the harnessing of aggressive energies for constructive purposes. Readers may* wish to consult "The School's Role in Promoting Sublimation" by Lili E. Peller (The Psychoanalytic Study of the Child, *International Universities Press, Inc., New York: 1956, 11, 437-449).*

ably does not matter too much what sort of thing they read. If comic books will induce them to read, let them read comic books. The "act" of reading at an early age can later become the "art" of reading. The collective fantasies expressed even in the most atrocious comic books are probably less anti-social than the individual fantasy that any child who has no means of socialization is capable of producing for himself. And a kind of socialization begins to work when the child participates in any kind of collective fantasy, however primitive. Sylvia Ashton-Warner in her book, "Spinster," describes how she taught Maori children of New Zealand to read.[Ed] At the start, they had no conception of what school was about. Day after day, month after month, they sat without learning to read—without, in fact, learning anything. But she found, when she came to know them well enough, that she could get at their fantasy life, and then connect a few words-to-be-taught with what she now knew to be their basic interests or fears. And thus a start was made. This kind of thing takes time, but is undoubtedly worth it.

The act of learning in school (or elsewhere) is essential to the development of the controlling processes—the ego processes which underlie the child's mastery of reality and of himself. This, I take it, is what classroom activity is mainly about. We teach facts about the real world so that the child can make predictions of what will happen, gain confidence in his ability to judge events, and learn to make decisions about what he is going to do. He builds his sense of independence on the basis of his confidence that he can make judgments for himself, and that these will work out well in the end. For this kind of development of the ego to occur, the child must have the experience of mastering harder and harder tasks; these can be school tasks or any others. The essential thing is that there be precise attention to the *grade* of the task: it must be hard enough to push the child along, to require new adaptations, but not so difficult that it will lead to failure, humiliation, and regression.

The big problem—and I don't know the answer to this—is how we can keep the young child's imaginative life going after he gets into the second or third grade, where he must concentrate on learning about "reality." A great many children lead a wonderful life of the imag-

Ed *Her book* Teacher *has also attracted wide attention (Simon and Schuster, New York, 1963; Bantam Books, #NM 1028, New York, 1964).*

ination until they reach school age. Once in school, they must meet the demands of a new and necessary discipline, which may lead them to suppress or dismiss altogether the earlier life of the imagination. The great task of the teacher is to develop the higher ego functions without doing so at the expense of the rich emotional life of the child.

SCHOOLS AND PERSONALITY DEVELOPMENT

In the realm of conscience-building and socialization, it is very important to recognize that external authority is necessary. During the primary school years, books and pragmatic instruction can be used to put before the child models of responsible social behavior. Here, again, cognitive functions would be used to develop personality in its more general aspects. But the more specific matter of judgment and enlightenment with respect to conscience seems to me to belong later in the school years. Possibly the last high school year is time enough for the individual to begin questioning the values according to which he was brought up, for up until now he has needed to believe firmly in certain values in order to inhibit the direct expression of the impulses of adolescence. But once adolescence is over, the time for deeper probing of his values is at hand. College, probably, is the time for him to gain the relativity with respect to values that is necessary to the greater enlightenment and hence eventual stability of conscience.

I said earlier that at various times in the life of the individual there are some unconscious maladaptive processes which influence what happens consciously. At such times we may feel the necessity of going in and finding out why the child has a problem, but it is by no means always wise to do that. What we can do instead is stimulate those parts of the personality which are not being influenced by the unconscious maladaptive process, and thus are still open to wholesome development. It is quite possible for the teacher to accent what can be developed, while ignoring parts of the personality that are foci of problems; indeed, this happens all the time. Teachers cannot wait for the clinical psychologist to straighten out a particular problem of the child before proceeding by educational means to attack the great developmental tasks.

I would argue on theoretical grounds that if the teacher does aim at developing those parts of the personality which are still open to experience—which are not under the influence of unconscious complexes—and this is done well enough, the relationship between the conscious and the unconscious parts of the personality can be changed, and the unconscious complexes may actually recede into relative insignificance. They may even wither on the vine, becoming irrelevant as the other parts of the personality expand.

This, then, is my belief: that ordinary educational procedures, even the most academic ones, can be vitally important in personality development. But if this transaction is to succeed, or succeed more often than it usually does, the educational work itself must be guided by psychological theory and psychological knowledge. So far, however, educational psychology of the kind I'm advocating here has not been highly developed. Much needs to be discovered about the conditions and processes by which personality changes are induced through the use of school materials and classroom activity. My hope then is that school psychologists, while not neglecting any of the other matters they are called upon to handle, will take some responsibility for developing the kind of theory and producing the kinds of facts that will enable us better to utilize the regular processes of education in the interests of personality development.

64/DAYDREAMS AND CHILDREN'S FAVORITE BOOKS[1]/ LILI E. PELLER *

. . . IN RECENT DECADES THE ESTEEM for writers of children's books has greatly risen, in line with the general tendency to relish a much wider range of productions in all fields of art (for instance, primitive, exotic, psychotic, and frankly amateurish art). In keeping with this trend, a publisher sometimes even brings out a story written and illustrated by a child. Such a book may be very appealing because its author is so genuine, so earnest, so involved in his own writing—but as a story it usually falls flat.

But a child can spin a daydream with such emotional intensity that he will remember it in later years; indeed, he may live his life under its spell. This is especially true when at a time of inner turmoil, he encounters his own, his private daydream woven into a story. Sometimes we discover only in analysis the strong grip that an early story has had on a person's life. Usually it is one scene of the story or one story character which is vested with emotional significance.

"The poet arouses in us emotions of which we hardly believed ourselves capable" (Freud, 1908). If the adult reader cherishes this ability of the poet, the child with his unlimited eagerness to savor life is wide open to the magic of the storyteller.

A fear or anxiety which remains covered up in everyday life may become broadly visible through the child's reaction to a story. But

[1] Paper presented at the Annual Meeting of the American Psychoanalytic Association in Chicago, May, 1957. A first version had been presented at the Hampstead Child Therapy Clinic, London, 1956.

* Lili Peller, Daydreams and children's favorite books, *The Psychoanalytic Study of the Child*, 1959, *14*, taken from 414-433. Reprinted by permission of International Universities Press, Inc., New York, and the author.

while a tale may frighten a child, it may give relief too. He discovers that he is not the only one in the world who harbors fears or hatred or spite, emotions that are socially unacceptable. Thus the recent well-meant endeavors to purge stories of all cruelties, of all mean feelings and of vengeance may actually increase a child's guilt feelings and the burden he carries unaided. . . .

I am going to discuss a number of typical childhood fantasies and some of the stories built on them.[Ed] Let us start with a plot intended for the very young.

THE FANTASY OF LOSS AND RETURN

A child loses his mother and, after dangerous adventures, is reunited with her. Any number of stories use this plot. Because it appeals to the youngest listener, the child in the story is often an animal child. This has the advantage that more gruesome adventures can be included. With an animal as the central figure, the storyteller can introduce the cannibalistic fears and fantasies of young children and thus increase the drama (see, e.g., *The Story about Ping, the Duckling; Peter Rabbit; Curious George, the Monkey*). It is the child who acts out, who runs away, but his leaving is often preceded by some fault or negligence of his mother (or protector) mentioned very casually, and hardly noticed by the reader—the story really gains momentum with the child's escapade.

Let us look at the best known story for very young children, *The Tale of Peter Rabbit*. His mother warns him not to go *near* Mr. McGregor's garden. She has hardly left on her shopping trip when Peter runs right into that forbidden territory. He finds it absolutely full of delicacies, young radishes and tender salad leaves, but Peter's happiness in stuffing himself is very short-lived. He is chased and almost caught and killed. Is it all Peter's fault? It looks this way, yet it never would have happened if his mother had not considered a shopping trip more important than looking after her children.

And so it goes also in the other stories. Curious George would not have ended up in jail had his protector not left him alone on their very first day in the big city where George was surrounded by gadgets tempting him to manipulate them. It is the mother who, by turn-

Ed Not all the story types discussed in the original are included in these excerpts.

ing her attention temporarily to other matters, loosens the bond between herself and the child (A. Freud, 1953). Even in this simplest type of story there is a conscious plot and another one which reaches consciousness for a brief moment, then sinks back to the preconscious or unconscious. Yet this part contributes to the story's emotional appeal as well as to the motivation and the plausibility of the story hero's conduct. In all art, essential parts remain on the unconscious or preconscious level, and the nursery tale is no exception.

In these stories for very young readers, animals feel, behave, and talk like human beings. But these fantastic elements are not essential; the very same daydream may also be expressed in a cogently realistic story; see e.g., *Oley, the Sea Monster*. Oley is a baby seal that gets picked up and carried away by a sailor while his mother dives for some food. An exciting adventure story follows, with funny and deeply moving events—but nothing that could not have happened in reality. The book even carries a map showing the route through the Great Lakes, the St. Lawrence and around Nova Scotia by which Oley swam back to his mother.

Tales of *fantasy* and realistic "true" stories are considered to be basically different, yet we find that every childhood fantasy can become the backbone for either type of story.

THE FANTASY OF THE REVERSAL OF ROLES

The young son (the small one, the simpleton), the shy one who always is left out of things, proves to be stronger than all his older brothers when a great danger arises. Thus he not only slays the dragon and wins the princess, he also rescues his friends or his father's kingdom—in short, he becomes the beloved and admired benefactor. This is the core of many fairy tales, in which it is often the third, the youngest son whom nobody has taken seriously, and who wins after his older brothers have failed.[3]

[3] Why is it usually the *third* son who wins? We may think of the symbolic significance of the number three (Abraham, 1923). However, reasons of plot construction offer another explanation. Were the story to speak of one older and one younger brother, the contest between them would resemble too closely the father-son contest, and thus conjure up the oedipal struggle; on the other hand, the account of deeds of a larger number of brothers might be too lengthy, too repetitious—three is the smallest crowd. Finally, the story of the youngest son who succeeds where his older brothers lost out may be a faint memory of archaic conditions where elder

This is the plot of *Hop o' My Thumb*, of John Ruskin's famous *The King of the Golden River*, and also of the Biblical legend of Joseph and his brothers. The contrast of who seems to be strong and powerful and who is small and helpless, and the sudden unexpected reversal of roles provide the spice of these stories. Again there are completely realistic stories with the same plot, for instance the French story *Moustachio*. Moustachio is the smallest dog in his village, indeed, ridiculously small. Yet on the day of the great hunt, he is the one who finds and holds the vicious wild boar at bay until his master comes and fires the deadly shot. The storyteller's skill, his use of relevant details, makes the improbable victory plausible. . . .

HEROIC TALE— OEDIPAL-LEVEL STORIES

In these tales the hero obtains the goals of oedipal wishes in a form which is acceptable to the ego of the latency child. What we know of other latency fantasies also applies here: their ingredients are akin to those which in stories, dramas, operas, and ballads appeal to an adult audience. The essentials of these fantasies have been presented by Freud (1908, 1909b), and its juvenile version was studied by Friedlaender (1942), whose work remains to be of basic importance.

The hero or the heroine lives with one parent or some relatives. Thus at the outset of the story the parents, or at least the parent of the same sex, have been eliminated without the hero's guilt. The grownups in the story accept the child hero as one of them, not as a child. The story depicts the hero's struggle against adverse circumstances and against the villain or villains. But being fearless, resourceful, and a paradigm of many virtues, his eventual triumph is assured.

Friedlaender mentions the following favorite books which use this fantasy: *David Copperfield, Jane Eyre, Treasure Island, Emil and the Detectives;* Anna Freud (1936) has already pointed to *Little Lord Fauntleroy*, and to various fairy tales. Friedlaender attributes the overwhelming popularity of *Jane Eyre* to the fact that in this story the oedipal wish attains a "relatively undisguised" fulfillment. Here I do not follow her. It is the very art of storytell-

---

sons were murdered or exiled while the youngest, born when the father's strength was declining, stood a better chance of becoming his heir.

ing that the fulfillment of the primal wish is achieved and at the same time skillfully veiled. Occasionally, it even remains barred from consciousness. There is only one other alternative left to the artist: a hero (or heroine) who attains undisguised gratification goes to his own destruction—like Oedipus. But Jane, after long and tragic trials and tribulations, eventually marries her man, and they live fairly happily ever after. Throughout the story, Jane is a very proper girl. I do not agree that in her story the oedipal fantasies "break through in almost bare-faced fashion." Yet Friedlaender is right in one point: the gratification in *Jane Eyre* seems more direct than, for instance, in *Treasure Island* or *David Copperfield*.

A remark of Freud helps us to understand *Jane Eyre's* seemingly more overt wish fulfillment. In his story the poet may incorporate the boy's version of the oedipal wish—centering on gratification of aggression and ambition—or the poet may build the story on the feminine counterpart and focus on direct libidinal gratification: a prince charming who leads the heroine home. But it is a difference of focus only—both versions contain or allude to both gratifications, the erotic and the ambitious one. . . .

THE STORIES FOR "HAVE NOTS"

This group may not seem to be a counterpart to the others mentioned so far, but rather a catch-all term for a number of types, namely, for all stories which owe their special appeal less to the tale they spin or to the story characters they bring to life than to the *milieu* they describe. This discrepancy disappears when we extend the meaning of the term "daydream" to indicate not only a narrative, a sequence of events, but also a static *tableau*, the vision of a blissful scene, which includes the daydreamer in his enjoyment of a coveted environment. The readers of these tales are recruited from the ranks of those who pine for an ambient not attainable to them in reality. Here we think of the story describing ways and joys of *teenagers* for those who are still too timid or too young for them; there are the stories of *school life*, i.e., life in a British public school for those who are too young, or, more often, who do not quite belong to the socioeconomic strata who can afford such a school (Orwell, 1939). There are *nature, mystery, adventure, big game* and *Wildwest* stories for those who are barred from these experiences in reality. One generation ago, youthful readers loved historical novels which took them into a romanticized past. Today, stories of space travel have partly replaced them.

Of course, all these stories have also a hero; he has satellites and adversaries; there is a plot, and the story may represent hack-writing or may be well done—in either event a great deal of the attraction is due to the coveted milieu into which the readers are transposed. This is their bait; and this formula is by no means restricted to juveniles but accounts for the popularity of many books, movies, and plays for all ages.

Books may give pleasure through more than one fantasy. Biographies enable the reader to identify with a father image. You have to be famous to rate a biography, and achieving fame can be translated into psychoanalytic concepts as achieving a flamboyant oedipal victory. But a well-written biography does more than this: by reporting personal anecdotes, by letting the reader in on trivial day-by-day incidents, it fosters in him the illusion of hobknobbing with the great and the mighty. This is our reason for mentioning biographies here among the "Have Not" stories. (Receiving factual information may of course be also highly pleasurable, but is outside our topic.)

I suspect that the countless "How-To-Do-It" books, pamphlets and magazines describing hobbies and skills of amateurs are cherished not only by the "doers," to whom they deliver technical information, but also (or mainly?) by the "idlers," for whom they substitute for the doing. Not only an imaginative tale, also a sober step-by-step account can incite and feed daydreams.

I have presented typical daydreams paraphrasing the important emotional constellations of childhood. There is the relationship of the little child to the protective and despotic pre-oedipal mother. The young child cannot fight her, nor oppose her—the drama is restricted to the possibility of escape and return or rescue. The Loss-and-Return fantasy is really an elaboration of the infant's earliest play activity, the peek-a-boo game. There the plot also consists of separation and reunion.

Several types of daydream mirror the oedipal tension. The Reversal-of-Roles fantasy deals with the relationship to older siblings and to the early father, experienced as fearfully big and strong. The Hero and Heroine fantasies refer more directly to the oedipal constellation. The Bad-Boy stories glorify open defiance of all father images. Actually both the Hero and the Bad-Boy stories tell of oedipal victory, but the bad boy's triumph is quickly attained and

short-lived, while the hero attains his goal the slow and arduous way. There are the fantasies of having a twin, an alter ego, or a most faithful companion; and finally the last-mentioned omnibus group which "sells" admission to the coveted but unattainable milieu. Thus daydreams born and fomented by all basic childhood constellations seem covered—but the best group of stories for the young child is still to be discussed.

THE EARLY TALE

I am speaking of such universal favorites as the *Christopher Robin* stories, *The Story of Dr. Dolittle*, the *Mary Poppins* books, and Grahame's *The Wind in the Willows*. In some respect, the books of *Babar, the Elephant* also belong here.

In all groups discussed so far we find books which are little masterpieces and others where the writer has learned the formula and uses it glibly. But in this last group I know of no such hack-writing. These are tales which cannot easily be imitated. If not handled by a literary master, the plot would fall apart, and there would not be left a story worth the telling.

In *Winnie—the Pooh*, for instance, there is a group of toy animals who for all intents and purposes are alive, although they are at the same time plain stuffed animals. Each one lives in his own house—but all are within easy walking distance from each other. They share adventures and expeditions and all kinds of pleasures and hardships. Winnie—the Pooh is not their leader, but ranks first in seniority, he is *primus inter pares*. And he is a conceited, greedy, but lovable toy bear. The real leader, the figure who turns up in emergencies, is Christopher Robin, the five-year-old to whom they all belong. Only a few lines of each chapter deal with C.R. in person, but when he is badly needed he is right at hand. The personality of each toy animal emerges clearly and so do the positive, the likeable as well as the weaker qualities of its character.

Now let us take a quick glance at *Dr. Dolittle*. He is an elderly, smallish, shy doctor. The drawings show him pot-bellied, bald, a rather ridiculous figure. His outstanding qualities are his simplicity and kindness. No part of the globe is too distant to travel to when he learns about sick animals in need of his magical cure. His home is in the English country side; orginally his sister kept house for him, but she became disgusted and left when the doctor refused to give up the crocodile who ate up the linoleum. As the tale begins, the good doctor lives all alone with his faithful animals, a parrot, a dog, a baby pig, an owl, a duck, and a monkey. These, his household companions, are introduced by name and drawn as individual characters. Besides them are nameless throngs of animals who move in and out of the story.

The central figure of another classic series is *Mary Poppins*, the governess whom the eastwind blows into the home of four children at number Seventeen Cherry Tree Lane. The pictures show her rather unkindly as an old-fashioned, bony spinster with quite shabby yet frilly clothing and accessories. She is at times harsh, moody, often snappy in her commands and answers—but she works magic and enjoys a terrific reputation with various mysterious personages. Her children have wonderful adventures and thus are willing to put up with her occasional bad days.

And, finally, *The Wind in the Willows* (*The Wind in the Reeds*, as it was originally called) tells the story of four devoted friends, Toad, Rat, Mole and Badger. Each one has his own house and each house is quite different from the others. Rat lives at the bank of the busy river. Toad is rich and keeps residence in a splendid mansion, Badger's ancient and many-chambered home is in the Wild Woods, and Mole has very modest ("compact," his friends call it) quarters underground. Among the friends there is continuous visiting, passing by and dropping in, and staying for hours and days and sumptuous meals. These casual visits alternate with adventures undertaken jointly by two or three of them. The Almighty Protector of this chummy group appears only once. He is the Piper-at-the-Gates-of-Dawn, whose presence is felt long before he is seen, whose sweet chant is heard before he appears as a faun-shaped figure. Yet his animals know that in distress he will be at their side.

The togetherness of these friends, their deep loyalty, fills the books and shows in their cozy visits as well as in their wild and glorious adventures. Their enemies are nameless and faceless flocks of animals. A few incidentally introduced humans stay at the fringe of the narrative and their feelings remain hazy and are not really woven into the story. They appear and disappear as their function in the story requires not growing into story characters.

Here are four obviously very diverse tales. They differ not only in plot, in characters, in style, they also appeal to different age groups and are far apart in their literary levels. What, then, do they have in common? In each story we find a Group of loyal friends and we find a Protector who can work magic (at least in the eyes of his entourage; whatever five-year-old Christopher plans or figures out appears as magic to his toy animals). Every member of this group has unique gifts and skills and foibles. In the animal stories there is usually one of a kind, one of a species, and animals who in reality could never live together, like

a badger and a toad, or a pig and a parrot, are intimates. No member of the circle is defined as either young or old, as male or female.[5] The magician-protector's sex is given, but he (or she) is of an age or appearance where genital maleness or femaleness is of little consequence. . . .

The magician-protector stays offstage or near the wings and the friends' actions and their feelings really carry the story. The character of each one of them is etched distinctly, although age and sex are left vague. In these tales *the two great dichotomies, male-female, old-young,* which pervade and shape our life and bring so much pressure upon the ego of the young child, are mostly nonexistent. These stories seem to say: "See what good times and how much adventure you can have if you just forget and ignore those things."

The friends in these stories are devoted to one another, yet their love is conflict-free. There is no jealousy. Let us see what else is absent. Family relations of all kinds are nonexistent or they are at the very fringe of the story, and the feelings of these incidental relatives for one another are lukewarm in comparison with the ardent loyalty and the intimacy welding the friends together. The exception here is a parent's love for its small, helpless baby. Kanga loves Roo, Otter loves Little Portly.

In all the chapters of contented home life or risky adventures nothing happens that would suggest a comparison between what Tom does and what Dick does, or between their appearance. And perhaps as a further assurance against the pressure of comparison, of jealousy and competition, most of them belong to different species. Who will compare a monkey with an owl or a mole with a toad? The members of the closely knit circle are not measured against one another. And more than this: their earlier self is not compared with their later self. They are the same people at the end of the story as they were when we first met them. This, too, is in sharp contrast to the hero of the oedipal tale, who at the close of the story is not only in different circumstances, but is

[5] Exception: the children in the *Mary Poppins* stories. And the general principle may as well be stated here: I am presenting a story structure which exists in the abstract, yet is violated in one or the other point in each story. In relation to the perfect fantasy each story is like a web torn in a different spot in every instance and thus the pattern, i.e., the basic daydream, can be reconstructed by bringing them side by side and comparing them.

changed, an "improved" person. The good and
the sly and bad people he met, the events he
went through, joy and sorrow, love and loneliness—have molded him. The endearing characters of Lofting's, of Milne's and of Grahame's
tale remain throughout the story what they
were at the very beginning. Each one is as
boastful or greedy, or as kind or gullible as
we found him when he first entered. This is
not because these stories, by and large, appeal
to younger children who are but little aware
of the passage of time. After all, heroes intended for a very young age group (e.g.,
Pinocchio or Bambi) grow up and change, and
this recasting of their inner self becomes an
essential part of the story. But the heroes of
the Early Tale are static characters.[6]

The reader of the oedipal story identifies
with the hero and with his success, and by
doing so he vicariously shares the hero's pressures. The charm of the Early Tale may be due
to their complete absence.

Frequently the characters of these stories
wear animal masks.[7] These are the masks of
animals rather than real animals. Not only do
they talk and wear clothes, but besides giving
them a few convincing and specific animal features, there is no attempt to present a biologically correct picture of their animal life. Why,
then, are these animal masks employed by the
writer? A human character who in a story is
not defined according to his approximate age
remains so vague, so insipid, that he does not
win our interest, and a human being whose sex
remains undefined arouses anxiety. In the Early
Tale the animals are depicted with just enough
authentic detail to screen the absence of those
features which are usually indispensable for
creating a plausible character, i.e., the missing
age and sex. *The animal mask supports the
mechanism of denial.* The paucity of concrete
features gives them a heraldic quality.

In the preoedipal phase the child is almost
unaware that there are men and women. The
difference he perceives is between him and the
adults, the persons who can fulfill his wishes or
deny them all. The world is divided into chil-

dren and grown-ups. In the oedipal phase he
is aware of sexual differences but likely to forget that other division which formerly loomed
so large, he is cocky enough to consider himself the equal of his parents. I know that I am
over-simplifying—yet basically this is correct:
from being innocent of one of the great dichotomies (male-female) the child turns to ignore
the other one (child-adult). Time and again,
however, this dichotomy is sharply brought to
his attention. He is only a child and thus can
neither be his mother's partner nor his father's
successful competitor. In his happy moments he
succeeds in denying that he is small and un-
equipped for being a lover, but painful experiences bring him brusquely back to reality. That
a child envies the grownups has always been
known, but Freud pointed to the direct and
gross male (or female) aspirations which go
with the wish to be big. These fantastic aspirations make the child's happy illusions and his
downfalls so intense and potentially traumatic.

At this point I thought I had discovered a
new way of looking at the oedipal constellation.
But then I happened to scan the last pages of
Little Hans's case history and came across the
daydreams he produced at the end of his analysis (Freud, 1909b). Hans has two "happiness
fantasies" ("*Glücksfantasien*"), which testify to
his newly-won ability to cope with the pressures in his life. The plumber comes in one
fantasy to screw off his buttocks and his penis
and to give him larger ones instead; in the
other, Hans has many children and takes them
to the toilet, wipes their behind, their "podl,"
in short, does everything a mother does with
her little children.

With these fantasies Hans has regained his
former cheerfulness. They provide the gratifications from which reality excludes him because
he is only a little boy. With the first fantasy
he denies the gulf separating the boy from the
grown man, while the second cancels the difference between male and female. The Early Tale
employs the opposite technique: the confining
and often painful dichotomies are blissfully absent or irrelevant for the story characters.

The Early Tale builds on the defense mechanisms of denial. A quick glance at another story
character may clarify what is being done here.
Peter Pan is a little boy who refuses to grow
up—that is, he is well aware of the difference
between old and young, but says NO to something he does not like, he *negates* the need to
grow up. The Early Tale goes one step further:
there nobody heard of such a thing as growing

---

[6] In the discussion in London, 1956, Dr. B. Lantos
pointed to their similarity with the inhabitants of the
Garden Eden whose serene life flowed along without
strife, murder, or sexuality.

[7] The Pogo characters of Walt Kelly, which use the
childish form of the comic strip to amuse adults and to
bootleg some biting social and political criticism, also are
animal masks, also one of a kind and nondescript in their
sex and age.

up. The animal friends are a delightful mixture of childishness and grownupness.[8]

At the core of every successful story there is a universal daydream. The tale begins, the curtain rises, the reader identifies with the hero, and enjoys experiences inaccessible to him in reality. The intensity and the grip of emotions he finds in the story would at times be painful in real life.

The pleasure yielded by a daydream is intense, yet definitely restricted. The storyteller makes the daydream articulate, hence communicable, and he makes it ego-syntonic, thereby changing and multiplying the enjoyment. The hack-writer takes the daydream and uses it pretty much "as is." The poet paraphrases and veils it, and he even destroys some of its easy and glib gratification.

Earlier studies had assumed that the story in which we meet our own daydream makes it fully conscious by lending words to it. I believe that essential parts of a story, of its plot, of the story characters' motivations and conflicts remain unconscious or preconscious and *for this very reason* arouse our emotions, our sympathy most effectully. Here a good children's story shares the dynamics of all art.

Many nursery tales employ magical features, i.e., denial in fantasy. Miracles happen with complete ease and make the story possible. The well-known traditional fairy tales are very old and come to us from a time when adults, too, believed in magic. In a preliterate world the laws of reality have less validity, they are less stringent for the reasoning of anyone, child or adult.

The storyteller, like the poet, must believe in the tale he spins. If he makes a conscious effort to write "for little children," his story is likely to sound concocted or it becomes pedantic. This may explain why the majority of fairy tales written today are so trite and syrupy. But recent decades have given us one type of story where fantastic happenings are closely interwoven with highly realistic and prosaic details which in a way deny the first denial. The reader is shuttled between the two, and this double denial may account for the story's ability to hold his interest.

The sincere modern fairy tale is at home in both the world of magic and denial in fantasy *and* in the well-observed world of sober, everyday reality.

We have discussed daydreams, paraphrasing important human relationships and aspirations, and we also took a close look at one type of contemporary fairy tales. Because these stories usually appeal to young children and because they remind us of a simple, carefree age, we called them "Early Tales." In these stories, problems of genital sexuality and the slow encroachments of death are eliminated. Yet thanks to the poet's art, the sutures where these powerful realities were cut out from the fabric of human life are invisible.

BIBLIOGRAPHY

JUVENILES AND NOVELS.

BARRIE, J. M. (1906), *Peter Pan.*

BRONTË, C. (1847), *Jane Eyre.*

BURNETT, F. H. (1886), *Little Lord Fauntleroy.*

COLLODI, C. (1880), *The Adventures of Pinocchio.*

DE BRUNHOFF, J. (1933), *Babar, the Elephant.*[Ed]

DICKENS, C. (1850), *David Copperfield.*

ETS, M. (1947), *Oley, the Sea Monster.*

FLACK, M. (1933), *The Story about Ping.*

GRAHAME, K. (1908), *The Wind in the Willows.*

KÄSTNER, E. (1929), *Emil and the Detectives.*

LOFTING, H. (1920), *The Story of Dr. Dolittle.*[Ed]

MILNE, A. A. (1926), *Winnie–the Pooh.*[Ed]

POTTER, B. (1902), *The Tale of Peter Rabbit.*[Ed]

REY, A. H. (1941), *Curious George.*[Ed]

RIGBY, D. (1947), *Moustachio.*

RUSKIN, J. (1851), *The King of the Golden River.*

SALTEN, F. (1926), *Bambi.*

STEVENSON, R. L. (1883), *Treasure Island.*

TRAVERS, P. (1934), *Mary Poppins.*[Ed]

PSYCHOANALYTIC AND GENERAL.

ABRAHAM, K. (1923), Two Contributions to the Study of Symbols. *Clinical Papers and Essays on Psychoanalysis.* New York: Basic Books, 1955.

BUXBAUM, E. (1941), The Role of Detective Stories in a Child's Analysis. *Psa. Quart.,* X.

FRAIBERG, S. (1954), Tales of the Discovery of the Secret Treasure. *This Annual,* IX.

FREUD, A. (1936), Chapter VI: Denial in Phantasy. *The Ego and the Mechanisms of Defense.* New York: International Universities Press, 1946.

Ed *First volume of a series.*

---

[8] Suppression is the conscious attempt to forget something, while repression refers to the unconscious mechanism. I am using negation and denial in a parallel fashion.

FREUD, A. (1953), On Losing and Getting Lost. Presented at the International Psychoanalytical Congress, London.

FREUD, S. (1906), The Relation of the Poet to Day-Dreaming. *Collected Papers*, IV. London: Hogarth Press, 1925.

FREUD, S. (1909b), Family Romances. *Collected Papers*, V. London: Hogarth Press, 1950.

FRIEDLAENDER, K. (1942), Children's Books and Their Function in Latency and Prepuberty. *Am. Imago*, III.

ORWELL, G. (1939), Boys' Weeklies, In *A Collection of Essays by George Orwell*. New York: Doubleday, 1954.

65/STAGES IN THE DEVELOPMENT OF THE SENSE OF REALITY/SANDOR FERENCZI°

IN FAIRY-TALES . . . PHANTASIES OF omnipotence are and remain the dominating ones. Just where we have most humbly to bow before the forces of Nature, the fairy-tale comes to our aid with its typical motives. In reality we are weak, hence the heroes of fairy-tales are strong and unconquerable; in our activities and our knowledge we are cramped and hindered by time and space, hence in fairy-tales one is immortal, is in a hundred places at the same time, sees into the future and knows the past. The ponderousness, the solidity, and the impenetrability of matter obstruct our way every moment: in the fairy-tale, however, man has wings, his eyes pierce the walls, his magic wand opens all doors. Reality is a hard fight for existence; in the fairy-tale the words "little table, be spread" are sufficient. A man may live in perpetual fear of attacks from dangerous beasts and fierce foes; in the fairy-tale a magic cap enables every transformation and makes us inaccessible. How hard it is in reality to attain love that can fulfill all our wishes! In the fairy-tale the hero is irresistible, or he bewitches with a magic gesture.

Thus the fairy-tale, through which grown-ups are so fond of relating to their children their own unfulfilled and repressed wishes, really brings the forfeited situation of omnipotence to a last, artistic presentation.

° Excerpt from Stages in the development of the sense of reality, in Sandor Ferenczi, *Sex in Psychoanalysis* (New York: Basic Books, Inc., 1950), pp. 238-239. Reprinted by permission.

66/WHY DO CHILDREN WATCH TELEVISION?[1]/

ELEANOR E. MACCOBY[*]

TELEVISION, AS WE KNOW, CAN BE deeply absorbing to children of all ages, but we know little about the reasons for this. A related problem is the question of why some children become enthusiastic television fans while others are uninterested or even bored. If educators and parents wish to guide the quantity and quality of TV-viewing in young children, they must know something about the motives which lie behind the childrens' interest in this medium.

To some, the answer may appear obvious: children like TV because the material presented on the TV screen is intrinsically interesting or exciting. But to say that a television program is "interesting" is to make a statement not only about the program but about the viewer. If it is interesting, it strikes a responsive chord in him—satisfies a particular need, provides wanted information, or perhaps offers release from general tension. When we attempt to understand the relationship of the child to his favorite TV programs, we are face-to-face with a larger question which is of great importance to present-day psychology: What are the functions of fantasy for the individual? The child spends much of his waking life in daydreaming, imaginative play, and exposure to mass media (fairy stories, comic books, radio, and TV). There have been several suggestions concerning the child's motives for this active fantasy life. The first is that fantasy provides a child with experience which is free from real-life controls so that, in attempting to find solutions to a problem, he can try out various modes of action without risking the injury or punishment which might ensue if he experimented overtly. Another function of fantasy is

as a distractor. Readers are doubtless all familiar with the impulse to pick up a detective story and thus temporarily escape from the pressures of real life. Similarly for children, if the environment imposes strain, we may assume the child will be motivated to "get away from it all" by immersing himself in fantasy. A third function of fantasy, which was emphasized by Freud in connection with his analysis of dreams, is wish-fulfillment. According to this point of view, fantasy provides an outlet for impulses which are not allowed free expression in real life. Supporting this view is the fact that young children take an especially great interest in stories depicting violence and sudden death (reflecting perhaps the inhibition of aggressive impulses in their daily life) while adolescents are more interested in themes of romantic love. The vicarious satisfactions provided by fantasy are presumably of a lower order than real-life satisfactions, so that fantasy outlets are chosen only as second-best solutions when real-life satisfactions are lacking.

The present study represents an effort to provide data bearing upon some of the above presumed functions of fantasy. Specifically, the following hypothesis is tested: children will spend more time watching television if they are highly frustrated in real life than if they are not. Obviously this prediction is made on the basis of either the distraction explanation of fantasy or the wish-fulfillment explanation. Of course, no implication is intended here that the desire to escape from an unpleasant real-life environment or vicariously obtain satisfactions which are denied in real life are the *only* reasons for children's interest in television. The present study is focused upon only one of many possible explanations of interest in television.

During the winter of 1951-52, two-hour interviews were conducted with 379 mothers residing in the greater-Boston metropolitan area. Each of these mothers had a child in kindergarten (about five and a half years old), and was asked to describe in detail her methods of training the child. Among other things, she was asked about methods and severity of punishment, permissiveness in the areas of sex,

[1] The material presented in this report is drawn from a larger study of identification in young children, conducted by the Laboratory of Human Development at Harvard University. The group primarily responsible for planning the study, gathering data, and analyzing are: Professor Robert R. Sears, former director of the Laboratory; Professor John W. M. Whiting, present director; and Drs. Harry Levin, Edgar L. Lowell, Eleanor E. Maccoby, and Pauline S. Sears. This investigation was supported by a research grant (M 461) from the National Institute of Mental Health, of the National Institutes of Health, Public Health Service.

[*] Eleanor E. Maccoby, Why do children watch television? *The Public Opinion Quarterly*, 1954, 18, (3), 239-244. Reprinted by permission.

dependency and aggression, and the nature and degree of restrictions imposed upon the child in connection with noise, neatness, going away from the house alone, etc. On the basis of the entire interview, the mother was rated on the degree of emotional warmth which characterized her relationship with the child. Each mother was also asked how much time each day the child watched television, on the average, and whether she attempted to impose any restrictions on the total amount of television he could see or upon any particular programs.

The median length of time which the children spend watching TV daily, according to the mothers' reports, was one and a half hours. There is reason to believe, from previous studies, that this may be an underestimate of the time the children actually spent watching television. For the following analysis, we must assume that even though most mothers probably underestimated their children's television time, the rank order has some validity, so that *differences* in amount of TV-watching among children from different kinds of home environments may be relied upon even if the absolute figures on hours of viewing may not.

A first approach to analyzing the study's hypothesis would be to correlate measures of frustration the child undergoes at home with his hours of television viewing. But both the number of hours of TV-watching and the frustrations experienced by the child are functions of social class, as are the attitudes of mothers toward television itself. Mothers in the upper brackets of the socio-economic scale more often impose restrictions on the number of hours their children may watch television, and the particular programs they may see, than do the mothers in the lower groups, and (perhaps in consequence) the children in the families from the lower socio-economic levels spend more time on the average watching television. At the same time, the lower-SES mothers are less permissive and more restrictive in general in their child-training practices than the mothers in the upper-middle class group. Because of these relationships, the analysis has been carried out separately for the two main social-class groups included in the study.[2]

Nine characteristics of the parents' treatment of the child were selected, each of these nine characteristics being presumably related to the amount of frustration the child experiences in his home environment. Each of the characteristics was then related to the amount of the child's daily television viewing, within the two social-class groups. The results are shown in Table 1.

Among the upper-middle class group, it appears that the more frustrating a child's home experiences, the more he watches television, a finding consistent with the prediction. Seven out of the nine measures of frustration employed show a relationship with TV-viewing in the expected direction (six of the differences being significant at less than the .05 level), and there is no instance in which frustration is associated with *low* TV-watching.[3] As for the magnitude of the relationships: the children who are coldly treated by their mothers watch television a half-hour more per day than the children who are warmly treated—an increase of nearly 50 per cent in the amount of TV-watching from one group to the other. Other measures show an increase of from 15 to 40 per cent in the amount of television watching with increases in frustration.

In the lower-class group, however, the situation is different. It is true that severe physical punishment and lack of permissiveness in the sex sphere appear to be associated with high interest in television. However, the children who are frustrated in the sense of being required to be neat, quiet and mannerly, and go to bed at a rigidly-enforced bedtime spend *less* time watching television than the children who are given more freedom in these matters. And six of the frustration measures show no relationship with TV-viewing.

How can one explain the fact that frustration is associated with extensive television-viewing in upper-middle-class children but not among the upper-lower-class children? A possible explanation lies in the differential patterns of TV-viewing among the parents in the two class groups. Previous research has shown that the adults in upper-middle homes spend considerably less time watching TV than do the adults in the lower socio-economic brackets. Possibly, the children in the lower-SES families, when

[2] Social class was measured in this study by giving a weight of two to a score on Warner's index of occupational status, and a weight of one to the family's annual income. Our "upper-middle" group is mainly business and professional families, who would be classed 1-3 on Warner's 7-pt. scale. Our "upper-lower" group is primarily skilled and semi-skilled workers' families, with some service and clerical occupations represented, and would fall in categories 4-7 on Warner's scale.

[3] It is not permissible to combine these probabilities statistically since the nine measures employed are not fully independent of one another.

TABLE 1 / MEAN NUMBER OF HOURS PER DAY OF TELEVISION VIEWING FOR CHILDREN SUBJECT TO VARYING DEGREES OF FRUSTRATION IN THE HOME.

CHARACTERISTICS OF HOME TRAINING OF CHILD	UPPER-LOWER CLASS			UPPER-MIDDLE CLASS		
	HOURS TV	NO. OF CASES	SIGNIFICANCE LEVEL[*]	HOURS TV	NO. OF CASES	SIGNIFICANCE LEVEL[*]
Punishment for aggression toward parents						
1 Mild	1.4	25		1.6		
2 Moderate	1.3	93	$t_{12:3} = 2.00$	1.6		
3 Severe	1.6	42	$p = <.03$	1.7		
Permissiveness of sex behavior in child						
1 Highly permissive	1.0	24		—		
2 Moderately permissive	1.4	59	$t_{1:34} = 2.23$	1.5	34	$t_{23:4} = 2.34$
3 Slightly permissive	1.5	52		1.5	46	
4 Not at all permissive	1.4	33	$p = <.02$	1.8	79	$p = <.01$
Mother's response to dependent behavior in child						
1 Positive, rewarding	1.3	74		1.7		
2 Neutral	1.4	37	$t_{1:3} = 1.88$	1.7		
3 Negative, punishing	1.5	57	$p = <.05$	1.6		
How far away from home is child allowed to go alone?						
1 Fairly far (across streets)	1.3	19		1.6	32	
2 Own block only	1.4	71		1.6	72	
3 Restricted to own yard	1.4	75		1.7	53	
How frequently mother checks on child's whereabouts						
1 Seldom or never	1.4	24		1.3	11	
2 Occasionally	1.4	67		1.7	65	
3 Fairly often	1.4	35		1.5	40	
4 Constantly	1.3	39		1.8	43	
Level of obedience demands						
1 Child not expected to obey promptly	1.2	43		1.6	52	
2 Moderate obedience demands	1.4	98	$t_{1:3} = 1.77$	1.7	76	
3 Child expected to obey instantly	1.6	26	$p = <.05$	1.6	30	
Level of demands for quiet, neatness, good table manners, and going to bed on time						
1 Few demands	1.1	44		1.9	37	
2 Moderate demands	1.4	72	$t_{1:3} = 2.27$	1.6	56	
3 Severe demands	1.5	52	$p = <.02$	1.6	67	
Extent of use of physical punishment						
1 Child seldom or never spanked	1.2	35		1.5	16	
2 Spanked occasionally	1.4	71	$t_{1:4} = 1.58$	1.5	50	$t_{12:4} = 1.88$
3 Spanked fairly often	1.4	40		1.7	53	
3 Spanked often	1.5	21	$p = <.06$	1.8	42	$p = <.04$
Affectional relationship: mother to child						
1 Extremely warm	1.1	22		1.2	9	
2 Quite warm	1.4	63	$t_{1:4} = 2.88$	1.7	50	
3 Matter-of-fact	1.4	54		1.5	57	
4 Cold	1.6	29	$p = <.01$	1.7	45	

[*] For these p values, a one-tailed test has been used, since the test is for a difference in a predicted direction. It should be noted that a t-test is not an ideal measure of the significance of differences here, since it was designed to test differences between two groups (usually an experimental and control group) and it is difficult to know what combinations of groups may be legitimately made for t-tests when there are more than two groups. Therefore, the individual p values in the above table should be interpreted with caution, and the meaning of the table should rest more upon the series of tests considered jointly.

they are frustrated, tend to escape to television. But when they are *not* frustrated, they do what their parents do: namely, watch television. To put it another way: if the parents of a lower-class child are permissive, warm and non-punitive with him, he tends to imitate them and to want to be with them, which makes him a TV fan, since that is what his parents are. If he does not have a warm relationship with his parents, he may seek television as an escape and a source of vicarious satisfaction. Thus, in the lower-class groups, the amount of frustration does not differentiate the children who are greatly interested in television from those who are not. In the upper-middle groups, however, the parents are busy doing other things. If the child is motivated to be like them and be near them, he will not spend as much time at television, while coldness on the part of the parents (along with other frustrations) will increase the attractiveness of television as an escape and a source of vicarious satisfaction.

It might be pointed out here that the relationship between the upper-middle-class child's interest in television and his home frustrations is perhaps even stronger than it appears in Table 1. For the mothers who are strict and non-permissive with their children tend to disapprove of television and place restrictions upon the amount of time their children may watch in a given day. This means that in the upper-middle class the frustrated children spend more time watching television despite the fact that their mothers make efforts to limit their exposure to television. As a matter of fact, an effort was made to analyze the relationship between television watching and the mothers' demands for quiet, orderliness, etc., holding constant both social class and the mother's restrictions on TV itself. While the number of cases for this analysis is small, it appears that among the upper-middle families, the children who are highly restricted at home spend the most time watch-

ing television, *except* when the mother places great and rigidly-enforced restrictions upon television itself, in which case, presumably the child seeks forms of vicarious satisfaction which are not directly restricted.

SUMMARY AND CONCLUSIONS

The extent of a child's interest in television has been studied as a symptom of a need for vicarious satisfaction through fantasy when the child is frustrated in his efforts to obtain satisfaction in real life. The findings are:

1. In the upper-middle class, the children who are highly frustrated in their current home life (subject to many restrictions and not treated permissively or warmly) spend the most time viewing television programs.

2. In the upper-lower class, there is little or no relationship between frustration and TV-viewing in children.

The differences between the classes has been interpreted as meaning that in the upper-lower class, where the parents themselves spend a good deal of time watching TV, there is more positive motivation for a child to watch television, so that a child will be drawn to it even in the absence of frustration because it is a dominant activity of the family circle. In the upper-middle class, the effects of frustration may be seen more clearly, because, in the absence of frustration, the child is drawn away from television.

67/THE STIMULATING VERSUS CATHARTIC EFFECTS OF A VICARIOUS AGGRESSIVE ACTIVITY/

SEYMOUR FESHBACH[*]

THE PRESENT STUDY IS CONCERNED with the complex effects of participation in a presumably vicarious aggressive activity upon subsequent aggressive behavior. A number of studies have demonstrated that the expression of aggression—whether directly or in symbolic form—results in a lowering of subsequent aggression (Berkowitz, 1960; Feshbach, 1955; Pepitone & Reichling, 1955; Rosenbaum & de Charms, 1960; Thibaut & Coules, 1952). However, there is also experimental evidence to the effect that aggressive activity has a stimulating effect upon the manifestation of other aggressive acts (Feshbach, 1956; Kenny, 1953); that is, aggression may breed aggression.

Since both possibilities—reduction and stimulation—have been experimentally observed, the pertinent issue then is under what conditions a vicarious aggressive act increases and under what conditions it decreases the probability of subsequent aggressive behavior. One such condition suggested by differences in procedure between the studies that obtained evidence of a cathartic effect and those demonstrating a stimulating effect is the emotional state of the subject at the time the aggressive act is performed; that is, if the subject is angry at the time he engages in the aggressive activity, he can then use the act to satisfy and thereby reduce his hostility.

The general hypothesis is suggested that in order for an activity to have drive reducing properties, components of the drive must be present or evoked during performance of the activity; that is, there must be some functional connection between the vicarious act and the original drive instigating conditions. While it is undoubtedly true that the vicissitudes of life will arouse hostilities that cannot be directly discharged, it does not follow that any indirect aggressive act will have the property of reducing hostility that has been evoked under markedly different circumstances. According to the present view, a child's anger toward its mother will not be reduced by an aggressive act toward a doll figure unless its anger toward the mother

has been aroused when the aggressive act is performed. The evocation of anger may not be a sufficient condition—the doll figure may have to be similar to the mother—but it is probably a necessary condition for drive reduction to take place.

If the subject is not hostile at the time of participating in an aggressive act, his subsequent aggressive behavior will not merely remain unaffected but is very likely to be increased. An increase in aggression following a vicarious aggressive act could result from a number of different processes: a reduction in inhibition or in aggression anxiety, reinforcement of aggressive responses, and finally conditioned stimulation of aggressive drive and/or aggressive responses.

On the basis of the foregoing considerations, the following hypotheses are proposed: Participation in a vicarious aggressive act results in a reduction in subsequent aggressive behavior if aggressive drive has been aroused at the time of such participation; if aggressive drive has not been aroused at the time of participation in a vicarious aggressive act, such participation results in an increase in subsequent aggressive behavior.

METHOD

The experimental procedure consisted of arousing a subject's aggressive drive before participation in a vicarious aggressive act or before participation in a neutral act and then obtaining measures of aggression subsequent to these interpolated activities. The variation in level of aggression was accomplished by means of an insult versus noninsult condition and the variation in the interpolated activity consisted of exposure to a fight film versus a neutral film.

SUBJECTS. The subjects were male college student volunteers who were assigned at random to one of the four treatment groups generated by the two experimental variables. One hundred and one subjects were used in the study, with approximately equal numbers in each experimental condition. The subjects were seen in small groups by the experimenter so that nine experimental sessions in all were held, three for the Noninsult Fight Film condition

[*] Seymour Feshbach, The stimulating versus cathartic effects of a vicarious aggressive activity, *Journal of Abnormal and Social Psychology*, 1961, 63, 2, 381-385. Reprinted by permission.

and two sessions for each of the other experimental conditions.

PROCEDURE.

Insult versus Noninsult conditions. Subject assigned to the insult groups were subjected to a number of unwarranted and extremely critical remarks. These comments essentially disparaged the intellectual motivation and the emotional maturity of the students.[1] [For example, the experimenter made such comments as, "Now I realize that you ——— College students, or should I say ——— College grinds, have few academic interests outside of your concern for grades. . . . If you will try to look beyond your own limited horizons, your cooperation will be useful. In other words, I'd like you to act like adults rather than adolescents. . . . Since the material will not be graded, there is no reason for you to cheat."Ed] Previous studies (Feshbach, 1955; Gellerman, 1956) have provided abundant evidence that this technique successfully arouses hostility toward an experimenter. Subjects assigned to the Noninsult condition were given standard test instructions.

Aggressive Film versus Neutral Film condition. Subjects in the Insult and Noninsult groups then witnessed either a Fight Film or a Neutral Film. The Fight Film consisted of a film clip of a rather exciting prize fight sequence taken from the motion picture *Body and Soul* while the neutral film depicted the consequence of the spread of rumors in a factory. The duration of each of the films was approximately 10 minutes.

As a rationale for the presentation of the film, the

TABLE 1 / A. MEAN AGGRESSIVE WORD ASSOCIATION RESPONSES OBTAINED UNDER EACH EXPERIMENTAL CONDITION.

DRIVE (D)	FILM (F)	
	FIGHT (F)	NEUTRAL (N)
Insult	24.5 (25)a	28.9 (21)
Noninsult	27.7 (29)	25.3 (25)

B. SUMMARY OF ANALYSIS OF VARIANCE OF AGGRESSIVE WORD ASSOCIATION RESPONSES.

SOURCE	SS	df	MS	F
D	8.93	1	8.93	
F	38.43	1	38.43	
DF	291.59	1	291.59	4.58°
Within	6,111.80	96	63.66	
Total	6,450.75	99		

a The word associations of one subject were not scored due to illegibility.

° $p < .05$.

[1] The author wishes to express his gratitude to Abraham Wolf for his competence and courage in carrying out this phase of the experiment.

subjects were told before the film was presented that they would be asked to judge the personality of the main character in the film. Following the completion of the film, each subject indicated his impression of the personality of the hero of the film on a questionnaire provided for that purpose.

Dependent Measures of Aggression. All subjects were given a modified association test which, in a previous study (Gellerman, 1956), had been shown to be sensitive to differences in the arousal of aggression. The test involves the presentation of five aggressive words interspersed among six neutral stimuli as follows: wash, choke, travel, massacre, walk, murder, relax, stab, sleep, torture, listen. The subjects are asked to give in written form a series of associations to each word. The stimuli are presented orally and also visually, the experimenter holding up a 5″ × 8″ card on which the stimulus word is printed. The subject's Aggression score is based on the number of aggressive word associations among the first 10 responses to each of the aggressive stimulus words. The maximum score that can therefore be obtained on this measure is 50.

Subsequent to the administration of the word association test, the first experimenter left the room having presumably completed the study. A second experimenter then entered and informed the subjects that the psychology department wished to assess students' opinions of the value of participating in psychological experiments. A questionnaire was then administered dealing with the subjects' attitudes toward the experiment. The questionnaire which consists of six items, each of which has six alternatives, is described in more detail in a previous study (Feshbach, 1955). It is scored so that the least aggressive choice for a particular item is given a score of 1 and the most aggressive choice, a score of 6.

RESULTS

By hypothesis, it was predicted that the Insult group exposed to the Fight Film would manifest *less* subsequent aggression on each of the two measures of aggression than the Insult group exposed to the Neutral Film while the Noninsult group exposed to the Fight Film would display *more* subsequent aggression than the Noninsult group exposed to the Neutral Film. The word association data bearing upon these predictions are presented in Table 1. The mean differences are in accordance with expectation, the Insult-Fight (IF) Film group responding with fewer aggressive associations than the Insult-Neutral (IN) Film group and the Noninsult-Fight (NIF) Film group responding with more aggressive associations than the Noninsult-Neutral (NIN) Film group. The results of an analysis of variance of the data indicate that the interaction between the Insult and the Film variable is statistically significant. The difference between the IF Film and the IN Film groups falls short of the 5% confidence level, the value of t being 1.9. The difference between the NIF Film and NIN Film groups yields a t value of approximately 1 which is clearly not significant.

The contrast between the IF Film and IN Film groups is more sharply delineated by a simple median split. The chi square for the fourfold table presented in Table 2 is 6.02 which yields a p value of $< .02$. The word association data, then, indicate that under conditions of anger-arousal, witnessing a fight film results in a lowering of aggression. However, the hypothesized stimulating effect of an aggressive film under nonaroused conditions is not borne out by the data.

The questionnaire data are presented in Table 3. Because of the lack of homogeneity of variance between the IN and NIF Film groups, separate comparisions were made between pertinent groups and, in these comparisions, the

variances of the respective distributions are not reliably different. As was the case with the word association data, the IF Film group displays significantly less aggression on the questionnaire than does the IN group. The difference between the Non-insult groups is not in the predicted direction but is small and unreliable.

The difference in subsequent aggressive attitudes between the insulted group exposed to the fight film and the insulted group exposed to the neutral film is further illustrated by a simple median split. The chi square for the fourfold table presented in Table 4 is 15.1, which is significant at less than the .001 level.

DISCUSSION

The experimental results are consistent with the hypothesis that the drive reducing effect of a vicarious aggressive act is dependent upon the aggressive state of the subject at the time of the vicarious aggressive activity. Witnessing the prize fight film resulted in a significant relative decrement in aggression in comparision to witnessing the neutral film only for those subjects in whom aggression had been previously aroused by the insulting comments of the experimenter. The predicted increase in aggression for the noninsulted subjects following exposure to the fight film did not occur, however. Each of these two outcomes warrants further comment.

With regard to the difference between the two Insult groups in subsequent aggression, a possible alternative to a catharsis or drive reduction hypothesis is one that assumes that guilt or revulsion stimulated by the fight film is the primary mechanism responsible for the lowered aggression. Berkowitz (1958, 1960) has strongly argued for such an explanation of a reduction in aggressive behavior following an aggressive act. However, it must be noted that the evidence for a guilt or inhibition process is most indirect and inferential.

With regard to the present study, the guilt alternative is certainly possible, although, for various reasons to be suggested below, not a likely one. If guilt arousal were a ubiquitous process, occurring whenever people are given the opportunity to indulge in aggressive fantasies, then the fight film should similarly have inhibited the aggressive response output of the Noninsult group. The possibility still remains that guilt arousal can account for the aggression reducing effects of fantasy under conditions where aggression has recently been stimulated, as in the Insult condition. As a check on whether

TABLE 2 / DISTRIBUTION OF AGGRESSIVE WORD ASSOCIATION RESPONSES FALLING ABOVE AND BELOW THE MEDIAN AS A FUNCTION OF INSULT FIGHT FILM AND INSULT NEUTRAL FILM TREATMENTS.

TREATMENT	<27	>27
Insult Fight Film	17	8
Insult Neutral Film	10	19

Note.$-\chi^2 = 6.02$; $p < .05$.

TABLE 3 / A COMPARISON OF MEAN SCORES ON THE AGGRESSION QUESTIONNAIRE.

INSULT-FIGHT (IF) ($N = 26$)	INSULT-NEU-TRAL (IN) ($N = 29$)	NONINSULT-FIGHT (NIF) ($N = 20$a)	NONINSULT-NEUTRAL (NIN) ($N = 25$)
M 14.6	19.5	13.7	15.0
s 3.72	3.90	2.52	2.95

Note.—IF—IN $= 4.7$; $p < .01$.

a One subject failed to complete questionnaire.

TABLE 4 / DISTRIBUTION OF AGGRESSION QUESTIONNAIRE SCORES FALLING ABOVE AND BELOW THE MEDIAN AS A FUNCTION OF INSULT FIGHT FILM AND INSULT NEUTRAL FILM TREATMENTS.

TREATMENT	< 17.5	> 17.5
Insult Fight Film	20	6
Insult Neutral Film	7	22

Note.$-x^2 = 15.1$; $p < .001$.

the lowered aggression of the IF Film group was due to some inhibitory factor, the word associations were scored for defensiveness. A previous study of the effects of inhibition upon aggressive word associations has shown that when inhibition is experimentally aroused, the number of aggressive responses decreases while the number of defensive responses increases (Gellerman, 1956). While, in the present study, a difference was observed in the number of aggressive associations, the difference between the two Insult groups in the number of defensive associations was negligible and insignificant. The absence of an increment in defensive responses, while not decisive since the experiment cited employed an inhibition procedure more closely resembling fear rather than guilt, is more consistent with a drive reduction rather than guilt explanation of the decrease in aggression following the exposure of the insulted subjects to the Fight Film.

The problem remains of accounting for the failure to obtain the expected increase in aggression in the Noninsult group. One possible reason is the limitation of the questionnaire instrument as a measure of aggression. Although one's preference for or attitude toward another person is frequently used as an index of aggression, as was the case in the present experiment, dislike and aggression are not equivalent dimensions. At the extreme, aversion and aggression are likely to be strongly correlated but within moderate ranges of feeling, the association between dislike and aggression may well be negligible. For this reason, the word association measure is probably a better instrument than the attitude questionnaire for detecting changes in aggression in the noninsulted groups. However, although the relative increment in aggressive associations following exposure of the Noninsult group to the Fight Film was in the predicted direction, it was not statistically significant. Whether this failure to obtain evidence of a stimulating effect of a vicarious aggressive activity under relaxed emotional conditions is due to inadequacies in the theoretical analysis or to limitations in the methods utilized cannot be ascertained from the present data.

On the other hand, the data consistently reflect the dependence of the drive reduction effect upon the arousal of aggression at the time the subject is engaging in the vicarious aggressive activity. Presumably vicarious aggressive acts do not willy-nilly serve as outlets for aggressive motivation. This latter process warrants further attention. Aggression is not an ever-present tension system pervading all of an individual's activities. Like other acquired motives, its appearance is very much dependent upon situational factors; and, the more specific the category of objects toward which the aggression is directed, the narrower is both the range of stimuli that can elicit the motivation and the range of situations that can serve as substitute outlets for the aggression.

What would appear to be a relatively simple matter—the effects of a vicarious aggressive activity upon subsequent aggressive behavior—is in actuality a quite complex process. The present study has examined the influence of the drive state of the organism upon this process. Beyond the requirement of replication in a variety of situations, further research is needed to establish the extent to which other variables determine the effects of so-called vicarious aggressive activities and to establish the precise mechanism by which the performance, direct or vicarious, of an aggressive act influences subsequent aggressive behavior.

SUMMARY

Studies of the effects of a presumably vicarious aggressive activity upon subsequent aggressive activity suggest that under certain conditions the activity will tend to increase, and under other conditions decrease, the probability of subsequent aggressive behavior. The purpose of this experiment was to study the effects of one such condition—namely, the emotional state of the subject at the time the vicarious aggressive activity is performed. Specifically, it was proposed that a vicarious aggressive activity results in a *reduction* in subsequent aggressive behavior if the subject is emotionally aroused at the time he is engaging in this activity, but if anger has not been aroused, the activity results in an *increase* in subsequent aggressive behavior. The two independent variables manipulated in the study consisted of an Insult versus Noninsult condition and an Aggressive Film versus Neutral Film condition. One hundred and one college students were assigned at random to the four treatment groups generated by the two experimental variables. The subjects met the experimenter in small groups so that nine experimental sessions in all were held. Subjects assigned to the Noninsult condition were given standard test instructions while subjects in the Insult groups were subjected to a number of unwarranted and extremely critical remarks. The subjects then witnessed either an Aggressive Film or a Neutral Film. The former consisted of a film clip depicting a prize fight sequence while the latter depicted the consequences of the spread of rumors in a factory. They were then administered a word association test and under the guise of a departmental assessment of the value of students' serving as experimental subjects, a second experimenter administered a questionnaire dealing with the subjects' attitudes toward the first experimenter and with their evaluation of the experiment. The degree of aggression manifested on the attitude questionnaire and the number of aggressive responses on the word association test constituted the dependent measures.

A significant interaction in the predicted direction was obtained for the Word Association measure—the Insult-Aggressive Film group responding with fewer aggressive associations than the IN Film group, and the Noninsult-Aggressive Film group responding with more aggressive associations than the NIN Film group. A similar significant difference between the two Insult groups was found on the attitude questionnaire, but the difference between the two Noninsult groups on this measure was unreliable and was not in the predicted direction.

The results were interpreted as being consistent with a drive reduction theory, although an inhibitory process (guilt arousal) cannot be excluded by the evidence at hand. The dependence of the *aggression* reducing effect of exposure to a film depicting violent activity upon the prior or simultaneous arousal of aggressive drive was stressed.

REFERENCES

BERKOWITZ, L. The expression and reduction of hostility. *Psychol. Bull.*, 1958, 55, 257-283.

BERKOWITZ, L. Some factors affecting the reduction of overt hostility. *J. abnorm. soc. Psychol.*, 1960, 60, 14-22.

FESHBACH, S. The drive-reducing function of fantasy behavior. *J. abnorm. soc. Psychol.*, 1955, 50, 3-11.

FESHBACH, S. The catharsis hypothesis and some consequences of interaction with aggressive and neutral play objects. *J. Pers.*, 1956, 24, 449-462.

GELLERMAN, S. The effects of experimentally induced aggression and inhibition on word association response sequences. Unpublished doctoral dissertation, University of Pennsylvania, 1956.

KENNY, D. T. An experimental test of the catharsis theory of aggression. Unpublished doctoral dissertation, University of Michigan, 1953.

PEPITONE, A., & REICHLING, G. Group cohesiveness and the expression of hostility. *Hum. Relat.*, 1955, 3, 327-337.

ROSENBAUM, M. E., & DE CHARMS, R. Direct and vicarious reduction of hostility. *J. abnorm. soc. Psychol.*, 1960, 60, 105-111.

THIBAUT, J. W., & COULES, J. The role of communication in the reduction of interpersonal hostility. *J. abnorm. soc. Psychol.*, 1952, 47, 770-777.

68/COMPULSIVITY, ANXIETY, AND SCHOOL

ACHIEVEMENT[1]/ JESSE W. GRIMES

AND WESLEY ALLINSMITH[*]

THE PROBLEM OF THE CHILD IN THE task of learning to read is of serious concern to psychologists, as well as to educators, parents, and children themselves. Among the many possible causes of reading retardation, some, such as physical handicaps or low intelligence, are obvious. Others are more subtle. Recent psychological research suggests that certain motivational and perceptual characteristics of children may interact with common techniques used in the teaching of reading. Individual differences in such factors as selective perception or emotional needs may dispose pupils to find that one or another method of teaching makes learning easier, more palatable, or more satisfying. The classroom procedure that is effective for some children may prove to be deleterious to the performance or development of others. If a clear-cut association can be shown between school achievement and an interaction of pupil personality and teaching method, the implications will be far-reaching for the psychology of learning and instruction as well as for teaching the specific skill of reading.

Each person restructures any stimulus into a unique pattern that fits his own expectations, conceptions, values, taboos, and wishes. Learning becomes a function of what the individual does to the material as well as of the actual content of the material. Studies of perceptual defense (Spence, 1957; Lowenfeld, 1956) and clinical observations of children with learning difficulties (Weisskopf, 1951) have given evidence of perceptual distortions that protect the individual from conscious recognition of unwanted or feared stimuli. Bruner (1951) emphasizes the factor of expectation, interpreting his research as evidence that the individual perceives by using a set of cues which he has learned from his particular experiences to associate with certain situations.

A child's personal reconstruction of stimuli in perception may be vastly different from reality as a consequence of his unique needs, anxieties, or ambitions. For instance, when a teacher kindly remarks, "I know you will do well," some children may perceive severe threat, perhaps unconsciously generalizing from earlier traumatic experiences when an authority figure demanded performance beyond their capacities. When a teacher attempts to be democratic and permissive, some other children's conflicts over making decisions in the absence of direction may cause them to perceive only disorganization, danger, and confusion. If the teacher as well as the child is unaware that what is seen or heard is not being interpreted realistically, it is impossible for the teacher to help the pupil perceive correctly.

It seems probable that one cannot teach a single lesson in a particular manner with any assurance that *all* children will have perceived the content as intended or will attend to it as hoped, free of crippling anxiety or other preoccupation. If almost all children are to be reached and some degree of unity established in the perception of a given fact or generalization, a differentiation of teaching methods may be required. Interest in these problems led to an investigation of ways in which reading is currently taught.

METHODS OF INSTRUCTION IN READING. There are two major schools of thought about the teaching of reading, and each group leans upon psychological principles to support the method advocated. Much controversy between the groups has been publicized in recent years, particularly as an aftermath of Flesch's *Why Johnny Can't Read* (1955) which provoked a rebuttal by Carroll (1956). A summary of the two systems is presented below.

One group would initiate reading instruction

[1] This investigation was part of a program of studies conducted at the Harvard Laboratory for Research in Instruction under the direction of Dr. John B. Carroll, who gave much help during the collection and analysis of data. We are grateful also to Celeste T. Forbes and to Dr. Beverly Allinsmith, Dr. Leonard M. Lansky, and Dr. Judy F. Rosenblith for their deft criticisms of the manuscript.

[*] Jesse W. Grimes and Wesley Allinsmith, Compulsivity, anxiety, and school achievement, *Merrill-Palmer Quarterly*, 1961, 7, 247-271. Reprinted by permission.

through systematic presentation of sounds and their letter symbols, and teaching for competence in the skill of "sounding out" the words encountered in reading. This "phonics" method is basically a system of rules; the child learns that the word symbols have been built from the letter elements in an orderly manner.

Most such systems begin with a limited number of letters. The children are drilled in the sound-letter associations. Syllables and words are built by the child through the use of known word elements, with new letters and letter combinations presented systematically, followed by drill, and then by usage in word attack. The phonics approach is usually followed by an emphasis upon thought-getting when the child actually begins to read, with whole words becoming automatically recognized *after* the child establishes the skill of word analysis. Proponents of the system argue that since the child has already acquired much of the spoken language, his greatest need in learning to read is to achieve mastery of the translation of the alphabetical symbols.

In contrast to the method in which phonics is emphasized from the outset, the "whole-word" or "look-and-say" approach to initial reading instruction has been advocated by many educators in recent decades and is in wide use throughout the United States. Instruction begins with narrative reading material. The child is taught to recognize whole word configurations in association, with meaning, thus developing a "sight vocabulary" through repetitive exposure to a limited but gradually expanding number of words.

The original "sight vocabulary" of 50 to 200 words is learned through memorization of total word forms with little or no attention to the alphabetical details of word construction. The words that are taught are chosen for their concept and interest value rather than in accordance with any designed plan for systematizing word recognition. The whole-word approach is *followed* by instruction in a variety of word attack skills including phonics, but the latter is taught incidentally, i.e., when the teacher perceives the need during the on-going process of reading for meaning. In the procedure, generalizations are made, and used later in attempts at word analysis, but there is seldom a systematic follow-through with isolated drills to establish the learning of one generalization at a time in an ordered fashion. Other word attack techniques accompanying the sight method encourage the child to make "trial responses" on unfamiliar words, i.e., to make intelligent guesses, on the basis of clues gained from pictures, text, or configuration.

Proponents of the whole-word method argue that since the only real objective of reading is to derive meaning from the printed words, skill in achieving this objective can best be attained through successful and rewarding experience in actual reading. They argue further that an early emphasis upon phonic analysis impedes the child in the process of thought-getting, and that the irregularities in spelling render this approach confusing. In contrast, advocates of phonics allege that many children taught with a sight emphasis cannot analyze new words effectively and do poorly in composition because they fail to differentiate nuances of spelling.

Of course individual teachers can be found who use a combination of techniques from both systems. Nevertheless, one emphasis has tended to exclude the other in many educational settings. The major differences between the two systems are found in (a) the timing of the introduction of phonics instruction; (b) the degree of systemization of phonics instruction; (c) the emphasis upon phonics as a basic tool in word attack; and (d) the encouragement of trial responses on the basis of clues other than letter-sound associations.

Many researchers have investigated the differential effectiveness of the two methods. The results are inconclusive and contradictory, often showing no significant differences in reading skill between groups taught one way and those taught another, but usually finding a substantial and about equal number of children in *both* systems who do not achieve satisfactorily in reading and whose under-achievement or relatively poor performance is not explained by the usual "causes" of school failure, such as low intelligence or clear-cut emotional problems. After reviewing the literature, Witty and Sizemore (1955) concluded that while differences in method of reading instruction may produce different qualities of reading skill, they are inconsequential when overall skill is judged. Others have voiced opinions that many children learn to read more successfully through the whole-word approach, but that certain children seem to make better progress through a systematic study of phonics.

INTERACTION OF PERSONALITY AND METHODS. This latter observation suggests that there may be an interaction between children's personality characteristics and methods of teaching. Until recently there has been almost no attempt through research to discover whether one teaching method may have been more effective than another for certain students because of the students' individual characteristics.

The few relevant studies, all within the past decade, have in every case dealt with college students. Wispe (1953), Smith, *et al.* (1956), and McKeachie (1958) have reported experiments which suggest that teaching methods interact with student personality characteristics. In all these experiments some students were placed in recitation or lecture sections where expectations were clearly defined, while other students were placed in seminar-like sections where they were free to establish objectives and course procedures. In one instance, Smith, *et al.*, the more highly structured sections were taught in a cold, impersonal, even punitive manner, while the unstructured sections were conducted in a warm, supportive, and permissive atmosphere. In all three instances, a type of student was identified who appeared to demand a high degree of structuring in the learning situation in order to make optimum progress. Wispe describes such students as personally insecure and dependent:

In the first place, this insecurity demands an abnormal amount of structuring of the situation, so that tensions arising out of the fear of doing the wrong thing can be reduced. . . . When this kind of student, who is disposed toward a highly dependent type of educational system, with desires for direction that cannot be met by any "normal" amount of instructor-structuring of the situation, is placed in a permissive section, the real conflict comes to the fore. Being intensely frustrated, and lacking the personal security to make the best of a bad situation this student becomes rigid, intropunitive, and vindictive in his evaluation of sections and instructors. To this student the permissive section meetings are "absolutely worthless," a place where intellectual confusion is heaped upon personal anxiety. (pp. 176-177)

Such reports suggest a promising method of attack on the problem at hand. The two methods of teaching reading described may be viewed as providing contrasting amounts of structure imposed in the definition of the task. From the above reports, two different pupil personality tendencies appear relevant: anxiety and compulsivity, tendencies for which there is much descriptive evidence in the literature. If an interaction does exist between teaching methods and these two personality types, we should find that highly anxious or highly compulsive children will perform successfully when exposed to one method of instruction while similar children will do less well or even fail when taught by the other method. Before making a prediction, we need to look at (a) structure in teaching, (b) the nature of anxiety and compulsivity.

STRUCTURE AS A DIMENSION IN THE TEACHING OF READING. Structure in teaching involves the availability of cues within the whole that give certainty of meaning, definiteness of form, or clearly understood expectations. Usually this means that material is presented sequentially in such a way that when new stimuli are introduced, the learner is able to recognize familiar elements and attack each problem on the basis of prior learning of fundamental skills, facts, or principles. In structured teaching, the child is made aware of all expectations through carefully defined rules; when new situations are presented, the child is prepared to act with certainty on the basis of previously taught information.[2]

We believe that the two methods of teaching reading provide different amounts of structure. The phonics method, because of its reliance upon rules, systematic arrangement, and provision for certainty in problem-solving, appears to represent a high degree of structuring. The whole-word method, particularly in its earlier stages, can be judged as relatively unstructured because of its lack of discipline in word attack, and its encouragement of "intelligent guessing" on the basis of loosely defined clues.

PERSONALITY TENDENCIES. Anxiety and compulsivity, the two personality characteristics chosen for the investigation of a possible interaction with methods, are discussed below to determine what evidence exists that would enable us to predict the direction of interaction.

Compulsivity. Fenichel (1945) describes the need for being systematic and for clinging to known routine and clear guide-rules as it occurs in the obsessive-compulsive, as well as the tendency of such persons to classify ideas rigidly in logical categories and to think in black and white terms. Meticulous preoccupation with small, insignificant details and with the letter

---

[2] "Structure," as a term long applied to educational practices, has recently taken on a special color as a result of Bruner's (1960) writings. He uses the term with a meaning which differs somewhat from ours. To him, structure is an attribute of the curriculum concerned with the sequence of the *conceptual principles* taught and their application to the mastery of later material. (We are using "structure" in a more traditional sense as referring to the clarity of procedure to be followed in a given task and the explicitness of the connections between one task and the next. This usage does not exclude Bruner's theme.)

of the law are noted in many cases with a frequent inability to see the forest for the trees.

Murphy (1947) offers a functional description of the compulsive personality: "Everything that is free, uncontrolled, spontaneous is dangerous. Papa will spank. Play safe; put the books back in the right place; rule the notepaper neatly; pay your bills on the first of the month; be good." (p. 748)

Frenkel-Brunswik (1952) pursued the task of demonstrating the inhibitory and paralyzing effects of harsh discipline upon the initiative and imagination of children. In homes with a rigid orientation she found that discipline was often based upon an expectation of the quick learning of external, superficial rules. Her description of the behavior of children from such homes is typical of the syndrome of compulsivity:

> In order to reduce conflict and anxiety and to maintain stereotyped patterns, certain aspects of experience have to be kept out of awareness. . . . The clinging to the familiar and precise detail can go hand in hand with the ignoring of most of the remaining aspects of the stimulus configuration, resulting in an altogether haphazard approach to reality. (pp. 487-489)

Children of this type exhibited an extreme intolerance of ambiguity. Ambiguity seems to be perceived as a warning of the uncertainty of continued well being and tends to evoke fear or anxiety. It is as though the individual would prefer to see anything "certain" rather than remain in a state of flux, often accepting superficial clarity at a cost of maladaptive behavior.

In summary, the compulsive person appears to have exaggerated conceptions about exactness and order, and is oriented motivationally and perceptually by these concerns. Compulsives are described as relatively rigid, preoccupied with small details, inhibited in spontaneity, conforming, perfectionistic, seeking certainty, and intolerant of the ambiguous or incongruous situation. Of course these adjectives apply in marked degree only to disordered personalities (or to some fairly well-adjusted people in periods of stress). But obsessive-compulsive *tendencies* can be observed in so many children who are clinically within the normal range that we found it possible to categorize our sample of "normal" public school pupils as relatively "high," "medium," or "low" in compulsivity. It seems logical to predict that the structured phonics program would facilitate school progress for children who show evidence of "high" compulsivity compared with similar children exposed to an unstructured whole-word reading program. The latter approach would probably be perceived by such children as disorganized and unsystematic, and they could be expected to have difficulty in complying with the requirement to guess in ambiguous situations.

Anxiety. Anxiety as a universal experience of human beings and as a factor in neurosis has long been recognized as a key psychological phenomenon, but only recently has there been a concentrated attack upon it as a personality variable in normal subjects. People measured as highly anxious have been shown to perceive more intense threat in a greater variety of circumstances (Heath, 1956). It appears that anxiety is a response to stress or to the perception of threat. When experienced at an optimum level for the subject, such anxiety *facilitates* problem-solving behavior (Sarason, 1957) but at an intense level it exerts a disorganizing effect (Castaneda, 1956), diminishing the powers of discrimination and thinking.

Korchin and Levine (1957) analyzed types of errors and rate of learning verbal material and found that the more anxious subjects differed little from non-anxious in the amount learned when dealing with simple and logically associated material, but that the differences were significant when difficult or unfamiliar material was presented, particularly if it was contradictory to previous knowledge. Their interpretation was, "In the situation in which the subject has to make a novel adjustment and cannot utilize existing behavior patterns, the possibility of failure and the consequent loss of self-esteem can further release anxiety and further reduce the subject's ability to develop appropriate behavior." (pp. 234-240) A similar point is made by Ausubel, *et al.* (1953).

Noll (1955) investigated the relation of anxiety to the learning and retention of verbal material. He found that the more difficult the task, the more difficult it was for highly anxious subjects to habituate to the learning situation, but that they were able to do so when required to master a series of tasks that aided in the structuring of the succeeding tasks. When task difficulty was thus structured, the anxious subjects performed as well as or better than the other group.

These findings seem directly applicable to the problem of this study, and justify forecasting the direction of an interaction between anxiety and methods of teaching beginning reading.

We predicted that if learning experiences are highly structured as in the phonics method of teaching reading, the child with high anxiety will make greater progress in school than similar children in the unstructured setting.

Thus the structured phonics approach should allow anxious children as well as compulsive children to do better than they would have with the unstructured, whole-word method.

RESEARCH PROCEDURE

SELECTION OF SCHOOLS REPRESENTING METHODS OF READING INSTRUCTION. Two city school systems chosen to be representative of the methods of instruction required for this study. Trained independent observers surveyed the methods of teaching primary reading throughout the two communities, using objective checklists. Classroom observations and studies of curricula were made in the first three grades, obtaining evidence of actual practices. In one system, all schools initiated reading through teaching the alphabet, using a systematic phonics program with phonics drill held separately from reading practice, and through an emphasis upon "sounding out" as the major word-attack tool. In the other school system all primary grade teachers were using the whole-word approach as the initial instructional technique followed by incidental phonics begun late in the first grade and continued throughout the primary grades. Objective categorizing of the data confirmed the classification of each school as structured or unstructured according to the dimension of structure discussed earlier in this paper.

Further differences were noted in the general conditions in the classrooms in the two school systems. In the structured schools, the classroom atmosphere was found to be more authoritarian and cold, the curriculum more traditional. In the unstructured schools, child expression and meaningful experience were emphasized throughout the curriculum, and the teachers were more democratic and permissive.

CONTROL OF SOCIO-ECONOMIC STATUS. It would have been desirable for the two communities to have differed only in respect to the variable being investigated: the degree of structure in teaching method. The structured schools were in an industrial city, with three-family tenement houses typical of the residential areas, but with one rather sizeable section of middle-class homes. The unstructured schools were in a large suburban community, predominantly middle- to upper-middle class, but fringed by an industrial area. In order to equate the samples on socio-economic status, we chose schools in both cities on the basis of socio-economic status of the neighborhoods. School principals and guidance workers made ratings of the various neighborhoods and the research team made independent observations of houses and dwelling areas. An objective scale was developed for rating school neighborhoods from

these data. Equal proportions of children in each city were drawn from upper-lower and lower-middle class neighborhoods.

SUBJECTS. Individual differences in maturation and the development of readiness for learning to read indicate that not until the third grade have most children had ample opportunity to demonstrate their capacity for school achievement. Therefore, third grade children were chosen as subjects for this study.

For purposes of sample selection only (individual tests were given later) we obtained group test scores of reading achievement and intelligence from school records of the entire third grade population in each school system.[3] The subjects for this study were randomly selected from stratified areas of the distribution, one third as under-achievers, one third medium, and one third over-achievers. Children whose reading scores were at least one standard deviation below the regression line of each total third grade school population were considered under-achievers for the purposes of sample selection. Over-achievers were at least one standard deviation above the regression line in their school system. The final sample was not significantly different from a normal distribution in regard to reading achievement or intelligence test scores. Twenty-four classrooms in twelve unstructured schools furnished 156 cases, 87 boys and 69 girls. Eight classrooms in three structured schools furnished 72 cases, 36 boys and 36 girls. Administrative restrictions necessitated the smaller sample size in the structured schools.

It was assumed that the sampling procedure was purely random with respect to the personality variables under investigation.

RATING SCALE OF COMPULSIVITY. An interview schedule of open-ended questions and a multiple choice questionnaire[4] were prepared, and one parent of each of the sample children was seen in the home. The parent was asked to describe the child's typical behavior in certain standard situations in which there was an opportunity to observe tendencies toward perfectionism in demands upon self and others, irrational conformity to rules, orderliness, punctuality, and need for certainty. The interviewers were instructed not to suggest answers and, as much as possible, to record the parents' actual words as they described the child's behavior in home situations.

The rating scale of compulsivity was constructed by first perusing the interview records, categorizing all evidence related to compulsivity, then arranging a

[3] In structured schools, the California Test of Mental Maturity was used as a measure of intelligence; in unstructured schools, the Kuhlmann-Anderson Intelligence Test. Reading achievement was recorded from scores on the Paragraph Meaning Subtest of Stanford Achievement Test, Form J, in both school systems.

[4] These and other instruments used in the study are given in the report of Grimes (1958) on which this article is partly based.

distribution on such information apart from the case records. Final ratings were made on the basis of a point system which was developed after studying the distributions of actual behaviors recorded and assigning weight values to each type of behavior that was deviant from the discovered norms. Children scoring high in compulsivity were those who gave evidence of tension or emotionality in situations where there was lack of organization or conformity to standards and expectations, or who made exaggerated efforts to achieve these goals.[5] The low compulsive child was one who appeared relatively unconcerned about such matters. For instance, the following statement was rated low in compulsivity, "She's naturally quite neat about things, but it doesn't bother her at all if her room gets messy. But she cleans it up very well when I remind her."

MEASUREMENT OF ANXIETY. Castaneda, *et al.* (1956) revised the Taylor Anxiety Scale for use with children. The Taylor Scale was adapted from the Minnesota Multiphasic Personality Inventory, with item selection based upon clinical definitions of anxiety. There is much research evidence (Taylor, 1956) to validate the use of the instrument in differentiating individuals who are likely to manifest anxiety in varying degrees. Reliability and validation work with the Children's Anxiety Scale by Castaneda, *et al.* demonstrated results closely similar to the findings with the adult scale. Although the Taylor Scale was designed as a group testing device, in this study it was individually administered by psychologically trained workers who established rapport and assisted the children in reading the items.[6]

RELATIONSHIP OF ANXIETY TO COMPULSIVITY. The question may be raised whether or not we are dealing with a common factor, in anxiety and compulsivity. The two ratings yield a correlation of +.04, which is not significantly different from zero; therefore, we

have measured two different characteristics. In theory, compulsive behavior is a way of diminishing anxiety, and one might expect a negative association except for the possibility that for many children the obsessive-compulsive defenses are not sufficient to quell the amount of anxiety they suffer. The issue of interaction between anxiety and compulsivity will be taken up later.

CRITERION MEASUREMENT. In the primary grades, reading permeates almost every aspect of school progress, and the children's early experiences of success or failure in learning to read often set a pattern of total achievement that is relatively enduring throughout the following years. In establishing criterion measurements, it was therefore thought best to broaden the scope beyond the reading act itself. The predicted interaction effect should, if potent, extend its influence over all academic achievement.

The Stanford Achievement Test, Form J, was administered by classroom teachers, consisting of a battery of six sub-tests: Paragraph Meaning, Word Meaning, Spelling, Language, Arithmetic Computation, and Arithmetic Reasoning. All of these subtests involve reading except Arithmetic Computation. Scores are stated in grade-equivalents on a national norm. The battery median grade-equivalent was used in data analysis in this study.

The Wechsler Intelligence Scale for Children was administered to each sample third grade child by a clinical worker. The relationship of intelligence test scores to school achievement is a well-established fact (in this case, $r = .506$ $p < .001$); therefore, in the investigation of the present hypothesis, it was necessary to control this factor.

The criterion score used in the statistical analysis is an index of over- or under-achievement. It is the discrepancy between the actual attained achievement test score and the score that would be predicted by the I.Q. For example, on the basis of the regression equation, a child with an I.Q. of 120 in this sample would be expected to earn an achievement test score of 4.8 (grade equivalent). If a child with an I.Q. of 120 scored 5.5 in achievement, his discrepancy score would be +.7, representing .7 of one year of over-achievement. A child with an I.Q. of 98 would be expected to earn an achievement test score of 3.5. If such a child scored 3.0, his discrepancy score would be −.5, representing .5 of one year of under-achievement. In this manner, the factors measured by the intelligence test were controlled, allowing discovered differences in achievement to be interpreted as resulting from other variables.

RESULTS

TEST OF INTERACTION OF COMPULSIVITY AND TEACHING METHODS. Tables 1 and 2 present the results of the statistical analysis of the data when compulsivity is used as the descriptive variable. Figure 1 portrays the mean achieve-

---

[5] In order to fit the theoretically-defined compulsive character we scored deviant behavior in either direction as compulsive: those whose need for orderliness was exaggerated, those who were rebelliously disorderly, and those who inconsistently oscillated between the extremes.

[6] The work of Alpert and Haber (1960) raises the question whether a test of situational anxiety specific to schooling, e.g., one of test-anxiety, might have been more appropriate and revealing than the Taylor Children's Scale of general anxiety used in the present study. Such an instrument was not available at the time these data were collected. Since that time the Sarason (1960) scale of test anxiety for children has been developed. It is interesting to note that even though Alpert and Haber found no correlation between the Taylor Scale and academic achievement with college students, Castaneda found significant negative correlations between the Taylor Children's Scale and achievement scores, foreshadowing one aspect of the results reported below. Perhaps the contradiction arises from an absence, among those gaining entrance to college, of students whose general anxiety inhibits rather than facilitates school performance.

TABLE 1 / THE EFFECT OF TEACHING METHOD ON SCHOOL ACHIEVEMENT OF CHILDREN RATED LOW, MEDIUM, OR HIGH IN COMPULSIVITY.

TEACHING METHOD	MEAN YEARS OF OVER- OR UNDER-ACHIEVEMENT						*t* RATIO HI VS. LOW
	LOW COMPULSIVITY		MEDIUM COMPULSIVITY		HIGH COMPULSIVITY		
	YEARS	N	YEARS	N	YEARS	N	
Structured	+.05	17	+.45	36	+.82	19	2.89a
Unstructured	−.28	42	−.36	57	−.12	56	.99
t-ratio	1.65a				4.15b		

a *p* < .01 (2 tail)
b *p* < .001 (1 tail)

TABLE 2 / ANALYSIS OF VARIANCEc OF HI VS. LOW COMPULSIVITY.

SOURCE OF VARIANCE	S.S.	d.f.	MEAN SQ.	F
Between method groups	40.73	1	40.73	17.12a
Between trait groups	21.51	1	21.51	9.04a
Interaction	9.26	1	9.26	3.89b
Error		131	2.38	

a *p* < .01 (2 tail)
b *p* < .05 (1 tail)
c Corrected for unequal frequencies.

ment scores of each sub-group graphically. First of all, as we had surmised, the highly compulsive children in the structured setting score significantly better ($p < .001$) on achievement than do similar children in the unstructured schools. It can be seen too that when we contrast levels of compulsivity within the structured schools, the high compulsive children do better ($p < .01$). No significant difference was found in achievement between high and low compulsive children within the unstructured school. The hypothesis of there being an interaction between compulsivity and teaching method was supported, in this case, at the .05 level.

While we had expected that compulsive children in the unstructured school setting would have difficulty when compared to those in the structured, we were surprised to find that the achievement of the high compulsives within the schools where the whole-word method is used in beginning reading compares favorably with that of the low compulsives.[7] Indeed their achievement scores were somewhat better on an absolute basis although the difference was not significant. We speculate that compulsives in the unstructured schools are under greater strain because of the lack of systemization in their school setting, but that their need to organize (for comfort) is so intense that they struggle to induce the phonic rules and achieve in spite of the lack of direction from the environment.[8]

[7] This could have been foretold from a careful reading of Frenkel-Brunswik (1952) or from listening to our colleague Dr. Leonard M. Lansky who anticipated that the compulsive person is one who is inclined to make blind stabs at any possible solution. One might then speculate that difficulty in guessing under lack of structure would occur only in the case of those compulsive children who were also highly anxious. The achievement of such children who are anxious is compared below with those compulsive children low in anxiety. The trend is in line with the expectation although it is not significant with the small number of cases.

[8] If this is true, we would expect that high compulsives in the unstructured schools would develop skill in phonics to a greater extent than the low compulsive children. Scores were available on a test of phonics skill, and again intelligence was controlled. Analysis revealed that high compulsives in unstructured schools learned phonics significantly ($p<.01$) more successfully than low compulsives.

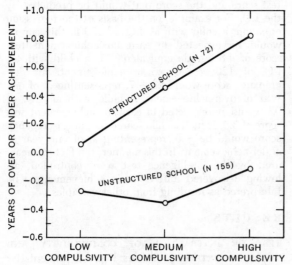

FIGURE 1 / GRAPH OF TEST RESULTS SHOWING MEAN SCHOOL ACHIEVEMENT OF CHILDREN CATEGORIZED AS TO COMPULSIVITY.

TABLE 3 / THE EFFECT OF TEACHING METHOD ON SCHOOL ACHIEVEMENT OF CHILDREN RATED LOW, MEDIUM, OR HIGH IN ANXIETY.

| TEACHING METHOD | MEAN YEARS OF OVER- OR UNDER-ACHIEVEMENT | | | | | | *t* RATIO HI VS. LOW |
| | LOW ANXIETY | | MEDIUM ANXIETY | | HIGH ANXIETY | | |
	YEARS	N	YEARS	N	YEARS	N	
Structured	+.39	27	+.43	27	+.60	18	.80
Unstructured	+.002	51	−.24	46	−.49	59	3.34[b]
t-ratio	2.07[a]				4.88[c]		

[a] $p < .05$ (2 tail)
[b] $p < .01$ (2 tail)
[c] $p < .001$ (1 tail)

TABLE 4 / ANALYSIS OF VARIANCE[c] OF HI VS. LOW ANXIETY.

SOURCE OF VARIANCE	S.S.	d.f.	MEAN SQ.	F
Between method groups	54.27	1	54.27	26.22[a]
Between trait groups	1.87	1	1.87	.90
Interaction	12.09	1	12.09	5.83[b]
Error		151	2.07	

[a] $p < .01$ (2 tail)
[b] $p < .01$ (1 tail)
[c] Corrected for unequal frequencies.

It is interesting to note that medium compulsives in the unstructured schools made the lowest achievement scores (though not significantly lower). Possibly their compulsivity was not strong enough to cause them to build their own structure.

Our conjecture is, then, that regardless of the manner in which school lessons are taught, the compulsive child accentuates those elements of each lesson that aid him in systematizing his work. When helped by a high degree of structure in lesson presentation, then and only then does such a child attain unusual success.

TEST OF INTERACTION OF ANXIETY AND TEACHING METHODS. The statistical analyses of achievement in relation to anxiety and teaching methods and the interactions of the two are presented in Tables 3 and 4. Figure 2 is a graph of the mean achievement scores of each group. As predicted, the highly anxious children in the unstructured schools score more poorly ($p < .001$) than those in the structured schools. The interaction effect, which is significant at the .01 level, can be seen best in the contrast of mean scores. While high anxiety children achieve significantly less well ($p < .01$) in the unstructured school than do low anxiety children, they appear to do at least as well as the average in the structured classroom.

The most striking aspect of the interaction demonstrated is the marked decrement in performance suffered by the highly anxious children in unstructured schools. According to the theory proposed, this is a consequence of the severe condition of perceived threat that persists unabated for the anxious child in an ambiguous sort of school environment. The fact that such threat is potent in the beginning reading lessons is thought to be a vital factor in the continued pattern of failure or underachievement these children exhibit. The child with high anxiety may first direct his anxiety-released energy toward achievement, but because his distress severely reduces the abilities of discrimination and memorization of complex symbols, the child may fail in his initial attempts to master the problem. Failure confirms the threat, and the intensity of anxiety is increased as the required learning becomes

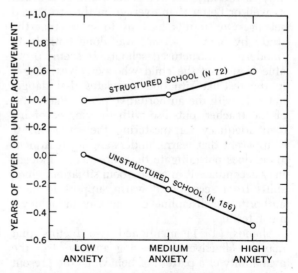

FIGURE 2 / GRAPH OF TEST RESULTS SHOWING MEAN SCHOOL ACHIEVEMENT OF CHILDREN CATEGORIZED AS TO ANXIETY.

more difficult, so that by the time the child reaches the third grade the decrement in performance is pronounced.

The individual with high anxiety in the structured classroom may approach the learning task with the same increased energy and lowered powers of discrimination. But the symbols he is asked to learn are simple. As shown earlier, the highly anxious individual may be superior in his memorizing of simple elements. Success reduces the prospect of threat and his powers of discrimination are improved. By the time the child first attacks the actual problem of reading, he is completely familiar and at ease with all of the elements of words. Apparently academic challenge in the structured setting creates an optimum of stress so that the child with high anxiety is able to achieve because he is aroused to an energetic state without becoming confused or panicked.

Sarason, *et al.* (1960), present evidence that the anxious child will suffer in the test-like situation, and that his performance will be impaired unless he receives supporting and accepting treatment from the teacher. Although the present study was not a direct replication of their investigations, the results do not confirm their conclusion. Observers, in the two school systems studied here, judged the teachers in the structured schools to be more impersonal and demanding, while the atmosphere in the unstructured schools was judged to be more supporting and accepting. Yet the highly anxious child suffered a tremendous disadvantage only in the unstructured school, and performed as well or better than average in the structured setting. Our results lead us to guess that the study by Sarason, *et al.*, was done entirely in "modern," unstructured schools. It seems probable to us that the child who perceives danger in the test-like situation associates that danger not only with the authoritative parent-like status of the teacher, but also with the degree of his own adequacy for mastering the situation. It is apparent that warm, understanding treatment alone does not mitigate that threat, and indeed, may accentuate it in a classroom situation which shifts from accustomed warm support to more authoritative discipline on the day of achievement testing.

Shands (1954) mentioned two factors that may be effective in relieving anxiety: (a) the availability of a pattern of behavior (the present authors assumed that a structured program should excel in offering a guide to behavior) and (b) the availability of a pattern of relationship, i.e., dependence upon some other person. Sarason, *et al.*, have concentrated on personal relationships and support as a means of allaying anxiety and presumably making it possible for the child to achieve. The present study shows that even in the absence of such support, the condition of structure is so potent that it will have a significant beneficial effect upon the achievement of the anxious child. But with support available and structure missing, the anxious child risks failure. The feeling the teacher imparts to such a child is evidently not so influential as the extent to which the teacher lets the child know exactly what is expected, and structures the learning in simple, logically-ordered steps. Of course teachers should not exacerbate children's anxiety, but it may be that they should be less concerned with allaying anxiety on the assumption that in doing so they are providing a sufficient condition for learning, and more concerned with teaching in a manner that allows the child to make optimum "use" of his existing anxieties.

Sarason, *et al.*, argue well that the influence of the teacher goes well beyond what is measured in an achievement test, and that the supportive and benign attitudes and behavior they recommend would have far-reaching effects in improving mental health. This is probably true as far as it goes, but the positive value of academic success cannot be discounted, nor can the seriously disruptive effects of school failure or underachievement. We then have to raise the question: Is there any reason why teachers cannot provide both conditions prescribed by Shands? Many complex interacting factors are at work in any classroom. While the results of a number of studies have indicated the rewarding advantages of warmth and friendliness on the part of the teacher, e.g., Withall's (1951) investigations have demonstrated that a greater degree of general progress can be expected in a warm, assuring climate, yet in the present study we find that such emotional support is of little avail in the absence of structure. This discovery enables us to postulate that if the highly anxious children in the structured schools had experienced a greater degree of warmth and security in interpersonal relationships, they might have made even greater gains as Sarason, *et al.*, would expect.

The implications of these findings may reach further. Interpretations of both psychoanalytic and non-directive concepts have led many workers in the fields of counseling and educational therapy as well as remedial reading to spend months—or even years!—in establishing a "proper" relationship, with no sense of urgency about actual instruction. Meantime the children continue to fail in school and their anxiety mounts. It is entirely possible too that when actual tutoring itself is conducted in an unstructured, non-directive way, it cannot meet certain needs of children whose symptoms include anxiety and loss of self-esteem through continued school failure. If ways can be found to accelerate educational progress through more directive and structured teaching without hampering the work of the psychotherapist, the time and professional investment often taken to treat learning difficulties might be reduced.

DIFFERENCES IN THE TOTAL SAMPLES. A highly significant difference was found between the two towns in the means of achievement criterion scores ($p < .001$), indicating that the structured school system was more successful in bringing about a generally higher level of student achievement. The magnitude of the difference in terms of grade equivalents as depicted in Figures 1 and 2 might at first seem spectacular, and an answer to the nation's prayer for guidance in furthering early school performance, but the differences call for qualification. We raise a question first about the causation of the differences, and then state our uncertainty whether such achievement is the most important goal for education at this level.

A possible factor other than teaching method in accounting for the differences may be cultural variations between the two communities. The attempt to equate socio-economic status may not have been sufficient, based as it was on house and dwelling area. Data established that incomes were lower in the structured school community, and interviewers gained the impression that a larger proportion of income was used there to keep up residence appearances, while certain cultural values seemed less highly prized than in the other community. It is possible that school achievement in primary grades, particularly skill development, is stressed to a greater extent in the homes of the structured school community. At the same time, the conditions ordinarily expected to motivate reading growth were found to be more prevalent in the homes of the unstructured school community: these homes contain more books, the parents read more to their pre-school children, they provide more tutoring, and have higher expectations for future academic and vocational attainments for their children. It appears that there may be two different types of achievement motivation in the two communities, and future research should control this factor.

If the achievement differences between systems are due to the differences in schooling methods, several questions may be asked regarding the desirability of such achievement, and whether or not it is attained at too great a cost. It is probable that more of the total school time in the structured schools was devoted to practice of skills, thereby producing students able to read, spell, and work arithmetic problems, but for all we know, less advanced in other areas of development. The general scholastic superiority in the structured schools of this study may possibly be attributed to this factor of extra practice.

The achievement test used in this study essentially measures skill in fundamental tool subjects, and does not measure the breadth of the child's understanding and behavior in other respects. For instance, we have no evidence about the creativity of one set of children or the other. We do, however, have scores on the California Test of Personality. Children in the unstructured schools scored higher ($p < .001$) than in the structured schools. This fact may indicate a greater degree of social adjustment.

It may be, too, that the attainment of skill proficiency is the only rewarding element in the school environment in these particular structured schools, i.e., perhaps the children find that they must achieve in the limited sphere of the three R's to gain any approbation.

Anderson, *et al.* (1956) found that systematic instruction resulted in faster initial progress in skill development but that after a few years, children taught by a technique emphasizing child expression and meaningfulness of each task caught up or surpassed those who continued in the systematized learning situation. Our results, then, do not necessarily point to a clear superiority of one method over another as a recommended approach for teaching *all* children. Our goal is to call attention to the possible need for creating methods of instruction attuned to the type of pupil, or for seeking a single method that does not handicap any pupils. Indications are that many primary grade children might be helped by a more formal structure in their earlier school learnings.

TEST OF INTERACTION OF ANXIETY AND COMPULSIVITY. The results of the study open up

TABLE 5 / MEAN ACHIEVEMENT AND FREQUENCIES ABOVE AND BELOW LOCAL MEDIANS OF CHILDREN CATEGORIZED ACCORDING TO COMBINATIONS OF HIGH AND LOW ANXIETY AND COMPULSIVITY.

| | STRUCTURED SCHOOLS | | | |
	HiComp-HiAnx	HiComp-LoAnx	LoComp-HiAnx	LoComp-LoAnx
Above local median	8	7	3	4
Below local median	0	7	8	9
Mean achievement criterion scores	+1.24	+.42	+.08	+.08

| | UNSTRUCTURED SCHOOLS | | | |
	HiComp-HiAnx	HiComp-LoAnx	LoComp-HiAnx	LoComp-LoAnx
Above local median	11	22	5	10
Below local median	11	11	16	11
Mean achievement criterion scores	−.22	+.16	−.68	−.14

TABLE 6 / NON-PARAMETRIC SIGNIFICANCE TESTS OF THE FREQUENCIES IN TABLE 5 (MOOD'S LIKELIHOOD RATIO TEST).

SCHOOL SYSTEM	GROUPS COMPARED	d.f.	χ^2
Structured	HiComp-HiAnx X HiComp-LoAnx X LoComp-HiAnx X LoComp-LoAnx	3	15.336[b]
Unstructured	HiComp-HiAnx X HiComp-LoAnx X LoComp-HiAnx X LoComp-LoAnx	3	9.834[a]

[a] $p < .03$ (2 tail)
[b] $p < .01$ (2 tail)

TABLE 7 / SIGNIFICANCE OF DIFFERENCES BETWEEN PERSONALITY CATEGORIES WITHIN EACH SCHOOL SYSTEM, TESTED BY CHI SQUARE CORRECTED FOR CONTINUITY. PROBABILITIES ARE TWO-TAILED.

| | STRUCTURED SCHOOLS | | UNSTRUCTURED SCHOOLS | |
	d.f.	χ^2	d.f.	χ^2
HiComp-HiAnx X HiComp-LoAnx	1	5.867[b]	1	1.528
LoComp-HiAnx X LoComp-LoAnx	1	.035	1	2.593
HiComp-HiAnx X LoComp-HiAnx	1	10.455[d]	1	3.154[a]
HiComp-LoAnx X LoComp-LoAnx	1	1.033	1	1.929
HiComp-LoAnx X LoComp-HiAnx	1	1.325	1	9.429[c]
HiComp-HiAnx X LoComp-LoAnx	1	9.692[d]	1	.024

[a] $p < .10$ [c] $p < .01$
[b] $p < .02$ [d] $p < .005$

several new questions, at least one of which can be investigated through further analysis of these data. When ratings in one personality factor are held constant, will the other factor exert a significant influence, or are the discovered differences a result of an interaction of anxiety and compulsivity such that neither has an effect without the other?

In this analysis, each school system, the structured and unstructured, is considered separately. Within each system four groups of children are studied: HiComp-HiAnx, HiComp-LoAnx, LoComp-HiAnx, LoComp-LoAnx. In order to obtain larger frequencies in each cate-

gory, the cutting point for each extreme group was moved closer to the median score on compulsivity and anxiety than in the previous three-way categorization. The resulting smaller medium groups were removed from consideration. This recategorization was done without reference to achievement scores, and the cutting points then set so that one third of the cases would fall in the excluded median group. The mean achievement score of each new group and the frequencies above and below the local medians are presented in Table 5. Results of non-parametric tests of significance of differences between groups are shown in Tables 6 and

7. Since the overall differences between groups in each school are significant as shown in Table 6, we may interpret each specific difference in terms of the personality categorization.

At once apparent is the successful academic performance of the HiComp-HiAnx children in the structured schools. As a group they are more than a year advanced in achievement! Apparently, when the school systematizes the learning experiences for such children in accordance with their need for orderliness, their anxiety is facilitating rather than disorganizing.[9]

This interpretation is supported by the comparable data of the other groups, each of which is significantly different from the HiComp-HiAnx. The HiComp-LoAnx children are evidently benefited by lesson structure in satisfying their need for organization but apparently lack some of the drive of the HiComp-HiAnx group.

In the unstructured school, the data again indicate an interaction of the two personality variables. The HiComp-LoAnx group makes the best record while the LoComp-HiAnx group does poorly, and the difference is significant at the .01 level. The child with low anxiety is evidently not threatened by the lack of structure, and if he has the organizational power to systematize his own learning tasks, he is able to master the achievement problem reasonably well. However, when little structure is provided in the school experiences, children with high anxiety and no personal drive to systematize for themselves are in serious trouble. The anxiety serves to disrupt problem-solving ability to a striking degree.

The same analyses were repeated but with sex held constant, and the results are closely similar to those shown above. We still find for both sexes the poor performance of LoComp-HiAnx in the unstructured school, and in the case of girls (there was a dearth of boys in the comparison) the marked high performance of HiComp-HiAnx in the structured school.

ALTERNATE INTERPRETATIONS OF STRUCTURE. What we have really shown definitively, of course, is merely that there are interactions among compulsivity, anxiety, and school system attended. The question is, what causes these findings. Although we have chosen the matter of structure in methods of teaching reading to account for the variations, there may, in fact,

be at least three meanings. a) The influence of teaching method may reflect *not* the structure of phonics but a generally-structured manner of teaching and classroom management if such existed in one school system more than another. Clarity of directions, explicitness about the applications of principles taught, and precise knowledge on the part of the child as to what is expected of him are characteristics of a structured manner of teaching. b) The findings of interaction between pupil personality and teaching method may be due to the structure provided in phonics, along with whatever structure through sequencing and rule-teaching may have existed in other subject-matter areas. c) Pupil personality may have been interacting with one or more attributes of teaching method other than the provision of structure.

We have no evidence that interpretation (c) is incorrect, but the concordance with personality theory of the interactions that we discovered leads us to reject it as an explanation of our findings. Our skepticism of interpretation (a) is less easy to defend: we made no measurements of structure in teaching manner. Yet it seems to us that structure of this type might be provided equally well by a teacher in either system.[10] During their three years in school, our 156 whole-word taught children had been taught by 87 different teachers, and our 72 phonics-taught children had experienced 31 different teachers. Individual differences among teachers must have been great in both school systems. We have considerable confidence that if structure in teaching manner had been constantly greater in one system than in the other, this fact would not have gone undetected by our team of observers.

The methods of teaching reading were accurately determined, and the structure of the phonics program was the only clear-cut difference that was found to be constant across school systems. Therefore, we feel justified in accepting interpretation (b) as an explanation of the interactions of personality tendencies with teaching methods. This does not rule out the possibility that if degree of structure in teaching manner were experimentally varied it would produce similar results. It seems prob-

---

[9] Their "overachievement" may of course mask serious neurotic problems by causing them to be regarded as model children.

[10] Earlier in this paper, it was mentioned that the team of observers had noted a more authoritarian and cold atmosphere in the structured schools. We do not consider this to be evidence of general structure in teaching manner. The more traditional curriculum that was also noted may or may not indicate a greater degree of structure in the organization of subject-matter.

able that structure provided by phonics[11] in conjunction with that in the whole classroom experience would produce even more striking benefits for highly anxious or highly compulsive children.

We must acknowledge an important caution about the provision of structure in teaching. The continuance of structuring too far in later schooling may perpetuate dependence upon those in authority positions. Because of this danger McKeachie (1951) wrote of structured techniques, ". . . we still may not grant that it is the most desirable method to be used in our educational system which has as its aim preparation for life in a democracy." We suggest that if particular children's desperate need for structure in certain types of learning can be satisfied during the early school years with failure prevented and their literacy assured, ways to reduce the need for continuance of such structure may be gradually introduced later.

ALTERNATE INTERPRETATIONS OF PERSONALITY CHARACTERISTICS. We have implied a causal relationship—that because of existing tendencies toward compulsivity or anxiety, a child may need structure in teaching. The reverse might be argued, that failure or success in learning to read contributed to or actually caused the personality characteristics that we observed. Since we have no personality measures of the children before they entered first grade, we cannot deny this possibility, but our examination of the results leads us to discount it as an explanation of the findings.

The reverse argument gains plausibility from the common observations that children who are retarded in reading often are emotionally maladjusted and that with wise remedial instruction and consequent success in learning to read, the signs of maladjustment may disappear. This is doubtless often true, but the argument is weakened if those signs are not the same as the ones measured by our instruments. And

indeed, the behaviors exhibited by pupils and recognized by teachers as maladjustment are not those revealed by our tests of compulsivity and anxiety. Each of our sample children was placed on a five-point scale of emotional adjustment by the first, second, and third grade teachers who had taught them. The scaled continuum ran from (1) well adjusted and secure, to (5) poorly adjusted, insecure, apprehensive. Teacher ratings were then compared with our measures of compulsivity and anxiety, and also with school achievement. Non-parametric analysis showed that teacher ratings of maladjustment were negatively related ($p < .05$) to school achievement, but not related to anxiety or compulsivity. Thus children's emotional reactions in the classroom are not indicative of the more subtle personality characteristics measured in our instruments, and the data do not confirm the supposition that the degree of school success actually causes the personality tendencies that we measured.

School failure will probably cause certain manifestations of emotional behavior in most children, but if we are reasoning soundly, it can hardly account for the interactions that we found. While low achievement in the unstructured school may heighten tension, it does not seem reasonable that high achievement would cause a *high* rating on the same test of anxiety for some children in the *structured* school! Also it is not reasonable that compulsivity, as measured by emotionality in certain home-like situations, would be changed substantially by variations of methods of teaching at school. Therefore, we feel justified in interpreting our data to mean that the differential in teaching methods (that we see in the structure provided in systematic phonics) interacts with personality characteristics such that highly anxious and/or highly compulsive children are helped in school achievement by the introduction of structure in teaching.

POSSIBLE APPLICATIONS. Do we seriously envisage the differentiation of teaching methods according to pupils' personality tendencies? Upon first hearing this suggestion, educators may throw up their hands in horror! But homogeneous grouping done by means of achievement or intelligence test scores is, after all, common practice. Already the skilled teacher tries as best he can to individuate instruction for certain pupils within his classroom based upon his intuitive judgments of personal needs. When

[11] Should further investigations show interpretation (b) to be valid, the needed structure might be provided by means other than the alphabetic or phonics approach. Brown (1958) describes a method in which the rules of pronunciation and spelling are defined to children early in their study of reading, but word recognition is used from the start for necessary words like "and" and "the," without which meaningful material cannot be read. Also, Richards and Gibson (1957) have prepared materials using a structured whole-word program, teaching the child in his first lessons to discriminate letter, sound, and meaning within closely similar sentences.

the results of studies like ours have hardened in the kiln of replication, they may foretell the wide use of personality tests to distinguish those children who will particularly benefit by increased structure (or other techniques) in their school experiences.

A final implication concerns those doing counseling or educational therapy with children afflicted by learning difficulties. In some cases where emphasis has been placed upon allaying anxiety, it may prove effective to provide concomitantly a high degree of structure in the remedial teaching.

SUMMARY

In this study we tested the hypothesis that there is an interaction between teaching method and pupils' personality characteristics in determining school achievement. We anticipated that highly anxious or highly compulsive children who are taught reading initially by "structured" methods stressing phonics will show more achievement by the third grade than similar children taught in other schools where the "unstructured" word recognition approach to beginning reading is used. Our expectation is supported by the findings.

We also examined the effects of personality variables with teaching method held constant. Under structured teaching, compulsive children do substantially better than less compulsive children, but compulsivity makes no difference in the unstructured settings. Anxiety, in contrast, makes no difference under structured conditions; it is in the unstructured settings that high anxiety impedes scholastic performance.

Anxiety and compulsivity, which are not correlated in our sample, interact with one another as well as with teaching method. Children who are both highly anxious *and* highly compulsive overachieve strikingly in the structured environment, and those who are highly anxious but *low* in compulsivity underachieve in the unstructured schools.

Thus choice of instructional methods makes a big difference for certain kinds of pupil, and a search for the "best" way to teach can succeed only when the learner's personality is taken into account.

REFERENCES

ALPERT, R., and HABER, R. N. Anxiety in academic achievement situations. *J. abnorm. soc. Psychol.*, 1960, *61*, 207-215.

ANDERSON, I. H., HUGHES, B. O., and DIXON, W. R. Relationships between reading achievement and method of teaching. *Univer. Michigan, sch. of educ. bull.*, 1956, 7, 104-108.

AUSUBEL, D. P., SCHIFF, H. M., and GOLDMAN, M. Qualitative characteristics in the learning process associated with anxiety. *J. abnorm. soc. Psychol.*, 1953, *48*, 537-547.

BROWN, R. *Words and things.* Glencoe, Ill.: Free Press, 1958, 78-79.

BRUNER, J. S. Personality dynamics and the process of perceiving. In R. Blake and G. Ramsey (Eds), *Perception: An approach to personality.* New York: Ronald, 1951.

BRUNER, J. S. *The process of education.* Cambridge, Mass.: Harvard Univer. Press, 1960.

CARROLL, J. B. The case of Dr. Flesch. *Amer. Psychologist*, 1956, *11*, 158-163.

CASTANEDA, A. Reaction time and response amplitude as a function of anxiety and stimulus intensity. *J. abnorm. soc. Psychol.*, 1956, 53, 225-228.

CASTANEDA, A., MC CANDLESS, B. R., and PALERMO, D. S. The children's form of the manifest anxiety scale. *Child develpm.*, 1956, 27, 317-326.

FENICHEL, O. *The psychoanalytic theory of neurosis.* New York: Norton, 1945.

FLESCH, R. *Why Johnny can't read.* New York: Harper, 1955.

FRENKEL-BRUNSWICK, ELSE. The inhibitory effects of an authoritarian home regime on the emotional and cognitive patterns of children. In J. Frosh, (Ed), *Annual survey of psychoanalysis* (Vol. 3). New York: Internat. Univer. Press, 1952.

GRIMES, J. W. The interaction of pupil personality with methods of teaching reading in determining primary grade achievement. Unpublished doctoral dissertation, Harvard Univer., 1958.

HEATH, D. H. Individual anxiety thresholds and their effect on intellectual performance. *J. abnorm. soc. Psychol.*, 1956, *52*, 403-408.

KORCHIN, S. J., and LEVINE, S. Anxiety and verbal learning. *J. abnorm. soc. Psychol.*, 1957, *54*, 234-240.

LOWENFELD, J., RUBENFELD, S., and GUTHRIE, G. M. Verbal inhibition in subception. *J. gen. Psychol.*, 1956, *54*, 171-176.

MC KEACHIE, W. J. Anxiety in the college classroom. *J. educ. Res.*, 1951, 55, 153-160.

MC KEACHIE, W. J. Students, groups, and teaching methods. *Amer. Psychologist*, 1958, *13*, 580-584.

MURPHY, G. Personality. New York: Harper, 1947.

NOLL, J. O. An investigation of the relation of anxiety to learning and retention. *Dissert. Abstr.*, 1955, *15*.

RICHARDS, I. A., and GIBSON, CHRISTINE M. *First steps*

in reading English. New York: Washington Square Press, 1957.

SARASON, I. G. Effect of anxiety and two kinds of motivating instructions on verbal learning. *J. abnorm. soc. Psychol.*, 1957, 54, 166-171.

SARASON, S. B., DAVIDSON, K. S., LIGHTHALL, F. F., WAITE, R. R., and RUEBUSH, B. K. *Anxiety in elementary school children.* New York: Wiley, 1960.

SHANDS, H. C. Anxiety, anaclitic object, and the sign function: Comments on early developments in the use of symbols. *Amer. J. Orthopsychiat.*, 1954, 23, 84-97.

SMITH, D. E. P., WOOD, R. L., DOWNER, J. W., and RAYGOR, A. L. Reading improvement as a function of student personality and teaching method. *J. of educ. Psychol.*, 1956, 47, 47-59.

SPENCE, D. P. A new look at vigilance and defense. *J. abnorm. soc. Psychol.*, 1957, 54, 103-108.

TAYLOR, JANET A. Drive theory and manifest anxiety. *Psychol. Bull.*, 1956, 53, 303-320.

WEISSKOPF, EDITH A. Intellectual malfunctioning and personality. *J. abnorm. soc. Psychol.*, 1951, 46, 410-423.

WISPE, LAUREN G. Evaluating section teaching methods in the introductory course. *J. educ. Res.*, 1951, 45, 162.

WITHALL, J. The development of the climate index. *J. educ. Res.*, 1951, 45, 93-100.

WITTY, P., and SIZEMORE, R. A. Phonics in the reading program: A review and an evaluation. *Elem. English*, 1955, 32, 355-371.

69/TEACHERS' AND CLINICIANS' ATTITUDES TOWARD THE BEHAVIOR PROBLEMS OF CHILDREN: A REAPPRAISAL[1]/ HARRY BEILIN°

THE CONTRAST BETWEEN CONTEMPO-rary American education and that of 40 or 50 years ago is striking in at least one respect, the influence of psychology, in particular, clinical psychology.[2] It would require little effort to detail the many and diverse ways teacher training, parent education and child care re-

flect the consequences of psychology's influence. The future historian will undoubtedly dwell upon the part played by E. K. Wickman's 1928 Commonwealth Fund monograph, "Children's Behavior and Teachers' Attitudes" in this development (43). Wickman's report, which contrasts teachers' and "mental hygienists'" attitudes toward the behavior problems of children evoked an assault upon the teacher's mode of dealing with children when it made evident that teachers attitudes were widely at variance with those of clinicians. The effect of its publication is still felt. The contiguity of events might suggest to some a causal relationship between widespread

[1] The author is indebted to Martin Hamburger and Louis Rosenzweig for their critical reading of this paper.

[2] Although the period following the first World War saw the impact of the testing movement and the effects of Behaviorism, it was not till the 1930's and 1940's that clinical psychology became a part of the child development and educational scene in a major way.

° Harry Beilin, Teachers' and clinicians' attitudes toward the behavior problems of children: a reappraisal, *Child Development*, 1959, *30*, 9-25. Copyright, 1959, by the Society for Research in Child Development, Inc. Reprinted with abridgement by permission of the Society and the author.

knowledge of the Wickman findings and the emergence of clinical psychology as a force in contemporary education. However, a more temperate and realistic appraisal would accept the ubiquitous penetration of psychology into American life and not as a condition unique to education. The impact of the monograph was in actuality only one of a series of challenges to the values and attitudes of educational personnel. But irrespective of its true role—whether as reflection, or as initiator of a Zeitgeist—the place of the Wickman study in education and child psychology has been significant and will probably continue to be.

Wickman's results, in the main, suggested that mental hygienists were primarily concerned with *withdrawing* and other nonsocial forms of behavior in children of elementary school age, whereas teachers of these same children were more concerned with *classroom management, authority,* and *sex problems.* The results influenced many (starting with Wickman) to urge teachers to adopt a hierarchy of attitudes closer to that of the clinician. This view presumed that the clinician's judgment should be accepted as the criterion for adequate and inadequate behavior. Few have challenged this thesis.

The intent of the present review is to examine what the result of 30 years of research suggests for continued acceptance of this point of view. To anticipate, it will be suggested that Wickman's findings be reinterpreted and his prescription for change in educational policy modified.

THE WICKMAN STUDY

The Wickman studies were begun in Minneapolis in 1924, but a more ambitious program was undertaken in Cleveland in 1925-1926, where the following was done:

1. In a single pilot school, teachers' characterizations of undesirable behavior, with indications of "sensitiveness" to their occurrence, were elicited by questionnaire.

2. Teachers' attitudes toward various types of problems were obtained by three measures (detailed in part below).

3. On rating scales, teachers noted their reactions to problems themselves, then to pupils in whom the problems were observed, and finally to the total adjustment of their pupils.

4. Subsequently, the teachers from 13 schools in six communities and two additional teacher groups enrolled in graduate school were studied using the rating scale method developed for the pilot study. The most important feature of this involved the rating of a number of behaviors obtained from the teachers' original freely-given characterizations of problem behavior. The results are reported as mean ratings and rankings of mean ratings.

5. Finally, 30 "mental hygienists" (8 psychiatrists, 4 psychologists, 13 psychiatric social workers and 5 teachers with social work background) from child guidance clinics in three cities were studied for their attitudes toward 50 of the same behaviors rated by teachers. The mean ratings and rankings of ratings were then contrasted and correlated with those of teachers.

The rating instructions for teachers stressed: (a) *present* problems, (b) "seriousness" of the problems or "difficulties" created by them, and (c) rapid responses to the rating scale. With clinicians, the emphasis was on (a) relevance of the problem behavior for *future* adjustment, (b) though "seriousness" and "difficulty" were retained, the focus was on the "importance" of the behavior, and (c) no time limit was imposed for response to the rating scale.

The principal results can be summarized as follows:

1. Teachers were most aware of overt and aggressive behaviors, inattention to school tasks, and behaviors which violated their standards of morality. They were much less concerned with behaviors indicative of social or emotional maladjustment not directly related to school routine.

2. Boys were reported more frequently than girls for behavior problems.

3. Teachers preferred the less active, more compliant behavior of girls to the more aggressive behavior of boys. Desirable conduct for teachers, then, took on the distinguishing characteristics of girl behavior.

4. "Mental hygienists" considered withdrawing and other nonsocial forms of behavior most serious and discounted the teachers' stress on antisocial behavior and violations of school rules.

5. There was a rank order correlation of −.22 between the rankings by mental hygienists of 50 behavior problems and the original Cleveland teachers' ($N = 28$) rankings of the same behaviors. The correlation was −.11 when the full sample was used ($N = 511$).

These findings were interpreted by Wickman in Thorndikian stimulus-response terms. The teachers distinguish, he said, between the attacking and withdrawing types of behavior problems. Their attitudes are principally determined, however, by the attacking nature of the child's conduct. The aggressive behaviors are identified and considered more serious because the teacher is aroused to counterattack by virtue of the frustration in him. On the other hand, the responses to withdrawing forms of behavior are modified by sympathy and protective feelings.

On the basis of these findings Wickman then proposed that:

1. Teachers' attitudes should be influenced to become more like the "ideal" clinicians. (Clinicians' attitudes are considered ideal because their judgments are (ostensibly) based upon knowledge of research in child adjustment.)

2. Teacher attitudes should be changed not by exhortation but by (a) information about child behavior through seminars and other learning experiences; and (b) practice in therapy with children.

3. Teachers' functions should be less concerned with intellectual learnings and more with life adjustment.

After the appearance of the 1928 monograph some serious limitations in method and conception were pointed out by G. Watson (50) in a critical note[3] which are as cogent now as when first offered. The majority of efforts to rectify the deficiencies have concerned only some of the criticisms. The others, however, may be of as great issue as those treated.

Watson's objections were:

1. *The procedures themselves are open to criticism.*

a. The directions given teachers and clinicians were not the same. Teachers were instructed to rank behaviors for *present* seriousness; clinicians, for *future* adjustment.

b. The time given to respond to the questionnaires was not identical. Teachers were under the control of the experimenter; clinicians were allowed an extended period to respond.

c. No definitions were given for the behavioral terms to be rated leaving to each subject the interpretation of the terms, and thus further reducing comparability of the results.

The issues raised by Watson's concern with methodology are intimately related to other criticisms.

[3] One writer has even wondered how the study could have been so widely and uncritically accepted with these limitations. The answer probably rests in the fact that its thesis was part of a powerfully developing movement.

2. *The choice of mental hygienists' attitudes toward the behavior problems of children as criterion for evaluating teachers' attitudes toward the same problems is open to question.*

The Wickman study and others that follow (though not all) accept the clinicians' judgments as a criterion either implicitly or explicitly. Watson observes that there is no reason to suppose clinicians to be "correct" and teachers not, rather than vice versa. Wickman is questioned for not even considering this possibility.

3. *There has been too ready an acceptance of a causal relationship between withdrawing behavior in childhood and maladjustment in adulthood.*

In addition to questioning whether the term "withdrawing" means the same thing to teachers and clinicians, Watson questioned whether withdrawing behavior in childhood is causally related to, or predictive of, maladjustment in adulthood. Although this is contended in more than one theoretical position, there was very little evidence for the validity of this claim in 1928, and little more is available now. In Watson's paper there is reference to a pilot study which, for all its limitations, casts some doubt on the aforementioned assumption.

THE LITERATURE

After the Watson critique there was concern for the validity of the results and replications were undertaken with one or another modification in design, ultimately making comparability difficult.[4]

The studies, in the main, fall into the following groupings according to procedures used:

A. *Studies employing descriptions of problem behavior.*
  1. Teacher nomination of children with problems, followed by description and classification of problem behaviors (3, 5, 16, 26, 41).
      a. In addition to all or part of the above, some use is made of a rating scale of problem behaviors (7, 14, 22, 23, 33, 40, 45, 46).
  2. Teacher description of problem behavior (with no reference to specific children) from which a rating scale is developed or the descriptions themselves are used (9, 10, 20, 32, 37, 39, 43).
  3. Children identified and described as problems by a social or therapeutic agency (6, 29).

[4] We shall consider all studies found that bear upon the problems focused on by Wickman and his critics in spite of the lack of comparability. Some studies are included which antedate Wickman because the data they offer are relevant.

B. *Studies employing the Wickman rating scales.*
  1. With Wickman's directions (1, 18, 31).
  2. With modifications of Wickman's directions
    (13, 17, 24, 34, 35, 36).

CONFIRMATION OF WICKMAN FINDINGS. . . . Holding the question of the validity of Wickman's methodology aside for the moment, [we would conclude from a number of studies (1, 7, 10, 12, 14, 15, 20, 31, 33, 39, 45, 46) that there is] considerable evidence to indicate agreement with Wickman's original findings. Furthermore, there has been an observable shift in the intervening years in the attitudes of teachers in the direction of being more like those of "mental hygienists." In spite of greater congruence, however, a sizable difference remains between the attitudes of teachers and clinicians toward behavior problems of children.

THE METHODICAL ISSUE. Modifications as a rule have aimed at introducing uniformity in the administration of the problem rating scales. This has meant either modifying the directions given clinicians or teachers so that both groups could respond under the same stimulus conditions. . . .
[From several studies (3, 13, 17, 24, 34, 35, 36, 40)] it appears that the differences in directions that were a part of the Wickman procedure quite clearly contributed to the differences demonstrated between teachers and mental hygienists. When this is controlled, however, differences still emerge and these are of the kind originally observed.
It is also apparent that there has been a change in the direction of greater congruence between the attitudes of teachers and clinicians. That that congruence is not consistent for all levels of teachers has been made explicit in recent studies. It is likely that differences between elementary and secondary teachers have always existed vis-à-vis the matters here reviewed, but, where teacher and clinician attitudes appear to be the same, differences in meaning may still attach to the behaviors.

TEACHER "EXPERTNESS." The specific criteria employed by teachers and clinicians in assessing maladjustment in children have been mentioned. As already indicated, most investigators have shown teachers to be most concerned with children's behaviors that are *aggressive, disruptive of school routines,* or generally reflecting *lack of interest in school activities.* In addition, teachers are, or have been, less concerned with *withdrawing* and other nonsocial behaviors. Some investigators have characterized this as indicative of a middle class value pattern; e.g., *stealing* is the teacher's consistent concern in Mac-Clenathan's (22) study. The emphasis upon these school disrupting traits has not been unanimous, however. Peck (26) found *undesirable personality traits* to be the greatest concern of the teacher, *regressive* traits somewhat less so, and *aggressive* behaviors least. Of only moderate import were *viola-*

tions of school work demands. Clark (9) differs from the usual view, too, in concluding that teachers are actually more annoyed by children's behaviors which annoy other children than by behaviors which affect teachers themselves.
In most of the cited studies it is implied or explicitly stated that the teacher is "wrong" in reacting as she does to the problems of children. Teachers have been criticized as untutored in the scientific facts concerning child development and are thus seen as generally being incapable of assessing children's adjustment.
Stewart (38) rejects this thesis. With 184 boys and 193 girls as subjects, a comparison was made between ratings of problem students and non-problem students. Identification was also attempted of those with and without "whole life" problems. From ratings of these youngsters she concludes that teachers are capable of distinguishing between problems as school problems or "whole life" problems. She insists that teachers possess much more insight into children's behavior than they are credited with by some investigators.
In spite of the few studies that report different patterns of teachers' attitudes, the hierarchy of attitudes seems to be quite close to Wickman's formulation. The Stewart report is important not so much because it rejects this hierarchy but rather in its highlighting the difference between clinicians and teachers as not being a matter of ignorance. What the difference is attributable to remains to be discussed.

SEX DIFFERENCES. There seems to be universal agreement that boys are more likely to be identified as maladjusted or behavior problems than girls (6, 7, 14, 15, 16, 18, 23, 25, 26, 29, 33, 43, 45, 47). The proportion of boys (in contrast to girls) so identified ranges in these reports from 66 to 88 per cent. Not only is there a difference in proportion but behaviors which form the bases for these identifications are in part different for each sex (5, 14, 43). Ullmann's (47) interpretation is of some interest. It is *not,* he says, that "desirable conduct for teachers takes the distinguishing characteristics of girl behavior as suggested by Wickman but rather teachers assign girls more favorable ratings because they lack awareness of the manner in which girls are making their adjustment" (p. 39). Ullmann explains that the boys' patterns of adjustment are more manifest to the observer, whereas girls deal with problems on an intrapsychic level. This interpretation is in the tradition of imputing lack of insight to teachers. Stewart's (38) results are again cogent. Her data do not suggest that teachers lack insight into their adjustment, but rather that they distinguish a different *kind* of adjustment for girls. Another study with young adults suggests the same (5). In this instance, sex differences in degree of adjustment are supplemented by differences in the types of behavior identified with the maladjustments of each sex.
Why should the nature of adjustment be different

for boys and girls? Whatever the *ultimate* reasons (whether biological or social), the temptation is to say that the differences, in an *immediate* sense at least, result from different *expectations*. It is evident from the cited studies that boys and girls are expected to act in prescribed ways in our culture. The reasons girls are considered better adjusted by teachers is that teachers have certain expectations of what good adjustment *in school* should be and the prescription for girls' adjustment is more consistent with these expectations than the prescription for boys' good adjustment. As Wickman makes evident, the teacher is concerned with getting what she is teaching "across," and behaviors which facilitate this are more likely to be valued. The behaviors of girls are of this kind.

This approach is more acceptable to us, from the evidence, than the interpretation that teachers' attitudes are based on a lack of sophistication.

There is some evidence that men and women teachers evaluate the problems of children differently. Women are found by one investigator to rate problem behaviors as more serious than do men (13). Another study (17) reports, however, that specific problem behaviors are treated differently by each sex. Men teachers consider *sex* problems as less serious than do women; women consider *appearance* and *destruction of property* as less serious than do men. Others (4, 37) report similar findings, although in the former case it is emphasized that the similarities are greater than the differences.

AGE AND GRADE INFLUENCES. The sixth grade appears to be modal for the nomination of children with problems, with the first and second grades offering the least. The fifth, seventh, and eighth grades also give the teacher some difficulty (16, 18, 23, 33). Differences in maladjustments of elementary and secondary school youngsters were reported early in the literature (16) and somewhat neglected till recently. Hildreth (16) observed that maladjusted elementary school children are more likely to be identified as *unstable, nervous,* or *shy*; the secondary school pupil, as *aggressive* or demonstrating *poor study habits*. Peck (26) finds the differential effect of sex of students in these identifications, however. Grade differences in problem type are reported by others as well (5, 36, 37). The differences found by Stouffer (36) have already been described. Griffiths (15) states that certain behavior difficulties (as reported by teachers and parents) increase with age; others decrease.

SOCIOECONOMIC STATUS. There are limited data relating socioeconomic status of the child to his identification as a problem. Levy (21) finds "socially high grade children have personality or emotional problems . . . children of lower classes have social problems" (p. 158). Yourman (46) reports a larger proportion of problem children are of lower socioeconomic status. Snyder (33) found that schools differentiated by their level of socioeconomic status

yielded different numbers of problems with more from the lower groups. There was no statistically significant difference, however, in socioeconomic status between a problem group and a control group.

The study by Griffiths (15) makes the most ambitious attempt to relate socioeconomic status to the identification of behavior problems. There were few significant differences among children of different socioeconomic levels in teachers' ratings of their problems. More differences appear, however, according to the parents' ratings and the child's own ratings. Griffiths concludes that some differences exist between middle socioeconomic level children and others. In particular, they are more submissive and less aggressive.

It is apparent that few data are available as to the relationship between socioeconomic status and the behavior problems of children.

DISCUSSION

The studies reviewed suggest strongly that differences in teachers' and clinicians' attitudes existed in 1927. From that time to the present changes appear to have taken place among teachers' attitudes so that they approximate more closely those of clinicians. There is some possibility that clinicians have tempered their evaluations as well.

Despite the shift toward congruence, teachers' attitudes remain different, and different in ways not dissimilar from what they were in Wickman's day. Why? First, let us recall that Wickman and others made much of this difference. It was suggested, even insisted, that the teacher should change. Such an injunction could rest only on the premise that the clinician's attitudes were more legitimate or more correct. This view was accepted though G. Watson was the first and not the last to question it. Watson's position was not that the clinician was necessarily incorrect or that he should not serve as a criterion. Rather, Wickman was chided for not even considering the alternatives to accepting the clinician as criterion. For Wickman, the virtue of choosing the clinicians' attitudes as an ideal was recommended by his expert knowledge of children's adjustment. Let us examine this claim.

For one, Wickman asked clinicians to rate behaviors in light of their possible future consequences. Would the clinician, with any validity, know the future consequences of the appearance of a behavior in childhood? The answer is doubtful. In 1927 there were few if any studies which had indicated with even low degrees of certainty the outcome in adolescence or adulthood of a child's particular behavior (e.g., *with-*

drawing behavior). In fact, if anything, there was some doubt that this could be done (27, 42). Evidence since then leads to even greater uncertainty (2, 19). According to some theories a withdrawn child is more likely to become maladjusted than one who is not. Yet the proof of how true this is and in what proportion for any population is almost nonexistent. Although it has been shown that in an adult *psychotic* group (44) there was a tendency for maladjustive behaviors to be present in childhood (information was obtained from retrospective reports), this tells us little about the prevalence of withdrawing behavior in a population of children or about the likelihood of such behaviors resulting in maladjustment, neurosis, or psychosis in adulthood.

However, there is a more important issue, in light of the functions of the therapist qua therapist: withdrawing behaviors present a problem to be dealt with at the time of their appearance. Such behaviors can be a basis for a visit to a therapist—in childhood as well as adulthood. The clinician is more likely to attempt some therapy than to postpone action till adolescence or adulthood (although, in some instances, this might reasonably be done). The clinician is often forced to act by immediate criteria; for he cannot wait for ultimate validation. It is thus part of his role as a therapist to be concerned about these behaviors. In essence, the behaviors with which a clinician is concerned are related to his status and the functions that accompany that status. If these behaviors were of equal relevance to the functions of the teacher, they would be equally valued. However, they are not. This has been so even in the period of "life-adjustment" programs and through the era of the "whole child," except possibly for some special groups of teachers. In spite of much pressure, teachers on the whole continue to be concerned with behaviors that facilitate or interfere with their teaching. A number of investigators recognize the difference in function between clinician and teacher (11, 16, 22, 31, 38, 42, 46) even though the teacher's role is not simple to define. It is, after all, a reflection of an educational philosophy. The prevailing philosophy of education in 1927, whether explicit or implicit, was oriented to the training of intellectual skills. In the interim the function of the teacher has broadened considerably to include training in social and other skills. There has been much pressure on the teacher to be a counselor and in some ways something of a psychotherapist as well—but, at the least, to focus more on the emotional life and adjustment of the child. The question of which role is "better" is a question of values. At present, the trend is back again toward the training of intellectual skills. The trend of increasing teacher sophistication in psychology will probably continue, and will probably not revert to the level of 1927. To urge (e.g., 35, 36) that the teacher's attitudes approximate the clinician's is unrealistic unless the teacher's role becomes one with the clinician—and this seems unlikely.

Other considerations recommend themselves as well. The teacher has a vital role in the socialization of the child. She is, after all, a culture carrier and to some extent a parental surrogate. Her own behaviors are significant in the child's development of self-control, character traits, values, and work habits. These functions are certainly as important as any. There is no question that the teacher needs to be aware of withdrawing and other undesirable personality characteristics. What is questioned is the need for the teacher to concern herself with them to the same extent and in the same way as the clinician.

To summarize, the difference reported by Wickman in attitudes toward the behavior problems of children should be interpreted as reflecting differences in the roles of teachers and clinicians and the discharge of functions of the role incumbents (8, 30). The efforts of many have been directed to alter the prescription of the teacher's role and performance in this role. This effort has in part been successful, as witnessed by the greater congruence in attitudes between teacher and clinician. In spite of the partial change in prescription, the teacher's role remains principally task-oriented; the clinician's, more adjustment-oriented. It seems unrealistic and possibly even undesirable to expect the teacher's behaviors reflected in her attitudes and values to become congruent with those of clinicians. Other results reviewed here are consistent with this thesis. The reported disparity between elementary and secondary teachers results from differences in role. The high school teacher is even more subject matter-oriented than the elementary school teacher. The greatest impact of the "child-oriented" or "life-adjustment" philosophy in turn has been in the elementary school. This has resulted in a modification of role prescription for the elementary school teacher which is reflected in greater similarity between the attitudinal hierarchies of elementary teachers and clinicians. The observed differences are due not only to the teacher's role but result from the actions of the children themselves. The pupil's role-related behaviors change with progress through school as the youngster assumes new responsibilities and loses old ones. Behavior differences are not only bound to their age but also their sex. The same behavior is not expected or demanded of boys and girls. The attitudes of teachers in turn will reflect differences in age and sex role expectations.

SUMMARY AND CONCLUSION

The studies concerning teachers' and clinicians' attitudes toward the behavior problems of children, which have emerged principally from the initiative of the Wickman 1928 monograph, are reviewed. The following conclusions are drawn:

1. Differences existed in 1927 between the attitudes of teachers and clinicians toward the behavior problems of children. This seems to have been true in spite of the methodological limitations of the Wickman study.

2. Since 1927 there has been a shift in the hierarchy of teachers' attitudes to approximate more closely those of clinicians. This shift is not due to an artifact of research methodology. Those studies which incorporate adequate controls and consistent instructions show even greater congruence between the attitudes of the two groups.

3. There has been some change in the attitudes of clinicians although this is based upon the conclusions of one study.

4. Criteria employed in evaluating the behavior problems of children differ for elementary and secondary school teachers.

5. More boys are identified as maladjusted than girls and the criteria of maladjustment (and adjustment) differ in part for each sex.

6. The sex of the teacher affects, in part, attitudes toward children's problems.

7. Studies of the relationship of socioeconomic factors to the evaluation of children's behavior problems are inadequately dealt with in the literature.

Differences in attitudes between teachers and clinicians are interpreted in the framework of role theory. The attitudinal hierarchies of teachers and clinicians are seen as reflecting their respective roles and the ways these roles influence the organization of their respective experiences. Wickman's findings of 1927 are interpreted as indicative of the role of the teacher in that era. The role expectations of teachers have changed. Replications of the Wickman study indicate these changes have re-

sulted in greater congruence between teachers' and clinicians' attitudes. It is suggested by virtue of the teachers' essential task-orientation and the clinicians' adjustment-orientation that complete or nearly complete congruence is not likely to be achieved.

The relationship of sex and age to attitudes toward behavior problems is also explained in the light of role theory.

REFERENCES

1. BAIN, W. E. A study of the attitudes of teachers toward behavior problems. *Child. Develpm.*, 1934, 5, 19-35.

2. BEILIN, H. The prediction of adjustment over a four-year interval. *J. clin. Psychol.*, 1957, 13, 270-274.

3. BEILIN, H. Effects of social (occupational) role and age upon the criteria of mental health. *J. soc. Psychol.*, 1958, 48, 247-256.

4. BEILIN, H., and WERNER, E. Sex differences among teachers in the use of criteria adjustment. *J. educ. Psychol.*, 1957, 48, 426-436.

5. BEILIN, H., and WERNER, E. Sex role expectations and the criteria of social adjustment for young adults. *J. clin. Psychol.*, 1957, 13, 341-343.

6. BLANCHARD, P., and PAYNTER, R. H. The problem child. *Ment. Hyg.*, 1924, 8, 26-54.

7. BOYNTON, P. L., and MC GAW, B. H. The characteristics of problem children. *J. juv. Res.*, 1934, 18, 215-222.

8. BRIM, O. G. The parent-child relation as a social system: 1. Parent and child roles. *Child Develpm.*, 1957, 28, 343-364.

9. CLARK, E. J. Teacher reactions toward objectionable pupil behavior. *Elem. Sch. J.*, 1951, 51, 446-449.

10. DEL SOLAR, C. *Parents and teachers view the child; a comparative study of parents' and teachers' appraisals of children.* New York: Bureau of Publications, Teachers College, Columbia Univer., 1949.

11. DAVIS, E. A., and MC GINNIS, E. *Parent education; a survey of the Minnesota program.* Minneapolis: Univer. of Minnesota Press, 1939.

12. DICKSON, V. E. Behavior difficulties that baffle teachers. *J. juv. Res.*, 1932, 16, 93-101.

13. ELLIS, D. B., and MILLER, L. W. Teachers' attitudes and child behavior problems. *J. educ. Psychol.*, 1936, 27, 501-511.

14. EPSTEIN, L. J. An analysis of teachers' judgments of problem children. *J. genet. Psychol.*, 1941, 59, 101-107.

15. GRIFFITHS, W. *Behavior difficulties of children as perceived and judged by parents, teachers and children themselves.* Minneapolis: Univer. of Minnesota Press, 1952.

16. HILDRETH, G. A survey of problem pupils. *J. educ. Res.,* 1928, *18,* 1-14.

17. HUNTER, E. C. Changes in teachers' attitudes toward children's behavior over the last thirty years. *Ment. Hyg.,* 1957, *41,* 3-11.

18. HURLOCK, E. B., and MC DONALD, L. C. Undesirable behavior traits in junior high school students. *Child Develpm.,* 1934, *5,* 278-290.

19. IVES, O. L. *A critique of teachers' ratings of high school boys as an indication of later neuropsychiatric rejection for the armed services.* New York: Bureau of Publications, Teachers College, Columbia Univer., 1949.

20. LAYCOCK, S. R. Teachers' reactions to maladjustments of school children. *Brit. J. educ. Psychol.,* 1934, *4,* 11-29.

21. LEVY, J. A quantitative study of the relationship between intelligence and economic status as factors in the etiology of children's behavior problems. *Amer. J. Orthopsychiat.,* 1931, *1,* 152-162.

22. MAC CLENATHAN, R. H. Teachers and parents study children's behaviors. *J. educ. Sociol.,* 1934, *7,* 325-333.

23. MC CLURE, W. E. Characteristics of problem children based on judgments of teachers. *J. juv. Res.,* 1929, *13,* 124-140.

24. MITCHELL, J. C. A study of teachers' and mental hygienists' ratings of certain behavior problems of children. *J. educ. Res.,* 1942, *36,* 292-307.

25. NEUMEYER, M. H. *Juvenile delinquency in modern society.* New York: D. Van Nostrand, 1949.

26. PECK, L. Teachers' reports of the problems of unadjusted school children. *J. educ. Psychol.,* 1935, *26,* 123-138.

27. PRESTON, G. H., and SHEPLER, W. MC L. A study of the problems of "normal" childen. *Amer. J. Orthopsychiat.,* 1931, *1,* 245-256.

28. ROGERS, C. R. The criteria used in a study of mental health problems. *Educ. res. Bull.,* 1942, *21,* 29-40.

29. ROGERS, C. R. Mental health findings in three elementary schools. *Educ. res. Bull.,* 1942, *21,* 69-79.

30. SARBIN, T. R. Role theory. In G. Lindzey (Ed.), *Handbook of social psychology.* Cambridge: Addison-Wesley, 1954, Pp. 223-258.

31. SCHRUPP, M. H., and GJERDE, C. M. Teacher growth in attitudes toward behavior problems of children. *J. educ. Psychol.,* 1953, *44,* 203-214.

32. SEIDMAN, J. M., and KNAPP, L. B. Teacher likes and dislikes of student behavior and student perceptions of these attitudes. *J. educ. Res.,* 1953, *47,* 143-149.

33. SNYDER, L. M. The problem child in the Jersey City elementary schools. *J. educ. Sociol.,* 1934, *7,* 342-352.

34. SPARKS, J. N. Teachers' attitudes toward the behavior problems of children. *J. educ. Psychol.,* 1952, *43,* 284-291.

35. STOUFFER, G. A. W., JR. Behavior problems of children as viewed by teachers and mental hygienists. *Ment. Hyg.,* 1952, *36,* 271-285.

36. STOUFFER, G. A. W., JR. The attitudes of secondary school teachers toward certain behavior problems of children. *Sch. Rev.,* 1956, *64,* 358-362.

37. STOUFFER, G. A. W., JR., and OWENS, J. Behavior problems of children as identified by teachers and compared with those reported by E. K. Wickman. *J. educ. Res.,* 1955, *48,* 321-331.

38. STEWART, N. Teacher's concepts of "behavior problems." In *Growing points in educational research.* Washington: American Educ. Res. Ass. Rep., 1949.

39. THOMPSON, C. E. The attitudes of various groups toward behavior problems of children. *J. abnorm. soc. Psychol.,* 1940, *35,* 120-125.

40. ULLMANN, C. A. *Identification of maladjusted school children.* Public Hlth. Monogr. No. 7. Washington: U. S. Govt. Printing Office, 1952 (Rev. 1957).

41. WANDT, E. Measurement and analysis of teacher's attitudes. *Calif. J. educ. Res.,* 1952, *3,* 10-13.

42. WATSON, G. A critical note on two attitude scales. *Ment. Hyg.,* 1933, *17,* 59-64.

43. WICKMAN, E. K. Children's behavior and teachers' attitudes. New York: Commonwealth Fund, 1928.

44. WITMER, H. L. Childhood personality and parent-child relationships of dementia praecox and manic depressive patients. *Smith Coll. Stud. Soc. Wk.,* 1934, *4,* 287-378.

45. YOUNG-MASTEN, I. Behavior problems of elementary school children: a descriptive and comparative study. *Genet. Psychol. Monogr.,* 1938, *20,* 123-181.

46. YOURMAN, J. Children identified by their teachers as problems. *J. educ. Sociol.,* 1932, *5,* 334-343.

47. U.S. CHILDREN'S BUREAU. *Juvenile court statistics, 1946-49.* Statistical Series No. 8 Washington: U.S. Govt. Printing Office, 1949.

70/THE TEACHER'S ROLE IN THE MOTIVATION OF THE LEARNER/PAULINE S. SEARS AND ERNEST R. HILGARD[*]

THE SIGNIFICANCE OF MOTIVATION for learning is usually assumed without question. On the one hand, the promise of reward or the threat of punishment provides means by which the teacher can keep the pupil at work; on the other hand, interest, curiosity, and self-selected goals keep the learner at work without pressure from the teacher. The teacher has a choice between using specific goals or enlisting self-activating motives, or perhaps employing some combination of these. The considerations that bear on what can or should be done are the present concern.

MOTIVATION IN LEARNING THEORY

The straightforward relationship between motivation and learning is not supported by experimental studies of learning as these are carried out and described by psychologists. One obstacle to experimentation is the uncertain distinction between learning and performance as they relate to motivation: It may be that learning (habit formation) arises through simple contiguous association, independent of motivation, while motivation affects the utilization of habit, that is, performance. For purposes, such as those of instruction, the distinction between learning and performance becomes somewhat less important, since what keeps the pupil performing is also likely to keep him learning. Still, if the distinction is important in theory it may also have some importance in practice. For example, some relatively low-pressure learning, such as browsing in a library, may be quite important, even though it goes on at a low level of motivation. When motivation is aroused, the results of this browsing may be capitalized on, thus providing an illustration in practice of the distinction that the experimentalists make in theory.

There is considerable turmoil within learning theory at the present time, as other chapters of the 1964 yearbook indicate. The once dominant need-drive-incentive theory, interpreting reinforcement as drive-reduction, has been under-going searching re-examination. The drives usually studied (hunger, thirst, pain) were always treated as aversive drives, from which relief was sought; now the "neglected drives" of curiosity, manipulation, activity, and achievement, which emphasize the positive side of something sought rather than the negative of something to be escaped, have come to the fore.[1][Ed]

Secondary reinforcements, that is reinforcing situations supposed to have been derived from primary ones based on primitive drives, turn out not always to be secondary at all, and their properties are quite complex. Lawrence and Festinger[2] have shown in a series of provocative experiments that small or intermittent rewards, if they are sufficient to keep an organism at the task, tend to yield responses more resistant to extinction than large and regular rewards; they attribute this to the "extra attractions" that have to be adduced to justify the amount of work expended for the slight reward obtained.

The drive theory itself has been subjected to criticism by those who see learning becoming attached to cue-stimuli, whether these cues are internal or external.[3] Thus we do not need a "doorbell-answering-drive" to make us respond to a ringing doorbell: the ringing bell is both cue and drive.

The literature on motivation has been summarized in a large number of recent books,

[1] Ernest R. Hilgard, "Motivation in Learning Theory," in *Psychology: A Study of a Science*, Vol. V. Edited by S. Koch. New York: McGraw-Hill Book Co., 1963.

[Ed] *See the first paper in this section by J. McV. Hunt (no. 58) for further documentation of this point.*

[2]. Douglas H. Lawrence and Leon Festinger, *Deterrents and Reinforcement: The Psychology of Insufficient Reward*. Stanford, California: Stanford University Press, 1962.

[3] For example, see William K. Estes, "Stimulus Response Theory of Drive," in *Nebraska Symposium on Motivation*, pp. 114-68 (Edited by Marshall R. Jones. Lincoln, Nebraska: University of Nebraska Press, 1958); and Evan R. Keislar, "A Descriptive Approach to Classroom Motivation," *Journal of Teacher Education*, XI (June, 1960), 310-15.

[*] Pauline S. Sears and Ernest R. Hilgard, The teacher's role in the motivation of the learner, *Theories of Learning and Instruction*, Sixty-third Yearbook of the National Society for the Study of Education, Part I, 1964, 182-209. Reprinted with abridgment by permission.

many of which have little to say about human motivation. One of the broader studies is that of Rethlingshafer,[4] which includes animal studies but is more particularly concerned with human motives.

Despite the uncertainty about the precise relationship between motivation and learning, the general importance of motivation in relation to the learner's absorption in his task, his resistance to distraction, his favorable attitudes toward school, can scarcely be denied. Thus, some problems of detail (e.g., that excessive motivation may in some cases hinder learning) need not confuse us or prevent our paying confident attention to motivation as important in classroom learning.

MOTIVES WHICH TEACHERS CAN UTILIZE OR AROUSE

A distinction has to be made between a motivational disposition and an aroused motive. A motivational disposition is a relatively enduring tendency to be prone to certain forms of motivational arousal, although at any one time that motive may be dormant. Thus, a person might be characterized as having a voracious appetite, which means that he is easily aroused by food; yet at any one time he may be satiated. Hunger is an aroused motive; the enduring characteristic of having a good appetite is a motivational disposition. In the same way some children are easily aroused to aggression, easily become dependent, or anxious. When so characterized, their motivational dispositions are being described.

SOCIAL MOTIVES: WARMTH AND NURTURANCE. Social motives have to do with one's relationships to other people. The desire to affiliate with others is one class of dependable human motivational dispositions found in parent-child relations, friendships, and as an important aspect of sex and marriage. Because the teacher is an adult, the affiliative motive often takes the form of dependency, that is, the child is the welcome recipient of the warmth and nurturance of the adult. There is evidence that such warmth and nurturance clearly relate to performances by young children on concept formation, memory, and maze performance, and affect the imitation of irrelevant behavior performed by adults. A nurturant adult, who then withdraws that nurturance, leads the child to make great efforts to

restore the warm interaction. Most of the experimental evidence comes from tests made over short periods of time, and it would be valuable to know how these relationships endure through time. These conclusions are supported by the studies of Hartup,[5] Rosenblith,[6] Bandura and Huston,[7] Gewirtz,[8] and Gewirtz and Baer.[9]

The investigations just mentioned are chiefly laboratory-type studies designed to examine the effect of manipulation of nurturant variables upon child behavior. That their conclusions have implications for the classroom can be documented by studies of teacher warmth and pupil behavior. For example, Cogan[10] found that warm and considerate teachers got an unusual amount of original poetry and art from their high-school students. Reed[11] found that teachers higher in warmth favorably affected pupils' interest in science. He found that the utilization of intrinsic interest by the teacher and the teacher's personal warmth were highly correlated; this would seem to justify some emphasis upon warmth of personality in the selection of teachers who are to be trained to make use of pupils' intrinsic motivation.

EGO-INTEGRATIVE MOTIVES: THE ACHIEVEMENT MOTIVE. A group of motives that serve to main-

[4] Dorothy Rethlingshafer, *Motivation as Related to Personality*. New York: McGraw-Hill Book Co., 1963.

[5] Willard W. Hartup, "Nurturance and Nurturance-Withdrawal in Relation to the Dependency Behavior of Preschool Children," *Child Development*, XXIX (June, 1958), 191-203.

[6] Judy F. Rosenblith, "Learning by Imitation in Kindergarten Children," *Child Development*, XXX (1959), 69-80. [See Section IV, no. 25 in this book.]

[7] Albert Bandura and Aletha C. Huston, "Identification as a Process of Incidental Learning," *Journal of Abnormal and Social Psychology*, LXIII (1961), 311-18.

[8] Jacob L. Gewirtz, "A Program of Research on the Dimensions and Antecedents of Emotional Dependence," *Child Development*, XXVII (1956), 206-21.

[9] Jacob L. Gewirtz and Donald M. Baer, "The Effect of Brief Social Deprivation on Behaviors for a Social Reinforcer," *Journal of Abnormal and Social Psychology*, LVI (1958), 49-56; Jacob L. Gewirtz and Donald M. Baer, "Deprivation and Satiation of Social Reinforcers as Drive Conditions," *Journal of Abnormal and Social Psychology*, LVII (1958), 166-72; Jacob L. Gewirtz, Donald M. Baer, and Chaya H. Roth, "A Note on the Similar Effects of Low Social Deprivation on Young Children's Behavior," *Child Development*, XXIX (1958), 149-52.

[10] Morris L. Cogan, "The Behavior of Teachers and the Productive Behavior of Their Pupils," *Journal of Experimental Education*, XXVII (December, 1958), 89-124.

[11] Horace B. Reed, "Implications for Science Education of a Teacher Competence Research," *Science Education*, XLVI (December, 1962), 473-86.

tain self-confidence and self-esteem have sometimes been referred to as ego-integrative motives. These have been variously characterized as motives of self-actualization[12] or of competence.[13] The achievement motive may be taken as a convenient representative of this group of motives, for it has been the subject of numerous investigations.

Our society is achievement-oriented, and it is not surprising that the desire to meet standards of excellence motivates some students. Any such motivational disposition is, however, quite complex, and without some clarification we confuse motives of social competition (the desire for prestige or power) with those of meeting standards of excellence in a skill or in scientific or artistic production. The earlier studies on level of aspiration, concerned more with aroused motives, have been supplemented by studies of persistent achievement motives, initiated by McClelland and his associates,[14] and since carried on by many others.[15]

Because the achievement motive is so obviously related to classroom behavior, we shall return to it in other contexts.

CURIOSITY AND OTHER COGNITIVE MOTIVES. Among the "neglected drives" that have more lately come to prominence we may recognize a group that can be called cognitive because they are concerned with "knowing" the environment or the relationships among things and ideas. Pavlov long ago recognized what he called a "What-is-it reflex," by which he referred to curiosity in animals. The exploratory motives have been reintroduced by Harlow;[16] Berlyne[17]

has brought out his own work and that of others in book form. This group of motives also includes manipulative motives[18] and activity motives.[19] These are related to what in the past have been called *intrinsic* motives, that is, motives that reside in the task itself rather than external to it (i.e., *extrinsic* motives, such as rewards or prizes).

These motives, too, are so important in school learning that further attention will be paid to them. All of these motives—social, ego-integrative, and cognitive—are open to manipulation in one way or another by the teacher. We turn now to how this may be done and what consequences can be expected.

THE SCHOOL ENVIRONMENT AND INSTRUCTIONAL PROCEDURES AS THEY BEAR UPON MOTIVATION

The general atmosphere of the school may determine which motives are aroused and, hence, which children will profit most from the school. This follows if some children respond more to one kind of motivation than to another; if all are to be served, some flexibility is essential. Within the general atmosphere the particular instructional methods and emphases also affect the utilization of motivational potential for learning. . . .

THE SCHOOL ENVIRONMENT AND ATMOSPHERE. It is well known that the socioeconomic backgrounds of the pupils affect their school motivation, particularly achievement motivation. This is well attested in numerous studies of subcultures within America, such as those of Rosen[20] and Strodtbeck.[21] To the extent that school success (and continuing in school) is associated with higher occupational level, vocational aspiration can often be taken as a measure of achievement motivation. While the father's oc-

[12] A. H. Maslow, *Motivation and Personality.* New York: Harper & Bros., 1954.

[13] R. W. White, "Motivation Reconsidered: The Concept of Competence," *Psychological Review*, LXVI (1959), 297-333.

[14] David C. McClelland, John W. Atkinson, Russell A. Clark, and Edgar L. Lowell, *The Achievement Motive.* New York: Appleton-Century-Crofts, 1953.

[15] For example, *Motives in Fantasy, Action, and Society* (Edited by John W. Atkinson. Princeton, New Jersey: Van Nostrand Co., 1958); and V. J. Crandall, "Achievement," in *Child Psychology*, pp. 416-59 (Sixty-second Yearbook of the National Society for the Study of Education, Part I. Edited by Harold W. Stevenson. Chicago: Distributed by University of Chicago Press, 1963).

[16] H. F. Harlow, "Learning and Satiation of Response in Intrinsically Motivated Complex Puzzle Performance by Monkeys," *Journal of Comparative and Physiological Psychology*, XLIII (1950), 289-94.

[17] D. E. Berlyne, *Conflict, Arousal, and Curiosity.* New York: McGraw-Hill Book Co., 1960.

[18] H. F. Harlow and G. E. McClearn, "Object Discrimination Learned by Monkeys on the Basis of Manipulation Motives," *Journal of Comparative and Physiological Psychology*, XLVII (1954), 73-76.

[19] W. F. Hill, "Activity as an Autonomous Drive," *Journal of Comparative and Physiological Psychology*, XLIX (1956), 15-19.

[20] Bernard C. Rosen, "Race, Ethnicity, and the Achievement Syndrome," *American Sociological Review*, XXIV (1959), 47-60.

[21] Fred L. Strodtbeck, "Family Interaction, Values, and Achievement," in *Talent and Society: New Perspectives in the Identification of Talent.* Edited by David C. McClelland *et al.* Princeton, New Jersey: D. Van Nostrand Co., 1958.

cupation has little relation to school success in the early grades, by the time the pupil reaches junior high school, his achievement is likely to be more related to his father's occupation than to his intelligence level.[22] These facts need to be recognized by the teacher; the inevitability of poor motivation on the part of those from lower occupational groups need not be accepted, but the need for special motivational efforts is obvious.

Let us suppose that a school wishes to stress problem-solving and creativity, in line with the current emphasis upon cognitive motives. How, then, can an atmosphere be created in which such motives will be aroused? The question has been studied by Shaftel, Crabtree, and Rushworth,[23] who point out that the teacher in dealing with the young child must do the following things: (a) make sure that the emotional climate of the classroom is suitable for the development of a healthy self-concept, (b) evoke problems when they are not immediately apparent to the children, (c) stimulate a problem-solving climate, which involves the process of search, rather than focusing on one right answer, and (d) plan a curriculum which stimulates problem-solving, by the use of experience units, construction activities, science experiments, group work, dramatic play, and role-playing.

A book by Taba[24] goes into specifics on the development of curricula and teaching methods which will release cognition and serve to satisfy cognitive needs. She makes use of some of the reflections about intelligence and experience recounted by Hunt,[25] and some of the observations of Piaget.[26] (The new interest in Piaget is evidenced in many places; a very able summary of his work has appeared.[27])

The old concept of ability grouping, as simplifying the task of the teacher, has been examined in a new light by Thelen.[28] He proposes that some teachers find given students, selected on the basis of the teacher's purposes, more "teachable" than others. When pupils are grouped in accordance with this criterion, the teacher tends to be more satisfied with his class, to like the pupils better, and to give them higher grades. The pupils, in turn, tend to be more orderly and more manageable, more co-operative, and more satisfied with the activities. They like each other better, and the class appears to be more cohesive than classes not selected on this basis. The achievement gains in these classes depended on the purposes of the teacher. When achievement was central among the teacher's purposes, these teachable groups did better. For some teachers achievement was not a central goal; their students did not do as well by achievement criteria.

ACTIVITIES CAPITALIZING ON COGNITIVE MOTIVATION. It is difficult to unravel those aspects of instruction that should be called motivational from those that are merely successful for whatever reason. It can be assumed that a kind of program that leads to spontaneous effort, to absorption in learning, and to results that yield the self-esteem that comes from reaching goals that are self-set by the learner must be well-grounded in appropriate motivation. In part, these results come about without direct concern for motivation through a kind of contagion of interest when problems are well set up, so that search leads to creative answers. Much of modern curriculum-planning concerns itself with the structure of knowledge and with the kind of thinking that is divergent rather than convergent; when conditions are appropriate, motivation appears to take care of itself.

Thus, major curricular studies in specific fields, such as the Biological Sciences Study Group[29] and the Physical Sciences Study Group,[30] try to get the student to learn not only content but also the strategy and approaches of

[22] Joseph A. Kahl, *The American Class Structure.* New York: Rinehart & Co., 1957.

[23] Fannie R. Shaftel, Charlotte Crabtree, and Vivian Rushworth, "Problem-solving in the Elementary School," in *Problems-approach in the Social Studies,* pp. 25-47. Edited by Richard E. Gross. Washington: National Education Assn., 1960.

[24] Hilda Taba, *Curriculum Development: Theory and Practice.* New York: Harcourt, Brace & World, 1962.

[25] J. McV. Hunt, *Intelligence and Experience.* New York: Ronald Press, 1961.

[26] Jean Piaget, *The Psychology of Intelligence* (London: Routledge & Kegan Paul, 1950); Jean Piaget, *The Origins of Intelligence in Children* (Translated by Margaret Cook. New York: International University Press, 1952).

[27] John H. Flavell, *The Developmental Psychology of Jean Piaget.* Princeton, New Jersey: D. Van Nostrand Co., 1963.

[28] Herbert A. Thelen, "Development of Educational Methods for Different Types of Students." Chicago: Department of Education, University of Chicago, 1960 (duplicated).

[29] Bentley Glass, "Renascent Biology: A Report on the AIBS Biological Curriculum Study," *School Review,* LXX (Spring, 1962), 16-43.

[30] Gilbert C. Finlay, "The Physical Science Study Committee," *School Review,* LXX (Spring, 1962), 63-81.

the scientist. In so doing, it is anticipated that as a by-product the student will wish to adopt a pattern of behavior conducive to productive thinking.

Suchman[31] has developed a program for training in inquiry skills with reference to science instruction. He conceives that some dissonance is necessary for development of such skills: a puzzling problem, a lack of structure. However, induction of relational constructs or discovery depends on existing conceptual systems in the child. Hunt[32] has suggested that controlling intrinsic motivation is a matter of providing an organism with circumstances that provide a proper level of incongruity with the residues of previous encounters with such circumstances that the organism has stored in his memory—the "problem of the match" between incoming information and that already stored.

Some experiments have been directed specifically to the problem of the conditions under which new ideas are freely developed. Torrance[33] divided all pupils in a university experimental school from the first to the sixth grade into four experimental groups at each grade level. Four conditions were created by two conditions of training and two sets of verbal instructions regarding output. The training conditions consisted in teaching two groups the principles for developing new ideas as suggested by Osborn,[34] while the other two groups, not taught any principles, were told that they would receive prizes for the best performance. The two sets of verbal instructions, combined with the two training conditions, were, first, a motivation to produce as many ideas as possible; second, a motivation to produce clever, original, and unusual ideas. In general, the results were in the expected direction: the special training in principles produced desired results beyond those produced by the promise of prizes, and the specific instructions to produce clever and unusual responses yielded more of them than the request for mere quantity of ideas. However, this was a short-range experiment and leaves unanswered the question:

Would a series or pattern of exercises or training produce a permanent change in thinking abilities or cognitive style of a student?

How a teacher can produce divergent rather than convergent thinking is well illustrated by some studies by Gallagher.[35] There appears to be a correspondence between the sorts of statements the teacher makes and those the students make, as these are studied at the junior high school level. Thus, the profile of divergent ideas produced by the students corresponds rather closely to the pattern set by the teacher. In those sessions during which the teacher asks for more divergent production, the percentages of student responses in this direction are correspondingly high. Only a slight increase in the teacher's percentage of divergent questions brings forth a large increase in divergent production by the student. A single question, such as "What would have happened were the United States colonized from the west coast to the east instead of vice versa?" can bring forth as many as 15 or 20 responses, each related to a divergent idea. This illustration points again to the close relationship between content and motivation: The motivation here is to keep curiosity alive, and the only motivational device needed is to ask the right questions, and not to stifle curiosity by sticking too closely to facts that are to be memorized.

The introduction of mechanical aids to instruction, such as audio-visual aids and teaching machines, raises interesting motivational questions. Part of the appeal of the teaching machine is to the manipulative motives, and at the least an active process is substituted for a passive one. Smedslund[36] analyzes the orienting response, the overt response, and the reinforcement, and decides that the teaching machine relies entirely on extrinsic motivation. His analysis is, however, incomplete, for the program of a teaching machine need by no means be cut-and-dried, and sustained only by the reward of "right." A well-designed teaching program brings out cognitive motivation, and provides the intrinsic satisfactions that come with competence. At least the learner knows that he is learning, a result, alas, that is often not yielded for some pupils in the same classrooms. The chief criticism of too gen-

[31] J. Richard Suchman, "Inquiry Training: Building Skills for Autonomous Discovery," *Merrill Palmer Quarterly*, VII (1961), 147-69.

[32] Hunt, *op. cit.*

[33] *Guiding Creative Talent.* Edited by Paul Torrance. Englewood Cliffs, New Jersey: Prentice-Hall, Inc., 1962.

[34] Alex F. Osborn, *Applied Imagination: Principles and Procedures of Creative Thinking.* New York: Charles Scribner's Sons, 1957.

[35] *A Report on a Conference of Research on Gifted Children.* Edited by James J. Gallagher. Washington: U.S. Department of Health, Education, and Welfare, U.S. Office of Education, Cooperative Research Branch, 1963.

[36] J. Smedslund, personal communication, 1961.

eral reliance on teaching machines is that the learning process is essentially sedentary and isolated, even though the learner is active in finding his way through the program. Much of creative search involves moving about and active interchange with others.

OBSERVED TEACHER INTERACTION WITH CHILDREN. Teacher behavior has such a strong effect upon pupil motivation that it is worthwhile to review some of the observational studies that show how this comes about. For purposes of this review, these interactions will be grouped under three topics: (a) *affective* interaction, in which emotional-attitudinal variables, those most often considered in connection with positive mental health, will be in the foreground; (b) *evaluative* interaction, in which the teacher judges and criticizes rewards, and punishes; and (c) *cognitive* interaction in which emphasis is essentially nonaffective and nonevaluative of achievement but encourages problem-solving, intellectual ferment, originality, and creativity.

Affective interaction between teacher and pupils. The teacher's responsibility for maintaining discipline in the classroom brings to the fore the affective consequences of various rewarding and punishing techniques, though these are by no means the only sources of affective influence of teachers upon students. Other aspects include the general warmth of the atmosphere that is created, the tolerance of some release of feeling on the part of the child, the protection of the individual egos, the satisfaction of individual needs. The techniques of control are, however, readily open to observation, and a number of studies have been directed toward them.

In an experiment in regular classrooms with eighth- and ninth-grade children, Kounin, Gump, and Ryan[37] studied the effects of three "desist techniques." Under one condition the teacher was punitive and intense. When a pretrained male student got up while slides were being shown and sharpened his pencil the teacher stalked toward him, saying, "Hey you, who do you think you are?" in a firm, irritated voice; put her arm on his shoulders in a gesture of pushing him into his seat and said, "Now sit down! If you ever do that again, I'll really make trouble for you."[38] A second condition involved a

matter-of-fact reprimand—i.e., "Don't do that again. Please sit down in your seat now." Under the third condition the teacher indicated her awareness of the behavior but did nothing about it. When the effects on the audience children were compared under the three conditions, the punitive technique was found to result in "the subjects' rating the *deviancy* as 'most serious,' the degree of *interference* with attention to the task as 'greatest,' the *teacher* as 'making too much of an issue' over the event, the experience 'most discomforting,' and the *teacher* 'best able to maintain order in a class of tough kids.' "[39] The simple reprimand resulted in the students reporting the highest ratings for teacher fairness and paying more attention to the lesson after witnessing the event. Under the "ignoring" condition, pupils rated the teacher highest in her liking for children but thought the misbehavior most likely to recur.

In another study,[40] three pairs of punitive versus nonpunitive first-grade teachers were selected from three elementary schools. The 174 children in these teachers' classrooms were individually interviewed about what they thought was "the worst thing to do in school" and were asked for their explanations of why these misconducts were bad. Regarding their responses as expressions of their preoccupations, it was concluded that children who have punitive teachers, as compared with children who have nonpunitive teachers, manifest more aggression in their misconducts; are more unsettled and conflicted about misconduct in school; are less concerned with learning and school-unique values; and show some, but not consistent, indication of a reduction in rationality pertaining to school misconduct. A theory that children with punitive teachers develop less trust of school than do children with nonpunitive teachers was also presented to explain some of the findings.

Some hypotheses concerning the types of social power that are exercised in classrooms were tested in a correlational study by Rosenfeld and Zander.[41] Among other findings were the following:

[37] Jacob S. Kounin, Paul V. Gump, and James J. Ryan, "Explorations in Classroom Management," *Journal of Teacher Education*, XII (June, 1961), 235-46.

[38] *Ibid.*, p. 237.

[39] *Ibid.*

[40] Jacob S. Kounin and Paul V. Gump, "The Comparative Influence of Punitive and Nonpunitive Teachers upon Children's Concepts of School Misconduct," *Journal of Educational Psychology*, LII (February, 1961), 44-49.

[41] Howard Rosenfeld and Alvin Zander, "The Influence of Teachers on Aspirations of Students," *Journal of Educational Psychology*, LII (February, 1961), 1-11.

1. Two forms of coercion by teachers are discriminated by students: disapproval of inadequate performance, and disapproval when the performance is as good as the student feels he can do. The first type has little effect on future aspiration or performance, while the second has a deleterious effect on both aspiration and future performance.

2. Two forms of reward are also discriminated by students. When rewards are showered indiscriminately, tendencies to accept the teacher's influence are lowered; when rewards are limited to adequate performances, the teacher's influence is increased.

The ways in which teachers exercise power, as indicated by these types of reward and punishment, have additional consequences in affecting the favorableness or negativeness of student attitudes toward the teacher and toward course content.

While rewarding and punishing behavior affect teacher influence, there are many other affective interactions between teachers and pupils. Della Piana and Gage[42] found, for example, that some pupils are more concerned about feelings and personal relationships, while others are mainly achievement-oriented. Classes made up predominantly of pupils of the first type tend to accept the teacher whom they like, and to reject the teacher whom they dislike, on personal grounds; classes composed of pupils of the second type pay less attention to teacher warmth in estimating their acceptance or rejection of particular teachers. It often turns out that what is important for one pupil is not important for another; this is one reason why cookbook formulas for good teaching are of so little use and why teaching is inevitably something of an art.

Another subtle influence of affective responsiveness of teachers has to do with creativity. A rather plausible principle from psychoanalysis is that creativity involves some freedom in the use of unconscious or preconscious processes. These processes tend to be less critical and more impulsive than the more rational and analytical processes, and hence are likely to call for some tolerance on the teacher's part. The process of partial or limited regression has been called "regression in the service of the ego" by Kris;[43] the importance of something similar has been stressed by Kubie,[44] who believes that too much emphasis upon convergent thinking in the early years leads to a neurotic distortion of the creative process. That is, the child becomes frightened or anxious over that part of the normal play of his own fantasy life which does not follow the "rules" of evidence and logic.

Thus Spaulding[45] found strong negative relations between the expression of creativity in elementary-aged children and teacher behavior characterized as formal group instruction, using shame as a punishment technique. Sears[46] has shown that there are positive correlations between creativity and teachers' rewarding by personal interest in the child's ideas, accompanied by a high frequency of listening to the child. Such teaching techniques probably provide an atmosphere in which the child can permit himself more leeway in expression of unconventional ideas without threat of devastating criticism. Torrance[47] has emphasized the pressures toward conformity, away from creativity, exerted by the peer group of classmates. Competition may increase such pressures. Teachers may be able to provide an atmosphere which reduces these pressures somewhat. It is interesting that, in the aforementioned Sears study, much the same teacher behavior which tended to be related to creativity in the children was also positively related to the degree in which children in the classroom liked one another. A peer group in which there are good feelings between the children probably is more tolerant of nonconformist behavior than one in which the children like each other less.

The competitive situation of the classroom is almost inevitably anxiety-provoking for some children, and the handling of this anxiety in one form or another becomes an important task for the teacher. There is a large literature on this topic, concerned both with anxiety in general and with the special anxieties arising in the

[42] G. M. Della Piana and N. L. Gage, "Pupils' Values and the Validity of the Minnesota Teacher Attitude Inventory," *Journal of Educational Psychology*, XLVI (March, 1955), 167-78.

[43] Ernest Kris, *Psychoanalytic Explorations in Art*. New York: International University Press, 1952.

[44] L. S. Kubie, *Neurotic Distortions of the Creative Process*. New York: Noonday Press, 1952.

[45] R. Spaulding, "Achievement, Creativity, and Self-concept Correlates of Teacher-Pupil Transactions in Elementary Schools." Urbana, Illinois: University of Illinois (U.S. Office of Education Cooperative Research Project No. 1352), 1963 (mimeographed).

[46] Pauline S. Sears, "The Effect of Classroom Conditions on Strength of Achievement Motive and Work Output of Elementary-School Children." In press, 1963.

[47] Torrance, *op. cit.*

test situation so often confronted in school.[48] The results are complex and, in some cases, contradictory. The subtlety of the relationships involved is well illustrated by a study by Sarason, Mandler, and Craighill[49] in which it was found that (a) low-anxious college students did better, in general, on a laboratory task than high-anxious subjects, and (b) pressure to complete the task improved the performance for low-anxious subjects, but did not do so for high-anxious ones. It appears that anxiety is interfering enough, without adding new components to it through pressure; low-anxious subjects, working without interference, can accept the exhortation to do better.

The interplay between anxiety and achievement has been studied by Flanders[50] in experimentally produced climates, characterized on the one hand as "learner-centered" and on the other as "teacher-centered." In the learner-centered climate the teacher was acceptant and supportive of the student and problem-centered in approach; in the teacher-centered climate the teacher was directive and demanding, often deprecating, in his behavior toward the individual. Anxiety was estimated from physiological measures (pulse rate, galvanic skin responses) and by the direction and intensity of movements of a lever operated by the students to indicate positive and negative feelings. The major conclusions were:

1. When a conflict arises, student behavior oriented to the handling of interpersonal anxiety takes precedence over behavior oriented toward achievement.

2. The "teacher-centered" behavior of directing, demanding, and using private criteria in deprecating a student leads to hostility to the self or the teacher, aggressiveness, or occasionally withdrawal, apathy, and even emotional disintegration.

3. The "learner-centered" behavior of accept-

ing the student, being evaluative or critical only by public criteria, and being usually supportive, elicited problem orientation, decreased interpersonal anxiety, and led to emotionally readjusting and integrative behavior.

In these days of emphasis upon cognitive processes, it is quite possible for the pendulum to swing too far, and hence to defeat the attainment of the very cognitive goals that are being sought. If cognition is made synonymous with achievement and competition for excellence, the concomitantly aroused anxiety may defeat the development of the very creativity and problem-solving orientation that is being sought. Hence the teacher's awareness of the affective interaction with pupils is as important in a curriculum directed toward cognition as one with other goals, such as those of social competence or personal adjustment. Much of the abstract discussion of educational goals overlooks the essential interrelatedness of low anxiety and high performance, and the need for teacher warmth if the climate to create is to be provided.

Evaluative interaction between teacher and *pupils.* As indicated in the foregoing section, teacher evaluation can be by private criteria or by public criteria; in the one case the evaluation is likely to be punitive and to arouse hostility; in the other case it is likely to be informative and hence lead to better learning.

A very interesting experiment was done by Page[51] with high school and junior high school students and a large number of teachers. The teachers graded objective tests of their students and then randomly assigned each paper to one of three groups. The group-one pupil was given back his paper with no comment except the mark. Each group-two pupil was given a stereotyped comment from excellent if his score was high to "let's raise this grade." Every C student, for example, received his mark with the notation, "perhaps try to do still better?" For group three, the teacher wrote a personal comment on every paper, saying whatever she felt would encourage that particular pupil. On the next objective test, groups two and three outperformed group one. The personalized comments seemed to have a greater effect than the standardized comments, but even a very short standard comment written on the paper produced measurable improvement. The greatest improvement was found in the failing students

[48] Seymour B. Sarason *et al.*, *Anxiety in Elementary-School Children* (New York: John Wiley & Sons, 1960); Britton K. Ruebush, "Anxiety," in *Child Psychology*, pp. 460-516 (Sixty-second Yearbook of the National Society for the Study of Education, Part I. Edited by Harold W. Stevenson. Chicago: Distributed by the University of Chicago Press, 1963).

[49] Seymour B. Sarason, George Mandler, and Peyton G. Craighill, "The Effect of Differential Instructions on Anxiety and Learning," *Journal of Abnormal and Social Psychology*, XLVII (April, 1952), 561-65.

[50] Ned A. Flanders, "Personal-Social Anxiety as a Factor in Experimental Learning Situations," *Journal of Educational Research*, XLV (October, 1951), 100-110.

[51] E. B. Page, "Teacher Comments and Student Performance," *Journal of Educational Psychology*, XLIX (1958), 173-81.

in group three, who received an encouraging personal note.

This study points up the motivational significance of evaluative practices that go beyond the indication of right or wrong answers. Personal interest of the teacher in the student's progress is shown to be effective.

[A paragraph about the work of Wickman and Beilin is here omitted because their work and the appropriate references are covered in Beilin's paper just preceding.]

Without reviewing further studies at this point, it is perhaps sufficient to point out that a teacher's evaluative activities go far beyond marking papers; they include attention to many experiences of success and failure, of expanded or restricted autonomy, of immediate and long-term goal-setting, of recognition of individual progress, and of attitudinal response to divergent behavior. These evaluative behaviors have the characteristics of positive and negative reinforcers, and, as such, are motivationally relevant to learning.

Cognitive interaction between teacher and pupils. To the extent that the teacher imparts skill and knowledge and teaches the approaches to solving problems and creating products that are both novel and valuable, he is having a cognitive interaction with pupils. This is the most readily understood purpose of teaching, but it is by no means easy to categorize the processes that are involved. They include methods, such as lecture, discussion, individual projects; they include content-related matters, such as structuring the problem and developing content-relevant understandings. Attempts at categorizing, such as those of Medley and Mitzel,[54] Smith,[55] and Wright and Proctor[56] are none too satisfactory, being either very general or at such a commonsense level as to have no element of newness in them. Thus, Wright and Proctor[57] classify the content of what teachers of mathe-

matics say to their pupils as promoting (*a*) ability to think, (*b*) appreciation of mathematics, and (*c*) curiosity and initiative. The effort to devise such categories has value, however, in that it calls attention to the fact that what the teacher says to the pupil goes beyond the exposition of subject matter.[58]

Spaulding,[59] using tape recordings from 21 elementary teachers, identified empirically components of teacher behavior similar to the more global behavior syndromes discussed by Anderson,[60] Withall,[61] and Lewin, Lippitt, and White.[62] Support was given to the prediction that self-concepts of children would be higher in classrooms in which the teacher was "socially integrative" and "learner supportive." Spaulding's description of the behavior found to be positively related to self-concept was as follows: "calm, acceptant transactions in general with private, individualized instruction and a concern for divergency, attention to task, and the use of task-appropriate procedures and resources."

However, a test of the predictions involving "democratic" teacher behavior[63] failed to gain support. Neither pupil self-concepts, achievement, nor creativity was found to be related to this pattern of behavior.

All of these pupil outcomes were positively correlated to a modest degree with the component described as follows: "business-like lecture method with insistence upon attention to task and conformity to rules of procedure."[64] In the case of scores on reading achievement, this

[54] Donald M. Medley and Harold E. Mitzel, "Measuring Classroom Behavior by Systematic Observation," in *Handbook of Research on Teaching*, pp. 247-328. Edited by N. L. Gage. Chicago: Rand McNally & Co., 1963.

[55] B. Othanel Smith, "A Study of the Logic of Teaching: A Report on the First Phase of a Five-Year Research Project." Washington: U.S. Office of Education, 1959 (duplicated).

[56] E. Muriel J. Wright and Virginia H. Proctor, *Systematic Observations of Verbal Interaction as a Method of Comparing Mathematics Lessons.* St. Louis, Missouri: Washington University (U.S. Office of Education Cooperative Research Project No. 816), 1961.

[57] *Ibid.*

[58] For problems of cognitive interactions as related to particular subject matters, see the chapters in the 1964 yearbook by Bruner on mathematics and by Carroll on reading. *The Handbook of Research on Teaching* (*op. cit.*) contains excellent comprehensive reviews of significant studies.

[59] Spaulding, *op. cit.*

[60] Harold H. Anderson, "Domination and Socially Integrative Behavior," in *Child Behavior and Development,* pp. 459-84. Edited by Roger G. Barker, Jacob S. Kounin, and Herbert F. Wright. New York: Mc-Graw-Hill Book Co., 1943.

[61] John Withall, "Development of a Technique for the Measurement of Socioemotional Climate in Classrooms," *Journal of Experimental Education,* XVII (March, 1949), 347-61.

[62] Kurt Lewin, Ronald Lippitt, and R. K. White, "Patterns of Aggressive Behavior in Experimentally Created 'Social Climates,'" *Journal of Social Psychology,* X (1939), 271-99.

[63] *Ibid.*

[64] *Ibid.,* p. 119.

correlation was strongly significant. Ryans[65] also found businesslike methods and warmth related to students' behavior. For elementary-school classes, high positive relationships were noted between observers' assessments of "productive pupil behavior" (e.g., assessments presumed to reflect pupil alertness, participation, confidence, responsibility and self-control, initiating behavior, and so on) and observers' assessments of previously identified patterns of teacher behavior which seemed to refer to understanding, friendly classroom behavior; organized, businesslike classroom behavior; and stimulating, original classroom behavior.

For secondary-school classes, low positive relationships appeared to obtain between productive pupil behavior and the above-named categories of teacher behavior, with a tendency for the stimulating, original teacher classroom-behavior pattern to show a slightly higher correlation with pupil behavior than the understanding, friendly or the organized, businesslike teacher behavior patterns.

A narrower definition of pupil task-oriented behavior was used by Sears.[66] Time samples of the percentage of time elementary-school children were attentive to the assigned task were found strongly related to teacher behavior. If children work steadily during a large proportion of class time, their teachers tend to give rewards in evaluative terms, to the group rather than to the individual, without show of interest in individual personalities. They tend to teach by statement and by giving of information. Thus the teacher behavior related to task-oriented work is very different from that associated with children's production of creative responses. It was also found that high frequencies of task-oriented behavior, as defined here, did not relate to achievement as reflected in test scores. The quiet, apparently industrious groups did not achieve more.

The teaching methods just described could be characterized as directive on the part of the teacher. Stern[67] has reviewed 34 studies (largely of college classes) comparing nondirective with directive instruction in influencing two types of learning outcome: (a) gain in achievement of cognitive knowledge and understanding, and (b) attitude change toward self or others. The following quotation summarizes the findings:

college

In general, it would appear that amount of cognitive gain is largely unaffected by the autocratic or democratic tendencies of the instructor. The majority of investigators who have attempted to measure differences in achievement report no particular advantage for either approach. . . . Regardless of whether the investigator was concerned with attitudes toward the cultural outgroup, toward other participants in the class, or toward the self, the results generally have indicated that non-directive instruction facilitates a shift in a more favorable, acceptant direction.[68]

However, in connection with student reactions to nondirective instruction, "at least as many students feel dissatisfied, frustrated, or anxious in a nondirective classroom as consider it valuable." Nondirective instruction, as practiced by some instructors, may be more laissez faire than learner-centered, and may arouse latent anxieties in students with precarious ego-strength. The next section considers the interaction of student predisposition and teaching method.

CHILD PERSONALITY, TEACHER PERSONALITY, AND THEIR CONSEQUENCES FOR THE MOTIVATION OF THE LEARNER

It has not been possible, in attempting to indicate some of the influences of teachers upon pupils, to avoid occasional mention of differences in pupils (and teachers) that affect the results, not entirely related to the specific classroom behavior of the teacher or specific instructional techniques. In this section we shall call attention more specifically to some of the personality factors that influence the acceptability of different methods of teaching.

PUPIL PERSONALITY AND THE CONDITIONS FAVORING ACHIEVEMENT. As one illustration, consider the differences between the independent, autonomous student and the one who is dependent-prone, that is, is likely to turn for support to adult authority. These relationships among students of eighth-grade geometry have been studied by Amidon and Flanders.[69]

[65] David G. Ryans, "Some Relationships between Pupil Behavior and Certain Teacher Characteristics," *Journal of Educational Psychology*, LII (April, 1961), 82-90.

[66] Sears, *op. cit.*

[67] George G. Stern, "Measuring Non-cognitive Variables in Research on Teaching," in *Handbook of Research on Teaching, op. cit.*, p. 427.

[68] *Ibid.*, p. 428.

[69] Edmund Amidon and Ned A. Flanders, "The Effects of Direct and Indirect Teacher Influence on Dependent-prone Students Learning Geometry," *Journal of Educational Psychology*, LII (December, 1961), 286-91.

The primary purpose of this study was to determine the effects of direct versus indirect teacher behavior and of clear versus unclear student perception of the learning goal on the achievement of eighth-grade geometry students. A specially trained teacher role-played both a very direct and a very indirect teacher in a laboratory situation involving 140 eighth-grade pupils, chosen from a larger population on the basis of high scores on a test of dependency proneness. All students were randomly assigned to one of the following four experimental treatments: direct teacher influence with clear goals, direct teacher influence with unclear goals, indirect teacher influence with clear goals, and indirect teacher influence with unclear goals.

Students in the various classifications were then compared on the basis of pre- and post-achievement tests in geometry. No differences were found between the clear-goal and unclear-goal treatments, indicating that in this study, at least, achievement of dependent-prone students was not affected by perception of the learning goal. An analysis of the direct and indirect treatments indicated that the children taught by the indirect teacher learned more than did the children taught by the direct teacher.

The results of this study take on additional meaning when compared with the results of Flanders[70] using the same experimental design. Flanders found no differences (among the four experimental conditions) in the total group of 560 students who ranged from very high to very low on the dependence scale. Apparently, dependent-prone students are more sensitive to types of teacher influence than are independent-prone students as measured by scores on the test for dependence proneness.

Whether or not a particular type of student can learn when he is exposed to a particular style of teaching has interested a number of researchers. Smith[71] and Wispe[72] have both shown that when students are classified by the use of personality test data, they respond differently to highly organized (versus loosely organized) classroom activities in a college remedial read-

ing course[73] and to college lecturing (versus group discussion) techniques[74] in Freshman sociology.

Asch,[75] Kagen and Mussen,[76] and Livson and Mussen[77] have studied the reactions of dependent-prone persons in various kinds of experimental situations. They concluded that dependent-prone individuals are more likely to comply with authority figures and conform to group pressures than the less dependent-prone. Their results suggest that a dependent-prone student might become overly concerned with following the suggestions and directions of a teacher and more dependent on support and encouragement.

Kagan, Sontag, Baker, and Nelson,[78] working from the Fels Institute longitudinal data, studied the 35 subjects who had gained the most on I.Q. retest, and the 35 who had lost the most. The ascending I.Q. group was characterized by independence, mastery, high need achievement, and curiosity. The descending I.Q. group showed dependence and an attitude that competition was not emotionally comforting. Thus, there seems to be a relation between motivational dispositions and the production represented by scores on an intelligence test. The more active and achievement-motivated subjects the data suggest, interact more effectively with their environment in ways which provide for increase in I.Q. Much of the teacher's interaction with pupils must be directed toward arousal of such motivation.

Gains in achievement for children of superior mental ability were found related, in Sears' study,[79] to various teacher behaviors which may provide such arousal. These included the frequency with which the teacher emphasizes the

[70] Ned A. Flanders, "Teacher Influence, Pupil Attitudes, and Achievement." Minneapolis: University of Minnesota (U.S. Office of Education Cooperative Research Project no. 397), 1960 (mimeographed).

[71] Donald E. P. Smith, "Fit Teaching Methods to Personality Structure," *High School Journal,* XXXIX (December, 1955), 167-71.

[72] Lauren G. Wispe, "Evaluating Section Teaching Methods in the Introductory Course," *Journal of Educational Research,* XLV (November, 1951), 161-86.

[73] Donald E. P. Smith, *op. cit.*

[74] Wispe, *op. cit.*

[75] Solomon E. Asch, "Effects of Group Pressure upon the Modification and Distortion of Judgments," in *Groups, Leadership, and Men.* Edited by H. Guetzkow. Pittsburgh: Carnegie Press, 1951.

[76] Jerome Kagan and Paul H. Mussen, "Dependency Themes on the TAT and Group Conformity," *Journal of Consulting Psychology,* XX (1956), 19-27.

[77] Norman Livson and Paul H. Mussen, "The Relation of Control to Overt Aggression and Dependency," *Journal of Abnormal and Social Psychology,* LV (1957), 66-71.

[78] Jerome Kagan, Lester W. Sontag, Charles T. Baker, and Virginia L. Nelson, "Personality and I.Q. Change," *Journal of Abnormal and Social Psychology,* LVI (1958), 261-66. [See Section IX, no. 53 in this book.]

[79] Sears, *op. cit.*

expanding and amplifying of ideas, giving of alternatives and possibilities rather than of straight statements of facts, and also the amount of listening to the child done by the teacher. These methods essentially stimulate but do not direct, and for bright children they seem to be effective in connection with achievement.

Another illustration of pupil personality as affecting responsiveness to teaching is that of Grimes and Allinsmith concerned with compulsivity and anxiety. . . . [A summary of the Grimes and Allinsmith material is here omitted because the original article is reprinted in this book (X, 68). Ed]

It appears that instructional methods make a difference for certain kinds of pupils, and a search for the preferred method of teaching can succeed only when consideration is given to the personality of the learner. On the other hand, many of the relationships cited are of only moderate size and based on selected samples of teachers. Definitive answers to questions of results of different instructional techniques await replication of new samples.

TEACHING PERSONALITY AND TEACHING EFFECTIVENESS. Heil, Powell, and Feifer[81] have related pupil achievement to interaction between teacher and pupil personalities. Three teacher and four pupil personality types were identified. The various teacher-pupil combinations were compared in terms of measures of pupil achievement, teacher knowledge, and classroom ratings. The well-integrated (self-controlling) teachers were the most effective with all types of students, whereas the weakly integrated (fearful) teachers were ineffective with everyone except the children identified as "strivers." The third type of teacher (turbulent) identified by these investigators is similar to a defensively intellectual person in using intellectualization as a mechanism of defense. The turbulent teachers were found to be effective with children who had been categorized as "conformers" or "strivers," particularly in mathematics and science achievement. They were ineffective with "opposers" and "waverers," two classroom-problem types requiring interpersonal skills to which these teachers were totally indifferent. The behavior of the "self-controlled teacher" suggests the importance

of consistency, structure, routine activities, and orderliness—especially for "opposing" or "wavering" (anxious) children. The criterion measure in this study was simply scores on achievement tests.

It was earlier pointed out that teacher warmth tends to be associated with the encouragement of creativity. Sears[82] found that teachers who like pupils tend to have pupils who like each other. Other aspects of teacher behavior related to the pupils' liking of each other include the manner in which such teachers use rewards and punishments. Rewards tend to be individualized, directed to the person, rather than to the group; punishments, however, are more often group-directed, hence reducing the sting of individual criticism. Children perhaps show liking for each other under these circumstances because the teaching techniques allow for social interchange without tension engendered by personal evaluation.

Thus, the teacher as a motivating agent operates in two interrelated ways. First, teacher personality and behavior act through a kind of contagion, in which the teacher becomes a model for appropriate behavior. The principles at work here are those of imitation and identification. Second, the teacher, as an administrator of rewards and punishments, wields power and creates a structure in which learning occurs. Here the principles are the more usual ones of positive and negative reinforcement. In addition, and in subtle ways, the child becomes an independent seeker and learner, satisfying his curiosity in his own ways and at his own pace.

The consequence of displaying interest in the individual child and his ideas, of acting in a warmly encouraging manner rather than in a critically evaluative one, is to produce a creative child, with a liking for the other children. The consequence of "efficient" teaching, in which the quiet industrious classroom is the goal, comes about through group methods and frequent evaluation, with a product neither high in conventional subject-matter achievement nor characterized particularly by new ideas or child-to-child affiliation. However, businesslike, well-organized teaching together with individualized attention to the student is associated with favorable learning outcomes, and structure appears to be favorable, at least on a short-term basis, for more anxious or dependent students. There are suggestions, however, that dependent students tend to become more dependent on au-

[81] L. M. Heil, Marion Powell, and I. Feifer, *Characteristics of Teacher Behavior Related to the Achievement of Children in Several Elementary Grades*. Washington: U.S. Department of Health, Education, and Welfare, Office of Education, Cooperative Research Branch, 1960.

[82] Sears, *op. cit.*

thority figures with directive teaching, and that
their achievement may be better in certain situations with less directive teaching.

SUMMARY AND CONCLUSIONS

The turmoil in learning theory at the present
time is reflected also in the uncertainty about
the relationship between motivation and learning. Some extreme positions assert that motivation affects only performance, not learning;
another viewpoint is that motivation is an irrelevant category, and that all learning is eventually
under the control of the stimulus. These uncertainties within the more abstract discussions of
learning theory need not detract from the practical importance of motivation in applied settings, where the distinction between learning
and performance becomes less important, and
where motivational dispositions are as relevant
as motivational arousal.

The kinds of motives that the teacher can
utilize and arouse are not the ones most often
studied in the animal laboratory (hunger, thirst,
and pain), but have more to do with personal
and social motives that characterize children
growing up in a particular culture. Even in the
laboratory there is a turn away from deprived
states to positive motives, such as activity, curiosity, and manipulation, to "hope" rather than
"fear" as fundamental. Among the motives that
the teacher necessarily uses in one way or another are the social (illustrated by warmth and
nurturance), the ego-integrative (illustrated by
the achievement motive), and the cognitive (illustrated by curiosity).

The school environment and atmosphere contribute to the arousal and support of particular
motives. (Various socioeconomic backgrounds
bring children to school with different expectations of achievement.) The ways in which pupils
are grouped may affect their teachableness by
given teachers. The ways in which the school is
set up will determine whether or not creativity
will be encouraged.

The current interest in making schools more
intellectually exciting can be described as an
effort to enhance and capitalize upon cognitive
motivation. Most of the new curricula more or
less take for granted that if students are free to
work out their own solutions to problems, if they
have an opportunity for divergent rather than
merely convergent thinking, intrinsic motivation
appears to be readily aroused.

Efforts to see how, in fact, teachers affect students have led to extensive observations of
teacher behavior, to attempts to relate this behavior to certain consequences in the behavior,
attitudes, and achievements of pupils. These
interactions are conveniently classified as affective, evaluative, and cognitive. Affective consequences arise through teacher efforts to maintain
control by way of reward and punishment;
many other affective consequences are related
to the anxieties created by the competitive situation in classrooms. Evaluation can be done
individually in such a manner as to threaten self-esteem, or it can be done according to group
standards and thus be less threatening. The non-academic behavior of students is of course evaluated, particularly in the effort to maintain
discipline; the judgment of severity of pupil problems tends today to conform more nearly to that
of clinicians than formerly. Cognitive interaction
of teachers and pupils lies at the heart of instruction. Some plausible conjectures about autocratic and democratic atmospheres do not
appear to be supported by some recent studies;
businesslike and matter-of-fact approaches tend
to yield achievement as well as creativity. At the
same time, support is given to nondirective approaches, apparently because they keep alive
the searching behavior important to divergent
thinking. Teachers who are insistent on quiet,
orderly behavior, who teach by informative
statements, produce task-oriented behavior favorable to convergent thinking; teachers who
show personal interest and who avoid critical
individual evaluation tend to favor the more
creative products of divergent thinking.

Child personality affects the ability to profit
from particular kinds of teaching. Compulsive
and anxious children respond differently from
those less compulsive and less anxious; for example, those high in these characteristics do
very well ("overachieve") in structured situations; those who are highly anxious, but low in
compulsivity, do poorly ("underachieve") in an
unstructured setting. Dependency tendencies
also affect the profit from particular kinds of
teaching. Hence, teachers must know their pupils and must be flexible in their approaches if
they are to have the most favorable results.

Teacher personality also has an influence on
teaching effectiveness. This is to be expected
because of the importance of the teacher as a
"model" for pupil behavior. In some comparisons
of self-controlling, fearful, and turbulent teachers, best results, by achievement measures, were
obtained by the self-controlled teachers. Another dimension—that of warmth—appears to af-

fect creativity, the warmer teachers encouraging divergent behavior. While perhaps there is little the teacher can do about his own personality, some self-awareness is no doubt helpful in avoiding extremes of unfavorable influence. Those responsible for teacher selection may be helped to make wiser choices when the results of some of these studies become better established.

The problems of motivation are so intertwined with problems of personality that an adequate account of motivation in relation to learning cannot rest solely on the findings of the learning laboratory. A classroom is a social situation, with a power structure, including peer relationships, and adult-child relationships; hence the most favorable motivational conditions need to take all of these factors into account, recognizing that the teacher is both model and reinforcer and, in ways not fully understood, a releaser of intrinsic motives.

XI/Specific Educational Implications

IN THIS SECTION WE PRESENT PAPERS WHICH FOCUS ON instructional issues and on cognitive learning as studied both in the laboratory and in the classroom. To varying degrees all of the determinants of behavior discussed in previous parts of the book affect the behaviors subsumed under the label "educational implications." Some psychologists, however, are interested in studying the conditions under which present cognitions occur without regard to the effects of group membership, constitution, intelligence, etc. The papers presented here will usually reflect this interest in cognition per se and/or in matters of direct relevance to the classroom.

The first two selections are by Jerome S. Bruner, Professor of Psychology and Director of the Center for Cognitive Studies at Harvard University. The first of these selections was Bruner's address to the American Psychological Association as its President. In the paper Bruner probes the relation between cognitive development and pedagogy and thus represents the dual concerns of this section. To convey a slightly different approach to similar problems, we cite here the opening section of a paper by N. L. Gage, Professor of Educational Psychology at Stanford University and editor of the extremely useful *Handbook of Research on Teaching* (Chicago: Rand McNally and Co., 1963).

What *must* (the teacher) do, if his behavior is to have the desired effect on the comprehension of his youngsters? How can the behavior of one person, a teacher, have an effect on another person's comprehension of a concept or principle? . . .

My answer, in very general terms, is that the teacher will manipulate the learner's environment, in accordance with the laws of logic and cognition, in the same way that he can influence another person's perceptions by manipulating the environment in accordance with the laws of perception. . . .

The teacher, by the same token, can compel us to comprehend concepts and principles, depending on whether the stimuli or ideas themselves exist in certain patterns, whether they have certain relationships to one another, and, of course, on whether the pupil has certain cognitive capacities, sets, and the like.[1]

Compare this with Bruner's statement

. . . Part of the failure of educational psychology was its failure to grasp the full scope of its mission. It has too readily assumed that its central task was the application of learning theory to education—or, in turn, the application of personality theory or of group dynamics or whatnot. In fact, none of these efforts produced a major contribution to educational practice largely because the task was not really one of application in any obvious sense, but of formulation. Learning theory, for example, is distilled from descriptions of behavior in situations where the environment has been arranged either for the convenience of observing learning behavior or out of a theoretical interest in some special aspect of learning—reinforcement, cue distinctiveness, or whatnot. But a theory of instruction, which must be at the heart of educational psychology, is principally concerned with *how* to arrange environments to *optimize* learning according to various criteria—e.g., to optimize transfer or retrievability of information or whatnot.[2]

[1] From N. L. Gage, Toward a cognitive theory of teaching, *Teachers College Record*, 1964, 65, 408-412 (p. 410). Reprinted by permission.

[2] From J. S. Bruner, Education as social invention, *The Journal of Social Issues*, 1964, 20, 21-33 (p. 32). Reprinted by permission.

In the second selection, Bruner shares with us some of his thinking about learning in present-day classrooms. His conclusions are based on both his laboratory research and his observations and experiments in schools.

For a further glance at problems in teaching see Bruner's *The Process of Education* (Harvard University Press, 1961). In this small book he sets forth his views of the conclusions reached by leading scholars and educators who attended the conference on new educational methods held in 1959 under the auspices of the National Academy of Science.

The third paper in this section summarizes a great deal of the evidence on a central topic of educational psychology, transfer of training. The paper is by Thomas C. Andrews of the University of Maryland and Lee J. Cronbach, Professor of Education and Psychology at Stanford University. Cronbach, a former President of the American Psychological Association and formerly at the University of Illinois, is a leading expert on psychological measurement and author of a widely used text in educational psychology. As an appetizer giving an idea of the scope of the problems of transfer we quote here the opening paragraphs of "Transfer of training in general education" by Lloyd G. Humphreys.

The expected outcomes of education do not always materialize. Time spent in training seems wasted when students are asked to use their learning in new situations. A group of children are taught multiplication combinations by rote alone. They later have great difficulty in utilizing their multiplication skills in long division. The graduates of a course in English literature, supposedly designed to promote literary appreciations, show no increase in either the quantity or the quality of their reading in comparison with their pre-course status. A Sunday-school teacher believes that she is engaged in moral training. Her charges acquire a great deal of biblical information, but there is no observable effect on their moral behavior. The information is also rather quickly forgotten. An instructor believes that his language course sharpens the intellect, but no generalized intellectual advantage can be observed in comparing his students with those of initially comparable ability who have had no language training. The claimed function of a laboratory course in physical science is to teach the scientific method. Not only does there seem to be no carry-over by the students to biological science or social science, but the skills and attitudes acquired are more those of the technician than of the scientist. It is claimed that geometry increases logical reasoning ability. The only measurable outcome of a traditional geometry course, however, is an increase in the ability to solve problems in geometry.

These problems are known in psychology as "transfer-of-training" problems; they were selected to dramatize the issue, since in each case someone expected transfer that did not occur. All of us make similar assumptions, either implicitly or explicitly, concerning possible transfer effects from our courses. Few of us attempt to check the validity of those assumptions. We need to know, first, whether transfer is possible in situations such as those described. Second, if transfer is possible, we need to know how to maximize it.

Questions such as the following pose similar problems: Does the usual music-appreciation course actually produce a change in the student's appreciation of music? If not, what can be done in the course to produce the desired change in student behavior? Do foreign-language courses promote international understanding? What are the transfer effects to later civilian status of compulsory military training for eighteen-year-olds? If these effects are undesirable, how can we change military training to promote desirable democratic objectives and still maintain our national security? How can we teach the graduates of our schools, as citizens of a democracy, to make intelligent choices concerning control of atomic energy, anti-vivisection legislation, protective tariffs, treatment of minorities, etc.?[3]

[3] From Lloyd G. Humphreys, Transfer of training in general education, *Journal of General Education*, 1951, 5, 210-216. Reprinted by permission.

The fourth paper is by Herbert G. Birch, of Albert Einstein College of Medicine and Yeshiva University, and Herbert S. Rabinowitz. It gives a rather dramatic example of the fact that transfer-of-training is not always beneficial or necessarily to be desired. One should remember the more general points made by Bruner in this connection.

The fifth article poses issues with respect to the organizational framework a person has on which he can "hang" new information. These issues are very important in terms of the problems of curriculum planning. The selection is by David P. Ausubel, a prolific author who does research at the Bureau of Educational Research and is Professor of Educational Psychology at the University of Illinois.

The sixth article questions some of the assumptions that underlie present-day achievement testing. Its author is Verner M. Sims, Professor of Education at the University of Alabama prior to his demise. The points he raised are very current. Compare them with the following quotation from Edward Joseph Shoben, Jr.

> . . . From such an analysis [as required for programming] . . . it might be possible to derive a curricular structure that would promote more in the amount of information learned and in the habits of reflective thought acquired than has heretofore been considered possible. Should such a state come to pass, individual differences will, of course, remain in learning outcomes. But these differences are more likely to be in how far various children go in completing a twelve-year course of study or in the branching directions they choose to follow in it. Parenthetically it may be noted that such an arrangement would have a decided implication for the meaning of grades. Ordinarily, a C, for example, currently implies that a pupil has less knowledge of a piecemeal sort in a whole segment of the curriculum (tenth grade social studies, for example) than a pupil with an A, more than a youngster receiving a D. Under the system envisioned here, the student with a C would have finished less work than his confrere with an A, but he would have achieved the same degree of competence at the point he has reached as his quicker colleague when he was at that point.[4]

In addition one should note that Sims's paper provides aid in understanding the complexities of evaluating new programs in teaching. The next article, also by Sims, is a brief discussion of the advantages and disadvantages of objective tests in the classroom.

The article which follows is addressed to a topic of tremendous concern today, the teaching of disadvantaged children. At the same time it makes keen observations about teaching in general. The article by Grimes and Allinsmith in Section X showed that children's school performance depended on the match between their personality characteristics and the type of teaching method used, thus rejecting the idea of a universally "good" method. The present article similarly rejects the notion of the universally "good" instructional approach. In addition it assumes that culturally disadvantaged children, though highly variable, are a describable pupil population in need of teachers uniquely "good" for them. The author, Dr. Miriam L. Goldberg, is at Teachers College, Columbia University.

[4] From E. J. Shoben, Jr., Viewpoints from related disciplines: learning theory, from the issue devoted to "What Shall the Schools Teach?" *Teachers College Record*, 1959, *60*, 272-282 (p. 279). Reprinted by permission.

The next paper is by Lumsdaine, mentioned in Section III, and Irving Janis, of Yale University. It concerns the effectiveness of communications designed to change people's ideas or beliefs. Although such communications are referred to as "propaganda," the possible implications for teachers in planning their classroom presentations are obvious. The book by Hovland, Lumsdaine, and Sheffield referred to in the article covers many other aspects of this area of psychology. Additional articles dealing with effectiveness of communication can be found in Section 4 of Maccoby, Newcomb, and Hartley, *Readings in Social Psychology* (Holt, 1958).

In recent years teaching machines have provoked both a great deal of work and a good deal of debate. The current models used (both theoretical and actual) are based on the earlier work of Skinner. Sidney L. Pressey, long at Ohio State University and now at the University of Arizona, is generally credited with being the first to devise a "teaching machine". As is frequently the case, the climate was not favorable at the time and not much development occurred. This is in marked contrast to what happened subsequent to Skinner's invention of a teaching machine. Pressey's recent article critical of the present ways such devices are being used may be consulted in the source footnoted here.[5] For an interesting critique by Pressey of current general problems in education, see his speech accepting the 1964 Edward Lee Thorndike Award.[6]

The last three articles in this book are devoted to the topic of new instructional methods. The first of these is by Charles S. Morrill, of the Mitre Corporation, and reviews the subject of teaching machines. Next comes a paper concerned with the problem of assessing the effectiveness of these new technologies of teaching. It provides further material on the problem of determing outcomes, a problem referred to in connection with one of Sims's articles above. This second paper is by Robert Glaser, Professor of Education and Psychology and Director of Research at the Learning Research and Development Center, University of Pittsburgh. In the final article Arthur W. Melton, of the University of Michigan, makes some thought-provoking and cautionary points with respect to the issues raised by teaching machines and programmed learning and to the problems of educational and psychological research generally. As such, it is a fitting epilogue to this collection.

[5] "A puncture of the huge 'programming' boom?" *Teachers College Record,* 1964, *65,* 413-418.

[6] "Two basic neglected psychoeducational problems," *American Psychologist,* 1965, *20,* 391-395.

71/THE GROWTH OF MIND[1]/JEROME S. BRUNER[*]

THESE PAST SEVERAL YEARS, I HAVE had the painful pleasure—and it has been both—of exploring two aspects of the cognitive processes that were new to me. One was cognitive development, the other pedagogy. I knew, as we all know, that the two were closely related, and it was my naive hope that, betimes, the relation would come clear to me. Indeed, 2 years ago when I first knew that in early September 1965 I would be standing here, delivering this lecture, I said to myself that I would use the occasion to set forth to my colleagues what I had been able to find out about this vexed subject, the relation of pedagogy and development. It seemed obvious then that in 2 years one could get to the heart of the matter.

The 2 years have gone by. I have had the privilege of addressing this distinguished audience (Bruner, 1964) on some of our findings concerning the development of cognitive processes in children, and I have similarly set forth what I hope are not entirely unreasonable ideas about pedagogy (Bruner, in press). I am still in a very deep quandary concerning the relation of these two enterprises. The heart of the matter still eludes me, but I shall stand by my resolve. I begin on this autobiographical note so that you may know in advance why this evening is more an exercise in conjecture than a cataloguing of solid conclusions.

What is most unique about man is that his growth as an individual depends upon the history of his species—not upon a history reflected in genes and chromosomes but, rather, reflected in a culture external to man's tissue and wider in scope than is embodied in any one man's competency. Perforce, then, the growth of mind is always growth assisted from the outside. And since a culture, particularly an advanced one, transcends the bounds of individual competence, the limits for individual growth are by definition greater than what any single person has previously attained. For the limits of growth depend on how a culture assists the individual to use such intellectual potential as he may pos-

sess. It seems highly unlikely—either empirically or canonically—that we have any realistic sense of the furthest reach of such assistance to growth.

The evidence today is that the full evolution of intelligence came as a result of bipedalism and tool using. The large human brain gradually evolved as a sequel to the first use of pebble tools by early near-man. To condense the story, a near-man, or hominid, with a slightly superior brain, using a pebble tool, could make out better in the niche provided by nature than a near-man who depended not on tools but on sheer strength and formidable jaws. Natural selection favored the primitive tool user. In time, thanks to his better chance of surviving and breeding, he became more so: The ones who survived had larger brains, smaller jaws, less ferocious teeth. In place of belligerent anatomy, they developed tools and a brain that made it possible to use them. Human evolution thereafter became less a matter of having appropriate fangs or claws and more one of using and later fashioning tools to express the powers of the larger brain that was also emerging. Without tools the brain was of little use, no matter how many hundred cubic centimeters of it there might be. Let it also be said that without the original programmatic capacity for fitting tools into a sequence of acts, early hominids would never have started the epigenetic progress that brought them to their present state. And as human groups stabilized tools became more complex and "shaped to pattern," so that it was no longer a matter of reinventing tools in order to survive, but rather of mastering the skills necessary for using them. In short, after a certain point in human evolution, the only means whereby man could fill his evolutionary niche was through the cultural transmission of the skills necessary for the use of priorly invented techniques, implements, and devices.

Two crucial parallel developments seem also to have occurred. As hominids became increasingly bipedal, with the freed hands necessary for using spontaneous pebble tools, selection also favored those with a heavier pelvic bony structure that could sustain the impacting strain of

[1] Address of the President to the Seventy-Third Annual Convention of the American Psychological Association, Chicago, September 4, 1965.

[*] Jerome S. Bruner, The growth of mind, *American Psychologist*, 1965, *20*, 12, 1007-1017. Reprinted by permission.

bipedal locomotion. The added strength came, of course, from a gradual closing down of the birth canal. There is an obstetrical paradox here: a creature with an increasingly larger brain but with a smaller and smaller birth canal to get through. The resolution seems to have been achieved through the immaturity of the human neonate, particularly cerebral immaturity that assures not only a smaller head, but also a longer period of transmitting the necessary skills required by human culture. During this same period, human language must have emerged, giving man not only a new and powerful way of representing reality but also increasing his power to assist the mental growth of the young to a degree beyond anything before seen in nature.

It is impossible, of course, to reconstruct the evolution in techniques of instruction in the shadow zone between hominids and man. I have tried to compensate by observing contemporary analogues of earlier forms, knowing full well that the pursuit of analogy can be dangerously misleading. I have spent many hours observing uncut films of the behavior of free-ranging baboons, films shot in East Africa by my colleague Irven DeVore with a very generous footage devoted to infants and juveniles. I have also had access to the unedited film archives of a hunting-gathering people living under roughly analogous ecological conditions, the !Kung Bushman of the Kalahari, recorded by Laurance and Lorna Marshall, brilliantly aided by their son John and daughter Elizabeth.[2] I have also worked directly but informally with the Wolof of Senegal, observing children in the bush and in French-style schools. Even more valuable than my own informal observations in Senegal were the systematic experiments carried out later by my colleague, Patricia Marks Greenfield (in press).

Let me describe very briefly some salient differences in the free learning patterns of immature baboons and among !Kung children. Baboons have a highly developed social life in their troops, with well-organized and stable dominance patterns. They live within a territory, protecting themselves from predators by joint action of the strongly built, adult males. It is striking that the behavior of baboon juveniles

is shaped principally by play with their peer group, play that provides opportunity for the spontaneous expression and practice of the component acts that, in maturity, will be orchestrated into either the behavior of the dominant male or of the infant-protective female. All this seems to be accomplished with little participation by any mature animals in the play of the juveniles. We know from the important experiments of Harlow and his colleagues (Harlow & Harlow, 1962) how devastating a disruption in development can be produced in subhuman primates by interfering with their opportunity for peer-group play and social interaction.

Among hunting-gathering humans, on the other hand, there is *constant* interaction between adult and child, or adult and adolescent, or adolescent and child. !Kung adults and children play and dance together, sit together, participate in minor hunting together, join in song and story telling together. At very frequent intervals, moreover, children are party to rituals presided over by adults—minor, as in the first haircutting, or major, as when a boy kills his first Kudu buck and goes through the proud but painful process of scarification. Children, besides, are constantly playing imitatively with the rituals, implements, tools, and weapons of the adult world. Young juvenile baboons, on the other hand, virtually never play with things or imitate directly large and significant sequences of adult behavior.

Note, though, that in tens of thousands of feet of !Kung film, one virtually never sees an instance of "teaching" taking place outside the situation where the behavior to be learned is relevant. Nobody "teaches" in our prepared sense of the word. There is nothing like school, nothing like lessons. Indeed, among the !Kung children there is very little "telling." Most of what we would call instruction is through showing. And there is no "practice" or "drill" as such save in the form of play modeled directly on adult models—play hunting, play bossing, play exchanging, play baby tending, play house making. In the end, every man in the culture knows nearly all there is to know about how to get on with life as a man, and every woman as a woman—the skills, the rituals and myths, the obligations and rights.

The change in the instruction of children in more complex societies is twofold. First of all, there is knowledge and skill in the culture far in excess of what any one individual knows. And so, increasingly, there develops an economical technique of instructing the young based heav-

2 I am greatly indebted to Irven DeVore and Educational Services Incorporated for the opportunity to view his films of free-ranging baboons, and to Laurance and Lorna Marshall for the opportunity to examine their incomparable archives. DeVore and the Marshalls have been generous in their counsel as well.

ily on *telling* out of context rather than *showing* in context. In literate societies, the practice becomes institutionalized in the school or the "teacher." Both promote this necessarily abstract way of instructing the young. The result of "teaching the culture" can, at its worst, lead to the ritual, rote nonsense that has led a generation of critics from Max Wertheimer (1945) to Mary Alice White (undated) of Teachers' College to despair. For in the detached school, what is imparted often has little to do with life as lived in the society except insofar as the demands of school are of a kind that reflect *indirectly* the demands of life in a technical society. But these indirectly imposed demands may be the most important feature of the detached school. For school is a sharp departure from indigenous practice. It takes learning, as we have noted, out of the context of immediate action just by dint of putting it into a school. This very extirpation makes learning become an act in itself, freed from the immediate ends of action, preparing the learner for the chain of reckoning remote from payoff that is needed for the formulation of complex ideas. At the same time, the school (if successful) frees the child from the pace setting of the round of daily activity. If the school succeeds in avoiding a pace-setting round of its own, it may be one of the great agents for promoting reflectiveness. Moreover, in school, one must "follow the lesson" which means one must learn to follow either the abstraction of written speech—abstract in the sense that it is divorced from the concrete situation to which the speech might originally have been related—or the abstraction of language delivered orally but out of the context of an ongoing action. Both of these are highly abstract uses of language.

It is no wonder, then, that many recent studies report large differences between "primitive" children who are in schools and their brothers who are not: differences in perception, abstraction, time perspective, and so on. I need only cite the work of Biesheuvel (1949) in South Africa, Gay and Cole (undated) in Liberia, Greenfield (in press) in Senegal, Maccoby and Modiano (in press) in rural Mexico, Reich (in press) among Alaskan Eskimos.

What a culture does to assist the development of the powers of mind of its members is, in effect, to provide amplification systems to which human beings, equipped with appropriate skills, can link themselves. There are, first, the amplifiers of action—hammers, levers, digging sticks, wheels—but more important, the programs of action into which such implements can be substituted. Second, there are amplifiers of the senses, ways of looking and noticing that can take advantage of devices ranging from smoke signals and hailers to diagrams and pictures that stop the action or microscopes that enlarge it. Finally and most powerfully, there are amplifiers of the thought processes, ways of thinking that employ language and formation of explanation, and later use such languages as mathematics and logic and even find automatic servants to crank out the consequences. A culture is, then, a deviser, a repository, and a transmitter of amplification systems and of the devices that fit into such systems. We know very little in a deep sense about the transmission function, how people are trained to get the most from their potential by use of a culture's resources.

But it is reasonably clear that there is a major difference between the mode of transmission in a technical society, with its schools, and an indigenous one, where cultural transmission is in the context of action. It is not just that an indigenous society, when its action pattern becomes disrupted falls apart—at a most terrifying rate—as in uncontrolled urbanization in some parts of Africa. Rather, it is that the institution of a school serves to convert knowledge and skill into more symbolical, more abstract, more verbal form. It is this process of transmission—admittedly very new in human history—that is so poorly understood and to which, finally, we shall return.

There are certain obvious specifications that can be stated about how a society must proceed in order to equip its young. It must convert what is to be known—whether a skill or a belief system or a connected body of knowledge—into a form capable of being mastered by a beginner. The more we know of the process of growth, the better we shall be at such conversion. The failure of modern man to understand mathematics and science may be less a matter of stunted abilities than our failure to understand how to teach such subjects. Second, given the limited amount of time available for learning, there must be a due regard for saving the learner from needless learning. There must be some emphasis placed on economy and transfer and the learning of general rules. All societies must (and virtually all do) distinguish those who are clever from those who are stupid—though few of them generalize this trait across all activities. Cleverness in a particular activity almost universally connotes strategy, economy, heuristics, highly generalized skills. A society must also place emphasis upon how one derives a course of action from what one has learned. Indeed, in an indigenous society, it is almost impossible to separate what one does from what one knows. More advanced societies often have not found a way of dealing with the separation of knowledge and action—probably a result of the emphasis they place upon "telling" in their instruction. All societies must maintain interest among the young in the learning process, a minor problem when learning is in the context of life and action, but harder when it becomes more abstracted. And finally, and perhaps most obviously, a society must assure that its necessary skills and procedures remain intact from one generation to the next—which does not always happen, as witnessed by Easter Islanders, Incas, Aztecs, and Mayas.[3]

Unfortunately, psychology has not concerned itself much with any of these five requisites of cultural transmission—or at least not much with four of them. We have too easily assumed that learning is learning is learning—that the early version of what was taught did not matter much, one thing being much like another and reducible to a pattern of association, to stimulus-response connections, or to our favorite molecular componentry. We denied there was a problem of development beyond the quantitative one of providing more experience, and with the denial, closed our eyes to the pedagogical problem of how to represent knowledge, how to sequence it, how to embody it in a form appropriate to young learners. We expended more passion on the part-whole controversy than on what whole or what part of it was to be presented first. I should except Piaget (1954), Kohler (1940), and Vygotsky (1962) from these complaints—all until recently unheeded voices.

Our neglect of the economy of learning stems, ironically, from the heritage of Ebbinghaus (1913), who was vastly interested in savings. Our nonsense syllables, our random mazes

[3] I have purposely left out of the discussion the problems of impulse regulation and socialization of motives, topics that have received extended treatment in the voluminous literature on culture and personality. The omission is dictated by emphasis rather than evaluation. Obviously, the shaping of character by culture is of great importance for an understanding of our topic as it bears, for example, upon culture-instilled attitudes toward the uses of mind. Since our emphasis is upon human potential and its amplification by culturally patterned instrumental skills, we mention the problem of character formation in passing and in recognition of its importance in a complete treatment of the issues under discussion.

failed to take into account how we reduce complexity and strangeness to simplicity and the familiar, how we convert what we have learned into rules and procedures, how, to use Bartlett's (1932) term of over 30 years ago, we turn around on our own schemata to reorganize what we have mastered into more manageable form.

Nor have we taken naturally to the issue of knowledge and action. Its apparent mentalism has repelled us. Tolman (1951), who bravely made the distinction, was accused of leaving his organisms wrapt in thought. But he recognized the problem and if he insisted on the idea that knowledge might be organized in cognitive maps, it was in recognition (as a great functionalist) that organisms go somewhere on the basis of what they have learned. I believe we are getting closer to the problem of how knowledge affects action and vice versa, and offer in testimony of my conviction the provocative book by Miller, Galanter, and Pribram (1960), *Plans and the Structure of Behavior.*

Where the maintenance of the learner's interest is concerned, I remind you of what my colleague Gordon Allport (1946) has long warned. We have been so concerned with the model of driven behavior, with drive reduction and the *vis a tergo* that, again, until recently, we have tended to overlook the question of what keeps learners interested in the activity of learning, in the achievement of competence beyond bare necessity and first payoff. The work of R. W. White (1959) on effectance motivation, of Harlow and his colleagues (Butler, 1954; Harlow, 1953) on curiosity, and of Heider (1958) and Festinger (1962) on consistency begins to redress the balance. But it is only a beginning.

The invention of antidegradation devices, guarantors that skill and knowledge will be maintained intact, is an exception to our oversight. We psychologists have been up to our ears in it. Our special contribution is the achievement test. But the achievement test has, in the main, reflected the timidity of the educational enterprise as a whole. I believe we know how to determine, though we have not yet devised tests to determine, how pupils use what they learn to think with later in life—for there is the real issue.

I have tried to examine briefly what a culture must do in passing on its amplifying skills and knowledge to a new generation and, even more briefly, how we as psychologists have dealt or failed to deal with the problems. I think the situation is fast changing—with a sharp increase in interest in the conversion problem, the problems of economy of learning, the nature of interest, the relation of knowledge and action. We are, I believe, at a major turning point where psychology will once again concern itself with the design of methods of assisting cognitive growth, be it through the invention of a rational technology of toys, of ways of enriching the environment of the crib and nursery, of organizing the activity of a school, or of devising a curriculum whereby we transmit an organized body of knowledge and skill to a new generation to amplify their powers of mind.

I commented earlier that there was strikingly little knowledge available about the "third way" of training the skills of the young: the first being the play practice of component skills in prehuman primates, the second the teaching-in-context of indigenous societies, and the third being the abstracted, detached method of the school.

Let me now become highly specific. Let me consider a particular course of study, one given in a school, one we are ourselves constructing, trying out, and in a highly qualitative way, evaluating. It is for schools of the kind that exist in Western culture. The experience we have had with this effort, now in its third year, may serve to highlight the kinds of problems and conjectures one encounters in studying how to assist the growth of intellect in this "third way."

There is a dilemma in describing a course of study. One begins by setting forth the intellectual substance of what is to be taught. Yet if such a recounting tempts one to "get across" the subject, the ingredient of pedagogy is in jeopardy. For only in a trivial sense is a course designed to "get something across," merely to impart information. There are better means to that end than teaching. Unless the learner develops his skills, disciplines his taste, deepens his view of the world, the "something" that is got across is hardly worth the effort of transmission.

The more "elementary" a course and the younger its students, the more serious must be its pedagogical aim of forming the intellectual powers of those whom it serves. It is as important to justify a good mathematics course by the intellectual discipline it provides or the honesty it promotes as by the mathematics it transmits. Indeed, neither can be accomplished without the other. The content of this particular course is man: his nature as a species, the forces that shaped and continue to shape his humanity. Three questions recur throughout:

What is human about human beings?
How did they get that way?
How can they be made more so?

In pursuit of our questions we explore five matters, each closely associated with the evolution of man as a species, each defining at once the distinctiveness of man and his potentiality for further evolution. The five great humanizing forces are, of course, tool making, language, social organization, the management of man's prolonged childhood, and man's urge to explain. It has been our first lesson in teaching that no pupil, however eager, can appreciate the relevance of, say, tool making or language in human evolution without first grasping the fundamental concept of a tool or what a language is. These are not self-evident matters, even to the expert. So we are involved in teaching not only the role of tools or language in the emergence of man, but, as a necessary precondition for doing so, setting forth the fundamentals of linguistics or the theory of tools. And it is as often the case as not that (as in the case of the "theory of tools") we must solve a formidable intellectual problem ourselves in order to be able to help our pupils do the same. I should have said at the outset that the "we" I employ in this context is no editorial fiction, but rather a group of anthropologists, zoologists, linguists, theoretical engineers, artists, designers, camera crews, teachers, children, and psychologists. The project is being carried out under my direction at Educational Services Incorporated, with grants from the National Science Foundation and the Ford Foundation.

While one readily singles out five sources of man's humanization, under no circumstances can they be put into airtight compartments. Human kinship is distinctively different from primate mating patterns precisely because it is classificatory and rests on man's ability to use language. Or, if you will, tool use enhances the division of labor in a society which in turn affects kinship. So while each domain can be treated as a separate set of ideas, their teaching must make it possible for the children to have a sense of their interaction. We have leaned heavily on the use of contrast, highly controlled contrast, to help children achieve detachment from the all too familiar matrix of social life: the contrasts of man versus higher primates, man versus prehistoric man, contemporary technological man versus "primitive" man, and man versus child. The primates are principally baboons, the prehistoric materials mostly from the Olduvai Gorge and

Les Eyzies, the "primitive" peoples mostly the Netsilik Eskimos of Pelly Bay and the !Kung Bushmen. The materials, collected for our purposes, are on film, in story, in ethnography, in pictures and drawings, and principally in ideas embodied in exercises.

We have high aspirations. We hope to achieve five goals:

1. To give our pupils respect for and confidence in the powers of their own minds

2. To give them respect, moreover, for the powers of thought concerning the human condition, man's plight, and his social life

3. To provide them with a set of workable models that make it simpler to analyze the nature of the social world in which they live and the condition in which man finds himself.

4. To impart a sense of respect for the capacities and plight of man as a species, for his origins, for his potential, for his humanity

5. To leave the student with a sense of the unfinished business of man's evolution

One last word about the course of study that has to do with the quality of the ideas, materials, and artistry—a matter that is at once technological and intellectual. We have felt that the making of such a curriculum deserved the best talent and technique available in the world. Whether artist, ethnographer, film maker, poet, teacher—nobody we have asked has refused us. We are obviously going to suffer in testing a Hawthorne effect[Ed] of some magnitude. But then, perhaps it is as well to live in a permanent state of revolution.

Let me now try to describe some of the major problems one encounters in trying to construct a course of study. I shall not try to translate the problems into refined theoretical form, for they do not as yet merit such translation. They are more difficulties than problems. I choose them, because they are vividly typical of what one encounters in such enterprises. The course is designed for 10-year-olds in the fifth grade of elementary school, but we have been trying it

out as well on the fourth and sixth grades better to bracket our difficulties.

One special point about these difficulties. They are born of trying to achieve an objective and are as much policy bound as theory bound. It is like the difference between building an economic theory about monopolistic practices and constructing policies for controlling monopoly. Let me remind you that modern economic theory has been reformulated, refined, and revived by having a season in policy. I am convinced that the psychology of assisted growth, i.e., pedagogy, will have to be forged in the policy crucible of curriculum making before it can reach its full descriptive power as theory. Economics was first through the cycle from theory to policy to theory to policy; it is happening now to psychology, anthropology, and sociology.

Now on to the difficulties. The first is what might be called *the psychology of a subject matter.* A learned discipline can be conceived as a way of thinking about certain phenomena. Mathematics is one way of thinking about order without reference to what is being ordered. The behavioral sciences provide one or perhaps several ways of thinking about man and his society —about regularities, origins, causes, effects. They are probably special (and suspect) because they permit man to look at himself from a perspective that is outside his own skin and beyond his own preferences—at least for awhile.

Underlying a discipline's "way of thought," there is a set of connected, varyingly implicit, generative propositions. In physics and mathematics, most of the underlying generative propositions like the conservation theorems, or the axioms of geometry, or the associative, distributive, and commutative rules of analysis are by now very explicit indeed. In the behavioral sciences we must be content with more implicitness. We traffic in inductive propositions: e.g., the different activities of a society are interconnected such that if you know something about the technological response of a society to an environment, you will be able to make some shrewd guesses about its myths or about the things it values, etc. We use the device of a significant contrast as in linguistics as when we describe the territoriality of a baboon troop in order to help us recognize the system of reciprocal exchange of a human group, the former somehow provoking awareness of the latter.

There is nothing more central to a discipline than its way of thinking. There is nothing more important in its teaching than to provide the

---

Ed *An effect often observed when new procedures are introduced. It consists of an increase in productivity, irrespective of changing conditions of work, because of improvement in mental attitude of the workers as a result of their being subjects in an experiment. For example, not only may production increase if lighting conditions are bettered, it may also increase if they are worsened. Because of discovery of this effect, we know that heightened performances of workers or students who are participants in a new plan or program may not be indicative of the long-term value of the innovation but may, in some cases, be solely the consequence of raised morale.*

child the earliest opportunity to learn that way of thinking—the forms of connection, the attitudes, hopes, jokes, and frustrations that go with it. In a word, the best introduction to a subject is the subject itself. At the very first breath, the young learner should, we think, be given the chance to solve problems, to conjecture, to quarrel as these are done at the heart of the discipline. But, you will ask, how can this be arranged?

Here again the problem of conversion. There exist ways of thinking characteristic of different stages of development. We are acquainted with Inhelder and Piaget's (1958) account of the transition from preoperational, through concrete operational, to propositional thought in the years from preschool through, say, high school. If you have an eventual pedagogical objective in mind, you can translate the way of thought of a discipline into its Piagetian (or other) equivalent appropriate to a given level of development and take the child onward from there. The Cambridge Mathematics Project of Educational Services, Incorporated, argues that if the child is to master the calculus early in his high school years, he should start work early with the idea of limits, the earliest work being manipulative, later going on to images and diagrams, and finally moving on to the more abstract notation needed for delineating the more precise idea of limits.

In "Man: A Course of Study," (Bruner, 1965) there are also versions of the subject appropriate to a particular age that can at a later age be given a more powerful rendering. We have tried to choose topics with this in mind: The analysis of kinship that begins with children using sticks and blocks and colors and whatnot to represent their own families, goes on to the conventional kinship diagrams by a meandering but, as you can imagine, interesting path, and then can move on to more formal and powerful componential analysis. So, too, with myth. We begin with the excitement of a powerful myth (like the Netsilik Nuliajik myth), then have the children construct some myths of their own, then examine what a set of Netsilik myths have in common, which takes us finally to Lévi-Strauss's (1963) analysis of contrastive features in myth construction. A variorum text of a myth or corpus of myths put together by sixth graders can be quite an extraordinary document.

This approach to the psychology of a learned discipline turns out to illuminate another problem raised earlier: the maintenance of interest.

There is, in this approach, a reward in understanding that grows from the subject matter itself. It is easier to engineer this satisfaction in mathematics, for understanding is so utter in a formal discipline—a balance beam balances or it does not: therefore there is an equality or there is not. In the behavioral sciences the payoff in understanding cannot be so obviously and startlingly self-revealing. Yet, one can design exercises in the understanding of man, too—as when children figure out the ways in which, given limits of ecology, skills, and materials, Bushmen hunt different animals, and then compare their predictions with the real thing on film.

Consider now a second problem: *how to stimulate thought in the setting of a school.* We know from experimental studies like those of Bloom and Broder (1950), and of Goodnow and Pettigrew (1955), that there is a striking difference in the acts of a person who thinks that the task before him represents a problem to be solved rather than being controlled by random forces. School is a particular subculture where these matters are concerned. By school age, children have come to expect quite arbitrary and, from their point of view, meaningless demands to be made upon them by adults—the result, most likely, of the fact that adults often fail to recognize the task of conversion necessary to make their questions have some intrinsic significance for the child. Children, of course, will try to solve problems if they recognize them as such. But they are not often either predisposed to or skillful in problem finding, in recognizing the hidden conjectural feature in tasks set them. But we know now that children in school can quite quickly be led to such problem finding by encouragement and instruction.

The need for this instruction and encouragement and its relatively swift success relates, I suspect, to what psychoanalysts refer to as the guilt-ridden oversuppression of primary process[Ed] and its public replacement by secondary process. Children, like adults, need reassurance that it is all right to entertain and express highly subjective ideas, to treat a task as a problem where you *invent* an answer rather than *finding* one out there in the book or on the blackboard. With children in elementary school, there is often a need to devise emotionally vivid special games, story-making episodes, or construction projects to reestablish in the child's mind his right not only to have his own private ideas but

[Ed] *For a further explication of this concept, see Section X, no. 61.*

to express them in the public setting of a classroom.

But there is another, perhaps more serious difficulty: the interference of intrinsic problem solving by extrinsic. Young children in school expend extraordinary time and effort figuring out what it is that the teacher wants—and usually coming to the conclusion that she or he wants tidiness or remembering or to do things at a certain time in a certain way. This I refer to as extrinsic problem solving. There is a great deal of it in school.

There are several quite straightforward ways of stimulating problem solving. One is to train teachers to want it and that will come in time. But teachers can be encouraged to like it, interestingly enough, by providing them and their children with materials and lessons that *permit* legitimate problem solving and permit the teacher to recognize it. For exercises with such materials create an atmosphere by treating things as instances of what *might* have occurred rather than simply as what did occur. Let me illustrate by a concrete instance. A fifth-grade class was working on the organization of a baboon troop—on this particular day, specifically on how they might protect against predators. They saw a brief sequence of film in which six or seven adult males go forward to intimidate and hold off three cheetahs. The teacher asked what the baboons had done to keep the cheetahs off, and there ensued a lively discussion of how the dominant adult males, by showing their formidable mouthful of teeth and making threatening gestures had turned the trick. A boy raised a tentative hand and asked whether cheetahs always attacked together. Yes, though a single cheetah sometimes followed behind a moving troop and picked off an older, weakened straggler or an unwary, straying juvenile. "Well, what if there were four cheetahs and two of them attacked from behind and two from in front. What would the baboons do then?" The question could have been answered empirically—and the inquiry ended. Cheetahs *do not* attack that way, and so we do not know what baboons *might* do. Fortunately, it was not. For the question opens up the deep issues of what might be and why it is not. Is there a necessary relation between predators and prey that share a common ecological niche? Must their encounters have a "sporting chance" outcome? It is such conjecture, in this case quite unanswerable, that produces rational, self-consciously problem-finding behavior so crucial to the growth of intellectual power. Given the materials, given some background

and encouragement, teachers like it as much as the students.

I should like to turn now to the *personalization of knowledge*. A generation ago, the progressive movement urged that knowledge be related to the child's own experience and brought out of the realm of empty abstractions. A good idea was translated into banalities about the home, then the friendly postman and trashman, then the community, and so on. It is a poor way to compete with the child's own dramas and mysteries. A decade ago, my colleague Clyde Kluckhorn (1949) wrote a prize-winning popular book on anthropology with the entrancing title *Mirror for Man*. In some deep way, there is extraordinary power in "that mirror which other civilizations still hold up to us to recognize and study . . . [the] image of ourselves [Lévi-Strauss, 1965]." The psychological bases of the power are not obvious. Is it as in discrimination learning, where increasing the degree of contrast helps in the learning of a discrimination, or as in studies of concept attainment where a negative instance demonstrably defines the domain of a conceptual rule? Or is it some primitive identification? All these miss one thing that seems to come up frequently in our interviews with the children. It is the experience of discovering kinship and likeness in what at first seemed bizarre, exotic, and even a little repellant.

Consider two examples, both involving film of the Netsilik. In the films, a single nuclear family, Zachary, Marta, and their 4-year-old Alexi, is followed through the year—spring sealing, summer fishing at the stone weir, fall caribou hunting, early winter fishing through the ice, winter at the big ceremonial igloo. Children report that at first the three members of the family look weird and uncouth. In time, they look normal, and eventually, as when Marta finds sticks around which to wrap her braids, the girls speak of how pretty she is. That much is superficial—or so it seems. But consider a second episode.

It has to do with Alexi who, with his father's help, devises a snare and catches a gull. There is a scene in which he stones the gull to death. Our children watched, horror struck. One girl, Kathy, blurted out, "He's not even human, doing that to the seagull." The class was silent. Then another girl, Jennine, said quietly: "He's got to grow up to be a hunter. His mother was smiling when he was doing that." And then an extended discussion about how people have to do things to learn and even do things to learn how to feel appropriately. "What would you do if you had to live there? Would you be as smart about getting along as they are with what they've got?" said one boy, going back to the accusation that Alexi was inhuman to stone the bird.

I am sorry it is so difficult to say it clearly. What I am trying to say is that to personalize knowledge one does not simply link it to the familiar. Rather one makes the familiar an instance of a more general case and thereby produces awareness of it. What the children were learning about was not seagulls and Eskimos, but about their own feelings and preconceptions that, up to then, were too implicit to be recognizable to them.

Consider finally the problem of *self-conscious reflectiveness*. It is an epistemological mystery why traditional education has so often emphasized extensiveness and coverage over intensiveness and depth. We have already commented on the fact that memorizing was usually perceived by children as one of the high-priority tasks but rarely did children sense an emphasis upon ratiocination with a view toward redefining what had been encountered, reshaping it, reordering it. The cultivation of reflectiveness, or whatever you choose to call it, is one of the great problems one faces in devising curriculum. How lead children to discover the powers and pleasures that await the exercise of retrospection?

Let me suggest one answer that has grown from what we have done. It is the use of the "organizing conjecture." We have used three such conjectures—what is human about human beings, how they got that way, how they could become more so. They serve two functions, one of them the very obvious though important one of putting perspective back into the particulars. The second is less obvious and considerably more surprising. The questions often seemed to serve as criteria for determining where they were getting, how well they were understanding, whether anything new was emerging. Recall Kathy's cry: "He's not human doing that to the seagull." She was hard at work in her rage on the conjecture what makes human beings human.

There, in brief, are four problems that provide some sense of what a psychologist encounters when he takes a hand in assisting the growth of mind in children in the special setting of a school. The problems look quite different from those we encounter in formulating classical developmental theory with the aid of typical laboratory research. They also look very different from those that one would find in an indigenous society, describing how children picked up skills and knowledge and values in the context of action and daily life. We clearly do not have a theory of the school that is sufficient to the task of running schools—just as we have no adequate theory of toys or of readiness building or whatever the jargon is for preparing children to do a better job the next round. It only obscures the issue to urge that some day our classical theories of learning will fill the gap. They show no sign of doing so.

I hope that we shall not allow ourselves to be embarrassed by our present ignorance. It has been a long time since we have looked at what is involved in imparting knowledge through the vehicle of the school—if ever we did look at it squarely. I urge that we delay no longer.

But I am deeply convinced that the psychologist cannot alone construct a theory of how to assist cognitive development and cannot alone learn how to enrich and amplify the powers of a growing human mind. The task belongs to the whole intellectual community: the behavioral scientists and the artists, scientists, and scholars who are the custodians of skill, taste, and knowledge in our culture. Our special task as psychologists is to convert skills and knowledge to forms and exercises that fit growing minds—and it is a **task ranging from how to keep children free** from anxiety to how to translate physics for the very young child into a set of playground maneuvers that, later, the child can turn around upon and convert into a sense of inertial regularities.

And this in turn leads me to a final conjecture, one that has to do with the organization of our profession, a matter that has concerned me greatly during this past year during which I have had the privilege of serving as your President. Psychology is peculiarly prey to parochialism. Left to our own devices, we tend to construct models of a man who is neither a victim of history, a target of economic forces, or even a working member of a society. I am still struck by Roger Barker's (1963) ironic truism that the best way to predict the behavior of a human being is to know where he is: In a post office he behaves post office, at church he behaves church.

Psychology, and you will forgive me if the image seems a trifle frivolous, thrives on polygamy with her neighbors. Our marriage with the biological sciences has produced a cumulation of ever more powerful knowledge. So, too, our joint undertakings with anthropology and sociology. Joined together with a variety of disciplines, we have made lasting contributions now that the emphasis is shifting to the problems of alleviating stress and arranging for a community's mental health. What I find lacking is an alignment that might properly be called the growth sciences. The field of pedagogy is one participant in the growth sciences. Any field of inquiry devoted to assisting the growth of effective human beings, fully empowered with zest, with skill, with knowledge, with taste is surely a candidate for this sodality. My friend Philip Morrison once suggested to his colleagues at Cornell that his department of physics grant a doctorate not only for work in theoretical, experimental, or applied physics, but also for work in pedagogical physics. The limits of the growth sciences remain to be drawn. They surely transcend the behavioral sciences cum pediatrics. It is plain that, if we are to achieve the effectiveness of which we as human beings are capable, there will one day have to be such a field. I hope that we psychologists can earn our way as charter members.

REFERENCES

ALLPORT, G. Effect: A secondary principle of learning. *Psychological Review*, 1946, *53*, 335-347.

BARKER, R. On the nature of the environment. *Journal of Social Issues*, 1963, *19*, 17-38.

BARTLETT, F. *Remembering*. Cambridge, England: Cambridge Univer. Press, 1932.

BIESHEUVEL, S. Psychological tests and their application to non-European peoples. *Yearbook of Education*. London: Evans, 1949. Pp. 87-126.

BLOOM, B., & BRODER, L. Problem solving processes of college students. *Supplementary Educational Monograph, No. 73*. Chicago: Univer. Chicago Press, 1950.

BRUNER, J. The course of cognitive growth. *American Psychologist*, 1964, *19*, 1-15.

BRUNER, J. Man: A course of study. *Educational Services Inc. Quarterly Report*, 1965, Spring-Summer, 3-13.

BRUNER, J. *Toward a theory of instruction*. Cambridge: Harvard Univer. Press, in press.

BUTLER, R. A. Incentive conditions which influence visual exploration. *Journal of Experimental Psychology*, 1954, *48*, 19-23.

EBBINGHAUS, H. *Memory: A Contribution to experimental Psychology*. New York: Teachers College, Columbia University, 1913.

FESTINGER, L. A theory of cognitive dissonance. Stanford: Stanford Univer. Press, 1962.

GAY, J., & COLE, M. Outline of general report on Kpelle mathematics project. Stanford: Stanford University, Institute for Mathematical Social Studies, undated. (Mimeo)

GOODNOW, JACQUELINE, & PETTIGREW, T. Effect of prior patterns of experience on strategies and learning sets. *Journal of Experimental Psychology*, 1955, *49*, 381-389.

GREENFIELD, PATRICIA M. Culture and conservation. In J. Bruner, Rose Olver, & Patricia M. Greenfield (Eds.), *Studies in cognitive growth*. New York: Wiley, in press. Ch. 10.

HARLOW, H., & HARLOW, MARGARET. Social deprivation in monkeys. *Scientific American*, 1962, November.

HARLOW, H. F. Mice, monkeys, men, and motives. *Psychological Review*, 1953, *60*, 23-32.

HEIDER, F. *The psychology of interpersonal relations*. New York: Wiley, 1958.

INHELDER, BARBEL, & PIAGET, J. *The growth of logical thinking*. New York: Basic Books, 1958.

KLUCKHORN, C. *Mirror for man*. New York: Whittlesey House, 1949.

KOHLER, W. *Dynamics in psychology*. New York: Liveright, 1940.

LEVI-STRAUSS, C. The structural study of myth. *Structural anthropology*. (Trans. by Claire Jacobson & B. Grundfest Scharpf) New York: Basic Books, 1963. Pp. 206-231.

LEVI-STRAUSS, C. Anthropology: Its achievements and future. Lecture presented at Bicentennial Celebration, Smithsonian Institution, Washington, D. C., September 1965

MACCOBY, M., & MODIANO, NANCY. On culture and equivalence. In J. Bruner, Rose Olver, & Patricia M. Greenfield (Eds.), *Studies in cognitive growth*. New York: Wiley, in press. Ch. 12.

MILLER, G., GALANTER, E., & PRIBRAM, K. *Plans and the structure of behavior*. New York: Holt, 1960.

PIAGET, J. *The construction of reality in the child*. New York: Basic Books, 1954.

REICH, LEE. On culture and grouping. In J. Bruner, Rose Olver, & Patricia M. Greenfield (Eds.), *Studies in cognitive growth*. New York: Wiley, in press. Ch. 13.

TOLMAN, E. Cognitive maps in rats and men. *Collected papers in psychology*. Berkeley & Los Angeles: Univer. California Press, 1951. Pp. 241-264.

VYGOTSKY, L. *Thought and language*. (Ed. & trans. by Eugenia Hanfmann & Gertrude Vakar) New York: Wiley, 1962.

WERTHEIMER, M. *Productive thinking*. New York & London: Harper, 1945.

WHITE, MARY A. The child's world of learning. Teachers College, Columbia University, undated. (Mimeo)

WHITE, R. W. Motivation reconsidered: The concept of competence. *Psychological Review*, 1959, *66*, 297-333.

72/LEARNING AND THINKING[1]/

JEROME S. BRUNER[*]

I

I HAVE BEEN ENGAGED, THESE LAST few years, in research on what makes it possible for organisms—human and subhuman alike—to take advantage of past learning in attempting to deal with and master new problems before them now. It is a problem with a deceptively simple ring to it. In pursuit of it, my colleagues and I have found ourselves observing children in schoolrooms, watching them learning. It has been a revealing experience.

We have come to recognize in this work that one of the principal objectives of learning is to save us from subsequent learning. This seems a paradox, but it is not. Another way of putting the matter is to say that when we learn something, the objective is to learn it in such a way that we get a maximum of travel out of what we have learned. A homely example is provided by the relationship in arithmetic between addition and multiplication. If the principle of addition has been grasped in its deeper sense, in its generic sense, then it is unnecessary to learn multiplication. For, in principle, multiplication is only repeated addition. It is not, as we would say in our curricula, another "unit."

Learning something in a generic way is like leaping over a barrier. On the other side of the barrier is thinking. When the generic has been grasped, it is then that we are able to recognize the new problems we encounter as exemplars of old principles we have mastered. Once over the barrier, we are able to benefit from what William James long ago called "the electric sense of analogy."

There are two interesting features in generic learning—in the kind of learning that permits us to cross the barrier into thinking. One of them is *organization;* the other is *manipulation.* If we are to use our past learning, we must organize it in such a way that it is no longer bound to the specific situation in which the learning occurred. Let me give an example from the history of science. It would have been possible for Galileo to have published a handbook for the distances

traversed per unit time by falling bodies. School boys for centuries thereafter could easily have been tortured by the task of having to remember the Galilean tables. Such tables, cumbersome though they might have been, would have contained all the necessary information for dealing with free-falling bodies. Instead, Galileo had the inspiration to reorganize this welter of information into a highly simplified form. You recall the compact expression $S = \frac{1}{2} gt^2$: it not only summarizes all possible handbooks but organizes their knowledge in a way that makes manipulation possible. Not only do we know the distances fallen, but we can use the knowledge for bodies that fall anywhere, in any gravitational field—not just our own.

One of the most notable things about the human mind is its limited capacity for dealing at any one moment with diverse arrays of information. It has been known for a long time that we can deal only with about seven independent items of information at once; beyond that point we exceed our "channel capacity," to use our current jargon. We simply cannot manipulate large masses of information. Because of these limits, we must condense and recode. The seven things we deal with must be worth their weight. A simple formula that can regenerate the distance fallen by any free body, past or future, is under these conditions highly nutritious for its weight. Good organization achieves the kind of economical representation of facts that makes it possible to use the facts in the future. Sheer brute learning, noble though it may be, is not enough. Facts simply learned without a generic organization are the naked and useless untruth. The proper reward of learning is not that it pleases the teacher or the parents, nor is it that we become "quiz kids." The proper reward is that we can now use what we have learned, can cross the barrier from learning into thinking. Are we mindful of these matters in our conduct of teaching?

What has been said thus far must seem singularly lacking in relevance to magic, to art, and to poetry. It appears to relate principally to the learning of mathematics, science, and the social studies. But there is an analogous point to be

---

[1] Paper presented to Massachusetts Council on Teacher Education, February 13, 1958.

[*] Jerome S. Bruner, Learning and thinking, *Harvard Educational Review*, 1959, 29, 184-192. Reprinted by permission.

made about the learning of the arts and literature. If one has read literature and beheld works of art in such a way as to be able to think with their aid, then one has also grasped a deeper, simplifying principle. The underlying principle that gives one the power to use literature and the arts in one's thinking is not of the order of a generic condensation of knowledge. Rather it is metaphoric in nature, and perhaps the best way of describing this class of principles is to call them guiding myths.

Let me take an example from mythology. Recall when you read for the first time the story of Perseus slaying the hateful Medusa. You recall that to look directly upon the Medusa was to be turned to stone. The secret of Perseus was to direct the killing thrust of his sword by the reflection of Medusa on his polished shield. It is an exciting story, full of the ingenuity that Hercules had taught us to expect. Beneath the story, beneath all great stories, there is a deeper metaphoric meaning. I did not understand this meaning for many years, indeed, not until my son asked me what the myth of Perseus "meant." It occurred to me that the polished shield might symbolize all of the devices by which we are able to take action against evil without becoming contaminated by it. The law suggested itself as one such device, enabling us to act against those who trespassed against morality without ourselves having to trespass in our action. I do not wish to hold a brief for my interpretation of the Perseus myth. But I would like to make one point about it.

Man must cope with a relatively limited number of plights—birth, growth, loneliness, the passions, death, and not very many more. They are plights that are neither solved nor by-passed by being "adjusted." An adjusted man must face his passions just as surely as he faces death. I would urge that a grasp of the basic plights through the basic myths of art and literature provides the organizing principle by which knowledge of the human condition is rendered into a form that makes thinking possible, by which we go beyond learning to the use of knowledge. I am not suggesting that the Greek myths are better than other forms of literature. I urge simply that there be exposure to, and interpretation of, literature that deals deeply with the human condition. I have learned as much from Charley Brown of *Peanuts* as I have learned from Perseus. The pablum school readers, stripped of rich imagery in the interest of "readability," stripped of passion in the errone-

ous belief that the deeper human condition will not interest the child—these are no more the vehicles for getting over the barrier to thinking than are the methods of teaching mathematics by a rote parroting at the blackboard.

II

I should like to consider now some conditions in our schools today that promote and inhibit progress across the barrier from learning to thinking. I should point out in advance that I am not very cheerful on this subject.

THE PASSIVITY OF KNOWLEDGE-GETTING. I have been struck during the past year or so, sitting in classrooms as an observer, by the passivity of the process we call education. The emphasis is upon gaining and storing information, gaining it and storing it in the form in which it is presented. We carry the remainder in long division so, peaches are grown in Georgia, transportation is vital to cities, New York is our largest port, and so on. Can the facts or the methods presented be mimicked? If so, the unit is at an end. There is little effort indeed which goes into the process of putting the information together, finding out what is generic about it. Long division is a skill, like threading a needle. The excitement of it as a method of partitioning things that relates it to such matters as subtraction is rarely stressed. One of the great inventions of man—elementary number theory—is presented as a cookbook. I have yet to see a teacher present one way of doing division and then put it squarely to the class to suggest six other ways of doing it—for there are at least six other ways of doing it than any one that might be taught in a school. So too with algebra. Algebra is not a set of rules for manipulating numbers and letters except in a trivial sense. It is a way of thinking, a way of coping with the drama of the unknown. Lincoln Steffens, in his *Autobiography*, complains upon his graduation from the University of California that his teachers had taught him only of the known, how to commit it to mind, and had done little to instruct him in the art of approaching the unknown, the art of posing questions. How does one ask questions about the unknown? Well, algebra is one technique, the technique for arranging the known in such a way that one is enabled to discern the value of an unknown quantity. It is an enriching strategy, algebra, but only if it is grasped as an extended instance of common sense.

Once I did see a teacher specifically encourage a class to organize and use minimal information to draw a maximum number of inferences. The teacher modeled his technique, I suppose, on the tried method of the storyteller. He presented the beginnings of the Whiskey Rebellion and said to his pupils, much in the manner of Ellery Queen speaking to his readers, "You now have enough to reconstruct the rest of the story. Let's see if we can do it." He was urging them to cross the barrier from learning into thinking. It is unhappily true that this is a rare exception in our schools.

So knowledge-getting becomes passive. Thinking is the reward for learning, and we may be systematically depriving our students of this reward as far as school learning is concerned.

One experiment which I can report provides encouragement. It was devised and carried out by the research group with which I am associated at Harvard in collaboration with teachers in the fifth grade of a good public school. It is on the unpromising topic of the geography of the North Central States and is currently in progress so that I cannot give all of the results. We hit upon the happy idea of presenting this chunk of geography not as a set of knowns, but as a set of unknowns. One class was presented blank maps, containing only tracings of the rivers and lakes of the area as well as the natural resources. They were asked as a first exercise to indicate where the principal cities would be located, where the railroads, and where the main highways. Books and maps were not permitted and "looking up the facts" was cast in a sinful light. Upon completing this exercise, a class discussion was begun in which the children attempted to justify why the major city would be here, a large city there, a railroad on this line, etc.

The discussion was a hot one. After an hour, and much pleading, permission was given to consult the rolled up wall map. I will never forget one young student, as he pointed his finger at the foot of Lake Michigan, shouting, "Yipee, *Chicago* is at the end of the pointing-down lake." And another replying, "Well, OK: but Chicago's no good for the rivers and it should be here where there is a big city (St. Louis)." These children were thinking, and learning was an instrument for checking and improving the process. To at least a half dozen children in the class it is not a matter of indifference that no big city is to be found at the junction of Lake Huron, Lake Michigan, and Lake Ontario. They were slightly shaken up transportation theorists when the facts were in.

The children in another class taught conventionally, got their facts all right, sitting down, benchbound. And that was that. We will see in six months which group remembers more. But whichever does, one thing I will predict. One group learned geography as a set of rational acts of induction—that cities spring up where there is water, where there are natural resources, where there are things to be processed and shipped. The other group learned passively that there were arbitrary cities at arbitrary places by arbitrary bodies of water and arbitrary sources of supply. One learned geography as a form of activity. The other stored some names and positions as a passive form of registration.

THE EPISODIC CURRICULUM. In a social studies class of an elementary school in a well-to-do suburb of one of our great eastern cities, I saw groups of twelve-year-old children doing a "project" on the southeastern states. Each team was gathering facts that might eventually end up on a map or a chart or some other graphic device. The fact-gathering was atomized and episodic. Here were the industrial products of North Carolina. There was the list of the five principal cities of Georgia. I asked the children of one team what life would be like and what people would worry about in a place where the principal products were peanuts, cotton, and peaches. The question was greeted as "unfair." They were gathering facts.

It is not just the schools. The informational environment of America seems increasingly to be going through such an atomization. Entertainment is in fifteen minute episodes on TV, to be taken while sitting down. The school curriculum is built of episodic units, each a task to itself: "We have now finished addition. Let us now move to multiplication." Even in our humor the "gag" threatens to replace the shrewd observer of the human comedy. I have seen an elementary school play fashioned entirely on a parody of radio commercials. It was a brave effort to tie the 10-second atoms together.

I do not wish to make it seem as if our present state of education is a decline from some previous Golden Age. For I do not think there has ever been a Golden Age in American public education. The difference now is that we can afford dross less well than ever before. The volume of positive knowledge increases at a rapid rate. Atomizing it into facts-to-be-filed is not likely to produce the kind of broad grasp that will be needed in the world of the next quarter century. And it is certainly no training for the higher education that more and more of our children will be getting.

I have not meant the above as a plea for the "central subject" or the "project" method of teaching. It is, rather, a plea for the recognition of the continuity of knowledge. One hears professional educators speak of "coverage," that certain topics must be covered. There are indeed many things that must be covered, but they are not unconnected things. The object of learning is to gain facts in a context of connectivity that permits the facts to be used generatively. The larger the number of isolated facts, the more staggering the number of connections between them—unless one can reduce them to some deeper order. Not all of them can be. Yet it is an ideal worth striving for, be it in the fifth grade or in graduate school. As Robert Oppenheimer put it in a recent address before the American Academy, "Everything cannot be connected with everything in the world we live in. Everything can be connected with anything."

THE EMBARRASSMENT OF PASSION. I should like to consider now the guiding myth. Let me begin with a summary of the young Christopher Columbus as he is presented in a popular social studies textbook. Young Chris is walking along the water front in his home town and gets to wondering where all those ships go. Eventually he comes back to his brother's cobbler shop and exclaims, "Gee, Bart, I wonder where all those ships go, whether maybe if they just kept going they wouldn't come back because the world is round." Bart replies with pleasant brotherly encouragement. Chris is a well-adjusted kid. Bart is a nice big brother. And where is the passion that drove this obsessed man across uncharted oceans? What impelled this Columbus with such force that he finally enlisted the aid of Ferdinand and Isabella over the protest of their advisors? Everything is there in the story except the essential truth—the fanatical urge to explore in an age of exploration, the sense of an expanding world. Columbus did not have a schoolboy's whim, nor was he the well-adjusted grownup of this account. He was a man driven to explore, to control. The justification for the pablum that makes up such textbooks is that such accounts

as these touch more directly on the life of the child.

What is this "life of the child" as seen by text writers and publishers? It is an image created out of an ideal of adjustment. The ideal of adjustment has little place for the driven man, the mythic hero, the idiosyncratic style. Its ideal is mediocentrism, reasonableness above all, being nice. Such an ideal does not touch closely the deeper life of the child. It does not appeal to the dark but energizing forces that lie close beneath the surface. The Old Testament, the Greek Myths, the Norse legends—these are the embarrassing chronicles of men of passion. They were devised to catch and preserve the power and tragedy of the human condition—and its ambiguity, too. In their place, we have substituted the noncontroversial and the banal.

Here a special word is needed about the concept of "expressing yourself," which is our conception of how one may engage the deeper impulses of the child. I have seen a book review class in a public school in which the children had the choice of reporting on any book they wished to choose, in or out of the school library, and where the discussion by the other children had to do entirely with the manner in which the reciting child presented his material. Nothing was said about the book in the discussion. The emphasis was on nice presentation, and whether the book sounded interesting. I have no quarrel with rewarding self-expression. I wonder simply whether it is not perhaps desirable, too, to make known the canons of excellence. The children in this class were learning to be seductive in their recounting; they were not concerned with an honest accounting of the human condition. The books they had read were cute, there was no excitement in them, none to be extracted. Increasingly the children in American elementary schools grow out of touch with the guiding myths. Self-expression is not a substitute. Adjustment is a worthy ideal, if not an ennobling one. But when we strive to attain it by shutting our eyes to the turmoils of human life, we will not get adjustment, but a niggling fear of the unusual and the excellent.

THE QUALITY OF TEACHERS. I do not wish to mince words. The educational and cultural level of the majority of American teachers is not impressive. On the whole they do not have a good grasp of the subject matter that they are teaching; courses on method will not replace the absent subject matter. In time and with teaching experience this deficiency is often remedied. But in so many cases there is no time: the turnover in the teaching profession as we all know is enormous; the median number of years of teaching before departure for marriage or motherhood is around three.

This leaves us with a small core of experienced teachers. Do we use them to teach the new teachers on the job? No. The organization of the school with respect to utilization of talent is something short of imaginative. It consists of a principal on top and a group of discrete teachers beneath her, and that is all. In large metropolitan high schools this is sometimes supplemented by having departments at the head of which is an experienced teacher. The communication that goes on between teachers is usually at a highly informal level and can scarcely be called comprehensive. It is usually about problem-children, not about social studies or mathematics or how to bring literature alive.

I would urge, and I believe that educators have taken steps in this direction, that we use our more experienced teachers for on-the-job training of less experienced, new teachers. I would also urge that there be established some means whereby the substantive topics taught in our elementary and high schools be included in some kind of special extension program provided by our eighteen hundred colleges and universities in the United States for the benefit of teachers. I am not speaking only of teachers colleges, but rather of all institutions of higher learning. Institutions of higher learning have a responsibility to the lower schools, and it can be exercised by arranging for continuous contact between those, for example, who teach history at the college level and those who are teaching history or social studies at the lower levels. And so, too, with literature or mathematics, or languages. To assume that somehow a teacher can be "prepared" simply by going through teacher training and then by taking courses on methods in summer school is, I think, fallacious. Often it is the case that the teacher, like her students, has not learned the material well enough to cross the barrier from learning to thinking.

III

It is quite plain, I think, that the task of improving the American Schools is not simply one of technique—however comforting it would be to some professional educators to think so. What is at issue, rather, is a deeper problem, one that is more philosophical than psychological or technological in scope. Let me put it in all innocence. What do we conceive to be the end product of our educational effort? I cannot help but feel that this rather overly simplified question has become obscured in cant. There is such an official din in support of the view that we are "training well-rounded human beings to be responsible citizens" that one hesitates to raise the question whether such an objective is a meaningful guide to what one does in classroom teaching. Surely the objective is worthy, and it has influenced the techniques of education in America, not always happily. For much of what we have called the embarrassment of passion can, I think, be traced to this objective, and so too the blandness of the social studies curriculum. The ideal, sadly, has also led to the standardization of mediocrity by a failure of the schools to challenge the full capacity of the talented student.

Since the war, there has been a perceptible shift in the problems being faced by schools and parents alike. It is the New Competition. Will Johnny and Sally be able to get into the college of their first choice or, indeed, into any college at all? The origins of the concern are obvious enough—the "baby bulge" has made itself felt. The results are not all bad, I would urge, or need not be. There are, to be sure, severe problems of overcrowding that exacerbate the difficulties already inherent in public education. And it is true that parental pressures for grades and production are increasing the proportion of children with "learning blocks" being referred to child guidance clinics.

But the pressures and the competition are also rekindling our awareness of excellence and how it may be nurtured. The shake-up of our smugness by the evident technical thrust of the Soviet Union has added to this awareness. Let me urge that it is this new awareness that requires shaping of expression in the form of a new set of ideals. Grades, admission to college, followed by admission to graduate school—these are surely not the ideals but, rather, the external signs.

Perhaps the fitting ideal is precisely as we have described it earlier in these pages, the active pragmatic ideal of leaping the barrier from learning into thinking. It matters not *what* we have learned. What we can *do* with what we have learned: this is the issue. The pragmatic argument has long been elaborated on extrinsic grounds, that the higher one has gone in the educational system the greater the economic gain. Indeed, at least one eminent economist has proposed that parents finance college education for their children by long-term loans to be repaid by the children on the almost certain knowledge that higher earning results from such education. All of this is the case, and it is indeed admirable that educational progress

and economic success are so intimately linked in our society. I would only suggest that the pragmatic ideal be applied also to the intrinsic aspects of education. Let us not judge our students simply on *what* they know. That is the philosophy of the quiz program. Rather, let them be judged on what they can generate from what they know—how well they can leap the barrier from learning to thinking.

73/TRANSFER OF TRAINING/THOMAS G. ANDREWS AND LEE J. CRONBACH*

ALL EDUCATIONAL EFFORTS AIM AT learning which can be transferred to new situations. Some of these new situations are to be met within the school curriculum; others are life situations outside the classroom. Ultimately it is to the latter type of situation that educational interest in transfer of training is pointed. When one practices a response to a specific stimulus situation, *learning* (*q.v.*) takes place. When a particular learning experience also influences an individual's ability to respond effectively to stimuli different in some ways from those he reacted to during learning, transfer of training is said to have taken place.

If transfer were not possible, it would be necessary to train the individual in every specific situation he will ever face. The mechanic who has learned to repair one tractor would have to begin learning anew on each new model, and the rifleman who is an expert with one weapon would begin as a novice when he changes to another.

There are several important psychological questions concerning transfer of training. For

educational purposes two of these questions are most important: To how wide a range of different situations will a particular learning transfer? What instructional methods promote the greatest degree of transfer? Transfer is apparent in impressive proportions in everyday life, but it cannot be taken for granted in all educational situations. The transfer problem is a question of degree and of the relative efficiency of educational or training procedures.

Individuals do not always transfer to the same extent from one learning experience to another. Research is required to establish how and when training will transfer. Will practice firing at towed targets improve the combat firing of an aerial gunner? Will study of logical propositions in mathematics improve reasoning about life problems? Will lectures on mental hygiene improve adjustment to frustrating situations? Will the study of Latin aid in mastering law? Such questions underlie all curriculum construction.

EMERGENCE OF THE TRANSFER PROBLEM. So long as the curriculum was supposed primarily to transmit knowledge of Western culture, the problem of transfer was not important. A man learned Latin, geometry, and natural history because these knowledges were the mark of an educated man. With the emergence of a less aristocratic notion of education in America during the 1800's there developed gradual acceptance of the axiom that the function of any teaching is to change behavior. The place of skill subjects such as reading and arithmetic was secure under this philosophy. Classical knowledge had less obvious value for everyday behavior and the classical subjects were defended on the ground that they strengthened certain mental faculties—reasoning, judgment, memory, will, etc. According to this *faculty psychology*, exercising a faculty by appropriate training developed the mind, and so improved behavior. Conventional school subjects were said to provide "mental discipline."

Experimental psychology began to challenge this theory of transfer when James (1890, pp. 666-668), about 1890, attempted to measure the effect of training on memory. He and his students timed their speed of memorizing passages from Victor Hugo's *Satyr*. Daily for a month or longer they memorized selections from another author, and then retested themselves on new passages from Hugo. According to the faculty theory, memorization of the classics develops the memory. James and his group found some improvement, but results were so slight as to throw into question the entire value of mental discipline. Further tests were made of transfer effects in memory, perception, reasoning, and other alleged faculties. These studies showed rather small transfer and were considered adequate to disprove the claims of formal discipline.

Transfer through specific habits was emphasized in the theory of Thorndike and Woodworth (1901), which replaced the faculty approach. Under this theory, curriculum makers sought to provide learning experiences which would give training in the particular skills, habits, and responses likely to be used in later life. Thus in citizenship training, study of political thought was superseded by training in how to mark a ballot, how to read editorials, and how to acquire facts specifically needed about current problems and in forming judgments about them.

More recent emphasis in education points to broader possibilities of transfer. In addition to habits and facts, school experiences engender attitudes and broad understandings which have great significance. Feelings of inadequacy fostered in school may transfer to an adult's performance on his job and to his methods of dealing with his children. A concept of fair dealing, learned in childhood, may reflect itself in an adult's marital relations, treatment of his employees, and attitudes on international affairs. Judd (1908) contributed to this viewpoint by showing experimentally that teaching meaningful general principles permits more effective transfer than a curriculum which is merely a collection of useful habits. Current methods of teaching for transfer are discussed at the end of this article.

METHODOLOGY

Studies of transfer have been pursued both in the laboratory and in classroom situations. The essential features of transfer as a psychological process are best studied in the experimental approach. By designing experiments in which the crucial variables are controlled, we can assess with considerable assurance the importance of each factor for transfer. In actual school situations, learning and transfer cannot be explained by such a simple formula as "so much presentation plus so much motivation plus so much generalization result in so much transfer." Changes in pupils come from a complex interaction of factors. To understand this interaction (e.g. why does presentation Z improve the work of some pupils but not others?) careful studies in the classroom are needed to supplement laboratory findings.

A crucial difficulty in studies of transfer has been the problem of assessing all outcomes of a learning experience. Results of instruction are usually thought of in terms of gains in knowledge or skill, and these are readily measured. Each instructional process, however, affects in many ways the personality, and attitudes of the pupil. If it is established that two procedures (e.g. study of civics vs. student self-government) produce equal gains in ability to reach logical decisions about new political questions, we still do not know their relative effect on such behavior as concern about political problems, tendency to vote on election day, and tendency to seek information on civic problems as they arise. We do not know whether the adult, capable as he is in reasoning as a result of the teaching, will have the confidence to follow his own thinking or will be swayed by partisan appeals. Few studies have attempted to evaluate the transfer effects of learning procedures in terms of these crucial but subtle concomitants.

Transfer may be positive (facilitating subsequent performance), negative (inhibitory), or mixed. Study of past political debates may produce some positively transferring effects, such as ability to interpret a new question in terms of its historical antecedents. It may produce such negative effects as an attitude that politics and civics are boring and to be thought about only under a teacher's compulsion. Study of the Latin verb *cedere* may lead to positive transfer in spelling the English *precede* but to negative transfer in spelling *supersede*. The usual experiment, in which "total" learning is measured by some test, can rarely disentangle such positive and negative outcomes. It is impossible to prove or demonstrate zero transfer, because an experimentally measured zero gain may represent cancelling positive and negative effects. Attempts to express amount of transfer on a scale from 0 to 100 per cent have been confusing, in the absence of an accepted operational definition of 100 per cent transfer (Woodworth, 1938, pp. 176-207).

The methodology of transfer investigations involves several important problems of control. The simplest and most fundamental experimental design involves the following steps: (a) Subjects are tested to determine their initial proficiency on the final task. (b) Two groups are equated, either as matched pairs or as total groups with equal means and equal variances. One of these groups is arbitrarily identified as the experimental group and the other as the control group. (c) The educational experience from which we expect transfer is now given to the experimental group. During this period of practice, the control group receives no training. (d) At the end of the period of practice, or some time later, both groups are retested on the final task, in which we expect the experimental group to have improved as a result of the intervening experience.

Such an experimental design may be represented by the following schema:

Experimental Group:

 Test on R_2; Training on R_1; Test on R_2

Control Group:

 Test on R_2; ....; Test on R_2
We would expect the control group, and also the experimental group, to better their performance on R_2 merely by virtue of their previous experience on R_2. Over a long period of time, maturational effects would also produce better scores in both groups. It is important to note that we may claim transfer effect only to

the extent that the two groups are accurately matched or equated in terms of their initial ability on the final task and on such additional relevant factors as intelligence, previous training, and motivation for taking the pretest. The methodology of transfer studies is like that for learning experiments in every respect save one, that gains are measured not on the practiced task but on a different performance. James's learning of poetry was shown by his better knowledge of the poetry he studied; the transfer to memory in general was tested by his ability to master new poetry.

Various modifications of the above procedure are used when we intend to compare different types of intermediate training. When no pretest on the final task is possible because neither group has skill in it at the outset (as in testing whether experience with one gun transfers to ability to assemble a different piece), we must equate groups on supplementary variables such as intelligence or mechanical aptitude. Attention should be drawn to two rather precise statistical controls which obviate the usual loss of individual subjects in forming groups. We may "match through regression" (Peters and Van Voorhis, 1940, pp. 463-468) or apply the Neyman-Johnson method (Butch, 1944). Both these methods, although complicated, are powerful tools. The Neyman-Johnson method has the added advantage of identifying differences in amount of transfer for different types of subjects. We should expect this method to be used more frequently in future studies.

STUDIES OF TRANSFER

The research on transfer may be summarized in terms of three significant questions:
1. What types of responses can be improved through transfer?
2. Do some school subjects possess greater "transfer value" than others, in terms of their effect on the pupil's general mental functioning?
3. What educational procedures produce the greatest amount of transfer?

1. CHARACTERISTIC TRANSFER EFFECTS. The first point of attack for research on transfer was to determine whether such broad mental powers as memory, observation, judgment, reasoning, and volition could be improved by training. Following the pioneer study of James (1890, pp. 666-668), Thorndike and Woodworth (1901) performed an important series of investigations. Their first experiments were designed to deter-

mine the transfer effects of training in observation and perceptual discrimination. Subjects practiced estimating areas of certain geometric figures. The investigators then determined the effects of this practice on the accuracy of estimation of figures not previously presented. The transfer effects were found to vary between 30 and 50 per cent of the gains on the practiced figures. Training in estimating lengths of lines, however, produced little or no improvement in estimating lines not previously presented. Improvement in the accuracy of estimating weights from an initial test to a final test, with an intervening practice period on a different set of weights, was found to be about 40 per cent of the efficiency gained with the material practiced. Such studies indicated that transfer was evident but by no means considerable.

In other experiments Thorndike and Woodworth found that practicing the cancellation of certain letters of the alphabet from material on a printed page increased the efficiency of cancelling other letters only by 25 per cent of the gain observed during the practice period itself. The same general result was found for the relative improvement in finding and cancelling parts of speech in prose material.

These experiments represented a critical attack on the claims of formal discipline and gave little encouragement to the concept of a general observational ability which could be improved significantly through training. Much of the transfer effect found by Thorndike and Woodworth was interpreted by them as due to the carrying over of specific methods and rules of procedure or to the similarity in the practiced and the tested material.

Following these studies on observational ability there was an emphasis on research directed at rather specific aspects of transfer, such as problems of bilateral transfer (cross education) and memory for specific elements, such as nonsense syllables. Swift (1903) found that there was approximately 66 per cent transfer of ball-tossing skill from the right hand to the left hand. Ebert and Meumann (1904) found that subjects made considerable transfer from learning nonsense syllables, mainly by becoming adapted to the experimenter, the task, and the laboratory conditions. Seemingly as a result of practicing the learning of nonsense syllables, the subjects investigated by Ebert and Meumann were improved in the learning of letters, numbers, prose, and poetry, as well as meaningless visually perceived forms. But when the experiment of Ebert and Meumann was repeated by

Reed (1917) with the use of a control group, it was found that any spread of ability from specialized memory practice is relatively small and undependable.

There were a large number of such investigations on specific learning functions early in the century and further analysis of the problems produced important interpretations. Thus, Swift noted in his experiment on ball-tossing that the method of handling the balls was carried over from one hand to the other. Dearborn (1909) showed that the "transfer" of Ebert and Meumann was largely due to gains made within the test series and the remainder was due to general improvement in orientation, attention, and technique of learning. Bray (1928), in a study of target-aiming transfer from hand to foot, found that methods, tricks, and modes of adjustment seem to be the primary media of transfer from one member to another.

An experiment by Sleight (1911) is somewhat representative of early attempts to identify the particular learnings transferred. He equated four groups of young girls on the basis of performance on several memory tasks. Each of three groups was given training in one task of memorizing either poetry, the substance of prose passages, or tables of measures and other quantitative data. Before, during, and after the practice period of 12 days, the subjects of the three experimental groups and one control group were measured on several kinds of learning, such as orally given names and dates, nonsense syllables, and series of letters. There were some gains and some losses, and in general Sleight's experiment showed no general improvement in memory attributable to practice.

It became evident that transfer produced little generalized improvement. In a study by Woodrow (1927), however, the interest was shifted to determine whether it was possible to train subjects so that the *techniques* of memorizing acquired during the training period will be used to advantage on later occasions. Two experimental groups and one control group were studied. All groups were tested to determine their initial memorizing ability. One experimental group had a total of about 3 hours of practice at memorizing with no special instruction or training. The other experimental group was given the same amount of time in training on several simple *rules* and how or when to use them. The practice time of this latter experimental group was spent in consciously applying these techniques. All three groups then took final tests which were like the inital tests and included poetry, prose, miscellaneous factual items, Turkish-English vocabulary, and little-known historical dates. The two experimental groups dealt only with nonsense syllables and with poetry during their practice and training periods. The results indicated that simple practice, with no special aid or set, produces little transfer, whereas the learning of memory techniques with intent to use them definitely transfers to the final memory test.

In the psychological domain of reasoning Barlow (1937) found that instruction in analysis, abstraction, and generalization produces appreciable transfer to problems requiring understanding and reasoning—e.g. getting the point of Aesop's fables.

In addition to investigations of transfer of particular capacities, there is a large amount of evidence that attitudes, emotional reactions, and habits of character can and do transfer. (See Attitudes; Character Education, in Monroe, 1950, pp. 77-84, 126-134.) Watson and Rayner (1920) called attention to the transfer of an emotional response in one of his experiments on conditioning. In a young child who had learned to fear a furry animal, the fear response readily transferred to other furry animals, cotton, wool, and Santa Claus whiskers.

A pioneering experiment on the transfer of moral or character habits was performed by Voelker (1921), who gave six groups of boys a series of initial tests of honesty or trustworthiness, such as not returning over-change, not returning borrowed property, cheating in scoring one's own examination paper, peeping in blindfold tests, and the like. Two of the groups were then given intensive Boy Scout work on trustworthiness, including discussions, learning of codes, and exhortations. In two other groups the regular Scout training was given, but there was far less emphasis on honesty. The remaining two groups served as controls and received no Boy Scout training and no training in trustworthiness. All of the six groups were retested with measures similar to those constituting the initial tests. Most progress had been made by the two Boy Scout groups which received the intensive training, and the least progress was made by the two control groups.

Such studies as that of Barlow and of Voelker have largely reversed the earlier conclusions that broad mental processes are relatively immune to transfer. The development of attitudes is demonstrated by an important experiment performed by Bond (1940) in a course in genetics which emphasized generalizations about racial characteristics. The training produced measurable changes not only in knowledge of facts but also in reduction of superstition and in improved ability to solve new problems in human genetics, and it significantly changed attitudes regarding imperialism, Jews, Italians, Latin Americans, and Orientals. Bond's method of teaching for transfer had greater effect for students in some ranges of intelligence and initial knowledge than for others. The study illustrates the significant advantages of the Neyman-Johnson technique for this type of research.

Transfer is also in question in the several investigations on the effect of nurture on general intellectual development. See Nature and Nurture, in Monroe (1950, pp. 772-777).

2. TRANSFER VALUE OF SCHOOL SUBJECTS. Proponents of various subjects, particularly the traditional ones, have been anxious to claim general mental improvement as an outcome of their subjects. The most important research on this problem is found in studies by Thorndike (1924), Brolyer, Thorndike, and Woodyard (1927), and Wesman (1945). Thorndike devised a plan for comparing the tested intelligence of pupils exposed to different school subjects. By working with thousands of cases, he was able to establish subgroups taking exactly the same subjects, except that one group took mathematics whereas the other took stenography or cooking. Similar groups permitted comparing the transfer values of each important pair of subjects. The final conclusions, which have been supported by later studies with similar technique, are that gains in intelligence as a result of following particular subjects are negligible and that the differences in effect on intelligence of particular subjects are far too small to be given weight in planning curriculums. This finding was startling to those who had confidence in the importance of classical subjects in producing superior intellects. Thorndike considered this widespread belief to be the result of uncontrolled observation, pointing out that if all the best pupils took classical subjects, those subjects would seem to be producing better graduates than other curriculums.

3. METHODS OF INCREASING TRANSFER. Much attention has been given to methods of promoting transfer. Judd (1908) trained two groups to throw darts at a target 12 inches under water. One group used a trial-and-error method, while

the other was taught the principles of refraction. When the target was moved to a depth of 4 inches, the former group was unable to adapt its previously acquired skill, but the group taught by generalizations adapted to the new conditions rapidly. Hamblen (1925) reached similar conclusions in studying the value of Latin for increasing ability to understand English derivatives. In classes where no special teaching for transfer was attempted, automatic transfer was negligible. Where teachers introduced many derivations, transfer was greater, but substantial improvement in dealing with unfamiliar derivations was obtained only where illustrative derivatives were related to rules and principles of derivation. Many other studies have confirmed the importance of conscious generalizing in other fields (Katona, 1940, Chaps. III and IV).

Other studies have brought out the importance of recognition in transfer. If the learner does not identify a problem as an opportunity to apply his knowledge, it will not transfer. Smith (1940) found that many pupils who, for example, were able to erect a perpendicular to a horizontal line could not construct a perpendicular to an oblique side of a triangle. He therefore proposed a teaching method in which responses were taught both in simple and complex settings, with specific teaching in methods of analyzing the complex problems. Significant gains in solving new complex problems were found. Fawcett (1938) developed a course in mathematics stressing "the nature of proof" rather than particular theorems. He helped pupils see the need for definitions, assumptions, and proofs in connection with problems from their everyday lives and made them aware of methods of proof. Tests showed that the group made normal progress on geometry itself and made impressive gains in ability to analyze nonmathematical reasoning about unfamiliar problems. The control groups, learning traditional geometry, did not show transfer to nonmathematical materials.

The reader is referred to more complete bibliographies and summaries for detailed listings of the thousand or so studies bearing on transfer (Coover, 1916; McGeoch, 1942, pp. 394-452; Norem, 1933, pp. 3-35; Sandiford, 1928, pp. 275-300; Stroud, 1946, pp. 555-597; Swenson, 1941). Attention may be drawn to the steady improvement in research technique shown in these studies. Earlier work was open to criticism for failure to use an adequate control group, small numbers of cases, emphasis on meaningless

learning unrelated to problems of school or life, training of such short duration that little transfer could be expected, failure to study long-term transfer effects, and failure to measure all types of outcomes. The reader must bear these criteria in mind in considering particular studies of transfer.

THEORIES OF TRANSFER

From time to time, as findings on transfer have accumulated, theories to account for the results have been advanced. With the exception of the initial theory of formal discipline, that practice develops mental strength, the subsequent theories may be considered successive refinements of a basic idea, rather than competing and incompatible notions. The most widely discussed theory is Thorndike's (1906, p. 243 f.) *theory of identical components*. When first proposed, under the name "identical elements," the theory sought to account for the fact that transfer was negligible unless the practiced task and the final task had a great deal in common. In keeping with his theory that each specific act of learning made use of a specific neural bond, Thorndike assumed that transfer was greatest when the practiced learning and the new learning had the largest number of bonds in common.

Association theory has been modified with the passage of time, as research has shown that the neural-chain theory is inadequate to account for learning. In its modern form, the theory of identical components states that the extent to which a response transfers to a new situation depends on the degree to which the new situation resembles the practiced one (Gibson, 1941). Situations may resemble each other in the specific configuration of the stimulus (*pêche* and *péché* are very similar, although one means *peach* and one means *sin*) or in the general character of the situation even though all details are different (as when a child transfers to an employer attitudes and anxieties learned in relation to his father).

If responses to new situations depend entirely on familiarity with the various components to be encountered, it is necessary for education to equip the pupil with responses to all the many components of the situations he will meet in life. This led to the "social utility" curriculum, which stressed the particular facts adults encountered after leaving school. This was a major advance, for it removed from arithmetic deliberately difficult fractions (e.g. 121/318, 23/79) which were supposed to provide mental development under the discipline theory, and replaced them with the limited number of fractions actually found in business, carpentry, and so on (3/8, 5/32, etc.). In social studies, topics and concepts which represented only general culture were eliminated in favor of the concepts represented in current live issues.

Unfortunately, the highly specific theory of identical components made the curricular task overwhelming, because of the large number of specific learnings needed to solve all future problems. Judd added greatly to the design of sound curriculums with his stress on a *theory of generalization* (Judd, 1908). This theory pointed out that a response could be generalized so that the learner would apply it to every new situation of a given type. One then need not practice with every important fraction, but merely learn the general principles of fractions. Mastery of general social and historical principles would equip the subject to attack new situations subsumed under those principles. One may readily combine the Judd and Thorndike theories by considering that one way in which two situations may have an "identical component" is by falling under the same generalization. For a curriculum based on generalization, it is necessary that the pupil learn generalizations explicitly and that he know where they can be applied.

Gestalt psychologists have made much of the fact that learning often is not applied to a new situation, no matter how nearly identical to an old one, because the subject does not recognize the familiar in the new situation. Such criticisms force one to rephrase the theory of transfer as follows: *Transfer of a previously acquired behavior-pattern to a new situation will occur whenever an individual recognizes the new situation as similar to the situation for which the behavior was learned.* We have therefore swung through a cycle, from blind assumption that transfer is widespread, through a period of skepticism when transfer was expected only in the narrowest specific knowledge and habits, to a theory which looks on transfer as common and to be expected, provided certain conditions are met.

IMPLICATIONS FOR EDUCATION

The educator may draw implications for curriculum and classroom practice from many of the studies in this area. One of the major contributions of the research has been to demonstrate that no particular school subject has, in itself, any magical transfer value. To argue for teaching geometry, Latin, or philosophy because it "develops the mind," "increases understanding of the common problems of modern and ancient civilization," or "strengthens the control of reason over emotion," is to ignore an indisputable body of evidence. To examine the likelihood of transfer, one must question not what school subject is offered but what responses the pupil learns. From a study of Latin, one can probably improve his English, or become aware of the problems of man and the state, or establish a lifelong enjoyment of Roman poetry, or become antagonistic to Latin, the teacher, the school, and "culture" in general. There is no superior subject matter for transfer, there are only superior learning experiences. No doubt, under skilled teaching, educational psychology, art, or cooking can be made the vehicle for developing reasoning, a sense of values, or superior study habits.

The teacher in any subject may choose between teaching for mastery of his narrow strip of subject matter and teaching for transfer to life beyond the algebra or the economics book. Transfer will not be automatic. The A student in algebra or economics will often fail to use his skills in problems outside the classroom unless the subjects have been taught for transfer. There are five major steps in teaching for transfer:

1. POINT OUT THE POSSIBILITY OF TRANSFER. If pupils expect that what they learn will help in later situations, they are most likely to use it when opportunity arises. The teacher can introduce specific materials illustrating life situations where the principles of the school subject are applicable: shortcut calculations based on algebra, hidden assumptions in the reasoning of advertisements for comparison with geometric postulates, and habits of dental care as an application of knowledge about bacteria. Instances of confusingly similar situations may be specifically pointed out to reduce negative transfer.

2. USE VARIED TEACHING MATERIALS, LIKE THOSE TO WHICH THE LEARNING IS EXPECTED TO TRANSFER. Beyond merely pointing out situations to which learning may transfer, the teacher should base the classroom work on life-like materials whenever possible. The more a pupil experiences the real situation, the more likely he is to recognize his next opportunity to respond to it. This principle is illustrated in the gradual reduc-

tion of verbalism in the schools, exercises with words being replaced by exercises with objects, charts, and motion pictures. The experience of conducting a student-body election has more in common with the experience of a citizen than does memorizing the life history of a bill introduced in Congress. The class which experiments on white rats learns more about the effect of nutrition on growth than the class which merely learns the verbal principles. If the algebra class works with the equations in s, a, and g, habits will not become sterotyped around the familiar x. The school can never provide experience with all important life situations and one must still teach for transfer beyond the materials studied.

3. DEVELOP MEANINGFUL GENERALIZATIONS. Each classroom topic can be thought of as something to be learned in itself or as an illustration of a broad principle. One may memorize Caesar's biography, or one may observe in it the consequences of concentrated power. One may learn how the gasoline engine operates, or one may derive from it princples applicable to all thermodynamic systems. One may do an arithmetic problem, or one may learn from it a general plan for all problem solving. It is these broader principles which make a particular learning most widely transferable. It is not enough, however, to present generalizations. They must be understood by the learner, not merely parroted.

4. PROVIDE PRACTICE IN APPLYING THE GENERALIZATION. An essential stage in transfer is recognizing a new situation as a special case of an old type. One cannot practice such recognition by drilling on a page of exercises, all of one labelled type. Practice is obtained by encountering a new situation in a setting which does not carry a sign identifying the generalization to be used. Some of the best experiences for transfer come through encountering algebra in the science text or science in the home-economics project. Any teacher can set up transfer experiences by introducing problems calling for application of generalizations in a context which forces the student to decide for himself what procedures or principles apply.

5. EVALUATE THE LEARNING EXPERIENCE BY DETERMINING HOW THE PUPIL'S BEHAVIOR IN NEW SITUATIONS IS CHANGED. Such evaluation stresses for the pupil that learning goes beyond memorizing and points out for the teacher his achieve-

ments and failures. Test materials requiring transfer of principles to new problems in most school subjects are illustrated in *The Measurement of Understanding* (National Society for the Study of Education, 1946).

In the long run transfer has reduced to a special case of the problem of learning. One learns the response one practices, if that response has satisfying consequences.

BIBLIOGRAPHY

SUMMARIES AND BIBLIOGRAPHIES

1. COOVER, J. E. "Formal Discipline from the Standpoint of Experimental Psychology." *Psychological Monograph*, No. 87, 1916, 255 pp.
2. MC GEOCH, J. A. *The Psychology of Human Learning.* Longmans, Green, 1942, pp. 394-452.
3. NOREM, C. M. "Transfer of Training Experiments Revalued." *University of Iowa Studies in Education*, Vol. 8, No. 6, 1933, pp. 3-35.
4. SANDIFORD, P. *Educational Psychology.* Longmans, Green, 1928, pp. 275-300.
5. STROUD, J. B. *Psychology in Education.* Longmans, Green, 1946, pp. 555-597.
6. SWENSON, E. J. *Retroactive Inhibition; A Review of the Literature.* University of Minnesota Press, 1941. 59 pp.

INVESTIGATIONS

7. BARLOW, M. D. "Transfer of Training in Reasoning." *J. Educ. Psychol.* 28:122-128, 1937.
8. BOND, A. D. *An Experiment in the Teaching of Genetics,* Teachers College, 1940, 99 pp.
9. BRAY, C. W. "Transfer of Learning." *J. Exper. Psychol.* 11:443-467, 1928.
10. BROLYER, C. R., E. L. THORNDIKE, and E. WOODYARD. "A Second Study of Mental Discipline in High School Studies." *J. Educ. Psychol.*, 18:377-404, 1927.
11. BUTSCH, R. L. C. "A Work Sheet for the Johnson-Neyman Technique." *J. Exper. Educ.*, 12:226-241; 1944.
12. DEARBORN, W. F. "The General Effects of Special Practice in Memory." *Psychological Bulletin*, Vol. 6, No. 1, 1909, 44 pp.
13. EBERT, E., and MEUMANN, E. "Uber einige Grundfragen der Psychologie der Ubungsphanomene in Berichte des Gedachtnisses." *Archive fur die gesamte Psychologie*, 4:1-232, 1905.

14. FAWCETT, H. P. "The Nature of Proof." *National Council of Teachers of Mathematics, Thirteenth Yearbook.* Teachers College, Columbia University. 1938.

15. GIBSON, E. J. "Retroactive Inhibition as a Function of Degree of Generalization Between Tasks." *J. Exper. Psychol.,* 28:93-115, 1941.

16. HAMBLEN, A. A. *The Extent to Which the Effect of the Study of Latin upon a Knowledge of English Derivations Can be Increased.* University of Pennsylvania, 1925, 81 pp.

17. HENRY, N. B. (Ed.) "The Measurement of Understanding." *Forty-fifth Yearbook Nat'l. Soc. Study of Educ., Part I,* University of Chicago Press, 1946, 338 pp.

18. JAMES, W. *Principles of Psychology,* Vol. 1, Holt, 1890, pp. 666-668.

19. JUDD, C. H. "The Relation of Special Training to General Intelligence." *Educ. Rev.,* 36:28-42, 1908.

20. KATONA, G. *Organizing and Memorizing.* Columbia University Press, 1940, Chaps. III and IV.

21. PETERS, C. C., and W. R. VAN VOORHIS. *Statistical Procedures and Their Mathematical Bases,* McGraw-Hill, 1940, pp. 463-468.

22. REED, H. B. "A Repetition of Ebert and Meumann's Practice Experiment on Memory." *J. Exper. Psychol.,* 2:315-346, 1917.

23. SLEIGHT, W. G. "Memory and Formal Training." *Brit. J. Psychol.,* 4:386-457, 1911.

24. SMITH, R. R. "Three Major Difficulties in the Learning of Demonstrative Geometry." *Mathematics Teacher,* 33:99-134, 1940.

25. SWIFT, E. J. "Studies in the Psychology and Physiology of Learning." *Amer. J. Psychol.,* 14:201-251, 1903.

26. THORNDIKE, E. L. *The Principles of Teaching,* A. G. Seiler, 1906, p. 243f.

27. THORNDIKE, E. L. "Mental Discipline in High School Studies." *J. Educ. Psychol.,* 15:1-22, 83-98, 1924.

28. THORNDIKE, E. L., and R. S. WOODWORTH. "The Influence of Improvement in One Mental Function upon the Efficiency of Other Functions." *Psychol. Rev.,* 8:247-261, 384-395, 553-564, 1901.

29. VOELKER, P. F. *The Function of Ideals and Attitudes in Social Education: An Experimental Study,* Teachers College, 1921, 126 pp.

30. WATSON, J. B., and R. RAYNER. "Conditioned Emotional Reactions." *J. Exper. Psychol.,* 3:1-14, 1920.

31. WESMAN, A. G. "A Study of Transfer of Training from High School Subjects to Intelligence." *Teachers College Contributions to Education, No. 909.* Teachers College, Columbia University, 1945, 82 pp.

32. WOODROW, HERBERT. "The Effect of Type of Training upon Transference." *J. Educ. Psychol.,* 18:159-172, 1927.

33. WOODWORTH, R. S. *Experimental Psychology,* Holt, 1938, pp. 176-207.

74/THE NEGATIVE EFFECT OF PREVIOUS EXPERIENCE ON PRODUCTIVE THINKING/ HERBERT G. BIRCH

AND HERBERT S. RABINOWITZ[*]

THE PART WHICH IS PLAYED BY PAST experience in human problem-solving behavior has long been a subject for experiment and discussion. Investigations viewing the evidence from different theoretical vantage points have arrived at diverse conclusions, which in some instances identify problem solving with trial-and-error learning (3), in other cases (1, 8) consider past experience in general as providing the raw materials out of which a problem-solving response may be fabricated, and on occasion some investigators have even neglected to consider the question of past experience as essential for a problem-solving theory (9). One of the reasons for the diversity of roles which have been accorded to past experience is that problem solving is by no means a unitary process. Although in all problem solving a solution is arrived at, the processes of behavior whereby the solution is achieved are of several different kinds. Maier (8) has served to clarify this issue by sharpening the often belabored distinction between *reproductive and productive thinking.* His discussion was developed in terms of the part which past experience may play in each type of performance. Reproductive thinking, Maier believes is characterized by the solution of problems by means of the existence of stimulus equivalences in the novel (or problem) situation and in the previously mastered situation. Thus, for him, reproductive thinking and transfer of training are to be considered closely similar if not identical phenomena. *Productive thinking,* however, is not merely the process of arriving at a solution through the direct application of previous learning. In productive thinking past experience is repatterned and restructured to meet current demands, and is thus the counterpart of reasoning as Maier has defined that term (6). In the present study we are concerned with the relation of past experience to the productive thinking process, and not with reproductive thinking.

Probably the studies which have contributed most directly to an understanding of the manner in which the background of past experiences influences the nature of human productive thinking are those of Maier (6, 7) and Duncker (2). Maier, in his examination of the relation between stimulus equivalence and reasoning (8), identified several ways in which past experience may affect problem-solving activities. Problem solving may be facilitated by equivalences which exist in the immediate problem situation and in past experience. Further, as he has shown elsewhere (6), and as Birch (1) has shown for the chimpanzee, the background of past learning represents an essential repertoire of behavior which must be available for restructuring when new situational demands develop. On the other hand, productive thinking is impossible if the individual is chained to the past. The past experience may become a hindrance and an obstacle which blocks productive thinking and reduces behavior to stereotyped and fruitless essays.

It is primarily with this negative effect which may be exercised by past experience that Duncker has dealt in his problem-solving experiments (2). In a series of situations designed to study what he terms "functional-fixedness," Duncker tried to determine the manner in which the previous utilization of an object for a dissimilar function in the *same problem context* affected its availability in subsequent problem solving, and found that such specific experience made the objects previously utilized in this manner significantly less available as instruments when the problem presented for solution was changed. Two weaknesses in experimental design limit the generality of the inferences which may be drawn from Duncker's results. In the first place, by using the same objective situation for both his "pre-utilization" experience and for his new problem-solving task, he makes it impossible to determine whether the difficulty in using a previously utilized object for the solution

[*]Herbert G. Birch and Herbert S. Rabinowitz, The negative effect of previous experience on productive thinking, *Journal of Experimental Psychology,* 1951, *41,* 121-125. Reprinted by permission.

of a new problem derives from the limitation of the functional properties of this object by the prior experience, from the establishment of false problem-solving directions, from the development of attitudes of completion ("over and done with") on the part of the S which effectively remove the already-used object from the field of activity, or from any of a variety of other effects. Secondly, in selecting the different tools which would be available to the Ss in their problem-solving activities, Duncker made no attempt to equate the instruments for different degrees of objective adequacy as tools in solving the problem. Obviously, if the objects in the "pre-utilization" group are objectively less adequate as tools than are the non-pre-utilized materials, the scales are weighted in favor of fewer solutions for the "pre-utilization" group. In not a few instances Duncker's problem situations may be criticized on these grounds, and the question arises as to whether his results derive as much from the pre-experimental object selection as from the effects of pre-utilization of the materials by the subjects.

To remove these impediments to interpretation of this aspect of the effects of previous experience on problem solving, it is necessary to study the problem under conditions in which the background of prior specific experience is obtained by the Ss in a situation remote from the crucial problem-solving task, and to contrast as problem-solving tools objects whose adequacy as instruments is objectively equal. The design of the present study stems from these considerations.

SUBJECTS AND PROCEDURE

Twenty-five students at the City College, New York, were used as Ss in this experiment. These Ss were divided into three groups, a control group and two experimental groups. The control group had 6 Ss, and the experimental groups contained 10 and 9 Ss, respectively.

As the crucial problem-solving task in this experiment, all Ss were required to solve the two-cord problem used extensively by Maier (7) in his studies of "direction" in problem solving. In this problem the S is required to tie together the free ends of two cords which are suspended from the ceiling to the floor of a corridor. The distance between the two cords is such that the S cannot reach one cord if the other is held. In our arrangement the problem could be solved

only if the S would tie a weight to the end of one of the strings and thus convert it into a pendulum which could be set swinging and then be caught on its upswing while the stationary cord was held. The two cords could then be tied together and the problem solved. In our situation only two objects could be utilized as weights. The first of these objects was an electrical switch and the second, an electrical relay. The conditions of pretest training involved the acquisition of differential prior experience with these objects by our Ss. The pretest training was conducted as follows:

Group S contained 9 Ss who were given the pretest task of completing an electrical circuit on a "bread-board" by using a *switch*, which had to be installed if the circuit were to be completed and controllable.

Group R consisted of 10 Ss who received pretest training in the completion of an identical circuit by the use of a *relay*, which is essentially a switch.

Group C, the control group, consisted of 6 engineering students with a wide variety of electrical experience. These Ss were given no pretraining. The Ss in groups R and S had had little or no experience with electrical wiring.

Shortly after having completed the pretesting tasks, the Ss were presented with the two-cord problem and asked to solve it by using the objects lying before them on a table. Only two objects were present, a *switch* and a *relay*, each identical with the ones used in the pretraining period.

Since the two-cord problem is very difficult to solve without the presentation of "direction"-producing hints, such hints were presented by E 9 min. after the presentation of the problem. The hints consisted in brushing against the string or strings and "accidentally" setting them swinging. Solutions were always achieved within 3 min. after the presentation of hints. All Ss were individually tested. Upon completing the two-cord problem, the Ss were asked why they had chosen either the switch or the relay as the pendulum weight.

RESULTS

The results reported will deal primarily with the nature of the choice of objects made by the Ss in the critical task situation. These data for all groups are shown in Table 1. The control group chose equally between the switch and the relay

TABLE 1 / FREQUENCY OF CHOICE OF OBJECTS IN PROBLEM SOLUTION.

GROUP	N	NO. USING RELAY	NO. USING SWITCH
Control (C)	6	3	3
Exper. (R)	10	0	10
Exper. (S)	9	7	2

as pendulum weights which might be utilized for the solution of the two-cord problem. These data indicate that for individuals with prior experience which is not heavily weighted in favor of either the switch or the relay, no significant difference exists between the objects in terms of their utility as tools in solving the two-cord problem.

The behavior of the Ss who had received specific pre-utilization experience with either the switch or the relay differed in a striking manner from the behavior of the Ss who had not received such experience. Those who had initially been trained to complete an electrical circuit with a relay never utilized this object as the pendulum weight for the solution of the two-cord problem. In every instance the Ss chose the switch, an object not previously manipulated, as the object which was to be converted into a pendulum bob in the solution of the two-cord problem. On the other hand, the Ss who had initially been trained to use a switch for the completion of an electrical circuit preponderantly chose the relay as the pendulum weight in solving the two-cord problem.

If the results on solving the two-cord problem for both the switch and relay pre-utilization groups are combined, it is found that 17 of the 19 Ss used that object with which they had had no pre-experimental training as the problem-solving tool. There are less than five chances in one hundred that such results could have occurred as the result of chance fluctuations in responding on the part of the Ss. It may, therefore, be inferred that the nature of the previous specific experiences of the Ss was influential in determining their problem-solving choices.

The replies which the Ss made to the question, "Why did you use the switch (or relay) as the pendulum weight?" further indicate that the pre-utilization experiences exercized a decisive effect upon their problem-solving efforts. Those Ss who used the switch as the pendulum weight in the two-cord problem offered varying reasons for its superiority over the relay as a pendulum

bob. They claimed that it was easier to attach, more compact, etc. The Ss who tended to use the relay as the pendulum bob in solving the two-cord problem proffered equally "good" reasons for their selection. The relay, they claimed, was easier to attach, heavier, etc. In both groups of Ss individuals became somewhat defensive when queried as to the reasons for their choices, and typically replied by prefacing their answers with the remark, "Anyone can see that this one is better as a pendulum weight." A number of Ss even went so far as to say, "Any *fool* can see that this one is better." Since these remarks are directed with equal vehemence at either the switch or at the relay, it is clear that the Ss were not advancing objective reasons for their choices, but were, rather, revealing the effects which their prior specific experience was having on their perceptions.

DISCUSSION

Although the present study was designed primarily to explore a neglected aspect of problem-solving behavior, it has some significance for problem-solving theory and provides clarifications for several important questions. In the first place, the results reveal that the question of the role played by past experience in productive thinking cannot receive a uniform answer until the nature of the past experience is clearly understood. Even though this study indicates that prior experience of a specific kind with a potential problem-solving tool effectively prevents this instrument from being used in problem solution, there is little doubt on the basis of other studies (1, 4) that a different kind of experience may enhance the value of an object as a tool in problem solving. Therefore, what appears to be important for problem solving is not that an individual's performance is dependent upon past experience per se, but rather that *different kinds* of experience are differentially effective in influencing the content of problem-solving behavior. Our results therefore are in accord with those of Katona (5), who found that *how* and *what* an individual learned and not simply *whether* he learned determined the amount of positive transfer effect that occurred in subsequent learning.

Perhaps the most interesting phase of our results concerns the manner in which the individual's previous experience influenced his perceptions. The pre-utilization experience apparently changed the perceived properties of the object previously used in a different context to such a degree that its problem-solving characteristic could not be readily seen. This change in perception was probably based on the manner in which the previous experience had emphasized the instrument as an *electrical object* and so made for extreme difficulty in perceiving it in terms of its general characteristic of *mass*, which is essential for pendulum construction. The kind of previous experience presented therefore functioned to limit the number of the properties of the object that could be perceived by the S.

These results suggest that there are two phenomenally describable kinds of learning that may be important in problem solving. The first variety of learning involves the acquisition by S of certain broad, nonspecific, general notions about the properties of the object or method experienced. This was undoubtedly the case in Birch's study of chimpanzee problem solving (1), where young chimpanzees who were initially capable of using a stick to take distant food into reach manifested this ability after a very short period of play with sticks. It is this general, broad, nonspecific experience which seems to provide the repertoire of experience essential for productive thinking.

A second type of learning involves the acquisition of experiences which convert the initial perception of broad general properties of an object into perceptions of specific limited functional characteristics. It is this second variety of learning which appears to have occurred in the pre-utilization experiences of the Ss in our study and to have produced what Duncker (2) refers to as "functional fixedness" in problem-solving perceptions. Such fixedness limits the range of perceptual organizations capable of being developed by the S and so interferes with problem solving.

SUMMARY

The present study was designed to investigate the effects of specific experience with objects in unrelated situations upon their utilizability as problem-solving instruments. The results revealed that specific prior experience limited the perception of object properties and made the experienced materials less available as problem-solving tools. These results are discussed in connection with Duncker's hypothesis of "functional fixedness," and as contributions to the general areas of transfer and of productive thinking.

REFERENCES

1. BIRCH, H. G. The relation of previous experience to insightful problem-solving. *J. comp. Psychol.*, 1945, 38, 367-383.
2. DUNCKER, K. *On problem-solving.* (Trans. L. S. Lees.) *Psychol. Monogr.*, 1945, No. 270.
3. GUTHRIE, E. R., and HORTON, G. P. *Cats in a puzzle box.* New York: Rinehart, 1946.
4. JACKSON, T. A. Use of the stick as a tool by young chimpanzees. *J. comp. Psychol.*, 1942, 34, 223-235.
5. KATONA, G. *Organizing and memorizing.* New York: Columbia Univ. Press, 1939.
6. MAIER, N. R. F. Reasoning in humans: I. On direction, *J. comp. Psychol.*, 1930, 11, 115-143.
7. MAIER, N. R. F. Reasoning in humans: II. The solution of a problem and its appearance in consciousness. *J. comp. Psychol.*, 1931, 12, 181-194.
8. MAIER, N. R. F. Reasoning in humans: III. The mechanisms of equivalent stimuli and of reasoning. *J. exp. Psychol.*, 1945, 35, 349-360.
9. WERTHEIMER, M. *Productive thinking.* New York: Harper, 1945.

75/THE USE OF ADVANCE ORGANIZERS IN THE LEARNING AND RETENTION OF MEANINGFUL VERBAL MATERIAL/

DAVID P. AUSUBEL*

THE PURPOSE OF THIS STUDY IS TO test the hypothesis that the learning and retention of unfamiliar but meaningful verbal material can be facilitated by the advance introduction of relevant subsuming concepts (organizers). . . . It is reasonable to suppose (Ausubel, Robbins, & Blake, 1957) that new meaningful material becomes incorporated into cognitive structure in so far as it is subsumable under relevant existing concepts. . . .

In the present study, appropriate and relevant subsuming concepts (organizers) are deliberately introduced prior to the learning of unfamiliar academic material, in order to ascertain whether learning and retention are enhanced thereby in accordance with . . . theoretical premises. . . .

METHOD

SUBJECTS. The experimental population consisted of 120 senior undergraduate students (78 women and 32 men) in four sections of an educational psychology course at the University of Illinois. All Ss were enrolled in one of eight teacher education curricula at the secondary school level. Students specializing in industrial education and in vocational agriculture were excluded from the study since they had received specific instruction in the topic covered by the learning passage. The experiment was conducted separately in each section as a required laboratory exercise and was performed during regularly scheduled class hours. In order to maximize ego-involvement, Ss were informed that after the data were processed their individual scores, as well as the class results, would be reported to them.

LEARNING PASSAGE AND TEST OF RETENTION. The learning material used in this study was a specially prepared 2,500-word passage[1] dealing with the metallurgical properties of plain carbon steel. Emphasis was placed on such basic principles as the

relationship between metallic grain structure, on the one hand, and temperature, carbon content, and rate of cooling, on the other. Important factual information (e.g., critical temperatures), however, was also included, and basic principles were also applied to such technological processes as heat treatment and tempering.

The metallurgical topic was chosen on the basis of being generally unfamiliar to undergraduates in liberal arts and sciences (i.e., not ordinarily included in chemistry courses), but still sufficiently elementary to be both comprehensible and interesting to novices with no prior background in the field. The criterion of unfamiliarity was especially crucial because the purpose of the study was to ascertain whether advance organizers could facilitate retention in areas of knowledge *new* to learners. By using unfamiliar material it was also possible to ensure that all Ss started from approximately the same baseline in learning the material. Empirical proof of unfamiliarity was sought, therefore, by administering the retention test on the steel passage to a comparable group of naive Ss who had *not* studied the material; but although this latter group of Ss made scores which, on the average, were only slightly and not significantly better than chance, it was evident from later analysis of the experimental data that scores earned by Ss who *had* studied the passage were related to both sex and field of specialization. Male students and majors in science and art were better able to learn and retain the steel material than were female students and majors in English, foreign languages, music, and the social sciences. Hence, the criterion of unfamiliarity was not completely satisfied, in as much as these differences undoubtedly reflected, in part, variability in relevant incidental experience influencing the learnability of the material.

Knowledge of the steel passage was tested by a 36-item multiple-choice examination with a corrected split-half reliability of .79. Test questions covered principles, facts, and applications, and were selected by an item analysis procedure from a larger population of items. Scores on the test showed a satisfactory range of variability and were distributed normally. Since it was intended as a power test, no time limit was imposed.

---

[1] Appreciation is expressed to Robert M. Tomlinson for assistance in the preparation of the learning passage.

* David P. Ausubel, The use of advance organizers in the learning and retention of meaningful verbal material, *Journal of Educational Psychology*, 1960, 51, 267-272. Reprinted with abridgement by permission.

PROCEDURE. It was first necessary to equate experimental and control groups on the basis of ability to learn an unfamiliar scientific passage of comparable difficulty. The passage used for this purpose was concerned with the endocrinology of human pubescence and was approximately 1,800 words long. Ss were given 20 minutes to read and study this material, and were tested immediately thereafter by a 26-item multiple-choice test with a corrected split-half reliability of .78. (The unfamiliarity of the material had been previously ascertained by administering the test to a comparable group of naive Ss who had not studied the passage, and obtaining a mean score only slightly and not significantly greater than chance.) Test scores on the pubescence passage were normally distributed and correlated .64 on a product-moment basis with test scores on the steel passage. F tests were performed on the variance ratios of the pubescence material test scores for all possible combinations of the four sections, and none approached significance at the .05 level of confidence. It was considered justifiable, therefore, to treat the retention scores of experimental and control groups on the steel passage as if derived, respectively, from one large class rather than from four separate sections.

Ss in each of the four sections were matched on the basis of test scores on the pubescence material and assigned to experimental and control groups. Experimental and control treatments were then administered simultaneously to experimental and control Ss, respectively, within each section. This procedure was possible because the two treatments consisted of studying identical appearing introductory passages differing only in content. The use of this procedure also provided the important methodological advantage of holding instructor, class, and situational variables constant for both groups. Each introductory passage of approximately 500 words was studied twice, 5 minutes each time, by the appropriate group of Ss. The two occasions were 48 hours and immediately before exposure to the main learning passage.

The experimental introductory passage contained background material for the learning passage which was presented at a much higher level of abstraction, generality, and inclusiveness than the latter-passage itself. It was designed to serve as an organizing or anchoring focus for the steel material and to relate it to existing cognitive structure. Principal emphasis was placed, therefore, on the major similarities and differences between metals and alloys, their respective advantages and limitations, and the reasons for making and using alloys. Although this passage provided Ss in the experimental group with relevant background concepts of a general nature, it was carefully designed not to contain specific information that would confer a direct advantage in answering any of the questions on the steel test. This latter criterion was tested empirically and shown to be warranted when a comparable group of Ss made only a

slightly better than chance mean score on the steel test after studying the introductory passage alone.

The control introductory passage, on the other hand, consisted of such historically relevant background material as the historical evolution of the methods used in processing iron and steel. This type of introductory material is traditionally included in most textbooks on metallurgy and is presumably intended to enhance student interest. In contrast to the introductory passage given to the experimental group, it contained no conceptual material that could serve as an ideational framework for organizing the particular substantive body of more detailed ideas, facts, and relationships in the learning passage.

It was methodologically necessary to provide this control treatment in order that any obtained difference between experimental and control groups could be attributed to the particular nature of the experimental introductory passage (i.e., to its organizing properties) rather than to its presence per se.

Both groups studied the steel passage for 35 minutes and took the multiple-choice steel test 3 days later. Since it was evident from a comparison of test scores on the steel and pubescence passages that scores on the steel test were related to Ss' sex and major field, it was necessary to hold these latter factors (as well as pubescence test scores) constant. Hence, it was no longer possible to use the originally matched pairs of Ss within each section. Sufficient Ss were also not available to rematch individual pairs of Ss on all three variables. By matching experimental and control Ss across sections, however, it was possible to equate two groups of 40 Ss each for sex, pubescence scores, and field of specialization. The crossing of sectional lines in this rematching procedure was justifiable in view of the intersectional homogeneity of variance.

RESULTS AND DISCUSSION

The mean steel test score of the experimental group was 16.7, as compared to 14.1 for the control group and a mean chance score of 7.2 (one-fifth of 36).[2] The standard deviations of the two groups were 5.8 and 5.4, respectively. The difference between the means[3] of the experimental and control groups was significant at the .05 level and nearly at the .01 level for a one-tailed test.

The obtained difference in retention between experimental and control groups, although statistically

[2] The distribution of steel test scores for both experimental and control groups did not deviate significantly from the norm. Appreciation is expressed to Pearl Ausubel for assistance in the processing of the data.

[3] The standard error of the difference for equated groups was calculated according to a method described by Edwards (1954, pp. 282-288).

TABLE 1 / RETENTION TEST SCORES OF EXPERIMENTAL AND CONTROL GROUPS ON LEARNING PASSAGE.

GROUP	TYPE OF INTRODUCTION	MEAN	SD
Experimental	Substantive	16.7	5.8
Control	Historical	14.1	5.4

Note.—Chance Score on the multiple-choice test of 36 items is 7.2. The difference between the means in this table is reliable at between the .05 and .01 level of confidence.

significant, would undoubtedly have been even greater if the learning passage used for matching purposes had been in the same subject matter field as the steel material (i.e., if the relationship between the two sets of scores were higher than that indicated by the correlation of .64 between the steel and pubescence scores.) Another experimental condition probably detracting from the difference between the two groups was the fact that the steel material was not completely unfamiliar to many Ss. Because of some prior general familiarity with the contents of the steel passage, many Ss already possessed relevant and stable subsuming concepts. These obviously rendered less significant the potential learning advantages conferable by advance organizers.

It could be argued, of course, that exposure to the experimental introduction constituted in effect a partial substantive equivalent of an additional learning trial. Actually, however, any substantive repetition was at most very indirect, since the introductory passage consisted of much more inclusive and general background material than was contained in the learning task itself, and also provided no direct advantage in answering the test items. Furthermore, according to behavioristic (interference) theory, prior exposure to similar but not identical learning material induces proactive inhibition rather than facilitation.

Advance organizers probably facilitate the incorporability and longevity of meaningful verbal material in two different ways. First, they explicity draw upon and mobilize whatever relevant subsuming concepts are already established in the learner's cognitive structure and make them part of the subsuming entity. Thus, not only is the new material rendered more familiar and meaningful, but the most relevant ideational antecedents are also selected and utilized in integrated fashion. Second, advance organizers at an appropriate level of inclusiveness provide optimal anchorage. This promotes both initial incorporation and later resistance to obliterative subsumption.

The appropriate level of inclusiveness may be defined as that level which is as proximate as possible to the degree of conceptualization of the learning task—relative, of course, to the existing degree of differentiation of the subject as a whole in the learner's cognitive background. Thus, the more unfamiliar the learning material (i.e., the more undifferentiated the learner's background of relevant concepts), the more inclusive or highly generalized the subsumers must be in order to be proximate. If appropriately relevant and proximate subsuming concepts are not available, the learner tends to use the most proximate and relevant ones that are. But since it is highly improbable, however, that we can count on the spontaneous availability of the most relevant and proximate subsuming concepts, the most dependable way of facilitating retention is to introduce the appropriate subsumers and make them part of cognitive structure prior to the actual presentation of the learning task. The introduced subsumers thus become advance organizers or anchoring foci for the reception of new material.

Even though this principle seems rather self-evident it is rarely followed in actual teaching procedures or in the organization of most textbooks. The more typical practice is to segregate topically homogeneous materials into separate chapters, and to present them throughout at a uniform level of conceptualization in accordance with a logical outline of subject matter organization. This practice, of course, although logically sound is psychologically incongruous with the postulated process whereby meaningful learning occurs, i.e., with the hierarchical organization of cognitive structure in terms of progressive gradations of inclusiveness, and with the mechanism of accretion through a process of progressive differentiation of an undifferentiated field. Thus, in most instances, students are required to learn the details of new and unfamiliar disciplines before they have acquired an adequate body of relevant subsumers at an appropriate level of inclusiveness.

As a result, both students and teachers are often coerced into treating meaningful materials as if they were rote in character, and students consequently experience unnecessary difficulty and reduced success in both learning and retention. The teaching of mathematics and science, for example, still relies heavily on rote learning of formulas and procedural steps, on recognition of stereotyped "type problems," and on mechanical manipulation of symbols. In the absence of clear and stable concepts which can serve as anchoring points and organizing foci for the incorporation of new meaningful material, students are trapped in a morass of confusion and have little choice but to rotely memorize learning tasks for examination purposes. The traditional historical introduction to new and primarily nonhistorical, subject matter concepts possibly enhances student interest, but lacks the necessary substantive content to serve this organizing function (see examples under *Procedure* section above).

The pedagogic value of advance organizers obviously depends in part upon how well organized the learning material itself is. If it contains built-in organizers and proceeds from regions of lesser to greater differentiation (higher to lower inclusiveness), rather than in the manner of the typical textbook or lecture presentation, much of the potential benefit derivable from advance organizers will not be actualized. Regardless of how well-organized learning material is, however, it is hypothesized that learning and retention can still be facilitated by the use of advance organizers at an appropriate level of inclusiveness. Such organizers are available from the very beginning of the learning task, and their integrative properties are also much more salient than when introduced concurrently with the learning material.

SUMMARY AND CONCLUSIONS

An empirical test was made of the hypothesis that the learning and retention of unfamiliar but meaningful verbal material could be facilitated by the advance introduction of relevant subsuming concepts (organizers). Experimental and control groups of 40 undergraduate Ss each were equated on the basis of sex, field of specialization, and ability to learn unfamiliar scientific material. The learning task consisted of a 2,500-word passage of empirically demonstrated unfamiliarity, dealing with the metallurgical properties of steel. On two separate occasions, 48 hours and immediately prior to contact with the learning task, experimental Ss studied a 500-word introductory passage containing substantive background material of a conceptual nature presented at a much higher level of generality,

abstraction, and inclusiveness than the steel material itself. This passage was empirically shown to contain no information that could be directly helpful in answering the test items on the steel passage. Control Ss similarly studied a traditional type of historical introduction of identical length. Retention of the learning material was tested 3 days later by means of a multiple-choice test. Comparision of the mean retention scores of the experimental and control groups unequivocably supported the hypothesis.

The facilitating influence of advance organizers on the incorporability and longevity of meaningful learning material was attributed to two factors: (*a*) the selective mobilization of the most relevant existing concepts in the learner's cognitive structure for integrative use as part of the subsuming focus for the new learning task, thereby increasing the task's familiarity and meaningfulness; and (*b*) the provision of optimal anchorage for the learning material in the form of relevant and appropriate subsuming concepts at a proximate level of inclusiveness.

The suggestion was offered that the greater use of appropriate (substantive rather than historical) advance organizers in the teaching of meaningful verbal material could lead to more effective retention. This procedure would also render unnecessary much of the rote memorization to which students resort because they are required to learn the details of a discipline before having available a sufficient number of key subsuming concepts.

REFERENCES

AUSUBEL, D. B., ROBBINS, LILLIAN C., and BLAKE, E., JR. Retroactive inhibition and facilitation in the learning of school materials. *J. Educ. Psychol.*, 1957, 48, 334-343.

EDWARDS, A. L. *Statistical methods for the behavioral sciences.* New York: Rinehart, 1954.

76/QUESTIONING SOME ASSUMPTIONS UNDERLYING CURRENT ACHIEVEMENT TESTING/VERNER M. SIMS*

THE VALUE OF ANY MEASUREMENT OF educational achievement must be judged ultimately in terms of the extent to which the measurement reveals information leading to a more intelligent prediction or control of the behavior of students. Commonly, however, we neither apply this criterion directly to our instruments nor to our measuring activity. Instead, in the testing which we do, we either consciously or unconsciously accept a chain of assumptions which stem from and presumably may be justified, either logically or experimentally, as supporting this ultimate purpose. The soundness of our measurement and its usefulness to education is, therefore, contingent on the validity of a set of assumptions which are implicit in our testing. It is the purpose of this paper to make explicit and to critically examine certain of the assumptions which seem to underlie current measurement of achievement.

1. Current measurement of achievement assumes that the value of a learning experience is indicated by increased ability (skill or knowledge) to cope with some situation or class of situations.

Achievement testing as presently practiced appears to be confined to the testing of ability. Standardized tests of achievement, whether subject tests or general tests, survey or diagnostic, whether tests of knowledge, skills, or understanding, or tests of ability to apply principles and interpret data, are all concerned with measuring what children *can* do. Teachers in their own testing and marking are concerned with measuring the same outcomes. If the teacher does attempt measurement of anything other than ability it is usually made clear to the pupils that "this test does not count." For teachers to permit anything other than achievement (interpreted as increased knowledge or ability) to influence their marks is commonly considered questionable practice.

The obvious conclusion to be drawn from an examination of current achievement testing is that the end of education is to increase the abilities of · pupils. Most of our educational theorists would not be willing, however, to accept any such conclusion. They would say, rather, that the end sought in teaching is changed behavior on the part of the learner; which is, of course, not the same thing as having the ability to do differently. Whether one *will* act so and so depends not only on whether he *can* do so but also on a complex of attitudinal-emotional-motivational factors which are generally neglected. Furthermore, it seems reasonable to assume that whether the learner will use his learning or not is a factor of the setting in which it is acquired. Not only the learner's own purposes and methods but those of his teacher will condition the kind and amount of use made of the learning.[1]

If the fundamental question in achievement testing is whether, in terms of the evidence at hand, one can predict that the learner will act differently in a certain class of situations, it would seem desirable that our testing comprehend more than the measurement of *ability*. Recognition of this assumption and acceptance of its limiting influence would, in the writer's opinion, lead to a revamping of many of our present approaches, to the designing of new instruments, and to a reinterpretation of many of our test findings. Tests might be designed, for example, to measure whether a child *would*, as well as could, read, reason or act in certain types of situations. Measures of the effectiveness of the use made of learnings might be developed. In time we might be able to describe (even quantitatively) the conditions under which learnings would or would not function.

2. Current measurement of achievement assumes that the value of a learning experience is indicated by growth in those directions toward which the learning (or teaching) activities are specifically pointed.

[1] The writer has developed this point at considerable length in an earlier article "Educational Measurements and Evaluation," *Journal of Educational Research*, September, 1944, pp. 18-24.

* Verner M. Sims, Questioning some assumptions underlying current achievement testing, *Educational and Psychological Measurement*, 1948, 8, 565-574. Reprinted by permission.

It seems fairly obvious that this assumption does underlie our testing. Typically, we test the value of drill in spelling by measuring the increase in ability to spell, the value of instruction in health by measuring the increase in knowledge and understandings relating to matters of healthful living, the value of a method of science instruction by measuring the increased ability to apply scientific principles, etc. We measure the child's growth and mark him on the achievement of the specific objectives which are set up for the course.

Superficially the soundness of this procedure would seem almost axiomatic; but the thoughtful reader will recognize immediately that it is justified only when many other things are accepted as "being equal," and without evidence to support this, one cannot always assume that such is the truth. If the increased ability to spell comes as a result of sacrifice in the ability to read, if it is accompanied by the acquisition of unfavorable attitudes toward spelling or toward school, if it furnishes an escape from real problems about which the children could and should be doing something directly, or if it merely results in pupils becoming increasingly better in a skill in which they are already *good*, one would certainly question the value of the learning experience. Yet evidence relating to such matters is commonly not made available. Such information is usually not even considered the concern of the tester.

If the "whole child" is involved in any learning experience, then inferences concerning the value of learning which ignore this fact are of questionable validity. Testing theory which neglects the fact forces the trained user to interpret his test results in conjunction with a large amount of "common sense," subjective and informal data, and encourages the untrained user to arrive at conclusions that are unsound.

3. Current measurement of achievement assumes that the value of a learning experience may be inferred from measures of the outcomes evident at some particular moment after learning, typically at the conclusion of a learning experience.

The test-teach-test formula describes the accepted procedure for evaluating the outcomes of learning. In practical classroom situations and in educational experimentation we test the value of method and the growth of children in such terms. Progress is assumed to be measured by noting the difference between initial and terminal test scores. Furthermore, in cases where there has been no previous formal training the first testing is commonly dispensed with, and the terminal test score becomes the measure of learning.

We do this although we know that learning is a form of growth the path of which is best expressed by a curve. If this is true, predicting later performance is a matter of projecting this curve into the future. We attempt to do this extrapolation by locating one point (in the case of terminal testing only) or at the best two points (in the case of initial-terminal testing) on the curve. Mathematically, this is not possible. With one point we can tell nothing about the curve, with two points the curve would need to be a smooth one the slope of which was known. These are conditions which are not met in practical teaching-testing situations, unless in the doubtful case where the concern is entirely with group averages. Certainly no individual's curve of learning is a "smooth one the slope of which is known." This implies that dependable predictions can be made only when we locate further points on the curve of growth.

Some educators will point out, however, that there is a correlation between such measures of progress and later performance. The fact is, the nature of these correlations is one of the reasons which cause the writer to question the soundness of this assumption. The size of the coefficients usually found between terminal tests and later achievement suggests that we may be dealing with little more than "the correlation between desirable traits." Reading age, at ten years, for example, is no more closely correlated with reading ability at 15 years than is general intelligence. In the writer's institution at least, terminal achievement on a standardized test of high-school algebra is not as closely correlated with success in college algebra as is general quantitative ability as measured by the *ACE Psychological Examination*. One is led to suspect that the only real justification for assuming that initial-terminal testing measures the value of a learning experience is found in the convenience and simplicity of the procedures which the assumption makes possible.

4. Current measurement of achievement assumes that the only sound interpretation of measures of achievement is through comparison with norms of some sort.

Educational measurement, as it has developed, is a "normative" science; that is, it attempts to develop norms of performance for groups of known (and described) status from which one may by comparison interpret measures of other groups or individuals. Standardized achievement testing is universally of this nature. Raw scores are to be interpreted in terms of age or grade norms, T-scores, scaled scores, or percentiles. The writer knows of no standardized achievement test which does not use this method of interpreting scores. In fact, the word "standardized" has come to refer not only to a standard testing procedure but to a test with "standards." Furthermore, very few tests propose any other method of interpretation. In teacher testing, too, the emphasis, as the testing experts would have it certainly, is in the same direction. In all text books concerned with the problem of marking with which the writer is familiar, teachers are encouraged to make relative interpretations, to "mark on the curve," to define an A as superior performance in the group; some even go as far as to recommend that promotion and non-promotion be determined on the basis of position in some group. Any teacher who proceeds otherwise today is apt to be labeled either old-fashioned or too "progressive."

The writer is not questioning the value of the interpretation of test scores in terms of norms. In the hands of a trained teacher, standard scores may serve many useful purposes. (The fact that they are too often misused, being accepted as goals of achievement, for instance, is also irrelevant to our purpose here.) Relative position in a class, as expressed by the kind of marks which specialists in measurement advocate, also has its uses. That which is being questioned is the assumption that the *only* valid interpretation of measures of achievement is through comparison with norms. For many school objectives and for many situations facing teachers, the writer contends that there are other perfectly valid interpretations possible and desirable. There are two cases in particular which seem worthy of comment.

First, in the case of some learnings, worthwhile interpretations may be made by comparing a child's performance with the demands of life (present or future). For example, we assume that a child needs to know how to add, and to know automatically, all the digit combinations. The fact that Johnny has mastered 50 per cent of these combinations, or 60 per cent, or 90 per cent, is valuable information for the teacher who is working with Johnny without regard to where he stands with reference to other children. In fact, the job which lies ahead for Johnny is just the same whether he is at the top, in the middle, or at the bottom of some group. Or, let us consider

writing or spelling. Johnny must write legibly (we assume), and whether his writing is legible, or not, can be determined without comparing him with other children. If we assume that the child should be able to spell the 1,000 most common words, or the 100 "spelling demons," then knowing that he can spell certain of these words has great meaning to Johnny and to his teacher, even though he is the only pupil she has ever had in class or even known. If there is anything wrong with this idea it is in the assumption concerning what he should know, not in the interpretation of the measurement.

Our whole system of prerequisites falls into the same category. If certain learnings are really needed to succeed in later work then tests which show whether the student has mastered these learnings have meaning which is independent of the performance of others. The same is true of learning in multitudinous fields. Particularly in the fields of attitudes and habits of action could illustrations be multiplied. The fact that a child throws rocks at Negro children every time he gets a chance, the regularity with which he brushes his teeth, or the extent to which he eats a balanced diet, all have meaning which is not determined by a normative score.

Secondly, many measurements may have meaning when interpreted in terms of the student's own educational-psychological make-up. Illustrated simply, the child who succeeds in mastering the mechanics of arithmetic but who cannot solve problems involving the same processes can be located without any normative interpretations. The student whose factual learning is entirely acceptable to the teacher but whose attitudes toward the same problems are not; the student whose emotional blockings prevent him from using his ability to reason sensibly on problems relating to labor unions; the student whose motivations are all in the direction of pleasing the teacher: these can all be identified without the use of norms, whether class norms or large group ones. The fact that the teacher's own experiences with students are involved in the judgments which she makes concerning the goodness or badness of such characteristics is aside from the point. Exactly the same value judgments are involved in the interpretation of tests which are provided with norms.

Insisting that measures of achievement have meaning only through comparison with norms must result in limiting the usefulness of educational measurements.

5. Current measurement of achievement assumes either that "appropriate" measurement is independent of one's theory of learning and of education, that current measurement concepts fit all current theories of learning and of education, or that there is only one acceptable theory of learning and of education.

When achievement testing techniques were first subjected to careful study, some three decades ago, the prevailing theory of learning was a narrow, "connectionist" one, expressed by Thorndike's stimulus-response formula, and the commonly accepted theory of education was that education is preparation for living. It is perhaps no accident, therefore, that our testing procedures so aptly fit these theories of learning and of education. In the meantime, however, in many quarters at least, other theories of learning and of education have come to be accepted, while our testing techniques remain relatively unchanged. (The only major change in achievement testing procedures that has taken place during the past two decades which the writer is able to identify is represented by Tyler's approach. Most of our testing seems to fit the theory that education is an accumulation of large numbers of relatively independent knowledges and skills, while Tyler's testing would seem to identify it as an accumulation of a large number of abilities to apply principles, interpret data, and reason logically, all of which are still relatively independent. It is not difficult to see in Tyler's work the influence of Judd's theory of "transfer through generalization" rather than Thorndike's "transfer of identical elements," but otherwise it fits perfectly an atomistic conception of learning as preparation.)

So far as the writer can find, no one working in the field of achievement testing has seriously considered the implications of insightful learning, or of organismic or "field" psychology for achievement testing procedures. Nor does anyone seem to have considered the possibility that other theories of education, such as the theory that education is a form of intelligent living which within itself constitutes an end, may demand different approaches to the matter of testing.

If one rejects the theory that learning consists of the acquisition of a large number of more or less simple and independent abilities, then one can justify present means of testing the outcomes of instruction only by assuming that the number of such abilities acquired is indicative of total learning. When the fundamental nature

of the differences among the several theories of learning and of education is considered it seems rather naive to accept such an assumption without any evidence to support it—even without trying to get evidence to support it. Can we assume, for example, that a child who showed no progress on a current standardized reading test during his first three years in school, and then, in his fourth year, without any special help, jumped from a reading age of seven years to almost eleven years, actually learned nothing about reading during the first three years?[2] How could one who denies that psychologically the whole is equal to the sum of the parts be expected to take to current tests of arithmetic, of social studies, of science? As long as we operate as though the end of education is the accumulation of a set of skills and knowledges which will be useful later, can we blame the "progressives" (who accept a quite different theory of education) if they reject our instruments in their entirety?

It does not seem unfair to say that the measurements experts have very subtly, although perhaps unconsciously, thrown their support to a particular theory of learning and of education. Would not an eclectic approach contribute to a greater serviceableness from the discipline? With our present lack of effort, can we presume to say that educational measurements have no contribution to make to those who hold to differing philosophies of education or belong to differing schools of psychology?

In summary, the attempt has been made in this paper to point out several assumptions which seem to be implicit in present-day measurement of achievement. The assumptions identified are those of which the writer is critical. In general, the basis of the criticism is the fact that through operating on the assumptions we restrict the usefulness of educational measurements. Whether or not the assumptions are defensible may, of course, be debated. If they do underlie our measurements, however, there can surely be no question concerning the worth of making them explicit, and the desirability of consciously recognizing them as assumptions. It may even be that simply accepting the assumptions for what they are would, in itself, result in some rather fundamental changes in our measuring activity and in the techniques of measurement finally developed.

[2] Reported by Willard C. Olson, "When Should My Child Learn to Read?" *University of Michigan School of Education Bulletin*, XIX (1947), 9.

77/OBJECTIVE TESTS AND TEACHERS'

MEASUREMENTS/VERNER M. SIMS*

NEW-TYPE, OBJECTIVE TESTS, DEVEL-oped in connection with group intelligence tests and quickly applied to standardized measures of achievement, were very naturally carried over by the teacher to the measurement of the results of her instruction. The modern teacher knows more about making objective tests than did the "measurements expert" of a few years ago, and the use of an essay examination is commonly taken as an indication of ignorance, laziness or antiquity. Like most movements in education our enthusiasm for the new precluded any serious attempts at rational evaluation, and to-day many teachers, supervisors, administrators and educational writers contend that all the teacher's testing should be of this sort. It does seem high time that we attempt a critical appraisal of these tests. Aside from any general criticism of the "objective" testing technique in other realms of human measurement, there seem to be conditions peculiar to the use of these tests as class-room tests that make the wisdom of their exclusive use appear very doubtful.

Typically, this method of examining places the individual in a large number of relatively narrow, rather simple and more or less isolated situations, assuming that the number of such situations adequately met is a measure of ability. For the teacher this means using true-false, completion, multiple-choice, etc., types rather than the traditional essay examination; and further it means testing on facts, single qualities, elementary relationships, in general what the psychologist would call "limited perceptions." Whether or not this is what it should mean to the teacher is more or less aside from the issue. Suffice it to say that not only in the hands of the teacher but also in the hands of experts (in our standardized tests) they are of this narrow nature. In fact, such authorities as Ruch, Russell and Odell point to this as the peculiar advantage of the new testing.

The theory supporting the use of such tests is that an extensive sampling of narrow items gives better measurement than an intensive sampling, where a few relatively complex situations are presented. At first glance the theory is very at-tractive, especially to the "measurement-conscious" teacher. Certainly it will give more reliable measurement than the intensive sampling; not only because the units are of necessity finer, but also, since the number of complex situations that can be presented must be limited, it is less sensitive to accidental inequalities in learning due to such things as absence, illness or temporary inattention. For the same reasons, other things being equal, it would presumably give more valid measurement. But, are other things equal in the case of the classroom tests?

To justify the use of objective tests for measuring the outcomes of instruction one must assume either (1) that the learning consists of a large number of more or less simple and independent habits or (2) that the number of such habits formed is indicative of total learning in the given field. In other words, when one tests knowledge by measuring ability to react to a large number of narrow items the assumption is either that knowledge is made up of the number of such items known or that knowledge is indicated by the number known.

Now, in certain school subjects (or at least in parts of certain subjects) the first assumption is, for all practical purposes, true. For example, in spelling, in number combinations, in vocabulary, the learning is essentially a matter of acquiring a large number of simple habits. In such subjects the extensive sampling would undoubtedly give reliable and valid measurement. Here good measurement would simply consist in making a random sampling long enough to be reliable.

In other subjects, in most subjects, the learning is not alone a matter of acquiring many isolated modes of response. It is primarily a matter of organizing and relating these responses into patterns. In such subjects learning is best conceived as a hierarchy of habits, the elementary facts being the lower order habits and the combinations, relations, organizations, integrations being the higher order habits. In these subjects the first assumption (that learning consists of simple and independent habits) would not be valid; consequently, one could justify interpreting the score on an objective test as a measure of

* Verner M. Sims, Objective tests and teachers' measurements, *School and Society*, 1932, *36*, 300-302. Reprinted by permission.

563

knowledge only on the basis of the second assumption, that it indicates knowledge. And it is this supposition that I question, particularly in the case of the teacher's own tests.

In the realm of intelligence testing, and in general achievement testing, the empirical evidence does seem to justify such assumption, for there is certainly a close relationship between scores on these tests and other measures of the ability or abilities being measured. But, if it be true in these fields, it is true only when the ability being measured develops and exists independent of its measurement; and in the case of the teacher's measurements one cannot postulate any such independent development or existence. To illustrate, if a child had been previously drilled on the answers to the items in an intelligence test one would hesitate to contend that performance on the test was indicative of general ability. Yet this is practically what happens in the case of the teacher's tests. The implication is not that she drills the class upon the items in the tests (although there is probably more of this than one would suppose) but that she unconsciously emphasizes the lower order habits to the exclusion of all others. The teacher who is to test for facts known will naturally come to lay stress upon facts. One could not imagine a teacher, testing month after month, year after year, on narrow, simple items, who did not eventually come to think of the acquistion of such habits as being the ends of instruction. This seems to be a very natural condition that one could avoid only by divorcing the testing from the teaching, which in this case is impossible, since the same person carries on both jobs.

If it is natural for the teacher to teach what she is going to test, it is just as natural for the student to study what he is going to be tested on. Our second assumption would be invalid, not only because the teacher is influenced by what she is to test on but also because the student is in like manner influenced. If we could assume that the student acquires knowledge, regardless of the method of testing, then to sample the lower order habits might give satisfactory measurement, but it is too far-fetched to imagine that the student will attempt to master the subject without any regard to approaching periods of reckoning. Among other things, he studies for the examination, and what he studies as well as the methods used will be determined in some measure by the type of test expected. Terry (in a study as yet unpublished) has investigated the methods of study used in preparing for different types of examinations, and he found that less than 4 per cent of some 250 students used the same methods in studying for the two types, essay and objective. What is more significant, he found that the average student in preparing for an objective test concentrated on details, on what he calls "small units," while in preparing for an essay examination attention was given mainly to "large units."

The ideal testing program would necessitate first a setting up of the objectives of instruction and then the development of instruments that would measure these ends; but, so long as we have such vague conceptions of what we are trying to teach, this intimate relation between teaching and testing and between studying and testing would suggest that for many subjects the use of objective tests to the exclusion of the essay will actually pervert the ends of instruction. In my opinion, the most satisfactory testing procedure for most school subjects would involve the supplementing of objective tests with essay questions definitely designed to measure these higher order habits of relationship and organization.

78/ADAPTING TEACHER STYLE TO PUPIL DIFFERENCES: TEACHERS FOR DISADVANTAGED CHILDREN[1]/ MIRIAM L. GOLDBERG[*]

IT HAS BECOME A CLICHÉ TO STATE that the major effects on pupil learning result from what goes on in the classroom. We recognize that what the teacher and the pupils do during the five or six hours a day when they are in direct contact with each other is the "compass of learning." And yet, until recently, little of our research has addressed itself to the teaching process. We have studied the achievement of pupils under various methods of instruction, we have described and theorized about the personality characteristics of teachers, we have explored various theoretical formulations about the nature of learning, and the effects of varying the administrative deployment of pupils and more recently of teachers have been investigated. We have examined the effects of class size, the functions of the administrator, the guidance counselor and other adjunct personnel of the school. But we still could not describe with any degree of accuracy what teaching is all about, what the teacher actually says and does in the process of teaching, and what effect this has on pupil learning.

Although little may be known about the teaching process in general, even less information is available on the "fit" between particular styles of teaching and the learning of particular pupil populations. This question looms especially large as one considers the problems of teaching children from depressed or disadvantaged areas; pupils who, thus far, have not been effectively "reached" by the teaching procedures to which they have generally been exposed. That various teaching procedures now in use are more or less effective with pupils from more affluent or academically motivating environments is undoubtedly true. But these same procedures, typically learned in teacher education programs, have rarely proved effective with disadvantaged youngsters.

Three assumptions underlie this paper: The first maintains that a pupil's learning is, in large measure, a function of the kind of teaching to which he is exposed. Thus, the extent to which a pupil masters a given set of academic tasks reflects not only his aptitudes and attitudes, but also the appropriateness of the particular approach by which he is taught.

The second assumption, implied by the title, rejects the notion of the universally "good" teacher, equally able to adapt his style to varying pupil populations, and substitutes a conception of a variety of "good" teachers, differentially suited (by temperament and training) to teaching differing groups of students.

The third assumption proposes that children from culturally disadvantaged backgrounds though highly variable, nevertheless represent a describable pupil population in need of teachers who are uniquely "good" for them.

The first portion of this paper presents some of the evidence in support of the first two assumptions, citing studies which point up the variety of teaching styles and their effects on pupil achievement in general and on the achievement of specific categories of pupils in particular. The remainder of the paper proposes a hypothetical model of the successful teacher of disadvantaged pupils and suggests how such a model may be approached.

STUDIES OF TEACHER PERFORMANCE

The last decade has witnessed a number of efforts to study the processes of teaching. The first consideration of most of the studies has been to describe and classify what the teacher and the pupils say and do during a class session. Some of the investigations have gone beyond the descriptive material into a study of the relationships between the teacher's style of performance and the learning patterns of children.

[1] A revision of a lecture presented at The Merrill-Palmer Institute, March, 1963.

[*] Miriam L. Goldberg, Adapting teacher style to pupil differences: teachers for disadvantaged children, Merrill-Palmer Quarterly of Behavior and Development, 1964, 10, 161-178. Reprinted by permission.

CATEGORIZING TEACHER STYLE. A variety of more and less structured classroom observations have yielded various classifications of teacher style. For example, Flanders (1960) classified teachers as those who more often exert "direct influence," through lecturing, giving directions or criticizing student's work, and those who more often exert "indirect influence" through clarifying feelings, providing praise and encouragement, developing and making use of student ideas and asking questions.

Medley (1962) divided the teacher's performance into three broad categories: (1) his means of controlling the class, (2) his approach to the content, and (3) the interpersonal climate he creates. In the "control" category fell such behaviors as eliciting large amounts of pupil response, maintaining a high degree of order or permitting a high degree of pupil initiative. "Approach to content" included such procedures as emphasizing individualization or using interesting, original devices and materials. The "class climate" category included the teacher's consideration for pupils' problems and feelings, the degree of support given to pupil statements and responses, and the frequency with which reproof and criticism were used.

More clearly defined, perhaps, are the three dimensions of teacher style suggested by Ryans (1963). The first is a personal dimension ranging from "friendly-warm-understanding to aloof-restricted." The second is a task dimension, ranging from "responsible-organized-business-like to unplanned-slipshod." The third describes the dynamic quality of the teacher's performance from "stimulating-informative to dull-routine." These categories are similar to those suggested by Warrener (1962), who drew his observations from social behavior in non-teaching leadership situations. His categories were: (1) "objective" work orientation, (2) "social relations" orientation, and (3) "subjective" personal, expressive orientation.

The dimensions suggested by Ryans are sufficiently independent of each other so that a teacher may be at a different point along that scale on each one. For example, one teacher may be characterized as warm, business-like, and stimulating; another as warm, business-like but dull; or one might even be seen as aloof, business-like and stimulating. Each dimension represents a continuum, and for most teachers there will be a characteristic point along its baseline.

CATEGORIZING VERBAL BEHAVIOR. The studies mentioned above have concentrated on the teacher's stance, his characteristic mode of behavior, the flavor of his performance, and his attitudes toward his task. Little attention was paid to the handling of content, the skill of questioning, the organization of material, and the like. For aspects of the teacher's work which relate to the processes of handling content, one must turn to the work of B. Othanel Smith and his associates (1963). Here, the concern has been with the "logical operations" of teaching; with discovering ". . . how concepts, norms, laws, etc., are introduced, analyzed and manipulated in the course of instruction" (Smith et al., 1963, p. 2). Using large samples of electrically taped classroom sessions, the verbal behavior of both teachers and pupils was categorized into 13 "major acts"—such as defining, stating, reporting, opining, explaining, comparing and contrasting, classifying, etc. Such analyses made possible the description of a teacher's characteristic performance through quantifying the frequency with which his verbal behavior falls into one or another of the various categories. Eventually, it should become possible to discover to what extent the differential frequencies are a function of a pervasive style of teaching, a response to the inherent logic of a particular subject or phase of it or a reflection of the particular group of pupils being taught.

RELATING TEACHER STYLE TO PUPIL ACHIEVEMENT. But the analyses of teaching styles and logical operations, significant though they may be in supplying needed systematic information on the teaching process, have only just begun to shed light on two crucial questions: (1) What difference do these ways of teaching make? Do pupils, in general, come out with different kinds or amounts of learning when taught by teachers using one or another approach to teaching? (2) Does a particular teacher's style have more or less the same effect on all pupils under his tutelage? If not, are there ways of determining the characteristics of pupils who would fare better under one teaching style than under another?

Working with junior high school classes in mathematics and social studies, Flanders (1960) related teaching style to pupil achievement and degree of dependence. He reported that when learning goals were unclear, as in a new task, lecturing and giving directions increased the dependence of students on the teacher and tended to lower achievement. In general, he found that patterns of "indirect influence" resulted in greater content mastery and in more positive attitudes toward school than did the "direct influence" procedures. However, in classes designated as superior—where pupils' achievement was greatest and attitudes toward the teacher were most favorable—there was an element of flexibility in the teacher's influence patterns not found in below-average classrooms. In superior classes, teacher behavior was less predictable, "shifting from domination and close supervision" on some occasions, to "indirect participation" at other times. These studies also suggest that for pupils who tend to be dependent upon teacher direction and unable to pursue work on their own, a high level of "direct influence"—lecturing, criticizing, giving directions—tends to be associated with lower achievement than is apparent when more independent pupils are exposed to similar "direct" teaching procedures.

In their study of "The Language of Teaching," Bellack and Davitz (1963) analyzed tape-scripts of high school social studies classes studying a unit in economics. They identified four basic Pedagogical Moves: structuring, soliciting, responding, and reacting which "describe the verbal maneuvers of students and teachers . . . and set the framework for the analysis of meaning communicated in the classroom." Although the first phase of this research is largely descriptive, as are most of the other analyses of the verbal behavior of teaching, the data analysis will be used not only to categorize and describe but also to relate the linguistic variables to student learning and attitude change. In subsequent phases, Bellack plans to address himself more intensively to studying the functions of the various Pedagogical Moves—the recurring patterns or "cycles" of moves characteristic of a given teacher, and the relation between patterns of teacher verbal behavior and student performance.

Of special interest to the major concern of this paper is the work of Heil and his associates (1960). They hypothesized that "in a particular class, the teacher's behavior will evoke a certain amount of achievement with children of a given set of feelings and level of intelligence." On the basis of assessment instruments, 5th and 6th grade pupils in a New York City school were divided into four personality categories: (1) Conformers—characterized by incorporation of adult standards, high social orientation, control over

impulses and emphasis on mature behavior; (2) Opposers—showing disturbed authority relationships, oppositional trends, pessimistic tone, intolerance of ambiguity and disappointment and frustration as central dynamics; (3) Waverers—described as anxious, ambivalent, fearful, floundering and indecisive, and (4) Strivers—showing marked drive for recognition, especially in school achievement, and exhibitionistic needs. The teachers were divided into three personality types—the Turbulent, the Self-controlling, and the Fearful.

Pupil achievement was contrasted for each pupil category under each teacher type. In general, when achievement was controlled for I.Q., the "strivers" achieved most, followed by the "conformers," then the "opposers" and showing least gains, the "waverers." Neither the "strivers" nor the "conformers" were significantly affected by teacher personality; but for the "opposers" and the "waverers," teaching style made a significant difference. For the last two groups, the "self-controlling" teachers, who maintained an orderly, workmanlike class, focused on structure and planning—but, at the same time, showed a sensitivity to children's feelings and emphasized interpersonal relations in the classroom—were most effective. The "turbulent" teachers—characterized by greater concern for ideas than for people, freedom of expression of strong feelings and attitudes, little patience with routine tasks, "sloppiness," and inconsistency—were more successful than either of the other types in teaching math and science. In the other subjects their success was limited to "strivers" and "conformers." The "turbulent" teachers were least successful with the "opposers" who evidenced the highest intolerance of ambiguity. The "fearful" teachers—anxious, dependent on the approval of supervisors and of the children, unable to bring structure and order to the teaching task, and highly variable in their behavior—were uniformly ineffective with all kinds of children except "strivers," who fared well regardless of the teacher.

TEACHABLE GROUPS. A quite different approach to the study of the relationship between teacher style and pupil learning is found in Thelen's (1961) recent work on the formation of "teachable" groups. Since the 1930's repeated efforts at assessing the effects of "homogeneous" versus "heterogeneous" grouping or, in more modern parlance, broad and narrow ability range groups, have produced meager results. The findings, though apparently inconclusive, are consistent in reporting that in the absence of deliberate curricular modifications, grouping, on the basis of ability, has no significant effects on pupil achievement. But all of the grouping efforts were predicated on the assumption that if the class group is "homogeneous" with respect to intelligence or reading level or achievement in a particular subject, then, *ipso facto*, such a group becomes more "teachable." A teacher in such a group would accomplish more with the pupils than would be the case where the range of ability was wide. What was left out of the equation of "teachability" was the teacher's style of working and his perception of the kinds of pupils with whom he tends to be most successful. From Thelen's (1961) work it would appear that I.Q. or achievement status are by no means the most significant determinants of the teacher's perception of "teachability." Thelen states that, in general ". . . teachers recognize four kinds of students: the good, the bad, the indifferent, and the sick. But the problem is that each teacher places different students in these categories, so that whatever is being judged is not primarily some characteristic of the student" (p. 226). He urges that ". . . the teachable students for one teacher may be quite different than for another, that the fit between teacher and teachable students primarily results in better meeting the teacher's most dominant needs . . . he is able with the teachable class to do more fully what he tries to do with his other classes . . . that successful grouping must take the teacher himself into account" (p. 220). Despite finding few differences in achievement between "teachable" and random groups, Thelen states: "We remain convinced that any grouping which does not in some way attempt to 'fit' students and teachers together can have only accidental success" (p. 221).

A significant implication of the studies of teacher characteristics, teaching process, and teachable groups is the recognition that variations in pupil attainment in the classroom are related to variations in teacher performance, and that a particular teacher affects different pupils differently. We are forced to question the stereotype of the "good teacher" and the "poor teacher," although there may be some few who would prove excellent for all pupils and many more who would be inadequate no matter what the assignment. Most teachers, however, vary in their effectiveness depending upon the characteristics of the pupils they confront, the opportunity to fulfill their expectations for themselves and for their class, the content of what they teach, and the extent to which the school provides them with what they perceive to be necessary facilitations.

TEACHERS FOR DISADVANTAGED CHILDREN

In discussing the problem of "teachable groups" Thelen (1961) points out that despite great individual differences in teachers' perception of who is teachable, there are some pupils—from 10 to 25 percent of the average school—whom *no* teacher includes among the teachable. His description of this group is reminiscent of what we know about the school behavior of children from disadvantaged areas, from city slums, and rural backwoods. Similarly, Heil's "opposers" and to some extent his "waverers" remind one of typical behaviors of disadvantaged children. In the great cities these children represent an increasing proportion of the total pupil population, far more than the 10 to 25 percent suggested by Thelen. And it is expected that by 1970 one out of every two pupils in large city schools will be "culturally disadvantaged."

The approach to the problem of staffing schools in depressed areas requires several sequential efforts. The first step is to gain broad public acceptance of the assumption that disadvantaged pupils, though widely variable in their abilities and personal characteristics, nonetheless represent a describable group. That is, they represent a group which, although it overlaps other groups in many ways, has unique characteristics, stemming from common backgrounds, values and experiences. The second step is to characterize the teacher who is successful with culturally disadvantaged pupils—successful because the pupils in his classes achieve better than similar pupils in other teachers' classes and have more accepting attitudes toward school, toward the teacher, and toward learning. The third step involves re-examinations of teacher selection and education for staffing disadvantaged area schools.

Since there are no systematic data on what such teachers do, it may be worth while to create a hypothetical model of the "successful teacher of disadvantaged children." Our model can be constructed of implications from available research on teacher behavior, insights from impressionistic observations, and inferences from investigations of the characteristics of disadvantaged pupils and their social world. It may well be that several models of successful teachers will be needed to account for the great variety of pupils within the disadvantaged population. What is suggested here is a general outline which may have to be refined and subdivided to achieve optimum "fit" between pupils and teacher.

HYPOTHETICAL MODEL OF THE SUCCESSFUL TEACHER OF DISADVANTAGED PUPILS. The teacher who is successful with any group of pupils is the one who respects the children in his classes and they, in turn, respect him. As teachers in slum schools look at their pupils, they see many children who are discouraged and defeated, even in the early grades, children who express their alienation from the school and the society it represents by aggressive acting-out behavior or by a kind of tuned-out lethargy and listlessness. There are frequent transgressions against the ethical, moral, and legal codes of society. Pupils seem to be making little effort to learn, show no desire to better themselves, to break out of the limits imposed upon them by their ignorance. The teacher may feel sorry for them, realizing the limiting circumstances of their lives. Or, he may be angered by their laziness, their lack of effort, believing that they could if they would, but they won't. Or, he may write them off as hopeless, too dumb to learn, taking up time and resources that could be better utilized by pupils with more ability and greater motivation.

But the successful teacher of disadvantaged children does respect his pupils—and not because he sees them through the rose-colored lenses of the romantic—finding "beauty" and "strength" where others see poverty and cultural emptiness. On the contrary, he sees them quite realistically as different from his children and his neighbors' children, yet like all children coping in their own way with the trials and frustrations of growing up. And he sees them, unlike middle-class children, struggling to survive in the ruthless world of their peers, confused by the conflicting demands of the two cultures in which they live—the one of the home and the street and the neighborhood, the other of the school and the society that maintains it.

Like the anthropologist, the successful teacher views the alien culture of his pupils not as a judge, but as a student. He understands the backgrounds from which the children come, the values placed on various achievements, the kind of work and life to which they aspire. He recognizes and understands the reasons for their unwillingness to strive toward future goals, where such efforts provide little reward in the present.

He knows that many of the children bear the scars of intellectual understimulation in their early years. Familiar with the home life of the children, he knows how rarely they are helped to name the things they see and feel and bear, to recognize similarities and differences, to categorize and classify perceptions, to learn the word for the object, and the phrases through which to express an idea or a feeling.

The successful teacher is aware of the various family structures from which the children come: The matriarchal family in which no father is present; the home where there are two parents, but both working; where one or both parents are able-bodied but out of work, recipients of relief; where the father is disabled and stays home while the mother works; where an extended family—grandparents, aunts, uncles, and other relatives—live together. This teacher has seen the physical conditions in which the children live: their lack of privacy, the poor facilities, the absence of basic amenities. He knows the kinds of jobs the parents have, their aspirations for themselves and for their children, and what role they attribute to the school in shaping their child's future.

The teacher is aware of the ethnic group membership of his pupils and how such membership shapes the child's image of himself and of his world. He knows something about the history, traditions and social structures of the various ethnic groups, their unique culture patterns, their status in American society, the blocks and frustrations which they confront, and their perceptions of what life has in store for them.

He knows that the language of his pupils is closely tied to the life they lead. While it may represent a complete lack or a distortion of acceptable English, he recognizes its functional qualities for the pupils. Though this language is not "the coin of the realm," it often represents the only known and acceptable medium of exchange in the child's home or neighborhood.

In addition to his knowledge about the child in his environment, the successful teacher has a sophisticated understanding of how a child's abilities are assessed and therefore a realistic perception of what these measurements describe and predict. He knows that native potential intelligence is, at least thus far, unmeasurable; that what tests measure is learned behavior, and that the learning results not only from the child's native ability but also from his total experience. Yet he realizes that many intellectual abilities, like some of those which enter into creative functioning are not measured by existing intelligence tests.

He is also aware that the tests provide a fairly accurate description of the child's present ability to handle academic material and, unless there is a significant expansion and reorganization of his experience, the tests will predict with fair reliability how the child will function academically in the future. The successful teacher accepts the test scores as a fair and valid measure of the child's present academic ability, while rejecting them as a measure of native intelligence.

These and many other anthropological and psychological data affect the style of the successful teacher of disadvantaged pupils. But while the anthropologist's task is to describe and compare behavior of various cultures, and the psychologist's to understand individual behavior, the teacher's job is to modify it. Therefore, he must use his knowledge about his pupils and the world in which they live to guide him as he attempts to open more and more doors for them, and to help them acquire the skills and knowledge with which to enter the new and open spaces which lie beyond. The successful teacher sees his task as preparing his pupils to make competent choices among potentially available alternatives. He is aware that with every passing year the rapidly automating economy affords fewer and fewer opportunities to the minimally educated, and more and more to the academically and technically trained, and he communicates this understanding to his pupils.

The successful teacher meets the disadvantaged child on equal terms, as person to person, individual to individual. But while he accepts, he doesn't condone. He sets clearly defined limits for his pupils and will brook few transgressions. He is aware that, unlike middle-class children, they rarely respond to exhortations intended to control behavior through invoking feelings of guilt and shame. He, therefore, sets the rules, fixes the boundaries, and establishes the routines with a minimum of discussion. Here he is impersonal, undeviating, strict, but never punitive. Within these boundaries the successful

teacher is businesslike and orderly, knowing that he is there to do a job. But he is also warm and outgoing, adapting his behavior to the individual pupils in his class. He shows his respect and liking for his pupils and makes known his belief in their latent abilities.

He realizes the danger of the "self-fulfilling prophecy" of expecting, and consequently finding a low level of achievement. He, therefore, lets each pupil know that he expects more than the pupils thinks he can produce—but his standards are not so high as to become too remote to strive toward, and the attempt fraught with frustration. He rewards each tiny upward step, alert to every opportunity for honest praise, and, as much as possible, withholds harsh criticism and censure when progress is slow or entirely lacking. Above all, he is honest. He doesn't sentimentalize, doesn't pretend that a pupil's work is good when it isn't, doesn't condone unacceptable behavior.

The successful teacher is also something of a showman, coming to his task with an extensive repertory of carefully constructed scripts and props into which he breathes a sense of drama and high interest to capture the imagination of his pupils and hold their attention.

His repertory is not only extensive, providing a great variety of materials and teaching procedures tailored to the learning patterns of his pupils, it is also carefully catalogued to allow him to find what he needs quickly and efficiently.

As do other successful teachers, our model teacher has extensive knowledge of the content of the subjects he teaches. In fact, he knows it so well, that he has no need to rely on study guides. Like the knowledgeable native, he guides his pupils through his country without a Baedeker, relying rather on his own familiarity with its terrain to take them to the important sights by paths and highways not often known to the less sophisticated.[Ed]

Like all composite portraits, this hypothetical model presents an idealized version of reality. The hypothetical teacher is described as a mature, well-integrated person who respects his difficult, unmotivated and apparently unteachable pupils. He communicates his respect by setting high but reachable expectations, by his impartial and consistent firmness and honesty, and by his warm personal regard for each individual. He combines the detached but

Ed *See the quotation from Allen following the article by Terman (IX, 56).*

completely accepting stance of the anthropologist observing cultural differences, with the active involvement and manipulative approach of the determined reformer, the educator, in the sense of one who *leads* his pupils *out* into the wider world. Though not a specialist in any one of the behavioral or social sciences, he gleans from each of them knowledge which helps him understand the behavior of his pupils, the meaning of their scores on tests of intelligence and aptitude, the realities of their present and future world, the demands which various social and vocational alternatives will make upon them. In addition, the model requires the teacher to have a wide repertoire of materials and procedures, the ability to devise new ways, to deviate from accepted procedures and courses of study—but always to be aware of the knowledges and skills the pupils must eventually acquire. If the hypothetical "successful teacher" were to be characterized in a single phrase it would be *ordered flexibility*.

EXAMINING THE HYPOTHETICAL MODEL. The sketch presented here needs to be examined on two counts. First, it represents a hypothetical model, derived from inference and deduced from theoretical concepts. Before it is accepted, it must be verified through systematic observation, classification, and comparison of successful and unsuccessful teachers in "slums and suburbs."

But if the model in whole or in part does fit reality, if the characteristics described in the portrait do in fact approximate the characteristics which distinguish the successful teacher of disadvantaged pupils, then we must ask: How are we to get such teachers? Although the ideal presumably represented by this characterization can act only as a remote goal, how can it be approached?

It is simply nonsense to suppose that, even if the entire pool of existing teachers were screened, one would find enough people who resemble the hypothetical model to staff even a small proportion of the depressed-area schools. We must, therefore, look to teacher education to produce new teachers more nearly in the image of the model and to reshape the styles of those already in service. We return to the question of teachability, but this time with reference to the teacher as a student.

APPROACHING THE MODEL THROUGH EDUCATION. To what extent are the attributes of the model teachable? At least three of the aspects are of a cognitive nature and, for the reasonably bright and motivated student, can probably be approached through instruction: (1) mastery of subject matter; (2) the acquisition of an understanding of the major concepts from the behavioral and social sciences and their relevance to teaching disadvantaged children; and (3) the development of a repertoire of teaching strategies which hold promise for working with disadvantaged pupils. But to accomplish these three purposes alone would require a considerable reorganization and revision of undergraduate and graduate programs of teacher education, both pre-service and in-service.

Developing New Courses. The development of appropriate courses would require the intensive collaboration of social and behavioral scientists, faculties of education, and successful classroom teachers. Out of such collaboration can grow not only curricula which would lead to a better understanding of the child in his environment, but also new strategies, new methods, new materials based on the empirical evidence provided by the social scientist and the practical wisdom of the teachers and educators. This has been successfully done in the development of some of the new curricula for the secondary and elementary schools.

Laboratory Experiences. Given increased understanding and a repertory of appropiate teaching methods, the teacher can approach his task with greater openness, with less prejudice, and above all, with less fear. But every young teacher needs a bridge by which to cross the chasm which separates "knowing about" from actually doing something. For the teacher confronted by a class of poorly motivated, often discouraged and difficult pupils, continuous assistance and reinforcement in the teaching situation are essential. In *Teachers for the Schools in Our Big Cities*, Harry Rivlin, Dean of Teacher Education of the City University of New York, outlined a variety of desired modifications in existing modes of teacher preparation for large city schools (Rivlin, 1962). He placed major stress on the importance of laboratory experiences, starting with observation, leading to limited participation, then to student teaching, and finally, to independent responsibility for instruction. At every stage, the future teacher, and then the newly appointed teacher to the difficult school, must work under close supervision, receiving both psychological and practical support from the college staff and from the master teachers in the schools.

Hunter College (Haubrick, 1962), in an effort to improve the preparation of teachers for depressed area schools, selected a group of students who expressed a willingness to remain as regularly appointed teachers in the same "most difficult" junior high schools in which they had accepted appointments as student teachers. As part of their training, they were seen more often than was customary by a member of the college faculty and worked closely with carefully selected cooperating teachers. They spent the last 10 weeks of their student teaching in full command of the class, under constant supervision. A number of these young men and women, in due course, took and passed the required examinations and were appointed as regularly licensed teachers to the same school in which they had taught as students. But the supervision and assistance continued, reinforcing their earlier learning and providing the needed support and encouragement.

Selection of Candidates. But so far, the discussion has not taken account of those less tangible, but perhaps most significant characteristics of our model: openness to and acceptance of differences in people, firmness and consistency, warmth and respect and, above all, flexibility. Can courses, laboratory experiences, or field work assignments be devised which will develop these characteristics? The descriptive material on teacher characteristics and teaching style referred to earlier sheds little light on the antecedents of the observed behavior. Do some teachers use more and others less "direct influence," for example, because they are, by nature, more or less directive as people? Were they ever so, from childhood on? Or, does their classroom behavior reflect their teacher training and education? Are some teachers relatively "unplanned" in their approach to teaching because they believe that too much planning restricts the participation of the pupils, and given evidence to the contrary, would become more organized and business-like? Or is their unplanned, "slipshod" approach to the classroom just one case of an unplanned and inconsistent approach to most life situations, a behavioral pattern unamenable to easy change through training?

There are no simple answers to this crucial question. Perhaps, the training of teachers for the several areas of special education may be a case in point. In each area of exceptionality, teachers are exposed to technical knowledge of the medical, social, and psychological aspects of the disability with which they will work. Further, the teachers are instructed in ways of changing the general curriculum and adjusting both content and method to their special groups (Mackie and Williams, 1959). Such training has prepared large numbers of teachers who are successful in working with pupils normally viewed as difficult or unteachable.

But teachers who enter special education do so voluntarily. In fact, they select the special area in preference to teaching normal children. Their own natural styles may thus be suited to the work they select and the training falls on fertile ground. It is probably beyond common sense to expect any training to make of the potential secondary school teacher with a passion for communicating the ideas of the physical sciences, a fine teacher of retarded adolescents. To attempt to retrain the elementary school teacher who thrives on the rapid progress, the quick wit, the deep probing, and ingenious responses of his gifted pupils into a successful teacher of the dull and lethargic would be equally foolhardy.

Consider also: (1) The man or woman threatened by ambiguity, unable to adapt readily to unexpected circumstances, who functions adequately only in a meticulously ordered world; or (2) the basically weak, dominated person who seeks in the classroom, perhaps unconsciously, the opportunity to prove his power by bending others to his will; or, further (3) the bigot who clothes his prejudices in psychological theories of ethnic or class inferiority and is convinced, before he enters a classroom, that for all but a few disadvantaged children, schooling beyond the very minimum is a waste of the taxpayers' money. Such prospective teachers may or may not be adequate for other teaching assignments—the compulsive character may well make a fine college professor somewhere —but they are probably not the kind of people who can be trained to fit the hypothetical model.

But then there are those prospective or practicing teachers who, although not completely free of prejudice, are yet not so bigoted as to resist attitudinal change in the face of new experiences. And some who may not be overly flexible in their approach are yet not immobilized by rigidity. Although somewhat at variance with the hypothetical model, the personalities, attitudes and values of some teachers would not be antithetical to those required by the model. For them we must assume, at least until proven wrong, that teacher education can produce greater consonance, better "fit" between what the pupils need in order to learn and what the teacher does in the act of teaching.

Developing Emotional Closeness. Since a considerable portion of teaching style derives from attitudes and values, teachers of disadvantaged children would need, in addition to cognitive learnings, experiences through which to come emotionally close to the feelings, the anxieties, the aspirations of slum children and through which to examine their own feeling and reactions. Such efforts might include role-playing in situations where the teacher alternately takes the part of the child as he copes with various school and out-of-school problems, and of the teacher responding to life-like classroom situations.

Teachers' feelings and values might also be involved and reshaped through the study of literary works. The novel and the short story which, at their best, provide a penetrating and illuminating exposition of life's fundamental conflicts, often have the power to transport the reader into the lives of people unlike himself but who, nonetheless, share with him many aspects of the human predicament. Books which deal with changing attitudes across generations, with the transition of immigrant groups from their original ghettos to the broader American Society, with adaptations to bicultural life, with the effects of early disability or severe deprivation on the behavior of the adult, with the universal problems of the adolescent as well as with those unique to a given time or place —these and many other literary themes might be used effectively. For the literary art is often able to create acceptance where direct contact may engender rejection or contempt. The "safe remove" of literature enables the individual to view the problems of others with greater openness, especially if his reading is geared toward exploring his own feelings as they become enmeshed with the feelings and strivings of others.

Such special efforts, though desirable for all teachers, are especially needed for teachers of the disadvantaged, since they most often come from backgrounds which provide little familiarity or personal involvement with the life which their pupils live.

In short, it is proposed that if the hypothetical model stands up under rigorous examination as embodying the characteristics, the "style" of the successful teacher of disadvantaged children,

then the idealized model can be approached (though rarely reached) through deliberate pre-selection, and by an expanded and reconstructed approach to pre-service and in-service teacher education. Given the relatively bright student or young teacher, not completely blocked by deeply rooted attitudes and personality structures antithetical to the desired characteristics, education may help shape him in the image of the model.

ATTRACTING TEACHERS TO DIFFICULT SCHOOLS. But even assuming that there are ways to prepare successful teachers for depressed area schools, why should bright young people want to enter such a vocation? The realities are against such a choice. Teachers today are in a seller's market. There are many more vacancies than candidates, especially at the elementary level and in the sciences and mathematics, and teachers can choose the district in which they want to work. Suburban schools, for example, afford amenities which urban schools so often lack. But above all, because of their size and organization, the suburban schools more often give the teacher a sense that he is a professional, that he is respected in his job and can successfully carry out what he has set out to do. He can teach children and, in most instances, they learn.

What inducement does the slum school offer? The children are difficult, in the perceptions of many teachers now in these schools they are "unteachable." The supervision is inadequate and often hostile. Principals and their assistants are constantly harassed by continuous teacher turnover, uncovered classes, disciplinary problems in the school, involvement with the police and the courts, lack of appropriate or even adequate books and materials. They have little time and less energy to give their teaching staffs the needed help and support. Teachers, frustrated by their inability to induce learning in their pupils, often having no place to turn for help, resort to discipline-maintaining rather than teaching activities. In this process, the teacher loses all sense of professional commitment. Many feel as did a very young woman when asked how long she had taught before leaving the field. She said, "I haven't taught a day in my life, but I served a three-year sentence in junior high school X."

What awaits them in depressed area schools is well known to prospective teachers. In fact, in 1962 better than a third of the new teachers appointed to Manhattan schools declined the appointment. Although they had prepared to teach, they apparently preferred almost any other kind of employment or none at all, to teaching in a slum school.

No matter how excellent the preparation of teachers of disadvantaged children may become, no matter how much assistance is given both to pre-service students and to beginning teachers, teaching in slum schools will remain a difficult, often frustrating and very taxing job—far more so than teaching in the unruffled surrounding of tree-lined suburbia. What, then, will induce young people to become candidates for a hard life, deliberately to choose the slum over the suburb?

Perhaps the answer to this question requires the addition of still another characteristic to our hypothetical model, one that is most difficult to teach—idealism, dedication to a cause, the desire to help the have-nots, to render service. That openness to commitment exists in many young people is confirmed by the large numbers who apply for the Peace Corps, prepare for missionary work, or choose to work in settlements, in hospital schools, and in special schools for disturbed or retarded or otherwise handicapped children. These young people feel that they are answering a call, and they rise to its demands. We have also witnessed such behavior (perhaps too often) in times of revolution and war, when young men and women have willingly gone into hardship and danger for what they believed in. How can this spirit be harnessed for teaching in difficult schools, in the "underdeveloped" areas of our own great cities? Is there, to paraphrase William James, an "educational equivalent of war?"

Perhaps each city needs to designate, as some have already begun to do, one or two schools in each depressed area which become service centers, open to view, for which teachers are carefully selected and in which they feel privileged to teach. Such schools could help to counteract the negative image now in the minds of prospective teachers. Those who are idealistic, who would like to perform a service, will see that there is hope; that the task, though difficult, can be done.

Helping the Teacher in Service. But even when colleges and universities have evolved the needed curricula and made them part of the total education of prospective teachers, when bright young people are motivated to enroll, even if the graduate programs incorporate the new developments into their courses for experienced teachers, the problem of staffing schools in depressed urban areas will be only slightly alleviated. Assistance must be given to the hundreds of thousands of teachers now serving in depressed-area schools. Obviously, no program of study can reach all teachers now in our schools through direct contact. But they could be reached and helped and encouraged by changing supervisory patterns, by re-educating existing supervisors where they may be amendable to such re-education, or by selecting from each school one teacher who comes closest to the model and exposing him to a special program. Such teachers could return to their schools as supervisors, master teachers, or team leaders. From them could be formed the corps of cooperating teachers responsible for training students.

Problems of School Organization. The problem of staffing disadvantaged-area schools must be attacked simultaneously on many fronts. We must confront the fact that teachers for difficult schools need special training. We must reshape the program of teacher preparation, attract capable young people to such programs and help them as they move through their apprenticeship into full professional status. And we must also provide a corps of trained master teachers and supervisors who will bring skills and hope to the hundreds of thousands of teachers now in service.

But there is still another front upon which the attack must be launched—making changes in the amenities and management of the schools. Some of these are easy changes to make, because they do not require devising new courses or reshaping attitudes and values. All that they require is some additional money— simple things like providing a safe parking place, a comfortable lunch and rest room; of giving the teacher, especially at the elementary level, some relief during the day. Each school must make provisions for removing the one or two most difficult children from regular classrooms so that classes may become more teachable, lessening the teacher's sense of frustration and enhancing his sense of fulfilling his professional responsibility.

Somewhat less simple are the needed changes in supervision. Additional supervisory personnel, both in the school and from affiliated teacher education institutions, need to be provided. The presence in each school of staff members— eventually trained in the new approaches—

whose sole responsibility would be to help teachers, unburdened by administrative or disciplinary matters, might prove especially helpful. Perhaps if the supervisory load is spread, principals will be less harassed, less afraid of trouble, less apt to reward the teacher who maintains a quiet classroom, and more respectful of the teachers as people and as professionals.

The solution of any problem requires first, a clear recognition and description of the problem; secondly, a concerted research and experimental effort; and thirdly, the implementation of what is already known or what is learned through systematic study. To approach a solution to the problem of staffing schools in disadvantaged areas and providing competent teachers to work with disadvantaged children requires the following steps: (1) Open recognition that slum schools and disadvantaged children need uniquely prepared teachers. (2) Systematic study of the personal qualities, knowledge, and skills needed for successful teaching in these situations. (3) Development and experimental testing of reconstructed teacher education programs, both on campus and in the field. (4) Screening of candidates to eliminate those students or young teachers now in service whose values and personality characteristics are in conflict with the desired teaching style. (5) Raising the status of the disadvantaged-area teacher to that of a high calling, by invoking all available reward systems. (6) Initiating systematic changes to make the schools more livable for the teacher, the teaching experience less frustrating, and the supervision more professional. Such efforts can go a long way toward raising the morale and the effectiveness of those presently teaching, and toward bringing into the teaching force many able young people who will not only come but will stay.

It is, of course, a romantic notion to suppose that even the best qualified teachers will, through their efforts alone, solve all the social problems which shape the lives of disadvantaged children. The work of other agencies in the community needs to be integrated with the work of the school. The more effective the school becomes, the more help both the child and the family will need to understand and accept his changed behaviors and increased academic success and aspirations. But if the presently disadvantaged child is not to be fettered by his ignorance, not to be relegated to the ranks of the unemployable in a society which provides increasing opportunities to the academically competent and has less and less room for the functional illiterate, then the school has a central role to play. And central to the school, to the development and achievement of the child is the teacher.

REFERENCES

BELLACK, A. A. The language of teaching: Relationships of the linguistic behavior of students and teachers in high school classrooms to student learning. Project proposal: Teachers College, Columbia Univer., 1963. (Dittoed)

FLANDERS, N. A. Teacher and classroom influences on individual learning. In A. H. Passow (Ed.), *Nurturing individual potential.* Washington: Ass. Supervis. & Curriclm. Develpm., NEA, 1964. Pp. 57-65.

HAUBRICK, V. F. Teachers for big-city schools. In A. H. Passow (Ed.), *Education in depressed areas.* New York: Bur. Publ., Teach. Coll., Columbia Univer., 1963. Pp. 243-261.

HEIL, L. M., POWELL, M., & FEIFER, I. Characteristics of teacher behavior related to the achievement of children in several elementary grades. New York: Author, May, 1960. (Mimeo)

MACKIE, R. P., & WILLIAMS, H. M. Teachers of exceptional children. *Rev. educ. Res.*, 1959, 29, 395-407.

MEDLEY, D. M. The development of classroom behavior dimension for teachers and pupils. Paper presented at the Amer. Ass. Advnmnt. Sci., 1962. (Mimeo)

RIVLIN, H. N. Teachers for the schools in our big cities. New York: Div. Teach. Educ., City Univer. New York, 1962.

RYANS, D. C. Characteristics of teachers: An informative systems approach to theory of instruction with special reference to the teacher. Paper presented at Amer. Educ. Res. Ass. symposium on *Theories of teaching*, February, 1963.

SMITH, B. O., MEUX, M., ET AL. *A study of the logic of teaching.* III. Urbana, Ill.: Bur. Educ. Res., 1963.

THELEN, H. A. Teachability grouping. Dept. Educ., Univer. Chicago, August, 1961. (Mimeo)

WARRENER, C. K. A classification of social achievement. Paper presented at Amer. Sociol. Ass., August, 1962. (Mimeo)

79/RESISTANCE TO "COUNTERPROPAGANDA" PRODUCED BY ONE-SIDED AND TWO-SIDED "PROPAGANDA" PRESENTATIONS/

ARTHUR A. LUMSDAINE AND IRVING L. JANIS*

IN SPECULATIVE DISCUSSIONS CON-cerning propaganda effects, the question has often been raised as to whether a persuasive communication is more effective when it concentrates exclusively on the arguments supporting the communicator's position or when it includes some discussion (and/or refutation) of the opposing arguments. Various propaganda strategists have put forth the claim that, in appealing for acceptance of any specific belief or policy, no opposing arguments should be discussed because mentioning rival ideas invites comparison, hesitation and doubt. But experimental evidence reported by Hovland, Lumsdaine and Sheffield indicates that this generalization is not likely to hold true when the audience initially disagrees with the views advocated by the communicator.[1] Their results clearly indicated that among members of the audience who were initially *opposed* to the communicator's position, a two-sided presentation (including mention of opposing as well as supporting arguments) was much more effective in producing opinion changes in the desired direction than was a one-sided presentation (which mentioned only arguments supporting the communicator's position). The one-sided presentation proved to be more effective only with those members of the audience who were already favorably disposed toward the communicator's position.

In the experiment reported by Hovland, Lumsdaine and Sheffield, the effects of the communications were measured only in terms of *immediate* changes in opinion; it was not possible to compare the effects of one-sided and two-sided communications in terms of "resistance" to the effect of subsequently presented counterarguments or "counterpropaganda." Accordingly, the present experiment was designed to extend the evidence by comparing the effectiveness of the two forms of presentation after part of the audience had been exposed to a second, counterpropaganda communication.[2]

DESIGN OF THE EXPERIMENT

The present experiment was conducted several months before President Truman announced that Russia had produced its first atomic explosion and was designed to compare the effects of two forms of a persuasive communication. Both forms consisted of a transcribed "radio program" in which the same communicator took the position that Russia would be unable to produce large numbers of atomic bombs for at least the next five years.

Program I, the one-sided presentation, contained only the arguments that supported this conclusion, such as the following: Russian scientists have not yet discovered some of the crucial secrets; they cannot learn all the "know-how" through espionage; even after they succeed in making their first A-bomb the Russians will be unable to mass produce the bombs because of insufficient uranium supplies.[3]

[2] This study was conducted at the Institute of Human Relations, Yale University, as part of a coordinated program of research on communication and opinion change, financed by a grant from the Rockefeller Foundation. The communication research program is under the direction of Professor Carl I. Hovland, to whom the authors are indebted for valuable suggestions and criticisms. The authors also wish to express their appreciation to Joseph A. Foran, Superintendent of Schools at Milford, Connecticut, and to the faculty of the Milford High School.

Many of the technical details concerning the way the present experiment was conducted have been described in an earlier publication which made use of data bearing on a different research problem. (Cf. I. L. Janis, A. A. Lumsdaine, and A. I. Gladstone, "Effects of Preparatory Communications on Reactions to a Subsequent News Event," *Pub. Op. Quart.*, 1951, XV, 487-518.)

[3] For a more detailed description of the content of the communications used in this experiment see the earlier publication by Janis, Lumsdaine, and Gladstone, *op. cit.*, p. 494.

[1] C. I. Hovland, A. A. Lumsdaine, and F. D. Sheffield, *Experiments on Mass Communication* (Princeton: Princeton University Press, 1949), pp. 201-227.

* Arthur A. Lumsdaine and Irving L. Janis, Resistance to "counterpropaganda" produced by one-sided and two-sided "propaganda" presentations, *Public Opinion Quarterly*, 1953, 17, 311-318. Reprinted by permission.

TABLE 1 / EXPERIMENTAL TREATMENTS.

	SEQUENCE OF EVENTS (SPRING 1949)		
GROUPS	MID-MAY	EARLY JUNE	JUNE, ONE WEEK LATER
A. *Not* exposed to counter-propaganda			
I. ($N = 36$)	Initial questionnaire	Program I	Final questionnaire
II. ($N = 52$)	Initial questionnaire	Program II	Final questionnaire
B. *Exposed* to counter-propaganda			
I. ($N = 60$)	Initial questionnaire	Program I	Counter-propaganda	Final questionnaire
II. ($N = 49$)	Initial questionnaire	Program II	Counter-propaganda	Final questionnaire

Program II, the two-sided presentation, contained the very same arguments presented in identical fashion, but also presented and discussed arguments for the other side of the picture. (These arguments were, for example: Russia has many first-rate atomic scientists; Russian industries have made a phenomenal recovery since the war; Russia has some uranium mines in Siberia.) The opposing arguments were interwoven into the relevant sections of the communication and in some instances no attempt was made to refute them.

The total content of both programs was designed to lead unambiguously to the conclusion that Soviet Russia would be unable to produce A-bombs in quantity for at least five years. Except for the presence of the opposing arguments, the two communications were identical: Program II was recorded first and Program I was constructed by simply deleting the opposing arguments from the tape recording.[4]

Four main experimental groups were used, each composed of several classrooms of high-school students in social-science courses. Classrooms were assigned at random to the different experimental treatments. In order to determine initial level of opinion, all groups were given an initial questionnaire as part of an independent "opinion survey" that was conducted several weeks before the experimental communications were presented. Two groups were then given the one-sided communication (Program I) and the other two groups were given the two-sided communication (Program II). The effects of

the communications were measured by a second questionnaire given about a week after the presentation of these communications. Just before the administration of the second questionnaire, however, two of the groups (one having received Program I and the other Program II) were exposed to a second transcribed radio program that was designed to function as "counterpropaganda." In this second communication (about 1300 words in length), the same issue was discussed by a different commentator who took the opposite position. He argued that Russia had probably already developed the A-bomb and within two years would be producing it in large quantities. Most of this communication consisted of playing up and elaborating the opposing arguments that had been mentioned earlier in Program II, but some new material was also introduced, including a description of four plants in Russia alleged to be producing A-bombs. This "counterpropaganda" communication was largely a one-sided presentation but contained a few sentences in which arguments stressed by the earlier communication were mentioned and then refuted.

The treatments administered to the four major experimental groups are summarized in Table 1. The initial and final questionnaires were also administered to a fifth group which received neither the original communication nor the counterpropaganda. This group was included as a control on amount of opinion change that could be attributed to outside causes which might have been operating during the interval between the two questionnaires. At the time when the other groups were being presented with Program I or II, this control group was given an irrelevant radio program on a completely different topic (social changes in postwar Italy).

[4] Programs I and II contained approximately 2,200 and 2,800 words respectively, the difference of 600 words being due solely to the addition of the opposing arguments in the two-sided presentation. The opposing arguments were selected partly on the basis of spontaneous arguments given in pretest interviews of high school students.

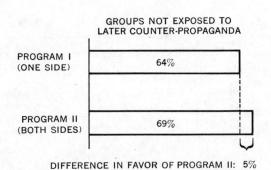
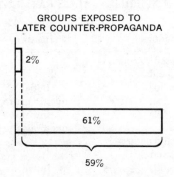

FIGURE 1 / COMPARISON OF THE EFFECTIVENESS OF PROGRAMS I AND II; CHANGES IN OPINIONS CONCERNING THE LENGTH OF TIME BEFORE RUSSIA PRODUCES LARGE NUMBERS OF A-BOMBS. (NET CHANGE IN THE POSITIVE DIRECTION.[a])

RESULTS OF THE EXPERIMENT

The main question designed to measure the effects of the communications was as follows: "About how long from now do you think it will be before the Russians are really producing *large numbers* of atomic bombs?" This "key" question was asked in both the initial questionnaire and the final questionnaire.

The *net change* for each group was calculated as the excess in percentage of subjects increasing their estimates over the percentage decreasing their estimates. The *net effect* of each program (or combination of programs) was taken as the net change for each experimental group minus the corresponding net change for the control group.

As in the previous experiment by Hovland, Lumsdaine and Sheffield, there was little overall difference in the effectiveness of the two programs for those groups that were *not* exposed

to counter-propaganda.[5] The main interest here is, however, attached to the results for the groups that were exposed to subsequent counterpropaganda, and to the comparison between these groups and those which received no coun-

[5] It will be recalled that in the previous experiment the one-sided communication was superior for those initially in favor of the commentator's position while the two-sided version was superior for those initially opposed; for the over-all results these two opposing effects virtually cancelled out, leaving little net difference in the *average* effectiveness of the two programs. For groups not receiving counterpropaganda in the present experiment, this same pattern of results was observed. However, the differences among subgroups with different initial points of view was not large enough to be reliable. This might be attributed to the fact that initial opinions were not as strongly held as those concerning the issue used in the earlier experiment. Alternatively, it may be supposed that the differences might have been significant in the second experiment had a larger number of cases been available for the small subgroups with different initial opinions.

[a] "Positive" changes refer to changes (from initial to final questionnaire) in the direction advocated by the communicator in Programs I and II—i.e., in the case of the key question, an increase in estimated number of years before Russia would produce large numbers of A-bombs. The probability values indicating the reliability of differences in Figure 1 and elsewhere in this article are based on the method described by Hovland, Lumsdaine and Sheffield (*ibid.*, p. 321). They are expressed in terms of one tail of the probability distribution.

The 2 percent net change for the group which received Program I and the later counterpropaganda was slightly smaller than the (nonsignificant) net change of 15 percent found in the control group, which had not been exposed to any of the communications. But the net-change value for each of the other three experimental groups shown in Figure 1 was reliably greater (at beyond the one percent confidence level) than the corresponding value for the unexposed controls and hence for these groups the net effect was "significant" in terms of the statistical tests used.

When the measures of net change were calculated independently for each classroom, the results on the key question were found to be highly consistent among the different classroom groups that had been randomly assigned to the experimental treatments. The percentage of net change was close to zero for each of the individual classrooms in the group which received the one-sided presentation followed by subsequent counterpropaganda. There was no overlap·between these net change values and the ones obtained from classrooms which received any of the other three experimental treatments. The probability of this outcome is less than one in a hundred, so that the general pattern of the results in Figure 1 can be considered reliable even in terms of a stringent test that counts each classroom group as a single observation.

terpropaganda. The pattern of results is quite clear-cut: for the subjects who were exposed to counterpropaganda, the two-sided presentation was decidedly superior to the one-sided presentation. The results for the key question are presented in Figure 1. After exposure to the counterpropaganda, the second-order difference between the net change for the two-sided presentation (61 percent) and that for the one-sided presentation (2 percent) is 59 percent and is statistically reliable at beyond the one-percent level of confidence.[6] The third-order difference between this 59 percent difference and the corresponding difference of only 5 percent for the groups not exposed to counterpropaganda is also reliable at beyond the 1-percent level.

Two supplementary questions were also included in the initial and final questionnaires: (1) "About how many atomic bombs would you guess Russia will have made by five years from now?"; (2) "About how long from now do you think it will be before Russia has made its *first* atomic bomb?" Unlike the key question, neither of these supplementary questions dealt directly with the main conclusion advocated by Programs I and II. Although the first supplementary question was worded so as to be pertinent to the main conclusion, it specified only a single-time point and relied upon each student's own conception of what figure would constitute a "large number" of A-bombs. (It should be noted that the programs did not refer to any specific number of A-bombs.) The second supplementary question did not deal with the main conclusion but covered an important subconclusion which was heavily emphasized by Programs I and II and which was subsequently opposed by the counterpropaganda.

Data derived from analysis of individual opinion changes on the two supplementary questions for the two groups which were exposed to the subsequent counterpropaganda are shown in Table 2. The results from both supplementary questions are in the same direction as those derived from the key question (see Figure 1). In the case of the first supplementary question the difference is not large enough to be statistically significant, but the findings for the second supplementary question again show that Program II was significantly more effective than Program I.

[6] For the two groups who were not exposed to subsequent propaganda, the results showed the same pattern as Figure 1; the differences between Programs I and II, although showing a slightly greater effect from Program II, are small and nonsignificant.

DISCUSSION

The evidence from this experiment supports the following general conclusions: Under conditions where the audience is subsequently exposed to counterpropaganda arguing in favor of the opposing position, a persuasive communication which advocates a definite position on a controversial issue is more effective in the long run if it presents and discusses the opposing arguments than if it presents only the arguments that support the communicator's conclusion.

The rationale leading to the expectation of superior effectiveness for the two-sided over the one-sided communication differs somewhat as between the present experiment and the earlier experiment reported by Hovland, Lumsdaine, and Sheffield. In the earlier experiment which was concerned with immediate effects, the explanation is essentially as follows: If a member of the audience has a strongly held "negative" opinion and is familiar with arguments supporting this opinion, presentation of a one-sided communication supporting the "positive" point of view will encounter a comparatively high degree of resistance. The listener's tendency to think of his own arguments will interfere with acceptance of (or even attention to) the arguments that the communicator is presenting. If, however, the communicator explicitly discusses the listener's own negative arguments, this source of interference is reduced. Moreover, the listener may be more impressed by the communication and less inclined to distrust the arguments as coming from a biased source if the communicator makes it clear that he has taken the negative arguments into account.

To explain the findings of the present experiment, which show differences in resistance to subsequent counterpropaganda, there is no need to introduce any assumptions about the audience's initially negative point of view. Our tentative explanation is as follows. Regardless of initial position, a convincing one-sided communication presenting only positive arguments will tend to sway many members of the audience farther in the direction advocated by the communicator. However, when these persons subsequently hear the opposite point of view, also supported by cogent-sounding arguments, their opinions tend to be swayed back in the negative direction, especially if the new arguments appear to offset the previous positive arguments. But if the initial communication is, instead, a two-sided one, it will already have taken into account both the positive and negative argu-

TABLE 2 / COMPARISON OF THE EFFECTIVENESS OF PROGRAMS I AND II FOR GROUPS EXPOSED TO SUBSEQUENT COUNTERPROPAGANDA.[a]

SUPPLEMENTARY QUESTIONS	NET CHANGE IN POSITIVE DIRECTION			
	Program I: "One side" (N = 60)	Program II "Both sides" (N = 49)	Difference in favor of Program II	p value[b]
No. of A-bombs Russia will have in 5 years	3%	16%	13%	.22
No. of years before Russia produces its first A-bomb	20%	51%	31%	.02

ments and still have reached the positive conclusion. When the listener is then subsequently exposed to the presentation of opposing arguments in the counterpropaganda, he is less likely to be influenced by them. He is not only familiar with the opposing point of view but has been led to the positive conclusion in a context in which the negative arguments were in evidence. In effect, he has been given an advance basis for ignoring or discounting the opposing communication and, thus "inoculated," he will tend to retain the positive conclusion.

In the preceding statement of the rationale for the superiority of the two-sided communication under the specified conditions, no explicit account has been taken of the manner and extent to which the opposing arguments should be introduced into the communication. In both the present study and the preceding one the opposing arguments were presented in a way that appeared most likely to achieve clear-cut effects, with no attempt at experimental variation of their content and arrangement within the communication. It is apparent, however, that a complete account of the factors determining the effectiveness of two-sided communications would have to deal systematically with the relative number and cogency of opposing arguments, the context in which they are introduced into the discussion, the extent to which they are explicitly refuted or merely overridden by implication, and so on. Experimental analysis of the effects of such factors remains an extensive area for future work.

[a] Based on opinion changes shown on two supplementary questions.

[b] The control group, which had not been given any relevant propaganda during the interval between the initial and final questionnaire, showed practically no opinion change on the first and second supplementary questions (net change of 2 percent and 1 percent, respectively). The experimental groups which had received Programs I and II, after exposure to the counterpropaganda, did not differ reliably from the control group on the first supplementary question (p values = .37 and .13 respectively) but showed sizeable differences on the second supplementary question (p values = .07 and <.01).

80/TEACHING MACHINES: A REVIEW[1]/

CHARLES S. MORRILL[2]*

THE SAME FORCES WHICH HAVE CHAR-acterized the evolution of general educational practices are inherent to the history of the new science of automated teaching. As a result of the expansion and multiplying complexities of political, economic, and social interests, there developed an ever increasing need for the rapid education of large numbers of people. New educational objectives demanded new methods of instruction, and the history of education is marked by many diverse attempts at establishing more efficient teaching procedures. Once again teaching methods must be reevaluated. Rigid adherence to the principle of personal teacher-student relationships no longer seems feasible—an instructional system more appropriate for present-day needs must be established. It is probable that the use of automated teaching devices can fill this need in the method of education. As Corrigan (1959) has suggested:

The automated teaching method has grown out of a pressing need. This need has been created by a twofold technical training problem. As advances in science and technology have been made, there has been an ever increasing demand for well-trained instructors; at the same time the availability of these trained persons has been diminishing. This situation is aggravated further by the increased scope and complexity of subjects, and the ever increasing ratio between number of instructors and students (p. 24).

CURRENT TRENDS IN AUTO-MATED TEACHING MACHINES

Current interest in the area of automated teaching machines is well illustrated by the simple index of frequency-per-year of published teaching machine articles. Fry, Bryan, and Rigney (1960) report that for the years prior to 1948 there are only 6 references, whereas through 1959 there were more than 50 reports published.

The grandfather of automated teaching machines is Sydney L. Pressey (1926, 1927), who designed machines for automated teaching during the mid-1920s. His first device was exhibited and described at the American Psychological Association (APA) meetings in 1924; an improved device was exhibited in 1925 at the APA meetings. Both forms of the apparatus automatically performed simultaneous administration and scoring of a test and taught informational and drill material. Pressey's device, about the size of a portable typewriter, presented material to the subject via a small window. Four keys were located alongside the apparatus. If the student activated a key corresponding to the correct answer, the machine advanced to the next item. If his response was incorrect, the machine scored an error and did not advance to the next item until the correct answer was chosen. The capacity of the drum was 30 two-line typewritten items; the paper on which the questions appeared was carried as in a typewriter.

In 1927, Pressey summarized his effort as follows:

The paper reports an effort to develop an apparatus for teaching drill material which (a) should keep each question or problem before the learner until he finds the correct answer, (b) should inform him at once regarding the correctness of each response he makes, (c) should continue to put the subject through the series of questions until the entire lesson has been learned, but (d) should eliminate each question from consideration as the correct answer for it has been mastered (p. 552).

In 1930, Peterson devised a self-scoring, immediate feedback device. The Chemo Card, as this device was later called, utilized the technique of multiple choice. A special ink was used by the student in marking his answer. The mark appeared red if the answer was incorrect; a dark color resulted if the answer was correct. Although Pressey's notions and the Chemo Card might have stimulated an interest in automated teaching techniques in the twenties, educators and researchers obviously were not at that time ready for this advanced con-

[1] The research reported in this document was supported by the Department of the Air Force under Air Force Contract AF-33-(600) 39852.

[2] The author wishes to acknowledge the valuable editorial assistance of Sylvia Pilsucki.

* Charles S. Morrill, Teaching machines: a review, *Psychological Bulletin*, 1961, 58, 363-375. Reprinted by permission.

cept of teaching. Automated teaching did not take hold.

In 1932, Pressey published an article describing a kind of answer sheet which could be scored by an automatic scoring device. This apparatus recorded errors by item, and thus provided the instructor with clues as to what questions needed further instruction. In 1934, Little experimented with this device as well as with the device originated by Pressey in 1926. His results favored the use of automated devices in contrast to regular classroom techniques.

The next appearance of automated teaching literature came a considerable number of years later. During World War II, the Automatic Rater was used by the Navy for training. This device projected a question on a small screen; the subject's response consisted of pushing one of five buttons.

In 1950, Pressey described a new automated device called the Punchboard. Multiple-choice questions were presented to the student. The key answer sheet inside the Punchboard contained holes opposite the correct answers only. If the answer was correct, the student's pencil penetrated deeply; if incorrect, the pencil did not penetrate the paper significantly. Angell and Troyer in 1948 and Angell in 1949 reported the results of using the Punchboard. Both studies suggested the superiority of this method over traditional classroom procedures.

In 1954, Skinner published "The Science of Learning and the Art of Teaching," which provided the basis for the development of his teaching machines. In this article, he stressed the importance of reinforcement in teaching and suggested teaching machines as a method of providing this needed reinforcement for the learner.

Reports concerning the Subject-Matter Trainer began to appear in 1955 (Besnard, Briggs, Mursch, & Walker, 1955; Besnard, Briggs, & Walker, 1955). This electromechanical device is a large multiple-choice machine used essentially for training and testing in the identification of components and in general verbal subject matter. Extensive research has been done with this device because of its considerable flexibility, i.e., it allows several modes of operation for self-instruction: variety of programmed subject matter, drop-out feature after items have been mastered, etc.

The Pull-Tab, used experimentally by Bryan and Rigney in 1956, was a device in which the subject received not only a "right" or "wrong" indication after his choice but also a somewhat detailed explanation of "why" a response was incorrect. In 1949, Briggs had found in experimenting with the Punchboard that learning is significantly enhanced by immediate knowledge of results. Bryan and Rigney's data illustrated that the combination of immediate knowledge of results plus explanation, if the student is in error, produced significantly higher scores on a criterion test than if no explanation had been given. The importance of this research from a historical point of view is that it investigated immediate knowledge of results as a factor existing on a continuum with varying degrees of effect. Up to this point any comparison involving the effectiveness of teaching machines had been one between classroom instruction and the "new" machine under consideration. In Briggs' and in Bryan and Rigney's research, however, we see the beginning of a concern, to become greater in the next few years, with the possible effects of specific variables and their interactions on learning.

The years 1957-58 mark the beginning of the period in which resurgent interest in teaching machines was initiated. Ramo's arguments (1957) reopened the consideration of automated techniques for classroom use. His article served as one of the more forceful attempts to alert educators to the needs and requirements for automated techniques in education. Skinner's continued interest (1958) served as the major catalyst in this area. In his article, he reviewed earlier attempts to stimulate interest in teaching machines and further explained that the learning process was now better understood and that this increased sophistication would be reflected in teaching machine technology. Skinner suggested that the most appropriate teaching machine would be that which permits the student to *compose* his response rather than to select it from a set of alternatives. On the basis of this philosophy and in conjunction with other principles of learning theory to which Skinner adheres, he designed a teaching machine with the following characteristics. The questions, printed on a disk, are presented to the student through a window. The student's response is written on a paper tape, which is advanced under a transparent cover when the student lifts a lever. At this point the correct answer appears in the window. If the student is correct, he activates the lever in one manner, which eliminates the item from the next sequence. If he is incorrect, the lever is activated in a different manner, thus retaining the item in the next sequence.

Holland (1960), a co-worker of Skinner's, has suggested several well-known learning principles that should be applied to teaching machine technology: immediate reinforcement for correct answers is a must, learned behavior is possible only when it is *emitted* and reinforced, gradual progression (i.e., small steps in learning sequences and reducing wrong answers) is necessary to establish complex repertoires, gradual withdrawal (fading or vanishing) of stimulus support is effective, it is necessary to control the student's observing and echoic behavior and to train for discrimination, the student should write his response. The Skinner machine does in fact employ these principles.

Ferster and Sapon (1958) described the Cardboard Mask, a most simple teaching machine which employs the principles which Skinner and Holland outline so clearly. This device is a cardboard folder containing mimeographed material which is presented one line at a time. The student, after writing his response on a separate sheet of paper, advances the paper in the mask, thereby exposing the correct response.

In 1958, a number of investigators interested in teaching machines recommended that the programmed material be a function of the student's response. This idea suggests that a "wrong" response may not necessarily be negative reinforcement and that both the "right" and "wrong" responses should modify the program. Rath and Anderson (1958) and Rath, Anderson, and Brainerd (1959) have suggested the use of a digital computer which automatically adjusts problem difficulty as a function of the response. Crowder's (1955, 1958, 1959) concept of "intrinsic programming" permits the response to alter the programming sequence.

During the last few years, researchers have been focusing their attention on investigating many of the variables which are pertinent to the design and use of teaching machines. The seemingly simple task of defining a teaching machine has been a serious problem to many authors (Day, 1959; Silberman, 1959; Weimer, 1958). Some definitions have made more extensive demands on teaching devices than others. Learning theorists (Kendler, 1959; Porter, 1958; Skinner, 1957; Spence, 1959; Zeaman, 1959) are now most outspoken concerning the application of theoretical concepts to teaching machine technology. Transfer of training, mediational processes, reinforcement, motivation, condition-

ing, symbolic processes, and language structure are but a few of these areas of interest.

There are indeed many other variables about which there is a divergence of opinion and about which experimental evidence is completely lacking or controversial. The reports of Skinner (1958), Israel (1958), Coulson and Silberman (1960), Fry (1959), and Stephens (1953) are all focused, at least in part, on questions related to response modes, e.g., multiple choice, construction of the response, responses with reinforcement, etc. Briggs, Plashinski, and Jones (1955) investigated self-paced vs. automatically paced machines. The importance of motivation in connection with teaching machines has been explored by Holland (unpublished), Mayer and Westfield (1958), and Mager (1959).

Essentially, the history of automated teaching is short—it started in the mid-twenties and was strenuously reactivated by the appearance of Skinner's 1958 article. Empirical investigations of many important issues in this field are just now beginning to appear. However, the necessity of developing automated teaching methods has been evident for many years.

GENERAL PROBLEM AREAS

DEFINITION. As in any new field, the first problem is one of definition. What is a teaching machine? Silberman (1959) says that a teaching device consists of four units: an input unit, an output unit, a storage unit, and a control unit. As such, this definition includes a broad category of devices, from the most simple to the most complex. Weimer (1958) goes beyond the device itself, stating that a teaching machine must present information to the student as well as test the student by means of a controlled feedback loop. Crowder (1960) insists that a teaching machine

must in some way incorporate two-way communication. That is, the student must respond to the information presented by the machine, and the machine must in turn recognize the nature of the student's response and behave appropriately (p. 12).

Perhaps the most inclusive definition is one given by Day (1959):

A teaching machine is a mechanical device designed to present a particular body of information to the student. . . . Teaching machines differ from all other teaching devices and aids in that they require the active participation of the learner at every step (p. 591).

Although the emphasis in some of the above concepts is different, together they give a rather complete description and, if you will, definition.

PROGRAMMING. The programming of subject matter for teaching machines is the most extensive and difficult problem in this new technology. Beck (1959) describes specific concepts which he thinks appropriate for programming a Skinner-type machine:

A student's responses may be restricted and guided in a great number of ways. These range from all types of hints . . . to simply presenting the response which it is desired a student acquire (p. 55).

Carr (1959) discusses in some detail the importance of programming in terms of learning efficiency and retention. Much of what he says remains open for empirical verification. Rothkopf (1960) has suggested that the development of programmed instruction suffers from two difficulties: a weak rational basis for program writing and inadequate subject-matter knowledge among program writers.

The extent to which any initial program needs revision is perhaps exemplified by the program in Harvard's course Natural Sciences 114. Holland points out that the first program of materials included 48 disks, each containing 29 frames, whereas a revision and extension of the program the following year included 60 disks of 29 frames each. Holland's objective was to extend the program and decrease the number of student errors. Crowder's (1960) programming objectives are different from Holland's. He states:

By means of "intrinsic programming" it [the program] recognizes student errors as they occur and corrects them before they can impede understanding of subsequent material or adversely affect motivation (p. 12).

Crowder considers it almost impossible to write a program which completely avoids error, and therefore he structures the program requirements on the probability of error. When an error is made, the next presentation explains the subject's mistake. Depending on the nature of the error and when it occurs, the subject may either return to the original question or enter a program of correctional material.

Another concept for programming is known as branching (Bryan & Rigney, 1959). Through branching, many possible routes are provided through which the subject can proceed, depend-

ing on the response. The subjects are allowed to skip certain material if they have demonstrated a knowledge of it. One study (Coulson & Silberman, 1960) suggests that under branching conditions subjects require less training time than under nonbranching conditions; however, results on the criterion test were not significantly different.

For certain kinds of subject matter, vanishing is still another concept for programming (Skinner, 1958). A complete or nearly complete stimulus is presented to the subject. Subsequent frames gradually omit part of the stimulus until all of it is removed. The subject is then required to reconstruct the stimulus.

To program verbal learning sequences, Homme and Glaser (1959) suggest the Ruleg. With this method, the written program states a rule and provides examples for this rule. In each case, either the rule or the example is incomplete, requiring the subject to complete it.

In a recent study Silverman (1960b) investigated methods of presenting verbal material for use in teaching machines. He recommended that further research involving the design and use of teaching machines should take into consideration the possible use of context cues as a means of facilitating serial rote learning. At the same time, however, he stated that continuous use of context cues as ancillary prompts should be avoided, since such prompts can interfere with learning.

The optimum size of steps and the organization of the programmed material are two formidable problems. Skinner (1958) states:

Each step must be so small that it can always be taken, yet in taking it the student moves somewhat closer to fully competent behavior (p. 2).

In order to determine the value of steps in a program, Gavurin and Donahue (1961) investigated the effects of the organization of the programmed material on retention and rate of learning. They state that the assumption that optimum teaching machine programs are those in which items are presented in a logical sequence has been validated for acquisition but not retention. The results of a study carried out by Coulson and Silberman (1959) indicated that small steps were more time consuming but resulted in statistically significant higher test scores on one of the criterion tests. Pressey (1959) in principle disagrees with Skinner's notion of short and easy steps, and he strongly suggests an experimental investigation of this question. Both rate of learning and retention (recall or recognition) are of critical concern.

The above discussion suggests several areas which are directly applicable to programming and which are under investigation and/or need further experimentation. Indeed, there are a number of unanswered questions in the programming complex, some of which have been suggested by Galanter (1959):

1. What is the correct order of presentation of material?

2. Is there an optimum number of errors that should be made?

3. How far apart (in some sense) should adjacent items be spaced?

4. Is experimentally controlled pacing more effective (in some sense) than self-pacing?

5. Is one program equally effective for all students?

6. What are the effects of using different programming techniques (branching, intrinsic programming, vanishing) in various subject-matter areas?

7. What criteria are most appropriate in the evaluation of student learning?

These questions are but a few of the intriguing and complex problems facing investigators in the new field of programming material for teaching machines. Answers to these questions will help not only the educator but also the engineer who is concerned with writing adequate specifications for the construction of teaching machines.

RESPONSE MODE. The kind of response that should be given by a subject has been a controversial question in the teaching machine field. Pressey's original machine (1926) required the subject to press a lever corresponding to his choice of answer. The format of the answers was multiple-choice. Skinner (1958) emphasized the necessity of having the subject *compose* (construct) the response. Skinner states:

One reason for this is that we want him to recall rather than recognize—to make a response as well as see that it is right. Another reason is that effective multiple-choice material must contain plausible wrong responses, which are out of place in the delicate process of "shaping" behavior because they strengthen unwanted forms (p. 2).

Coulson and Silberman (1960) investigated this question of multiple-choice vs. constructed response by using *simulated* teaching machines—human beings were used instead of automatic

control mechanisms. Their results indicated that the multiple-choice response mode required significantly less time than the constructed response mode and that no significant difference was obtained between response modes on the criterion test. Further, they reported that no significant differences were obtained among the experimental groups on the multiple-choice criterion subtest or on the total (multiple-choice plus constructed response) criterion test. Fry (1959) has discussed this response-mode question along with other variables, and he has carried out extensive research concerning constructed vs. multiple-choice response modes. The results of his study favor the use of constructed response when recall is the objective of the learning.

In addition to the basic controversy (which needs much more investigation) between multiple-choice and constructed responses, there are several "variations on the theme" which are evident. Stephens (1953) has recommended that every wrong answer in a multiple-choice question appear as a correct choice for another item. He calls this program "inside alternatives." His data indicate that there was no difference between control and experimental groups on a criterion test using either nonsense syllables or Russian unless each right choice appeared as a wrong alternative for the three subsequent items. The use of prompts in general has been shown to be an effective technique in automated teaching (Cook, 1958; Cook & Kendler, 1956; Cook & Spitzer, 1960).

Using learning booklets, Goldbeck (1960) investigated the effect of response mode and learning material difficulty on automated instruction. The three response modes used were: overt response (the subject was required to construct a written response), covert response (the subject was permitted to think of a response), and implicit response (the subject read the response which was underlined). Goldbeck states:

Learning efficiency scores, obtained by dividing quiz scores by learning time, showed that the implicit (reading) response condition produced significantly more efficient learning that the overt response condition. The covert response condition fell between the other conditions in learning efficiency (p. 25).

Concerning quiz-score results, the overt response group

performed significantly poorer than the other response mode groups at the easy level of difficulty. Performance of the overt response group improved significantly at the intermediate difficulty level to the extent that it exceeded the performance of all other groups (pp. 25-26).

Goldbeck concludes that

doubt is cast upon the assumption that the best learning is achieved by use of easy items and requiring written constructed responses (p. 26).

To the author's knowledge, the use of an oral response in conjunction with the Skinner teaching machine and its effect on learning rate and retention have not been reported in the literature. Furthermore, the importance of response mode as a function of reinforcement must be specified. Israel (1958) has suggested that natural and artificial reinforcement may affect the subjects' learning. A most comprehensive analysis of response-mode and feedback factors has been reported by Goldbeck and Briggs (1960).

The general area of reinforcement suggests problems related to the drop-out feature of teaching machines. Pressey's (1927) original machine dropped items after the correct answer had been given twice. Skinner's machines at the Harvard Psychological Laboratory also have the drop-out feature, although the commercially available machines based on Skinner's design do not incorporate this feature. With reference to a study carried out at Harvard, Holland (unpublished) reported significantly superior performance when the drop-out feature was used.

If items are dropped, the sequence of items is of course changed. How important is the sequence? If items should be dropped, by what criterion of learning can one justify omitting an item from the sequence? If items are not dropped and the criterion for the learning procedure is a complete run (i.e., once through the sequence without error), what is the effect upon retention? Being correct is positive reinforcement; thus, some items under these circumstances will receive a greater amount of positive reinforcement than others. What would be the effect of additional reinforcements with or without drop-out? Again, a plethora of problems and a paucity of answers!

Response time, another important variable, has been investigated by Briggs, Plashinski, and Jones (1955). Their study suggests that there is no difference between self-paced and automatically paced programs as determiners of response time. However, the problem of pacing

for individual items is still a recent one and needs further research. Another aspect of response time—the distribution of practice—has been studied extensively since Ebbinghaus' investigation in 1885. For example, Holland (unpublished) states that in an experiment at Harvard "a few students completed all the disks in a small number of long sessions while others worked in many short sessions. . . . Apparently the way practice was distributed made little difference" (p. 4). Nevertheless, the distribution of practice, like the problem of pacing, is yet a subject of controversy, with most investigations favoring some form of distributed practice (Hovland, 1951).

The above section outlines briefly some of the major problems associated with the variables affecting response mode. Although some of the variables have already been investigated, these and others, together with their interactions, need further research.

KNOWLEDGE OF RESULTS. There are many peripheral problems related to teaching machines, one of which is the effect of immediate knowledge of results on learning. Angell (1949), using a multiple-choice punchboard technique, found that "learning is significantly enhanced by immediate knowledge of results." Briggs (1949), also using the Punchboard, confirmed these results. Bryan and Rigney (1956) noted superior performance when subjects were given knowledge of results, specifically, an explanation if the answer was incorrect. This last study was later expanded by Bryan, Rigney, and Van Horn (1957), who investigated differences between three kinds of explanation given for incorrect response. None of the three types of explanation proved to be superior in teaching the subjects. Because of their controvertible results, the above studies demonstrate that, although immediate knowledge of results appears to be effective in the learning process, this problem contains many facets which need more empirical data.

MOTIVATION. One of the many reasons given for the effectiveness of teaching machines is that the student's motivation is increased. Psychologists and educators have realized for some time that the motivation variable ranks very high among those variables pertinent to learning. In 1958 and 1959, Holland surveyed the use of the teaching machine in classes at Harvard. He found that most students felt that they would have gotten less out of the course if the machines had not been used, that most students preferred to have machines used for part of the course, and finally that most students felt that the teaching machine was used by the instructor "to teach me as much as possible with a given expenditure of my time and effort." During a field tryout of the Subject-Matter Trainer in the Semi-automatic Ground Environment System, Mayer and Westfield (1958) observed that "motivation to work with the trainer is high." The supervisory as well as the operational personnel encouraged the use of this training technique.

Mager (1959) suggests that motivation and interest are a function of the percentage of correct responses. He observed that in two young subjects negative feelings for learning mathematics in the usual classroom situation did not transfer to learning mathematics by means of a teaching machine.

The cause of this phenomenon is perhaps best explained by the subjects' statement that, because they were able to understand the programmed material, it did not seem to be mathematics at all. This interesting relationship between comprehension and motivation needs further investigation.

EQUIPMENT. There are many inexpensive models of teaching machines which will soon hit the consumer market. For much of this equipment, there is very little experimental evidence which supports the various designs. As previously pointed out, Holland has collected data which support the efficiency of the drop-out feature in a teaching machine; yet commercial models presently available do not incorporate this feature, presumably because of its high cost. Generally, it seems that production is now and will continue to be out of phase with much of the research which has provided necessary teaching machine specifications. Moreover, because of their expense, it is likely that some very important features will be omitted in manufacture.

The methods of displaying programmed material, another unexplored problem area, must be investigated so as to provide the design engineer with requirements based on empirical findings. The display problem is less acute, perhaps, with material for the elementary school than it is with programs designed to teach maintenance procedures and aspects of the biological sciences.

The use of computer controlled teaching machines has been recommended by many authors (Coulson & Silberman, 1959; Skinner, 1958).

Utilizing a central computer, with many programs capable of adapting to individual needs and of providing stimulus materials to 50 or more students simultaneously, is a feasible notion for large-scale training programs. With a computer, the display problem again becomes a major issue. Training in pattern recognition, information handling, and display interpretation are but a few appropriate areas which should be studied. The alternate modes of presentation become more extensive as computer capacity increases. In the case of certain kinds of subject matter, a computer generated, pictorial display of information may be a more effective presentation than other display techniques. Future research must solve these problems in equipment design.

TEACHING MACHINES AND OTHER TECHNIQUES. The use of automated teaching devices may be optimized, perhaps, if there is a proper balance between this technique and other compatible teaching methods. What percentage of a course should be machine taught? What subject matter is best suited to automated devices? If classroom courses were as carefully and thoughtfully programmed as some of the programs currently being prepared for teaching machines, might some of the advantages of machines diminish? Perhaps some of the apparent advantages of teaching machines are no more than methods of illustrating correctable classroom techniques! It might well be that the instructor's enthusiasm and inspiration, a factor supposedly dominant in higher education, is vital in mastering a particular subject-matter area, will creativity in certain students be harmed by extensive education via the machine? Again, consideration of the use of a teaching machine, the subject matter, the program the level of education, and the techniques used in combination with the teaching machine provide a fertile field for experimentation. As of now, questions in this area remain unanswered. Silverman (1960a) has presented an excellent, detailed discussion of problems inherent in this new technology of automated teaching and the current trends in the field.

PROBLEMS OF APPLICATION

The most obvious problems in the attempt to use automated teaching techniques have been outlined in the previous section. There is still much of the unknown associated with techniques, machines, programming, etc. to be eliminated before a direct solution to a particular training problem can be specified. Many alternatives exist, the best of which has not yet been determined. In addition to these voids, there is a serious lack of definition in the objectives of many training programs.

What is the objective of a particular automated course or program? From a pragmatic point of view, what are the criteria by which a specific educational program can be evaluated? For example, the objectives might range from the teaching of rote tasks to the presentation of more abstract material. Needless to say, the techniques for both teaching and evaluating learning could be substantially different in each case. The purpose of teaching, the objective of an educational program, must be initially defined. Only then will the concepts *learning* and *teaching* be meaningful in a particular context.

After definition, the next step is to determine what subject matter will provide the student with the necessary information. It is at this point that the major pitfall in education is likely to appear. Even though many training programs do not have a defined objective, their course content is nonetheless prescribed, and the text and/or materials used in previous, nonautomated courses become the prime source of material for an automated teaching program. To program an automated teaching machine with presently available materials might well result only in a more efficient method of teaching the wrong material!

The third step requires decisions in the selection of appropriate teaching techniques. Answers to questions involving programming, choice of teaching machine, learning procedures, pacing, and response modes are still not known.

The fourth and last step requires an evaluation of the selected automated teaching method in terms of the originally established objectives. Conventional methods of instruction should be compared with the innovative methods by means of a specific set of criteria, e.g., in terms of training time, job performance, retention of learned information, etc.

The questions confronting the researcher in teaching machine technology are one example of the broader questions of man-machine interrelation. Data pertinent to the principles of human engineering, the optimum man-machine interaction, the degree to which the machine can perform functions formerly allocated to man, and the appropriate allocation of functions between man and machine will be provided by a research program investigating teaching machines. Inade-

quate attention to any of the above-mentioned steps will result in failure to provide the needed answers in a field which may increase training effectiveness and reduce training costs.

REFERENCES

ANGELL, G. W. The effect of immediate knowledge of quiz results on final examination scores in freshman chemistry. *J. educ. Res.*, 1949, *42*, 391-394.

ANGELL, G. W., and TROYER, M. E. A new self-scoring test device for improving instruction. *Sch. Soc.*, 1948, *67*, 84-85.

BECK, J. On some methods of programming. In E. H. Galanter (Ed.), *Automatic teaching: The state of the art.* New York: Wiley, 1959. Pp. 55-62.

BESNARD, G. G., BRIGGS, L. J., MURSCH, G. A., and WALKER, E. S. Development of the subject-matter trainer. *USAF Personnel Train. Res. Cent. tech. Memo.*, 1955, No. ASPRL-TM-55-7.

BESNARD, G. G., BRIGGS, L. J., and WALKER, E. S. The improved subject-matter trainer. *USAF Personnel Train. Res. Cent. tech. Memo.*, 1955, No. ASPRL-TM-55-11.

BRIGGS, L. J. The development and appraisal of special procedures for superior students and an analysis of the effects of knowledge of results. *Abstr. Doctoral Dissertations, Ohio State U.*, 1949, No. 58.

BRIGGS, L. P., PLASHINSKI, D., and JONES, D. L. Self-pacing versus automatic pacing of practice on the subject-matter trainer. *USAF Personnel Train. Res. Cent. lab. Note*, 1955, No. ASPRL-LN-55-8.

BRYAN, G. L., and RIGNEY, J. W. An evaluation of a method for ship-board training in operations knowledge. *U. Sth. Calif. Electronics Personnel Res. Group tech. Rep.*, 1956, No. 18.

BRYAN, G. L., and RIGNEY, J. W. Current trends in automated tutoring and their implications for naval technical training. *U. Sth. Calif. Dept. Psychol. tech. Rep.*, 1959, No. 29.

BRYAN, G. L., RIGNEY, J. W., and VAN HORN, C. An evaluation of three types of information for supplementing knowledge of results in a training technique. *U. Sth. Calif., Electronics Personnel Res. Group tech. Rep.*, 1957, No. 19.

CARR, W. J. Self-instructional devices: A review of current concepts. *USAF WADC tech. Rep.*, 1959, No. 59-503.

COOK, J. O. Supplementary report: Processes underlying learning a single paired-associate item. *J. exp. Psychol.*, 1958, *56*, 455.

COOK, J. O., and KENDLER, T. S. A theoretical model to explain some paired-associate learning data. In G. Finch and F. Cameron (Eds.), *Symposium on Air Force human engineering, personnel, and training research.* Washington, D.C.: National Academy of Sciences-National Research Council, 1956. Pp. 90-98.

COOK, J. O., and SPITZER, M. E. Supplementary report: Prompting versus confirmation in paired-associate learning. *J. exp. Psychol.,* 1960, *59,* 275-276.

CORRIGAN, R. E. Automated teaching methods. *Automated teach. Bull.,* 1959, *1*(2), 23-30.

COULSON, J. E., and SILBERMAN, H. F. Proposal for extension of automated teaching projects. *Sys. Develpm. Corp. field Note,* 1959.

COULSON, J. E., and SILBERMAN, H. F. Effects of three variables in a teaching machine. *J. educ. Psychol.,* 1960, *51,* 135-143.

CROWDER, N. A. The concept of automatic tutoring. *USAF Personnel Train. Res. Cent. organizational Pap.,* 1955.

CROWDER, N. A. *An automatic tutoring book on number systems.* Vol. 1. Timonium, Md.: Hoover Electronics Co., 1958.

CROWDER, N. A. Automatic tutoring by means of intrinsic programming. In E. H. Galanter (Ed.), *Automatic teaching: The state of the art.* New York: Wiley, 1959. Pp. 109-116.

CROWDER, N. A. The "tutor." *J. Amer. Soc. Train. Dir.,* 1960, *14*(5), 12-17.

DAY, J. H. Teaching machines. *J. chem. Educ.,* 1959, *36,* 591-595.

FERSTER, C. B., and SAPON, S. M. An application of recent developments in psychology to the teaching of German. *Harv. educ. Rev.,* 1958, *28,* 58-69.

FRY, E. B. Teaching machine dichotomy: Skinner versus Pressey. Paper presented at American Psychological Association, Cincinnati, September 1959.

FRY, E. B., BRYAN, G. L., and RIGNEY, J. W. Teaching machines: An annotated bibliography. *Audio Visual commun. Rev.,* 1960, *8,* Suppl. 1, 1-80.

GALANTER, E. H. The ideal teacher. In E. H. Galanter (Ed.), *Automatic teaching: The state of the art.* New York: Wiley, 1959, Pp. 1-11.

GAVURIN, E. I., and DONAHUE, V. M. Logical sequence and random sequence. *Automated teach. Bull.,* 1961, *1*(4), 3-9.

GOLDBECK, R. A. The effect of response mode and learning material difficulty on automated instruction. *Amer. Inst. Res. tech. Rep.,* 1960, No. AIR-328-60-IR-124.

GOLDBECK, R. A., and BRIGGS, L. J. An analysis of response mode and feedback factors in automated instruction. *Amer. Inst. Res. tech. Rep.,* 1960, No. AIR-328-60-IR-133.

HOLLAND, J. G. Teaching machines: An application of principles from the laboratory. In Proceedings of the Educational Testing Service Invitational Conference, October 1959. *The impact of testing on the educational process.* Princeton, N. J.: Educational Testing Service, 1960.

HOMME, L. E., and GLASER, R. Problems in programming verbal learning sequences. Paper presented in symposium on research issues in study of human learning raised by developments in automated teaching methods, American Psychological Association, Cincinnati, September 1959.

HOVLAND, C. I. Human learning and retention. In S. S. Stevens (Ed.), *Handbook of experimental psychology.* New York: Wiley, 1951. Pp. 613-689.

ISRAEL, M. L. Skinnerian psychology and educational redesign. Paper read in symposium, American Psychological Association, Washington, D. C., September 1958.

KENDLER, H. H. Teaching machines and psychological theory. In E. H. Galanter (Ed.), *Automatic teaching: The state of the art.* New York: Wiley, 1959. Pp. 177-185.

LITTLE, J. K. Results of use of machines for testing and for drill upon learning in educational psychology. *J. exp. Educ.,* 1934, *3,* 45-49.

MAGER, R. F. Preliminary studies in automated teaching. *IRE Trans. Educ.,* 1959, *E-2,* 104-107.

MAYER, S. R., and WESTFIELD, R. L. A field tryout of a teaching machine for training in SAGE operations. *USAF Cambridge Res. Cent. tech. Memo.,* 1958, No. OAL-TM-58-16.

PETERSON, J. C. A new device for teaching, testing, and research in learning. *Trans. Kans. Acad. Sci.,* 1930, *33,* 41-47.

PORTER, D. Teaching machines. *Harv. Grad. Sch. Educ. Ass. Bull.,* 1958, *3*(1), 1-5.

PRESSEY, S. L. A simple apparatus which gives tests and scores—and teaches. *Sch. Soc.,* 1926, *23,* 373-376.

PRESSEY, S. L. A machine for automatic teaching of drill material. *Sch. Soc.,* 1927, *25,* 549-552.

PRESSEY, S. L. A third and fourth contribution toward the coming "industrial revolution" in education. *Sch. Soc.,* 1932, *36,* 668-672.

PRESSEY, S. L. Development and appraisal of devices providing immediate automatic scoring of objective tests and concomitant self-instruction. *J. Psychol.,* 1950, *29,* 417-447.

PRESSEY, S. L. Certain major psycho-educational issues appearing in the conference on teaching machines. In E. H. Galanter (Ed.), *Automatic teaching: The state of the art.* New York: Wiley, 1959. Pp. 187-198.

RAMO, S. A new technique of education. *Engng. sci. Mon.,* 1957, *21* (October), 17-22.

RATH, G. J., and ANDERSON, NANCY S. The IBM research center teaching machine project: I. The teaching of binary arithmetic. II. The simulation of a binary arithmetic teaching machine on the IBM 650. Paper presented at USAF Office of Scientific Research symposium on teaching machines, University of Pennsylvania, December 8-9, 1958.

RATH, G. J., ANDERSON, NANCY S., and BRAINERD, R. C. The IBM research center teaching machine project. In E. H. Galanter (Ed.), *Automatic teaching: The state of the art.* New York: Wiley, 1959. Pp. 117-130.

ROTHKOPF, E. Z. A do-it-yourself kit for programmed instruction. *Teach. Coll. Rec.*, 1960, *62*, 195-201.

SILBERMAN, H. F. Introductory description of teaching machines (physical characteristics). Paper read in symposium on automated teaching, Western Psychological Association, San Diego, California, April 1959. (Abstract)

SILVERMAN, R. E. Automated teaching: A review of theory and research. USN Training Device Center, 1960. (ASTIA AD-241 283) (a)

SILVERMAN, R. E. The use of context cues in teaching machines. USN Training Device Center, 1960. (ASTIA AD-238 777) (b)

SKINNER, B. F. The science of learning and the art of teaching. *Harv. educ. Rev.*, 1954, *24*, 86-97.

SKINNER, B. F. *Verbal behavior.* New York: Appleton-Century-Crofts, 1957.

SKINNER, B. F. Teaching machines. *Science*, 1958, *128*, 969-977.

SPENCE, K. W. The relation of learning theory to the technology of education. *Harv. educ. Rev.*, 1959, *29*, 84-95.

STEPHENS, A. L. Certain special factors involved in the law of effect. *Abstr. Doctoral Dissertations, Ohio State U.*, 1953, No. 64.

WEIMER, P. K. A proposed "automatic" teaching device. *IRE Trans. Educ.*, 1958, *E-1*, 51-53.

ZEAMAN, D. Skinner's theory of teaching machines. In E. H. Galanter (Ed.), *Automatic teaching: The state of the art.* New York: Wiley, 1959. Pp. 167-176.

81/INSTRUCTIONAL TECHNOLOGY AND THE MEASUREMENT OF LEARNING OUTCOMES: SOME QUESTIONS[1]/ROBERT GLASER[*]

EVALUATION OF THE EFFECTIVENESS

of teaching machines and programmed learning, and of broadly conceived instructional systems, has raised into prominence a number of questions concerning the nature and properties of measures of student achievement. In the evaluation of instructional systems, the attainment of subject matter knowledge and skill as well as other behavioral outcomes must, of course, be considered, but the remarks in this paper will be restricted primarily to the measurement of subject matter proficiency, as it may be defined by recognized subject matter scholars.

Achievement measurement can be defined as the assessment of terminal or criterion behavior; this involves the determination of the character-

[1] Symposium address presented at meetings of American Educational Research Association, Chicago, February 1963. This paper is concerned with student educational achievement; however, similar notions have been expressed with respect to the human component in man-machine systems in R. Glaser and D. J. Klaus (1962).

[*] Robert Glaser, Instructional technology and the measurement of learning outcomes: some questions, *The American Psychologist*, 1963, *18*, 519-521. Reprinted by permission.

istics of student performance with respect to specified standards. Achievement measurement is distinguished from aptitude measurement in that the instruments used to assess achievement are specifically concerned with the characteristics and properties of present performance, with emphasis on the meaningfulness of its content. In contrast, aptitude measures derive their meaning from a demonstrated relationship between present performance and the future attainment of specified knowledge and skill. In certain circumstances, of course, this contrast is not quite so clear, for example, when achievement measures are used as predictor variables.

The scores obtained from an achievement test provide primarily two kinds of information. One is the degree to which the student has attained criterion performance, for example, whether he can satisfactorily prepare an experimental report, or solve certain kinds of word problems in arithmetic. The second type of information that an achievement test score provides is the relative ordering of individuals with respect to their test performance, for example, whether Student A can solve his problems more quickly than Student B. The principal difference between these two kinds of information lies in the standard used as a reference. What I shall call criterion-referenced measures depend upon an absolute standard of quality, while what I term norm-referenced measures depend upon a relative standard. Distinctions between these two kinds of measures have been made previously by others (Flanagan, 1951; Ebel, 1962).

CRITERION-REFERENCED MEASURES

Underlying the concept of achievement measurement is the notion of a continuum of knowledge acquisition ranging from no proficiency at all to perfect performance. An individual's achievement level falls at some point on this continuum as indicated by the behaviors he displays during testing. The degree to which his achievement resembles desired performance at any specified level is assessed by criterion-referenced measures of achievement or proficiency. The standard against which a student's performance is compared when measured in this manner is the behavior which defines each point along the achievement continuum. The term "criterion," when used in this way, does not necessarily refer to final end-of-course behavior. Criterion levels can be established at any point in instruction where it is necessary to obtain infor-

mation as to the adequacy of an individual's performance. The point is that the specific behaviors implied at each level of proficiency can be identified and used to describe the specific tasks a student must be capable of performing before he achieves one of these knowledge levels. It is in this sense that measures of proficiency can be criterion-referenced.

Along such a continuum of attainment, a student's score on a criterion-referenced measure provides explicit information as to what the individual can or cannot do. Criterion-referenced measures indicate the content of the behavioral repertory, and the correspondence between what an individual does and the underlying continuum of achievement. Measures which assess student achievement in terms of a criterion standard thus provide information as to the degree of competence attained by a particular student which is independent of reference to the performance of others.

NORM-REFERENCED MEASURES

On the other hand, achievement measures also convey information about the capability of a student compared with the capability of other students. In instances where a student's *relative* standing along the continuum of attainment is the primary purpose of measurement, reference need not be made to criterion behavior. Educational achievement examinations, for example, are administered frequently for the purpose of ordering students in a class or school, rather than for assessing their attainment of specified curriculum objectives. When such norm-referenced measures are used, a particular student's achievement is evaluated in terms of a comparison between his performance and the performance of other members of the group. Such measures need provide little or no information about the degree of proficiency exhibited by the tested behaviors in terms of what the individual can do. They tell that one student is more or less proficient than another, but do not tell how proficient either of them is with respect to the subject matter tasks involved.

In large part, achievement measures currently employed in education are norm referenced. This emphasis upon norm-referenced measures has been brought about by the preoccupation of test theory with aptitude, and with selection and prediction problems; norm-referenced measures are useful for this kind of work on correlational analysis. However, the imposition of this kind of thinking on the purposes of achievement measurement raises some question, and concern with instructional technology is forcing us toward the kind of information made available by the use of criterion-referenced measures. We need to behaviorally specify minimum levels of performance that describe the least amount of end-of-course competence the student is expected to attain, or that he needs in order to go on to the next course in a sequence. The specification of the characteristics of maximum or optimum achievement after a student has been exposed to the course of instruction poses more difficult problems of criterion delineation.

THE USES OF ACHIEVEMENT MEASUREMENT

Consider a further point. In the context of the evaluation of instructional systems, achievement tests can be used for two principal purposes. First, performance can be assessed to provide information about the characteristics of an individual's present behavior. Second, achievement can be assessed to provide information about the conditions or instructional treatments which produce that behavior. The primary emphasis of the first use is to discriminate among individuals. Used in the second way, achievement tests are employed to discriminate among treatments, that is, among different instructional procedures by an analysis of *group* differences.

Achievement tests used to provide information about *individual* differences are constructed so as to maximize the discriminations made among people having specified backgrounds and experience. Such tests include items which maximize the likelihood of observing individual differences in performance along various task dimensions; this maximizes the variability of the distribution of scores that are obtained. In practical test construction, the variability of test scores is increased by manipulating the difficulty levels and content of the test items.

On the other hand, achievement tests used primarily to provide information about differences in treatments need to be constructed so as to maximize the discriminations made between *groups* treated differently and to minimize the differences between the individuals in any one group. Such a test will be sensitive to the differences produced by instructional conditions. For example, a test designed to demonstrate the effectiveness of instruction would be constructed so that it was generally difficult for those taking it before training and generally easy after training. The content of the test used to differentiate

treatments should be maximally sensitive to the performance changes anticipated from the instructional treatments. In essence, the distinction between achievement tests used to maximize individual differences and tests used to maximize treatment or group differences is established during the selection of test items.

In constructing an achievement test to differentiate among *individuals* at the end of training, it would be possible to begin by obtaining data on a large sample of items relating to curriculum objectives. Item analysis would indicate that some test items were responded to correctly only by some of the individuals in the group, while other items were answered correctly by all members of the group. These latter 1.00 difficulty level items, since they failed to differentiate among individuals, would be eliminated because their only effect would be to add a constant to every score. The items remaining would serve to discriminate among individuals and thus yield a distribution of scores that was as large as possible, considering the number and type of items used.

On the other hand, if this test were constructed for the purpose of observing *group* instead of individual differences, the selection of items would follow a different course. For example, where instruction was the treatment variable involved, it would be desirable to retain test items which were responded to correctly by all members of the post-training group, but which were answered incorrectly by students who had not yet been trained. In a test constructed for the purpose of differentiating groups, items which indicated substantial variability within either the pre- or post-training group would be undesirable because of the likelihood that they would cloud the effects which might be attributable to the treatment variable.

In brief, items most suitable for measuring individual differences in achievement are those which will differentiate among individuals all exposed to the same treatment variable, while items most suitable for distinguishing between groups are those which are most likely to indicate that a given amount or kind of some instructional treatment was effective. In either case, samples of test items are drawn from a population of items indicating the content of performance; the particular item samples that are drawn, however, are those most useful for the purpose of the kind of measurement being carried out. Hammock (1960) has previously discussed such a difference.

The points indicated above reflect the achievement measurement concerns that have arisen in my own work with instructional technology. There is one further point which must be mentioned, and that is the use of diagnostic achievement tests prior to an instructional course. It appears that, with the necessity for specifying the entering behavior that is required by a student prior to a programed instructional sequence, diagnostic assessment of subject matter competence must take on a more precise function. This raises the problem of developing an improved methodology for diagnostic achievement testing. In this regard, researchers using programed instructional sequences to study learning variables point out that prior testing influences learning, and that this effect must be controlled for in determining the specific contribution of programing variables. In an instructional sense, however, the influence and use of pretesting is an important variable for study since it is not the terminal criterion behavior alone which dictates required instructional manipulations, but the differences between entering and terminal behavior. Furthermore, pretesting of a special kind may contribute to "motivation" by enhancing the value of future responses; there is some indication that this may be brought about by prior familiarity with future response terms (Berlyne, 1960, pp. 296-301) or by permitting some early aided performance of the terminal behavior eventually to be engaged in (Taber, Glaser, & Schaefer, 1963, Ch. 3).

In conclusion, the general point is this. Test development has been dominated by the particular requirements of predictive, correlational aptitude test "theory." Achievement and criterion measurement has attempted frequently to cast itself in this framework. However, many of us are beginning to recognize that the problems of assessing existing levels of competence and achievement and the conditions that produce them require some additional considerations.

REFERENCES

BERLYNE, D. E. *Conflict, arousal, and curiosity.* New York: McGraw-Hill, 1960.

EBEL, R. L. Content standard test scores. *Educ. psychol. Measmt.*, 1962, 22, 15-25.

FLANAGAN, J. C. Units, scores, and norms. In E. T. Lindquist (Ed.), *Educational measurement.* Washington, D. C.: American Council on Education, 1951, Pp. 695-763.

GLASER, R., & KLAUS, D. J. Proficiency measurement: Assessing human performance. In R. Gagne (Ed.), *Psychological principles in system development.* New York: Holt, Rinehart & Winston, 1962. Pp. 421-427.

HAMMOCK, J. Criterion measures: Instruction vs. selection research. *Amer. Psychologist*, 1960, 15, 435. (Abstract)

TABER, J. I., GLAZER, R., & SCHAEFER, H. H. *A guide to the preparation of programmed instructional materials.* Reading, Mass.: Addison-Wesley, in press.

82/SOME COMMENTS ON "THE IMPACT OF ADVANCING TECHNOLOGY ON METHODS IN EDUCATION"/A. W. MELTON*

The following comments were made by Dr. Melton following an address by Dr. Ramo at the Annual Convention of the American Psychological Association, Cincinnati, September 1959. Dr. Melton has indicated that these comments also apply to the 1957 paper of Dr. Ramo, which is reprinted on pages 367-81 of [Lumsdaine and Glaser].

MY COMMENTS WILL RELATE PARTICU-larly to Dr. Ramo's suggestions regarding the application of engineering technology to education, with specific reference to teaching machines. I am sure that the "brave new world" of automated education described so graphically and hopefully by Dr. Ramo captures the imagination of all of us. This is not to say that all thinking men will be pleased with the prospect of this extension of mechanistic science and engineering to the moulding of minds through the marriage of behavioral science and electronics engineering. Surely, some humanists will see the work of the devil in his effort to automate education, just as they have seen the work of the devil in some applications of nuclear physics. However, the worries of these people who cherish the old order and fear the new will not be mine, nor do I think they should be psychology's. Nevertheless, I can remain calm in the face of this impending educational revolution, and I think that you should remain calm, only if we assume that, in addition to engineering feasibility, there will be two guiding considerations in the development and use of automated aids to human learning of the complex sorts involved in the production of educated men and women. The first of these considerations relates to educational objectives; the second relates to the development of the science and technology of psychology.

First, with respect to the educational objectives, I interpret Dr. Ramo's interests to be the promotion of an educational technology which can be employed as an efficient means toward whatever educational objectives our society defines as "good." When viewed as a technology for achieving a higher level of education in more people in less time and with lesser brain-power cost, if not manpower cost, I see no possible basis for worry. However, I do see a basis for worry if there is failure to recognize that a taxonomy of educational objectives reveals many objectives other than the acquisition of knowledges and skills. I refer, of course, to such objectives as the inculcation of socially acceptable attitudes and motivations; the inculcation of motivation to achieve, to create, to invent, to think independently; and the development of skills in interpersonal relations.

When viewed against this background of educational objectives which literally encompasses the whole spectrum of behaviors associated with the concept of the civilized man, it is clear that the initial successes of automated education will be in the achievement of knowledges and skills. In fact, many mechanical aids to such achievement have already been devised and used extensively. It is now clear that the state of the art in engineering is adequate to support much more complicated types of knowledge and skill acquisition than the simple rote-learning and problem-solving aspects of reading, writing, and arithmetic, and so we are now witnessing attempts to automate language, higher mathematics, the fundamentals of science, history, etc. But, let it not be forgotten that there is the problem of appropriate *utilization* of these knowledges and skills by the individuals who will possess such elegant mental furniture as a gift from electronic engineering. Such individuals must be intellectually curious, inventive, and ingenious; they must be socially and emotionally mature in the employment of their intellectual talents; and above all they must be motivated to perform their roles in our ever more complex society. What I am attempting to say is: Let us *not* consider the goals of this

* A. W. Melton, Some comments on "The impact of advancing technology on methods in education" by Dr. Simon Ramo, September 1959, unpublished, in A. A. Lumsdaine and Robert Glaser, Editors, *Teaching Machines and Programmed Learning: A Source Book.* Washington: Department of Audiovisual Instruction, NEA, 1960. Reprinted by permission. The article by Melton originally appeared in *Harvard Educational Review*, 1959, 29, 96-106.

educational technology to be merely, for example, the attainment of mastery of differential calculus in the greatest number of people in the shortest possible time; instead, let us be sure to consider also the techniques for improving the motivation of individuals for the attainment and appropriate use of such knowledge and the techniques for accelerating the acquisition of attitudes and social habits that are just as necessary for the advancement of our society as are those skills.

Some of you will perceive, I am sure, that I am a bit worried lest automated education become a fad, to take its place alongside progressive education, the mental testing movement, and the guidance movement. By putting automated education in such company I mean no offense to it or to progressive education, mental testing, or educational guidance; but I do mean to say that all represent piecemeal approaches to the technology of education, all represent emphases on some educational objectives to the exclusion of other equally valid objectives, and that all represent applications of psychological science that have been—or, in the case of automated education, might be—adopted and lavishly supported by our society while the furtherance of the basic knowledge and theory on which they should be grounded has been forced to scrounge for itself. Which leads me to the plea that—this time, at least—we attempt to anchor this new component of the technology of education in the complete system of educational objectives and in the science of psychology. Let us keep always before us the full range of educational objectives that is defined, in the last analysis, in terms of the desired behavior of the whole person in our society—let there be no exclusive emphasis on the perfection of intellectual skills at the one extreme, nor on the encouragement of individual initiative and originality at the other extreme, but *rather* an emphasis on both of these as well as all other desired characteristics of the whole educated man, as revealed by our taxonomy and systematic integration of educational objectives. Also, and with comparable emphases, let us plant this new component of the technology of education (machine aids to learning) firmly in the science of psychology, and use the goals of the technology as justification for the liberal support by our society for advancement of basic knowledge and theory in areas of psychology most necessary for valid decision-making within the technology.

My principal concern has to do with the second of these exhortations; that is, the support of basic psychological science in a manner and to a degree appropriate to the emphasis given automated education. Perhaps I am a "worry wart," but I can see the managers of resources in our society, as well as some starry-eyed educators and psychologists, being carried away by the imaginativeness and insightfulness of the concept of automated education, and forgetting our counsel that contemporary psychology is able to give only first approximations as answers to questions about the processes and programming of human learning which are quite critical in the engineering of education. As a consequence, I can publicly cringe at the thought that millions may well be appropriated for such technological efforts, with the usual 1 percent, or one-tenth of 1 percent, for fundamental research in psychology in support of the improvement of the technology. Why am I gun shy on this point? Those of you who know the history of psychological research in the Air Force personnel and training effort over the past ten years will understand. In the context of the Personnel and Training Systems of the Air Force, it was recognized about 1950 that a technology was needed, and *feasible*, for anticipating the tasks that human beings would perform in new weapon systems, like the ballistic missile systems, and for specifying, far in advance of even the prototype model, what the specific selection, training, and on-the-job management techniques for the production and maintenance of these human components should be. Thus, the technology promised the delivery of the essential human components of a weapon system concurrently in time with the delivery of the equipment components.

After a period of confusion and poor communication, the very simple *idea* of extracting information about human tasks from the *designs* of future weapon systems and using such information to establish the special procedures for selection and training of men to perform those anticipated tasks finally caught on, and was properly recognized as an essential step in the production of an operational weapon-system. Consequently, millions of dollars are now being spent annually by the Air Force in implementing this procedure for defining what is now appropriately called the Personnel Subsystem of each new weapon system. But somewhere along the line a warning of the psychologists who devised this technology was forgotten. Lost somewhere along the line was their warning that the technology that could be supported by contemporary psychological science was primitive —only a first approximation—and that substantial support of certain critical areas of fundamental psychological science should proceed concurrently with the initial implementations of the technology, if the technology were to become reliable and effective. Such support was not only not increased within the Air Force; it was drastically decreased. Now we are witnessing the elaborate employment of a technology by the Air Force, but with the scientific underpinning on starvation rations. One is reminded of the disembodied grin of the Cheshire cat, and the whole affair would be the source of some sardonic humor if the consequences were not so serious for our long-range security, for the viability of the important technology which was introduced into the Air Force, and for our science.

Now, this is not the only case where enthusiasm for a psycho-technology has been coupled with relative apathy for its scientific foundations. I think here again of mental testing, progressive education, guidance, visual education. My concern is that this not be the history of the next ten years in the automation of teaching. This is neither the time nor the place for me to discuss the details of the basic research that should receive support. . . . It is important to note, however, that psychologists and educators are currently joining forces in thinking about the objectives of education and about the developments in basic knowledge and theory of learning that are necessary to support these objectives. These efforts will come to naught if the resources for the development of basic knowledge do not represent some substantial and continuing proportion of the total resources applied to the application of engineering technology to education.

In summary, I believe that the full exploitation of electronic engineering in a radical revision of the technology of education is an essential condition for achieving effective control over the learning process. I am, therefore, a willing partner to Dr. Ramo's enthusiasms and prognostications. At the same time, I think we will be fostering an abortive and potentially harmful fad—and certainly a very costly fad— if we fail to temper our exploitation of gadgetry in terms of clearly formulated educational objectives, only some of which will be promoted by such gadgetry. Which is to say that the educational objective to be achieved should determine the use of such devices, rather than the availability of the device determining, or limiting, the objective. This matching of educational methods and media to the components of an intricate system of objectives is no simple exercise and will tax the talents of psychologists and educators for many years to come. One principal reason why this is so is that the scientific understanding of human behavior, and especially the scientific understanding of the learning, motivation, and performance aspects of human behavior, can provide only first approximations to answers to critical questions involved in the statement of educational objectives and to critical questions involved in the design of a teaching machine.

From this line of thought I derive my second plea—or "warning," if you will—that some substantial proportion of the resources employed in the exploitation of engineering for the benefit of education be allocated to basic and applied research on the learning process, on human motivation, and on related problems of human behavior. If this is not done, the fruits of this imaginative adaptation of engineering technology to the technology of education will be largely wormy and rotten, and only occasionally fit for human consumption. In view of the high economic cost of the automation of education, such occasional pay-off cannot be afforded, and might well result in abandonment of the whole idea. On the other hand, if the definition of educational objectives and the advancement of basic knowledge and theory in psychology can move forward at an accelerating pace to match the pace of engineering applications to education, I am prepared to view the new technology of education which Dr. Ramo has so forcefully described, as a conceptual "break-through" of the first magnitude, and as a unique opportunity for the educator, psychologist, and engineer to work together for a technology that will make the new world *much* braver than Huxley ever imagined.

Index

Abe, C., 410, 418
Ability, testing of, 387–391 (see also Achievement)
Ability factors, 383–386
    and environmental influences, 387–391
    psychological origins of, 386–387
Abraham, K., 461, 471, 475
Acceleration, 404–405
Accomplishment, sense of, 294–296
Achievement:
    and age, 403–404
    and creativity, 413–414
    desire for, in children, 309
    and experience of success and failure, 434–436
    measurement of, 590–593
    and personality, 517–519
    related to change in IQ, 393–397
    and school environment, 510–511
    and social mobility, 188, 191–192
    and teacher style, 566–567
    testing of, 559–562
Achievement imagery, 239–242
Achievement motivation, 238–239, 243, 282–283, 509–510
Ackerman, N. W., 187, 199
Acquired drives, 90–91
Acquisition of behavior, 92–93, 125, 359
Action, and theory, 124
Activity, and competence, 302–304
Adelson, J., 133, 186, 199, 288
Adjustment, problems of:
    and children's textbooks, 360–361
    leading to banality, 540
    sex differences in, 503–504
Adler, A., 8
Adolescence:
    and genital stage, 304–306
    and identity, 295–296
    normality in, 334
    psychoanalytic study of, 328–334
    rate of physical maturation in, 71–79
Adolescents:
    heterosexuality in, 262
    planning curricula for, 324–328
    problems of, 288
    studied in kibbutzim, 257–264
Adorno, T. W., 199, 265, 266, 271
Adult social reinforcement, 99–106
Affect, reversal of, 331–332
Affective interaction, 513–515
Affiliation, and critical periods, 312–316

Affiliation imagery, 239–241, 242
Affiliation motivation, 238–239, 243
Age, chronological:
    and achievement, 403–404
    as determinant of behavior, 285–288
    limitations of, 374
    and perceptual-motor development, 68
    related to problem behavior, 504
Age periods, 81–86
Aggression:
    and anxiety, 369
    attitude of teachers toward, 365, 368–369
    and change in IQ, 393–397
    control of, 140–147, 248
    and counter-aggression, 368–369
    and intellectual blocking, 456–457
    and punishment, 140–147, 363
    relation to dependency, 255
    and sex role, 354
    socialization of, 140–147
    sources of, in home, 144–147
    studied in kibbutzim, 252–253
    vicarious expression of, 481–484
Aichhorn, A., 331, 334
Alexander, W. P., 462
Allee, W. C., 54
Allen, F. L., 408, 570
Allen, K. E., 101, 102, 106
Allen, L., 81, 86
Allinsmith, W., 178, 230, 233, 421, 445, 449, 486, 519, 525
Allport, F. H., 124, 129
Allport, G. W., 5, 124, 129, 287, 335, 339, 388
Alpert, R., 491, 499
Amatruda, C. S., 317, 356
Ambiguity, intolerance of, 489
Ames, L. B., 356
Amidon, E., 517
Anal conflicts, 454–456
Anal stage, 300, 304
Anastasi, A., 32, 45, 47, 52, 54, 373, 387, 391
Anderson, H. H., 365, 370, 435, 516
Anderson, I. H., 494, 499
Anderson, J. E., 80, 86
Anderson, N. S., 583, 589, 590
Andrews, T. G., 524, 542
Angell, G. W., 582, 586, 588
Animal research, 54–56
    and drive, 302
Anthropology, and study of sex roles, 341, 343
Antisocial behavior, and teachers' attitudes, 501, 503

Antisocial needs, 363–364
Anxiety:
    and aggression, 141–142
    and apathy, 336–337
    and creativity-intelligence distinction, 417
    defense against, 331–333
    interaction of, with compulsivity, 488, 495–497
    and learning, 489–490, 493–495
    and punishment for aggression, 141–142
Approval, use of by teachers, 365–370
Aronfreed, J., 107, 109, 115, 118, 437, 443
Arsenian, S., 52
Asceticism, in adolescence, 333
Asch, S. E., 518
Ashton-Warner, S., 468
Association theory, 87, 547
Associational processes, 410–412
Atkinson, J. W., 199, 239, 240, 242, 244, 398, 510
Attachment, 312–315 (see also Filiative behavior; Imprinting)
Attention, and problem behavior, 100–106
Attitudes, toward behavior problems, 500–506
Attneave, F., 321
Ausubel, D. P., 263, 489, 499, 525, 555, 558
Authoritarianism, and prejudice, 265–266, 269–271, 273
Autonomy:
    child's attainment of, 291–293
    lack of, in children's textbooks, 361
    and social mobility, 188, 193–195

Bach, G. R., 368, 369, 370
Back, K., 210
Bacon, M. K., 237, 342, 343
Baer, D. M., 88, 99, 103, 106, 184, 186, 438, 443, 509
Bagley, W. C., 210
Bain, W. E., 506
Baines, C., 307, 426
Baker, C. T., 86, 158, 374, 393, 394, 397, 398, 518
Baker, R., 308
Baldwin, A. L., 157
Bales, R. F., 166, 178, 348, 349
Bandura, A., 106–109, 116–118, 132, 150, 157, 159, 161, 163, 165, 166, 421, 437, 443, 509
Banks, R. K., 115, 118
Barker, R. G., 47–48, 51, 52, 283, 421, 434, 516, 535, 536

Barlow, M. D., 546, 549
Barrett-Lennard, G. T., 28, 30
Barrie, J. M., 475
Barron, F., 410, 418
Barry, H., III, 237, 342, 343
Bartlett, F., 530, 536
Baruch, D. W., 133
Bass, B. M., 266, 271, 438, 443
Bayley, N., 33, 79, 80, 83–86, 387, 388, 392, 398, 401
Beach, F. A., 21, 32, 35, 42, 50, 52, 368, 370, 425, 431
Beck, J., 584, 588
Behavior:
    influence of setting on, 201–203
    maintenance of, by reinforcement, 93–96
    and maturation, 285
    theories of, 89–91
    typical, 285
Behavior change, 125
Behavior problems:
    changing attitudes toward, 500–506
    teachers' perception of, 501–504
Behaviorism, as a philosophy of science, 11–18
Beilin, H., 422, 500, 506, 516
Belief congruence, 274, 277, 281
Beliefs, and race prejudice, 274, 277, 281
Bellack, A. A., 575
Beloff, J. R., 86
Bendix, R., 272
Benedict, R., 288, 345, 348, 449
Berg, J. A., 438, 443
Berkeley Growth Study, comparisons with, 80–86
Berkowitz, L., 443, 481, 483, 485
Berlyne, D. E., 307, 425, 426, 431, 510, 593
Bernfeld, S., 304, 307, 329, 334
Bernstein, B., 229, 233
Besnard, G. G., 582, 588
Bettelheim, B., 269–271
Bexton, W. H., 425, 426, 431
Bibring, G. L., 330
Bieri, J., 157
Biesheuvel, S., 388, 391, 529, 536
Bijou, S. W., 99
Bilingualism, 48
Binet, A., 373, 375, 378
Bing, E., 132, 148
Bingham, W. vanD., 383, 391, 399, 400
Biological determinants of behavior, 31
Birch, H. G., 80, 86, 525, 551, 554
Bischof, L. G., 373
Bishop, B. M., 185, 186
Bixtenstein, V. E., 115, 118
Blaine, G. B., 336, 339
Blake, E., 55, 558
Blake, R., 499
Blakeley, W. P., 218
Blame, use of by teachers, 365–370
Blanchard, P., 462, 506
Blewett, D. B., 86
Blin, Dr., 375–377
Blink response, 64
Bliss, E., 432
Blocksma, D., 211
Bloom, B., 533, 536
Bloom, B. S., 388, 391
Blough, D. S., 14, 18, 95
Bond, A. D., 546, 549
Books for children:

and childhood fantasies, 470–475
    typical early tales, 472–475
Borek, E., 34
Bornstein, B., 455, 457, 462
Bossom, J., 70
Bowlby, J., 311, 313, 314, 316, 317
Boynton, P. L., 506
Brackbill, G. A., 52
Brackbill, Y., 314, 317
Bradburn, W. M., 157
Bradway, K., 398
Brady, J. V., 95
Brainerd, R. C., 583, 590
Brandt, H. F., 435
Bray, C. W., 545, 549
Breese, F. H., 157
Breland, K., 92
Brewer, J. E., 365, 370
Bridgman, L., 380
Bridgman, P. W., 11, 13, 18
Briggs, L. J., 582, 583, 586, 588, 589
Brill, A. A., 307, 431
Brim, O. G., 506
Broder, L., 533, 536
Brody, S., 64, 70
Brolyer, C. R., 546, 549
Bronfenbrenner, U., 159, 166, 178
Bronte, C., 475
Brown, D. G., 165, 166, 178, 237, 342, 349, 350, 355, 356
Brown, R., 499
Brown, W. M., 462
Bruner, J. S., 5, 19, 264, 272, 286, 287, 318, 319, 321, 415, 418, 459, 462, 463, 486, 488, 499, 516, 523, 524, 527, 533, 536, 537
Brush, E. S., 107, 118
Bryan, G. L., 581, 582, 584, 586, 588, 589
Buell, J. S., 101, 102, 106
Buhler, K., 425, 431
Bunker, H. A., 431
Burlingham, D., 329, 334, 427, 431
Burnett, F. H., 475
Burt, C., 386, 392, 403
Burton, R. V., 178
Butler, R. A., 302, 304, 425, 426, 431, 530, 536
Butsch, R. L. C., 544, 549
Buxbaum, E., 453, 462, 475
Byrne, D., 274, 275, 279, 281, 282

Caldwell, B. M., 32, 33, 40, 286, 310, 314, 317
California Adolescent Growth Study, 71–79
California Growth Studies, 32–33
Cameron, I., 588
Cameron, L. J., 334
Campbell, B. A., 308
Campbell, D. T., 384, 392
Cane, V. A., 88, 107
Cannon, W. B., 425, 431
Caplan, G., 464
Carmichael, L., 317
Caron, A. J., 158
Carr, W. J., 584, 588
Carroll, J. B., 486, 499, 516
Cartwright, D., 166
Cash, W. J., 270, 271
Casler, L., 64, 70
Castaneda, A., 489, 491, 499
Castle, P., 63, 70
Castner, B. M., 356
Cattell, P., 314, 317

Cattell, R. B., 81, 86, 384, 389, 392, 402, 460, 462
Centers, R., 266, 272
Chall, J., 240, 244
Chance, J. R., 79
Character Education Inquiry, 357
Charles, M. S., 53
Charters, W. W., 235
Chein, I., 266, 267, 272
Chess, S., 80, 86
Chidester, L., 455, 462
Child, I. L., 53, 90, 91, 237, 342, 343, 357, 427, 431
Child, the:
    desire for achievement in, 309
    and intellectual efficiency, 451
Child-rearing:
    in different cultures, 50–51
    and expression of aggression, 144–147
    related to aggression and dependency, 141–142
    and theories of learning, 119–121
Choice, child's right to, 292
Christenson, P. R., 410, 418, 419
Christie, R., 266, 271, 272
Church, R. M., 107, 115, 118
Church attendance, and intolerance, 267–268, 270
Clark, E. J., 503, 506
Clark, R. A., 199, 239, 244, 398, 510
Clarke, A. C., 356
Classroom:
    mental health situation in, 214–216
    socio-emotional structure in, 211–212
    success in, 434–436
Classroom instruction, and science of learning, 121–122
Classroom learning:
    influence of the group upon, 204
    and problems of mental health, 211–216
Cline, V. B., 410, 418
Clinical psychology, and modern education, 500–506
Cliques, in the classroom, 205
Coch, L., 210
Cochran, W. G., 366
Cogan, M. L., 509
Cognitive abilities:
    and child-rearing practices, 148–158
    and IQ, 393–394
Cognitive development:
    in animals, 42–44
    in children, 41–42
    and interaction situation, 154–157
    nonintellective factors in, 450–461
    and pedagogy, 527–536
    role of mother in, 156–157
Cognitive interaction, 516–517
Cognitive motivation, 511–513
Cognitive-perceptual factors in development, 427–428
Cole, M., 529, 536
Colleges, and later achievement of graduates, 405–406
Comic books, 218–224
Common sense, and genius, 407
Competence, 300–309
    and ego psychology, 303–304
    as fitness or ability, 301–304

Competence (*cont.*):
    and psychosexual stages, 300–309
    sense of, 303
Competence model, of development, 301
Competition:
    lack of, in children's books, 473
    related to change in IQ, 393–397
    and social mobility, 187
Compulsivity:
    interaction of, with anxiety, 495–497
    and learning, 488–489, 491–493
Conant, J. B., 423, 431
Conceived values, 24–26
Concept Mastery Test, 401
Concepts:
    of conservation, 319–323
    development of, 318, 323–324
    of magnitude and order, 318–324
Conceptualizing activities, 414–416
Conditioned reinforcer, 92–93
Conditioning: (*see also* Reinforcement)
    and conditioned response, 89–90
    and conditioned stimulus, 89–90
    and trauma theory of anxiety, 429–430
Conflict:
    and conscience, 445–449
    and moral needs, 448–449
Conformity:
    and intolerance, 270–271, 273
    and teacher approval, 368–369
Conn, J. H., 356
Conscience:
    and conflict, 445–449
    defined, 445
    development of, 293–294
    relation to guilt, 294
    and superego, 445, 448
Conservation, concept of, 319–324
Constitutional factors:
    in IQ change, 397
    in rearing, 57–59
Constriction of personality, 294
Contiguity theory, 90
Contingencies of reinforcement, 94–97
Cook, J. O., 585, 588, 589
Cook, M., 308, 433, 511
Cooley, C. H., 423, 431
Coons, E. E., 115, 118
Coover, J. E., 547, 549
Copying behavior, 179
Cordova, F. A., 52
Corey, S. M., 287, 324
Correlation techniques, 3–4
Corrigan, R. E., 581, 589
Cottrell, L. S., 125, 129
Coules, J., 481, 485
Coulson, J. E., 583, 584, 585, 587, 589
Counter-aggression, by teacher, 368–369
Counterpropaganda, 576–580
Countertransference, 21
Course of study, problems in constructing, 532–536
Cox, C. C., 402, 407, 408
Cox, G. M., 366
Crabtree, C., 511
Craig, W., 41
Craighill, P. G., 514
Crandall, V. C., 116, 118

Crandall, V. J., 116, 118
Creative process, elements of, 410–411
Creativity:
    correlation with IQ, 410
    and intelligence, 409–411
    and task orientation, 410–411
    and teacher behavior, 514
    tests of, 409
    as unitary dimension, 409–410
Crick, F. H. C., 34
Crises, in normal personality development, 335–339
Criterion-referenced measures of achievement, 591
Critical period hypothesis, 310–312
Critical periods, 36–37, 285, 310–316
Cronbach, L. J., 384, 392, 423, 431, 524, 542
Cross-Cultural Files, 51
Cross-cultural studies:
    of intelligence, 387, 389–391
    of masculine role preference, 351
    of sex, 343–348, 351
Crowder, N. A., 583, 584, 589
Crying and whining, 101–102
Cultural change, 238–239, 241–243
    in sex-role patterns, 354–355
Cultural deprivation:
    psychological meaning of, 227–229
    and school learning, 226–232
    and teacher style, 565–575
Cultural deviance, and intolerance, 270–271, 273
Cultural influence, on personality, 358–360
Cultural islands, 206
Cultural transmission, requisites of, 529–531
Cultural values, expressed in children's readers, 238–239, 241–243
Cunningham, R., 352, 356
Curiosity, about nature:
    and motivation, 510
    related to change in IQ, 393–397
Curriculum:
    for adolescents, 324–326
    enrichment of, for the gifted, 405
    episodic quality of, 439–540
    problems in development of, 532–536
    and student development, 324–325

Dale, E., 240, 244
Dameron, L. E., 353
Dann, S., 236
Darcy, N. T., 52
Darwin, C., 19, 23
Dashiell, J. F., 426
David, P. R., 53
Davidson, H. H., 258, 263
Davidson, K. S., 417, 419, 500
Davis, A., 52, 227, 265, 270, 272, 284, 398
Davis, D. R., 158
Davis, E. A., 506
Davis, W., 408
Davis, W. A., 368, 370
Davitz, J. R., 79, 567
Day, J. H., 583, 589
Daydreams:
    reflected in children's books, 469–475

universal, 475
Dearborn, W. R., 545, 549
Deboer, J. J., 224
DeBrunhoff, J., 475
deCharms, R., 235, 238, 481, 485
Defense mechanisms:
    adolescent, 331–333
    against anxiety, 331–333
    against guilt, 447–448, 449
    against impulses, 333
    and inner conflict, 447–449
Defensiveness, in classroom, 215
Defensive identification, 180
Defensive identification hypothesis, 171–173, 175–177
De Groat, A. F., 366, 370
Deignan, H. G., 356
DeKruif, P., 462
Delayed instinct, 40
Delayed reward, 437–443
Delinquency, and failure in school, 295
DellaPiana, G. M., 514
Del Solar, C., 506
Demkow, L. F., 115, 118
Democracy, fostered in classroom, 207
Democratic strategist, role of teacher, 208
DeMontaigne, M., 121
Denenberg, V. H., 70, 430, 431
Dennis, W., 388, 392, 428, 431
Dependency:
    and nurturance, 509
    observations of, in children, 253–255
    related to aggression, 255
    and social mobility, 188, 193–195
    and teacher influence, 518
    and verbal ability, 154
Deprivation:
    cultural, 226–233
    and sexual behavior, 136–139
    and social responsiveness, 136–139
Deutsch, H., 305, 307
Deutsch, Martin, 227–229, 231, 233
Deutsch, Morton, 210
Development:
    cognitive and perceptual factors in, 427–428
    emotional, 300
    role of education in, 464–469
    stages of, 285, 289–299
    theories of, 465–469
Development schedule, 39
Developmental identification, 180
Developmental identification hypothesis, 167–168, 171–178
Developmental periods, 80–86
Developmental tasks, of adolescence, 326–328
Developmentalism, 289
Devinney, L. C., 264, 272
DeVore, I., 528
Dickens, C., 475
Dickson, V. E., 506
Dinitz, S., 356
Disadvantaged children, teachers for, 565–575
Disapproval, use of by teachers, 365–370
Discipline:
    and guilt, 446
    and intermittent reinforcement, 95–96
    in kibbutzim, 248
    in rearing, 57–59

Displacement, 454–459
Distler, L., 160, 166, 170–172, 178
Dixon, W. R., 499
Dobzhansky, T., 46, 52
Dodge, R., 400
Dollard, J., 7, 89, 91, 126, 129, 179
  186, 265, 270, 272, 425, 432
Dominance, of teachers, 365
Donahue, V. M., 584, 589
Dorr, M., 199
Doubt of self-worth, 292–293
Douglas, V., 212, 216
Douvan, E., 133, 186, 282–284,
  288
Downer, J. W., 500
Downward mobility, 188
Driesch, H., 35
Drives:
  acquired, 90–91
  in adolescence, 328–329
  aversive and neglected, 508
  and competence, 301–302
  Freudian theory of, 300–301,
    302
  naming of, 425
  revision of theory of, 302–304
Duncker, K., 551, 552, 554
Durkin, K., 282
Dyadic units of behavior, 125–129
Dybwad, G., 218
Dyk, R. B., 388, 392
Dynes, R. R., 356

Ebbinghaus, H., 530, 536, 586
Ebel, R. L., 591, 593
Ebert, E., 80, 86, 545, 549
Echelberger, E., 213, 216
Eckblad, G., 426, 431
Education:
  and adolescents, 324–328
  automation of, 581–588
  for disadvantaged children, 565–
    575
  and factors related to learning,
    537–542
  for the gifted, 405
  mechanical aids to, 512–513
  and prejudice, 269, 271
  and psychoanalysis, 225
  relationship to psychology, 121–
    122
  role of in development, 464–
    469
  social psychology of, 357–364
  and testing for achievement, 559
  and transfer of training, 543–
    549
Educational objectives, 594–596
Educational psychology, changing
  concepts of, 204–207
Edwards, A. L., 79, 556, 558
Edwards Personal Preference
  Schedule, 73–76
Eells, K., 231, 233, 283, 284
Effectance, 303
Efficacy, feeling of, 303
Ego, in adolescence, 328–329,
  331–333
Ego-integrative motives, 509–510
Ego process in learning, 464–469
Ego strength, and delayed grati-
  fication, 437
Ego structure:
  psychoanalytic theory of, 303–
    304
  and social mobility, 197–199
  and work, 305–306
Eichorn, D. H., 80, 86, 310, 341
Eisenstadt, S. N., 262, 263

Elam, S. L., 230, 233
Elliott, O., 54, 317
Ellis, D. B., 506
Elzi, A., 356
Emmerich, W., 178
Emmet, W. C., 158
Emotional attachments, and homeo-
  static needs, 428–429
Endler, N. S., 425, 431
Energy level, and social mobility,
  188, 190–191
English, O. S., 98, 133, 463
Enrichment of environment, and
  visual-motor development, 65–
  66
Environment:
  and ability factors, 387–391
  and cognitive development, 41–
    44
  and heredity, 31, 45–53
  methodological approaches to,
    49–53
Environmental event, 126–128
Environmental factors:
  behavioral, 48–49
  and IQ, 48–49, 388–389, 393–
    397
  organic, 47–48
  in rearing, 57–59
Epstein, L. J., 506
Erickson, M. C., 284
Erikson, E. H., 8, 81, 86, 286, 301,
  303, 305–307, 339
Eron, L. D., 263
Escalona, S., 80, 86
Estes, W. K., 508
Ethnographic reports, 343
Ets, M., 475
Evaluation, locus of, 24–27 (see
  also Valuing process; Values)
Evaluative interaction, 515–516
Evans, R. I., 274, 282
Evolution, 20
Examinations, 563–564 (see also
  Tests)
Existentialism, 8–9
Expectancy, in social interaction,
  127
Experiencing, as a value, 26–30
Exploration, and competence, 302–
  304
Expressiveness, and creativity, 416–
  417
Externalization, 264, 265, 269–271,
  273
Extinction, and tantrums, 98–99

Face-to-face groups, 201
Factor theory, 373
Faigin, H., 133, 236, 245, 256
Failure:
  fear of, 187
  and inhibition, 457–458
  and level of aspiration, 434–436
Fairy stories, 363–364, 472–475,
  476
Falkner, F., 80, 86
Family structure, and social mobility, 189, 196–197
Fantasy:
  in childhood, 294
  in children's books, 470–475
  in fairy tales, 472–475
  functions of, 477
  of omnipotence, 476
  related to rearing, 294
  in television, 477
Fantz, R. L., 32
Farber, I. E., 430, 431

Farrell, M., 356
Faterson, H. F., 388, 392
Fauls, L. B., 353, 356
Fawcett, H. P., 547, 550
Federn, P., 333, 334
Feifer, I., 519, 575
Feminine protest, 353–354
Feminine role:
  depicted in school readers, 361–
    362
  preference for, 167–178
Fenichel, O., 317, 449, 488, 499
Ferenczi, S., 332, 422, 476
Ferguson, G. A., 386, 392
Ferster, C. B., 93, 94, 97, 583, 589
Feshbach, S., 422, 481, 482, 485
Festinger, L., 124, 125, 127, 129,
  210, 426, 427, 431, 508, 530,
  536
Fiction, latent meaning in, 422
Fighting, 140
Filiative behavior, in humans, 312–
  316
Finch, G., 588
Finlay, G. C., 511
Fisher, R. A., 398
Fiske, D. W., 384, 392
Fiske, M., 219, 224
Flack, M., 475
Flanagan, J. C., 591, 593
Flanders, N. A., 514, 517, 566, 575
Flavell, J. H., 285, 511
Fleming, E., 264
Flesch, R., 486, 499
Flescher, I., 410, 418
Flexibility:
  in sex-role learning, 354
  of teachers, 571–573
Flugel, J. C., 447, 450
Foley, J. P., Jr., 47, 52, 54
Forgays, D. G., 428, 431
Forgays, J. W., 428, 431
Forgus, R. H., 52, 53, 428, 431
Fox, R., 211
Fraiberg, S., 475
Frank, F., 319–321
Frank, J., 219, 224
Frank, L. K., 356
Frazier, A., 77, 79
Freeman, T., 333, 334
Freedman, D. G., 32, 54, 57, 88,
  311, 317
Freedman, S., 70
French, J. R. P., 160, 166, 210
Frenkel-Brunswik, E., 199, 265,
  271, 489, 492, 499
Freud, A., 8, 159, 166, 236, 287,
  304, 307, 328, 334, 426, 431,
  450, 462, 470, 471, 475, 476
Freud, S., 7, 8, 12, 13, 19–23, 96,
  120, 121, 124, 129, 131, 159,
  166, 178, 180, 236, 286, 287,
  300, 304, 306, 307, 351, 425–
  428, 431, 437, 443, 462, 469,
  471, 476
Friedlaender, K., 471, 476
Friedman, G. A., 239, 244
Friendliness, and prejudice, 277–
  279
Friendship, as sign of mental
  health, 213
Fromm, E., 8, 180, 301, 306, 308,
  373, 447, 450
Frustration:
  correlated with watching TV,
    477–480
  and expression of aggression,
    144–147
Fry, E. B., 583, 585, 589

Fuller, J. L., 33, 49, 53
Functional autonomy, 10
Functional fixedness, 551, 554
Future perspective, 263 (*see also* Time perspective)

Gage, M. L., 235
Gage, N. L., 514, 516, 523
Gagne, R., 593
Galanter, E., 386, 392, 585, 588, 589, 590
Galinsky, M. D., 157
Gall, H. S., 243, 244
Gallagher, J. J., 512
Gallup, G., 356
Gallwey, M., 106
Galton, F., 12, 18, 54
Garcia, J., 265, 272
Gardner, B., 265, 270, 272
Gardner, M., 265, 270, 272
Gardner, R. W., 158
Gates, A. I., 52
Gavurin, E. I., 584, 589
Gay, J., 529, 536
Geber, M., 80, 86
Gellerman, S., 482, 484, 485
Gendlin, E. T., 26, 27, 30
General intelligence:
    and creativity, 409–410
    g factor, 383–384
    in the gifted, 402–403
    as unitary faculty, 386
Generalization, 90
Genes, 46–47, 49
Genetic factors, and IQ, 387–388, 397
Genetics:
    influence of, on human behavior, 31–33
    of intelligence, 54–57
    of personality, 54–57
    reading in, 33–34
    related to social behavior, 54–55
    studies in, 54–57
Genital stage, 304–306
Genius, early identification of, 402–403
Gesell, A., 39, 66, 285, 286, 314, 317, 356, 374
Gestalt psychology:
    and stimulus situation, 205
    theory of learning, 90
Getzels, J. W., 409, 410, 414, 418
Gewirtz, J. L., 184, 186, 314, 317, 509
Gibson, C. M., 498, 499
Gibson, E. J., 547, 550
Gifted children:
    acceleration of, 404–405
    as adults, 401–402, 405
    enrichment for, 405
    study of, 401–408
Gillespie, J. M., 339
Gilligan, C., 437, 438, 444
Gjerde, C. M., 507
Glaser, R., 88, 121, 122, 526, 584, 589, 590, 593, 594
Glass, G., 511
Glazer, N., 238, 244
Glazer, R., 593
Gleser, G. C., 385, 392, 423, 431
Glock, C. Y., 275
Glover, E., 462
Goals:
    group determination of, 207
    of kibbutzim adolescents, 262–263
    as levels of aspiration, 434–436
    selection of, in childhood, 294

Goethals, G. W., 230, 233
Gold, M., 211, 212, 216
Goldbeck, R. A., 585, 586, 589
Goldberg, M. L., 374, 525, 565
Goldenson, R. M., 356
Goldfarb, W., 236, 313, 317, 428, 431
Goldman, J. R., 430, 431
Goldman, M., 499
Goldstein, K., 8
Gonick, M. R., 52
Good, S., 116, 118
Goodenough, D. R., 388, 392
Goodenough, E. W., 352, 356
Goodenough, F. L., 365, 370
Goodnow, J., 533, 536
Goodrich, H. B., 406, 408
Goodwin, E., 317
Gordon, K., 400
Gorer, G., 216, 353, 356
Gottesman, I., 81, 85, 86
Gottlieb, G., 312, 317
Gough, H. G., 178, 199, 265, 272
Gowan, J. C., 410, 419
Graham, F. K., 314, 317
Grahame, K., 472, 474, 475
Gray, P. H., 312–314, 317
Gray, S. W., 356
Greenbaum, J. J., 406, 408
Greenblum, J., 268, 269, 270, 272
Greenfield, P. M., 528, 529, 536
Greening, T. C., 449
Griffiths, R., 314, 317
Griffiths, W. J., Jr., 430, 432, 504, 507
Grimes, J. W., 422, 486, 490, 499, 519, 525
Grinder, R., 288
Gross, R. E., 511
Group dynamics:
    and mental health, 211–215
    related to educational psychology, 205–207
    teacher understanding of, 208
Group-factor theory, 384–386
Group membership:
    and social behavior, 248–249
    social class, 282–284
    sub-cultural, 264–271
Group values, 250–251
Gruenberg, S. M., 462
Guess Who? 365–367, 370
Guetzkow, H., 518
Guhl, A. M., 54
Guidance, psychological models for, 6–10
Guidance Study, comparisons with, 80–86
Guiding myths, 538, 540
Guilford, J. P., 230, 233, 384, 386, 387, 410, 413, 418, 419, 432
Guilt:
    beginning of, in childhood, 293–294
    and conflict, 447–449
    defenses against, 446–448, 449
    inhibitions caused by, 456
    intensity of, 446
Gump, P. V., 513
Gumpert, M., 454, 462
Gurney, N. L., 53
Guthrie, E. R., 87, 90, 91, 129, 554
Guthrie, G. M., 499
Guttman, N., 92, 95, 384

Habel, K., 317
Haber, R. N., 491, 499
Haeckel, E. H., 21

Hafez, E. S. E., 431
Hagen, E. E., 243, 244
Haggard, E. A., 231, 233, 398
Haggerty-Olson-Wickman Behavior Rating Schedule, 213, 216, 220
Haldane, J. B. S., 52
Hall, C. S., 430, 432
Hall, J. A., 356
Halverson, H. M., 356
Hamblen, A. A., 547, 550
Hamburger, V., 311, 317
Hamilton, G. V., 124, 130
Hammock, J., 493, 592
Handling, and visual-motor development, 64–65
Handy, G. D., 356
Hanfmann, E., 536
Harding, J., 266, 267, 272
Hardyck, J. A., 237, 274
Harlow, H. F., 33, 40, 70, 85, 86, 132, 134, 136, 302, 308, 310, 315, 316, 317, 425, 428, 432, 510, 528, 530, 536
Harlow, M. K., 33, 40, 132, 134, 528, 536
Harrell, R. F., 50, 52
Harris, D. B., 166, 178, 265, 272
Harris, F. R., 88, 99–103, 106
Harsh, C. M., 117, 118
Hart, B. M., 101, 102, 106
Hart, H., 242, 244
Hartley, E. L., 143, 210, 237, 244, 266, 272, 284, 288, 526
Hartley, R., 352, 353, 356
Hartman, L., 373
Hartmann, L., 8, 301
Hartshorne, H., 364
Hartup, W. W., 99, 184, 186, 509
Harvey, O. J., 432
Hathaway, S. R., 79
Haubrick, V. F., 572, 575
Havel, J., 266, 272
Havens, J., 337, 339
Havighurst, R. J., 52, 195, 199, 310, 317, 368, 370, 398
Hayes, C., 35, 43, 44
Hayes, K., 35, 43, 44
Hayes, M. L., 365, 370
Haynes, H., 62, 70
Heath, D. H., 489, 499
Heathers, L. B., 79
Hebb, D. O., 2, 34, 38, 50, 52, 229, 233, 386, 387, 388, 392, 426–430, 432
Heider, F., 530, 536
Heider, G. M., 80, 86
Heil, L. M., 519, 567, 568, 575
Hein, A., 64, 70
Heinroth, O., 429, 432
Heisler, F., 219, 224
Held, R., 32, 38, 60, 62–65, 70
Hellmuth, J., 233
Helmholtz, L. von, 20
Helper, M. M., 168, 178
Helson, H., 426, 430, 432
Hendrick, I., 425, 432
Hendry, C. E., 210
Henry, N. B., 550
Henry, W. E., 261, 263
Herbert, J. J., 117, 118
Hereditary factors, 45–47
Heredity:
    and behavioral differences, 54–57
    and environment, 31, 45–53
    methodological approaches to, 49–53
Hermann, I., 458, 462

Heroic tales, and fantasy, 471
Heron, W., 425, 426, 431, 433
Herrnstein, R. T., 14, 96
Hertzig, M., 80, 86
Hertzmann, M., 388, 392
Herzberg, F., 158
Hess, E. H., 310, 311, 313, 314, 317
Heteronomy, 448
Heterosexuality, in adolescents, 262
Hildreth, G., 504, 507
Hilgard, E. R., 88, 422, 427, 432, 435, 508
Hill, W. F., 510
Himmelweit, H. T., 216, 217
Hindley, C. B., 80, 86
Hirsch, J., 49, 52
Hobson, J. R., 158
Hoch, P. H., 317, 431
Hoffman, M. L., 118, 199
Hogan, R. A., 350, 356
Holland, J. G., 538, 584, 586, 589
Hollenberg, E., 130
Holmes, F. B., 430, 432
Holt, E. B., 7
Holzman, P. S., 158
Homeostatic needs, 428–429
Homme, L. E., 584, 589
Homunculus, 12
Honzik, M. P., 32, 33, 80, 81, 83, 85, 86
Hoppe, F., 434
Horney, K., 8, 301, 308, 462
Horowitz, F. D., 99, 106
Horton, G. P., 554
Horwitt, M. K., 52
Hostility:
    causes of, 332
    in classroom, 215
Houghton, L. J., 238, 244
Hoult, T. F., 219, 224
Hovland, C. I., 438, 443, 526, 578, 579, 586, 589
Howard, K. I., 314, 317
Hsu, F. L. K., 450
Hudson, W., 388, 392
Hughes, B. O., 499
Hull, C. L., 87–91, 126, 127, 129, 130, 425, 432
Human Relations Area Files, 342
Humphreys, L. G., 384, 392, 524
Hunter, E. C., 507
Hunt, J. McV., 60, 69, 229, 233, 286, 386, 392, 421, 423–433, 508, 511, 512
Hurlock, E. B., 352, 356, 365, 370, 507
Huston, A. C., 161, 163, 165, 166, 509
Hyman, H. H., 264, 266, 272
Hymovitch, B., 428, 432
Hypothetical model, of teacher, 568–571

Id, in adolescence, 328, 330, 333
Identical components, theory of, 547
Identification:
    defensive, 180
    developmental, 180
    with group, 248–249
    and sex role, 167–178, 353
Identification theories, 179–180
Identificatory learning, theories of, 159–160
Identity, child's sense of, 296–297
Idiot, 375
Ilg, F. L., 356

Imagination:
    of the child, 294
    in learning, 466–467
Imbecile, 375
Imitation:
    learning by, 179–186, 437–438
    matched-dependent, 179
Imprinting, 41
    and emotional attachments, 429
    in human infants, 312–314
Incentives: (see also Motivation; Reinforcement)
    material and non-material, 284
    and social class, 282–284
Incongruity, and avoidance of dissonance, 426–427
Independence: (see also Autonomy)
    in adolescents, 262
    child's attainment of, 291–293
    and nonverbal ability, 154
    training for, 248
Index of Status Characteristics, 283
Individual differences:
    and creativity-intelligence distinction, 409–418
    and development, 285–286
Indulgence, in rearing, 57–59
Industry, sense of, 295, 305
Inferiority:
    feelings of, 295
    freedom from, and success, 295, 407
    related to sex, 362
Informational interaction, 426–427
Inhelder, B., 323, 533, 536
Initiative, child's sense of, 293–294
Injury, and aggression, 140–141
Inner-direction, 238–239
Instinct, 39–40
Instinctive responses, 39–41
Instincts, Freud's theory of, 300
Instruction, role of teacher in, 207–208, 508–521
Instructional procedures, and motivation, 510–517
Instructional technology, and learning outcomes, 590–593
Instrumental learning, 302
Integration toward goals, 407
Integrity, achievement of, 298–299
Intellectual blocking, emotional factors in, 451–461
Intelligence:
    changes in, 393–397
    and creativity, 409–418
    as determinant of behavior, 373–374
    evolution of, 527
    and exceptional achievement, 402–403
    as fundamental faculty, 380
    measurement of, 381
    modified by selection, 55
    and personality factors, 450–461
Intelligence-creativity distinction:
    and anxiety, 417
    and conceptualizing activities, 414–416
    and expressiveness, 416–417
    psychological correlates, 413–414
Intelligence quotient (IQ):
    changes in, 393–397
    constancy of, 41–42
    as predictive, 402
    related to TV viewing, 217
Intelligence testing:
    limitations of, 450

need for, 375–377
pioneer work in, 373
Intelligent behaviors, 373, 450
Interaction:
    of personality and teaching methods, 487–488
    of persons, 125–129
    of organism and environment, 426–427
    of teacher and children, 513–517
Interaction situation, 154–157
Intermittent reinforcement, 93–96
Internalization of standards:
    as conscience, 445–449
    and social mobility, 188, 192–193
Interpersonal model, of development, 301
Interpersonal relationships:
    of the adolescent, 297–298
    and modification of Freudian theory, 301, 303–304
Intimacy, sense of, 297–298
Intolerance of ambiguity, 489
Introjected values, 25–26
Introspection, 12–16
Inversion, 353–354
Invisibility, and surreptitious gratification, 459–460
Irvine, E. E., 256
Irvine, S. H., 389, 392
Isaacs, N., 426
Isaacs, S., 286, 309
Iscoe, I., 86, 166
Isolate play (see Solitary play)
Israel, M. L., 583, 586, 589
IT Scale for Children (ITSC), 168–169, 350–351
Ives, O. L., 507

Jackson, P. W., 409, 410, 414, 418
Jackson, T. A., 554
Jacobsohn, E., 462
Jahoda, M., 187, 199, 266, 271
James, W., 9, 537, 543, 544, 550, 574
Janis, I. L., 438, 443, 526, 576
Janowitz, M., 269, 270, 271
Jaynes, J., 50, 52, 310, 311, 317
Jenkins, D. H., 204, 210
Jenks, C., 226, 233
Jennings, H. H., 213, 216
Jersild, A. T., 430, 432
Johnson, C., 240, 244
Johnson, M. K., 100, 103, 106
Jones, D. L., 583, 586, 588
Jones, E., 329, 334, 460, 462
Jones, H. E., 33, 72, 79, 80, 86
Jones, M. C., 33, 72, 79
Jones, M. R., 118, 166, 244, 443, 508
Jones, R. M., 225
Jones, V., 357, 364
Judd, C. H., 543, 546, 548, 550, 562
Judgment, as intelligence, 380
Jung, C. G., 8

Kagan, J., 40, 80–85, 156, 159, 166, 178, 374, 393, 415, 418, 518
Kahl, J. A., 227, 233, 511
Kalhorn, J., 157
Kallmann, F. J., 51, 52
Kamin, L. J., 115, 118
Kanfer, F. H., 437, 444
Kanner, L., 356
Kaplan, B. A., 258, 263
Kaplan, L., 369, 370

602

Karas, G. G., 70
Karp, S. A., 388, 392
Kastner, E., 475
Katan, M., 333, 334
Katan-Angel, A., 330, 331, 334
Katona, G., 547, 550, 553, 554
Keislar, E. R., 508
Keller, F. S., 89
Keller, H., 380
Kelley, C. S., 100, 103, 106
Kelley, H. H., 438, 443
Kelly, C. A., 119, 121
Kelly, G. A., 427, 432
Kelly, W., 474
Kendler, T. S., 583, 585, 588, 589
Kennedy, W. A., 282, 284
Kenney, H., 321
Kenny, D. T., 481, 485
Kent, M., 158
Kessen, W., 426, 433
Keys, N., 404, 408
Kinder, E. F., 39
King, J. A., 53, 54, 317
Kite, E. S., 375, 378
Klatskin, E. H., 342
Klaus, D. J., 590, 593
Klein, E., 462
Klein, G. S., 158
Klein, M., 159, 166, 462
Klett, C. J., 398
Kluckhohn, C., 534, 536
Knapp, L. B., 507
Knapp, R. H., 406, 408
Knobloch, H., 53
Koch, S., 30, 432
Kogan, N., 374
Köhler, W., 530, 536
Korchin, S. J., 489, 499
Kounin, J. S., 284, 513, 516
Kris, E., 306, 308, 514
Krogman, J., 229, 233
Kubie, L. S., 225, 514
Kuckenberg, L., 158
Kunst, M. S., 456, 457, 463
Kupers, C. J., 437, 443
Kutner, B., 266, 272

Laforgue, R., 462
Lambert, N. M., 464
Landauer, K., 457, 460, 462
Landis, O., 232, 233
Landreth, C., 99, 106
Lange-Eichbaum, W., 407, 408
Language, related to social learning, 91
Lansky, L. M., 492
Lantos, B., 474
Latency period, 300, 304
Latent meanings, 422
Lawrence, D. H., 508
Laycock, S. R., 507
Lazarsfeld, P. F., 224
Lazarus, R., 463
Learned, J., 354
Learned, W. S., 404, 408
Learning:
   advance organizers of, 555–558
   and cultural deprivation, 226–233
   and drives, 301–302
   etiology of failures in, 451–461
   generic, 537–538
   and group phenomena, 205–207
   by imitation, 179–186
   of logical operations, 566
   and meaningfulness, 556–558
   objective tests of, 563–564
   observational, 108–109, 117
   and past experience, 551–554

primary, 89–90
by reinforcement, 92–93, 508
secondary, 90–91
social, 91
stages in, 55
and teaching machines, 512–513, 581–588
and technology of educational methods, 121–122, 594–596
and tests of achievement, 559–562
theories of, 89–91, 508–509
theories, reflected in child-rearing, 119–121
transfer of, 542–549
Learning curves, 93
Leat, M., 107, 118, 437, 444
Lees, L. S., 554
Lehman, H. C., 403, 408
Lepkin, M., 158
Level of aspiration, 434–436
Levi-Strauss, C., 533, 534, 536
Levin, H., 132, 133, 140, 147, 150, 158, 169, 172, 178, 356, 390, 392, 477
Levine, E. M., 342, 357
Levine, S., 70, 430, 432, 489, 499
Levinger, G., 160, 166
Levinson, B. M., 158
Levinson, D. J., 199, 265, 271
Levy, D. M., 57, 59, 156, 158
Levy, J., 504, 507
Levy, S., 264
Lewin, K., 124, 125, 126, 130, 434, 516
Lewis, D. J., 410, 419
Lewis, H. B., 388, 392
Libido:
   in adolescence, 330–333
   and emotional attachments, 428–429
   Erikson's restatement, 303–304
   Freud's theory of, 300–301
   model of development, 301
Liebert, R. M., 437, 444
Lighthall, F. F., 417, 419, 500
Likert scales, 265
Lilienfeld, A. M., 53
Lindquist, E. T., 591, 593
Lindsley, O. R., 95
Lindzey, G., 272, 430, 431, 432, 507
Linton, H. B., 158
Lippitt, R., 210, 211, 212, 216, 516
Lipset, S. M., 272
Lisonbee, L. K., 77, 79
Liss, E., 462
Little, J. K., 582, 589
Livson, N., 518
Locus of evaluation, 24–27
Logical contradiction, 323–324
Loevinger, J., 53, 88, 119, 133
Lofting, H., 474, 475
Longitudinal studies, 51, 80–86
Lorand, S., 462
Lorenz, K., 41, 50, 53, 54, 312, 317, 429, 432
Lorge, I., 463
Lorge-Thorndike Intelligence Test, 220
Loss and return, fantasy of, 470
Low, W. P., 356
Lowell, E. L., 199, 239, 244, 398, 477, 510
Lowenfeld, J., 486, 499
Luchins, A. S., 53
Luckiesh, M., 219
Lumsdaine, A. A., 88, 121, 122, 525, 576, 578, 579, 594

Luther, M., 286
Lykken, D. T., 432
Lyman, H. B., 5
Lynn, D. B., 78, 79, 178
Lynn, K. S., 199

McArthur, C. C., 336, 339
McCandless, B. R., 168, 178, 398, 499
McCarthy, D., 148, 158, 463
McClearn, G. E., 510
McCleary, J., 463
McClelland, D. C., 191, 199, 238, 239, 243, 244, 395, 398, 510
MacClenathan, R. H., 507
McClure, W. E., 507
Maccoby, E. E., 132, 133, 140, 143, 149, 150, 158–160, 166, 169, 172, 178, 237, 288, 356, 390, 392, 422, 477, 526, 536
McDonald, L. C., 507
MacDonald, M. W., 354, 356
McDougall, W., 124, 130, 425, 432
Macfarlane, J. W., 80, 81, 83, 86
McGaw, B. H., 506
McGeoch, J. A., 547, 549
McGhie, A., 334
McGinnies, E., 459, 463
McGinnis, E., 506
McGraw, M., 285, 310, 317, 374
McGuffey, W. H., 240, 244
Machover, K., 388, 392
McKeachie, W. J., 488, 498, 499
McKee, J. P., 84, 86, 178
McKelvey, R. K., 428, 432
Mackie, R. P., 572, 575
McKinley, J. C., 79
Mackinnon, W. J., 266, 272
McNemar, Q., 277, 282, 384, 392
Magaret, G. A., 435
Mager, R. F., 583, 587, 589
Magnitude, perception of, 319–323
Maher, B. A., 444
Mahler-Schoenberger, M., 453, 459, 460, 463
Mahrer, A. R., 437, 444
Maier, N. R. F., 551, 552, 554
Main, T., 210
Maintenance of behavior, by reinforcement, 93–96, 442–443
Maladjustment, teachers' attitude toward, 501, 504–506
Mandler, G., 514
Manipulation:
   and competence, 302–304
   factor in generic learning, 537
Marcuse, H., 306, 308
Marshall, L., 528
Marston, A. R., 437, 444
Marston, M.-V., 317
Martin, B., 107, 118
Martin, W. E., 178, 265, 272
Marx, M. H., 428, 432
Masculine protest, 351–352
Masculine role:
   depicted in school readers, 361–362
   preference for, 167–178, 351–353
Maslow, A., 8, 510
Masochism, 453
Mason, D. J., 79
Mason, W. A., 136
Mass media:
   comic books, 218–224
   effects of, on children, 216–218
   television, 216–218, 477–480

Matarazzo, R. G., 314, 317
Matched-dependent imitative behavior, 179
Maternal behavior, 39–40
Maternal care, and development of trust, 290–291
Maternal conditions, and personal-social development, 137–139
Maturation:
  and behavior, 285
  in learning, 90
  and readiness, 374
  and sense of integrity, 298–299
Maturation rate, in adolescence, 71–79
Maturity, and children's textbooks, 361
May, M. A., 364
Mayer, S. R., 583, 587, 589
Maze learning ability, 49
Mead, G. H., 423, 432
Mead, M., 288, 341, 345, 348, 354, 356, 463
Mechanical aids to learning, 512–513 (see also Teaching machines)
Medawar, P., 34
Medley, D. M., 516, 566, 575
Mednick, S. A., 410, 419
Meehl, P. E., 79
Meeker, M., 283, 284
Mees, H. L., 106
Meier, G. W., 70
Meissner, P. B., 388, 392
Melton, A. W., 88, 121, 526, 594
Melzack, R., 53
Memorization, as test of intelligence, 380
Menninger, K. A., 455, 462
Mental health, and social structure in classroom, 211–216
Mental hygienists, and behavior problems of children, 501–502
Mental states, 14–16
Mentalistic formulations, 11–18
Merrill, R. M., 79
Metapelet, 247–248
Methodological approaches, to study of environmental and hereditary factors, 49–53
Methods in education, and technology, 594–596
Metzner, R., 437, 444
Meumann, E., 545, 549
Meux, M., 575
Meyer, D. R., 425, 432
Meyer, W. J., 342, 356
Mezei, L., 107, 118, 437, 444
Mierke, K., 428, 432
Mikaelian, H., 70
Miles, C. C., 347, 349
Miller, D. R., 212, 216, 445, 449
Miller, G. A., 386, 392, 530, 536
Miller, J. G., 317
Miller, L. W., 506
Miller, N. E., 7, 88–91, 115, 118, 124, 126, 130, 179, 186, 302, 308, 425, 432, 456, 463
Milne, A. A., 474, 475
Milner, E. A., 51, 53, 153, 158
Milner, P., 302, 308
Milton, O., 265, 272
Miner, J. B., 228, 233, 400
Minnesota Multiphasic Personality Inventory (MMPI), 73–76
Mischel, W., 421, 437, 438, 443, 444
Mitchell, J. C., 369, 370, 507

Models:
  for development, 301
  for identification, 159–166
  in observational learning, 108–109, 179–180
  symbolic vs. live, 437–438
  for teachers, 568–571
Modes:
  and competence, 304
  of response, 424–425
Modiano, N., 529, 536
Moeller, G. H., 235, 238
Moltz, H., 313, 317
Monadic unit of behavior, 125–129
Monroe, W. S., 542, 546
Montagu, M. F. Ashley, 34
Montessori, M., 100
Montgomery, K. C., 302, 308, 425, 432
Moore, B. V., 383, 391
Moore. O. K., 232, 233
Moore, T., 80, 86
Moral teaching imagery, 239–242
Moral values:
  and personality, 445–449
  and social mobility, 188, 192–193
  as sources of conflict, 448
Moray House test of intelligence, 405
Morgan, L., 12
Moron, 375
Morrill, C. S., 526, 581
Morris, C. W., 24, 30, 274, 282
Morrison, H. W., 160, 166
Morse, W. C., 96, 204
Moss, H., 80–85, 158, 219, 415, 418
Mother, rejection of by adolescent, 329–330
Mother surrogates, 136–138
Motivation: (see also Incentives)
  for achievement, 509–510
  cognitive, 511–513
  in the group, 206–207
  in learning theory, 508–509
  and performance, 90, 508
  and reinforcement, 96
  and teaching machines, 512–513, 586–587
Motives:
  cognitive, 510
  differing by sex, 361–362
  ego-integrative, 509–510
  and the school, 357
  social, 509
Mowrer, O. H., 107, 108, 115, 118, 159, 160, 166, 177, 178, 425, 428, 432
Muller, H. J., 34
Multiple factor theory of intelligence, 383–386
Munsinger, H. L., 426, 433
Murdock, G. P., 345–347, 348
Murphy, G., 447, 450, 489, 499
Murphy, L. B., 80, 86, 255, 256
Murray, H. A., 124, 130, 258, 260, 263, 364, 425, 460, 463
Mursch, G. A., 582, 588
Mussen, P., 33, 72, 79, 88, 132, 160, 166, 167, 170, 171, 172, 178, 389, 392, 518
Mutual regulation:
  and autonomy, 292
  and competence model, 304–306
Myers, A. K., 302, 308
Myerson, L., 52
Myrdal, G., 264, 272

Nair, P., 321
Negative reinforcement, 95
Neilon, P., 80, 86
Nelson, V. L., 86, 158, 374, 393, 394, 397, 398, 518
Neo-Freudians, 301, 304
Nest-building, 39–40
Neumeyer, M. H., 507
Newcomb, T. M., 125, 130, 143, 210, 237, 244, 284, 288, 526
Neyman-Johnson method, 544, 546
Nielsen, G. S., 86, 392
Nietz, J. A., 240, 244
Nightmares, 294
Nissen, H. W., 40, 42, 425, 427, 433
Noll, J. O., 489, 499
Nonverbal ability:
  antecedents of, 153–154
  and dependency-independence, 154
Norem, C. M., 547, 549
Norms, and tests for achievement, 560–561
Norm-referenced measures of achievement, 591–592
Nowlis, H. H., 428, 433
Nowlis, V., 255, 256
Nursery, as a community, 309
Nurturance:
  defined, 364
  and dependency, 509
  and the parental sense, 298
  in textbooks, 361
Nyswander, M., 210

Oakland Growth Study, comparisons with, 80–86
Objective tests (see Tests)
Objective value, 24
Observational learning, 108–109, 117, 437–438
Obsessive-compulsive tendencies, 489
Occupation, and sex role, 352–353
Odell, M. O., 563
Oden, M. H., 401, 408
Ogle, K. N., 18
Ojemann, R., 365, 369, 370
O'Kelly, L. I., 426
Olden, C., 463
Olds, J., 302, 308
Olson, W. C., 365, 371, 562
Olver, R. R., 415, 418, 536
Operative values, 24
Oppenheim, A. N., 216, 217
Oppenheimer, R., 540
Oral conflict, 454–456
Oral stage, 304
Order, perception of, 318–319
Orderliness of development, 36, 39, 285
Organization, in generic learning, 537
Organizer substances, 36–37, 311
Organizers, and learning, 535, 555–558
Orlansky, H., 427, 433
Ort, R. S., 356
Orwell, G., 316, 471, 476
Osborn, A., 512
Osgood, C. E., 425, 433
Other-direction, 238–239, 447
Owens, J., 507

Page, E. B., 514
Pain, avoidance of, 302
Palermo, D. S., 499

Parent-child relations:
in adolescence, 331–332
and children's sex-role preferences, 167–168
Parental attitude:
and child-rearing, 119–120
and children's intellectual efficiency, 451–452
and repression of aggression,
142–147
Parental personality, and children's
sex-role preferences, 167–178
Parental sense, and nurturance, 298
Parenthood, and theories of learning, 119–121
Parke, R. D., 88, 107, 108, 109,
111, 116, 117, 118
Parker, R. G., 242, 244
Parsons, T., 125, 130, 159, 160,
166, 178, 244, 342, 347, 349,
353, 356
Pasamanick, B., 50, 53
Passion for learning, 540
Passivity:
in education, 538–539
related to change in IQ, 393–397
represented in textbooks, 362
and social reinforcement, 103–
104
Passow, A. H., 575
Pathology, in adolescence, 330–333
Patrick, J. R., 264, 272
Pavlov, I., 89–91
Payne, D. E., 178
Paynter, R. H., 506
Pearlin, L. I., 268, 269, 270, 272
Pearson, G. H. J., 98, 133, 463
Pearson Product Moment Correla-
tion, 3
Peck, L., 503, 504, 507
Pedagogy:
and cognitive development, 527–
536
and curriculum, 532–536
Peller, L. E., 422, 465, 467, 469
Penfield, W., 13
Pepitone, A., 481, 485
Perception:
of magnitude, 319–323
of order, 318–319
selectivity in, 486
Performance:
on ability tests, 387–389
and motivation, 90, 508–509
and personality theory, 125
and reinforcement, 93–96
Permissiveness, and aggression,
142–147
Persistence toward goals, 407
Personal-social development, and
early deprivation, 134–139
Personality:
attributes of health in, 289–299
and changes in IQ, 393–397
and dyadic experience, 126–129
and group membership, 206
influence of textbooks on, 357–
364
in late adolescence, 71–79
and moral force, 445–449
and motivation, 517–520
related to use of intelligence,
406–407, 450–461
stages in development of, 289–
299
theory of, 123–130, 423–430
traits, 423–425
Personalization of knowledge, 534–
535

Persons, S., 52
Persuasive communication, 576,
579–580
Peters, C. C., 544, 550
Peterson, J. C., 581, 589
Petrullo, L., 178
Pettigrew, T. F., 158, 236, 264,
265, 271, 272, 273, 533, 536
Phonics, 487
Piaget, J., 42, 64, 66, 70, 251, 256,
285, 286, 303, 308, 318, 320,
323, 374, 386, 388, 392, 427,
429, 433, 511, 530, 533, 536
Piers, G., 119
Pintler, M. H., 368, 369, 371
Plashinski, D., 583, 586, 588
Plasticity:
of sensorimotor development,
60–70
of tissue development, 36–37
Play, as exploration, 302–303
Polansky, N., 212, 216
Polt, J. M., 317
Porter, D., 583, 589
Porteus, S. D., 186
Porteus Maze Test, 180
Positive reinforcement, 95
Positivism, 6–8
Postman, L., 459, 462, 463
Potentiality for action, 125
Potter, B., 475
Potter, E. H., 342, 357
Powell, M., 519, 575
Praise, use of by teachers, 365–
370
Prediction:
of adolescent upset, 329–330
of behavior, 80–86
Prejudice:
and beliefs, 274, 277, 281
determinants of, 264–271, 274–
281
and friendliness, 277–279
and social distance, 279–281
Prenatal factors, 50
Pressey, S. L., 404, 408, 526, 581,
582, 584, 585, 586, 589
Preston, G. H., 507
Pribram, K. H., 386, 392, 530, 536
Primary learning, 89–90
Proactive man, 6–8
Problem behaviors:
and social reinforcement, 99–
106
and teachers' attitudes, 501–504
Problem finding behavior, 533–534
Problem solving, and past experience, 553–554
Proctor, V. H., 516
Programming, in teaching machines, 584
Projection, 460–461
Propaganda:
effectiveness of, 576
one-sided vs. two-sided, 579–580
resistance to, 578–580
Proshansky, H., 266, 272
Protestant ethic, 238
Prothro, E. T., 264, 265, 272, 390,
392
Prothro, J. W., 265, 272
Psychoanalysis:
and adolescence, 328
and children's literature, 422
and developmental theory, 285
and education, 225
and emotional development,
300–306
Psychoanalytic theory:

applied to adolescence, 328–334
and delayed gratification, 443
and stages of emotional development, 300–301, 303–306
Psychometric performance, and
personality factors, 450–451
Psychosexual stages, 285
and White's concept of competence, 300–309
Punishment:
and aggression, 141–147
and anxiety, 141–142
and initiative, 294
as negative reinforcement, 95
of parents by children, 452–453
of self, 453
timing of, 107–108, 115–118

Rabban, M., 178, 352, 356
Rabin, A. I., 236, 257, 263, 264,
288
Rabinowitz, H. S., 525, 551
Radke, M. J., 365, 368, 371
Rage, expression of, 140
Rajaratnam, N., 385, 392, 423, 431
Ramo, S., 582, 589, 594, 596
Ramsay, A. O., 312, 317
Ramsey, G., 499
Rapaport, D., 197, 199
Rate of maturation, and personal-
ity, 71–79
Rath, G. J., 583, 589, 590
Rationalism, 9–10
Rau, L., 149, 158
Raven, B., 160, 166
Raygor, A. L., 500
Razran, G. H. S., 428, 433
Reaching, visually directed, 63–64
Reaction formation, 449
Reactive man, 6–8
Read, K. H., 99, 106
Readiness, and critical period
hypothesis, 310
Reading:
correlated with compulsivity,
491–493
and imagination, 467
importance of, 467–468
methods of teaching, 486–487
and structure, 488
Reading ability, and comic books,
219, 223
Reality, and fantasy, 476
Reality practice, 206
Rearing conditions, and monkey
behavior, 134–139
Reber, A., 109, 115, 118
Redl, F., 120, 121, 210, 212, 216
Reed, H. B., 509, 545, 550
Reed, M. F., 365, 370
Reflectiveness, 535
Regression, 333
Reich, L., 529, 536
Reichling, G., 481, 485
Reinforcement, 92–97
contingencies of, 93–96
effects of, on child behavior, 99–
106
as incentive, 282–284
removal of, 98–99
schedules of, 93–96
and shaping of behavior, 93
theory of learning, 89–91
Rejection, in classroom, 214–215
Renner, K. W., 442, 444
Resistance, and critical periods,
311–312
Resistance to deviation, 111–117
Response, conditioned, 89–90

Response inhibition, and timing of
    punishment, 107–109
Rethlingshafer, D., 509
Retinoscope, 63
Reversal of roles, in fantasy, 470–
    471
Rewards:
    acquired, 90–91
    delayed, 437–438, 442–443
Rey, A. H., 475
Reymert, M. L., 431
Rheingold, H. L., 314, 317
Richards, I. A., 498, 499
Richards, T. W., 398
Richman, J., 309
Riesen, A., 38, 39, 64, 65, 70, 310
Riesman, D., 238, 239, 242, 243,
    244, 447, 450
Riessman, F., 227, 233
Riess, B., 40
Rigby, D., 475
Rigney, J. W., 581, 582, 584, 586,
    588, 589
Rindlisbacher, A., 243, 244
Risley, T. R., 106
Riviere, J., 307, 308
Robbins, L. C., 555, 558
Roberts, M., 356
Robinson, M. Z., 199
Roby, T. B., 308
Rogers, C. R., 5, 8, 23, 24, 30, 427,
    433, 507
Rokeach, M., 280, 281, 282
Role:
    changes in, by teacher, 209–210
    of teachers, 207–209
Ronge, P. H., 356
Roper, E., 264, 266, 272
Rorschach Test, 257–258, 394–397
    use of, as research instrument,
    397
Rose, A. M., 271, 272
Rosen, B. C., 510
Rosen, S., 211
Rosenbaum, M. E., 481, 485
Rosenberg, B. G., 178
Rosenblith, J. F., 132, 179, 186,
    509
Rosenfeld, H., 513
Rosenstein, A. J., 424, 431
Rosenzweig, S., 264, 428, 433
Ross, D., 107, 118, 132, 159, 166,
    437, 443
Ross, H. W., 314, 317
Ross, S. A., 107, 118, 132, 159, 166,
    437, 443
Rostow, W. W., 243, 244
Roth, C. H., 509
Rothkopf, E. Z., 584, 590
Rubenfeld, S., 499
Ruch, F. L., 563
Ruebush, B. K., 417, 419, 500, 515
Rugg, H., 411, 419
Rushworth, V., 511
Ruskin, J., 475
Rutherford, E., 89, 132, 167
Ryan, J. J., 513
Ryans, D. C., 566, 575
Ryans, D. G., 517

Sacks, J. M., 264
Sadism, 456–457
Sait, E. M., 435
Salama, A. A., 430, 433
Salten, F., 475
Samelson, B., 264, 272
Sanchez-Hidalgo, E., 356
Sandiford, P., 547, 549

Sanford, F., 128
Sanford, N., 199, 265, 271, 422,
    464
Sapon, S. M., 583, 589
Sarason, S. B., 393, 417, 419, 494,
    500, 514
Sarason, I. G., 489, 491, 500
Sarbin, T. R., 507
Sarnoff, I., 199
Schacter, S., 210
Schaefer, E. S., 83–86, 387, 388,
    392
Schaefer, H. H., 593
Schedule of reinforcement, 93–96
Schein, E. H., 179, 186
Scheinfeld, A., 345, 349, 356
Schiff, H. M., 499
Schilder, P., 305, 308
Schlosberg, H., 432
Schmideberg, M., 463
Schmidt, V., 463
School discipline, 95–96
School environment, and motiva-
    tion, 510–517
School learning:
    and background deficiencies,
    229–231
    and cultural deprivation, 226–
    232
Schools:
    and children's motives, 357
    conditions related to learning in,
    229–232
    and personality development,
    468–469
    and sense of achievement, 295–
    296
Schramm, W., 216
Schrier, A. M., 18
Schrupp, M. H., 507
Schwartz, N., 179, 186
Schwarz, P. A., 387, 389, 392
Schwesinger, G. C., 53
Scott, J. P., 32, 49, 53, 54, 310–313,
    316, 317, 373
Scott, R. B., 51, 53
Scott, T. H., 425, 426, 431
Scott, W. D., 400
Searle, L. V., 49, 53, 54
Sears, P. S., 178, 255, 256, 365,
    371, 436, 477, 508, 514, 517,
    518, 519
Sears, R. R., 88, 90, 91, 123, 130,
    133, 140, 145, 147, 150, 158,
    159, 166, 167, 169, 172, 178,
    255, 256, 310, 353, 356, 368,
    369, 371, 390, 392, 422, 477
Secondary learning, 90–91
Secondary reinforcement, 508
    theory of identificatory learning,
    160
Secularization, 238, 242
Seidenberg, B., 266, 272
Seidman, J. M., 507
Selectivity, in perception, 486
Self-confidence:
    and social mobility, 188, 195
    and success, 407
Self-conscious reflectiveness, 535
Self-control:
    and delay of reward, 437–438
    development of, 292–293
    and social learning theory, 443
Self-evaluation, 460
Self-expression, 540
Self-observation, 14–17
Self-punishment, 453
Self-rejection, and social mobility,
    195

Semmelweis, J. S., 458
Senden, M. von, 38
Senn, M. J. E., 34, 348
Sensitive periods, 311–312 (see
    also Critical periods)
Sensitivities, zonal, 304
Sensorimotor coordination, 60–70
Sensorimotor development, 60–70
Sentence Completion Test, 258–
    259
Setting:
    and assessment of creativity,
    410–411
    and behavior, 201–203
    school, and motivation, 510–517
Severity of punishment, for aggres-
    sion, 142–147
Seward, G. H., 354, 356
Sex:
    and adolescents, 327
    awareness of, 349–350
    education in, 456
Sex differences:
    in aggression, 365, 368–369
    in behavior problems, 503–504
    and prejudice, 266, 270
    in socialization, 343–348
    and teachers' approval, 365–370
    variations in degree of, 345–348
Sex roles:
    and adult adjustment, 353–354
    in a changing culture, 349–355
    convergence of, 354–355
    inversion of, 353–354
    and masculine role preference,
    351–353
    patterns of, 353
    preference for, 167–168, 350–
    353
    reflected in children's textbooks,
    361–362
Sex training, in kibbutzim, 248
Sexton, P., 227, 233
Sexual behavior, 40–41
Sexual development: (see also
    Libido)
    in adolescence, 327
    Freud's theory of, 300
Shaftel, F. R., 511
Shame:
    in child-rearing, 292–293
    and doubt, 292–293
    versus guilt, 446–447
Shands, H. C., 494, 500
Shaping up of behavior, 93
Sharing, 250, 251
Shaw, F. J., 356
Sheatsley, P. B., 264, 266, 272
Sheehan, J. G., 97
Sheffield, F. D., 302, 308, 526, 576,
    578, 579
Shepler, W. McL., 507
Sherman, J. A., 438, 443
Sherriffs, A. C., 178
Shirley, M. M., 80, 86
Shoben, E. J., 132, 525
Sibling rivalry, 457
Sidman, M., 95, 115, 118
Siegel, S., 59, 186, 244
Siegman, A. W., 79
Sigel, I. E., 231, 233, 415, 418
Sight vocabulary, 487
Significance, of data, 3–5
Silberman, H. F., 583, 584, 585,
    587, 589, 590
Silverberg, W. V., 301, 308
Silverman, R. E., 584, 587, 590
Simmons, K., 86
Simon, T., 373, 375, 378

Sims, V. M., 264, 272, 526, 559, 563
Sinclair, M., 323
Singer, J. L., 443, 444
Situational influences on behavior, 424–425 (*see also* Setting)
Sizemore, R. A., 487, 500
Skard, Ase, 80, 86
Skinner, B. F., 5, 7, 11, 87, 88, 90, 91, 92, 97, 129, 526, 582–587, 590
Sleeper effect, 85
Sleight, W. G., 545, 550
Smedslund, J., 512
Smith, B. O., 516, 566, 575
Smith, C. U., 265, 272
Smith, D. E. P., 488, 500, 518
Smith, M. B., 237, 264, 272, 274
Smith, P. W., 274, 282
Smith, R. R., 547, 550
Smith, W. D., 353, 356
Snyder, L. H., 53
Snyder, L. M., 504, 507
Snyder, M. M., 86
Snyder, W., 365, 371
Social adjustment:
  in the classroom, 211–216
  as a factor in prejudice, 264–265, 269–271
Social behavior:
  and creativity, 413–414
  of young children in kibbutzim, 245–256
Social class:
  and behavior problems in children, 504
  as environmental factor, 48
  and incentive, 282–284
  and social pressure, 435–436
  and teacher relationships, 368
  and TV, 217, 478–480
Social control, 250–251
Social deprivation, 134–137
Social distance, and prejudice, 279–281
Social ethic, 238
Social interaction, and personality theory, 125–129
Social learning, 91
  growing emphasis on, 205
Social mobility:
  dynamics of, 197–199
  factors in, 187–189
  and prejudice, 268–269, 270
  theory of, 186–189
Social motives, 509
Social participation, 249–250
Social play, 102–103
Social power theory, of identificatory learning, 160
Social pressures, and level of aspiration, 435–436
Social psychology:
  of assessment situation, 410–411
  of education, 357–364
  theory of, 123–130
Social reinforcement, 99–106
Social releasers, 54
Social stimulation, 35, 126–129
Social structure, in the classroom, 211–214
Socialization:
  of aggression, 140–147
  in kibbutzim, 247–248
  sex differences in, 343–348
Sociocultural factors, 264–265
  in prejudice, 269–271, 273
Solitary play, 102–103
Solomon, R. L., 107, 115, 118, 432

Somatopsychological relationships, 47–48, 51
Sontag, L. W., 80, 86, 158, 374, 393, 394, 397, 398, 518
Sparks, J. N., 507
Spaulding, R., 514, 516
Spearman, C., 386, 387, 402, 463
Spemann, H., 37
Spence, D. P., 158, 486, 500
Spence, K. W., 88, 90, 91, 583, 590
Sperry, M., 130
Sperzer, E. Z., 219, 224
Spiro, M. E., 256, 264, 348, 349
Spitz, R., 35, 42, 44, 313, 317, 388, 392, 429, 433
Spitzer, M. E., 589
Spoerl, D. T., 53
SRA Junior Inventory, 220
Standards, and conscience, 445, 447–448 (*see also* Norms)
Standing, E. M., 100, 106
Stanford Achievement Test, 220, 491
Stanford-Binet Test, 394, 401
Stanton, F. N., 224
Star, S. A., 264, 272
Statistical significance, 2–4
Statistics, 2–4
Status envy theory, of identificatory learning, 159–160
Staub, E., 437, 444
Stein, D. D., 237, 274
Stellar, E., 432
Stendler, C. B., 178
Stephens, A. L., 583, 585, 590
Stevens, S. S., 13, 18, 91, 589
Stevenson, H., 86, 166, 515
Stevenson, R. L., 475
Stewart, N., 503, 507
Stimulus, 89–90
Stimulus deprivation, 228–229
Stimulus substitution, 89–90
Stoddard, G. D., 450, 463
Stoke, S. M., 178
Stott, D. H., 388, 392
Stouffer, G. A. W., Jr., 504, 507
Stouffer, S. A., 264, 272
Strachey, J., 463
Strauss, M. A., 238, 244
Strodtbeck, F. L., 510
Strong, E. K., 400
Stroud, J. B., 547, 549
Structure, as dimension in teaching, 488, 497–498
Subnormal children:
  diagnosis of, 378–381
  education of, 375
Success:
  in the classroom, 434–436
  and sense of accomplishment, 295
  and social mobility, 187
  underlying factors of, 406–407
  and use of superior intelligence, 406–407
Suchman, E. A., 264, 272
Suchman, J. R., 512
Suci, G. J., 425, 433
Sullivan, H. S., 301, 305, 308
Superego:
  in adolescence, 329–330
  and guilt, 447–448
Surrogate mothers, 136–138
Sutton-Smith, B., 178
Swanson, G. E., 212, 216, 244, 445, 449
Swenson, E. J., 547, 549
Swift, E. J., 545, 550
Sylvester, E., 456, 457, 463

Symbolic models, vs. live models, 438

Taba, H., 226, 228, 229, 230, 233, 237, 374, 511
Taber, J. I., 593
Tagiuri, R., 178
Tanenbaum, S., 369, 371
Tannenbaum, P. H., 425, 433
Tantrums, 98–99
Taylor, J. A., 79, 491, 500
Taylor, K. W., 100, 106
Taylor Manifest Anxiety Scale, 73–76, 491
Teachable groups, 567–568
Teacher:
  attitudes of, 368–369
  attitudes of, toward behavior problems, 500–506
  and difficult schools, 573–575
  for disadvantaged children, 565, 575
  effectiveness of, 519–520
  expertness of, 503
  interaction of, with children, 513–517
  quality of, 540–541
  roles of, 207–209, 505–506, 508–521
  and social adjustment of pupils, 214–215
  training of, 571–573
  warmth of, 509
Teacher approval, 365–370
Teacher style, 565–575
Teacher-pupil relationships, 204, 207–209, 214–215
  supplemented by machines, 581
Teaching machines:
  current trends in, 581–583
  defined, 583–584
  equipment, 587
  and knowledge of results, 586
  and motivation, 512–513, 586–587
  and problems of application, 587–588
  programming for, 584
  and response mode, 585–586
Technology of education, 594–596
Television:
  and fantasy, 477
  as scapegoat, 216–218
Tensions, in groups, 206
Terman, L. M., 347, 349, 356, 374, 399, 408, 570
Terminology, confusions of, relating to intelligence, 375–377
Terrell, G., Jr., 79, 237, 282, 283, 284
Tests:
  of achievement, 404–405, 559–562
  classification of, 381
  of creativity, 409
  for exceptional children, 400, 404–405
  norms for, 560–561
  objective, 563–564
  related to theories of learning, 562
  uses of, 379
  validation of, 379
Textbooks, and motivation, 357–364
Thelen, H. A., 511, 567, 568, 575
Thema, 358

Thematic Apperception Test (TAT), 259–262, 394–397
use of, as research instrument, 397
Thematizing, 415–416
Theory, criteria of, 123–125
Therapeutic relationship, 26, 28
Therapy, and the teacher, 208–209
Thibaut, J. W., 210, 481, 485
Thinking:
development of, 42
divergent and convergent, 511–512
reproductive and productive, 551
as a step beyond learning, 538, 539
and transfer, 551
Thomas, A., 80, 86
Thomas, L., 108, 118
Thomas, W. I., 423, 433
Thompson, C., 301, 308, 507
Thompson, C. E., 507
Thompson, G. G., 342, 365, 366, 370
Thompson, H., 356
Thompson, W. R., 53, 54, 428, 433
Thomson, G. H., 386, 392, 403, 405
Thorndike, E. L., 90, 91, 93, 399, 400, 543–550, 562
Thorndike, R. L., 410, 419
Thorpe, W. H., Jr., 429, 432, 433
Thurstone, L. L., 373, 383, 387, 400, 403
Thurstone Tests of Primary Mental Abilities, 403
Time perspective, and social mobility, 188, 192
Timing of punishment, and response inhibition, 107–108, 115–118
Tinbergen, N., 54
Tissue transplant, in embryo, 36–37
Toilet training, 247–248
Tolman, E. C., 87, 90, 91, 126, 129, 399, 530, 536
Tomlinson, R. M., 555
Torrance, E. P., 410, 419, 512, 514
Tradition-direction, 238
Traits:
identification of, 401–402
as personality dimensions, 424
Transfer of training:
characteristic effects of, 544–546
historical background of, 542–543
implications of, 548–549
methods for increasing, 546–547
methodology of, 543–544
theories of, 547–548
Transference, 21
Trauma theory of anxiety, 429–430
Travers, P., 475
Triandis, H. C., 274, 279–282
Trow, W. C., 204
Troyer, M. E., 582, 588
Trust, sense of, 290–291
Tryon, R. C., 49, 52, 53, 54, 56
Tuddenham, R. D., 82–86, 365, 371
Turner, W. S., 84, 86
Twin studies, 51
Tyler, L. E., 562

Uhr, L. M., 317
Ullman, A. D., 115, 118
Ullman, C. A., 403, 507
Uniformity, among adolescents, 296
Uniqueness, of associates, 410–412

Universal values, 28–30
Upward mobility, 187
Uzgiris, I. C., 429, 432

Vakar, G., 530, 536
Value directions, 28–30
Values, 23–30
conceived, 24–26
cultural, 238–239, 241–243
expressed in children's readers, 238–244
group, 250–251
introjected, 25–26
operative, 24
universal, 28–30
Valuing process, 23–30
Vance, P., 216, 217
Van Horn, C., 586, 588
van Sommers, P., 14, 18
Van Voorhis, W. R., 544, 550
Verbal ability:
antecedents of, 151–153
and dependency-independence, 154
and sex-role identification, 153
Verbal stimulation, 151–154
Vernon, P. E., 237, 373, 383, 384, 387, 389, 392, 403
Viki, 35, 43, 44
Visual accommodation, 62–63
Visual attention, 61–62, 66–69
Visual-motor development, 61–69
Visual perception, 37–39
Visual pursuit, in infants, 314
Visually-directed reaching, 63–64
Voelker, P. F., 546, 550
Vogel-Sprott, M. D., 115, 118
Volkart, E. H., 423, 433
Vygotsky, L., 530, 536

Wagenheim, L., 316, 317
Waite, R. R., 417, 419, 500
Walker, E. S., 582, 588
Wallach, M. A., 158, 374, 409, 419
Walters, R. H., 88, 107, 108, 109, 111, 115–118, 150, 157, 437, 438, 443, 444
Wandt, E., 507
Wapner, S., 388, 392
Warkany, J., 311, 317
Warmth, of teacher personality, 509
Warner, W. L., 283, 284, 478
Warrener, C. K., 566, 575
Watson, G., 503, 504, 507
Watson, J. B., 546, 550
Watson, J. M., 242, 244
Watson, R. I., 310, 317
Way of thinking, of a discipline, 532–533
Weaning, 446
Weatherley, D., 32, 33, 71, 79, 288
Webb, E., 463
Weber, M., 238, 244
Wechsler, D., 412, 419, 451, 463
Wechsler Tests, 374
Weimer, P. K., 583, 590
Weisskopf, E., 421, 450, 463, 486, 500
Wellmann, B. L., 398
Wells, F. L., 400
Werner, E., 506
Werner, H., 285
Wertham, F., 219, 224
Wertheimer, M., 528, 536, 554
Wesman, A. G., 546, 550
West, J., 178
Westfield, R. L., 583, 587, 589
Whalen, C. K., 437, 443
Whipple, G. M., 400

White, B. L., 32, 38, 60, 62, 63, 70
White, L., Jr., 356
White, M. A., 528, 536
White, R., 8, 33, 70
White, R. K., 210, 516
White, R. W., 264, 272, 286, 300, 308, 426, 433, 510, 530, 536
White House Conference on Education, 227, 286
Whiting, B. B., 389, 392
Whiting, J. W. M., 1, 50, 53, 87, 89, 90, 91, 115, 159, 166, 255, 256, 347, 348, 389, 392, 448, 477
Whyte, L. L., 27, 30
Whyte, W. H., 238, 244
Wickman, E. K., 369, 500–507, 516
Wiesley, M., 282
Wilcoxon, F., 182, 186
Wilkinson, F. R., 365, 369, 370
Wilkinson, M., 365, 371
Williams, C. D., 87, 98
Williams, E., 428, 433
Williams, H. H., 572, 575
Williams, J. R., 51, 53
Williams, K., 432
Williams, K. A., 428, 433
Williams, R. M., 264, 272
Williams, S. B., 428, 433
Wilson, K. V., 283, 284
Wilson, J. T., 35
Wilson, R. C., 410, 419
Wineman, D., 120, 121
Winston, H. C., 432
Winterbottom, M. R., 158, 243, 244
Wish fulfillment, 477
Wispe, L. G., 488, 500, 518
Withall, J., 494, 500, 516
Withdrawal, and maladjustment, 501–502
Witkin, H. A., 158, 388, 392
Witmer, H. L., 507
Wittenborn, J. R., 260, 261, 264
Witty, P., 219, 224, 408, 487, 500
Wolf, M. M., 88, 99–103, 106
Wolfe, K. M., 219, 224
Wolff, P. H., 314, 317
Wong, T. J., 274, 279, 281, 282
Wood, B. D., 404, 408
Wood, R. L., 500
Woodrow, H., 545, 550
Woodworth, R. S., 53, 543, 544, 545, 550
Woodyard, E., 52, 546, 549
Woolsey, C., 70
Worden, O., 426
Work:
and competence, 305–306
and reward for effort, 359
Wortis, J., 97
Wright, E. M. J., 516
Wright, H. F., 51, 52, 284, 516
Wright, J. C., 418
Wulff, J. J., 308
Wundt, W., 21
Wyer, R. S., 79

Yarrow, L. J., 64, 70, 313, 315, 316, 317
Yerkes, R. M., 54
Young, W. C., 54
Young-Masten, I., 507
Yourman, J., 504, 507

Zander, A. F., 204, 210, 513
Zeaman, D., 583, 590
Zipf, S. G., 160, 166
Zubin, J., 317, 431

608